THE ROUTLEDGE HANDBOOK OF ENVIRONMENTAL MOVEMENTS

This handbook provides readers with up-to-date knowledge on environmental movements and activism and is a reference point for international work in the field. It offers an assessment of environmental movements in different regions of the world, macrostructural conditions and processes underlying their mobilization, the microstructural and social-psychological dimensions of environmental movements and activism, and current trends, as well as prospects for environmental movements and social change.

The handbook provides critical reviews and appraisals of the current state of the art and future development of conceptual and theoretical approaches as well as empirical knowledge and understanding of environmental movements and activism. It encourages dialogue across the disciplinary barriers between social movement studies and other perspectives and reflects upon the causes and consequences of citizens' participation in environmental movements and activities. The volume brings historical studies of environmentalism, sociological analyses of the social composition of participants in and sympathizers of environmental movements, investigations by political scientists on the conditions and processes underlying environmental movements and activism, and other disciplinary inquiries together, while keeping a clear focus within social movement theory and research as the main lines of inquiry.

The handbook is an essential guide and reference point not only for researchers but also for undergraduate and graduate teaching and for policymakers and activists.

Maria Grasso is Professor at the School of Politics and International Relations, Queen Mary University of London, UK.

Marco Giugni is Professor at the Department of Political Science and International Relations and Director of the Institute of Citizenship Studies (InCite) at the University of Geneva, Switzerland.

THE ROUTLEDGE HANDBOOK OF ENVIRONMENTAL MOVEMENTS

Edited by Maria Grasso and Marco Giugni

Routledge
Taylor & Francis Group

LONDON AND NEW YORK

First published 2022
by Routledge
2 Park Square, Milton Park, Abingdon, Oxon OX14 4RN

and by Routledge
605 Third Avenue, New York, NY 10158

Routledge is an imprint of the Taylor & Francis Group, an informa business

British Library Cataloguing-in-Publication Data
A catalogue record for this book is available from the British Library

Library of Congress Cataloging-in-Publication Data
Names: Grasso, Maria T. (Maria Teresa), 1984– editor. |
Giugni, Marco, editor.
Title: The Routledge handbook of environmental movements /
edited by Maria Grasso and Marco Giugni.
Other titles: Handbook of environmental movements
Description: Abingdon, Oxon ; New York, NY : Routledge, 2022. |
Series: Routledge international handbooks | Includes bibliographical
references and index.
Identifiers: LCCN 2021034821 (print) | LCCN 2021034822 (ebook) |
ISBN 9780367428785 (hardback) | ISBN 9781032171524 (paperback) |
ISBN 9780367855680 (ebook)
Subjects: LCSH: Environmentalism—Case studies.
Classification: LCC GE195 .R677 2022 (print) | LCC GE195 (ebook) |
DDC 363.7—dc23
LC record available at https://lccn.loc.gov/2021034821
LC ebook record available at https://lccn.loc.gov/2021034822

ISBN: 978-0-367-42878-5 (hbk)
ISBN: 978-1-032-17152-4 (pbk)
ISBN: 978-0-367-85568-0 (ebk)

DOI: 10.4324/9780367855680

Typeset in Bembo
by Apex CoVantage, LLC

CONTENTS

Contents

FIGURES

TABLES

CONTRIBUTORS

Jon Agnone is the director of People Analytics at Tableau. Dr. Agnone is also an affiliate assistant professor with the University of Washington's Department of Sociology, faculty associate with the University of Washington's Harry Bridges Center for Labor Studies, faculty affiliate with the University of Washington's eScience Institute, and director and co-founder of the Northwest Social Research Group. He has authored multiple published scholarly and policy reports on social movements and economic inequality, has presented to technical and non-technical professional, policy, and academic audiences and has become enamored with the power of Tableau to bring data to life for non-technical audiences.

Elia Apostolopoulou is a human geographer and a political ecologist. She is a senior researcher at the University of Cambridge and an editor of Dialogues in Human Geography. Her research is guided by radical research on human and urban geography, political economy, and political ecology and focuses on various aspects related to the uneven production of nature and space within and beyond cities. Her monograph on the links between offsetting, urbanization and inequality was published in 2020 by Springer-Palgrave and her co-edited volume on the right to nature, social movements and environmental justice in 2019 by Routledge.

Florencia Arancibia is a CONICET Researcher at Universidad Nacional de San Martín-CENIT. She received her PhD from SUNY Stony Brook in 2015. Her research interests include science and technology, political sociology, environment, and social movements. Her doctoral dissertation on the conflict over pesticide use in Argentina is published in several journals, including *Science as Culture*, *Journal of Land Use Change*, *Technology in Society*, and *Sociology Compass*. Her current research continues her focus on environmental-health conflicts, agriculture, and social movements-experts' partnerships in Latin America. She has received fellowships from the National Science Foundation (US), the Inter-American Foundation, and Fulbright.

Dena Arya is a doctoral candidate at Nottingham Trent University, working on 'What role does economic inequality play in how young people participate in environmental politics in the UK?' Her research intersects social policy, political economy, and youth political culture, involving empirically investigating young environmental protesters through ethnography, interviews, and focus groups. She has published on young environmental activists and on research about young people during the COVID-19 lockdown in the UK. Previously, she worked for over a decade in the youth and community sector and is currently tutoring BA undergraduates in social policy at the University of Nottingham.

Philip Balsiger is professor of sociology at the University of Neuchâtel, Switzerland. Bringing together social movement studies and economic sociology, his research has in particular analyzed the contentiousness of markets, sustainable consumption, and moral valuation in markets. He is the author of *The Fight for Ethical Fashion* (Routledge, 2016), co-editor of *The Contested Moralities of Markets* (Emerald, 2019), and has published in outlets such as *Social Movement Studies*, *Socio-Economic Review*, and *Journal of Consumer Culture*.

Valerie Berseth is a doctoral candidate in sociology at the University of British Columbia. Her research examines environmental politics and governance, social and environmental applications of genomic science, climate change adaptation, Indigenous-settler relations, and natural resource management. Her SSHRC-funded dissertation investigates wildlife conservation in the context of Pacific salmon.

Benjamin Bowman is a lecturer in youth justice at the Department of Sociology, Manchester Metropolitan University, and a member of the Manchester Center for Youth Studies (MCYS). Benjamin is co-convener and treasurer of the young people's politics specialist group Political Studies Association (PSA). His research is on young people's everyday politics and the opportunities for social change in contemporary democracy. He has worked extensively with young people, including young activists, and is part of the international working group on the Existential Toolkit for Climate Educators, Rachel Carson Center, Munich, Germany.

Carl Cassegård is professor of sociology at the University of Gothenburg, Sweden. He is a cultural sociologist and social movement researcher whose present research concerns the environmental movement. He is the author of *Toward a Critical Theory of Nature: Capital, Ecology, and Dialectics* (2021), *Youth Movements, Trauma and Alternative Space in Contemporary Japan* (2014), and *Shock and Naturalization in Contemporary Japanese Literature* (2007), as well as numerous essays and articles. He has also co-edited *Climate Action in a Globalizing World* (2017).

Ondřej Císař is professor of sociology at Charles University and also works as the editor-in-chief of the Czech edition of *Czech Sociological Review* at the Institute of Sociology of the Academy of Sciences of the Czech Republic in Prague. His primary research interest is in protest, social movements, civil society, political mobilization, and the future of democracy.

Joel E. Correia is an assistant professor in the Center for Latin American Studies at the University of Florida. He holds a PhD in geography from the University of Colorado Boulder. Correia's research investigates intersections between Indigenous politics, land rights, socio-environmental (in)justice, and law in the context of extractive development and Latin America, with a particular focus on Paraguay and the Gran Chaco. His research is published in journals such as *Geoforum*, *Journal of Peasant Studies*, and *Journal of Latin American Geography*. He is currently completing his first book, *Disrupting the Patrón*, an ethnography of Indigenous environmental justice.

Joost de Moor is an assistant professor of political science at the Center for European Studies and Comparative Politics at Sciences Po Paris. He has published on social movements, political participation, and environmental politics in various academic journals, such as *Theory and*

Society, Environmental Politics, Mobilization, Social Movement Studies, and the *International Journal of Urban and Regional Research*. His work studies how political, urban, and ecological contexts shape strategies in environmental movements. His PhD dissertation (University of Antwerp) dealt with the composition and causal mechanisms of political opportunity structures. More recently, his work has focused on lifestyle politics, the depoliticization of environmental activism, and activism on climate mitigation and adaptation.

Mario Diani is professor of sociology at the University of Trento. His main contributions focus on social network approaches to social movements and collective action. Recent books on the topic include *The Cement of Civil Society* (Cambridge University Press, 2015) and *Multimodal Political Networks* (Cambridge University Press, 2021, with D. Knoke, J. Hollway, and D. Christopoulos). The third edition of *Social Movements: An Introduction*, co-authored with D. della Porta, appeared for Blackwell in 2020. His articles have appeared in major journals including *American Sociological Review, American Journal of Sociology, Theory and Society, Social Networks, Sociological Review*, and *Mobilization*, among others.

Salpie Djoundourian is an associate professor of economics in the Adnan Kassar School of Business at the Lebanese American University. Djoundourian holds a PhD in economics from Louisiana State University, an MSc in economics, and a BS in international trade and finance. Her primary area of expertise is applied microeconomics, with an emphasis on environmental and natural resource economics and public finance. She is actively involved in academic research and scholarly work as well as consultancy work for reputable organizations in both the private and public sectors. Her research appeared in *Public Choice, Journal of Economic Policy Reform, Environment, Development and Sustainability*, and *Transportation Research*, among others.

John Drury is professor of social psychology at the University of Sussex. His work focuses on collective behavior – in emergencies, protests, and social movements, as well as at festivals and music and sports events. He has published over 100 peer-reviewed journal articles on these and other topics, including events such as the 2011 English riots, the London bombings of 7 July 2005, the Hillsborough disaster, and the 2010 Chile earthquake. He is currently researching collective responses to hostile threats and how COVID-19 mutual aid groups can be sustained. He heads the Crowds & Identities group at the University of Sussex.

Linda Etchart has lectured in human geography at Kingston University, London, since 2014. She has taught development studies, social and political geography, international political economy, security, and gender studies, specializing in Latin America. From 2001 to 2004, she was a consultant at the Commonwealth Secretariat in London, in the area of gender and conflict transformation, post-conflict reconstruction, and human rights in Africa. Recent Publications include, with Rawwida Baksh, Elsie Onubogu, and Tina Johnson (eds) (2005), Gender Mainstreaming in Conflict Transformation: Building Sustainable Peace (London: Commonwealth Secretariat), and, with Leo Cerda (2020), "Amazonians in New York: Indigenous Peoples and Global Governance" in *City: Analysis of Urban Trends, Culture, Theory, Policy, Action*; forthcoming (2022) *Global Governance of the Environment, Indigenous Peoples and the Rights of Nature in Latin America: Extractive Industries in the Ecuadorian Amazon*. London: Palgrave Macmillan. She is a contributor to *Voices of Latin America: Social Movements and The New Activism*, edited by Tom Gatehouse (Latin America Bureau/Practical Action, 2019).

Helena Flam is professor emeritus at the Institute of Sociology at the University of Leipzig, where she taught between 1993 and 2017. She gained her degrees at the University of Lund in Sweden (1976) and Columbia University in New York City (1983). Her affiliation with the Swedish Collegium for Advanced Study in Uppsala led to the publication of *States and Antinuclear Movements* in 1994. She has contributed to social movements, political, and organizational studies, playing a pioneering role in the European sociology of emotions. Her most recent publications on German, Hong Kong, Japanese, and US lawyers show how the collective mobilization of professionals and social movements can jointly be studied.

Francesca Forno is associate professor of sociology at the University of Trento. Francesca's research interests include political consumerism and sustainable community movement organizations (SCMOs). A special focus in these areas is on the consequences of the spread of market-based forms of action for citizens' participation and mobilization. Her work has appeared in the following journals, among others: *The Annals of the American Academy of Political and Social Science*, *The Journal of Consumer Culture*, *International Journal of Consumer Studies*, *South European Politics and Society*, *European Societies*, *British Food Journal*, *The Annals of the Feltrinelli Foundation*, and anthologies published by Oxford University Press, Wiley-Blackwell, Routledge, and Zed Books.

Scott Frickel is professor of sociology and environment and society at Brown University and founding editor of the Nature, Society, and Culture book series for Rutgers University Press. His research and teaching focus broadly on the intersection of nature, knowledge, and politics. He has published over 50 articles and chapters, as well as five books, most recently, with James R. Elliott, *Sites Unseen: Uncovering Hidden Hazards in American Cities*, winner of the Robert E. Park Book Award for 2020. A new co-authored book, *Residues: Thinking through Chemical Environments*, will be published in 2021.

Marco Giugni is professor at the department of political science and international relations and director of the Institute of Citizenship Studies (InCite) at the University of Geneva, Switzerland. His research interests focus on social movements and political participation protests, social exclusion, and the participation of disadvantaged and discriminated groups, such as the unemployed and immigrants. He has participated in and coordinated numerous research projects. Publications include 12 books, 14 edited collections, and about 150 journal articles and book chapters. In addition, he has edited or co-edited a number of special issues for scholarly journals. Since 2006, he has been European Editor of *Mobilization*.

Maria Grasso is professor at the School of Politics and International Relations at Queen Mary University of London, UK. She is European Editor of *Mobilization* and author of *Generations, Political Participation and Social Change in Western Europe* (Routledge, 2016); *Street Citizens: Protest Politics and Social Movement Activism in the Age of Globalization* (Cambridge University Press, 2019, with Marco Giugni); and *Living with Hard Times: Europeans in the Great Recession* (ECPR Press, 2021, with Marco Giugni). Her papers have appeared in *British Journal of Political Science*, *European Journal of Political Research*, *International Political Science Review*, *European Political Science Review*, *Electoral Studies*, and other journals.

Robyn Gulliver (PhD UQ, 2020) is a researcher at the University of Queensland and a multi-award winning environmentalist, writer, and scholar who has served as an organizer and leader of numerous local and national environmental organizations. Born in New Zealand, she has spent the last decade advocating for and writing about environmental issues for activist groups, local councils, not-for-profit organizations, and academia. Her research focuses on the antecedents and consequences of environmental and pro-democracy activism. Upcoming publications include *The Advocates, Civil Resistance against Climate Change,* and *The Psychology of Effective Activism.*

David J. Hess is a professor in the sociology department at Vanderbilt University, James Thornton Fant Chair in Sustainability Studies, and director of Environmental and Sustainability Studies. His research and teaching are on societal and policy dimensions of science, technology, energy, and the environment. He focuses on public accountability, local and state energy policy, civil society, coalitions, and social movements. He is the recipient of the Robert K. Merton Prize, the Diana Forsythe Prize, the Star-Nelkin Prize, and the General Anthropology Division Prize for Exemplary Cross-Field Scholarship.

Hiroshi Honda is professor of political science on the faculty of law, Hokkai-Gakuen University in Sapporo. He holds an MA in social sciences (University of Amsterdam) and a PhD in law (Hokkaido University). A pioneer of comparative political research on anti-nuclear movements in Japan, his research interest is in the intersection of political parties, labor movement, and other social movements. Major publications (in Japanese language): *Anti-nuclear Movement and Politics in Japan,* Sapporo: Hokkaido University Press, 2005 and *Comparative Politics of Phasing-out of Nuclear Power,* Tokyo: Hosei University Press, 2014.

Joanna K. Huxster, PhD, is an assistant professor of environmental studies at Eckerd College. Her research addresses public understanding of science, environmental issues, and climate change, with a focus on effective climate change communication.

Anders Hylmö is a researcher at Lund University School of Economics and Management, and part time senior researcher at NIFU, Oslo. His research interests span the sociology of science, research and innovation policy, and social movement studies. Current work focuses on innovation studies, research governance and evaluative practices across research settings.

Ana Isla is a professor emerita, Brock University, Canada. She is the author of *The "Greening" of Costa Rica: Women, Peasants, Indigenous People and the Remaking of Nature,* University of Toronto Press, and editor of *Climate Chaos: Ecofeminism and the Land Question,* Inanna Publications & Education Inc., Toronto.

Erik W. Johnson is an associate professor of sociology at Washington State University. His research focuses on the emergence, development, and institutional outcomes of environmental movements. Collaborative research projects examine change over time in public environmental concern and the developing field of environmental crime. Johnson's research has appeared in journals such as *Social Forces, Environmental Sociology, Mobilization, Environment and Behavior, Nonprofit and Voluntary Sector Quarterly,* and *Social Problems.*

Anastasia Kavada is a reader in media and politics in the School of Media and Communication at the University of Westminster. Her research explores the use of digital media by social movements and non-governmental organizations, focusing on processes of participatory democracy as well as on organizing, coordination, and the construction of a collective identity. Anastasia is course leader of the MA in Media, Campaigning and Social Change and co-leader of the Arts, Communication and Culture Research Community.

Erick Lachapelle is an associate professor in the department of political science at the University of Montreal. He is the principal investigator for the Canadian Surveys on Energy and the Environment (CSEE). He has written widely on climate change public opinion in Canada and the United States and has published articles in *Global Environmental Politics*, *Energy Policy*, *Environmental Politics*, *PLoS ONE*, *Policy Studies Journal*, *Climate Policy*, *Review of Policy Research*, and *Canadian Journal of Political Science*, among other journals.

Peter Lentini is associate professor of politics and international relations and founding director of the Global Terrorism Research Center (GTReC), Monash University. He is also the milestone coordinator of the Social and Political Sciences Graduate Research Program, School of Social Sciences, Monash University. His research focuses on comparative radical, extremist, and terrorist movements; new religious movements; and Russian domestic politics. Monash University has provided him with awards and commendations for research-industry partnerships, higher degree by research supervision, and small-group teaching.

Jasmine Lorenzini is research fellow at the Institute of Citizenship Studies at the University of Geneva, where she works on food activism, political participation, and social movement activism. In her doctoral research, she worked on youth long-term unemployment and its impact on economic, social, and political inclusion. Together with Marco Giugni and other colleagues, she wrote two books on this topic (*Jobless Citizens* and *Young People and Long-Term Unemployment*). During her postdoctoral research, she worked on protest in times of economic crisis. She edited a book with Hanspeter Kriesi and others on this topic (*Contention in Times of Crisis*).

Winnifred R. Louis (PhD, McGill, 2001) is a professor in the School of Psychology at the University of Queensland. Her research interests focus on the influence of identity and norms on social decision-making. She has studied this broad topic in contexts from politics and community activism to health and environmental choices. She is a fellow of the Society for the Psychological Study of Social Issues, a fellow of the Society for Personality and Social Psychology, and a fellow of the Australian Psychological Society.

Amanda Machin is currently a researcher at the PPE Institute for Social and Institutional Change (ISIC) at the University of Witten/Herdecke, and a visiting fellow at the Centre for Social Investment, Heidelberg University in Germany. Her research focuses on environmental politics, radical democracy and sustainability transformation, and her books include *Society and Climate: Transformations and Challenges* (World Scientific, 2019, co-authored with Nico Stehr); *Against Political Compromise: Sustaining Democratic Debate* (Routledge, 2017, co-authored with Alexander Ruser); and *Negotiating Climate Change: Radical Democracy and the Illusion of Consensus* (Zed Books, 2013). The forthcoming book *Bodies of Democracy: Modes of Embodied Politics* will be published by Transcript later in 2021.

Marjolaine Martel-Morin is a PhD candidate in political science at the University of Montreal. Her research is concerned with climate change communication and psychology, with a focus on assessing how different audience segments respond to framing strategies in Canada.

Angela G. Mertig is a professor of sociology at Middle Tennessee State University (Murfreesboro, Tennessee, US). She earned her MA (1990) and PhD (1995) in sociology from Washington State University (Pullman, Washington, US). She has published extensively on the American environmental movement and public attitudes toward the environment, animals, and natural resource management. She specializes in environmental sociology; animals and society; social movements; social research methods, particularly survey research; and statistics.

Lyle Munro MA (ANU); PhD (Monash) was a lecturer and research associate in Sociology at Monash University and Federation University of Australia (Gippsland campus in Victoria) from 1990 until the advent of the coronavirus in 2020. He is the author of *Compassionate Beasts: The Quest for Animal Rights* (Praeger, 2001); *Confronting Cruelty: Animals, Moral Orthodoxy and the Challenge of the Animal Rights Movement* (Brill, 2005); and *Man is the Cruelest Animal: Essays on the Human-Animal Link* (Common Ground, 2021). *Life Chances, Education and Social Movements* (Anthem Press, 2019) highlights the existential threats of pandemics and climate change to human and non-human animals.

Gerry Nagtzaam is an associate professor at the Faculty of Law, Monash University. His research focuses on the intersections between international environmental law, international relations, politics, history, and economics. He has written a number of well-received books on topics including international environmental treaties and their normative treatment, nuclear waste disposal in democratic states, and international environmental legal regime evolution. He has also written extensively on the concept of ecoterrorism, including "From Environmental Action to Ecoterrorism: Towards a Process Theory of Environmental" and *Animal Rights Oriented Political Violence* (Edward Elgar Publishers, 2017).

Eugene Nulman is the author of *Climate Change and Social Movements: Civil Society and the Development of National Climate Change Policy* and numerous articles about social movements and the climate change movement. These include publications in *Third World Quarterly*, *Environmental Politics*, *European Journal of Social Theory*, *Current Opinion in Environmental Sustainability*, and *Journal of Youth Studies*. Eugene Nulman is senior lecturer in sociology at Birmingham City University.

Sylvie Ollitrault, is senior researcher at CNRS and a member of the center of research UMR 7050 ISP-Paris Nanterre-Ecole Normale supérieure. Her field of research is green activism (political party, NGO, social movements). She has published several articles and books on the green movement, collective action. and civil disobedience. She published, with Graeme Hayes and Isabelle Sommier, *Breaking the Laws* (Amsterdam University Press, 2019, https:// cv.archives-ouvertes.fr/sylvie-ollitrault). She is also involved in research networks on Green politics.

Louisa Parks PhD is associate professor in political sociology at the University of Trento's School of International Studies and Department of Sociology and Social Research. She is the author of *Benefit-sharing in Environmental Governance: Local Experiences of a Global Concept*, published in 2020 by Routledge, and *Social Movement Campaigns on European Policy: In the Corridors and in the Streets*, published in 2015 by Palgrave Macmillan. She has published work on transnational social movements and their impacts, civil society participation in the European Union, the environmental activism of Indigenous peoples and local communities around benefit sharing, and the Convention on Biological Diversity.

Phaedra C. Pezzullo is an associate professor at the University of Colorado Boulder in the College of Media, Communication, and Information. She is an award-winning author on environmental communication and environmental justice, with more recent work focusing on global creative climate communication, US public advocacy for just transitions, and green communication in China. She has been an invited speaker internationally, including at the Université de Paris-Sorbonne in France and Fudan University in Shanghai, China. Deeply dedicated to public engagement, she works and consults with ENGOs and governments for a more sustainable and just world. For more information, see https://phaedracpezzullo.com/.

Sarah Pickard is a senior lecturer in British politics and society at the Université Sorbonne Nouvelle – Paris 3 and board member of its CREW (EA 4399) research laboratory. She is a convenor for the Political Studies Association (PSA) Young People's Politics specialist group and a vice president of the International Sociological Association (ISA) Sociology of Youth research committee. Her research focuses on contemporary youth electoral and non-electoral political participation, especially emerging forms of engagement and activism in relation to environmental issues and Do-It-Ourselves (DIO) politics. Her monograph *Politics, Protest and Young People* (501 pages) was published with Palgrave Macmillan in 2019.

Clare Saunders is professor in environmental politics in the Environment and Sustainability Institute and Department of Politics at the University of Exeter. Her work on social movements is published widely in journals ranging from *British Journal of Sociology* to *Comparative Political Studies*. When COVID stresses and strains die down, she hopes to finish the second edition of her book on environmental networks with Bloomsbury Academic Press. She is also co-editor in chief of the journal *Social Movement Studies*.

Ellen Griffith Spears is a professor in the interdisciplinary New College and the department of American studies at the University of Alabama. She teaches environmental history and policy with a focus on social movements in the US South in a global context. She is affiliated faculty in UA's department of gender and race studies. Her book *Rethinking the American Environmental Movement Post-1945* (Routledge Press, 2019) reconsiders US environmentalism in the context of broader social justice movements. Spears's 2014 book, *Baptized in PCBs: Race, Pollution, and Justice in an All-American Town* (University of North Carolina Press), won several awards.

Doug Specht is a chartered geographer and a senior lecturer in the School of Media and Communication at the University of Westminster. His research examines how knowledge is constructed and codified through digital and cartographic artefacts, focusing on development issues in Latin America and sub-Saharan Africa.

Suzanne Staggenborg is professor of sociology at the University of Pittsburgh. The author of numerous articles and books on the dynamics of social movements, she is the 2019 winner of the John D. McCarthy Award for Lifetime Achievement in the Scholarship of Social Movements and Collective Behavior. Her recent work focuses on the environmental movement. Her latest book, entitled *Grassroots Environmentalism*, was published in Cambridge University Press's Contentious Politics series in October 2020. With David S. Meyer, she is co-editor of the Cambridge Elements series on contentious politics.

Phia Steyn is a lecturer in African history and African environmental history at the University of Stirling. She has published a range of articles and chapters within the broad field of African environmental history on themes such as environmentalism in apartheid South Africa, Southern African foodways, and the exploration and exploitation of petroleum in Nigeria. She is currently working on two projects looking at the environmental impact of war and the environmental crises in the late-nineteenth-century Orange Free State republic.

Håkan Thörn is full professor of sociology at the University of Gothenburg. His research is concerned with social movements, globalization, and power, and he has published a number of articles and books on these topics, including *Climate Action in a Globalizing World: Comparative Perspectives on Environmental Movements in the Global North* (co-edited, 2017); *Contemporary Co-housing in Europe: Towards Sustainable Cities?* (co-edited, 2020); *Urban Uprisings: Challenging Neoliberal Urbanism in Europe* (co-edited, 2016) and *Anti-Apartheid and the Emergence of a Global Civil Society* (Second edition, 2009).

David B. Tindall is a professor of sociology at the University of British Colombia; where he studies and teaches about contention over environmental issues. His research examines the environmental movement and environmentalism in Canada, media coverage of climate change discourse and other environmental topics, climate change politics and policy networks, and public opinion about climate change and other environmental issues. Currently, he is investigating the role of social networks in fostering climate action, including the relative importance of virtual and non-virtual ties.

Chie Togami is a PhD candidate at the University of Pittsburgh whose research interests span environment, gender, social movements, and political sociology. Her current research includes a cross-national comparative study of climate change movements in the United States and the UK, as well as an ongoing study of citizen science and the politics of air pollution in Pittsburgh, PA.

Sara Vestergren is lecturer in social psychology at Keele University. Sara holds a PhD in psychology from Linköping University, Sweden. Sara's research focuses on collective action and collective behavior, with the main focus on participation in collective action, protests, and activism. Sara has previously studied participation in both left-wing and environmental movements. She is currently researching social movement participation in various protest and activist contexts, including the environmental movement, focusing on dimensions such as biographical consequences, leadership, and long-term psychological changes.

Stefan Wahlen is professor of "food sociology" at the University of Giessen in Germany. Stefan is interested in (food) consumption and eating cultures as well as in the socio-political organization of consumption. His research has been published, among other places, in the *International Journal of Consumer Studies*, *Journal of Consumer Culture*, *Journal of Consumer Policy*, and the *Journal of Cleaner Production*. He has been guest editor (with Mikko Laamanen) for a special issue on "Lifestyle, Consumption and Social Movements" at the International Journal of Consumer Studies. He is further a board member of the European Sociological Association's (ESA) research network for the sociology of consumption.

Mattias Wahlström is associate professor of sociology at the department of sociology and work science, University of Gothenburg. His publications on various aspects of social movements, protest, repression, and political violence can be found in a wide spectrum of scientific journals, including *Global Environmental Politics*, *New Media & Society*, *Mobilization*, *Sexualities*, *Terrorism and Political Violence*, and *Theory and Society*. He recently published the internationally comparative study *Pride Parades and LGBT Movements*, co-authored with Abby Peterson and Magnus

Wennerhag (Routledge, 2018). Contemporary climate mobilization is one of his main current research foci.

Magnus Wennerhag is professor in sociology at the School of Social Sciences, Södertörn University, Sweden. His research mainly concerns social movements, political participation, social stratification, climate protests, political violence, and sociological theory.

Susilo Wibisono (PhD UQ, 2021) is a researcher at the Social Change Lab in the School of Psychology, University of Queensland, Australia. As a lecturer at the Islamic University of Indonesia, Susilo published on the social psychology of religiosity (in Indonesian), before beginning a PhD in 2016 on religious collective action, working with Professors Winnifred R. Louis and Jolanda Jetten. Currently, he is studying extremism and effective activism in contexts including Indonesia, Australia, and Oceania.

Fengshi Wu is associate professor in political science and international relations at the School of Social Sciences, University of New South Wales, Sydney, Australia. She has published extensively on environmental politics, state-society relations, and global governance with the empirical focus on China and Asia and is the inaugural series editor of *Environment and Society in Asia*, Amsterdam University Press. She also currently serves on the board of the International Society for Third-Sector Research. Her edited book *China's Global Conquest for Resources* (Routledge, 2017) examines political and socio-economic impacts of China's overseas investment in and acquisition of natural resources.

ACKNOWLEDGMENTS

We are very grateful to all the authors for their contributions and interesting chapters. We are also very grateful to Andrew Mould and Egle Zigaite for their support.

1

ENVIRONMENTAL MOVEMENTS WORLDWIDE

Maria Grasso and Marco Giugni

Environmental movements: heterogeneous, transforming, and institutionalizing

Research on social movements generally tends to focus on specific movements or – at times – a given movement family. Moreover, comparative analyses are becoming increasingly common. In this regard, environmental movements are perhaps one of the most often studied social movements. The wider social movement literature abounds with books and articles dealing with different aspects of environmental movements. Such attention has translated into historical studies of environmentalism, sociological analyses of the social composition of participants and sympathizers of environmental movements, investigations by political scientists on the conditions and processes underlying environmental movements and activism, and still other forms of disciplinary inquiries. Many of these works are reviewed in this *Handbook*, which aims to bring together these different outlooks while maintaining a clear focus within social movement theory and research in terms of the main lines of inquiry. In this way, *The Routledge Handbook of Environmental Movements* provides an introduction to and overview of the different aspects relating to this field of studies, ranging from assessments of environmental movements in different regions of the world to the macrostructural conditions and processes underlying their mobilization and the microstructural and social-psychological dimensions of environmental movements and activism, to finish with discussions of current trends as well as future prospects for environmental movements and social change.

In this way, *The Routledge Handbook of Environmental Movements* aspires to become a reference point for international work in the field. To do so, it aims to provide critical reviews and appraisals of the current state of the art and indicate pathways for future development of conceptual and theoretical approaches as well as bringing together up-to-date evidence and empirical knowledge and understanding of environmental movements and activism. In doing so, it aims to encourage dialogue across the disciplinary barriers between social movement studies on the one hand and other perspectives on the other and to engage with, and reflect upon, the causes and consequences of citizens' participation in environmental movements and activities.

One difficulty when dealing with a specific movement or movement family is a definitional one: What do we mean by environmental movements? Intuitively, this seems like an easy question to answer, and each of us has perhaps a good idea of what environmental movements are

1   DOI: 10.4324/9780367855680-1

in our mind. However, when it comes to delimiting the object of study from a scientific point of view, this can become somewhat less clear cut. Therefore, we believe it is a good idea at this stage to provide one from the outset. In a social movement perspective and following a general understanding of what movements are (Diani, 1992), an environmental movement

> may be defined as a loose, noninstitutionalized network of informal interactions that may include, as well as individuals and groups who have no organizational affiliation, organizations of varying degrees of formality, that are engaged in collective action motivated by shared identity or concern about environmental issues.
>
> (Rootes, 2004: 610)

However, since definitions are always debatable and depend to some extent on the theoretical perspective that one adopts, this one should not be taken as final, but more modestly as a compass that can guide us in our investigations as well as guide the reader through the various chapters included in the volume. It is not necessarily adopted in all the chapters, but it serves to keep the rudder straight while sailing between the various aspects of environmental movements throughout the volume.

When it comes to environmental movements, the main problem lies perhaps more in setting a thematic boundary than in the analytical definition as such. The distinction between environmental and anti-nuclear or anti-nuclear power movements is particularly telling in this regard. Sometimes movements in opposition to nuclear power plants are included as part of a broader environmental movement; at times, they are treated as if they were separate. Similarly, some movement branches – such as, for example, the climate or climate change movement, the animal rights movements, or the environmental justice movement – are sometimes considered as part of environmental movements but other times as distinct movements. Furthermore, some scholars speak of environmental movements, whereas others prefer to call them ecology movements. We should also note the metaphorical term "Green movements", which is sometimes used in the literature to refer to our subject matter, although this term is most often used with reference to political parties rather than in relation to social movements.

As we discuss at more length elsewhere (Giugni and Grasso, 2015), environmental movements share three main features: they are heterogeneous, they have profoundly transformed themselves, and they have generally become more institutionalized. All three aspects also come out clearly from the chapters included in this volume. Of course, many other features could be mentioned as well, which will also be addressed in the *Handbook*. Yet these three seem to characterize the movements quite well. Environmental movements are far from being monolithic entities. Rather, they are extremely heterogeneous. They display a wide variety of actors and organizations (from local and loosely structured to national and supranational professionalized organizations), issues and goals (covering all dimensions of environmental protection and related issues such as justice), strategies (from the most moderate to radical forms of action), and finally in terms of effects as well. This heterogeneity amounts to both a strength and a weakness. Insofar as the movement has multiple options for mobilizing, it can be seen as a strength. However, heterogeneous movements can have more trouble coalescing around a shared collective identity.

Another key fact is that environmental movements have profoundly transformed. This can be seen in the shift from conservationism to more politically oriented movement streams but also, in the short term, in the emergence of new actors and issues as well as new ways of framing the problems of the environment. While not entirely a voluntary process, this capability for change may have in fact contributed to the movements' survival, despite the ebbs and flows of patterns of mobilization along with the strong organizational structures characterizing them compared also to other movements.

Moreover, environmental movements have also become strongly institutionalized. This can be seen in how they are now a constitutive part of contemporary societies. The general public and policy makers are very concerned with the environment and are increasingly sensitive to environmental problems. This awareness raising is also the major impact of environmental movements. Environmental actors have also institutionalized. The formation of Green parties is a clear sign of this, as is the incorporation of environmental organizations in policy networks. However, institutionalization has not touched upon the movements completely. Some examples, such as the anti-nuclear energy movements, are much less institutionalized. Moreover, this process has occurred to a greater extent in some countries, given also the different political opportunity structures.

The *Handbook* is structured along six parts. Part 1 looks at the history, status, and prospects of environmental movements in different regions of the world. Part 2 examines a number of key issues and movement sectors. Part 3 deals with the macrostructural conditions and processes relating to the rise and mobilization of environmental movements. Part 4 addresses the microstructural and social-psychological dimensions of environmental movements and activism. Part 5 focuses on the consequences and outcomes of environmental movements. Finally, Part 6 offers a prospective outlook on environmental movements, looking at some recent trends and how they might influence environmental activism in the future. Each part includes a varying number of chapters written by leading scholars in the field. This introduction maps the terrain for the chapters to follow by pointing out the core issues they address and, above all, by briefly presenting the content of the chapters. We do so along the six-fold thematic structure of the *Handbook*.

Part 1: Environmental movements around the world

Much, if not most, of the literature on environmental movements focuses on the Western world, in particular on Western Europe (see, for example, Rootes, 2003) and North America. Indeed, the first environmental organizations appeared there, such as, for example, the American Society for the Prevention of Cruelty to Animals, which is perhaps the first environmental organization ever, created in the US in 1866. This shows that environmental movements have longstanding historical roots. Similarly, one could argue, along with Inglehart (1977), that the post-materialist or, more broadly, progressive values that underly the rise of the modern environmental movements – the more "politicized" ones – first appeared in Western societies in the wake of the protest wave of the 1960s and 1970s and then spread to other parts of the world. Yet this by no means implies that environmental movements are non-existent or marginal actors in other parts of the world. Quite the contrary, examples of strong mobilizations in favor of environmental protection and other environment-sensitive issues can be found across the globe.

Part 1 of the *Handbook* looks at environmental movements in different parts of the world, allowing us to avoid the "Western-centrism" that has often characterized the study of social movements in general. Eight chapters form this part of the volume, corresponding to eight different regions. Chapter 2, by Sylvie Ollitrault, provides an overview of environmental movements in Western Europe. Chapter 3, by Ondřej Císař, looks at the other side of what once was called the Iron Curtain and focuses on the development of environmental activism and protest in Central Eastern Europe after 1989. This chapter shows in particular important variations of the movements' protest agenda across countries, more specifically in four Eastern European countries – namely, the Czech Republic, Slovakia, Poland, and Hungary – arguing that cross-country differences in protest agendas depend on what issues the mainstream political parties are competing on.

North America, the other area where much work on environmental movements has been focused, is discussed in Ellen Griffith Spears's Chapter 4. This critical reflection on the state of the movements in two major countries of North America (the US and Canada) reveals both distinct national trends and significant correspondences. Although the rise of post-materialist values and issues, which has often been associated with the rise of environmental movements as well as other "modernity-critical" movements, was said to have first developed in Western societies (Inglehart, 1977), protest and activism on the environment have also occurred elsewhere. The other chapters in this part of the *Handbook* clearly show that environmental movements are by far not limited to Europe and North America. Thus, for example, Joel E. Correia shows in Chapter 5 that Latin America has a long tradition of social mobilization to protect the environment, including emblematic protests against deforestation in the Amazon, oil extraction in Ecuador, and dam construction in Chile, which have galvanized grassroots resistance movements and captured international attention. This overview points also to the increasing levels of violence that threaten social-environmental movements in this part of the world.

Chapter 6, by Fengshi Wu, examines environmental movements in Asia. This comparative analysis covering a wide range of countries in East, Central, and Southeast Asia unveils the relationship between (domestic) political regimes and the rise, development, and outcomes of environmental movement. Chapter 7, by Salpie S. Djoundourian, focuses on the Arab world – the Middle East and North Africa (MENA) – a region where economic and social concerns usually overshadow environmental concerns. Yet, as this review shows, environmental movements and activism have also emerged in the Arab world. The chapter points in particular to the fact that, given Islam's reach as a state religion, academics and environmentalists are seeking inspiration from Islam to mobilize the environmental movement.

The last two chapters in this part of the volume look at experiences in Africa and in Oceania. Phia Steyn examines environmental movements in Africa in Chapter 8, focusing on the most recent developments. The chapter covers a brief historical overview of the movements' contexts, issues, microstructures, and future prospects. Then, Chapter 9, by Robyn Gulliver, Susilo Wibisono, and Winnifred R. Louis, turns to environmental groups across the four regions of Oceania – Melanesia, Micronesia, Polynesia, and Australasia. The chapter examines the different environmental issues that groups focus on, their different strategies for promoting environmental behaviors, and the different mobilization tactics employed to gain supporters.

Part 2: Issues and movement sectors

As we mentioned earlier, environmental movements are heterogenous collective actors. They are formed by different actors and organizations, often adopting very different protest tactics and strategies. Furthermore, although the social profiles of the most committed activists are perhaps similar, people mobilizing on environmental issues come from different social backgrounds and are driven by different motivations. Environmental protests and movements address a wide range of issues, from nature protection and conservation to nuclear energy, extractivism, climate change, animal rights, alternative consumption, environmental justice, and still other issues. This is also what makes delimiting the boundaries of these movements challenging at times.

The chapters in Part 2 of the *Handbook* account for such a heterogeneity in terms of the issues addressed by the movements. Without claiming exhaustivity, they cover some of the key issues and movement sectors. The part quite naturally starts with Chapter 10 on environmental conservation, by Angela G. Mertig, as it forms the first strand of environmental concerns historically. This chapter discusses the meaning of environmental conservation, its historical background, contemporary features, and mobilization. The chapter looks at environmental conservation, illustrating this through the example of the US and other cases internationally. Chapter 11, by Helena Flam and Hiroshi Honda, examines the anti-nuclear movements as well as their historical transformations in the US where they started and also in Europe and a few Asian countries. This movement sector is often characterized by a strong degree of politicization of the struggles against the use of nuclear power. Chapter 12, by Ana Isla, looks at the impact of extractive activities and the large number of natural resources it removes. Centered on ecofeminist perspectives, it evaluates global capital's ecological management in North, Central, and South America.

In recent years in particular, environmental concerns have often come to be framed in terms of climate change. Eugene Nulman examines this aspect in Chapter 13 on climate change, an issue that has played a major role in recent environmental mobilizations, especially thanks to the strong involvement of pupils and students in the so-called Friday for Future demonstrations as well as other events. As the chapter shows, the climate change movement is a heterogenous network of formal organizations, informal groups, and individuals working to address the issue of global warming and its various effects, caused by greenhouse gas emissions. The chapter provides a very brief outline of the history and different aspects of the climate change movement, with a focus on campaigns in the Global North.

Animal rights, arguably one of the issues that has spurred the most radical and sometimes even violent forms of protesting, is examined by Lyle Munro in Chapter 14. This chapter describes the motivations and campaigns of Australian animal rights activists and shows the importance of the movement in helping reduce greenhouse emissions by a reduction in or elimination of meat in our diets. The existential threats of climate change and pandemics such as COVID-19 are discussed in the context of China's exploitation of animals. The chapter advocates the necessity of a mass movement of animal rights and environmental groups along with public health advocates to persuade governments to adopt more humane policies and sustainable practices. These aspects are discussed by Jasmine Lorenzini in Chapter 15. This is a broad topic that may include a variety of different, though related, aspects, from the more traditional political consumerist activities (boycotting and buycotting) to broader issues concerning food activism and lifestyle activism (de Moor, 2017). The chapter focuses on how political consumerism contributes to shaping citizens' relation to politics. It asks how political consumerism shapes citizens' democratic imagination; examines how food activism proposes to transform the economy, the state, and society; and explores alternatives to political consumerism in the environmental movement.

Food activism does not only rely on individualism, consumerism, and private property but also has deeper implications for economic justice, social equality, and democracy (Alkon and Guthman, 2017). Indeed, environmental concerns have come to be articulated in terms of justice, leading, for example, to the emergence in the US of an environmental justice movement in the 1980s as a response to existing disparities in the burden of environmental degradation and pollution facing minority and low-income communities. Phaedra C. Pezzullo discusses this dimension in Chapter 16 on environmental justice and climate justice. This chapter retraces the origin of the movement and how articulating new vocabularies such as "environmental racism" was critical to its initial period of mobilization, then examines environmental justice critiques of the environmental movement and the period of institutionalization, and finally identifies how climate justice reaffirms and reinvents environmental justice.

An overview of issues and sectors of environmental movements would not be complete without reference to the important role played by Indigenous movements in this context. Linda Etchart fills this gap in Chapter 17, exploring the relationship between Indigenous peoples and nature, their spiritual beliefs with regard to man's place in the environment, and the significance of their worldview in the light of the struggle to keep global temperatures below 1.5% above pre-industrial levels. The chapter discusses the intersection of Indigenous and environmental movements and in particular how relationships and collaborations have evolved, leading to global networks of environmental activism. It looks at North and South America, aiming to highlight the voices of Indigenous representatives within Indigenous environmental movements and within the global movement against climate change.

Part 3: Macrostructural conditions and processes

With Part 3, the *Handbook* moves from accounts of environmental movements and their activities in different regions of the world and on different issues to conditions for their emergence and the processes underlying their mobilization. Scholars of social movements often operate an analytical distinction between macro conditions and micro dynamics (Klandermans, 1997; Snow, 2004). Accordingly, this part deals with the macrostructural conditions and processes underlying the mobilization of environmental movements; Part 4 is devoted to the microstructural and social-psychological dimensions of environmental activism.

While treated together, the chapters in this section of the book in fact deal with two aspects that, analytically, should be kept separate in spite of being related to each other. On the one hand, we must consider the conditions under which environmental movements emerge and mobilize. Such conditions may vary considerably from one context – whether national or local – to another, thereby providing different sets of opportunities for the emergence and mobilization of the movements. In the field of social movement studies, this is an aspect that has been notoriously emphasized by political opportunity theorists (Kriesi, 2004). At its best, it considered the influence of conjunctures – events and processes, as well as encounters between the social movements and their opponents – on the emergence, mobilization, and outcomes of the social movement contestation (Flam, 1994; Kriesi et al., 1995; see also Chapter 11). The latter have stressed above all the structural aspects of the context, looking at the role of political-institutional opportunities while cultural aspects have often been overlooked, at least as features of the broader context for the emergence and mobilization of social movements. Therefore, both the political context (McAdam and Tarrow, 2019) and the cultural context (Jasper and Polletta, 2019) should be considered when examining the macrostructural conditions for the emergence and mobilization of environmental movements.

Social movements, however, are not only constrained by macro-level conditions such as political opportunity structures or cultural frames. One should also consider meso-level conditions that structure the context for the emergence of mobilization of social movements in general and environmental movements more specifically. Here, we refer to organizational networks – that is, the web of connections between social movements organizations – but also between them and other kinds of organizational actors, which may provide the resources needed to mobilize but could also create some barriers to mobilization. Indeed, networks can either facilitate or inhibit mobilization and play a key role in recruiting movement participants (Crossley and Diani, 2019). At the same time, social movement organizations continue to be of vital importance for social movements, contributing to their internal dynamics (Walker and Martin, 2019). Furthermore, movement organizations may also act as powerful "political entrepreneurs" by framing environmental issues in a certain way – for example, as social problems requiring political solutions rather than being "natural" and inevitable – as the "framing" literature has shown (Benford and Snow, 2000; Snow, 2004; Snow et al., 2019). This, in turn, facilitates movements' mobilization.

This part of the *Handbook* deals with both the structural and cultural conditions of environmental movements and the processes underlying their mobilization. The first three chapters deal with the political and cultural context of environmental movements as well as their organizational networks. Chapter 18, by Joost de Moor and Mattias Wahlström, focuses on the political context, the traditional terrain of political process theorists. This chapter discusses the relationship between political context and environmental movements using the concept of political opportunity structure, which captures a broad range of elements in the political context that may impinge on mobilization, strategies, and the outcomes of environmental movements. The chapter illustrates the theoretical arguments through the recent example of the climate movement, showing how variations over time in political opportunity structures on the international level produced changes in the movements' strategies. Moreover, the chapter points to the limitations of a view that puts too much emphasis on such structural conditions. The cultural side of environmental movements' context is examined in Chapter 19 by Scott Frickel and Florencia Arancibia. To do this, the chapter turns to the relationship between environmental movements and environmental knowledge by focusing on the role of experts and expertise. The chapter focuses on empirical and strategic questions concerning how expert mobilization into environmental movements is organized; the conditions under which they are more likely; and effects on science, environmental conflict, and socioecological change more broadly.

More broadly, Chapter 20, by Mario Diani, looks at environmental movements' organizational networks or, in his own terms, the interdependence of multiple actors and the systems of relations that bind them in broader patterns. This is a fundamental aspect to study for making sense of collective action and its forms and emergence, including those linked to environmental movements. The chapter provides the conceptual tools to explore the relational patterns that link groups and associations interested in environmental issues to each other, generating more complex forms of organizing – or "modes of coordination". The chapter furthermore also looks at multiple relational levels, from inter-organizational alliances to co-memberships to identity mechanisms. This is aimed at assessing, importantly, to what extent practical exchanges between environmental actors match mutual recognition on the symbolic level.

Once in motion, a movement follows a given trajectory and undergoes certain processes, which are in part influenced by the very same macrostructural conditions – both political and cultural – but also by their own internal logics and dynamics. Research has often focused on social movement organizations to depict how they evolve over time. From this perspective, Kriesi (1996) has offered a helpful framework, suggesting that four aspects must be considered in the analysis of organizations' development: organizational growth and decline, internal structuring, external structuring, and goal orientations and action repertoires. Concerning the transformation of goal orientations and action repertoires, he proposed a typology combining two criteria: whether the organization has a constituency or client orientation and whether there is direct participation by the organization's constituency or a lack thereof. The combination of these two criteria yields four possible trajectories, depending on whether more emphasis is put on one or the other aspect: institutionalization, involution, commercialization, and radicalization.

Although meant to describe the possible trajectories of social movement organizations, rather than entire movements, this distinction between four main processes is also helpful for studying the development over time of social movements as a whole. More specifically, three chapters address three of these four trajectories or processes, which are particularly relevant for environmental movements: radicalization, institutionalization, and commercialization. Gerry Nagtzaam and Pete Lentini look at radicalization in Chapter 21. This chapter focuses more specifically on the Radical Environmental and Animal Liberation Movement (REALM). It addresses the issue of REALM actors' radicalization, arguing that REALM radicalization shares broad similarities with other radical, extremist, and terrorist radicalization but also that they diverge significantly with respect to the ideological and tactical positions on the use of violence, the emphasis that they place on the value of life, and how social networks reinforce the values of life and non-violence as both irrevocable in theory and in practice.

Håkan Thörn examines in Chapter 22 the apparently contradictory process of institutionalization. The latter is only apparently opposed to radicalization, as both processes may well take place – and often do so – at the same time within a given movement, although not necessarily by the very same movement organizations. The chapter also shows how recent developments associated with globalization, neoliberalism, and ecological modernization have transformed the field of environmental politics profoundly, calling for a re-conceptualization of movement institutionalization and arguing that a key dimension of current climate activism, affecting how institutionalization is shaped today, is a politics of responsibility. Philip Balsiger discusses in Chapter 23 paths towards commercialization, examining the relationship of environmental movements to markets. The chapter argues that the question of the relation of environmentalism to the capitalist market economy divides the movement and that there are historically two branches in the movement: a transformative, radical, anti-capitalist branch and a reformative branch advocating green capitalism. The chapter further examines the position of each branch with regard to commercialization.

Part 4: Microstructural and social psychological dynamics

Research on social movements has paid much attention to the microstructural and social psychological dynamics underlying participation in social movements and protest activities. Referring more specifically to street demonstrations, elsewhere we distinguished between three interrelated layers of explanatory factors for participation in social movements, which apply more generally to participation in social movements and protest activities: mobilizing context, microstructural dynamics, and social psychological dynamics (Giugni and Grasso, 2019). Leaving the mobilizing context aside – we considered this aspect in the previous section – the other two aspects reflect two broad approaches to the study of social movements from a micro-level perspective.

A longstanding tradition in social movement research stresses the importance of the structural dimension of movement participation. This includes a variety of aspects referring to the determinants of participation in environmental movements and the microstructural dynamics of environmental activism. Two such aspects seem particularly relevant here. On the one hand, the first aspect refers to social class and, more generally, to the social bases of environmental movements and activism. Scholarship on social movements has examined the role of social class as an important structural component of movement participation (della Porta, 2015; Eder, 1993, 2013; Kriesi, 1989; see Eidlin and Kerrissey, 2019, for a general discussion). The role of social class has been put at center stage in particular by new social movement theory.

Scholars in this research tradition have stressed the fact that the new issues and movements that arose in the 1970s and 1980s – especially those relating to environmental protection – were the sign of the mobilization of "middle class radicals" (Parkin, 1968). On the other hand, one of the most consistent findings of research on micromobilization is that individual participation in social movements rests on people's previous embeddedness in social networks (Corrigall-Brown, 2013). Discussions of environmental activism must take such "mobilizing structures" into account and study the recruitment process through which people are brought into environmental activism. This means looking into the collective vehicles through which people mobilize and engage in collective action (McAdam et al., 1996) and, above all, the social networks and ties that support and facilitate mobilization (Diani, 2004). These aspects have been stressed in particular by resource mobilization theorists.

Social movement scholars have also paid a great deal of attention to the social psychological factors facilitating or preventing participation (van Stekelenburg and Klandermans, 2013). Accordingly, discussions of environmental movements and activism would not be complete without reference to the psychological dynamics of participation in demonstrations. This includes a variety of aspects such as identity (Hunt and Benford, 2004), ideology (Snow, 2004), emotions (Goodwin et al., 2004; Flam and King, 2005), motivations (Klandermans, 2015), commitment (Erickson Nepstad, 2013), and still others. Of particular importance here is the role of political attitudes and values as predispositions favoring – or preventing – engagement in environmental movements. Research has shown in this regard that committed environmental activists tend to have a strong left-libertarian value orientation. In addition, consideration should also be given to the ways in which specific framing processes may favor participation in social movements. As we mentioned earlier, the ways in which environmental problems are framed – for example, by environmental organizations – is of outmost importance. At the micro level this reflects on smaller or greater changes that one gets involved in environmental movements and activities.

All these microstructural and social psychological dynamics may support people's participation in environmental movements and lead some to become environmental activists, sometimes with strong degrees of commitment. However, as several chapters in this volume attest, environmentalism has changed over time in many respects. One such change is that environmentalism takes on an increasing importance in people's everyday life. Today, environmental concerns do not necessarily lead to voting for a Green Party candidate, becoming a member of an environmental organization, or participating in some kind of protest activity on these issues. They are often expressed in a number of everyday practices – starting from political consumerism to forms of alternative living – that reflect new forms of political opposition to mainstream predominant cultural norms and values (Haenfler et al., 2012). This does not mean that those individuals who act in an "environmentally friendly" manner in their everyday life do not also take part in more "traditional" protest activities, but simply that the terrain for political opposition about the environment has, at least in part, shifted its focus.

Part 4 of the *Handbook* turns to the microstructural and social psychological dynamics underlying environmental activism. The first three chapters in this part look at some of the micro-level characteristics that have been shown to account for participation in social movement activities and therefore are also important for environmental movements. Magnus Wennerhag and Anders Hylmö examine in Chapter 24 the role of social class in engagement in environmental movements. The chapter focuses more specifically on the class composition of environmental movements and environmental movement organizations. It discusses the possible causes and consequences of this composition, including the role of class-related framings and demands in environmental movements. David B. Tindall, Valerie Berseth, Marjolaine Martel-Morin, and Erick Lachapelle look in Chapter 25 at political values and socialization. They show empirically the importance of values for environmental activism by examining variables such as the new ecological paradigm scale, post-materialist values, identification with the environmental movement, and participation in environmental movement activities.

The next two chapters deal with two of the key micro-level processes through which people are driven to participate in social movements and protest activities, including those carried out by environmental movements: recruitment through social networks and framing. Chapter 26, by Clare Saunders, examines the role of social networks and recruitment, with a thematic focus on climate change and a territorial one on the United Kingdom, but looking at different types of environmental action. The chapter focuses on the role of networks in recruiting activists to climate change mobilizations and examines the relative importance of personal networks, indicators of social capital, and organizational memberships as recruitment tools in four types of activism: climate change marches, school strikes, movements using civil disobedience, and pro-environmental behavior. On the other hand, Chapter 27 by Louisa Parks, turns to the role of framing in environmental movements. It distinguishes between studies of how social movements frame environmental issues and more internally oriented processes and studies of how the issue framings of environmental movements match up with others at large in society. The chapter suggests that reading framing processes in broader perspectives might contribute to debates about the role of framing processes for environmental movements – and social movements more generally – and to the continued and crucial debate on inclusion and deliberation in a model of ecological democracy.

Chapter 28, by Chie Togami and Suzanne Staggenborg, looks at the role of gender, an aspect too often neglected by scholars of social movements. The chapter examines the ways in which gender influences the mobilization of environmental movements, showing that gender dynamics are connected to several related processes occurring at different levels – macro, meso, and micro – which affect the mobilization of environmental movements. The role of gender in environmental movement recruitment and participation, ideology and framing, and tactics is analyzed. Next up, Chapter 29, by Francesca Forno and Stefan Wahlen, discusses an increasingly relevant aspect in theories of social movements and political participation: namely, everyday life as an important "locus for change" from which to understand contemporary mobilization and politicization. The chapter focuses on the interplay between everyday life and environmentalism, first by discussing in general terms everyday life and its implication for collective action. Then it examines why, how, and when everyday practices started to be increasingly utilized as a way to address environmental problems. Finally, it looks at the extent to which practices of everyday life can give rise to and support different forms of mobilization on individual as well as collective levels as well as across different scales.

Part 5: Consequences and outcomes

The outcomes and consequences of social movements have long been a neglected aspect of this field of study (Giugni, 1998). This is no longer true; since the late 1990s, research on how collective mobilizations and protest activities may – or may not – bring about social and political change has flourished (Bosi et al., 2016). Such increasing attention paid to this aspect has also benefitted our knowledge of the effect of environmental movements, although much remains to be done in this field. Part V of the *Handbook* tries to fill this gap by looking at different kinds of effects of the movements.

Research on the consequences of social movements is typically divided into three main broad types: political, biographical, and cultural (Giugni, 2008). Broadly speaking, these refer, respectively, to effects of movement activities that alter the political environment, effects on the life course of individuals who have participated in movement activities, and effects on their broader cultural environment. Of these, political consequences are by far the ones that have most often been studied by scholars of social movements. Even more narrowly, the bulk of research in this field has dealt with policy effects: that is, effects on legislation or other policy changes. This is especially true when it comes to the impact of environmental movements, as works on other kinds of effects are very rare in this case. Yet even studies of the policy effects of environmental movements still remain rather sparse, and most focus on anti-nuclear energy (see cross-national comparative analyses by Flam, 1994; Kolb, 2007; Midttun and Rucht, 1994, among others). This is perhaps because these effects are more tangible and easy to measure – for example, through a decrease in the number of nuclear power plants built or the percentage of electricity produced through nuclear energy in a given nation – rather than on environmental movements in their broader meaning (Rucht, 1999) or by comparing both anti-nuclear energy and ecology movements (Giugni, 2004).

The chapters in Part 5 of the *Handbook* all deal with the consequences and outcomes of environmental movements and activism. While they obviously cannot cover the full range of potential consequences, taken together, they address all three types of outcomes most often considered in the social movement literature. Chapter 30, by Erik W. Johnson and Jon Agnone, deals with policy and legislative outcomes. This chapter applies Gamson's (1990) classical distinction between acceptance and new advantages, firstly, to discuss how environmental movements effect policy and legislative outcomes and secondly, to illustrate this through the case of climate change policy in the US. Yet, though crucial, influencing policy is not the only way through which social movement may have an impact. Also important is the extent to which they are able to influence public opinion (Burstein, 2014). This aspect is addressed by Joanna K. Huxster in Chapter 31, which explores the relationship between environmental movements, public opinion, and environmental attitudes from an interdisciplinary perspective. Although few empirical studies exist on the environmental movement's direct influence on public opinion, the chapter hypothesizes that this relationship might work by outlining the potential avenues and barriers to shifting environmental attitudes that relate to the actions of the movements.

Chapter 32, by David J. Hess, shifts the focus from political to cultural outcomes. This is a very broad category, including a wide variety of different kinds of potential effects not always easy to identify and delimit (Earl, 2004). This chapter examines the role of environmental movements in scientific, technological, and industrial change, all particularly relevant areas for movements mobilizing around environmental concerns. The chapter argues that attention to the material and epistemic dimensions of environmental movements is central to understanding the problem of outcomes, and it adopts a "sociotechnical perspective" on these dimensions. This approach includes the construction of new analytical categories and questions, such as the comparative analysis of industrial transition movements, the politics of design, and undone science.

The final chapter in this part of the *Handbook*, Chapter 33 by Sara Vestergren and John Drury, looks at biographical consequences of environmental activism. In a way, these can also be seen as a particular type of cultural outcome, as they often consist in changing or keeping alive certain attitudes and values of participants in social movement activities. However, unlike the previous type, which take place at the macrostructural level, here we are dealing with the micro, individual level. The chapter examines the range of biographical changes, such as changes in consumption behaviors and increased well-being, that may emerge as a result of environmental activism and activism in general. It shows that participation in environmental activism can have a profound effect on the lives of those participating, suggesting that perceived supportive interactions and relationships with other environmental activists are important for such biographical consequences to endure over time.

Part 6: Environmental movements in the twenty-first century

Environmental movements and activism have evolved greatly over time, transforming themselves in several ways. From the early days of the nineteenth century, when the focus was on nature conservation and preservation, moving into the politicization of ecology in the 1960s and 1970s to more recent strands including environmentalism and lifestyle politics, environmental justice and green democracy, the range of actors and organizations involved, and the tactics and strategies adopted, as well as the issues addressed, have broadened considerably. The movements have also shifted their scale from the local to the national and finally to the worldwide scale, leading to what some have called "global ecology" (Finger, 1992; Lipschutz and Conca, 1993; McCormick, 1989). However, on the other hand, the formula "think globally, act locally" (Rucht, 1993) – which remains an important mantra for environmental activists – seems to suggest that while environmental problems are inherently global, responses to them are perhaps best implemented at the local level.

The last part of the *Handbook*, Part 6, looks at some recent trends and how they will influence environmental activism in the future. Among the more recent developments in the features of environmental movements and activism is no doubt the increasing presence and involvement of the youngest generation. Started in the summer of 2018 as an individual "school strike" enacted by the now-world-famous, then-15-year-old Swedish schoolgirl Great Thunberg, a unprecedented wave of strikes and mass demonstrations – known as "Fridays for Future", as they were mostly held on that day of the week, at least initially. Since then, they have spread worldwide and taken place at the global level involving millions of young people around the world protesting against climate change and pushing the political authorities – the "adults" – to act with great urgency to bring effective solutions (see de Moor et al., 2020; Wahlström et al., 2019 for comparative analyses of some of the demonstrations). To be sure, these protests are not only attended by pupils and students. However, the latter are seen as their initiators and play a key role in the movements, and this has been reflected by the particularly high numbers of very young people in protests, at least in some countries.

In this respect, Chapter 34, by Sarah Pickard, Benjamin Bowman, and Dena Arya, discusses the specificities of young people's involvement in environmental movements in the twenty-first century. More specifically, it addresses why and how there has been a growth in youth-led environmental activism and young people's involvement in the current environmental movements – including in the more radical branch using civil disobedience of the UK Extinction Rebellion – as well as outcomes and the likely future of their environmental activism. They argue that, while young people form a specific generational unit and some are using what they call "Do-It-Ourselves" (DIO) politics in their environmental activism, they are not a homogeneous group. The future of their environmental activism will depend partly on political and policing reactions.

Partly related to the strong involvement of the youngest in the movements, another key feature of environmental movements and activism is the increasingly important role played by the net and online forms of activism. This holds for social movements more generally, leading some to speak of a "logic of connective action" – a clever allusion to and transformation of the title of Olson's (1965) seminal *Logic of Collective Action* – meaning that the rise of a personalized digitally networked politics in which diverse individuals address common problems that, for some can be seen as replacing or supplementing a more traditional network environment made of direct contacts and ties (Bennett and Segerberg, 2013). Chapter 35, by Anastasia Kavada and Doug Specht, examines the role of digital media in environmental activism by focusing on processes of organization and the rapid formation of collectives. Their chapter shows, while also pointing to the limitations of these tools, how activists and environmental movements have utilized social media, digital maps, memes, and other kinds of visual communication and leveraged the affordances of these tools in the fight for the environment.

Just like social movements in general do not simply perform the function of opposing or promoting certain issues or changes – be they political, social, cultural – so to do environmental movements more specifically also raise broader issues linked to the meaning of democracy and its future as well as the ideal organization of society. Amanda Machin examines in Chapter 36 a recurring feature of green movements: their emphasis on democracy. The chapter, however, stresses that there is no necessary connection between democratic means and environmental ends. It delineates a green democratic imaginary that enables and shapes discussions of democracy between greens characterized by six dimensions: decentralization, inclusion, passion, participation, protest, and rupture – in turn highlighting the connections and contradictions of these dimensions and their appearance in relation to various green movements.

Relatedly, Chapter 37 by Elia Apostolopoulou examines the emergence of various social-environmental movements mobilizing against the increasing neoliberalization of nature, space, and the commons and opposing environmental, social, and spatial injustices and the undemocratic character of socio-spatial and social-environmental change often putting up barriers against the relentless capitalist exploitation of public spaces and socio-natures within and beyond cities. Finally, Chapter 38 by Carl Cassegård, the last chapter in this part and final chapter of the entire *Handbook*, offers an enticing outlook toward the future of environmental movements.

References

Alkon, Alison Hope, and Julie Guthman. 2017. *The New Food Activism Opposition, Cooperation, and Collective Action.* Berkeley: University of California Press.

Benford, Robert D., and David A. Snow. 2000. "Framing Processes and Social Movements: An Overview and Assessment." *Annual Review of Sociology* 26: 611–640.

Bennett, Lance W., and Alexandra Segerberg. 2013. *The Logic of Connective Action: Digital Media and the Personalization of Contentious Politics.* Cambridge: Cambridge University Press.

Bosi, Lorenzo, Marco Giugni, and Katrin Uba. 2016. "The Consequences of Social Movements: Taking Stock and Looking Forward." Pp. 3–37 in Lorenzo Bosi, Marco Giugni, and Katrin Uba (eds.), *The Consequences of Social Movements.* Cambridge: Cambridge University Press.

Burstein, Paul. 2014. *American Public Opinion, Advocacy, and Policy in Congress: What the Public Wants and What It Gets.* Cambridge: Cambridge University Press.

Corrigall-Brown, Catherine. 2013. "Participation in Social Movements." Pp. 900–905 in David A. Snow, Donatella della Porta, Bert Klandermans, and Doug McAdam (eds.), *The Wiley-Blackwell Encyclopedia of Social and Political Movements.* Oxford: Blackwell.

Crossley, Nick, and Mario Diani. 2019. "Networks and Fields." Pp. 151–166 in David A. Snow, Sarah A. Soule, Hanspeter Kriesi, and Holly J. McCammon (eds.), *The Wiley Blackwell Companion to Social Movements.* Second edition. Oxford: Wiley Blackwell.

della Porta. 2015. *Social Movements in Times of Austerity: Bringing Capitalism Back Into Protest Analysis.* Cambridge: Polity Press.

de Moor, Joost. 2017. "Lifestyle Politics and the Concept of Political Participation." *Acta Politica* 52: 179–197.

de Moor, Joost, Katrin Uba, Mattias Wahlstrom, Magnus Wennerhag, and Michiel De Vydt (eds.). 2020. *Protest for a Future II: Composition, Mobilization and Motives of the Participants in Fridays For Future Climate Protests on 20–27 September, 2019, in 19 cities around the world.* Retrieved from: https://osf.io/asruw/

Diani, Mario. 1992. "The Concept of Social Movement." *Sociological Review* 40: 1–25.

Diani, Mario. 2004. "Networks and Participation." Pp. 339–359 in David A. Snow, Sarah A. Soule, and Hanspeter Kriesi (eds.), *The Blackwell Companion to Social Movements.* Oxford: Blackwell.

Earl, Jennifer. 2004. "The Cultural Consequences of Social Movements." Pp. 508–530 in David A. Snow, Sarah A. Soule, and Hanspeter Kriesi (eds.), *The Blackwell Companion to Social Movements.* Oxford: Blackwell.

Eder, Klaus. 1993. *The New Politics of Class: Social Movements and Cultural Dynamics in Advanced Societies.* London: Sage.

Eder, Klaus. 2013. "Social Class and Social Movements." Pp. 1179–1182 in David A. Snow, Donatella della Porta, Bert Klandermans, and Doug McAdam (eds.), *The Wiley-Blackwell Encyclopedia of Social and Political Movements*. Oxford: Blackwell.

Eidlin, Barry, and Jasmine Kerrissey. 2019. "Social Class and Social Movements." Pp. 517–536 in David A. Snow, Sarah A. Soule, Hanspeter Kriesi, and Holly McCammon (eds.), *The Wiley-Blackwell Companion to Social Movements*. Second edition. Oxford: Wiley Blackwell.

Erickson Nepstad, Sharon. 2013. "Commitment." Pp. 229–230 in David A. Snow, Donatella della Porta, Bert Klandermans, and Doug McAdam (eds.), *The Wiley-Blackwell Encyclopedia of Social and Political Movements*. Oxford: Blackwell.

Finger, Matthias (ed.). 1992. *The Green Movement Worldwide*. Greenwich, CT: JAI Press.

Flam, Helena (ed.). 1994. *States and Anti-Nuclear Movements*. Edinburgh. Edinburgh University Press

Flam, Helena, and Debra King (eds.). 2005. *Emotions and Social Movements*. London. Routledge

Gamson, William A. 1990. *The Strategy of Social Protest*. Second edition. Belmont, CA: Wadsworth.

Giugni, Marco. 1998. "Was if Worth the Effort? The Outcomes and Consequences of Social Movements." *Annual Review of Sociology* 24: 371–393.

Giugni, Marco. 2004. *Social Protest and Policy Change: Ecology, Antinuclear, and Peace Movements in Comparative Perspective*. Lanham, MD: Rowman and Littlefield.

Giugni, Marco. 2008. "Political, Biographical, and Cultural Consequences of Social Movements." *Sociology Compass* 2: 1582–1600.

Giugni, Marco, and Maria T. Grasso. 2015. "Environmental Movements in Advanced Industrial Democracies: Heterogeneity, Transformation, and Institutionalization." *Annual Review of Environment and Resources* 40: 337–361.

Giugni, Marco, and Maria T. Grasso. 2019. *Street Citizens: Protest Politics and Social Movement Activism in the Age of Globalization*. Cambridge: Cambridge University Press.

Goodwin, Jeff, James M. Jasper, and Francesca Polletta. 2004. "Emotional Dimensions of Social Movements." Pp. 413–432 in David A. Snow, Sarah A. Soule, and Hanspeter Kriesi (eds.), *The Blackwell Companion to Social Movements*. Oxford: Blackwell.

Haenfler, Ross, Brett Johnson, and Ellis Jones. 2012. "Lifestyle Movements: Exploring the Intersection of Lifestyle and Social Movements." *Social Movement Studies* 11: 1–21.

Hunt, Scott A., and Robert D. Benford. 2004 "Collective Identity, Solidarity, and Commitment." Pp. 433–458 in David A. Snow, Sarah A. Soule, and Hanspeter Kriesi (eds.), *The Blackwell Companion to Social Movements*. Oxford: Blackwell.

Inglehart, Ronald. 1977. *The Silent Revolution: Changing Values and Political Styles Among Western Publics*. Princeton, NJ: Princeton University Press.

Jasper, James M., and Francesca Polletta. 2019. "The Cultural Context of Social Movements." Pp. 63–78 in David A. Snow, Sarah A. Soule, Hanspeter Kriesi, and Holly J. McCammon (eds.), *The Wiley Blackwell Companion to Social Movements*. Second edition. Oxford: Wiley Blackwell.

Klandermans, Bert. 1997. *The Social Psychology of Protest*. Oxford: Blackwell.

Klandermans, Bert. 2015. "Motivations to Action." Pp. 219–230 in Donatella della Porta and Mario Diani (eds.), *The Oxford Handbook of Social Movements*. Oxford: Oxford University Press.

Kolb Felix. 2007. *Protest and Opportunities: The Political Outcomes of Social Movements*. Frankfurt: Campus Verlag.

Kriesi, Hanspeter. 1989. "New Social Movements and the New Class in the Netherlands." *American Journal of Sociology* 94: 1078–1116.

Kriesi, Hanspeter. 1996. "The Organizational Structure of New Social Movements in a Political Context." Pp. 152–184 in Doug McAdam, John D. McCarthy, and Mayer N. Zald (eds.), *Comparative Perspectives on Social Movements: Political Opportunities, Mobilizing Structures, and Cultural Framings*. Cambridge: Cambridge University Press

Kriesi, Hanspeter. 2004. "Political Context and Opportunity." Pp. 67–90 in David A. Snow, Sarah A. Soule, and Hanspeter Kriesi (eds.), *The Blackwell Companion to Social Movements*. Oxford: Blackwell.

Kriesi, Hanspeter, Ruud Koopmans, Jan Willem Duyvendak, and Marco Giugni. 1995. *New Social Movements in Western Europe*. Minneapolis: University of Minnesota Press.

Lipschutz, Ronnie D., and Ken Conca (eds.). 1993. *The State and Social Power in Global Environmental Politics*. New York: Columbia University Press.

McAdam, Doug. 1996. "Conceptual Origins, Current Problems, Future Directions." Pp. 23–40 in Doug McAdam, John D. McCarthy, and Mayer N. Zald (eds.), *Comparative Perspectives on Social Movements:*

Political Opportunities, Mobilizing Structures, and Cultural Framings. Cambridge: Cambridge University Press.

McAdam, Doug, and Sidney Tarrow. 2019. "The Political Context of Social Movements." Pp. 17–42 in David A. Snow, Sarah A. Soule, Hanspeter Kriesi, and Holly J. McCammon (eds.), *The Wiley Blackwell Companion to Social Movements.* Second edition. Oxford: Wiley Blackwell.

McCormick, John. 1989. *Reclaiming Paradise: The Global Environmental Movement.* Bloomington: Indiana University Press.

Midttun, Atle, and Dieter Rucht. 1994. "Comparing Policy Outcomes of Conflicts Over Nuclear Power: Description and Explanation." Pp. 383–415 in Helena Flam (ed.), *States and Anti-Nuclear Movements.* Edinburgh: Edinburgh University Press.

Olson, Mancur. 1965. *The Logic of Collective Action.* Cambridge, MA: Harvard University Press.

Parkin, Frank. 1968. *Middle Class Radicalism: The Social Bases of the British Campaign for Nuclear Disarmament.* Manchester: Manchester University Press.

Rootes, Chris. 2003. *Environmental Protest in Western Europe.* Oxford: Oxford University. Press.

Rootes, Chris. 2004. "Environmental Movements." Pp. 600–640 in David A. Snow, Sarah A. Soule, and Hanspeter Kriesi (eds.), *The Blackwell Companion to Social Movements.* Oxford: Blackwell.

Rucht, Dieter. 1993. "'Think Globally, Act Locally'? Needs, Forms and Problems of Environmental Groups' Internationalization." Pp. 75–95 in D. Liefferink, P. Lowe, and A. P. J. Mol (eds.), *European Integration and Environmental Policy.* London: Belhaven.

Rucht Dieter. 1999. "The Impact of Environmental Movements in Western Societies." Pp. 204–224 in Marco Giugni, Doug McAdam, and Charles Tilly (eds.), *How Social Movements Matter.* Minneapolis: University of Minnesota Press.

Snow, David A. 2004. "Framing Processes, Ideology, and Discursive Fields." Pp. 380–412 in David A. Snow, Sarah Soule, and Hanspeter Kriesi (eds.), *The Blackwell Companion to Social Movements.* Oxford: Blackwell.

Snow, David A., Rens Vliegenthart, and Pauline Ketelaars. 2019. "The Framing Perspective on Social Movements: Its Conceptual Roots and Architecture." Pp. 392–410 in David A. Snow, Sarah A. Soule, Hanspeter Kriesi, and Holly J. McCammon (eds.), *The Wiley Blackwell Companion to Social Movements.* Second edition. Oxford: Wiley Blackwell.

van Stekelenburg, Jacquelien, and Bert Klandermans. 2013. "The Social Psychology of Protest." *Current Sociology* 61: 886–905.

Wahlström, Mattias, Piotr Kocyba, Michiel De Vydt, and Joost de Moor (eds.). 2019. *Protest for a Future: Composition, Mobilization and Motives of the Participants in Fridays For Future Climate Protests on 15 March, 2019 in 13 European Cities.* Retrieved from: https://osf.io/asruw/

Walker, Edward T., and Andrew W. Martin. 2019. "Social Movement Organizations." Pp. 167–184 in David A. Snow, Sarah A. Soule, Hanspeter Kriesi, and Holly J. McCammon (eds.), *The Wiley Blackwell Companion to Social Movements.* Second edition. Oxford: Wiley Blackwell.

PART 1

Environmental movements around the world

2

ENVIRONMENTAL MOVEMENTS IN WESTERN EUROPE

From globalization and institutionalization to a new model of radicalization in the twenty-first century?

Sylvie Ollitrault

Western Europe has witnessed the emergence of environmental awareness and played an important role in the global structuring of environmental protest (Dalton, 1994). While the United States and North America carried representations of nature bound to their history, inventing the idea of wilderness and forms of conservation of the environment (Eder, 1996), Western Europe has under the effects of its own history colonialism, industrial revolution, rural exodus, urbanization and demographic densification of its cities, carried claims, and interests for the environment that marked the history of world ecology (Ollitrault, 2008).

Is it to say that the invention of the environment in the industrial era has had the effect of homogenizing the question of its protection in Western Europe? The reality is more complex, especially because this part of the continent begins at the level of the North Pole and ends at the gates of Africa: the populations are not more or less constrained by the environment, but their relationship with nature and agricultural production is subject to differences in climate, agricultural production, and the effects of industrialization. Following Stein Rokkan's seminal typology (1971), political interests are subject to social and economic conditions, but we will add, in the case of ecological movements, the cultural effects of the relationship to the environment via religion (Catholicism, Protestantism) and the question of economic differences between nature as a source of production and nature as an element of well-being. This chapter does not aim to exhaustively identify all the factors distinguishing the differences in the implantation of the ecological movements in the political landscape or to detail each national situation, but rather the ambition is to present the broader contemporary tendencies as regards claims related to the ecological movement and to the questioning of its place within globalization.

The aim of this chapter is to describe the history of the environmental movement in Western Europe, including the impact of colonization and of the globalization of environmental conservation. The actors are varied, from local groups to global scientific networks (Dalton, 1994); environmental themes are tied to the mindsets and values of each context. Western Europe is vast, and differences exist from Sweden to Greece. After the Second World War, the expansion

 DOI: 10.4324/9780367855680-3

of international institutions (UN) and the European Union supported the birth of green politics. It should not be forgotten that the main leaders of environmental thought were European (British, German, or Swedish) and that the major networks (IUCN-WWF) were based in Switzerland, with UNESCO in Paris. The major NGO groups were first located in London or Paris, whereas Germany had its own Green Party by the end of the 1970s (Rucht and Roose, 2003; Roose, 2014).

History of the structuring of the environmental movement in Western Europe

In this history section, we are going to present two aspects of this structuring: namely, in a first step, the awareness via the first organizations for the protection of nature and the first sensitivities with respect to the question of the conservation of the environment or those of animal well-being. In a second step, following Russell Dalton's typology (1994), we will examine the first interconnection of common interests by networks allowing to put the question of nature *largo sensu* on the national and international agendas. It is necessary in particular to insist on the importance of the investment of scholars, the first naturalists and, in parallel, the first mobilizations related to industrial pollution, which changed the relationship with the environment.

The question of nature in Europe is linked to the intellectual history that had a globalized effect on the perceptions outside of man. Thus, Descartes, by reifying nature, also allowed the setting aside of its singularity and gave man (human beings) authority and prerogatives over the whole of this universe. The environment was conceived of as being at the service of man. This utilitarian perception of nature had consequences, including on economic perceptions. Thus, an Englishman, Malthus, worried about the effects of overpopulation on resources because his population lived on an island. When the Puritan migrants left on the Mayflower, the representation was that of the Bible and the search for a lost paradise. This conception was at the heart of the ways of thinking about the conservation of nature as God's work. Thus, in the seventeenth and eighteenth centuries, a way of thinking emerged that still has an important value today: of the environment (with its non-human beings) at the service of the human being either as a material resource (survival) or as an immaterial resource (divine work, well-being, artistic inspiration). Today, this grammar of representation remains present in international negotiations. Either the environment is perceived as a stock, a resource (management of fisheries, biodiversity, or even the climate) essential to human life or survival, or it is recognized for its own characteristics, in this case for aesthetic or heritage reasons, referring to an idea of artistic or religious beauty (e.g., UNESCO World Heritage).

Another dynamic appeared at the end of the eighteenth century and throughout the twentieth century, in particular in Great Britain, the German states, and France: the idea of a redeeming nature, even allowing the re-education of beings perverted by the new civilization (i.e., the industrial era) leading to the collapse of certain family, rural, and local values. Many movements of utopian socialism suggested a return to nature in the way of Jean Jacques Rousseau, including ways to create more egalitarian societies, putting the human being in the center of his own interests and not in the service of a new capitalist system dominating them socially and economically. In this dynamic, a movement called Romantic or pre-Raphaelite in Great Britain exalted nature as a space for resourcefulness. Moreover, industrial societies started to count their populations and to think about them in terms of birth rates and longevity, and in turn, this led to a reflection on public health. Often doctors associated with sociologists or even philanthropists developed hygienic concerns. The idea of large urban parks, as in London, was a direct result of this thinking, which wanted the poor working classes to get some fresh air, to play sports, and to avoid alcoholism and even moral decadence. The National Trust in Great Britain, which promoted the protection of built and unbuilt heritage, represents this dynamic, in contrast to the utopian socialists, of a "paternalistic" protection of the environment in the sense of nature being good for human beings and their well-being without questioning the capitalist system. It was a question, as Michel Foucault analyzes, of protecting the bodies to better increase the productivity of the workers. However, from this dynamic was born the idea of leisure, good for the rest and the well-being of the worker, with the idea of the observation of nature, of sport, and of the activities allowing the population to move away from practices unworthy from a moral point of view and bad for the public health (alcoholism, violence, sexuality outside marriage). From this period, we can note how the movement for the protection and organization of natural spaces in our European cities comes directly from this sensitivity to reorganize the urban space for the purpose of policies of protection of the moral and physical health of the populations.

At the same time, revolts or protests can arise among the population, often rural or related to agriculture or fishing, on the occasion of industrial pollution. Let us mention the one that took place in the middle of the nineteenth century in Prussia, which led Bismarck to mobilize a scientist, Karl Möbius, following the sudden disappearance of oysters from the shore of the Baltic (Ollitrault, 2008). In this context, the first ecological study in the contemporary sense was conducted: that is to say, the scientist managed to demonstrate that the disappearance of the oysters was linked to the modification of the aquatic environment due to industrial pollution: i.e., the discharge of chemicals into the water. This study allowed for the visibility of antagonistic interests regarding the use of the environment, and the state began to carry out studies and to reflect on the beginnings of public policies in the sense of carrying out a reflection on the uses. In France and Great Britain, the protests were more often rural, but peasant protests could target the new factories, rejecting fumes or effluents or poisons in the waters (e.g., leading to poisoned cattle or sickness in the population). This proto-history, often referred to as peasant or worker revolts, must be related to contemporary environmental questionings. For it seems obvious that the cause of the protests was environmental before being social or economic: e.g., wages. The very first legislations framing the implantations of factories were born at the beginning of the nineteenth century, a little everywhere in the European states to regulate the effects on nature and people of these new processes. Here again, nature was protected as a resource, and the struggles were more for reasons of use than for intrinsic protection of the environment.

A last dynamic common to the Western states – in particular, France, Great Britain, and Germany but also the whole of this part of the world – was the creation of natural history museums. Two aspects in particular are relevant with respect to this phenomenon: the institutionalization of the natural sciences, which became sciences of the observation of nature and of the development of knowledge of living beings receiving strong state support, and the organization of the zoos to represent the diversity of living beings with the importation of species from other continents. Science historians agree that this institutionalization is closely linked to colonization, to the circulation of knowledge among Europeans (the first congresses appeared) and to a growing sense of injustice among its scholars, who saw species and nature disappear due to hunting or human depredations, often of colonial origin. The real paradox is that the feeling of the limits of colonization and even of the misdeeds came from the agents of colonization since the scientists participated in the movement and traveled, and even Darwin, a great traveler, built his theory without escaping the European mentality of the time, which claimed to know and understand the world. This was at the same time a product of the Enlightenment, with the implementation of learned tools for understanding the world (taxonomy, various classifications, the counting of living things) and a form of discovery of otherness that put Europe back into the world, leading to important questioning of the effects of civilization on spaces (falsely) represented as virgin, wild.

In this context, the first associations for the conservation of nature were born in the middle of the nineteenth century, and, as Dalton rightly points out, the first wave of mobilization in favor of nature for itself because of its singular value appeared. This wave allowed the promotion of the idea of the national park, first born in the United States and, in the same period, notably also in South Africa, Congo, Kenya, and France, concerning the protection of birds (Sept Iles, in Brittany). More and more, the question of animal stocks, in particular wild animals (whales, etc.), was going to be regulated as much because of the international character of said resource and the rivalries between fishermen from different states as it was by those associations starting to carry out awareness campaigns or even lobbying. In particular, in Great Britain, the mobilization for the protection of birds was very strong, to the point of going to Parliament. At the same time, associations protesting against cruelty to domestic animals were born in Europe and demanded legislation punishing actions of this sort. In Germany, Great Britain, and even in Scandinavia, a movement promoting vegetarianism and even a return to organic farming that refused to use pesticides was beginning to take hold. This dynamic can be linked to puritanical body hexes or to a cult of the healthy body. It should be noted that at that time, these sensitivities and even these associative movements were stronger in Northern Europe than in Southern Europe, which was more preoccupied with poverty and backwardness in terms of industrialization and, more generally, solving social problems by migrating (Italy, Spain, Portugal) to North and South America, while other European states (particularly England, Ireland, Scandinavia, and Germany) were less supportive of exporting their population to the Americas at the beginning of the twentieth century.

During this period, environmentalist consciousness was born without creating real protests, as would be the case with the protests of workers, who were fighting against the effects of the new methods of work organization generated by capitalism. If mobilizations are organized in the countryside, they focus on questions of defending their work, as in Ireland or Great Britain, where the poorest people were evicted from the countryside. On the other hand, the middle classes, including those with altruistic, humanistic messages, were beginning to develop a sensitivity and a reflection that was conducive to promoting the importance of protecting nature because of the resources or benefits it provides, or even because of its aestheticism.

We are no longer in the era of proto-mobilization: i.e., the creation of a feeling of injustice toward nature and the questioning of the excesses of an industrial society that forgets the preservation of human and non-human beings or their quality of life. The movement of the Romantics, utopian socialism, and even the sometimes religious branches of Puritanism created this soil which was to give rise to the first movements for the protection of nature and its political expression through lobbying in its favor.

The birth of the second wave of environmentalist protest

Between 1900 and 1945, the structuring of European and North American networks began to slowly become institutionalized thanks to the network of naturalists. While the structuring accelerated before the First World War, the interwar period marked a time of loss of momentum at the beginning of the century. Indeed, the scholars had aged, and the generational relay was not established in a very clearly tense context. The League of Nations (LON) could not be the relay of this transnational institutionalization. However, this proto-history of transnational organization in favor of nature conservation was accompanied by an acceleration in the number of international treaties dealing with nature conservation issues. Little by little, more and more national parks were created, notably in Sweden, the first in Europe (Dalton, 1994) in 1909.

It was the period after the Second World War that constituted the period of institutionalization of the environmental NGOs (Giugni and Grasso (2015) under the effect of the structuring of the International Union of Conservation of Nature (IUCN) born in 1949 with Switzerland as the seat. From this period, the issue of environmental conservation was on the agenda of states via international networks and the rise in power of the supranational structuring of intergovernmental organizations such as UNESCO and even FAO or the WHO. These structures are going to be important supports for the "environmental" cause (Doherty and Doyle, 2008, 2013) by articulating themselves as in service of either conservation or the fight against hunger or health issues.

The mobilization of public opinion was crucial, and it was in its wake that the WWF was born. The importance of this NGO, still central from a global point of view, was that it was as much a part of environmental management (an actor in conservation policy at the global level) as at the European level. Of European origin (Swiss-British in particular), it had spun off local groups in each European state and participated in the creation of a globalized conservation narrative while managing numerous private and public funds in order to deploy conservation actions. In the spectrum of large NGOs known worldwide, it has been the pivot of many international negotiations both at the UN and European (European Union) levels. It has supported many conservation policies, whether it be the application of the European Natura 2000 directive or the management of parks in Africa or Asia. The fact that this NGO is located in Switzerland also marks the fact that the international organization has a strong presence in Europe and generates a form of international militancy in the main European states. In this way, it joined the large North American NGOs such as the Sierra Club in the international arena.

The real breakthrough came at the end of the 1960s, with the politicization of nature conservation and a change in the scale of protection, from sectoral to global. In order to understand what happened in Europe, particularly on the side of the institutionalization of NGOs, the multiplication of green social movements, and the appearance of political parties, it is essential to understand the changeover that took place in the baby-boomer years. The mobilizations were resolutely political in Europe: against colonial wars, against capitalism, against fascism (present in Portugal, Spain, and Greece) in the context of a Europe cut in two by the Cold War. The question of environmental protection intersected with that of pacifist and anti-nuclear mobilizations. It was this melting pot that crossed Europe and gathered activists who were as much contesting the developments destroying the environment, the local life of rural territories, and exceptional landscapes as the rise of a growing militarization of society or the use of nuclear energy with long-term effects on human life and nature.

From this time of large gatherings, the logo of the ecologists with the sunflower and the slogans emerged, socializing the first political staff investing itself either in the ecologist associations or in the political parties. The influence of North American activism was also felt through the establishment of local groups of two NGOs: Friends of the Earth and Greenpeace. Friends of the Earth, from the opening of its first branches in London and Paris, played a role in supporting new ways of campaigning for the protection of planet earth by attracting a new generation of young activists (Ollitrault, 2008; Doherty and Doyle, 2013), who were ready to use the media, non-violent direct action, and protests that aimed to emphasize feelings of moral outrage (Berny, 2009). Their means appeared new, and in the landscape of European environmentalist associations, the use of the media, of counter-expertise, changed the registers of action and gave a transnational tone to the whole repertoire of environmentalists. More and more, local groups in many medium-size cities were emerging, and at the local level, they led environmentalist struggles with the same logo and way of managing their image. In Germany, the number of associations was increasing, and they linked to an alternative and countercultural left, which was experimenting with new ways of living, including anti-patriarchal and feminist values.

The networking of all these actors was remarkable because activists circulated, trained, and acculturated themselves at the time of the mobilizations. It was not uncommon at anti-nuclear rallies to see activists from other states coming to reinforce the ranks. The circulation of ideas on environmental protection intensified through alternative media, newspapers, and book translations. "Ecology" became a generic term, as did the term "green movement" (Rootes, 2013b) to gather the forces that still expressed themselves in the majority of the states in associative form.

If the ecologists thought that they could influence the issues and debates by presenting candidates in elections, the electoral systems were rarely in their favor, especially in France and Great Britain. German ecology succeeded in entering the scene at the end of the 1970s while being divided between the fundis and the realos as to the degree of openness to alliances and negotiation with other states. The anti-nuclear position in a state strongly marked by the Cold War (Berlin Wall) or even pacifism in addition to a position of environmental protection strongly marked the left of the political formation. However, in many European states, ecology was not necessarily positioned on the left, and it could also be perceived as neither left nor right. This debate was present in the majority of the ecologist formations, even if the political militants came very clearly from the associative world (environmental protection, anti-nuclear, feminist), often countercultural and emerging from the educated middle classes, which the sociologists classify as among the supporters of post materialism and post industrialism.

After the fall of the Berlin Wall, under the pressure of the multiplicity of mobilizations in favor of environmental protection, Green parties became actors in many European countries, with sometimes contrasting but real implementations and with the important role of the European Parliament, which gathered the forces of the Green parties and allowed thanks to its mode of vote, to elect Green members of parliament, who become important spokespersons for ecology. Once again, political ecology can have influence, thanks to a European and international structuring beyond the national contexts, whereas each state has its specificities, which are not always necessarily favorable to a strong partisan implantation of the Greens (Ollitrault, 2014).

It can be observed that states such as Germany saw the establishment of Green parties much earlier than other states such as Great Britain. Although both countries are Protestant and have had an ecological or environmentalist consciousness since the middle of the nineteenth century, it is remarkable that the structures of political opportunities diverge. Britain remains a highly centralized state with an electoral system that is not very favorable to new parties and even less so to minority parties. The two-party system has been a brake on the emergence of Green politics, as it has in France. The French Greens were more successful in local elections and those with proportional representation. In Germany, the federal system has allowed the emergence of the Green party.

So if we have to admit that there is a Europe of the North and South with cultural differences, attitudes toward nature that depend strongly on their level of industrialization and even on the rural exodus, this has transformed the way people look at their environment, which is less about survival or a resource and more about conservation for its intrinsic qualities or an awareness of the effects of pollution on health. However, there are also obstacles linked to the institutional system, the party structures, and the possibility or otherwise of building alliances. In France, on the other hand, since the creation of the Greens, the party has had to create alliance strategies, particularly with the Socialist Party, which has sometimes limited its own demands.

The European Parliament can offer a space of autonomy in particular to the Green parties, which, in their national space, are either in the minority or caught in the stranglehold of alliances.

NGOs' influence on the global issues

Since the first international conference of Stockholm on the environment in 1972, under the aegis of the United Nations, interest in the environment has risen on the international agendas and through a top-down effect that has supported the institutionalization of its protection at the national level: new ministries, the creation of dedicated administration, and the impulse of novel legislation. The associations, often hyper-sectorialized or still spread over the national territories in a relatively anarchic way, are organizing themselves with national and international networks. Exchanges between these structures are becoming more formalized, and the largest NGOs, the older WWFs or the newer, more demanding and politicized ones, are orchestrating awareness and protest campaigns. The phenomenon is relatively homogeneous throughout Western Europe, which moreover relays international campaigns, sometimes coming from the United Nations or from their American colleagues, clearly more powerful in terms of budget and media initiative. It was also at this time that Greenpeace began its first expeditions against nuclear testing, whaling, and the slaughter of baby seals.

At the same time, the European community, the future European Union, created the European Environment Agency and supported environmental policies by relying on the learned expertise of NGOs (Berny, 2013a). For, in order to understand the dynamics of the institutionalization of environmental NGOs in Western Europe, it is important to emphasize that their repertoire of actions reflects the skills of activists who come from the scientific world or from amateurs of nature protection particularly invested in its intimate knowledge. We find the features of an epistemic community, which, in the context of putting an interest on the agenda, relies as much on symbolic capital (scholars sometimes recognized internationally), social capital (circulation in elite circles, allowing the sensitization of decision-makers), and strong cultural capital (scientists). Additionally, much depends on the scale of mobilization; at the local level, the social profiles will be less elitist but very well anchored in the social networks (associations, intellectual elite, access to the resources of the decisions of the local governance).

The scholarly expertise and their capacity to organize knowledge that legitimizes decisions in the face of other industrial and technical interest groups means that NGOs and local associations, almost everywhere in Europe, became institutionalized over the decade from 1970 to 1980 by investing in spaces for consultation and participatory democracy and even, as in France, by strongly demanding it.

During the 1970s and 1980s, the birth of the green movement was part of the institutional routines for organizing a public policy sector that was independent of health, agriculture, or technical sectors such as construction and industry. In this context, the environment became a transversal sector in the different scales of public policies, which did not occur without disturbing the sectoral policies. It should also be remembered that most environmental standards are European in origin, often created thanks to the activism of NGOs and the work of the Greens in the European Parliament, and are then integrated into national legislation with varying degrees of speed. Then, when the majority of the states of the Mediterranean coast (Portugal, Spain, Greece) joined the European community, that had the effect of integrating them not only into a model of democratic transition but also into the concert of the new standards of governance of public policies of which the environment is a part. In this framework, the associations, including weak or more recent ones with respect to environmental protection, gradually felt supported by Europe and became able to legitimize themselves.

After the fall of the Berlin Wall, the European Union reinforced its institutionalization with the Maastricht Treaty, but another event marked the period to the point of giving the general look of contemporary mobilizations in environmental matters: the Rio Earth Summit in 1992. This planetary event, which brought together most of the NGOs, created and supported environmental interests that are still relevant today, such as the fight against global warming, the protection of biodiversity and Indigenous peoples, and the Rio Declaration, which promotes sustainable development policies at the national level. The European NGOs participated in this summit and, above all, began to intensify their relations, including with NGOs from the South, on issues of reflection on a different kind of globalization. While the first politicization of the green movement was built around the question of nuclear energy and pacifism contesting the rise of conflict between the two blocs (USA/USSR), the current problematization revolves around denouncing the threat of an exclusively economic globalization that ignores environmental, social, and economic issues. Sustainable development is a public policy frame of reference that responds in part to this concern by accompanying and reducing the economic, environmental, and social costs, but not all NGOs agree with this approach. Some of them are beginning to think about another kind of globalization and are joined by groups that are challenging capitalism – the model that emerged victorious from the Cold War and the fall of the Eastern bloc – head-on. The counter-summits appeared as a mode of action, seducing a new generation of activists who built direct, media-oriented modes of action, with a strong circulation between the places of mobilization. If these traits are common to their predecessors of the 1970s, their use of the internet is intense, and collaborations are carried out in strongly horizontal networks, which means that the modes of action can be large gatherings as well as sporadic or surprise occupations. As episodes of violence are not uncommon (Seattle in 1999, Genoa in 2001),[1] more and more rituals of interaction with police forces are being organized between non-violent direct action and provocation. The European states are familiar with these demonstrations, which can end in urban guerrilla warfare and change the grammar of the environmentalists' demonstrations, which until now have been generally non-violent, often on the very sites that needed to be protected from development (Plogoff, Creys Malville, etc.) Suddenly, it is the summits of the G7 that become the protesting target (Ollitrault, 2008; Hayes and Ollitrault, 2019).

More and more groups, less numerous but very organized, claim a more radical ecology denouncing a particular violence towards animals (Animal Liberation) or pollution (Earth First). The disturbances are more sporadic but intense; their mode of action, often inspired by the forms of North American militancy, wants to be closer to nature to the point of positioning themselves with the suffering of the non-living (to tie themselves to a tree to prevent a bulldozer from operating, to deliver animals from vivisection centers). These illegal operations are repressed, but most European states are aware of this new mode of action, which sometimes clashes with well-established traditions (e.g., bullfighting or hunting). In this dynamic, Western Europe is challenged by real cultural struggles on the choice to reintroduce the bear or the wolf against the sheep farmers or traditional hunting. So much so that in the early 2000s, a Hunting, Fishing, and Traditions party (*Chasse Peche Nature et traditions*) was organized in France, linked by Italy, Greece, and Spain, which ran for election and presented Europe as being under the influence of ecologists (Ollitrault, 2014). In this framework, the European Union became the target of movements claiming other practices of nature more rural and traditional, including being respectful of nature but not being within the canons of the ecologists, seen as urban, intellectual, and subservient to international standards or even to the North of Europe. The old traditions versus a form of globalization of values and representations of good attitude toward the environment cuts the society into two sides, with economic and social effects (rural people lost the control of their local economy, and the urban are more and more present through tourism or new norms of behavior). This cleavage has provoked an anti-European resentment instrumentalized against the ecologists, who are seen as allies of this transnational globalization.

At the end of the period from the 1990s to 2010, we observe in Western Europe environmental NGOs that are often critical, with differentiated levels of opposition to a liberalization of markets and a capitalism that instrumentalizes the environment for profit and disregards its integrity, even leading to the loss of all humanity (e.g., global warming); protest movements of small, highly structured groups that put the defense of life at the center of their preoccupations to the point of denying all divergent interests; and a "ruralist" protest movement that opposes a globalization that denies their values and local specificities by presenting ecologists as scapegoats for this evolution.

Civil disobedience: radicalism and institutionalization

Civil disobedience is a means of action calling for illegal acts in order to denounce a situation or legislation that is unjust or iniquitous or ignores the rights of a minority or group (Hayes and Ollitrault, 2019). The green movements have used it since the beginning, with Greenpeace being strongly inspired by these practices to highlight nuclear tests or hunting or to denounce an unjust situation with regard to the protection of the environment or of animal species while making public opinion its witness. In this dynamic, the campaigns rely on moral outrage and on the sensitivity of Western public opinion, which is capable of being in support against governments or the incriminated companies (Hayes and Ollitrault, 2019).

Many thinkers mobilized by the political theory of environmentalists inspire these modes of collective action. The first one was Henry David Thoreau, who influenced as much the philosophy as the forms of contestations carried out by the ecologists. Moreover, in France, José Bové, a farmer alter-globalist environmentalist since the 1970s, has carried this mode of non-violent direct action by dismantling a McDonald's in Millau then by mowing down GMO crops with the support of Greenpeace France. This mode of action appeals to ecologists who adhere to the non-violent mode because of their ideology of respecting the living, whether human or non-human. In France, the influence of left-wing Catholicism is very significant, especially in a union strongly invested in ecological struggles: the *Confédération paysanne* (Hayes, 2007). The influence of the Quakers or the Plowshares of the Protestant branches, invested in humanitarian and environmental causes, is significant in the sense that, as for Greenpeace at its beginnings, the tone is one of radical commitment, even to the point of imprisonment, but respecting strict non-violence. Thus, occupations, obstructions, and illegalities multiply, but the stake is that the police stop them, and a trial allows them to plead their cause as well as to defend their point of view. Lawyers are specializing in the protection of activists everywhere.

Since the beginning of the 21st century, Western Europe as well as the USA (11 September 2001) have been experiencing a wave of terrorist attacks that have led to increased security. In this way, demonstrations and radical actions are under the effect of stricter laws, and in France, especially after the wave of attacks in 2015, the state of emergency has made it challenging to run some demonstrations, even peaceful ones, in the face of more severe repression. The death of activists (Remy Fraisse in 2014) and the inflicting of severe and disabling injuries (loss of eyes or limbs) have gradually transformed the demonstrating milieu in France to the point that even non-violent marches can become very violent and end in clashes with the police. At the same time, anti-capitalist groups – more violent and more provocative with police – that are increasingly present at demonstrations are often blurring the non-violent message of environmentalists, who are increasingly mobilizing in the face of the climate emergency.

It is the climate emergency and the feeling that governmental actions are not up to the global stakes that motivate the young generation and also part of Extinction Rebellion, which emerged in Great Britain and has made non-violent actions and calls for civil disobedience a ritual since the mid-2010s. Thus, Greta Thunberg, a young Swedish activist, has been able to breathe new life into a generation of youth born within this century who demand action on behalf of their generation, threatened by the effects of their deteriorating environment. If her calls are heard around the world, in Western Europe, young people have certainly taken to the streets to strike for the climate by disobeying, in the sense of leaving their high schools or schools.

This mobilization joins and breathes new life into an NGO movement that is experiencing a crisis due to its broader institutionalization (Giugni and Grasso, 2015) and a strong feeling among activists that lobbying actions at the international level do not rapidly advance decision-making. The register of urgency also has the effect of reinvigorating mobilization by taking radical actions in the name of the very survival of humanity. Thus, the exhausted environment becomes an issue for itself and for the population. Due to globalization and the effects of the circulation of information, activists can stage desertification in Africa or the rising waters in the Pacific to make people aware of the climate issue at the European level. Moreover, numerous hot summers, changes in the landscape, droughts in Western European countries, and the melting of ice in the North are symptoms and facts that can be opposed by public opinion, which has been seduced by the discourse but still needs to be won over to change its practices.

In this light, the ecological habits that have always been exemplary by following an organic or healthy consumption tend to spread among the educated urban middle classes with new practices (farms in cities, organic gardens, etc.). But the countercultural places have taken a new rise with the relocalization of struggles following the failure of the Copenhagen conference on global warming in 2008. In France, the Zone à Défendre (ZAD) was born, linked to occupation or even squats in rural areas, with the development of protest and countercultural spaces that are meant to be self-managed and a laboratory of ecological thoughts. In these squats, which are half ecological, half libertarian and anti-capitalist, a way of thinking and acting is organized, promoting new ways of thinking about ecology: veganism, alternative housing, eco-feminism, or the animal rights cause. In these spaces, many activists from many European countries can circulate and socialize as youth tends to become radicalized in the face of the institutionalization of NGOs or political parties, including green ones.

In this context, the political and administrative authorities observe these spaces as being places of radical militants who, moreover, refuse any form of consultation and can slow down or hinder the progress of new large developments (airports, shopping centers, highways). In France, for example, the Tarnac group has been prosecuted for terrorism. Thus, following the North American legislation on eco-terrorism, in France and Western Europe, certain radical forms of environmental protest fall into this category, while many activists use civil disobedience to make themselves heard and inform public opinion of the climate emergency through court cases. This tendency towards radicalization and illegality gives a new tone to environmental movements, which calls for large-scale citizen mobilizations.

This resurgence of social movements corresponds as much to a real anxiety of the populations regarding their environmental future as to the social effects of the new capitalism that is making employees, including the middle classes, more precarious. (See, for example, the Yellow Vests in France in 2018–19). In Western Europe, the issue of joining environmental justice and social justice is paramount, especially as Green political parties must reposition themselves in the face of the rise of the Far Right. In Austria, for example, the Green Party has become a major political force in opposing the rise of these extremes. This democratic issue in a context of internal and external security issues, the so-called migrant crisis of 2015, which has been seen to have weakened Germany, is furthermore at the heart of the new political deal of the Greens, who are often protectors of fundamental freedoms and welcome and protect migrants. In this liberal opening, we must add the support of the LGBT and trans minorities, which makes this type of party, with respect to the spectrum of European political parties, culturally liberal and politically leftist (for example, with respect to the limitation of the effects of capitalism on the environment and populations).

The crisis linked to the COVID pandemic has put the question of environmental health back at the heart of the agendas of many countries across Europe and allows ecologists to think about the crisis of broader systems from a global point of view by affirming the link between the degradation of biodiversity (possibly at the origin of the mutation generating the COVID virus) and the effects on the populations. Another notion, that of One Health, appears to encompass health and environment issues in a single theme. In this last phase, we see in many European countries the multiplication of citizens' movements ready to invest in climate change with the support of networks calling for civil disobedience, a political movement that has become institutionalized and takes charge of social and economic interests beyond strictly environmental issues and national boundaries, As ecological issues are placed on the agenda, they have opened up spaces for dialogue, stimulated new legislation, and initiated urban policies that are more respectful of norms that avoid pollution. National characteristics remain, and the European Union is keeping a watchful eye on countries that are slow to transform their environmental practices. However, this institutionalization does not prevent a rise in concerns among citizens faced with global environmental issues that raise fears for the well-being and even the survival of populations.

Conclusion

The green movements of Western Europe have been at the heart of the development of environmental awareness and the circulation of knowledge, expertise, and even militant networks since the beginning of the nineteenth century, and they have created an environmental interest that has gone from the sectoral to the planetary scale. These networks have opened up to questions of North/South relations and those of equality and justice beyond the mere conservation of the environment. The driving effect of the institutional construction of the European Union has made it possible to homogenize public policies on the environment and to support the structuring of social movements, particularly in countries where environmental awareness in the sense of conservation is low. It is important to remember Europe is very diverse, with different institutional and partisan systems that do not always allow for the support of Green political parties. Nevertheless, European cities are taking more and more environmental measures and sometimes have Greens elected as mayors (such as in France and Germany).

On the other hand, since the last decade, some green movements have tended to become more radical in their positions and their modes of action, too, sometimes, often under the effect of the closure of the systems that only open the negotiations on bases that cannot satisfy a new militant generation motivated by the urgency of the stakes related to the degradation of the environment and global warming. These movements heed the calls for civil disobedience, support for the idea of economic degrowth, the protection of animals, and a drastic change in the relationship with consumer society. For them, the issue goes beyond ecological questions by including social concerns and the redistribution of wealth. In this context, in terms of the cycles of protest (Tarrow, 1994), we can conclude that Western Europe is in a new wave of ecological protest supported by a militant generation inventing a way of life and criticizing in a more radical way the effects of capitalism on the planet.

Note

1 The first massive demonstrations against globalization of the markets with urban riots and the birth of the anti-globalization protest sector.

Bibliography

Berny, N. (2009, May) "Mastering national contextual challenges: The institutionalisation of LPO and Greenpeace France compared", *Environmental Politics*, 18 (3), pp. 371–390.

Berny, N. (2013a) "Building the capacity to play on multilevel policy processes: French environmental movement organizations and the European Union", *Social Movement Studies*, 12 (2/3), pp. 298–315.

Berny, N. (2013b) "Europeanization as organizational learning: When French environmental movement organizations play the EU multilevel policy game", *French Politics*, 11 (2/3), pp. 217–240.

Dalton, R.J. (1994) *The Green Rainbow: Environmental Groups in Western Europe*. New Haven, CT: Yale University Press, 305p.

Diani, M. (1995) *Green Networks: A Structural Analysis of the Italian Environmental Movement*. Edinburgh: Edinburgh University Press, 221p.

Doherty, B. and Doyle, T. (2006) "Beyond borders: Environmental movements and transnational politics", *Environmental Politics,* 15 (5), pp. 697–712.

Doherty, B. and Doyle, T. (2013) *Environmentalism, Resistance and Solidarity: The Politics of Friends of the Earth International*. London: Palgrave Macmillan.

Doyle, T. and MacGregor, S. (Eds.). (2014) *Environmental Movements Around the World: Shades of Green in Politics and Culture*. Santa Barbara, CA: Praeger.

Eder K. (1996) *The Social Construction of Nature*. London: Sage.

Giugni, M. and Grasso, M.T. (2015) "Environmental Movements: Heterogeneity, Transformation, and Institutionalization", *Annual Review of Environment and Resources*, 40, pp. 337–361.

Hayes, G.A. (2007) "Collective action and civil disobedience: The anti-GMO campaign of the Faucheurs volontaires", *French Politics*, 5, pp. 293–314, 22 p.

Hayes, G.A. and Doherty, B. (2015) The courts: Criminal trials as strategic arenas. In: Duyvendak, J.W. and Jasper, J.M. (Eds.). *Breaking Down the State: Protestors Engaged*. Amsterdam: Amsterdam University Press, pp. 27–51, 25 p. (Protest and Social Movements).

Hayes, G.A. and Ollitrault, S. (2019) *Breaking Laws: Violence and Civil Disobedience in Protest*. Sommier, I., Hayes, G.A. and Ollitrault, S. (Eds.). Amsterdam: Amsterdam University Press, 274 p. (Protest and Social Movements)

Jordan, A. (Dir.). (2012) *Environmental Policy in the EU: Actors, Institutions and Processes*. London: Routledge.

Ollitrault, S. (1998) The transnational repertoire. *La Lettre de la Maison Française d'Oxford*, Maison Française d'Oxford, 1999, Séminaire" Analysing Social Movements", 10, pp. 57–70.

Ollitrault, S. (2001) "French green activists: Experts in action", *Revue Française de science politique*, 1 (1–2), pp. 105–130. doi: 10.3917/rfsp.511.0105

Ollitrault, S. (2008) *Militer pour la planète*. Rennes: PUR.

Ollitrault, S. (2012) "Derrière la rhétorique de la crise écologique, les crises économiques? Origine et diffusion du cadre de la crise écologique en France (1974–2009)", *Modern & Contemporary France*, 20 (2), pp. 221–236. doi: 10.1080/09639489.2012.665573

Ollitrault, S. (2014) The green movement in France: History, ideology and action repertoire. In: Doyle, T. and MacGregor S. (Eds.). *Environmental Movements Around the World: Shades of Green in Politics and Culture,* vol. 2. Santa Barbara, CA: Praeger. Westport: ABC-Clio, S. 95–117.

Ollitrault, S. and Hayes, G. (2011) *The French Environmental Movement in the Era of Climate Change: The Case of Notre Dame des Landes*. Green Politics section, Panel on The National Politics of Climate Change – ECPR General Conference, August 2011, Reykjavik, Iceland. ⟨halshs-00794155⟩.

Pickerill, J., Krinsky, J., Hayes, G., Gillan, K. and Doherty, B. (2014) *Occupy! A Global Movement*. London: Routledge.

Rokkan, S. (1971) "Nation-building: A review of models and approaches", *Current Sociology*, 19 (3), pp. 7–38.

Roose, J. (2014) The institutionalization of environmentalism in German society. In: Doyle, T. and McGregor, S. (Hg.). *Environmental Movements around the World: Shades of Green in Politics and Culture*, vol. 2. Westport: ABC-CLIO, S. 23–44.

Rootes, C. (Ed.). (2013a) *Environmental Protest in Western Europe*. Oxford: Oxford University Press.

Rootes, C. (2013b) "From local conflict to national issue: When and how environmental campaigns succeed in transcending the local", *Environmental Politics*, pp. 95–114. Routledge Journals. doi: 10.1080/09644016.2013.755791

Rootes, C. (2013c) The environmental movement in Great Britain. In *Environmental Movements Around the World: Shades of Green in Politics and Culture*. Santa Barbara, CA; Denver, CO; and Oxford: Praeger.

Rucht, D. and Roose, J. (2003) Germany. In: Rootes, C. (Ed.). *Comparative Politics Environmental Protest in Western Europe*. New York: Oxford University Press, pp. 80–108.

Seel, B., Paterson, M. and Doherty, B. (2000) *Direct Action in British Environmentalism*. London: Routledge.

Tarrow, S. (1994) *Power in Movement, Social Movements and Contentious Politics*. Cambridge: Cambridge University Press.

3

RHAPSODY IN GREEN

Environmental movements in East Central Europe

Ondřej Císař

Introduction

This chapter focuses on the development of environmental activism and protest in East Central Europe after 1989. The chapter mostly surveys the situation and existing research on the Czech Republic, Slovakia, Hungary, and Poland and, when relevant, refers also to the wider group of East European countries. Many aspects and instances of environmental movement mobilization that have been observed in East Central Europe have been addressed in systematic analyses of movements and environmental movement organizations (EMOs). The environmental movement has been extensively researched since 1989 (for example Hicks, 1996; Fagan, 2004, 2005; Jehlička et al., 2005; Carmin and VanDeveer, 2005; Fagan and Carmin, 2011; Jehlička and Jacobsson, 2021).

The chapter is mostly organized in a chronological order. The years of post-communist development are divided into several time periods derived from the extant literature. Environmental movements evolved considerably in these different periods and responded to the opportunities and threats specific to each one. When applicable, the discussion is organized around the most important scholarly debate or controversy in the given period, reflecting the problems of importance at that time. The chapter thus deals with the most important debates in the research on environmental movements in several time periods.

The first section describes the situation before 1989, as environmental movements had formed by the 1980s even under the region's undemocratic regimes. The second section focuses on the first post-1989 period, which was in many ways unique and specific but which also introduced factors that have continued to shape the situation of EMOs ever since. Post-1989 environmental activism has been shaped by both the national and the international – especially the European – political contexts. Therefore, the third section discusses the role that these contexts played in the mobilization of environmental activism and especially the effects that Europeanization had during the pre-accession period up to 2004. This section focuses especially on the debate over the effects of EU funding on environmentalism, and it also distinguishes the different forms of environmental mobilization. The fourth section presents a debate on the post-accession period in the development of environmental activism. The fifth one discusses the most recent debates on the effects that the mobilization of new environmental groups centered on the issue of climate change have had. Since social movements operate within a broader

DOI: 10.4324/9780367855680-4

political space, the last section summarizes the available research on the interactions between (environmental) social movements and other important organizations in democratic politics, especially political parties.

Against communism: the pre-1989 period

Movements and mobilizations, including environmental ones, did not appear out of the blue at the end of the 1980s when the old regimes collapsed. Fully fledged social movements, such as Solidarity in Poland and dissident anti-regime platforms in other communist countries, such as Charter 77 in Czechoslovakia, existed and received some scholarly attention even before 1989 (Sarre and Jehlička, 2007). In that period, autonomous non-state collective actors were discussed in the writings of dissident authors, such as Václav Havel (Czechoslovakia), György Konrád (Hungary), and Adam Michnik (Poland), and they were primarily concerned with human and civil rights, not granted by the undemocratic socialist regimes (Císař, 2018).

The pre-1989 anti-communist activist network did not just focus on the narrowly understood issue of human rights but concerned itself also with various aspects of the regime's functioning. Given the negative impact of communist regimes on the state of the environment, these aspects were framed by activists as human rights–related problems and, more specifically, as a violation of the right to live in a clean environment. Accordingly, in Eastern Europe, the issue of environmental degradation first gained political salience in the 1980s due the efforts of dissident groups, which highlighted the issue alongside the other problems connected to the socialist regimes. As a result, environmental mobilization had become an important part of the anti-communist struggle in many East European countries well before the regimes ultimately collapsed: "environmental problems united activists within the Bloc, especially on Slovak-Hungarian, Czech-Polish, and Czech-German lines. . . . [T]he first group to notice the problem and react with clear statements was Charter 77" (Szulecki, 2011: 288).

Alongside anti-regime activists, there also existed official organizations, most of them devoted to conservation and focused on the so-called "small ecology" issues. Such organizations were tolerated and even recognized by the communist regimes, as long as they defined themselves as non-political organizations concerned with pollution rather than challenging the regime. Some of them, nevertheless, provided a platform on their fringe for the political mobilization of anti-regime activists, especially from the young generation (Jehlička, 2001: 81–84; Fagan, 2004: 61–66).

By the end of the 1980s, environmental issues acquired more power to mobilize as they increasingly resonated with the everyday experience of some sections of the population. For example, some of the demonstrations that came to mark the end of the communist regime in Czechoslovakia, especially the ones that took place in the environmentally damaged regions of North Bohemia and Prague, were in fact primarily organized to voice environmental demands (Fagan, 2004). In Poland, almost half the population was unhappy with the state of the environment from as early as 1980, a grievance that was voiced by environmental groups in the country, which visibly developed and became highly popular during the 1980s (Kimla, 2016; Szulecka and Szulecki, 2019). In Hungary, environmental groups became one of the most important forces of anti-regime mobilization, so much so that by the mid-1980s, the regime was unable to control them (Buzogány, 2016: 407). The plan to build the Gabcikovo-Nagymaros Dam on the Danube became the most important campaign. Various groups participated in it, and a link was thereby formed between human rights, the environment, and support for democracy (Pickvance, 1998).

Post-revolutionary activism: the early 1990s

After the collapse of the region's communist regimes, some prominent anti-regime environmental activists of the communist era joined the ranks of the post-communist political elite and even came to occupy executive positions in the first democratically elected governments (see Jehlička, 2001; Fagan, 2004; Szulecka and Szulecki, 2019). Drawing on Fagin's study (2000) of the development of the Czech environmental movement, the early 1990s can be labelled a time of "post-revolutionary radicalism and activism", when environmental activists began working for state institutions and enjoyed influence over them. Activist organizations at that time, however, were not consolidated and were not fully able to utilize the opportunities open to them. In other words, while the political opportunity structure was open, activist organizations lacked the effective organizational capacity to take advantage of it.

Once the pre-1989 environmental activists began working for state institutions, they were involved in introducing new environmental legislation in post-communist countries (Pleines and Bušková, 2007; Szulecka and Szulecki, 2019). For many activists and citizens alike, this meant that the contentious strategies of claims making used in the past lost their legitimacy under the conditions of open democratic institutions: "contentious forms of politics – strikes, civil disobedience and mass demonstrations – were increasingly delegitimized by the liberal elite and mainstream media as a counterproductive activity" (Szulecka and Szulecki, 2019: 8). Although anti-regime collective mobilization before 1989 was understood as a legitimate form of political expression when it was aimed at non-democratic regimes, it started to be seen as illegitimate once the old regimes had been toppled. In the view of the political mainstream, collective action and protest have no place in a democratic polity, which is supposed to be shaped by regular elections only (see Fagan, 2004). To put it bluntly, the "spectre of Joseph Schumpeter" was haunting post-communist Europe: while protest is the way to confront a non-democratic regime, it is no way to address political problems in the conditions of democracy. According to this understanding, which largely still applies in the post-communist political mainstream, protest is a sign of a non-democratic problem; it is not part of a standard democratic solution (see Císař, 2013a). In Hungary, the first shock from democratic contention occurred early, just six months after the first elections in October 1990: the government responded violently to a taxi blockade triggered by increased petrol prices (Buzogány, 2016: 409).

The result was the gradual delegitimization of contentious environmental action soon after the regimes collapsed and even the end of open opportunities for activism in some of these countries (Fagan, 2004; Szulecka and Szulecki, 2019). Many of the dissidents who had begun working for state institutions left them; governments put human rights and environmental issues on the back burner; and activist organizations were refused access to the policy process (Fagin, 2000; Frič, 2001). The fact that in 1995, three environmental advocacy organizations were included on a state intelligence services' list of subversive organizations in the Czech Republic is a good illustration of the state's adversarial attitude toward political activists (Fagan, 2004: 87).

As soon as environmental organizations were unable to find any partners within the political system, they started to employ strategies that would get them media attention. This was especially the case of newly established activist organizations, whose numbers exploded after 1989 and that often had close ties to transnational partners and were able to draw on imported protest know-how (Císař, 2010; Szulecka and Szulecki, 2019). Also, the groups continued cooperating among themselves. According to some accounts, they even increased their advocacy capacity, which they were able to utilize later. External influences, resources, information, and know-how from the West played an important role in the process of the capacity building of local EMOs.

In the first half of the 1990s, these organizations were supported by American and European state and non-state actors. From the end of the 1990s, European Union (EU) funds became the most important source of funding. Some of the most active supporters of civil society in post-communist Europe were US-based private foundations, such as the Rockefeller Brothers Fund, the Charles Stewart Mott Foundation, the Ford Foundation, the Andrew W. Mellon Foundation, Atlantic Philanthropies, the Catherine T. MacArthur Foundation, and, most important among them, George Soros's Open Society Fund and its network. As post-communist countries came closer to becoming EU members (the post-communist countries of East Central Europe became full EU members in 2004), EU funds assumed a much greater role (Císař, 2013b). The "Americanization" of post-communist EMOs was replaced by their "Europeanization", which further intensified trends that had already begun in the early 1990s, namely institutionalization, organization capacity building, and professionalization.

In the 1990s, there was an enormous increase in the number of formally registered advocacy organizations (understood as NGOs) in post-communist Europe, including the EMOs that form the environmental movement. However, some researchers argued that they were not capable of serving as a platform for broader (networked) social movements (Fagan, 2004, 2005; McMahon, 2001). Other researchers, by contrast, claimed that some of these organizations actually fared much better than others in terms of their capacity to cooperate with other organizations and coordinate their advocacy strategies. Tarrow and Petrova (2007) even came up with a new label – *transactional activism* – to conceptually capture the strategic cooperation of these groups. In fact, in reference to post-communist countries, Tarrow and Petrova seem to draw on the well-established resource-mobilization argument that social movements unable to tap into existing pools of potential followers substituted "thick mobilization infrastructures" with "thin" ones (McCarthy, 1987). The notion of transactional relations is generally used to denote an actor's ability to engage with other relevant (collective) actors by exchanging information and resources, building coalitions around different projects, and collaborating with other organizations and even public sector institutions (see also Císař and Navrátil, 2015).

The debate on international capacity building: the pre-accession period

As has already been discussed elsewhere (Císař, 2010, 2020), when it came to the resources for environmental activism, which were indeed instrumental to the capacity building of environmental groups after the fall of communism, public funding was not made available to advocacy-oriented organizations and was only channeled to "apolitical conservation projects pursued by the older EMOs" (Fagan, 2004: 91). The newly established organizations had thus to apply for support from various foreign funding agencies; in fact, they "became [the] favourites of various US and West European backed funders" to help build post-communist civil society (Sarre and Jehlička, 2007: 353; see also Jehlička, 2001; Mendelson and Glenn, 2002; Henderson, 2002, 2003; Fagan, 2004; Císař, 2010). As a result, external funding became the single most important source of money for these new organizations (Carmin et al., 2008).

The general result of the dependency on foreign funding, according to the traditional interpretation of this dependency, was the immediate de-radicalization of the environmental movement (Fagin and Jehlička, 1998; Fagin, 2000; Jehlička, 2001; Fagan and Jehlička, 2003; Fagan, 2004, 2005). This interpretation asserts that by providing funds, external donors were actually contributing to a process whereby local political elites co-opted social movements. It contends that the external dependency of social movement organizations led to their professionalization, which "siphons movement activists from grassroots organizing, thereby diverting them from their original goals and demobilizing the movements" (Jenkins, 1998: 212). As Fagan and Jehlička (2003: 54) argue, "the dependency of . . . EMOs on the state and on foreign donors for funding acts as a constraint on their political adventure and mediates their interaction with the political process".

Viewed this way, the process of cooptation had begun in the early 1990s. However, as EU funding gained momentum in the second half of the decade, the pressure for further moderation and "institutional procedures – lobbying, consulting on draft legislation, researching and writing reports and opinions, attending public meetings" increased even more (Hicks, 2004: 225). According to critics, EU funding only reinforced the already-established relations of donor dependency. Although the EU's funding strategy differed considerably from the earlier funding by emphasizing the long-term sustainability of NGOs, it nevertheless perpetuated the old pattern by continuing to distribute assistance through project-based mechanisms (Fagan, 2005). As a result, instead of presenting an alternative to the mainstream liberal market-based view of environmental protection, the environmental movement embraced the liberal view and strove to become a recognized voice in the public debate. These organizations "were keen to demonstrate their professionalism as well as their proximity to the policy process and the media" (Fagan, 2004: 99). At the same time, the quality of EMOs' expertise "in some areas surpassed that of public administration, especially in nature conservation, renewable energy, transport, energy efficiency, water and waste management" (Szulecka and Szulecki, 2019: 10, writing on Poland, but the argument can be read more generally).

And there was a price to be paid for their increasing influence. They had to abandon protest in favor of policy making and lobbying, which in turn demanded increasing professionalization on their part. They lost the ability to set their agendas independently. In order to become eligible for funding, campaign goals had to fit the donors' preferences (Hallstrom, 2004; Bell, 2004; Hicks, 2004). Instead of social movements, public interest groups mushroomed in the region. In terms of their action repertoire, these organizations preferred cooperation with political elites to more contentious forms of protest and action (Carmin and Hicks, 2002). Hence, the popular mobilizations that accompanied the collapse of the regimes at the end of the 1980s gave way to a more institutionalized and moderated form of "interest politics".

A competing stream of research (Stark et al., 2006; Bruszt and Vedrés, 2008, 2013; Císař, 2010; Císař and Vráblíková, 2013; Císař and Navrátil, 2015) demonstrated that external dependency is not necessarily a de-politicizing force. In other words, even if social movement organizations are channeled toward professionalization by external donors, they can still function as a platform for effective and contentious political activism. If the domestic political context and prevailing ideological climate are generally not conducive to the goals of EMOs, international patronage may actually lead to their increased autonomy and even radicalization vis-à-vis domestic conditions. In fact, it was the dependency on foreign money that actually enabled some EMOs to swim against the current of domestic public opinion and political authorities and voice an agenda that would otherwise never find its way into the public debate, such as the campaigns against nuclear energy in the region.

The requirements and policies of the EU also helped legitimize the demands of many activist groups in the eyes of domestic political elites that would not otherwise have acknowledged them as relevant political problems. This was especially true of groups fighting various types of discrimination, but the influence of the EU was visible also in the case of the environmental movement (Fagan, 2005; Börzel and Buzogány, 2010; Buzogány, 2016; Szulecka and Szulecki, 2019). The EU contributed to the recognition of these organizations as legitimate participants in the political process and created additional opportunities for them (Cent et al., 2014). As a result, it opened up access points for non-state actors in the structure of state institutions. The process of Europeanization, which started with the accession process at the end of the 1990s and has continued since the accession of candidate countries to the EU in 2004, generally helped make the political system more open to environmental activists (Börzel and Buzogány, 2010).

In addition, national EMOs' connections to partner organizations in Brussels created new opportunities for them to "put pressure on their government both via European institutions as well as through mobilizing international public opinion" (Buzogány, 2016: 411). They also helped them in the transfer of knowledge. As Borzel and Buzogány have summed up (2010: 726–777), EMOs in "Hungary, Poland and Romania greatly benefited from their transnational and EU-level networks that supplied them with policy expertise and resources". Similar results have been reached by research on the transnational cooperation of Czech social movement organizations: "Taking into account other factors, it is not EU funding, but representation in Brussels that determines SMOs' lobbying [on a transnational level]" (Císař and Vráblíková, 2013: 153).

While the mainstream groups gradually professionalized their activities, more radically oriented activists opted for strategies of direct action, such as, in the late 1990s, blockading nuclear powers stations and organizing street parties (Novák, 2017; Binka, 2009). Probably the most visible example internationally was the participation of environmental activists in the protests against the joint meeting of the International Monetary Fund and World Bank in Prague in 2000. In order to organize protests against this summit, a loose organizational platform was established in 2000, but preparatory work had started as early as the summer of 1999. The platform was established as a local coordinating structure, but after the events in Seattle in late 1999, which sparked a resurgence in transnational anti-capitalist mobilization, the platform's activities became more internationalized in the lead-up to the summit in 2000 (Welsh, 2004). Foreign activists brought with them necessary resources in the form of experience and protest know-how. As a result, even the more radical groups were shaped by influences from abroad in terms of ideational, and at times, even material and human resources diffused under the conditions of deepening globalization. In fact, some of these groups formed part of the global anti-capitalist resistance: i.e., the so-called alter-globalization movement (Piotrowski, 2017).

After EU accession

In conformity with the results of research on social movement mobilization in the West, EU accession was expected to provide East European social movements with additional opportunities to mobilize at the supranational level and even bypass the national government if needed (Börzel and Buzogány, 2010). First, as the accession process itself demonstrated, international institutions influence national political opportunities: "Changes in the international context can, by altering political and economic conditions, and/or perceptions of those conditions, change the opportunities for activists within a country" (Meyer, 2003: 20). For example, if a social movement organization is attempting to push through its agenda, the likelihood of success increases if this agenda is in line with EU-recognized standards. International institutions shape domestic opportunities, creating new access points for some actors and closing them for others, and provide domestic actors with resources they would not otherwise be able to obtain (for example, Börzel and Buzogány, 2010; Císař and Vráblíková, 2010).

Second, the influence of the EU not only changes the domestic rules of the game and redistributes the available resources in domestic political arenas; it also enables SMOs to expand the scope of their activities and enter into interaction either with European institutions directly or with EU-supported networks of non-governmental organizations. As already pointed out by the theory of multilevel governance in the mid-1990s, the political process in the EU is characterized by the interlinking of subnational, national, and European institutions, which allows political actors at different levels to interact, establish various types of coalitions, and diffuse their political message across borders (Imig and Tarrow, 2001; Börzel and Buzogány, 2010).

More recent research has questioned the notion that the accession of post-communist countries to the EU had any uniform or progressive effect on environmental activism (Szabó and Márkus, 2015; Císař and Navrátil, 2021). While before accession, the EU worked as an integration magnet for all political agencies that supported the issue of environmental protection, compelling them to conform to EU demands, the post-accession period in some countries was marked by the end of this influence in politics in general and in environmental protection in particular. In post-accession Hungary, when the EU no longer worked as an "integration magnet", this was followed by "the dissolution of the governmental Agency for Environment, and by diminishing the influence of the public voice in technology and investment planning and implementation" (Szabó and Márkus, 2015: 36). There was a similar attempt to limit the rights of activists to participate in the process of approving new investment projects in the Czech Republic.

Reinforced by the financial crisis of 2008, public opinion, in Hungary and Poland especially, shifted from the more liberal worldviews of the 1990s, including tolerance for environmental protection, toward a more conservative, authoritarian, and materialist stance (Szabó and Márkus, 2015; Szulecka and Szulecki, 2019: 12). While the gradual process of EU accession had concealed a relatively deep cultural cleavage between liberals and conservatives and served as a general integration magnet, turning even conservatives into pro-European and seemingly liberal forces up until the moment of accession, after accession, these fault lines were revealed (Vachudova and Hooghe, 2009). As a result, the issue of environmental protection and climate change even more (see later in this chapter) have become an even bigger part of the recently intensifying cultural wars in the region (Caiani and Císař, 2019).

Although EU influence generally diminished, this does not mean political activism disappeared. Rather, the nature of its relation to the EU became more diverse and variegated across campaigns, depending on available resources and on how activists in a particular campaign evaluated the situation. Several ways in which Europe was "used" or deployed by campaign organizers and their opponents in post-accession conflicts have recently been identified. Among the different ways in which the EU was strategically used, the following stand out: as the subject of framing. as a standard-setter and authority over the national government (part of a boomerang effect), as an arbiter to refer to in disputes, as a means to amplify protest, as a tool to legitimize the status quo, as a source of resources for activists, and as an agenda setter for climate action. These strategies appeared in different combinations in different campaigns, depending on how the situation was evaluated by the parties involved in the particular conflict (Císař and Navrátil, 2021).

New climate activism

Although the environmental movement has been around for a long time, it is going through a visible transformation right now. This is mostly due to the mobilization of newly established political actors, such as Fridays for Future (FFF) and Extinction Rebellion (XR), which focus on the pressing issue of climate change and its social consequences. These new agencies have helped transform not only the public discourse but also the environmental movement, both globally and in particular political contexts, including East Central Europe. FFF evolved out of one school strike initiated by Greta Thunberg, starting in August 2018, into a globally coordinated protest action, mostly involving schoolchildren but with the clear ambition to also attract adults (de Moor et al., 2020b). XR started several months later, in October 2018, when British activists assembled in London to publicize a Declaration of Rebellion against the UK government, and in subsequent weeks, thousands of protesters blocked five major bridges across the Thames (ibid.). In response to these events, national branches started to be formed in many countries around Europe and the world. Although these two actors differ in many respects, they share a deep discontent with the political elite as well as with established environmental groups and movements. They therefore came up with an innovative action repertoire – school strikes and civil disobedience, respectively – to raise awareness about the urgency of the climate crisis.

Several global climate strikes have already been organized by FFF since the first one on 15 March 2019, and they have also taken place in East Central European countries. In September 2019, FFF organized a week of actions and demonstrations across the world, with over 6,000 events in 185 countries that attracted 7.6 million participants (de Moor et al., 2020a: 7; the remainder of this paragraph draws on the same source, pp. 8–30). The size of the main demonstrations in Eastern Europe was comparatively small, but around 3,000 protesters gathered in Budapest, and 12,000 protested in Warsaw. While in Scandinavia (except Denmark) and West European countries, the demonstrations also managed to attract a significant number of adults, the demonstrations in Eastern Europe were dominated by youngsters. The average FFF protester is young and female, and females outnumbered males in all the East European cities studied – Bucharest, Budapest, Prague, and Warsaw. On average, almost half of all young people learned about the demonstrations on social media, and one-fourth through interpersonal networks. Greta Thunberg played an important role in sparking the interest of both young and older protesters in climate change across most of the researched cities. In general, there was a significant lack of trust in the capacity of governments to solve the coming environmental problems, and only Scandinavian countries displayed somewhat larger shares of people trusting the government.

Actions by FFF and XR in East Central European countries immediately led to conflict within the environmental movement and with society as a whole. Within the movement, this conflict has mostly hinged on the strategies used by XR, which has on several occasions targeted transportation lines and crossings, including lines of public transportation. In the eyes of the established groups, these strategies are ill conceived because they alienate ordinary people who use public transport, while they miss the real target, such as the big fossil-fuel industry and its representatives. Further, XR has been accused of fragmenting the existing networks of the environmental movement, attracting mostly educated metropolitan elites unable to understand the needs of the working class.

In Eastern Europe, XR has been criticized for copying the strategies of the British chapter and applying them in a completely different social context. Moreover, since the issue of climate change has already been articulated by local groups, such as We Are the Limits in the Czech Republic, some critics argue that the new activists are overlooking what has already been achieved by home-grown groups in getting the issue of climate on the agenda (for examples from South East Europe, see Velicu, 2019). As early as 2016, We Are the Limits got involved in an event organized by the Ende Gelände movement blocking a coal mine in Germany. This was one of the largest recent civil disobedience protests in Germany and was framed as activism against global climate change. After that, the We Are the Limits network announced its intention to use civil disobedience in their Czech protests and declared itself a part of the climate justice movement (Císař and Navrátil, 2021).

While the liberal-leaning part of the political spectrum began showing support for these activities, especially the ones organized by FFF and its symbol, Greta Thunberg, these groups became the target of conservatives, who see them as extreme and lacking in useful suggestions.

Accordingly, student protests and the XR's blockades are regularly accused of doing nothing more than criticizing and being disruptive and of being unable to put forth any concrete measures that should be taken to avoid the negative consequences of the climate crisis. Ageism often comes into play, when students are framed as inexperienced, insufficiently educated, and naïve. A population survey fielded in the Czech Republic in the autumn of 2019 revealed that society was divided in its support for FFF, with more than 40% of the respondents supporting and the same proportion not supporting the students who were protesting (CVVM, 2019). Support was stronger among younger, more educated, and better positioned people; voters of liberal parties; and people on parental leave and was weaker among older and less educated people and voters of conservative parties. There was strong disapproval (more than 70%) of protests taking place instead of teaching. Political elites have sometimes adopted a strategy of cooptation by meeting the young protesters' representatives while they do not make any substantive concessions to them in their actual policies.

Environmentalism in the political space and in the context of other political issues

Taking into account the most important theoretical debates on social movements in post-communist Europe, the chapter has reviewed the development of the environmental movements in East Central Europe from the 1980s on (cf. Giugni and Grasso, 2015). However, social movements do not exist in a political vacuum but are part of a broader field of democratic politics. Specifically, social movements interact with other political actors and struggle over various issues with them.

As a result, contemporary democracies show considerable differences in the issue composition of their protest politics, which moreover tends to remain relatively stable over time. Issue composition has been debated in the literature on post-communist protest since the beginning of the 1990s. The research available at that time underscored the economic character of protests. Although there were no really big social conflicts related to the transformation during the first post-communist years in East Central Europe (Greskovits, 1998), the available data show that when mobilization did occur, it primarily concerned transformation-related (i.e., economic) issues. Thus, Ekiert and Kubik's (2001: 130) study of Polish protest in the period of 1989–93 showed that "protesters' demands had a predominantly economic character. Poles protested *mostly* to improve their standard of living".

However, the systematic study of protest events in the Czech Republic between 1993 and 2005 (five years were selected for actual coding: 1993, 1996, 1999, 2002, 2005) showed that Czech protesters' protest issues were the very opposite in character (Císař, 2010, 2013b; this paragraph draws on these two sources). While Ekiert and Kubik found almost none of the "post-materialist" issues commonly associated with the new social movements in Poland in the early 1990s, these issues, counted as the sum of environmental and human rights–related claims, made up one-third of all protest issues in the Czech Republic during the studied period. The results of this study of protest events indicate that environmental activists have been the single most visible activist group in the post-communist Czech Republic since the beginning of the 1990s. They were the organizers of nearly a quarter of all events; only self-organized popular protest, which accounts for a third of all events, surpassed them. Self-organization is based on "individual" organizational effort: i.e., protest in this category is not sponsored by any formal organization or informal group. As a result, regarding organized political activism, environmentalists fared best in terms of the frequency of collective action.

Environmentalists also substantially contributed to the prevalence of post-materialist claims among protest issues in the Czech Republic in the period under study. In terms of mobilization and protest, Czechs have concentrated much more on the environment (and human rights) than on economic and social welfare issues. Environmental issues formed the single most represented category of political claims in Czech public discourse (23% of all publicly expressed demands; for more, see Císař, 2010). Later research, which covered all the years in the country from 1993 to 2017, found that environmental protest accounted for 12% of the national protest agenda, mostly due to a drop in its frequency in the post-accession period (Císař et al., 2018). Comparatively, however, this was still almost twice as much as in Hungary in the same period (data until 2015).

Starting from this observation on the variability of the protest agenda across countries, a comparative project focused on protest issues in four East Central European countries – the Czech Republic, Slovakia, Poland, and Hungary – between 1993 and 2010 (see Císař and Vráblíková, 2019; the remainder of this section draws on the same source). In countries like the Czech Republic and, to a lesser extent, Slovakia, the vast majority of protests have been mobilized around socio-cultural issues, such as human rights, peace, nuclear power, or the environment, and only a tiny portion of protest has focused on economic issues. At the opposite extreme, protest in Hungary and, to a lesser extent, Poland usually has a strongly economic character, and it voices demands relating to material redistribution and social policy. What lies behind these cross-country differences in the protest agenda?

In addition to other factors (e.g., social structure, historical legacies, and external events) that determine which specific issues are contested in a given society, the types of issues that are salient in national protest depend on what issues the mainstream political parties are competing on – or, in other words, on the content and strength of the master-issue dimension. Research into niche political parties has revealed a substitutive effect; where the stronger a specific master-issue dimension (either economic or socio-cultural) is in party politics, the less salient that issue dimension is in protest politics. This substitutive effect results from the tendency of party politics to reduce political conflict to single-dimension equilibrium. This then decreases the importance of other issue dimensions and relegates the contest over secondary, niche issues to the realm of policy-seeking strategies, with protest being a common type of this political strategy. In party systems where single-dimension equilibrium does not exist and the master-issue dimension is weaker, the same dynamics result in a more convergent relationship between party and protest politics and a greater similarity between the protest- and party-system agendas.

The content and the strength of the master-issue dimension vary in the selected four countries. The results show that in the Czech Republic, where the master-issue dimension has remained steadily and strongly economic, protest has been predominantly socio-cultural. In Poland between 1993 and 2001 and Hungary between 1993 and 2006, the master-issue dimensions are strongly socio-cultural, while protest is predominantly economic. There is no single-dimension equilibrium in party politics in Slovakia or in post-2001 Poland, and mainstream parties (in the two countries) compete on both economic and socio-cultural issues. Consequently, the substitutive dynamics between party and protest politics is weaker, and the issue agendas in party and protest arenas are here more alike.

Other studies also expect a substitutive relationship between protest and party politics and suggest that the institutionalization of political conflict means that it no longer takes place in the protest arena (Kriesi et al., 1995, Koopmans et al., 2005). However, those studies do not distinguish between the master and secondary status of the dimensions of political conflict and expect that this substitutive effect can result from all the issues that are being articulated in the party arena or can result from the mere presence of different parties in parliament, regardless of what their master or secondary/niche position is. For instance, this theory would imply that a niche Green party in parliament (that competes on the secondary-issue dimension in most party systems) would have the effect of reducing environmental protest in the streets. In contrast, the new theory emphasizes the crucial importance of distinguishing between the issues articulated by the mainstream parties and the issues taken up by niche parties and protest actors. For example, the strongly one-dimensional nature of Czech party politics centered mainly on economic issues has not been weakened by the presence of niche parties in parliament seeking to compete on socio-cultural issues, such as the Green Party (2006–10).

Based on this theory, environmental protest in the region is likely to increase in relation to the ever-growing amount of recognition given to the issue of the climate crisis. Since the mainstream political parties have thus far been lagging behind in incorporating the new climate agenda into their programs and public discourse, niche parties and protest movements could come to play a central role in highlighting the pressing nature of the issue and even possible solutions to it. A series of events has already occurred that shows a new climate justice movement is gradually becoming mobilized in East Central Europe.

The work on this chapter was supported by the Charles University Research Programme Progress Q18: *Social Sciences*. While working on the text, the author was a fellow at the Center for Advanced Studies of Southeastern Europe at the University of Rijeka.

References

Bell, G. (2004). Further Up the Learning Curve: NGOs from Transition to Brussels. *Environmental Politics* 13(1): 194–215.

Binka, B. (2009). *Zelený extrémismus*. Brno: MUNI Press.

Börzel, T. A. and Buzogány, A. (2010). Environmental Organisations and the Europeanisation of Public Policy in Central and Eastern Europe: The Case of Biodiversity Governance. *Environmental Politics* 19(5): 708–735.

Bruszt, L. and Vedrés, B. (2008). The Politics of Civic Combinations. *Voluntas: International Journal of Voluntary and Nonprofit Organizations* 19(2): 140–160.

Bruszt, L. and Vedrés, B. (2013). Associating, Mobilizing, Politicizing: Local Developmental Agency from Without. *Theory and Society* 42(13): 1–23.

Buzogány, A. (2016). From Democratization to Internationalization: Studying Social Movements in Hungary. In O. Fillieule and G. Accornero (eds.) *Social Movement Studies in Europe: The State of the Art*. New York, Oxford: Berghahn, 403–418.

Caiani, M. and Císař, O. (eds.) (2019). *Radical Right Movement-Parties in Europe*. London and New York: Routledge.

Carmin, J., Albright, E., Healy, R. and Teich, T. (2008). *Environmental NGOs in Central and Eastern Europe. Summary of Survey Findings*. Cambridge, MA: MIT.

Carmin, J. and Hicks, B. (2002). Triggering Events, Transnational Networks, and the Development of Czech and Polish Environmental Movements. *Mobilization: An International Quarterly* 7(3): 305–324.

Carmin, J. and VanDeveer, S. (eds.) (2005). *EU Enlargement and the Environment: Institutional Change and Environmental Policy in Central and Eastern Europe*, London and New York: Routledge.

Cent, J., Grodzińska-Jurczak, M. and Pietrzyk-Kaszyńska, A. (2014). Emerging Multi-level Environmental Governance: A Case of Public Participation in Poland. *Journal for Nature Conservation* 22(2): 93–102.

Císař, O. (2010). Externally Sponsored Contention: The Channelling of Environmental Movement Organisations in the Czech Republic after the Fall of Communism. *Environmental Politics* 19(5): 736–755.

Císař, O. (2013a). Post-Communism and Social Movements. In D. Snow, D. della Porta, B. Klandermans, and D. McAdam (eds.) *Encyclopaedia of Social and Political Movements*, vol. 3. London: Blackwell, 994–999.

Císař, O. (2013b). The Diffusion of Public Interest Mobilization: A Historical Sociology View on the Advocates without Members in the Post-Communist Czech Republic. *East European Politics* 29(1): 69–82.

Císař, O. (2018). Social Movements after Communism. In A. Fagan and P. Kopecký (eds.) *Routledge Handbook of East European Politics*. London and New York: Routledge, 184–196.

Císař, O. (2020). Diffusion of Social Movements in Eastern Europe. In C. F. Fominaya and R. Feenstra (eds.) *Routledge Handbook of Contemporary European Social Movements*. London and New York: Routledge, 237–250.

Císař, O. and Navrátil, J. (2015). Promoting Competition or Cooperation? The Impact of EU Funding on Czech Advocacy Organizations. *Democratization* 22(3): 536–559.

Císař, O. and Navrátil, J. (2021). Political Agency in the Context of a Multilevel Polity: Post-Accession Environmental Protest in the Czech Republic. MS.

Císař, O., Navrátil, J. and Vráblíková, K. (2018). Protest Event Analysis in East Central Europe. Dataset.

Císař, O. and Vráblíková, K. (2010). The Europeanization of Social Movements in the Czech Republic: The EU and Local Women's Groups. *Communist and Post-Communist Studies* 43(2): 209–219.

Císař, O. and Vráblíková, K. (2013). Transnational Activism of Social Movement Organizations: The Effect of European Union Funding on Local Groups in the Czech Republic. *European Union Politics* 14(1): 140–160.

Císař, O. and Vráblíková, K. (2019). National Protest Agenda and the Dimensionality of Party Politics: Evidence from Four East-Central European Democracies. *European Journal of Political Research* 58(4): 1152–1171.

CVVM. (2019). *Česká veřejnost o stávkách za klima – říjen 2019*. Retrieved from: https://cvvm.soc.cas.cz/media/com_form2content/documents/c2/a5047/f9/oe191119.pdf

de Moor, J., De Vydt, M., Uba, K. and Wahlstrom, M. (2020b). New Kids on the Block: Taking Stock of the Recent Cycle of Climate Activism. *Social Movement Studies*, online first, https://doi.org/10.1080/14742837.2020.1836617

de Moor, J., Uba, K., Wahlstrom, M., Wennerhag, M. and De Vydt, M. (eds.) (2020a). *Protest for a Future II: Composition, Mobilization and Motives of the Participants in Fridays for Future Climate Protests on 20–27 September, 2019, in 19 Cities Around the World*. Retrieved from: https://gup.ub.gu.se/publication/290509

Ekiert, G. and Kubik, J. (2001). *Rebellious Civil Society: Popular Protest and Democratic Consolidation in Poland, 1989–1993*. Ann Arbor: University of Michigan Press.

Fagan, A. (2004). *Environment and Democracy in the Czech Republic. The Environmental Movement in the Transition Process*. Cheltenham, Northampton: Edward Elgar.

Fagan, A. (2005). Taking Stock of Civil-Society Development in Post-Communist Europe: Evidence from the Czech Republic. *Democratization* 12(4): 528–547.

Fagan, A. and Carmin, J. (eds.) (2011). *Green Activism in Post-Socialist Europe and the Former Soviet Union*. London: Routledge.

Fagan, A. and Jehlička, P. (2003). Contours of the Czech Environmental Movement: A Comparative Analysis of *Hnuti Duha* (Rainbow Movement) and *Jihoceske matky* (South Bohemian Mothers). *Environmental Politics* 12(2): 49–70.

Fagin, A. (2000). Environmental Protest in the Czech Republic: Three Stages of Post-Communist Development. *Czech Sociological Review* 8(2): 139–156.

Fagin, A. and Jehlička, P. (1998). Sustainable Development in the Czech Republic: A Doomed Process? In S. Baker and P. Jehlička (eds.) *Dilemmas of Transition: The Environment, Democracy and Economic Reform in East Central Europe*. London, Portland: Frank Cass, 113–128.

Frič, P. (2001). Společensko politický kontext aktuálního vývoje neziskového sektoru v ČR. In P. Frič and R. Goulli (eds.) *Neziskový sektor v České republice. Výsledky mezinárodního srovnávacího projektu Johns Hopkins University*. Praha: Eurolex Bohemia, 73–125.

Giugni, M. and Grasso, M. T. (2015). Environmental Movements in Advanced Industrial Democracies: Heterogeneity, Transformation, and Institutionalization. *Annual Review of Environment and Resources* 40(1): 337–361.

Greskovits, B. (1998). *The Political Economy of Protest and Patience: East European and Latin American Transformations Compared*. Budapest: CEU Press.

Hallstrom, L. (2004). Eurocratising Enlargement? EU Elites and NGO Participation in European Environmental Policy. *Environmental Politics* 13(1): 175–193.

Henderson, S. (2002). Selling Civil Society: Western Aid and the Nongovernmental Organization Sector in Russia. *Comparative Political Studies* 35(2): 139–167.

Henderson, S. (2003). *Building Democracy in Contemporary Russia. Western Support for Grassroots Organizations*. Ithaca and London: Cornell University Press.

Hicks, B. (1996). *Environmental Politics in Poland: A Social Movement Between Regime and Opposition.* New York: Columbia University Press.

Hicks, B. (2004). Setting Agendas and Shaping Activism: EU Influence on Central and Eastern European Environmental Movements. *Environmental Politics* 13(1): 216–233.

Imig, D. and Tarrow, S. (eds.) (2001). *Contentious Europeans. Protest and Politics in an Emerging Polity.* Lanham, Boulder, New York, Oxford: Rowman and Littlefield.

Jehlička, P. (2001). The New Subversives – Czech Environmentalists after 1989. In H. Flam (ed.) *Pink, Purple, Green: Women's, Religious, Environmental, and Gay/Lesbian Movements in Central Europe Today.* Boulder, CO: East European Monographs, 81–94.

Jehlička, P. and Jacobsson, K. (2021). The Importance of Recognizing Difference: Rethinking Central and East European Environmentalism. *Political Geography* 87: 102379.

Jehlička, P., Sarre, P. and Podoba, J. (2005). The Czech Environmental Movement's Knowledge Interest in the 1990s: Compatibility of Western Influences with pre-1989 Perspectives. *Environmental Politics* 14(1): 64–82.

Jenkins, C. J. (1998). Channeling Social Protest: Foundation Patronage of Contemporary Social Movements. In W. W. Powell and E. Clemens (eds.) *Private Action and the Public Good.* New Haven and London: Yale University Press, 206–216.

Kimla, P. (2016). Polish Environmental Movements during the Political Transformation (1980–1989). *Ecology and Safety* 10: 463–472.

Koopmans, R., Statham, P., Giugni, M. and Passy, F. (2005). *Contested Citizenship: Immigration and Cultural Diversity in Europe.* Minneapolis, London: University of Minnesota Press.

Kriesi, H., Koopmans, R., Duyvendak, J. W. and Giugni, M. (1995). *New Social Movements in Western Europe: A Comparative Analysis.* Minneapolis: University of Minnesota Press.

McCarthy, J. D. (1987). Pro-Life and Pro-Choice Mobilization: Infrastructure Deficits and New Technologies. In M. N. Zald and J. D. McCarthy (eds.) *Social Movements in an Organizational Society.* New Jersey: Transaction Publishers, 49–66.

McMahon, P. (2001). Building Civil Societies in East Central Europe: The Effects of American Non-governmental Organizations on Women's Groups. *Democratization* 8(2): 45–68.

Mendelson, S. and Glenn, J., eds. (2002). *The Power and Limits of NGOs.* New York: Columbia University Press.

Meyer, D. (2003). Political Opportunity and Nested Institutions. *Social Movement Studies* 2(1): 17–35.

Novák, A. (2017). *Tmavozelený svět. Radikálně ekologické aktivity v České republice po roce 1989.* Praha: SLON.

Pickvance, K. (1998). *Democracy and Environmental Movements in Eastern Europe: A Comparative Study of Hungary and Russia.* London and New York: Routledge.

Piotrowski, G. (2017). *In the Shadow of the Iron Curtain: Central and Eastern European Alterglobalists.* Bern: Petr Lang.

Pleines, H. and Bušková, K. (2007). Czech Environmental NGOs: Actors or Agents in EU Multilevel Governance. *Contemporary European Studies* 2(1): 37–50.

Sarre, P. and Jehlička, P. (2007). Environmental Movements in Space-Time: The Czech and Slovak Republics from Stalinism to Post-Socialism. *Transactions of the Institute of British Geographers* 32(3): 346–362.

Stark, D., Balázs, V. and Bruszt, L. (2006). Rooted Transnational Publics: Integrating Foreign Ties and Civic Activism. *Theory and Society* 35(3): 323–349.

Szabó, M. and Márkus, E. (2015). Civil Society in Hungary. In C. Schreier (ed.) *Years Later: Mapping Civil Society in the Visegrád Countries.* Stuttgart: Lucius and Lucius, 9–58.

Szulecka, J. and Szulecki, K. (2019). Between Politics and Ecological Crises: (De)legitimization of Polish Environmentalism. *Environmental Politics*, online first.

Szulecki, K. (2011). Hijacked Ideas: Human Rights, Peace, and Environmentalism in Czechoslovak and Polish Dissident Discourses. *East European Politics and Societies* 25(2): 272–295.

Tarrow, S. and Petrova, T. (2007). Transactional and Participatory Activism in the Emerging European Polity: The Puzzle of East Central Europe. *Comparative Political Studies* 40(1): 74–94.

Vachudova, M. and Hooghe, L. (2009). Postcommunist Politics in a Magnetic Field: How Transition and EU Accession Structure Party Competition on European Integration. *Comparative European Politics* 7(2): 179–212.

Velicu, I. (2019). De-growing Environmental Justice: Reflections from Anti-mining Movements in Eastern Europe. *Ecological Economics* 159: 271–278.

Welsh, I. (2004). Network Movement in the Czech Republic: Peturbating Prague. *Journal of Contemporary European Studies* 12(3): 321–337.

4

THE "TAR WARS" AND CLIMATE JUSTICE ACTIVISM IN NORTH AMERICA

A transboundary movement linking the US and Canada

Ellen Griffith Spears

Introduction

The vast oil sands in Canada's western province of Alberta form an epicenter of the global contest over energy and climate. Though just one focal point in a vast array of environmental activism in North America, the Tar Sands campaign and related pipeline protests reveal the vigor and interconnectedness of the contemporary movements in the United States and Canada. These campaigns illuminate the rise of climate justice activism; its increasingly transnational character; its diverse constituencies, alliances, and strategies; its opponents; and its limitations, as well as its strengths. Today's climate justice movement has focused and revitalized environmentalism within both countries and bolstered ties with climate activists around the globe.

In the fight for a socially just climate policy, activists are taking on a formidable adversary, "the largest integrated energy market in the world". The two nations' combined energy trade in 2011 exceeded 100 billion US dollars (Bird and Heintzelman, 2018: 175). That energy regime generates a significant portion of the climate-warming greenhouse gases that now surround and imperil the planet. According to 2016 data from the World Resources Institute, Canada and the United States have the highest per capita greenhouse gas emissions (GHGs) as measured in metric tons of carbon dioxide. US emissions comprise 13% of global GHGs, a much higher percentage than Canada's 1.51%; only China at 26% emits more GHGs (Ge and Friedrich, 2020). In addition, the conflict over energy affects the production and distribution of food, the condition of water supplies, deforestation, biodiversity, disease ecology and public health, and every other aspect of life.

In the latter third of the twentieth century, with growing globalization, US and Canadian fossil-fuel extraction and energy markets became increasingly interdependent. The US and Canada share the longest land border between two nations anywhere in the world. US-based multinationals are among the largest investors in the Tar Sands and other Canadian energy projects. Pipelines carrying Canadian crude and natural gas from the US crisscross both nations on their way to buyers around the globe.

 DOI: 10.4324/9780367855680-5

The Tar Sands campaign reveals that North American environmentalism likewise has grown increasingly intertwined in a transboundary network. Deepening exploitation of the land through extreme extraction places Indigenous rights and Native sovereignty at the center of the rise in climate justice activism. A convergence with the Black Lives Matter movement against state-sanctioned racial violence in the US sharpens the questions facing traditional environmental organizations, whose constituencies have long been predominantly white (Pellow, 2016). As a result, climate justice activism in these campaigns is more widely understood as needed not only to protect the earth from warming but also to protect water resources, support Indigenous sovereignty, and demand racial justice. Activists are exercising an increased level of militance, through direct action and civil disobedience (Takach, 2017: 3), challenging unjust relationships between peoples and lands.

Over the course of the twentieth century, environmental reforms in each nation served to expand both the role of the state and democratic public participation in environmental decision-making. By the 1980s, neoliberalism, privatization, and deregulation became features of governance in both countries. Movement activists in both countries have fought retrenchment, even as neoliberal opponents hammered away at government services, undermining what was once global leadership in environmental protection.

Historically, the conservation movement

Cross-boundary collaborations regarding nature protection have a long history. From the first North American Conservation Conference in 1909 that brought together delegates from the US, Canada, and Mexico in Washington, DC, conservationists conceived of their work as international. Spurred by extensive deforestation, diminution of wildlife, and water pollution, key forerunners of contemporary North American environmental movements "initiated continental cooperation on resource allocation", writes historian Ian Tyrrell (Tyrrell, 2015: 5). Led by conservationist US President Theodore Roosevelt, the elites who convened in the East Room of the White House in February 1909 understood their role as protectors of nature to serve national identity, economic advancement, and the supremacy of Anglo-Saxon peoples, notes Tyrrell (Tyrrell, 2015: 63).

Roosevelt's vision was built upon a history of colonization and conquest that the US and Canada share. Settler colonialism has depended on extractive industries – timber, the fur trade, minerals, and fossil fuels – as primary tools for nation building, with devastating consequences for Indigenous populations and their environments. Each nation followed patterns of assimilation, cultural displacement, and annihilation toward the Native populations (Wotherspoon and Hansen, 2013: 26; Estes, 2019: 16). Both countries are steeped in white supremacy (Johnson, 2013: 26; Adams, 1989), which shaped their conservation policies.

The creation of national parks in the two countries followed similar and overlapping paths, driven by economic development and tourism. In Canada, the Rocky Mountains Park Act of 1887, which established what is now Banff National Park, echoed language from the 1872 act that created Yellowstone. The Dominion Forest Reserves and Parks Act of 1911 made way for parks across Canada; the Organic Act establishing the US national park system passed Congress in 1916. Progressive Era conservationists in the US countenanced, even advanced, an agenda that trampled Indigenous rights. Park designations dispossessed Native populations. As environmental historians Ted Binnema and Melanie Niemi explain, "aboriginal people were excluded from national parks in the interests of game conservation, sport hunting, tourism, and Indian assimilation" (Binnema and Niemi, 2006: 724).

Early binational collaboration took the form of the International Boundary Waters Treaty, signed in 1909, which established the International Joint Commission to mediate boundary disputes over the use and quality of shared waters. Several years in negotiations, the treaty was as much an effort to secure US economic interests, notes Tyrrell, as it was an example of "cooperative internationalism" (Tyrrell, 2015: 171).

Wilderness protection and wildlife preservation campaigns developed along parallel lines, though conservation groups generally formed later in Canada, perhaps due to the country's relative abundance of wildlife. By the mid-1910s, as the new science of ecology emerged, hunters and bird protection advocates alike realized that they could not maintain species populations without a cross-border agreement between the US and Canada that protected birds and waterfowl along their migration routes. The 1916 Migratory Birds Convention enacted seasonal hunting limits. Aboriginal people hunting for subsistence were exempted, though this provision was often contested and later all but eliminated (Loo, 2006: 23, 47).

Nature conservationism as advocated by elite white men such as Teddy Roosevelt molded early twentieth-century conservation policy but was not the only underpinning of modern environmentalism in either country. Early work, less acknowledged, often by women and by labor leaders and consumer advocates, focused on municipal sanitation and safe conditions in workplaces (Gottlieb, 2005; Spears, 2019). Navajo people in the US Southwest protested the New Deal era culling of goats and sheep essential to their livelihood (Weisiger, 2009); African Americans practiced agroecology on fields they worked and lands they owned in the American South (Hersey, 2011). In Canada, Native people had long "rationalized and regulated" wildlife trapping and hunting to sustain animal populations as well as humans (Loo, 2006: 49) But after World War II, a more broad-based public health–oriented environmentalism expanded to take in concerns over nuclear fallout, pesticide poisoning, urban pollution, acid rain, and damage to the ozone layer. Constituencies expanded among middle-class white activists, and cross-boundary contacts increased. However, longstanding conservation groups such as the Sierra Club, the National Audubon Society, and the Wilderness Society, with adherents in both countries, largely failed to include people of color or to address their environmental concerns.

Conservation concerns broaden after World War II

With the sharp rise after World War II of fossil fuel usage – not only as energy but as pesticides, other chemicals, and consumer products, especially plastics – the environmental impact of these commodities mounted. Environmental advocates increasingly turned their attention to the damage traceable to fossil fuels. *Silent Spring*, the influential text by Rachel Carson that decried the effects on wildlife and human health of DDT and other organochlorine chemicals, built upon and generated ecology-oriented health activism in multiple locales around the globe, including in Canada (Carson, 1962). The 1967 Canadian Broadcasting Company's (CBC) television program "The Air of Death", by Larry Gosnell, also served as a wake-up call in Canada, sparking the formation of Toronto-based Pollution Probe (1969) and Group Action to Stop Pollution (GASP). In the film, doctors and activists from the US and Canada, including Hazel Henderson from New York City's Citizens for Clean Air, spelled out the health consequences of polluted air (O'Connor, 2015: 19).

Pollution Probe spawned branches in multiple cities around Canada. As in the US, professionalization (i.e., hiring and training paid staffs) and institutionalization (establishing nonprofit entities and significant fundraising operations) transformed what had been ad hoc volunteer environmental groups, though the process was uneven (Gottlieb, 2005). Tactics diverged, with some groups maintaining radical protest politics and others moderating their demands, choosing lobbying and negotiation over street demonstrations and direct action (Guigni and Grasso, 2015: 347). Serious negotiations for a US-Canada energy compact were underway by 1970, and Pollution Probe's Energy and Resources Project, which later spun off to focus on lobbying and education, urged hundreds of environmental groups in both countries to join them in opposing it. The group campaigned across borders, explains historian Ryan O'Connor, realizing that "a continental energy pact would fuel American growth with Canadian energy and resources" (O'Connor, 2015: 81).

Additional translocal connections included Canadian activists' support for the Love Canal Homeowners Association and other grassroots groups near Niagara Falls that took on the federal EPA and the State of New York in the 1978 campaign to redress a dioxin-laden chemical disaster (O'Connor, 2015: 8; Gibbs, 1982; Blum, 2008). On Canada's western coast, in British Columbia, US expats and Canadians in Vancouver founded the now-global direct-action organization Greenpeace in 1971. Greenpeace used direct-action tactics to challenge nuclear tests in the Pacific and attempted to block whaling and the seal hunt. The latter were economically significant Canadian pursuits that put the group at odds with Indigenous sealers (Zelko, 2014: 110). At times, Canadian activists directly engaged US policy, testifying against harp sealing at the US congressional hearings that led to the passage of the US Marine Mammal Protection Act of 1972 (Zelko, 2014: 113).

Air and water pollution also prompted cross-boundary activism. Pollution Probe advocated reductions in phosphate pollution in the Great Lakes, measures adopted when the two countries signed the Great Lakes Water Quality Agreement in 1972 (O'Connor, 2015: 59–60). Unfortunately, when acid rain, mainly originating in the US, caused ecological and health impacts largely felt in Canada, US President Ronald Reagan used a now-familiar tactic – denying scientific findings – to back out of a pledge he had made to Canadian Prime Minister Pierre Trudeau to enforce US pollution rules to alleviate acid rain (Parr, 2018: 7).

International collaboration resulted in the multilateral 1987 Montreal Protocol on Substances that Deplete the Ozone Layer, one of the most successful international environmental agreements to date. The treaty yielded practical steps to remediate damage to the ozone layer, the upper atmosphere that shields the earth from harmful ultraviolet rays from the sun. Friends of the Earth and the Sierra Club had campaigned as early as 1970 against superjets that spewed ozone-depleting exhaust (Cook, 1990: 334). The Montreal Protocol, signed by 197 nations, established binding targets for reducing ozone-depleting chlorofluorocarbons (CFCs). Especially important for the pact's success was the continued work of grassroots activists in both countries. After the agreement was signed, Friends of the Earth-Canada, Greenpeace Action, Clean Water Action, the National Toxics Campaign, and the US Public Interest Research Group mobilized the shopping public to stop buying CFC-containing products (Cook, 1990: 336). Enforcement of the treaty led to reductions in CFCs, visible contraction in the holes in the ozone layer, and notable health benefits – reductions in skin cancer rates and the incidence of cataracts (U.S. EPA, 2017: 6; Velders et al., 2007).

The anti-CFCs campaign established working relationships across borders and showed greater global cooperation was possible just as the seriousness of the climate crisis was coming more sharply into view. In 1988, NASA scientist James Hansen warned the US Congress that the planet was inexorably warming due to increased carbon in the earth's atmosphere. The trend was due to human actions, especially the longstanding and widespread dependence on non-renewable carbon-based fuels (Hansen, 1988; Shabecoff, 1988).

Fossil fuel interdependence

A Canadian entrepreneur drilled the first North American oil well in Ontario, Canada, in 1858, a year before the first US well at Titusville, Pennsylvania (Smil, 2017: 246). However, Canadian oil production did not grow significantly until after World War II, when it was celebrated for what Canadian writer and filmmaker Geo Takach calls "the ingenuity, hard work, and masculinity of resource extraction" in the context of the Cold War (Takach, 2017: 30).

Ten years later, Conservative Prime Minister John G. Diefenbaker (1957–63) articulated his "Northern Vision", in which Canada's Northern Territories were "the keystone of Canada's survival, development, and identity", explains environmental historian Tina Loo (Loo, 2006: 127). On- and offshore oil reserves in the region became central to that vision and have long been key environmental battlegrounds. By the 2000s, the Tar Sands region of Alberta took center stage in the energy drama.

Enhanced integration of the two markets dates to the US-Canada energy compact of the late 1960s, as post-war nation building and national renewal heightened the two nations' dependence on non-renewable fossil fuels. The Cold War exacerbated global competition for resources. A wave of anti-colonial independence movements around the globe marked a shift in the global politics of oil. With the founding of the Organization of Petroleum Exporting Countries (OPEC) in Baghdad in September 1960, US leaders came to view Canadian oil as crucial to US energy security, writes political scientist Angela V. Carter, serving "as a secure, reliable, and geographically proximate supplier of oil resources" (Carter, 2014: 30). Encouraged by free trade pacts, the economic integration of the two markets grew, and by 2017, Alberta became the source of one-fourth of US oil supplies (Takach, 2017: 45).

Climate change and climate justice

Informed by global assessments of the climate impact of fossil fuels, as compiled by the Intergovernmental Panel on Climate Change (IPCC) beginning in 1988, and as deliberated at the annual global meetings held pursuant to the United Nations Framework Convention on Climate Change signed at the Earth Summit in Rio de Janeiro, Brazil, in 1992, transboundary activism to stem the climate threat grew. The Climate Action Network formed in 1989, and by 2020 was a worldwide network with more than 1,300 participating non-governmental organizations. Canada's Climate Action Network/Réseau Action Climat (CAnet.org) lobbies on climate policy and chooses NGO members of Canadian delegations to international climate negotiations (Olive, 2016: 237).

As awareness increased, existing environmental organizations adopted climate projects, and hundreds of new climate-focused groups formed. Among the new groups is 350.org, founded at Middlebury College in Vermont by US writer and ecologist Bill McKibben and colleagues and students in 2008. The group's name referred to 350 parts per million, the level of carbon dioxide in the atmosphere regarded as "safe". (Global measurements had passed 400 million ppm by 2016) (Jones, 2017). By 2020, 350.org had developed links with global grassroots groups in 188 countries. In collaboration with Canadian environmentalist and author Naomi Klein and others, 350.org and many other groups helped shift the climate debate (Russell et al., 2014: 170).

As the climate movement expanded, attention focused more directly on disproportionate exposure of specific groups to environmental hazards, a condition that is being exacerbated by climate warming. At an international scale, the adopting of the Bali Principles of Climate Justice in 2002 marked greater emphasis on the impact of warming on developing nations and marginalized peoples. Indigenous groups, communities of color, and low-income neighborhoods are most deeply affected by environmental pollution and often lack access to healthful amenities, such as parks, health-care facilities, and other social goods. Often traced in the US to the landmark battle against the siting of a hazardous PCB landfill in an African American neighborhood in Warren County, North Carolina, in 1982 (McGurty, 2007), the environmental justice paradigm calls for distributive justice: that is, an end to disparate treatment. Environmental justice activists also demand procedural justice and the inclusion of marginalized populations in environmental decision-making, as well as the equitable enforcement of environmental laws (Martínez-Alier, 2002).

At the root of environmental racism is violence, argues critical environmental justice scholar David Pellow (Pellow, 2016). "Slow violence", literary scholar Rob Nixon termed the gradual accretion of poisons in marginalized bodies (Nixon, 2011). Society and mainstream environmental groups must recognize the intersectional nature of oppression, oppose the devaluation of Black lives, and practice a "politics of solidarity", Pellow argues (Pellow, 2016: 12). By the 2010s, the locus of attention shifted from the work of national organizations based in the countries' respective capitals to more decentralized, often local, place-based work, led by communities of color and Indigenous groups. Transboundary and translocal ties increased as a more intersectional environmentalism arose.

The Tar Sands: a hub for climate justice activism

As oil has ever more tightly linked the two nations' economies and their respective environmental movements, the Tar Sands region has anchored a network that extends via pipelines and other tentacles throughout Canada to the US and the rest of the globe. The Tar Sands venture is likely the world's greatest investment of capital in one project and the globe's largest industrial undertaking (Takach, 2017: 3). These operations highlight the costs of human technological interventions in nature, their geopolitical context, and the ecological damage and social consequences that ensue.

All fossil fuels release harmful byproducts that are hazardous to human health and surrounding ecosystems during extraction and use. However, the bitumen crude taken from the Tar Sands since 1967 has been dubbed "the dirtiest oil on the planet" (Takach, 2017: 3; Nikiforuk, 2010). Toxic and polluting, the Tar Sands oil is also "corrosive", making pipelines especially vulnerable to leaks (Lukacs, 2014: 78). Extracting bitumen is an energy-intensive enterprise that "generates two to four times more greenhouse gases than extracting conventional oil" (Takach, 2017: 7). Extraction expanded rapidly in the early 2000s. As a result, vast swaths of Indigenous lands in western Canada have been scraped of vegetation and wildlife, disrupting ways of life and livelihoods.

US firms exercise significant power over Tar Sands operations. The Oil Sands Leadership Initiative, an industry compact, includes ConocoPhillips, Nexen, Shell, Statoil (a Norwegian company), Suncor Energy, and Total (Klein, 2014: 246). Industry officials acknowledge 52% ownership by US corporations and 15% by non-Canadian, non-US companies (Skuce, 2012; Natural Resources Canada, 2012). Foreign ownership has steadily increased since 2006, complicating both regulation and accountability (Carter, 2014: 29) and making cross-boundary activism a necessity.

Anti-extraction campaigns form a vital element of the climate movement. Pipelines are a key target for climate activists because pipeline proponents aim to embed a distribution network that solidifies national and corporate commitments to a fossil-fuel energy delivery system for decades to come. Climate advocates oppose extending oil and gas infrastructure for this very reason: to do so perpetuates fossil fuel dependence and delays the necessary shift to renewables. The Tar Sands oil cannot be distributed without pumping capacity, so the pipeline fight is crucial to keeping the dirty oil in the ground. Transport of oil is subject to bottlenecks, which makes the transportation routes vulnerable to blockades and other protests (Weis et al., 2014: 16).

Tar Sands Blockade, "an all-volunteer horizontal, consensus-based organizing collective" launched in 2012, focused its efforts on the local communities affected by "tar sands mining, transportation, and refining" (Tar Sands Blockade, 2016). Pipelines "provoke resistance by projecting serious eco-health risks onto ever more regions" (Weis et al., 2014: 17). In addition to alarm about climate change, fear of contamination of water supplies by chemicals used at the site and concern about oil spills along the pipeline route motivated opposition from many landowners, who also balked at excessive use of eminent domain to benefit a private company (Tar Sands Blockade, 2016).

Pipeline opponents employ multiple creative strategies, including mass mobilizations, educational campaigns, lobbying state and municipal entities, blockades, and litigation. On Earth Day 2013, Montreal's streets filled with 50,000 people, marching in opposition to transporting Tar Sands oil through Quebec (Lukacs, 2014: 81). The following April, marching under the slogan, "Reject and Protect", Athabascan and Beaver Lake Cree First Nations along with fellow Canadian Neil Young and the Cowboy-Indian Alliance joined a climate action in Washington, DC, against the Keystone XL pipeline being built to carry Tar Sands oil (Narine, 2015). In September 2014, the People's Climate March brought 400,000 people to New York and more than 2,000 climate actions swept the globe.

Other creative strategies include American author Terry Tempest Williams's attempt to purchase auctioned drilling leases to prevent extraction (Schimel, 2016). Some groups have pressured secondary targets. The US-based Natural Resources Defense Council (NRDC) pushed US and Canadian airlines to commit to not using Tar Sands oil (Klein, 2014: 248). Activists launched a broad coalition effort, the "Keep It in the Ground" campaign, as researchers reported that 85% of Tar Sands crude must stay in the ground to keep global warming under the 2° Celsius rise scientists deem necessary to prevent catastrophic harm (McGlade and Ekins, 2015: 190).

The coalition of opponents to Tar Sands extraction is broad. Catholic opposition in Fort McMurray has been important; one local priest said that current modes of extraction "cannot be morally justified" (Haluza-DeLay, 2014: 42). First Nations spokespersons define the meaning of the fight. Beaver Lake Cree Nation member Crystal Lameman explains that the Tar Sands extractors' assault on Indigenous land and bodies is "a complete dismissal of legal and ethical duties to protect our waters, our one true Mother [earth], and the ecosystems that life depends on" (Lameman, 2014: 120). Tar Sands operations have brought loss of caribou habitat and contamination of water supplies, she explains. Oil spills have killed birds and other wildlife. Medicinal plants understood through Indigenous knowledge are disappearing. A corollary to the violence against the land is the exploitation of women. With large numbers of transient male workers, residents near Fort McMurray and other oil sands extraction sites report an alarming increase in violence against women and in the disappearances of Indigenous women (Awâsis, 2014: 255).

Lameman emphasizes the failure of the oil sands industry to meet the minimum international standards of "free, prior and informed consent" (PRIC). Nevertheless, "First Nations rights are arguably some of the most important rights in the Canadian legal landscape and certainly the most powerful environmental rights in the country", Lameman points out. "We will always have an inherent right to the land with the ability to sustain ourselves in a meaningful

Transnational Climate Resistance

Resistance to the climate, ecological, and public
health impacts of extreme extraction of fossil fuels
extends along pipeline routes from the Tar Sands in
Alberta, Canada, and throughout the United States.

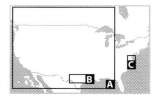

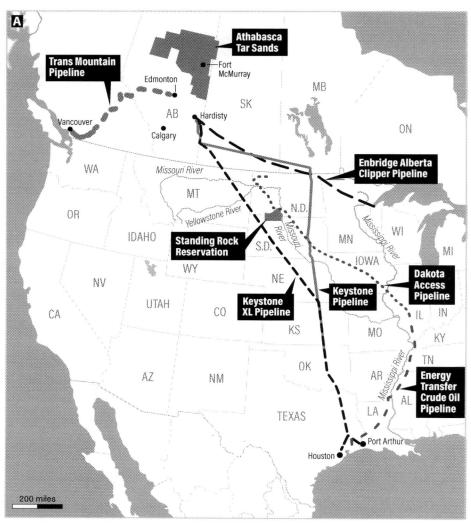

Figure 4.1　Transnational climate resistance

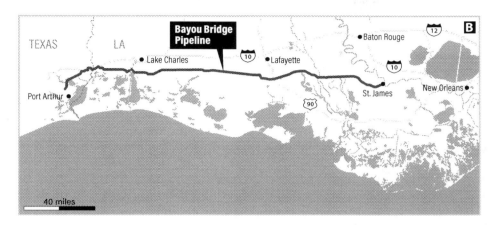

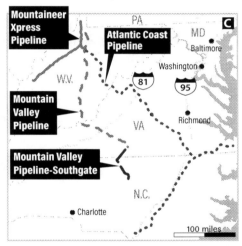

A An alliance of green groups, Latinx and Mexican-American communities, farmers, conservative landowners, and Indigenous groups have opposed pipelines that transport Tar Sands oil from Alberta to multiple refineries and ports in the U.S. and Canada.

B The Bayou Bridge Pipeline cuts through ecologically sensitive landscapes on its route from Port Arthur, Texas, to the majority African American St. James Parish in Louisiana.

C In 2020, activists succeeded in halting two major pipelines, the Atlantic Coast Pipeline and the Mountain Valley Pipeline-Southgate.

Maps by Charles Jones / icjdesign.com. Sources: A: Natural Resources Defense Council, "What is the Keystone XL Pipeline?"; KeystoneXL.com/maps; Gordon Jaremko, "Trans Mountain Pipeline Detour to Increase Construction Costs," Shale Daily, December 30, 2020; B: Tristan Baurick, "Bayou Bridge Pipeline is now complete, after years of controversy," NOLA.com, The Times-Picayune, March 27, 2019; C: Jimmy Davidson, Appalachian Voices.

Figure 4.1 (Continued)

way" (Lameman, 2014: 122–123). The Athabasca Chipewyan First Nation and the Beaver Lake Cree Nation have filed numerous lawsuits, attempting to block further incursions on First Nations lands in Alberta (Coats, 2014: 274).

Indigenous women like Lameman have played leading roles in intersectional environmental activism. Idle No More, an initiative by First Nations women in central Canada, was stimulated in part by the Harper administration's efforts in 2012 to limit public input and roll back environmental regulation. Both an organization and a movement, Idle No More spread its spirit and tactics around Canada and within the US, with actions including "hand drums and jingle dresses . . . flash mob round dances", hunger strikes, spiritual walks, and blockades of roads and railroads (Klein, 2014: 381).

European public opinion and activism against accepting Tar Sands crude have provided useful leverage in Canadians' battle to resist extreme extraction (Engler, 2014: 55–56; Takach, 2017: 38). The UK Tar Sands Network formed in 2009, raising the profile of the issue in the United Kingdom. Tar Sands opponents mounted an art exhibition in Trafalgar Square in London, demonstrated at the Spanish port of Bilbao against Tar Sands shipments, and held an "oil orgy" at a Canada-Europe Energy Round Table in London in 2011 (UK Tar Sands Network, 2011). Canada's Harper government fought back, using its diplomats as advocates for Tar Sands crude (Engler, 2014: 57ff.). However, lobbying at the EU successfully forestalled European acceptance of Tar Sands oil until 2019 (Global Climate Finance, 2019).

A crucial link in the industry's distribution infrastructure, TransCanada's (now TC Energy's) Keystone XL pipeline was designed to bring oil sands crude from Hardisty, Alberta, to Steele City, Nebraska. An unprecedented alliance of green groups, Latinx and Mexican American communities, farmers, conservative landowners, and US and Canadian Indigenous groups formed to protest the proposed route, which threatens the Ogallala aquifer, tribal lands, and

Figure 4.2 Activists launched a broad coalition effort, the "Keep It in the Ground" campaign.

Midwestern farmlands. The Cowboy-Indian Alliance brought together progressive white farmers from Bold Nebraska and Dakota Rural Action. In March of 2014, the Oglala Sioux Tribal President Bryan Brewer declared war on the Keystone XL pipeline (Estes, 2019: 34, 26–27).

After the US Congress failed in 2010 to pass a climate change bill, the American Clean Energy and Security Act, several Washington, DC–based national organizations began prioritizing grassroots work (Bagley, 2013). Local and regional organizations stepped up. In the Midwest, the Great Plains Tar Sands Resistance network linked organizations in education, lobbying, and direct action to block TransCanada's pipeline expansion efforts (Weis et al., 2014: 17). Individuals, some identified with Earth First!, chained themselves to concrete to halt construction. Diverse groups rallied against Keystone XL, including the:

> Sierra Club – Red Earth Group, Sooner Utilities, Stop Fracking Payne County, Our Earth, Idle No More – Central Oklahoma, Grand Riverkeeper/Lead Agency, the Society to Protect Indigenous Rights & Indigenous Treaties (S.P.I.R.I.T.), Clean Energy Future OK, Oklahoma Sierra Club, Center for Conscience in Action, Green Party of Oklahoma, and the Oklahoma IWW.
>
> (Common Dreams, 2014)

Militant direct action against TransCanada's Keystone XL pipeline accompanied other forms of non-violent protest. Earlier, an 80-day sit-in along Keystone's southern route had been brutally quashed, and that pipeline was already in operation as the protests of the proposed northern route heightened (Estes, 2019: 34). In summer 2011, more than 1,200 people, many of whom had never previously participated in civil disobedience, were arrested in front of the White House for protesting KXL (Klein, 2014: 139; Russell et al., 2014: 171). Nearly 50 members of the US House of Representatives petitioned then–Secretary of State John Kerry to reject the pipeline; the Department of State was required to issue clearance because the project crossed the international border (Feldman, 2010). Canadian Prime Minister Stephen Harper lobbied Obama to support the pipeline project (Engler, 2014: 62). However, though the Obama administration long vacillated on Keystone XL, President Obama eventually denied approval for the northern leg of the line in December 2015 (Klein, 2014: 140; Estes, 2019: 40). The Trump administration green-lighted KXL but was reversed by President Joe Biden on his first day in office in January 2021, a decision that blocked further construction.

Indigenous leadership at Standing Rock, North Dakota

Indigenous communities contribute little to climate-impacting greenhouse gases but are often among those most vulnerable to water and air pollution, sea-level rise, more frequent and more severe storm systems, and extreme extraction (Olive, 2016: 241). Groups such as the Indigenous Environmental Network (IEN) have expanded on the environmental justice paradigm to link climate, land, and Indigenous sovereignty. Climate and anti–fossil fuel extraction movements, many led by Indigenous activists, surged in 2009, marking unprecedented growth in transboundary collaboration. Unsurprisingly, however, Indigenous groups do not always agree about oil and gas mining. Fifty-one Indigenous groups support the ongoing Trans Mountain pipeline project through British Columbia (Olive, 2016: 240).

The fight over the Dakota Access Pipeline (DAPL) at Standing Rock, North Dakota, became emblematic of the anti-pipeline movement as media attention peaked in 2016 in the waning days of the Obama administration. The NO DAPL fight showed the power of unified Indigenous resistance against dominant industrial actors and the militarized force of the state and federal government. The land had been that of a confederation of seven member tribes, Oceti Sakowin, whose members live on both sides of the 49th parallel in Saskatchewan and North and South Dakota (Olive, 2016: 49). However, unlike Keystone XL, DAPL took a domestic route only and did not require State Department review. Moreover, with DAPL licensed under Nationwide Permit 12, the Texas firm financing the project, Energy Transfer Partners, managed to bypass Clean Water Act and National Environmental Policy Act requirements (Estes, 2019: 42–43). The route would cut through sites sacred to the Standing Rock Sioux and would run under the Missouri River, the tribe's water source. Standing Rock has special significance as the site at which the American Indian Movement and others founded the International Indian Treaty Council in 1974, attended by 5,000 people representing 97 Indigenous nations (Estes, 2019: 223). The land is classified as culturally sensitive under the National Historic Preservation Act (Estes, 2019: 43).

When residents of the majority-white state capital city of Bismarck complained that the initial route might put that city's water supply at risk, the pipeline was rerouted near the Standing Rock tribes' ancestral territory. The danger to drinking water was "a threat to Standing Rock's sovereignty", writes historian Nick Estes (Estes, 2019: 44). "Water is Life" became the Water Protectors' refrain. Their concerns were well-founded. The Dakota Access Pipeline has been riddled with predictable leaks and spills – five in the first six months of operation. Nevertheless, operators sought to double the flow to 1.1 million barrels per day (Estes, 2019: 43–44; Soraghan, 2020; O'Connell, 2019).

The #NoDAPL campaign in 2016 brought together 300 Indigenous and First Nations groups from the US and Canada, who were joined by allies from environmental groups, farmers, and laborers, including young people and military veterans. Two encampments established near the proposed pipeline route attracted as many as 12,000 protestors to join Native American Water Protectors. Indigenous women were leaders in the #NoDAPL resistance (Estes, 2019: 83). As in Alberta, gender violence accompanied the pipeline construction camps (Estes, 2019: 79–82).

The campaign faced harsh state reaction. Police and troopers inflicted brutal repression. Icy water sprayed on protestors in winter, the bombardment with sound, and especially the attack dogs were reminiscent of the violent police crackdowns against civil rights protesters and the treatment of Black Lives Matter marchers (Estes, 2019: 63, 90). (Moreover, in the wake of the Standing Rock and Tar Sands protests, at least 13 US states and the provincial government of Alberta have enacted laws criminalizing protests that target critical infrastructure) (Black, 2020; Shea, 2020). Finally, under the mounting pressure and with intervention from the Obama White House, the Army Corps denied the DAPL permit on December 4, 2016, pending a more thorough environmental assessment. The victory was significant, if fleeting.

The anti-pipeline campaign extended deep into the US South, where Gulf Coast residents already faced devastating environmental losses due to the oil industry and extreme weather events. The region was still recovering from the levee failures after Hurricane Katrina in 2005, when five years later, a British Petroleum (BP) oil rig exploded in the Gulf of Mexico, killing 11 oil workers and discharging nearly five million barrels of crude oil into the inland sea. In 2017, Louisiana activists learned that Energy Transfer Partners and Phillips 66 planned to pump North Dakota crude through fragile ecosystems and vulnerable populations in their state. The Bayou Bridge pipeline route included the predominantly low-income African American industrial town of St. James along "Cancer Alley", the chemically contaminated stretch between Baton Rouge and New Orleans, and included 11 of the top 20 census tracts with the highest cancer risk in the nation (US EPA, 2014). Activists established the L'eau Est La Vie protest camp, directly invoking the "Water is Life" slogan of the DAPL activists. Students Organizing

Against Racism, the Green Club, and other groups at Tulane University held a teach-in. Louisiana landowners filed several suits to block the pipeline through the environmentally sensitive Atchafalaya Basin along the proposed 160-mile Bayou Bridge pipeline. An appeals court found that the Bayou Bridge Pipeline Company had "trampled" on the rights of residents and awarded damages, but the pipeline was completed and opened in 2019 (King, 2020).

At every step, climate activists faced vigorous and well-financed opposition. Oil and gas industrialists had long attempted to subvert and undermine environmental laws that had passed the US Congress in the 1970s with bipartisan support. In the early 1990s, the Global Climate Coalition, an industry group formed by petrochemical giants, including Exxon, Shell, Amoco, and Texaco, and major automakers GM, Ford, and Chrysler derailed standards for greenhouse gas emissions and worked to torpedo the 1996 climate negotiations at Kyoto. By 2002, as outright climate denialism became less tenable, the coalition had folded, but new entities formed, fueled by large sums from unidentified donors. These opponents targeted environmental activists through a barrage of media campaigns, greenwashing their climate-intensive products, and, especially when conservatives held national political power, through the arms of government. Similar efforts were underway in Canada, as the Stephen Harper government (2006–15) initiated significant reversals of federal environmental legislation, and Canadian oil interests lobbied across borders and sued to block California's fuel standards (Engler, 2014: 60–61).

One target of these anti-environmental campaigns was science itself. In Canada, activists responded to the Harper government's assault on the science of environmental protection with a "Death of Evidence" march to Parliament Hill in 2012 (Lakanen, 2018: 558). Until Exxon Mobil was outed in 2015 by the *Los Angeles Times* as having made internal decisions based on clear knowledge of climate warming, the company funded advertising campaigns denying the reality of climate change (Jennings et al., 2015).

The Obama, Trudeau, and Trump Years

Fossil fuels still dominate the energy grid, accounting for 86% of the world's primary energy in 2015, only a 4% decline since 1990 (Smil, 2017: 295, citing the *BP Statistical Review of World Energy* 2016). To climate activists' dismay, the Obama administration pursued an "all of the above" energy policy, which included funding for renewables, but also supported nuclear and robust oil and gas extraction. By mid-2014, writes energy historian Vaclav Smil, the US had re-emerged as "the world's largest producer of oil, thanks to dramatic increases in shale oil production through hydraulic fracturing" (Smil, 2017: 366). Nevertheless, anti-extraction coalitions claimed victories during the second Obama administration, including the temporary halt of Keystone XL and the denial of the Dakota Access Pipeline permit, which briefly blocked construction.

The prospects for environmental reform in the US sank, however, with the election of Donald J. Trump in 2016. Trump replaced the "energy independence" national security framework with a nationalistic call for "energy dominance". Trump appointed opponents of environmental protection to every major administration post. Nevertheless, when Trump announced in June 2017 his plan to pull out of the Paris Climate Accord, "22 states, 550 cities, and 900 companies", cities, and states pledged to keep GHG reduction commitments (Climate Action Tracker, 2020). Twenty-five states had joined the US Climate Alliance as of late 2020 (US Climate Alliance, 2020).

In Canada, sharp differences exist, even among those who favor climate mitigation. The Pan-Canadian framework, which includes carbon pricing as a centerpiece, supported by Justin Trudeau's Liberal Party, is evident in the Greenhouse Gas Pollution Pricing Act, passed by

Parliament in 2018 (Olive, 2016: 232–233). The Indigenous Environmental Network and the Climate Justice Alliance oppose carbon pricing as a strategy, concerned that creating a market for carbon will perpetuate fossil-fuel dependence and fail to reduce carbon emissions at their source (Gilbertson, 2019). Conservative provincial leaders challenged the Act's national carbon pricing system (Olive, 2016: 233; Stefanovich, 2020). The Supreme Court of Canada upheld the Act in March 2021.

The disastrous environmental impacts of Trumpism – following a long conservative assault on the US environmental movement's gains – shape fortunes for human health and nature worldwide. However, environmentalists took heart from a series of victories in the US in the summer of 2020, made possible by their efforts: winning further review of the Keystone XL (Farah, 2020) and DAPL pipelines (Fortin and Friedman, 2020) and halting proposed Atlantic Coast and Mountain Valley Southgate pipelines (Anchondo et al., 2020; Skibell, 2020).

Racial justice reckoning

The racial justice reckoning in the United States that followed the murder of George Floyd in Minneapolis, Minnesota, on 25 May 2020 and the countless other racial murders and beatings that resulted in greater public notice to police brutality in the US spread to many sectors. The rise in Indigenous and Black activism augurs a potentially "transformative resurgence" in environmental activism, argues Canadian scholar Ingrid R. G. Waldron (Waldron, 2018: 19). Many environmental organizations, including the US Climate Action Network, representing 180 organizations, issued statements supporting the Black Lives Matter movement. The Stop the Money Pipeline campaign focused in 2020 on protecting minority communities affected by the fossil fuel industry (Banks, 2020).

The mounting US movement to end Black inequality and injustice toward people of color raised renewed questions to environmental organizations, which have largely failed to diversify their staffs and program focus or to deal with their long legacy of white privilege. In 1990, the Southwest Organizing Project and dozens of co-signers challenged major US environmental organizations over lack of diversity in staffing and failure to tackle environmental injustice (Fears and Mufson, 2020; Taylor, 2018). Still today, a failure to examine and redress the impact of whiteness in the traditional environmental movements in both countries has hindered success (Curnow and Helferty, 2018). In summer 2020, the Sierra Club took the modest but significant step of denouncing preservationist icon and club founder John Muir for his racist Progressive Era denigration of the Native peoples displaced from Yosemite National Park (Merchant, 2003: 382; Brune, 2020). The 2020 protests have opened space for more robust action by the environmental movement to act in solidarity to address institutional racism within the movement's ranks and in the broader society.

COVID-19 has had a dramatic effect on the oil and gas industry, shutting down wells and leaving workers without jobs or health insurance. In North Dakota alone, oil companies closed 7,500 wells in the first half of 2020 and all but halted new drilling (Bolstad, 2020). Pipeline construction is nevertheless moving forward in some locales. "By barreling forward with construction [of the KXL pipeline] during a global pandemic", Sierra Club's Beyond Dirty Fuels campaign associate director Catherine Collentine told *E&E News* in April 2020, "TC Energy [formerly TransCanada] is putting already vulnerable communities at even greater risk" (Anchondo, 2020).

In Canada, the oil fields became a hot spot for COVID-19 transmission. In April and May 2020, the disease spread from a fly-in, fly-out work camp in Kerl, 70 kilometers north of Fort McMurray (McIntosh, 2020). However, the Canadian Parliament, sensitive to the climate consequences of government COVID-relief programs, attached climate provisions to COVID-19 loans in its bailout of the country's largest companies (Cusick, 2020). By contrast, the Trump administration undercut efforts to require COVID-protective measures in workplaces.

While former Harper government and Trump administration actions to deny science, gut environmental laws, and reverse climate-ameliorative measures have enduring impacts, the long arc of energy usage is moving away from fossil-fuel dependence. As is true globally, young people are transforming the movement. Vigorous campus-based fossil-fuel divestment campaigns led primarily by students have now yielded nearly 1,250 organizations with divestment commitments worth $11 trillion. Responding to pressure and market forces, educational institutions, large charitable entities, and other investors have divested from fossil-fuel stocks (Cadan et al., 2019; Mangat, 2018: 188).

The Biden administration moved quickly in early 2021 to reverse the damage of the Trump years, rejoining the Paris Climate Accord; restoring EPA monitoring and enforcement; rejecting oil and gas drilling on public lands, including in the Arctic National Wildlife Refuge; and blocking unnecessary pipelines. Biden's January 2021 revocation of the cross-boundary permit for the Keystone XL pipeline undergirded a momentous win for the 10-year campaign by the coalition of Indigenous groups, environmental organizations, climate advocates, and landholders seeking to halt the pipeline. On 9 June 2021, amid rising protests of other pipeline projects, TC Energy terminated Keystone XL (*E&E News* staff, 2021).

US environmentalists will find more room to rebuild during a Democratic administration, though advocates have often found it challenging to win gains with Democrats in office, especially when Congress is sharply divided. Anti-environmental forces persist that were able to capitalize on what the Trump administration allowed them to do. And leaders in several of Canada's western provinces remain allied with extractive industry against setting robust climate goals. Even among Democrats, moderates diverge from supporters of a Green New Deal, who seek to link renewable energy jobs with forceful climate action. Nevertheless, under extreme threat, a heterogeneous, intersectional climate justice movement representing a multiplicity of voices has built power in both countries based on a politics of solidarity that supports Indigenous rights and racial justice; much will depend on such a movement building the alliances necessary to lead and sustain a transformative resurgence.

Thanks to the volume editors and University of Alabama American Studies colleague Jolene Hubbs for insightful comments.

References

Adams, H. (1989) *Prison of Grass: Canada from A Native Point of View*. Saskatoon: Fifth House Publishers.

Anchondo, C. (2020) KXL Decision Reignites Climate Fight. *E&E News*, April 1.

Anchondo, C., Swartz, K. E. and Northey, H. (2020) Decision to Kill Atlantic Coast Project Upends Natural Gas. *E&E News*, July 6.

Awâsis, S. (2014) Pipelines and Resistance Across Turtle Island. In T. Black et al. (eds.), *A Line in the Tar Sands*. Toronto, ON, Canada; Oakland, CA: PM Press.

Bagley, K. (2013) To Defeat Keystone, Environmental Movement Goes from Beltway to Grassroots. *Inside Climate News*, May 23.

Banks, B. (2020) George Floyd Protests: Climate Advocacy Groups Join Demonstrations. *E&E News*, June 2.

Binnema, T. T. and Niemi, M. (2006, October) 'Let the Line be Drawn Now': Wilderness, Conservation, and the Exclusion of Aboriginal People from Banff National Park in Canada. *Environmental History* 11: 724–750.

Bird, S. and Heintzelman, M. (2018) Canada/US Transboundary Energy Governance, 175–199. In S. Brooks and A. Olive (eds.), *Transboundary Environmental Governance Across the World's Longest Border*. East Lansing: Michigan State University Press.

Black, M. (2020) Alberta Bill Targeting Blockade Protesters Passed into Law. *TVNewsEdmonton.ca*, June 17.

Black, T., Russell, J. K., D'Arcy, S. and Weis, A. J. (2014) *A Line in the Tar Sands: Struggles for Environmental Justice*. Toronto, Ontario, Canada; Oakland, CA: PM Press.

Blum, E. D. (2008) *Love Canal Revisited: Race, Class, and Gender in Environmental Activism*. Lawrence: University Press of Kansas.

Bolstad, E. (2020) Hope Outlasts Prosperity in Town Flattened by Oil Bust. *E&E News*, July 27.

Brown, M. (2020) U.S. Supreme Court Deals Blow to Keystone Oil Pipeline Project. *The Washington Post*, July 6.

Brune, M. (2020) Pulling Down Our Monuments. *Sierra Club*, July 22.

Cadan, Y., Mokgopo, A. and Vondrich, C. (2019) $11 Trillion and Counting. *Fossilfree.org*.

Carson, R. (1962) *Silent Spring*. Boston: Houghton Mifflin.

Carter, A. V. (2014) Petro-Capitalism and the Tar Sands, 23–35. In T. Black et al. (eds.), *A Line in the Tar Sands*. Toronto, ON, Canada; Oakland, CA: PM Press.

Climate Action Tracker. (2020) USA, https://climateactiontracker.org/countries/usa/, accessed July 28, 2020.

Coats, E. (2014) What Does It Mean to Be a Movement? 267–278. In T. Black et al. (eds.), *A Line in the Tar Sands*. Toronto, On, Canada; Oakland, CA: PM Press.

Common Dreams. (2014) Pipeline Construction Under Lake Thunderbird Sparks Rally. *Common Dreams Newswire*, December 17, www.commondreams.org/newswire/2014/12/17/pipeline-construction-under-lake-thunderbird-sparks-rally, accessed July 30, 2020.

Cook, E. (1990) Global Environmental Advocacy: Citizen Activism in Protecting the Ozone Layer. *Ambio* 19: 334–338.

Curnow, J. and Helferty, A. (2018) Contradictions of Solidarity: Whiteness, Settler Coloniality, and the Mainstream Environmental Movement. *Environment and Society: Advances in Research* 9: 145–163.

Cusick, D. (2020) Canada is Offering COVID-19 Aid to Some of the Country's Largest Companies – So Long As They Disclose Their Climate Impacts. *E&E News*, May 13.

E&E News staff. (2021) Keystone XL is Dead. Now What? *E&E News*, June 10.

Engler, Y. (2014) Canadian Diplomatic Efforts to Sell the Tar Sands, 55–63. In T. Black et al. (eds.), *A Line in the Tar Sands*. Toronto, ON, Canada; Oakland, CA: PM Press.

Estes, N. (2019) *Our History is the Future: Standing Rock versus the Dakota Access Pipeline, and the Long Tradition of Indigenous Resistance*. London; New York: Verso.

Farah, N. H. (2020) 'A Big Deal': Keystone XL Ruling Could Threaten Other Pipelines. *E&E News*, April 22.

Fears, D. and Mufson, S. (2020) Liberal, Progressive and Racist? The Sierra Club Faces Its White-Supremacist History *The Washington Post*, July 22.

Feldman, S. (2010) U.S. Politicians Oppose 2,000-Mile Oil Sands Pipeline. *The Guardian*, June 24, 2010.

Fortin, J. and Friedman, L. (2020) Dakota Access Pipeline to Shut Down Pending Review, Federal Judge Rules. *The New York Times*, July 6.

Ge, M. and Friedrich, J. (2020) 4 Charts Explain Greenhouse Gas Emissions by Countries and Sectors. *World Resources Institute*, February 06.

Gibbs, L. M. (1982) *Love Canal: My Story* told to Murray Levine. Albany: State University of New York Press.

Gilbertson, T. (2019) *Carbon Pricing: A Popular Education Toolkit for Community Resistance*. Bemjdi, MN: Climate Justice Alliance and the Indigenous Environmental Network.

Global Climate Finance. (2019) First Shipment of Canadian Tar Sands Heads Towards EU Shores. *Global Climate Finance*, November 29, https://globalclimatefinance.org/news/first-shipment-of-canadian-tar-sands-heads-towards-eu-shores/, accessed July 30, 2020.

Gottlieb, R. (2005) *Forcing the Spring: The Transformation of the American Environmental Movement*, 2nd ed. Washington, DC: Island Press.

Guigni, M. and Grasso, M. T. (2015) Environmental Movements in Advanced Industrial Democracies: Heterogeneity, Transformation, and Institutionalization. *Annual Review of Environment and Resources* 40: 337–361.

Haluza-DeLay, R. (2014) Assembling Consent in Alberta: Hegemony in the Tar Sands, 36–44. In T. Black et al. (eds.), *A Line in the Tar Sands*. Toronto, ON, Canada; Oakland, CA: PM Press.

Hansen, J. (1988) Congressional Testimony. *U.S. Senate Committee on Energy and Natural Resources*, June 23.

Hersey, M. D. (2011) *My Work is That of Conservation: An Environmental Biography of George Washington Carver*. Athens: University of Georgia Press.

IEN (Indigenous Environmental Network) (2020) www.ienearth.org/

Jennings, K., Grandoni, D. and Rust S. (2015) How Exxon Went from Leader to Skeptic on Climate Change Research. *Los Angeles Times*, October 23.

Johnson, W. (2013) *River of Dark Dreams: Slavery and Empire in the Cotton Kingdom*. Cambridge, MA: Belknap Press of Harvard University Press.

Jones, N. (2017) How the World Passed a Carbon Threshold and Why It Matters. *Yale360*, January 26.

King, P. (2020) Judges: La. Pipeline 'Trampled' Landowner Rights. *E&E News*, July 17.

Klein, N. (2014) *This Changes Everything: Capitalism vs. the Climate*. New York: Simon & Schuster.

Lakanen, R. (2018) Dissent and Descent: Tracing Canada's Environmental Governance from Regulatory Beginnings to Dismissal and Reversals by the Harper Government. *Local Environment* 23, no. 5: 549–564.

Lameman, C. (2014) Kihci Pikiskwewin – Speaking the Truth, 118–126. In T. Black et al. (eds.), *A Line in the Tar Sands*. Toronto, ON, Canada; Oakland, CA: PM Press.

Loo, T. M. (2006) *States of Nature: Conserving Canada's Wildlife in the Twentieth Century*. Vancouver: UBC Press.

Lukacs, M. (2014) Canada's Eastward Pipelines, 76–83. In T. Black et al. (eds.), *A Line in the Tar Sands*. Toronto, ON, Canada; Oakland, CA: PM Press.

Mangat, R., Dalby, S. and Patterson, M. (2018) Divestment Discourse: War, Justice, Morality and Money. *Environmental Politics* 27, no. 2: 187–208.

Martínez-Alier, J. (2002) *The Environmentalism of the Poor: A Study of Ecological Conflicts and Valuation*. Northampton, MA: Edward Elgar Publishing.

McGlade, C. and Ekins, P. (2015, January 8) The Geographical Distribution of Fossil Fuels Unused When Limiting Global Warming to 2°C. *Nature* 517: 187–190.

McGurty, E. M. 2007. *Transforming Environmentalism: Warren County, PCBs, and the Origins of Environmental Justice*. New Brunswick, NJ: Rutgers University Press.

McIntosh, E. (2020) 'Alberta didn't Contain It': COVID-19 Outbreak at Oilsands Camp. *Canada's National Observer*, May 13.

Merchant, C. (2003, July) Shades of Darkness: Race and Environmental History. *Environmental History* 8, no. 3: 380–394.

Narine, S. (2015) Indigenous Action Played Key Role in Keystone Rejection. *Windspeaker*, December 2015.

National Energy Policy Development Group, Committee on Science. (2001) Report to the U.S. House of Representatives, May 23.

Natural Resources Canada. (2012) Analysis of the ForestEthics Report on Foreign Investment in the Tar Sands, https://archive.org/stream/516798-nrcan-forest-ethics-oilsands-foreign-ownership/516798-nrcan-forest-ethics-oilsands-foreign-ownership_djvu.txt, accessed July 10, 2020.

Nikiforuk, A. (2010) *Tar Sands: Dirty Oil and the Future of a Continent*. Vancouver/Berkeley: Greystone Books; David Suzuki Foundation.

Nixon, R. (2011) *Slow Violence and the Environmentalism of the Poor*. Cambridge, MA: Harvard University Press.

O'Connell, P. M. (2019) Dakota Access Pipeline Owners Want to Pump More Oil through Illinois. *Chicago Tribune*, December 26, 2019.

O'Connor, R. (2015) *The First Green Wave: Pollution Probe and the Origins of Environmental Activism in Ontario*. Vancouver: UBC Press, The University of British Columbia.

Olive, A. (2016) *The Canadian Environment in Political Context*. Toronto: University of Toronto Press.

Parr, A. (2018) *Birth of a New Earth: The Radical Politics of Environmentalism*. New York: Columbia University Press.

Pellow, D. (2016) Toward a Critical Environmental Justice Studies: Black Lives Matter as an Environmental Justice Challenge. *DuBois Review: Social Science Research on Race* 13: 221–236.

Russell, J. K., Capato, L., Leonard, M. and Breaux, R. (2014) Lessons from Direct Action at the White House to Stop the Keystone XL Pipeline, 166–180. In T. Black et al. (eds.), *A Line in the Tar Sands*. Toronto, ON, Canada; Oakland, CA: PM Press.

Schimel, K. (2016) How the Keep It in the Ground Campaign Came to Be. *High Country News*, July 19.

Shabecoff, P. (1988) Global Warming Has Begun, Expert Tells Senate. *The New York Times*, June 24.

Shea, D. (2020) Balancing Act: Protecting Critical Infrastructure and Peoples' Right to Protest. *National Conference of State Legislatures*, July 21.

Skibell, A. (2020) 'Unnecessary.' N.C. Deals Major Blow to Pipeline Project. *E&E News*, August 12.

Skuce, N. (2012) Who Benefits? An Investigation of Foreign Investment in the Tar Sands. *ForestEthics*, May 10.

Smil, V. (2017) *Energy and Civilization: A History*. Cambridge, MA: The MIT Press.

Soraghan, M. (2020) Trail of Spills Haunts Dakota Access Developer. *E & E News*, May 26.

Spears, E. G. (2019) *Rethinking the American Environmental Movement Post-1945*. New York: Routledge.

Stefanovich, O. (2020) Court is to Render a Decision at a Later Date. *CBC News*, July 23.

Takach, G. F. (2017) *Tar Wars: Oil, Environment and Alberta's Image*. Edmonton, Alberta, Canada: The University of Alberta Press.

Tar Sands Blockade. (2016) https://tarsandsblockade.org/

Taylor, D. E. (2018) *Diversity in Environmental Organizations: Reporting and Transparency*. Report No. 1. University of Michigan, School for Environment and Sustainability, January 2018.

Tyrrell, I. R. (2015) *Crisis of the Wasteful Nation: Empire and Conservation in Theodore Roosevelt's America*. Chicago: The University of Chicago Press.

UK Tar Sands Network. (2011) "Oil orgy" Invades Energy Summit. *UK Tar Sands Network*, October 11, www.no-tar-sands.org/illicit-_oil-orgy_/, accessed July 30, 2020.

U.S. Climate Alliance. (2020) www.usclimatealliance.org/, accessed July 29, 2020.

U.S. EPA. (2014) National Air Toxics Assessment. *National Cancer Risk by Tract*, www.epa.gov/national-air-toxics-assessment/2014-nata-assessment-results#nationwide, accessed October 20, 2020.

U.S. EPA. (2017) Stratospheric Ozone Protection: 30 Years of Progress and Achievements, November, www.epa.gov/sites/production/files/2017-12/documents/mp30_report_final_508v3.pdf, accessed July 28, 2020, 6.

Velders, J. M., Andersen, S. O., Daniel, J. S., Fahey, D. W. and McFarland, M. (2007, March 20) The Importance of the Montreal Protocol in Protecting Climate, *PNAS* 104, no. 12: 4814–4819.

Waldron, I. (2018) *There's Something in the Water: Environmental Racism in Indigenous and Black Communities*. Winnipeg; Black Point: Fernwood Publishing.

Weis, T., Black, T., D'Arcy, S. and Russell, J. K. (2014) Introduction, 1–22. In T. Black et al. (eds.), *A Line in the Tar Sands*. Toronto, ON, Canada; Oakland, CA: PM Press.

Weisiger, M. L. (2009) *Dreaming of Sheep in Navajo Country*. Seattle: University of Washington Press.

Wotherspoon, T. A. and Hansen, J. (2013) The 'Idle No More' Movement: Paradoxes of First Nations Inclusion in the Canadian Context. *Social Inclusion* 1, no. 1: 21–36.

Zelko, F. (2014) Blood on the Ice: The Greenpeace Campaign Against the Harp Seal Slaughter, 107–127. In M. Armiero and L. Sedrez (eds.), *A History of Environmentalism: Local Struggles, Global Histories*. London; New York: Bloomsbury Academic.

5

GEOGRAPHIES OF LATIN AMERICAN SOCIAL-ENVIRONMENTAL MOVEMENTS

Defending territories and lifeways in the face of violent extractivism

Joel E. Correia

Introduction

There is a long tradition of social mobilization to protect the environment in Latin America. Emblematic struggles over deforestation in the Amazon (Hecht and Cockburn, 1989), oil extraction in Ecuador (Sawyer, 2004), and dam construction in the Chilean Patagonia (Patagonia Sin Represas, n.d.) have galvanized grassroots resistance movements and captured international attention. Beyond spurring global awareness about environmental degradation, the efforts of different movements across Latin America have been instrumental in reimagining what constitutes "the environment" and how it should be protected. The work of grassroots movements that work to defend life and territory – like Paro Civico in Buenaventura, Colombia; Kawsak Sacha of Sarayaku, Ecuador; or the Zapatistas of Chiapas, Mexico – show the demands for justice and well-being are always social-environmental. Scholars such as Martinez-Alier (2007) and Wittman (2009) take a different approach by employing Marxian-influenced analyses of development as a metabolic process that further show that extractivism in Latin America is always social-environmental. Together, popular movements and academic studies in, of, and from Latin American compel critical reflection about how legacies of extractivism shape notions of "the environment" and with what effects on racialization, inequality, and (in)justice.

Rather than frame movements as merely *environmental* or *social*, the dynamics and demands of such movements are social-environmental. I employ the term *social-environmental* movements in this chapter to draw attention to popular uses of the concept in Latin America (see, e.g., Leff, 1998; Cubero, 2019). Few are the days that people mobilize merely to protect "the environment". People mobilize to protect community well-being and maintain relations in, and to, territories (Ulloa, 2016; Haesbaert, 2020). I argue that Latin American territorial movements must be understood as social-environmental, striving for the protection of all life rather than the bifurcation of the "social" from the "environmental" through which extractive logics and colonial capitalism operate. Thinking with ontologies that do not bifurcate environment

 DOI: 10.4324/9780367855680-6

from society is more than a mere discursive or theoretical argument; it is an act that has profound material impacts on justice, governance, conservation practice, social difference, and life – broadly construed (see, e.g., Porto-Gonçalves and Leff, 2015). It should come as no surprise then that Latin American social-environmental movements have instrumentally informed recent academic debates.

A rich body of scholarship engages social-environmental movements. Yet drawing boundaries around what constitutes such movements is a fraught task (see, e.g., Inclán, 2018) that relies on how one defines "the environment" and what constitutes a "movement". Given my critical training in human geography, I approach this analysis with attention to the fact that movements are not coherent homogenous entities but struck through with internal differences (Wolford, 2010: 10) that are shaped by place-based processes (Oslender, 2016: 25–27) and transscalar networks. Thus, this chapter focuses primarily on grassroots or community-based movements and less so on transnational initiatives driven by donor organizations that may influence community-level organizing. The works I engaged for this review mainly derive from geographers, anthropologists, and sociologists whose research attends to community-based responses to social-environmental change. Yet I also engage gray literature and online platforms that counter-map social-environmental movements across Latin America because some of the most powerful and transformative thinking on social-environmentalism emanates from the grounded struggles and lives of people who demand the protection of their lifeways. I also explicitly draw from works by scholars and movements in, of, and from Latin America to bring such analyses into conversation with English-language scholarship because important contributions written in Spanish and Portuguese are often left out of publications in English.[1] The chapter provides readers with an overview of empirical issues, theories, challenges, and successes that animate social-environmental mobilization in Latin America.

My survey of the literature derives from the following methodology. Drawing from a search methodology inspired by Da Silva et al. (2018), I identified relevant peer-reviewed journal articles, books, and book chapters through keyword searches using the Web of Science database that generated 352 results between the years 1990 and 2020. After reviewing titles, abstracts, and keywords of the search results, I culled results that were not pertinent to this study. Additional searches were conducted using Google Scholar to identify other works pertinent to specific themes or topics that my Web of Science search may have missed. I organized and coded the articles using NVivo qualitative data analysis software to run keyword searches and word frequency tests. The results allowed me to identify possible trends or topics in the literature I may not have intuited, aside from my familiarity with the topic. The articles and sources reviewed here are representative, though not exhaustive, of the pertinent scholarship and reporting on social-environmental movements in the region. The rest of this chapter attends to important historical and scalar dynamics to provide a grounding for readers not familiar with Latin America, then offers an appraisal and schematic "mapping" of prominent movements with suggestions for future research.

I map social-environmental movements across three axes. First, I show that European colonialism in Latin America created structures of extractive relations that persist to the present, ultimately influencing the emergence of social-environmentalism. Second, the chapter evaluates new and ongoing efforts to map social-environmental conflicts in Latin America and consequently provides an overview of key trends and concerns reported by activists and academics. Next, I assess one of the most concerning issues confronting social-environmental movements today – increasing violence against movement actors. The section structure illustrates historical and current literature alongside key topics that provide the reader with a foundation for further research.

Extractivism and the emergence of social-environmental movements

Many scholars situate the nascence of "modern" environmental movement with the publication of Rachel Carson's *Silent Spring* (1962). Some go so far as to suggest Carson's work spurred an "environmental awakening" in the United States (Dunlap and Mertig, 1991; Heiskanen, 2006) that inspired the first Earth Day in 1970, often reiterated as an origin story for global environmental movements (Acuña, 2007). Although Carson's book and the popular mobilizations that led to the first Earth Day are important waypoints in the emergence of a new global political ecology that foregrounded environmental concerns, Peet et al. (2011) and Martinez-Alier et al. (2016) argue that there is a much deeper history to environmentalism in Latin America (see also D'Amico and Agoglia, 2019). It is a history rooted in responses to metabolic exchange between the territories and colonies of the "New World" and European powers of the time like Spain and Portugal. A region shaped by extractive relations, the natural resources of Latin America have long been the target of transnational interests transformed over time vis-à-vis colonialism, imperialism, and capitalism in their many variants (Paulson, 2012; Mollett, 2016).

The title of Uruguayan journalist Galeano's (1971) classic *Las Veinas Abiertas de América Latina* (*Open Veins of Latin America*) strikes at the core of colonialism qua extractivism in Latin America. Galeano frames the relationship between Latin America, Europe, and the United States as one built on the violence of Indigenous genocide, African slavery, and the extraction of resources to enrich colonial powers. This foundational violence, he argued, helped shape social, political, and spatial structures that continue to subject Latin America to exploitative relations whereby the environment is seen as a resource for the accumulation of wealth in so-called "core economies".[2] Indeed, Indigenous peoples across América, or the Americas – otherwise known as Turtle Island and Abya Yala – have defended their territories or sought to reclaim ones that have been appropriated for more than 500 years. Indigenous marginalization and the establishment of mestizo racial orders based on European-era colonial land grabs endure via contemporary resource extraction.[3]

Ensuing politics of land and resource distribution compounded inequality along racial and class lines to shape the emergence of social-environmental movements. The rise of authoritarian governments across Latin America in the twentieth century built from colonial legacies of extractive relations and land tenure inequality (Grosfoguel, 2008). Military strongmen often came to power vis-à-vis their willingness to leverage private industry for personal gain, with the implicit or explicit support of the United States, from Guatemala and El Salvador to Chile and Argentina. While the wave of authoritarianism in Latin America from the 1950s to the 1980s was frequently framed as a struggle to quell the spread of communism, military regimes helped maintain trade relations and private control over natural resource extraction (Grandin, 2006). Not surprisingly, social-environmental movements that challenged the ill effects of land tenure inequality, extractivism, or contamination were uncommon during the authoritarian period because popular mobilizations were often construed as communist and could result in torture or death (Carvalho de Oliveira and Florentin, 2019). Despite threats of state violence, robust resistance networks formed within countries and across the region to denounce human rights violations. The history of human rights activism in response to authoritarianism is not only credited with helping bring an end to those oppressive regimes but also as fundamental to visions of social-environmentalism where claims for citizenship within a democratic state have often been mediated by demands for resource access and environmental well-being as a form of justice (see, e.g., Engle, 2010). Carruthers (2008: 9) observed that with the transition to democracy new social movements exploded across the region in "'rhizomatic' fashion . . . demonstrating connection, heterogeneity, and multiplicity. Thus, a diverse mosaic of existing popular struggles with an unmistakably environmental cast has evolved throughout Latin America". The intersection of Indigenous rights movements and environmental activism played a crucial role in shaping imaginaries that animated social-environmentalism in Latin America during region-wide transitions to democracy, often stereotyping Indigenous peoples as "ecologically-noble savages" (Conklin and Graham, 1995; Ramos, 1998; Blaser, 2010).

The turn to democracy in Latin America during the late 1980s and 1990s mapped onto the deepening and broadening of neoliberal political economic reforms. Thus, the evolution of social-environmentalism cannot be disentangled from the rollout of neoliberalism and its effects on social well-being and environmental governance. Military dictatorships sowed the seeds of neoliberalism through the 1970s. Yet the Latin American debt crisis of the 1980s spurred large-scale interventions by international financial institutions like the World Bank (Petras and Veltmeyer, 2007), with sweeping economic reforms that had a dramatic impact on the governance of natural resources (Liverman and Vilas, 2006), the privatization of public goods (Harvey, 2005), and the expansion of extractivism and commodity exports to fuel growth (Perreault and Martin, 2016). In the wake, popular movements vehemently decried what they saw as unfettered neo-colonialism that ushered in a new phase in the history of extractive relations that had long shaped the region and its international relations (Bebbington and Batterbury, 2001; Caldeira, 2015). While mobilizations gathered in the streets to protest structural adjustment policies, globalization, and environmental change (Roberts and Thanos, 2003; Perreault and Valdivia, 2010), high-level negotiations like the 1992 Conference on Environment and Development in Rio de Janeiro began to reshape policy and hegemonic discourses (D'Amico and Agoglia, 2019) on the environment with lasting implications for the future of social-environmentalism in the region (Leff et al., 2003).

Before proceeding further, I would be remiss not to pause on how "sustainability" discourse advanced in the 1992 Rio Declaration provided an important reference for the emergence of social-environmental movements – both for and against this agenda. Souza (2018: 104) suggests the Declaration proved a moment where "[p]rotection of the environment and the right to a healthy environment became the path to strengthening social inclusion. The synthesis, after all, translated to a new and creative term that gained space from that point to the future – socioenvironmental". Indeed, notions of social-environmentalism have become both a juridical tool to protect biocultural diversity and a core tenet of many Indigenous movements in Brazil (Silveira and Camargo, 2018). Moreover, Latta and Wittman (2012) argue that social-environmental movements advance claims that seek to protect humans and the biophysical systems that sustain their well-being. Yet critics of sustainability discourse argue that the notion does little to de-center growth-oriented development but instead objectifies "environmental services" as quantifiable, fungible, and exchangeable commodities that perpetuate histories of extractivism and racialized dispossession (Escobar, 1998; Toledo et al., 2015; Lapegna, 2016). That is to say, Euro-modern ontologies (Latour, 1993) that frame *the environment* as a realm apart from humans have been fundamental in constructing "natural resources" (Escobar, 1996) to be exploited via "sustainable development" (Blaser, 2010) in ways that facilitate the logics of extractive capitalism (Gómez-Barris, 2018; D'Amico and Agoglia, 2019). The globalization of environmental concerns vis-à-vis the United Nations and new World Bank sustainable development initiatives in the late 1990s thus facilitated what many call the "neoliberalisation of nature" (Heynen and Robbins, 2005) and new forms of enclosure in the name of conservation (Peet et al., 2011).

Popular resistance to neoliberal reforms shifted the pendulum left in the 2000s with the "pink tide" and embrace of new presidents across South America, from Venezuela to Argentina (Lapegna, 2015; Pellegrini and Ribera Arismendi, 2012). The new political conjuncture was first hailed as *post*-neoliberal but rapidly revealed a neoextractive imperative that sparked new social-environmental movements in defense of people and place (Svampa, 2019; Yates and Bakker, 2014; Barzola and Baroni, 2018). Despite state discourses of commitments to the rights of nature and social justice, the TIPNIS conflict in Bolivia (Hirsch, 2019) and failure to ensure protections in Yasuni, Ecuador, are but two examples that show the limits of the left turn to disrupt enduring extractive imperatives (Villalba-Eguiluz and Etxano, 2017). Popular resistance to extractivism is clearly not new in Latin America. However, new technologies have changed how movements and their allies render social-environmental struggles visible, something to which I now turn.

Counter-mapping and social-environmental movements

The dynamic nature of grassroots socio-environmental movements makes them a moving target for researchers seeking to analyze mobilizations at a scale beyond singular case studies or on a time horizon shorter than peer-review processes dictate. However, several recent scholar-activist initiatives have created repositories that track and document the prevalence and different types of social-environmental conflict in the Americas through counter-mapping that provides a rich dataset to evaluate. *Counter-mapping* (Peluso, 1995; Bryan, 2018) promises to write against state cartographic authority by shifting authorship to the hands of whoever can map. The proliferation of web-based mapping platforms and technology as well as geospatial data have thus created new tools many social-environmental movements use to document and display human rights abuses and injustice to counter environmental violence.

Perhaps the most well-known counter-mapping project of this sort is the Environmental Justice Atlas (https://ejatlas.org), an open-access crowd-sourced project that currently documents 3,165 cases of environmental conflicts globally (Temper et al., 2015). "The EJ Atlas collects these stories of communities struggling for environmental justice . . . to make these mobilizations more visible, highlight claims and testimonies" (EJAtlas, n.d.). Temper et al. (2018: 576) explain the project methodology and its explicit effort to track what they call ecological distribution conflicts, "when communities refuse to be polluted, to be contaminated, displaced and erased and decide to mobilize and rise up in social opposition". At the time of this writing, over 900 cases documented are in Latin America and the Caribbean (see Table 5.1.), classified into nine broad categories from fossil fuels and energy justice to biomass and land conflicts. More than just a catalogue of conflicts, each registered case includes data that has enabled scholars to analyze trends in focused social-environmental movements across the region (Temper et al., 2018). The availability of the data and its quality has enabled robust comparative case study analyses within single countries (Teran-Mantovani, 2017), at the sub-regional scale like the Andes (Pérez-Rincón et al., 2017), or region wide with Central America (Navas et al., 2018), opening new avenues for the generation of social-environmental movement theory (Rodriguez-Labajos et al., 2019).

While EJAtlas is a global repository, several other counter-mapping initiatives shift the scale of analysis by focusing solely on Latin America as a region. Tierra de Resistentes tracks social-environmental conflicts in ten Latin American countries (see https://tierraderesistentes.com/en). A movement in and of themselves, the project involves more than 50 expert journalists, photographers, videographers, and computer developers who have been documenting social conflicts regarding the environment with 2,367 cases recorded between 2009 and 2019. Although violence is implicit in the issues covered by the EJAtlas, Tierra de Resistentes explicitly tracks violence against social-environmental movement actors. This project reflects an increasingly worrisome trend of physical violence against, and criminalization of, Latin

American social-environmental movements (see, e.g., Bacallao-Pino, 2016; Munoz and Vil-lamar, 2018; Szablowski and Campbell, 2019).

Other counter-mapping projects focus on single countries, yet survey cross-sector issues. The Mapa de Conflictos Envolvendo Injustiça Ambiental e Saúde no Brasil[4] (http://mapa-deconflitos.ensp.fiocruz.br) has 605 documented cases that track conflicts across sectors, detailing how social-environmental change produces specific harms to human health. Leveraging public health data alongside media reporting and follow-up research, the platform provides specific data, a narrative summary to contextualize the case, and links to supporting information. Da Rocha et al. (2018) argue that this project has been instrumental in helping movements on the ground and as an advocacy tool to raise awareness about social-environmental change and injustice within Brazil. Utilizing a single-country focus, Observando a Goliat[5] (http://obser-vandoagoliat.com) examines neoextractivism in Mexico by examining energy and mining. The database and map draw from over 1,000 newspaper reports of conflicts related to neoextractivism from 2006 to 2019, complemented with a juridical analysis of industry regulation and 40 in-depth key informant interviews. Project members Zaremberg et al. (2018) argue that despite regulations calling for participatory processes to minimize the negative impacts of extractive industries on affected communities, there is a disjuncture between the implementation of consultation practices and legal mandates to include such measures. Such findings resonate with studies by Perreault (2015), Bebbington (2012), and Walter and Urkidi (2017) that collectively show how the lack of free, prior, and informed consent processes is a central concern that animates Indigenous social-environmental movements across Latin America. Observando a Goliat shows that a lack of meaningful participatory processes, prior consultation, and implementation of pertinent laws correlates with high incidences of violence in the context of the documented social-environmental conflicts. As others have noted (Middeldorp, 2016; Acosta and Martinez, 2019), lack of meaningful consultation processes often impels affected communities to resist development while on the other hand industry actors often employ extra-legal measures to implement their projects (Lakhani, 2020).

The four counter-mapping projects I just discussed are distinct in their respective methods, specific foci, and data. The criteria used to document or classify something as a qualifying conflict varies across platforms as do the presentation of supporting information and conclusions derived. Yet some preliminary trends emerge from a quick assessment of the frequency and type of environmental conflicts reported. Mining, hydrocarbons, and the energy sector stand out across platforms as priority areas for social-environmental mobilization, followed by land conflicts that encompass agricultural production, forestry, and livestock. The third major area of concern centers on dams, hydroelectric projects, and water management. For those familiar with the political ecologies of social-environmental movements in Latin America, these findings are not surprising and are well represented in extant literature (Fisher, 1994; Wolford, 2007; Perreault, 2008; Valdivia, 2008; Bebbington et al., 2008; Asher and Ojeda, 2009; Schapper et al., 2020; *inter alia*). The four projects also point to other empirical issues that warrant further attention: namely, the impact of narco-trafficking, the uneven effects of climate change, and urban movements – issues I address in the conclusion. Before doing so, I want to highlight one of the most urgent problems members of Latin American social-environmental movements now face – violence and criminalization.

Social-environmental movements in an era of increasing violence

Latin America is now the deadliest region of the world for environmental defenders. The human rights organization Global Witness (www.globalwitness.org) tracks the murder of

Table 5.1 Frequencies of documented socio-environmental conflicts documented across four counter-mapping projects.

Data Source	Dataset Scale	Sector where conflict occurred	Frequency
EJAtlas	Global database and mapping project.	Mineral ores and building material extraction	315
	Data displayed was filtered to Latin America.	Biomass and Land Conflicts (Forests, Agriculture, Fisheries Livestock Management)	151
		Water management	131
		Fossil fuels and climate justice/energy with	119
		Infrastructure and built environment	64
		Waste management	62
		Industrial and utilities conflicts	34
		Biodiversity and Conservation Conflicts	28
		Tourism/recreation	19
		Nuclear	11
Tierra de Resistentes	Latin America, focusing on: Argentina, Bolivia, Brazil, Colombia, Ecuador, Guatemala, Honduras, México, Perú, Venezuela.	Agribusiness	755
		Logging	387
		Mining	376
		Infrastructure	240
		Hydropower	175
		Drug trafficking	131
		Hydrocarbons	77
		Energy	57
		Forestry	31
		Real estate speculation	15
		Hunting/trafficking of biodiversity	11
		Fishing	17
		Waste	8
		Tourism	1
Mapa de Conflictos envolvendo Injustiça Ambiental e Saúde no Brasil	National, only Brazil.	Actions by government entities	350
		Monocultures	173
		Public policy and environmental legislation	127
		Mining and steel production	110
		Dams and hydroelectric	101
		Actions by the Judiciary or and/or Public Ministry	93
		Livestock	82
		Real estate speculation	76

(Continued)

Table 5.1 (Continued)

Data Source	Dataset Scale	Sector where conflict occurred	Frequency
		Forestry	73
		Transportation networks (water, road, train tracks, terminals)	62
		Chemical and petrochemical industry	46
		Fishing and aquaculture	30
		Creation of protected areas	30
		Pipelines	26
		Tourism industry	25
		Landfills, incinerators, recycling sites	16
		Agro-toxics	15
		Energy and nuclear reactors	12
		Petroleum or gas transport	12
		Thermoelectric	11
		Other industries	9
		Civil construction	7
		Charcoal	6
		Transgenics	6
		Petroleum or gas refining	5
		Agroindustry	4
		Petroleum or gas exploration	4
		Missionary work	3
		Wind energy	3
		Shipyards	3
		Irrigation	3
		Inter-basin water transfers	3
		Commercial extractivism	2
		Transmission lines	2
		Mega-events	2
		Narco-trafficking	1
		Navigation	1
Observando a Goliat	National, only México.	Mining	85
		Oil fields and wells	36
		Hydroelectric	34
		Gas pipelines	19
		Wind farms	13

Source: Table elaborated by author with data from EJAtlas (https://ejatlas.org), Tierra de Resistentes (https://tierraderesistentes.com/en), Mapa de Conflictors Envolvendo Injustiça Ambiental e Sáudade no Brasil (http://mapadeconflitos.ensp.fiocruz.br), and Observando a Goliat (http://observandoagoliat.com).

"environmental defenders"[6] globally. Their reporting shows that physical violence against social-environmental movements has been rising in the last five years (Global Witness, 2019). The murders of high-profile activists Berta Cáceres of Honduras in 2016 and Isidro Baldenegro López of Mexico in 2017 are well-known hallmarks of this violent trend. Both were awarded the Goldman Environmental Prize in recognition of their longstanding activism to defend the environment and rights of their respective communities. Cáceres confronted dam construction that would have displaced Lenca peoples from their lands. Baldenegro López confronted large-scale illegal logging in Tarahumara territories. During a workshop on Indigenous and Afro-descendant environmental justice I hosted in 2019, Francia Márquez, 2018 Goldman Environmental Prize recipient from Colombia, told me that her life is regularly threatened for her work to defend Afro-Colombian territorial rights in opposition to mining. Mere days after the workshop, a paramilitary group with links to private industry attempted to assassinate Márquez and fellow activists. Though several people sustained injuries, fortunately, no one was killed.[7] Such examples underscore the prevalence of violence against well-known social-environmental movement leaders.

The recent increases in violence and criminalization is alarming, but unfortunately, violence against environmental defenders in Latin America is not new (Bebbington, 2018). The slaying of Brazilian rubber tapper and community organizer Chico Mendes in 1988 and that of nun Dorothy Stang in 2005 for opposing deforestation in the Amazon are but two commonly cited examples that also captured international attention (Gomes et al., 2018). Rather than merely outliers or examples of spectacular violence, each of these cases is indicative of the trend that Global Witness and projects like Tierras de Resistentes continue to document. There is a qualitative and quantitative difference in the prevalence of violence against social-environmental defenders in the last decade – more are being targeted and criminalized for resisting extractivism and demanding reparations for wrongs that result.

Responding to the increasing violence, a handful of recent studies have grappled with the available data to assess the situation. Poulos and Haddad (2016: 2) assembled a database comprising 175 "grassroots environmental protests" from over 35,472 periodicals spanning from 1965 to 2013 from the "most comprehensive databases of media coverage available" from which they found two key findings: 1) incidents of violence against environmental defenders have been increasingly reported over the study period globally, and 2) Latin America stands out as the region with the greatest violent repression of "marginalized" environmental defenders. Working with data from Global Witness, Butt et al. (2019) show that international supply chains are increasingly connected to the use of extra-judicial means to keep them operating at all costs. Middeldorp and Le Billon (2019) contend that a resurgence of authoritarian populism in the region tracks closely onto the increased criminalization of environmental defenders via manipulation of legal norms to persecute them (see also Munoz and Villamar, 2018). Navas et al. (2018), on the other hand, note that violence against environmental defenders is not always physical; the emotional and psychological toll from threats of violence and impunity for those responsible for the violence is equally pernicious. Some analysts contend that only high-profile cases of such violence get tracked (Butt et al., 2019), and others suggest the actual picture is much more alarming (Grant and Le Billon, 2019). Because most deaths of environmental defenders are recorded by non-governmental human rights organizations working with limited resources (United Nations Human Rights Council, 2018), available data are likely incomplete and fail to capture the full scope of the problem.

Who is responsible for the increased violence? Scholarship and recent reporting show that mercenaries and company employees are sometimes involved in such violence (Poulos and Haddad, 2016). Yet an alarming amount of violence comes from state actors working in close collaboration with private industries or, perhaps better put, in the service of those industries (Middeldorp, 2016; Szablowski and Campbell, 2019; Zhouri et al., 2019). Moreover, legal reforms criminalizing protests increasingly target social-environmental movements across the region (Birss, 2017; Atiles-Osoria, 2014; Tanner, 2011). The prevalence of criminalizing environmental defenders and corruption in criminal justice systems, to say nothing of direct physical violence, has become so alarming that the Inter-American Commission on Human Rights held a special session in September 2019 to document the how extra-judicial means intersect with the criminalization of protest to imperil human rights defenders in the region (CEJIL, 2019).

Efforts to track and stop violence against environmental defenders are laudable given the paucity of comprehensive data on the problem as it manifests across the region and seemingly low interest by states in preventing such violence. It is impossible, however, to calculate the number of lives lost or harmed due to the adverse effects of everyday environmental change driven by an extractive imperative. Extractivism-induced contamination of vital resources like air and water (Perreault, 2012; Radonic, 2015; Akchurin, 2020), the siting of dumps or factories in economically marginalized neighborhoods (Carruthers, 2008; Ontiveros et al., 2018), and the effects of land dispossession on Indigenous and *campesino* communities at the fore of agrarian frontiers (Hetherington, 2020; Leguizamón, 2020) are quotidian forms of environmental injustice that undermine well-being and sometimes result in death. Rather than the explosive, spectacular violence that comes from the gun of a private security force dispossessing people of land (Correia, 2019) or the site of a mega-development project that garners international outcry (Silva et al., 2018), everyday environmental injustice embodies "a violence the occurs gradually and out of sight, a violence of delayed destruction that is dispersed across time and space, an attritional violence that is typically not viewed as violence at all" (Nixon, 2011: 2). Extractivism in its many guises incites slow and at times spectacular violence that animates movements in defense of territory and well-being.

Conclusion

The extractive imperatives motivating Galeano's (1971) blistering critique in the *Open Veins of Latin America* have undeniably changed the geographies of social-environmental relations. Indeed, the very logics of racialized dispossession forged during centuries of extractive relations create the conditions of possibility for the current criminalization and violence against actors who stand in the way of development. Despite such threats, social-environmental movements maintain vibrant and enduring efforts to defend their territories and well-being (Bratman, 2015; Abers, 2019; Silva, 2016). In this chapter, I traced the outlines of social-environmentalism in Latin America by following trends in foundational studies and using those to highlight current issues driving activism and research. Enduring concerns like the effects of extractivism, land tenure inequality, and the siting of new infrastructure projects warrant continued research because those sectors are still highly relevant, perhaps even more so as Latin America continues to urbanize, and per-capita income rises alongside demands for goods and resources. Yet the counter-mapping initiatives and literature surveyed here also point to other dynamics that call for greater attention.

Of these, narco-trafficking, climate justice, urbanization, and the rights of nature are urgent. Geographers are investigating relationships between narco-trafficking and deforestation in Central America (McSweeney et al., 2017; McSweeney et al., 2018; Devine et al., 2018), contesting claims that forest degradation is driven by Indigenous and *campesino* communities (Ybarra, 2018). These studies suggest more research can be done to investigate how the narcotics trade intersects with social-environmental change across the region. A robust body of research has followed the evolution of climate change mitigation strategies and social responses to the implementation of such projects in Latin America (Santelices and Rojas, 2016; Borras et al., 2012; Rojas Hernández, 2016). Yet as the calls to act on climate change become more urgent, a focus on how demands for just transitions and climate justice are translated into new actions is an important area for future research (Alves and Mariano, 2018; Torres et al., 2020). Urban issues are another area largely under-represented in the extant literature on social-environmentalism in Latin America. Given that the region is majority urban and continues to urbanize, I was surprised to find that less than 15% of the articles I assessed mentioned the term "urban" while even fewer explicitly focused on urban issues. The paucity of work in this area is evident in the focus of my review. Interestingly, though, several counter-mapping platforms did address urban themes, which suggests a disconnect between currently published studies and crowd-sourced information on social-environmental conflicts. Though I focused on violence and threats in this review, it bears noting that Latin American social-environmental movements have been instrumental in driving the judicialization of the rights of nature, exemplified in the Ecuadorian and Bolivian constitutions. However, the guarantee and implementation of such rights are fraught with contradictions (Valladares and Boelens, 2017; Kinkaid, 2019) and are yet another important area for continued research. Finally, I would be remiss not to suggest that there is a pressing need to understand how COVID-19 and the global pandemic have impacted, and will likely continue to shape, social-environmental movements in Latin America. The effects of mandatory quarantines as well as the exercise of legislative acts to spur economic growth through extractivism in several countries suggest new challenges for social-environmental movements in the years to come.

Latin American movements in defense of life and territory provide are extremely heterogenous yet draw our attention to the ways that demands for justice are always social-environmental. Indeed, the partition of society from environment has animated destructive logics of extractive development, racialization, and inequality that have given rise to the popular resistance movements I discussed in this chapter. Like many movements in industrial democracies (Giugni and Grasso, 2015), contemporary Latin America is animated by social-environmental movements. Yet my review shows two alarming trends that are distinct – the expansion of unfettered extractivism and the increased frequency of violence against environmental defenders. Building from longstanding traditions of popular mobilizations for justice, be it from land appropriations or human rights violations driven by authoritarian regimes, social-environmental movements in Latin America provide an important counter to the expansion of extractive frontiers. However, demands for justice are now being met with more violence. Ongoing efforts like those to ratify the United Nations Escazú Agreement and increased attention by the Inter-American Commission on Human Rights are welcome. But given the routinized and increasing levels of violence, it is exceedingly crucial that engaged scholars foster partnerships in conversation with community partners to support their struggles through critical research in the defense of threatened territories and lifeways.

Notes

1 Quotations included in this chapter from works originally published in a language other than English were translated to maintain fidelity of the meaning in the original language rather than to provide a direct translation.
2 See also Gunder-Frank (1966) and Escobar (1995).

3 See Cusicanqui (1991), Mallon (2005), Grandin (2011), Mollett (2016), and Mora (2017) for key examples.
4 Map of Conflicts Involving Environmental Injustice and Health in Brazil.
5 Observing Goliath.
6 Butt et al. (2019, 742) define environmental defenders as "people engaged in protecting lands, forests, water and other natural resources. This includes community activists, members of social movements, lawyers, journalists, non-governmental organization staff, indigenous peoples, members of traditional, peasant and agrarian communities, and those who resist forest eviction or other violent interventions".
7 For media coverage of the attack, see https://news.mongabay.com/2019/05/goldman-prize-winner-survives-armed-attack-on-afro-colombian-social-leaders/.

References

Abers, Rebecca. 2019. Bureaucratic activism: Pursuing environmentalism inside the Brazilian state. *Latin American Politics and Society*, 61, 21–44. https://doi.org/10.1017/lap.2018.75.

Acosta, Henry B., and Martinez, Jorge E. C. 2019. Extractivism, law and social conflict in Colombia. *Revista Republicana*, 143–170. http://dx.doi.org/10.21017/rev.repub.2019.v26.a63.

Acuña, Isáias. T. 2007. Ambientalismos y ambientalistas: Una expresión del ambientalismo en Colombia. *Ambiente & Sociedade*, x, 45–60. https://doi.org/10.1590/S1414-753X2007000200004.

Akchurin, Maria. 2020. Mining and defensive mobilization explaining opposition to extractive industries in Chile. *Sociology of Development*, 6, 1–29. https://doi.org/10.1525/sod.2020.6.1.1.

Alves, Marcelo. W. F. M., and Mariano, Enzo. B. 2018. Climate justice and human development: A systematic literature review. *Journal of Cleaner Production*, 202, 360–375. https://doi.org/10.1016/j.jclepro.2018.08.091.

Asher, Kiran, and Ojeda, Diana. 2009. Producing nature and making the state: Ordenamiento territorial in the Pacific lowlands of Colombia. *Geoforum*, 40, 292–302. https://doi.org/10.1016/j.geoforum.2008.09.014.

Atiles-Osoria, José M. 2014. The criminalization of socio-environmental struggles in Puerto Rico. *Oñati Socio-Legal Studies*, 4, 85–103. https://ssrn.com/abstract=2381607.

Bacallao-Pino, Lázaro M. 2016. Agents for change or conflict? Social movements, democratic dynamics, and development in Latin America. *Voluntas*, 27, 105–124. https://doi.org/10.1007/s11266-015-9574-2.

Barzola, Erika J., and Baroni, Paola A. 2018. El acercamiento de China a América del Sur. Profundización del neoextractivismo e incremento de conflictos y resistencias socioambientales. *Colombia Internacional*, 93, 119–145. http://dx.doi.org/10.7440/colombiaint93.2018.05.

Bebbington, Anthony. 2018. Rural social movements: Conflicts over the countryside. In *The Routledge Handbook of Latin American Development*. Cupples, J., Palomino-Schalscha, M., and Prieto, M. Eds. New York: Routledge, 321–331.

Bebbington, Anthony, Bebbington, Denise, Bury, Jeffery, Lingan, Jeannat, Munoz, Juan P., and Scurrah, Martin. 2008. Mining and social movements: Struggles over livelihood and rural territorial development in the Andes. *World Development*, 36, 2888–2905. https://doi.org/10.1016/j.worlddev.2007.11.016.

Bebbington, Anthony J., and Batterbury, Simon. 2001. Transnational livelihoods and landscapes: Political ecologies of globalization. *Cultural Geographies*, 8, 369–380. https://doi.org/10.1177%2F096746080100800401.

Bebbington, Denise. H. 2012. Consultation, compensation and conflict: Natural gas extraction in Weenhayek territory, Bolivia. *Journal of Latin American Geography*, 11, 49–71. www.jstor.org/stable/24394812.

Birss, Moira. 2017. Criminalizing environmental activism. *NACLA Report on the Americas*, 49, 315–322. https://doi.org/10.1080/10714839.2017.1373958.

Blaser, Mario. 2010. *Storytelling Globalization from the Chaco and Beyond*. Durham, NC: Duke University Press.

Borras Jr., Saturnino. M., Franco, Jennifer C., Gómez, Sergio, Kay, Cristóbal, and Spoor, Max. 2012. Land grabbing in Latin America and the Caribbean. *Journal of Peasant Studies*, 39, 845–872. https://doi.org/10.1080/03066150.2012.679931.

Bratman, Eve. 2015. Passive revolution in the green economy: Activism and the Belo Monte dam. *International Environmental Agreements-Politics Law and Economics*, 15, 61–77. https://doi.org/10.1007/s10784-014-9268-z.

Bryan, Joe. 2018. Counter-mapping development. In *The Routledge Handbook of Latin American Development*. Cupples, J., Palomino-Schalscha, M., and Prieto, M. Eds. New York: Routledge, 263–272.

Butt, Nathalie, Lambrick, Francis, Menton, Mary, and Renwick, Anna. 2019. The supply chain of violence. *Nature Sustainability*, 2, 742–747. https://doi.org/10.1038/s41893-019-0349-4.

Caldeira, Teresa, P. 2015. Social movements, cultural production, and protests São Paulo's shifting political landscape. *Current Anthropology*, 56, s126–136. https://doi.org/10.1086/681927.

Carruthers, David R. 2008. The globalization of environmental justice: Lessons from the U.S.-Mexico border. *Society & Natural Resources*, 21, 556–568. https://doi.org/10.1080/08941920701648812.

Carvalho de Oliveira, Nathalia C., and Florentin, Carlos G. 2019. Hydroelectric dams and the rise of environmentalism under dictatorship in Brazil and Paraguay (1950–1990). In *Environmentalism Under Authoritarian Regimes: Myth, Propaganda, Reality*. Brian, S., and Pál, V. Eds. New York: Routledge, 51–74. https://doi.org/10.4324/9781351007061.

CEJIL (Centro por la Justicia y el Derecho Internacional). 2019. Inter-American Commission on Human Rights holds special hearing on environmental defenders under attack. 27 September. Accessed 10 November 2019 at www.cejil.org/en/inter-american-commission-human-rights-holds-special-hearing-environmental-defenders-under-attack.

Conklin, Beth. A., and Graham, Laura A. 1995. The shifting middle ground: Amazonian Indians and eco-politics. *American Anthropologist*, 97, 695–710. www.jstor.org/stable/682591.

Correia, Joel. E. 2019. Soy states: Resource politics, violent environments and soybean territorialization in Paraguay. *The Journal of Peasant Studies*, 46, 316–336. https://doi.org/10.1080/03066150.2017.1384726.

Cubero, María E. P. 2019. La participación ciudadan de los movimientos socioambientales en América Latina. *Revista Colombiana de Sociología*, 42, http://dx.doi.org/10.15446/rcs.v42n1.73023.

Cusicanqui, Silvia. R. 1991. Aymara past, Aymara future. *Report on the Americas*, 25, 18–45. https://doi.org/10.1080/10714839.1991.11723133.

D'Amico, María P., and Agoglia, Ofelia. 2019. La cuestión ambiental en disputa: el ambientalismo hegemónico y la corriente ambiental critica. Lecturas desde y para América Latina. *Revista Colombiana de Sociologia*, 42, 97–116. http://dx.doi.org/10.15446/rcs.v42n1.73247.

Da Rocha, Diogo F., Porto, Marcelo F., Pacheco, Tania, and Leroy, Jean Pierre. 2018. The map of conflicts related to environmental injustice and health in Brazil. *Sustainability Science*, 13, 709–719. https://doi.org/10.1007/s11625-017-0494-5.

Da Silva, Sven, Tamás, Peter A., and Kampen, Jarl K. 2018. Articles reporting research on Latin American social movements are only rarely transparent. *Social Movement Studies*, 17, 736–748. https://doi.org/10.1080/14742837.2018.1499511.

Devine, Jennifer A., Wrathall, David, Currit, Nate, Tellman, Beth, and Langarica, Yunen R. 2018. Narco-cattle ranching in political forests. *Antipode*, 52, 1018–1038. https://doi.org/10.1111/anti.12469.

Dunlap, Riley E., and Mertig, Angela G. 1991. The evolution of the U.S. environmental movement from 1970 to 1990: An overview. *Society & Natural Resources*, 4, 209–218. https://doi.org/10.1080/08941929109380755.

EJAtlas. n.d. Frequently asked questions. What is the project about? Accessed 1 November 2020 at https://ejatlas.org/about.

Engle, Karen. 2010. *The Elusive Promise of Indigenous Development: Rights, Culture, Strategy*. Durham, NC: Duke University Press.

Escobar, Arturo. 1995. *Encountering Development: The Making and Unmaking of the Third World*. Princeton, NJ: Princeton University Press.

Escobar, Arturo. 1996. Construction nature: Elements for a post-structuralist political ecology. *Futures*, 28, 325–343. https://doi.org/10.1016/0016-3287(96)00011-0.

Escobar, Arturo. 1998. Whose knowledge, whose nature? Biodiversity, conservation, and the political ecology of social movements. *Journal of Political Ecology*, 5, 53–82. https://doi.org/10.2458/v5i1.21397.

Fisher, William H. 1994. Megadevelopment, environmentalism, and resistance: The institutional context of Kayapó indigenous politics in central Brazil. *Human Organization*, 53, 220–232. www.jstor.com/stable/44127176.

Galeano, Eduardo. 1971. *Las venas abiertas de América Latina*. Madrid: Siglo XXI.

Giugni, Marco, and Grasso, Maria, T. 2015. Environmental movements in advanced industrial democracies: Heterogeneity, transformation, and institutionalization. *Annual Review of Environment and Resources*, 40, 337–361.

Global Witness. 2019. Enemies of the state? How governments and business silence land and environmental defenders. www.globalwitness.org/en/campaigns/environmental-activists/enemies-state/.

Gomes, Carlos V. A., Alencar, Ane, Vadjunec, Jacqueline M., and Pacheco, Leonardo M. 2018. Extractive reserves in the Brazilian amazon thirty years after Chico Mendes: Social movement achievements, territorial expansion and continuing struggles. *Desenvolvimento e Meio Ambiente*, 48, 74–98. http://dx.doi.org/10.5380/dma.v48i0.58830.

Gómez-Barris, Macarena. 2018. *The Extractive Zone: Social Ecologies and Decolonial Perspectives*. Durham, NC: Duke University Press.

Grandin, Greg. 2006. *Empire's Workshop: Latin America, the United States, and the Rise of the New Imperialism*. New York: Owl Books.

Grandin, Greg. 2011. *The Last Colonial Massacre: Latin America in the Cold War*. Chicago: University of Chicago.

Grant, Hollie, and Le Billon, Philippe. 2019. Growing political: Violence, community forestry, and environmental defender subjectivity. *Society & Natural Resources*, 32, 768–789. https://doi.org/10.1080/08941920.2019.1590669.

Grosfoguel, Ramón. 2008. Developmentalism, modernity, and dependency theory in Latin America. In *Coloniality at large: Latin America and the Postcolonial Debate*. Moraña, M., Dussel, E., and Járegui, C. A. Eds. Durham, NC: Duke University Press, 307–334.

Guha, R. 2000. *Environmentalism: A Global History*. New York: Longman.

Gunder-Frank, Andre. 1966. The development of under development. *Monthly Review*, 18, 4–17.

Haesbaert, Rogério. 2020. Território(s) numa perspectiva latino-americana. *Journal of Latin American Geographers*, 19, 141–151. http://doi.org/10.1353/lag.2020.0007.

Harvey, David. 2005. *A Brief History of Neoliberalism*. Oxford: Oxford University Press.

Hecht, Susanna, and Cockburn, Andrew. 1989. *The Fate of the Forest: Developers, Destroyers, and Defenders of the Amazon*. London: Verso.

Heiskanen, Eva. 2006. Encounters between ordinary people and the environment: A transdisciplinary perspective on environmental literacy. *Journal of Transdisciplinary Environmental Studies*, 5, 1–13.

Hetherington, Kregg. 2020. *The Government of Beans: Regulating Life in the Age of Monocrops*. Durham, NC: Duke University Press.

Heynen, Nick, and Robbins, Paul. 2005. The neoliberalization of nature: Governance, privatization, enclosure and valuation. *Capitalism Nature Socialism*, 16, 5–8. https://doi.org/10.1080/104557505020 00335339.

Hirsch, Cecilie. 2019. Between resistance and negotiation: Indigenous organisations and the Bolivian state in the case of TIPNIS. *Journal of Peasant Studies*, 46, 811–830. https://doi.org/10.1080/03066150.20 17.1394846.

Inclán, María. 2018. Latin America, a continent in movement but where to? A review of the social movement's studies in the region. *Annual Review of Sociology*, 44, 535–551. https://doi.org/10.1146/annurev-soc-073117-041043.

Kinkaid, Eden. 2019. "Rights of nature" in translation: Assemblage geographies, boundary objects, and translocal social movements. *Transactions of the Institute of British Geographers*, 44, 555–570. https://doi.org/10.1111/tran.12303.

Lakhani, Nina. 2020. *Who Killed Berta Cáceres? Dams, Death Squads, and an Indigenous Defender's Battle for the Planet*. London: Verso.

Lapegna, Pablo. 2015. Popular demobilization, agribusiness mobilization, and the agrarian boom in post-neoliberal Argentina. *Journal of World-Systems Research*, 21, 69–87. https://doi.org/10.5195/jwsr.2015.523.

Lapegna, Pablo. 2016. Genetically modified soybeans, agrochemical exposure, and everyday forms of peasant collaboration in Argentina. *Journal of Peasant Studies*, 43, 517–536. https://doi.org/10.1080/0306 6150.2015.1041519.

Latour, Bruno. 1993. *We Have Never Been Modern*. Trans. Porter, C. Cambridge, MA: Harvard University Press.

Latta, Alex, and Wittman, Hannah. 2012. *Environment and Citizenship in Latin America: Nature, Subjects and Struggles*. New York: Berghahn Books.

Leff, Enrique. 1998. *Saber Ambiental: Sustentabilidad, Racionalidad, Complejidad, Poder*. México D.F.: Siglo Ventiuno Editores.

Leff, Enrique, Argueta, Arturo, Boege, Eckart, and Gonçalves, Carlos W. P. 2003. Más allá del desarrollo sostenible: La construcción de una racionalidad ambiental para la sustentabilidad. Una vision desde América Latina. *Medio Ambiente y Urbanización*, 59, 65–108. https://doi.org/10.1630/0326785041834793.

Leguizamón, Amalia. 2020. *Sees of Power: Environmental Injustice and Genetically Modified Soybeans in Argentina*. Durham, NC: Duke University Press.

Liverman, Diana M., and Vilas, Silvina. 2006. Neoliberalism and the environment in Latin America. *Annual Review of Environment and Resources*, 31, 327–363. https://doi.org/10.1146/annurev.energy.29.102403.140729.

Mallon, Florencia E. 2005. *Courage Tastes of Blood: The Mapuche Community of Nicolás Ailío and the Chilean State, 1906–2001*. Durham, NC: Duke University Press.

Martinez-Alier, Joan, 2007. Social metabolism and environmental conflicts. *Socialist Register*, 43.

Martinez-Alier, Joan, Baud, Michiel, and Sejenovich, Héctor. 2016. Origins and perspectives of Latin American environmentalism. In *Environmental Governance in Latin America*. DeCastro, F. Hogenboom, B., and Baud, M. Eds. New York: Palgrave Macmillan, 29–48. https://doi.org/10.1057/9781137505729.

McSweeney, Kendra, Richani, Nazih, Pearson, Zoe, Devine, Jennifer, and Wrathall, David J. 2017. Why do narcos invest in rural land? *Journal of Latin American Geography*, 16, 3–29. https://doi.org/10.1353/lag.2017.0019.

McSweeney, Kendra, Wrathall, David J., Nielsen, Erik A., and Pearson, Zoe. 2018. Grounding traffic: The cocaine commodity chain and land grabbing in eastern Honduras. *Geoforum*, 95, 122–132. https://doi.org/10.1016/j.geoforum.2018.07.008.

Middeldorp, Nick. 2016. Minería, Resistencia y repression en Honduras: Entre la ley y la impunidad. *Cuadernos de Antropologia Social*, 26, 69–89. http://revistas.ucr.ac.cr/index.php/antropologia/article/view/26488.

Middeldorp, Nick, and Le Billon, Phillipe. 2019. Deadly environmental governance: Authoritarianism, eco-populism, and the repression of environmental and land defenders. *Annals of the American Association of Geographers*, 109, 324–337. https://doi.org/10.1080/24694452.2018.1530586.

Mollett, Sharlene. 2016. The power to plunder: Rethinking land grabbing in Latin America. *Antipode*, 48, 412–432. https://doi.org/10.1111/anti.12190.

Mora, Mariana. 2017. *Kuxlejal Politics: Indigenous Autonomy, Race, and Decolonizing Research in Zapatista Communities*. Austin: University of Texas.

Munoz, Echart, and Villamar, María D. C. V. 2018. Resistencias y alternativas al desarrollo en América Latina y Caribe: Luchas sociales contra el extractivismo. *Relaciones Internacionales-Madrid*, 141–163. https://doi.org/10.15366/relacionesinternacionales2018.39.008.

Navas, Grettel, Mingorria, Sara, and Aguilar-González, Bernardo. 2018. Violence in environmental conflicts: The need for a multidimensional approach. *Sustainability Science*, 13, 649–660. https://doi.org/10.1007/s11625-018-0551-8.

Nixon, Rob. 2011. *Slow Violence and the Environmentalism of the Poor*. Cambridge, MA: Harvard University Press.

Ontiveros, Letyizia S., Munro, Paul G., and Zurita, Maria L. M. 2018. Proyectos de muerte: Energy justice conflicts on Mexico's unconventional gas frontier. *Extractive Industries and Society*, 5, 481–489. https://doi.org/10.1016/j.exis.2018.06.010.

Oslender, Ulrich. 2016. *The Geography of Social Movements: Afro-Colombian Mobilization and the Aquatic Space*. Durham, NC: Duke University Press.

Patagonia Sin Represas. n.d. Patagonia Sin Represas! Una campaña de educación pública. Consejo de Defensa de la Patagonia Chilena. www.patagoniasinrepresas.cl/final/dinamicos/libro_campana_PSR.pdf.

Paulson, Susan. 2012. Land-claims: Racialized environmental struggles in Latin America. In *Ecology and Power: Struggles Over Land and Material Resources in the Past, Present, and Future*. Hornborg, A., Clark, B., and Hermele, K. Eds. New York: Routledge, 262–273.

Peet, Richard, Robbins, Paul, and Watts, Michael. 2011. *Global Political Ecology*. New York: Routledge.

Pellegrini, Lorenzo, and Ribera Arismendi, Marco O. 2012. Consultation, compensation and extraction in Bolivia after the 'left turn': The case of oil exploration in the north of La Paz department. *Journal of Latin American Geography*, 11, 103–120. www.jstor.org/stable/24394814.

Peluso, Nancy L. 1995. Whose woods are these? Counter-mapping forest territories in Kalimantan, Indonesia. *Antipode*, 24, 383–406. https://doi.org/10.1111/j.1467-8330.1995.tb00286.x.

Pérez-Rincón, Mario, Vargas-Morales, Julieth, and Crespo-Marín, Zulma. 2017. Trends in social metabolism and environmental conflicts in four Andean countries from 1970 to 2013. *Sustainability Science*, 13, 635–648. https://doi.org/10.1007/s11625-017-0510-9.

Perreault, Tom. 2008. Custom and contradiction: Rural water governance and the politics of usos y costumbres in Bolivia's irrigators' movement. *Annals of the Association of American Geographers*, 98, 834–854. https://doi.org/10.1080/00045600802013502.

Perreault, Tom. 2012. Dispossession by accumulation? Mining, water and the nature of enclosure on the Bolivian altiplano. *Antipode*, 45, 1050–1069. https://doi.org/10.1111/anti.12005.

Perreault, Tom. 2015. Performing participation: Mining, power, and the limits of public consultation in Bolivia. *The Journal of Latin American and Caribbean Anthropology*, 20, 433–451. https://doi.org/10.1111/jlca.12185.

Perreault, Tom, and Martin, Patricia. 2016. Geographies of neoliberalism in Latin America. *Environment and Planning A: Economy and Space*, 37, 191–201. https://doi.org/10.1068%2Fa37394.

Perreault, Tom, and Valdivia, Gabriela. 2010. Hydrocarbons, popular protest and national imaginaries: Ecuador and Bolivia in comparative context. *Geoforum*, 41, 689–699. https://doi.org/10.1016/j.geoforum.2010.04.004.

Petras, James, and Veltmeyer, Henry. 2007. Neolberalism and imperialism in Latin America: Dynamics and responses. *International Review of Modern Sociology*, 33, 27–59. www.jstor.org/stable/41421287.

Porto-Gonçalves, Carlos, and Leff, Enrique. 2015. Political ecology in Latin America: The social reappropriation of nature, the reinvention of territories and the construction of an environmental rationality. *Desenvolvimento e Meio Ambiente*, 35, 65–88. https://doi.org/10.5380/dma.v35i0.43543.

Poulos, Helen M., and Haddad, Mary A. 2016. Violent repression of environmental protests. *Springerplus*, 5, 230. https://dx.doi.org/10.1186%2Fs40064-016-1816-2.

Radonic, Lucero. 2015. Environmental violence, water rights, and (un) due process in northwestern Mexico. *Latin American Perspectives*, 42, 27–47. https://doi.org/10.1177%2F0094582X15585111.

Ramos, Alcidia R. 1998. *Indigenism: Ethnic politics in Brazil*. Madison: University of Wisconsin.

Roberts, J. Timmons, and Thanos, Nikki D. 2003. *Trouble in Paradise. Globalization and Environmental Crises in Latin America*. London: Routledge.

Rodriguez-Labajos, Beatriz, Yanez, Ivonne, Bond, Patrick, Greyl, Lucie, Munguti, Serah, Ojo, Godwin, and Overbeek, Winfridus. 2019. Not so natural an alliance? Degrowth and environmental justice movements in the global south. *Ecological Economics*, 157, 175–184. https://doi.org/10.1016/j.ecolecon.2018.11.007.

Rojas Hernández, Jorge. 2016. Society, environment, vulnerability, and climate change in Latin America. *Latin American Perspectives*, 43, 29–42. https://doi.org/10.1177%2F0094582X16641264.

Santelices Spikin, Andrea, and Rojas Hernández, Jorge. 2016. Climate change in Latin America. *Latin American Perspectives*, 43, 4–11. https://doi.org/10.1177/0094582X16644916.

Sawyer, Suzana. 2004. *Crude chronicles: Indigenous politics, multinational oil, and neoliberalism in Ecuador*. Durham, NC: Duke University Press.

Schapper, Andrea, Unrau, Christine, and Killoh, Sarah. 2020. Social mobilization against large hydroelectric dams: A comparison of Ethiopia, Brazil, and Panama. *Sustainable Development*, 28, 413–423. https://doi.org/10.1002/sd.1995.

Silva, Eduardo. 2016. Patagonia, without dams! Lessons of a David vs. Goliath campaign. *Extractive Industries and Society*, 3, 947–957. https://doi.org/10.1016/j.exis.2016.10.004.

Silva, Eduardo, Akchurin, Maria, and Bebbington, Anthony J. 2018. Policy effects of resistance against mega-projects in Latin America: An introduction. *European Review of Latin American and Caribbean Studies*, (106), 27–47. http://doi.org/10.32992/erlacs.10397.

Silveira, Edson Damas, and Camargo, Serguei Aily. 2018. *Socioambientalismo de fronteiras: Direito indígena e ambiental*. Vila Nova de Gaia: Juruá.

Souza, M. A. 2018. Finaciando o movimento socioambiental na América do Sul: Um novo olhar. In *Filantropia de justiça social, sociedade civil e movimentos sociais no Brasil*. Hopstein, G. Ed. Rio de Janeiro: E-papers, 101–118. www.e-papers.com.br/produtos.asp?codigo_produto=2986&promo=0.

Svampa, Maristella. 2019. *Las fronteras del neoextractivismo en América Latina: Conflictos socioambientales, giro ecoterritorial y nuevas dependencias*. Zapopan: Calas Maria Sibylla Merian Center. http://calas.lat/sites/default/files/svampa_neoextractivismo.pdf.

Szablowski, David, and Campbell, Bonnie. 2019. Struggles over extractive governance: Power, discourse, violence, and legality. *The Extractive Industries and Society*, 6, 635–641. https://doi.org/10.1016/j.exis.2019.06.009.

Tanner, Lauri R. 2011. Kawas v. Honduras – protecting environmental defenders. *Journal of Human Rights Practice*, 3, 309–326. https://doi.org/10.1093/jhuman/hur020.

Temper, Leah, del Bene, Daniela, and Marinez-Alier, Joan. 2015. Mapping the frontiers and front lines of global environmental justice: The EJatlas. *Journal of Political Ecology*, 22, 256–278. https://doi.org/10.2458/v22i1.21108.

Temper, Leah, Demaria, Federico, Scheidel, Arnim, Del Bene, Daniela, and Martinez-Alier, Joan. 2018. The global environmental justice atlas (EJatlas): Ecological distribution conflicts as forces for sustainability. *Sustainability Science*, 13, 573–584. https://doi.org/10.1007/s11625-018-0563-4.

Teran-Mantovani, Emiliano. 2017. Inside and beyond the petro-state frontiers: Geography of environmental conflicts in Venezuela's Bolivarian revolution. *Sustainability Science*, 13, 677–691. https://doi.org/10.1007/s11625-017-0520-7.

Toledo, Victor, Garrido, David, and Barrera-Bassols, Narciso. 2015. The struggle for life socio-environmental conflicts in Mexico. *Latin American Perspectives*, 42, 133–147. https://doi.org/10.1177%2F0094582X15588104.

Torres, Pedro H. D., Leonel, Aana L., de Araújo, Gabriel P., and Jacobi, Pedro R. 2020. Is the Brazilian national climate change adaptation plan addressing inequality? Climate and environmental justice in a global south perspective. *Environmental Justice*, 13, 42–46 https://doi.org/10.1089/env.2019.0043.

Ulloa, Astrid. 2016. Feminismos territoriales en América Latina: Defensas de la vida frente a los extractivismos. *Nómadas*, 45, 123–139.

United Nations Human Rights Council. 2018. *Attacks Against and Criminalization of Indigenous Peoples Defending Their Rights (No. A/HRC/39/17).* Report of the Special Rapporteur on the Rights of Indigenous Peoples. UN Human Rights Council, Geneva.

Valdivia, Gabriela. 2008. Governing relations between people and things: Citizenship, territory, and the political economy of petroleum in Ecuador. *Political Geography*, 27, 456–477. https://doi.org/10.1016/j.polgeo.2008.03.007.

Valladares, Carolina, and Boelens, Rutgerd. 2017. Extractivism and the rights of nature: Governmentality, 'convenient communities' and epistemic pacts in Ecuador. *Environmental Politics*, 26, 1015–1034. https://doi.org/10.1080/09644016.2017.1338384.

Villalba-Eguiluz, C. Unai, and Etxano, Iker. 2017. Buen vivir vs development (ii): The limits of (neo) extractivism. *Ecological Economics*, 138, 1–11. https://doi.org/10.1016/j.ecolecon.2017.03.010.

Walter, Mariana, and Urkidi, Leire. 2017. Community mining consultations in Latin America (2002–2012): The contested emergence of a hybrid institution for participation. *Geoforum*, 84, 265–279. https://doi.org/10.1016/j.geoforum.2015.09.007.

Wittman, Hannah. 2009. Reworking the metabolic rift: La Vía Campesina, agrarian citizenship, and food sovereignty. *Journal of Peasant Studies*, 36, 805–826. DOI: 10.1080/03066150903353991.

Wolford, Wendy. 2007. Land reform in the time of neoliberalism: A many-splendored thing. *Antipode*, 39, 550–570. https://doi.org/10.1111/j.1467-8330.2007.00539.x.

Wolford, Wendy. 2010. *The Land is Ours Now: Social Mobilization and Meanings of Land in Brazil*. Durham, NC: Duke University Press.

Yates, Julian S., and Bakker, Karen. 2014. Debating the post-neoliberal turn in Latin America. *Progress in Human Geography*, 38, 62–90. https://doi.org/10.1177%2F0309132513500372.

Ybarra, Megan. 2018. *Green Wars: Conservation and Decolonization in the Maya Forest*. Oakland: University of California.

Zaremberg, Gisela, Torres Wong, Marcela, and Guarneros-Meza, Valeria. 2018. Descifrando el desorden: instituciones participativas y conflictos en torno a megaproyectos en México. *América Latina Hoy*, 79, 82–102. https://doi.org/10.14201/alh20187981102.

Zhouri, Andréa, Oliviera, Raquel, Zucarelli, Marcos, and Vasconcelos, Max. 2019. Violence, memory and new forms of resistance: The Samarco disaster in the Eio Doce. *Revista Pos Ciencias Sociais*, 16, 51–68. http://dx.doi.org/10.1590/1809-43412017v14n2p081

6

ENVIRONMENTAL MOVEMENTS IN ASIA

Divergent relationship with political liberalization

Fengshi Wu

Introduction

As in other regions across the globe, public awareness of environmental degradation and climate change and social mobilization for environmental protection have been on the rise in Asia in recent decades. The Goldman Environmental Prize, a most reputable award to honor "grassroots environmental heroes", has since 1990 recognized 180 distinguished environmentalists around the world such as Wangari Muta Maathai from Kenya (winner in 1991), who later became the first African woman Nobel prize winner in 2004. By 2019, one-sixth of the Goldman awardees were from the greater Asia region.[1] As a result, an increasing number of publications have emerged that either explore environmental activism and movements in a single Asian country or compare such movements across countries within the Asian region. However, scholarly effort is still limited in conceptualizing environmental movements in Asia – their origins, developments, and impacts – as a whole and possibly identifying an "Asian way" of environmental struggle and policy advocacy. This lacuna in the existing literature in a way is not surprising and may accurately indicate the high level of intra-regional diversity in Asia. As the largest continent on the planet, Asia is home to diverse cultures, peoples, polities, and ecosystems. Therefore, it makes theoretical sense to study a sub-region, or a cluster of countries in Asia. For example, the Northeast Asia cluster (Japan, South Korea, mainland China, and Taiwan) and the Central Asia cluster (Kazakhstan, Kyrgyzstan, Tajikistan, Uzbekistan, and Turkmenistan).

Given this research background, this chapter focuses on the impact of political liberalization on the rise of environmentalism as a main form of broad social mobilization in contemporary Asia and approaches the topic in the following steps. It first introduces a theoretical inquiry on the relationship between political regime and transition and the development of modern environmental movements in the Asian context. Keeping the intra-regional diversity in mind, case selection for this research is guided by both the call for broad coverage of Asia and the logic of comparative politics so that findings from the cases will be able to generate a level of theoretical discussion. After presenting the empirical evidence from the specific Asian countries, the chapter endeavors to offer discussion of not only the shared patterns of the dual transition of politics and environmental movement in the focused countries but also the key intervening factors that contribute to the incongruent development of the opening up of the political system and, on

DOI: 10.4324/9780367855680-7

the other hand, of the development of environmental movements. The chapter concludes with suggestions for future studies on the topic.

Environmental movement and political liberalization: research context

Political liberalization in this research is conceptualized as a continual spectrum, not defined by the presence or lack of democratization (Brynen et al., 1995: 3–6). Essentially, political liberalization entails the expansion of the public sphere where ordinary citizens can become self-organized and participate in public affairs and collective decision-making without substantial interference by the state and political authorities, which can include a broad range of activities and informal institutional formations. Democratization, in comparison, is marked by more definite and formal political events and institution building such as general elections and independence of the judicial system. It is particularly important for students of social mobilization in the Asian context to note that political liberalization and public participation in policy making can happen without the concomitant ticking of all the conceptual boxes of democratization occurring, and, vice versa, having general elections and formal democratic institutions in some contexts does not lead to better protection of civil or political liberties (Bell et al., 1995). As the following case analysis of some longstanding non-democratic states in Asia will show, public space for activism, policy advocacy, and social mobilization in the name of nature conservation and mitigation of environmental crisis have been opened up, which in turn has led to significant changes in politics and policy making in a broader scope.

To compare environmental movements across cases more systematically, the research emphasizes two aspects: one, the scope of the movements, particularly whether there is any form of linking up across localities and small-scale initiatives or protests that *transcend* specific social ties, causes, and victimhood or solidarities and two, the *transformative* potential of such movements, which could lead the movements to aspire to and achieve broader public and environmental good. A transformative environmental movement, as a type of "new social movement" broadly defined (Inglehart, 1977; Offe, 1985, cited in Ku, 1996: 159–161), promotes new political ideas and ideologies that aim at comprehensive and sustainable changes in politics, economics, and culture while not limited to solving the immediate environmental problems and assisting pollution victims.

Unlike their counterparts in post–World War II Western democratic societies, leaders of environmental activism and movements in the rest of the world often find themselves caught in more complex political struggles against several interconnected fundamental issues such as decolonization and nation building, economic development and global market integration, and political stabilization and post-conflict reconciliation. Environmentalist narratives do not always synchronize well with the chorus of multiple concurrent socio-political transformations. Existing scholarship on the topic outlines at least three possible trajectories of environmental movements and governance building in the vast developing world: ecological modernization, authoritarian environmentalism, and environmental democracy.

Scholars of ecological modernization theory emphasize the possible synergy between the state, regardless of its regime type, and civil society and the balance between economic taking off and environmental protection for newly independent and/or post-conflict countries (e.g., Carter and Mol, 2006). It is not just possible but also necessary that state-led reforms and bottom-up activism go in tandem to reshape and modernize a country's environmental governance. In sharp contrast, scholars of environmental authoritarianism remain cautious, if not doubtful, about the governments in developing countries, especially under an authoritarian regime, and their initial acceptance of environmental activism and willingness to enhance environmental governance. For example, some observe that taking a lead in developing renewable energy and constructing a domestic narrative on climate change has made the Chinese Communist Party (CCP) more resilient at home, more assertive on the global stage, and even more popular in neighboring countries (Beeson, 2010; Gilley, 2012). Finally, the framework of environmental democracy highlights that environmental protection hinges on social justice, human rights, rule of law, and other key elements of modern democratic systems, and therefore, a full-fledged environmental movement will eventually usher in more fundamental political development and demand for democratization. Case evidence of regime change and social mobilization from the former Soviet Union, South Korea, Taiwan, and Brazil in the past decades suggests that environmental activism in authoritarian regimes ultimately converges with broad resistance and pro-democracy movements (Weiner, 1999; Hochstetler, 2000; Schreurs, 2002). The environmental democracy theory and authoritarian environmentalism challenge, from two angles, the hypothesis that environmental movements can coexist and co-evolve with authoritarian rule in the long run, which is highly relevant to understand the current trends in Asia.

Instead of testing or eliminating any of these theoretical lenses, this research incorporates all three lines of logic in the following comparative analysis to best present the status of ongoing political struggles related to environmental movements in Asia. Given the high level of diversity in political, economic, historic, and cultural terms, the "Asian experience" may well be plural and represent variations and various combinations of the three noted patterns. Limited in length, this research selected eight cases to both broaden geographical coverage and control political structural variation (Table 6.1). Cases were first selected across three main sub-regions of Asia – East Asia, Central and Inner Asia, and Southeast Asia. Then, for each sub-region, one or two representative case(s) of both authoritarianism and democracy were chosen. Most of the democratic cases are young and fresh out of pro-democracy movement and transition, and they offer a unique research opportunity to observe the co-evolvement of political liberalization and environmental movements.

From South Korea to Mongolia: many fates of environmental movements

The case analysis for this research starts with South Korea as it demonstrates the co-evolution of the environmental movement and political structural change to a great extent. Politics in the

Table 6.1 Political context of environmental movements in contemporary Asia

Sub-region	Cases	Political context
Northeast Asia	China (mainland)	Communist regime, political liberalization without democratization since 1978
	Japan	Democracy with one dominant party since 1945
	South Korea	Democratic transition and consolidation since the late 1990s
Southeast Asia	Indonesia	Democratic transition since 1998
	Singapore	Electoral authoritarian regime since 1965
	Vietnam	Communist regime, political liberalization without democratization since 1986
Inner and Central Asia	Kazakhstan	Electoral authoritarian regime since independence in 1991
	Mongolia	Democratic transition since early 1990s

southern half of the Korean peninsula has experienced a sea change from authoritarian rule after the devastating war in the 1950s to a consolidated democracy in the new millennium. Environmental protesters and activism leaders, first triggered by internationally reported pollution and health crises in Seoul, such as the case of "Onsan illness", later became a crucial force in the broad spectrum of social resistance and the pro-democracy movement from the 1980s to 1990s. Umbrella organizations such as the Anti-Pollution Movement Association and Korean Federation for Environmental Movement and critical non-governmental organizations (NGOs) such as the Pollution Research Institute provided necessary leadership (e.g., Yul Choi, 1995 Goldman Prize winner) for the environmental movement and anti-regime resistance as well.

According to Ku (1996), the environmental movement in South Korea had already achieved structural transformation, expanded beyond victim-based social organizations, and transcended to incorporate more broad political claims and goals by the end of the 1980s. After the democratic transition, like their counterparts in other young democracies such as Taiwan and Brazil, Korean environmental activists gradually got elected or appointed into the governing administration. Nevertheless, new generations of movement leaders have emerged, and the original bottom-up mobilizational momentum has been retained. In December 2005, the news of farmers from South Korea jumping in the waters at the Victoria Harbor, Hong Kong, made front pages around the world and marked the history of a global-scale anti-WTO, anti-globalization, and pro-environment movement. Korean activists have creatively used public spectacles to popularize their environmental causes, from local river conservation and anti-nuclear power plants to climate change and a green lifestyle (Wu and Wen, 2015: 109–110). It can be argued that the push and pull from both pro-environment politicians within the state system and broad-based environmental activism and resistance outside the state together contribute to the rise of "developmental environmentalism" and the "green economy", as new national-level policy narratives in contemporary South Korea (Death, 2015; Kim and Thurbon, 2015).

Japan, the next-door neighbor of South Korea, is a rare case of stable constitutional monarchy and democracy, though dominated by the Liberal Democratic Party, in Asia. After World War II, Japan's industrialization took off swiftly, and, in turn, environmental accidents and pollution soared to the degree that Tokyo suffered the world's worst air pollution in the early 1960s. Resistance by pollution victims and mass protests, sometimes highly contentious, against pollution broke out in Tokyo and across the country at that time.[2] The Japanese state eventually responded by the 1970 "pollution diet", a package of multiple national-level laws, and the establishment of the state environmental agency in the following year. This wave of social mobilization not only engendered a generation of environmental activists and movement leaders but also led to the transformation of the overall governance structures in post-war Japan (Schreurs, 2003). Furthermore, Japanese environmentalists such as Ui Jun, who attended the NGO forum and staged demonstrations to expose Japan's domestic pollution problems at the United Nation's Conference on Human Development in Stockholm in 1972, also pioneered transnational advocacy networks in Asia after they learned from fellow Asian NGO leaders and activists at the Conference about the environmental damages created by Japanese industries overseas (Avenell, 2017).

However, the transformative power of the first wave of the environmental movement in Japan gradually receded, and public contestation against state and corporate power evolved into other forms of activism led by community-based associations, local environmentally friendly politicians, and a pro-environmentalism circle of "soft elite" – technocrats and academicians – embedded in all levels of formal environmental governance, most of whom took part in the environmental protests in the 1960s (Wu and Wen, 2015: 106–108). The downside of Japan's "quiet", though "far from impotent", environmentalism is that at the national level, it has become "politically marginalized" over time (Mason, 1999: 188). This partially explains why even after the Fukushima nuclear disaster, which spurred anti-nuclear protests around the world and led to major policy shifts in Germany, environmental civil society and protests in Japan were not able to thwart then Prime Minister Abe, who authorized the resumption of the nuclear power sector. Although the anti-nuclear movement sustains, it would require more than a "business as usual" type of social mobilization in post-Abe Japan to break down the pro-nuclear state-corporate coalition, which has a long history in the country (Valentine and Sovacool, 2010).

In contrast to South Korea and Japan, the political structure in China for the past seven decades has remained authoritarian and centered on the CCP *nomenklatura*. Nevertheless, civil society and social activism were sprouting after the death of Chairman Mao in 1976 and during the early years of the "Open and Reform" era, which became evident with all the events leading to the Tian'anmen anti-corruption and pro-democracy protests in 1989. In the wake of the state's repression, resulting in an international embargo and a diplomatic freeze, the Chinese society was silenced, and the space of civil society shrank. It was not until the year 1994 that a group of Beijing-based university professors, intellectuals, and environmentalists established the first environmental NGO, Friends of Nature, to openly conduct public education programs on wildlife conservation, recycling, and environmental protection. In the next 25 years, the environmental activism community not only survived the communist rule but also, in relative terms, thrived, with a broad geographic spread of NGOs and networks, a high level of international support, and a large number of successful cases of public campaign and policy advocacy (Steinhardt and Wu, 2016; Dai et al., 2017; Dai and Spires, 2018). According to the China Environmental Organization Map, there are over 2,000 active grassroots environmental NGOs across the country.[3] The anti–large dam campaign to protect the Nu River (upstream of the Mekong River), led by an international award–winning Chinese environmentalist, Wang Yongchen, and a transnational network of activists from China, Southeast Asia, Japan, North America, and Europe, is one of the most reported examples of the expanding environmental movement in China, which started in 2004 and continues today.[4]

A main quality of the environmental NGO community in China is the high level of inter-organizational connections and a relatively strong sense of "having peers" and social belonging across localities and/or issue specializations (Wu, 2017). There are by now tens of nationwide and broadly focused networks, such as the China Zero Waste Alliance, targeting recycling and sustainable urban civil waste management (Lu and Steinhardt *forthcoming*); the public pollution-monitoring network centered around the Institute for Public and Environmental Affairs, the mangrove alliance along China's southern coastal regions, and the loose alliance of various "river stewardship" groups along the Yangtze River supported by the Alibaba Foundation. Memberships in these resourceful alliances and networks often overlap, which further strengthens social solidarity within the environmental activism community. A connected and effective NGO community with leadership and shared visions has been argued as a major explanation for the emergence of public interest–oriented, large-scale environmental protests and partially explains why and how the Chinese environmental movement by and large has been able to sustain its capacity and relevance in spite of a series of restrictive regulations and policy changes since Xi Jinping took power in 2012 (Wu and Martus, 2021).

Sharing many political structural features with neighboring China, Vietnam also embarked on systematic reforms, "Doi Moi", in 1986 and subsequently witnessed the revival of associational lives and prototype civil society organizations (Wells-Dang, 2012). Locally rooted and single-incident-focused protests at the community level, in a way, are not something completely new to Vietnamese society, partially due to a long history of labor activism. The anti-bauxite campaign in 2009, which emerged rather incidentally as a response to the central government's planning, led to widespread criticism and activism by ordinary citizens, religious communities, and even political elites. Despite its minor policy impact, this campaign is viewed by many as "one of the most significant expression of public dissent against the single-party state since the end of the Vietnam War" (Morris-Jung, 2011, as cited in Ortmann, 2017: 154) and marked a new page of environmentalism in the country. Between 2010 to 2015, at least 14 protests against various pollution incidents and development projects took place across the country, ranging from landfill construction, cement plants, and coal power plants to steel and textile mills, all of which amassed hundreds, sometimes thousands, of local participants (Ortmann, 2017: 139).

However, establishing NGOs outside the Vietnamese Communist Party system and developing independent environmental and professional capacities are new to Vietnamese society. With support from international donors and NGOs and occasional empathy from the reformist wing of the Vietnamese state, environmental NGOs and activism networks have emerged and continued to grow in numbers in the last decade (Wells-Dang, 2010). Like their counterparts in China, many of these NGOs seek formal and informal ties with the authorities to survive and be exempted from political suppression and devote most of their energy to developing expertise in specific areas, such as the Vietnam Association for Conservation of Nature and Environment – one of the oldest of its kind, established in the 1980s (Vu, 2019).

In more recent years, the introduction of Facebook and other types of social media has ushered in a new wave of environmental activism and social mobilization, in which cross-locality networking and collective actions become more possible. The "tree movement" in Hanoi in 2015, sharing many characteristics with the new social movements in other parts of the world, where young netizens and social media play a critical role and no specific social movement organization can be identified as the sole leader, has prompted scholars such as Vu (2017) to argue for "more deliberative and accountable politics in the same country [Vietnam] in the long run". The ongoing anti–Formosa steel plant movement, triggered by the massive fish death along Vietnam's central coasts in 2016, is the most significant case so far and in many ways has pushed the political redlines, with multiple large-scale protests taking place in main cities across the country, including in both Ha Noi and Ho Chi Minh City. Although the government reacted to the protests and activism harshly by quickly arresting over 100 environmentalists, Catholic priests, bloggers, and concerned citizens, the movement has been able to maintain parts of its momentum and even inspired other anti-pollution protests over the years (Nguyen and Datzberger, 2018).

Moving on to the other side of the Southeast Asian region, the archipelago country, Indonesia, has gone through a crisscross process of political liberalization and democratization in the past decades. Social mobilization and localized resistance already were on the rise at the peak of the authoritarian rule by Suharto in the 1970s, similar to the South Korean case. However, more than their Korean counterparts, Indonesian environmental activists and technocrats were able to carve out more political space and in many ways aided resistance in other social sectors, particularly the agrarian movements and student movements, which became critical forces in the ousting of Suharto at the end of 1990s (Peluso et al., 2008).

Much of the start of environmentalism in post-independence Indonesia can be attributed to a single politician and environmentalist, Emil Salim (Minister of Development Supervision and the Environment from1978 to1983 and Minister of Population and the Environment from 1983 to1993), who founded the first nationwide environmental NGO in the country, Indonesian Forum for Environment (*Wahana Lingkungan Hidup Indonesia*, WALHI). Since its beginning, WALHI has been the flagship organization for all environmentalists and NGOs and played the critical role of providing leadership and protection for bottom-up initiatives. In the broad context that the American government was tolerant toward Suharto's regime during the Cold War, environmental NGOs from the West, such as the World Wildlife Fund (WWF), were permitted to operate in Indonesia since the end of the 1970s, which incidentally provided an extra boost to the emergence of domestic environmentalism in the country (Nomura, 2007: 500). By the late 1990s, environmental NGOs and activism had developed in Indonesia far beyond major cities and reached the Outer Islands. Environmental civil society has grown steadily in the post-1998 *reformasi* era in Indonesia, not merely in quantity but also in quality, measured by their increasing presence in formal politics and policy-making processes and, more importantly, their commitment to public accountability, representation, and intra-organizational democracy (Nomura, 2007: 508–513).

Being one of the most climate-vulnerable countries and home to some of the last remaining large-scale rainforests on the planet, Indonesia has become a hot destination for international donors and funding agencies in recent decades. Some of these funding opportunities – e.g., the WWF, mentioned earlier, and the small-grant program of the Global Environment Facility in the 1990s (or even earlier) – have provided much-needed support to local environmental activism. However, experts observe the double-sided impact of the significant flow of zest and funds from international realms to local Indonesian communities, channeled through decentralized, sometimes excessively fragmented and contradictory, domestic political institutions (Gellert, 2010). Furthermore, Jokowi's leadership, coupled with the resurgent political Islam, has introduced new twists to post-transition Indonesian politics, which will affect the future trajectories of environmentalism in the country. For example, based on interview evidence, Nilan (2020) has found that many young Indonesian environmental activists base their environmentalist commitments "firmly on their Muslim faith", seeing themselves as *khalifah* – God's lieutenants on earth. The deep impact on environmental governance and outcomes of this companionship between Islam faith and environmentalism in Indonesia remains to be seen.

Singapore, a city-state situated at the heart of Southeast Asia, may seem to be an outlier case in this study; nevertheless, it exemplifies a few underlining patterns of environmental politics shared by many Asian societies. The concept of the electoral authoritarian state – repeated incumbent successes enabled by unfair elections and sustained by mostly authoritarian political institutions (Morse, 2012: 162) – best captures politics in Singapore under the continuous rule by the People's Action Party (PAP), with the premiership passed from the father to the son of the Lee family since 1965. Given this context, there are three different types of environmentalism, not necessarily merged yet, active in contemporary Singapore. First, an ultimately anti-authoritarian, moral-environmental movement started by the Nature Society Singapore (NSS), which has protested many PAP developmentalist ideologies and policies since the late 1980s. Back then, concerned with government-led large-scale infrastructure projects, a group of NSS members, including scientists and amateur naturalists, "embarked on detailed area surveys, drew up conservation proposals and lobbied the government". These initiatives marked the policy advocacy turn of the organization (Goh, 2001). Second, resembling the government-organized and sponsored NGOs (GONGOs) in China and Vietnam, particularly at the local levels, Singapore has a vast network of residential community–based "people's associations" that are becoming more proactive in implementing environmental related policies. Some even argue that these community associations have pushed environmental protection beyond what the policy makers may have originally envisioned, when conditions are met (Han and Tan, 2019). Last, but not least, mirroring the trends in other parts of the world, a new wave of social activism, mainly driven by the youth and facilitated by social media, is fast growing and calls for fundamental change in environmental thinking and policy making, which has the potential to mobilize across sectoral boundaries and bring about more broad socio-political transformations (LJY, 2019).

Student movements have a strong track record of tipping off authoritarian figures and shaking existing political systems in Singapore's neighboring regions, including China, Taiwan, South Korea, the Philippines, Indonesia, and most recently Hong Kong. Therefore, experts shall watch closely whether and how young greenies in Singapore grow their social outreach and merge with both the senior generation of environmental activists and community-rooted associational leaders. A first public demonstration for more progressive climate actions took place on 21 September 2019, and over 2,000 citizens attended with enthusiasm, which could be a milestone in Singapore's environmental movement or even the beginning of the dual transformation exemplified by the South Korean experience, as the general election in the following July ushered in a batch of non-PAP, young, women, minority, and progressive politicians as the newest members of the parliament and marked a historically low popular vote for PAP.

During the first decade after its independence in 1991, the environmental NGO community, which share the origins with the anti-nuclear movement in the former Soviet Union and Eastern Europe, thrived in Kazakhstan with sufficient support from the UN, EU, and international NGOs (Weinthal and Luong, 2002). As Nazarbayev's government evolved, the green civil society in Kazakhstan shrank in terms of overall scale and quality. According to the director of the Association for the Conservation of Biodiversity of Kazakhstan (ACBK) – the largest conservation NGO in the country – despite the significant decline, there is still a decent-size, loosely connected community of environmental NGOs and activists in today's Kazakhstan, particularly in Almaty and Astana.[5] These NGOs, such as GS and ACBK, have reached out to local communities and victim groups and successfully leveraged their resources not only to alter the outcomes of state-backed development projects but also to contribute to environmental law enforcement and policy implementation. In some specific policy areas, environmental NGOs have been invited and/or permitted to participate in formal policy making and implementation processes (Soltys, 2013).

Since its independence, Kazakhstan has joined many international environment-related agreements (e.g., the Aarhus Convention on the Access to Information, Public Participation in Decision-making and Access to Justice in Environmental Matters) and enacted a large body of environmental regulations to formally ensure public participation in environmental governance (Cherp, 2000). This legal-political background is critical to understanding the partial success of some environmental NGOs' advocacy work and local resistance to large developmental projects. Almaty-based Green Salvation (GS), the largest and most reputable environmental law NGO in the country, for example, has always exercised its legal rights to access environmental information and even initiated and won court hearings and suits against both governmental agencies and industries, which led to the slowing down or even cancellation of economic projects that could have significant detrimental ecological and social impacts.[6] Coalitions of activists inside and beyond the country have used Kazakhstan's official membership and signatory status in international environmental treaties as leverage to launch transnational policy advocacy and assert pressure on various governmental agencies (Weinthal and Watters, 2010).

Unlike Kazakhstan, the other landlocked inner-Asian country, Mongolia, went through a swift transition to democracy with mass protests and hunger strikes concentrated in the capital city, Ulaanbaatar, during the period from the end of the 1980s to the first half of the 1990s. However, the old political ecology has not fundamentally changed since then, as the former Communist Party metamorphosized itself into the Mongolian People's Party and held on to public appeal and political power. Along with the regular elections, power shifts between the two leading parties, and subsequent reshufflings of the central administration, Mongolia has had many rounds of changes of environmental regulatory agencies, which has fundamentally weakened the credibility and capacity of environmental law and policy enforcement institutions.

The widespread corruption and power abuse (Boone et al., 1997) further exacerbates the low effectiveness of governance across the board and, in turn, contributes to the highly contentious forms of environmental activism, yet with little sustaining policy impact even when the activism and public protest succeeded.

Evidence from Mongolia's mining and water sectors illustrates this vicious circle. Several different ministries share the responsibility of regulating water use and conservation in the country, suffering from the lack of effective horizontal coordination. With rare exceptions, water activism in Mongolia is highly localized and isolated, carried out usually by lone activists with no support network and often in a highly contentious manner instead of institutionalized public participation. One of the high-profile cases took place in 2010 when Ts. Munkhbayar was reported to have used firearms at the properties of the (Canadian) Centerra Gold and (Chinese) Puraam mining companies to protest their violation of local laws that prohibit mining near water sources. Ts. Munkhbayar was later sentenced to 12 years in jail for his action.

Many international NGOs have worked closely with local nomadic communities resisting mining projects, contributing to the decline of the total percentage of land licensed to mining in recent years. However, scholars argue that such transnational networks have had unintended consequences that may further fragment Mongolian society and politics due to the ideological gaps between the local communities and the international NGOs (Byambajav, 2015). This is an ongoing trend, not exclusive to Mongolia, that needs more systematic studies and will be touched upon again in the next section.

Comparative discussion

The many routes of environment-related resistance and movements in contemporary Asia (summarized in Table 6.2) have offered an opportunity to explore the relationship between political opening up and democratic transition and the emergence and outcome of environmentalism. The main finding of the research is that political liberalization is a necessary, though not sufficient, condition for a broad and transformative environmental movement to emerge and sustain. While there are encouraging cases, notably South Korea and Indonesia, where political reforms and environmental movements have worked out in tandem, the majority of the cases studied here, and in Asia in general, present non-optimal co-evolution where strong social activism and contention related to over-exploitation of natural resource and ecosystems in fact have led to political stalemate or made it hard for local environmentalism to grow broad political relevance. There is strong evidence from post-totalitarian China, authoritarian Vietnam, and electoral-authoritarian Singapore to indicate that some level of political reform and opening up for public participation, NGO development, and transnational civic linkages has made it possible for environmental activists to break the taboo and become the frontrunners of social mobilization, pubic campaigns, and policy advocacy. However, after the initial breakthrough, the trajectory of environmental movements in these non-democratic countries remains uncertain: it could further take off like in South Korea and Indonesia or wither away like in Kazakhstan and Mongolia.

Flipping the equation, mounting evidence from this study points to the pattern that environmental activism and social mobilization have played a critical role in the long, often interrupted journey of political liberalization and democratization in Asian societies. In pre-transition South Korea and Indonesia and current China, Vietnam, and Singapore, the environmental sector hosts some of the most vibrant and broadest networks of activists and NGOs to the extent that

Table 6.2 Environmental movements in selected Asian countries

Case	Timeline	Scope	Transformative impact
China (mainland)	Emerged in the mid-1990s	Nationwide networks, campaigns	Mostly reactive with early signs of transformative potential
Japan	Emerged in the 1960s	Notable nationwide networks with a large number of strong and localized environmental movements	Significant transformative impact in the 1960s and 1970s, but now less so
South Korea	Emerged together with the pro-democracy movement in the 1980s	Many nationwide broad associations and networks	Has been transformative throughout the democratization process
Indonesia	Emerged in the early 1970s under dictatorship	Mostly local movements and groups, but there are notable nationwide associations and networks	Contributing to transformative politics with movements from other sectors
Singapore	Became publicly visible since the 1990s	Mostly localized initiatives	Mostly reactive initiatives
Vietnam	On the rise since the 2000s	Limited nationwide events	Reactive and localized
Kazakhstan	Shared origins with the anti-nuclear and environmental movement in the Soviet Union and East European countries in the 1980s (or earlier)	Mostly locally rooted protests and campaigns, some but not many nationwide networks	Had the potential to be transformative in the 1990s, but now mostly reactive and in decline
Mongolia	Became present since the 1990s	Mostly localized, issue specific initiatives	Not transformative and in decline

other dissidents and activists, promoting more politically sensitive causes such as human rights, minority rights, and labor rights, would strategize and embed themselves in the environmental activism circles. Because of their shared roots in the widespread anti-nuclear protests in the former Soviet Union, environmental activists were among the most prominent pro-democracy social leaders and organizers in the first decade of independent Kazakhstan. Politics in the first few decades of post-war Japan was mostly democratic in name, and the sweeping anti-pollution protests in the 1960s and effective policy advocacy achieved by leading environmentalists in the 1970s generated a significant impact on the Japanese political system to allow for more accountability, transparency, and public participation in the future.

Returning to the three conceptual trajectories of political-environmental dual development, particularly in an authoritarian context, case evidence presented here could suggest that all three are relevant to understanding environmental movements in Asia, and, within a single case, it is often the case that a particular trajectory is more visible at a time but subject to changes. Having mapped out this character of the environmental-political dual transformation, this research encounters a more intriguing question: Why would the initial synergy between political liberalization and the environmental movement evolve and diverge into two different paths? (See Figure 6.1) For example, this synergy has sustained and produced a mutually reinforcing relationship between democratic institutional building and the continuation of effective environmental movement in the case of South Korea and, to a less degree, also in Indonesia. However, in other cases, particularly Kazakhstan, China, Singapore, and even Japan, elements of authoritarian environmentalism can be found where the authoritarian state or anti-reform political forces have been able to absorb social pressure and reap parts of the success of the environmental movement to strengthen their own legitimacy and social control, which in turn has taken a heavy toll on the further growth of the environmental activism community. In some of the most disappointing scenarios, such as the case of Mongolia, there is a vicious circle between political reform and activism, where successful environmental activism has little impact on policy and institutional changes, and constant reshuffling of environmental bureaucracies cancels out policy modifications made by previous environmental activism and advocacy.

Borrowing a literary metaphor from the opening line of the novel *Anna Karenina*, "Happy families are all alike; every unhappy family is unhappy in its own way", this research has found that environmental movement and political liberalization can go well in tandem, but when they fall out, as is very often the case in contemporary Asia, the causes are quite different. The rest of this section will discuss two relevant factors that could break the initial co-evolution of the opening up of political participation and the rise of environmental activism and lead to a deviant and regressive pathway, drawing on the case evidence from Asia.

First and foremost, the pressure of economic growth and the environmental costs of joining the global markets. Most Asian countries are overachievers in economic growth measured by global standards: for example, the "dragons and tigers" in the second half of the twentieth century[7] and China, to some extent Kazakhstan, and increasingly Vietnam since the new millennium. However, they lag behind when it comes to environmental protection. According to the Environmental Performance Index (EPI) published periodically by the Yale Center of Environmental Law and Policy, five out of the eight cases highlighted in this chapter on average in the past two decades have been in the bottom 50th percentile (Table 6.3).

To reduce poverty, embarking on industrialization and competing in global markets have not only dominated most Asian governments' agendas but also become a quasi-ideology and mega-narrative affecting Asian societies' collective consciousness, which diverts public attention

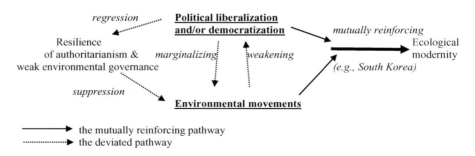

Figure 6.1   Two pathways of the dual evolution of political liberalization and environmental movements

from any other major socio-political tasks including, but not limited to, environmental protection. Moreover, this developmentalist mindset does not give way to democratic transition (Kim and Thurbon, 2015). As their main mandate is to respond to what the voters want, politicians in young democracies often find themselves even more pressed to boost the economy and find themselves less incentivized to strengthen environmental protection or align with environmentalists and pollution victims. When the massive fish death happened in 2016, local governments and politicians in central coastal Vietnam reacted to protests with harsh suppressive measures, fearing the resistance would lead to the departure of large foreign investments from Taiwan and, in turn, economic loss for the whole province. Many local governments across China, particularly in the rural area, are caught in the same quandary and in between lucrative business deals and development projects and environmental disasters and community grievances in the aftermath.

The tale of the two central- and inner-Asian cases, Kazakhstan and Mongolia, further sheds light on the significant impact of the drive to jump-start the national economy by rapidly selling natural resources to the global markets in the process of establishing regulatory institutions both effective and responsive to the demands of environmental movements, especially in newly independent or transitioned developing countries. Even though Mongolia has seen some of the most courageous "water worriers" and impressive campaigns against mining pollution, these efforts have not been fruitful in terms of producing institutional changes to actually halt polluting practices, mainly due to the rampant corruption and close ties between political elites and the mining industry and, probably more devastatingly, the fact that Mongolia's national economy is heavily dependent on mineral exports. A similar pattern can be found in Kazakhstan's petroleum and increasing hydropower industries, but to a much less extent as its national economic structure is much more diversified and growth less contingent on resource extraction and export. For example, increasing investment from China in leasing agricultural lands and food production eventually urged the Kazakhstan central government to withdraw a law that permits foreigners to lease land (Sternberg et al., 2017).

Another important, yet so far understudied factor that has contributed to the divergent patterns of environmental movements in Asia is transnational advocacy and global civil society networks (Keck and Sikkink, 1998). In the context of climate change and ecological degradation

Table 6.3 Global rankings of environmental performance

Country	2006	2010	2020
China (mainland)	94	121	120
Indonesia	79	134	116
Japan	14	20	12
Kazakhstan	70	92	85
Mongolia	115	142	147
Singapore	n/a	28	39
South Korea	42	94	28
Vietnam	99	85	141

Note: Data extracted from Environmental Performance Index (EPI) 2006, 2010, and 2020 report (available at https://epi.yale.edu/downloads). For each round of the survey, both the total number of countries and the measurements vary.

in the twentieth century, environmental activism in individual countries and societies is increasingly linked to global-level mobilization, governance building, and narrative construction. Asia is not an exception in this respect. In fact, external non-state agencies and donors have been present and even influential in some Asian communities for a relatively long period due to the colonial history and great power penetration during the Cold War. More recent decades have seen the rise of transnational advocacy networks in which local activists and small-scale community resistance have reached out to form new partnerships and solidarity with well-endowed and positioned NGOs, foundations, and other institutions in Washington, DC; New York; Oxford; Tokyo; Taipei; Amsterdam; and more.

Related to the rise of such solidarity-based and value-laden transnational advocacy networks, at least two issues have emerged that further complicate the relationship between the political authorities and the environmental civil society in Asian countries. One, in the wake of the Color Revolutions in the former Soviet space and the Arab Spring in 2012, many governments in the developing world are becoming suspicious of, if not antagonistic toward, foreign NGOs, charities, and foundations. Political authorities in China, India, Myanmar, Cambodia, Indonesia, and more recently Hong Kong have introduced new laws, regulations, visa policies, and more to tighten up the monitoring and control over international NGOs' activities, seeing international NGO networks as one source of anti-regime, pro-democracy public sentiments and social mobilization. The other, internal disparities, in terms of either materialistic power or discursive knowledge within the transnational networks, between local and international NGOs further affect domestic state-society relations. At times, such disparities can have unintended ramifications that are detrimental to local communities. For example, the "brain drain" of local experts as observed in transnational environmental networks working in China (Litzinger, 2004) and divisive impacts caused by external donors on local communities in Indonesia (Gellert, 2010) and Mongolia (Byambajav, 2015), as discussed earlier.

Conclusions

Environmental movements and environmental activism are on the rise in Asia, even though a majority of the states in the region are not stable democracies. This research has found that opening up the political system and deepening public participation in politics are critical for the early development of the environmental movement, yet not enough for the movement to sustain and become effective in the long run. Only few Asian societies, markedly South Korea and Indonesia, have seen continuous growth of the environmental movement after the fundamental political regime shift. For countries like Kazakhstan, Mongolia, or even Japan, the initial golden opportunity for the environmental movement and broad social mobilization to push for more sustained political liberalization has been missed, and environmental activism has been either mostly absorbed into the formal state apparatus or sidelined.

The research further found that the ideological urgency of economic development has contributed to the divergence of political reform and environmental movement in many Asian countries, even more so in young democracies. With rare exceptions, marketization and integration into the global economic system, managed by often unstable, if not corrupt, elected politicians, have taken a toll on the environment. Outstanding as a region, Asian countries are overachievers in economic development while lagging in environmental performance. In addition, attention and assistance from international agencies and environmental NGOs to Asian countries has not been consistently effective in supporting bottom-up activism and facilitating collaboration between the state and society in environmental protection. Instead, well-intended international NGOs often find themselves caught in problematic political entanglements, which can result in the unintended weakening of environmental governance in the recipient country.

Limited by space, this research cannot explore in greater depth and more systematically the intertwined relationship between political liberalization, economic development, transnational activism, and bottom-up environmental movements. Further studies on the topic could employ various methods, qualitatively or quantitively, to expand case numbers and enhance the understanding of the relationships across these important factors.

Acknowledgments

Interviews conducted in Kazakhstan for this chapter were supported by the Ministry of Education, Singapore, under Tier-1 Grant number RG154/15.

Notes

1 Asia here includes geographic Central, Inner, and Western Asian regions (e.g., Siberia, the Russian Far East, and the Asian parts of the Middle East): www.goldmanprize.org/about/, last accessed 15 August 2020.
2 Four major public campaigns broke out in the 1960s against the construction of the Narita Airport and demanded compensation for the victims of the Itai-Itai cadmium poisoning, Minamata and Niigata mercury disease, and Yokkaichi asthma incidents.
3 www.hyi.org.cn/go/, last accessed 1 September 2019.
4 https://gt.foreignpolicy.com/2016/profile/wang-yongchen?df8f7f5682, last accessed 9 September 2020.
5 Interview at the office of ACBK in Astana, 8 July 2016.
6 Office visit and interview in Almaty, 7 July 2016.
7 Dragons – Japan, South Korea, Taiwan, and Hong Kong; Tigers – Philippines, Malaysia, Singapore, and Thailand.

References

Avenell, S. 2017. Transnational Environmental Activism and Japan's Second Modernity. *Asia-Pacific Journal-Japan Focus*, *15*(14), 1–18. https://apjjf.org/-Simon-Avenell/5055/article.pdf

Beeson, M. 2010. The Coming of Environmental Authoritarianism. *Environmental Politics*, *19*(2), 276–294.

Bell, D.A., Brown, D., Jayasuriya, K. and Jones, D.M. 1995. *Towards Illiberal Democracy in Pacific Asia*. London: Palgrave Macmillan.

Boone, P. et al. 1997. Mongolia's Transition to a Democratic System. In Woo, W.T. (ed.), *Economies in Transition: Comparing Asia and Eastern Europe*. Cambridge, MA: MIT Press.

Brynen, R., Korany, B. and Noble, P. eds. 1995. *Political Liberalization and Democratization in the Arab World* (Vol. 1). Boulder, CO: Lynne Rienner Publishers.

Byambajav, D. 2015. The River Movements' Struggle in Mongolia. *Social Movement Studies*, *14*(1), pp. 92–97.

Carter, N.T. and Mol, A.P.J. 2006. China and the Environment: Domestic and Transnational Dynamics of a Future Hegemon. *Environmental Politics*, *15*(2), 330–344.

Cherp, O. 2000. Environmental Impact Assessment in the Republic of Kazakhstan. In Bellinger, E.G. (ed.), *Environmental Assessment in Countries in Transition*. Budapest and New York: CEU Press, pp. 63–71.

Dai, J. and Spires, A.J. 2018. Advocacy in an Authoritarian State: How Grassroots Environmental NGOs Influence Local Governments in China. *The China Journal*, *79*(1), pp. 62–83.

Dai, J., Zeng, F. and Wang, Y. 2017. Publicity Strategies and Media Logic: Communication Campaigns of Environmental NGOs in China. *Chinese Journal of Communication*, *10*(1), pp. 38–53.

Death, C. 2015. Four Discourses of the Green Economy in the Global South. *Third World Quarterly*, *36*(12), pp. 2207–2224.

Gellert, P.K. 2010. Rival Transnational Networks, Domestic Politics and Indonesian Timber. *Journal of Contemporary Asia*, *40*(4), pp. 539–567.

Gilley, B. 2012. Authoritarian Environmentalism and China's Response to Climate Change. *Environmental Politics*, *21*(2), pp. 287–307.

Goh, D.P. 2001. The Politics of the Environment in Singapore? Lessons from a "Strange" Case. *Asian Journal of Social Science*, *29*(1), pp. 9–34.

Han, H. and Tan, A.K. 2019. From Messengers to Partners in Governance: Discussion of the Evolving Roles of Singapore's Grassroots Organizations through the Case of the Active Mobility Policy. 동남아연구 *(Southeast Asia Journal)*, *29*(1), pp. 151–192.

Hochstetler, K. 2000. Democratizing Pressures from Below? Social Movements in the New Brazilian Democracy. In Kingstone, P. and Power, T.J. (eds), *Democratic Brazil: Actors, Institutions, and Processes*. Pittsburgh, PA: University of Pittsburgh Press, pp. 167–184.

Inglehart, R. 1977. *The Silent Revolution: Changing Values and Political Styles Among Western Publics* (1st edition). Princeton, NJ: Princeton University Press.

Keck, M. and Sikkink, K. 1998. *Activists Beyond Borders*. Ithaca: Cornell University Press.

Kim, S.Y. and Thurbon, E. 2015. Developmental Environmentalism: Explaining South Korea's Ambitious Pursuit of Green Growth. *Politics & Society*, *43*(2), pp. 213–240.

Ku, D.W. 1996. The Structural Change of the Korean Environmental Movement. *Korea Journal of Population and Development*, pp. 155–180.

Litzinger, R. 2004. The Mobilization of Nature: Perspectives from North-West Yunnan. *China Quarterly*, *178*, pp. 488–504.

LJY. 2019. Why We Should Rally Against the Garden City. *Equality and Democracy: Singaporean Political Theory in Action (Online Journal)*, available at https://equalitydemocracy.commons.yale-nus.edu.sg/2019/12/10/1174/ accessed 10 September 2020.

Lu, J. and Steinhardt, H.C. forthcoming. Alliance Building Among Environmental Non-Governmental Organizations in China. *Modern China*. (manuscript provided by the authors).

Mason, R.J. 1999. Whither Japan's Environmental Movement? An Assessment of Problems and Prospects at the National Level. *Pacific Affairs*, pp. 187–207.

Morris-Jung, J. 2011. *Prospects and Challenges for Environmental Politics: The Vietnamese Bauxite Controversy*. Paper presented at the "Vietnam Update" Conference at Australian National University, November 17–18, Canberra.

Morse, Y.L. 2012. The Era of Electoral Authoritarianism. *World Politics*, *64*, pp. 161–198.

Nguyen, T.D. and Datzberger, S. (2018) The Environmental Movement in Vietnam Frontier of Civil Society Activism? *Challenging Authoritarianism Series, The Transnational Institute*, available at www.tni.org/es/node/24106 accessed 15 August 2020.

Nilan, P. 2020. Muslim Youth Environmentalists in Indonesia. *Journal of Youth Studies*, online first, DOI: 10.1080/13676261.2020.1782864.

Nomura, K. 2007. Democratisation and Environmental Non-Governmental Organisations in Indonesia. *Journal of Contemporary Asia*, *37*(4), pp. 495–517.

Offe, C. 1985. New Social Movements: Challenging the Boundaries of Institutional Politics. *Social Research*, *52*(4), pp. 817–868.

Ortmann, S. 2017. *Environmental Governance in Vietnam: Institutional Reforms and Failures*. New York: Springer.

Peluso, N.L., Afiff, S. and Rachman, N.F. 2008. Claiming the Grounds for Reform: Agrarian and Environmental Movements in Indonesia. *Journal of Agrarian Change*, *8*(2–3), pp. 377–407.

Schreurs, M.A. 2002. Democratic Transition and Environmental Civil Society: Japan and South Korea compared. *The Good Society*, *11*(2), pp. 57–64.

Schreurs, M.A. 2003. *Environmental Politics in Japan, Germany, and the United States*. Cambridge, UK: Cambridge University Press.

Soltys, D. 2013. Challenges to the Institutionalisation of Environmental NGOs in Kazakhstan's Corporatist Policy Arena. *Journal of Contemporary Asia*, *44*(2), pp. 342–362.

Steinhardt, H.C. and Wu, F. 2016. In the Name of the Public: Environmental Protest and the Changing Landscape of Popular Contention in China. *The China Journal*, *75*(1), pp. 61–82.

Sternberg, T., Ahearn, A. and McConnell, F. 2017. Central Asian 'Characteristics' on China's New Silk Road: The Role of Landscape and the Politics of Infrastructure. *Land*, *6*(3), p. 55.

Valentine, S.V. and Sovacool, B.K. 2010. The Socio-Political Economy of Nuclear Power Development in Japan and South Korea. *Energy Policy*, *38*(12), pp. 7971–7979.

Vu, A.N. 2019. NGO-Led Activism Under Authoritarian Rule of Vietnam: Between Cooperation and Contestation. *Community Development*, *50*(4), 422–439.

Vu, N.A. 2017. Grassroots Environmental Activism in an Authoritarian Context: The Trees Movement in Vietnam. *Voluntas*, *28*(3), 1180–1208.

Weiner, D. 1999. *A Little Corner of Freedom. Russian Nature Protection from Stalin to Gorbachev*. Berkeley: University of California Press.

Weinthal, E. and Luong, P.J. 2002. Environmental NGOs in Kazakhstan. In Mendelson, S.E. and Glenn, J.K. (eds), *The Power and Limits of NGOs*. New York: Columbia University Press, pp. 127–152.

Weinthal, E. and Watters, K. 2010. Transnational Environmental Activism in Central Asia: The Coupling of Domestic Law and International Conventions. *Environmental Politics*, *19*(5), pp. 782–807.

Wells-Dang, A. 2010. Political Space in Vietnam: A View from the 'Rice-Roots'. *The Pacific Review*, *23*(1), pp. 93–112.

Wells-Dang, A. 2012. *Civil Society Networks in China and Vietnam: Informal Pathbreakers in Health and the Environment*. New York: Palgrave Macmillan.

Wu, F. 2017. Having Peers and Becoming One: Collective Consciousness Among Civil Society Actors in China. *Journal of Contemporary China*, *26*(106), pp. 564–576.

Wu, F. and Martus, E. 2021. Contested Environmentalism: The Politics of Waste in China and Russia. *Environmental Politics*, *30*(4), pp. 493–512.

Wu, F. and Wen, B. 2015. Nongovernmental Organizations and Environmental Protests. In *Routledge Handbook of Environment and Society in Asia*. London: Routledge, pp. 105–119.

7

MIDDLE EAST AND NORTH AFRICA

Civil society and environmental activism in the Arab world

Salpie S. Djoundourian

Introduction

During the last decade, the Arab countries of the Middle East and North Africa (MENA) region witnessed a wave of pro-democracy protests, uprisings, economic crises, and armed rebellions. The Jasmine Revolution of 2010 in Tunisia, followed by the 2011 uprisings and revolutions in Egypt, Yemen, Syria, Bahrain, and Libya gave rise to the Arab Spring. Acemoglu et al. (2018) argue that the lack of adequate economic opportunities for an increasingly educated population in the Arab world may explain the uprisings. Demonstrators in the Arab Spring had a variety of demands, including political freedom, respect for human rights, better economic conditions, and leadership and/or regime changes in respective countries; however, they faced violent responses and crackdowns by authorities. By the end of February 2011, Tunisia had ousted its leader but failed to solve the economic problems of unemployment and inflation that were the main drivers of the Tunisian Revolution. Egypt, Libya, and Yemen also realized leadership changes but also failed to end the conflicts and resolve the economic hardships. Egypt is relatively stable; Libya continues to struggle; the Bahrain, Yemen, and Syria uprisings escalated to large-scale regional conflicts and wars. The governments' harsh responses transformed peaceful demonstrators into activists engaged in violent street protests and various forms of civil disobedience. Prior to the Arab Spring, the existence and efficacy of the civil society in the Middle East were highly contested. With the rare exception of a significant and successful uprising and protest movement in Lebanon in 2005, most scholars documented the size and evolution of organized social movements in the Middle East rather than spontaneous protest dynamics (see Kandil, 1995). The Arab Spring caught scholars and policy makers off guard since most of the structural characteristics of organized networks were missing in the presence of the complex dynamics of leaderless (or leaderful) movements (Volpi and Clark, 2019). The many protests across various countries shared common characteristics, including spontaneity and emotional behavior, as protesters mobilized in unexpected ways.

Economic and social concerns usually overshadow the environmental concerns of communities in the Arab world. A huge body of theoretical and empirical literature promotes the "affluence hypothesis" and presents ample evidence that the level of national per capita income influences the level of environmental concern expressed by the population (see the literature on Environmental Kuznets Curve: e.g., Beckerman, 1992; Seldon and Song, 1994;

DOI: 10.4324/9780367855680-8

Grossman and Krueger, 1995; Stern et al., 1996; Duroy, 2005; Djoundourian, 2011; Baalbaki and Marrouch, 2020). The Arab Spring will probably not go in history as a pro-environmental movement, but more as a political economic disenchantment movement, although in some of the countries, environmental degradation may have been one of the motives for at least some demonstrations. Boutros (2015) argues that the repeated protests in the suburbs of Beirut since 1997 reflect the ongoing public demand to resolve the garbage crisis. In 1997, the crisis erupted after the government closed down an overflowing landfill in a highly populated area in the heart of the city and unsuccessfully attempted to establish alternative landfill sites. Finally, the government was able to establish a new landfill site in another populated suburb of the city, despite the local community's resistance to the choice of the location, the traditional NIMBY (not in my backyard) syndrome. In the absence of a sustainable solution to the crisis, the new landfill created more problems, given its location and the fact that it was not properly designed to handle the enormous amount of waste generated in the region. In 2015, the garbage crisis erupted again when a group of 40 residents from around the landfill site organized a protest that eventually led to the closure of the controversial landfill. The authorities failed to develop and implement a timely contingency plan to replace the overflowing garbage site; as a result, dumping and burning waste on the streets became widespread. A garbage crisis dubbed "a national health crisis" by Human Rights Watch led to the mobilization of dozens of local NGOs.[1] Organized and not-so-organized protests marked the daily calendar of events all across the country for extended periods, with limited effect on public policy. The "You Stink" movement, which was the Lebanese version of the Arab Spring, started as a response to the garbage crisis, rallying members of civil society organizations and various environmental and human rights groups. "You Stink" soon became a reference to the civic movement against the sectarian political system that had failed to resolve many of the gripping economic problems in the country for decades, including the garbage crisis. The leadership of the movement consisted mainly of young, educated, urban activists with experience in political mobilization and social movements from earlier campaigns, including the 2005 uprising against the Syrian occupation. The "You Stink" movement against the country's political elite, according to some analysts, may have been the genesis of the October 2019 revolt. Fakih et al. (2020) argue that had policy makers paid closer attention to how their citizens perceived the existing public institutions, they may have averted the uprisings. Although the government did not respond well to the demands of the civil society, one interesting outcome of the movement was the establishment of recycling activities across the country, based on non-governmental social initiatives. More than 45 local recycling centers started operations with the objective of reducing the amount of waste going to landfills, while creating jobs for Lebanese and refugees.[2] Live Love Organization is one such social enterprise that solicits donations and pledges to kick-start the Live Love Recycle Project.[3] Recycle Beirut is another start-up business that aims to clean the city and create jobs.[4] Recycling junk through using it as the primary resource in art projects flourished as a new industry in the country.

Duroy (2005) demonstrates that the level of subjective well-being and the level of income equality have direct effects on awareness while economic affluence has, at best, a marginal influence on environmental awareness and no direct impact on environmental behavior. In general, there is a divergence between the body of literature assessing the political and socioeconomic history and evolution of the Arab region and scholarly work exploring environmental issues within larger social, political, and historical contexts. The Arab Spring may be reflective of the "environmentalism of the poor" clearly echoed in other environmental movements around the globe, combining concerns for the environment with more visible concerns for social and economic justice (Ramachandra, 2000).

Environmental pressure groups thrive and multiply on the premise that they are able to influence legislations that aim to improve society's well-being. Giugni and Grasso (2015) define environmental movements as "networks of informal interactions that may include individuals, groups, and organizations engaged in collective action motivated by shared identity or concern about environmental issues". They suggest that a good way of gauging the strength of environmental movements is to examine their impact on public policy and the government's response to the collective concerns of their members. They further argue that even if environmental movements are unsuccessful in affecting policy, at the very least, they raise public awareness and influence public opinion. Globally, environmental pressure groups are able to pass substantial legislation, resist counter forces, and reduce targeted pollutants (Everett and Peplies, 1992). Some claim that environmental movements had the most enduring influence on politics of all the social movements that emerged in the late 1960s (Rootes, 1999).

Environmental movements resort to different means in different countries and usually evolve over time. Giugni and Grasso (2015), in a comprehensive review of environmental movements in advanced democracies, concluded that these movements are heterogeneous. They present a wide variety of actors, issues, strategies, and outcomes. Djoundourian (2011) argues that the mere presence of an environmental ministry is a preliminary indicator of environmental awareness and engagement. Using various indicators of environmental performance, including the total number of international environmental agreements signed, ratified, or accessed by individual governments, the paper concludes that the Arab world is on par with the developing world in its environmental performance. In another paper, Djoundourian (2007) assesses the evolution of the government's environmental engagement by reviewing the commitments it made to the local, regional, and international communities and arguing that an increase in such commitments is an indicator of environmental activism. She uses the total number of established environmental groups and the activities they engage in to spread awareness as indicators of the private sector's involvement in environmental activism.

This chapter is an attempt to review and evaluate social and environmental movements and activism in the Arab world. The next section investigates the pertinent literature on civil society organizations in the Arab world, including both social and environmental organizations as well as the types of activities they engage in, aiming throughout to identify the prevalence of the environmental movement and the importance of environmental issues in Arab communities.

Social and environmental activism over time

The formation and evolution of civil society organizations in the Arab world may allow a better understanding of the Arab Spring and the recent changes in the MENA region. An excellent reference on the size and efficacy of civil society in the Arab world is that of Kandil (1995), a volume published by the World Alliance for Citizen Participation (CIVICUS) as part of a series of publications on citizen participation in voluntary organizations across the world. Historically, according to Kandil (1995), the educated class and the religious leaders, particularly in Egypt, Iraq, Lebanon, Syria, and Tunisia, as well as the traditional elite and the members of royal families in Jordan and Morocco, initiated and sponsored the civil, religious, and royal societies, associations, and organizations in the Arab world. While charity, philanthropy, and social care characterized the rationale for the formation of the private voluntary organizations in the early stages, community-led organizations engaged in activities supporting development, human rights, and environmental protection gradually evolved.

Huge disparities exist across the Arab countries in terms of socio-economic, political, and developmental needs; accordingly, the scope of activities and the target groups that civil society organizations support differ significantly. For instance, in the absence of government services, the civil society was instrumental in Lebanon during the civil war (1975–92). They focused on social issues such as provision of first aid training, helping communities cope with water and food shortages, moving the injured to the hospitals, and maintaining a minimum level of social order in a country characterized by chaos. The civil society in Lebanon reclaimed its prominent role after the most tragic explosion in the commercial port of Beirut that shook the city and almost destroyed it completely. Experts referred to the Beirut explosion of 4 August 2020 as a miniature nuclear explosion, the third-largest recorded blast in the history. It resulted in around 200 deaths (many are still missing), more than 5,000 injuries, total and partial destruction of commercial and residential property, and the displacement of hundreds of thousands of people. The civil society, represented by hundreds of heterogeneous groups, were able to convince the international community that they should be entrusted with the management of disaster relief funds that dozens of countries pledged since they were carrying the burden of all emergency response efforts. In Sudan, the emergency conditions resulting from the 1998 famine led to the establishment of organizations providing food and emergency support services. In countries where unemployment rates are high, such as Palestine, organizations that provide vocational training are active; where poverty rates are high, as in Yemen, charitable organizations provide assistance in cash and in kind; the degree of democratization in the political system determines the nature of organizations that can exist and evolve.

Bayat (2000) examines the extent to which activism by, or on behalf of, grassroots groups (mainly the urban poor) contributed to social change and policy change in Middle Eastern countries. He identifies the various types of activisms that are commonly used in the region at the urban grassroots level, including urban mass protests, organized labor, social and political Islam, NGOs, and the "quiet encroachment strategy" of the urban poor. He examines the strategies that activists in the region pursue to defend their rights and improve their lives. While most of his analysis revolves around poverty and the urban poor, Bayat gives few examples of community mobilization campaigns in the 1970s, against industrial pollution created by smelter plants that caused major health and environmental problems in a low-income community in Cairo, using traditional strategies of communication within the community as well as modern tactics such as engaging the media, lobbying politicians, and accessing the court system as means of registering opposition. He also presents instances in which communities relied on the "quiet encroachment strategy" to solve their problems. For example, in Beirut, during the civil war, many displaced families occupied vacant homes as thousands of people from the south moved to the southern suburb of the city, building illegal settlements that currently make up 40% of housing in the area, dramatically changing the social landscape of the city for the next few decades.

Bayat (2000, 2002) describes the mixed results of urban protests in the Middle East. He evaluates the riots that erupted during the 1980s in response to various austerity measures, including cuts in subsidies introduced by governments to reduce budget deficits. Arab protestors considered such measures as violations of the social contract between the states and the masses. In some cases, governments revoked the policies they implemented (Egypt in 1977, Tunisia and Morocco in 1984, Sudan in 1985, Algeria in 1988, and Jordan in 1989), and in other cases, they resulted in political reforms (Algeria, Jordan, and Tunisia in 1990s); yet in other cases, they resorted to violence to curb the protests (especially if the protests were localized, as in remote cities in Egypt). During the 1990s, the region witnessed growth of welfare NGOs and "social Islam" as a substitute for organized government in provision of services to the masses. The collapse of the state during the civil war in Lebanon (1975–90) and after the Iraqi invasion of Kuwait in 1990 contributed to the rise and empowerment of various social and religious organizations. The current Islamist movements in the Arab world articulate the concerns and struggles of the underprivileged urban societies. In his review of the extant literature on Middle East politics, Diwan (2013) argues that political Islam was once one of the main organized opposition movements against autocracy, secularism, unpopular foreign alliances, and corruption, and it was at times severely repressed and operated largely outside the formal system. Islamist movements contribute to social welfare by direct provision of services, such as health care, education, and financial aid, as well as involvement in community development and social networks, most of which are established in local, non-governmental mosques. Trade unions represent a sustained institution through which working people defend their rights or exert pressure on economic elites and governments to bring about social change.

Hawthorne (2005) identifies and explores four phases of development and growth of civil society in the Arab region. The first phase, the period prior to European penetration, consisted mainly of community-based self-help groups, guilds, and religiously oriented charitable and educational institutions. The European colonialism period followed, with the emergence of "modern" forms of associative life, such as professional associations, trade unions, secular charities, cultural clubs, and Islamist organizations such as the Muslim Brotherhood. A restricted phase three emerged after the Arab countries got their independence. During this period, independent civic activity was tightly controlled as civil society organizations were transformed into state-dominated institutions or were repressed. According to Hawthorne, the Arab region currently enjoys a more liberal and diversified civil society. Hawthorne argues that many Arab governments began to implement limited economic and political liberalization as a way of staying in power. She identifies five broad sectors for civil society, including the Islamic sector, non-governmental service organizations, membership-based professional organizations, mutual aid societies that foster solidarity and companionship, and pro-democracy associations.

Mikhail (2013), in his book *Water on Sand: Environmental Histories of the Middle East and North Africa*, published in 2012, demonstrates the intimate connection between people and environment that shaped the political, economic, and social history of the region. The book, with a collection of essays, represents the holistic environmental history of a region where nearly all political powers based their rule on the management and control of natural resources, and nearly all individuals were in constant communion with the natural world.

Makdissi (2012) explores the evolution of environmentalism in Lebanon since its independence in 1943. He presents evidence suggesting that the Lebanese society, operating within the contexts of sectarianism and (neo)liberalism, responded to environmental threats with distinct strands of environmentalism that briefly coalesced into a coherent national environmental movement in the immediate post–civil war period, before declining and ultimately fragmenting. He argues that the first strand of the movement, rooted in liberal civil society, began in the 1960s and represented elite concerns about the disappearance of nature. The Republic's first president was a founding member and the head of the Lebanese Friends of the Tree Association that was created in the early 1930s. The Tree Day Celebrations were symbolic gestures to celebrate the importance of nature. The early elite environmental "pioneers" established the Lebanese League for Bird Preservation. The second strand of social environmentalism was that of the poor originating in the social and sectarian periphery of the post-colonial state that advocated for equitable redistribution of natural resources and public services in Lebanon. The third and perhaps less pronounced, but no less important, strand of environmentalism emerged in Lebanon during its civil war to confront emergencies in an ad hoc and temporary manner to overcome the absence and inability of the Lebanese government to protect its citizens in times of war and local environmental catastrophe. Rapid and unplanned urbanization led the way to unprecedented environmental degradation. Rivers, springs, and groundwater resources were compromised by the unregulated discharge of raw sewage and other waste and effluents dumped by households, farmers, and industries. Meanwhile, the number of registered environmental NGOs has hugely increased in the post-war years, reaching roughly 300 organizations. Moreover, since 2001, 16 academic and research institutions have been established to specifically address various environmental issues. Lebanon also hosts the main pan-Arab environmental magazine, *al-Bi'ah wa al-Tanmiyya* (*Environment and Development*). In line with greater public knowledge and awareness of the environment, official discourse has also changed as key national environmental issues such as quarrying, water resource and solid waste management, and energy policies have become highly politicized. Indeed, Lebanon now boasts two recently established green parties, although with no parliamentary representation yet.

The processes of mobilization, demobilization, and remobilization of civil society movements are well illustrated in Geha's (2019) examination of the wave of environmental protests that occurred in Lebanon in the summer of 2015. The "You Stink" movement, discussed earlier, mobilized citizens around the message that the real stink came from the corruption and incompetence of politicians. The movement was forced to demobilize in 2015; however, it later regrouped and entered the political arena in the 2016 municipal elections under the electoral list entitled Beirut Madinaty (Beirut My City). Following the municipal elections, the movement and its networks once again remobilized and entered the 2018 parliamentary elections.

Community engagement in civil and environmental activism

The Arab world, with prevailing authoritarian regimes, is witnessing a growing number of organizations representing the civil society. Observers attribute the increase in the number of such organizations and the scope of the activities in which they are involved as necessary precursors to the political transitions toward democratization that are taking place in the region (Cavatorta and Durac, 2010; Durac, 2015). Mass citizen mobilization across the Arab region during 2010 and 2011 resulted in a sense of empowerment for civil society organizations. The young Arabs who took to the streets and voiced their dissatisfaction with the ruling elites became an inspiration for many on the northern shore of the Mediterranean to protest against the austerity measures and economic policies pursued by their respective governments (Cavatorta, 2012). In the uprisings' immediate aftermath, and in response to the events, some governments introduced a number of legal and constitutional amendments aimed at improving respect for individual freedoms, particularly the freedoms of association, expression, and peaceful assembly. However, according to observers, more recently, the authorities introduced restrictions under the pretext of the rising threat of terrorism and a more turbulent political atmosphere. A recent CIVICUS Monitor Watch List added Lebanon and Iraq to the countries where there is a serious and rapid decline in civic space. The CIVICUS Monitor rates the conditions for civil society or civic space globally, using a set of universally accepted rules, which allow people to organize, participate, and communicate with each other freely and without hindrance. According to the Monitor, the distribution of the world's population in the civic space in 2020 is as follows: 3% in *open*, 14% in *narrowed*, 16% in *obstructed*, 40% in *repressed*, and 27% in *closed*. The Monitor indicates that the majority of people living in the Arab world face repressed or closed systems. Jordan, Lebanon, Morocco, and Tunisia are the only Arab countries that enjoy unobstructed civic space.[5]

Arab non-governmental organizations (NGOs) have grown in number and prominence in the last two decades. This proliferation is often interpreted as a sign of burgeoning independent civic activity and perhaps as the source of peaceful democratic change. However, Hawthorne (2005) reveals that the bulk of Arab civil society is made up of organizations, associations, and movements that support the status quo, advocate conservative reforms, or are simply apolitical.

For example, armed conflicts, along with government neglect and ineffective management of the environment, characterized the Lebanese reality during the 15-year civil war (1975–90). NGOs and other civic groups across the country supported communities by providing medical care to the injured; provision of essential services, including food and water; and maintaining a minimum level of social order in a country devastated by war and chaos. Post-war Lebanon emerged as a weak state unable to provide basic services and inflicted with a host of economic and environmental problems. Land erosion and degradation, intrusion of seawater into ground and spring water resources, solid waste discharge into coastal waters and soil, coastal water pollution due to unmonitored and untreated garbage dumps, and air and noise pollution created by the overuse of diesel-fueled generators are only a few of the problems Lebanon and its people had to deal with. These problems, along with the fragile government, promoted the emergence of humanitarian societies to provide much-needed basic support to the communities. Haddad (2012) argues that the success of the civil society organizations may have been a factor in weakening the fragile government even further. Post-war Lebanon witnessed an exponential growth in NGOs that filled the gap and substituted for the government services. These NGOs proved to be an absolute necessity for the community in need of immediate relief efforts post Beirut port explosion.

In Bahrain, the first attempt at forming modern NGOs started over a century ago, with limited success. In 1919 Al-Adabi Club (the Literary Club) was established to exchange views and to enhance cultural debate, but within the same year, it was dismantled by the authorities when members started debating political issues. Currently, the Labor and Social Affairs Ministry recognizes 138 NGOs in addition to numerous community centers, mosques, and assembly halls. However, these social centers are under close governmental control. The Labor and Social Affairs minister is empowered by law to dissolve any club or society, to attend any meeting, to demand permission for any function performed by the association, and to punish any person objecting to orders. Brutal government repression followed the peaceful protests in Bahrain during February and March 2011, leaving dozens of demonstrators dead.

According to publicly available data from Arab.org, the total number of NGOs in the Arab regions listed in their databank is 3,799. Arab.org is the NGO portal that compiles data from the member countries of the League of Arab States. According to the portal, there are approximately 222,000 national civil society organizations and even more uncounted local associations across the Arab world. Table 7.1 presents a summary of data, albeit grossly underreported, on registered NGOs and the scope of their operation. There seems to be a wide range of variation in the total number of NGOs listed across the countries. The civil society seems to expand and diversify in relatively more democratic countries such as Egypt, Jordan, Lebanon, and Tunisia. Tunisia tops the list with over 1,000 registered NGOs, followed by Lebanon with 783 and Palestine with 428. On the other hand, in Iraq and Libya, the civil society is not highly developed, but the political system allows the establishment of community-based organizations while closely monitoring their activities. Comoros, on the other hand, reports only three NGOs followed by Libya with eight and Djibouti with eleven. The scope of activities that these organizations are involved with include general advocacy, environmental engagement, developmental issues, animals rights, finance, health care, food provision, people with special needs, relief work, faith based, and education. Most of the organizations listed engage in multiple activities. For instance, the environmental NGOs engage in traditional activities targeting nature and wildlife conservation, promoting biodiversity, animal rights, and organized awareness campaigns, among others. Sowers (2020) reports that environmental activism is growing across the MENA region, despite concerted efforts by states to stifle the civil society. Expanding educational opportunities coupled with variety of new means of communication are allowing for the development

Table 7.1 Total number and type of NGOs in selected Arab countries

NGOs	Algeria	Bahrain	Djibouti	Egypt	Jordan	KSA	Kuwait	Lebanon	Morocco	Oman	Palestine	Qatar	Syria	Tunisia	UAE
Total number registered	154	69	11	244	262	65	57	783	45	48	428	41	46	1,009	108
Environmental	**10**	**4**	**1**	**22**	**10**	**2**	**3**	**73**	**10**	**2**	**27**	**2**	**5**	**73**	**11**
• **Biodiversity**	4	0	1	4	5	1	2	13	2	0	4	1	4	15	7
• **Conservation**	5	1	1	13	7	1	3	31	4	2	15	2	4	51	5
• **Animals**	2	4	1	6	4	1	2	19	1	1	6	2	3	13	7
• **Animal Welfare**	1	4	1	3	1	1	2	7	1	0	1	1	1	4	5
• **Wildlife Conservation**	2	2	1	4	4	1	2	18	1	1	6	2	3	12	6
• **Hunting**	0	2	0	1	0	1	2	1	1	0	1	1	1	1	0

Source: Compiled by author from the Arab NGO Network

of small-scale, informal, and localized activism, in parallel to the more established ENGOs and their coordinated campaigns. Tunisia and Lebanon stand out in the Arab world with a total listing of 73 ENGOs each. However, Lebanon, with a population 6.8 million scores, 11 ENGOs per million people compared to 6 ENGOs per million for Tunisia, with a population 11.6 million. The number of ENGOs conveys important information concerning community interest and engagement in environmental issues. These numbers reconcile with Hawthorne (2005) reporting that Lebanon has the "most diverse and active civil society in the region". ENGOs in Jordan, for example, made a leap toward becoming a change engine in the society by establishing the Jordanian Federation for Environmental NGOs. The Federation includes a mix of old and new NGOs seeking to engage in participative governance and policy advocacy to create social impact (Al-Zuby, 2019).

The Arab world is also home to a few regional environmental organizations, including the Arab Forum for Environment and Development (AFED), the Arab Network for Environment and Development (RAED), the Arab NGO Network for Development (ANND), the Center for Environment and Development in the Arab Region and Europe (CEDARE), and the Mediterranean Strategy for Sustainable Development (MSSD). These organizations actively promote environmental awareness, advocate for social and economic rights, and lobby for prudent environmental policies and action. AFED publishes an annual flagship report on the state of the Arab environment and runs a comprehensive environmental information portal in Arabic (see www.afedmag.com). RAED has held an observer status in the League of Arab States since 1995. CEDARE helps build human resources and institutional capacity, advances applied research and environmentally friendly technologies, and acts as a catalyst for joint action between the Arab region, Europe, and the international community. MSSD provides a regional response to the sustainable development agenda and SDGs for Mediterranean countries.

Individual engagement and activism in civil society

Against all adversities, individuals in the Arab world, especially the young, are actively seeking change and better opportunities. The Arab Spring was just a manifestation of the accumulated anger and discontent against the authoritarian regimes and oppression. Generations of immigrants and asylum seekers tell stories of economic and political hardships that obliged them to seek refuge in other countries. The systematic "brain drain" that characterized the region is indicative of economic hardship and lack of local opportunities in many countries in the Arab world. However, the current generation is keen about staying in their countries because of the harsh realities of the time. Most Arab immigrants and students experience discrimination in the countries where they escape to traditionally to enjoy basic human rights and proper government support and education. The World Value Survey allows gauging individual interest in issues of concern to the general public, through inquiry about active participation in civil society organizations, including environmental, political, professional, religious based, etc. Tables 7.2 and 7.3 present some pertinent statistics from the available surveys for the Arab countries. Wave 6 of the World Value survey administered in 2013 included 11 Arab countries. At least 1,000 individuals from each country participated in the survey that included a unified set of questions. Table 7.2 reveals the proportion of respondents who claim to have membership in civil society organizations. Individual engagement in civil society varies significantly across countries and types of organizations. At least 10% of respondents in more than 50% of the countries report membership in religious organizations, with Kuwait leading the way with almost 23%. It is interesting to note that respondents from North Africa are the least engaged in religious groups. In Egypt, for instance, only 17 people out of 1,523 stated that they are members in such organizations. Religious organizations support the notion of social interdependence in both Christianity and Islam. Islam, the religion of the majority of people in the Arab region, advocates charity and voluntarism as important pillars of the faith. "Zakat", or almsgiving, one of the five pillars of Islam, obliges Muslims to help the public in general and the closer community members and family in particular with financial and other forms of support as a measure of solidarity and faith. Most Arab countries include Christians as minorities, with varying levels of rights and privileges. Christianity is most common in Lebanon, a country characterized by plurality with 18 officially acknowledged religious sects. Christian faith-based organizations are active in supporting many societal needs, including the provision of educational institutions, charitable organizations, special care and support for orphanages, handicapped facilities. and supporting the general social welfare of the community.

Membership in sports or other recreational organizations as well as art, music, or educational organizations is popular across the Arab countries, with almost one-fourth of respondents from Lebanon claiming individual active membership in such organizations. In fact, Lebanon stands out as an outlier in terms of individual engagement in social networks. With few exceptions, Lebanese respondents claim more active engagement in civil society organizations than any other nationality in the Arab world.

Membership in environmental organizations is not a common engagement activity for the sampled individuals. Lebanese respondents come ahead in this category with 16% claiming active membership in such organizations, followed by Qatari respondents with 13%. Table 7.3 reveals significant differences in the various indicators of political activism across individuals in the Arab world. A survey question inquiring whether the interviewee contributed financially to any ecological organization in the past two years, revealed that around 17% of Kuwaitis responded affirmatively, followed closely with Qataris and the Lebanese, with 16.3% and 15.3%, respectively. The survey results revealed that 15.8% of the Lebanese respondents, 11.6% of the Qataris, and 10.7% of the Kuwaitis confirmed participation in environmental protests within the last two years. A large proportion of respondents across the Arab world indicated interest in politics, ranging between 15% of the Moroccans and 70% of the Egyptians. These results reconcile with and provide, at the very least, credibility for the occasional survey results conducted by the Arab organizations. For example, a recent survey of individuals in the Arab world revealed that 73% of the respondents were ready to participate in environmental awareness campaigns,

Table 7.2 Individual engagement in civil society organizations, by country

Membership in organizations (% of total sample)	Algeria	Egypt	Iraq	Jordan	Kuwait	Lebanon	Libya	Morocco	Palestine	Qatar	Tunisia
Church or Religious	8.33	1.12	10.00	10.75	22.79	22.25	9.48	3.25	17.60	18.87	1.58
Sport or recreational	11.33	0.20	6.42	8.25	21.11	25.25	17.41	8.58	17.20	21.42	5.48
Art, music or educational	6.42	0.20	3.50	5.42	12.20	24.00	10.75	4.67	12.60	13.68	3.90
Labor Union	3.92	0.20	2.42	5.25	–	17.25	11.45	2.50	12.60	–	1.91
Political party	3.10	1.38	3.08	4.83	–	22.17	6.76	3.17	18.80	–	1.74
Environmental	**2.33**	**0.20**	**1.58**	**5.33**	**9.06**	**16.42**	**9.10**	**1.42**	**8.40**	**13.11**	**0.75**
Professional	2.83	0.39	3.92	7.33	19.03	17.25	10.89	3.58	10.70	–	1.83
Charitable or humanitarian	5.67	0.79	8.83	9.33	23.41	20.75	18.72	2.33	12.80	21.79	1.08
Consumer	1.92	0.13	1.17	4.50	12.43	12.83	8.87	1.00	6.60	11.98	0.50
Self-help or mutual aid group	2.67	0.20	4.33	5.92	11.28	17.00	11.87	2.17	8.00	18.02	0.41
other	2.50	0.20	0.17	0.58	3.07	1.67	7.04	4.67	4.40	9.06	0.08
Sample Size	1,200	1,523	1,200	1,200	1,303	1,200	2,131	1,200	1,000	1,060	1,205

Source: Prepared by author from the World Value Survey, Wave 6

Table 7.3 Indicators of political activism, by country

Percentage of respondents who have	Algeria	Egypt	Iraq	Jordan	Kuwait	Lebanon	Libya	Morocco	Palestine	Qatar	Tunisia
Contributed to an ecological organization	8.2	2.4	4.8	8.0	17.1	15.3	9.7	2.4	4.6	16.3	2.8
Participated in environmental protests	3.9	0.8	3.0	2.8	10.7	15.8	9.5	3.3	5.1	11.6	2.1
Interested in politics	36	70	46.5	39.4	61	54	60.7	15	60	69	42
signed or would sign a petition	26.4	5	31.4	14.8	30.8	40.5	20.7	12.7	37	0	25
At least once signed a petition	6.3	0	12.6	5.2	12.4	7.1	5.16	3.6	8.5	–	5.0
joined or would join a boycott	27.2	7.3	27.6	14.7	0	36.4	21.5	12.3	43.5	0	20
At least once joined a boycott	2.3	0.5	3.3	5.5	–	5.3	5.36	2.4	8.7	–	2.5
Attended or would attend peaceful protests	40.2	7.1	38.4	11.4	0	45.8	47.6	17.8	51.5	0	31
At least once attended a protest	6	2.2	10.1	4.2	–	10.3	27.8	8.5	18.8	–	10.5
Joined or would join strikes	38.6	3.4	26.7	7.3	0	40.2	20.4	17.1	45.6	0	22
At least once joined a strike	10.6	0.8	3.5	2.3	–	8.8	5.7	6.6	13.3	–	4.0
Joined or would join any other protest	34.8	2.6	30	7.6	0	36	21.0	0	41	0	19
At least once joined any other protest	3	0	3.7	2.3	–	5.9	3.6	–	6.7	–	1.0
Sample Size	1,200	1,523	1,200	1,200	1,303	1,200	2,131	1,200	1,000	1,060	1,205

Source: Prepared by Author from the World Value Survey, Wave 6

and 65% were willing to comply with environmental legislation, in response to a question about personal initiatives they were ready and willing to take to protect the environment. Furthermore, in terms of willingness to pay, 45% of respondents stated that they would accept government taxes to protect the environment, but only 20% were willing to pay donations to an environmental protection fund (see AFED, 2017).

Further inquiry into activism and willingness to participate in various political activities revealed that, with few exceptions, at least 10% of all respondents signed or would sign a petition. Palestinians are more likely to join a boycott, attend a peaceful demonstration, join a strike, or join any other protest, with 8.7% of respondents stating participation in a boycott and 18.8% in a peaceful protest, at least once. The surveyed Kuwaitis and Qataris have never joined nor would they join any boycott, protest, or strike. The Egyptian respondents seemed to be reserved for some reason: either the sample was biased, or the respondents were not feeling at ease.

Concluding remarks

The review of environmental movements in the Arab world highlights the growing role of the civic society in the region. However, the driving force behind their active role is mainly socio-economic and humanitarian concerns of the communities and rarely environmental issues. The young Arabs are actively seeking economic and political reforms in an attempt to improve their well-being by demanding better employment opportunities locally in order to eliminate the "brain drain" from the Middle East.

Across the world, community leaders, politicians, and scientists are rallying to combat climate change by designing policies to either mitigate the production of greenhouse gases or adapt to environmental degradation. The Arab world suffers disproportionately from the environmental and economic challenges of climate change. Given Islam's reach as a state religion, academics and environmentalists are seeking inspiration from Islam to mobilize the environmental movement (Bodetti, 2019). Muslim proponents of eco-theology believe that they have a personal and spiritual obligation to curb the spread of environmental degradation because Islam encompasses not only humanity but also nature. Countries of the MENA that have already expressed support for environmental protection by engaging in both mitigation and adaptation efforts to combat climate change can strengthen their environmental policies by looking into the teachings of Islam. As the world's fastest-growing religion, Islam can play an important role in the environmental movement. Before the end of the twenty-first century, Muslims are expected to outnumber Christians, the world's current largest religious denomination; as such, environmental activists in the Arab world will have the opportunity to appeal to and reach a larger audience than their Buddhist, Christian, Hindu, and Jewish counterparts.

Notes

1 https://civilsociety-centre.org/party/social-movement-responding-lebanese-garbage-crisis.
2 www.lebtivity.com/p/recycling-lebanon.
3 https://www.kickstarter.com/projects/livelove/live-love-recycle-lets-reduce-lebanons-waste-crisi
4 www.recyclebeirut.com/.
5 https://monitor.civicus.org/.

References

Acemoglu, D., Hassan, T.A., & Tahoun, A. (2018). The Power of the Street: Evidence from Egypt's Arab Spring. *The Review of Financial Studies*, 3, 1–42.

AFED. (2017). Arab Environment in 10 Years. In N. Saab (Ed.), *The 2017 Annual Report of Arab Forum for Environment and Development*. Beirut, Lebanon: Technical Publications.

Al-Zuby, R. (2019). Environmental NGOs as a Trigger for Social Good- a Jordanian Perspective. *ECOMENA*, November 11. www.ecomena.org/environmental-ngos-jordanian-perspective/ accessed June 10, 2020.

Baalbaki, R., & Marrouch, W. (2020). Is there a Garbage Kuznets Curve? Evidence from OECD Countries. *Economics Bulletin, AccessEcon*, 40(2), 1049–1055.

Bayat, A. (2000). *Social Movements, Activism and Social Development in the Middle East*. Civil Society and Social Movements Program, Paper Number 3, November 2000, UNRISD.

Bayat, A. (2002, February). Activism and Social Development in the Middle East. *International Journal of Middle East Studies*, 34(1), 1–28. Cambridge University Press. www.jstor.org/stable/3880166 accessed January 06, 2020.

Beckerman, W. (1992). Economic Growth and the Environment: Whose Growth? Whose Environment? *World Development*, 20, 481–496.

Bodetti, A. (2019). Islam and Environmentalism, *Lobe log*, May 10. https://lobelog.com/islam-and-environmentalism/ accessed June 24, 2020.

Boutros, J. (2015). Garbage Crisis in Lebanon – 1997: Same Policy, Repeated History. *The Legal Agenda*. https://legal-agenda.com/en/article.php?id=3102 accessed June 24, 2020.

Cavatorta, F. (2012). Arab Spring: The Awakening of Civil Society. A General Overview. In *European Institute of the Mediterranean Yearbook*, 75–81. Barcelona: European Institute of the Mediterranean.

Cavatorta F. & Durac, V (2010). Civil society and democratization in the Arab World: The dynamics of activism. Routledge.

Diwan, I. (2013). Understanding Revolution in the Middle East: The Central Role of the Middle Class. *Middle East Development Journal*. www.worldscientific.com.

Djoundourian, S. (2009). Environmental Movement in Lebanon. *Environment, Development and Sustainability*, 11, 427–438. Springer Publisher, online publication date: 8 November 2007.

Djoundourian, S. (2011). Environmental Movement in the Arab World. *Environment, Development and Sustainability*, 13, 743–758.

Durac, V. (2015). Social Movements, Protest Movements and Cross-Ideological Coalitions – The Arab Uprisings Re-Appraised. *Democratization*, 22(2), 239–258. doi: 10.1080/13510347.2015.1010809

Duroy, Q. (2005). *The Determinants of Environmental Awareness and Behavior*. Working Papers in Economics. New York: Department of Economics, Rensselaer Polytechnic Institute.

Everett, M., & Peplies, P (1992, Winter). The Political Economy of Environmental Movements: U.S. Experience and Global Movements. *Environmental Values*, 1(4), 297–310.

Fakih, A., Makdissi, P., Marrouch, W., Tabri, R.V., & Yazbeck, M. (2020). *Confidence in Public Institutions and the Run up to the October 2019 Uprising in Lebanon*. IZA Discussion Papers 13104. Bonn, Germany: Institute of Labor Economics (IZA).

Geha, C. (2019). Politics of a Garbage Crisis: Social Networks, Narratives, and Frames of Lebanon's 2015 Protests and Their Aftermath. *Social Movement Studies*, 18(1), 78–92. doi: 10.1080/14742837.2018.1539665.

Giugni, M., & Grasso, M. (2015). Environmental Movements in Advanced Industrial Democracies: Heterogeneity, Transformation, and Institutionalization. *The Annual Review of Environment and Resources*, 40, 337–361. doi: 10.1146/annurev-environ-102014-021327 accessed May 13, 2020.

Grossman, G., & Krueger, A. (1995). Economic Growth and Environment. *Quarterly Journal of Economics*, 110(2), 353–377.

Haddad, T. (2012). *The Role of Civil Society in a Fragmented and a Weak Arab State: Developing or Fragmenting the State?* Analyzing the Mujtama Ahli, Mujtama Taefi and Mujtama Madani in Lebanon, PhD Dissertation, Libera Università Internazionale degli Studi Sociali.

Hawthorne, A. (2005). Is Civil Society the Answer? In T. Carothers and M. Ottaway (Eds.), *Uncharted Journey: Promoting Democracy in the Middle East*, 81–114. Carnegie Endowment for International Peace. http://www.jstor.org/stable/j.ctt6wpjng.8.

Kandil, A. (1995). Civil Society in the Arab World: Private Voluntary Organizations. *CIVICUS*.

Makdissi, K. (2012). The Rise and Decline of Environmentalism in Lebanon. In A. Mikhail (Ed.), *Water on Sand: Environmental Histories of the Middle East and North Africa*. Print publication date: 2012 Print ISBN-13: 9780199768677 Published to Oxford Scholarship Online: January 2013. doi: 10.1093/acprof:oso/9780199768677.001.0001.

Mikhail, A., Ed. (2013). Water on Sand: Environmental Histories of the Middle East and North Africa. Print publication date: 2012 Print ISBN-13: 9780199768677 Published to Oxford Scholarship Online: January 2013. doi: 10.1093/acprof:oso/9780199768677.001.0001.

Ramachandra, G. (2000). *Environmentalism: A Global History*. New York: Longman.

Rootes, C. (1999). Environmental Movements: From the Local to the Global. *Environmental Politics*, 8(1), 1–12. doi: 10.1080/09644019908414435.

Seldon, T.M., & Song, D. (1994). Environmental Quality and Development: Is There a Kuznets Curve for Air Pollution Emissions?" *Journal of Environmental Economics and Management*, 27, 147–162.

Sowers, J.L. (2020). *Environmental Activism in the Middle East: Prospects and Challenges, Humanities Futures*. Durham, NC: Franklin Humanities Institute.

Stern, D.I., Common, M.S., & Barbier. E.B. (1996). Economic Growth and Environmental Degradation: The Environmental Kuznets Curve and Sustainable Development. *World Development*, 24, 1151–1160.

Volpi, F., & Clark, J.A. (2019). Activism in the Middle East and North Africa in Times of Upheaval: Social Networks' Actions and Interactions. *Social Movement Studies*, 18(1), 1–16. doi: 10.1080/14742837.2018.1538876 accessed June 9, 2020.

8

AFRICAN ENVIRONMENTAL MOVEMENTS

Africans saving Africa themselves

Phia Steyn

Introduction

The contemporary environmental movement in Africa is as diverse as the continent and its people. There are thousands of smaller-scale environmental organizations working across the continent on a variety of environmental issues in an attempt to address current and future environmental, social, and economic problems and challenges. It is in many respects a young movement that is rooted in the inability of post-colonial African states to address the multitude of challenges facing rural and urban populations after independence and to bring development and economic growth that benefitted more than just the privileged ruling classes, the prolonged droughts of the 1970s and 1980s and accompanying hardships, and the dismal socio-economic conditions created by widespread structural adjustment programs in the 1980s. The general failure of the African state to provide for even the most basic needs of too many of its citizens during the independence era proved to be fertile ground for grassroots and community organization around socio-economic and environmental issues. While the first three decades of independence sowed the seeds of environmental activism, the post–Cold War period with its demand for more democratic governance in Africa created the political space in the 1990s and 2000s within which environmental organizations could operate. The final piece of the puzzle to slot into place in the 1990s was the shift in focus away from national-level planning to development agencies working directly with local communities in international development projects in African countries. International aid organizations required local partners at the community level, and this resulted in the creation of a plethora of non-governmental organizations (NGOs), most of which addressed a variety of related socio-economic, health, and environmental issues. It is from this diverse pool of grassroots, community, and NGO activities that the contemporary environmental movement in Africa emerged to take on governments, society, big business, and international capital, in order to create better current and future environments in which to live.

This does not imply that Africa had no environmental movements before independence or the perfect storm of the 1990s. On the contrary, some of the most important African environmental activists, such as the legendary Wangari Maathai of Kenya in East Africa, started their activism decades before, and NGOs such as South Africa's Wildlife and Environment Society have been in existence since the 1920s. Additionally, the foundations of African environmental management were not only laid during the colonial era, but the views and corresponding actions

DOI: 10.4324/9780367855680-9

that underpinned these environmental initiatives also continued to dominate governmental and mainstream environmental management in Africa until the 1990s. The contemporary African environmental movement did not start from new; it built upon, reacted against, and greatly expanded on what had come before. Consequently, it is important to begin this discussion by briefly focusing on the history of the African environmental movement up till independence (c.1960) before considering the growth, development, and expansion of this movement during the post-colonial era. The latter discussion will be organized into three chronological periods: independence until the early 1970s; the ecological and economic crises of the 1970s and 1980s; and the post–Cold War period, which will include a discussion of the current African environmental movement.

Historical roots of the post-colonial African environmental movement

The modern environmental movement is a global phenomenon in which developments at an international level have both guided and inspired actions at national and even continental levels, whether by governments, organizations, or individuals. African environmental movements developed within this international context, especially in terms of governmental environmental management and the types of issues NGOs adopted into their environmental agendas. Consequently, it is important to plot the historical development of African environmental movements against the backdrop of the global environmental movement.

The immediate roots of the modern environmental movement date back to the conservation movement of the second half of the nineteenth century, which focused mainly on air pollution and the conservation of particular areas, fauna, and flora (McCormick, 1989: viii–ix). The conservation agenda was very influential at the onset of colonial rule in Africa at the end of the nineteenth century for two reasons in particular. Firstly, the era of the Great Hunt in the second half of the nineteenth century and the resulting huge quantities of related exports had decimated wildlife resources across Southern, Central, and Eastern Africa. The belief existed that if big game hunting was to survive, which was an important source of revenue in the early colonial period, wildlife with the highest economic value had to be protected against uncontrolled hunting. Following the 1900 London Convention for the Preservation of Wild Animals, Birds, and Fish in Africa, the creation of game reserves became a popular method to both protect and conserve wildlife in many African colonies. These would later be transformed into national parks following the 1933 London Convention Relative to the Preservation of Fauna and Flora in their Natural State (MacKenzie, 1987: 41–61; MacKenzie, 1997: 25–166; Beinart and Hughes, 2007: 58–75; Maddox, 2006: 139–153). Secondly, the conservation agenda provided the justification for colonial governments to alienate large tracks of forested areas with valuable resources from local communities in the name of conservation. Once these areas became part of the colonial network of forest reserves, the colonial government and its agents were able to exploit these resources for profit on the global markets (Neumann, 1997: 45–68; Lanz, 2000: 99–120).

The original purpose of the conservation agenda in the early years of colonial rule was the conservation of fauna and flora in order to ensure the continuation of exploitation of these resources to create revenues for struggling colonial economies. It entailed demarcating specific areas as game and forest reserves and led to the exclusion and often the eviction of local communities who had lived in these areas for centuries and who depended on these resources for their livelihoods. Overnight, hunters became poachers who could be prosecuted under colonial laws (Carruthers, 1993: 11–22; Carruthers, 1995). And in many colonies, such as German

Tanganyika where the hunting of bush pigs was prohibited, Africans lost the right to defend their fields and property against protected wildlife (Sunseri, 1997). It was the start in Africa of what Brockington (2015: 2) has termed "fortress conservation". He describes this as "a practice of exclusion. . . . It is about restricting access to nature in order that that nature is protected. That can require force and is often unwelcome for the people who were accustomed to use those resources" (Brockington, 2015: 2). Local communities became the enemies of conservation and would remain demonized by the conservation community until the 1980s when community-based conservation projects in Namibia and Zimbabwe such as the Purros Project demonstrated that fauna and flora conservation thrived when local communities had ownership in projects, parks, and reserves (Koch et al., 1990: 27–29). The creation of national parks from the 1920s onward merely entrenched the notion that in Africa, fauna and flora had to be protected from local African communities. By then, the only shooting allowed in many protected areas, as is made clear in the commentary of a 1937 film clip on the Kruger National Park in South Africa by British Pathé, was the shooting of photographs by (European) tourists visiting the areas (British Pathé, 1937).

Fauna and flora conservation in British colonial Africa was strongly promoted by the influential Society for Protection of Wild Fauna of the Empire. Created in London in 1903, this society played a key role in lobbying the British and colonial governments in Africa to implement comprehensive conservation programs. Local NGOs concerned with conservation were also created. In South Africa, for example, the Transvaal Game Protection Association was re-established after the Boer War ended in 1902. In 1925 this group disbanded, and its members went on to create the Wildlife Protection Society of South Africa in 1926. It is known today as the Wildlife and Environment Society of South Africa and is considered the largest environmental organization in Africa. The mainstream environmental movement in Africa at this stage was largely composed of, and supported by, white Europeans, often residing outside Africa (Pringle, 1982: 60–161; Carruthers, 1995). African communities were mostly vilified as squanderers of the African environment. This stereotype was challenged by the Native Farmers Association, which was founded in 1918 in South Africa in the Eastern Cape. Its founders, Davidson Don Tengo Jabavu and Rev. JE. East, an African American missionary, set out to address the widespread environmental decline and poverty in the rural Eastern Cape and focused on agricultural, socio-economic, and political issues (Khan, 1989: 3–5; Khan, 1992: 275; Khan, 1997: 439–459).

The Native Farmers Association was ahead of its time in many ways, especially in terms of their focus on soil conservation. The latter would become the last pillar of the conservation agenda in colonial Africa (along with fauna and flora conservation) from the 1930s onward. Given the centrality of farming to traditional African life, colonial soil conservation strategies directly affected a much larger percentage of the African populations in colonies than fauna and flora conservation did. It resulted in colonial interference in everyday African work and life at levels never experienced before, with Africans being instructed on every aspect of farming. Worse still were the unpopular soil conservation works that required back-breaking manual labor to create soil breaks and terraces, the planting of thousands of trees, and controversial culling programs to reduce the number of livestock in African reserves. The colonial authorities opted to blame Africans for the poor soil conditions in the reserves and implemented forms of planned agriculture such as the betterment schemes in Southern Africa to remedy the situation, often ignoring the fact that the over-exploitation of resources resulted from overcrowding caused by colonial land and settlement policies (Beinart, 1984; Anderson, 1984). In many areas, this situation created fertile ground for anti-colonial agitation, none more so than in Tanzania and Malawi, where local opposition to soil conservation works played a key role in mobilizing

Africans' opposition to colonial rule in the 1950s (Maack, 1996: 152–169; Lonsdale, 1968: 119–146; Tangri, 1968: 142–161). In South Africa, despite widespread opposition to betterment schemes, the soil conservation agenda created for a brief period the political space for the founding of the country's second Black environmental NGO. The African National Soil Conservation Association (ANSCA) was founded in 1953 with Sam Motsuenyane as organizing secretary and W.B. Ngakane as president because the national soil conservation NGO, the National Veld Trust (1943), was a whites-only organization, which made Black participation impossible within the context of apartheid (Khan, 1997: 439–459).

Soil conservation was a very real concern for the colonial governments in Southern and Central Africa who met in Goma in the then Belgian Congo in 1948 at an Inter-African Conference to discuss soil and land utilization. This conference led to the establishment of the Southern African Regional Commission for the Conservation and Utilization of the Soil (SARCUSS). It was Africa's first regional governmental environmental body and focused on scientific cooperation to address problems associated with the conservation and utilization of natural resources. SARCUSS continued to exist up till the 1990s, when it was transformed into the Food, Agriculture and Natural Resources Directorate of the Southern African Development Community (SADC) after the demise of apartheid in South Africa (Rabie, 1973: 290; Steyn, 2018: 877, note 53). A continent-wide initiative led to the establishment of the Commission for Technical Cooperation in Africa South of the Sahara (CTCA) in 1954, which was absorbed in 1964 into the recently established Scientific, Technical and Research Commission of the Organization of African Unity (founded 1963) (Ogundere, 1972: 259–260). Both these and other bodies created in Africa after 1945 were strongly influenced by the prevailing belief that Western science would solve the numerous environmental challenges that Africa faced, mostly without the input and consultation of the Africans who lived in the environments that had to be "saved". This belief in the supremacy of Western science and, by implication, Western scientific experts, to the detriment of local African environmental knowledge, survived decolonization and would continue to result in government neglect of African environmental needs into the independence era.

The post-colonial African environmental movement

More of what went before, 1960–c. 1972

African independence around 1960 coincided with the onset of the United Nations' Decade of Development. In Africa this would translate into more of what had come before: the continuation of environmental and development practices initiated in the colonies after the Second World War. Hodge (2007) has vividly described this process in the British colonies, where many of the colonial development planners and scientific experts in charge of these projects in the late colonial period were employed by post-colonial African states as *the* environmental and developmental experts.

An important long-term consequence of this process was the continuation of situating the scientific knowledge of Africa, its people, and its environments outside the continent, mostly in the West. This practice was further entrenched through the development of closer relations between independent African states and the Organization of African Unity (OAU), with international organizations such as the Food and Agriculture Organization (FAO), UNESCO, and the International Union for the Conservation of Nature (IUCN). Many of the key environment-related initiatives on the continent north of Southern Africa (where SARCUSS was taking the lead) were held under the auspices of these and other international organizations.

Even *the* centerpiece of African environmental management up till the 1990s, the 1968 African Convention for the Conservation of Nature and Natural Resources, was written by representatives of FAO, UNESCO, and the IUCN at the request of the OAU. This Convention was the successor to the 1900 and 1933 London Conventions and bound signatories to the conservation, protection, utilization, and development of all natural resources along scientific principles (Van der Linde, 2002: 102–105; Ruppel, 2018: 214–125; Ogundere, 1972: 258–265). It would take decades before building the necessary institutional scientific capacity within African states would become a priority, along with recognizing that traditional African environmental knowledge had a place alongside Western science.

Governmental environmental management in Africa was further boosted by developments at the international level, in particular the preparatory processes for the United Nations Conference on the Human Environment (UNCHE, Stockholm, June 1972). The African Regional Seminar on the Human Environment was held in August 1971 in Addis Ababa under the aegis of the UN Economic Commission for Africa. This meeting and African states' subsequent participation in UNCHE made two important contributions to the global environmental agenda: firstly, it emphasised the fact that many environmental problems in developing countries resulted from the lack of development, and secondly, they succeeded in linking the oppressive apartheid policy in South Africa and colonial regimes in Southern Africa with the region's environmental problems (McCormick, 1989: 90–105). One of the most tangible outcomes of UNCHE was the creation of the UN Environment Program (UNEP). It became the first UN agency to be headquartered in the developing world and was set up in Nairobi, Kenya, in 1973 (McCormick, 1989: 106–124).

Despite the siting of UNEP in Africa, governmental commitment to environmental management and addressing the multitude of environmental problems of their urban and rural communities remained very limited on the continent. Governance in post-independence Africa was characterized by centralized ruling parties, increasing military involvement in politics after 1963, and the emergence of authoritarian leaders who displayed little tolerance for political opposition and even less for social organizations operating independently. As Larmer (2010: 225) notes, grassroots development initiatives operating outside government control and direction were often repressed and sometimes even banned. The fate of the Ruvuma Development Association in Tanzania in the 1960s is a good case in point. Ruvuma was set up in the early 1960s by a small group of people inspired by Julius Nyerere's early writing on ujamaa. This introduced the concept of villagization in 1962 and led to the creation of a number of independent development schemes across Tanzania. By the time Nyerere issued the Arusha Declaration in February 1967, which formally introduced ujamaa across the whole country, Ruvuma consisted of 16 villages and was the most successful development association in the country. Both its success and its independence were Ruvuma's undoing. Nyerere did not approve of the fact that some groups were growing at a faster rate than others, while ujamaa made state-directed development mandatory. Consequently, the Ruvuma Development Association was banned in September 1967 and its assets confiscated. Ujamaa's attempts to control Tanzanians' interaction with and use of local environments was strikingly expressed in the forced relocation figures: 13 million people were forcibly moved between 1969 and 1975, 11 million in 1974 and 1975 alone (Coulson, 1977: 87–96; Shao, 1986: 223, 232). Hrabanski (2010: 284), on the other hand, has demonstrated how the Senegalese cooperative movement that organized peasants over a variety of sectors from fishermen to groundnut farmers became an instrument of state power post-independence. Under state direction, these cooperatives became the controllers of rural development and, by implication, gained control over the profitable rural groundnut economy.

The situation was very different in South Africa. The country had, and continues to have, the most developed NGO sector of the African environmental movement, working on a variety of conservation issues, while local communities started to organize both locally and nationally around air, water, and soil pollution. Most South African NGOs pursued very narrow environmental agendas, often confining themselves to single issues such as anti-litter campaigns and soil conservation. In contrast to most of their continental counterparts, most environmental NGOs in South Africa worked very closely with the apartheid government, freely accepted the ban on multiracial membership, and, like the government, refused to accept that the environment was fundamentally a political issue. Additionally, most NGOs, such as the Wildlife Society, the Southern Africa Nature Foundation, and the Endangered Wildlife Trust willingly acceded to governmental requests in 1974 to establish a single coordinating council (the Habitat Council) that would become the main organization the government would deal with. The net result of these developments was that the environment remained essentially a white issue in South Africa that showed little interest in the environmental challenges and problems that Black, colored, and Indian South African communities faced (Steyn, 2002).

Up until the 1970s, the African environmental movement had a slow start. Rural movements that played important roles in the independence struggles became stifled by overbearing, controlling post-colonial states. The increasing totalitarian nature of African politics further reduced the political space for the non-governmental sector of the African environmental movement to oppose the government. Positive developments did take place in terms of environmental policy developments, and with the aid of international organizations, many African governments developed a more comprehensive understanding of what proper environmental management entailed, and some even adopted conservation and pollution control measures. Implementing these measures, however, would take many more years.

The ecological and economic crises of the 1970s and 1980s

The momentum generated by UNCHE and the creation of UNEP in 1972 did not last long in Africa. Most African states continued to experience some form of political instability in the 1970s and 1980s, which diverted state attention from developing proper environmental management structures while also limiting the political space within which NGOs could operate in their countries. Matters were made worse by the deterioration of the ecological base of many African countries owing to extreme and multi-year droughts that led to widespread crop failures and food shortages, which, in turn, caused famine, malnutrition, mass migration, and deaths. Drought is a regular phenomenon in Africa but the extreme droughts in 1972–73 and 1983–84 were particularly memorable because they were continental in nature (Masih et al., 2014: 3635). In Ethiopia alone, for example, almost 8% of the population had experienced starvation by 1974, and it is estimated that more than 200,000 people had died. Livestock mortality was also very high, and about 80% of cattle, 50% of sheep, 30% of camels, and 30% of goats in the regions of Welo, Tigray, Eritrea, and Haverge died between 1973 and 1974 (Koehn, 1979: 51; Kiros, 1991: 184).

The 1970s droughts created widespread concern for desertification in Africa and led in 1977 to the convening of the UN Conference on Desertification in Nairobi. Shortly before the conference, Wangari Maathai launched the "Save the Land Harambee" tree-planting project of the National Council of Women of Kenya. This project started as small ceremonial tree plantings on 5 June 1977, when seven trees were planted at Kamukunju grounds in Nairobi. After the UN conference, the decision was made to transform this project into a massive, women-led afforestation campaign that would soon thereafter become known as the Green Belt Movement

(GBM). The GBM focused on empowering rural women and promoting tree planting, agro-forestry among peasant farmers, soil conservation, and environmental education. It was very successful and received corporate funding from Mobil Oil (Kenya) and support from the Kenya Department of Forestry, UNEP, and numerous international NGOs. Consequently, it grew exponentially in the 1980s, in no small part due to the work of Maathai and by 1991 employed an office staff of 40 along with a field staff of about 750. By 1992, the GBM could boast that 10 million trees had been planted and had survived, and more than 80,000 women had partici-pated in their projects. Maathai was awarded the Right Livelihood Award in 1984, the Africa Prize in 1991, and in 2004 the Nobel Peace Prize for her work in the GBM and contributions made to empower women in Kenya (Michaelson, 1994).

Greening projects also started on a much smaller scale in South Africa in the late 1970s to address some of the environmental and socio-economic problems associated with the lack of urban planning and services provision in African townships during the apartheid era. The first African environmental NGO operating in the urban areas was founded by Japtha Lekgheto in Soweto in 1978. Called the National Environmental Awareness Campaign, it set out to promote environmental awareness, clean up areas that lacked waste removal services, and open a recrea-tional center for youth in Dobsonville Park. In the 1980s, a number of NGOs also embarked on promoting and developing food gardens, making use especially of trench gardening techniques, tree planting, and environmental education in some African townships in numerous locations in South Africa. These included Abalimi Bezekhaya ("Planters of the Home") in Nyanga and Khayelitsa outside Cape Town; the Africa Tree Centre in Edendale in Natal; Natsoc in the Cape Flats; and Ecolink in Gazankulu, KaNgwane, and Lebowa (Steyn, 2002: 143–144).

The 1980s also saw the development of community involvement in formal nature conserva-tion and the management of protected areas, which stood in direct opposition to the prevailing fortress conservation model. This process started in the small village of Purros in the arid north-west of Namibia in the early 1980s. With funding from the South African Endangered Wildlife Trust, Garth Owen-Smith and Margaret Jacobsohn started working with the local community of Purros to stop illegal poaching of wildlife in the area. This initially entailed appointing com-munity rangers who were accountable to the local community and later expanded to involve whole communities in nature conservation and to develop the necessary mechanisms to ensure local communities benefited directly from tourists who visited the areas (Steyn, 2002: 139). By the end of the 1980s, Owen-Smith and Jacobsohn had founded the Integrated Rural Develop-ment and Nature Conservation (IRDNC) NGO, which played a key role in the promotion and support of community-based conservation in Namibia post-independence in 1990. By 2020, the IRDNC formally supported almost 50 of the 86 registered communal conservancies in the country (IRDNC, 2020). Community-based conservation was not confined to Namibia in the 1980s. In Zimbabwe the government made provision for community involvement in the management and exploitation of local natural resources in the amended Parks and Wildlife Act in 1982. This program, called the Communal Areas Management Programme for Indig-enous Resources (CAMPFIRE), launched in 1988 when the Nyaminyami District Council was granted the necessary authority to start managing and exploiting their local wildlife resources to their own benefit. By 1989, 11 districts had signed up to this program (Alexander and McGregor, 2000: 606–608). The development of community-based conservation was very important since it challenged prevailing beliefs that local communities were the enemies of conservation and should be kept out of protected areas. In some countries such as South Africa, it further challenged the established practice that people should make room for conservation through forced removals, such as the removal of the Makelele community from the Kruger National Park in 1969 and the Bakgatla community when the Pilanesberg National Park was created in 1979. Community-based conservation has expanded from its small beginnings in the 1980s into extensive programs in many African countries. It is, however, not without problems as Alexander and McGregor (2000), for example, note in relation to CAMPFIRE in the Nkayi and Lupane districts in Zimbabwe, and many authors have documented in terms of the processes involved in creating the Great Limpopo Transfrontier Park in Southern Africa.

The 1980s were also marked by the so-called African debt crisis. The immediate origin of this crisis dated back to the impacts of the 1973 oil crisis and the subsequent increase in foreign debt by both oil importing and oil exporting African states. The total foreign debt of sub-Saharan Africa increased from US $14.8 billion in 1974 to US $50 billion in 1980, US $87 billion by 1983, and US $138 billion by 1987. This led to extraordinarily high debt-to-service ratios for some African countries: in 1983, it was almost 150% in the Sudan, 80% in Togo, between 40% and 50% in the Ivory Coast, and 40% in Uganda and Guinea. The global debt-to-service ratio in 1982 was 29%. In order to survive, many African countries turned to the International Monetary Fund (IMF) and the World Bank, which imposed neoliberal structural adjustment programs (SAPs) as preconditions for their help. In 1978 only 2 African countries had IMF agreements; by 1987 this number had increased to 25 countries. In 1986 and 1987 alone, about US $1 billion was transferred annually from Africa to the IMF to repay loans. The debt crisis had a profound impact on Africans. SAPs and other conditions imposed by the IMF, the World Bank, and other international lenders typically included demands to reduce public expenditure (through the removal of subsidies on basic foods and services, the reduction of the government workforce, and the privatization of services such as water), the implementation of neoliberal trade, devaluation of national currencies, increasing foreign export earnings, and increases in taxes and levies. The net result was a drastic increase in poverty levels and the general failure of most African states to provide even the most basic of needs to their citizens (Danso, 1990; Callaghy, 1984; Basu and Stewart, 1995).

As Obi (2005: 3) and Larmer (2010: 255) note, it was within this context that the new social movements started to emerge in Africa in the 1980s. These movements varied greatly in their actions, from NGOs working toward local solutions to socio-economic and environmental problems such as food gardens, to politically oriented environmental NGOs such as Earthlife Africa, which took issue with the mismanagement of the South African environment by the apartheid government (Steyn, 2002) to popular protests against the removal of state subsidies such as the Bread Riots in Tunisia in 1983–84 (Dakhli, 2021). It is from this widespread dissatisfaction with the established order and the numerous socio-economic, environmental, and political problems Africans were confronted with on a daily basis that the current African environmental movement emerged in the post–Cold War era.

While most African governments paid little attention to the socio-economic and environmental challenges of their citizens for most of the 1980s, they could not ignore the international publicity generated by cases of toxic waste dumping in Africa by developed countries. Two incidents in 1988 provided the much-needed wake-up call for African governments to be more attentive to environmental problems: the dumping of 15,000 tons of toxic incinerated ash from Philadelphia in the open air by a Norwegian waste company on the Guinean island Kassa and the Koko Port toxic waste incident in Nigeria, which involved an Italian waste company dumping 8,000 leaking barrels filled with toxic and chemical waste on land they hired from an unsuspecting Koko farmer for only US $100 per month. The practice of dumping toxic waste from the developed world in African countries with poor environmental laws and regulations was widespread in the 1980s, and by the early 1990s, over 50 incidents had already been documented by Greenpeace International. These included the case of mercury poisoning of soil and water resources associated with Thor Chemicals in Cato Ridge in South Africa – the country with the most sophisticated governmental environmental management system and best-developed environmental NGO sector on the continent. Greenpeace played a particularly important role in highlighting the problems associated with toxic waste disposal in Africa and acted as a crucial source of information and guidance for African countries as they participated in global negotiations that led to the adoption of the 1989 Basel Convention on the Transboundary Movement of Hazardous Waste. Since the Basel Convention only regulated this trade and did not make it illegal, 12 African states adopted the Bamako Convention on the Ban of Import into Africa and the Control of Transboundary Movements of Hazardous Waste within Africa in 1991. Despite continent-wide outrage over the practice of toxic waste dumping in Africa, governments were slow to ratify the Bamako Convention, which only came into force on 22 April 1998, after 13 states had ratified it (Van der Linde, 2002: 107–108; Clapp, 1994; Steyn, 2002: 150–151).

The African environmental movement in the post–Cold War era

The African environmental movement exploded in the post–Cold War period. In the past 30 years, it has grown from perhaps a few thousand NGOs to tens of thousands of NGOs focusing on a plethora of socio-economic and environmental issues. Governmental environmental management also drastically expanded and improved in this period, and many states now have some sort of institutional capacity to address and manage environmental issues at the national level. The flourishing of the African environmental movement has been made possible by a number of developments such as the "discovery" of rural and urban communities by development agencies who started to cooperate with local NGOs in their projects, global pressures on African governments to democratize and open up political spaces within which opposition groups could legally operate, and the promotion of Indigenous and minority rights by global agencies and NGOs. More than anything, the new global order has been characterized by the promotion of environmental and human rights, stimulated in no small part by the 1992 UN Earth Summit that led to the formal adoption of sustainable development as *the* developmental model for the future. Under the auspices of the UN, the implementation of sustainable development on local, national, and international levels has become a major concern for all stakeholders involved, including NGOs working at local, national, regional, continental, and international levels. The global sustainable development agenda was expanded in the late 1990s to include poverty reduction as the third pillar of development, while the adoption of the Kyoto Protocol in 1997 ensured that climate change developed as a global concern in its own right. The various regional, continental, and international meetings hosted by the UN and other agencies, such as the 2002 World Summit on Sustainable Development (WSSD, held in Johannesburg, South Africa) and the annual Conference of the Parties (COP) meetings of the UN Framework Convention on Climate Change, held since 1995, not only ensured that the environment in its broadest sense remained a central global issue but also created numerous opportunities for civil society to meet, mobilize, and organize around socio-economic, political and environmental issues. As Death (2010: 555) noted, for example, the street protests held outside the formal WSSD meetings in 2002 in Johannesburg were the largest in the country's history since the end of the apartheid era.

The example of environmental activists standing up to their governments and/or big business, often with the aid of international NGOs, in the early 1990s did much to inspire others to follow suit. Wangari Maathai, for example, became a vocal opponent of the authoritarian Kenyan president Daniel arap Moi after he announced plans to build a skyscraper in Nairobi's Uhuru Park in 1989. Maathai mobilized her extensive international connections both to pressure Moi into abandoning these plans and to protect herself and the GBM against Moi's backlash (Michaelson, 1994: 552–554). In South Africa, a new era of environmental activism followed the founding of Earthlife Africa in 1988. This organization was instrumental in demonstrating that the environment was a deeply political issue that belonged on the anti-apartheid struggle agenda, owing to the fact that most African communities in South Africa were subjected to unhealthy rural and urban environments as a direct consequence of apartheid policies. They adopted a very wide environmental agenda that included traditional green issues such as nature conservation and animal rights, as well as "brown" issues focusing on industrial and urban pollution, lack of basic services in African townships, water and electricity provision, mining, and agrochemicals, to name but a few. Their successes included forcing the South African government to suspend the annual seal harvesting at Kleinsee in 1991, forcing Thor Chemicals to cease operating in the county in the mid-1990s, and their extensive research into Sasol's operations, in cooperation with Groundwork, that provided the necessary evidence that this multinational was indeed one of *the* major polluters in South Africa. As Cock (2014: 187–188) argues, Earthlife Africa has been exceptionally skilled at globalizing local struggles in South Africa and acts on four interrelated fronts: namely, through research, making policy interventions, targeted protest action, and developing capacity at community level.

Perhaps the best-known example of an African environmental struggle that has been globalized is that of the Ogoni in Nigeria. This ethnic minority group of less than a million people, in a country with an estimated population of well over 200 million, inhabits an oil-rich area in the Niger Delta in Eastern Nigeria. Oil production by a subsidiary of Shell International commenced in Ogoniland in 1958, and in the decades that followed, the Ogoni were subjected to a range of environmental problems associated with the oil industry, such as regular oil spills; oil leakages from faulty and aging equipment; and constant gas flaring that caused widespread soil, water, and air pollution. Under the leadership of Ken Saro-Wiwa, the Movement for the Survival of the Ogoni People (MOSOP) embarked on a sustained campaign in 1991 to address the environmental, political, and socio-economic marginalization of the Ogoni people at the hands of the Nigerian federal government and Shell International. Greenpeace and other environmental and human rights NGOs took up their struggle on an international level and directed their activism at Shell International in the United Kingdom and the Netherlands. Saro-Wiwa and MOSOP succeeded in bringing oil production in Ogoniland to a halt in 1993, and Saro-Wiwa was internationally recognized for his activism when he was awarded the Goldman Environmental Prize in 1993 and the Right Livelihood Award in 1994. Unfortunately, the Ogoni's international connections could not save the lives of Saro-Wiwa and his eight fellow Ogoni, who were found guilty on spurious grounds for the murder of four Ogoni leaders and were executed by the Nigerian military government in November 1995 (Obi, 2005; Steyn, 2014).

The Ogoni struggle was hugely significant and can be regarded as a watershed in at least two ways. Firstly, it provided the other oil-producing communities in Nigeria, such as the Isoko Community Oil Producing Forum, with a blueprint on how to articulate their grievances against the federal government and the oil companies operating in their territories. This resulted in the destabilization of the Niger Delta well into the 2010s as this region descended into cycles of activism, militancy, and repression. Secondly, this struggle made a significant contribution to the adoption of corporate social responsibility programs by multinational companies from the late 1990s onward. Sustained international scrutiny of the Nigerian oil industry into the twenty-first century ensured that multinational oil companies were not able to get away with simply implementing greenwashing programs as was the norm in the 1990s. Instead, they had to make good on their promises and contribute in meaningful and measurable ways to the development of local oil-producing communities in the country (Steyn, 2014). Developments in corporate social responsibility have not been confined to the oil sector, and there has been a great push to promote resource exploitation that is more environmentally and socially responsible. Conservation International, the Botanical Society of South Africa, and Fauna & Flora International, for example, have worked in partnership with Rio Tinto, Anglo Base Metals, and De Beers in South Africa, Guinea, and Madagascar to conserve biodiversity in the areas in which the mining companies operate (Smuts, 2010).

Writing on the South African environmental movement in 2004, Cock (2004: 1–2) noted that it "has no coherent centre and no tidy margins; it is an inchoate sum of multiple, diverse, uncoordinated struggles and organizations". The same holds true for the wider environmental movement in Africa. It consists of a bewildering array of organizations ranging from large established NGOs that form part of international networks such as Greenpeace Africa and the World Wildlife Fund to smaller organizations like Trees4Goals started by Lesein Mutunkei in Nairobi when he was just 12 years old. Every time Mutunkei, a keen footballer, scores a goal in a football match, he and his teammates plant 11 trees. His goal is to convince FIFA to make Trees4Goals global (BBC, 2018). The vast majority of environmental struggles on the continent are local and address specific issues, though many organizations link up with others in larger networks that often transcend national boundaries. The African Biodiversity Network, for example, operates in 12 countries, where they promote indigenous knowledge and biodiversity protection and work to improve governmental agricultural policies and legislation. The climate justice movement has increased the opportunities for local organizations to link up with other climate activists across the continent, such as through the Panafrican Climate Justice Alliance, which consists of over 1,000 organizations operating in 48 countries and demonstrated their ability to act together during a pandemic when a collective calling themselves the African Climate Justice Groups issued a statement on COVID-19 in May 2020 (African Climate Justice Groups, 2020). Given the gerontocratic nature of power and authority across most of Africa, perhaps the most significant new development in the past two decades has been the mobilization of youth to fight for climate justice. Across the continent, the most vocal climate activists and strikers are young people, such as teenagers Yola Mgogwane (South Africa), Venessa Nakate (Uganda), and Nkosi Nyathi (Zimbabwe) (Mogoatlhe, 2020), who all work toward creating greater community awareness of the problems associated with climate change, pollution, and general environmental neglect while also calling on their respective national governments to pay constructive attention to these issues. Nakate, in particular, has been operating on the international level in cooperation with Greta Thunberg and other prominent climate activists, participating in the youth petition to the United Nations in 2019 and attending Davos in 2020, where she was subjected to racial discrimination by a US news agency, the Associated Press, who cropped her out of a photo with taken with four of her fellow youth climate activists (Evelyn, 2020).

Concluding thoughts

The African environmental movement has come a very long way since the colonial era and its dominant conservation agenda. The key feature of environmental movements on the continent is diversity – diversity in all aspects, from people involved and issues addressed to the scope and size of NGOs. It consists of tens of thousands of NGOs, ranging from those run by individuals to groups of all sizes, operating on all levels from micro-local levels all the way to national and continental levels. While there are still many African NGOs with conservation agendas reminiscent of the colonial era, the contemporary African environmental movement is predominantly concerned with brown environmental issues such soil, water and air pollution, lack of basic services, and the impact of global climate change on African livelihoods. The other striking feature of the African environmental movement is its age: it is still a young, growing movement with thousands of small, localized NGOs that often need to cooperate with large international NGOs to achieve their goals, while truly continent-wide environmental NGOs are still to emerge. However, advances in technology along with capacity building at local community levels in the past 30 years have significantly reduced historic inequalities in access to current scientific and environmental knowledge, management, and organizational skills. The development of social media has meant that African environmental activists now have global reach in ways that never existed before, while also being able to mobilize popular support for their causes through social media platforms. As a young movement, it is not without its troubles, as attested by the implosion of the Environmental Justice Networking Forum in South Africa in the 2000s, owing to infighting after a decade of activism. Yet the movement has grown to such an extent that future research should concentrate on producing detailed country studies such as those that Cock (2004, 2014) and Death (2014) have produced on South Africa and numerous more new studies on the climate justice movement and youth environmental activism to truly do it justice.

References

African Biodiversity Network. Available at: https://africanbiodiversity.org/

African Climate Justice Groups. (2020) *Climate justice for Africa: A new Africa is possible.* 7 May. Available at: www.africaclimatejustice.org/

Alexander, J. and McGregor, J. (2000) Wildlife and politics: CAMPFIRE in Zimbabwe. *Development and Change*, 31 (3), pp. 605–627.

Anderson, D. (1984) Depression, dust bowl, demography and drought: The colonial state and soil conservation in East Africa during the 1930s. *African Affairs*, 83, pp. 321–343.

Basu, A. and Stewart. F. (1995) Structural adjustment policies and the poor in Africa: An analysis of the 1980s. In: F. Stewart, ed. *Adjustment and poverty: Options and choices.* London: Routledge, pp. 61–79.

BBC. (2018) *Kenya football teen plants trees for goals*, 25.10.2018. Available at: www.bbc.co.uk/news/av/world-africa-45876475

Beinart, W. (1984) Soil erosion, conservationism and ideas about development: A Southern African exploration, 1900–1960. *Journal of Southern African Studies*, 11 (1), pp. 52–83.

Beinart, W. and Hughes, L. (2007) *Environment and empire.* Oxford: Oxford University Press.

British Pathé. (1937) *Kruger Park issue title – wait for it!* Available at: www.britishpathe.com/video/kruger-park-issue-title-wait-for-it

Brockington, D. (2015) *The enduring power of fortress conservation in Africa.* Available at: https://centredestudisafricans.org/wp-content/uploads/2015/11/Brockingtonfinal.pdf

Callaghy, T.M. (1984) Africa's debt crisis. *Journal of International Affairs*, 38 (1), pp. 61–79.

Carruthers, E.J. (1993) 'Police boys' and poachers: Africans, wildlife protection and national parks, the Transvaal 1902 to 1950. *Koedoe*, 36 (2), pp. 11–22.

Carruthers, E.J. (1995) *The Kruger National Park: A social and political history.* Pietermaritzburg: University of Natal Press.

Clapp, J. (1994) Africa, NGOs, and the international toxic waste trade. *The Journal of Environment & Development*, 3 (2), pp. 17–46.

Cock, J. (2004) *Connecting the red, brown and green: The environmental justice movement in South Africa.* Durban: University of KwaZulu-Natal. Available at: https://ccs.ukzn.ac.za/files/Cock%20Connecting%20the%20red,%20brown%20and%20green%20The%20environmental%20justice%20movement%20in%20South%20Africa.pdf

Cock, J. (2014) The challenge of ecological transformation in post-apartheid South Africa: The re-emergence of an environmental justice movement. In: M.C. Dawson and L. Sinwell, eds. *Contesting transformation: Popular resistance in twenty-first century South Africa.* London: Pluto Press, pp. 183–200.

Coulson, A. (1977) Agricultural policies in mainland Tanzania. *Review of African Political Economy*, 4 (10), pp. 74–100.

Dakhli, L. (2021) The fair value of bread: Tunisia, 28 December 1983–6 January 1984. *International Review of Social History*, 66 (S29), pp. 41–68.

Danso, A. (1990) The causes and impact of the African debt crisis. *The Review of Black Political Economy*, 19 (1), pp. 5–21.

Death, C. (2010) Troubles at the top: South African protests and the 2002 Johannesburg Summit. *African Affairs*, 109 (437), pp. 555–574.

Death, C. (2014) Environmental movements, climate change, and consumption in South Africa. *Journal of Southern African Studies*, 40 (6), pp. 1215–1234.

Evelyn, K. (2020) Outrage at whites-only image as Ugandan climate activist cropped from photo. *The Guardian*, 25 January. Available at: www.theguardian.com/world/2020/jan/24/whites-only-photo-uganda-climate-activist-vanessa-nakate

Hodge, J.M. (2007) *Triumph of the expert: Agrarian doctrines of development and the legacies of British colonialism.* Athens: Ohio University Press.

Hrabanski, M. (2010) Internal dynamics, the state, and recourse to external aid: Towards a historical sociology of the peasant movement in Senegal since the 1960s. *Review of African Political Economy*, 37 (125), pp. 281–297.

IRDNC. (2020) Tribute to Garth Owen-Smith, African conservationist (commentary). *Mongabay: News & Inspiration from Nature's Frontline*, 18 April. Available at: https://news.mongabay.com/2020/04/tribute-to-garth-owen-smith-african-conservationist-commentary/

Khan, F. (1989) The role of history in understanding current South African attitudes to conservation. *Southern African Journal of Environmental Education*, 10, pp. 3–5.

Khan, F. (1992) Davidson Don Tengo Jabavu: Pioneer South African environmental activist. *African Wildlife*, 46 (6), p. 275.

Khan, F. (1997) Soil wars: The role of the African National Soil Conservation Association in South Africa, 1953–1959. *Environmental History*, 2 (4), pp. 439–459.

Kiros, F.G. (1991) Economic consequences of drought, crop failure and famine in Ethiopia, 1973–1986. *Ambio*, 20 (5), pp. 183–185.

Koch, E., Cooper, D. and Coetzee, H. (1990) *Water, waste and wildlife: The politics of ecology in South Africa.* Johannesburg: Penguin Books.

Koehn, P. (1979) Ethiopia: Famine, food production, and changes in the legal order. *African Studies Review*, 22 (1), pp. 51–71.

Lanz, T.J. (2000) The origins, development and legacy of scientific forestry in Cameroon. *Environment and History*, 6, pp. 99–120.

Larmer, M. (2010) Social movements in Africa. *Review of African Political Economy*, 37 (125), pp. 251–262.

Lonsdale, J.M. (1968) Some origins of nationalism in East Africa. *The Journal of African History*, 9 (1), pp. 119–146.

Maack, P.A. (1996) 'We don't want the terraces!': Protest and identity under the Uluguru land usage scheme. In: G. Maddox, J. Giblin and I.N. Kimambo, eds. *Custodians of the land: Ecology and culture in the history of Tanzania.* London: James Currey, pp. 152–169.

MacKenzie, J.M. (1987) Chivalry, social Darwinism and ritualized killing: The hunting ethos in Central Africa up to 1914. In: D. Anderson and R. Grove, eds. *Conservation in Africa: People, policies and practice.* Cambridge: Cambridge University Press, pp. 41–61.

MacKenzie, J.M. (1997) *The empire of nature: Hunting, conservation and British imperialism.* Manchester: Manchester University Press.

Maddox, G.H. (2006) *Sub-Saharan Africa: An environmental history.* Santa Barbara, CA: ABC-CLIO.

Masih, I. et al. (2014) A review of droughts on the African continent: A geospatial and long-term perspective. *Hydrology and Earth System Sciences*, 18 (9), pp. 3635–3649.

McCormick, J. (1989) *The global environmental movement: Reclaiming paradise.* London: Belhaven Press.

Michaelson, M. (1994) Wangari Maathai and Kenya's Green Belt Movement: Exploring the evolution and potentialities of consensus movement mobilization. *Social Problems*, 41 (4), pp. 540–561.

Mogoatlhe, L. (2020) *Defend the planet: 5 youth activists who are demanding urgent climate action in Africa.* Available at: www.globalcitizen.org/en/content/youth-climate-change-activists-in-africa/

Neumann, R.P. (1997) Forest rights, privileges and prohibitions: Contextualising state forestry policy in Tanganyika. *Environment and History*, 3 (1), pp. 45–68.

Obi, C.I. (2005) *Environmental movements in Sub-Saharan Africa: A political ecology of power and conflict.* Civil Society and Social Movements Programme Paper nr 15. Geneva: United Nations Research Institute for Social Development.

Ogundere, J.D. (1972) The development of international environmental law and policy in Africa. *Natural Resources Journal*, 12 (2), pp. 259–260.

Panafrican Climate Justice Alliance. Available at: www.pacja.org/

Pringle, J.A. (1982) *The conservationists and the killers: The story of game protection and the Wildlife Society of Southern Africa*. Cape Town: T.V. Bulpin and Books of Africa (Pty.) Ltd.

Rabie, M.A. (1973) Soil conservation and the law. *The Comparative and International Law Journal of South Africa*, 6(2), pp. 145–198.

Ruppel, O.C. (2018) Environmental law in the Africa Union. In: O.C. Ruppel and E.D. Kam Yogo, eds. *Environmental law and policy in Cameroon: Towards making Africa the tree of life*. Baden-Baden: Nomos, pp. 119–137.

Shao, J. (1986) The Villagization Program and the disruption of the ecological balance in Tanzania. *Canadian Journal of African Studies/Revue Canadienne des Études Africaines*, 20 (2), pp. 219–239.

Smuts, R. (2010) *Are partnerships the key to conserving Africa's biodiversity? Four partnership case studies between mining companies and conservation NGOs*. Arlington, VA: Conservation International.

Steyn, P. (2002) Popular environmental struggles in South Africa, 1972–1992. *Historia*, 47 (1), pp. 125–158.

Steyn, P. (2014) Oil, ethnic minority groups and environmental struggles against multinational oil companies and the federal government in the Nigerian Niger Delta since the 1990s. In: M. Armiero and L. Sedrez, eds. *A history of environmentalism: Local struggles, global histories*. London: Bloomsbury, pp. 57–81.

Steyn, P. (2018) Apartheid South Africa's participation in United Nations-organised international environmental initiatives in the 1970s: A reassessment. *Journal of Contemporary History*, 53 (4), pp. 861–884.

Sunseri, T. (1997) Famine and wild pigs: Gender struggles and the outbreak of the Maji Maji War in Uzaramo (Tanzania). *Journal of African History*, 38 (2), pp. 235–259.

Tangri, R.K. (1968) The rise of nationalism in colonial Africa: The case of colonial Malawi. *Comparative Studies in Society and History*, 10 (2), pp. 142–161.

Van der Linde, M. (2002) African responses to environmental protection. *The Comparative and International Law Journal of Southern Africa*, 35 (1), pp. 99–113.

9

RISING TIDES AND DIRTY COAL

The environmental movement in Oceania

Robyn Gulliver, Susilo Wibisono, and Winnifred R. Louis

Introduction

Oceania is a continent defined by diversity and distance. The region is known for remarkable feats of ocean exploration which saw Aboriginal Australian settlement of Australia tens of thousands of years ago and connected and united communities from Tahiti to the Cook Islands to New Zealand during the great Polynesian migration. Yet it is also home to the most geographically isolated areas on the planet, brimming with biological diversity of outstanding global importance while suffering from a history of human-induced over-exploitation and extinction (Chape, 2006, p. 27). Each of the four Oceanian regions faces extreme environmental pressures. The South Pacific Islands (SPI) – composed of Micronesia, Melanesia, and Polynesia – have all experienced dramatic population growth in the last 50 years, leading people to move to more vulnerable coastal areas (Rudiak-Gould, 2013), reducing food security, and creating a dependency on migration and remittances to maintain the economy (Connell, 2015).

The continent also faces multiple environmental crises. In Micronesia, the Marshall Islands, Kiribati, and Tuvalu are three of the four sovereign states (along with the Indian Ocean atoll the Maldives) to face un-inhabitability and even non-existence because of rising sea levels due to climate change (Barnett & Adger, 2003). In Melanesia, the Papua New Guinean Panguna copper mine has killed all life in the Jaba River while phosphate mining in Palau, Makatea, Naura, and Banaba has destroyed much of each island's surface (see McNeill, 2015). Logging, overfishing, and the depletion of biological diversity continue to degrade many Polynesian islands while many traditional environmental stewardship behaviors have ebbed (Connell, 2015). Australia and New Zealand have also experienced widespread environmental decline since colonization. New Zealand has experienced major loss of forest cover (Wolf et al., 2021), and Australia has the highest extinction rate of mammal species globally (ICUN, 2018) while simultaneously maintaining its position as one of the world's largest coal exporters and climate polluters (Parra et al., 2019).

Yet coexisting with these challenges is a vibrant, diverse, and highly active environmental movement, consisting of well over 3,000 environmental groups and over 1,000 campaigns, organizing more than 40,000 events undertaken in the last decade alone (Gulliver et al., 2021a). Oceania has led the way in addressing environmental issues of critical importance. In 1985, the South Pacific Nuclear Weapon Free Zone was established. The Micronesian Challenge,

 DOI: 10.4324/9780367855680-10

signed in 2006 with the support of politicians, Pacific Island communities, and large transnational organizations including The Nature Conservancy and the World Wildlife Fund, sought to "effectively conserve at least 30% of the near-shore marine and 20% of the forest resources across Micronesia by 2020" (Gruby, 2017; Micronesia Challenge, 2006). South Pacific Island leaders have taken a prominent role in shaping international climate policies. Environmental activists across the continent are increasingly speaking out for environmental justice and for coordinating continent-wide actions challenging the legitimacy of colonial and corporate interests in driving environmental degradation.

How has this rich and complex environmental activism ecosystem emerged across the continent, and how has the movement helped achieve these positive outcomes? In this chapter, we examine the characteristics of environmental activism in Oceanian to respond to this question. In doing so, we follow Giugni and Grasso's (2015) definition of a movement: a collection of individuals who share a collective identity, interact in a loose network of organizations with varying degrees of formality, and engage voluntarily in collective action motivated by shared concern (see also Diani, 2003). Before considering how the movement formed and thrived, it must be noted that in Oceania, several barriers have hindered its development. First, a collective environmental identity is challenging to foster over the vast distances between islands, where isolation is the norm. Second, low population densities, poverty, and the effects of military occupation, dispossession, and corporate extractivism (Shewry, 2017b), have made networks of organizations difficult to create and even more challenging to sustain. Third, as a result of these characteristics, environmental concerns and grievances have been primarily local in nature and response.

How movements emerge, grow, and succeed have long fascinated scholars, with decades of research identifying three factors that can explain movement dynamics and outcomes: mobilization structures (Edwards et al., 2018), framing processes (Snow et al., 2018), and political opportunities (McAdam & Tarrow, 2018). Utilizing a large empirical database on Oceanian environmental groups, campaigns, and events (data and the protocol of search are available at https://osf.io/4s8e2), we examined the trajectory of Oceanian environmental activism focusing on these three factors. We argue that the Oceanian environmental movement has succeeded due to bottom-up, rather than top-down approaches. Localized activism has allowed the emergence of a complex ecosystem of distinct mobilizing structures, from national conservation organizations to grassroots direct action collectives. The localized nature of environmental activism in Oceania has also enabled framing of environmental concerns to align with the values and norms of the diverse communities found across the continent. Finally, local activism has enabled environmentalists to maximise their opportunities to influence and obtain power through the varying political opportunities open to them in different contexts. In the following sections, we consider each of these dynamics in turn.

Diversification of mobilization structures 1880–2021

Mobilization structures refer to the resources and processes that enable movements to persist, connect, and mobilize individuals in collective action (McAdam et al., 1996; Moser, 2007). In remote expanses such as Oceania, these resources – whether financial, human, or otherwise – can be challenging to acquire, yet they are critical for supporting the structures that enable effective participation (McCarthy & Zald, 1977; Tilly, 1978). In sociological and political analyses, they enable individuals to participate in activism, increase groups' capacity to mobilize more frequently, increase network connections, gain media attention, and lobby power holders (Andrews & Caren, 2010; see also Dalton et al., 2003). From a psychological perspective, mobilization structures both reflect and channel important social identities, which allow individuals to experience a sense of connection with each other and with the natural world that enables collective action (Fielding et al., 2008; Fielding & Louis, 2020; Milfont et al., 2020). Today across Oceania, we see a highly complex range of mobilization structures, ranging from transnational organizations (e.g., 350.org), pan-Pacific non-governmental organization (NGO) alliances (e.g., The Coral Triangle Initiative) and local conservation organizations (e.g., Marshall Islands Conservation Organisation). At the local level, there are sustainability groups (e.g., Transition Towns), which focus on building community self-reliance and climate resilience (Barr & Pollard, 2017), radical action collectives (e.g., Extinction Rebellion), and intersectional collectives such as the Pacific Urgent Action Hub for Ecological Justice. However, it took many decades for this rich and vibrant mobilization ecosystem to grow. The conditions that first prompted more diverse mobilization structures can be traced back to the rise of anti-nuclear sentiment.

Nuclear testing galvanized public opinion from the 1960s to the 1990s, fostering the first truly transnational mass mobilization on shared grievances across the continent. Prior to the 1960s, Oceanian communities had been characterized by their ability to adapt to and mitigate against environmental forces in isolation, fostered through intricate rituals and protocols around access and use of environmental resources (Keown, 2018). Adapting to environmental forces had been an essential mechanism to ensure continuous supplies of food and water and survival after natural disasters (Luetz & Nunn, 2020). These localized solutions worked: measures such as population control and forced migration to other islands (Chape, 2006) enabled the almost-unbroken occupation of most of these islands for centuries (Luetz & Nunn, 2020; McNeill, 2015).

At the advent of the colonial era, Aboriginal communities experienced the loss of between 80% and 96% of their population through massacre, sexual abuse, and disease (Harris, 2011). New Zealand embarked on a colonial war, and the South Pacific Islands were overrun with mining and military interests. To the colonizers, there was a widespread presumption that the removal and replacement of indigenous species, and sometimes Indigenous populations, by invasive plants, animals, and colonists, was inevitable or even desirable (Galbreath, 2002; Harris, 2011). Yet despite the violence and turmoil wrought by colonization, there is some evidence that concerns around environmental issues emerged swiftly. For example, fears regarding the extinction of New Zealand species were shared by Māori as far back as 1863 (see Galbreath, 2002). From as early as the 1880s, groups in Australia formed to preserve and record the native flora and fauna, while in New Zealand, scenery preservation societies, beautifying societies, and New Zealand Native Associations expressed support for protection of bush scenery and native birds. These conservation-focused groups continued to emerge well into the 1960s, often achieving substantial conservation outcomes in Australia and New Zealand. These primarily related to the excise of land for protection, with the world's second national park established in New South Wales, Australia, in 1879 and Resolution Island gazetted in New Zealand in 1881.

However, this particular "European solution to the problem" (Mills, 2009, p. 686) failed to ignite any sense of shared grievance across the wider Oceanian regions. Similarly, the plight of many smaller islands experiencing the wholesale extraction of their mineral resources (beginning as early as 1895 with phosphate mining in Nauru) did not trigger larger regional mobilization at the time. The lackluster island economies, denial of self-determination under colonial powers (Keown, 2018), and small island populations meant there were few grassroots organizations to raise awareness, mobilize people, and drive the long-term success of movements (McAdam, 2017).

The lack of shared grievances and suitable mobilization structures changed dramatically once awareness of nuclear testing grew. This testing began in 1946 and eventually spread across the South Pacific to Bikini Atoll, the Gilbert Islands, Tahiti, and Australia. While secrecy ensured that news of forced displacements and extensive radiation poisoning emerged slowly, mobilization first began in existing local church, community, and student organizations (George, 2011). By the early 1970s, new mobilizing structures were formed to advocate specifically against nuclear testing, such as Against Testing on Mururoa (ATOM) and the Nuclear Free and Independent Pacific (NFIP) collective, composed of church groups, trade unions, and community and environmental organizations at the Pacific Concerns Resource Center (Penjueli, 2015). The first Friends of the Earth group began in 1971 in Adelaide, Australia, following which diversification of mobilization structures continued apace through the development of a multiplicity of collectives and campaigns. The Australian anti-uranium collective began in 1976 and Campaign Again Nuclear Energy in 1974 (Walker, 2016), while in New Zealand, the Campaign for Nuclear Disarmament (CND) began in 1959 in Christchurch (Locke, 1992).

The second benefit of this diversification of mobilization structures was its ability to foster diverse action repertoires (e.g., see Porta & Rucht, 2002), fueling a massive growth in activism across the continent. We see evidence of this growth and diversification from as early as 1964 with the Australian "Peace Marches" (Garner, 1964). Action repertoires broadened, with events such as the annual "Bike ride against uranium", blockades against uranium shipping port facilities in Sydney and Darwin, and boycotts of French products (Wittner, 2009). In New Zealand, a 1963 petition "No Bombs South of the Line" gained 80,000 signatures – the largest petition since the equal rights petition of 1893 (Shoraka, 2017). The Greenpeace flagship boat *Rainbow Warrior* sailed into multiple ports before being bombed and sunk in Auckland Harbor by French government–supported saboteurs. Resistance continued across South Pacific islands well into the 1990s, with members of Vahine To'a ("warrior women to protect the land") occupying the Tahitian International Airport in 1995. By 1978, a complex and diverse movement structure had been developed (Wittner, 2003), with anti-nuclear activists working in newly formed local groups supported by transnational groups such as Greenpeace and Friends of the Earth.

There were a number of benefits to the expanded mobilization structure that characterized this newly emerged modern environmental movement. Local groups facilitated mobilization of the population in centers across wider geographical areas, the expansion of concern to other environmental issues, and increased networking between groups. For example, in 1974 at the height of the anti-nuclear protest in Australia, a campaign on public transportation was undertaken in a collaboration between Friends of the Earth, the Plumbers and Gasfitters Union, Australian Railways Union, Australian Federated Union of Locomotive Employees, the Cyclist Protection Committee, the Bowden Brompton Anti-freeway Group, and the Radical Technology Group (Walker, 2016). In New Zealand, a surge of new local environmental groups emerged (e.g., Ecology Action, Taranaki Clean Sea Action, Native Forests Action Council) (Downes, 2000; Mills, 2009; O'Brien, 2015), many of which supported radical direct action against native forest logging (O'Brien, 2013b). Indeed, the "Save Manapouri Campaign" against increased hydroelectric energy has been positioned as the beginning of the modern environmental movement in New Zealand (O'Brien, 2013a), similar to the Franklin River Blockade in Australia, which successfully stopped the damming of Tasmania's Franklin River in 1983.

Changing mobilization structures also formed to focus on political, extra-institutional, and cultural strategies for effecting change. For example, in 1972, the world's first national Green Party (the Values Party) was founded in New Zealand, while in Australia, a string of campaigns using blockades, sit-ins, and camps persisted from the 1960s to the 1990s. These grassroots radical actions generated substantial media coverage (Hutchins & Lester, 2006) and enjoyed widespread support from other environmental groups (Hartman & Darab, 2014) while sustaining long-term direct action tactics such as Australia's longest running anti-logging forest blockade at Goolengook in Victoria between 1997 and 2002 (Lines, 2003). In smaller Pacific islands, alongside anti-nuclear riots and demonstrations, a wide range of protest literature and art developed, including that of Kanaky (Indigenous New Caledonian) writer Déwé Gorodé, who also founded the Kanak independence movement Groupe 1878 after a 1974 sit-in at local law courts (Keown, 2018).

Yet despite these continent-wide patterns of change, we do not see the same trajectory of grassroots mobilization specifically directed toward environmental issues to the same extent in the South Pacific Islands. Ongoing struggles against attempts by colonial powers to violently undermine nuclear-free struggles meant that ecological issues became intricately connected to colonization and its practices (Shewry, 2017b). Organizations in Palau, for example, sought protection of their unique nuclear-free constitution from 1981 to 1993, which was ultimately unsuccessful (George, 2011). Similarly, in Papua New Guinea, activism against mining has led to the creation of landowner groups and alliances with international NGOs. However, limited responses from either mines or the state have resulted in longstanding grievances, which continue to cause environmental and social problems (Walton & Barnett, 2008).

Some researchers have argued that island populations have been too small and poor to focus on environmental change issues (e.g., McNeill, 2015). Indeed, during this period, many Pacific Islands were experiencing increasing levels of poverty, exacerbated by growing inequality and worsening health standards (Bryant-Tokalau, 1995), which may have influenced reduced protest activity (Dalton et al., 2010). These factors together may help explain the emergence, then apparent decline, of transnational activism that occurred during the anti-nuclear protests. It was the surge of localized environmental activism seeking solutions to climate change that would support the re-emergence of an Oceanian-wide environmental movement in the twenty-first century.

The influence of localized message framing on action repertoires

The climate crisis is a global issue of substantial importance to Pacific regions, like that of nuclear testing (Fry & Tarte, 2016). Yet the responses of communities and political representatives to climate messaging across the four Oceanian regions have been complex and varied. For example, South Pacific Island leaders have taken a prominent role in shaping international climate policies such as the Paris Climate Agreement (Mcleod et al., 2019). Many Pacific states have established ambitious migration and conservation targets of their own, despite their minimal contribution to climate emissions (Hoad, 2015; Ourbak & Magnan, 2018). Yet Australia remains the only country to have repealed a carbon-pricing scheme, with climate change destabilizing and deposing prime ministers (Beeson & McDonald, 2013). Australia also continues to support fossil fuel exports while ignoring calls from Pacific Island neighbors to engage in meaningful emission reductions projects (Climate Action Tracker, 2020). A high degree of political polarization on environmental issues has supported persistent gridlock and reluctance to act (Fielding & Hornsey, 2016; Hornsey et al., 2016).

Examining how climate change issues are framed and communicated by environmental activists in the different Oceanian regions can help shed light on these different responses. Framing refers to the way in which movements define issues, motivate participants, appeal to the public, and legitimize their struggle (Moser, 2007). Frames can help elicit sympathy and create meaning (Benford & Snow, 2000) and can influence the psychological responses of activism participants, bystanders, and other groups, including the opponents (Gulliver et al., 2021b).

Furthermore, frames that embody a group's values and interests are more likely to exert influence (Steffens et al., 2013). Across Oceania, groups have framed and delivered climate change messaging through disparate mobilization structures available in the different national contexts. This localization of frames has enabled messaging about the climate crisis to be more effectively tailored to local norms and identities.

From a social psychological perspective, groups' norms (their rules or standards for behavior) define the actions that are considered appropriate and enacted in local contexts (Fielding & Louis, 2020; Louis et al., 2020; Milfont & Schultz, 2016). Grassroots groups make decisions in the context of international and transnational norms for action that may align or conflict with local political, religious, and cultural values and standards. When environmental messages communicate norms that conflict with audiences' standards and values, backlash rather than action may occur (McDonald et al., 2013; Smith et al., 2012). When frames for environmental action are aligned with local norms, communicated by trusted insiders (Ross et al., 2014), and fulfill activists' needs (Cooke et al., 2016), action is more likely to follow and to strengthen the social identities for actors' subsequent actions (Lauren et al., 2016).

In the South Pacific context, while there was a lull in grassroots organizing in the 1990s (Titifanue et al., 2017), localized messaging about climate change began emerging quickly by 2000, when church-based organizations began encouraging community action on climate. Organizations such as the Pacific Conference of Churches implemented advocacy programs for social and environmental justice (Harris, 2014), while the United Church of Christ shared stories of local impacts of climate change as early as 2004 (Rudiak-Gould, 2013). Research on the impact of this framing found that messages that originated from religious leaders and engaged with spiritual beliefs were most influential, whereas climate messages that clashed with the community's spiritual agenda were met with hostility (Luetz & Nunn, 2020; Nunn, 2017).

Climate change messaging framing also influenced action repertoires. Across Melanesia, Micronesia, and Polynesia, groups have leaned heavily on the role of performative art in raising awareness and building support for action. Examples include the "Water is Rising" tour (2011), and *Moana: The Rising of the Sea*, alongside other forms of song, poetry, documentaries, and museum collaborations (McNamara & Farbotko, 2017; Steiner, 2015; Keown, 2018). These activities often involve collaborations between groups. For example, the 2014 Madang Wansolwara ("One People One Ocean") dance involved poets, musicians, yam farmers, landowners, and theologians from more than nine Pacific nations.

The longstanding belief in a balanced relationship between humans and the environment has also played a central role in how Indigenous Pacific protest responses have emerged (e.g., Hau'Ofa, 2008; Keown, 2018). A protracted legal campaign by Māori in New Zealand to have the Whanganui River, understood to be an ancestor of the local community, granted legal personhood, is one powerful example of how spiritual beliefs have shaped action choices. The success of this legal battle in 2020 has not only delivered a powerful symbolic victory but also entitled the Whanganui River to legal guardianship and concrete protection from harm, pollution, and degradation, inspiring emulation by other Indigenous groups worldwide.

Some researchers have argued that a resistance to conceptualization of advocacy as forms of "protest" in some Pacific island communities may also have affected how environmental issues are communicated (e.g., Rudiak-Gould, 2013; Shewry, 2017b). In the Marshall Islands, for example, neither grassroots participation nor protest were seen as part of the Marshall Islands Conservation Society's modus operandi (Rudiak-Gould, 2013, p. 141). Widespread civil resistance was utilized in the anti-nuclear struggle, such as the 1979 occupation of eight Marshall Islands by 500 people who had been forcibly removed due to US nuclear testing (Wittner, 2009). However, some activists disavow the concept of "protest" as a term suggesting rejection or opposition without solutions (Shewry, 2017b). At the same time, grassroots groups beyond the advocacy-oriented religious and conservation organizations continue to form, boosted by the use of informational technology tools and platforms, which have acted as a catalyst for mobilizations (Titifanue et al., 2017). In the South Pacific, online coordination enabled a surge of new groups, such as the Kiribati Climate Action Network, Project Survival Pacific in Fiji, and the Pacific Climate Warriors, to collaborate and advocate for climate action.

This reduced emphasis on contentious politics and engagement in protest activities (e.g., della Porta & Diani, 2009; McAdam et al., 2003) has resulted in climate and conservation messaging emanating from new, regionally driven partnerships. For example, prominent new regional institutions such as the South Pacific Forum (1971) and the South Pacific Regional Environmental Programme (1982) have fostered a more inclusive bottom-up approach in which islands take a greater role in addressing issues (Tarte, 2014). Indeed, the Forum has been highly active and successful in its advocacy for prohibitions on drift-net fishing, nuclear testing, and dumping of radioactive waste, as well as leading new international treaties on resource protection (Fry, 1994).

Transnational conservation NGOs and intergovernmental organizations have connected to support local conservation-based groups, which now dominate the movement mobilization structure in the Pacific Islands and also play a heavy role in conservation programs in Australasia. These organizational structures do not fit the definition of contentious politics, given their role in fostering on-the-ground conservation projects and private pro-environmental behaviors rather than adversarial protest (see Dalton, 2015, Stern, 2000). However, groups supporting these projects are highly active in mobilizing communities on environmental issues. For example, there has been a substantial growth in programs such as the Locally Management Marine Area Network (LMMAN), oriented to the challenge to conserve 30% of Micronesian near-shore resources and 20% of forest resources by 2020 (Chape, 2006). Advocates have used locally based mobilization to establish new protected areas, develop climate-smart development plans, and implement climate-smart agriculture (Mcleod et al., 2019). Often working in tandem with large, well-resourced transnational conservation organizations such as The Nature Conservancy, decades of local resilience, restoration, and adaptation projects have been led by groups such as Tenkile Conservation Alliance (Papua New Guinea) and the Guam Nature Alliance.[1]

However, while similar partnerships and programs have emerged in Australasia (e.g., Landcare Australia, which supports local groups of volunteers to undertake on-the-ground sustainable land management projects), a resistance to implementing urgent responses to climate change within the political sphere persists, particularly in Australia. To consider why this might be so, we turn now to examining the influence of political opportunities in mobilizing and sustaining environmental activism across Oceania.

Changing political opportunities from colonization to the present day

The diverse experiences of environmental groups in Oceania over the last two centuries provide extensive data to identify how political opportunities – the means by which groups can make claims against authorities (Meyer, 2004) – have influenced the movement's trajectories. The degree of political openness or closeness in each nation is likely to affect environmental activists' ability to gain political influence (Almeida & Stearns, 1998; Louis et al., 2020). Our data supports the view that political openness has influenced both the type of groups that have emerged and the action repertoires they use. New Zealand provides an indicative example.

With the signing of Treaty of Waitangi in 1840 between the British Crown and some Māori tribes, Māori were guaranteed full "sovereignty" (*tino rangatiratanga* in Māori) over their lands, forests, fisheries, and "other properties". Yet, in practice, compulsory acquisition of Māori land fueled widespread land-rights protests (Mills, 2009), and it took the establishment of the Waitangi Tribunal before a political process was established by which grievances could be heard. The effects of the Waitangi Tribunal in providing a forum to seek responses and redress regarding environmental issues have been significant. For example, by 1982, the Motunui-Waitara claim successfully stopped development of a waste discharge pipeline, and in 1983, the Kaituna claim won hearings against sewerage effluent discharge into a river, and a broader claim by the Waikato-Tainui people against the despoliation of Manukau Harbour succeeded.

The ability of environmental groups to raise issues within the New Zealand political arena was further advanced with the introduction of a mixed-member proportional voting system, which enabled greater political representation for minor parties (O'Brien, 2012). Following this, the introduction of the Resource Management Act in 1991 devolved powers to local councils. These three political characteristics have facilitated the decentralization of environmental groups, grounding grassroots coalitions in local community concerns while enabling the survival of umbrella organizations (Downes, 2000). This political openness flowed onto diversified mobilization structures and action repertoires, with O'Brien's (2012) analysis of environmental protests between 1997 and 2010 finding increasing protest levels, particularly those organized by grassroots groups (as opposed to more professionalized NGOs).

Conversely, our data indicates that while messaging around conservation and environment is becoming increasingly engrained in Pacific governance and community practices, this is not the case in Australia (Fielding & Hornsey, 2016; Hornsey et al., 2016). Political resistance has led some small atoll islands to express increasing frustration with Australian intransigence and complicity in both driving down emissions targets (Fry & Tarte, 2016) and defeating emissions control policies (O'Malley, 2014). Even within Australia, despite widespread public concern about climate change by 2019 (The Australia Institute, 2020), opportunities to prioritize environmental issues in policy have been repeatedly stymied. Ineffective environmental laws and crackdowns on the activities of advocacy organizations such as Greenpeace and 350.org demonstrate the willingness of governments to undermine environmental advocacy capacity and reduce activists' ability to engage in political and public discussions (e.g., Murray, 2019).

While opportunities to engage in the political processes in Australia remain available, the political resistance to change may have helped foster the substantial growth in civic groups focusing on climate change. By 2020, more than 730 Australian online groups were actively mobilizing against climate change across the country, well over 4,000 were active on other environmental issues, and more than 36,000 environmental actions had been organized between 2010 and 2019 alone (Gulliver et al., 2021a). In addition, action at state and local levels seems to be increasing in response to federal inaction. For example, a growing number of local councils are engaging with climate issues, such as through declarations of a "climate emergency" (see https://climateemergencydeclaration.org/).

This political context may have also influenced action repertoires, with a growth in radical action tactics – such as blockades and sit-ins – observable, especially since 2018 (Gulliver et al., 2021a). Indeed, some research suggests the frequency of radical action may be influenced by the openness or closedness of political structures (Meyer, 2004). This growth of radical action supports the argument that increased repression can sometimes lead to increased disruptive protest (Louis et al., 2020). In addition to attempts to restrict radical tactics such as those used by the grassroots climate action group Extinction Rebellion (see Gulliver et al., 2021a), we can see these effects in the case of Sea Shepherd. This transnational organization has used direct-action tactics against whaling and overfishing in Australian water since 1977 due to international polit-ical gridlock in developing and enforcing marine regulations. As a result, Sea Shepherd has been labelled variously as "terrorists", "vigilantes", and a "pirate organization" (Berube, 2021).

The effects of even more closed political opportunities can be seen in Oceanian countries riven by mining and corporate extractivism. Communities experiencing resource extractiv-ism frequently engage in resistance, particularly in local communities where people are more dependent on natural resources for their livelihoods and where opportunities to mediate con-flict are minimal (Walton & Barnett, 2008). Papua New Guinea is particularly indicative of this process as mining accounts for a large share of both national exports and gross domestic product and has also been held responsible for disrupting traditional practices and exacerbating social problems (Walton & Barnett, 2008). Conflict has persisted in areas such as the Ok Tedi mine (Kirsch, 2007) and the Misima and Lihir mines (Macintyre & Foale, 2004). Some researchers have argued that the root causes of these conflicts are the unequal distribution of benefits and the slow development of dispute resolution arenas, with the lack of power for communities to redress harm, increasing the risk that violent resistance may erupt (Walton & Barnett, 2008). Additional effects of closed political systems can be seen in islands that have endured military coups (e.g., Fiji in the 1980s and 1990s) and long-running violent resistance struggles (e.g., West Papua), while the substantial militarization of Guam has exacerbated environmental decline while perpetuating the longstanding oppression of the Indigenous Chamarro people (Aguon, 2021). These factors have hampered the development of regional identities and networks that could mobilize to advance self-determination and environmental sustainability (Keown, 2018).

In spite of the difficulties experienced by environmental organizations across the conti-nent, whether through government attacks on advocacy activities or unequal access to political power, our data on Australian environmental groups indicates that there has been a large rise in the number of grassroots groups focusing on local issues in the last 15 years. Before 2005, a total of 87 of the 195 groups (45%) in our database formed on the basis of focusing on local issues. In contrast, after 2005, more than 300 local groups were formed, compared with 101 groups focusing on environmental issues at the regional, state, or national level.

There are a number of reasons that may help explain this disparity. These local grassroots groups may have more freedom to engage in civil resistance activities and do not require stable funding or access to political processes as do more established NGOs (Zchout & Tal, 2017). These characteristics may enable them to overcome some of the barriers to political influence experienced by larger and more professionalized organizations (Dalton et al., 2003). However, these groups can have a heavy reliance on volunteer labor to organize actions and build groups (Gulliver et al., 2020). To support these new cadres of volunteers, numerous specialist organiza-tions and programs have emerged, supporting activism training and education (e.g., the Com-mons Social Change Library in Australia and the Pacific Pawa Up Fellowship by the Pacific Climate Warriors), legal services (e.g., Blue Ocean Law in Guam), and support for funding, promotion, and research (e.g., Climate Media Center and the Climate Council).

Another innovation emerging across Oceania is the rise of distributed network campaigns (see Mogus & Liacas, 2016 for a detailed overview). These campaigns are structured around a centralized professional organization that supports local grassroots groups, each working to influence power holders in their own local areas. A recent analysis of the Divestment and Stop Adani distributed network campaigns in Australia indicate that this structure enables the effi-cient development and sharing of campaign strategies, increased volunteer capacity to organize actions, and increased resources for targeting multiple power holders (Gulliver et al., 2021a). In the face of government resistance, we also see evidence that many groups have successfully pivoted to target corporate entities (Gulliver et al., 2019). In sum, this data suggests that the

Oceanian environmental movement has proven able to adapt and mobilize on environmental issues by responding specifically to localized political contexts.

The future of environmental activism in Oceania

The Oceanian environmental movement today is a diverse, vibrant, and highly active ecosystem composed of myriad local groups connected through regional umbrella organizations, transnational alliances, and distributed network campaigns. This ecosystem was built over a long journey overcoming the tyranny of distance and impacts of colonization. This chapter has examined three factors that have influenced this evolution: the diversification and growth of mobilization structures, the impact of localized framing and action repertoires, and the effects of the political context in influencing action repertoires and mobilization structures.

Our analysis indicated that shared grievances built on localized concerns were highly effective in creating the mobilization structures that drove the growth of anti-nuclear activism in the 1960s. However, since that time, there has been a slow uptake in prioritizing environmental justice and anti-colonial perspectives. There are positive signs that groups are now increasingly seeking to incorporate calls for environmental justice within their messaging and action (Schmidt, 2012), while Islanders are proactively responding to climate change (Luetz & Nunn, 2020; Walshe & Stancioff, 2018). In tandem with these calls for justice, the movement for Indigenous rights across Oceania has boosted organizing and activism skills. In New Zealand, for example, the Māori land rights movement in the 1980s educated a wave of young Māori who now demand justice and the right to self-determination (Mills, 2009). In Australia, new Indigenous-led organizations (e.g., SEED) support struggles to recognize and retain traditional owners' land rights. We suggest that prioritizing support for organizations seeking environmental justice and developing unifying narratives for socially just, sustainable societies is an important direction of future research and movement growth.

We also highlighted the importance of localized message framing and political opportunities in understanding the trajectories and characteristics of environmental activism across the four Oceanian regions. Differing levels of political openness and responsiveness influence divergent action repertoires: in Australia, new groups have formed to undertake radical action in response to non-responsive federal systems and imbalanced corporate power, whereas in other countries, there is a relative preference for non-contentious environmental advocacy supported by political action on environmental issues. These dynamics warrant further empirical analysis. We suggest that broad-based environmental coalitions using multiple action repertoires on multiple environmental issues may be able to help reduce polarization (e.g., in Australia), in conjunction with shaping message framing in ways that resonate with greater numbers of the population. This is particularly important given that new threats, such as deep-sea mining (Shewry, 2017a), are continually emerging. Responding effectively to these threats will require groups to collaborate across large distances, secure financial resources, and maintain influence in political decision-making against corporate interests. Maintaining capacity in smaller island NGOs to undertake this work also remains challenging, with environmentalists who rise through the ranks often recruited into other jobs or abroad (McLeod et al., 2019).

Despite these challenges, our overview of the Oceanian environmental movement demonstrates its power to adapt, evolve, and persist. As local mobilization structures adapt to the challenges of mitigating and responding to climate change, new action repertoires are enabling both local action and international coordination while capitalizing on the political opportunities available to effect change. In Oceania, as elsewhere in the world, the calls of environmental movements for change, balance, and recognition of our connection to nature are being listened to by new generations. Our analysis demonstrates that the Oceanian environmental movement is not only using its power to amplify those calls but also effecting meaningful environmental change in thousands of local communities scattered across its vast ocean reaches.

Note

1 Further information on each group in the chapter is available in the environmental group database on the Open Science Framework: https://osf.io/4s8e2.

References

Aguon, J. 2021. *The properties of perpetual light*. Mangilao, Guam: University of Guam Press.

Almeida, P., & Stearns, L. B. 1998. Political opportunities and local grassroots environmental movements: The case of Minamata. *Social Problems, 45*(1), 37–60.

Andrews, K. T., & Caren, N. 2010. Making the news: Movement organizations, media attention, and the public agenda. *American Sociological Review, 75*(6), 841–866.

Barnett, J., & Adger, W. N. 2003. Climate dangers and atoll countries. *Climatic Change, 61*(3), 321–337.

Barr, S., & Pollard, J. 2017. Geographies of transition: Narrating environmental activism in an age of climate change and 'peak oil'. *Environment and Planning A: Economy and Space, 49*(1), 47–64.

Beeson, M., & McDonald, M. 2013. The politics of climate change in Australia. *Australian Journal of Politics and History, 59*(3), 331–348.

Benford, R. D., & Snow, D. A. 2000. Framing processes and social movements: An overview and assessment. *Annual Review of Sociology, 26*(1), 611–639.

Berube, C. 2021. *Sea Shepherd: The evolution of an eco-vigilante to legitimized maritime capacity builder*. Rhode Island: CIWAG Maritime Irregular Warfare Studies.

Bryant-Tokalau, J. J. 1995. The myth exploded: Urban poverty in the Pacific. *Environment & Urbanization, 7*(2), 109–130.

Chape, S. 2006. *Review of environmental issues in the pacific region and the role of the pacific regional environment programme*. Workshop and Symposium on Collaboration for Sustainable Development of the Pacific Islands: Towards Effective e-Learning Systems on Environment, Okinawa, 27–28 February 2006.

Climate Action Tracker. 2020. *Australia country summary*. https://climateactiontracker.org/countries/australia/

Connell, J. 2015. Food security in the island Pacific: Is Micronesia as far away as ever? *Regional Environmental Change, 15*(7), 1299–1311.

Cooke, A. N., Fielding, K. S., & Louis, W. R. 2016. Environmentally active people: The role of autonomy, relatedness, competence and self-determined motivation. *Environmental Education Research, 22*(5), 631–657.

Dalton, R. J. 2015. Waxing or waning? The changing patterns of environmental activism. *Environmental Politics, 24*(4), 530–552.

Dalton, R. J., Recchia, S., & Rohrschneider, R. 2003. The environmental movement and the modes of political action. *Comparative Political Studies, 36*(7), 743–772.

Dalton, R. J., Van Sickle, A., & Weldon, S. 2010. The individual-institutional nexus of protest behaviour. *British Journal of Political Science*, 51–73.

della Porta, D., & Diani, M. 2009. *Social movements: An introduction*. Hoboken, NJ: John Wiley & Sons.

Diani, M. 2003. Leaders or brokers? Positions and influence in social movement networks. In Diani, M. (Ed.), *Social movements and networks: Relational approaches to collective action*, pp. 105–122. Oxford: Oxford University Press.

Downes, D. 2000. The New Zealand environmental movement and the politics of inclusion. *Australian Journal of Political Science, 35*(3), 471–491.

Edwards, B., McCarthy, J. D., & Mataic, D. R. 2018. The resource context of social movements. In *The Blackwell companion to social movements*, pp. 79–97. Hoboken, NJ: Blackwell Publishing Ltd.

Fielding, K. S., & Hornsey, M. J. 2016. A social identity analysis of climate change and environmental attitudes and behaviors: Insights and opportunities. *Frontiers in Psychology*, 7.

Fielding, K. S., & Louis, W. R. 2020. The role of social norms in communicating about climate change. In Holmes, D., & Richardson, L. (Eds.), *Research Handbook on communicating climate change*. Northampton, MA: Edward Elgar Publishing.

Fielding, K. S., McDonald, R., & Louis, W. R. 2008. Theory of planned behaviour, identity and intentions to engage in environmental activism. *Journal of Environmental Psychology, 28*(4), 318–326.

Fry, G. 1994. International cooperation in the South Pacific: From regional integration to collective diplomacy. In Axline, W. A. (Ed.), *The political economy of regional cooperation*, pp. 136–177. London: Printer Press.

Fry, G., & Tarte, S. 2016. *The new Pacific diplomacy*. Canberra: ANU Press.

Galbreath, R. 2002. Displacement, conservation and customary use of native plants and animals in New Zealand. *New Zealand Journal of History, 36*(1), 36–50.

Garner, G. 1964. *Women with Ban the Bomb banner during Aldermaston Peace March, Brisbane, 1964*. Brisbane: Fryer Library, University of Queensland.

George, N. 2011. Pacific women building peace: A regional perspective. *The Contemporary Pacific, 23*(1), 37–72.

Giugni, M., & Grasso, M. T. 2015. Environmental movements in advanced industrial democracies: Heterogeneity, transformation, and institutionalization. *Annual Review of Environment and Resources, 40*(1), 337–361.

Gruby, R. L. 2017. Macropolitics of Micronesia: Toward a critical theory of regional environmental governance. *Global Environmental Politics, 17*(4), 9–27.

Gulliver, R. E., Fielding, K. S., & Louis, W. 2020. The characteristics, activities and goals of environmental organizations engaged in advocacy within the Australian environmental movement. *Environmental Communication, 14*(5), 614–627.

Gulliver, R. E., Fielding, K. S., & Louis, W. R. 2019. Understanding the outcomes of climate change campaigns in the Australian environmental movement. *Case Studies in the Environment* (2019), *3*(1), 1–9.

Gulliver, R. E., Fielding, K. S., & Louis, W. R. 2021a. *Civil resistance against climate change*. Washington, DC: International Center on Nonviolent Conflict. Available at: https://www.nonviolent-conflict.org/ blog_post/civil-resistance-against-climate-change-insights-from-australia/

Gulliver, R. E., Wibisono, S., Fielding, K. S., & Louis, W. R. 2021b. *Psychology of effective activism*. Cambridge: Cambridge University Press.

Harris, J. 2011. Hiding the bodies: The myth of the humane colonisation of Aboriginal Australia. *Aboriginal History Journal, 27*, 79–104.

Harris, U. S. 2014. Communicating climate change in the Pacific using a bottom-up approach. *Pacific Journalism Review, 20*(2), 77–96.

Hartman, Y., & Darab, S. 2014. The power of the wave: Activism Rainbow region-style. *M/C Journal, 17*(6).

Hau'Ofa, E. 2008. *We are the ocean: Selected works*. Honolulu: University of Hawaii Press.

Hoad, D. 2015. Reflections on small island states and the international climate change negotiations (COP21, Paris, 2015). *Island Studies Journal, 10*(2), 259–262.

Hornsey, M. J., Harris, E. A., Bain, P. G., & Fielding, K. S. 2016. Meta-analyses of the determinants and outcomes of belief in climate change. *Nature Climate Change, 6*(6), 622–626.

Hutchins, B., & Lester, L. 2006. Environmental protest and tap-dancing with the media in the information age. *Media, Culture & Society, 28*(3), 433–451.

ICUN. 2018. *The IUCN red list of threatened species*. https://goo.gl/xo5vA4

Keown, M. 2018. Waves of destruction: Nuclear imperialism and anti-nuclear protest in the indigenous literatures of the Pacific. *Journal of Postcolonial Writing, 54*(5), 585–600.

Kirsch, S. 2007. Indigenous movements and the risks of counterglobalization. *American Ethnologist, 34*(2), 303–321.

Lauren, N., Fielding, K. S., Smith, L., & Louis, W. R. 2016. You did, so you can and you will: Self-efficacy as a mediator of spillover from easy to more difficult pro-environmental behaviour. *Journal of Environmental Psychology, 48*, 191–199.

Lines, B. 2003. Portrait with background: Today's conservation activists. *People and Place, 11*(1), 25–33.

Locke, E. 1992. *Peace people : A history of peace activities in New Zealand*. Christchurch: Hazard Press.

Louis, W. R., Thomas, E. F., McGarty, C. A., Lizzio-Wilson, M., Amiot, C. E., & Moghaddam, F. M. 2020. The volatility of collective action: Theoretical analysis and empirical data. *Advances in Political Psychology*. https://doi.org/https://doi.org/10.1111/pops.12671

Luetz, J. M., & Nunn, P. D. 2020. Climate change adaptation in the Pacific Islands: A review of faith-engaged approaches and opportunities. *Managing Climate Change Adaptation in the Pacific Region*, 293–311.

Macintyre, M., & Foale, S. 2004. Politicized ecology: Local responses to mining in Papua New Guinea. *Oceania*, 74(3), 231–251.

McAdam, D. 2017. Social movement theory and the prospects for climate change activism in the United States. *Annual Review of Political Science*, 20, 189–208.

McAdam, D., McCarthy, J. D., & Zald, M. N. 1996. *Comparative perspectives on social movements: Political opportunities, mobilizing structures, and cultural framings.* Cambridge: Cambridge University Press.

McAdam, D., & Tarrow, S. 2018. The political context of social movements. In *The Wiley Blackwell companion to social movements*, pp. 17–42. Hoboken, NJ: John Wiley & Sons.

McAdam, D., Tarrow, S., & Tilly, C. 2003. Dynamics of contention. *Social Movement Studies*, 2(1), 99–102.

McCarthy, J. D., & Zald, M. N. 1977. Resource mobilization and social movements: A partial theory. *American Journal of Sociology*, 82(6), 1212–1241.

McDonald, R. I., Fielding, K. S., & Louis, W. R. 2013. Energizing and de-motivating effects of norm-conflict. *Personality and Social Psychology Bulletin*, 39(1), 57–72.

Mcleod, E., Bruton-Adams, M., Förster, J., Franco, C., Gaines, G., Gorong, B., James, R., Posing-Kulwaum, G., Tara, M., & Terk, E. 2019. Lessons from the Pacific Islands – Adapting to climate change by supporting social and ecological resilience. *Frontiers in Marine Science*, 6, 1–7.

McNamara, K. E., & Farbotko, C. 2017. Resisting a 'Doomed' fate: An analysis of the Pacific Climate Warriors. *Australian Geographer*, 48(1), 17–26.

McNeill, J. R. 2015. Of rats and men: A Synoptic environmental history of the Island Pacific. *The Face of the Earth: Environment and World History*, 5(2), 76–130.

Meyer, D. S. 2004. Protest and political opportunities. *Annual Review of Sociology*, 30, 125–145.

Micronesia Challenge. 2006. *Declaration of Commitment: "The Micronesia Challenge."* Palau: Office of Environmental Response and Coordination (OERC). Available at: http://palau.chm-cbd.net/micronesia-challenge/declaration-commitment-micronesia-challenge

Milfont, T. L., Osborne, D., Yogeeswaran, K., & Sibley, C. G. (2020). The role of national identity in collective pro-environmental action. *Journal of Environmental Psychology*, 72, 101522.

Milfont, T. L., & Schultz, P. W. 2016. Culture and the natural environment. *Current Opinion in Psychology*, 8, 194–199.

Mills, K. 2009. The changing relationship between Māori and environmentalists in 1970s and 1980s New Zealand. *History Compass*, 7(3), 678–700.

Mogus, J., & Liacas, T. 2016. *Networked change. How progressive campaigns are won in the 21st century.* Australia: The Commons: Social Change Library.

Moser, S. C. 2007. In the long shadows of inaction: The quiet building of a climate protection movement in the United States. *Global Environmental Politics*, 7(2), 124–144.

Murray, I. 2019. Looking at the charitable purposes/activities distinction through a political advocacy lens: A trans-Tasman perspective. *Oxford University Commonwealth Law Journal*, 19(1), 30–54.

Nunn, P. D. 2017. Sidelining God: Why secular climate projects in the Pacific Islands are failing. *The Conversation*, 17 May 2017. Available at: https://theconversation.com/sidelining-god-why-secular-climate-projects-in-the-pacific-islands-are-failing-77623

O'Brien, T. 2012. Environmental protest in New Zealand (1997–2010). *The British Journal of Sociology*, 63(4), 641–661.

O'Brien, T. 2013a. Fires and Flotillas: Opposition to offshore oil exploration in New Zealand. *Social Movement Studies*, 12(2), 221–226.

O'Brien, T. 2013b. Fragmentation or evolution? Understanding change within the New Zealand environmental movement. *Journal of Civil Society*, 1–13.

O'Brien, T. 2015. Social control and trust in the New Zealand environmental movement. *Journal of Sociology*, 51(4), 785.

O'Malley, N. 2014. Australia is a Pacific Island: It has a responsibility. *The Canberra Times*, 21.

Ourbak, T., & Magnan, A. K. 2018. The Paris Agreement and climate change negotiations: Small Islands, big players. *Regional Environmental Change*, 18(8), 2201–2207.

Parra, P. Y., Hare, B., Hutfilter, U. F., & Roming, N. 2019. *Evaluating the significance of Australia's global fossil fuel carbon footprint.* Melbourne: Climate Analytics.

Penjueli, M. 2015. Civil society and the political legitimacy of regional institutions: An NGO perspective. *Diplomacy*, 65.

Porta, D., & Rucht, D. 2002. The dynamics of environmental campaigns. *Mobilization: An International Quarterly*, 7(1), 1–14.

Ross, V. L., Fielding, K. S., & Louis, W. R. 2014. Social trust, risk perceptions and public acceptance of recycled water: Testing a social–psychological model. *Journal of Environmental Management, 137*, 61–68.

Rudiak-Gould, P. 2013. Climate change and tradition in a small island state: The rising tide. In *Climate change and tradition in a small Island state: The rising tide*. Oxfordshire: Routledge.

Schmidt, A. 2012. Justice in the public climate debate. *24th International Climate Policy PhD Workshop in Freiburg*. Available at http://www.klimacampus.de/uploads/pics/Schmidt_-Justice_in_the_Public_Climate_Debate_fullpaper-final.pdf.

Shewry, T. 2017a. Going fishing: Activism against deep ocean mining, from the Raukumara Basin to the Bismarck Sea. *South Atlantic Quarterly, 116*(1), 207–217.

Shewry, T. 2017b. Introduction. *South Atlantic Quarterly, 116*(1), 170–173.

Shoraka, M. 2017. *New Zealand declares nuclear free zone 1963–1985*. Global Nonviolent Action Database.

Smith, J., Louis, W. R., Terry, D. J., Greenaway, K. H., Clarke, M. R., & Cheng, X. 2012. Congruent or conflicted? The impact of injunctive and descriptive norms on environmental intentions. *Journal of Environmental Psychology, 32*(4), 353–361.

Snow, D. A., Vliegenthart, R., & Ketelaars, P. 2018. The framing perspective on social movements: Its conceptual roots and architecture. In *The Wiley Blackwell companion to social movements*, pp. 392–410. Hoboken, NJ: John Wiley & Sons.

Steffens, N. K., Haslam, S. A., Ryan, M. K., & Kessler, T. 2013. Leader performance and prototypicality: Their inter-relationship and impact on leaders' identity entrepreneurship. *European Journal of Social Psychology, 43*(7), 606–613.

Steiner, C. E. 2015. Empowerment in the face of climate change in the pacific. *The Contemporary Pacific, 27*(1), 147–180.

Stern, P. C. 2000. New environmental theories: Toward a coherent theory of environmentally significant behavior. *Journal of Social Issues, 56*(3), 407–424.

Tarte, S. 2014. Regionalism and changing regional order in the Pacific Islands. *Asia and the Pacific Policy Studies, 1*(2), 312–324.

The Australia Institute. (2020). *Climate of the Nation*, June.

Tilly, C. 1978. *From mobilization to revolution*. Boston: Addison-Wesley.

Titifanue, J., Kant, R., Finau, G., & Tarai, J. 2017. Climate change advocacy in the Pacific: The role of information and communication technologies. *Pacific Journalism Review, 23*(1), 133–149.

Walker, C. 2016. *30 years of creative resistance*. Australia: The Commons: Social Change Library.

Walshe, R. A., & Stancioff, C. E. 2018. Small Island perspectives on climate change. *Island Studies Journal, 13*(1), 13–24.

Walton, G., & Barnett, J. 2008. The ambiguities of environmental conflict: Insights from the Tolukuma Gold Mine, Papua New Guinea. *Society and Natural Resources, 21*(1), 1–16.

Wittner, L. S. 2003. The forgotten years of the world nuclear disarmament movement, 1975–78. *Journal of Peace Research, 40*(4), 435–456.

Wittner, L. S. 2009. Nuclear disarmament activism in Asia and the Pacific, 1971–1996. *The Asia Pacific Journal, 7*(25), 1–11.

Wolf, C., Levi, T., Ripple, W. J., Zárrate-Charry, D. A., & Betts, M. G. 2021. A forest loss report card for the world's protected areas. *Nature Ecology and Evolution, 5*(4), 520–529.

Zchout, S. L., & Tal, A. 2017. Conflict versus consensus strategic orientations among environmental NGOs: An empirical evaluation. *Voluntas, 28*(3), 1110–1134.

PART 2

Issues and movement sectors

10

ENVIRONMENTAL CONSERVATION

Angela G. Mertig

Introduction

At first glance, the idea of environmental conservation is very broad. If conservation is the act of protecting something (a resource) so that current as well as future users can use or appreciate that thing, then environmental conservation would seem to entail much of what occurs within environmental movements around the globe. Indeed, throughout the history of environmental movements globally, the term has taken on numerous meanings, especially among the public as well as those who take part in environmental movements. These different meanings have included protection (with only limited human use) of natural land areas and of wild and native species, direct management (with higher levels of allowable human use) of land areas and species, promotion of environmentally sustainable economic activities, and the practice of environmentally friendly behaviors in one's household.

Some of these meanings would seem to contradict each other. Namely, a significant difference occurs between protecting (with limited human use) natural areas and species and allowing for greater use through direct management. This distinction reflects an often contentious and ongoing debate about the appropriate emphasis within environmental protection efforts, also known as the "people versus parks dispute" (Büscher and Fletcher, 2020: 1). Movement scholars, at least in the US and from a "Western" (or Global North) perspective more generally, have typically referred to the idea of protection with only limited human use as "preservation", while the term "conservation" has often been more narrowly reserved for those protective activities that allow for greater human use and management. Even so, at least within the US, both preservation and conservation ideas have frequently been lumped together under the moniker of "the conservation movement". In this chapter, I focus on this definition of environmental conservation: namely, movements that have focused on the preservation (protected, limited use) and conservation (managed, greater use) of natural areas and species.

As a sector within environmental movements, environmental conservation developed as one of the earliest approaches to addressing environmental issues, and it remains a key component of contemporary environmental movements. The development of environmental conservation has a particularly long and accomplished history within the United States, which is the primary focus here. Undoubtedly, numerous conservation-type activities have occurred throughout the world and throughout history, but the approach to conservation that developed in the US has

 DOI: 10.4324/9780367855680-12

significantly influenced how conservation has been undertaken in other areas of the world within the last two centuries (Büscher and Fletcher, 2020; Western, 2020).

In this chapter, I begin by providing an overview of how environmental conservation developed within the United States. I then turn to discussing how this sector fits within the contemporary US environmental movement, focusing specifically on key organizations that have developed over time to address conservation issues. While I focus largely on what are considered "mainstream" conservation organizations, I briefly discuss a handful of organizations that deliberately operate outside the mainstream movement (i.e., groups that are typically labelled "radical" in terms of their tactics and ideology). Because the US model of environmental conservation has heavily influenced the development of global environmental conservation efforts, I briefly discuss how the social justice issues that have plagued US environmental conservation efforts have had significant implications for environmental conservation globally. This leads to the final section of the chapter, in which I discuss broad developments in environmental conservation globally, with a specific emphasis on Western Europe as well as countries in the Global South.

Historical development of environmental conservation in the US

The notion of environmental conservation developed in the US with the growth of what is known as the conservation movement (CM), which started roughly around the turn of the nineteenth to the twentieth century. The movement as a whole was a negative reaction to the typical early-American approach to the natural world, with its laissez faire treatment and frequently wanton over-exploitation of natural resources (Petulla, 1977; Kline, 2011). Although the CM included preservationist as well as conservationist approaches to the treatment of natural resources, from the beginning, there were important, and often conflictual, distinctions between these two ideas and those who espoused them.

Even before the beginning of the CM, there were individuals who raised concern about over-exploitation of natural resources in the US. However, these expressions of concern grew in intensity and frequency as America grew more urbanized, industrialized, and settled (Petulla, 1977; Nash, 1982; Kline, 2011). The earliest voices for protecting the environment tended to be preservationist in orientation. Often voiced by intellectuals, arguments for protecting the environment were couched in religious and spiritual terms that were increasingly appealing to the general American public as fears grew about how urbanization and industrialization would transform the structure and morality of society. Early preservationists were heavily influenced by the Romantic movement of the early 1800s and the related movement of Transcendentalism (Kline, 2011). Beginning as a literary movement in Europe, the Romantic movement spread to the US, espousing beliefs in the natural world as a source of inspiration, imagination, creativity, freedom, and beauty (Petulla, 1977). Romanticism had a strong influence on Transcendentalism, which protested dominant religious strains in the early to mid-1800s in the US. Transcendentalists promoted communion with God through nature, arguing that people needed to get out of over-developed cities (Nash, 1982). Likewise, numerous reform movements in the early 1800s blamed social evils, such as crime and alcohol abuse, on industrialization and urbanization; the solution to such evils was to put people back in nature. Nature, therefore, needed to be preserved as a refuge for humanity.

In 1890, the US Census declared that the US frontier was closed; there was no longer a clear "frontier line" distinguishing settled and unsettled portions of the continent. The frontier was a potent symbol to the young American nation, denoting limitless resources, rugged individualism, and freedom (Nash, 1982). According to the "Frontier Thesis", espoused by historian Frederick Jackson Turner shortly after the closing of the frontier, the frontier, and the wild nature contained on the frontier, were uniquely American phenomena, which laid the foundation for American democracy. The declaration of the "end" of the frontier was, on the one hand, a symbol of progress, but it was also a forceful symbol of loss. The combination of the closing of the frontier, high rates of industrialization and urbanization, and rapid depletion of initially vast resources, such as the extinction of the passenger pigeon and the near extinction of the bison, fueled growing efforts to preserve and protect nature. The progressive movement at the turn of the twentieth century further amplified these concerns by advocating reform of people's living conditions; protecting nature was seen as central to improving the condition of humanity (Petulla, 1977).

The Conservation Movement

The CM sprang from the social context of the closing of the frontier, increasing urbanization and industrialization, and increasing public spiritual and social concerns about these changes. From the beginning, the CM in the US was split into two broad camps: preservationists and conservationists (Hays, 1959; Nash, 1982). This distinction remains, at least to some degree, within the contemporary environmental movement (i.e., organizations can be considered more preservationist or more conservationist in overall orientation). Preservationist-oriented organizations and activists have focused their efforts on setting aside protected areas (e.g., parks, forests, wilderness areas) and protecting wildlife and their habitats from human use. From the preservationist perspective (or social movement "frame"; see, e.g., Snow et al., 1986), it is vital to protect wilderness and wildlife because nature is "an important component in supporting both the physical and spiritual life of humans" (Brulle, 2000: 98). Preservationists, particularly contemporary ones, have also focused on the importance of preservation for the sake of nature itself as well as for the "ecological services" that nature provides to human society. Conservationism emphasizes stewardship of natural resources and their continued use for "the greatest good to the greatest number" of people (Pinchot, 1910). This utilitarian philosophy was meant, through government regulation and scientific management, to overcome extensive misuse of natural resources embodied in the laissez faire approach to natural resources that dominated US history to this point.

Early preservationist interests within the CM were led by naturalist and writer John Muir, who was instrumental in establishment of Yosemite National Park (California) in 1890. (Previously, Yellowstone [Wyoming, 1872] was established as the first national park, largely due to scientific curiosity about its geothermal activity. As noted by Western 2020, this was the first time that any nation had set aside land as a national park.) Like previous preservationists, Muir often couched his concern for the environment in spiritual terms, referring to stones as altars and to Yosemite as a temple. In 1892, Muir organized the first social movement organization (SMO) devoted to preserving wild lands, the Yosemite Defense Association (soon renamed the Sierra Club). A key activity of the group was to sponsor hiking trips to the mountains to enlist people's support for their protection. Initially limited to the San Francisco area, the club has since become one of the foremost environmental organizations in the nation, focusing on numerous issues in addition to preservation of land. Several other prominent preservationist organizations also formed during this time, including the New York Zoological Society (renamed the Wildlife Conservation Society in 1993 to more accurately reflect the broader emphasis it had since developed) and forerunners of the National Audubon Society (named after John James Audubon), which has been devoted heavily to bird protection. Preservationist goals became institutionalized in the US National Park Service (NPS, 1916), whose purpose has been to preserve natural beauty and facilitate recreation in the national parks. The first director of the NPS became an early leader of the National Parks Conservation Association (1919), a preservation organization founded to promote the expansion and protection of the US National Park System.

Although organized activities on behalf of preservationism began somewhat earlier than organization on behalf of conservationism (Brulle, 2000), the latter had greater success in having its ideas associated closely with the larger movement (hence, the term "conservation" movement). Conservationist interests, led by Gifford Pinchot, the nation's first professional forester, had less organized public support; however, they were very successful at getting their agenda incorporated into new government agencies – largely due to the close relationship between Pinchot and President Theodore Roosevelt (Hays, 1959). Conservationist ideas were institutionalized in the form of the US Forest Service and the Bureau of Reclamation, both of which focus on "multiple use" of resources, as opposed to the NPS, which preserves land purely for recreational or aesthetic purposes.

Despite obvious intersections between preservation and conservation, they represent distinct ideologies that have led to conflicts throughout the history of environmentalism in the US. Preservationists and conservationists came into direct opposition, for example, in the struggle over damming the Hetch Hetchy river valley inside Yosemite National Park, a battle that lasted from 1908 to 1913. Conservationists and developers led by Gifford Pinchot urged that the dam be created to provide water to San Francisco, which had been ravaged by an earthquake in 1906, while John Muir and other preservationists decried despoliation of a beautiful valley inside a national park (Nash, 1982). President Roosevelt, a great believer in conservation and a friend to both Muir and Pinchot, ultimately sided with Pinchot, and the valley eventually was dammed.

After the heyday of the CM and the subsequent battle over the Hetch Hetchy dam, conservationist and preservationist issues diminished considerably in the public eye. However, despite the advent of two world wars and the Great Depression, these issues did not entirely disappear. Conservationist causes were prominent in the administration of President Franklin Roosevelt, who initiated several programs as part of his New Deal to address the social devastation of the Great Depression as well as several contemporaneous environmental disasters, including massive flooding and the loss of topsoil in Oklahoma and adjacent states during the Dust Bowl. Two important conservationist-oriented organizations also began at this time: the Izaak Walton League (1922) and the National Wildlife Federation (1936). While both organizations were founded by sportsmen eager to protect natural resources for recreational uses (Mitchell, 1989), the latter has moved substantially beyond purely conservationist causes, becoming one of the country's largest environmental organizations.

Preservationism was also being advanced during this time. Aldo Leopold, a forester who later became America's first professional wildlife manager, successfully initiated the idea of granting wilderness status to undeveloped portions of the National Forests. In the 1930s, he developed a philosophy termed "the land ethic", which promoted the idea that humankind is part of nature rather than its master. In 1935, he and another forester, Robert Marshall, organized the Wilderness Society, which continues to be a strong advocate for preservation of wilderness (Nash, 1982). Other preservationist organizations that developed during this time were Defenders of Wildlife (1947; initially Defenders of Furbearers) and the Nature Conservancy (1951; initially the Ecologists Union). Both the Wilderness Society and the Sierra Club successfully fought against two dam projects in the 1950s and 1960s, one in Dinosaur National Monument (Colorado/Utah) and one in the Grand Canyon (Arizona). Preservationists went on to influence passage of the Wilderness Act of 1964, which immediately protected nine million acres of federally owned wilderness. These successes garnered greater public attention for preservationist causes at a critical point in American history; greater public attention to the efficacy of collective action helped fuel development of the contemporary environmental movement in the late 1960s.

Environmental conservation and the contemporary US environmental movement

The shift from the CM to what is considered the contemporary environmental movement marked an important ideological change in US environmental consciousness. Contemporary environmentalism encompassed a much broader set of concerns than either conservationism or preservationism (Mertig et al., 2002). Even so, these earlier concerns did not disappear. If anything, the new ideology of environmentalism was grafted onto the older agenda, augmenting rather than displacing it (Brulle, 2000; Johnson, 2006). Older organizations that had developed during the CM era gradually evolved to incorporate both older and newer concerns. The older organizations, especially those that were more preservationist in orientation, actually fared quite well in terms of drawing supporters and resources, despite general ideological transformation in the movement (Carmichael et al., 2012). While numerous new environmental organizations sprouted during this time, they also eventually added the more traditional foci to their repertoires. The older organizations were also immensely helpful to newer environmental organizations, providing an important source of encouragement, strategies, activists, and resources (Mitchell, 1989; Mitchell et al., 1992). The focus of environmental conservation has thus remained an integral part of the contemporary environmental movement.

Environmental conservation continued to resonate strongly with the general public even though other environmental issues appeared to take center stage at this time. For instance, a large oil spill off the California coast in 1969 (the Santa Barbara oil spill) generated concerns not only about pollution of waters and beaches but also about damage to wildlife, as the media presented pictures of oil-soaked birds and dying animals. Due in part to increases in education, affluence, and leisure time after WWII, people were spending more time outdoors, prompting many to revere and then fight for landscapes threatened by development (Gale, 1972). In fact, preservationist organizations such as the Sierra Club had been sponsoring nature trips since their inception in order to recruit members and enlist supporters for protecting natural areas (Faich and Gale, 1971). Concern about conservation/preservation of natural areas and species has thus remained important in mobilization efforts during the contemporary environmental movement.

The contemporary movement was ushered in with important legislative and policy changes. Prior to 1970, the federal government's role in environmental issues and policy had been mostly that of public lands manager (Kraft and Vig, 2003). This role aided both conservationist and preservationist causes as the government set aside some public land for full protection from human uses and other land for multiple use, including government-regulated activities such as logging and mining. In the 1970s, however, the federal government began to take on a greater role by passing a plethora of legislation and developing environmental policy in line with the broader agenda of contemporary environmentalism. Well-publicized laws, such as the National Environmental Policy Act (1969) and the Clean Air Act (1970), were aimed directly at mitigating environmental damage, but conservation/preservation issues were also important in policy and legislative initiatives at this time. Among the best-known examples are the Endangered Species Act (1973) and the Alaska National Interest Lands Conservation Act (1980), which promoted wildlife protection and set aside a vast portion of Alaska for protection (Vig and Kraft, 2003).

The contemporary environmental movement is probably one of the largest social movements in the US in terms of organizations, memberships, and resources (Brulle, 2000). Literally thousands of groups and organizations in the US work for environmental causes (Kempton et al., 2001). Many are relatively short lived, small, of only local or regional scope, or focused on specific topics. Such groups provide critical support to environmental conservation and preservation efforts in the US and even internationally. Brulle (2000) estimates total membership of environmental organizations in the US to be somewhere between 19 and 41 million. He notes that there are over 1,000 such organizations commanding budgets in excess of $100,000.

Despite the large number of organizations overall, a relatively small set of organizations comprises what is commonly known as the core or "mainstream" of the US environmental movement (Bosso, 2005). These organizations are typically national or international in scope; have relatively large memberships; garner substantial resources, including membership revenues and grants from government, foundations, and corporations; and often wield considerable name recognition and political power. Despite occasional dips in memberships and resources, the number of these organizations and the size of their memberships has generally remained strong (Mitchell et al., 1992; Bosso, 2005). As a testament to the continuing importance of environmental conservation and preservation within the movement, preservationist organizations, among all organizations involved in the US environmental movement, generally have the highest net worth and the largest annual incomes and are among those groups with the largest memberships and staffs. One of the preservationist organizations, the Nature Conservancy, stands out for its formidable monetary heft. Brulle (2000) notes that the Nature Conservancy actually distorts analyses of movement resources as it commands a substantial portion of the income received by all environmental organizations (roughly 30%) and an even larger portion of their assets (66%).

Mainstream conservation and preservation organizations in the US

Most major national environmental organizations in the US can be considered "hybrids" in that they address a host of issues that run the gamut from traditional (conservation and preservation) to more contemporary environmental concerns (e.g., pollution and toxic waste; see, for example, Johnson, 2006). As noted earlier, the older and more traditionally conservationist and preservationist organizations now spend considerable time and effort on broader environmental issues, and the newer organizations also devote substantial resources to conservation- and preservation-type issues. While distinctions in focus have become considerably blurred for many of these organizations, environmental organizations in the US can still be usefully distinguished in terms of primary philosophy and program focus (Brulle, 2000). Table 10.1 lists the large national organizations most commonly considered preservationist or conservationist in orientation (Brulle, 2000; Mertig et al., 2002; Mertig, 2007). Most of these organizations began prior to the advent of contemporary environmentalism and are direct or slightly delayed products of the earlier CM.

As can be seen in Table 10.1, in 1960, the membership of conservation/preservation organizations was quite small, probably fewer than 150,000 members combined; today, most of these organizations individually have substantially more than 150,000 members. While there is likely some overlap in membership across organizations, their total membership is nevertheless considerable. Some of the organizations (e.g., Sierra Club, National Audubon Society, National Wildlife Federation) also have hundreds of chapters or affiliates nationwide, which adds to their influence at local, regional, and national levels. Since the 1960s, most of the older organizations have also made significant shifts toward greater professionalization and bureaucratization,

Table 10.1 Major environmental conservation/preservation organizations in the United States[1]

Organization	Year Founded	Estimated membership (in thousands)			Budget (Million $US)
		1960	1990	2008	2008
Sierra Club	1892	15	560	550	43
Wildlife Conservation Society	1895	4	34	105	95
National Audubon Society	1905	32	600	600	44
National Parks Cons. Assoc.	1919	15	100	300	17
Izaak Walton League	1922	51	50	40	3
The Wilderness Society	1935	(10)	370	255	17
National Wildlife Federation	1936	na	975	4,400*	96
Defenders of Wildlife	1947	21	80	180	7
Nature Conservancy	1951	2	600	1,000	245
World Wildlife Fund	1961	--	940	1,200	60
Rainforest Alliance	1986	--	18	19	9
Conservation International	1987	--	55	70	50

1 Membership information for 1960 and 1990 reported in Mertig (2007). Membership and revenue information for 2008 taken from Swarthout (2008). Numbers in parentheses are estimates; na=not available.
* National Wildlife Federation changed its definition of membership, which now includes all those enrolled in its school programs (Bosso, 2005). Bosso (2005) estimates the Federation's 'actual' membership in 2003 to be 650,000.

seeking substantial growth in membership and resources and significant shifts in organizational structure and staffing (Mitchell, 1989). The Izaak Walton League is unique, however, as it did not focus on recruiting a mass membership; it continued recruiting through its chapter structure rather than using newly developed direct-mail techniques, maintaining a fairly constant membership size over time (Mitchell et al., 1992). Interestingly, membership growth of preservationist groups since the 1970s has been more pronounced, on average, than that of other prominent national environmental groups. While some preservationist organizations (e.g., the Wilderness Society) have experienced small membership losses in recent years, others, such as the Nature Conservancy and the World Wildlife Fund, have grown substantially.

Although all these organizations continue to focus heavily on more traditional issues of conservation and preservation, over time, they have incorporated an even more diverse array of issues. For instance, the Sierra Club started to incorporate more contemporary environmental issues (such as pollution and overdevelopment) into its agenda in the mid-1960s (Mitchell, 1989). Similarly, the Izaak Walton League added water pollution to its agenda early on, being the first of the older organizations to do so (Mitchell, 1989). Defenders of Wildlife was initially concerned about the mistreatment of individual animals (in fur trapping and at roadside zoos) but has widened its concerns to include habitat and wildlife protection (Mitchell, 1989; Mitchell et al., 1992). Likewise, the Wildlife Conservation Society, initially founded as a zoological society, began working on a more expansive agenda as early as the 1940s (Mertig, 2007).

These organizations have also broadened geographically. While the older organizations (pre-1960) all started as regional- or national-level organizations (e.g., the Sierra Club initially focused on the Sierra Nevada mountains of California), they have grown more internationally focused. Indeed, two of these older organizations are among the top four BINGOs (Big

International Non-Governmental Organizations) in terms of size and influence (Wildlife Conservation Society; Nature Conservancy) (Hance, 2016; Larsen, 2016). The newest organizations listed in Table 10.1 deliberately began as internationally focused organizations (e.g., Conservation International began when several members of the Nature Conservancy concluded it was not international enough) (Mitchell et al., 1992). Two of these organizations are the other two groups identified as being among the top four BINGOs (World Wildlife Fund, which is affiliated with the Swiss-based BINGO World Wide Fund for Nature; Conservation International) (Hance, 2016). Hence, of the top four BINGOs, three are US-based organizations, and the fourth has a large affiliate in the US. According to Hance (2016), "together these four groups employ over ten thousand people in nearly a hundred countries and have a collective annual income of around $2 billion".

"Radical" conservation/preservation organizations in the US

The organizations listed in Table 10.1 are considered "mainstream" environmental organizations in the US. As such, their tactical choices are relatively traditional and non-controversial, including research, education, litigation, and lobbying activities. (The Nature Conservancy also engages in the relatively unique tactic of purchasing land to ensure its protection.) However, there are some organizations that use more "radical" approaches. In addition to engaging in some of the tactics used by mainstream organizations, these groups employ direct-action tactics usually considered too extreme by the mainstream. Greenpeace, an organization focused on a broader contemporary environmental agenda (and hence not listed in the table), is typically considered the pioneer of direct-action techniques, such as plugging effluent pipes and steering inflatable rubber boats between whalers and whales. However, groups such as Earth First! (EF!), founded in 1980; Sea Shepherd Conservation Society (founded in 1977); and Earth Liberation Front (ELF) (founded in 1992) have gone even further, condoning property damage and sabotage. They have contaminated fuel for bulldozers used at logging operations, nailed spikes into trees to hinder potential timber sales, rammed drift-net ships, and committed arson at a ski resort (Manes, 1990; Scarce, 1990). In fact, Paul Watson, founder of Sea Shepherd, was ousted from Greenpeace, a group he helped co-found, for being too radical. The radical groups target property, taking pains to ensure that people are not physically harmed by their activities. Because of their direct challenge to property rights, all these groups have come under the watchful eye of the Federal Bureau of Investigation. Indeed, ELF was designated in the early 2000s as a top US domestic terrorist group (Wall Street Journal, 2001).

Radical groups often justify their actions through the ideology of "deep ecology". In contrast with "shallow" ecology, the term radicals use for the anthropocentric worldview of mainstream organizations – even preservationist ones – deep ecology revolves around a biocentric ethic and a passionate self-identification with nature (Manes, 1990; Scarce, 1990; Devall, 1992). Rather than protecting the environment for the sake of humans, radicals seek to protect nature for nature's own sake. In this sense, they take environmental preservation even further than most earlier preservationists, who argued that nature needed protection for the aesthetic, recreational, or even ecological interests of humans. Activists' identification with nature – solidified through frequent contact with wilderness and rituals like the "Council of All Beings" – is thought to transform them from activists working to protect nature to nature working to protect itself (Devall, 1992).

Organizationally, radical groups attempt to avoid the professionalization and bureaucratization they despise in mainstream organizations (Scarce, 1990). Likewise, they operate on significantly smaller budgets and have substantially fewer members than mainstream organizations.

Membership size is often difficult to determine for these groups, especially for ELF, which has operated almost entirely in a covert manner. EF! may have as many as 10,000 to 15,000 members nationally and worldwide (Mitchell et al., 1992; Wall, 1999) while Sea Shepherd has around 35,000 members (Swarthout, 2008). In 2008, Sea Shepherd reported revenue of $500,000 while revenues for EF!, which can only be estimated from subscription income for its journal, were roughly $85,000 in 2005 (EF! Journal, personal communication).

US environmental conservation and social justice issues

Before getting into a brief discussion of how environmental conservation efforts have developed internationally, it is important to broach the subject of how social justice issues have played out within the US environmental movement. The US model of environmental conservation has had significant sway in the development of international efforts. Therefore, social justice issues that have played significant roles within the US have not only infiltrated US versions of environmental conservation but have also necessarily influenced global efforts at environmental conservation. Some critics contend that historic and contemporary racism, as well as classism and sexism, make national and global efforts at environmental conservation not only socially problematic but also environmentally ineffectual (see, e.g., Kashwan, 2020).

The historical development of the CM in the US has had classist, racist, and sexist undertones from its very beginning (Taylor, 2016). White, urban elites comprised the vast bulk of those who advocated for conservation and preservation throughout the heyday of the CM. Recently, at least three of the early conservation/preservation organizations have acknowledged the racist backgrounds of their founders (Sierra Club, Wildlife Conservation Society, National Audubon Society) (Kashwan, 2020; WCS, 2021). After coming under fire within the past few decades for being staffed and led predominantly by white males, numerous environmental organizations, including those focused largely on conservation and preservation, have attempted to increase the proportion of women and people of color they employ (Dowie, 1995). Their efforts have had mixed results thus far (Green 2.0, 2020). It should also be noted that the membership base for most of the environmental conservation/preservation organizations, like environmental organizations more broadly, has also tended to be drawn from the wealthier sectors of society and to be largely white (Dowie, 1995). As is the case for many SMOs within the US, members tend to be highly educated and are typically above average in income and occupational prestige (Morrison and Dunlap, 1986).

In addition to the historical background and contemporary makeup of these organizations, the fundamental framing of conservation in the US has racist and classist implications. Because environmental conservation within the US has been heavily focused on preservation, particularly of pristine wilderness areas, it has often been given the label of "fortress conservation" (Büscher and Fletcher, 2020; Kashwan, 2020). In this model, when an area is designated for protection, any human inhabitants are to be removed (at least eventually, if not immediately), and any prior human uses (usually already minimal in order to warrant designation as a protected area) are extensively limited or completely stopped. As Büscher and Fletcher (2020: 15) note, "the North American wilderness area stood as the main model for the global expansion of protected areas in the nineteenth and twentieth centuries" (see also Western, 2020). This exclusionary approach to environmental protection has garnered extensive critique, especially from Indigenous peoples, rural communities, and other groups of people who have been displaced for development of protected areas. Often, displaced people were already engaging in effective conservation practices within the areas that have now become off limits to them (Kashwan, 2020). This has especially been the case in the Global South, where the US model has been championed by BINGOs; other large international conservation organizations, such as the World Conservation Union (IUCN) (Markham and van Koppen, 2007); and many other US-based organizations operating internationally, as well as "corrupt government officials and commercial tourism and safari operators" (Kashwan, 2020: 5). Indeed, Büscher and Fletcher (2020) argue that much of mainstream contemporary conservation efforts, based on the classic North American model, go hand in hand with capitalism, promoting conservation activities that significantly enhance social inequities, minimally (if at all) protect the environment, and extensively boost capitalist interests.

Environmental conservation beyond the US

Environmental conservation has become a significant international phenomenon. While global conservation efforts have had a predominant focus on North American–style conservation, there are no doubt numerous exceptions, and there is certainly a greater breadth and variety of activities than can be fully discussed here. In this section, I provide an overview of how environmental conservation efforts have developed around the world, focusing specifically first on Western Europe and then on the Global South.

Environmental conservation in Western Europe

Given the strong historical connections between the US and Western Europe, it is not surprising that there are significant parallels in how environmental conservation has developed in these areas. Both the US and Western European nations share a predominant framing of conservation as protection of "relatively untouched areas" (Markham and van Koppen, 2007: 3). Of course, the definition of "relatively untouched" necessarily varies given vast differences in types and availability of areas that could be protected. As Markham and van Koppen (2007: 3) note: "Particularly in densely settled European nations, nature protection has also focused on protecting traditional and scenic rural landscapes of cultivated fields, hedgerows, woodlots and managed forests". Hence, within Western Europe, environmental conservation has included a much greater emphasis on protection of "cultural and often agricultural landscapes" (Büscher and Fletcher, 2020: 14) than has occurred in the US. Because of these differences, it should also be noted that the strong distinction between preservation and conservation that has dominated environmental protection efforts in the US., particularly early on, has not been a predominant theme within Western Europe (Van Koppen and Markham, 2007). Environmental protection efforts within Western Europe have, from the onset, been focused on protection and management of lands and species that allowed for continued human use (similar to "pure" conservation in US history).

There have also been substantial parallels in the historical development of environmental conservation organizations in the US and Western Europe. Both areas witnessed the beginning of conservation efforts and development of the first organizations devoted to environmental conservation in the late nineteenth century, continuing into the early twentieth century; likewise, both saw a second "wave" of environmental conservation as part of a larger, broader environmental movement that began in the 1960s and 1970s (Van Koppen and Markham, 2007). The initial development of conservation concerns in both areas had strong ties to Romanticism and was strongly motivated by both scientific and aesthetic interests. During the second wave, older conservation organizations gained in support and membership in both areas, expanding their agendas to incorporate broader environmental concerns, and, in both areas, newer environmental organizations also incorporated more traditional conservation issues. Environmental conservation organizations, like organizations in the broader environmental movements, have likewise undergone substantial professionalization and bureaucratization in both the US and Western Europe, with the latter benefitting substantially from support from the European Union (Markham and van Koppen, 2007; Van Koppen and Markham, 2007). National environmental conservation organizations are among the largest organizations in the environmental movements in the US and Western Europe.

Yet another parallel is the development of a radical flank of environmental conservation groups. Indeed, growth of a radical flank is typical within successful social movements (see, e.g., Haines, 1984). For instance, there have been numerous EF! actions within the UK and other Western European countries (as well as in Eastern Europe and Australia) (Wall, 1999). Even more recently, development of Extinction Rebellion, beginning in 2018 with a "Declaration of Rebellion against the UK government", has promoted the spread of direct, non-violent action in the interest of environmental protection throughout Europe and beyond (Extinction Rebellion, 2021).

Environmental conservation in the Global South

While conservation in the Global South has been strongly influenced by the model of conservation developed in the US and other areas of the Global North, there are also important distinctions. The movement within the North has been strongly driven by large, bureaucratic SMOs, with extensive access to and expertise in media dissemination and scientific and legal deliberations (Guha and Martinez-Alier, 1997). The movement within the South, at least at local or regional levels, has typically had less access to such resources and has typically heavily involved peasants and Indigenous communities (see, e.g., Guha and Martinez-Alier, 1997; Kashwan, 2017; Munck, 2020). Large organizations (e.g., BINGOs) working in the Global South have typically come from outside the countries in which they do their conservation work and, while helpful in many ways, have also been heavily criticized for being ineffective and perpetuating social inequities (Larsen, 2016; Shanee, 2019).

The context of conservation efforts has also differed significantly. Historically, conservation began in the US after or while original inhabitants of natural areas were removed from the land; in contrast, conservation in the Global South has ordinarily occurred "alongside people" (Western, 2020: 173), albeit often not in ways conducive to social justice. Conservation in the North, particularly in the US, therefore, has largely occurred apart from (and despite) the livelihoods not only of conservationists but also of anyone who might have been living on and using the land. Conservation efforts in the South have often developed as an integral component of the lives and livelihoods of those who use the land (Guha and Martinez-Alier, 1997). Local social movement actors in the South are often not just fighting to protect natural areas and species but also fundamentally fighting to protect their own livelihoods and communities and to gain or maintain access to and control over natural resources. As Guha and Martinez-Alier (1997: 19) point out, Northern-style wilderness protection has its counterparts in the South, but it comes "typically from [people with] patrician backgrounds, and. . . [has] shown little regard for the fate of human communities". Outside actors, such as BINGOs, are often critiqued for discussing rights of peasants and Indigenous peoples only when it serves the end of conservation rather than it being important in and of itself (Kashwan, 2017). Many places designated as key areas for conservation by BINGOs are replete with social inequities (e.g., repression, poverty, insecure land tenure), and despite local fights to promote socially inclusive conservation efforts, conservation, especially when promoted by governments and BINGOs, remains highly exclusionary (Kashwan, 2017; Thing et al., 2017; Shanee, 2019).

Despite being in the "post-colonial era", most countries in the Global South are still encumbered by the impacts of colonialism. While the first wildlife reserves in Africa, for instance, date back to the late 1800s and the first parks to the early 1900s, the 1950s saw a spurt of conservation activity among colonial governments who feared "that approaching African independence might spell doom for wildlife" (Western, 2020: 172). Additionally, after gaining independence, national leaders throughout much of Africa took control over territories, eventually designating them as reserves in order to gain support from international agencies and conservation organizations (Kashwan, 2017). Conservation practices, at least by governments and large, often outside conservation organizations, began and continue to operate in fairly exclusionary ways in many African countries (Brockington and Scholfield, 2010; Matusse, 2019; Musavengane and Leonard, 2019). Although governments within many African countries have extensive sway over conservation, the influence of BINGOs, such as the World Wide Fund for Nature and the Wildlife Conservation Society, has grown substantially since decolonization (Brockington and Scholfield, 2010). While the African Wildlife Foundation, a fairly influential NGO, is headquartered within Africa (Kenya) and several NGOs active in sub-Saharan Africa hail from other African countries (predominantly from South Africa), almost half of the organizations active in sub-Saharan Africa are based in the Global North (23% based in the US) (Brockington and Scholfield, 2010).

Post-colonial leaders in numerous Asian countries, as occurred in Africa, also centralized control over their hinterlands (Kashwan, 2017). Despite recent efforts in many of these countries to develop more inclusionary conservation practices, the legacy of "fortress conservation" handed down from the Northern (US) model of conservation and colonial governance remains (see, e.g., Thing et al., 2017; Foggin, 2018). Because local communities in many nations in the Global South are heavily reliant upon and have already been acting as stewards of natural resources, they frequently find themselves conflicting with governmental and BINGO-driven conservation efforts. Guha and Martinez-Alier (1997) argue that this has led in many places (they especially note this happening in India) to an even greater emphasis on direct action (often viewed as more "radical" by mainstream organizations) by local social networks and villages (e.g., the Chipko movement). There are, however, instances when outside conservation interests are credited with playing more positive roles, such as in Taiwan (likely due to greater economic development; see, e.g., Wang and Hosoki, 2016) and in former countries of the Soviet bloc (e.g., Kazakhstan), where international organizations have assisted local NGOs in politically fluctuating and often still authoritarian contexts (Wu, 2021). Interestingly, China, despite governmental efforts to promote greater and more inclusive conservation, has recently made it more difficult for international conservation organizations to support the growing number of national NGOs (Dai and Spires, 2020).

Conservation efforts in Latin America face many of the same issues as other areas of the Global South. Despite growing emphasis globally on inclusion of indigenous and peasant communities, these communities are often still kept out of conservation planning and from their traditional lands and practices (see, e.g., Shanee, 2019; Azcona et al., 2020). Even so, throughout Latin America, locals, peasants, Indigenous groups, and even trade unionists are heavily involved in local fights to conserve natural resources (Munck, 2020). BINGOs and other international NGOs are greatly involved in Latin American conservation efforts, often being sought out by but also heavily critiqued by local NGOs for their tendency to overlook the importance of local communities (Shanee, 2019). However, Munck, (2020: 109) argues that a new "social movement discourse has emerged in Latin America . . . the Buen Vivir discourse. . . [that] translates poorly into English as 'living well'". He states that this new grassroots philosophy not only opposes Western notions of how nations should develop but also defines "a new relationship between nature and humanity . . . in which community values and respect for nature take priority" (Munck, 2020: 109–110). While a few Latin American governments have incorporated these priorities in their constitutions (e.g., Ecuador, Bolivia), he notes that these governments (similar to those of other countries in the Global South) continue to take actions that contradict these tenets. Even so, he holds out hope for this new philosophy, stating that "nevertheless, it breaks the Northern grip on development theory and the dominant approach to ecology, which, for all its ostensible globalism, is mainly North-centric" (Munck, 2020: 111). Indeed, this fight to redefine environmental conservation more broadly and in tune with both nature and the rights of human communities is shared throughout the Global South and is increasingly being advocated by organizations and activists in both the North and South.

Conclusion

As demonstrated throughout this volume, environmental movements overall are extremely heterogeneous, have undergone significant transformations, and have become core institutionalized aspects of numerous societies. Environmental conservation, as a key early segment of environmentalism, shares these characteristics. Not only is it highly heterogeneous in topical scope, tactics utilized, and organizational/activist composition, but it has also faced important transformations over time and become institutionalized around the globe.

Environmental conservation remains an influential sector within environmental movements, globally as well as within the US and in numerous (if not most) countries. Indeed, future research should focus more heavily on how conservation efforts have been occurring in non-Western/non–Global North contexts. Ultimately, environmental conservation, while ostensibly a broad concept, has been narrowly defined. The approach to conservation that developed in the US (and was paralleled to a great degree in Western Europe) has had a significant – some would say constraining and problematic – impact on how conservation has unfolded elsewhere. While there have likely been substantial positive impacts in terms of expanding the amount of area set aside as protected, there have also been substantial negative impacts through expansion of social inequities, and, as some critics have alleged, this model may not have effectively led to environmental protection. The current exorbitant rate of extinctions, habitat loss, and environmental degradation, coupled with growing social injustices, demand that we address these issues.

It should also be noted that much of the conservation discussion has centered on large-scale, typically government-backed protection of large swaths of public land and natural features. Yet there is growing interest in private land conservation, particularly in the Global North (US, Canada, Europe, Australia) but also in parts of the Global South (e.g., Latin America) (Johnson, 2014; Stein, 2015). Additional research is needed on how efforts at private land conservation are occurring around the globe and whether this can effectively aid in larger goals of environmental conservation while also addressing social justice issues that have plagued typical approaches to conservation.

Büscher and Fletcher (2020) discuss how contemporary conservation efforts globally have increasingly become split between those more amenable to incorporating human groups and uses into management of areas and species (referred to as "new conservationists") and those who have doubled down on the fortress conception of conservation ("neoprotectionists"). They propose an alternative approach ("convivial conservation") that builds upon "positive aspects in both radical proposals" (Büscher and Fletcher, 2020: 158). Ultimately, to paraphrase their argument, it is time to rethink environmental conservation.

References

Azcona, Ivett, Erin Estrad Lugo, Ana Arce Ibarra and Eduardo Baltazar. 2020. Meanings of Conservation in Zapotec Communities of Oaxaca, Mexico. *Conservation and Society*. 18 (2), 172–182. doi: 10.4103/cs.cs_18_135.

Bosso, Christopher J. 2005. *Environment, Inc.: From Grassroots to Beltway*. Lawrence: University Press of Kansas.

Brockington, Dan and Katherine Scholfield. 2010. The Work of Conservation Organisations in Sub-Saharan Africa. *The Journal of Modern African Studies*. 48 (1), 1–33. doi: 10.1017/S0022278X09990206.

Brulle, Robert J. 2000. *Agency, Democracy, and Nature: The U.S. Environmental Movement from a Critical Theory Perspective*. Cambridge, MA: MIT Press.

Büscher, Bram and Robert Fletcher. 2020. *The Conservation Revolution: Radical Ideas for Saving Nature Beyond the Anthropocene*. London, UK: Verso.

Carmichael, Jason T., J. Craig Jenkins and Robert J. Brulle. 2012. Building Environmentalism: The Founding of Environmental Movement Organizations in the United States, 1900–2000. *Sociological Quarterly*. 53 (3), 422–453. doi: 10.1111/j.1533-8525.2012.01242.x.

Dai, Jingyun and Anthony J. Spires. 2020. Grassroots NGOs and Environmental Advocacy in China. In Esarey, A. et al. eds. *Greening East Asia: The Rise of the Eco-developmental State*. Seattle: University of Washington Press.

Devall, Bill. 1992. Deep Ecology and Radical Environmentalism. In Dunlap, R. E. and Mertig, A. G. eds. *American Environmentalism: The U.S. Environmental Movement, 1970–1990*. Philadelphia: Taylor and Francis, 51–62.

Dowie, Mark. 1995. *Losing Ground: American Environmentalism at the Close of the Twentieth Century*. Cambridge: MIT Press.

Extinction Rebellion. 2021. *Extinction Rebellion*. Viewed 19 February 2021. https://rebellion.global/.

Faich, Ronald G. and Richard P. Gale. 1971. The Environmental Movement: From Recreation to Politics. *Pacific Sociological Review*. 14 (3), 270–287. doi: 10.2307/1388642.

Foggin, J. Marc. 2018. Environmental Conservation in the Tibetan Plateau Region: Lessons for China's Belt and Road Initiative in the Mountains of Central Asia. *Land*. 7 (2), 52. doi: 10.3390/land7020052.

Gale, Richard P. 1972. From Sit-In to Hike-In: A Comparison of the Civil Rights and Environmental Movements. In Burch, W. R., Cheek, N. H. and Taylor, L. eds. *Social Behavior, Natural Resources and the Environment*. New York: Harper and Row, 280–305.

Green 2.0. 2020. *Report Card*. Viewed 18 December 2020. www.diversegreen.org/2019-transparency-report-card/.

Guha, Ramachandra and Juan Martinez-Alier. 1997. *Varieties of Environmentalism: Essays North and South*. London, UK: Earthscan.

Haines, Herbert H. 1984. Black Radicalization and the Funding of Civil Rights: 1957–1970. *Social Problems*. 32 (1), 31–43. doi: 10.2307/800260.

Hance, Jeremy. 2016. Has Big Conservation Gone Astray? *Mongabay: News & Inspiration from Nature's Frontline*. Viewed 1 March 2021. https://news.mongabay.com/2016/04/big-conservation-gone-astray/.

Hays, Samuel. 1959. *Conservation and the Gospel of Efficiency*. Cambridge, MA: Harvard University Press.

Johnson, Erik. 2006. Changing Issue Representation among Major United States Environmental Movement Organizations. *Rural Sociology*. 71 (1), 132–154. doi: 10.1526/003601106777789800.

Johnson, Laura A. 2014. *An Open Field: Emerging Opportunities for a Global Private Land Conservation Movement*. Cambridge, MA: Lincoln Institute of Land Policy.

Kashwan, Prakash. 2017. *Democracy in the Woods: Environmental Conservation and Social Justice in India, Tanzania, and Mexico*. New York: Oxford University Press.

Kashwan, Prakash. 2020. American Environmentalism's Racist Roots have Shaped Global Thinking about Conservation. *The Conversation*. Viewed 10 September 2020. https://theconversation.com/american-environmentalisms-racist-roots-have-shaped-global-thinking-about-conservation-143783.

Kempton, Willett, Dorothy C. Holland, Katherine Bunting-Howarth, Erin Hannan and Christopher Payne. 2001. Local Environmental Groups: A Systematic Enumeration in Two Geographical Areas. *Rural Sociology*. 66 (4), 557–578. doi: 10.1111/j.1549-0831.2001.tb00084.x.

Kline, Benjamin. 2011. *First Along the River: A Brief History of the US Environmental Movement*. 4th edition. New York: Rowman and Littlefield.

Kraft, Michael E. and Norman J. Vig. 2003. Environmental Policy from the 1970s to the Twenty-First Century. In Vig, N. J. and Kraft, M. E. eds. *Environmental Policy: New Directions for the Twenty-First Century*. Washington, DC: Congressional Quarterly, 1–32.

Larsen, Peter B. 2016. The Good, the Ugly and the Dirty Harrys of Conservation: Rethinking the Anthropology of Conservation NGOs. *Conservation & Society*. 14 (1), 21–33. doi: 10.4103/0972-4923.182800.

Manes, Christopher. 1990. *Green Rage: Radical Environmentalism and the Unmaking of Civilization*. Boston: Little, Brown.

Markham, William T. and C. S. A. (Kris) van Koppen. 2007. Nature Protection in Nine Countries: A Framework for Analysis. In Van Koppen, C. S. A. and Markham, W. T. eds. *Protecting Nature: Organizations and Networks in Europe and the USA*. Northampton, MA: Edward Elgar, 1–33.

Matusse, Anselmo. 2019. Laws, Parks, Reserves, and Local Peoples: A Brief Historical Analysis of Conservation Legislation in Mozambique. *Conservation and Society*. 17 (1), 15–25. doi: 10.4103/cs.cs_17_40.

Mertig, Angela G. 2007. The 'Nature' of Environmentalism: Nature Protection in the USA. In Van Koppen, C. S. A. and Markham, W. T. eds. *Protecting Nature: Organizations and Networks in Europe and the USA*. Northampton, MA: Edward Elgar, 239–262.

Mertig, Angela G., Riley E. Dunlap and Denton E. Morrison. 2002. The Environmental Movement in the United States. In Dunlap, R. E. and Michelson, W. eds. *Handbook of Environmental Sociology*. Westport, CT: Greenwood Press, 448–481.

Mitchell, Robert Cameron. 1989. From Conservation to Environmental Movement: The Development of the Modern Environmental Lobbies. In Lacey, M. J. ed. *Government and Environmental Politics: Essays on Historical Developments Since World War Two*. Washington, DC: The Wilson Center Press, 81–113.

Mitchell, Robert Cameron, Angela G. Mertig and Riley E. Dunlap. 1992. Twenty Years of Environmental Mobilization: Trends Among National Environmental Organizations. In Dunlap, R. E. and Mertig, A. G. eds. *American Environmentalism: The U.S. Environmental Movement, 1970–1990*. Philadelphia: Taylor and Francis, 11–26.

Morrison, Denton E. and Riley E. Dunlap. 1986. Environmentalism and Elitism: A Conceptual and Empirical Analysis. *Environmental Management*. 10 (5), 581–589. doi: 10.1007/BF01866762.

Munck, Ronaldo. 2020. *Social Movements in Latin America: Mapping the Mosaic*. Newcastle upon Tyne, UK: Agenda Publishing.

Musavengane, Regis and Llewellyn Leonard. 2019. When Race and Social Equity Matters in Nature Conservation in Post-apartheid South Africa. *Conservation and Society*. 17 (2), 135–146. doi: 10.4103/cs.cs_18_23.

Nash, Roderick. 1982. *Wilderness and the American Mind*. 3rd edition. New Haven, CT: Yale University Press.

Petulla, Joseph M. 1977. *American Environmental History: The Exploitation and Conservation of Natural Resources*. San Francisco: Boyd and Fraser.

Pinchot, Gifford. 1910. *The Fight for Conservation*. Garden City, NY: Harcourt, Brace.

Scarce, Rik. 1990. *Eco-Warriors: Understanding the Radical Environmental Movement*. Chicago: Noble Press.

Shanee, Noga. 2019. Reclaim Conservation: Conservation Discourse and Initiatives of the *Rondas Campesinas*, North-Eastern Peru. *Conservation and Society*. 17 (3), 270–282. doi: 10.4103/cs.cs_18_6.

Snow, David A., E. Burke Rochford, Jr., Steven K. Worden and Robert D. Benford. 1986. Frame Alignment Processes, Micromobilization, and Movement Participation. *American Sociological Review*. 51 (4), 464–481. doi: 10.2307/2095581.

Stein, Peter. 2015. *The Global Reach of Land Trust Organizations*. Cambridge, MA: Lincoln Institute of Land Policy.

Swarthout, Kristy A. ed. 2008. *Encyclopedia of Associations: National Organizations of the U.S.* 45th edition. Detroit: Gale Group.

Taylor, Dorceta E. 2016. *The Rise of the American Conservation Movement: Power, Privilege, and Environmental Protection*. Durham, NC: Duke University Press.

Thing, Sudeep Jana, Roy Jones and Christina Birdsall Jones. 2017. The Politics of Conservation: Sonaha, Riverscape in the Bardia National Park and Buffer Zone, Nepal. *Conservation and Society*. 15 (3), 292–303. doi: 10.4103/cs.cs_15_2.

Van Koppen, C. S. A. (Kris) and William T. Markham. 2007. Nature Protection in Western Environmentalism: A Comparative Analysis. In Van Koppen, C. S. A. and Markham, W. T. eds. *Protecting Nature: Organizations and Networks in Europe and the USA*. Northampton, MA: Edward Elgar, 263–285.

Vig, Norman J. and Michael E. Kraft (eds). 2003. *Environmental Policy: New Directions for the Twenty-First Century*. Washington, DC: Congressional Quarterly Press.

Wall, Derek. 1999. *Earth First! and the Anti-Roads Movement*. London, UK: Routledge.

Wall Street Journal. 2001. *The Boy Who Cried 'ELF'*. Dow Jones & Company. Viewed 17 December 2020. www.wsj.com/articles/SB982110611254960728.

Wang, Cheng-Tong Lir and Ralph Ittonen Hosoki. 2016. From Global to Local: Transnational Linkages, Global Influences, and Taiwan's Environmental NGOs. *Sociological Perspectives*. 59 (3), 561–581. doi: 10.1177/0731121416648936.

WCS. 2021. *Wildlife Conservation Society*. Viewed 7 March 2021. www.wcs.org/.

Western, David. 2020. *We Alone: How Humans have Conquered the Planet and Can Also Save It*. London, UK: Yale University Press.

Wu, Fengshi. 2021. Relevance in a State of Flux: Civil Society and Environmental Protection in Kazakhstan. In Spires, A. and Ogawa, A. eds. *Civil Society and Authoritarian States in Asia*. London, UK: Routledge. Forthcoming.

11

ANTI-NUCLEAR MOVEMENTS IN THE US, EUROPE, AND ASIA

Helena Flam and Hiroshi Honda

Introduction

With the horrific consequences of the US nuclear bombs dropped on Hiroshima and Naga-saki freshly in mind, the first post–World War II anti-nuclear movements were directed against nuclear weapons. At this time, several governments aspiring to assert their power in the inter-national competition sought to redefine atomic power as peaceful, while launching R&D pro-grams on the military and civilian uses of atomic energy. In 1953, US President Dwight D. Eisenhower, in his "Atoms for Peace" speech to the UN General Assembly, listed the US, Can-ada, and the UK, as well as the Cold War enemy, the Soviet Union, as the nuclear powers of the time (IAEA). And, indeed, it was the USSR that built the first successful nuclear power plant (NPP) in Obninsk in 1954. In contrast, the early, malfunctioning US NPP had to be closed.

Initially, the Western bloc (North America, Western Europe, Japan, and Australia) and the Eastern bloc (the USSR and its satellites and client states) monopolized nuclear technologies. No East-West nuclear trade took place (Szarka, 2017). Later, the emerging economies – Iran, Iraq, India, and Pakistan – joined, Iran already in the late 1950s. The 1970 UN Non-Proliferation Treaty, Article IV, granted a right to all countries to do research and produce and use nuclear energy for peaceful purposes. By 2011, the year of the Fukushima accident, six countries gen-erated 70% of the world's nuclear power: the US, France, Russia, South Korea, Japan, and Germany (Hindmarsh and Priestley, 2017). By 2020, 31 countries had nuclear energy programs.

Rapid construction of NPPs from the 1950s through the 1980s was blocked by their costs and failures, and anti-nuclear social movements' capacity to mobilize public opinion and some political parties as allies, especially after the Three Mile Island (TMI) accident in 1979 in the US and the Chernobyl accident in 1986 in Ukraine. Still, in 1989, China signed an agreement to build an NPP in Pakistan.

In the 1990s, nuclear energy was reframed as a climate-friendly alternative to fossil fuels, and a nuclear giant, France, began pushing for the "nuclear renaissance". Even though popular and expert mobilization for stopping climate change in the long term undermined anti-NPP discourses, the "nuclear renaissance" did not materialize: about 60 states expressed interest to the International Atomic Energy Agency in the 2000s, but no new construction took place, and France only sold one NPP to Finland. Its problems in Finland let South Korea win a contract with the United Arab Emirates in 2010 – the first case of an emerging economy winning a tender from a newcomer country (Szarka, 2017). The Fukushima disaster in Japan in 2011 put

 DOI: 10.4324/9780367855680-13

a definite end to the "nuclear renaissance". Many countries confirmed their abstention from, moratorium on, or phasing out of their NPPs. Apart from Japan and Germany, the nuclear energy giants, such as France, Russia, South Korea, and the US, remained set on their course.

This chapter traces the development of the anti-nuclear movements in the US, Europe, and Asia. Several country case studies highlight specific policy and movement trends. Reflecting the state of the art, little is said about the authoritarian Russia and totalitarian China, two states that continue their ambitious NPP programs, facing, respectively, local (sometimes successful) and regional mobilization (Stsiapanau, 2017; Tarasova, 2017; Fang, 2017). Theoretical issues are discussed next and in the conclusion. Hiroshi Honda authored the text on Asia, and Helena Flam the remainder of this text.

Theorizing anti-nuclear movements

Competing models have been proposed to explain the successes and failures of anti-nuclear movements. They include some of the following elements: energy (import) dependence; costs sunk in the NPPs; dependence on nuclear power; strength of the anti-nuclear mobilization; (political) culture; direction of public opinion; direct contestation opportunities, widely known, following Kitschelt (1986), as "political opportunity structures", such as basic citizen rights; local veto rights; contestation relying on referenda or courts; movement alliances with the political parties or elites; and, later, the access of Green parties to political power.

Early research focused on the anti-nuclear movements in single states (Price, 1982). Later, it turned comparative. To explain state policies, it stressed the importance of either differing political cultures (Joppke, 1993) or state institutions or the interactive effects of encounters between the movements and the states (Kitschelt, 1986; Jasper, 1990: Rüdig, 1990; Flam, 1994; Kriesi et al., 1995; O'Neil, 1999). Separate and joint effects of protest, mobilized public opinion, and political allies on nuclear energy policy (spending) were also investigated (Giugni, 2007). Much more than Kitschelt, other authors stressed the role contingent factors and events have played in the sequence-for-sequence development of protest mobilization, political decisions, and policies concerning nuclear energy (cf Rüdig, 1990; Flam, 1994; Kriesi et al., 1995; O'Neil, 1999; Giugni, 2004; Müller and Thurner, 2017). The encounter and the processual approach shared much in common since they paid heed to the history of how movement discourses, their issue framing, and their identities refract the institutional context and government responses to the movement strategies and actions (Flam, 1994; Kriesi et al., 1995). This chapter echoes these approaches, although at times it leaves methodological nationalism behind to highlight international and transnational connections.

Anti-nuclear movements in the US and Europe

US

The US anti-nuclear protests at times included and at times moved between anti-militarist and anti-NPP mobilization. Although between 1945 and Eisenhower's speech, the US conducted 42 nuclear test explosions, the anti-nuclear protests against nuclear weapons testing, which took place at the Nevada Test Site (NTS), started in 1957, a few years after the NTS had been selected for this purpose in 1950 by the Atomic Energy Commission (AEC, 1946–1975). At the height of the Cold War in 1961, about 100,000 women in 100 cities marched against nuclear weapons, brought together by the Women's Strike for Peace, launching their anti-nuclear campaign. By the late 1980s, the NTS became a major anti-nuclear protest site in the US.

The first successful anti-NPP mobilization emerged in 1958, directed against an NPP project in Bodega Bay, north of San Francisco. In 1977 the anti-nuclear protest shifted for a couple of years to the energy issues. It received much public attention when 3,000 protesters from the Clamshell Alliance non-violently occupied the NPP in Seabrook, New Hampshire, and the Abalone Alliance held the first blockade at the Diablo Canyon Power Plant in California. In March of 1979, the TMI accident – a partial meltdown of one reactor and a leak of radioactive gases and iodine at the nuclear generating station – alarmed activists and the general public alike. That year, anti-nuclear protest peaked. For example, in April, 30,000 people marched in San Francisco for shutting down the Diablo Canyon Power Plant, while in June, about 40,000 people attended a protest rally at Diablo Canyon itself. New regulations for the nuclear industry contributed to the decline of the reactor construction program, discouraging further investments in the already-problematic nuclear energy power sector.

In 1982, the largest US and worldwide anti-nuclear protest took place – 1,000,000 people demonstrated in New York City against nuclear weapons and for an end to the Cold War arms race. In contrast, protest events against NPPs had declined below their pre-1979 level by 1980, and after the intensified mobilization following the Chernobyl nuclear plant accident in 1986, anti-nuclear mobilization disappeared from the media radar in the early 1990s (Giugni, 2007; Litmanen, 1998). The Fukushima NPP disaster of 2011 had no discernible impact on the United States Nuclear Regulatory Commission (USNRC) (1975–present, a successor to the AEC, both long criticized for collusion with the nuclear sector). In 2012, it licensed the construction of two additional reactors at the Vogtle Electric Generating Plant, but this was the first approval it made in over 30 years since the TMI accident (Rascoe, 2012). A dozen environmental and anti-nuclear groups sued unsuccessfully to stop this project. Many post-Fukushima applications for new reactors were suspended or cancelled while protesters targeted old NPPs, especially those with a Fukushima-like design. In 2013–14, several old reactors were closed or sued by state authorities. Still, today the US has the most nuclear reactors in the world: 96 out of 449 (WEF). Starting in 2019, the USNRC plans to extend operating licenses to about 20 plants for an unprecedented number of years, making new construction unnecessary.

The US stores the world's largest inventory of used nuclear fuel in pools or dry casks at 75 sites in 33 states (Kinsella, 2017). Although the Church Rock uranium mill spill in New Mexico in 1979 released more radioactivity than the TMI accident and contaminated Navajo County, Arizona, and the Navajo Nation, it did not receive comparable public attention. Today, hundreds of abandoned mines present environmental and health risks to the Navajo Nation and many communities in Utah, Colorado, New Mexico, and Arizona. Instead, the contestation has long focused on Yucca Mountain, designated by Congress in 1987 as the sole geologic repository for the US high-level radioactive nuclear waste. Even though the involvement of the Western Shoshone Nation in these protests had already begun in 1984, it was cast in anti-militarist terms (Futrell and Brents, 2003). First when the Western Shoshone formed the Shundahai Network with other activists in 1994 and connected to environmental, peace, justice, and Indigenous land rights communities across the globe, the protest focused on non-violent opposition to all nuclear weapons programs at the NTS and nuclear waste dumping at Yucca Mountain and the Skull Valley Reservation in Utah, taking up anti-extractivist issues.

Europe

Letting the EU stand as Europe's proxy, it can be said that the EU imports 55% of its energy, making it the largest energy importer in the world (WNA, 2020a: 1–3). In 2018, its demand for electricity was supplied by nuclear power (26%), fossil fuels and biomass (46%), renewables (28%) and hydro (12%). Currently, 15 of the 27 EU member states operate a total of 109 nuclear power reactors, generating over 25% of its electricity. Located in the EU-neighbor states, 53 Russian and Ukrainian and 4 Swiss units account for about 15% to 20% of the electricity in Europe (WNA, 2020a: 4).

The development and expansion of the nuclear energy programs began in the 1950s. However, no new NPPs have been constructed in the Netherlands since 1973 and in Belgium, Germany, Spain, Sweden, or the UK since the mid-to-late 1980s (Thurner et.al., 2017: 7). Only France and Finland have expanded their nuclear programs.

In 2020, France operated 58 reactors and stood for 50% of the EU's nuclear electricity (WNA, 2020a: 4–5). The UK had 15 reactors. Belgium, Spain, and Sweden each operated 7 reactors, and Germany and the Czech Republic had 6 reactors each. Finland, Hungary, and Slovakia ran 4 units, Bulgaria and Romania 2 units, and the Netherlands and Slovenia each 1 unit. Only Finland and four East European countries plan new units.

As in the US, in some European countries, anti-nuclear protest interwove anti-militarist and anti-NPP elements. Below the media radar, the first to protest against NPP in the 1950s were, for example, French and German farmers, worried about the landscape and the radioactive destruction of the soil and the crops. Urban and student protesters, some influenced by the US expertise and protests, joined them in the late 1960s. NPPs became framed as a threat to human life and health. The successful conclusion of protests in Wyhl in Germany in 1974–75, which included marches, protest camps, and an administrative court case against the NPP construction, became legendary. It is said to have inspired many anti-nuclear movements across Europe and beyond.

The European anti-nuclear movements developed and peaked in the 1970s, most losing their momentum in the 1980s. Along with the Chernobyl accident, they left a noticeable imprint on their governments and their nuclear policies. To offer some examples: while Austria pioneered nuclear exit/ban (1978, confirmed 1997), Sweden pioneered a phase out (1980) and Spain a moratorium on further construction (1984, confirmed 1994). In the Netherlands, a new NPP project was shelved (1986) and in 1994, a phase-out decision taken. Italy abandoned its NPP and construction plans between 1987 and 1990 (see Flam, 1994). The Swiss anti-nuclear movement stopped the construction of an NPP in 1988 and, in a 1990 referendum, achieved majority support for a 10-year construction moratorium. The Austrian, Swedish, Italian, and Swiss anti-nuclear movements also made themselves heard in referenda that curtailed government nuclear plans. In Spain, the socialist government took an anti-nuclear stand, while in the Netherlands, the Chernobyl disaster made pro-nuclear government parties turn around on the issue, heeding the anti-nuclear movement and its political party allies. The anti-nuclear movements led to the establishment of many new research centers and ministries. They helped Green parties gain parliamentary seats in Austria, France, Germany, Italy, and Switzerland.

Comparative research helps account for some counterintuitive outcomes. The pioneering French anti-nuclear energy movement was one of the strongest in Europe. Its mobilizing capacity notwithstanding, it failed to influence its government. The explanation for this failure includes a few crucial points: the centralized-militarized French state, controlling the mass media and the nuclear sector, set on asserting French sovereignty in relationship to Germany, the US, and NATO and the pro-nuclear stand of the French left-wing parties (Litmanen, 1998). In this context, a protest event proved decisive in causing the movement's demise. About 60,000 protesters marched against the Creys-Melville NPP in 1977. The march turned into a violent confrontation with the police – one demonstrator died, and several were hurt. The government-propagated view that the violence was caused by invading German hooligans caused the movement to lose its public legitimacy and its momentum. Lacking cohesion and political allies, it never recovered. The French Greens did not succeed like their counterparts in Germany, Switzerland, and Austria.

The case of the first state to pioneer a phase-out program in 1980, Sweden (followed by, for example, Holland in 1994 and Germany in 2001), is also counterintuitive. Its anti-nuclear movement emerged in the early 1970s and caused a heated nationwide controversy when it confronted pro-nuclear business, state, trade union, and Social Democratic forces. Moreover, the Swedish phase-out program was adopted in the absence of a Green party, which first emerged in 1981. Between 1980 and 2009, Sweden moved between phase-out and phase-in policy elements, reflecting the shifting outcomes of the tug of war between its pro-nuclear and anti-nuclear forces, wherein its (in principle) pro-nuclear and anti-nuclear political parties unexpectedly switched fronts. This applies to the initially wholeheartedly pro-nuclear Social Democratic (ruling) Party, which turned about, allowed the referendum on the issue after the TMI accident in 1979, and supported the initial phase-out decision in 1980 as well as to the Center (formerly Farmers') Party, which turned anti-nuclear in the 1973 elections but announced its pro-nuclear stand in 2005. The anti-nuclear Green Party endorsed some pro-nuclear policies in 2016, after it had formed coalition governments with the Social Democrats since 2014 despite its minority status. Sweden exemplifies a group of countries characterized by policy reversals – a research subject coming into its own (see Berengäs, 2009; Müller and Thurner, 2017). For this reason, it is worthy of a closer inspection.

Surprisingly, given its hydropower resources, Sweden was the largest per-capita importer of oil in the world in the 1970s. In 1973, Sweden, with its population at a mere eight million, embarked on one of the world's most ambitious nuclear energy programs: 24 nuclear reactors by 1990. However, as a result of an early anti-nuclear social movement and the Center Party's (and Left Party's) electoral positioning against it, the Center Party could join a coalition government in 1976, Social Democrats lost a clear government majority for the first time in 44 years, and Swedish plans dwindled down to 12 nuclear reactors by 1985, approved by parliament in 1979 (Flam, 1994; Berengäs, 2009). Between 1973 and 1980, the NPP issue came to dominate the national agenda. Contestation involved the local population and public officials and several flaring-up nationwide debates. The ruling Social Democratic Party saw significant internal opposition, anti-nuclear demonstrations and marches with between 2,000 and 7,000 protesters, and reversing national opinion polls. A Royal Energy Commission did not manage to neutralize the issue. The heated controversy culminated in a referendum in 1980, following the TMI accident, in which the phasing out of nuclear energy within 10 years received about 39% of the vote, although two additional referendum alternatives, each also calling for phasing out and 12 reactors before stating their differences, introduced much ambivalence and unduly split the vote among three referendum alternatives (Flam, 1994). Despite the referendum having only an advisory role, in the same year, the parliament approved a plan to phase out NPP by 2010. However, reactor construction continued until 1985.

By 2008, Sweden's NPPs supplied 45% and hydropower about 47% of its electricity. Biofuel and wind power were insignificant. Following the Chernobyl accident of 1986, the first effective phase-out plan came in 1988, when the Social Democrat–led government set 1995–96 as its beginning, marked by closing two nuclear reactors (Flam, 1994, Berengäs, 2009). In 1991, a center-right governing coalition overturned this decision because of sharp criticism from industry and labor unions pinpointing the high costs. But in 1992, after an incident at Barsebäck, all five reactors (and a reactor at Oskarsham) were ordered down for reconstruction. Acting against a parliamentary energy commission's report of 1995, in 1997, the Swedish parliament agreed to shut down two of Barsebäck reactors in 1998 and 2001. After another tug of war between the anti-nuclear and nuclear forces, two Barsebäck reactors were closed in 1999 and 2005. In 2006, following an incident at a Forsmark NPP, three reactors were closed (cf WNA 2020b).

A new center-right coalition government, including the Center Party (which, surprisingly, turned pro-nuclear in 2005, pinpointing that a phase out by 2010 would not allow the country to meet the national demand for energy) was voted into office in 2006. Sweden gradually abandoned all aspects of the phase-out policy in 2009 in the context of the "nuclear renaissance" and the post-Kyoto stress on reducing greenhouse gas emissions (Berengäs, 2009). Further, its non-confrontational, pro-environmental experts were included in deliberative institutions while vibrant local protest remained unconnected and kept invisible by the media, and official emphasis on NPP profitability and security limited discursive opportunities of effective contestation (Tarasova, 2017). Public opinion favored nuclear energy (Berengäs, 2009; Holmberg, 2020). In 2009, the Alliance government reversed the phase-out policy, envisioning the construction of a maximum of 10 reactors at the existing NPP sites; granting permits to replace reactors at the end of their technological and economic life; annulling the 1997 Nuclear Phase-Out Act; and lifting prohibition against new construction in the 1984 Nuclear Activities Act (Berengäs, 2009). However, the government would not finance Sweden's NPPs and would continue to impose an output tax introduced in the late 1990s. In 2009, this policy affected Sweden's 10 operating nuclear reactors in Oskarshamn (3), Forsmark (3), and Ringhals (4).

In 2010, Swedish Greenpeace protested the phase-in by invading the Forsmark NPP. After the Fukushima disaster of 2011, a large majority opposed nuclear power, and Greenpeace protested in Ringhals and Forsmark in 2012, since they did not meet European stress tests, but to no avail. However, a 2015 "commercial" decision closed down two reactors at Ringhals in 2019 and 2020 for lack of profit. Another political turnabout came in 2016 after the Red-Green government was reshuffled. It phased out the output tax by 2019, which by then amounted to one-third of the nuclear energy production costs. Ringhals 2, operating with mishaps since 1975, was closed in 2019, although the Swedish pro-nuclear parties pressed the Social Democratic–led coalition government to engage in pro-nuclear policy. In 2020, Sweden had seven active reactors at its three NPP – Forsmark (three), Oskarshamn (one), and Ringhals (three), where a plant due to be shut down in 2020 was still operating! (IAEA-SE, 2020).

As the Swedish case also shows, the early achievements of many Western European anti-nuclear movements explain in part why mobilization declined in most of the European countries in the 1990s, returning only briefly after the Fukushima accident in 2011 (cf. Thurner et al., 2017: 14–18). Germany constitutes an exception to the rule since it has featured a steady, sizeable mobilization against radioactive waste deposit transports and destination from the mid-1990s and was already mobilizing on the issue in the 1970s as not just its demonstrations in Germany but also its cooperation with the Australian anti-uranium movement and the related Aboriginal fight for land rights show (Milder, 2014, Kirchhof, 2014).

From the late 2000s, mainly Austria, Germany, and Switzerland have shown continuous high mobilization against nuclear energy policies, encouraged by multiple contestation possibilities (referenda, courts, federal structures) and by the institutionalized Greens, who are the strongest in Europe (compare to Thurner et al., 2017). Government nuclear power policies also play a crucial role as triggers of protest. Taking Germany as an example, large protests had little influence on federal policies until the Red-Green government came to power in 1998. Its phase-out decision (2001) was about to be reversed by a conservative government (2009–10), causing, for example 120,000 protesters to form a 120-kilometer-long human chain between the NPPs at Krummel and Brunsbuttel in 2010. Ostensibly, it was the Fukushima disaster of 2011 that made the government abandon its generous agreements with the nuclear sector, yet it had to be aware that, at the time, more than 100,000 people in hundreds of places participated in the so-called quiet demonstrations. In March 2011, 250,000 participants demonstrated against nuclear energy in Berlin, Cologne, Hamburg, and Munich. Two months later, Merkel's coalition government revived the phase-out plan without abolishing the fuel tax and, surprisingly, returned to fossil energy (the so-called double *Energiewende*) (WNA, 2019). Germany has shut down 8 of its 17 reactors and pledged to close the rest by the end of 2022. But the phase-out has been hindered by court cases fought by the nuclear sector. The radioactive disposal issue remains. Moreover, Germany draws 12% of its electricity from seven reactors while over 40% comes from coal (mostly lignite), making mobilization for renewable energy crucial.

Current EU policies in the energy area can be interpreted as a long-term achievement of the European anti-nuclear movements, the Greens, and their political allies. Since at least 2015, the EU has aimed at decreasing its dependence on energy imports and fossil fuels while increasing its reliance on renewables, with the overall aim of reducing its CO_2 emissions and contributing to a better climate (WNA, 2020a). The 2019 elections to the EU parliament were marked by the social movement's and Greens' enormous push for climate change (and against extreme right-wing parties and movements). In 2019, the European Commission announced the framework for the EU's Green New Deal, followed in 2020 by related documents and the European Green Deal, which do not offer any funds to help finance construction of new NPP (Lowry, 2020).

Anti-nuclear Movements in Asia

As of July 2020, 31 countries in the world operate 408 nuclear reactors, excluding 31 long-term halted ones. In a broader sense of Asia, state commitment to atomic energy continues in South Asia (India, Pakistan, Bangladesh) and the Middle East (Turkey, Iran, UAE). In contrast, Vietnam cancelled its nuclear projects with Russia and Japan. China stays committed to expanding atomic energy while its contribution to electricity generation has remained lower than its wind energy. China has 47 operating reactors, and South Korea has 22 while Taiwan is working only 4 units. Since the severe accident of 2011, Japan's nuclear fleet has dwindled down from 54 to around 9 (WNISR, 2020).

This section compares the anti-nuclear movements in Japan, Taiwan, and South Korea because they share a centralized yet liberal democratic political system that can, in principle, be responsive to issues raised by social movements. All three opted for nuclear power by relying on the United States as their major Cold War ally. They have also at least once over the past 10 years announced their will to phase out nuclear energy.

Japan

When Japan started nuclear development, the dominant party rule began, following the merger of conservative parties into the Liberal Democratic Party (LDP) in 1955. A powerful state-industry complex formed out of the Ministry of International Trade and Industry; nine private utilities monopolizing regional electricity markets; and the industrial groups, each with a flagship manufacturer (Toshiba, Hitachi, Mitsubishi). Tokyo Electric Company ordered its first nuclear plant at the Fukushima No.1 (Daiichi) site in the 1960s. Japan came to have the third-largest capacity of nuclear power next to the United States and France by 1985. But its atomic contribution to electricity production never went beyond the peak of 31% in 1997. The Fukushima disaster hindered all the overseas NPP projects by Japanese companies. The share of nuclear energy in electricity generation fell from 26% in 2010 to 0% in 2014. It had recovered only to 6.4% in 2018 (IEA, 2017–2019).

The liberal democratization of Japan immediately after World War II and the growing awareness of the atomic bomb casualties enabled an early start-up of an anti-nuclear weapon movement. The nationwide campaign against nuclear tests attracted more than 30 million signatures in 1955 following the radioactive fallout from US hydrogen bomb tests in the South Pacific in 1954. The initiatives of housewives fearful of food contamination by fallout soon gave way to leftist peace campaigns, which led to a split along partisan lines (Higuchi, 2008). And the LDP government was successful at disseminating a discourse on the peaceful use of nuclear energy, allegedly separable from the military use.

Among the Ban-the-Bomb campaign organizations establishing themselves in the 1960s, the Japan Congress against A- and H-Bombs began to frame the contamination caused by discharges from US military submarines as a pollution issue amid the growing protests against industrial pollution. The Japan Socialist Party (JSP) and the public sector unions behind the Congress began to help local groups mobilize against NPP around 1972. The Congress also helped establish the Citizens' Nuclear Information Center (CNIC) as the counter-expert institute in 1975. Together, they initiated a network of anti-nuclear groups from around the country and overseas (Honda, 2005: 78–88, 124–125).

Though the first wave of mobilization had declined by the mid-1980s, the Chernobyl accident of April 1986 gave it another impetus. With imported food items found contaminated in January 1987, CNIC and consumer cooperatives started radiation measurements (Kimura, 2016). The new mobilization wave gradually emerged among urban women in their 30s and 40s. However, the size and action repertoire of the mobilization was moderate. Even the biggest demonstration attracted only 20,000 in 1988. The petition campaigns gained much greater support. The campaign for a bill to abolish nuclear energy collected three million signatures from 1989 to 1991 (Honda, 2005: 203, 223), and the petition to the prefectural assembly attracted a million signatures in 1988: it demanded a referendum on the start of the first NPP in Hokkaido, the northernmost of Japan's four main islands. A series of accidents at nuclear facilities in the late 1990s and the early 2000s caused critical attitudes among governors of prefectures hosting nuclear facilities. A local referendum partly succeeded in aborting a new NPP (Hasegawa, 2004: 147–163).

But the LDP rule continued, except for a brief period between the summers of 1993 and 1994. The overall political opportunity structures were thus closed. The situation changed in 2009 when the Democratic Party of Japan (DPJ), which had formed from the mainstream of the JSP and other moderate forces in 1996, came to power for the first time.

A month after the Fukushima Daiichi (No.1) Plant exploded in March 2011, anti-nuclear demonstrations reappeared nationwide, reflecting a moderate resurgence of social movements throughout the 2000s. All 54 reactors located in 13 prefectures were stopped by spring 2012. Approval by the unstable government led by the DPJ to restart two reactors provoked protests in front of the prime minister's official residence and the Diet building every Friday beginning in March. They reached an unprecedented (organizer-provided) number of 200,000 participants by the end of June.

The DPJ administration sought ways of turning away from the pro-nuclear policy it had taken over from its conservative predecessors. In June 2012, two bills passed the Diet: a bill establishing a stricter regulator of nuclear facilities and a bill requiring the state to support voluntary evacuees and those remaining in a higher radiation dose area (Löschke, 2018). The DPJ-led cabinet finally proclaimed an Innovative Energy and Environmental Strategy in September 2012, aiming to abolish nuclear power in the 2030s.

These measures, combined with a public majority opposing re-activation of the reactors, constrained the pro-nuclear LDP when it returned to power in December 2012. It therefore has tried to make the damages from the accident invisible (Kimura, 2016) and has half-heartedly promoted renewable energy, favoring coal-fired power plants inland and overseas.

Taiwan

Taiwan had built six reactors, all operated by the state-owned utility Taipower, at three sites by 1985 (Hsiao et al., 1999: 255). Most of the atomic power plants were built close to the nation's capital, Taipei, causing much public concern. The fourth NPP at Lungmen near Taipei has long been under construction with no prospect of starting operation. But Taiwan, with its economy dominated by small- and medium-sized enterprises (Liu, 2015: 64), did not gain the capability to build NPP on its own. Power liberalization from the mid-1990s allowed independent power providers to sell electricity to Taipower. The private business has since increasingly opposed the completion of the fourth plant. Taipower's alteration of the original design and unwarranted assembly quality also raised concerns (Ming-sho Ho, 2014: 968–970). Nuclear energy provided 13.4% of the electricity in 2019, compared with its maximum share of 41% in 1988 (WNISR, 2019: 302).

Environmental protests rose in the 1970s in Taiwan (Liu, 2015). As in South Korea, liberal democratization in Taiwan coincided with the Chernobyl accident and helped organize anti-nuclear movements. With the termination of martial law in July 1987, victims of nuclear energy mobilized to have their voices heard. In December 1987, the Indigenous people of the small offshore island of Lanyu protested against dumping nuclear waste. In March 1988, Kongliao residents rose to oppose the fourth nuclear plant. In the 1990s, anti-nuclear demonstrations in Taipei City emerged, reaching a peak of more than 20,000 participants in 1994 (Ming-sho Ho, 2014: 971–972).

The Fukushima accident happened when the conservative Kuomintang Party (KMT) returned to power in 2008 and turned upon social movement activists. Facebook became a new mobilizing tool available to student activists. This accounts for the unprecedented anti-nuclear demonstration of March 2013, in which 200,000 participants protested in four big cities (Ming-sho Ho, 2014: 966, 975–976).

The local elections opened in the 1950s for competition, and the national legislature followed by steps starting in 1969 (Liu, 2015: 100). Fifty-five KMT and six opposition legislators proposed suspending the fourth nuclear plant project in 1985. After the Chernobyl accident, opposition politicians founded the Democratic Progressive Party (DPP) in September 1986 and adopted an anti-nuclear policy. Throughout the 1990s, the DPP built up its stronghold in and around Taipei. From 1994 to 1998, DPP incumbents supported local opposition by sponsoring four unofficial referendums on the fourth NPP in the national capital area (Ming-sho Ho, 2014: 970–971).

After the 2000 presidential election victory, the DPP, led by Chen Shui-bian, announced the end of the fourth NPP. However, the KMT-led opposition kept its parliamentary majority. In a compromise, the DPP government allowed the construction of the fourth NPP to resume in February 2001 while promising a national referendum. The DPP did not keep this promise, even though the referendum was finally legalized as a valid decision-making procedure in 2003 (Ming-sho Ho, 2014: 972–973).

Reacting to the Fukushima disaster, the DPP reverted to its previous anti-nuclear stance. In her unsuccessful presidential campaign of 2012, Tsai Ing-wen of the DPP proposed finishing the remaining construction work without putting the fourth NPP into operation (Ming-sho Ho, 2014: 978). After she finally became president in May 2016, she declared a goal of nuclear phase out by 2025. The Electricity Act Amendment of January 2017 legalized this goal. Pro-nuclear activists won a referendum in November 2018 to delete the target of 2025 from the Act, but the deadlines for extending operations of reactors had already passed by the time the referendum was held (WNISR, 2019: 105–107). Tsai Ing-wen won re-election in January 2020.

South Korea

Like Taiwan, South Korea made an initial decision to opt for nuclear power under the authoritarian regime, though its intention to acquire military capacity was rejected by the US (Richardson, 2017: 5; Ming-sho Ho, 2014: 968).

The close link between the state-owned corporations and the privately owned conglomerates known as *chaebol* played a crucial role in the nuclear industry's rapid development (Andrews-Speed, 2020: 47). The first commercial NPP began operations in 1978. The Korea Hydro & Nuclear Power Company owns all the nuclear units located at four sites. Nuclear power supplied 26.2% of the electricity in 2019, less than half of its maximum of 53.3% in 1987 (WNISR, 2020: 172). Because of the security concerns with North Korea, South Korean governments also justified atomic development with nationalistic discourses (Lee et al., 2018: 187). But since an overly aggressive tone was not appropriate for a divided nation (O'Neil, 1999: 180), the government framed the NPP construction as part of economic growth, technological modernization, and rural development. The state-owned KEPCO (Korea Electric Power Corporation) secured the first major international contract in 2009 to construct four reactors for the United Arab Emirates (UAE) (Richardson, 2017: 9).

Environmental protests staged by subsistence farmers and fishermen up to the 1980s were generally weak. The government redressed grievances by handing out cash collected from polluting factories and resettling victims (Liu, 2015: 85–87). Out of four sites, Younggwang (later renamed Hanbit) is the only site on the western side of the Korean Peninsula. It is near the city of Kwangju, where citizen protest met violent repression in 1980. The first reactor unit there was about to initiate a commercial operation after the Chernobyl accident. Several accidents occurred at Younggwang between 1987 and 1989, causing seashore pollution by thermal discharge from the plant. The compensation campaign began in 1988, and the government had to make concessions to the fish-raising industries (Lee et al., 2018: 191–192). The active social movement sector, including religious groups and farmers' unions, remained confined to the region.

The major issue for the South Korean anti-nuclear movement from the late 1980s to the 1990s was the candidate sites for a central nuclear waste repository. Occasional militant protest pushed the South Korean government to abandon 12 candidate sites (Hsiao et al., 1999: 263; Richardson, 2017: 6).

Following the Fukushima accident, the anti-nuclear movement underwent a moderate resurgence. Activists targeted existing plants, especially the lifetime extensions of the oldest reactors. Residents of the candidate sites of new plants at Samcheok and Yeongdeok also held an unofficial referendum in October 2014 and November 2015. The national government dismissed the result as non-binding (Richardson, 2017: 7–8). But a series of nuclear industry scandals kept mobilizing the anti-nuclear sentiment, starting with a station blackout of an old reactor in February 2012: whistle-blowing uncovered corrupt practices involving falsified testing reports on plant components, which resulted in the indictment of 100 individuals from the nuclear industry (Andrews-Speed, 2020: 54).

Compared with Taiwan, electoral politics did not provide any significant chances to the opposition forces in the authoritarian era of South Korea. Local self-government ended in 1961, and elections were mere instruments for securing power to the regime.

The military junta needed no party machinery equivalent to Taiwan's KMT rule (Liu, 2015: 66, 116). Even after the democratic transition, political parties found it difficult to challenge the nuclear power program widely seen as a nationalist project (Hsiao et al., 1999: 262). The National Assembly responded to the Fukushima accident merely by passing a bill establishing the Nuclear Safety and Security Commission in June 2011 (Richardson, 2017: 9).

A significant policy change came with President Moon Jae-In in 2017 with a campaign pledge to phase out nuclear energy. He organized a public debate commission, which allowed the construction work on Units 5 and 6 of Shin Kori (Kori No. 2) to continue while dropping plans for constructing six new reactors, including those at Samcheok and Yeongdeok. In December 2017, the administration approved the Basic Plan for Long-term Electricity Supply and Demand. According to it, nuclear power capacity would peak in 2022, before declining toward phase out by 2080 (WNISR, 2018: 85–87, 2019: 97–98). The ruling Democratic Party won the national election of 2020.

These case studies underscore the importance of the institutionalization of nuclear technologies constituted by the material presence of the nuclear sector and the way a nation legitimizes nuclear energy for contestation outcomes (O'Neil, 1999). Political opportunity structures, created primarily by party politics but also through other channels of expressing dissent, such as referendums, also play a role.

Japan was the first to succeed in institutionalizing nuclear energy. On the one hand, the atomic bombings in 1945 and the radioactive fallout from the hydrogen bomb tests in 1954 helped establish the Ban-the-Bomb movement, aided by the leftist parties and labor unions active within a broader wave of post-war peace and democratization movements. On the other hand, the conservative elites transformed the burgeoning consciousness of radioactive contamination from the fallout into public acceptance of a peaceful use of atomic power to achieve economic growth. The long-term LDP dominance and the rivalry among opposition parties guaranteed a stable development of Japan's nuclear industry.

The Fukushima accident of 2011 discredited the nuclear policy community and its ability to administer dangerous technology. The government by the center-left party urged a significant change in Japan's nuclear energy policy. But the return of the conservative LDP to power and vested interests have caused a policy standstill. Still, most of the gigantic Japanese nuclear sector, once comprising more than 54 reactors, was forsaken.

Taiwan and South Korea, both divided nations, could not take on overly nationalistic overtones in promoting nuclear energy, even under the authoritarian regimes. Each of them instead sought to institutionalize nuclear power as emblematic of the nation's mastery of an advanced technology that could contribute to economic development amid the oil crisis in the 1970s (O'Neil, 1999: 180).

Given the economy dominated by small- and medium-sized enterprises, Taiwan eventually failed to foster a viable domestic nuclear industry. While the atomic contribution to electricity production once reached a relatively high level, the reactors' location near the nation's capital undermined popular support for nuclear energy. Environmental protests in the 1970s merged with the liberal democratization movement of the 1980s. Receiving further impetus from the Chernobyl accident, the anti-nuclear movement emerged and identified nuclear energy as an artifact of the authoritarian regime. The newly instituted electoral competition helped the Democratic Progressive Party become a movement ally. The Fukushima accident also coincided with a resurgence of the protest movement in the late 2000s. Further, the DPP was repeatedly able to assume government power. Riding a tailwind from the disaster in Japan, it reverted to the phase-out path.

With the help of oligopolistic business groups and the state-owned utility, South Korea, under the authoritarian regime, succeeded in generating a nuclear industry capable of building 26 reactors and embarking on plant export. Environmental protests composed of subsistence farmers and fishermen were generally weak. The government legitimized the NPP as part of economic modernization and rural development. Even after the transition to liberal democracy, the two competing political party blocs remained aloof from the issue of nuclear energy. But the Fukushima accident facilitated anti-nuclear protests. The industry scandals in recent years caused widespread doubts about the ability of the nuclear policy community. They opened the way for the progressive political leaders to take up the phase out, but in a very long-time frame.

Conclusion

As the body of the text showed, the general trend is for the old NPPs to be phased out, closed, or replaced while upgrading the (seemingly) most secure NPPs. Anti-nuclear movements operating in competitive democratic systems have contributed to this trend. Equally important were the administrative, technological, and financial failures of the nuclear industry itself. Neither these failures nor variations in the national taxation of NPPs are sufficiently taken into account in the literature on the successes of anti-nuclear movements (see the literature review in Giugni and Grasso, 2015). Of the NPP giants, only France, Russia, and China still pursue their expansionist policies.

Turning to research gaps, anti-nuclear protest in Southern and Eastern Europe, Russia, and China has received little attention. Studies of Asian movements are advanced for Japan, South Korea, and Taiwan and also include India (Srikant, 2009) and Turkey (Temocin, 2018). Research on nuclear waste includes Asian nations to a limited extent (Brunnengräber et al., 2018). Hard to find is literature on civic activism against uranium mining and its use for commercial and military purposes. Possible reasons are the uneven location of unexhausted uranium ores (Kazakhstan, Canada, Australia, Southern Africa) and the hidden nature of uranium trade and production. More research and new methods are called for to fill these research gaps.

A return to the case study approach highlights the traditional rural women's protest participation at Wyhl in Germany (Engels, 2002) and the interlacing of the early anti-nuclear French and West German movements, whereby the causes of the movement violence and state repression are cast in a new light (Tompkins, 2016).

Although the comparative approach has not lost any of its appeal, today the emphasis is on how the media and policy discourses constrain movement contestation and thus restrict the chances of policy changes (compare Giugni and Grasso, 2015). Discursive and political opportunities (DOS and POS) are the main explanatory factors in a study of the Swedish, Polish, and Russian anti-nuclear movements, media, and policies (Tarasova, 2017) and in a collective volume highlighting the effects of past policy programs and present-day (diffusion) effects of the nuclear accidents in Fukushima on distinct national discourses, state policies, and protests (Hindmarsh and Priestley, 2017). Comparative political science research focused on Europe tests alternative hypotheses to account for differences in policy outcomes (Müller and Thurner, 2017). It singles out the institutionalization of the Green parties to explain policy reversals as well as the continued high mobilization in Austria, Germany, and Switzerland (see Thurner et al., 2017). However, leaving the confines of methodological nationalism, the role of the geographical proximity of such country clusters should also be investigated to pay heed to the interdependent government decisions as well as to protest diffusion and movement coalition building across borders.

Abandoning methodological nationalism allows us to see early transnational connections between various European movements, their networking and NGO initiating, and also their early attempts to engage the European institutions and non-European movements (Tompkins, 2016; Kirchhof and Meyer, 2014; Kirchhof, 2014; Milder, 2014; Meyer, 2014). It thus reverses the view of the anti-nuclear movements as being intensely local (Giugni and Grasso, 2015). Contrary to the "intense localism" thesis developed for environmental movements, the European anti-nuclear protesters were inspired by their US predecessors, who combined public discourses with demonstrations and court contestation, to then witness European protest in Wyhl, Germany, be catapulted to prominence as a worldwide exemplary. Since 2011, the weekly Tokyo protests have become focal. The protester endurance seems effective in keeping the NPP shut down. Multi-sited, multi-scalar research, stressing international and transnational cooperation, diffusion, and boomerang and ping-pong effects, as well as their blockages, is much called for. It should highlight these not just among the anti-nuclear movements but also among the nation-states on whose territories they develop. Expanding the geographical analytical scope and bringing up to date our knowledge about how anti-nuclear movements networked across borders and sought to hook up with international and transnational institutions would vastly enrich our knowledge.

References

Andrews-Speed, Philip (2020) 'South Korea's nuclear power industry: Recovering from scandal,' *Journal of World Energy Law and Business* 13: 47–57. DOI: 10.1093/jwelb/jwaa010

Berengäs, Johan (2009) *Sweden Reverses Nuclear Phase-out Policy*. Available at: www.nti.org/analysis/articles/sweden-reverses-nuclear-phase-out/

Brunnengräber, Achim, M.R. Di Nucci, A.M.I. Losada, L. Mez, and M. Schreurs, (eds.) (2018) *Challenges of Nuclear Waste Governance: An International Comparison*. Volume II. Berlin: Springer.

Engels, Jens Ivo (2002) 'Gender Roles and German Anti-Nuclear Protest: The Women of Wyhl,' in Bernhardt, Christoph (ed.) *Le demon modern: la pollution dans les sociétés urbaines et industrielles d'Europe*. Clermont-Ferrand: Presses univ. Blaise Pascal, 407–422.

Fang, Xiang (2017) 'China's Civil Nuclear Power Development: Shifts from Government to Risk Governance,' in Hindmarsh, Richard and Rebecca Priestley (eds.) *The Fukushima Effect*. London: Routledge, 82–100.

Flam, Helena, (ed.) (1994) *States and Anti-Nuclear Movements*. Edinburgh: Edinburgh University Press.

Futrell, Robert and Barbara G. Brents (2003) 'Protest as Terrorism? The Potential for Violent Anti-Nuclear Activism,' *American Behavioral Scientist* 46 (6): 745–765.

Giugni, Marco (2004) *Social Protest and Policy Change: Ecology, Anti-Nuclear and Peace Movements in Comparative Perspective*. Lanham, MD: Rowman & Littlefield.

Giugni, Marco (2007) 'Useless Protest? A Time-Series Analysis of the Policy Outcomes of Ecology, Anti-nuclear, and Peace Movements in the United States, 1977–1995,' *Mobilization* 12 (1): 53–77.

Giugni, Marco and Maria T. Grasso (2015) 'Environmental Movements: Heterogeneity, Transformation, and Institutionalization,' *Annual Review of Environment and Resources* 40. DOI: 10.1146/annurev-environ-102014-021327

Hasegawa, Koichi (2004) *Constructing Civil Society in Japan: Voices of Environmental Movements*. Melbourne: Trans Pacific Press.

Higuchi, Toshihiro (2008) 'An Environmental Origin of Antinuclear Activism in Japan, 1954–1963. The Government, the Grassroots Movement, and the Politics of Risk,' *Peace & Change* 33 (3): 333–367. DOI: 10.1111/j.1468-0130.2008.00502.x

Hindmarsh, Richard and Rebecca Priestley, (eds.) (2017) *The Fukushima Effect*. London: Routledge.

Holmberg, Sören (2020) Swedish Opinion on Nuclear Power 1986–2019. The Research Project Swedish Opinions on Environment, Energy and Climate Change (EECC), publicerad av Energimyndigheten, SOM-Institutet, Göterborgs Universität (by courtesy of the author, per email on 7/31/2020).

Honda, Hiroshi (2005) *Datsu Genpatsu no Undo to Seiji* (Anti-Nuclear Movement and Politics in Japan). Sapporo: Hokkaido University Press.

Hsiao, Hsin-Huang Michael, Hwa-Jen Liu, Su-Hoon Lee, On-Kwok Lai and Yok-Shiu F. Lee (1999) 'The making of Anti-Nuclear Movements in East Asia: Movements Relationships and Policy Outcomes,' in Lee, Yok-Shiu F. and Alvin Y. So (eds.) *Asia's Environmental Movements: Comparative Perspectives*. Armonk, NY: M. E. Sharpe, 252–268.

IAEA (International Atomic Energy Agency) (n.d.) *Atoms for Peace Speech*. Available at: www.iaea.org/about/history/atoms-for-peace-speech

IAEA-SE (2020) Available at: https://pris.iaea.org/pris/CountryStatistics/CountryDetails.aspx?current=SE

IEA (International Energy Agency) (2017–2019) *World Energy Balances*. Paris: OECD.

Jasper, James (1990) *Nuclear Politics: Energy and the State in the United States, Sweden and France*. Princeton, NJ: Princeton University Press.

Joppke, Christian (1993) *Mobilizing against Nuclear Energy: A Comparison of Germany and the United States*. Berkeley: University of California Press.

Kimura, Aya Hirata (2016) *Radiation Brain Moms and Citizen Scientists. The Gender Politics of Food Contamination after Fukushima*. Durham, NC: Duke University Press.

Kinsella, William J. (2017) 'A Question of Confidence: Nuclear Waste and Public Trust in the United States after Fukushima,' in Hindmarsh, Richard and Rebecca Priestley (eds.) *The Fukushima Effect*. London: Routledge, 223–246.

Kirchhof, Astrid Mignon (2014) 'Spanning the Globe: West-German Support for the Australian Anti-Nuclear Movement,' *Historical Social Research* 39 (1): 147, 254–273.

Kirchhof, Astrid Mignon and Jan-Henrik Meyer (2014) 'Global Protest Against Nuclear Power: Transfer and Transnational Exchange in the 1970s and 1980s', *Historical Social Research* 39 (1): 165–190.

Kitschelt, Herbert (1986) 'Political Opportunity Structures and Political Protest: Anti-Nuclear Movements in Four Democracies,' *British Journal of Political Science* 16: 57–85.

Kriesi, Hanspeter et al. (1995) *New Social Movements in Western Europe: A Comparative Analysis*. Minneapolis: University of Minnesota Press.

Lee, Sang-Hun, Jin-Tae Hwang and Jungpil Lee (2018) 'The Production of a National Riskscape and Its Fractures: Nuclear Power Facility Location Policy in South Korea,' *Erdkunde* 72 (3): 185–195. DOI: 10.3112/erdkunde.2018.02.07

Litmanen, Tapio (1998) 'International Anti-Nuclear Movements in Finland, France and the United States,' *Peace Research* 30 (4): 1–19.

Liu, Hwa-Jen (2015) *Leverage of the Weak: Labor and Environmental Movements in Taiwan and South Korea*. Minneapolis: University of Minnesota Press.

Löschke, Ayaka (2018) 'Civil Society Advocacy after Fukushima. The Case of the Nuclear Disaster Victims' Support Law,' in Chiavacci, David and Julia Obinger (eds.) *Social Movements and Political Activism in Contemporary Japan: Re-Emerging from Invisibility*. London: Routledge, 156–176.

Lowry, David (2020) *EU Recovery Plan Goes Green and Excludes Nuclear*. Available at: https://energytransition.org/2020/06/eu-recovery-plan-goes-green-and-excludes-nuclear/ (Accessed: 29 July 2020).

Meyer, Jan-Henrik (2014) ''Where Do We Go from Wyhl?' Transnational Anti-Nuclear Protest Targeting European and International Organizations in the 1970s,' *Historical Social Research* 39 (1): 212–235.

Milder, Stephen (2014) 'Between Grassroots Activism and Transnational Aspirations: Anti-Nuclear Protest from the Rhine Valley to the Bundestag, 1974–1983,' *Historical Social Research* 39 (1): 191–211.

Ming-sho Ho (2014) 'The Fukushima Effect: Explaining the Resurgence of the Anti-Nuclear Movement in Taiwan,' *Environmental Politics* 23 (6): 965–983. DOI: 10.1080/09644016.2014.918303.

Müller, Wolfgang C. and Paul W. Thurner (2017) 'Understanding Policy Reversals and Policy Stability', in Thurner, Paul W. and Wolfgang C. Müller (eds.) *The Politics of Nuclear Energy in Western Europe*. Oxford: Oxford Scholarship Online.

O'Neil, Patrick H. (1999) 'Atoms and Democracy: Political Transition and the Role of Nuclear Energy,' *Democratization* 6 (3): 171–189. DOI: 10.1080/13510349908403626

Price, Jerome (1982) *The Anti-Nuclear Movement*. Boston: Twayne Publishers.

Rascoe, Ayesha (2012) 'U.S. Approves First New Nuclear Plant in a Generation,' *Reuters*, February 9. Available at: www.reuters.com/article/us-usa-nuclear-nrc-idUSTRE8182J720120209

Richardson, Lauren (2017) 'Protesting Policy and Practice in South Korea's Nuclear Energy Industry', *The Asia-Pacific Journal* 15 (21–24): 1–17. Available at: https://apjjf.org/2017/21/Richardson.html (Accessed: 18 October 2020).

Rüdig, Wolfgang (1990) *Anti-Nuclear Movements: A World Survey of Opposition to Nuclear Energy*. Harlow: Longman.

Srikant, Patibandla (2009) *Koodankulam Anti-Nuclear Movement: A Struggle for Alternative Development?* Working Paper 232. The Institute for Social and Economic Change, Bangalore.

Stsiapanau, Andrei (2017) 'Nuclear Exceptionalism in the Former Soviet Union after Chernobyl and Fukushima,' in Hindmarsh, Richard and Rebecca Priestley (eds.) *The Fukushima Effect*. London: Routledge, 121–140.

Szarka, Joseph (2017) 'France, the Nuclear Revival and the Post-Fukushima Landscape,' in Hindmarsh, Richard and Rebecca Priestley (eds.) *The Fukushima Effect*. London: Routledge, 203–222.

Tarasova, Ekaterina (2017) *Anti-Nuclear Movements in Discursive and Political Contexts*. Between Expert Voices and Local Protest. Södertörns Högskola, Stockholm. Högskolans Skrifter. Huddinge: Södertörn Doctoral Dissertations, 1652–7399; 131.

Temocin, Pinar (2018) 'Framing Opposition to Nuclear Power: The Case of Akkuyu in Southeast Turkey,' *Asian Journal of Peacebuilding* 6 (2): 353–377. DOI: 10.18588/201811.00a047

Thurner, Paul W. et al. 2017. 'Conflict Over Nuclear Energy,' in Thurner, Paul W. and Wolfgang C. Müller (eds.) *The Politics of Nuclear Energy in Western Europe*. Oxford: Oxford Scholarship Online.

Tompkins, Andrew (2016) *Better Active than Radioactive! Anti-Nuclear Protest in 1970s France and West Germany*. Oxford: Oxford University Press.

WEF (World Economic Forum) *These Countries have the Most Nuclear Reactors*. Available at: www.weforum.org/agenda/2019/11/countries-that-have-the-most-nuclear-power-alternative-energy-electricity-climate-change/

WNA (2019) *Nuclear Power in Germany*. Available at: www.world-nuclear.org/information-library/country-profiles/countries-g-n/germany.aspx (Accessed: 1 August 2020).

WNA (World Nuclear Association) (2020a) *Nuclear Power in the European Union*. Available at: www.world-nuclear.org/information-library/country-profiles/others/european-union.aspx (Accessed: 30 July 2020).

WNA (World Nuclear Association) (2020b) *Nuclear Power in Sweden*. Available at: www.world-nuclear.org/information-library/country-profiles/countries-o-s/sweden.aspx (Accessed: 18 October 2020)

WNISR (2018–2020) *The World Nuclear Industry Status Report*. Edited by Mycle Schneider and Antony Froggatt. Paris: Mycle Schneider Consulting. Available at: www.worldnuclearreport.org/ (Accessed: 18 October 2020).

12

EXTRACTIVISM IN THE AMERICAS' INDIGENOUS

The land of resisters

Ana Isla

Introduction

The geographical scope of this chapter on extractivist movements is place-based processes on the Americas' continents (North, Central, and South). It argues that Indigenous peoples' life experience re-values the work of reproduction and reconnects our connection with nature, with others, and with our bodies to regain a sense of wholeness in our life. Four questions are addressed: how extractivism has been organized; how women's movements against violence in their territories defy extractivism; how Indigenous peoples' movements against oil and mining have become involved in contesting global trends as well as national and local policies supporting them; and why potential extractivist conflicts are looming in Amazonia. Focusing on single countries, the chapter examines violence against bodies and territories by oil and by mining and dams.

An ecofeminist framework is used to question the message that the "green economy" and so-called sustainable development can in any way create social and gender equality, reduce poverty, confront ecological destruction, and combat climate change. Instead, this perspective shows how extractivism can be understood as robbery of bodies and territories in a new phase of capital accumulation in which extractive industries intensify – from enclosures for wind power, mining and metals, carbon, oil, natural gas, soya, sugar cane, oil palm, corn, and meat to include forests, natural vistas, etc. – directly contributing to the ethnocide of Indigenous peoples, dispossessing the peasantry, expropriating the soil, and destroying ecosystems while at the same time creating conditions for human rights violations and increasing violence against women.

Global governance: from neoliberal development to sustainable development

In North America, the large-scale drivers of climate change, made by coal, oil, gas, and cement in large corporations, remain unaddressed while the restructuring of the Third World capacities to accommodate the corporations has been the concern, including of the United Nations.

On the other hand, in Latin America, neoliberal restructuring was initiated in 1982, during the debt crisis. Countries were forced to open up even more to market-centered policies, so-called neoliberal development. Since then, US banks have been using International Monetary

DOI: 10.4324/9780367855680-14

Fund (IMF) stabilization and World Bank (WB) structural adjustment policies (SAP) to reorganize internal social production and reproduction of the indebted world to favor the penetration of transnational capital. Restructuring implies setting up a new model of accumulation, new patterns of investment and saving, new income distribution, and the creation of capital in new ways (Isla, 1993).

Further restructuring was developed at the Earth Summit in 1992 in Rio de Janeiro as development and environment were linked together under Agenda 21 and offered sustainable development (SD) as a cure for social and environmental crises. SD was defined as "development that meets the needs of the present without compromising the ability of future generations to meet their own needs" (WCED, 1987: 8). Economists from the World Bank proposed that the ecology must be embedded in the economic system through the price system: that is, the ecology requires a fully monetized world in order to be protected. That meant that the atmosphere, oceans, land, forests, mountains, biological diversity, ecosystems, fresh water, etc. needed to be priced. Governments/states were seen as responsible for organizing SD. Following this logic, the World Bank developed "genuine" savings measures that "broaden the usual national account definitions of assets to include Natural Capital, minerals, energy, forest resources and the stock of atmospheric CO_2" (Hamilton, 2001).

At the Earth Summit 2002, held in Johannesburg, responsibility for SD was transferred to corporations and their shareholders. The United Nations (UN) advocated for "a new way of governing the global commons . . . partnership that may include non-government organization, willing governments and other stakeholders" (The Johannesburg Summit Test: What Will Change?). The commons were defined as existing within the so-called development, with its unacknowledged structures of dominance to serve the institutions of development whose *raison d'etre* is restructuring Third World capacities and social-natural relations to accommodate transnational capital expansion (Goldman, 1998, 47).

At the Earth Summit 2012, again in Rio de Janeiro, the "green economy" was unmistakably publicized as the process to eradicate poverty and subsequently objectified goods (water) and services (forests), which are now traded in financial markets. The Kyoto Protocol (1987) initiated the payment for environmental services (PES) that later evolved into reduction of emissions from deforestation and forest degradation (REDD), REDD+ (focused on the forests of indebted countries), and the European emissions trading systems (ETS) programs, using global markets to manage the forest as an environmental service. A number of dollars are paid for each hectare of forest.

In brief, the triumph of corporate-driven globalization resulted in the imposition of global control over the commons – land, water, biodiversity, rivers, lakes, oceans, atmosphere, forest, and mountains – at every level of global governance. The next section examines the consequences of this restructuring on women.

Critiques by ecofeminists: enclosure, "unwaged labor," "greening"

Ecofeminism regards nature and gender as deeply interrelated so that the one cannot be emancipated without the other. They have focused on the sphere of reproduction and locate the origins of oppression in the interconnected systems of patriarchy, colonialism, and capitalism. (Mellor, 2010; Bennholdt-Thomsen and Mies, 1999; Merchant, 1983, 2005; Federici, 2009; Shiva, 1989). As new forms of enclosure in the name of SD were defined, Federici describes the witch hunt in Europe as a process of devaluation of women and as part of the enclosure of the commons. With the enclosure, the social aspects of a community and its autonomy were eliminated. This produced a new sexual division of labor, redefined in relation to men, as wives, daughters, mothers, and widows, all of whom "hid their status of workers, while giving men free access to women's bodies, their labour, and the bodies and labour of their children". The witch hunt-controlled women's knowledge and female sexuality.

At the center of the ecofeminist analysis is the knowledge that capitalist patriarchy creates an intersecting domination against all "unwaged" labor. Mies (1986) saw housewifization as one aspect of a system of exploitation that embraced the low-paid or unpaid labor of women, destruction of the natural environment, and colonization of the resources and knowledge of Indigenous people around the world. Mies (1986) argues that housewifization is an ideology and method to define some human beings and nature as having no value. They are called feminized or "resourced" – that have to be appropriated, exploited, raped, extracted, and destroyed.

Salleh (2004) uses the term "meta-industrial class" to describe all invisible reproductive labors (mothers, peasants, and Indigenes) whose unwaged labor sustains natural processes but is exploited by the capitalist markers. Salleh (2004) argues that the meta-industrial class is the historical agent par excellence in the struggle for life who may be able to begin steps toward liberation and subsistence living.

My own research on the "green" economy disputes the message that sustainable development (SD) can in any way create social and gender equality, reduce poverty, confront ecological destruction, or combat climate change (Isla, 2015). Instead, it shows that extractivism as SD can be understood as a new phase of the accumulation of global capital. "Greening" denotes the massive expropriation of territories, depredation and contamination of the soil, and dispossession of the workers through the monetization of nature that requires the devaluing of all other forms of social existence, transforming skills into deficiencies, commons into resources, knowledge into ignorance, autonomy into dependency, and men and women into commodified labor-power whose needs require the mediation of the markets (Isla, 2015). Therefore, viewed through the lens of ecofeminism, these aspects of "greening" come together to wage war on women, subsistence producers, and nature by formulating a new kind of domination based on poverty and unsustainability.

Women's movements against violence against bodies and territories by extractivism

Extractive projects deepen the power relations of gender, causing greater inequalities toward women and childhood, and alter the cycles that reproduce life, which implies greater control and violence toward women's bodies. Latin America ecofeminists revealed that

> When there is conflict in the territories, we feel pain that materialize directly in the body and specifically in the women's bodies. We think of the body as our first territory and we recognize the territory in our bodies: when the places we inhabit are violated, our bodies are affected, when our bodies are affected, the places we inhabit are violated. We understand the body as a political territory to defend.
>
> (Colectivo Miradas Criticas, 2017)

The region is raged with anti-systemic movements, including the anti-femicide movement. In Canada, between 2012 and 2013, a movement called Idle No More against resource exploitation on First Nations territories was launched. It demanded respectful consultation on land claims, treaties, water protection, and resource sharing. The movement points out that the treaties between First Nations and the British Crown cannot be altered or broken by either side. It argues that the theft of land and resources by the state and corporations has already left us and our non-human relatives with lands and waters poisoned and deepened inequality between Indigenous people and the settler society.

Canada, Amnesty International acknowledged that "[t]he scale and severity of violence faced by Indigenous women and girls in Canada . . . constitutes a national human rights crisis" (AI, 2014). Around 1,200 Indigenous women and girls are missing or murdered. In 2016, the federal government responded to this call by initiating the National Inquiry into Missing and Murdered Indigenous Women and Girls: "Experts and knowledge keepers spoke to specific colonial and patriarchal policies that displaced women from their traditional roles in communities and governance and diminished their status in society, leaving them vulnerable to violence" (MMIWG, 2016).

Aboriginal people suffered genocide as a result of state and institutional racism. It was exposed first in the Truth and Reconciliation Commission (TRC) (2015), which confronted and documented the deliberate genocide of Aboriginal people by the government of Canada, through Canada's residential schools system during the nineteenth and twentieth centuries. TRC brought attention to the abuse, trauma, and torture that took place in many residential schools. Second, the "sixties scoop" of Indigenous children refers to a practice of taking children from their families of birth and their subsequent adoption into predominantly non-Indigenous, white, middle-class families, resulting in children losing their language, culture, and identity. These policies have been called "cultural genocide": this means the assimilation of Indigenous people to cease their existence as distinct legal, social, cultural, religious, and racial entities in Canada.

In Latin America, an ecofeminist manifest revels that "Corporations leave us traces of pain because they break our community relations, if they extract water, land, or poison our spaces that we inhabit, they harm our body" (Colectivo Miradas Criticas, 2017). The arrival of men – workers of extractive companies, state employees, and the military – to the territories causes most of the spaces to be occupied by them. Spaces of community use are monopolized by them, generating new power relations and leaving out of them women, girls, and boys. As a result, their bodies, like the land, begin to be controlled, objectified, appropriated, and violated. When the territory is masculinized, women are continually exposed to intimidation, harassment, sexual assault, and other types of violence by oil and mining workers, security, the military, and the paramilitary, as in Colombia and Mexico. We know that when territories are militarized, female bodies are used as military objects and objectives; they are used for humiliation and as bargaining chips.

As oil and mining expanded, Indigenous, Black, and rural women saw that their children had various health ailments and began to organize *encuentros* (gatherings) against mining. They gather information and acted together in the defense of their territories and their human rights by challenging their states and justice systems, which do not work for the common good or for the right to life. By 2005, these women had declared themselves in rebellion and in open opposition to the robbery and predation committed by transnational oil and mining companies (Ecuador, 2007). As a result, violence is directed at them, and they are harassed, stigmatized, disappeared, and murdered.

The mark of extractivism on women's bodies is expressed in the number of women assassinated or disappeared. For instance, the latest report from the Gender Equality Observatory of the UN Economic Commission for Latin America and the Caribbean (ECLAC) reveals that, in 2019, at least 4,640 femicides took place in the region, noting that it is in the state where high levels of impunity, repression, and rape by state agents occur. The violence that runs through the continent is derived from military dictatorships, the way the United States and Canada protect their extractive corporations by bribing or running over governments, and with the help of the notorious School of the Americas, also known as the School of Assassins (SOA Watch, n.d.).

In 2015, in Argentina, due to the lack of judicial response to femicide, women created a movement called Ni una Menos [(No One (Woman) Less], which means that another woman does not die; that cannot be tolerated! It paved the way for "Un Violador en Tu Camino" ("A Rapist on Your Path") by the Chilean group Las Tesis, which began as a street act in the midst of the commemoration of a new International Day against Gender Violence and the social outbreak in Chile in 2019. The message of the lyrics says that "patriarchy is a judge who criticizes us for being born and our punishment is the violence that you already see". It claims, "The repressive state is a male rapist" before concluding that "the rapist is you". The movement "Ni una Menos" and the lyrics of "A rapist on Your Way" have crossed borders and, in some cases, have been modified according to the context of each country or city where they have been replicated.

In Mexico, 3,752 women were killed in 2020 (AI, 2021). Mexican women denounced femicide in "Song without Fear":

> Let the State, the skies, the streets tremble
> Let the judges and the judiciary tremble
> Women's calm was rekindled
> They scared us, but We Grew Wings
> For all the compas [compañeras] marching in Reforma [where the government house is located]
> For all the girls fighting in Sonora
> For the Comandantas battling for Chiapas
> For all the mothers looking [for their disappeared children] in Tijuana
> We sing without fear, we ask for justice
> We scream for every missing
> Let it resound loudly "We Want Each Other Alive!" [Nos Queremos Vivas]
> Let the femicide fall with force.

In sum, these women have become a global symbol of women's repudiation of the misogynist violence, gendered discrimination, and destruction of the planet. Focusing on single countries, the following sections examine violence against territories, first by oil and second by mining.

Oil extractivism: violence against territories and Indigenous people's movements

The scientific consensus is that human beings are a geologic force that are causing climate change. For the past 150 years, hydrocarbons have been the most important source of energy for industrial capitalism, but the consequences of their use are changing the climate. However, North America is reluctant to make changes.

In Western Canada, there is a strong conflict where the Athabasca River Basin contains one of the world's largest bitumen reserves. Currently, the landscape is marked by deforestation, strip mines, wastewater ponds, pipelines and roads, refineries, energy-generation facilities, and moving machines. This area houses the Enbridge Northern Gateway Pipeline (ENGP), which consists of two parallel pipelines between an inland terminal in Alberta and a marine terminal in British Columbia, each with a length of 1,177 kilometers. Competing projects are Kinder Morgan Energy Partners and TransCanada's Keystone XL pipeline, cancelled lately by the United States' new administration. Enbridge, line 5, is in a legal battle to avoid another close down of a crude-oil pipeline. (McCarten, 2021)

The Athabasca River Basin, however, is first and foremost the homeland of the Cree, Dene, and Metis peoples. They see pipelines as another wave of colonial violence. Furthermore, the lands of Wet'suwet'en Nation were never entered into formal treaties with the Canadian government. In 1997, the Supreme Court stated that these lands are to be governed by Indigenous laws. Consequently, across Canada, First Nations and non-Indigenous people are in solidarity with the Wet'suwet'en Nation (Federman, 2020). Together, they have targeted these projects, the government review processes, pension funds, and financial institutions (Black Toban et al., 2014). In 2014, the British Columbia Civil Liberties Association (BCCLA) filed a complaint against the RCMP for spying on climate organizations and Indigenous nations opposed to oil and gas projects. As the struggle continued, in December 2018, Wet'suwet'en people and their supporters set up a checkpoint to block various construction projects, and "Canadian police were prepared to shoot Indigenous defenders blockading construction of a natural gas pipeline" (Dhillon and Parrish, 2019). In February 2019, the Royal Canadian Mounted Police started raiding protesters' monitoring posts. These raids brought action across Canada in support of the Wet'suwet'en Nation. National corporations such as VIA Rail and CN Rail were blocked to cancel or halt all trains, creating shortages of goods from coast to coast, to call attention to its plight. In 2020, after six years, the Civilian Review and Complaints Commission (CRCC) released its final report, in which it details countless examples of RCMP monitoring and spying on individuals who were opposed to pipeline projects and creating secret profiles on organizers. Despite this, the CRCC found most of these RCMP activities "reasonable" (Harsha Walia, executive director).

One of the largest Indigenous uprisings in recent history, in the United States, consisted of blocking the Dakota Access Pipeline, an 1,886-kilometer-long underground oil pipeline project. Many in the Standing Rock tribe and surrounding communities considered the pipeline a threat to the region's drinking water and a harm to tribal members' right to fish, hunt, and gather, as well as a contamination source of the water supply used to irrigate surrounding farmlands.

The protests began in early 2014 and intensified in 2016 in reaction to the government's approval to construct the Energy Transfer Partners' Dakota Access Pipeline. The youth who organized a direct-action group and social media campaign to stop the pipeline called themselves ReZpect Our Water (Estes and Dhillon's, 2019). Inspired by these youth, several adults established a water protectors' camp as a center for direct action, cultural preservation, and defense of Indigenous sovereignty. The movement decreased in 2017 when ex-President Trump authorized the Army Corps of Engineers to take action. As a result, police launched a crackdown against Indigenous communities and their supporters (Treaties Still Matter, 2016). In July 2018, Red Fawn Fall, a young political prisoner arrested during the movement, was sentenced to 57 months in prison by the federal court. At least five other water protectors faced federal charges carrying prison sentences.

The Amazon has huge reserves of oil and gas that lie beneath its landscape. In Ecuadorean Amazonia, in 1964, Texaco, a US company, arrived to prospect oil. When Texaco pulled up in 1994, it left behind rusted plexus of pipes, hundreds of open oil pits, and billions of gallons of toxic wastewater dumped into the region. In 2003, a trial against Chevron, which had bought Texaco's liabilities, began in Ecuador. In the lawsuit, the natives and the lawyers brought evidence of land and water pollution with toxic waste and 4,000 kilometers with residue from the extraction of crude oil. Children died; women had miscarriages due to water laced with toxins. The waste caused the destruction of fish, jungle animal, and Indigenous peoples. Unprotected by the state, five Indigenous communities (Waorani, Kichwa, Secoya, Siona, and Cofan), with different languages, traditions, customs, and territories, joined forces to fight together (Zaitchik, 2014). Now the Indigenous peoples who have lived there for generations are scrambling for survival.

In 2011, Steven Donziger, a human rights lawyer, won $9.5 million from the giant Chevron for dumping oil in the Ecuadorian Amazonia. Chevron refuse to pay or clean up the land. In 2018, the Permanent Arbitration Court in The Hague ruled that the trial against Chevron was invalidated by corruption and that the oil company was exonerated from any liability. It issued an arbitration order requiring Ecuador to set aside the sentence handed down by its courts against the multinational company. In addition, Chevron countersued in New York and blocked the Ecuador's Supreme Court decision from being enforced on US soil. Since then, Donziger has been under house arrest for 600 days, disbarred, and his bank account frozen after a federal judge drafted charges for refusing to surrender his cell phone and computer. Furthermore, the federal judge appointed a private law firm with Chevron ties to prosecute Donziger in the name of the state (Democracy Now, May 11, 2021).

Oil production in the Peruvian Amazon was initiated during the first peak oil in the 1970s when a military dictatorship granted illegal rights to Occidental Petroleum Company for the use of the commons. Guided by global capital, Fujimori's administration (1990–2001) changed the constitution in 1993, eliminating the inalienable character of Indigenous communal land, removing the imprescriptibly character of perpetual right, and seizing the land, arguing abandonment.

By 2003, Indigenous peoples in oil production areas had initiated several uprisings due to the destruction of their subsistence economies. In 2008, three Indigenous groups, living on three rivers disturbed by Petroleum Concession Block 1AB, joined to protest against soil degradation as well as poor wages in an oil remediation program, leading to arrests in 2008 and legal proceedings in 2009. Here is what happened: On 20 March 2008, more than 1,000 community members, including women and children, congregated at an abandoned airport in Andoas town. They hoped to discuss their issues with any institution of the government interested in solving the low payments and the deteriorating living conditions resulting from the oil economy. With oil spills and water contamination, they had lost their traditional economy based on common grounds. Several of their young children were dying from contamination while their teenaged children were forced to sell their bodies to oil workers as prostitutes. Instead, their protest placed them into the Judicial Court of Loreto in 2009. They were cleared when the court verdict recognized Indigenous people's collective rights in opposition to state criminalization (Isla, 2019).

In sum, Canada and the United States are intensive carbon users and are the most aggressive promoters of continued fossil fuel combustion; subsequently, Aboriginal people endure the continuous colonial dispossession and contamination. In Ecuador and Peru, the law defines protest as organized crime, and land and water protectors are killed.

Mining and dams extractivism: violence against territories and Indigenous' people movements

Minerals have been the basic inputs of industrial production. In the mineral economy, subsoil resources and water are the primary means of accumulation. Governments and corporations, using the concept of sustainable development, claim that agriculture and mining can harmoniously coexist. But mining is a fundamentally unsustainable activity that destroys ecosystems through massive deforestation, poisoning water and lagoons, turning land into deserts, increasing traffic, polluting rivers, and draining chemical sludge and heavy metals into inhabited valleys. Moreover, mining corporations pay few income taxes and little for the massive amounts of water and energy they use.

Furthermore, to expand mining, capital needs to destroy the self-reproducing capacity of individuals and communities; therefore, it has generated the most conflicts because access to water for cultivation and livestock is distorted by extractive activities and even more by the effects of climate change. Communities resist violent and corrupt incursions of government and military-backed companies and investors operating in many sectors. Pressured by Indigenous activists, since 1989, the International Labor Organization has recognized the ancestral rights of Indigenous peoples. But in a deregulated framework, there is no community right to reject mining investments, and therefore, the most tragic outcomes of mining projects occur when rural communities refuse to become stakeholders in what they perceive as the plunder and contamination of their lands and resources. Consequently, civil unrest is the only option left to those who do not want mining in their areas or territories (Coumans, 2010).

Binks-Collier (2020) examines the ongoing landmark Hudbay Minerals lawsuits in Canada. In 2004, Skye Resources, a Vancouver-based mining company, was granted permission by the government to begin work in a large area in northeastern Guatemala that was home to at least 20 Maya Q'eqchi' communities, including Lote Ocho. Earlier that year, Skye had bought the rights to the open-pit Fenix nickel mine, located near the majority-Maya town of El Estor, from the Canadian mining company INCO. Skye had also bought INCO's 70% share of its subsidiary, EXMIBAL, which Skye then renamed CGN. But the deal also saw Skye acquire the long-festering, unresolved disputes over land left by INCO and EXMIBAL's violent past. (As an example, between 2006 and 2008, CGN dispatched helicopters to terrorize those living on the land.)

The CGN campaign culminated in two waves of evictions targeting several Indigenous villages on 8, 9, and 17 January 2007. Eleven women from Lote Ocho were allegedly gang-raped by police officers, soldiers, and CGN's security during the last eviction. Consequently, 11 women have been suing Hudbay Minerals Inc., a Toronto-based mining company that bought Skye in 2008, acquiring Skye's legal liability. Five were pregnant at the time; four miscarried, and one, three days from her due date when she was allegedly gang-raped, said in a deposition that she gave birth to a stillborn who "was all blue or green". Then, men from all three groups (soldiers, police, and CGN security) splashed gasoline over the makeshift huts and the women's tattered clothing and set them ablaze. Marriages were irreparably ruined. The impoverished community eventually split and drifted apart as some members accepted jobs at CGN. Supported by Rights Action (Archives), the litigation, seeking justice, continues in Canada and Guatemala.

In Honduras, the 1998 mining law erased any distinction between exploration and exploitation concessions, legalized open-pit cyanide mining, permitted forced expropriation in the case of conflict, reduced taxes on mining, and established no limits on water use and no closure requirements for abandoned mines. However, by 2004, an organized coalition had forced the president to reject more than 60 mining concessions solicited and suspend new concessions by executive decree, pending the passage of a new mining law (Bebbington, Fash and Rogan 2018). In addition, the Supreme Court unanimous ruled in 2006 that 13 articles of the 1998 law violated the "fundamental right to harmonic conviviality with the environment and to sustainable development" (Bebbington, Fash and Rogan 2018).

Consequently, by 2007, Comte Ambientalista del Valle de Siria – organized by communities around San Andrés, concessioned to the Canadian Greenstone Resources Limited, and San Martín, concessioned to the Canadian Goldcorp – enlisted scientific studies on problems such as cyanide usage and spills and associated fish kills. They denounced health problems, such as skin infections, respiratory illness, sexual and psychological violence, and *feminicidio* (www.ocmal.org/3661/#more-102). Also in 2007, the government passed a new general water law, promoting private hydroelectric dams. Between mining and dams, hundreds of defenders of freshwater resources have been killed and many others silenced. Among the dead in 2016 was Berta Caceres, murdered for leading a grassroots campaign to prevent a private energy company, Desarrollos Energéticos Sociedad Anónima, from building a hydroelectric dam in Agua Zarca. Furthermore, since September 2019, at least seven Garifuna leaders have been killed, and in 2020, five Garifuna from the Land Protection Committee were abducted (Bu), while an Indigenous man, Feliz Vasquez, was assassinated.

In Costa Rica, people from the town of Bellavista organized resistance to Bellavista Mining, a Canadian Company, to secure clean water and maintain livelihoods in agriculture and fishing. The Miramar Front in Opposition to Mining (Miramar Front) in Miramar City made its concerns public when they realized that the water and energy used by mining corporations was the same water and energy expropriated from their subsistence production, resulting in destroyed economies. Miramar Front involved municipalities and other local community members in acts of defiance against the national government's decision to expand mining. They were on the streets, defending their rights to clean water and a secure livelihood. Bellavista Mining resorted to legal intimidation to stop the protests and took women leaders to court. By 2006, 16 municipalities had fought fiercely against the destruction of their communities and ecologies. As a result of community activism, several mining projects have been stalled, and local opposition to mining won a case in the courts, cancelling the contract of Industrias Infinito S.A in Crucitas, and the decision was upheld by the Supreme Court in 2011 (Isla, 2002).

In Peru, struggles for environmental justice are spread. The first movement against mining was in Tambogrande, Piura, when Fujimori's government granted Manhattan Minerals, a Vancouver-based corporation, 10 mining concessions, totaling 89,000 hectares, for an open pit. Under Tambogrande lies a deposit of a million ounces of gold and silver, copper and zinc that the company wants to excavate.

Over 70,000 people in the area earn their living from agriculture (limes, mangos, and avocados). The community in Tambogrande actively campaigned, nationally and internationally, arguing that the use of explosives could damage their homes, consume farmland, destroy the valley of San Lorenzo, contaminate the San Lorenzo Irrigation Project and the groundwater, and alter flora and fauna; cyanide and mercury pose health risks. When disagreements between locals and the corporation increased, the mayor collected signatures among the eligible voters on a petition calling for Manhattan's immediate departure. Despite of multiple ways of saying no to the project, the company embarked on a confrontation path.

In 1999, a coalition of farmers was organized. Soon after, a group of unidentified persons set fire to Manhattan's machines. Months later, offices were ransacked, and trucks and machinery were burned. The collective protest torched the first section of model homes that the company planned to give to displaced families. In 2001, the main leader of the Defense Front was killed in his organic lime grove farm by two hooded men. Since then, persecutions have increased against the leadership of the Defense Front and their families. The confrontation attracted activist supporters from Canada and Europe. In 2002, the Tambogrande municipality held a referendum on whether or not to allow mining in the area; 94% said "No to mining". The government of the day made clear that a municipal referendum did not have legal weight. Due to the success of the struggle, in 2003, it was publicly announced that Manhattan Minerals had lost its main concessions under Tambogrande on a technicality (Isla, 2003).

In Argentina, The Tratado de Integracion y Complementacion Minera entre Chile and Argentina, a treaty signed in 1997, converted an area in the Andes into a new country with its own laws, regulations, and administration (Rodriguez, 2009). The most relevant experience of self-convening in San Juan was in Jachal. Barrick Gold's Veladero and Pascua (Chile) and Lama (Argentina) projects extract gold, silver, and copper in the Biosphere Reserve of San Guillermo, 5,000 meters above sea level. The Veladero project is 375 kilometers from San Juan. As a result, social movements emerged in San Juan Province and towns located at the foot of the Andes. The women, organized in Madres Jachaleras, declared themselves Autoconvocadas and, supported by the Federacion de Viñateros y Productores Agropecuarios, disputed the policies of the governor of San Juan Province and declared "No to the Mine". The strategy used, assemblies and marches, denounced the local political accomplices of the mining company and warned that it was a looting of common goods because "They come for Gold, and They come for Everything". The "No to the Mine" became a slogan of collective struggle, and the self-convened were prosecuted. Furthermore, two non-binding public trials took place, one in Chile (2006) and another in Argentina (2007), where the public rejected and expelled Barrick and all other mining corporations.

Developing movements against ecosystem services in South America

Scientific theories have highlighted that forest vegetation absorbs and stores carbon that might otherwise trap heat in the atmosphere, driving up temperatures and speeding up climate change. Absorbing carbon dioxide (CO_2) from the overflowing waste of industrial countries to reduce the greenhouse effect has become part of the sustainable development agenda.

At the Climate Change Convention held in Kyoto in 1997, industrial countries proposed the creation of mechanisms to reduce greenhouse gas emissions. A key concept in the "green economy" is payment for ecosystem services (PES), which is a voluntary transaction in which a buyer from the industrial world pays a supplier for a well-defined environmental service, such as a patch of forest or a form of land use, and that supplier effectively controls the service that ensures his supply (Fatheuer, 2014, 46). The Convention on Climate Change (CCC) extended PES to countries and industries that manage to reduce carbon emissions to levels below their designated amount. They would be able to sell their credits to other countries or industries that exceed their emission levels. The creation of a global market in carbon dioxide, focused on the forest of indebted countries, has been expropriating Indigenous people's territories. However, it is also relevant to emphasize that the measure of emission absorption of carbon gases is not really possible since forests are living organisms that breathe and are dynamic and complex systems, so measurements are always estimates. Again, this program is problematic as Indigenous and peasant users of the land are described as the most important agents of deforestation.

PES conflicts with the Indigenous Amazonia's experience. Spanish and Portuguese colonization and evangelization incorporated them into global commerce, and the early twentieth century boom in rubber also linked them to industrial capitalism. These experiences made them among the first inhabitants rejecting and resisting colonization and capitalism to this day. They stuck steadfast to their forested ecosystems, and their mode of production is characterized by its high degree of autonomy and freedom in the organization of work. Sociability is obtained in the interaction between human beings (group work) and in the synergy with the elements of the biophysical environment where the dialogue with the rest of nature follows the rhythm given by the cultural system based on common rights usages. They do not divide life in two periods —utilitarian work and pleasant leisure; their activities bring together the useful and the pleasant, and life is built in the exercise of solidarity, according to social rights and obligations

(Gashe and Vela, 2012). Their economy survived, despite of being under intense development pressure by oil, mining, cocoa plantations, navigation, deforestation, etc.

In the 1980s, Brazil's marginalized rubber tapper communities were losing land to timber companies and cattle ranchers. Chico Mendes proposed the creation of extractive reserves to allow forest peoples to live sustainably. His assassination in 1988 sparked worldwide attention to the plight of the Amazon's forest communities. In 2007, the government laid the groundwork for Acre's program, the State System of Incentives for Environmental Services (SISA), by dividing all land into zones. With a basic framework, SISA developed programs pricing forests, biodiversity, water, soil, climate, and traditional/cultural knowledge. In the Acre Amazon region, two REDD+ programs under international guidelines outlined by the World Wildlife Fund (WWF), the International Union for the Conservation of Nature (IUCN), the Federal University of Acre (UFAC), the Amazon Environmental Research Institute (IPAM), the Woods Hole Research Center, Brazilian Agriculture Research Corporation (EMBRAPA), and the German Agency for International Cooperation (GTZ) in collaboration with local governments have disenfranchised Indigenous people and converted skills into deficiencies.

The program did not help people live with or obtain their livelihood from the forests. On the contrary, restrictive measures were imposed on *seringueiros* (rubber tappers). With respect to the Indigenous Peoples of Acre, despite written promises, REDD+ money was never utilized for the urgently needed titling of Indigenous lands that still have not been demarcated, creating incentives for outsiders to further dispossess Indigenous People. Meanwhile, large-scale livestock and agribusiness, logging industry activities, land grabbers, and miners who threaten Indigenous Peoples' territories and forests managed to proceed (WRM, 2020). Instead, the commodification of the processes of natural and social reproduction (water, carbon sequestration, and biodiversity knowledge) leads to the further alienation of people from the rights to their natural surroundings. It puts the burden of mitigating carbon emissions on communities that have not created the ecological crisis.

Indigenous organizations and social groups of Acre have denounced REDD+ for 1) violations of land and collective territory rights as Indigenous people have no land title, deepening territorial conflicts, and 2) violations of the rights of the peoples in REDD+-occupied territories to subsistence and traditional activities, such as traditional agriculture and fishing, which have been reduced or eliminated, depriving communities of their livelihood. As a result, entire families have moved to the periphery of the cities, forcing some of their children into prostitution (Faustino and Furtado, 2014).

Currently, in the Amazonas region of Peru, one of the several REDD+ programs/agreements is the Norway and Germany join declaration of intent to reduce deforestation and greenhouse gas emissions. The program is administered by the WWF Inc. The NGO claims that getting money now is a matter that cannot be postponed because a decent life is not possible without funding. To integrate Indigenous communities into the global economy, AIDESEP (an Indigenous federation) and organizations involved in REDD+ as agents of capital have created a concept called Articulation with Identity, meaning that some principles of Indigenous culture are included in the agreement (Espinoza, 2016). PES is incorporating Indigenous people into microenterprises.

However, this perspective conflicts on two fronts. On one hand, in a capitalist society, there is a legitimate desire to have a better income to improve the quality of life; on the other hand, it means reviewing, modifying, or even eliminating some of the characteristics of Indigenous peoples, culture, and livelihood. Then, if these organizations want to integrate Indigenous peoples into the global economy, they will have to transform biodiversity through agro-exportation because that is what brings profit. But this scheme collides with the recognition that forest loss is a key factor in climate change. Furthermore, the NGO's insistence that, to better integrate Indigenous people into markets, the "flexibilization" of the concept of territory was needed, creating the possibility that other figures could be incorporated into the forest, such as private property, modalities of rental of communal lands, or invitation to third parties for use or exploitation of resources. Since the territory constitutes the most important social and cultural asset for Indigenous peoples, if territories are rented, REDD+ become REDD+-based offsets, as such, they do not represent emission reduction; instead, they represent another, ostensibly lower-cost means by which firms can meet their emissions quota, allowing polluting industries to continue or even expand the corporate operations that ruin forests and the climate (Isla, forthcoming 2021).

The Amazonian rainforest, due to its role in regulating the climate of the hemisphere and the enormous amounts of carbon it stores in the subsoil, is key for the planet in the face of climate change. Scientists say that Amazonia's forests are giant rain machines that produce and recycle water that evaporates from the Atlantic. Amazonia's trees take up moisture from the soil and transpire it, lifting it into the atmosphere. A tree can pump up to 1,000 liters of water per day. Trees also produce aromatic substances, aerosols, whose particles become condensation nuclei of water vapor in an ecosystem where dust particles are virtually absent. Without them, the clouds would be completely sterile. However, the destruction of Amazonia's commons by global deforestation and climate change are wrecking this wonderful machine, putting the regional climate at risk.

Conclusion

Giugni and Grasso (2015) argue that environmental movements in the advanced industrial democracies have become strongly institutionalized at two levels: environmental issues, because the general public and policy makers are today more concerned with the environmental problems, and environmental actors, which is evident in the increasing incorporation of environmental organizations in policy networks. This latest perception is echoed in this piece.

This chapter has reviewed literature on extractivist movements of Indigenous peoples in the Americas (North, Central, and South) from an ecofeminist perspective. It selected a variety of countries, organizations, networks, and strategies; highlighted three extractivist movements: women/gender, oil, and mining; and forecasted developing movements against environmental service in the Amazonia's region. The historical context is the political ecology of sustainable development stemming, from three previous Earth Summits (1992, 2002, 2012) and Conventions on Climate Change, which bear direct intervention of states and NGOs over local inhabitants and their commons. Therefore, signed international consultations (Convention 169, UN Declaration on the Rights of Indigenous People, and other United Nations resolutions) become meaningless.

In detailing the gendered processes of enclosure, housewifization, and greening, I have tried to expose some of the fallacies of green capitalism and corporate-defined sustainable development.

A sustainable development that prioritizes multinational organizations and large environmental NGOs engaged in enormous projects is showing its tendency toward the dispossession of the very means of survival of people who follow the rhythm of nature. Rural women, Indigenous people, and peasants have demonstrated that the politics of SD are not separated from their everyday life, and when they protest, they are assassinated or disappeared by the police and their undercover agents and, in some countries, also by paramilitaries.

What distinguishes these extractivist movements is that their local struggles reach across borders, involving activists around the world in a truly "globalized" campaign against the worst aspects of sustainable development and corporate globalization. These movements want to change the system to stop the rapacious dependence of the so-called "developed societies" on the resources and labor of the so-called "underdeveloped" other. New theoretical concepts and practices to interrupt the human and planetary crises are imperative.

References

Amnesty International. (2014) *Violence Against Women and Girls in Canada.* https://www.amnesty.ca/sites/amnesty/files/iwfa_submission_amnesty_international_february_2014_-_final.pdf

Amnesty International. (2021) *Violence Against Women and Girls.* www.amnesty.org/en/countries/americas/mexico/report-mexico/ (accessed April 14, 2021).

Bebbington, Anthony Benjamin Fash, and John Rogan. (2018) *Socio-Environmental Conflict, Political Settlements, and Mining Governance: A Cross-Border Comparison, El Salvador and Honduras.* www.researchgate.net/publication/329459588_Socio-environmental_Conflict_Political_Settlements_and_Mining_Governance_A_Cross-Border_Comparison_El_Salvador_and_Honduras (accessed October 22, 2020).

Bennholdt-Thomsen, Veronika, and Maria Mies. (1999) *The Subsistence Perspective: Beyond the Globalized Economy.* New York: Zed Books.

Binks-Collier, Max. (2020) *Evicting Lote Ocho. How a Canadian Mining Company Infiltrate the Guatemala State.* https://theintercept.com/2020/09/26/hudbay-skye-canada-mining-guatemala/ (accessed October 18, 2020).

Black Toban, Stephen Darcy, Weis Tony, and Kan Joshua (Eds.). (2014) *A line in the Tar Sands: Struggles for Environmental Justice.* Canada: Between the Lines.

Colectivo Miradas Criticas del Territorio desde el Feminismo. (2017) "Mapeando el cuerpo-territorio. Guia metodologica para mujeres que defienden su territorios" *Ecofeminism*, Publicaciones y material multimedia. www.accionecologica.org/mapeando-el-cuerpo-territorio-guia-metodologica-para-mujeres-que-defienden-sus-territorios/ (accessed October 20, 2020).

Coumans, Catherine. (2010) "Alternative Accountability Mechanisms and Mining: The Problems of Effective Impunity, Human Rights and Agency" *Canadian Journal of Development Studies*, Vol. 30, No. 1–2, pp. 27–48.

Dhillon, Jaskiran, and Will Parrish. "Exclusive: Canada Police Prepared to Shoot Indigenous Activists, Documents Show" *The Guardian*, December 20, 2019. www.theguardian.com/world/2019/dec/20/canada-indigenous-land-defenders-police-documents (accessed November 18, 2020).

Dhillon, Jaskiran, and Will Parrish. "Exclusive: Canada Police Wet'suwet'en Nation's Ancestral Lands Show Commanders Argued for 'Lethal Overwatch'" *The Guardian*. www.theguardian.com/world/2019/dec/20/canada-indigenous-land-defenders-police-documents (accessed December 12, 2019).

ECLAC. (2020) *Gender Equality Observatory.* https://oig.cepal.org/en/indicators/femicide-or-feminicide (accessed December 18, 2020).

Ecuador. (2007) *Declaracion del Encuentro de los Pueblos por la Vida.* www.ocmal.org/3665/#more-106 (accessed November 20, 2020).

Espinoza, Roberto. (2016) "REDD+ Indígena Amazónico (RIA/Indigenous REDD+) Progress and Challenges" *UNREDDY: A Critical Look at REDD+ and Indigenous Strategies REDDY for Comprehensive Forest Protection*, pp. 14–17. www.climatealliance.org/fileadmin/Inhalte/7_Downloads/Unreddy_EN_2016-02.pdf (accessed November 18, 2020).

Estes, Nick, and Jaskiran Dhillon (Eds.). (2019) *Standing with Standing Rock: Voices from the #NoDAPL Movement (Indigenous Americas).* Minneapolis, London: University of Minnesota Press.

Fatheuer, T. (2014) *Nueva Economia de la Naturaleza. Una Introduccion Critica.* Berlin: Heinrich Böll Foundation. Print.

Faustino, Cristiane, and Fabrina Furtado. (2014) *Economía Verde, Pueblos de los Bosques y Territorios: Violaciones de derechos en el estado de Acre, Informe preliminar de la Misión de Investigación e Incidencia.* Rio Branco, Brazil. Dhesca: Plataforma de Dereitos Humanos, Economicos, Sociales, Culturais e Ambientas.

Federman, Adam. "Revealed: US Listed Climate Activist Group as 'Extremists' Alongside Mass Killers" *The Guardian*, 13 January 2020. www.theguardian.com/environment/2020/jan/13/us-listed-climate-activist-group-extremists

Federici, Silvia. 2009. *Caliban and the Witch: Women, the Body and Primitive Accumulation*. New York, NY: Automedia.

Gashe, Jorge, and Napoleon Vela. (2012) Instituto de Investigaciones de la Amazonia Peruana, Iquitos, Peru. (Tomo 1).

Giugni Mario, and Maria Grasso. (2015) "Environmental Movements in Advanced Industrial Democracies: Heterogeneity, Transformation, and Institutionalization" *Annual Review on Environment and Resources*, Vol. 40, pp. 337–361.

Goldman, Michael. (1998) "Inventing the Commons: Theories and Practices of the Commons' Professional" in *Privatizing Nature: Political Struggles for the Global Commons*. Ed. Michael Goldman. New Brunswick, NB: Rutgers University Press.

Hamilton, Kirk. (2001) *Genuine Savings, Population Growth, and Sustainable Economic Welfare*. Paper presented at the Natural Capital, Poverty and Development Conference, Toronto, 5–8 September.

Idle No More. https://idlenomore.ca (accessed November 18, 2020).

Isla, Ana. (1993) "The Debt Crisis in Latin America: Un Example of Unsustainable Development" *Canadian Woman Studies*, Vol 13, No. 3, pp. 65–68.

Isla, Ana. (2002) "A Struggle for Clean Water and Livelihood: Canadian Mining in Costa Rica in the Era of Globalization" *Canadian Woman Studies*, Vol. 21/22, No. 4/1, pp. 148–154.

Isla, Ana. (2003) "The Politics of Sustainable Development. A Subsistence View Women and Sustainability: From Rio de Janeiro (1992) to Johannesburg (2002)" *Canadian Woman Studies*, Vol. 23, No. 1. pp. 6–16.

Isla, Ana. (2015) *The "Greening" of Costa Rica. Women, Peasants, Indigenous People and the Remaking of Nature*. Toronto: University of Toronto Press.

Isla, Ana. (2019) "Indigenous Andoas Uprising: Defending Territorial Integrity and Autonomy in Peru" in *Climate Chaos. Ecofeminism and the Land Question*. Ed. Ana Isla. Toronto: Inanna Publications & Education Inc., pp. 94–124.

Isla, Ana. (Forthcoming) "The 'Greening': Stretching Biopiracy" in *Handbook on Latin America and the Environment*.

McCarten, James. *Canada Warns Michigan Oil Line Shutdown Could Undermine U.S. Ties*. www.ctvnews.ca/politics/canada-warns-michigan-oil-line-shutdown-could-undermine-u-s-ties-1.5423101 (accessed May 12, 2021).

Mellor, Mary. (2010) *The Future of Money: From Financial Crisis to Public Resources*. New York: Pluto Press.

Merchant, Carolyn. (1983) *The Death of Nature: Women, Ecology and the Scientific Revolution*. San Francisco: Harper and Row.

Merchant, Carolyn. (2005) *Radical Ecology*. New York and London: Routledge.

Mies, Maria. (1986) *Patriarchy and Accumulation on a World Scale: Women in the International Division of Labour*. London: Zed Books.

(MMIWG) National Inquiry into Missing and Murdered Indigenous Women and Girl. (2016) www.mmiwg-ffada.ca/final-report/ (accessed December 12, 2020).

Rights Action. *Archives – Hudbay Mineral* (INCO, SKYE Resources, Solway Investment Group). https://rightsaction.org/hudbay-minerals-archives

Rodriguez, Javier. (2009) '*Vienen por el ORO vienen por todo. Las invasiones mineras 500 años después*'. Argentina: Ediciones Ciccus.

Salleh, Ariel. (2004) "Global Alternatives and the Meta-Industrial class" in *New Socialisms: Futures Beyond Globalization*. Eds. Robert Albritton, Shannon Bell, and Richard Westra. London, England: Routledge, pp. 201–211.

Shiva, Vandana. (1989) *Staying Alive: Women, Ecology, and Development*. London: Zed Books.

SOA Watch. (n.d.) http://soaw.or/home/ (accessed April 23, 2021).

"The Johannesburg Summit Test: What will change?" U.N. Feature Story, Johannesburg, Summit 26 August-4 September 2002. New York, 25 September.

Treaties Still Matter. 2016. *The Dakota Access Pipeline*. https://americanindian.si.edu/nk360/plains-treaties/dapl (accessed December 8, 2019).

Truth and Reconciliation Commission of Canada. (2015) www.trc.ca (accessed April 15, 2021).

WCED (World Commission on Environment and Development). (1987) *Our Common Future*. New York: Oxford University Press.

WRM (World Rainforest Movement). (2020) *Deforestation in the Amazon and the REDD money keeps coming to Brazil*. https://wrm.org.uy/articles-from-the-wrm-bulletin/section1/deforestation-in-the-amazon-and-the-redd-money-that-keeps-coming-to-brazil/

Zaitchik, Alexander. (2014). Meet the Amazon Tribespeople Who Beat Chevron. . . https://grist.org/climate-energy/meet-the-amazon-tribespeople-who-beat-chevron-in-court-but are-still-fighting-for-clean-water/ (accessed May 14, 2018).

13

CLIMATE CHANGE MOVEMENTS IN THE GLOBAL NORTH

Eugene Nulman

Introduction

The climate change movement, similar to the environmental movement as a whole, as pointed out in the introduction to this *Handbook*, is a heterogenous network of formal organizations, informal groups, and individuals working to address the issue of global warming and its various effects, caused by greenhouse gas emissions. The movement consists of organizations and campaigns that focus on a broad range of prognoses and diagnoses of climate change, often coming together to mount pressure on government and corporate actors.

The establishment of a climate change movement was gradual. When the scientific community first began seriously debating climate change, the complexity of the issue delayed activism. Scientific consensus began to form years prior to the first efforts of social movement actors to tackle the issue. However, it was partially the work of some environmentalists that led to the issue becoming a matter of political discussion, although this was not enough to secure much early action on the part of states. Even after the issue became a key topic among environmental scientists and an international summit was established to work toward a climate treaty, many environmental organizations ignored the issue due to its global scale and delayed effects. Despite the limited role activists played in these early years, it can be argued that prior activism – from the student movement to the environmental movement – created a "cognitive praxis" to enable climate change to eventually become an issue political actors and the public could conceptualize and understand.

Later, in a context in which early political negotiations on climate change were often hampered by the United States and the United Kingdom, and the general public was becoming increasingly aware of the issue, environmental organizations began mobilizing around climate change. Environmentalists mobilized public concern and used their own expertise to push policymakers to increase their pledges during negotiations. The international negotiations, known as Conferences of the Parties (COPs), highlighted divisions among movement organizations concerning their stance on equity between the developed and greenhouse gas–emitting countries in the Global North and those in the Global South. "Climate justice" became the term used for advocating for the serious incorporation of the concerns of less-developed countries and their populations. Climate justice activists formed their own network due to their differences with other members of the climate change movement.

DOI: 10.4324/9780367855680-15

In addition to campaigns at the international level, which often targeted the sites of negotiations and increasingly included acts of civil disobedience and other forms of protest, climate change campaigns and organizations also addressed the policies and practices of the governments and populations of individual countries. In the case of Friends of the Earth and the UK, for example, such mobilization and the availability of dynamic political opportunities led to the enactment of the Climate Change Act 2008. In other cases, localized mobilization around climate change often focused on material sites of ongoing or growing greenhouse gas emissions, such as the Keystone XL oil pipeline and Heathrow Airport. More recently, there has been an upsurge in climate protests led by young, school-aged children and civil disobedience–oriented protesters, whose framing of the issue focuses on reshaping the future and avoiding extinction. This chapter expands on this very brief history of the different aspects of the climate change movement, with a focus on campaigns in the Global North.

Climate change as a political issue

Concerns about greenhouse gases going into the atmosphere, primarily from the burning of fossil fuels, had been a topic of scientific debate for decades prior to mobilization on the issue (see Soroos, 2002; Zillman, 2009). Climate change featured as a minor component in wider investigations into environmental concerns and policy with government-backed research units helping further the scientific knowledge of global warming. By 1979, climate change became an issue pressing enough to demand a global scientific summit, the World Climate Conference, which was held in Geneva.

Indeed, a few months after the Conference, climate change became an international political issue, but not as one may have expected. Just one month after taking office, the new Prime Minister of the United Kingdom, Margaret Thatcher, attended the G7 Summit in Tokyo. On the eve of the summit, Thatcher remarked that "[we] should also be worried about the effect of constantly burning more coal and oil because that can create a band of carbon dioxide round the earth which could itself have very damaging ecological effects" (Moore, 2013: 448). Evidently, the issue was raised during the G7 meeting, as was acknowledged in the Summit Declaration (Nulman, 2015: 10), but it only formed a small part of the discussion, which was primary concerned with the increased price of oil, thus leading to a decision to reduce oil imports across the countries and to replace them with other sources. Ironically, the primary source of energy being advocated was coal.

It would take more than 10 years after the first World Climate Conference before an international conference working toward a treaty on climate change took place. This conference, the Second Climate Conference, was held in Geneva in the fall of 1990. In the decade in between, movement organizations had a mixed record in placing climate change on the agenda. Rafe Pomerance of Friends of the Earth was one of the first movement entrepreneurs on the issue, first bringing the issue to the attention of policymakers (see Rich, 2019: 13–14; Weart, 2020) and later testifying before the US House Committee on Science and Technology that government must act by funding further research, protecting low-lying coastal areas, and promoting energy efficiency and conservation (Pomerance, 1984 [2017]: 141–144).

However, most environmental movement organizations at that time failed to incorporate climate change into their activist work. The issue was daunting in scale and lacked the immediate impact that generated the publicity and public outrage of "backyard" issues such as Love Canal or Three Mile Island. For Friends of the Earth in the US, climate change's "insubstantiality made it difficult to rally the older activists" (Rich, 2019: 98). For the Sierra Club, the criteria of international campaigns were achievable goals around "clear and discrete" problems with regulatory solutions and increased public interest, as opposed to issues that were "too exotic" or "overly technical" (McCloskey, 1982 [2017]: 121–122). This left out climate change at that time. Pomerance himself left Friends of the Earth due to issues of making climate change an area of importance for the organization (Rich, 2019: 98). The pressures on environmental organizations in the US caused by the Reagan administration's destruction of environmental gains made climate change a second-tier issue.

While those early years of mild climate change activism played a small but important role in the politicization of the issue, some have argued that movements had made it cognitively easier to engage politicians and the public with the message of climate change that has since become well understood and accepted. Jamison (2010) argues that movements helped shape the context and knowledge base by which scientists and others were able to communicate their concerns about the climate. The environmental movement of the 1970s developed a "cognitive praxis" of holism that allowed for the systematic thinking needed to connect fossil fuel burning with future climate events and changes. Cognitive praxis is the interpretive framework developed by, used within, and espoused through social movements (Eyerman and Jameson, 1998: 19), and the modern environmental movement itself was arguably developed through the cognitive praxis of the student movements of the 1960s, which provided a space for critiquing the misuses of science and technology (Jamison, 2004: 67). Thus, movements facilitated climate science reaching the general public through the shared understanding of interconnectedness and the importance of the natural world. Beyond the cognitive framework, the networks, resources, and skills of movement organizations and activists helped facilitate the dissemination of scientific knowledge regarding climate change to the public and to policymakers (see, e.g., Rich, 2019).

Early international climate change negotiations and activism

In 1988, the Canadian government sponsored the World Conference on the Changing Atmosphere, which attracted delegates from nearly 50 countries. The event called for the establishment of an international framework to deal with the issue alongside greater research and monitoring of climate change (Soroos, 2002: 126; Zillman, 2009). It closed with a call for a comprehensive and holistic international solution. The following year, an event to create a framework on "the law of the atmosphere" addressing climate change, along with acid rain and ozone depletion (Bodansky, 1994: 53), failed to come to a resolution because of the lack of US support (Macdonald and Smith, 1999–2000: 110). The US preferred to have more scientific evidence before entering negotiations (Bodansky, 1994: 54), though they later changed their position following pressure from other countries.

The Intergovernmental Panel on Climate Change (IPCC) was established by the UN in 1988 and tasked to

> prepare a comprehensive review and recommendations with respect to the state of knowledge of the science of climate change; the social and economic impact of climate change, and potential response strategies and elements for inclusion in a possible future international convention on climate.
>
> (Hecht, 2018: 102)

This was less powerful than the proposed global environmental organization backed by the International Court of Justice and a result of political maneuvering by the US and UK (Cass, 2006: 24–26).

From the public perspective, by January 1989, climate change was making headlines. *TIME* magazine had a "planet of the year" issue featuring an article on climate change (Lemonick, 1989; Dessler and Parson, 2010: 23–24), and opinion polls were showing that climate change had become an important public concern (Weart, 2004: 116–117). It was at this point that a social movement began to mobilize around the issue.

In 1989, dozens of environmental organizations met in Hanover, Germany, to discuss climate change (Weart, 2011: 72) and coordinate lobbying efforts for the Second World Climate Conference that would take place the following year (Lipschutz and McKendry, 2011: 375). With the lead from Greenpeace International and the Environmental Defense Fund, the meeting resulted in the establishment of a coordinated network called Climate Action Network (CAN) (Weart, 2011: 72). The network started off with 63 environmental non-governmental organizations (ENGOs) from 22 countries in the Global North (Newell, 2000, 126; Rahman and Annie, 1994: 246) and was a body by which these organizations could discuss policy positions, share strategies, and develop common platforms to achieve the goal "to keep global warming as below 2°C as possible" (Lipschutz and McKendry, 2011: 375).

Attempts at lobbying policymakers to establish a strong framework for action at the Second World Climate Conference was not particularly successful. Intense debate among delegations led to the Ministerial Declaration failing to assign any specific targets, leaving only broad principles of equity and sustainability. A framework treaty was delayed until 1992, when national delegations would meet for the United Nations Conference on Environment and Development (UNCED), known as the Earth Summit (Nulman, 2015: 13–15).

The Intergovernmental Negotiating Committee for a Framework Convention on Climate Change (INC) was established by the UN General Assembly and tasked with holding meetings prior to the Earth Summit to prepare the framework that was due to be discussed. In preparation, NGOs prepared draft texts that could be agreed on as the basis of negotiation (Bodansky, 1994: 62). At the INC meetings themselves, ENGO were formally incorporated in the process through a platform for NGOs to make a single, collective statement to the delegations (INC, 1991: 11), despite their internal disagreements (Rahman and Annie, 1994: 251–252).

Ultimately, NGOs were only given a symbolic role in the formal negotiations (Faulkner, 1994: 231), and even the draft texts provided by the NGOs prior to the meeting failed to result in a negotiating text being adopted (Bodansky, 1994: 62). Thus, NGOs had to do most of the work behind the scenes. Individual ENGOs attempted to influence the meetings by communicating with policymakers who were keen to speak with organizations that had expertise on the issue due to the scientific complexity of climate change (see Rahman and Annie, 1994: 251). In the end, this proved somewhat useful as "the most controversial issues were not even brought to the main forum of negotiations after consultations between the delegates and the NGOs" (ibid.).

CAN also attempted to influence the meetings through the publication of *ECO*, a daily newsletter that summarized the debates taking place and made suggestions from the perspective of the NGOs (ibid.: 249). *ECO* has been sustained throughout each year's negotiations and was "the most widely read source of information on the negotiations" (Dowdeswell and Kinley, 1994: 129; see also Betsill, 2008). Outside these formal spaces of negotiations, ENGOs were bringing climate change to the attention of the public, with Greenpeace publishing the book *Global Warming: The Greenpeace Report* and Friends of the Earth raising awareness through local groups across countries (Rahman and Annie, 1994: 245).

NGOs were pushing for commitments for rapid, effective, and meaningful reductions of greenhouse gases and that these commitments should be made by developed countries who had historically produced emissions. The latter demand seemed firmly rooted into the framework, but the former was rejected by the US and UK delegations, leading to an INC that was weak. In addition, flexibility mechanisms, which allow countries to offset emissions using carbon sinks such as forests or through investing in greenhouse gas–reduction projects in other countries, were included in the INC (ibid: 266–269), though not all ENGOs were opposed to this, such as CAN Europe, a regional subnetwork of CAN (Chasek et al., 1998: 12).

The arms-length treatment of NGOs continued in the Earth Summit, an international conference that was meant to lead to government action on the issue of climate change. The Summit included 172 countries, over 115 heads of state or government, 9,000 members of the press, and thousands of NGOs (Adams, 2001: 80). The UNCED Secretariat helped organize a gathering of non-governmental organizations alongside the Summit, known as the Global Forum. The Forum "was a mixture of extensive NGO networking, street fair, trade show, political demonstration, and general events" (Parson et al., 2010). Here, 18,000 people participated in what some referred to as a counter-summit because, while it may have been helpful in coordinating NGO responses or generating publicity for the issue, it also served to remove the NGOs from the formal conference of government delegations where the real negotiations were taking place. This was not just a symbolic separation but a physical one as the Global Forum was established over 20 miles away from the Earth Summit (Nulman, 2015: 14; Parson et al., 2010).

The Earth Summit became the vehicle for countries to sign up to the UNFCCC, which only included a general commitment to stabilize emissions at 1990 levels by 2000. The general commitment was not specific enough to make the Convention legally binding, again a product of US disagreement (Little, 1995). Nevertheless, the UNFCCC provided the framework for negotiating stronger commitments in the future.

Conference of the Parties

Following the Earth Summit, a series of negotiations to create a legislative framework that would prevent or reduce global warming was announced. These were the Conferences of the Parties, with the first conference (COP1) taking place in Berlin in 1995. There, many ENGOs supported the position of the Alliance of Small Island States (AOSIS), which advanced a draft protocol calling on certain rich and middle-income countries to cut CO_2 emissions to 20% below 1990 levels by 2005 (Nulman, 2015: 15). Enough countries disagreed with the proposal that the NGOs had to sit down alongside a group of 72 countries to redraft the policy known as the Green Paper. In the end, however, the influence of key states and their opposition to making significant changes in their emissions, especially in an asymmetric way relative to their political opponents, overshadowed the work of the NGOs. They decried the final outcome, the Berlin Mandate, as " 'soft' at best" (Earth Negotiations Bulletin, n.d.).

In an attempt to increase their impact at the COPs, environmental organizations and other NGOs formed into networks such as the KILMAFORUM '95 during COP1 and the Kiko Forum organized for COP3 in Kyoto, Japan. These networks facilitated communication between the NGOs as well as communicating to the general public, especially via the news media (Muller-Kreanner, n.d.). The Kiko Forum was initiated a year before COP3 and grew from a network of 46 organizations to 225 by the time of the negotiations. This network organized demonstrations, a petition, and hundreds of public workshops. NGO participation in the Kyoto Protocol was dominated by ENGOs from the Global North, with large delegations from some of the largest ENGOs such as World Wide Fund for Nature (WWF), Greenpeace, and Friends of the Earth (Betsill, 2008: 46). Many ENGOs continued to coordinate their efforts under the CAN umbrella, which regionalized its collective lobbying efforts into eight sections: Africa, Australia, Central and Eastern Europe, Europe/United Kingdom, Latin America, South

Asia, Southeast Asia, and the United States/Canada. As a network, CAN had four objectives for an agreement made at COP3: reducing greenhouse gas emissions 20% below 1990 levels by 2005 for industrialized countries, strong review and compliance mechanisms, not including emissions trading as a mechanism to meeting reduction commitments, and not including sinks that absorb emissions to offset reductions (ibid: 46–47).

As access to the negotiations for ENGOs was limited, some had to engage in subterfuge to try to achieve these results. There are reports of searching through rubbish bins to find documents and lurking in hallways to overhear the conversations of delegates (ibid: 47–49). What leverage the ENGOs did have largely came from their expertise on the issue while government delegates had little specific knowledge.

The COP3 negotiations led to the creation of the Kyoto Protocol, a compromise position between the US and the EU that was only arrived at in the final hours of an additional, unscheduled day of negotiations (ibid: 45). The Protocol's first commitment was an aggregate 5.2% reduction of greenhouse gas emissions (based on 1990 levels) by 2012, with individual targets for each country. This was a far cry from what CAN had called for when they supported a 20% reduction by 2005 as outlined in the AOSIS proposal. Largely, ENGOs failed to influence the overall outcome of the negotiations but did have some impact on the positions taken by certain national delegations (Rahman and Annie, 1994; Corell and Betsill, 2001: 98; Betsill, 2008: 60–61).

The Kyoto Protocol only came into effect in 2005 after being ratified by Russia in the last months of 2004. Organizations such as the WWF and Greenpeace worked hard to push for Russia to ratify, but the decision was only made after substantial political concessions were granted by the international community (Tipton, 2008; Henry and Sundstrom, 2007). By 2007, the Protocol was already looking weak as Japan and Canada both expressed concerns about the targets. NGOs began to address these concerns and provide these countries with the political motivations to stay in the agreement. In addition, new climate movement organizations and networks, such as the Global Call for Climate Action (TckTckTck) and the Climate Justice Network, formed (Nulman, 2015: 18–19).

Every year's international negotiations were met with protests of some form or another calling for greater action to be taken and to remove aspects of the policy that activists believed were commodifying the environment or preventing real decarbonization from occurring. Following the Kyoto Protocol, which set emissions targets through 2012, these protests increased, particularly as the next wave of negotiations was cooling to the idea of significant targets, and some countries were failing to meet their targets set in the Kyoto Protocol. The next step beyond Kyoto was to be discussed at COP15 in Copenhagen. These decisions were meant to provide commitments for the period following 2012, and activists geared up to impact the negotiations. Between 20,000 and 30,000 NGO observers participated in the COP, the largest number of any Conference of the Parties to date (Fisher, 2010: 12; also see Climate Action Network, 2009b). Even more people gathered outside the negotiations to demonstrate the lack of progress on mitigating climate change. Between 60,000 and 100,000 protesters demonstrated for "system change, not climate change" (Nulman, 2015: 20), putting pressure on the NGO observers inside the negotiations, with Friends of the Earth International, Avaaz, and TckTckTck having their observer statuses revoked (Fisher, 2010: 15). Some have argued that the mobilization outside the hall was central to the passage of the Copenhagen Accord (Rietig, 2011), which, while still deemed weak by many, was stronger than nothing.

The Copenhagen Accord was a non-binding statement endorsing a continuation of the Kyoto Protocol, acknowledging the importance of preventing an increase in global temperatures of 2° Celsius and agreeing to establish new emission targets at a later date, failing to set out targets itself. While protest efforts had waned until 2015, large NGOs continued to attend the COPs to push for change. Progress was slow, and commitments were weak. Wealthy countries had even failed to provide poor countries with the funding to adapt to climate change at COP19 in 2013, provoking NGOs such as WWF, Friends of the Earth, and Greenpeace to walk out of the conference (Nulman, 2015: 20).

The next set of targets were set to be agreed at COP 21 in Paris in 2015. Two weeks prior to the conference, terrorist attacks occurred in Paris, causing martial law to be imposed on the city and a state of emergency ban on demonstrations. Climate movement organizations had been planning to make the demonstrations in Paris the largest ever for any COP, expecting 200,000 participants. Despite the restrictions, thousands still participated in physical and symbolic protests such as covering the area where marchers were to demonstrate with more than 20,000 shoes (Orr, 2016: 26)

Climate justice

The early phases of international negotiations to deal with climate change featured a division across national delegations that was to some extent replicated across NGOs. Specifically, NGOs and delegates from the Global North differed in their approach to addressing the problem relative to their Global South counterparts. For those in the Global South, equity, sustainability, and development were all crucial components of the conversation around climate change. Countries in the Global North had been historically the ones emitting the most greenhouse gases; their populations continue to contribute a larger proportion of greenhouse gas emissions per capita through their lifestyles and consumption patterns; in addition, countries in the Global North have more wealth to offset the damage done by climate change. This tension was noticeable during INC meetings where NGOs from the Global South, although under-represented in the process, pushed for initiatives around global equity – arguing against the concept of joint implementation, against the proposed financial mechanism for the subsequent treaty, and in favor of per capita entitlements (for more, see Rahman and Annie, 1994). The voices that were calling for such a just transition rooted in equity labelled this perspective "climate justice".

Further differences emerged in 1997 when the first international network on climate change, Climate Action Network, advocated the "minor, incremental emissions reductions augmented by carbon trading related offsets" (Bond, 2011). Climate justice activists were making much stronger demands, such as calls for 50% greenhouse gas emissions cuts by 2020, and opposed carbon trading (Bond, 2011). It was not only NGOs from the Global South that took the climate justice position. For example, the US-based organization CorpWatch was also an early climate justice organization. Established in 1996 to address issues of corporate accountability, the organization published a report entitled "Greenhouse Gangsters vs. Climate Justice", in which they defined climate justice as "holding fossil fuel corporations accountable for the central role they play in contributing to global warming" using solutions that would not "fall hardest on low income communities, communities of color, or the workers" (Bruno et al., 1999: 3). This was one of the first acknowledged uses of the concept, and it followed from the idea of the environmental justice movement that looked at the intersections between environmental problems and inequalities (Tokar, 2013). For CorpWatch, corporations and the elites proposed "false solutions" to the climate change problem.

In 2000, the year after they published that report, CorpWatch and other organizations from around the world converged at the first Climate Justice Summit, which coincided with the COP6 held in The Hague (Warlenius, 2018: 36), demonstrating how wide ranging and well networked the movement had become. Approximately 500 activists from around the world participated in that Summit (Chawla, 2009). Discussions were held by the climate justice activists, but the Climate Justice Summit also enabled protests, which occurred inside and outside the official negotiations. Having presented fake conference passes, some activists stormed into a closed negotiating session. Others, equipped with a banner reading "Carbon Trading: Profits ✓ Progress X", got into the main conference area and put the banner on display for all the delegates to see. Two women even entered a press conference with a lead US negotiator and threw a cream pie in his face (Whitehead, 2014; Loong, 2000). Meanwhile, inside the negotiations, other NGOs such as WWF, Greenpeace International, and Climate Action Network South Asia distanced themselves from these actions as they were busy trying to assert whatever political capital they had to affect the final wording of policy documents and delegation positions (Loong, 2000: 19). That summit in 2000 "was a turning point for [climate justice's] prominence in the climate change movement" (Whitehead, 2014).

CorpWatch was also part of a consortium of 28 environmental, civil rights, and environmental justice organizations based in the United States. These organizations included the Deep South Center for Environmental Justice, the Black Leadership Forum, and Communities for a Better Environment. The consortium was called the Environmental Justice and Climate Change Initiative (EJCCI), and in 2001, they developed the "10 Principles for Just Climate Change Policies in the US" (Newton, 2009: 102–103).

1 Stop cooking the planet
2 Protect and empower vulnerable individuals and communities
3 Ensure just transition for workers and communities
4 Require community participation
5 Global problems need global solutions
6 The US must lead
7 Stop exploration for fossil fuels
8 Monitor domestic and international carbon markets
9 Caution in the face of uncertainty
10 Protect future generations

The following year, the United Nations organized a World Summit on Sustainable Development, which was held in Johannesburg. Prior to this, they held a final preparatory meeting in Bali, where NGOs also got together and developed the Bali Principles of Climate Justice, which sought to push for climate justice to be incorporated into any international agreement that would be discussed in the World Summit. Crafted by organizations that included CorpWatch, Greenpeace International, Third World Network, and the Indigenous Environmental Network (Pezzullo and Cox, 2018: 292), the Bali Principles of Climate Justice echoed the Environmental Justice Principles that were developed in 1991 at the People of Color Environmental Justice Leadership Summit in Washington, DC, and transposed them onto issues of climate change. The Bali Principles further articulated the meaning of climate justice by specifically affirming Indigenous rights and democratic responsibilities of states and curtailing corporate power within the context of policies to reduce greenhouse gas emissions. The Bali Principles also brought up the notion of the ecological debt that was owed by the Global North and transnational corporations to the Global South. This was the debt of benefiting from the environmental destruction that has negatively impacted the Global South. Some have argued that the Bali Principles of Climate Justice were crucial in reframing climate change for the general public from an issue that was purely scientific and technical to one that was rooted in human rights and ethics (Agyeman et al., 2007: 119). The Bali Principles of Climate Justice were adopted at the 2002 Earth Summit and endorsed by 14 organizations from different parts of the world. The introduction to the document called on the international community to participate in the Climate Justice Summit held in New Delhi in parallel with the COP8 meeting.

At COP8, details of the Kyoto Protocol were being negotiated at the UNFCCC, and activists organized a coalition of groups under the umbrella Indian Climate Justice Forum. This was a space not just for development and environmental organizations, but for ordinary men and women in India to have their voices heard. In total, the Forum had over 1,500 participants from over 20 countries and 17 states in India. Protests were organized, including the largest climate justice protest in history up to that point, which, despite being unpermitted, included more than 5,000 demonstrators (Khastagir, 2002).

At the end of COP8, no new emissions reductions were proposed, but the conference ended with the Delhi Ministerial Declaration on Climate Change and Sustainable Development, which meagerly stated that "Parties have a right to, and should, promote sustainable development". The movement countered this declaration with one of their own. The Delhi Climate Justice Declaration placed the poor and marginalized at the front and center while rejecting market-based approaches, concluding with the line "Our World is Not for Sale!"

Campaigns for local and national climate change policies

While some organizations campaigned for greater efforts to be made in curbing climate change and making a more just transition within the international negotiations, others were working hard to influence national and local policies. To explore this further, we will take the campaigns in the United Kingdom as examples. In the UK, local campaigns included attempts at stopping an airport expansion, getting organizations to divest from fossil fuel companies, and forcing policy makers to enact their own emissions targets above and beyond those demanded through international negotiations.

One campaign by the climate change movement in the UK included involvement in a local struggle against airport expansion. Heathrow Airport, the largest airport in the country, was looking to expand by adding a third runway. Due to a range of concerns including aviation emissions, national organizations and local groups formed a network to campaign to stop the expansion project, which would have made Heathrow Airport the single largest greenhouse gas emitter in the UK (Nulman, 2015: 33). Local activists against noise pollution were joined by direct action–oriented climate change protesters, and while the different segments did not always see eye to eye, working together helped bridge the ideological gaps between the more anti-capitalist climate campaigners and the local community. By taking advantage of dynamic political opportunities, together, the campaigners were successfully able to fend off the Conservative-led government from approving the airport's expansion (Nulman, 2015), at least at the time of writing.

A divestment campaign was created by 350.org and others who came together to form a campaigning organization called Fossil Free, which began by pressuring local government pension funds to freeze any new investments into fossil fuels and divest from fossil fuel public equities and corporate bonds. In 2015, two national Friends of the Earth groups, Platform, 350.org, and Community Reinvest joined forces to produce a report that detailed how such UK pension schemes were funding the fossil fuel industry. The report noted that £14 billion of local government pension funds were being invested in fossil fuel corporations, and it called on councils to divest from these companies and reinvest in renewable energy, public transport, and social housing. Along with local activist groups, Fossil Free was able to use protests, petitions, and publicity to get the Environment Agency Pension Fund, the Waltham Forest Pension Fund, and the South Yorkshire Pension Fund to announce their divestment plans within two years of the report being published (Lander, 2017: 9).

Before Fossil Fuel was pushing businesses and local councils to divest, Friends of the Earth had launched a campaign to get the UK government to push through national legislation calling on 80% emissions reductions in the UK by 2050. This campaign was known as the Big Ask Campaign, and Friends of the Earth called on its local groups to campaign on the issue while on the national level, the organization lobbied the main political parties, pushing them to a adopt the policy. Activists on the ground were asked to get members of the public to sign postcards calling on their Member of Parliament to sign up to support the policy. Their campaign coincided with an attempt by the center-right Conservative Party, under the leadership of David Cameron, to rebrand away from its "nasty party" image by adopting green positions. The public pressure and the political expedience led the Conservative Party to adopt the climate change policy, generating political competition on the issue. Soon, the Labour government was pressured into adopting the legislation so as not to be outflanked by the traditionally less environmentally friendly Conservatives. The Big Ask campaign featured protests, petitions, and publicity stunts in which other campaigning groups, including a network of over 100 organizations called Stop Climate Chaos, participated. The campaign was also supported by a number of environmentally conscious Members of Parliament as well as celebrities such as Radiohead frontman Thom Yorke, who became a Friends of the Earth spokesman on the issue (Nulman, 2015).

These examples demonstrate the multi-level and organizational networking and campaigning that occurs within the climate movement. From the local to the national level, a variety of campaigning groups networked together or supported each other's campaigns to drive reforms in an effort to mitigate climate change.

For larger organizations, their efforts were spread across international-level policy change as well as local and national policy changes. We can look at the WWF as one example that managed to campaign on issues across international and local campaigns. WWF, a conservation organization working in 100 countries with support of over five million members, could be found in the halls of the UNFCCC, but it was also playing a role in calling for mayors of cities in the US to make changes in their jurisdictions. Together with the ICLEI-Local Governments for Sustainability, the National League of Cities, and the US Green Building Council, they formed the Resilient Communities for America campaign in 2013 (ICLEA, n.d.).

Recent climate mobilization around the world

A relatively recent wave of mobilization around the issue of climate change has hit the world head on in the last few years. From Indigenous communities protecting their lands from the fossil fuel industry to global strikes by students worried about the world they will inherit to campaigns recognizing that climate change may lead to extinction, movements have mobilized, particularly due to the failures of international negotiations and stagnant policy change.

In 2016 in the United States, following the precedent of the XL Pipeline protests of 2012, environmental and Indigenous activists gathered at camps near a location where a crude oil transport was being constructed, known as the Dakota Access Pipeline (DAPL). Thousands had gathered to demonstrate against the risks of the pipeline to the health of the nearby Indigenous communities, the destruction of their land, and the continuation of the use of fossil fuels. The #NoDAPL movement had to withstand brutal treatment from private security and generated enough pressure to force President Obama and his administration to delay the project in order to undertake an impact assessment, leading to further delays that some perceived would financially ruin the project. A decision was made not to allow the project to continue on the route originally planned, but that decision was reversed soon after Donald Trump took office (see Whyte, 2017), providing further evidence of the importance of dynamic political opportunities for such victories.

In 2018, a 15-year-old Swedish girl, Greta Thunberg, refused to go to school until the Swedish general elections as a protest of climate inaction. This triggered others to join her, leading to school strikes that spread across many countries. A day of climate strikes by school-aged children was declared for 15 March 2019, and on that day, an estimated 1.6 million students across over 120 countries went on strike from school in protest. These strikes sometimes became regular occurrences, when students would either leave early or not attend school on Friday in support of the strikes, often gathering together to hold demonstrations. These became referred to as Fridays for Future or Climate Strikes (Jung et al., 2020).

In 2018 in the United Kingdom, activists formed an organization called Extinction Rebellion (XR), which framed the issue of climate change as leading to human extinction and thereby called on people to engage in non-violent civil disobedience that would lead to arrests in an attempt to force policy change before it was too late. In particular, the organization called on the government to act by communicating the urgency of the ecological emergency, reaching net-zero emissions by 2025, and following the decisions of a government-created Citizens' Assembly on climate and ecological justice.

Local XR chapters were formed, and within them, small affinity groups of activists were organized to take actions of civil disobedience that would create enough disruption to push through policy change. Mass actions were planned on strategic days when people could be mobilized for substantial amounts of time, and demonstrations were planned primarily in London, where they would have the most strategic disruptive impact on government and businesses while also providing the news media an easy opportunity to cover the action. These protests, coupled with the Climate Strikes, pushed the UK government, under the leadership of Conservative Prime Minister Theresa May, to declare a climate emergency, but at the time of writing, the demands of XR have not been met. XR continued to push for their demands during the COVID-19 lockdowns, holding local socially distanced protests.

Conclusion

A movement that was slow to begin mobilizing, in part due to the delayed impacts of climate change, is now acting with urgency to address a potentially existential crisis. Scientists and activists alike believe policymakers have failed to develop effective national and international mechanisms for curbing greenhouse gas emissions, and data continues to suggest that we have gone past key thresholds that indicate that the world will no longer be in a position to prevent significant harms from climate change. Indeed, when compared with various climate models, our position at the time of writing suggests that we are on the trajectory predicted by the models with more worrying consequences.

In 2009, many climate activists framed the Copenhagen COP as the international community's last chance to mitigate climate change. The mobilization for that conference often framed the prognosis as dire and urgent. Having failed to attain the desired results, that language briefly subsided. The most recent wave of protests reignited the call for urgent action and describes climate change as an extinction-level event. As I write, fires continue to blaze on the West Coast of the United States, having already burned millions of acres, causing air quality to dip to dangerous levels across Oregon, Washington, and California; five tropical cyclones are presently in the Atlantic Ocean at the same time – a phenomenon only recorded once before; a

70-square-kilometer glacier has broken off an ice sheet in Greenland. Activists have increasingly used record-breaking temperatures and extreme weather events to highlight the growing risks that climate change poses, especially as such events are increasing in frequency.

While these events occur, the world is also facing a pandemic, which makes predicting the trajectory of the climate change movement particularly difficult. However, COVID-19 has not prevented climate change protests and widespread civil disobedience from taking place. It is possible that if protest actions continue to grow, they can disincentivize governments in key countries such as the United States from sitting on their hands. This would enable the world to take substantial steps toward minimizing the damage of climate change and working toward adapting to the changes we can no longer prevent.

References

Adams, W. M. (2001) *Green Development: Environment and sustainability in the Third World*, London: Routledge.

Agyeman, J., Doppelt, B., Lynn, K., and Hattic, H. (2007) 'The Climate-Justice Link: Communicating Risk with Low-Income and Minority Audiences', in Moser, S. C., and Dilling, L. (eds) *Creating a Climate for Change: Communicating Climate Change and Facilitating Social Change*, Cambridge: Cambridge University Press, pp. 119–138.

Betsill, M. M. (2008) 'Environmental NGOs and the Kyoto Protocol Negotiations: 1995 to 1997', in Betsill, M. M., and Corell, E. (eds) *NGO Diplomacy: The Influence of Nongovernmental Organizations in International Environmental Negotiations*, Cambridge, MA: The MIT Press, pp. 43–66.

Bodansky, D. (1994) 'Prologue to the Climate Change Convention', in Mintzer, I. M., and Leonard, J. A. (eds) *Negotiating Climate Change: The Inside Story of the Rio Convention*, Cambridge: Cambridge University Press, pp. 45–74.

Bond, P. (2011) *Politics of Climate Justice: Paralysis Above, Movement Below*, Presented to the Gyeongsang University Institute of Social Science, Jinju, 27 May.

Bruno, K., Karliner, J., and Brotsky, C. (1999) *Greenhouse Gangsters vs Climate Justice*. www.corpwatch.org/sites/default/files/Greenhouse%20Gangsters.pdf

Cass, L. R. (2006) *The Failures of American and European Climate Policy: International Norms, Domestic Politics, and Unachievable Commitments*, Albany: State University of New York Press.

Chasek, P., Downie, D. L., Baumert, K. Clark, S., Tosteson, J., Bissell, L., Hjerthen, J., Hjerthen, J., Jayaraman, B., Karkus, E., Leahy, J., and Mulder, G. (1998) 'European Union Views on International Greenhouse Gas Emissions Trading', Columbia University School of International and Public Affairs Environmental Policy Studies Working Paper 3. Columbia University, 18 May 1998.

Chawla, A. (2009) 'Climate Justice Movements Gather Strength', in Starke, Linda (ed.) *2009 State of the World: Confronting Climate Change*, London: Earthscan, pp. 119–121.

Climate Action Network. (2009b) 'Outrage over Lockout', *ECO, CXXII*(11): 4.

Corell, E., and Betsill, M. M. (2001) 'A Comparative Look at NGO Influence in International Environmental Negotiations: Desertification and Climate Change', *Global Environmental Politics*, 1(4): 86–107.

Dessler, A. E., and Parson, E. A. (2010) *The Science and Politics of Global Climate Change: A Guide to the Debate*, Cambridge: Cambridge University Press.

Dowdeswell, E., and Kinley, R. J. (1994) 'Constructive Damage to the Status Quo', in Mintzer, I. M., and Leonard J. A. (eds) *Negotiating Climate Change: The Inside Story of the Rio Convention*, Cambridge: Cambridge University Press, pp. 113–128.

Earth Negotiations Bulletin. (n.d.) *Adequacy of Commitments*. https://enb.iisd.org/vol12/1221013e.html

Eyerman, R., and Jameson, A. (1998) *Music and Social Movements: Mobilizing Traditions in the Twentieth Century*, Cambridge: Cambridge University Press.

Faulkner, H. (1994) 'Some Comments on the INC Process', in Mintzer, I. M., and Leonard, J. A. (eds) *Negotiating Climate Change: The Inside Story of the Rio Convention*, Cambridge: Cambridge University Press, pp. 229–238.

Fisher, D. R. (2010) 'COP-15 in Copenhagen: How the Merging of Movements Left Civil Society Out in the Cold', *Global Environmental Politics*, 10(2): 11–17.

Hecht, A. D. (2018) *Making America Green and Safe: A History of Sustainable Development and Climate Change*, Newcastle upon Tyne: Cambridge Scholars Publishing.

Henry, L. A. and Sundstrom, L. M. (2007) 'Russia and the Kyoto Protocol: Seeking an Alignment of Interests and Image', *Global Environmental Politics*, 7(4): 47–69.

ICLEA. (n.d.) *Biggest US Cities Setting Unprecedented Emissions Reductions Goals to Fight Climate Change*. https://icleiusa.org/biggest-us-cities-setting-unprecedented-emissions-reductions-goals-to-fight-climate-change/

INC. (1991) *Report of the Intergovernmental Negotiating Committee for a Framework Convention on Climate Change on the Work of its First Session*, Document A/AC.237/6, [internet site]. http://unfccc.int/resource/docs/a/06.pdf Accessed 10 August 2014.

Jamison, A. (2004) *The Making of Green Knowledge: Environmental Politics and Cultural Transformation*, Cambridge: Cambridge University Press.

Jamison, A. (2010) 'Climate Change Knowledge and Social Movement Theory', *WIREs Climate Change*, 1(6). https://doi.org/10.1002/wcc.88

Jung, J., Petkanic, P., Nan, D., and Hyun Kim, J. (2020) 'When a Girl Awakened the World: A User and Social Message Analysis of Greta Thunberg', *Sustainability*, 12(7): https://doi.org/10.3390/su12072707

Khastagir, N. (2002) 'The Human Face of Climate Change', *Global Policy Forum*, 4 November. www.globalpolicy.org/component/content/article/211/44309.html

Lander, R. (2017) *Fuelling the Fire: A New Report on the Local Government Pension Scheme and Fossil Fuels*. https://631nj1ki9k11gbkhx39b3qpz-wpengine.netdna-ssl.com/uk/wp-content/uploads/sites/3/2017/11/Councils-Fuelling-the-Fire-Online-1.3.pdf

Lemonick, M. D. (1989) 'Global Warming Feeling the Heat the Problem: Greenhouse Gases Could Create a Climatic Calamity', *Time*, 133(1): 36–41.

Lipschutz, R. D., and McKendry, C. (2011) 'Social Movements and Global Civil Society', in Dryzek, J. S., Nordgaard, R. B., and Schlosberg, D. (eds) *The Oxford Handbook of Climate Change and Soci Little, Paul E. (1995) 'Ritual, Power and Ethnography at the Rio Earth Summit', Critique of Anthropology, 15(3): 265–288.ety*, Oxford: Oxford University Press, pp. 369–383.

Little, P. E. (1995) 'Ritual, Power and Ethnography at the Rio Earth Summit', *Critique of Anthropology*, 15(3): 265–288.

Loong, Y. (2000) 'COP6 denounced as "trade-fair" by activists', in *Dissenting Voices*. https://issuu.com/platform-london/docs/dissenting_voices_cop_6_climate_tal

MacDonald, D., and Smith, H. A. (1999–2000) 'Promises Made, Promises Broken – Questioning Canada's Commitments to Climate Change', *International Journal*, 55(1): 107–124.

McCloskey, M. (1982 [2017]) 'Criteria for International Campaigns', in Howe, J. P. (ed.) *Making Climate Change History*, Seattle: University of Washington Press, pp. 121–122.

Moore, C. (2013) *Margaret Thatcher: The Authorized Biography, Volume One: Not for Turning*, London: Penguin.

Muller-Kreanner. (n.d.) *Klima Forum'95*. www.casa1988.or.jp/katudou/aanea/osaka2-e/0315-7-sascha.htm

Newell, P. (2000) *Climate for Change: Non-state Actors and the Global Politics of the Greenhouse*, Cambridge: Cambridge University Press.

Newton, D. E. (2009) *Environmental Justice: A Reference Handbook*, 2nd Edition, Denver: ABC-CLIO.

Nulman, E. (2015) *Climate Change and Social Movements: Civil Society and the Development of National Climate Change Policy*. London: Palgrave Macmillan.

Orr, S. K. (2016) 'Institutional Control and Climate Change Activism at COP 21 in Paris', *Global Environmental Politics*, 16(3): 23–30.

Parson, E. A., Haas, P. M., and Levy, M. A. (2010) 'A Summary of the Major Documents Signed at the Earth Summit and the Global Forum', *Environment: Science and Policy for Sustainable Development*, 34(8): 12–36.

Pezzullo, P. C., and Cox, R. (2018) *Environmental Communication and the Public Sphere*, 5th Edition, Los Angeles: SAGE.

Pomerance, R. (1984 [2017]) 'Testimony Before the House Committee on Science and Technology, February 28, 1984', in Howe, J. P. (ed.) *Making Climate Change History*, Seattle: University of Washington Press, pp. 141–144.

Rahman, A., and Annie, R. (1994) 'A View from the Ground Up', in Mintzer, I. M., and Leonard, J. A. (eds) *Negotiating Climate Change: The Inside Story of the Rio Convention*, Cambridge: Cambridge University Press, pp. 239–273.

Rich, N. (2019) *Losing Earth: The Decade We Could Have Stopped Climate Change*, London: Picador.

Rietig, K. (2011) *Public Pressure versus Lobbying – How Do Environmental NGOs Matter Most in Climate Negotiations?*, Centre for Climate Change Economics and Policy, Working Paper No. 79, Grantham Research Institute on Climate Change and the Environment, Working Paper No. 70. London, UK: Grantham Research Institute on Climate Change and the Environment, London School of Economics and Political Science.

Soroos, M. S. (2002) 'Negotiating Our Climate', in Spray. S. L., and McGlothlin, K. L. (eds) *Global Climate Change*, Lanham, MD: Rowman & Littlefield Publishers.

Tipton, J. E. (2008) 'Why Did Russia Ratify the Kyoto Protocol? Why the Wait? An Analysis of the Environmental, Economic, and Political Debates', *Slovo*, 20(2): 67–96.

Tokar, B. (2013) 'Movements for Climate Justice in the US and Worldwide', in Dietz, M., and Garrelts, H. (eds) *Routledge Handbook of the Climate Change Movement*, Abingdon, UK: Routledge, pp. 131–146.

Warlenius, R. (2018) 'Climate Debt: The Origins of a Subversive Misnomer', in Jacobsen, S. G. (ed.) *Climate Justice and the Economy: Social Mobilization, Knowledge and the Political*, New York: Routledge.

Weart, S. (2011) 'The Oxford Handbook of Climate Change and Society', in Dryzek, J. S., Norgaard, R. B., and Schlosberg, D. (eds) *The Oxford Handbook of Climate Change and Society*, Oxford: Oxford University Press, 67–81.

Weart, S. (2020) *The Discovery of Global Warming*. https://history.aip.org/climate/Govt.htm#L_0498

Weart, S. R. (2004) *The Discovery of Global Warming*, Cambridge, MA: Harvard University Press.

Whitehead, F. (2014) 'The First Climate Justice Summit: A Pie in the Face for the Global North', *The Guardian*, 16 April. www.theguardian.com/global-development-professionals-network/2014/apr/16/climate-change-justice-summit

Whyte, K. P. (2017) 'The Dakota Access Pipeline, Environmental Injustice, and U.S. Colonialism', *REDINK*, 19(1): 154–169.

Zillman, J. W. (2009) 'A history of climate activities', *WMO Bulletin*, 58(3): 141–150.

14

ANIMAL RIGHTS AND ANTI-SPECIESISM

Lyle Munro

Introduction

The chapter explains the importance of the two concepts in the chapter's title. In discussing the idea of animal rights, the term "animal" applies to non-human animals, in contrast to the rights of human animals, although the latter will also be mentioned in the discussion. Furthermore, in accordance with common usage, non-human animals will be referred to in most cases simply as animals. The strategies and tactics of the worldwide APM – sometimes referred to by activists as the animal movement and, more commonly, as the animal rights movement by the public – vary according to the movement's various branches or sub-groups (see Figure 14.1).

Speciesism, a concept first coined by Richard Ryder in 1989, was popularized and defined by Singer (1975: 7) as "a prejudice or attitude of bias toward the interests of members of one's own species and against those of members of other species". For the animal movement, anti-speciesism is meant to imply that its campaigns are akin to movements against racism, sexism, and classism, sociology's most analyzed social problems.

Speciesism and anti-speciesism

While anti-speciesism is what motivates animal protectionists worldwide, speciesism remains a controversial topic among scholars, in the media, and in public discussions on the welfare of animals. Speciesist attitudes and actions are seen by committed activists as a moral issue because if it means that animals can be eaten by humans – arguably the worst atrocity as it denies animals the right to life – then anything can be done to them. Speciesism, however, is a word rarely used by animal protectionists in Australia, the UK, or the USA, where the terms animal "cruelty", "abuse", "exploitation", and "oppression" are preferred to the awkward-sounding neologism. Nonetheless, the practice of speciesism, argues Sanbonmatsu (2014: 31), is so deeply embedded in human consciousness that it "constitutes one of the fundamental existential structures of human life".

Sanbonmatsu maintains that we "need" to kill animals in order to sustain the idea that "the human" defines our civilization (39). He describes humans as animals of bad faith, by which he means we do have a choice about how we treat animals – compassionately or cruelly, as sentient beings or as commodities – but we choose the latter out of self-deception. This form of

 DOI: 10.4324/9780367855680-16

denial is most evident, he believes, in the increasing global expansion of industrialized animal agriculture, which harms the biosphere and imperils life itself, a prospect that Hamilton (2010) warns is "a requiem for our species". While Hamilton's dismal diagnosis offers little hope for our collective ability to change the way we treat the natural world, Sanbonmatsu (2014: 43) sees a glimmer of hope in that the existential threats we face may give birth to a legitimation crisis for speciesism.

As I hope to demonstrate in this chapter, there are signs that people do care about the suffering of animals and have the means to end the worst practices should they decide to do so. To take one example, Johnson et al. (2019) asked a representative sample of Australians (n = 1999) in an online survey about how we should respond to emerging infectious diseases (EIDs). In the "discrete choice experiment", the participants (mean age 45.3 years, 57% male) indicated their priorities in relation to the One Health idea of the interconnectedness of human, animal, and environmental health. The results surprised the academic team:

1   Food security
2   Animal welfare
3   Economic development
4   Environmental health
5   Community cohesion
6   Personal autonomy
7   Free trade
8   Travel

The team's most unexpected finding was that participants were willing to accept extra cases and more deaths from an outbreak of EIDs if food security and animal welfare were not threatened (p. 168). The study began in 2016, well before the current coronavirus between late 2019 and 2020, so it is possible that the results might now be different. What is certain, however, is that governments and people worldwide will need to rethink how animals suffer and die in factory farms and concentrated animal feeding operations (CAFOs), in slaughterhouses, in feedlots, in wet markets, during wildlife trafficking, and in the live animal export trade. As the lethal COVID-19 crisis has shown, the health and well-being of humans, animals, and the environment are inextricably interconnected.[1] For the moment, I describe the animal protection movement (APM) with a focus mainly on Australia, where the modern animal liberation movement originated following the publication of Singer's (1975) *Animal Liberation: A New Ethics for Our Treatment of Animals*.

The main branches of the worldwide APM include the Radical Animal Liberation Front (RALM), which is shown as separate from the three mainstream branches. The reason for this is that the RALM is not (as yet) widely supported by the public due to its reputation for violence. It will be observed that Animal Liberation and Animal Rights share some of the same characteristics, although the latter demands more from its members in its advocacy of a strict abolitionist agenda. Animal Liberation's pragmatic approach to the protection of animals means that it supports, for example, subsistence hunting but not sport hunting and traditional, open farming but not factory farming. Animal Welfare's respectability as the oldest organization in the APM attracts people who accept the status quo: that is, a moderate concern for animals that Clark (1997) calls the moral orthodoxy – that animals matter, but not as much as humans. This is speciesism as defined by Singer (1975).

Francione (1996), the influential American animal rights theorist, insists there are only two relevant branches of the animal movement: namely, new welfarism and animal rights. However,

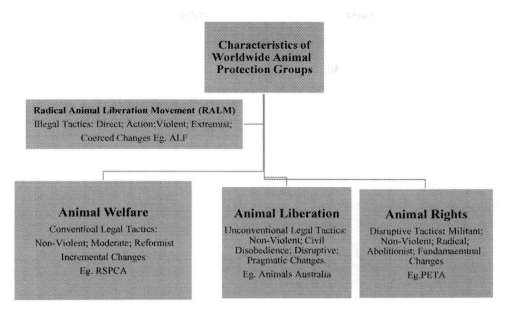

Figure 14.1 Characteristics of the worldwide animal protection movement

his characterization of the animal movement is not in accord with the testimonies of animal protectionists I have interviewed in Australia, the UK, and the US. Also, it does not match their professed dietary habits: animal welfarists (mostly meat eaters), animal liberationists (predominantly vegetarian), and animal rightists (committed vegans).

This brings us to the topic of anti-speciesism, a cause that unites the majority of committed activists in the worldwide animal movement. It is a cause criticized by the sociologist Alan Wolfe, who sees animal rights and environmental campaigns as threats to humanism and "one more nail in the coffin of anthropocentrism" (1993: 11).

Anti-speciesism and the APM's goal of ending animal cruelty

Related to speciesism – the idea that humans are superior to non-human animals – anthropocentrism presumes humans have dominion over nature, a belief that poses an even greater problem for the planet than speciesism. Until quite recently, environmentalists were at odds with animal protectionists over their understanding of what matters: that is, the death and suffering of individual animals versus the extinction of whole species of flora and fauna. Activists in both movements have recently acknowledged the existential threat presented by the climate crisis and thus recognize the necessity of being friends in solidarity; this was the case in Australia in the 1930s when preservationists acknowledged needing "sentimental" animal defenders as allies in preventing the destruction of the Australian bush – the natural habitat of the iconic koala or "bush baby", as the animal protectors labelled it (MacCulloch, 1993).

The following section describes a number of anti-cruelty campaigns prosecuted by the three mainstream groups in Australia along with a sample of activist testimonies and motivations.

Animal welfare: Dr. Bidda Jones

The RSPCA is the quintessential animal welfare organization whose strategy of working within institutional politics has meant that it has a moderate, reformist agenda designed to achieve incremental changes in legislation affecting animals. Garner (2006: 161) suggests that while the RSPCA's failure to reject speciesism is philosophically flawed, it makes sense strategically "to focus on reforms improving the treatment of animals which do not compromise significant human interests, and to engage in campaigns to try and shift perceptions on what is regarded as unnecessary suffering" (Garner, 2006: 161). Most people see the RSPCA as primarily concerned with the welfare of cats, dogs, and horses, a perception that may have changed with the organization's involvement in Australia's live animal export controversy, to be discussed shortly.

Bidda Jones (RSPCA Australia's chief scientist) qualifies as an animal welfarist rather than as an animal liberation or rights advocate. Like most Australians, she is not a vegetarian, but like most decent people, she is repelled by animal cruelty:

> I'm not vegetarian. It's partly because as a zoologist, I've always thought that the idea that it's intrinsically wrong for an animal to eat another animal is unrealistic, if not slightly bizarre.
>
> (Jones, 2016)

When it comes to animal abuse, Jones's views are in accord with public opinion in Australia, at least when people are made aware of the suffering and death of Australian animals in the live animal export trade to Asia and elsewhere (Munro, 2014).

In 2011, the Australian Broadcasting Commission (ABC) – in collaboration with the RSPCA's Bidda Jones and Animal Australia's Lyn White – produced an investigative report by the popular *Four Corners* program called "A Bloody Business" that shone a light on the abuse of Australian cattle in a number of Indonesian abattoirs. The visual images and sound effects of the gross mistreatment of the animals by some of the workers outraged the public and forced the government to place a temporary ban on the trade to Indonesia. The program achieved the largest audience response in the 50-year history of *Four Corners*.[2]

The scale of animal slaughter worldwide is suggested in the title of Pachirat's (2011) *Every Twelve Seconds* while the subtitle – *Industrialized Slaughter and the Politics of Sight* – recalls Kean's (1998) observation that by shining a light on animal suffering, animal protectionists from the nineteenth century onward have used the tactic of visualizing animal suffering and death to expose the hidden cruelties in factory farming, field sports, animal vivisection, and abattoirs.

In the weeks following "The Bloody Business" exposé, thousands of people demanded a ban on the trade.[3] However, the ban was short lived; after a month of grievance claims (financial losses and livelihood concerns) from the farming lobby, the Labor government was compelled to back down and allow the trade to resume, albeit with a number of allegedly improved animal welfare provisions.

In the next section, I discuss the early Animal Liberation branches established in Australia in response to Singer's (1975) widely read manifesto, which many believe launched the modern animal movement. Two of the founders of the movement in Australia are profiled next so as to provide an insight into their motives.

Animal liberation: Christine Townend

Seven Animal Liberation branches were established in Australia between 1976 and 1982 in response to Singer's (1975) *Animal Liberation*. The earliest were in NSW (1976) and Victoria

(1978), set up by Christine Townend and Patty Mark, respectively. Four decades on, Townend is still active in the movement as a writer, artist, and mentor. She has described the growth of the movement in Australia and the early opposition to it from farmers' groups and the rural press, which was, unsurprisingly, critical of the "animal libbers". Townend and her fellow advocates took pains not to retaliate, hoping they would be seen as respectable moderates in the tradition of the venerable RSPCA (Townend, 1981). In 1976, Animal Liberation (NSW) in Sydney was the first in the world to put Singer's ideas on the ethical treatment of animals into practice. What is particularly noteworthy about Townend's stance on animal protection is the argument she makes for seeing animals as part of the commons which we all share; the commonwealth of human and non-human animals alike is arguably a more realistic idea than the related notions of animal personhood and a call for a Zoopolis (Donaldson and Kymicka, 2011). Townend (2013) says she wants the right to see animals unmolested and free:

> Although intangible, the human–animal relationship belongs to us all and the natural evolution of this relationship cannot occur when animals are locked in sheds, where their basic behavioural needs are denied and human contact with the creatures is reduced to a minimum.

Animal rights: Patty Mark

Patty Mark, the founder of Animal Liberation Victoria (ALV) in 1978, like Christine Townend, is a Singer disciple. Mark's story also reveals a life devoted to improving the lives of animals, a commitment that has seen her arrested and jailed for her novel style of activism. Her conflicts with the law and her imprisonment were because she raised the level of her activism from a moderate form of bearing witness to a more provocative style of animal rights activism that involves illegal trespass. She has been a prominent exponent of "open rescue", in which activists seek to liberate captive animals without attempting to avoid detection.[4] Open rescuers "rely on video footage to not only show the deplorable conditions they find the animals in but also the importance of the immediate care and attention given to neglected and enslaved animals in great need" (Cronin, 2016). Mark got involved with open rescue in the early 1990s after seeing footage of "dead and dying hens sinking in their own faeces . . . struggling to access water". Seeing the suffering of these birds was the motivation for Mark's rescue mission, which involved a camera crew documenting the factory farm conditions in which billions of animals worldwide are kept. Mark has said that it is no fun sitting in factory farms waiting to be arrested (more than a dozen times) for trespass, something she finds nerve racking but necessary:

> What do you do? . . . You've gone to the police, you've gone to the Minister, you've gone to the RSPCA, you've done everything legally viable, and nobody does anything. Then I think I have a moral responsibility to individually go in and help those animals.
>
> (Munro, 2005: 137)

The reference to the RSPCA is significant as activists seek to shame the organization for allegedly failing to do its job. For activists like Mark, becoming a vegan is the single most important decision an individual can make to end animal exploitation. She acknowledges, however, that a vegan lifestyle is not for everyone and that most people are unlikely to change their diet after witnessing footage of animal suffering.

Improving the lives of animals

It has been suggested that animal rights would be taken more seriously if the argument for moral egalitarianism was replaced by "a much more (morally and politically) acceptable version of animal rights based on the sentience of animals and not their personhood" (Garner, 2010: 128). Most people are willing to see animals as sentient beings, rather than as persons or indeed property as our laws frame them, yet most are not willing to take up the movement's challenge to "Go Veg", such is the addiction to meat and dairy products.

There is a chance, however slim, that the appetite for eating animals could well be perceived as an unacceptable risk, given the COVID-19 pandemic of 2019–21. If and when we become more aware of the unsanitary, stress-inducing environments in which animals live and die in live animal markets in several countries in Asia and elsewhere, we might be persuaded to investigate how our supermarket meat is produced. To inquire into animal husbandry practices in factory farms wherever they exist – particularly in Australia, China, and North America – means asking if the most basic welfare needs of animals are being met, and if not, does this mean sick and stressed animals slaughtered for their meat pose a major health hazard for consumers? The basic needs are:

1   Freedom from thirst, hunger and malnutrition
2   Freedom from discomfort and exposure
3   Freedom from pain, injury and disease
4   Freedom from fear and distress
5   Freedom to express normal behavior[5]

It should be blatantly obvious that thousands of animals in the intensive confinement of a factory farm have few if any of these basic needs satisfied. The next section focuses on where the largest number of animals suffer and die, unnecessarily, according to animal protectionists and, increasingly, entrepreneurs, who are working on alternative animal-free meat and dairy products (Hughes, 2020).

The long shadow of industrialized animal agriculture

Aysha Akhtar MD – a neurologist and public health specialist – argues that our treatment of animals is linked to emerging infectious disease (EID) epidemics that threaten the lives of people and animals as well as contributing to environmental destruction and global warming (2012: 129). In line with Akhtar's scientific research, intensive farming and the treatment of animals occur in abattoirs, feedlots, illegal animal trafficking, the live animal export trade, and live animal markets/wet markets. My approach is to explain these issues sociologically, as social problems – defined simply as things society would be better off without (Passmore, 1980) – that are therefore amenable to social or political solutions. The negative impacts of the industrial scale of animal food production is taken up next.

CAFOs: concentrated animal feeding operations

If we think of meat production in the context of Figure 14.2, the conversion of animals to meat has three main impacts. Here I rely on the various contributors to *The CAFO Reader*, edited by Imhoff (2010).

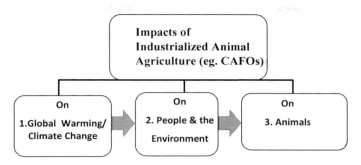

Figure 14.2 Impacts of industrialized animal farming

1 Global warming/climate change

Industrialized animal farming is labelled "factory farming" by animal activists while the meat industry refers to its practices as "intensive agricultural farming". The term widely used in the US, concentrated animal feeding operations (CAFOs), more accurately describes meat production than terms that suggest the animals live on what we generally imagine as open farms. Whatever label is preferred, the process of converting animals – beef and dairy cows, pigs, sheep, broiler chickens, and laying hens – to meat and other animal products is responsible for the death and suffering of billions of animals annually; it has been suggested that if cows were a country, that country would be the third largest greenhouse gas emitter after China and the US (Foer, 2019).

Statistics on the consequences of climate change or global warming are strongly contested by different interest groups in this long-running controversy; it may be more useful to focus on the descriptive arguments from social and climate scientists, which are arguably more readily understood by the public. Before moving to these qualitative analyses, I note some easily digested statistics produced by Labao and Stofferahn (2008), who reviewed 51 social-scientific studies over some eight decades. Their literature review found that industrialized farming was regarded as having an overwhelmingly negative impact by 82% or 42 of the studies, compared to only 3 studies that reported largely beneficial effects for the planet.

The most destructive impacts of CAFOs on the earth's climate were identified by Imhoff and his collaborators (2010) as the already-mentioned greenhouse gas emissions, the transportation of live and dead animals, and deforestation and compaction, as well as the fertilizer factor, which involves the manufacture, planting, harvesting, processing, and transporting of feed to the factory farms.

If cows were rotated through paddocks and ate fresh green grass, it is estimated the animals would produce 20% less methane (FAO, 2006: 107–108). In CAFOs, thousands of animals produce tons of manure that is difficult to dispose of and often ends up in waterways or causes air pollution, accompanied by an unbearable stench affecting people unfortunate enough to be living in the vicinity. *The CAFO Reader* notes that pigs raised by Smithfield Foods in the US produce three times the excrement that humans do, which means a half million hogs in one Smithfield factory in Utah have the distinction of generating more shit than 1.5 million humans.

The arrows in Figure 14.2 indicate the impact of climate change on both human and non-human animals, a scenario well described by Thornes (2016: 81), who cites a World Wildlife

Fund (WWF) report that noted of the 3,000 or so species of vertebrate animals, just over half became extinct between 1970 and 2010; while only 7% of that number can be attributed to climate change, the percentage is tipped to increase if and when habitats are destroyed due to an increase in human population and land acquisition encroaching on animal habitats.

2 People and the environment

A host of diseases have been linked to CAFOs and live animal markets, where both domestic and wild animals are slaughtered for food and medicinal purposes.[6] Intensive animal agriculture has caused the spread of harmful viruses, epidemics, and pandemics, including avian flu, severe acute respiratory syndrome (SARS), the Ebola virus (Greger, 2010; Guterl, 2012; Karesh and Cook, 2005; Schlosser, 2001; Swabe, 1999; Walters, 2014),[7] and most recently, the coronavirus.[8].

Throughout history, pandemics have posed existential threats to our survival as a species. Whatever the future holds post COVID-19, it is surely clear that the worst abuses of animals, especially in food production, are no longer acceptable for ethical, ecological, and health reasons. The risks in consuming animal products have been shown to include cancer, heart disease, obesity, and diabetes, which could be prevented by people converting to a plant-based diet (Akhtar, 2012). Friedrich (2019) has called for the replacement of animal meat products by a plant-based diet – and, in due course, by cell-based meat, which is still in the development stage – and which, as vegans, vegetarians, and animal activists have long argued in their "Go Veg" campaigns, is a safer and healthier option than animal-based products. Friedrich notes the serious consequences of feeding antibiotics to food animals, resulting in super-bugs that killed thousands of individuals in North America in 2018 and rendered antibiotics ineffective.[9]

The health risks of consuming contaminated animal products are almost certainly the most powerful incentive for an individual's conversion from a carnivore to a vegetarian or vegan. In the current COVID-19 crisis, as yet, there has been virtually no serious discussion in the mass media in Australia or elsewhere of the unethical treatment of animals confined in CAFOs, killed in abattoirs, or in other stress-inducing environments, such as wildlife in captivity. In the global media's framing of the crisis as a health and economic crisis, only the lives and livelihoods of people have featured. This is unsurprising, as demonstrated by Arcari's (2019) review of 15 major international and Australian reports on climate change, sustainability, and food security, in which animals are only mentioned if their meat is thought to compromise food safety.

As mentioned earlier, Sanbonmatsu (2014: 43) suggests that the scale of industrialized agriculture's impact on the biosphere might well be seen as an existential threat to our collective existence, thereby posing a legitimation crisis for speciesism. But will "the hog squeal of the universe" (Sinclair, 1906) that disturbed the author of *The Jungle* more than a century ago be heard, much less silenced? Much will depend on how we weigh up the costs (to the health of the environment upon which all species depend) and our appetite for meat.

3 The suffering of animals

It is unlikely that genuine improvements in the treatment of animals in the live export trade, as discussed earlier, have been achieved; we only know that the insatiable demand for meat in countries like Indonesia and elsewhere is increasing at a faster rate than the vegetarian or vegan alternatives. Knowing this means animal protectionists need public support for their anti-cruelty campaigns to succeed. As noted earlier, in the study by Johnson et al. (2019), animal cruelty is high on the list of atrocities that Australians are not prepared to accept in silence. Why, then, did the moral crusade against live exports only achieve minor improvements in animal welfare?

The activists succeeded in providing a supportive climate for "consensus mobilization" but were unable to manage the related concept of "action mobilization" – concepts explained by Klandermans (1984) – that translates to a well-organized protest and a continuous media blitz that no government could easily ignore. Although it did put the government and the meat industry in the hot seat for a brief time, the campaign petered out in the absence of a wider conversation including animal liberation and rights rather than animal welfare – the media's main frame – along with veganism, vegetarianism, and the environmental and health consequences of a meat diet (Pendergrast, 2015).[10]

Ethical choices associated with food consumption – rather than health considerations – are of most concern to animal protection advocates and activists; as sentient beings, animals feel pain when sick or abused, as was the case in the live export trade. And it was the cruelty exposed in "the Bloody Business" that alarmed the public. In the most recent and surely the most alarming crisis in recent global history, the consequences of how we treat animals have been graphically revealed in the coronavirus calamity being experienced worldwide.

In the next section, I focus on the pandemic and what it reveals about the human-animal link in its most hazardous form.

The trafficking of wildlife: life and death in live animal markets

Many commentators believe the global coronavirus pandemic originated in a "wet market" in Wuhan, China (see Appendix). Whatever the origin and cause of the virus turn out to be, it is certain that human interactions with animals in CAFOs, slaughterhouses, feedlots, etc. – where huge numbers of animals are confined – is a health risk to anyone in close contact with the animals (Hollenbeck, 2016: 44–46). In the case of live animal markets, the dangers posed by an outbreak of zoonotic or animal-based diseases are even greater, given the generally unsanitary environment and the poor condition of captive, stressed animals living and dying in close proximity to people. Animal waste – feces and urine – inevitably comes into contact with animal body parts in the multi-species environment of these crowded markets where traders and their customers are susceptible to infection and are likely to spread the viruses.

According to Orenstein (2020: 2) – a zoologist, lawyer, and consultant to the Humane Society International (HSI) – live animal markets should be closed immediately in order to prevent the "practical certainty" of another coronavirus-based disease. It will take many months before we know what the results of any inquiry into the origins of COVID-19 will be and how governments will act to prevent it from re-emerging in one form or another.

We do know that the illegal trafficking of wild and exotic animals is hugely profitable for those involved; for example, the massively poached pangolin from Borneo (and elsewhere) is believed by devotees of traditional Chinese medicine (TCM) to have healing powers in its scales; the scales sell for US$1,000 per kilogram and a live pangolin for US$1,000 (Jaclin, 2016: 412). China's wildlife-farming operations are valued at US$74 billion and its wild-meat markets at US$7.1billion, with over one million employees. Emerging infectious diseases (EIDs) have long been linked to markets that sell many different species of domestic, wild, and exotic animals for human consumption and for TCM. "From ivory to pangolin scales, totoaba bladders to shark fins, [China] has a ravenous appetite for wildlife products" (Nuwer, 2018). Evidently, only the adored giant panda in China escapes the dinner table in a country where subsistence farming and poverty put all manner of beasts, wild and domestic, at risk of being used for food or for TCM.

According to Woodward (2020), the Chinese Communist Party (CCP) in early February 2020 banned the breeding, trading, and eating of wild animals, a ban that, given the profits and the gustatory and medicinal pleasures claimed, will need exceedingly strict measures of regulation and enforcement to succeed, especially in China, where animal welfare and animal rights are foreign concepts (Li, 2006). Only a concerted and sustained effort by governments, public health authorities, scientists, social movement activists, and NGOs is likely to lead to a change of heart regarding the treatment of animals in China.

While China is not the only country where outbreaks of zoonotic diseases are likely to originate, it is the most at risk, given the size of the population (1.5 billion) it needs to feed. According to Li and Davey (2013: 49), there are signs of potential change in China with the emergence of environmental NGOs and a new generation of young animal rights activists who use social media – Weibo, the equivalent of Twitter – to initiate actions against animal cruelty, such as blocking trucks loaded with malnourished, sick dogs en route to dog-meat markets. These small protests will need to be dramatically magnified if activists are to succeed in banning live animal markets in China. At the time of writing, the most recent analysis of China's mistreatment of animals is Li's (2021) *Animal Welfare in China*, based mainly on Chinese sources rather than conventional Western perspectives. He describes the worst examples of animal exploitation in modern China and the reasons that might explain some of them while noting that the ancient Chinese dynasties, in stark contrast to today, advocated the compassionate treatment of animals.

Pollan (2010), among many others, has argued that without a complete overhaul of the industrial food system, the risks to the environment and public health will only worsen. This would mean the gradual downsizing of CAFOs in North America, Australia, China, and elsewhere, as well as live animal markets in Asia and in countries engaged in wildlife trafficking. The threats and solutions regarding the latter are clearly illustrated in Figure 14.3.

"Go veg": the dietary future of humankind?

The easier and more palatable alternative would be a mass conversion to vegetarianism, which Elias (1978) predicted will be the dietary future of humankind. There are an increasing number of vegetarian advocates who call for an ethical diet that does not include meat; vegans go further in insisting on a diet that is completely free of dairy and meat products. However, a vegetarian lifestyle would appeal to a broader range of people given that it is less restrictive in food choices than its strict and demanding cousin.

Ethical vegetarianism involves people's conversion to a meat-free diet because it reduces animal cruelty while pragmatic vegetarianism is based on consumer awareness of the risk of eating contaminated meat; both these motivations are radical insofar as they represent a boycott of meat products, which ultimately makes a huge dent in the ideology of speciesism. The subversive potential of vegetarianism occurs when defects in food regulations are revealed that shock consumers into converting to a vegetarian (or vegan) diet (Frank, 2004). It is also evident, according to Hughes (2020), that animal-free dairy products and plant-based meats are increasingly on the menu, for example at Hungry Jack's in Australia. She notes how the food-animal industry is fighting back with what it ridicules as a "vegan fantasyland" of animal-free foods. Hughes, on the other hand, explains why the Australian dairy industry "is already in deep cow manure", with New Zealand's dairy products – its most valuable export – likely to be in much less demand in 20 to 25 years, with the consumption of synthetic milk sold worldwide. Healthy food is an issue on which animal protectionists could unite in common cause with public health, consumer, food security, environmental, and other like-minded groups to promote a vegetarian or vegan lifestyle.

Figure 14.3   Wildlife trafficking and live animal markets: threats and solutions

Source: Global Wildlife Conservation (www.wcs.org)

For such a mass movement to be mobilized, the public first needs to be convinced about the many negative consequences of the intensive confinement and abuse of animals that have been identified in this chapter. Additionally, as Akhtar (2013) argues, there is the need to include animal protectionism in public health policies as well as the importance of educating the public that EIDs are linked to the cruel treatment of animals.[11]

At the time of writing, the Chinese Communist Party's (CCP) failure to alert the world immediately to a virus outbreak in Wuhan is seen as the most likely reason for the initial spread of the coronavirus globally; while the facts of the matter can only be determined by a trusted authority, we can be certain that our ill treatment of food animals has severe consequences for the health of our species.

I have argued the case for a mass movement – of environmentalists, animal protectionists, vegetarians, vegans, public health and food security advocates, consumers, and ordinary citizens – to confront the political and economic interests that seek to maintain the status quo at the expense of life on our planet.[12] Finally, as previously noted, the iconic Australian koala has since the early nineteenth century proven to be an animal whose tribulations – whether being skinned for its fur or suffering and dying by the thousands in bushfires – have aroused the public's sympathy. For many people, the plight of suffering animals is often what drives them to take action against the forces that support speciesism and its twin, anthropocentrism. I leave the last words attributed to the late animal rights philosopher Regan (1985): "Philosophy can lead the mind to water but only emotion can make it drink".

Conclusion

Like many other aspects of our lives, it has taken COVID-19 to compel us to consider our relations with and our treatment of animals. Abattoirs and meat works in many countries, including developed economies such as Germany and Australia, have been revealed as hot spots for spreading the coronavirus. While there has been much publicity on slaughterhouses and their infected workers, very little media attention has been given to the thousands of wet and live animal markets or the trade in exotic wildlife, particularly in countries in Asia and Africa. The well-known animal rights slogan "Meat is Murder" now carries a new and grim message in the era of a global pandemic.

This chapter argued the case for a common cause movement capable of confronting animal industries, particularly in the food and agriculture sectors, where billions of animals are sacrificed for human consumption. Vegetarianism has long been advocated as the alternative to meat eating. A vegetarian diet adopted widely on a gradually increasing scale would reduce greenhouse emissions, improve human health, and reduce the numbers of animals raised for food. While vegetarianism has a long history and only a minority of followers worldwide, the current pandemic will surely induce many more people to "Go Veg" or significantly reduce their consumption of meat.

The APM has historically used the defense of individual animals as its *raison d'être*, with little recognition of the environmental movement's campaigns to protect wildlife species as a whole. The time is now opportune for the APM to emphasize much more the health risks of excessive meat consumption in campaigns that include environmental concerns as well as the animal movement's seminal issues of anti-speciesism and the rights of non-human animals.

Appendix

Notes on COVID-19

On 17 January 2020, the Chinese government admitted the pandemic virus could be transmitted from person to person, At the time, between 60,000 and 70,000 Chinese citizens were travelling to and from Wuhan – where the virus allegedly originated – to the USA; on 21 January, the first case of the virus was recorded in Seattle, while Australia documented its first case on 25 January.

Cao (2020) blames the recent outbreak of the COVID-19 virus on the live animal markets or wet markets in China. Following an outbreak of an infectious disease, Chinese authorities have from time to time closed the worst offenders for health reasons, only to reopen them again. According to Crimmins (2020), the CCP is unlikely to permanently close the offending markets where the risks to global public health are an ever-present threat.

Actman (2019) notes how the belief in TCM goes back to the third century BC and is practiced in more than 180 countries, most predominantly in Southeast Asia, where ivory, rhino horns, pangolin scales, tiger bones, and bile from sun and moon bears are prized. The scale of the trade is therefore vast and difficult to control given the massive profits involved, despite the fact that TCM is arguably ineffective and possibly dangerous to consumers, as suggested by Fritz Sorgel, head of the Institute for Biomedical and Pharmaceutical Research in Frankfurt, Germany (cited by Cross, 2019).

A number of graphic photographs by Fritz Hoffmann (in Actman, 2019) picture some of the animals and animal parts sold at a market in Guangzhou, China; these include deer parts such as penises, antlers, and tendons, as well as sea horses – some 20 million animals traded annually according to *National Geographic* – sold as TCM apparently for treating erectile dysfunction. According to Standaert (2020), the trade in wild and exotic animals for TCM was valued in 2019 at AU\$74 billion in China alone and was endorsed by the WHO as a legitimate medical practice, thus proving the complicity of the WHO in facilitating the illegal trade in wildlife. President Xi Jinping has been known to promote TCM as superior to Western medicine, and it is therefore imperative that the risks of further pandemics via the spread of zoonotic diseases are highlighted as existential threats by grassroots activists and advocacy organizations supported by medical scientists, virologists, and epidemiologists.

Notes

1 The One Health concept seeks to address global health problems such as zoonotic diseases that are transmitted from animals to humans – an approach based on the idea that humans, animals, and the environment are interconnected and therefore share the risks of disease outbreaks (Bidaisee and Macpherson, 2014). It has been estimated that 75% of emerging infectious diseases (EIDs) come from animals (Woodward, 2020; Akhtar, 2013).
2 According to Villanueva (2018: 205), Animals Australia's website recorded more than a million messages demanding the banning of the trade; this was an unprecedented response, vastly outnumbering the expression of grievances recorded in the combined results of Australia's two leading environmental organizations, the Australian Conservation Foundation and the Wilderness Society.
3 An online petition to the Australian Parliament attracted some 200,000 signatories, and some members of parliament confessed they had received more emails demanding action than on any issue in their experience.
4 Villanueva (2018) has suggested Patty Mark's open rescue is an Australian tactical innovation that was adopted briefly in the US and more permanently in Europe. Open rescue, in contrast to undercover investigations, means that activists want to be identified and their trespassing and subsequent arrest by the police witnessed by the media in the hope that the plight of the animals in distress will resonate with the public.
5 Originally proposed by John Webster (1994), professor of animal husbandry (University of Bristol), the five freedoms specify what people responsible for farming animals are expected to observe as best practice.
6 In China it has been estimated that the number of animals in CAFOs has increased exponentially from less than 5% of the country's domestic animals in 1980 to more than 50% in 2010. Wet markets are said to exist in several countries outside China; however, the largest number of public places where wild and domestic animals are slaughtered for human consumption and traditional medicines is in China (Hou et al. (2013).
7 See Munro (2019: 175–178) for the arguments of these authors who expose the dark side of the animal-human link.
8 Cao (2020) www.abc.net.au/radionational/programs/sciencefriction/covid-19,-chinas-wet-markets-and-bats/12119458. The podcast panel includes David Hayman from Massey University and Hume Field from the Eco-health Alliance. Field, a veterinarian, said the dangerous mixing of species in these wet markets was "a no brainer". See also Cao (2015), *Animals in China: Law and Society*.
9 Friedrich (2019). "The Next Global Agricultural Revolution", a TED talk with transcript available. Friedrich features in *Speciesism: The Movie* directed by Mark Devries. The cast in the feature-length

film released in 2013 includes Friedrich and other animal activists and advocates such as Peter Singer, Temple Grandin, Richard Dawkins, and Steven Best.

10 For a detailed description of the "backlash" against the animal rights campaign, see Jones (2016) and Lindsay's (2020) condemnation of the Australian government's animal welfare legislation as a sham. He states that the weak regulatory system "allows our animals to be mercilessly subjected to barbaric and unconscionable treatment" and leaves the policing of the trade to unofficial volunteer activists in Animals Australia.

11 Akhtar (2013) notes that since 1980, of the 175 pathogens that have emerged or re-emerged, three-quarters come from animals. She includes the growth in the wildlife trade as one of the most important contributors to these viruses.

12 See Munro (2019) for why and how education and social movements are essential in protecting our individual and collective life chances against the threat of climate change and pandemics.

References

Actman, Jani (2019) 'Traditional Chinese Medicine and Wildlife', *National Geographic*, 27 February, accessed 4 July 2020.

Akhtar, Aysha (2012) *Animals and Public Health: Why Treating Animals Better is Critical to Human Welfare*, Houndmills, UK and New York: Palgrave Macmillan.

Akhtar, Aysha (2013) 'The Need to Include Animal Protection in Public Health Policies', *Journal of Public Health Policy*, 34: 549–559. doi: 10.1057/ jphp.2013.29.

Arcari, Paula (2019) 'Normalised Human-Centric Discourses of Meat and Animals in Climate Change, Sustainability and Food Security Literature', *Agriculture and Human Values*, 34: 69–86.

Australian Broadcasting Commission (ABC) (2011) 'A Bloody Business', *Four Corners*, Sydney: ABC.

Bidaisee, Satesh and Calum Macpherson (2014) 'Zoonosis and One Health: A Review of the Literature', *Journal of Parasitology*, 2014. doi: 10.1155/2014/874345.

Cao, Deborah (2015) *Animals in China: Law and Society*, London: Palgrave Macmillan.

Cao, Deborah (2020) *Covid-19, China's Wild Wet Markets, Pangolins and Bats – is it us or Them?* A Podcast Hosted by Natasha Mitchel. www.abc.net.au/radionational/programs/sciencefriction/covid-19,-chi-nas-wet-markets-and-bats/12119458 accessed 5 April 2020.

Clark, Stephen (1997) *Animals and Their Moral Standing*, London: Routledge.

Crimmins, Francine (2020) 'The Complex Role of Wet Markets and Global Health', *Medical Republic*, posted by Crimmins on 14 May 2020 and accessed 5 July 2020. www.http://medicalrepublic.com.au/the-complex-role-of-wet-markets-and-global-health/28850.

Cronin, Keri (2016) *Patty Mark – Fierce and Fearless: Patty Mark's Unique Approach to Animal Liberation*. www.unboundproject.org/currentstories/patty-mark/.

Cross, David (2019) 'Chinese Traditional Medicine is a scourge on exotic wildlife', *Sustainabilitytimes.com/* 5 August 2019, accessed 4 July 2020.

Donaldson, Sue and Will Kymicka (2011) *Zoopolis: A Political Theory of Animal Rights*, New York: Oxford University Press.

Elias, Norbert (1978) *The Civilising Process: The History of Manners* Vol. 1, Oxford: Blackwell.

FAO (2006) *Livestock's Long Shadow*, Rome, UN: The Food and Agricultural Organisation.

Foer, Safran Jonathan (2019) *We are the Weather: Saving the Planet Starts at Breakfast*, London: Hamish Hamilton.

Francione, Gary (1996) *Rain Without Thunder: The Ideology of the Animal Rights Movement*, Philadelphia: Temple University Press.

Frank, Joshua (2004) 'The Role of Radical Animal Activists as Information Providers to Consumers', *Animal Liberation Philosophy and Policy Journal*, 2: 1–13.

Friedrich, Bruce (2019) 'The Next Global Agricultural Revolution', a TED talk with transcript available. Friedrich features in *Speciesism: The Movie* directed by Mark Devries.

Garner, Robert (2006) 'Animal Welfare: A Political Debate', *Journal of Animal Liberation and Ethics*, 1: 161–174.

Garner, Robert (2010) 'Animals, Ethics and Public Policy', *The Political Quarterly*, 81 (1): 123–130.

Greger, Michael (2010) *Bird Flu: A Virus of Our Own Hatching*, New York: Lantern Books.

Guterl, Fred (2012) *The Fate of the Species: Why the Human Race May Cause Its Own Extinction and How We Can Stop It*, New York: Bloomsbury.

Hamilton, Clive (2010) *Requiem for a Species: Why We Resist the Truth About Climate Change*, London: Earthscan.

Hollenbeck, James (2016) 'Interaction of the Role of Concentrated Animal Feeding Operations (CAFOs) in Emerging Infectious Diseases (EIDs)', *Infection, Genetics and Evolution*, 38: 44–46.

Hou, Y., L. Ma, Z. L. Gao, F. H. Wang, J. T. Sims, W. Q. Ma, and F. S. Zhang (2013, July–August) 'The Driving Forces for Nitrogen and Phosphorus Flows in the Food Chain of China, 1980 to 2010', *Journal of Environmental Quality*, 42: 962–971. doi: 10-2134/jeq 2012.0489.

Hughes, Lesley (2020, March) 'The Milk of Human Genius: On the End of the Cow and the Future of Food', *The Monthly*, 164: 44–50.

Imhoff, Daniel (2010) *The CAFO Reader: The Tragedy of Industrial Animal Factories*, Berkeley and Los Angeles: University of California Press.

Jaclin, David (2016) 'Poached Lives, Traded Forms: Engaging with Animal Trafficking around the Globe', *Social Science Information*, 55: 400–425.

Johnson, Jane, Kirsten Howard, Andrew Wilson, Michael Ward, Gwendolyn Gilbert and Chris Degeling (2019) 'Public Preferences for One Health Approaches to Emerging Infectious Diseases: A Discrete Choice Experiment', *Social Science and Medicine*, 228: 164–171. https:/doi.org/j.socscimed.2019.03.013.

Jones, Bidda (2016) *Backlash: Australia's Conflict of Values Over Live Exports*, Braidwood: Finlay Lloyd Publishers.

Karesh, William and Robert Cook (2005) 'The Human-Animal Link', *Foreign Affairs*, 84: 38–50.

Kean, Hilda (1998) *Animal Rights: Political and Social Change in Britain Since 1800*, London: Reaktion Books.

Klandermans, Bert (1984) 'Mobilization and Participation: Social-Psychological Expansions of Resource Mobilization Theory', *American Sociological Review*, 49: 583–600.

Labao, Linda and Curtis Stofferahn (2008) 'The Community Effects of Industrialized Farming: Social Science Research and Challenges to Corporate Farming Laws', *Agriculture and Human Values*, 25: 219–240.

Li, Peter (2006) 'The Evolving Animal Rights and Welfare Debate in China: Political and Social Impact Analysis', in Jacki Turner and Joyce D'Silva (eds) *Animals, Ethics and Trade: The Challenge of Animal Sentience*, London and Sterling VA: Earthscan, pp. 111–128.

Li, Peter (2021) *Animal Welfare in China: Culture, Politics and Crisis*, Sydney: Sydney University Press.

Li, Peter and Davey, Gareth (2013) 'Culture, Reform Politics, and Future Directions: A Review of China's Animal Protection Challenge', *Society & Animals: Journal of Human-Animal Studies*, 21: 34–53.

Lindsay, Stuart (2020, June) 'The Conservative Case Against Live Animal Exports', *Quadrant*, 28–32.

MacCulloch, Jennifer (1993) *Creatures of Culture: The Animal Protection and Preservation Movements in Sydney, 1880–1930*, Unpublished PhD Thesis, University of Sydney.

Munro, Lyle (2005) *Confronting Cruelty: Moral Orthodoxy and the Challenge of the Animal Rights Movement*, Leiden and Boston: Brill.

Munro, Lyle (2014) 'The Live Animal Export Controversy in Australia: A Moral Crusade Made for the Mass Media', *Social Movement Studies: Journal of Social, Cultural and Political Protest*. doi: 10.1080/14742837.2013.874524.

Munro, Lyle (2019) *Life Chances, Education and Social Movements*, London and New York: Anthem Press.

Nuwer, Rachel (2018) 'The Key to Stopping the Illegal Wildlife Trade: China', *The New York Times*, Science Times at 40. 19 November, 2018.

Orenstein, Ronald (2020) 'Wildlife Markets and Covid-19', *Humane Society International*, Washington, DC, pp. 1–21.

Pachirat, Timothy (2011) *Every Twelve Seconds: Industrialized Slaughter and the Politics of Sight*, New York: Putnam.

Passmore, John (1980) *Man's Responsibility for Nature: Ecological Problems and Western Traditions*, London: Duckworth.

Pendergrast, Nick (2015) 'Live Animal Export, Humane Slaughter and Media Hegemony', *Animal Studies Journal*, 4: 99–125.

Pollan, Michael (2010, May) 'The Food Movement, Rising', *The New York Review of Books*, 1–6. http://michaelpollan.com/articles-arcvhive/the-food-movement-rising

Regan, Tom (1985) 'The Case for Animal Rights', in Peter Singer (ed.) *In Defence of Animals*, New York: Harper & Row Publishers.

Ryder, Richard (1989) *Animal Revolution: Changing Attitudes Towards Speciesism*, Oxford: Basil Blackwell.

Sanbonmatsu, John (2014) 'The Animal of Bad Faith: Speciesism as an Existential Project', Chapter 3 in Atsuko Matsuoka and John Sorenson (eds) *Critical Animal Studies: Thinking the Unthinkable*, Toronto: Canadian Scholars Press.

Schlosser, Eric (2001) *Fast Food Nation: The Dark Side of the All-American Meal*, Boston: Houghton Mifflin.

Sinclair, Upton (1906) *The Jungle*, New York: The Vanguard Press.

Singer, Peter (1975) *Animal Liberation: A New Ethics for Our Treatment of Animals*, New York: Random House.

Standaert, Michael (2020) 'China Signals End to Dog Meat Consumption by Humans', *The Guardian* (Australian edition). www.theguardian.com accessed 10 April.

Swabe, Johanna (1999) *Animals, Disease and Human Society*, London: Routledge.

Thornes, Tobius (2016) 'Animals and Climate Change', *Journal of Animal Ethics*, 6 (1): 81–88.

Townend, Christine (1981) *A Voice for the Animals: How Animal Liberation Grew in Australia*, Kenthurst NSW: Kangaroo Press.

Townend, Christine (2013) *Freeing the Human-Animal Relationship*. www.kosmosjournal.org/article/freeingthehumananimalrelationship.

Villanueva, Gonzalo (2018) *A Transnational History of the Australian Animal Movement, 1970–2015*, London: Palgrave Macmillan.

Walters, Mark Jerome (2014) *Seven Modern Plagues and How We are Causing Them*, Washington, DC: Island Press.

Webster, John (1994) *Animal Welfare: A Cool Eye Towards Eden*, Oxford: Blackwell Science Ltd.

Wolfe, Alan (1993) *The Human Difference: Animals, Computers and the Necessity of Social Science*, Berkeley: University of California Press.

Woodward, Aylin (2020) 'China Just Banned the Trade and Consumption of Wild Animals: Experts Think the Coronavirus Jumped from Live Animals to People at a Market', *Business Insider Australia*, 26 February.

15

POLITICAL CONSUMERISM AND FOOD ACTIVISM

Jasmine Lorenzini

Some citizens refuse to buy brands that do not comply with specific environmental or social norms, others buy fair-trade clothes or join community-supported agricultural projects, and still others adapt their whole lifestyle to avoid consuming animal products. Whatever form it takes, citizens increasingly use their purchasing power to support and advance a variety of political values, such as environmental protection, animal rights, fair working conditions, and child-free labor. Political consumerism is a central mode of political participation that has attracted much scholarly attention in the last decades. Some scholars view political consumerism as a way to mobilize citizens who are disconnected from politics and who seek individualized modes of action (Bennett, 2012; Stolle and Hooghe, 2011). Others criticize political consumerism for its narrow understanding of politics based on individual interests (Johnston, 2008), for draining resources away from other political actions (Berglund and Matti, 2006), and for reinforcing the power of ever-expanding markets (Jacques, 2016). Environmental researchers point to the narrow understanding of social change that accompanies political consumerism (Maniates, 2001). They show how corporations highjack the concept of sustainability through green consumption (Dauvergne and LeBaron, 2014) and how they influence the environmental movement through financial support (Assadourian, 2016). Altogether, these studies enquire about the capacity of political consumerism to bring about social change in the face of multiple environmental challenges. Yet political sociologists devote limited attention to question the democratic imagination that these forms of action carry. Hence, the following research question guides the reflections presented in this chapter: how political consumerism contributes to shaping citizens' relation to politics. To answer this question, I argue that we need to distinguish different forms of political participation that broadly fall under the label of political consumerism in order to examine specific conceptions of citizens' participation and democratic social change that prevail in each action form.

The hybrid consumer-citizen is a central actor in contemporary democracies. Ever-expanding markets shape individuals' everyday life across multiple life spheres. Want to cook a meal for your friends? Hire a chef. Want to graduate? Pay someone to write your thesis. Want a baby? Rent a uterus. Want to become president? Invest millions in a political campaign. In advanced capitalism, everything appears to be for sale, and this phenomenon does not spare democratic life (Sandel, 2000). Commodification processes affect democracies at different levels, influencing the selection of elected representatives but also the shape of public policies (Bartels, 2009;

DOI: 10.4324/9780367855680-17

Crouch, 2004; Hacker and Pierson, 2010). The neoliberal state serves primarily the interest of the economy since growth is the ultimate goal of governments, the one goal that constitutes their *raison d'être* (Brown, 2015). Social solidarities are dismantled in favor of individualism, personal responsibility, and family values (Harvey, 2007). Public policies are increasingly written in terms of services offered to customers, not in terms of public services (Schneider and Ingram, 2005). Together, all these transformations affect citizens' democratic imagination – how they understand social problems, as well as their capacity and tools for action. In a world where everything seems to be for sale, citizens imagine their participation in terms of donating money to political groups or parties and buying eco-friendly, fair, local products. Focusing on the environmental movement, Szasz (2007) refers to this phenomenon as the inverted quarantine. Individuals feel threatened by growing air, water, and soil pollution so they buy goods that "insulate" them from these harmful environmental conditions, such as bottled water, organic fruit, and suntan lotion. The quest for commercial solutions to environmental (social or political) problems takes place at the individual level *and* at the collective level. Social movements use market-based strategies to gain leverage on politics. They organize boycott campaigns (Balsiger, 2014) and create labels (Bartley et al., 2015) or small-scale food networks (Graziano and Forno, 2012). The environmental movement is no exception; major organizations in the movement encourage and engage in political consumerism (Dauvergne and LeBaron, 2014; Jacques, 2016). However, multiple forms of participation are available for consumer-citizens. It is worth understanding the democratic implications of each such form of participation as they vary in their relationship to the market – some actions seek to influence markets while others try to bypass or overcome markets.

In the first part of the chapter, I define political consumerism as forms of action that refer to buying or refusing to buy products and services for political reasons. These political acts commodify political values – citizens buy goods and services that correspond to their ideological views. Citizens can financially support projects that offer alternatives to the mainstream market: for instance, fair-trade goods, organic food, or local services. However, other forms of political consumerism have a broader scope – people who engage in community-supported agriculture often give time and work to the project; people who refuse to eat meat embrace a broader political project. In these cases, political consumerism is more far reaching and not reducible to a mere commodification of political values. Thus, I argue that the meaning and the scope of political consumerism change depending on the specific forms that it takes. Studying a broader set of action forms allows identifying those action forms that move away from purely market-based mechanisms of monetary exchanges with profit-seeking goals. In order to expand the concept of political consumerism while maintaining conceptual clarity, I introduce the concept of food activism to distinguish different forms of market-based activism that aim at transforming food production, distribution, and consumption.

In the second part of the chapter, I examine the different forms of social change foreseen by specific forms of food activism. I build on the idea of real utopias (Wright, 2010) and different conceptions of social change (Lofland, 1993). Wright (2010) proposes to start with a critical diagnostic of the existing situation to develop alternatives that defend emancipatory and democratic goals. Real utopias enable transformations by expanding our imaginaries. One key element in his approach is the focus on the interplay of state, economic, and social power. Hence, to assess the transformative potential of food activism, one needs to assess its understanding of social change in the economic realm (transformation of capitalist modes of consumption and production), in the political realm (transformation in the understanding of the state's role and democratic institutions), and in society (collective action capacity of different groups). Building on Erik Olin Wright's work on real utopias,

I ask how food activism in its different forms proposes to transform the economy, society, and politics.

In the third part, I ask to what extent the environmental movement uses political consumerism to advance its goals and highlight four alternatives. Voluntary simplifiers and ecofeminists challenge prevailing divisions between production and consumption, they highlight the core value of reproductive work, and they place the subsistence economy central stage. In addition, commoners and freegans enlarge the action repertoire of the environmental movement through strategies of direct action and resistance, as well as collective processes of decision-making. Hence, a variety of relations to production and consumption transpire and enrich our democratic imaginaries. In the conclusion, I return to the consumer-citizen debate, and I emphasize promising forms of citizenship and democratic social change that appear in market-based forms of activism.

Political consumerism and food activism

At the beginning of the twenty-first century, Michele Micheletti (2003) coined the term "political consumerism" to refer to citizens' attempt to influence politics through their consumption choices. Micheletti refers to political consumerism as an individualized collective form of political participation. This term highlights that these actions are performed at the individual level in a flexible way, which, at first, appear disconnected from any political group. Yet most boycott campaigns result from social movement activism (Balsiger, 2010). A political group organizes and calls the action. Beyond the individualized action, there is a collective agency. Similarly, buying products for political reasons results from collective organization and action. In a complex world, individuals are not able to assess modes of production and distribution or to evaluate the impact of consumption in order to choose between one product and another solely on their own. Labels guide their choices; they reduce the complexity of markets characterized by long chains of transformation. Political groups (Balsiger, 2016) and consumers' organizations (Lang and Gabriel, 2005) set up and promote labels to help individuals acquire information about the products and services that they buy.

Forms of political consumerism

Although the most common and well-known forms of political consumerism are buying or refusing to buy products for political reasons, it is important not to limit political consumerism to these actions (Littler, 2005). Researchers have expanded the scope of the concept to include: 1) actions that require a long-lasting commitment such as community-supported agriculture, 2) actions that mark a rupture with the market such as voluntary simplicity, and 3) actions that question the consumer culture: for instance, culture jamming. What is markedly different in these other forms of participation?

Community-supported agriculture brings together consumers and producers in a long-lasting economic relationship. Consumers pay in advance for the food that producers will grow, produce, and/or transform for them. This guarantees a stable income to the producers and shortens food chains. Thus, consumers gain more traction on the food that they eat. It is part of an action mode that includes different food collectives, such as participator supermarkets (Zitcer, 2017b), solidarity purchase groups (Forno et al., 2015), and community-supported agriculture (Dubuisson-Quellier and Lamine, 2004; Graziano and Forno, 2012; Hassanein, 2008).

Voluntary simplicity seeks to reduce consumption altogether; practitioners work less and earn less (Lorenzen, 2012; Schor, 1998). This means that they have more time to produce their own food – either growing food or buying raw products and cooking at home. In addition, they engage in exchanging goods and services. Voluntary simplicity creates social connections within groups where people share goods and services free of charge – one hour of work being exchanged for another hour of work or one good for another – and where they discuss trade-offs and build collective solutions to problems they face in their everyday lives (Lorenzen, 2014). Voluntary simplicity is a form of lifestyle politics – the transformation of different dimensions of one's life to adjust to specific political values (Micheletti and Stolle, 2012).

Lastly, culture jamming transforms advertisement to make people think about their social environment (Carducci, 2006). Subverting advertisement allows us to see what becomes invisible as part of our taken-for-granted everyday life. So many public spaces are rented to advertisers that commercial messages are omnipresent in the streets, on public transport, and online. They shape how we think and relate to the world around us.

These forms of action all have an indirect relationship to markets; thus, some researchers consider that they are part of political consumerism. However, this creates conceptual problems. Are all these actions specific forms of political consumerism or, rather, different forms of participation? I suggest that we refer instead to market-based activism, to include all the political actions that question mainstream economic, social, and political engagements within markets, and use the concept of political consumerism to refer only to boycotting and buying products for political reasons – the individualized collective action forms (Micheletti, 2003).[1]

What is wrong with political consumerism?

As the concept of political consumerism gained more traction, it became an important mode of political participation (Teorell et al., 2006; Van Deth, 2014). This means that citizens have additional means to have their voices heard in the political realm. Political consumerism is one form of action in a diversified action repertoire (Willis and Schor, 2012). In addition, it might even be a way to enter politics – a gateway to politics (de Moor and Verhaegen, 2020). As such, political consumerism might offer opportunities to mobilize citizens who would otherwise be disconnected from politics. However, increased attention to and usage of political consumerism resulted in a critical reading of this action form. Political consumerism offers a narrow understanding of politics based on individual interests and commodified dissent (Maniates, 2001). In so doing, it might be draining resources away from other political actions and reinforcing the power of ever-expanding markets. In short, prevailing critiques point to four problematic aspects of political consumerism: 1) the unequal access to political consumerism due to purchasing power, 2) the crowding out of other forms of participation by these "easy" or "light" forms of political action, 3) the commodification of political values, and 4) the retreat of the state (see Lorenzini, 2019 for a discussion).

In this chapter, I want to focus on what political consumerism does to citizens' democratic imagination. Citizenship is based on thinking, talking, and practicing (Perrin, 2009). This means that citizens learn about political participation and experiment with it to be(come) active citizens. So what is wrong with political consumerism when we consider how it informs citizens about democratic thinking, talking, and practicing? Buying or refusing to buy is a form of political action that uses consumers' purchasing power to have an influence on politics. In terms of thinking, talking, and practicing, the key message is that individuals engage in politics with their money, and that politics, like many other goods and services in a capitalist economy, is for sale. Another example of critique addressed to political consumerism relates to labels. One of the problems is that labels promote passive information and do not promote active learning (Boström and Klintman, 2019). Individuals rely on labels and take them at face value since they have limited or no information about the criteria used to give the label, how compliance with the norms and values promoted is guaranteed, and how independent the label is from the firm that sells the product.

Is it possible to overcome the shrinking of citizens' political imagination that political consumerism sustains? I argue that we can recognize the existence of a more vivid democratic imagination, perhaps even expand it, if we 1) consider a broader range of action forms that fall in the category of market-based activism but cannot be narrowed down to political consumerism and 2) examine critically the understandings of social change that prevail in each of these action forms.

Food activism – focusing on a single issue to expand our understanding of social change

Focusing on one issue – namely, contention around food – allows seeing the richness and diversity of actions associated with consumption. Food activism includes all action forms that aim at transforming food production, distribution, and consumption (Reichman, 2014). It includes political consumerism but goes beyond this form of action since it covers actions that establish long-term relationships between producers and consumers, as well as actions that aim to bypass the market. Food activism includes political consumerism, food collectives, and lifestyle politics (Lorenzini, 2019).

Political consumerism, in this case, means either refusing to buy or buying specific food for political reasons. For instance, boycotting a brand that has damaging environmental modes of production, that does not respect workers' rights, or that sells genetically modified products. Buycotting, in turn, refers to the act of buying products for political reasons: for instance, choosing products that correspond to specific labels, are produced locally, or comply with the social and solidary economy. Food collectives include participatory supermarkets, where consumers not only shop but also work to fill in the shelves, make orders, or work as a cashier (Zitcer, 2017a). It also covers community-supported agriculture, where citizens buy in advance a certain amount of vegetables, fruit, cereals, or other goods produced by local farmers (Forno et al., 2015; Hassanein, 2008). Lastly, lifestyle politics includes forms of action that require important changes in citizens' everyday lives – for instance veganism (Ophélie, 2016), voluntary simplicity (Lorenzen, 2012), or freeganism (Barnard, 2011). In these cases, citizens commit to a lifestyle that sets them apart from prevailing modes of consumption and require that they adapt their everyday life – not only refusing to buy some goods (e.g., meat, non-essential goods) but also changing their lives in terms of work, sociability, and political activism.

This fine-grained distinction of political actions that fall into the broad category of market-based activism and that are associated with transformation of the food system allows thinking about the kind of transformations that they propose. In the next section, I introduce the concept of real utopias and different understandings of social change to examine in more detail each form of market-based activism.

Real utopias and social change – the transformative potential of political actions

Eric Olin Wright proposed the concept of real utopias "to provide empirical and theoretical grounding for radical democratic egalitarian visions of an alternative social world" (Wright, 2010: 1). The core idea is that what we envision as "real" alternative possibilities depends on our capacity to imagine a different reality – different models of organizing society. Research on citizens' participation shows that our democratic imagination is fairly limited (Perrin, 2009). People see politics as remote from their everyday life and consider that they have few means of action. In addition, scholars pointed at the pervasive influence of market-based logics in our everyday life (Gibson-Graham, 2006). It is difficult to imagine any exchange and practices that fall outside the reach of markets. Yet our everyday life rests heavily on non-monetary exchanges if only for most of care work – providing food, shelter, and love in the realm of family life and friendship.

In order to build real utopias, the first step, according to Wright, is to identify how institutions limit our possibility to act differently. Furthermore, a key idea relates to the balance between three domains of power: the state, the economy, and society. The state includes the institutions that create binding rules, and state power refers to "the effective capacity to impose rules and regulate social relations over territory" (Wright, 2010: 119). The economy is the "the sphere of social activity in which people interact to produce and distribute goods and services" (Wright, 2010: 119). Economic power depends on economically relevant resources that actors control. Lastly, society is the domain of voluntary associations and interactions between individuals. Power in this case depends on the capacity for collective action. In the democratic ideal, state power is subordinated to social power. However, in recent years, critiques have pointed to the increasing concentration of power in the hands of a few elected representatives (Crouch, 2004). Key processes, in these regards, relate to the government growing power over the parliament (Rosanvallon, 2015) and the move from representative to responsible governments (Mair, 2013). Others pointed at the growing influence of economic power over politics (Purcell, 2003, 2009) and how, in a neoliberal state, the core task of the state is to support economic growth (Brown, 2015).

Conceptions of social change also shape the transformative potential of different forms of political participation. Lofland (1993) identified different conceptions of social change that coexist in the American peace movement. Conceptions of social change include two aspects. First, the end state – an assessment of what is wrong with the current situation and the definition of political objectives. Second, the means to get there – how to construct alternatives to the current state of affairs, identifying behaviors resulting in social change. Lofland distinguishes six theories of social change: 1) transcender theory, 2) educator theory, 3) intellectual theory, 4) politician theory, 5) protest theory, and 6) Prophet theory. Transcender theories argue that change happens because ideas spread; underpinning this conception is the idea of threshold – once a large number of people adhere to an idea, it changes the overall society. The goal is to trigger epochal change through rational thinking. Educator theory builds on the communication of facts and reasoning to accompany change. Similar to transcenders, they believe in the power of fact, but they consider that change is slow and incremental. Intellectual theory shares the core beliefs of educator theory; however, in this case, the process of change runs from intellectuals to educators, enlightened politicians, and broader audiences. The change is again slow and incremental. These conceptions resemble Serge Moscovici's theory of conversion (1980). An avant-garde first experiments with a new idea, then the idea spreads out in the private realm until it becomes the new mainstream mode of action. The politician theory of social change is the predominant conception of social change in society. The goal is to build majorities in the parliament, and therefore pragmatic policies are required to win over the elites. In this theory of social change, realism, feasibility, and compromise prevail. These first four theories are conventional forms of action, they rely on knowledge and information, and they demand trust in public authorities. The downside of these conventional action forms is that public authorities can easily ignore them. In response to these "weak" modes of action, some peace activists adopted an understanding of social change based on a more confrontational approach, using protest to disrupt the course of action and force authorities to consider their claims. These form the protest theories of social change. Lastly, prophet theory relies on the idea of regeneration at the individual level. Prophet theory seeks profound inner transformations. In this case, people change their overall lifestyle and are ready to engage in a marginal lifestyle to pursue their ideals. I use these ideal types to highlight the specific conceptions of social change that prevail in different forms of food activism.

Transformative potential of food activism

To apply these ideas to the study of food activism, I first consider the proposed balance of power between the state, the market, and society. Second, I examine the kind of social transformations that are likely to result from each form of action. Third, I discuss the conception of social change that characterizes each mode of food activism. I summarize these reflections in Table 15.1.

In political consumerism, political actions take place directly on the market. They seek to transform how firms produce goods and services, forcing them to comply with different values and norms. These actions seldom appeal to the regulatory role of the state. They directly target enterprises (Soule, 2009). Society has a role to play inasmuch as social movement seek to create new norms for the consumption of goods and services. They contribute to the moralization of markets (Balsiger, 2019). The transformations associated with political consumerism imply a commodification of political values since new norms for the production of goods and services add to their financial value. In addition, they imply some degree of individualization and privatization of responsibility since consumers and firms are responsible for engaging in changing prevailing modes of consumption and production. Lastly, this mode of action creates inequalities with a two-tier market offering goods and services that follow higher or lower social and environmental standards of production (Friedmann, 2005). In order to do so, social movement organizations run boycott campaigns or provide information through labels. These pursue two different goals, each associated with a specific conception of social change. In the case of a boycott, social change is close to a protest theory of social change. Protest claims are set on the market, not addressed to the state. Social movements seek to disrupt the normal course of action to force firms to take into account their demands. They are seldom able to weight on their market share or on their financial situation. Having this sort of impact would require mobilizing millions of consumers (Friedman, 2002). Hence, they rely mostly on the threat and the damage they might cause to the image of the firm (King, 2016). In the case of labels, which facilitate consumption choices, social movements rely on a learning process – they teach consumers how

Table 15.1 Specific forms of food activism and the role of the state, the economy, and society

	Political consumerism	*Food collectives*	*Lifestyle politics*
Locus of change	Market (+ society)	Society (+ market)	Society
Prevailing types of transformations	Commodification Individualization Privatization Inequalities	Small-scale Trust-enhancing Community-based	Experimental New narratives
Conceptions of social change	Education and protest theory	Prefigurative	Transcender and Prophet theory

to buy products that comply with social or environmental norms. In this case, we are closer to the education theory of social change.

Turning to food collectives, the main locus of change is society. Food collectives are organizations or informal groups that bring together food consumers and producers to create alternative food chains. Innovations take the form of advanced payment for the production of food through contractual relations between producers and consumers (Dubuisson-Quellier and Lamine, 2004; Hassanein, 2008); direct interactions between consumers and producers to define the quality, quantity, and types of good exchanged (Forno et al., 2015; Graziano and Forno, 2012); and participatory labelling or quality control (Koensler, 2020). The kind of transformations that prevail in food collectives are small-scale innovations that build on and contribute to developing trust. Scaling up is a key feature of capitalism and contributes to the creation and expansion of new markets (Tsing, 2017). Successful food collectives might expand or offer models for larger firms to copy. Therefore, the key locus of change is society, and the market is a second locus of change in the case of food collectives. In addition, these projects create communities of like-minded citizens. However, it is important to note here that food collectives may involve heterogeneous sets of members – with more or less engaged participants – and that they might compromise with some of their core values as they attract more members. For instance, participatory supermarkets face problems related to the inclusion of different types of participants (Zitcer, 2017b). It is difficult to tie food collectives to a theory of social change that Lofland identified in the peace movement. In this case, social change is more directly connected to collective action and takes place within groups that experiment with alternatives. It comes closest to a prefigurative understanding of social change (Yates, 2015). Luke Yates identifies five steps in the process associated with prefigurative social change: experimentation, circulation of political perspectives, production of new norms and conducts, material consolidation, and diffusion. In this conception, the collective plays a central role as experimenter of alternatives, but also in disseminating these alternatives, thanks to new material arrangements that facilitate the practice of these alternatives.

Lastly, lifestyle politics are laboratories of social change. The main locus of change is society; engaged citizens seek to create new values and practices that transform how we relate to the world around us. In these actions, food plays an important role but is not the sole or the most important issue of contention. Vegan citizens seek to develop new narratives and practices associated with the respect of animal rights and welfare (Giroux and Larue, 2019). They advocate not eating meat, eggs, dairy, or other animal products, but they also defend animals' right to live freely in good conditions. Voluntary simplifiers aim at reducing their environmental footprint thanks to minimal consumption. They reduce their consumption of manufactured goods, energy, and land. In the case of food, the main question relates to the quality of food (e.g., local, organic, seasonal). In so doing, voluntary simplifiers experiment with changes in their everyday life, but they also constantly deliberate with themselves and others about the choices that have to be made to reduce their consumption of natural resources (Lorenzen, 2012). Lifestyle politics offers experimental practices and creates new narratives about food. Transcender or prophet theories of social change come closest to lifestyle politics.

Market-based activism in the action repertoire of environmental movements

In the environmental movement, different practices are associated with market-based activism. Among them are political consumerism and the consumption of goods that either "protect" the environment or individually "protect" from environmental hazards. In addition, the boundaries between civil society organizations and corporations are blurring as these two types of actors collaborate to set up labels or to develop "sustainable" practices. Lastly, I present alternatives to market-based activism that stem from the environmental movement. These social movements question the core principles of a consumerist society. Voluntary simplifiers seek to reduce their engagement in production and consumption; they seek alternative sources of meaning in their lives. Similarly, ecofeminists highlight the value of a subsistence economy as an alternative to the division between paid productive and unpaid reproductive work but also as a way to establish satisfiers that fill different needs at once. Freegans value decommodified food (i.e., food that is considered as waste by mainstream food chains, and, therefore, is no longer a valued and valuable commodity) and aim to avoid paid work. Lastly, commoners seek collective modes of production, consumption, and decision-making processes. Each offers material and ideational alternatives that point at social transformation.

Political consumerism in the environmental movement

Maniates (2001) shows how limited our democratic imagination is when it comes to solving environmental issues. Even environmental students have difficulties envisioning forms of action that go beyond planting a tree, riding a bike, or changing a light bulb. Maniates argues that this individualized and commodified understanding of social change prevents any large-scale transformation. Szasz (2007) coined the term "inverted quarantine" to discuss how people move from collective action to individual sheltering from environmental hazards. Szasz documents how people sought individual solutions to collective problems instead of turning to protest and other forms of activism. Sometime in the 1980s, people began to buy bottled water instead of drinking tap water because they feared pollution of their drinking water (Szasz, 2007). During approximately the same period, the sales of organic food began to rise (Guthman, 2014 [2004]). Julie Guthman shows how, as it expanded and became more mainstream, organic food became a commodity that adds value to goods and increases the profits of large corporations. Friedmann (2005) even defines the current food regime as a corporate environmental food regime: a two-tier food regime in which those who can afford to, pay higher prices to gain access to healthy food while those who are too poor to do so are left with the cheap, unhealthy, industrial alternatives.

The increased use of political consumerism in the environmental movement is linked to protest waves and broader changes in social movements' action repertoires. As the state became less effective in responding to social movement demands, social movement organizations turned to the corporate world to set their claims (Soule, 2009). At the turn of the twenty-first century, the global justice movement set in motion a global protest wave. However, as it failed to materialize any major transformations, it triggered a turn to political consumerism and activism focused on private lives (Forno, 2019). Social movements that engage in market-based transformations – the moralization of markets – are heterogeneous. They include both radical actors who seek major transformations and moderate ones who seek compromise and collaboration with corporations (Balsiger, 2019). Processes of market moralization are associated with the creation of brands or labels to identify goods produced in compliance with stricter environmental or social norms.

Reinventing production and consumption – voluntary simplicity and ecofeminism

Etzioni (1999) argues that voluntary simplicity builds around three core principles: 1) free will and the deliberate choice to live a simple life (not due to necessity or poverty), 2) clear focus on changing and reducing consumption at the individual or household level, and 3) an attempt to possess fewer material goods accompanied by a quest for meaning (engaging in fulfilling activities and finding meaning in one's life). Voluntary simplifiers are more than downshifters who reduce their working time to earn less and spend less (Schor, 1998). They seek to consume less, and their concerns are driven by environmental awareness, the search for small scales of action that build community ties, a willingness to engage in self-determination, and self-realization (Elgin and Mitchell, 1977). Although it builds on individual action, it offers a promising understanding of the interplay between consumption and production. Rather, it redefines production as consumption – the consumption of time, human energy, creativity, natural resources (Maniates, 2017). As such, it offers the premises of alternative modes of production that consume less human and environmental capital.

Voluntary simplifiers question the relation to paid work and consumption. Ecofeminists interrogate, more generally, the division of work between productive and reproductive work in capitalist economies and defend a subsistence economy. An economic model focused on working to provide for one's needs – subsistence economy – growing food, hunting, wood picking, etc., that prevailed in pre-capitalist societies (Federici, 2004). Federici (2004) shows the centrality of taking over women's reproductive work during the establishment of capitalism. Marx highlighted the importance of primitive accumulation for capitalism. Federici (2004) identifies three key dimensions in this primitive accumulation: 1) concentration of land and capital (enclosure), 2) dispossessing workers of their means of production, and 3) controlling women's body and reproductive work (to ensure the reproduction of life and, therefore, of the workforce). The last element is the key contribution of ecofeminists to the study of capitalism and its emergence. Growth-based societies do not recognize the value of female unpaid reproductive labor and, more generally, the work related to self-production. Subsistence work does not add to the GDP; thus, it is easily discarded and considered irrelevant. This devaluation of (female) reproductive work is at the core of capitalism. Although these activities are vital for society (and for capitalism), they do not contribute to a narrow understanding of the economy (Mies and Shiva, 1993). More generally, Mies and Shiva (1993) highlight that capitalism threatens the environment because it fails to see the value of the economy of nature and subsistence, while both are vital for human survival. Capitalism's myopic focus on growth and the dismissal of reproductive work as non-contributive to growth are the core problems in the ecofeminist perspective. Hence, their alternative builds around the development and strengthening of a subsistence perspective.

The subsistence perspective contends that in consumerist societies, people satisfy most of their needs on the market – through consumption. However, consumption is a "pseudo-satisfier"; it produces little to no satisfaction. For instance, shopping is a quest for love and recognition, which cannot be obtained on the market. When fundamental needs are satisfied in non-commercial ways, they are often reciprocal – satisfiers exist for both giver and receiver. This is the case if someone helps a friend move out of his old house, when a father takes care of his children, or when a women cooks for her family. This is what Maria Mies and Vandana Shiva call the "subsistence way". The changes they seek require a turn to small-scale synchronized modes of production and consumption that enhance participatory decision-making within social groups.

Resisting commodification and transforming decision-making – freeganism and the commons

Voluntary simplicity and ecofeminism build on prefigurative understandings of social change – they are forms of lifestyle politics in which individuals, households, or communities engage in alternative modes of production and consumption. Furthermore, they redefine what producing and consuming mean. Yet there is only a limited protest agenda. Freeganism and its ties to anarchism offer a glimpse of a more protest-and-resistance understanding of social change.

Freeganism "is a combination of the words 'free' and 'vegan', and the philosophy behind freeganism is a fusion of both" (Barnard, 2011: 421). Freegans "protest over-consumption by abstaining from consuming anything that must be purchased" (Barnard, 2011: 421). In this movement, activists aim to work as little as possible because paid employment is the cornerstone of a consumerist society. Yet many freegans are not able to live without engaging in paid work. Those who live in a city need to pay rent for their housing, and this forces freegans to engage in some paid work. Alex Barnard (2011) argues that dumpster diving – the art of seeking edible food waste to feed oneself – plays a central part in the movement because it gives visibility to the movement and offers opportunities to engage in discussion with passers-by or invited participants. Freegans are close to anarchist movements. Ferrell (2014) studies scrounging practices and defines them "not only as alternative economic practice, but as a distinctively oppositional practice to legal regulation, mainstream politics, and consumerism" (Ferrell, 2014: 301). In this sense, they are akin to anarchist movements that seek to disavow existing structures of power and authority.

What are the alternatives to the existing oppressive structures of power and authority? Commoners oppose and resist laws that limit the possibilities for people to come together in communities and to own collectively the means of their subsistence economy. In addition, the commons are characterized by a two-step process: commoning and governing the common. Thus, the common is the result of a struggle by the plurality to acquire a good and to give meaning to that good (De Angelis, 2017). The commons are not specific products or goods; rather, they are the end result of a collective process of decision-making. Therefore, commons offer opportunities to create active citizens – individuals who take an active part in all the decisions related to the usage, management, and maintenance of common goods: that is, goods that have utility for collective entities. De Angelis (2017: 63) writes "to claim something as a common good in the context of a social struggle 'gives awareness to people, produces active citizenship, and therefore overcomes the passive consumerist model'". Many food collectives include collective decision-making processes; however, they fall short of envisioning and practicing the ideals of the commons.

Conclusion

In this chapter, I asked how political consumerism shapes citizens' democratic imagination. I examined how food activism proposes to transform the economy, the state, and society. On the other hand, I explored alternatives to political consumerism in the environmental movement.

First, I proposed to expand the concept of political consumerism to include different forms of actions that are tied to the market but not necessarily seeking changes directly on the market. Political consumerism builds a narrow democratic imagination associated with individualized modes of action, the privatization of goods and services, which foster inequalities. In this case, social change is understood in terms of education and protest. Yet, protest refers mostly to setting claims directly on the market. The state is absent in this conception of social change. The state's limited role is also striking in the other two modes of action. In food collectives, social change happens in society within small collectives. It enhances trust and reinforces communities, but it focuses only on small-scale projects. Lastly, lifestyle politics builds social change in society through experimental practices that seek to create new narratives about the good life within small communities.

Second, I scanned the environmental movement in search of alternatives to political consumerism. I identified four avenues of social change that depart from political consumerism and that propose an understanding of social change that redefines existing divisions between production and consumption, but also between production and reproduction. In these movements, social change is associated with a more-or-less radical break away from capitalism's core principles. Voluntary simplifiers work less and consume less, while ecofeminists defend a subsistence economy as the core provider of well-being for all. The subsistence economy offers satisfiers that address multiple needs at once outside the realm of market exchanges. Furthermore, freeganism and the commons expand democratic imagination beyond prefigurative politics and individual changes. Both freegans and commoners resist laws, institutions, and social practices that create structures of authority and power. They constitute sites for citizens to engage in critical thinking and participatory decision-making processes.

Note

1 In her original definition, Micheletti included petitions in addition to boycotts and buycotts, which I do not consider here.

References

Assadourian, Erik. 2016. "Converting the Environmental Movement into a Missionary Religious Force." Pp. 247–268 in *New Earth Politics*, edited by Simon Nicholson and Sikina Jinnah. Cambridge, MA: MIT Press.

Balsiger, Philip. 2010. "Making Political Consumers: The Tactical Action Repertoire of a Campaign for Clean Clothes." *Social Movement Studies* 9(3):311–329.

Balsiger, Philip. 2014. "Between Shaming Corporations and Promoting Alternatives: The Politics of an "Ethical Shopping Map." *Journal of Consumer Culture* 14(2):218–335.

Balsiger, Philip. 2016. "Tactical Competition and Movement Outcomes on Markets." P. 237 in *The Consequences of Social Movements*, edited by Lorenzo Bosi, Marco Giugni, and Katrin Uba. Cambridge: Cambridge University Press.

Balsiger, Philip. 2019. "The dynamics of 'Moralized Markets': A Field Perspective." *Socio-Economic Review*, online first.

Barnard, Alex V. 2011. " 'Waving the Banana' at Capitalism: Political Theater and Social Movement Strategy among New York's 'Freegan' Dumpster Divers." *Ethnography* 12(4):419–444.

Bartels, Larry M. 2009. *Unequal Democracy: The Political Economy of the New Gilded Age*. Princeton, NJ: Princeton University Press.

Bartley, Tim, Sebastian Koos, Hiram Samel, Gustavo Setrini, and Nik Summers. 2015. *Looking Behind the Label: Global Industries and the Conscientious Consumer*. Bloomington, IN: Indiana University Press.

Bennett, W. Lance. 2012. "The Personalization of Politics: Political Identity, Social Media, and Changing Patterns of Participation." *The ANNALS of the American Academy of Political and Social Science* 644(1):20–39.

Berglund, Christer, and Simon Matti. 2006. "Citizen and Consumer: The Dual Role of Individuals in Environmental Policy." *Environmental Politics* 15(4):550–571.

Boström, Magnus, and Mikael Klintman. 2019. "Can We Rely on 'Climate-Friendly' Consumption?" *Journal of Consumer Culture* 19(3):359–378.

Brown, Wendy. 2015. *Undoing the Demos: Neoliberalism's Stealth Revolution*. New York: Zone Books.

Carducci, Vince. 2006. "Culture Jamming: A Sociological Perspective." *Journal of Consumer Culture* 6(1):116–138.

Crouch, Colin. 2004. *Post-Democracy*. Cambridge: Polity Press.

Dauvergne, Peter, and Geneviève LeBaron. 2014. *Protest Inc.: The Corporatization of Activism*. Cambridge: Polity Press.

De Angelis, Doctor Massimo. 2017. *Omnia Sunt Communia: On the Commons and the Transformation to Postcapitalism*. London: Zed Books.

de Moor, Joost, and Soetkin Verhaegen. 2020. "Gateway or Getaway? Testing the Link Between Lifestyle Politics and Other Modes of Political Participation." *European Political Science Review* 12(1):91–111.

Dubuisson-Quellier, Sophie, and Claire Lamine. 2004. "Faire le marché autrement. L'abonnement à un panier de fruits et de légumes comme forme d'engagement politique des consommateurs." *Sciences de la société* (62):144–167.

Elgin, Duane, and Arnold Mitchell. 1977. "Voluntary Simplicity." *The Co-Evolution Quarterly* 3(1):4–19.

Etzioni, Amitai. 1999. "Voluntary Simplicity: Characterization, Select Psychological Implications, and Societal Consequences." Pp. 1–26 in *Essays in Socio-Economics*. Berlin, Heidelberg: Springer.

Federici, Silvia. 2004. *Caliban and the Witch*. Brooklyn, NY: Autonomedia.

Ferrell, Jeff. 2014. "Scrounging and Reclaiming." *The Routledge Companion to Alternative Organization* 295–307.

Forno, Francesca. 2019. "Protest, Social Movements, and Spaces for Politically Oriented Consumerist Actions – Nationally, Transnationally, and Locally." Pp. 69–88 in *The Oxford Handbook of Political Consumerism*, edited by Magnus Boström, Michele Micheletti, and Peter Oosterveer. Oxford: Oxford University Press.

Forno, Francesca, Cristina Grasseni, and Silvana Signori. 2015. "Italy's Solidarity Purchase Groups as 'Citizenship Labs'." Pp. 67–88 in *Putting Sustainability into Practice: Advances and Applications of Social Practice Theories*, edited by Emily Huddart Kennedy, Maurie J. Cohen, and Naomi T. Krogman. Cheltenham: Edward Elgar.

Friedman, Monroe. 2002. *Consumer Boycotts: Effecting Change through the Marketplace and Media*. New York, NY: Routledge.

Friedmann, Harriet. 2005. "From Colonialism to Green Capitalism: Social Movements and Emergence of Food Regimes." Pp. 227–264 in *New Directions in the Sociology of Global Development*, edited by Frederick H. Buttel, and Philip McMichael. Bingley, UK: Emerald Group Publishing Limited.

Gibson-Graham, Julie Katherine. 2006. *A Postcapitalist Politics*. Minneapolis: University of Minnesota Press.

Giroux, Valéry, and Renan Larue. 2019. *Le véganisme*. Paris: Presses Universitaires de France.

Graziano, Paolo R., and Francesca Forno. 2012. "Political Consumerism and New Forms of Political Participation: The Gruppi di Acquisto Solidale in Italy." *The ANNALS of the American Academy of Political and Social Science* 644(1):121–133.

Guthman, Julie. 2014 [2004]. *Agrarian Dreams: The Paradox of Organic Farming in California*. Oakland: University of California Press.

Hacker, Jacob S., and Paul Pierson. 2010. *Winner-Take-All Politics: How Washington Made the Rich Richer – and Turned Its Back on the Middle Class*. New York, NY: Simon and Schuster.

Harvey, David. 2007. *A Brief History of Neoliberalism*. New York, NY: Oxford University Press.

Hassanein, Neva. 2008. "Locating Food Democracy: Theoretical and Practical Ingredients." *Journal of Hunger & Environmental Nutrition* 3(2–3):286–308.

Jacques, Peter J. 2016. "Autonomy and Activism in Civil Society." Pp. 221–246 in *New Earth Politics*. Cambridge, MA: MIT Press.

Johnston, Josée. 2008. "The Citizen-Consumer Hybrid: Ideological Tensions and the Case of Whole Foods Market." *Theory and Society* 37(3):229–270.

King, Brayden G. 2016. "Reputation, Risk, and Anti-corporate Activism." in *The Consequences of Social Movements*, edited by Lorenzo Bosi, Marco Giugni, and Katrin Uba. Cambridge: Cambridge University Press.

Koensler, Alexander. 2020. "Prefigurative Politics in Practice: Concrete Utopias in Italy's Food Sovereignty Activism★." *Mobilization: An International Quarterly* 25(1):133–150.

Lang, Tim, and Yiannis Gabriel. 2005. "A Brief History of Consumer Activism." Pp. 39–53 in *The Ethical Consumer*, edited by Rob Harrison, Terry Newholm, and Deirdre Shaw. London: Sage.

Littler, Jo. 2005. "Beyond the Boycott." *Cultural Studies* 19(2):227–252.

Lofland, John. 1993. *Polite Protesters: The American Peace Movement of the 1980s*. Syracuse, NY: Syracuse University Press.

Lorenzen, Janet A. 2012. "Going Green: The Process of Lifestyle Change." *Sociological Forum* 27(1):94–116.

Lorenzen, Janet A. 2014. "Convincing People to Go Green: Managing Strategic Action by Minimising Political Talk." *Environmental Politics* 23(3):454–472.

Lorenzini, Jasmine. 2019. "Food Activism and Citizens' Democratic Engagements: What Can We Learn from Market-Based Political Participation?" *Politics and Governance* 7(4):131–141.

Mair, Peter. 2013. *Ruling the Void: The Hollowing of Western Democracy*. London: Verso.

Maniates, Michael. 2017. "Excerpts from "In Search of Consumptive Resistance: The Voluntary Simplicity Movement"." Pp. 177–188 in *Environment and Society*, edited by Christopher Schlottmann, Dale Jamieson, Colin Jerolmack, Anne Rademacher, and Maria Damon. New York: NYU Press.

Maniates, Michael F. 2001. "Individualization: Plant a Tree, Buy a Bike, Save the World?" *Global Environmental Politics* 1(3):31–52.

Micheletti, Michele. 2003. *Political Virtue and Shopping: Individuals, Consumerism, and Collective Action*. New York: Palgrave Macmillan.

Micheletti, Michele, and Dietlind Stolle. 2012. "Vegetarianism – A Lifestyle Politics?" pp. 127–147 in *Creative Participation. Responsibility-Taking in the Political World*, edited by Michele Micheletti and Andrew S. McFarland. Boulder and London: Paradigm Publishers.

Mies, Maria, and Vandana Shiva. 1993. *Ecofeminism*. New York, NY: Zed Books.

Moscovici, Serge. 1980. "Toward A Theory of Conversion Behavior." Pp. 209–239 in *Advances in Experimental Social Psychology*, edited by Leonard Berkowitz. New York: Academic Press.

Ophélie, Véron. 2016. "(Extra)ordinary Activism: Veganism and the Shaping of Hemeratopias." *International Journal of Sociology and Social Policy* 36(11/12):756–773.

Perrin, Andrew J. 2009. *Citizen speak: The Democratic Imagination in American Life*. Chicago: University of Chicago Press.

Purcell, Mark. 2003. "Citizenship and the Right to the Global City: Reimagining the Capitalist World Order." *International Journal of Urban and Regional Research* 27(3):564–590.

Purcell, Mark. 2009. "Resisting Neoliberalization: Communicative Planning or Counter-Hegemonic Movements?" *Planning Theory* 8(2):140–165.

Reichman, Daniel. 2014. "Information and Democracy in the Global Coffee Trade." Pp. 159–173 in *Food Activism: Agency, Democracy, and Economy*, edited by Carole Counihan and Valeria Siniscalchi. London: Bloomsbury Publishing.

Rosanvallon, Pierre. 2015. *Le bon gouvernement*. Paris: Le Seuil.

Sandel, Michael J. 2000. "What Money Can't Buy: The Moral Limits of Markets." *Tanner Lectures on Human Values* 21:87–122.

Schneider, Anne L., and Helen M. Ingram. 2005. *Deserving and Entitled: Social Constructions and Public Policy*. Albany: State University of New York.

Schor, Juliet B. 1998. *The Overspent American. Why We Desire What We Don't Need*. New York: Basic Books.

Soule, Sarah A. 2009. *Contention and Corporate Social Responsibility*. Cambridge: Cambridge University Press.

Stolle, Dietlind, and Marc Hooghe. 2011. "Shifting Inequalities: Patterns of Exclusion and Inclusion in Emerging Forms of Political Participation." *European Societies* 13(1):119–142.

Szasz, Andrew. 2007. *Shopping Our Way to Safety: How We Changed from Protecting the Environment to Protecting Ourselves*. Minneapolis: University of Minnesota Press.

Teorell, Jan, Mariano Torcal, and José Ramon Montero. 2006. "Political participation. Mapping the terrain." Pp. 334–357 in *Citizenship and Involvement in European Democracies: A Comparative Analysis*, edited by Jan W. van Deth. London: Routledge.

Tsing, Anna Lowenhaupt. 2017. *Le champignon de la fin du monde: Sur la possibilité de vie dans les ruines du capitalisme*. Paris: La Découverte.

Van Deth, Jan W. 2014. "A Conceptual Map of Political Participation." *Acta Politica* 49(3):349–367.

Willis, Margaret M., and Juliet B. Schor. 2012. "Does Changing a Light Bulb Lead to Changing the World? Political Action and the Conscious Consumer." *The ANNALS of the American Academy of Political and Social Science* 644(1):160–190.

Wright, Erik Olin. 2010. *Envisioning Real Utopias*. London: Verso.

Yates, Luke. 2015. "Rethinking Prefiguration: Alternatives, Micropolitics and Goals in Social Movements." *Social Movement Studies* 14(1):1–21.

Zitcer, Andrew. 2017a. "Buying in Bulk: Food Cooperatives and Their Pursuit of Justice." Pp. 181–205 in *The New Food Activism. Opposition, Collaboration, and Collective Action*, edited by Alison Hope Alkon and Julie Guthman. Oakland: University of California Press.

Zitcer, Andrew. 2017b. "Collective Purchase: Food Cooperatives and Their Pursuit of Justice." Pp. 181–205 in *The New Food Activism. Opposition, Cooperation, and Collective Action*, edited by Alison Hope Alkon and Julie Guthman. Oakland: University of California Press.

16

ENVIRONMENTAL JUSTICE AND CLIMATE JUSTICE

Phaedra C. Pezzullo

The movement for environmental justice was born when a new vocabulary emerged. As one Chicana woman who later became a movement leader testified: "I heard words like. . . 'environmental racism'. Somebody put words, names, on what our community was experiencing" (Augustine, 1993). The environmental justice movement created not only a new discourse for amplifying grassroots voices but also a compelling critique how the "environment" was too often misunderstood without a robust notion of justice.[1]

Twenty years later, a related discourse was articulated by transnational grassroots advocates: climate justice. At a Climate Justice Summit during COP6, India-based TRAC Climate Justice coordinator and spokesperson for the International Climate Justice Network Amit Srivastava linked local and global struggles:

> [T]he environmental disasters created by the oil industry in places like Nigeria, Louisiana, and Ecuador add up to a looming global catastrophe called climate change. What's more, the process of corporate-led globalization is amplifying the climate crisis.
>
> (CorporateWatch, 2000)

Stories of everyday people around the world experiencing the worst costs of environmental degradation – often called "frontline communities" – began establishing a broader pattern in which governments and transnational corporations were treating their bodies and land as disposable in the pursuit of extractivist petroculture. Lands spoiled, bodies ill, and now the precarity of the planet itself was beginning to threaten all life on earth – with the Global South being hit, as the movement adage goes, "first and worst". This is the "cruel irony" of climate injustice: those who contribute the least to creating greenhouses gases are the ones who are feeling the impacts first and worst (Pezzullo and Cox, 2021).

Environmental movements, as this volume attests, are not singular, isolated, or static. Like ecosystems themselves, once we delve into the histories of environmental advocacy, we discover social movements are multi-faceted, interconnected, and dynamic. This chapter revisits the story of origin for the environmental justice movement, when key issues of "environment" and "racism" became linked in the public imaginary. Next, it turns to the environmental justice critique of the environmental movement and a redefinition of "environment". Then it summarizes the institutionalization of environmental justice and the emergence of climate justice,

 DOI: 10.4324/9780367855680-18

including contemporary reluctance among some environmentalists to center justice as a key issue.

Mobilization: the birth of the environmental justice movement

The "birthplace", "symbolic center", and "milestone" of the environmental justice movement was Warren County in the state of North Carolina, US, due to the following story of origin (Pezzullo, 2001). As historical context, 1970 marked the institutionalization of the environmental movement in the US, establishing the US Environmental Protection Agency (EPA) and several landmark laws aimed at providing environmental protections (for the workplace, water, air, endangered species, and more). In 1976, the Toxic Substances Control Act was passed as an attempt to regulate harmful chemicals, including polychlorinated biphenyls ("PCBs").[2]

Naming "environmental racism"

In 1978, a truck drove along 210 miles of roads across 14 counties in the state of North Carolina. Out of the back of the truck leaked oil contaminated with PCBs. Shortly after, people began reporting foul odors and health complications. An investigation by the state identified Ward Transformer Company as the responsible party, and it pled guilty to paying three men to illegally dispose of 31,000 gallons of toxic PCB-laden waste for US$75,000 (Freudenberg, 1984: 182–183). The three men were New York residents Robert Burns and his two sons, Randy and Timothy ("3 Plead Guilty," 1979).

Although the state was able to identify and hold accountable the culprits, it was left with the burden of cleanup (Bullard and Wright, 1992: 41). It chose one of the counties, Warren County, to site a landfill, and the EPA approved the decision in 1979.

> Warren County, however, did not meet two of the EPA's guidelines:
> 1) that the bottom of the landfill be at least 50 feet above the groundwater and 2) that the site be located where there are "thick, relatively impermeable formations such as large-area clay pans". The high water table in Warren County would allow only a 7 foot difference and samples showed only small amounts of clay present within the highly permeable soil.
>
> (Labalme, 1987: 3)

Given these discrepancies, in 1981, Warren County sued the state of North Carolina and the EPA but lost, since the judge ruled the EPA had the right to waive its own guidelines (*Warren County v State of North Carolina*).

Residents then asked if their community was chosen for political reasons. "Warren County [was] the poorest county in the state with a per capita income of around $5,000 in 1980. Its population [was] 65% black" (Geiser and Waneck, 1994: 50). One Italian American resident, Ken Ferruccio, began sending out press releases calling for civil disobedience in the tradition he invoked as Henry David Thoreau's, claiming: "It's an environmental issue as well as a human rights issue because you're discriminating against a community by threatening it with toxic chemicals" (Labalme, 1987: 24). These efforts led to the creation of a multi-racial alliance.

An African American resident, Reverend Luther Brown, convinced African American Reverend Leon White of the United Church of Christ to support their struggle. White (as well as

Dollie Burwell, another African American resident) contacted well-known African American civil rights leader Reverend Benjamin Chavis.[3] The civil rights non-governmental organization NAACP (National Association for the Advancement of Colored People) then became involved. A second lawsuit, *NAACP v. Gorsuch*, lost, the first in the nation to be filed for "discriminatory intent" of environmental waste (No. 82–768-CIV-5. E.D.N.C. Aug. 10, 1982). The federal court rejected it on the grounds that there was not sufficient evidence that the state intended to discriminate. This ruling reinforced that racist intent is challenging to prove (although there are exceptions, such as the 1991 World Bank memo reprinted in Pellow, 2007); it also led future endeavors to a focus on disproportionate impacts (establishing racist patterns rather than motives).

Subsequently, the state started moving the contaminated soil into Warren County in 1982. In response, residents and African American civil rights allies and leaders – including Chavis, Reverend Joseph Lowery (Southern Christian Leadership Conference), and Walter E. Fauntroy (a non-voting member of Congress from the nation's capital, then chairman of the Congressional Black Caucus) – engaged in six weeks of civil disobedience. Creating an international media spectacle through direct action, this intersectional, intergenerational alliance laid their bodies in the middle of the road to deter the trucks and raise awareness. Five hundred and twenty-three arrests were made (Labalme, 1987: 5). "The PCB-landfill decision became the shot heard around the world" (Bullard, 2020).

The state claimed the PCB landfill was created for "the public good" (Labalme, 1987). Yet the protesters' principled stance and political pressure moved the governor to make the promise to detoxify the landfill "when and if technologically feasible" with feedback from a working group, including input from Warren County residents (Hunt, 1982). This statement became vital to lobbying efforts that eventually did lead to the detoxification of the landfill in 2003 when Hunt once again was governor.[4]

Although the alliance failed to stop the landfill, they achieved other successes. First, the protests in Warren County gave birth to a vocabulary that articulated or linked waste and race.[5] The phrase "environmental racism" was a neologism that soon became a powerful way for people to make sense of their experiences and resist these inequities (Pezzullo, 2001). Naming environmental racism, then, articulated civil rights and environmental traditions to create a discourse that drew upon but exceeded these predecessors. This "marriage of civil rights activism with environmental concerns" led Warren County to become known as the birthplace of environmental justice.

Warren County also motivated and underscored the significance of several studies that provided empirical evidence of systemic inequalities in US policies and practices related to toxic and solid waste (for example, see Bullard and Wright, 1987; Lavelle and Coyle, 1992). Notably, African American sociologist Robert D. Bullard (1983) already had begun to study the solid waste siting patterns in the Texas city of Houston.[6] The next year, at the request of Fauntroy, the US Government Accounting Office (GAO) conducted a study of the racial and economic demographics of communities surrounding hazardous waste landfills (GAO, 1983). Then the United Church of Christ Commission for Racial Justice commissioned an even more comprehensive landmark report of empirical evidence of environmental racism, authored principally by Chinese American Charles Lee (*Proceedings*, 1987).[7]

Second, Warren County galvanized a radical critique of a narrower understanding of "environment", which too often signified a place distinct from one's everyday life (such as public lands for outdoor recreation) or separate from humans (in which we somehow are imagined as a species outside nature). Categories of "built" and "natural" environments began to break down for many more people, as Warren County sparked an awareness that the environment is wherever people are because we are part of the environment. As African American environmental justice activist Dana Alston later stated:

> For us, the issues of the environment do not stand alone by themselves. They are not narrowly defined. Our vision of the environment is woven into an overall framework of social, racial and economic justice. The environment, for us, is where we live, where we work, and where we play.
>
> (*Proceedings*, 1991: 103)

This expanded notion of "environment" mattered, as Italian American environmental justice scholar and advocate Giovanna Di Chiro (1996: 303) argues, transforming "the possibilities for fundamental social and environmental change through processes of redefinition, reinvention, and construction of innovative political and cultural discourses".

Further, "Warren County challenged the common assumption that waste must be made and, therefore, it has to go somewhere" (Pezzullo, 2001: 8). If the state no longer imagined certain people to be disposable, then where could we place certain hazards? If the environment was not only where we created things but also where those objects and the associated waste went afterward, how might our environmental decisions change?

Finally, the voices of those most impacted by environmental degradation or crisis were amplified. The aforementioned statement by the governor had recognized that the voices of the residents of Warren County were left out of the decision-making process. Not only was a pattern of distributive injustice established, but also a pattern of procedural injustice: that is, excluding communities from meaningful engagement about environmental decisions most directly impacting their lives. As Alston (1990) emphasized: "We speak for ourselves".

As individual communities began sharing similar stories, a period of mobilization occurred for the next decade. In 1990, the Indigenous Environmental Network or IEN (www.ienearth. org/) and the Southwest Network for Environmental and Economic Justice (www.sric.org/voices/2004/v5n2/sneej.php) were founded. In 1993, the Asian Pacific Environmental Network or APEN was established (https://apen4ej.org/). In 1999, the National Black Environmental Justice Network was founded (www.nbejn.com/).

Critiquing the environmental movement and redefining "environment"

Mobilization also included a critique of environmental movements. Environmental and environmental justice movements generally differed in significant ways over whose voices mattered, what issues were relevant to the "environment", and what counted as environmental epistemologies (or ways of knowing), "including racism, classism, and sexism, as well as conceptual, rhetorical, historical, evaluative, and cultural differences" (Pezzullo and Sandler, 2007a: 7). Repeatedly, before and after the Warren County protests, the elitist racism, classism, and sexism of the environmental movement clashed with the predominantly people of color–, working class–, and women-led environmental justice movement.

In 1973, the EPA commissioned a study of environmental organizations after critiques of elitism; the study found environmental organizations primarily were staffed by "middle-class, professional, white, married men in their thirties" (quoted in McGurty, 1997: 303). There also were countless stories of grassroots communities reaching out to environmental organizations and being told their issues were not environmental issues. Consider, for example, testimony from activists trying to stop a solid waste incinerator in Los Angeles in the mid-1980s:

> These issues were not deemed adequately "environmental" by local environmental groups such as the Sierra Club or the Environmental Defense Fund. . . . They were informed that the poisoning of an urban community by an incineration facility was a "community health issue", not an environmental one.
>
> (Di Chiro, 1996: 299)

"[E]ventually, environmental and social justice organizations such as Greenpeace, the National Health Law Program, the Center for Law in the Public Interest, and Citizens for a Better Environment would join [the] Concerned Citizens' campaign to stop" the proposed facility; however, this initial reluctance reflects a broader pattern (Di Chiro, 1996: 527 note 2). A growing rift was felt in these moments of hesitation, exclusionary agendas, and uneven responses.

In 1990, a damning public letter was sent by the Gulf Coast Tenant Leadership Development Project to the national environmental organizations (then called the "Group of Ten"):

> Although environmental organizations calling themselves the "Group of Ten" often claim to represent our interests, in observing your activities it has become clear to us that your organizations play an equal role in the disruption of our communities. There is a clear lack of accountability by the Group of Ten environmental organizations towards Third World communities in the Southwest, in the United States as a whole, and internationally.

While the mobilization around "environmental justice" expanded in less than a decade beyond state and ethnic boundaries within the US, this letter also identifies the role of the US environmental movement in failing to support Third World nations through debt-for-nature swaps and more.[8]

The same year, Bullard (1990) edited the first of many books establishing environmental justice studies. Often in collaboration with Bullard, environmental justice sociologists African American Bunyan Bryant and European American Paul Mohai held the first academic conference on environmental justice in 1990 at the University of Michigan, which then led to the first environmental justice undergraduate and graduate degree programs in 1992 (Mohai, 1990; Bryant, 1995).

In 1991, academics and grassroots leaders hosted the First National People of Color Environmental Leadership Summit in Washington, DC. As noted, the definition of "environmental justice" expanded beyond disproportionate toxic burdens, as Chavis defined it:

> racial discrimination in environmental policymaking, the enforcement of regulations and laws, the deliberate [or unintentional] targeting of communities of color for toxic waste facilities, the official sanctioning of the life-threatening presence of poisons and pollutants in our [people of color] communities, and the history of excluding people of color from leadership of the environmental movement.
>
> (quoted in Grossman, 1994: 278)[9]

Notably, Bullard (1992: 21) re-articulated a broader agenda that remains among the priorities of environmental justice visions of freedom and abolition today: "[e]nvironmental racism is an

extension of the institutional racism which touches every aspect of our society, including housing, education, employment and law-enforcement".

This more robust understanding of environmental justice was articulated collectively by the
delegates at the Summit in the Principles of Environmental Justice (available widely, including
at www.ejnet.org/ej/principles.html). The preamble and 17 principles outline fundamental
environmental values and beliefs, as well as rights of access to mother earth, as well as all her
interdependent species, and protection from environmental harms, including toxins, hazards,
and radioactive waste, as well as discrimination, destruction, and exploitation.

The Summit provided a reminder that while Warren County was significant, the movement
was drawing on cultural resources that had existed long before. Not only were decolonial Indigenous rights linked to the movement, but also, for example, Latinx farmworker anti-pesticide
advocacy and the fact that civil rights leader Martin Luther King, Jr., was killed while organizing sanitation workers in 1968. Further, intersectional perspectives were voiced by participants,
which involved all 50 states, plus Puerto Rico, Brazil, Canada, Chile, Ghana, the Marshall
Islands, Mexico, and Nigeria. By then, environmental justice had become a uniting discourse
for diverse traditions and struggles beyond Warren County and the US.

Conversations about how environmental justice and environmental movements could work
together continued. Notably, in 1996, the Jemez Principles of Organizing were established
(www.ejnet.org/ej/jemez.pdf). At the Second National People of Color Environmental Leadership Summit in 2002, the Principles of Collaboration were written (Pezzullo and Sandler,
2007b). After a decade of mobilization, environmental justice was beginning to transform not
only environmental movements but also environmental policy.

Institutionalization: environmental justice recognition

The life cycle of a social movement long has been narrated through four stages: 1) emergence,
2) mobilization, 3) institutionalization, and 4) decline, which is due to a range of reasons,
including cooptation, repression, success, and/or failure (Tilly, 1978). As Marco Giugni and
Maria T. Grasso (2015: 347) have argued, environmental movements largely have been institutionalized, though not evenly and not necessarily resulting positively:

> Open opportunity structures – for example in terms of privileged access to politi-
> cal decision-making arenas and increasing integration of environmental movement
> organizations into policy networks – often result in both a moderation of the action
> repertoires (which in some cases can go as far as a total abandonment of protest activi-
> ties) and a progressive institutionalization of environmental movements.

For these reasons, institutionalization always signals both success and potential precarity,
although a movement might bridge, as Giugni and Grasso (2019) argue, institutional and extra-
institutional politics or electoral behavior and protest politics. The history of the US-based
environmental justice movement, however, suggests one way a movement may continue to
reaffirm and reinvent itself once achieving institutionalization, to avoid the pitfalls of assimilation or marginality.

In the US, environmental justice was institutionalized in the 1990s. The Congressional Black
Caucus met with the EPA in 1990, which then formed an environmental equity working
group. Out of those sustained efforts, in 1993, the National Environmental Justice Advocacy
Council (NEJAC) was established, which provided advice on environmental justice challenges
(such as toxic pollution public health risks, urban revitalization, and eventually climate change),

as well as solutions (such as meaningful public participation, community grants for capacity building and economic revitalization, monitoring of air quality, and emergency preparedness). The polyvocality of environmental justice was critical, and accordingly, members of NEJAC initially included, but were not limited to, Chicano/a and Latino/a/x and labor community organizers José Bravo, Richard Moore, and Baldemar Velásquez; African American sociologists Bryant, Bullard, and Beverly Wright; Jean Sindab, African American director of environmental and economic justice/hunger concerns for the National Council of Churches; Indigenous leaders, such as Gail Small, Cindy Thomas, and Sam Winder; previously noted principle author from the Toxic Wastes and Race Report, Lee; Peggy Saika, founding executive director of APEN; Velma R. Veloria, Filipino American union organizer and Washington state legislator; and a multi-ethnic group of lawyers.[10] One year later, European American US President Clinton issued Executive Order 12898, which mandated that all governmental offices coordinate for environmental justice efforts. Environmental justice was to become a consideration by the government for assessing environmental decision making, and increasing numbers of environmental justice advocates were being heard by elite decision makers.

Yet environmental racism and injustice continued. In a study of staff working for the EPA, European American environmental justice scholar Jill Harrison (2019: 202) provides evidence that while some staff imagine themselves as environmental justice advocates attempting to transform the state culture from within, others in the EPA remain resistant to including environmental justice as part of the purview of their scope of work. She also found that environmental justice remains under-authorized to regulate and fund material environmental justice changes.

Despite institutionalization, "environmental justice" has held off the expected social movement stage of termination. Notably, the language of "environmental justice" and "environmental racism" have remained a resource for a range of contemporary struggles. For example, when the US government diverted an oil pipeline from a predominantly white community through Indigenous lands, water protectors at Standing Rock reaffirmed many of the original environmental justice principles, including, but not limited to, the sacredness of mother earth, Indigenous sovereignty, the fundamental right to clean water, the right to be involved in environmental decision-making assessment, and the right to be free from discrimination (IEN 2018–2019; Enzinna, 2016; Nagle, 2018; Cagle, 2020). Networks like APEN (2020) are celebrating 25 years of meaningful organizing. More recently, the NAACP (2020) published a report and organized around equity as it relates to the coronavirus, reaffirming principles that public policy should be based on justice for all peoples and involve frontline communities in public participation processes and access to quality health care for all. And the NEJBN reconnected in 2020, reaffirming its original mission as new contexts arose, such as the COVID-19 global pandemic (www.nbejn.com/).

Reinvention: the rising of climate justice

In addition to reaffirmation, the environmental justice movement has reinvented itself in relation to the climate crisis. Since its emergence, climate justice has enabled advocates not only to name injustices but also to underscore and foster a broader ethic of care. Again, like the tributaries of environmental justice, many movements led to the articulation of "climate justice".

Articulating "climate justice"

Arguably, the first use of "climate justice" in print was by the San Francisco–based Transnational Resource and Action Center (TRAC) in 1999 (Dorsey, 2007). That document was written as the organization was in dialogue with the International Climate Justice Network (www.climatejusticenetwork.org/) and in solidarity with many grassroots struggles to address what this term names. Further, the Global South already had begun to make arguments about the inequity of climate negotiations as "environmental colonialism" (Agarwal and Narain, 1991).

Citing who is "hardest hit", who "have to fight harder for a fair share of resources and protections", and the cruel irony of climate change (among other factors), TRAC (1999: 5) argued: "climate change is likely to be the biggest environmental justice issue ever". TRAC's (1999: 3) definition of climate justice included seven main platforms, including preventing global warming, assisting impacted communities, and fostering a just transition. While community redress and regeneration remained pivotal, emphasis was placed on transnational organizations accountable for climate damage. The report, for example, outlined how the fossil fuel industry had established a pattern of five *D*s: deny, delay, divide, dump, and dupe (11).

TRAC thanks environmental justice advocates and networks, including the Southwest Network for Environmental and Economic Justice, the IEN, and the Just Transition Consortium. Further, to quote TRAC at length:

> The ranks of those fighting for Climate Justice are filled by democracy movements struggling against oil interests around the world. They include communities polluted by refineries and working for environmental justice in the United States, as well as Indigenous people trying to maintain their cultures and their lands. Residents of smog-filled cities, and students seeking to reign in unaccountable university investments all can be advocates for Climate Justice. Activists working to generate democratic control over corporations and to reverse the destructive dynamics of globalization, along with those fighting the environmentally destructive policies of the World Bank and the World Trade Organization, are also advocates of Climate Justice.
>
> (6)

Arguably, the desire to reinvent environmental justice to emphasize allies in global democratic struggles and university campaigns reflects not only a call for retributive justice but also a desire to deter the tactic of "divide" by broadening the list of allies for even wider mobilization.

Notably, climate justice benefits from ancient knowledges. The report, for example, foregrounded climate science and frontline epistemologies or ways of knowing matter. In addition to addressing "Climate Change Is Real", they quoted the Albuquerque Declaration of Indigenous Peoples:

> Indigenous prophecies are dovetailing with scientific projections. What we have known and believed, you now also know. The Earth is in disequilibrium. Plants are disappearing, animals are dying and the weather itself – the rain, the wind, and fire – react against human activities.
>
> (TRAC, 1999: 7)

As with environmental justice, therefore, articulating climate justice was informed by many cultural traditions and exceeded any one voice. Indian environmental scholar and activist Vandana Shiva already was working in solidarity with the Chipko movement on biodiversity (from which the name "tree huggers" was inspired) in 1972, had founded ENGO Navdanya in 1991 to support farmers, and was articulating related critiques of global industries and institutions that were eroding local rights (Shiva, 1994; India Development Review, 2019). In the 1990s, Nigerian Ogoni Indigenous people were protesting the exploitation by Shell of their land and culture (Bob, 2010; Saro-Wiwa, 1996). In 1997, Kenyan environmental scholar and activist Wangari Maathai founded the Green Belt Movement, advocating for equity, justice, and democracy through planting trees (Maathai, 2003). Indigenous movements in Ecuador and Bolivia also were arguing for the rights of nature in relation to human rights (Chuji et al., 2019). The list could go on.

Climate justice, therefore, is more accurately understood as a discourse that emerged as part of a broader set of movements that link social and economic justice with transnational corporate accountability, democratic values, and ecological values within specific contexts.

Today, the leading US climate justice coalition is the Climate Justice Alliance (https://climatejusticealliance.org), which formed in 2013. They bring together over 70 frontline communities, including familiar organizations such as APEN, IEN, Southwest Organizing Project, and the NAACP, as well as many more. In the call to move from an extractive economy to a regenerative one, the Climate Justice Alliance articulates their struggle as one that has emerged from the environmental justice movement:

> The EJ movement emphasizes bottom-up organizing, centering the voices of those most impacted, and shared community leadership. Building on these histories, members of the Climate Justice Alliance, many of whom are rooted in the environmental justice movement, have adapted the definition of Just Transition to represent a host of strategies to transition whole communities to build thriving economies that provide dignified, productive and ecologically sustainable livelihoods; democratic governance and ecological resilience.

Perhaps what is most noticeably different in contemporary articulations of climate justice is the increased focus on not just crises worth reacting against but also meaningful networks of care worth nurturing. This vision includes feeding and growing collective sacredness, regeneration, ecological and social well-being, and cooperation.

Early environmental justice activists also were motivated by caring for their health, as well as that of their families and communities. They, as noted in the previously quoted preamble to the Principles of Environmental Justice, were committed to honoring principles of restorative (healing) justice, including their

> interdependence to the sacredness of our Mother Earth; to respect and celebrate each of our cultures, languages and beliefs about the natural world and our roles in healing ourselves; . . . to promote economic alternatives which would contribute to the development of environmentally safe livelihoods.

Building off that foundation, a greater set of networks and practices is being established to show the value of care to climate justice, which challenges neoliberal values of individualism and disposability. Historically, caretaking and care work often have been placed on women and people of color (such as domestic labor, nursing, teaching, elder care, childcare), yet an ethic of care embraces and values that labor (Whyte and Cuomo, 2015). "There are several phrases circulating in environmental discourse today that attempt to capture this sentiment, including the goal of not just surviving but thriving and the mission of not just bouncing back from a disaster, but bouncing forwards. These discourses aim to foster a world that exceeds reactionary practices" (Pezzullo, 2017), "fostering an ethic of care about our global interdependence and interconnection" (Pezzullo, 2020). As Canadian journalist and advocate Naomi Klein (2019) claims: "Care work is climate work," which she notes often involve low-carbon labor on the frontlines of the climate crisis "systematically undertheorized by emission reduction specialists."

For example, in the aftermath of climate-related disasters, frontline communities have established networks of care.[11] Notably, Klein (2007) has outlined how disaster capitalism is a post-disaster pattern in which corporations and governments take advantage of the shock of a disaster's aftermath by using such tragedies to advocate for a neoliberal agenda of free-market exploitation. European American (with Puerto Rican heritage) environmental justice scholar and advocate Catalina M. de Onís (2018, 2021) has argued that while longstanding relations of what she calls "energy coloniality" and "energy privilege" were exacerbated in 2017 after Hurricane María made landfall in Puerto Rico, grassroots networks such as Coquí Solar are installing solar energy by working with service-learning projects for local engineering students. Likewise, after Hurricane Sandy hit New York City, grassroots organization UPROSE launched the Sunset Park Climate Justice Center to engage public participation about how to adapt and mitigate climate disasters, organizing and training block captains, monitoring environmental conditions, and building a map of their network to design a resiliency plan (see www.uprose.org/climate-justice).

Climate justice care work exceeds disaster response. As Di Chiro (2020) writes about intersectional networks of care she is involved in: "Collectivist and solidarity economies are proliferating in Philadelphia as evidenced by hundreds of local, democratically organized cooperatives focusing on food, housing, energy, health care, childcare, credit unions, and schooling" (325). The Oakland-based Movement Generation Justice & Ecology Project also organizes low-income communities and communities of color to work toward, for example, Black liberation, reparation, and land reform; climate worker trainings; and just transition in an age of COVID-19 (https://movementgeneration.org/). Likewise, care networks have emerged to provide mutual aid since the COVID-19 pandemic, calling for a "Just Recovery" (Climate Justice Alliance, 2018; Klein, 2020). Further, care networks are proliferating beyond the US; consider, for example, the New Zealand–based Center for Culture-Centered Approach to Research and Evaluation (www.massey.ac.nz/~wwcare/), which emphasizes the importance of voice and public participation in decision making related to public health.

Conclusion: what difference "justice" makes to environmental movements

Despite the successes, tensions remain. Lauded climate successes sometimes greenwash (Pezzullo, 2003, 2020, 2021) and carewash (The Care Collective, 2020). Consider, for example, the Unjust Transition Award, which was created by the Sierra Club (the oldest US-based environmental NGO) and presented by Bullard in 2015 at COP21 in Paris, France. The award recognized the French-based company Renault-Nissan for labor violations at the Canton, Mississippi, US, plant, where batteries for the electric vehicle the Nissan Leaf are built. Despite global excitement over the Leaf, predominantly Black workers were organizing for rights, and labor organizers were arguing that technological innovations are not indicators of climate success if worker and civil rights are not prioritized.[12]

Reminiscent of environmental justice conflicts with the environmental movement, climate justice also appears to create controversy for some (500 Women Scientists Leadership. 2020). For example, while European American climate scientist Michael Mann (2019a) advocates for diversity in climate communication and is not new to controversy for strong climate action arguments, he expresses reluctance about "justice" as a key climate term. In a review of Klein's (2019) book, *On Fire: The Burning Case for a Green New Deal*, Mann (2019b) writes:

> I share her concern over each of these societal afflictions, but I wonder at the assertation that it's not possible to address climate change without solving all that plagues us. . . . Saddling a climate movement with a laundry list of other worthy social programmes risks alienating needed supporters (say, independents and moderate conservatives) who are apprehensive about a broader agenda of progressive social change.

Mann's review provoked debate on #ClimateTwitter, with one side agreeing with Mann that climate action appears to carry enough baggage on its own and the other side claiming we can't separate climate, economic, and social justice goals (Morano, 2019). In response, Klein (2019) tweeted: "I respect MM as a scientist and appreciate his courage. But he overtly states: 'It's advisable to decouple economic justice and environmental issues'. That is an argument ★against★ climate justice and it's divisive".

Opponents of environmental and climate justice exacerbate these fissures to their benefits. Consider how Chevron worked with a public relations firm to send out the following message to journalists: "[E]nvironmental organizations, composed of predominantly white members, are backing radical policies like the Green New Deal which would bring particular harm to minority communities". Arguing that the growing popularity of the Green New Deal in the US has "got to have big polluters worried", African American environmental justice scholar David Naguib Pellow pointed out the hypocrisy of this public relations frame: "If you're perpetuating climate disruption, as Chevron is, then you're also perpetuating racial injustice" (Hiar, 2020). This insight underscores how climate inaction is an injustice; however, debates continue about whether justice should be a key issue.

African American environmental justice and climate justice organizer Reverend Lennox Yearwood (2020) of the Hip Hop Caucus eloquently expresses how articulating these issues matters:

> We cannot achieve climate justice without racial justice and we cannot achieve racial justice without climate justice. The right to breathe clean air, drink clean water, access healthy and safe food, and live in a safe environment, is the civil and human rights struggle of this century.

Likewise, African American climate justice scholar and Green New Deal advocate Rhianna Gunn-Wright emphasizes:

> People will often get kind of upset about how broad it is. *We're talking about climate, why do you have to talk about racial injustice? Why can't we just quote-unquote focus on climate?* But the input determines the outcome.
>
> (Goodman, 2020)

Such articulations illustrate how some argue justice is a necessary, not secondary, key issue for environmental movements.

Beyond defining key terms, events, and figures, this chapter develops three claims. First, rhetorical neologisms were foundational to the emergence of environmental justice. The origin story of Warren County became known as such for naming "environmental racism" and articulating civil rights with environmental issues. This new vocabulary fostered a broader imaginary that mobilized one of the most successful social movements of the twentieth century, which quickly gained momentum through grassroots networks, academic research, and policy achievements. That discourse also led to systemic changes in the lives of frontline communities, the environmental movement, and policymakers – though the struggle is not over.

Second, while institutionalization of a social movement can lead to termination, in the case of environmental justice, it provided an opportunity for a reaffirmation and reinvention. Environmental justice has remained relevant due to reaffirmation of the movement's initial principles and a reinvention through the transnational discourse of climate justice. With crises and care networks growing, the movement for environmental justice continues to regenerate, as will the movement for climate justice (consider, for example, emergent discourses of a just transition and Green New Deal).

Finally, "justice" as a key term continues to transform and be resisted by contemporary environmental movements. Tensions still emerge when justice is or is not included in environmental law, advocacy, policy, and networking. One would hope that environmental movements born of ecological systems thinking – that is, how elements including water, air, plants, and animals are interdependent for survival – would embrace social systems thinking. We now know racial inequality and coloniality are constitutive of environmental degradation as well as the converse: racial justice and decoloniality are constitutive of a more sustainable future. If we consider the difference justice makes to environmental movements, we may discover new ways to reaffirm and reinvent what and for whom we care once again.

Acknowledgments

The author thanks Giovanna Di Chiro for reading an earlier draft.

Notes

1 The first half of this chapter focuses on the story of origin of the environmental justice movement in the US, and, therefore, claims of its impacts also are US-centric. Broader patterns of environmental injustice using related discourses, such as "environmentalism of the poor", are transnational (Pellow, 2007; Martinez-Alier et al., 2016) and exceed this history. Even within the US, previous related movements existed, such as Indigenous decolonial protests since the founding of the US, the United Farmworkers' mid–twentieth century struggle to protect farmworkers through reducing pesticides, and Martin Luther King Jr.'s assassination in 1968 when he was organizing sanitation workers; these are just some of the more notable predecessors. Luke W. Cole and Sheila R. Foster (2001: 20) thus suggest it is more useful "to think metaphorically of the movement as a river, fed over time by many tributaries", such as the civil rights movement, the anti-toxics movement, academics, Native American struggles, the labor movement, and, of course, the environmental movement.
2 Health consequences of PCBs received international attention in 1968 after contaminated rice (*yusho*) in Japan led to mass poisoning (Masuda, 1985). PCBs were banned in the US in 1979.
3 Chavis was with civil rights leader Martin Luther King, Jr. when he was assassinated in 1968. They were scheduled to visit a high school in Wilmington, North Carolina. In 1971, the United Church of Christ sent Chavis to give a talk and work in solidarity with local anti-segregationists. Subsequently, firebombs and murders took place; Chavis was one of ten wrongly convicted (as "the Wilmington Ten"), which was protested by Amnesty International and civil rights leaders, including James Baldwin. In 1978, Governor Hunt commuted their sentences; in 1980, the courts voided the convictions due to prosecutorial misconduct. Chavis's presence in Warren County two years after Hunt commuted his sentence was significant, although they were not pardoned until 2012 (Hines, 2014).
4 Like most environmental justice scholars, I consider myself a scholar-activist. I conducted participant observation fieldwork of the Joint Warren County/State PCB Working Group for six months in 1996. Subsequently, I conducted in-depth interviews, lobbied with the community, and created outreach materials they used, which eventually helped with successful detoxification of the landfill. For more,

see Pezzullo, 2001; de Onís and Pezzullo, 2018; Pezzullo and de Onís, 2018. The state had issued US$18 million to detoxify the landfill by the end of 2003 (Rawlins, 2003).

5 By "articulate", I reference what cultural studies scholar Stuart Hall theorizes as "the form of the connection that can make a unity of two different elements, under certain conditions. . . . [A] linkage which is not necessary, determined, absolute, and essential for all time" (Grossberg, 141; Pezzullo, 2007). This pattern of environmental injustice and racism speaks to the hegemonic social imaginary of "appropriately polluted spaces": that is, cultural geographies where both the environmental pollution and the people (as "social pollution") are envisioned as expendable, separate, and "relatively invisible to white citizens and centers of power" (Higgins, 1994: 252).

6 The first lawsuit to challenge a waste facility under civil rights was filed in 1979, and the lawyer for the plaintiffs was Bullard's wife at the time, African American attorney Linda McKeever Bullard; she encouraged him to conduct research to help build her case (*Bean vs. Southwest*).

7 To see the twentieth anniversary report, which shows even greater patterns of inequity, see Bullard et al., 2007.

8 The "Big Ten" to which they refer began meeting during intense US anti-environmental backlash in the 1990s to help support each other and build their capacity. These nonprofit organizations included Defenders of Wildlife, the Environmental Defense Fund, Greenpeace, the National Audubon Society, the National Wildlife Federation, the Natural Resources Defense Council, the Nature Conservancy, the Sierra Club, the Wilderness Society, and the World Wildlife Fund.

9 In 1994, Chavis was fired from the NAACP for a series of reasons involving secrecy and a difference of political opinion, as well as hiding financial payment to resolve a sexual misconduct claim (Bock, 1994). Since, Chavis became a national director of the Million Man March in 1995 and co-founded the Hip-Hop Summit Action Network.

10 African American John Hall, head of the Texas Natural Resource Conservation Commission, initially was appointed chair but stepped down for Moore after grassroots activists expressed concern (Lester et al., 2001: 47).

11 Radical networks of care are not new. For more on the Black Panther movement's breakfast programs as an exemplar, as well as contemporary trans legal networks, see Spade, 2020.

12 At COP21 in Paris, as I was meeting with the first Black president of the Sierra Club, Aaron Mair, he was approached by Dean Hubbard, then labor director of the Sierra Club, who wanted Mair to meet Brad Markell, the executive director of the American Federation of Labor and Congress of Industrial Organizations (AFL-CIO), the largest federation of unions in the US. That meeting and our subsequent discussions led to the creation of the award. Unfortunately, the union vote was unsuccessful, even after Mair and many others protested in the region. The press release for the award is available at https://content.sierraclub.org/press-releases/2015/12/first-ever-unjust-transition-award-goes-renault-nissan.

References

3 plead guilty to dumping PCB's in North Carolina. 1979, June 5. *New York Times*. Section A, 19. Retrieved from www.nytimes.com/1979/06/05/archives/3-plead-guilty-to-dumping-pcbs-in-north-carolina.html

500 Women Scientists Leadership. 2020, June 6. Silence is never neutral; neither is science. *Scientific American*. Retrieved from https://blogs.scientificamerican.com/voices/silence-is-never-neutral-neither-is-science/

Alston, Dana. 1990. *We speak for ourselves: Social justice, race, and environment*. Washington, DC: Panos Institute.

APEN. 2020. Celebrating 25 years of environmental justice. *APEN: Asian Pacific Environmental Network*. Retrieved from https://apen4ej.org/celebrating-25-years-of-environmental-justice/

Agarwal, Anil, and Sunita Narain. 1991. *Global warming in an unequal world: A case of environmental colonialism*. New Delhi: Centre for Science and Environment.

Augustine, Rose Marie. 1993, October 21–24. *Environmental justice: Continuing the dialogue* [Cassette recording]. Recorded at the Third Annual Meeting of the Society of Environmental Journalists, Durham, NC.

Bean v. Southwestern Waste Management Corp. Civ. A. No. H-79–2215. December 21, 1979. Retrieved from https://law.justia.com/cases/federal/district-courts/FSupp/482/673/2095959/

Bob, Clifford. 2010. *The marketing of rebellion: Insurgents, media, and international activism*. Cambridge, UK: Cambridge University Press.

Bock, James. 1994, August 22. The downfall of Dr. Benjamin F. Chavis. *The Baltimore Sun*. Retrieved from www.baltimoresun.com/news/bs-xpm-1994-08-22-1994234108-story.html

Bryant, Bunyan, ed. 1995. *Environmental Justice: Issues, Policies, and Solutions*. Washington, DC: Island Press.

Bullard, Robert D. 1983. Solid waste sites and Black Houston community. *Sociological Inquiry*, 53.2–3: 273–288.

Bullard, Robert D. 1990. *Dumping in dixie: Race, class, and environmental justice*. Boulder, CO: Westview Press.

Bullard, Robert D. 1992, June. Politics of race and pollution: An interview. *Multinational Monitor*, 22–25.

Bullard, Robert D. 2020, June 4. Environmental justice for all. *National Humanities Center*. Retrieved from http://nationalhumanitiescenter.org/tserve/nattrans/ntuseland/essays/envjust.htm

Bullard, Robert D., Paul Mohai, Robin Saha, and Beverly Wright. 2007. *Toxic wastes and race at twenty 1987–2007: Grassroots struggles to dismantle environmental racism in the United States*. Cleveland, OH: United Church of Christ Justice and Witness Ministry. Retrieved from www.nrdc.org/sites/default/files/toxic-wastes-and-race-at-twenty-1987-2007.pdf

Bullard, Robert D., and Beverly H. Wright. 1987. Environmentalism and the politics of equity: Emergent trends in the black community. *Mid-American Review of Sociology*, 12: 21–37.

Bullard, Robert D., and Beverly H. Wright. 1992. The quest for environmental equity: Mobilizing the African-American community for social change. *Society and Natural Resources*, 3: 301–311.

Cagle, Alison. 2020, March 25. Standing Rock Tribe wins in court after years of perseverance. *EarthJustice*. Retrieved from https://earthjustice.org/blog/2020-march/standing-rock-tribe-wins-in-court-after-years-of-perseverance

Chuji, M., G. Rengifo, and E. Gudynas. 2019. Buen Vivir. In A. Kothari, A. Salleh, A. Escobar, F. Demaria, and Alberto Acosta, Eds., *Pluriverse: A post-development dictionary*. New Dehli, India: Tulika Books.

Climate Justice Alliance. 2018. *A just recovery is the only way forward in North Carolina*. Retrieved from https://cjaour-power.medium.com/a-just-recovery-is-the-only-way-forward-in-north-carolina-944b31234786

Cole, Luke. W., and Sheila R. Foster. 2001. *From the ground up: Environmental racism and the rise of the environmental justice movement*. New York: New York University Press.

Corporate Watch. 2000, November 19. *Alternative summit opens with call for climate justice*. Press release. Retrieved from https://web.archive.org/web/20160419205823/www.corpwatch.org/article.php?id=333

de Onís, Catalina M. 2018. Fueling and delinking from energy coloniality in Puerto Rico. *Journal of Applied Communication Research*: 1–26.

de Onís, Catalina M. 2021. *Energy islands: Metaphors of power, extractivism, and justice in Puerto Rico*. Berkeley, CA: University of California Press.

de Onís, Catalina M., and Phaedra C. Pezzullo. 2018. The ethics of embodied engagement: Ethnographies of environmental justice. In Ryan Holifield, Jayajit Chakraborty, and Gordon Walker, Eds., *Routledge handbook of environmental justice*. London: Routledge, pp. 231–240.

Di Chiro, Giovanna. 1996. Nature as community: The convergence of environment and social justice. In W. Cronon, Ed., *Uncommon ground: Rethinking the human place in nature*. New York: Norton, pp. 298–320.

Di Chiro, Giovanna. 2020. Mobilizing 'intersectionality' in environmental justice research and action in a time of crisis. In Brendan Coolsaet, Ed., *Environmental justice: Key issues*. London: Routledge, pp. 316–333.

Dorsey, Michael. 2007, June. Climate knowledge and power: Tales of skeptic tanks, weather gods, and sagas for climate (in)justice. *Capitalism Nature Socialism*, 18.2: 7–21.

Durlin, Marty. 2010, February 1. The Group of 10 respond. *High Country News*. Retrieved from www.hcn.org/issues/42.2/the-group-of-10-responds

Enzinna, Wes. 2016, December 6. How Standing Rock sparked a national movement toward environmental justice. *Grist*. Retrieved from https://grist.org/justice/how-standing-rock-sparked-a-national-movement-toward-environmental-justice/

Exchange Project. 2006. Real people–real stories. Afton, NC (Warren County). Retrieved from https://exchangeproject.unc.edu/files/2018/08/Real-People-Afton-long-story-07-0426.pdf

Freudenberg, N. 1984. *Not in our backyards! Community action for health & the environment*. New York: Monthly Review Press.

GAO. 1983. *Siting of hazardous waste landfills and their correlation with racial and economic status of surrounding communities*. Retrieved from www.gao.gov/assets/150/140159.pdf

Geiser, K., and G. Waneck. 1994. PCBs and Warren County. In R. D. Bullard, Ed., *Unequal protection*. San Francisco: Sierra, pp. 43–52.

Giugni, Marco, and Maria T. Grasso. 2015. Environmental movements in advanced industrial democracies: Heterogeneity, transformation, and institutionalization. *Annual Review of Environment and Resources*, 40: 337–361.

Giugni, Marco, and Maria T. Grasso. 2019. *Street citizens: Protest politics and social movement activism in the age of globalization*. Cambridge: Cambridge University Press.

Goodman, J. 2020, July 29. Want to fix the climate crisis? Start listening to Black people. *Bloomberg Green*. Retrieved from www.bloomberg.com/amp/news/articles/2020-07-29/want-to-fix-the-climate-crisis-start-listening-to-black-people?__twitter_impression=true

Grossberg, Lawrence. 1996. On postmodernism and articulation: An interview with Stuart Hall. In David Morley and Kuang-Hsing Chen, Eds., *Stuart Hall: Critical dialogues in cultural studies*. New York: Routledge, pp. 1–150.

Grossman, Karl. 1994. The people of color environmental summit. In Robert D. Bullard, Ed., *Unequal protection: Environmental justice and communities of color*. San Francisco: Sierra Club Books, pp. 271–297.

Harrison, Jill Lindsey. 2019. *From the inside out: The fight for environmental justice within government agencies*. Cambridge, MA: MIT Press.

Hiar, Corbin. 2020, June 18. Slip-up reveals Chevron ties to architect of climate attack. *E&E News*. Retrieved from www.eenews.net/stories/1063407645

Higgins, Robert R. 1994, Fall. Race, pollution, and the mastery of nature. *Environmental Ethics*, 16: 251–264.

Hines, Elizabeth. 2014. Wilmington Ten. *Encyclopedia Britannica*. Retrieved from www.britannica.com/topic/Wilmington-Ten

Hunt, James B. 1982, October 20. "Open Letter" to the people of Warren County.

IEN. 2018–2019. Stand with standing rock. *Indigenous Environmental Network*. Retrieved from www.ienearth.org/stand-with-standing-rock-no-dapl/

India Development Review. 2019. In conversation with Dr. Vandana Shiva: Chipko taught me humility. *Feminism in Media*. Retrieved from https://feminisminindia.com/2019/10/15/vandana-shiva-interview-chipko-movement/

Klein, Naomi. 2007. *The shock doctrine: The rise of disaster capitalism*. New York: Picador.

Klein, Naomi [@NaomiAKlein]. 2019, November 7. *Twitter*. Retrieved from: https://twitter.com/naomiaklein/status/1192465899145576448

Klein, Naomi. 2019, November 14. Care work is climate work: A series on the Green New Deal. Retrieved from www.youtube.com/watch?v=SdQPyGxLLUA

Klein, Naomi. 2020, October 1. A message from the future II: The years of repair. *The Intercept*. Retrieved from https://theintercept.com/2020/10/01/naomi-klein-message-from-future-covid/

Labalme, Jenny. 1987. *A road to walk: A struggle for environmental justice*. Durham, NC: The Regulator Press.

Lavelle, M., and M. Coyle. 1992, September 21. Critical mass builds on environmental equity. *The National Law Journal*. Washington Briefs Sec., 5.

Lester, James P., David W. Allen, and Kelly M. Hill. 2001. *Environmental injustice in the United States: Myths and realities*. Boulder, CO: Westview Press.

Maathai, Wangari. 2003. *The Green Belt Movement: Sharing the approach and the experience*. Herndon, VA: Lantern Books.

Mann, Michael E. 2019a, June 12. On the importance of diversity in climate communication. *Blog*. Retrieved from https://michaelmann.net/content/importance-diversity-climate-communication

Mann, Michael E. 2019b, September 18. Radical reform and the Green New Deal. *Nature*. Retrieved from www.nature.com/articles/d41586-019-02738-7 Lantern Books.

Mann, Michael E. 2021. *The new climate war: The fight to take back our planet*. New York: Public Affairs.

Martinez-Alier, Joan, Leah Temper, Daniela Del Bene, and Arnim Scheidel. 2016. Is there a global environmental justice movement? *The Journal of Peasant Studies*, 43.3: 731–755.

Masuda, Y. 1985. Health status of Japanese and Taiwanese after exposure to contaminated rice oil. *Environmental Health Project*, 60: 321–325.

McGurty, Eileen Maura. 1997, July. From NIMBY to Civil Rights: The origins of the environmental justice movement. *Environmental History*, 2.3: 301–323.

Mohai, Paul. 1990. Black environmentalism. *Social Science Quarterly*, 71.4: 744–765.

Morano, Marc. 2019, November 7. Update: Holthaus apologizes. *Climate Depot*. Retrieved from www.climatedepot.com/2019/11/07/warmist-eric-holthaus-disses-michael-mann-hes-not-your-climate-hero-hes-a-gatekeeper-declares-mann-constantly-promotes-his-own-work-even-when-women-are-more-qualified/

NAACP. 2020, April 3. *Coronavirus equity considerations*. https://naacp.org/wp-content/uploads/2020/04/Coronavirus-Equity Considerations.pdf

Nagle, Mary Kathryn. 2018, January 20. Environmental justice and tribal sovereignty: Lessons from Standing Rock. *The Yale Law Journal*, 127. Retrieved from www.yalelawjournal.org/forum/environmental-justice-and-tribal-sovereignty

Nieves, E. 2020, June 18. Q&A: A pioneer of environmental justice explains why he sees reason for optimism. *Inside Climate News*. Retrieved from https://insideclimatenews.org/news/18062020/robert-bullard-black-environmental-justice-network-relaunch

Pellow, David Naguib. 2007. *Resisting global toxics: Transnational movements for environmental justice*. Cambridge, MA: MIT Press.

Pezzullo, Phaedra C. 2001, Winter. Performing critical interruptions: Rhetorical invention and narratives of the environmental justice movement. *Western Journal of Communication*, 64.1: 1–25.

Pezzullo, Phaedra C. 2003. Resisting "National Breast Cancer awareness month": The rhetoric of counterpublics and their cultural performances. *Quarterly Journal of Speech*, 89.4: 345–365.

Pezzullo, Phaedra C. 2007. *Toxic tourism: Rhetorics of travel, pollution, and environmental justice*. Tuscaloosa: University of Alabama Press.

Pezzullo, Phaedra C. 2017. Environment. In *The* Dana Cloud, Ed., *Oxford research encyclopedia of communication and critical studies*. Vol. 1. Oxford: Oxford University Press.

Pezzullo, Phaedra C. 2020. Between crisis and care: Projection mapping as creative climate advocacy. *Journal of Environmental Media*, 1.1: 59–77.

Pezzullo, Phaedra C., and Robert Cox. 2021. *Environmental communication and the public sphere, 6th ed.* Newbury Park, CA: Sage.

Pezzullo, Phaedra C., and Catalina M. de Onís. 2018. Rethinking rhetorical field methods on a precarious planet. *Communication Monographs*, 85.1: 103–122.

Pezzullo, Phaedra C., and Ronald Sandler. 2007a. Environmental justice and environmentalism: Revisiting the divide. In Sandler, Ronald and Phaedra C. Pezzullo, Eds., *Environmental justice and environmentalism: The social justice challenge to the environmental movement*. Cambridge, MA: MIT Press, pp. 1–24.

Pezzullo, Phaedra C., and Ronald Sandler. 2007b. Conclusion: Working together and working apart. In Ronald Sandler and Phaedra C. Pezzullo, Eds., *Environmental justice and environmentalism: The social justice challenge to the environmental movement*. Cambridge: MIT Press, pp. 309–320.

1987 Proceedings: The First National People of Color Environmental Leadership Summit, Washington, DC, October 24–27, 1991. Distributed by the United Church of Christ Commission for Racial Justice.

Rawlins, W. 2003, November 11. Dump's days fade. *The News & Observer*, B5.

Saro-Wiwa, Ken. 1996. *A month and a day: A detention diary*. London: Penguin Books.

Shiva, Vandana. 1994. Conflicts of global ecology: Environmental activism in a period of global reach. *Alternatives: Global, Local, Political*, 19.2: 195–207.

Southwest Organizing Project. 1990, March 15. Letter to the executives of national environmental organizations. Unpublished.

Spade, Dean. 2020. Solidarity not charity: Mutual aid for mobilization and survival. *Social Text* 142, 38.1: 131–151.

The Care Collective. 2020. *The care manifesto: The politics of interdependence*. London: Verso.

Tilly, Charles. 1978. *From mobilization to revolution*. Reading, MA: Addison-Wesley.

TRAC. 1999. *Greenhouse Gangsters vs. Climate Justice*. Retrieved from www.corpwatch.org/sites/default/files/Greenhouse%20Gangsters.pdf

Warren County v State of North Carolina, et al, No. 79–560-CIV-5 (E.D.N.C. Nov. 25, 1981).

Whyte, Kyle P., and Chris Cuomo. 2015. Ethics of caring in environmental ethics: Indigenous and feminist philosophies. In S. M. Gardiner and A. Thompson, Eds., *The Oxford handbook of environmental ethics*. Oxford: Oxford University Press, pp. 234–247.

Yearwood, Rev Lennox. 2020, June 22. Climate justice is racial justice, Racial justice is climate justice. *Shondaland*. Retrieved from www.shondaland.com/act/a32905536/environmental-justice-racial-justice-marginalized-communities/

17

INDIGENOUS MOVEMENTS

Linda Etchart

The territories of the world's Indigenous peoples, which cover 38 million square kilometers of land over 87 countries, occupy 24% of land worldwide and contain 80% of the world's biodiversity (World Bank 2005; Fa et al. 2020). Indigenous peoples occupy the sites of precious natural resources, and it is they, it is argued, who protect forests vulnerable to the encroachment of modernity. The World Resources Institute claimed in 2014 that community forests around the globe of 513 million hectares stored 37 billion tons of carbon, 29 times the annual carbon footprint of the world's passenger vehicles (Stevens et al. 2014).

It is Indigenous peoples who have been on the frontline in defending the environment against development projects, agribusiness, mining, and hydroelectric dams; Indigenous individuals constituted 40% of the 212 environment defenders killed worldwide in 2019 (Global Witness 2020). Indigenous protestors suffer disproportionate levels of incarceration and cases of violence against them (Global Witness 2018; Sengupta 2018; Scheidel et al. 2020).

Who are Indigenous peoples?

Indigenous peoples are generally defined by the United Nations as those who have chosen to remain marginalized in former European colonies.

> *Indigenous* communities, *peoples* and nations are those which, having a historical continuity with pre-invasion and pre-colonial societies that developed on their territories, consider themselves distinct from other sectors of the societies now prevailing on those territories, or parts of them.
>
> (United Nations Department of Economic and Social Affairs [UNDESA] 2020)

According to the International Labor Organization (ILO), there are approximately 476.6 million Indigenous people in the world, belonging to 5,000 different groups, in 90 countries worldwide (International Labor Organization (ILO) 2020).

The ILO distinguishes Indigenous peoples from *tribal* peoples, who do not necessarily have their roots in the place in which they reside. The criterion the ILO uses for tribal peoples, as well as for Indigenous peoples, is that their social, cultural. and economic conditions differ from

DOI: 10.4324/9780367855680-19

Figure 17.1   Alicia Cawiya, Patricia Nenquihui, and Ena Santi, International Women's Day march, Puyo, Ecuador, 8 March 2016

Photo: Mike Reich.

other sections of the national community. Their status is regulated wholly or partially by their own customs or traditions or by special laws or regulations.

The UN Department of Social and Economic Affairs (UNDESA) avoids specificity in its definitions (Castellino and Doyle 2018), although it applies the label "Indigenous" to communities that governed themselves before a period of invasion, colonization, or settlement and live within territories where nation-states, such as New Zealand or Canada, are more widely recognized internationally as sovereign (Anaya 2004).

The roots of the United Nations Declaration on the Rights of Indigenous Peoples (UNDRIP) of 2007, the enactment of which was a groundbreaking moment in the history of Indigenous peoples, and which was 40 years in the making, are to be found in the mobilization of tribal peoples on the African continent in the 1970s (Anaya 2009). The institutional origins of the UNDRIP lie in the 1977 International NGO Conference on Discrimination against Indigenous Populations in the Americas, held at the Palais des Nations in Geneva and attended by spokespeople of representatives from 60 indigenous nations from 15 countries and the creation of the Working Group on Indigenous Populations by the UN Economic and Social Council in 1982 (Anaya 2009: 10–11), which was replaced by the United Nations Permanent Forum on Indigenous Issues (UNPFII), founded in the year 2000. The UNPFII welcomes the participation of Indigenous and tribal peoples from all continents, thereby blurring the boundary between the formerly colonized and the never colonized (UNPFII 2018).

The necessity of attachment to place to qualify for classification as Indigenous has been eroded over time in two ways: first, in that peoples of African descent in Latin America, for example, have been awarded special legal status equal to that of Indigenous peoples in the twenty-first century in some countries (Moreno-Tabarez 2020), and second, although many individuals and families of rural Indigenous peoples rooted in ancestral territory have, over time, moved to urban areas, thereby in social terms losing their Indigenous status (Wade 2010), they nevertheless began to reclaim Indigenous identity in the second decade of the twenty-first century as a means of honoring their roots and enabling them to participate in social movement mobilization.

The significance of discussions around Indigenous/mestizo/African ethnicity is that assertion of "identity" may be a useful tool for the purpose of claiming rights and as a mechanism for political organization (see Giugni and Grasso 2015) and that those identities are not fixed, can be fluid, and change over time, which gives them greater reach (Escobar 2008); groups with different identities, moreover, can learn from each other's experiences and build new alliances to address collective environmental concerns (Moreno-Tabarez 2020: 29), not least within the Black Lives Matter movement in 2020 (Kelley 2020). Trans-ethnic alliances are also important in Brazil, where Indigenous and mixed Afro-descendant communities were able to overcome long-standing differences to collaborate in resisting illegal logging and gold mining and in demarcating land in 2017 in Montanha Mangabal in the state of Pará, such that "old enemies" came together (Torres and Branford 2018: 151–153). It is notable, also, that one of the first successful court rulings in favor of "tribal" land and environmental defenders took place at the Inter-American Court of Human Rights (IACtHR) in 2007, after a seven-year struggle on the part of 60 villages comprising the 55,000 "maroon" Afro-descendant Saramakan people of Suriname (Price 2012).

In its 2019 report, the Intergovernmental Science-Policy Platform on Biodiversity and Ecosystem Services (IPBES)[1] proposed that Indigenous peoples have been the most effective vehicle in preventing habitat and therefore biodiversity loss, even in protected areas, and that they have contributed to limiting deforestation. The IPBES noted that Indigenous lands and livelihoods are under continued pressure from resource extraction, commodity production, mining and transport, and energy infrastructure, as well as agriculture, forestry, and fishing practices (IPBES 2019: 6).

Fa et al. determined that 36% of the world's intact forest landscapes (IFLs) were within Indigenous peoples' lands, "making these areas crucial to the mitigation action needed to avoid catastrophic climate change" (2020:1). The authors endorsed the IPBES's conclusion that IFL loss rates are lower in Indigenous peoples' lands than on non-Indigenous lands and that therefore, recognition of Indigenous peoples' rights, including land tenure rights, will prevent deforestation in order to keep global warming below 2°C above pre-industrial levels. Intact forest landscapes are regarded as "critical strongholds for the protection of indigenous and rural cultures and livelihoods, as well as being irreplaceable in terms of biodiversity conservation and provision of ecosystem services" (Fa et al. 2020: 1).

Indigenous peoples' relationship to nature

From an Indigenous perspective, man's relationship to nature is not instrumental: man and nature are one. In the words of Oklahoma Ponca elder Casey Camp Horinek (2020): "We are part of a sacred circle of life", where "we consider ourselves as nature protecting itself" (ibid.). Camp Horinek's words echo those of Luther Standing Bear of the Oglala Sioux of Dakota (c.1868–1939) of the early twentieth century:

> The American Indian is of the soil, whether it be the region of forests, plains, pueblos or mesas. He fits into the landscape, for the hand that fashioned the continent also fashioned the man for his surroundings. He once grew as naturally as the wild sunflowers; he belongs just as the buffalo belongs.
>
> (quoted in Running Press 1994: 18)

The concept of man's living in harmony with nature was central to the World People's Conference on Climate Change and the Rights of Mother Earth, held in the Bolivian city of Cochabamba on 20–22 April 2010 and attended by 55,000 people from around the world (Hope 2017). The outcome of the conference, the Universal Declaration of the Rights of Mother Earth, inspired by indigenous cosmologies, was signed on 22 April 2010 (Global Alliance for the Rights of Nature 2020).

The UN General Assembly Declaration on Harmony with Nature 70/208 of 2015 took note of the Cochabamba Declaration and demonstrated a willingness on the part of the signatory governments to take an avowedly "interdisciplinary" "holistic" approach (Article 7) that integrated "scientific work" and "use of *traditional knowledge* [emphasis added]" as means to protect the environment (United Nations 2020), thereby implicitly acknowledging the contribution that Indigenous peoples can make to preventing climate change.

The question of traditional knowledge is taken up by Colombian scholar Arturo Escobar in *Territories of Difference* (2008), where he examines the relationship between Indigenous cosmologies, (de)colonization and modernity, and their implications for social movement mobilization, building upon his earlier work that questioned the development paradigm (1995).

The work of Arturo Escobar (1995, 2010) can be situated in the Foucauldian post-development school of social theorists, alongside Gustavo Esteva (1992), Bruno Latour (1993), Eduardo Viveiros de Castro (2013), Tirso Gonzalez (2015), and Boaventura de Sousa Santos (2018) in questioning the nature/culture distinction of Western epistemology.

In his interpretation of non-Western worldviews, Viveiros de Castro, like Latour, challenges the binary opposition of human and animal. In Viveiros's conceptualization of Amazonian thought, the "gods, animals, the dead, plants, meteorological phenomena, and often objects or artefacts as well – equipped with the same general ensemble of perceptive, appetitive, and cognitive dispositions" (2013: 23) together form a soul, which could be described as an ecosystem. For Viveiros de Castro, "All animals and cosmic constituents are intensively and virtually persons, because all of them, it does not matter which, can reveal themselves to be (transform into) a person" (ibid.: 24), which in some sense confers personhood on creatures, such as sharks, and on natural phenomena such as rivers, endowing them with rights formerly held only by humans.

Possibilities for the upholding of the rights of nature through legislation were expressed by Christopher Stone in 1972, within *Should Trees Have Standing? Toward Legal Rights for Natural Objects*, but it was the work of economist Joan Martínez Alier, *Environmentalism of the Poor* (2002), (and Martínez Alier et al. 2011) and later Alberto Acosta (2017) – former Ecuadorean Minister of Mines and Energy, who incorporated the rights of nature into the Ecuadorean constitution of 2008 – who expressed an understanding of the centrality of indigenous and peasant knowledge and activism in protection of the environment and the achievement of environmental justice. Martínez Alier (2002) highlighted the success of the Chipko movement in the Himalayas, which began with a women's uprising against logging in 1974, Indigenous mobilizations against the Narmada dams in India in the 1980s, and the struggles of the Ogoni and Ijaw peoples against Royal Dutch Shell in the Niger Delta in the 1990s.

Acosta and Martínez Abarca (2018) argue that the non-capitalist alternative modes of collective living envisaged and practiced by Indigenous peoples in the philosophies of *buen vivir/vivir bien* that are integrated into the Ecuadorean and Bolivian constitutions, respectively, are shared by other communities in Latin America – by the Mapuche in Chile; the Guaraní and Kuna peoples in Argentina, Brazil, Paraguay, and Colombia; and in various forms in other countries: in the African continent as *ubuntu* and as *svadeshi swaraj* and *apargama* in India. The authors present *buen vivir/vivir bien* in the Amazon and Andes as a form of resistance to colonialism on the part of those who have been able to remain "at the margins of modern-day capitalism" (ibid.: 132).

Colonization, modernity, resistance, and Indigenous environmentalism

Within the Indigenous philosophy of *sumak kawsay* (in Kichwa) /*buen vivir* ("plenitude") (Gudynas 2011), the foundation of the new Ecuadorian Constitution of 2008 and the Bolivian Constitution of 2009, in the latter under the label *vivir bien* (*suma qamaña*) in Aymara, the enactment of the rights of nature declares itself to be a decolonization of thought, of people, of territories, and of the mind, in a spirit that recalls the decolonization of thought envisaged in the work of Eduardo Galeano in *Open Veins of Latin America* (1977) and the Kenyan Kikuyu novelist and social theorist, Ngugi Wa Thiong'o (1986).

Similarly, Boaventura de Sousa Santos, in *Epistemologies of the South* (2018), contextualizes the subordination of Indigenous knowledge within the framework of conquest and colonization:

> The destruction of knowledge (besides the genocide of indigenous people) is what I call epistemicide: the destruction of the knowledge and cultures of these populations, of their memories and ancestral links and their manner of relating to others and to nature. Their legal and political forms – everything – is destroyed and subordinated to the colonial occupation.
>
> (2016: 18)

From the first days of European empires, Indigenous communities resisted colonizers, engaging in local alliances and confederations in order to increase strength in numbers to defend territory, culture, and livelihoods (Newson 1995; Whyte 2016; Etchart 2019). In the late twentieth and early twenty-first centuries, Indigenous communities continued to form alliances – national, regional, and global – with the support of institutions such as United Nations agencies and non-governmental organizations associated with both human rights and the environment, thereby contributing to framing debates, legitimizing the work of (I)NGOs, and becoming part of a "global ecology" movement (Giugni and Grasso 2015: 341).

The empowerment of Indigenous communities in the 1970s (Wearne 1996; Anaya 2009; King 2016; Estes 2019) and their increased political mobilization and profile grew in parallel with the rise of social movements in the North and South in the same period. Networks of movements that proliferated through the 1980s and 1990s included the anti-globalization movements of the 1990s (Waterman 2001; Fisher and Ponniah 2003; Smith and Smythe in Smith et al. 2015); the Occupy movement (Harvey in Sitrin and Azzellini 2014), and the climate action movements of the second decade of the 2000s, in which Indigenous leaders began to take a leading role (Etchart and Cerda 2020).

A key player in the anti-globalization movement of the 1990s was the Indigenous Zapatista Army of National Liberation (EZLN), first created in the forests of Lacandón, Chiapas, in southern Mexico in 1983. The Zapatistas engaged in an uprising against the Mexican government on 1 January 1994, the day that the first North Atlantic Free Trade Agreement (NAFTA) came into effect. Led by Sub-Comandante Marcos, a university professor from Mexico City, EZLN claimed 150,000 hectares of land on which it constructed an alternative communal mode of existence to provide well-being, agriculture, health, and education systems in the absence of the state (Earle and Simonelli 2004). Its appearance coincided with the dawn of the age of the worldwide web, which transformed the Zapatista movement into one of the first global movements of the internet age. The movement became an inspiration for Indigenous mobilization across the planet, most importantly in Latin America, where its alternative development philosophy resonated with *sumak kawsay/suma qamaña* of the Amazonian and Andean First Nation peoples (Ramonet 2001; Hardt 2004; Earle and Simonelli 2004).

On a global level, the expansion and consolidation of global environmental movements in the 1990s can be attributed in large part to the use of the internet as a means of communication. The internet became an organizational tool for the anti-globalization protests that surrounded the annual World Trade Organization (WTO) conferences, starting with the battle of Seattle in 1999, attended by 40,000 activists from across the continents (Kaldor 2000; Seoane and Taddei 2002) and was vital to the organization of the annual World Social Forum (WSF) (Fisher and Ponniah 2003), a Southern initiative, within which protection of the environment was a key component and in which Indigenous peoples came to play a role.

The World Social Forum (WSF) movement grew in opposition to the World Economic Forum (WEF) of global leaders that took place every year at Davos in Switzerland from 1971, the purpose of the WSF being to set up a "counter-summit". The first World Social Forum took place in Porto Alegre, in the south of Brazil, in January 2001, with 20,000 participants from 100 countries (Smith and Smythe in Smith et al. 2015). Although Bleiker (2002) characterized the anti-globalization movements as a new kind of politics beyond the control of the nation-state, transnational or global movements were not in themselves new and had existed from the early days of the European empires (Fryer 1988), but the forging of links among Indigenous communities in the USA, Canada, Australia, and New Zealand, as well as Latin America, with Northern environmental movements, constituted a sea change.

The World Social Forum (WSF) in Mumbai, India, in 2004, attracted 115,000 participants, including 30,000 Indigenous *adivasis* and marginalized *Dalits* (Smith and Smythe in Smith et al. 2015); 90% of the participants were from India, demonstrating the logistical problem of organizing transnational conferences for individuals and collectivities with limited financial resources. Paradoxically, the success of the World Social Forum meetings over time weakened their impact, as the sheer size of the gatherings rendered them unmanageable. Indigenous representatives constituted a very small percentage of the participants: 2% in Porto Alegre, Brazil, in 2005, for example. As a response to their increasing invisibility at WSF meetings, indigenous groups decided to set up a separate forum of their own within the Porto Alegre 2005 Forum, but this only increased their marginalization (ibid.).

By then, the WSF had lost momentum, and it was felt that open debate with so many actors was not leading to collective action. One strategy was to decentralize: the 2006 World Social Forum was polycentric, held in Bamako, Mali, as well as in Caracas, Venezuela (Ramonet 2001). The headquarters were moved to Nairobi in 2007 (Smith and Smythe in Smith et al. 2015).

At the World Social Forum in the Amazon city of Belém, Brazil, 27 January–1 February 2009, Indigenous communities came from all over Brazil, with President Luis Ignacio "Lula" da Silva spurning the G7 at Davos to attend the conference. In Belém, there were 133,000 participants from 12 countries, including 1,900 Indigenous attendees representing 190 ethnic groups, as well as 1,400 *quilombos* of African descent (Osava 2009). In the same week, a meeting of the Pan-Amazon Forum (PASF) – established in 2002 (Campos 2009) – was organized to promote the value of Indigenous livelihoods and culture for alternative social development projects (Milcíades Peña and Davies 2014). There had been criticism that decision making within the World Social Forum structures had been dominated by a "highly mobile cosmopolitan elite of scholar-activists" (Stephansen 2013: 106); hence, the Pan-Amazon Forum was to include poor urban dwellers to engage in their own knowledge production around local struggles and to continue to build regional relationships.

The Quebec August 2016 World Social Forum attracted 150,000 people, with 35,000 foreign participants from 125 countries. The hosting of the forum in Quebec was significant in terms of the acknowledgment of Quebec as the Indigenous territory of the Mohawk people, though there were few Indigenous speakers, notwithstanding the presence of Bertita Cáceres, daughter of Berta Cáceres, a Lenca environmentalist and activist who had been murdered in Honduras in March of that year (World Social Forum Collective 2016).

Influence of Indigenous environmental movements on global non-governmental and intergovernmental institutions and the private sector

In the early days of the global environmental movements, dating back to the 1970s, Indigenous communities were often viewed not only as an obstacle to development by governments and intergovernmental institutions (Guha and Martínez Alier 1997; Blaser et al. 2004), but a number of Northern environmental NGOs also considered them a danger to forests and biodiversity. Several environmental projects, sponsored by Northern NGOs and Southern governments working in collaboration with governments of the Global North, resulted in the displacement, expulsion, and, in effect, ethnic cleansing of indigenous communities (Guha and Martínez Alier 1997; Büscher and Fletcher 2016). By the 2000s, however, the environmental tide had turned in favor of forest peoples, who began to be courted as allies by conservation agencies.

For their part, Indigenous communities seized the opportunity to garner support from conservation agencies, both within state apparatuses and outside and from within intergovernmental agencies, foundations, and philanthropic entities. Individuals and groups within networks of institutions could pressure state representatives within intergovernmental organizations as well as influence governments directly (Sikkink 2011). This is a point made by Brysk in 1996: that Indigenous communities were able to turn "weakness into strength", using international actors and funding to exert pressure on their own hitherto unresponsive governments to convince them to institute domestic reform (1996: 38).

Tying Indigenous land rights claims to environmental and climate change campaigns continued as an effective strategy in the 2000s. Indigenous communities often rejected UN-sponsored carbon trading schemes and reducing emissions from deforestation and forest degradation (REDD+) programs, which they viewed as detrimental to their interests (Indigenous Environmental Network 2013; Reyes García et al. 2019; Schroeder et al. 2020), but they were able to exert some leverage by negotiating their way into REDD+ decision-making procedures (Wallbott 2014). Many Indigenous communities endorsed the call to keep fossil fuels in the ground to protect their own water and land resources from being contaminated, to maintain territorial sovereignty and integrity, to prevent the construction of roads, to prevent the poaching of wildlife, and to protect wildlife habitat (Etchart and Cerda 2020). Coalitions of indigenous confederations within and across borders were essential, as Indigenous communities were small, had limited resources to challenge armed state forces who had the monopoly of violence within the territory of the state, and had less power than urban or even rural trade unions with which to challenge state or private entities.

The participation of Indigenous peoples in the United Nations and intergovernmental agencies

The importance of traditional (Indigenous) knowledge to global efforts to protect the environment was initially raised in the discussions that led to the creation of the International Union for the Protection (later Conservation) of Nature (IUPN/IUCN),[2] in 1948–50, although in practice, Indigenous peoples were sidelined from intergovernmental environmental policy making for another 40 years (López Rivera 2020).

By the 1970s, the gradual expansion of Indigenous movements and the appearance of their representatives on the global stage had led to their inclusion in international conferences, to the extent that the 1987 UN (Brundtland) Report of the World Commission on Environment and Development, *Our Common Future*, called for greater consultation of Indigenous peoples in global environmental governance (World Commission on Environment and Development 1987).

Despite the recommendations of the Brundtland Report, Indigenous peoples were marginalized from the United Nations Conference on Environment and Development (UNCED), which took place in Rio de Janeiro, Brazil, 3–14 June 1992, and where, in response to their exclusion, they hosted parallel gatherings. The World Conference of Indigenous Peoples on Territory, Environment and Development, held on 30 May 1992 at Kari'Oca, a village on the outskirts of Rio, resulted in the signing of the 1992 Kari'Oca Declaration and the Indigenous Peoples Earth Charter, the first global Indigenous declarations focusing on the environment (Indigenous Peoples Earth Charter 1992; López Rivera 2020).

Following the adoption in 1997 of the Kyoto Protocol to reduce global greenhouse gas emissions, Indigenous peoples' representatives began to push for engagement in climate change agreements, but they continued to be excluded from decision making (Glennie 2014; Etchart 2017). Indigenous rights were largely "annexed" out of the principal outcome documents of the COP21 Climate Summit in Paris in December 2015, where Indigenous leaders staged their own side events and presented their own platform, fronted by the International Indigenous Peoples Forum on Climate Change (IIPFCC), founded in 2008 (Cultural Survival 2015; Etchart 2017; IIPFCC 2020; Doolittle 2010).

In its December 2015 report, the Indigenous Peoples' Center for Documentation, Research and Information (DOCIP) reiterated the link between climate change and the rights of Indigenous peoples, stating that "Indigenous peoples have been making this link for several decades, taking center stage in its promotion" (DOCIP 2015: 3).

At the Sixteenth Session of the United Nations Permanent Forum on Indigenous Issues (UNPFII), 24 April to 5 May 2017 in New York, the ILO once again declared that Indigenous peoples had a critical role at the forefront of climate action. At the conference, Indigenous peoples presented themselves as key players in the achievement of sustainable development goals (SDGs) 13, 14, and 15, which include combating climate change, sustainably managing forests, and halting biodiversity loss. Indigenous networks continued to work within the International Union for the Conservation of Nature (IUCN), which comprised 1,400 governmental, non-government, and Indigenous organizations by 2020 (IUCN 2020). IUCN conferences themselves provided a platform for Indigenous representatives to build on their existing movements, improve their tactical repertoires (Giugni and Grasso 2015: 344), and strengthen their own networks.

Besides Northern NGOs that have supported Indigenous peoples' rights, such as Survival International (founded 1969), Cultural Survival (1972), and Land is Life (1992), Indigenous networks emerged on their own without the mediation of Northern organizations. The International Work Group on Indigenous Affairs (IWGIA) was established in 1968, and the World Council of Indigenous Peoples was created in 1974 under the leadership of the Canadian indigenous leader Secwépemc Shuswap George Manuel (Dahl 2009; Manuel and Posluns 2018 [1974]). The Indigenous Environmental Network, based in Minnesota, USA, founded in 1990, led by Tom Goldtooth (Dine' and Dakota) has been at the forefront of indigenous environmental movements.

Indigenous networks in the typology created by Kahler (2009) have to be considered networks as agents rather than networks as structures, as they are intentional and aimed at advocacy in order to build global support in defense of Indigenous interests. Networks composed of members of Indigenous communities are themselves networked into epistemic communities of scholars and networks of NGOs, which, in turn, are networked into governmental, non-governmental, and intergovernmental communities and networks (Sikkink 2011). The network of networks enables Indigenous communities and organizations to achieve the publicity they need (ibid.: 230; World Bank 2008) in view of their limited numbers and resources in the context of the triumvirates of power against which they are aligned, characterized by Arundhati Roy, with reference to India, as the "iron triangle" (1999: 24), a confluence of private, state, and military interests.

Indigenous environmental mobilizations in India

In India, as in Latin America, when local or national government agencies have embarked upon development projects in rural areas, Indigenous or tribal peoples have often been displaced. The Narmada Sarda Sarovar Dam, completed in 2019, claimed the cultures of the Sikka, Surung, Neemgavan, and Domkhedi people, who constituted 57.6% of those displaced by the dam (Roy 1999). Indigenous and other affected groups came together in 1986 to protest the dam, and by 1989, 50,000 protestors were mobilized and demonstrating. In early 1991, 6,000 demonstrators, including hunger strikers, had succeeded in halting work on the dam through mobilizing the international press, which persuaded the main sponsors, the World Bank, to announce a review of the project, from which it subsequently withdrew. The dam went ahead – without support from the World Bank – at the cost of the lives and livelihoods of both Indigenous and non-Indigenous communities (Guha and Martínez Alier 1997; Roy 1999).

In the South West of India, in Karnataka state north of Kerala, *adivasis* (Indigenous people) were evicted from the Nagar Hole National Park in the 1990s (Ravi Raman 2004), when they were designated as encroachers, while the state government continued to allow timber extraction to take place. The state had negotiated lease agreements with the Taj Group of Hotels for eco-development projects with the support of the World Bank. The *adivasis* mobilized against the government and challenged them in the courts: the high court ruled in 1997 that the assignment of forest land to the Taj Group was in violation of the laws of conservation and wildlife (Dowie 2009).

Indigenous environmental movements in Africa

In parts of Africa, as in India, the designation of wild areas as national parks by governments has resulted in the dispossession and displacement of forest dwellers from their ancestral homelands. The case of the Sengwer tribal peoples of the Embobut Forest in the Cherangany Hills of the North Rift Valley of Kenya is one example of a community that has allied itself with Indigenous communities in other parts of the world and with intergovernmental organizations and INGOs to generate support for upholding their rights to their territories and respect for their guardianship of natural resources (Chepkorir Kuto 2016). The area was declared a protected public forest in 1954 and a national park in 1961, although the colonial administration had granted the Sengwer permits to remain. The first evictions began in the 1970s (Amnesty International 2018).

In December 2013, personnel of the Kenya Forest Service (KFS) entered the forest, demolished the homes of the forest dwellers, and evicted all the families living there (Langat 2018). Around 5,000 families were displaced over time (Orosa 2019). Their experience illustrates the tensions around Indigenous occupation of protected areas: financing to the Kenyan government to protect the forest came from the World Bank and the European Union. When abuses of tribal peoples came to light from their cases being taken up by INGOs, including Amnesty International, as well as an Avaaz petition that collected 950,000 signatures (Vidal 2014), the European Union, which was funding a €31 million program to reforest the area, withdrew its support. The 2014 World Bank investigation confirmed that evictions were commonplace and were causing social unrest in the area (Vidal 2014; Orosa 2019).

In Africa, Indigenous communities sought recourse at the African Court on Human and Peoples' Rights in Arusha, Tanzania, in an attempt to secure rights to traditional lands (Langat 2018), as was the case of the Ogiek people of Kenya. Although the Kenyan Constitution of 2010 states that "Community land shall vest in and be held by communities identified based on ethnicity, culture or similar community of interest" (IWGIA 2017), mass evictions of the Ogiek from the Mau Forest began in 2009 by the Kenyan Forest Service. The Ogiek took their case to the African Commission on Human and Peoples' Rights (ACHPR), which issued preliminary provisional measures to protect them (Kobei 2015), but illegal land transactions continued. In 2016, there were evictions of 300 families, whose homes were destroyed (IWGIA 2017). The case was transferred to the African Court on Human and Peoples' Rights, and a verdict in favor of the Ogiek People's rights was made in 2017 under the African Charter and international law.

Despite these apparent successes, the IWGIA reported that evictions were still occurring in 2019 in the case of both the Sengwer and the Ogiek peoples, with governments unable or unwilling to uphold their rights under local or international law. These examples demonstrate the significance to Indigenous peoples of state, regional, and international law, as well as their limitations: the institutionalization of the rights of Indigenous peoples and associated rights of nature into law are only a first step. Intergovernmental and non-governmental organizations continue to have a role, meanwhile, in attempts to hold states to account in the protection of Indigenous peoples and the environment.

First Nations of North America

Nick Estes, citizen of the Lower Brule Sioux tribe and professor of American Studies at the University of New Mexico, has documented the history of the North American First Nation peoples' loss of their lands at the hands of colonizers dating back to the arrival of the Mayflower in 1620 (Estes 2019). He traces First Nations' resistance to invaders through to the Standing Rock protests of 2016–17 that were aimed at preventing the construction of the 1,712-mile Dakota Access oil pipeline that was planned to cut through "unceded territory of the Fort Laramie Treaty" (Estes 2019: 2), traversing four states.

The 2016–17 North Dakota Standing Rock protests, involving Indigenous peoples of the Americas and their non-Indigenous allies, brought together all seven nations of the Dakota-, Nakota-, and Lakota-speaking peoples for the first time in seven generations (Estes 2019:2). The Standing Rock protests drew Indigenous environmental activists from across the Americas, enabling land defenders to develop pan-continental solidarity networks to mount global protests on social media. Indigenous communities have been among the most active protestors on the ground against expansion of the extractive industries (Scheidel et al. 2020), with increasing numbers of Indigenous women, such as Ecuadorians Alicia Cawiya (see Figure 17.1) and Nemonte Nenquimo of the Huoarani people, Gloria Ushigua of the Sápara, and Patricia Gaulinga of the Sarayaku Kichwa, taking up leadership roles (Sempértegui 2019; Lake 2020; Etchart, forthcoming 2022; Nenquimo 2021) and attracting the attention of the Western mainstream media. Casey Camp Horinek led the Ponca Nation to become the first tribe in the state of Oklahoma to adopt the Rights of Nature Statute in 2006 and to pass a moratorium on fracking on tribal lands. In 2020, Indigenous environmental networks linked land defenders from Alaska to Patagonia, with the support of international NGOs and institutions that included the Women's Earth and Climate Action Network (WECAN), which united Indigenous women environment defenders from Alaska, from the Brazilian and the Ecuadorian Amazon, and from the Itombwe forest region of the Democratic Republic of Congo (Lake 2020).

Conclusion

This chapter has demonstrated how the strength of Indigenous environmental movements has increased exponentially since the 1990s, in parallel with the rise of environmental movements in non-Indigenous populations.

Global Indigenous environmental movements have become the vanguard of climate change activism, particularly in the context of the failure of state governments to agree to and comply with international accords aimed at limiting greenhouse gas emissions. Indigenous environmental movements have become champions of the rights of nature, now an integral part of national law in a number of countries, out of which juridical decisions have been made that have supported Indigenous territorial and cultural claims. Direct action and social media campaigns by Indigenous nations have brought about small victories for Indigenous communities and nature against the expansion of fossil fuel and mining frontiers. Power inequalities have remained, however, that threaten the survival of Indigenous peoples and of the wild places they protect.

By 2020 economic incentives as a result of public pressure had led to a shift toward more ethical and environmental social and governance (ESG) investment and sustainable business practices in Europe and North America. Yet despite pronouncements of the rise of "woke capitalism" (Douthat 2018), efforts at curtailing the influence of fossil fuel and mining lobbyists in resisting government regulation had proven ineffectual. At a time when regulatory agencies were still in the early stages of establishing metrics to measure carbon emissions, Indigenous environmental defenders on the ground continued to forfeit their lives in their efforts to protect nature for future generations.

Notes

1 IPBES Intergovernmental Science-Policy Platform on Biodiversity and Ecosystem Services (IPBES) is an independent intergovernmental body established by states to strengthen the science-policy interface for biodiversity and ecosystem services for the conservation and sustainable use of biodiversity, long-term human well-being, and sustainable development. It was established in Panama City on 21 April 2012 by 94 Governments. It is not a United Nations body. However, at the request of the IPBES Plenary and with the authorization of the UNEP Governing Council in 2013, the United Nations Environment Program (UNEP) provides secretariat services to IPBES.

2 Created in 1948, the World Conservation Union (IUCN) comprises 84 States, 108 government agencies, more than 800 NGOs, and around 10,000 scientists and experts from 147 countries. Its mission is

to influence, encourage, and assist societies throughout the world to conserve the integrity and diversity of nature and to ensure that any use of natural resources is equitable and ecologically sustainable. It has 1,000 staff located in 62 countries, with headquarters in Gland, Switzerland.

References

Acosta, Alberto. 2017. "Post-extractivism: From discourse to practice – reflections for action." *International Development Policy*. No. 9, 77–101. https://journals.openedition.org/poldev/2356. Accessed 2 June 2020.

Acosta, Alberto, and Martínez Abarca, Mateo. 2018. "Buen vivir: An alternative perspective from the peoples of the global South to the crisis of capitalist modernity." In Satgar, V. ed. *The Climate Crisis: South African and Global Democratic Eco-socialist Alternatives*. Johannesburg: Wits University Press, 131–147.

Amnesty International. 2018. "Kenya: Sengwer evictions from Embobut Forest flawed and illegal." www.amnesty.org/en/latest/news/2018/05/kenya-sengwer-evictions-from-embobut-forest-flawed-and-illegal. Accessed 27 August 2020.

Anaya, James. 2004. *Indigenous Peoples in International Law*. New York: Oxford University Press.

Anaya, James. 2009. *International Human Rights and Indigenous Peoples*. New York: Aspen/Wolters Kluwer.

Blaser, Mario, McRae, Glenn, and Feit, Harvey A. eds. 2004. *In the Way of Development: Indigenous Peoples, Life Projects and Globalization*. London: Zed.

Bleiker, Roland. 2002. "Politics after Seattle: Dilemmas of the anti-globalisation movement." *Pacifica Review*, Volume 14 (3). October. https://journals.openedition.org/conflits/1057. Accessed 5 November 2020.

Brysk, Alison. 1996. "Turning weakness into strength: The internationalization of Indian rights." *Latin American Perspectives*, Volume 23 (2), 38–57.

Büscher, Bram, and Fletcher, Robert. 2016. "Why E O Wilson is wrong about how to save the Earth." aeon.co/ideas/why-e-o-wilson-is-wrong-about-how-to-save-the-earth. Accessed 12 July 2020.

Camp Horinek, Casey. 2020. "The condor and the eagle." *Sierra Club Zoom*. 7 July. www.facebook.com/pg/thecondorandtheeaglethefilm/posts. Accessed 1 November 2020.

Campos, Luíz Arnaldo. 2009. "Pan-Amazon social forum." Escritório do FSM 2009 em Belém. http://external.assaif.org/fsm2009/www.fsm2009amazonia.org.br/fspa-1/memory/pan-amazon-social-forum-historic. Accessed 30 October 2020.

Castellino, Joshua, and Doyle, Cathal. 2018. "Who are indigenous peoples?" In Hohmann, J., and Weller, M. eds. *The United Nations Declaration on the Rights of Indigenous Peoples: A commentary*. Oxford: Oxford University Press, Part I(1).

Chepkorir Kuto, Milka. 2016. "Sengwer women's experience of evictions and their involvement in the struggle for Sengwer land rights." Moreton in the Marsh: Forest Peoples Programme.

Cultural Survival. 2015. "'Annexed': The rights of Indigenous peoples in the UN climate change conference 2015." 16 December. www.culturalsurvival.org/news/annexed-rights-indigenous-peoples-un-climate-change-conference-2015. Accessed 3 November 2020.

Dahl, Jens. 2009. *IWGIA: A history*. Copenhagen: International Work Group for Indigenous Affairs (IWGIA). www.iwgia.org/images/publications//0015_IGIA_-_a_history.pdf. Accessed 13 July 2020.

De Sousa Santos, Boaventura. 2018. *The End of the Cognitive Empire: The Coming of Age of Epistemologies of the South*. Durham, NC, and London: Duke University Press.

DOCIP. 2015. *see* Indigenous Peoples' Centre for Documentation, Research and Information.

Doolittle, Amity. 2010. "The politics of indigeneity: Indigenous strategies for inclusion in climate change negotiations." *Conservation & Society*, Volume 8 (4), 286–291.

Douthat, Ross. 2018. "The rise of woke capitalism." *New York Times*. 28 February

Dowie, Mark. 2009. *Conservation Refugees: The Hundred Year Conflict between Global Conservation and Native Peoples*. Boston: MIT Press.

Earle, Duncan, and Simonelli, Jean. 2004. "The Zapatistas and Global Civil Society: Renegotiating the Relationship." *Revista Europea de Estudios Latinoamericanos y del Caribe*, Volume 76. April.

Escobar, Arturo. 1995. *Encountering Development: The Making and Unmaking of the Third World*. Princeton, NJ: Princeton University Press.

Escobar, Arturo. 2008. *Territories of Difference: Place, Movements, Life*. Durham, NC: Duke University Press.

Escobar, Arturo. 2010. "Latin America at a crossroads: Alternative modernizations, post-liberalism, or postdevelopment?" *Cultural Studies*, Volume 24 (1), 1–65.

Estes, Nick. 2019. *Our History is the Future: Standing Rock versus the Dakota Access Pipeline, and the Long Tradition of Indigenous Resistance.* New York: Verso.

Esteva, Gustavo. 1992. "Development." In Sachs, W. ed. *Development Dictionary: A Guide to Knowledge as Power.* London: Zed.

Etchart, Linda. 2017. "The role of indigenous peoples in combating climate change." *Palgrave Communications,* Volume 3 (1), 1–4.

Etchart, Linda. 2019. "Indigenous peoples and the rights of nature." In Gatehouse, T. ed., *Voices of Latin America: Social Movements and the New Activism.* London: Latin America Bureau/Practical Action, 97–119.

Etchart, Linda. 2022, forthcoming. *Global Governance of the Environment, Indigenous Peoples and the Rights of Nature in Latin America.* London: Palgrave Macmillan.

Etchart, Linda, and Cerda, Leo. 2020. "Amazonians in New York: Indigenous peoples and global governance." *City: Analysis of Urban Change, Theory and Action,* Volume 24 (1–2), 5–21. https://rsa.tandfonline.com/eprint/UXYQDVP6BIEMF9ZED2GQ/full?target=10.1080/13604813.2020.1739440. Accessed 18 May 2020.

Fa, John, E., Burgess, Neil, Leiper, Ian, Molnar, Zsolt, Watson, James, E.M., Potapov, Peter, Evans, Tom D., Fernández-Llamazares, Alvaro, Duncan, Tom, Wang, Stephanie, Austin, B. J., Robinson, Cathy J., Malmer, Pernilla, Zander, Kerstin K., Jackson, Micha V., Ellis, Erle, Brondizio, Eduardo S., and Garnett, Stephen T. 2020. "Importance of Indigenous Peoples' lands for the conservation of Intact Forest Landscapes." *Frontiers in Ecology and the Environment.* January, 1–6. www.researchgate.net/publication/338412873_Importance_of_Indigenous_Peoples%27_lands_for_the_conservation_of_Intact_Forest_Landscapes. Accessed 14 January 2020.

Fisher, William F., and Ponniah, Thomas. 2003. *Another World is Possible: Popular Alternatives to Globalization at the World Social Forum.* London: Zed Books.

Fryer, Peter. 1988. *Black People in the British Empire.* London: Pluto.

Galeano, Eduardo. 1977. *Open Veins of Latin America: Five Centuries of the Pillage of a Continent.* New York: Monthly Review Press, first published 1971.

Giugni, M., and Grasso, M.T. (2015) "Environmental movements: Heterogeneity, transformation, and institutionalization." *Annual Review of Environment and Resources,* Volume 40. https://dx.doi.org/10.1146/annurev-environ-102014-021327.

Glennie, Jonathan. 2014. "Why are indigenous people left out of the sustainable development goals?" *Guardian.* 14 August.

Global Alliance for the Rights of Nature. 2020. "Universal declaration of rights of mother earth." Universal Declaration of Rights of Mother Earth – The Rights of Nature.

Global Witness. 2018. "At what cost? Irresponsible business and the murder of land and environment defenders in 2017." https://wrm. org.uy/articles-from-the-wrm-bulletin/recommended/at-what-cost-irresponsiblebusiness-and-the-murder-of-land-and-environmental-defenders-in-2017. Accessed 12 December 2019.

Global Witness. 2020. "Environmental activists defending tomorrow." www.globalwitness.org/en/campaigns/environmental-activists/defending-tomorrow/. Accessed 29 July 2020.

Gonzalez, Tirso. 2015. "An indigenous autonomous community-based model for knowledge production in the Peruvian Andes." *Latin American and Caribbean Ethnic Studies* 10(1), 107–133.

Gudynas, Eduardo. 2011. "Buen Vivir: Today's Tomorrow." *Development.* Volume 54 (4), 441–447.

Guha, Ramachandra, and Martínez Alier, Joan. 1997. *Environmentalism of the Poor.* Oxford: Earthscan.

Hardt, Michael. 2004. "Today's Bandung." In Mertes, T. ed. *A movement of movements: Is another world really possible?* London: Verso.

Harvey, David. 2014. "Preface." In Sitrin, Marina, and Azzellini, Dario. eds. *They can't represent us.* London: Verso.

Hope, Jessica. 2017. "The constraints of an 'ironic scholar': Negotiating critical engagement with indigeneity and nature conservation." *Geoforum,* Volume 78, 74–81.

Indigenous Environmental Network. 2013. "REDD+: A pathetic REDD package." 28 November. https://www.ienearth.org/a-pathetic-redd-package/. Accessed 18 November 2021.

Indigenous Peoples' Centre for Documentation, Research and Information (DOCIP). December 2015 report. Update no 110. https://cendoc.docip.org/collect/upd_en/index/assoc/HASHdd09.dir/Upd110_eng.pdf. Accessed 4 November 2020.

Indigenous Peoples Earth Charter. 1992. UNESCO. www.lacult.unesco.org/lacult_en/docc/Kari-Oca_1992.doc. Accessed 5 December 2019.

Intergovernmental Science-Policy Platform on Biodiversity and Ecosystem Services (IPBES). 2019. "Global assessment report on biodiversity and ecosystem services." https://ipbes.net/global-assessment Accessed 8 July 2020.

International Indigenous Peoples Forum on Climate Change (IIPFCC). 2020. "Local communities and indigenous peoples platform." UNFCCC. https://unfccc.int/topics/local-communities-and-indigenous-peoples-platform/the-big-picture/introduction-to-lcipp/chronology-local-communities-and-indigenous-peoples-platform-lcipp#eq-2. Accessed 13 July 2020.

International Labor Organization (ILO). 2020. "Who are the indigenous and tribal peoples?" www.ilo.org/global/topics/indigenous-tribal/WCMS_503321/lang – en/index.htm. Accessed 8 July 2020.

International Union for the Conservation of Nature (IUCN). 2020. "Members." Accessed 6 July 2020. www.iucn.org/about/union/members.

International Work Group for Indigenous Affairs (IWGIA). 2017. "Support to the Ogiek peoples shall ensure implementation of historic African Court ruling." www.iwgia.org/en/kenya/3281-implementation-of-african-court-ruling. Accessed 13 July 2020.

Kahler, Miles. 2009. "Networked politics agency, power, and governance." In Kahler, M. ed. *Networked Politics: Agency, Power and Governance*. Ithaca, NY: Cornell University Press, 1–12.

Kaldor, Mary. 2000. "'Civilising' globalisation: The implications of the 'battle' for Seattle." *Millennium*, Volume 29 (1), 103–140.

Kari-Oca Declaration. 1992. www.dialoguebetweennations.com/IR/ english/KariOcaKimberley/intro.html. Accessed 5 December 2019.

Kelley, Hilton. 2020. "The condor and the eagle." Zoom hosted by Sierra Club. 2 July. www.facebook.com/SierraClub/videos/765943267549114. Accessed 5 November 2020.

King, Jonathan C. H. 2016. *Blood and Land: The Story of Native North America*. London: Allen Lane.

Kobei, Daniel. 2015. "Statement on behalf of Ogiek peoples' development program at the 57th ordinary session of the African commission on human and people's rights." 4–18 November. Banjul, Gambia. https://minorityrights.org/wp-content/uploads/2015/03/OPDP-STATEMENT-2015.pdf. Accessed 13 July 2020.

Lake, Osprey Orielle. 2020. Zoom webinar "Women for forests and future generations: Defending communities from pandemics and climate chaos." 27 August. www.youtube.com/watch?v=bQ_PWtj8FzE&feature=youtu.behttps:// www.wecaninternational.org/.

Langat, Anthony. 2018. "Amid ongoing evictions, Kenya's Sengwer make plans to save their ancestral forest." *Mongabay*. news.mongabay.com/2018/09/amid-ongoing-evictions-kenyas-sengwer-make-plans-to-save-their-ancestral-forest. Accessed 13 July 2020.

Latour, Bruno. 1993. *We Have Never Been Modern*. Boston: Harvester Wheatsheaf.

López-Rivera, Andrés. 2020. "Blurring global epistemic boundaries: The emergence of traditional knowledge in environmental governance." *Global Cooperation Research Papers* 25. Duisburg: Käte Hamburger Kolleg/Centre for Global Cooperation Research (KHK/GCR21).

Manuel, George, and Posluns, Michael. 2018 [1974]. *The fourth world: An Indian reality*. Minneapolis: University of Minnesota Press.

Martínez Alier, Joan. 2002. *The environmentalism of the poor: A study of ecological conflicts and valuation*. Cheltenham: Edward Elgar.

Martínez Alier, Joan, Healy, Hali, Temper, Leah, Walter, Mariana, Rodriguez-Labajos, Bea, J.-F. Gerber, and Conde, Marta. 2011. "Between science and activism: Learning and teaching ecological economics with environmental justice organisations." *Local Environment*, Volume 16 (1), 17–36.

Milcíades Peña, Alejandro, and Davies, Thomas R. 2014. "Globalisation from above? Corporate social responsibility, the workers' party and the origins of the world social forum." *New Political Economy*, Volume 19 (2), 258–281.

Moreno-Tabarez, Ulises. 2020. "Towards Afro-Indigenous ecopolitics: Addressing ecological devastation in Costa Chica." *City: Analysis of Urban Change, Theory and Action*, Volume 24(1–2), 22–34, March.

Nenquimo, Nemonte. 2021. "This is my message to the Western world: Your civilization is killing life on Earth." *Guardian*. 12 October. This is my message to the western world – your civilisation is killing life on Earth | Amazon rainforest | The Guardian. Accessed 12 March 2021.

Newson, Linda. 1995. *Life and death in colonial Ecuador*. London and Norman: University of Oklahoma Press.

Orosa, Pablo. 2019. "Kenya's Embobut forest: Attacks and evictions in the name of conservation?" 28 August. Accessed 13 July 2020.

Osava, Mario. 2009. "World social forum: Stateless peoples defend diversity." Inter Press Service. www.globalissues.org/news/2009/02/02/506. Accessed 10 July 2020.

Price, Patricia L. 2012. "Race and ethnicity: Latino/a immigrants and emerging geographies of race and place in the USA. *Progress in Human Geography,* Volume 36(6), 800–809.

Ramonet, Ignacio. 2001. "Marcos marche sur Mexico." *Le Monde Diplomatique.* March.

Ravi Raman, K. 2004. "Muthanga: A spark of hope." In Kapferer, B. ed. *State, sovereignty, war: Civil violence in emerging global realities.* Oxford: Berghahn Books.

Reyes-García, Victoria, Fernández-Llamazares, Alvaro, McElwee, Pamela, Molnár, Zsolt, Öllerer, Kinga, Wilson, Sarah J., and Brondizio, Eduardo S. 2019. "The contributions of Indigenous Peoples and local communities to ecological restoration." *Restoration Ecology: The Journal for the Society for Ecological Restoration,* Volume 27 (1), 1–6.

Roy, Arundhati. 1999. "The greater common good." *Frontline,* Volume 16 (11), 22 May–4 June, 1–30. https:// pdfs.semanticscholar.org/3c5f/96784453dbf163ae528a62f09ee5359f3941.pdf. Accessed 8 July 2020.

Running Press. 1994. *Native American wisdom.* Philadelphia and London: Running Press.

Scheidel, Arnim, Del Bene, Daniela, Liu, Juan, Navas, Grettel, Mingorría, Sara, Demaria, Federico, Avila, Sofía, Roy, Brototi, Ertör, Irmak, Tempe, Leah, Martínez Alier, Joan, 2020. "Environmental conflicts and defenders: A global overview." *Global Environmental Change* 63, 1–12. June. Accessed 5 November 2020.

Schroeder, Heike, Di Gregorio, Monica, Brockhaus, Maria, and Thuy Thu, Phamf. 2020. "Policy learning in REDD+ Donor Countries: Norway, Germany and the UK." *Global Environmental Change* 63. July. Accessed 5 November 2020.

Sempértegui, Andrea. 2019. "Indigenous women's activism, ecofeminism, and extractivism: Partial connections in the Ecuadorian Amazon." *Politics and Gender.* July. 1–28.

Sengupta, Somini. 2018. "She stands up to power. Now, she's afraid to go home." *New York Times,* 3 May. www.nytimes.com/2018/05/03/world/asia/hurman-rights-philippines.html Accessed 5 November 2020.

Seoane, José, and Taddei, Emilio. 2002. "From Seattle to Porto Alegre: The anti-neoliberal globalization movement." *Current Sociology,* Volume 50 (1), 99–122.

Sikkink, Kathryn. 2011. "The power of networks." In: Kahler, M. ed. *Networked politics: Agency, power and governance.* Ithaca, NY: Cornell University Press.

Smith, Peter, and Smythe, Elizabeth. 2016. "(In) Fertile ground: Social forum activism in its regional and local dimensions." In Smith, J., Reese, E., Byrd, S., and Smythe, E. eds. *Handbook on world social forum activism.* London and New York: Routledge, 29–49.

Stephansen, Hilde C. 2013. "Starting from the Amazon: Communication, knowledge and politics of place in the World Social Forum." *Interface: A Journal for and about Social Movements,* Volume 5 (1): 102–127. May.

Stevens, Caleb, Winterbottom, Robert, Reytar, Katie, and Strong, A. 2014. "Ecuador shows why communities and the climate need strong forest rights." World Resources Institute, September. www.wri. org/publication/securing-rights-combating-climate-change. Accessed 6 July 2020.

Stone, Christopher. 1972. *Should trees have standing? toward legal rights for natural objects.* Los Altos, CA: William Kaufmann.

Torres, Mauricio, and Branford, Sue. 2018. *Amazon Besieged by dams, soya, agribusiness and landgrabbing.* Rugby/Latin America Bureau: Practical Action.

United Nations. 2020. Harmony with Nature Resolution A/RES/74/224 adopted by the General Assembly on 19 December 2019, updated from 2015. www.un.org/pga/74/wp-content/uploads/ sites/99/2020/02/A_RES_74_224_E.pdf. Accessed 5 November 2020.

United Nations Department of Economic and Social Affairs (UNDESA). 2020. "Indigenous peoples at the United Nations." www.un.org/development/desa/indigenouspeoples/about-us.html. Accessed 8 July 2020.

United Nations Permanent Forum on Indigenous Issues (UNPFII). 2017. Sixteenth Session 24 April to 5 May. "Indigenous speakers in permanent forum decry governmental abuse of traditional lands, natural resources, urge respect for self-governing systems." 26 April. www.un.org/press/en/2017/hr5353.doc. htm Accessed 5 November 2020.

United Nations Permanent Forum on Indigenous Issues (UNPFII). 2018. Permanent Forum on Indigenous Issues Seventeenth session New York, 16–27 April 2018. www.un.org/development/desa/indig-enouspeoples/unpfii-sessions-2/2017-2.html. Accessed 5 November 2020.

Vidal, John. 2014. "World Bank accuses itself of failing to protect Kenya forest dwellers." *Guardian.* 29 September. www.theguardian.com/global-development/2014/sep/29/world-bank-kenya-forest-dwellers. Accessed 13 July 2020.

Viveiros de Castro, Eduardo. 2013. "Cannibal metaphysics: Can anthropology do philosophy? Amerindian perspectivism." *Radical Philosophy* 182. December.

Wa Thiong'o, Ngugi. 1986. *Decolonising the mind: The politics of language in African literature.* Oxford: James Currey.

Wade, Peter. 2010. *Race and ethnicity in Latin America.* London: Pluto Press.

Wallbott, Linda. 2014. "Indigenous peoples in UN Redd+ Negotiations: 'Importing power' and lobbying for rights through discursive interplay management." *Ecology and Society,* Volume 19 (1), 21.

Waterman, Peter. 2001. *Globalization, social movements & the new internationalisms.* 2nd edn. London: A&C Black.

Wearne, Phillip. 1996. *The return of the Indian: Conquest and renewal in the Americas.* Philadelphia: Temple University Press.

Whyte, Kyle P. 2016. "Indigenous environmental movements and the function of governance institutions." In Gabrielson, T., Hall, C., Meyer, J., and Schlosberg, D. eds. *Oxford handbook of environmental political theory.* Oxford: Oxford University Press, 563–580.

World Bank (International Bank for Reconstruction and Development). 2005. OP 4.10 – Indigenous Peoples. BP 4.10 – Indigenous Peoples. https://policies.worldbank.org/sites/ppf3/PPFDocuments/ 3905Operational%20Manual%20-%20OP%204.pdf. Accessed 6 July 2020.

World Bank (International Bank for Reconstruction and Development). 2008. "The role of Indigenous peoples in biodiversity conservation: The natural but often forgotten partners." Claudia Sobrevila. May. http://documents1.worldbank.org/curated/en/995271468177530126/pdf/443000WP0BOX321ons ervation01PUBLIC1.pdf. Accessed 9 November 2020.

World Commission on Environment and Development. 1987. *Brundtland report: Our common future.* https://sustainabledevelopment.un.org/content/documents/5987our-common-future.pdf. Accessed 13 July 2020.

World Social Forum Collective. 2016. "Activity report world social forum Montreal August 9–14 2016." fsm2016.org/wp. content/uploads/2017/01/RAPPORT_FSM2016_anglais.pdf. Accessed 9 July 2020.

PART 3

Macrostructural conditions and processes

18

ENVIRONMENTAL MOVEMENTS AND THEIR POLITICAL CONTEXT

Joost de Moor and Mattias Wahlström

Introduction

Amid sometimes fierce theoretical debates, there is nevertheless broad scholarly agreement that social movements are shaped by their political context. Environmental movements are no exception in this respect. In this chapter, we discuss the relationship between political context and environmental movements using the concept of the political opportunity structure (POS). While environmental movements' contextual embeddedness has been studied from a variety of angles, including "political culture" (e.g., Jamison et al. 1991), POS has been by far the most prolific approach in the social movement literature. For better or worse, it captures a broad range of elements in the political context, thus meriting our full attention here.

In the following, we therefore begin by teasing out the central aspects of the POS and discuss what the main mechanisms are, through which POSs influence movements. We argue that a better understanding of those mechanisms is needed to make sense of some of the contradictory findings in previous studies and to provide a more robust theoretical framework. Here, a first argument we introduce is that scholars should consider how movements draw conclusions about the POS from narrated experiences of interactions with government institutions and how these narratives are embedded in collective identities.

Thereafter, we turn to a literature review of how various political contexts have impacted the mobilization, strategies, and outcomes of environmental movements. A second argument we introduce is that while much work has been done on the effect of input structures (governmental institutions' openness to movement demands), differences in output structures (the capacity of governmental institutions to produce change) have been overlooked.

Finally, we use recent climate movement mobilizations as an example to demonstrate these two arguments. We show how variations over time of (perceived) POSs on the international level changed movement strategies. However, introducing our third main argument, we also suggest that the wave of climate protests at the end of the 2010s – prominently represented by Fridays For Future and Extinction Rebellion – seemed to be strongly driven by a widespread sense of moral obligation to protest. This moral focus may render political opportunities less central.

 DOI: 10.4324/9780367855680-21

Political opportunity structures and social movements

During the last decades, "political opportunities" and "political opportunity structures" (POS) have been the predominant concepts used to theorize the effect of political contexts on social movements. However, there are persistent disagreements about either what aspects of the POS are most consequential or how they shape mobilizations. In his original formulation of the term "structure of political opportunities", Eisinger described it as "elements in the environment [that] impose certain constraints on political activity or open avenues for it", which he specifies as "the openings, weak spots, barriers, and resources of the political system itself" (1973: 11–12). Since the term "structure" has been associated with the more stable aspects of the political context, some authors have preferred the term "political opportunities" to capture also its sometimes volatile elements (e.g., Tarrow 1998: 77).

Following Koopmans's definition of political opportunities as "options for collective action, with chances and risks attached to them" (1999: 97), we argue that an "opportunity" can only exist in relation to specific goals and aims of a political actor (Goodwin and Jasper 1999; Meyer and Minkoff 2004). Nonetheless, it can be maintained that there are elements of the political sphere that condition political opportunities. Such elements may be structural in the sense that they are beyond the direct influence of movement actors. Some are rigid and only slowly changing, if at all (such as election systems and a degree of governmental decentralization), while others are potentially more volatile (such as elite allies in power and divisions among elites). Whether a combination of such elements provides sufficiently good chances to constitute an opportunity can only be determined by movement actors considering if and how to take political action.

Some authors have had very broad notions of what constitutes the POS, including such factors as societal myths, zeitgeist, and media discourse (e.g., Gamson and Meyer 1996). In order to maintain some consistency with the (admittedly still broad) mainstream of POS research, we think that the term "POS" should be reserved for opportunity structures related to governmental institutions. This way, POS is distinguished from other relevant contextual factors influencing movements, such as discursive opportunity structures (Koopmans and Olzak 2004), legal opportunity structures (Hilson 2002), and corporate opportunity structures (King 2008; Wahlström and Peterson 2006). McAdam and Tarrow highlight the following aspects of a regime which affect what political opportunities contenders might perceive:

> (1) the multiplicity of independent centers of power within the regime; (2) its openness to new actors and movements; (3) the instability of current political alignments; (4) the availability of influential allies or supporters; (5) the extent to which the regime suppresses or facilitates collective claims; and (6) changes in these properties.
>
> (2018: 21)

These aspects largely meet our definition of structures as "existing independently" and "being beyond the direct influence of movement actors", while varying in their stability. The more volatile factors are often related to the configuration of the more stable ones. For instance, the Green Party often presents a significant elite ally for environmental movements that can be voted in or out of office, but the party's electoral chances are determined by stable factors like the proportionality of the electoral system.

While much research on POSs has focused on the national level, research has also dealt with different levels of POS, including city, municipality, and international political opportunity structures (IPOS) (van der Heijden 2006). A basic distinction is furthermore made between input structures – which condition a political actor's access to a polity – and output structures – the capacity of a governmental institution to implement policies. While the former has drawn by far the most attention, the latter may be as important for explaining variation in environmental mobilizations. For example, international organizations such as the UN may be relatively open to environmental demands but have been rather weak in implementing and enforcing environmental policy (van der Heijden 2006), motivating various climate movement groups to ignore the institution and target presumably more powerful actors like fossil fuel companies (de Moor 2018; de Moor and Wahlström 2019).

There has been a longstanding debate regarding the causal mechanisms bringing about the various effects of POS on mobilizations. Some argue that objective conditions belonging to the POS can have a direct effect on mobilizations, regardless of the extent to which they are known by activists. In some cases, movements may be "consistent champions" (Meyer 2004) that experience political impact when the POS opens up. It is easy to imagine a movement mobilizing a campaign initially unaware of the presence of a new ally in the political system who eventually facilitates the realization of its demands. Similarly, Koopmans (2005) has proposed an "evolutionary" model, according to which the POS provides a habitat that determines which mobilizations and which repertoires of action "survive" competition over scarce mobilization resources.

However, with respect to movement strategies and levels of mobilization, it seems that the most widely held position is that POSs need to be perceived and interpreted by movement actors in order to have an effect on them (McAdam 1999; Meyer and Minkoff 2004). Yet it has rarely been specified why POSs sometimes would, and other times would not, be perceived and acted upon (de Moor and Wahlström 2019). People may learn about changes in the POS through various sources, but to assess whether such changes really constitute an opening or closure of opportunity, one needs to interact with the state and draw conclusions from those experiences (or, as noted by Wall [1999], interpret other organizations' interactions with the state). We have argued elsewhere (de Moor and Wahlström 2019) that experiences of such interactions are constructed, retained, and transformed into strategies through collective narration in which common conceptions of actors, causal connections, and projected developments are constructed. This perspective highlights that when a collective actor decides what conclusions to draw from prior interactions with the state, this is not a matter of simple cost-benefit analysis. Other considerations may include what narrative seems most convincing and fits other processes. For instance, narratives about the POS are more likely to affect strategies if they match ongoing processes of collective identity formation.

The relation between environmental movements and the POS

We have so far not focused on environmental movements, but several of the key early contributions to the literature on POS in fact relate to them (e.g., Kitschelt 1986; Rucht 1990; Kriesi et al. 1995). Findings on environmental movements were therefore central to shaping POS theory. In this section, we explore these foundational insights in greater detail, taking into account a number of distinctive features of the relation between the POS and environmental movements.

Historical overview of research on POS and environmental movements

Building on prior work on the impact of the political context of other movements, Kitschelt (1986) appears to have been the first to apply an explicit POS perspective on environmental movements – the anti-nuclear movement in France, Sweden, the US, and West Germany. Kitschelt considered both input and output structures to explain tactical variations between anti-nuclear movements in four countries. Where input structures were open, like in Sweden and the US, strategies focused on using those institutional openings through assimilative strategies like lobbying. By contrast, where input structures were closed, like in France and West Germany, more confrontational outsider strategies like demonstrations and civil disobedience were used. In the US, output structures were weak and therefore open to challengers, so activists maintained assimilative strategies even in the implementation phase of the nuclear policies. Meanwhile, Swedish 1970s anti-nuclear activists found few opportunities to influence the country's strong output structure.

In direct response to Kitschelt, Rucht (1990) analyzed anti-nuclear movements in the same cases (except Sweden), arguing that Kitschelt's POS model was overly simplistic and could not accurately explain strategic variations. While recognizing the value of considering input and output structures to explain more or less assimilative strategies, Rucht argued that "the concept of political opportunity in its present form can only serve as a starting point for a more sophisticated analysis which includes a broader range of explanatory variables" (1990: 218–219). These variables include transnational diffusion of strategies, the effect of socio-cultural conditions on the tactical repertoire that activists can draw from, time-specific factors affecting changes in the POS over time, varying perceptions of the same "objective" POS, and the interpretation of the meaning of a conflict. These considerations have remained influential in debates on POS.

Kriesi et al. (1995) later analyzed social movements' politicization of the Chernobyl nuclear disaster in four countries, showing that the exclusive French state disabled successful mobilization, whereas the weak Swiss and German states were more open to mobilization but did not provide the same opportunities for substantive success as the strong and inclusive Dutch state. Similarly, Van der Heijden (1997) studied the institutionalization[1] of environmental movements in France, Germany, the Netherlands, and Switzerland, arguing that differences in degrees of institutionalization were attributable to POS factors such as centralization of the state and degree of repression toward the movement. Rootes (1999), in contrast, argued that there is little consistency in the relation between stable features of the political context and environmental movement institutionalization: for instance, pointing to the then-increasing number of radical environmental groups in Great Britain, previously dominated by large institutionalized organizations.

Continuing the discussion about environmental movement institutionalization, Dryzek et al. (2003) published the seminal study *Green States and Social Movements*, comparing France, Norway, the US, and Germany. They were careful to point out the difference in their approach from POS. While their first dimension (inclusive–exclusive) resembles that of input structures, they contrast their second dimension (active–passive) to that of output structures. Where the latter refers to "the state's ability to impose its agenda on society", (Dryzek et al. 2003: 19), the former looks at whether the state takes a proactive stance on (environmental) issues. In effect, while France, for example, was considered "strong" by Kitschelt and Kriesi et al., it is "passive" for Dryzek et al. Still, the authors find common ground with the previous studies when they conclude that inclusive states lead to greater institutionalization, adding an important critical note that access does not equate to influence, but often rather cooptation.

Reflecting some more conceptual criticisms of POS in the same period (e.g., Goodwin and Jasper 1999; Rootes 1999), several publications from the late 1990s onward questioned the usefulness of POS. For example, the influential comparative study on *Environmental Protest in Europe* edited by Rootes (2003) echoed some of the criticisms articulated by Rucht (1990). The study concluded that "Strictly structural factors, political institutional arrangements foremost among them, explain little if any of the variation in the patterns of environmental protest among the seven states we have considered" (Rootes 2003: 22). Instead, "It is the contingent and conjunctural dimensions of political opportunities rather than the truly structural ones that best explain the patterns we have observed" (Rootes 2003: 23).

Since then, we have witnessed discussions about the use of POS per se (Doherty and Hayes 2012), the relevance of variations over time or space (Shriver and Adams 2010; Sarre and Jehlička 2007), and perceived or objective POSs (Saunders 2009). For instance, considering the strategic diversity among environmental groups that exist within the single POS of the UK, Saunders (2009) argued that the POS cannot determine strategies per se. However, she did find that the POS affects how groups relate to each other (see also Di Gregorio 2014; Heikkila et al. 2019; Poloni-Staudinger 2009). That is, while those excluded by the POS develop more collaborative strategies to compensate for unfavorable contextual conditions, those included can afford to remain more isolated. Yet despite these critiques and qualifications, the concept of POS – with all its variations – has continued to inspire research up until the present. We have identified a number of prominent themes and sub-fields that have dominated discussions on environmental movements.

Contemporary comparisons – on different geographic levels

While POS is a concept that is mainly applied to democracies, there are also a number of studies that use it to capture the political context for environmental movements in undemocratic contexts. China appears to be the most commonly studied country (Xie and van der Heijden 2010), but there are also comparative studies of non-democracies. In a comparison of the varying presence of environmental non-governmental organizations (ENGOs) in 71 autocracies, Böhmelt (2014) proposes regime type as a crucial factor, tying it primarily to the level of repression. He shows that one-party states, due to lower levels of (overt) repression, more often have active ENGOs, especially compared to military and personalist regimes.

In addition to studies comparing the effects of country-level POS on mobilization and strategies, a good number of studies focus on sub-national variation. For example, McCright and Clark (2006) compared the impact of varying POSs on environmental mobilization in 257 American communities, finding only weak effects of institutional dimensions of local POS on movement activity level. They instead emphasized the positive mobilizing effects of the activity of other movements and the activity levels of individual citizens, thereby including factors that clearly fall outside the typical definitions and operationalizations of POS.

The impact of local POSs on environmental mobilization has in many instances been studied by comparing resistance to infrastructural projects. Carmin (2003) found that openings in the POS – in terms of elite allies, political representation, divisions among elites, and political access – led to higher levels of individual participation against environmental exploitation through building projects. McAdam and Boudet (2010) compared large infrastructural projects in the "developing world", finding that Western funding of the projects and public consultation appeared to be necessary conditions for mobilization, increasing the chance of mobilization when combined with some level of environmental (or other) threat, whereas broader and more stable aspects of the POS on the national level had no discernible impact on the incidence of mobilizations. In apparent contrast, a study of resistance against mining projects in Sweden (Zachrisson and Beland Lindahl 2019) found that movements were mobilized when the state offered little or no access to influencing the decisions about mining projects. Apparently, factors like public consultations can have rather different effects on movements across different contexts.

International political opportunities and the growing importance of output structures

Sticking with questions of levels of government, the environmental movement is one of the movements most profoundly affected by the globalization of politics – as a result of the global nature of the problems it addresses and the international governmental organizations (IGOs) that have emerged in response to them. Graubart (2004) was one of the first to shift attention to the impact of the international level on environmental movement strategies, which was shortly after further developed by van der Heijden (2006). Van der Heijden argues that open formal structures and integrative formal elite strategies increase the frequency of NGOs using "conventional" strategies, whereas closed formal structures and exclusive elite strategies increase "unconventional" protest. Importantly, he points out that the IPOS for different social movements are tied to different international governmental institutions, depending on their jurisdiction and the issues they deal with. Concurrently, Derman (2014) argued that the relative favorability of the IPOS presented by the UN for working on climate justice can be used to explain transnational climate justice advocacy. Poloni-Staudinger (2008) adds that environmentalists' decision to act at the international level should be understood as a function of the national POS as well: the less favorable it is, the more likely groups are to explore opportunities at the transnational level (see also Henry et al. 2019). Similarly, Cassegård and colleagues (2017) argued that climate movement strategies should be seen as emerging out of a back-and-forth between acting in national and transnational contexts.

The discussion on IPOSs has also affected how output structures are understood and how central they might be for explaining movement activity. While Kitschelt mainly considered output structures as opportunities to exert influence during the implementation phase of policies, more recent studies on the transnational level (e.g., van der Heijden 2006; de Moor and Wahlström 2019) have considered output structures in terms of whether a polity is able to get things done, including the fulfillment of protesters' demands. It has been argued that output structures therefore rather determine *which* actors movements will target, whereas input structures are more decisive for *how* those actors should be targeted (de Moor 2016). Output structures have arguably become more important to explain the targets of environmental movements given the persistent inability of states to effectively address major environmental concerns like climate change, opening debates about which other, arguably more powerful actors (e.g., companies) should be targeted.

Perceived opportunities

A different approach to comparing the impact of "objective" features in different polities is to compare the strategic consequences of different groups' or individual activists' perceptions of the POS. Ergas (2010) demonstrated the importance of perceived opportunities and constraints for shaping how ecovillages pursue their goals. De Moor et al. (2017) similarly argued that perceived opportunities – output structures in particular – shape Belgian lifestyle activists' choice to engage with the state or not: if the state is perceived to be unable to solve environmental problems, they refrain from making demands to it.

While some stress the importance of rational evaluation of political opportunities by which activists learn to "read" the POS (Hadden 2018), we have argued for the importance of interaction and storytelling between groups. In our case study of the climate movement's mobilization around COP21, we found that perceiving the UNFCCC as incapable of getting things done motivates disengagement from targeting international climate negotiations (de Moor and

Wahlström 2019). However, we challenged the rationalist "perception model" by stressing the importance of learning about POSs through the experience of interacting with a polity (see also Shriver and Adams 2010) and the role of narratives in developing strategies to respond to experienced opportunities or constraints (see also Hadden 2017).

Opportunities changing over time

Many studies testing POS theory do so by comparing countries or regions. However, some study the impact of changes in POS over time, either by following long time periods or by studying the impact of major societal transitions. Further emphasizing that there is no obvious positive relationship between an open POS and environmental mobilization in the US, a study by Carmichael et al. (2012) showed that between 1900 and 2000, there was even a weak *negative* relationship between the founding of US environmental organizations and the presence of political allies such as a democratic Congress and/or a president sympathetic to the ideas of the movement. A prominent sub-group of diachronic POS studies concern Eastern Europe over the period of its transition to post-socialism. A considerable number of studies have looked at the impact of the collapse of the Soviet Union on environmentalist strategies, including the shift from organizing collective action to reproducing one's own organizations under hostile conditions in Russia (Yanitsky 2012) and Czechoslovakia (Shriver and Adams 2010) and the rise of contentious action in response to opportunities opened by a weakening Soviet Union, followed by institutionalization and internationalization (Carmin and Fagan 2010).

POS and movement outcomes

Finally, some studies connect POS and environmental movement outcomes. (See Chapter 30 by Johnson and Agnone for a discussion on outcomes.) On the one hand, studies indicate that POSs affect chances for movement success (Rootes and Nulman 2015). For instance, based on a study of anti-nuclear campaigners in China, Sheng (2019) argues that elite fragmentation and decentralization can increase the number of entry points for movements and consequently their success (see also Zhang 2018). Research on the US has shown the importance of having elite allies in power – particularly Democrats – to ensure the success of environmental campaigning (e.g., Kemberling and Roberts 2009; Giugni 2006). On the other hand, changes in POSs themselves are often depicted as important movement outcomes in the form of "structural effects" (Kitschelt 1986). For instance, Almeida and Stearns (1998) argue that a national anti-pollution movement in Japan put pressure on the national government to take pollution into account by challenging its legitimacy in this area, which made it increasingly costly to repress challengers, which, in turn, opened up opportunities for local campaigns. Such structural changes can, in turn, contribute to substantive movement successes (Zhang 2018).

POS and the climate movement

Our literature review in the previous section shows the relevance of POS as a concept for studying environmental movements but perhaps also confirms the challenge in drawing generalizable conclusions from this research. The latter is perhaps not so surprising given the diverse contexts to which POS has been applied and its many different operationalizations. In this final section, we discuss how our two main arguments made so far – about the importance of output structures and movement narratives – apply to the contemporary climate movement. We furthermore use the case to introduce our third and final argument that as movements become less "instrumental", the POS becomes less central to their strategic considerations. Specifically, we look at the climate movement's historic mobilization around the 2015 Paris Climate Summit (COP21) and the more recent mobilizations by Fridays for Future and Extinction Rebellion.

The Copenhagen narrative and the mobilization around COP21

The 2015 mobilization around COP21 was an iconic moment in the history of the climate movement. In analyzing how POSs affected this mobilization, a story of the failed COP15 Copenhagen Summit in 2009 kept recurring in strategic discussions. Copenhagen had – both inside and outside the climate movement – raised great expectations of delivering a crucial step forward in the global effort to address climate change but delivered an equally great disappointment when it failed. At least that was the dominant "Copenhagen narrative" – moderated and streamlined to unify the climate movement behind a new strategy. The following example illustrates both the key storyline and its (desired) strategic implications:

Interviewer: Do previous experiences with the COP affect how you are mobilizing for COP21?

> Respondent: Yes, definitely. . . . Alternatiba is actually answering [to] the . . . consequences of COP15 in Copenhagen where movements adopted a strategy of saying: "Yes this is the COP of the last chance", and thought that by massively mobilizing people, they could obtain this dream agreement, you know. And then it didn't work. And after that, the climate movement in Europe completely collapsed . . . And so Alternatiba said: "Yes, we need to change this strategy for COP21 and avoid saying it's . . . the COP of the last chance.
>
> (Interview Alternatiba 2015)

This story clearly emphasizes the contextual dependency of the climate movement's (lack of) success and, more specifically, how it was constrained by the weakness of the UN's output structure. Yet while there was broad agreement on this narrative, closer examination showed that it left out conflicting interpretations of what had caused the Copenhagen defeat, instead telling a unified story to identify today's climate movement as having learned from defeat and being on its way to greater success. For instance, some interviewees challenged the idea that everyone had believed that Copenhagen could deliver a great policy victory, instead emphasizing that the climate justice movement itself had failed to develop a strategy that could mobilize sufficiently for its cause, thus understating the role of the POS.

While most of these disputes remained in the background, disagreements on the future-oriented part of the narrative could not be fully resolved, creating a deep cleavage within the climate mobilization around COP21. It was in particular the online-based campaign group Avaaz (representing one of the most resourceful groups in the coalition) that strongly disagreed on the strategic conclusions drawn from the dominant narrative. One interviewee explained:

> We took Copenhagen as far as we could take it in that moment. . . . And our community was growing massively after Copenhagen. Donating more money than ever before, people were sharing our campaign more than ever before. . . . So, where is the sense of movement collapse coming from? . . . So, we get to Lima [COP20 2014] . . . and there's a presentation from the French groups that the COP is going to be a failure and we have to mobilize at the end of the COP and we shouldn't make it about the

COP because we could have the final word and signal to where the movement needs to go next. And we were like, uhm, what?!

(Interview AVAAZ 2015)

By disagreeing on the nature and the causes of the Copenhagen failure, Avaaz proposed an alternative narrative. This narrative did not so much challenge the perception of the POS during COP15, as downplay its importance by emphasizing the movement's ability to mobilize masses and the strength that lies in that, regardless of the POS. This resonates with Gamson and Meyer's (1996) argument that POSs are often framed to support pre-existing strategic preferences.

While the coalition that mobilized for COP21 remained intact, this disagreement did lead to a clear split in the strategic plans (de Moor 2018). Those adhering to the dominant Copenhagen narrative advocated a strategy that would symbolize the movement's skepticism about the ability of the COP to produce a meaningful outcome. For some, this meant mobilizing during the COP but focusing on corporate targets like fossil fuel companies and banks supporting them. Others mobilized at the end of the conference to symbolize that they were not trying to influence its outcome. Those who challenged this narrative argued that it was still useful to target the COP and that the movement merely had to mobilize enough people to drive up pressure on government leaders to do the right thing. To exert this pressure in a timely fashion, they would mobilize at the beginning of the summit. The latter strategy was criticized for its short-sightedness as it arguably prioritized the mobilization of as many participants as possible with an overly optimistic narrative that would inevitably lead to disappointment like in Copenhagen and, subsequently, a similar pattern of demobilization. To involve people in climate action for the long run, the dominant belief was that an honest, more somber presentation of expectations would be more successful. This disagreement crystalized in a split mobilization, in which those adhering to a story of favorable political opportunities at COP21 mobilized during the first weekend of the summit and those adhering to a story of lacking opportunities mobilized elsewhere or during the last weekend.

Ultimately, these plans were disrupted entirely when France introduced a state of emergency after the 15 November terrorist attacks in Paris, just two weeks before the Summit (Wahlström and de Moor 2017), indicating a dramatic and fast closure of opportunities in the form of a demonstration ban. However, the case still shows how narrated perceptions of the POS, and of output structures in particular, affected mobilization and strategy in the climate movement. We believe this case also shows that this version of the POS approach can bridge the structure-agency duality. It is possible to identify actual conditions "out there" that affect the degree of success of a mobilization, but experiences have to be made by the movement in interaction with these conditions and then interpreted to guide strategy. Different strategies among movement factions do not show the lack of impact of structure – only that it is not deterministic.

FFF and XR: a new narrative?

If the Copenhagen narrative motivated a widespread desire to move activism beyond attempts to influence (especially international) policy-making processes, more recent climate mobilizations suggest that this narrative, or at least its impact, has changed. Since late 2018, climate activism has taken a new turn with the emergence of new campaigns in the form of FFF and XR. While the former is mainly characterized by its non-confrontational tactics of school strikes and mass demonstrations, the latter opts for non-violent civil disobedience to disrupt public life and force stronger climate action. Yet they have in common that they primarily target governmental institutions – either at the local and national levels or at the international level, such as during the 2019 Climate Summits in New York and Madrid (de Moor et al. 2020b). This represents a clear break from recent trends toward direct action campaigns like Ende Gelände, which in Germany organizes massive occupations of coal mines, to instead focusing on demanding action from state governments.

How can we make sense of this shift, particularly from a POS point of view? Does this shift mean that FFF and XR are more optimistic about the ability of states to get things done, or do they share the skepticism of previous climate movements but draw different strategic conclusions from this? While more research is needed to answer these questions in full, some recently collected data indicates that the latter option provides a more convincing explanation.

During 2019, we participated in a research collaboration that collected protest-survey data at various large-scale FFF and XR demonstrations around the world, giving us representative data on how activists perceived states' ability to address environmental issues like climate change. (For details on the studies, see Wahlström et al. 2019; de Moor et al. 2020a; Saunders et al. 2020.) The data show widespread skepticism regarding governments' ability to address main environmental challenges, thus indicating that output structures were still perceived to be weak. Specifically, very few respondents agreed with the statement "Governments can be relied upon to solve our environmental problems". As Figure 18.1 shows, this is true across FFF demonstrations in various countries, and comparable data show a very similar picture at XR demonstrations in the UK (Saunders et al. 2020).

There are considerable variations between countries, but interestingly, there seems to be no direct correlation between "objective" indicators of environmental performance and these perceptions. While perceived capacity seems to be higher in some countries that are indeed known as environmental leaders (e.g., Sweden, but here we also find considerable internal differences), it is low in other "leading" countries (e.g., Germany) and relatively high in some laggards (e.g., Hungary) (see Liefferink et al. 2009). What seems to matter more is an overall perception of states as weak on environmental performance.

While we cannot directly compare these quantitative findings to the qualitative findings of our COP21 study, we can cautiously conclude that there has not been a radical shift away from perceiving states' output structures as weak. It is therefore more likely that what has changed is how activists draw strategic conclusions from these perceptions. Here we present some working hypotheses as to what might be going on.

A first possibility is that the capacity of the state to get things done is no longer framed as a given contextual determinant but as something that social movements can influence. Previous studies suggested that while social movements may believe that they can force governments to listen, they might not believe they can force them to become more capable (de Moor 2016). However, capacity to act is to some degree the result of political decisions (e.g., the amount of tax a state decides to collect can affect the extent to which it can address societal problems), and movements can and do challenge these decisions. For instance, Thörn and Svenberg (2017) argue that environmental movements sometimes oppose neoliberal processes by which states shift responsibility for addressing environmental challenges to market actors and civil society, demanding instead that states take more responsibility themselves. Such views may contribute to the current re-responsibilizing of the state (see also chapter 22 by Thörn). In POS terms, we could thus argue that not only input structures can be seen as movement outcomes (see earlier in this chapter), but that output structures can be as well. We also see this reflected in the argument expressed by multiple climate activists that states' far-reaching reactions to the COVID-19 pandemic prove that – if willing – governments could deploy similarly strong measures in response to the climate crisis.

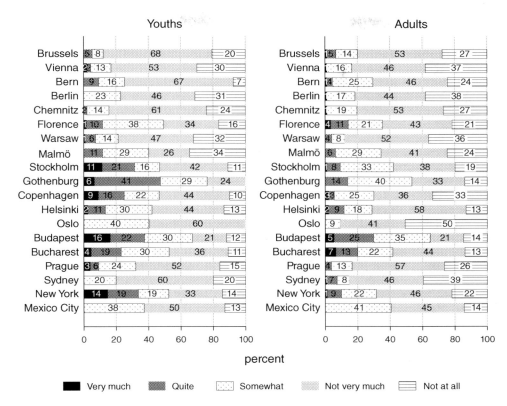

Figure 18.1 Degree of agreement with the statement "Governments can be relied upon to solve our environmental problems" among youth and adult participants in Fridays for Future demonstrations 20–27 September 2019.

Source: Reproduced under a Creative Commons BY-NC License 4.0 from de Moor et al. (2020a).

A second possibility is that we are witnessing a shift not so much in *how* POSs matter for FFF's and XR's strategies, but *whether* they matter. As discussed earlier, POSs are considered to be especially important for "instrumental movements", and changes in this regard may make perceived POSs less relevant to inform strategies in today's climate campaigns. While our survey data clearly show that participants in FFF and XR demonstrations have relatively strong instrumental motivations (Wahlström et al. 2019; de Moor et al. 2020a; Saunders et al. 2020), slogans and messages from within these campaigns also suggest a sense of moral obligation. Between 70% and 80% in most locations of the FFF protest survey agreed or strongly agreed that they participated because "felt morally obliged to do so". Instead of asking which potential target has the greatest capacity and willingness to make things change, governments are addressed based on their moral responsibility to protect the people – today and in the future – from existential threats posed by climate change. This is, for instance, illustrated by Greta Thunberg's famous speech at the UN Climate Summit in New York 2019:

> People are suffering. People are dying. Entire ecosystems are collapsing. We are at the beginning of a mass extinction, and all you can talk about is money and fairy tales of economic growth. How dare you?

The need for citizens to pressure governments into taking up this responsibility is framed in similarly moral terms, as illustrated by an elderly XR protester who was photographed wearing a sign saying, "I am a rebel so that I can look my grandchildren in the eye". In the face of existential crises, instrumental discussions about political opportunities seem to loose force, making room for unconditional demands for action – no matter what the circumstances. A Swedish activist recently explained to us that for XR, "bravery" is a key virtue, referring to the tenacity to keep fighting despite having the odds stacked against you.

Conclusion

The impact of political contexts on environmental movements has been a productive field of research for several decades now. Much of the early work in the area was preoccupied with comparisons of developments in the environmental movement in different countries, in particular different degrees of institutionalization (see also Giugni and Grasso 2015). Lately, focus seems to have increasingly shifted toward both local variations and international political opportunity structures. The latter represents the globalized framing of the climate issue and the concomitantly globalized mobilization. The complex governance of this issue has presented challenges for movement actors to accurately identify political opportunities and highlighted the need for studying activists' perceptions of the POS and how those perceptions are translated into movement strategies.

We have sought to make three main contributions to the already-rich literature on environmental movements and POS: 1) while input structures have received the most attention, output structures seem to merit as much attention – especially in a context in which states' capacity to act on society's main environmental challenges has become questionable; 2) narratives may present a key mechanism to link POS and strategies, and narrated opportunities need to be understood as entangled in wider movement processes, including collective identity formation; and 3) the relevance of POS can vary over time – even within movements – depending on the instrumental or moral orientation of the movement. Applying these ideas to some of the most recent climate movement mobilizations, we can conclude that new narratives facilitate a re-responsibilizing of the state, which may ultimately result in the strengthening of output structures, thus rendering the state's POS more favorable for environmental movements. At the same time, whether and how the POS is relevant to environmental movements remain questions that merit ongoing academic scrutiny.

Note

1 According to van der Heijden (1997), institutionalization is defined by three processes: 1) organizational growth, 2) internal institutionalization (e.g., professionalization, bureaucratization, and centralization), and 3) external institutionalization (the action repertoire of the movement). Cf. chapter 22 by Thörn's.

References

Almeida, Paul, and Stearns, Linda B. 1998. Political Opportunities and Local Grassroots Environmental Movements: The Case of Minamata. *Social Problems*. **45**(1), 37–60.

Böhmelt, Tobias. 2014. Political Opportunity Structures in Dictatorships? Explaining ENGO Existence in Autocratic Regimes. *The Journal of Environment & Development*. **23**(4), 446–471.

Carmichael, Jason T., Jenkins, J. Craig, and Brulle, Robert J. 2012. Building Environmentalism: The Founding of Environmental Movement Organizations in the United States, 1900–2000. *The Sociological Quarterly*. **53**(3), 422–453.

Carmin, JoAnn. 2003. Resources, Opportunities and Local Environmental Action in the Democratic Transition and Early Consolidation Periods in the Czech Republic. *Environmental Politics.* **12**(3), 42–64.

Carmin, JoAnn, and Fagan, Adam. 2010. Environmental Mobilisation and Organisations in Post-Socialist Europe and the Former Soviet Union. *Environmental Politics.* **19**(5), 689–707.

Cassegård, Carl, Soneryd, Linda, Thörn, Håkan and Wettergren, Åsa. 2017. *Climate Action in a Globalizing World: Comparative Perspectives on Social Movements in the Global North.* London: Routledge.

de Moor, Joost. 2016. *The Two-Dimensional Structure of Political Opportunities: A Quantitative and Mixed-Methods Analysis of the Effect of Political Opportunity Structures on Nonelectoral Participation.* PhD dissertation, University of Antwerp. Available at: www.academia.edu/27723402/The_Two_Dimensional_Structure_of_Political_Opportunities_PhD_Dissertation_Joost_de_Moor.

de Moor, Joost. 2018. The 'Efficacy Dilemma' of Transnational Climate Activism: The Case of COP21. *Environmental Politics.* **27**(6), 1079–1100.

de Moor, Joost, Marien, Sofie, and Hooghe, Marc. 2017. Why are Some Lifestyle Activists Avoiding State-Oriented Politics While Others are not? A Case Study of Lifestyle Politics in The Belgian Environmental Movement. *Mobilization.* **22**(2), 245–264.

de Moor, Joost, and Wahlström, Mattias. 2019. Narrating Political Opportunities: Explaining Strategic Adaptation in the Climate Movement. *Theory & Society.* **48**(3), 419–451.

de Moor, Joost, Uba, Katrin, Wahlström, Mattias, Wennerhag, Magnus and De Vydt, Michiel, eds. 2020a. *Protest for a Future II: Composition, Mobilization and Motives of the Participants in Fridays For Future Climate Protests on 20–27 September, 2019, in 19 Cities around the World.* Available at: https://osf.io/asruw/.

de Moor, Joost, De Vydt, Michiel, Uba, Katrin, and Wahlström, Mattias. 2020b. New Kids on the Block: Taking Stock of the Recent Cycle of Climate Activism. *Social Movement Studies.* https://doi.org/10.1080/14742837.2020.1836617.

Derman, Brandon B. 2014. Climate Governance, Justice, and Transnational Civil Society. *Climate Policy.* **14**(1), 23–41.

Di Gregorio, Monica. 2014. Gaining Access to the State: Political Opportunities and Agency in Forest Activism in Indonesia. *Social Movement Studies.* **13**(3), 381–398.

Doherty, Brian, and Hayes, Graeme. 2012. Tactics, Traditions and Opportunities: British and French Crop-Trashing Actions in Comparative Perspective. *European Journal of Political Research.* **51**(4), 540–562.

Dryzek, John S., Downes, David, Hunold, Christian, Schlosberg, David, and Hernes, Hans-Kristian. 2003. *Green States and Social Movements: Environmentalism in the United States, United Kingdom, Germany, and Norway.* Oxford: Oxford University Press.

Eisinger, Peter K. 1973. The Conditions of Protest Behaviour in American Cities. *American Political Science Review.* **67**(1), 11–28.

Ergas, Christina. 2010. A Model of Sustainable Living: Collective Identity in an Urban Ecovillage. *Organization & Environment.* **23**(1), 32–54.

Gamson, William A., and Meyer, David S. 1996. Framing Political Opportunity. In: McAdam, Doug, McCarthy, John D., and Zald, Mayer N. eds. *Comparative Perspectives on Social Movements. Political Opportunity Structures, Mobilizing Structures, and Cultural Framings.* Cambridge: Cambridge University Press, 275–290.

Giugni, Marco. 2006. Useless Protest? A Time-Series Analysis of the Policy Outcomes of Ecology, Antinuclear, and Peace Movements in the United States, 1977–1995. *Mobilization.* **12**(1), 53–77.

Giugni, Marco, and Maria Grasso. 2015. Environmental Movements: Heterogeneity, Transformation, and Institutionalization. *Annual Review of Environment and Resources.* **40**, 337–361.

Goodwin, Jeff, and Jasper, James M. 1999. Caught in a Winding, Snarling Vine: The Structural Bias of Political Process Theory. *Sociological Forum.* **14**(1), 27–54.

Graubart, Jonathan. 2004. Legalizing' Politics, 'Politicizing' Law: Transnational Activism and International Law. *International Politics* **41**, 319–340

Hadden, Jennifer. 2017. Learning from Defeat: The Strategic Reorientation of the U.S. Climate Movement. In: Cassegård, C., Soneryd, L., Thörn, H., and Wettergren, Å. eds. *Climate Action in a Globalizing World.* London: Routledge, 125–148.

Hadden, Jennifer. 2018. The Relational Sources of Advocacy Strategies : Comparative Evidence from the European and US Climate Change Sectors. *Policy Studies Journal.* **46**(2), 248–268.

Heikkila, Tanya, Berardo, Ramiro, Weible, Christopher M., and Yi, Hongtao. 2019. A Comparative View of Advocacy Coalitions: Exploring Shale Development Politics in the United States, Argentina, and China. *Journal of Comparative Policy Analysis: Research and Practice.* **21**(2), 151–166.

Henry, Laura A., Sundstrom, Lisa M., Winston, Carla, and Bala-Miller, Priya. 2019. NGO Participation in Global Governance Institutions: International and Domestic Drivers of Engagement. *Interest Groups & Advocacy.* **8**(3), 291–332.

Hilson, Chris. 2002. New Social Movements: The Role of Legal Opportunity. *Journal of European Public Policy.* **9**(2), 238–255.

Jamison, Andrew, Eyerman, Ron, Cramer, Jacqueline, and Læssøe, Jeppe. 1991. *The Making of the New Environmental Consciousness: A Comparative Study of Environmental Movements in Sweden, Denmark and the Netherlands.* Edinburg: Edinburgh University Press.

Kemberling, Melissa, and Roberts, J. Timmons. 2009. When Time is on their Side: Determinants of Outcomes in New Siting and Existing Contamination Cases in Louisiana. *Environmental Politics.* **18**(6), 851–868.

King, Brayden. 2008. A Social Movement Perspective of Stakeholder Collective Action and Influence. *Business & Society.* **47**(1), 21–49.

Kitschelt, Herbert. 1986. Political Opportunity Structures and Political Protest: Anti-Nuclear Movements in Four Democracies. *British Journal of Political Science.* **16**(1), 57–85.

Koopmans, Ruud. 1999. Political. Opportunity. Structure. Some Splitting to Balance the Lumping. *Sociological Forum.* **14**(1), 93–105.

Koopmans, Ruud. 2005. The Missing Link between Structure and Agency: Outline of an Evolutionary Approach to Social Movements. *Mobilization.* **10**(1), 19–33.

Koopmans, Ruud, and Olzak, Susan. 2004. Discursive Opportunities and the Evolution of Right-Wing Violence in Germany. *American Journal of Sociology.* **110**(1), 198–230.

Kriesi, Herbert, Koopmans, Ruud, Duyvendak, Jan Willem, and Giugni, Marco G. 1995. *New Social Movements in Western Europe: A Comparative Analysis.* Minneapolis: University of Minnesota Press.

Liefferink, Duncan, Arts, Bas, Kamstra, Jelmer, and Ooijevaar, Jeroen. 2009. Leaders and Laggards in Environmental Policy: A Quantitative Analysis of Domestic Policy Outputs. *Journal of European Public Policy.* **16**(5), 677–700.

McAdam, Doug. 1999. *Political Process and the Development of Black Insurgency, 1930–1970.* 2nd Edition. Chicago: University of Chicago Press.

McAdam, Doug, Boudet, Hilary Schaffer, Davis, Jennifer, Orr, Ryan J., Scott, W. Richard, and Levitt, Raymond E. 2010. "Site Fights": Explaining Opposition to Pipeline Projects in the Developing World. *Sociological Forum.* **25**(3), 401–427.

McAdam, Doug, and Tarrow, Sydney. 2018. The Political Context of Social Movements. In: D.A. Snow, S.A. Soule, H. Kriesi, and H.J. McCammon. eds. *The Wiley Blackwell Companion to Social Movements.* 2nd Edition. Chichester: John Wiley and Sons Ltd, 17–42.

McCright, Aaron M., and Clark, Terry N. 2006. The Political Opportunity Structure of the Environmental Movement in U.S. Communities. In: McCright, A.M., and Clark, T.N. eds. *Community and Ecology: Dynamics of Place, Sustainability, and Politics.* Amsterdam: Elsevier, 199–240.

Meyer, David S. 2004. Protest and Political Opportunities. *Annual Review of Sociology.* **30**, 125–145.

Meyer, David. S., and Minkoff, Debra C. 2004. Conceptualizing Political Opportunity. *Social Forces.* **82**(4), 1457–1492.

Poloni-Staudinger, Lori M. 2008. The Domestic Opportunity Structure and Supranational Activity: An Explanation of Environmental Group Activity at the European Union Level. *European Union Politics.* **9**(4), 531–558.

Poloni-Staudinger, Lori M. 2009. Why Cooperate? Cooperation among Environmental Groups in the United Kingdom, France, and Germany. *Mobilization.* **14**(3), 375–396.

Rootes, Chris A. 1999. Political Opportunity Structures: Promise, Problems and Prospects. *La Lettre de la maison Française d'Oxford.* **10**, 75–97.

Rootes, Chris A. (Ed.). 2003. *Environmental Protest in Western Europe.* Oxford: Oxford University Press.

Rootes, Chris A., and Nulman, Eugene. 2015. The Impacts of Environmental Movements. In: Donatella della Porta and Mario Diani. eds. *The Oxford Handbook of Social Movements.* Oxford: Oxford University Press, 729–742.

Rucht, Dieter. 1990. Campaigns, Skirmishes and Battles: Anti-Nuclear Movements in the USA, France and West Germany. *Industrial Crisis Quarterly.* **4**(3), 193–222.

Sarre, Philip, and Jehlička, Petr. 2007. Environmental Movements in Space-Time: The Czech and Slovak Republics from Stalinism to Post-socialism. *Transactions of the Institute of British Geographers.* **32**(3), 346–362.

Saunders, Clare. 2009. It's not Just Structural: Social Movements are not Homogenous Responses to Structural Features, but Networks Shaped by Organisational Strategies and Status. *Sociological Research Online.* **14**(1).

Saunders, Clare, Doherty, Brian, and Hayes, Graeme. 2020. A New Climate Movement? Extinction Rebellion's Activists in Profile. *CUSP Working Papers Series,* **25.** Available at: www.cusp.ac.uk/ themes/p/xr-study/.

Sheng, Chunhong. 2019. Petitioning and Social Stability in China: Case Studies of Anti- Nuclear Sentiment. *Voluntas.* **30**, 381–392.

Shriver, Thomas E., and Adams, Alison E. 2010. Cycles of Repression and Tactical Innovation: The Evolution of Environmental Dissidence in Communist Czechoslovakia. *Sociological Quarterly.* **51**(2), 329–354.

Tarrow, Sydney. 1998. *Power in Movement: Social Movements and Contentious Politics.* Cambridge: Cambridge University Press.

Thörn, Håkan, and Svenberg, Sebastian. 2017. The Swedish Environmental Movement: Politics of Responsibility between Climate Justice and Local Transition. In: Cassegård, C., Soneryd, L., Thörn, H., and Wettergren, Å. eds. *Climate Action in a Globalizing World.* New York: Routledge, 193–216.

van Der Heijden, Hein A. 1997. Political Opportunity Structure and the Institutionalisation of the Environmental Movement. *Environmental Politics.* **6**(4), 25–50.

van Der Heijden, Hein A. 2006. Globalization, Environmental Movements, and International Political Opportunity Structures. *Organization and Environment.* **19**(1), 28–45.

Wahlström, Mattias, and Peterson, Abby. 2006. Between the State and the Market: Expanding the Concept of 'Political Opportunity Structure'. *Acta Sociologica.* **49**(4), 363–377.

Wahlström, Mattias, and de Moor, Joost. 2017. Governing Dissent in a State of Emergency: Police and Protester Interactions in the Global Space of the COP. In: Cassegård, C., Soneryd, L., Thörn, H., and Wettergren, Å. eds. *Climate Action in a Globalizing World.* New York: Routledge, 57–80.

Wahlström, Mattias, Kocyba, Piotr, De Vydt, Michiel, and de Moor, Joost, eds. 2019. *Protest for a Future: Composition, Mobilization and Motives of the Participants in Fridays For Future Climate Protests on 15 March, 2019 in 13 European Cities.* Available at: https://osf.io/xcnzh/.

Wall, Derek. 1999. Mobilising Earth First! in Britain. *Environmental Politics.* **8**(1), 81–100.

Xie, Lei X., and van der Heijden, Hein A. 2010. Environmental Movements and Political Opportunities: The Case of China. *Social Movement Studies.* **9**(1), 51–68.

Yanitsky, Oleg N. 2012. From Nature Protection to Politics : The Russian Environmental Movement 1960–2010. *Environmental Politics.* **21**(6), 922–940.

Zachrisson, Anna, and Beland Lindahl, Karin. 2019. Political Opportunity and Mobilization: The Evolution of a Swedish Mining-Sceptical Movement. *Resources Policy.* **64**, 101477.

Zhang, Yang. 2018. Allies in Action: Institutional Actors and Grassroots Environmental Activism. *Research in Social Movements, Conflicts and Change.* **42**, 9–38.

19

MOBILIZING ENVIRONMENTAL EXPERTS AND EXPERTISE

Scott Frickel and Florencia Arancibia

Introduction

Social movement scholars have been studying environmental movements' ubiquitous but often fraught relationship to science for three decades. In *Social Movements: A Cognitive Approach*, Ron Eyerman and Andrew Jamison (1991) argued that social movements are important cultural producers of new knowledge and held out environmental movements' "knowledge interests" grounded in basic assumptions and topical research areas of systems ecology and other environmental fields in illustration of their claim (see also Jamison et al. 1990). Published the same year, Steven Yearley's *The Green Case* (1991) drew attention to the "uneasy alliance" between environmentalists, who claim political authority in protecting nature, and environmental scientists, who claim epistemic authority in knowing nature. Both books identified – and complicated – this chapter's central focus on the mobilization of environmental experts and expertise.[1]

Of course, the challenge of mobilizing science is not specific to environmental movements, nor is expert activism a role reserved for ecologists and other environmental scientists. Physicists, including Einstein and Oppenheimer, marched against the bomb (Smith 1965), and engineers protested the war in Vietnam (Wisnioski 2012). Biologists and reproductive health specialists joined forces with the women's movement (Clarke 1998). Physicians and urban planners organized against the racial and class politics of urban redevelopment (Hoffman 1989), biomedical experts allied with AIDs activists to transform clinical trial protocols (Epstein 1996), and geneticists support the work of anti-racist movements (Bliss 2012). Scientists regularly engage in social movement politics to varying degrees and always have.

Yet the relationship between environmental movements and environmental knowledge calls out for special attention. Environmental politics nearly always involve epistemic contests over what is known or unknown about nature and who gets to speak for it. This observation locates scientists and other professional experts at the center of struggles over environmental justice, wilderness preservation, climate change, GMOs, animal rights, and any of the other myriad themes taken up by environmental movements around the world. Experts – and thus a politics of expertise – are never far from the center of environmental movements.[2]

Thus, review articles with a broad focus on science, knowledge, and social movements regularly showcase environmental research (Breyman et al. 2017; Frickel and Arancibia 2021; Ottinger et al. 2017). A growing stream of books, journal articles, and special issues also focus,

DOI: 10.4324/9780367855680-22

more specifically, on environmental "expert activism" (Allen 2003) and "lay-expert collaborations" (Brown 2007; Sannazzaro 2014), especially, although not exclusively, involving grassroots environmental health and justice movements (Kroll-Smith et al. 2000; Ottinger and Cohen 2011). Other works cover related topics such as alternative ecological rationalities, environmental valuation languages articulated by activists (Martínez Alier 2002), and hybrid types of knowledge (Vessuri 2004). Even so, the mobilization of environmental experts and expertise remains poorly understood. Basic information about its organization, dynamics, and impact is lacking, even as expert activism mounts amidst a cascade of global crises, from climate change to the anti-science agendas of right-wing populist governments to the COVID-19 pandemic (Fisher 2018).

We attribute the knowledge gaps in part to the fact that students of social movements are not the primary producers of this research, which derives mostly from science and technology studies (STS) and, to a lesser extent, from environmental history and environmental sociology. One consequence has been that the full arsenal of analytical theories and methods used to study environmental movements (Giugni and Grasso 2015) has not, to date, been trained on mobilization processes among environmental experts as a distinct social group. The lacuna represents a missed opportunity to refine and extend meso- and micro-level social movement theory. Thus, we see every motivation to close the gap and offer this chapter as a reflexive call for research action on this understudied topic.

As such, in the following, we do not attempt anything like a comprehensive review of existing research. Rather, we tailor our discussion of extant work in ways that highlight what we see as areas of "undone science" as it applies to our topic (Hess 2016). We also are not so much concerned with the normative question of whether scientists and other experts should become involved in politics (which is how scientists often frame the issue). Instead, our focus is with the empirical and strategic questions concerning how expert mobilization into environmental movements is organized and what effects the mobilization of expertise has on environmental science, on environmental conflict, and on socioecological change more broadly.

We use the term "expert" in the traditional academic sense of individuals working in occupations that require advanced graduate or professional training. "Expertise" refers to the constellation of resources associated with being an expert. These resources include not only specialist knowledge but also access to and close familiarity with specialized technologies and practices; professional societies and communication networks; and institutional experiences, know-how, and status not typically available to others outside the field. This usage does not deny the importance of "lay experts" or "local knowledge" in shaping environmental conflict or as organizing tools for environmental movements. However, we view the distinction as important analytically.

We begin by describing conceptual and methodological challenges in studying experts in environmental movements. Next, we present a case study of experts and expertise in Argentina's ongoing pesticide conflict to highlight some of the gaps in current knowledge. A third section distills several lessons from the case study, and our concluding section identifies useful directions for future research.

From experts in movements to the mobilization of expertise

Most of what we know about environmental expert activism comes from case studies generated through archival research, participant observation, interviews, and document analysis. This work has been extremely generative (for a review, see Arancibia 2016). In broad strokes, extant studies depict environmental experts mobilizing on behalf of nature within their own disciplines (Frickel 2004; Shostak 2013), professional associations (Kinchy 2006), and in what Kelly Moore (2008) has called "public interest science organizations". The latter include older groups, ranging from the liberal Union of Concerned Scientists to the more radical Science for the People (both established around 1969) (Moore 2008) to newer groups emphasizing digital technology, like the Environmental Data and Governance Initiative in the US and Canada (est. 2016) (Dillon et al. 2017) and larger networks like Unión de Científicos Comprometidos con la Sociedad y la Naturaleza de América Latina in Latin America (UCCSNAL) (Feeney 2019).

Disciplinary and technical expertise is also a cornerstone of environmental movements (Hayes 1987; Yearley 1991). Many of the more well-funded environmental movement organizations (EMOs) have built in-house scientific capacity for data collection and analysis (Jamison 2001). Smaller organizations also rely on scientific experts. They might recruit PhD-level scientists onto advisory boards or form partnerships with scientists at area universities to gain greater access to resources that would otherwise be out of reach. An early example from the United States is the storied partnership between West Harlem Environmental Action (WE ACT for Environmental Justice) and researchers at the Mailman School of Public Health at Columbia University (Shepard et al. 2002).

Mobilizing environmental scientists comes with clear risks for experts themselves and for social movements. It can invite culture clash within EMOs (Cable et al. 2005) and provoke "backfire" when scientists' research and advocacy threaten industry and state priorities (Martin 2007). But expert activism can also bring clear advantages to environmental groups and movements. Dozens of studies have documented scientists working with environmental movements to design research, collect and analyze data, translate and disseminate technical knowledge, engage in political lobbying and petitioning, provide expert testimony throughout legal proceedings, and more (e.g., McCormick 2009).

Important as this scholarship is, much of it proceeds from, or implicitly reinforces, one or more of three limiting assumptions. The first limiting assumption is that environmental scientific or professional expertise within the movement (i.e., the bank of resources accessible to expert activists) is not only inherently valuable and potentially consequential for understanding movement processes and outcomes, but also more valuable, relatively speaking, than local or indigenous knowledge. Experts hold specialized knowledge and resources that many EMOs would not otherwise have access to, and thus, *ceretis paribus*, the more experts collaborating with environmental movements, the better. A second limiting assumption is that expert activists are relatively rare among their professional peers. Research tends to treat as exceptional those experts who risk their reputations by wielding expertise as a weapon in the service of environmental movements. A third limiting assumption is that experts mobilize primarily as individuals rather than as collectives. Political activism is a risky and thus deeply personal decision for anyone (Delborne 2008). For scientists, such decisions involve the additional risk of negative sanction from the scientific community for failing to remain "above" politics. The three assumptions are interrelated, insofar as the relative scarcity of mobilized experts (second assumption) compounds the inherent value of their expertise (first assumption) but also compounds the risk to individual experts (third assumption).

To the best of our knowledge, none of these limiting assumptions have been assessed empirically, raising important questions about their validity. What if one or more of the assumptions, if not wrong, are at least contextually dependent on social conditions or factors that we do not fully understand? For example, expert activism might undermine movement success as often as aid it. Perhaps expert activism is more common than we realize, just less visible and so more difficult to measure. Or maybe it is better to view expert mobilization as a process of collective action, rather than as a consequence of individual risk taking. Unfortunately, the general knowledge we would need to judge which set of assumptions is more or less valid, and under what conditions, does not exist.

The next section summarizes an empirical case that pushes against some of the limiting assumptions we have identified in the extant literature. Our analysis of the case is preliminary, relying on prior published research and early-stage data from an ongoing longitudinal study of expert mobilization in Argentina's pesticide conflict, which emerged in 2001 and continues today.

Experts and expertise in Argentina's pesticide conflict

Argentina is the world's third-largest producer and exporter of genetically modified (GM) soy. A key factor in Argentina's rise as an agricultural powerhouse is Roundup Ready Soy, a biotechnology developed in the 1990s by Monsanto that pairs GM seeds with intensive use of glyphosate-based pesticides. Aided by the absence of federal laws regulating pesticides (Paz Belada 2017),[3] Argentina's rapid shift to agricultural biotechnology has had major economic consequences for the country (Teubal 2006, 2008), but also growing ecological and public health consequences for communities located near soybean fields and most directly at risk from "pesticide drift" (Leguizamón 2014). In response, citizen mobilizations against spraying of glyphosate and other pesticides have emerged and spread across Argentina and in several other countries, including France (Jouzel and Prete 2014), the Philippines (Nikol and Jansen 2020), Sri Lanka (Bandarage 2013), and the United States (Harrison 2011).

To date, published research on anti-pesticide activism in Argentina highlights a case of "popular epidemiology" (Brown 1992) involving Las Madres de Ituzaingó, a group of women who first called attention to a rash of illnesses impacting their neighborhood on the outskirts of Ciudad Córdoba in 2001 (Carrizo and Berger 2009; Arancibia and Motta 2019). Hoping to shed light on the nature of the illnesses afflicting their community, Las Madres designed a simple health survey and went door to door collecting information from neighbors. While their results revealed a geographic pattern of impacted households and illness complaints, including an alarming number of cancers, local government officials ignored the group's unpublished findings (Carrizo and Berger 2009). Nationally, the scientific community had yet to recognize the scope of the problem raised by Las Madres. Few Argentinian scientists were studying the environmental and health effects of pesticides; effectively, an Argentinian field of pesticide effects research did not exist.

Recognizing that they lacked legitimacy to speak on questions related to public health and science, Las Madres developed alliances with a local biologist, clinical physician, epidemiologist and a public health expert who directed the municipal Sub-Secretary of Health (Arancibia and Motta 2019). Over the next few years, these lay-expert alliances produced several environmental and epidemiological studies, each one showing that Ituzaingó Anexo residents faced exposure to pesticides and heavy metals in higher doses than accepted by international limits (Montenegro 2002, 2003) and also identified a local cancer cluster (Carrizo and Berger 2009). Still, little changed on the ground. While the municipal legislature in the City of Cordoba acceded to community pressure as early as 2002 by enacting protective ordinances restricting pesticide use in the Ituzaingó Anexo area, soy producers routinely violated the ordinances without consequence. And although the Madres' alliances with experts produced publicly credible data supporting the movement's demands, the experts also encountered intense pressure and sanction from employers and government officials for their work with Las Madres (Arancibia and Motta 2019). One lost his job. Another had his work censored. Both walked away from the conflict. Overall, health conditions in the neighborhood worsened.

Throughout the initial period of protest, actions organized by Las Madres remained localized as neighborhood activists and allied experts engaged in a tug-of-war battle of evidence and counter-evidence with the municipal and provincial governments. The scale of activism broadened when Las Madres traveled to the capital city of Buenos Aires in 2005 to meet with a group of intellectual activists, El Grupo de Reflexión Rural (GRR). Founded in the mid-1990s by intellectuals representing different disciplines, including agronomic engineering, ecology, economics, and sociology. GRR operated as a discursive space for debate and analysis of the impacts of global capitalism in Argentina and as a forum for organizing opposition to an industrial model of agriculture based on the export of transgenic commodities. For GRR, Las Madres' concerns about pesticides illustrated the larger food systems problem.

In 2006, Las Madres and GRR co-launched the Stop the Sprayings campaign, organizing public talks, film screenings, and workshops "to raise consciousness"[4] in hundreds of rural villages and towns across Argentina's GM-soy-producing areas (Arancibia 2013). The campaign gained early support from other social movements and environmental NGOs around the country and, as it progressed, prompted grassroots organizing in many of the communities they visited. Soon, new neighborhood assemblies modelled on the national campaign began popping up across the countryside and in towns and cities.[5] Taking names like Stop Spraying Córdoba and Stop Spraying Junín, the new organizations replicated Las Madres' strategy of combining popular epidemiology and evidence mobilization with more traditional protest tactics. These assemblies also organized provincial gatherings once or twice a year called Encuentros de Pueblos Fumigados (Sprayed Villages' Gatherings) to knit bonds and increase political coordination among impacted communities and to build provincial social movements. When the campaign ended in 2009, it could claim at least two tangible outcomes that illustrate how partnerships between activists and mobilized experts were helping expand the terrain, intensity, and tactical repertoire of the conflict.

The campaign's first tangible outcome was a book, *Pueblos Fumigados* (Rulli 2009), 4,000 copies of which were printed and distributed by GRR.[6] Reflecting the campaign's mobile strategy of grassroots education and embrace of popular epidemiology, the book combined rural activists' first-hand experiences of struggle against pesticide use with reviews of the scientific literature on pesticide effects research. The book also included the first clinical observations of pesticide-related illnesses compiled by health experts from affected areas and a chapter describing legal tactics for challenging pesticide spraying (Rulli 2009). As the book spread with the campaign, a steady uptick in new legal and judicial challenges were filed in impacted villages and towns (Aranda 2015; Cabaleiro 2020), illustrating the campaign's second tangible outcome: the growing mobilization of legal expertise alongside scientific, medical, and public health expertise across GM-soy-producing regions.

The steadily increasing roster of lawyers, scientists, physicians, and other health experts represented incipient nodes in an expanding network of experts mobilized by the struggle. Six physicians, seven scientists, and at least one lawyer were involved in local pesticide conflicts when the Stop the Sprayings campaign began in 2006, including four from Ituzaingó Anexo. Our research identifies at least 28 additional experts who joined the movement as the campaign developed over the next three years. Most were physicians working in clinical care and dealing with patients from GM-soy-producing areas. Roughly a dozen pursued academic activities at national universities, and a few worked with environmental NGOs. Connected to one another mainly through the Stop the Sprayings campaign, most experts gave talks on the toxic effects of pesticides to non-academic audiences and asked that local government officials take action.

Despite the growing numerical and geographic spread of the movement during these years, experts from rural and peri-urban areas remained somewhat isolated from one another and, acting alone, had little leverage over local governments, rural producers, and agribusiness. Their arguments about the dangers of pesticide exposure and their requests for local regulation to curb unrestricted spraying were easily ignored or silenced, and the validity of their clinical observations or scientific research was often challenged. Some had their studies scuttled by supervisors; others faced censorship, withdrawal of funds, reprimands, and threats. The network of experts, while growing and expanding the movement's reach, remained relatively ineffective as a mechanism for regulatory and legal change. Still anchored geographically to rural and peri-urban agricultural areas, the movement begun by Las Madres had yet to attract the attention of the country's large urban populations or gain visibility on the national political scene.

This situation changed when new experimental findings from the laboratory of Dr. Andrés Carrasco, a prestigious embryologist in Buenos Aires, appeared on the front page of *Página 12*, one of Argentina's leading national newspapers (Aranda 2009).[7] The article explained that glyphosate exposure caused malformations in frog embryos and likely caused developmental abnormalities *in utero* in humans.[8] This was the first such study published in Spanish and the first study published in the mass media; its message reached into the homes of millions of Argentinian readers.[9] Overnight, Carrasco's study sparked intense public conversation and became a critical turning point in Argentina's pesticide conflict (Arancibia 2013; Motta and Alasino 2013). Yet, like other experts before him, Carrasco became the target of fierce backlash from national government officials, mayors, academic administrators, industry, and even the US Embassy. He endured censorship and harassment but also threats of physical violence, robbery, forced resignation, and career sabotage (Arancibia 2015).

The actions against Carrasco reinforced the movements' need to expand and strengthen ties among mobilized experts. The conditions for mobilization were also changing. Pesticide effects research was now gaining traction within Argentina's scientific community and beyond (Sosa et al. 2019). Published studies of the biological and environmental effects of glyphosate and other pesticides surged from Argentinian laboratories and field sites, registering a more than five-fold increase over the previous decade (from 6.1 articles per year during 1990–99 to 28.4 per year during 2000–09; see Figure 19.1). An Argentinian field of pesticide effects research was emerging in parallel with a less visible, socially "submerged" network of experts gradually mobilizing against the use of agricultural pesticides (Frickel et al. 2015).

The first meeting of Physicians of Sprayed Villages convened in August 2010 at the National University of Córdoba, four months after publication of Carrasco's glyphosate effects study. Organized by Medardo Ávila Vázquez, a physician with experience in the Ituzaingó Anexo protests and the Stop the Spraying campaign, the meeting brought together 160 participants, including experts from six universities and grassroots activists representing 10 of Argentina's 23 provinces. The meeting was a political-academic hybrid, partly focused on diffusing knowledge about the adverse health effects of pesticides and partly an attempt to influence public health and agrarian policy. At the meeting, 23 health experts formed Red Universitaria de Ambiente y Salud – Médicos de Pueblos Fumigados (REDUAS) (University Network for Public Health and Environment – Physicians of Sprayed Villages). Although short lived, REDUAS was the first formal network of health experts involved in the pesticide conflict. The network sought to draw public attention to the "undone science" of pesticide effects (Motta and Arancibia 2016; see also Hess 2016) and to coordinate the efforts of expert activists involved in different local and isolated anti-pesticide protests. Immediately, REDUAS began issuing public statements demanding that national authorities restrict pesticide spraying and calling researchers, students, and impacted citizens to join the network.

The second meeting of Physicians of Sprayed Villages took place the following year at the National University of Rosario in conjunction with a larger event, the First Conference on

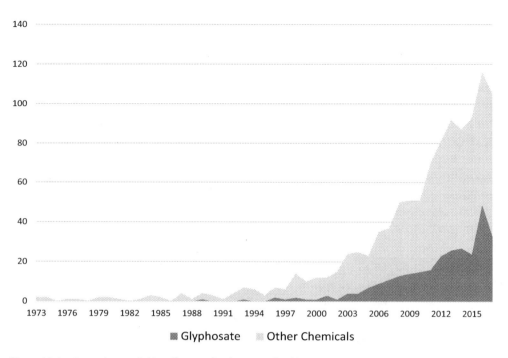

Figure 19.1 Argentina pesticide effects studies by year of publication (1973–2017)

Source: Scopus. Title-abstract-keyword search string: "Glyphosate" OR "pesticides"; country affiliation: Argentina

Socio-Environmental Health. Conference organizers included medical school professors and program administrators from the university and several environmental and anti-GMO organizations. One of the groups, the Center of Nature Protection (CEPRONAT), had also supported the Stop the Sprayings campaign a few years earlier.[10] The Conference became the first of a set of conferences that have been held biannually since 2011 in the city of Rosario, Argentina. The conferences have attracted increasingly larger and more diverse audiences, among them experts from a range of environmental, health and social sciences who are engaged in various socio-environmental conflicts in Argentina and regionally (Arancibia and Albea 2022). The conferences operate as mobilization contexts for expert recruitment and for coordinating future actions that gradually reinforced a growing national network of experts mobilized against the spraying of pesticides and for a change of agrarian model. In fact, it was at the third conference (in 2015) that the regional network of experts involved in environmental conflicts of Latin America – Unión de Científicos Comprometidos con la Sociedad y la Naturaleza de América Latina (UCCSNAL) – was established.

Actions coordinated among the networked experts varied. Some delivered public talks or made statements on the illegality of glyphosate and other pesticides use under Argentinian law.[11] Others challenged the methodology that regulatory agencies used to classify the toxicity of pesticides. Still others gave expert testimony in some of the more than 70 judicial hearings on the pesticide conflict that have occurred to date in provincial courts (Cabaleiro 2020). Most emblematic of the impact the expert network is having on Argentinian society are the "sanitary camps" organized four times a year by professors and graduate teaching assistants from the National University of Rosario School of Medicine.

Integrated into the medical school's teaching curriculum as a requirement for the MD degree, the camps are five-day epidemiological field studies in which the students use health surveys to collect morbidity and mortality information in small rural communities that lack official epidemiological public health data. Professors assess students' medical knowledge, diagnosis capacity, and community-engagement skills. On the last day, students present the main results to the community, and a few weeks later, a written report is given to residents and local health workers. Since 2010, the program has sponsored 40 sanitary camps in five provinces and has amassed epidemiological data for more than 100,000 people – data used to document the human health impacts of pesticide poisoning in the media, legislative bodies, and courts and for use by local Stop the Sprayings groups and other EMOs. Expert activists and others have mobilized this growing body of knowledge in numerous local, provincial, and national anti-pesticide actions (Verzeñassi and Vallini 2019). Their demands for legal and regulatory change receive additional empirical support from among many of the nearly 700 pesticide effects studies published by Argentinian researchers since 2010 (Figure 19.1).

Lessons from Pueblos Fumigados

Four key points about the epistemic politics of environmental movements emerge from the foregoing analysis of Pueblos Fumigados. First, while the extant literature offers examples of high-profile "dissident" scientists like Dr. Andrés Carrasco, who risk their reputations and careers to speak scientific truth to industrial and state power (for a review, see Delborne 2016), few studies investigate how expert mobilization is actually organized. What is clear in the Argentinian case, but which we suspect is also true for many environmental movements, is that expert mobilization often occurs through networks, and, in turn, expert activism creates networks. These are fundamental processes and deserve focused scholarly attention.

Second, conceptualizing expert mobilization as an ongoing collective (i.e., network) process, rather than as a collection of episodic events impacting individual researchers, raises important questions about the dynamic and scalar nature of expert activism. How does the organization of expert activism change over time and across space as the contentious politics of environmental movements ebb and flow? Research focused on the activism of individual experts or specific moments of expert mobilization may miss the dynamism of expert mobilization operating at higher scales of social, temporal, and spatial organization. For example, initially, expert mobilization against pesticides was highly localized, hinging mostly on personal alliances that Las Madres de Ituzaingó had forged with a handful of nearby physicians, public health researchers, and biologists. A decade later, expert mobilizations had formalized as a network anchored in the organizational resources of the National University of Rosario and counting more than 60 experts representing villages, towns, and cities across the country, united by their vocal opposition to pesticide spraying. Our analysis highlights the importance of a longer-term and geographically broad perspective for capturing the dynamics of expert mobilization as the pesticide conflict expands or contracts and as expert networks are created, merge, expand, or fracture.

Third, the Argentinian pesticide conflict also illustrates how disciplines, professions, and other knowledge systems structure opportunities for, and impediments to, expert mobilization. The experts we are tracking in our larger study represent a wide range of disciplinary and professional domains, including biology, agroecology and agro-engineering, medicine, law, epidemiology, environmental health, social work, and education. They also occupy a similarly diverse range of occupational settings where experts' knowledge claims are advanced and contested. These include municipal and provincial courts, city council hearings, federal regulatory agencies, rural health clinics, urban medical schools, public schools, and university departments.

Moreover, the network's composition has changed over time. During the Stop the Sprayings campaign, physicians dominated the network. Since the advent of the biannual Conference of Socio-Environmental Health in 2011, academic faculty with teaching appointments at various universities have become more prominent. A network perspective on expert mobilization overcomes the tendency to center analysis within one or another organization or institutional setting or to focus on one pre-defined type of expertise, thereby missing the hybrid expertise that develops when networks straddle disciplinary, professional, and occupational fields (Hess and Frickel 2014).

Finally, our longitudinal study of Pueblos Fumigados highlights important but understudied impacts of expert mobilization. Networks that link community and environmental activists with academic, government, and clinical researchers and other professionals can alter the social structure of knowledge formations and can inspire epistemic innovation (Eyal 2013). Citizen-science alliances (Brown 2007) and agroecological practices (Sarandon and Marasas 2017) are good examples of new kinds of knowledge formations resulting from expertise flowing into and through communities. Expertise carried by such networks can also move "upstream" into professional communities found in medical and agronomic schools, law firms, health clinics, and university laboratories. In Argentina, for example, the sanitary camps have reshaped medical school curriculum at the National University of Rosario while dozens of legal challenges against pesticides are creating new bodies of environmental law and legal strategy. More, the cumulative mobilization of experts against pesticides has helped nurture new judiciary praxis crystalized in 72 court rulings (Cabaleiro 2020), as well as a rapidly growing body of home-grown research on the biological and health effects of pesticides (Sosa et al. 2019). A scientific field that was essentially non-existent in the country prior to 2001 is now generating nearly 90 published studies annually. We need more research that examines not just how experts impact social movements but, as Eyerman and Jamison (1991) reminded us three decades ago, how social movements make knowledge *and* knowledge makers.

Directions for future research

We conclude with five general suggestions for future research. Our suggestions broadly align with general themes of environmental movement research focused on resources, political opportunities, networks, and identities (Giugni and Grasso 2015) while pushing standard models of collective action to consider how epistemic communities mobilized into environmental movements change environmental politics in unique and unexpected ways. Our suggestions also underscore the importance of casting a wide net around efforts to capture empirical data on a research topic whose subjects are often difficult to identify and whose scale, heterogeneity, and dynamism remain poorly understood.

From the outset, future research on experts and social movements needs to deal with a definitional problem that underlies much of the extant research, including this chapter. The definitional problem arises from the fact that STS research on expertise has at least three dimensions, involving people, identities, and practices. In studying expert activism, what kinds of people should count as experts? What kinds of knowledge should count as expertise? What scientific or professional practices should qualify as activism? Answers to these questions do not easily converge around uniform concepts. For example, are the public statements of an academic biologist on behalf of an EMO an example of expert activism when the statements are not informed by her scientific training? One approach for resolving the problem is to develop *a priori* definitions and proceed accordingly with one's research. This approach will produce knowledge that may be over-determined by one's normative definitions and reproduce the categorical ambiguities that characterize recent debates about the fuzzy nature of expertise (e.g., Collins and Evans 2007).

Another, we think better, approach may be to treat the definitional problem(s) as a set of empirical questions and design research strategies aimed at capturing a wide variety of people, identities, and practices and then look for patterns across diverse samples of each. While this second approach may be more challenging to design and execute, it is also more likely to build a solid empirical foundation for future research. For example, rather than debating the question of "what counts" as expert activism, research might instead focus on what researchers, professionals, and others who work with SMOs actually do and what types of knowledge they produce and mobilize (Eyal et al. 2010). Because contentious politics is context dependent, the form and impact of expert environmental activism will likely vary depending on where it occurs – in street protests, at community meetings, at legislative hearings, in courtrooms or laboratories, at professional conferences, or in many other settings. Understanding the political value of *expert* activism requires not that researchers dilute the term with definitional ambiguity, but rather that we take in the full scope of experts' identities, roles, and actions.

Following from this point, we also need to attend more systematically to the political contexts of expert activism and the conditions under which it is more or less likely to occur. Where do expert activists come from, and how are they mobilized? It will be important to study the mobilization pools that contribute expert activists and the processes of expert recruitment, including attention to shifting opportunities and threats. For example, consider that the inaugural March for Science, held in April 2017 in Washington DC, attracted higher proportions of PhDs and MDs than other mass protests organized in response to the 2016 United States presidential election, yet by far most of those marching were not scientists or doctors (Fisher 2018; see also MacKendrick 2017). Consider also that the Trump administration proposed shockingly large budget cuts to federal agencies that fund and produce environmental and medical research, and yet, for the most part, actual reductions were not as deep as many initially feared, nor did the cuts impact research fields uniformly. Some fields, including aerospace, biomedicine, engineering, and materials science saw resources increase under Trump's "anti-science" policy agenda. Understanding how changing structures of political opportunity and threat encourage or impede expert activism can help social movements accurately target "mobilizable" segments of the scientific or professional communities and maximize potential for expert recruitment (see Frickel 2018; Frickel and Rea 2020).

We also need more research on how expert activism is organized across organizational fields. As our study of Argentina's pesticide conflict suggests, the organizational structure of expert activism bridges social movement, political, medical, legal, and scientific fields, raising important questions about the role of networks in mobilizing experts and in generating and circulating expert knowledge that emerges in response to movement demands. Network studies of environmental movements (see, e.g., the chapters by Mario Dani and Clare Saunders in this volume) illustrate the analytical power of a network perspective. To date, however, researchers have not used these same tools to study the structure and dynamics of expert networks as they intersect with environmental movements (although see Frickel et al. 2015 and Arancibia 2016) or the production of expertise through environmental movement networks, as Eyal and colleagues (2010) have shown in the case of autism research. Indeed, Eyal's (2013) thesis that expertise exists as a property of networks, one that may include the constellation of knowledge, practices, resources, and conceptual arrangements among all network contributors – professionals and laypersons alike – allows for the relational analysis of the diversity of social movement knowledge formations that we seek to highlight in our larger study (see also Arancibia and Motta 2019; Vessuri 2004). The network organization of expert activism represents an area of untapped research potential for scholars and of strategic potential for environmental movements.

We end by echoing the *Handbook* editor's call for international research on environmental social movements "worldwide" (Grasso and Giugni, this volume). In particular, we note the imperative need to study the mobilization of experts and expertise in diverse regions of the world. To date, most research on the relationships between environmental movements, experts, and expertise has been developed by European and North American scholars. This has given us a distorted view of expert activism and its extent, dynamics, and impacts around the world. A robust theory of expert activism in environmental conflicts will require empirical research that extends beyond the Global North. We need more research that focuses on societies where environmental mobilization can mount with greater intensity and assume very different organizational forms, as illustrated by the cascading conflicts brought on by intensive, industrial-scale mining, logging, agriculture, and dam construction in many parts of Asia, Africa, and South America. The industrial development model, dubbed *neo-extractivismo* in Latin America (Svampa 2015), is rampant and has created massive social and ecological disruption. These regions of the world are brimming with the very kinds of expert activism we think are important (Motta and Arancibia 2016). Middle- and lower-income countries are also where environmental movements may benefit most from social movement studies that generate knowledge about experts and expertise that is as diverse and valuable as the ecosystems and human cultures they seek to protect.

Notes

1 The link between social resistance and knowledge traces at least to Gramsci's (1971) theory of cultural counter-hegemony (especially the potential of the "good sense" developed in everyday life and the role of organic intellectuals) (Cox 2014). Today, an extensive literature documents the "cognitive praxis" (Eyerman and Jamison 1991) of a wide range of social movements from around the world (e.g., Choudry and Kapoor 2010; Schroering 2019). Related literatures, building from Latin American critical pedagogy, feminist theory, and critical race theory reframe cognitive praxis as "knowledge from below" (Harding 1995; Lucena et al. 2019) and social movements as carriers of new "epistemological reflexivities" (Lozano 2018; Mejías Sandia and Suárez 2017).

2 Indeed, the politics of experts and expertise reaches inside academic circles where the meaning and operationalization of these terms are contested, as we note in the concluding section.

3 The only national law in place regulates the management of empty pesticide containers (ARGENTINA, 2016). The authority to regulate pesticide use, application, and commercialization is decentralized and held by provincial and municipal governments (Paz Belada 2017).

4 Interview with GRR representative (Arancibia, Buenos Aires, 29 November 2011).

5 Neighborhood assemblies became especially visible in Argentina after the 2001–2002 socio-economic crisis in which conventional political representation was challenged and discredited as never before (Svampa 2009). A new model of political organizing, neighborhood assemblies broke with traditional vertical forms of political representation and promoted direct democracy based on open and horizontal relationships among activists, with no leaders or representatives.

6 GRR sent one copy to the National Ministry of Health and another to Argentina's president, each accompanied by a letter warning of the critical situation faced by rural and peri-urban communities and requesting urgent federal-level action. Neither letter elicited a public response.

7 At the time, Carrasco ran the molecular embryology lab at the National University of Buenos Aires and led the research department at the national Ministry of Defense.

8 The malformations were cranial, cerebral, intestinal, and cardiovascular.

9 The same study was published a year later in the international peer-reviewed journal *Chemical Research in Toxicology*: Paganelli A., Gnazzo V., Abosta H., López, SL., Carrasco, A. 2010. "Glyphosate-based herbicides produce teratogenic effects on vertebrates by impairing retinoic acid signaling". *Chemical Research in Toxicology* 23 (10): 1586–1595.

10 Other organizing groups were the Ecologic Forum of Paraná, a grassroots social organization, and Red por una América Latina Libre de Transgénicos (Network for a Latin America Free of GMO).
11 Article 4 of the National Environmental Law 25675 states, "The absence of conclusive scientific proof or information should not be used as a reason for postponing effective measures to prevent environmental degradation".

References

Allen, Barbara. 2003. *Uneasy Alchemy: Citizens and Experts in Louisiana's Chemical Corridor Disputes*. Cambridge, MA: MIT Press.

Arancibia, Florencia. 2013. Challenging the bioeconomy: The dynamics of collective action in Argentina. *Technology in Society* 35(2),72–92.

Arancibia, Florencia. 2015. The struggle to restrict pesticide use: The confluence of social movements and a network of expertise. PhD dissertation, Department of Sociology, State University of New York at Stony Brook.

Arancibia, Florencia. 2016. Rethinking activism and expertise within environmental health conflicts. *Sociology Compass* 10(6), 477–490.

Arancibia, Florencia, and Javier Albea. 2022. Los Congresos de Salud Socio Ambiental: construcción de redes y movilización de saberes, unpublished manuscript.

Arancibia, Florencia, and Renata Motta. 2019. Undone science and counter-expertise: Fighting for justice in an Argentine community contaminated by pesticides. *Science as Culture* 28(3), 1–26.

Aranda, Darío. 2009. El tóxico de los campos. *Pagina 12*, April 13.

Aranda, Darío. 2015. *Tierra Arrasada*. Buenos Aires: Sudamericana.

Bandarage, A. 2013. Political economy of epidemic kidney disease in Sri Lanka. *SAGE Open* 3(4), 1–13.

Bliss, Catherine. 2012. *Race Decoded: The Genomic Fight for Social Justice*. Palo Alto, CA: Stanford University Press.

Breyman, Steve, Nancy Campbell, Virginia Eubanks, and Abby Kinchy. 2017. STS and social movements: Pasts and futures. In U. Felt, R. Fouché, C.A. Miller, and L. Smith-Doerr, eds. *Handbook of Science and Technology Studies*. Cambridge, MA: MIT Press, 289–318.

Brown, Phil. 1992. Toxic waste contamination and popular epidemiology: Lay and professional ways of knowing. *Journal of Health and Social Behavior* 33, 267–281.

Brown, Phil. 2007. *Toxic Exposures: Contested Illnesses and the Environmental Health Movement*. New York: Columbia University Press.

Cabaleiro, Fernando. 2020. *Praxis Jurídica Sobre Los Agrotóxicos En La Argentina*. Tercera Ed. Ciudad Autónoma de Buenos Aires: Naturaleza de Derechos.

Cable, Sherry, Tamara Mix, and Donald Hastings. 2005. Mission impossible? Environmental justice activists' collaborations with professional environmentalists and with academics. In David N. Pellow and Robert J. Brulle, eds. *Power, Justice, and the Environment : A Critical Appraisal of the Environmental Justice Movement*. Cambridge, MA: MIT Press, 55–75.

Carrizo, Cecilia, and Mauricio Berger. 2009. *Estado Incivil y Ciudadanos Sin Estado: Paradojas Del Ejercicio de Derechos En Cuestiones Ambientales*. Cordoba: Narvaja Editor.

Choudry, Aziz, and Dip Kapoor. 2010. *Learning from the Ground Up*. New York: Palgrave Macmillan.

Clarke, Adele E. 1998. *Disciplining Reproduction: Modernity, American Life Sciences, and "the Problems of Sex"*. Berkeley and Los Angeles: University of California Press.

Collins, Harry, and Robert Evans. 2007. *Rethinking Expertise*. Chicago: University of Chicago Press.

Cox, Laurence. 2014. Movements making knowledge: A new wave of inspiration for sociology? *Sociology* 48(5), 954–971.

Delborne, Jason. 2008. Transgenes and transgressions: Scientific dissent as heterogeneous practice. *Social Studies of Science* 38(4), 509–541.

Delborne, Jason. 2016. Suppression and dissent in science. In T. Bretag, ed. *Handbook of Academic Integrity*. Singapore: Springer, 943–956.

Dillon Lindsey, Walker Dawn, Shapiro Nicholas, Underhill Vivian, Martenyi Megan, Wylie Sara, Lave Rebecca, Murphy Michelle, Brown Phil, and Environmental Data and Governance Initiative. 2017. Environmental data justice and the Trump Administration: Reflections from the environmental data and governance initiative. *Environmental Justice* 10(6), 186–192.

Epstein, Steven. 1996. *Impure Science: AIDS, Activism, and the Politics of Knowledge*. Berkley and Los Angeles: University of California Press.

Eyal, Gil. 2013. For a sociology of expertise: The social origins of the autism epidemic. *American Journal of Sociology* 118(4), 863–907.

Eyal, Gil, Brendan Hart, Emine Onculer, Neta Oren, and Natashia Rossi. 2010. *The Autism Matrix*. London: Polity Press.

Eyerman, Ron, and Andrew Jamison. 1991. *Social Movements: A Cognitive Approach*. University Part: Pennsylvania State University Press.

Feeney, Ingrid Elizabeth. 2019. Ciencia digna: The Latin American movement for a 'pueblo-centric' science. *Science for the People* 22(1), n.p.

Fisher, Dana R. 2018. Scientists in the resistance. *Sociological Forum* 33(1), 247–250.

Frickel, Scott. 2004. *Chemical Consequences: Environmental Mutagens, Scientist Activism, and the Rise of Genetic Toxicology*. New Brunswick: Rutgers University Press.

Frickel, Scott. 2018. Political scientists. *Sociological Forum* 33(1), 234–238.

Frickel, Scott, and Florencia Arancibia. 2021. Environmental Science and Technology Studies. In Beth Caniglia, Andrew Jorgenson, Stephanie Malin, and Lori Peek, and David Pellow, eds. *International Handbook of Environmental Sociology*. London: Routledge, in press.

Frickel, Scott, and Christopher Rea. 2020. Drought, hurricane, or wildfire? Assessing the Trump Administration's anti-science disaster. *Engaging Science, Technology and Society* 6, 66–75; DOI:10.17351/ests2020.297.

Frickel, Scott, Rebekah Torcasso, and Annika Anderson. 2015. The organization of expert activism: Shadow mobilization in two social movements. *Mobilization* 21(3), 305–323.

Giugni, Marco, and Maria T. Grasso. 2015. Environmental movements in advanced industrial democracies: Heterogeneity, transformation, and institutionalization. *Annual Review of Environmental Resources* 40, 337–361.

Gramsci, Antonio. 1971. *Selections from the Prison Notebooks of Antonio Gramsci*, edited by Q. Hoare and G. Nowell-Smith. New York: International Publishers.

Grasso, Maria T., and Marco Giugni. 2021. Environmental movements worldwide. This volume.

Harding, Sandra. 1995. 'Strong objectivity': A response to the new objectivity question. *Synthese* 104(3), 331–349.

Harrison, Jill Lindsey. 2011. *Pesticide Drift and the Pursuit of Environmental Justice*. Cambridge, MA: MIT Press.

Hayes, Samuel P. 1987. *Beauty, Health and Permanence: Environmental Politics in the United States, 1955–1985*. Cambridge: Cambridge University Press.

Hess, David J. 2016. *Undone Science: Social Movements, Mobilized Publics, and Industrial Transitions*. Cambridge, MA: MIT Press.

Hess, David J., and Scott Frickel. 2014. Introduction: Fields of knowledge and theory traditions in the sociology of science. *Political Power and Social Theory* 27(August), 1–30. Special issue on *Fields of Knowledge: Science, Politics, and Publics in the Neoliberal Age*, Scott Frickel and David J. Hess, guest editors.

Hoffman, Lily M. 1989. *The Politics of Knowledge: Activist Movements in Medicine and Planning*. Albany, NY: SUNY Press.

Jamison, Andrew. 2001. *The Making of Green Knowledge: Environmental Politics and Cultural Transformation*. London: Cambridge University Press.

Jamison, Andrew, Ron Eyerman, Jaqueline Cramer (with J. Laessoe). 1990. *The Making of the New Environmental Consciousness: A Comparative Study of the Environmental Movements in Sweden, Denmark, and The Netherlands*. Edinburgh: University of Edinburgh Press.

Jouzel, Jean Noël, and Giovanni Prete. 2014. Devenir victime des pesticides. Le recours au droit et ses effets sur la mobilisation des agriculteurs phyto-victimes. *Sociologie Du Travail* 56(4), 435–453.

Kinchy, A. J. 2006. On the borders of post-war ecology: Struggles over the Ecological Society of America's Preservation Committee, 1917–1946. *Science as Culture* 15(1), 23–44.

Kroll-Smith, Steve, Phil Brown, and Valerie J. Gunther. 2000. Knowledge, citizens and organizations: An overview of environments, diseases, and social conflict. In Steve Kroll-Smith, Phil Brown, and Valerie J. Gunther, eds. *Health and Illness: A Reader in Contested Medicine*. New York: New York University Press, 9–28.

Leguizamón, Amalia. 2014. Modifying Argentina: GM soy and socio-environmental change. *Geoforum* 53, 149–160.

Lozano, Arribas Alberto. 2018. Knowledge co-production with social movement networks. Redefining grassroots politics, rethinking research. *Social Movement Studies* 17(4), 451–463.

Lucena, Hadassa Monteiro de Albuquerque, João Carlos Pereira Caramelo, and Severino Bezerra da Silva. 2019. Popular education and youth: The social movement as an educational space. *Cadernos de Pesquisa* 49(174), 290–315.

MacKendrick, Norah. 2017. Out of the Labs and into the Streets: Scientists get political. *Sociological Forum* 32(4), 896–902.

Martin, Brian. 2007. *Justice Ignited: The Dynamics of Backfire.* New York: Rowman & Littlefield.

Martínez Alier, Juan. 2002. *The Environmentalism of the Poor: A Study of Ecological Conflicts and Valuation.* Cheltenham, UK: Edward Elgar.

McCormick, Sabrina. 2009. *Mobilizing Science: Movements, Participation and the Remaking of Knowledge.* Philadelphia: Temple University Press.

Mejias Sandia, Carlos, and Pablo Suarez. 2017. Configurando nuevos movimientos sociales Latinoamericanos en el esapcio de requesbrajamiento epistemico-colonial. *Reflexiones* 96(1), 97–108.

Montenegro, Raúl. 2002. *Ituzaingo, Plaguicidas En Suelo. Informe de Prensa. Cordoba.* Córdoba, Argentina.

Montenegro, Raúl. 2003. *Informe Sobre Los Posibles Contaminantes Que Habrían Provocado La Alta Morbi-Mortalidad Registrada En Barrio Ituzaingo Anexo. Establecimiento de Los Contaminantes Principales y de Sus Rutas.* Córdoba.

Moore, Kelly. 1996. Organizing integrity: American science and the creation of public interest organizations, 1955–1975. *American Journal of Sociology* 101, 1592–1627.

Moore, Kelly. 2008. *Disrupting Science: Social Movements, American Scientists, and the Politics of the Military, 1945–1975.* Princeton, NJ: Princeton University Press.

Motta, Renata, and Nadia Alasino. 2013. Medios y política en la Argentina: las disputas interpretativas sobre la soja transgénica y el glifosato. *Question* 1(38), 323–335.

Motta, Renata, and Florencia Arancibia. 2016. Health experts challenge the safety of pesticides in Argentina and Brazil. In J. M. Chamberlain, ed. *Medicine, Risk, Discourse and Power*, vol. 1. New York: Routledge, 179–206.

Nikol, Lisette J., and Kees Jansen. 2020. The politics of counter-expertise on aerial spraying: Social movements denouncing pesticide risk governance in the Philippines. *Journal of Contemporary Asia* 50(1), 99–124.

Ottinger, Gwen, Javiera Barandiaran, and Aya Kimura. 2017. Environmental justice: Knowledge, technology and expertise. In U. Felt, R. Fouche, C. Miller, and S.-D. Laurel, eds. *Handbook of Science and Technology Studies*, 4th ed. Cambridge, MA: MIT Press, 1029–1057.

Ottinger, Gwen, and Benjamin R. Cohen, eds. 2011. *Technoscience and Environmental Justice: Expert Cultures in a Grassroots Movement.* Cambridge, MA: MIT Press.

Paganelli, Alejandra, Victoria Gnazzo, Helena Acosta, Silvia L. López, and Andrés E. Carrasco. 2010. Glyphosate-based herbicides produce teratogenic effects on vertebrates by impairing retinoic acid signalling. *Chemical Research in Toxicology* 23(10), 1586–1595.

Paz Belada, Alejandro. 2017. *Regulación de Los Agroquímicos En La Argentina: Hacia Una Ley General de Presupuestos Mínimos Regulatorios.* Licenciatura thesis, Universidad de San Andrés. Victoria, Buenos Aires, Argentina.

Rulli, Jorge Eduardo. 2009. *Pueblos Fumigados: Los Efectos de Los Plaguicidas En Las Regiones Sojeras.* Buenos Aires, Argentina: Del nuevo extremo.

Sannazzaro, Jorgelina. 2014. Citizen cartography, strategies of resistance to established knowledge and collective forms of knowledge building. *Public Understanding of Science* 25(3), 346–360.

Sarandon, Santiago, and Mariana Edith Marasas. 2017. Brief history of agroecology in Argentina: Origins, evolution, and future prospects. *Agroecology and Sustainable Food Systems* 41(3–4), 238–255.

Schroering, Caitlin. 2019. Producción de resistencia y conocimiento: Movimientos sociales como productores de teoría y praxis. *Revista CS* (29), 73–102.

Shepard, P.M., M.E. Northridge, S. Prakash, and G. Stover. 2002. Preface: Advancing environmental justice through community-based participatory research. *Environmental Health Perspectives* 110(Supplement 2, April), 139–140.

Shostak, Sara. 2013. *Exposed Science: Genes, the Environment, and the Politics of Population Health.* Berkeley and Los Angeles: University of California Press.

Smith, Alice Kimball. 1965. *A Peril and a Hope: The Scientist's Movement in America, 1945–47.* Cambridge, MA: MIT Press.

Sosa, Beatriz, Exequiel Fontans-Álvarez, David Romero, Aline da Fonseca, and Marcel Achkar. 2019. Analysis of scientific production on glyphosate: An example of politicization of science. *Science of the Total Environment* 681, 541–550.

Svampa, Maristella. 2009. Protesta, movimientos sociales y dimensiones de la acción colectiva en América Latina. *Nomadas* (20), 112–126.

Svampa, Maristella. 2015. Commodities consensus: Neoextractivism and enclosure of the commons in Latin America. *South Atlantic Quarterly* 114(1), 65–82.

Teubal, Miguel. 2006. Expansión del modelo sojero en la Argentina: De la producción de alimentos a los commodities. *Realidad Económica* (220), 71–96.

Teubal, Miguel. 2008. Soja y agronegocios en la Argentina: La crisis del modelo. *Labvoratorio/n Line* (22), 5–7.

Verzeñassi, Damián, and Alejandro Vallini. 2019. *Transformaciones En Los Modos de Enfermar y Morir En La Región Agroindustrial.* Rosario.

Vessuri, Hebe. 2004. La hibridización del conocimiento. La tecnociencia y los conocimientos locales a la búsqueda del desarrollo sustentable. *Convergencia* 11(35), 171–191.

Wisnioski, Matthew. 2012. *Engineers for Change: Competing Visions of Technology in 1960s America.* Cambridge, MA: MIT Press.

Yearley, Steve. 1991. *The Green Case: A Sociology of Environmental Arguments, Issues and Politics.* New York: Harper Collins.

20

FROM ENVIRONMENTAL (MOVEMENT) ORGANIZATIONS TO THE ORGANIZING OF ENVIRONMENTAL COLLECTIVE ACTION

Mario Diani

Like most (possibly all) social movements, environmental movements are highly heterogenous and internally complex. They consist of multiple actors, linked to each other through various types of connections, defining their cause in different (sometimes very different) ways. They also consist of broad sets of actions, from those with a very local focus to others encompassing multiple localities across the globe, in which participate actors who may identify with the movement's goals to variable degrees. Several chapters in this *Handbook* provide ample illustrations of these features (for an overall assessment of the literature, see Giugni and Grasso, 2015).

This remark is, of course, far from original. From different angles, social movement theorists have long recognized that movements should not be treated as if they were specific coherent actors, let alone specific organizations (Melucci, 1996; Oliver, 1989; Tilly and Tarrow, 2007). The late Alberto Melucci (1996) was particularly vocal in pointing out that one cannot assume the existence of a movement from the presence of collective actions on a certain set of issues; to the contrary, how a multiplicity of diverse actors (individuals and organizations) come to display some degree of coordination and solidarity and to be recognized by outsiders (for all their differences) as an entity with some agentic capacity represents an important problem in its own right. Moreover, this is not a purely theoretical problem as it affects our ability to interpret contemporary conflicts, differentiating, for example, local NIMBY phenomena from larger-scale collective challenges.

This chapter attempts to elaborate on this intuition by making two logically connected points. First, it highlights the risk of jumping to conclusions about the existence of "environmental movements" from the existence of actors interested in environmental issues or of public events addressing those issues. Of course, you cannot have environmental movements without organizations interested in the environment or actions addressing it, but the opposite is far from granted. Collective action on environmental issues may actually be coordinated in a number of ways, not all reducible to a social movement dynamic. The concept of "mode of coordination" (Diani, 2015, 2012) captures this complexity of form. Some of these forms do not even require

 DOI: 10.4324/9780367855680-23

a central role for organizations; hence, the shift suggested in the title from "organization", conceived as a bounded, goal-oriented unit with some internal rules, to "organizing", i.e., the mechanisms through which agents coordinate their actions even in the absence of formal rules and boundaries (Ahrne and Brunsson, 2011). As we shall see, recent literature on environmental collective action provides several illustrations of this multiplicity of modes of coordination. They may be found, albeit with variable emphasis, within any environmental collective-action field – i.e., within any set of voluntary actors (individuals as well as organizations) interacting with a view to generating collective good (Diani, 2015, pp. 12–13).

Second, the chapter tries to go beyond the simple recognition of environmental movements' "diversity" by discussing, more precisely, *how* diversity and heterogeneity may shape interactions in specific settings: do ideological and cultural differences between environmental organizations (better: between organizations mobilizing on environmental issues) represent an obstacle to cooperation or not? Under what conditions do these become an obstacle? Likewise, do different issues constitute different clusters of collective action within larger fields of environmental organizations, or do they get merged into broader agendas?

How to address diversity: the aggregative approach

Analysts of environmental politics have long recognized the internal diversity of contemporary environmentalism (Dalton, 1994; Rudig, 1990). This holds regardless of whether they were looking at the individuals (individuals concerned about the environment, possibly willing to engage in activism), organizations (groups or associations promoting collective action on environmental issues), or the political process (public events addressing environmental issues through various combination of pressure and protest politics). However, most studies have followed what we could define as an "aggregative" approach: namely, "a reductionist view of social structure as the sum of the properties of its discrete components, be they individuals, organizations, or events" (Diani, 2015, p. 2).

At the individual level, studies drawing upon survey data have searched for the main characteristics of environmental activists and sympathizers, in terms of standard socio-demographic variables as well as cultural orientations, background of political experiences, or styles of participation. Some studies (Barkan, 2004; Park and Raridon, 2017) have focused on the latter, differentiating, for example, between active participants ("gladiators" involved in associational life and protest activities) and less committed ones ("spectators", only willing to give money and sign petitions). Other studies have looked at the factors that account for involvement in lifestyle activism as opposed to political activism (e.g., de Moor et al., 2017 on Belgium; Pichardo et al., 1998 on the USA) or at the differences and similarities between waves of environmental activism (see, e.g., Hayes et al., 2020 on Extinction Rebellion activists in the UK). Sometimes, the exercise has taken a broad, comparative look, exploring differences in individual profiles across countries (e.g., Mertig and Dunlap, 2001). According to a recent review, most works looking at individual data seem to focus on values or, when they look at organizations, on how membership in environmental groups facilitates commitment to larger causes (Giugni and Grasso, 2015). Whatever the specific research question, the focus of these studies is on the properties of individuals and their distribution and variation across time and/or territory. Sometimes this takes a descriptive twist (addressing questions such as "Are there more environmental activists in country A or B?"), other times a more explanatory one (e.g., "What traits encourage activists to adopt certain styles of action?"), but still, the properties of "the movement" can be reconducted to the properties of its activists or supporters.

Likewise, various studies have highlighted the heterogeneity of environmental organizations (Andrews et al., 2016; Andrews and Edwards, 2005; Brulle et al., 2007; Dalton, 1994). They have started by identifying organizations that matched the profile of an environmental group (usually because of their issue priorities or their claimed identity) and have proceeded to look at the distribution of their properties. The relative weight of specific organizational formats, action repertoires, or conceptions of environmentalism has enabled analysts to reach conclusions about the nature of environmental movements in specific contexts or at different points in time. Once again, a profile of "the movement" has been derived from the aggregation of the properties of the units (in this case, the organizations) that were associated with it (by analysts in the first place, but also by observers in general).

Finally, similar remarks apply to many studies that take public collective events as the fundamental unit of analysis for the exploration of movement dynamics. While protest event analysis has been designed with the aim of enabling the analysis of social movements as series of events developing over time (Koopmans, 2004), when looking at specific movements, emphasis has fallen on the distribution of the properties of the events associated with a specific issue. In the case of environmental movements, this has meant tracing the changing proportion over time of events of a confrontational rather than peaceful nature or the nature of the specific issues addressed. This has enabled, for example, mapping the evolution of environmentalism in Europe between the 1970s and the 1980s in relation to other "new social movements" of that period (Kriesi et al., 1995). From this perspective, all the protest events addressing environmental issues have been taken as illustrations of the environmental movement; the properties of the latter have been derived from the aggregation of the properties of the single events. More recently, a similar aggregative approach has been taken by analysts looking at the global distribution of conflicts over environmental justice issues, and the existence of global EJ movement has been assessed by looking at the properties of those events (Martinez-Alier et al., 2016; Temper et al., 2018).

All the studies mentioned so far are surely valuable. When analyzing collective processes, it is absolutely vital to get a clear picture of their constitutive elements, be they individuals, organizations, or events. However, by jumping to conclusions on the "environmental movement" on the basis of the properties of the individuals ready to act on environmental problems, of the organizations mobilizing on environmental issues, or of collective events on those very same issues, we risk missing another crucial component of collective action: namely, its being the result of the interdependence of multiple actors and events: hence, the need to look at the systems of relations that bind those elements in broader patterns. For example, while environmental activism may attract people with both moderate and radical orientations, the extent to which people with different profiles collaborate with each other rather than operating in fragmented niches, oblivious to each other, deeply affects the nature of the collective process. Likewise, the extent to which inter-organizational alliances are shaped by differences in agendas, cultural approaches, or preferences regarding repertoires of action tells a lot about the nature of a movement: organizational populations with similar characteristics may display very different relational patterns (Diani, 2015). As for events, we may well have a similar number of events on environmental issues in different localities, but they may take on very different meanings, depending on whether there are connections between them or not. In the latter case, an aggregation of not-in-my-backyard protests will hardly authorize us to speak of an environmental movement, which we might well do if the very same events were framed by their promoters as part of broader collective-action campaigns (Diani and Kousis, 2014).

While few of the authors cited so far would question the importance of exploring the interdependence between the elements of collective action, the development of a relational perspective beyond specific, limited case studies is hampered by methodological and practical difficulties. Conceptually, approaches to social movements have swung between two poles. Some have treated movements as unitary actors in the context of much broader analyses of social change (e.g., Arrighi et al., 1989). As for researchers oriented to more limited and context-dependent explorations, they may have found it easier and more intuitive to treat environmental movements (or movements in general) as sets of individuals, organizations, or events than to think of them as complex systems of interactions. The former approach certainly enables researchers to refer more easily to the environmental movement by associating it to specific activists, associations, or episodes (one can contact WWF, Friends of the Earth, or even Extinction Rebellion, but cannot contact "the environmental movement"). Moreover, our research tools are often geared toward collecting data on the properties of our single units of analysis rather than on their interdependence. Whether through questionnaires or interviews, information on the properties of individuals or organizations is easier to collect than information on their contacts and the relations in which they are involved (Robins, 2015, chap. 6). Likewise, while it is relatively easy to acquire information on the main features of public events (size, targets, goals, levels of confrontation, etc.) through available sources, especially the media (Hutter, 2014), it is much more difficult to gauge to what extent single events are connected in larger-scale campaigns (Diani et al., 2010; Diani and Kousis, 2014). Still, for all the difficulties, looking at environmental movements from a relational perspective is worth the effort. In this vein, the next sections offer some suggestions to that end.

Network forms of organizing: emergence and implications

Taking a relational perspective means first of all recognizing that collective action on environmental issues is by no means the preserve of actors with a distinct environmentalist profile. Often, social actors do mobilize on specific problems without identifying with environmentalism at large or even framing these as "environmental". For example, protests against the construction of new motorways may be driven by not-in-my-backyard, non-environmental concerns and be totally disconnected from larger environmental campaigns; conversely, actors with a clear environmental identity may also get engaged in actions with a different focus, e.g., human rights.

In order to capture the complexity of environmental collective action, it may be useful to refer to the concept of "field". An environmental field may be defined, with a slight adaptation of DiMaggio and Powell's (1983, p. 148) classic definition, as the set of actors – individuals and organizations – that "constitute a recognized area of institutional life". Actors are "recognized" when they are legitimated to act and speak on environmental issues, but also when they relate to each other in distinct ways. By engaging in a multiplicity of activities and events, actors build on previously existing ties and also create new connections. This contributes to the definition of the boundaries of the field.

One should note that by prioritizing relations over actors' features, the focus moves away from environmental "organizations" to the "organizing" (e.g., Ahrne and Brunsson, 2011) of environmental collective action. As argued extensively elsewhere (Diani, 2015), through their exchanges, individuals and organizations create complex webs that are not purely contingent or random. Instead, they generate structures that may be less stable than those of formal organizations and lack some of their formal properties (such as neat boundaries between members and sympathizers) yet nonetheless provide opportunities to coordinate and somehow monitor behavior. They correspond, in other words, to specific, network forms of organizing (Ahrne and Brunsson, 2011).

Network structures may also stretch to intersect different networks – i.e., to constitute "networks of networks" – addressing partially different issues. A recent study analyzed 436 advocacy organizations from 75 countries, variably involved in 10 transnational advocacy networks combining environmental with economic and other social concerns (Hervé, 2014). By being involved in more than one network, some organizations acted as brokers between densely connected sets of groups with a different focus, illustrating the ultimate connectedness of sectors of collective action operating at the transnational level. A particular role in that regard was played by different branches of Friends of the Earth (Hervé, 2014, p. 405; see also Doherty and Doyle, 2013).

Regardless of whether their focus is domestic or transnational, the emergence of environmental networks is far from straightforward. While social actors have been found to have a tendency to build connections with similar alters (McPherson et al., 2001), the basis for similarity may change substantially. Sometimes it consists of general approaches to environmental issues, like the conservation versus political ecology divide. Other times, organizations may engage more with groups with a similar profile in terms of formalization and resources. Whatever the basis for homophily, it's difficult to find a balance between the tendency to form tightly knit, homogeneous clusters and the need to develop some commonality between heterogeneous organizations (Di Gregorio, 2012; Diani, 1995; Levkoe, 2014; Levkoe and Wakefield, 2014). Attempts to constitute extensive and cohesive environmental networks may be particularly difficult in countries where other political cleavages are very salient, at times even violently so: for example, the nationalist cleavage in the Basque country until the early 2010s (Ciordia Morandeira, 2020). Similarly difficult is negotiating the tensions between the accounts of movement networks as horizontal, equalitarian modes of coordination and their persistent tendency to reproduce hierarchical patterns of relations (Diani, 2003; Luxton and Sbicca, 2020).

It's important to recognize the importance of dynamic changes in network composition and configuration. In terms of organizational models, a reduction in the levels of activism promoted by national organizations does not necessarily result in the demise of collective action in general. For example, having emerged in the 1960s to oppose large-scale development projects, the New Zealand environmental movement enjoyed relative success in the 1970s and 1980s, which led to institutionalization and a decline in its contentiousness. However, this seems to have been compensated for by the growth of local, community-based initiatives, focused on issues more closely connected to local quality-of-life issues (O'Brien, 2013). In terms of network structures, some analysts have suggested that the best balance between the strength of ties one organization is involved in and the amount of diversity of their contacts might vary at different phases of the policy process: weak ties might prevail in the early and late phases of an issue cycle (coupled respectively with high and low diversity of relationships) while stronger ties might be more effective when an issue is most salient yet with a trend toward diminishing network diversity (Sommerfeldt and Yang, 2017).

Network configurations may affect in significant ways the dominant traits of environmental collective action and its outcomes. An analysis of transnational climate change NGOs working in the European Union, focused on the years 2008 and 2009, found that organizations' positions within larger networks and their exposure to their peers' influence accounted for their tactical choices better that traditional accounts based on organizational characteristics (Hadden and Jasny, 2019). Network influences have also been detected in relation to the outcomes of mobilizations. For example, a large scale analysis of conflicts over mining, drawing upon data from the *Environmental Justice Atlas* (https://ejatlas.org/) suggested that perceptions of success for environmental justice campaigns increased when 1) local mobilizations were promoted by large, dense coalitions, and 2) local organizers also enjoyed connections to civil society organizations

(COS) operating on a larger scale in a core-periphery dynamic. Moreover, COS also acted as connectors between different local campaigns through their multiple involvements (Aydin et al., 2017). Along similar lines, a study of the anti-fracking Global Frackdown network showed how some local groups with a global outlook may play a key role in connecting major transnational NGOs, operating in a broker capacity, with the smallest groups with a strictly local focus (Hopke, 2016). This study well illustrates how informal networks, based on mobile arrangements, may represent an alternative to formal organizing as reflected in traditional NGOs. Extensive informal alliances and the resulting networks may actually represent a way for grassroots, activist groups to avoid cooptation and fragmentation of the protest sector (Sumner and Wever, 2015).

Analyzing network structures

Despite recurrent claims to the contrary (Bourdieu, 1992, p. 199; Fligstein and McAdam, 2012), social network analysis (henceforth, SNA) has repeatedly contributed to the analysis of fields in a number of settings (Crossley, 2015; Diani, 2015; Osa, 2003). Environmental organizational fields are no exception to this trend, having been analyzed in reference to both online and offline connections (Ackland and O'Neil, 2011; Ansell, 2003; Di Gregorio, 2012; Diani, 1995; Saunders, 2013), occasionally in creative dialogue with post-modern theory (Sun et al., 2017). It is also possible, however, to bring individuals into the picture and explore the network patterns that connect environmental activists and sympathizers to each other. Their contribution to the organizing of environmental collective action will be explored in a specific section later in this chapter. First, we first turn to looking at inter-organizational networks.

Organizations in fields: boundaries and resource exchanges as basic mechanisms

One key issue in the analysis of fields is the definition of their boundaries. Similarly to other cases, the boundaries of environmental fields do not usually overlap with those of environmental movements. Even if we restrict ourselves to voluntary collective action, ruling out for-profit organizations and public agencies with a stake in environmental policy, we still face a variety of actors interested in environmental problems and promoting environment-related initiatives and campaigns. Some researchers have drawn the boundary between "field" and "movement" by including within movements only actors that display certain characteristics: in particular, promoters of extra-institutional action (e.g., Doherty, 2002). Others have taken a more inclusive path. Looking at British local environmentalism, Saunders (2013) has questioned the opportunity to differentiate neatly between interest or pressure groups and social movement organizations (SMOs), suggesting that both might play a role in environmental activism and campaigns. (See Hadden, 2015, p. 180 for a similar point in relation to climate change activism.) Saunders has also pointed to the role of residents' associations. They may not be perceived as primarily environmental by virtue of their profile, but they are still very much involved in local environmental networks (Saunders, 2013, p. 40). Although Saunders (2013, pp. 28–29) prefers to speak of environmental networks rather than movements, her approach is consistent with the one proposed here (see also Diani, 1995), in that what defines "membership" in a network/movement are not the actors' traits but their involvement in specific joint actions. For example, while animal rights groups seem (at least, seemed) to operate largely outside environmental networks in the UK, they were found to be much more integrated in the movement in other countries, including Italy (Diani, 1995).

While the boundaries of a field are difficult to conceive in the absence of specific inter-actions, the question remains whether such interactions are sufficient to define a distinctive movement. One could argue that sustained interactions between different groups do not indicate automatically an environmental movement dynamic in the absence of a specific movement identity: if, in other words, actors do not share a representation of themselves as part of a collective entity that transcends the boundaries of any single group and binds them together (albeit with variable intensity) as part of a larger collective subject (the "move-ment"). In the absence of that, one might be more properly witnessing instances of coali-tional collective action, primarily driven by pragmatic, instrumental goals. For example, a study of the environmental field in Milan in the mid-1980s showed that some organizations cooperated on a regular basis yet without sharing any environmental identity (Diani, 2012, p. 120). The development of identities, bringing together actors with different backgrounds and perspectives, has also been explored in relation to online dynamics. For example, Ack-land and O'Neil (2011) looked at the websites of 161 environmental organizations across the globe and explored the network mechanisms of reciprocity and transitivity binding them together.

At the same time, the very use of the concept of identity in relation to broad organizational populations has been questioned. Saunders (2013, chap. 7) in particular has argued that one should speak of identity in relation to clearly identifiable groups or organizations rather than larger and more vague sets of actors. This position is explicitly critical of Diani's (1992, p. 8) view of movements as "networks of informal interactions between a plurality of individuals, groups and/or organizations, engaged in political or cultural conflicts, on the basis of shared collective identities". Whatever our position on this particular issue, we have to recognize that even organizations that work together on shared goals and are conventionally represented in public discourse as a "movement" may be deeply divided on the basis of ideological or cultural principles. At times the depth of divisions may fragment networks in such a way as to render it difficult to speak of "environmental movements" as a relatively cohesive sector. Rather than on actors' immutable traits, levels of fragmentation between environmental groups seem to be sub-ject to change, with the evolution of political opportunities playing a major role in that regard. Looking at Milanese environmentalism in the 1980s, Diani (1995), for example, showed the relative integration of conservation and political ecology organizations in the 1980s, con-trasting this with the divisions of the 1970s, a political phase in which the left-right cleavage was still salient. He suggested that the opening of political opportunities for environmental activism, brought about by the crisis of class-based interpretations of politics, also facilitated greater dialogue between different currents of environmentalism. Other analyses, however, suggested otherwise. Looking at the mobilizations around the Copenhagen climate change summit of 2009, Hadden (2015) showed that climate change activism revolved around the precarious relation between more technical-oriented environmental NGOs and more radical groups focusing on climate justice as a slogan. In particular, she argued that the expansion of political opportunities changed the population of the organizations that mobilized on climate change, attracting

> a more diverse group of organizations – representing environmental NGOs, devel-opment NGOs, global justice organizations, and radical social movements. . . . This resulted in a divided network with two main components, rarely engaging in shared action: groups engaging in conventional climate advocacy and those adopting a con-tentious climate justice approach.
>
> (Hadden, 2015, p. 10)

The criteria defining the boundaries of a field, as well as of its internal components, also affect the nature and the probability of ties between different actors. While exchanges of resources may on occasion be driven by purely instrumental considerations, shared issue priorities are rarely the only drive behind alliance building. Most of the time, interests combine with cultural orientations in affecting alliance building. Exploring the link between religion and environmentalism in the US, Ellingson and co-authors (2012, p. 276) discovered that the core positions in a network of 83 organizations were occupied by interfaith or ecumenical organizations, while Buddhist and eco-spirituality groups were entirely disconnected from the rest of the field. Looking at Indonesian forest activist organizations, Di Gregorio (2012) also illustrated the complex relation between values and ties. While organizations holding similar versions of environmentalism were more likely to exchange, it was also possible to identify "discourse coalitions" that brought together actors with different values, yet who were compatible enough to support sustained cooperation. Di Gregorio's (2012) work highlights the importance of framing activities that create bridges between organizations with different approaches and value stances. This role is often taken up by members of the elites, who build on their personal prestige and technical competences to connect groups across traditional political divides. This was the case, for instance, of scientists in the early phases of the emergence of the Italian environmental movement back in the 1970s (Diani, 1995) as well as, more recently, in the case of citizens' actions on solid waste management in Tunisia (Loschi, 2019). By drawing upon personal resources, influential individuals managed to forge collective identities that somehow cut across previous social and political cleavages (Loschi, 2019, p. 108). Bridging work has been particularly important in facilitating connections between fields that have traditionally struggled to engage in mutual collaboration, such as environmentalism and labor. Exploring a rare instance of such a link, the Wisconsin Labor-Environmental Network (WLEN), active throughout the 1980s and early 1990s, Obach (1999, p. 47), showed how cooperation between those sectors may be driven by different principles: sometimes instrumental, other times oriented to negotiated compromise between actors holding divergent views, but also at times implying "a heightened sensitivity to one another's concern".

Identity markers and issue priorities may combine differently in shaping the structure of exchanges within civil society. They may, in particular, define specific sectors in which social movement dynamics are more significantly at play. In order to illustrate this logic of analysis, let's refer to data collected among civic organizations in Bristol, UK, in the early 2000s. Out of 134 organizations interviewed, 88 (54%) claimed to be interested in at least two out of a list of eleven environmental issues, identified through factor analysis (Diani, 2015, pp. 41–42). At the same time, only 43 organizations (32%) identified as environmental, of which three were actually single-issue, very specific ones. All in all we got a quite complex picture, with 32 organizations (24%) showing a non-occasional interest in the environment but holding other primary identities (Table 20,1).

Figure 20.1 portrays the field consisting of all organizations interested in at least two environmental issues. The size of nodes is proportional to the range of issues addressed. White circles indicate organizations with no environmental identity; black triangles are environmental movement organizations. As the size of the nodes suggests, several non-environmental organizations share an interest in several issues; however, their position in that sector of the civil society network is either isolated or largely peripheral in relation to a core that consists instead of groups with an environmental identity. Data suggest that a mere interest in environmental issues is much less salient in terms of alliance patterns than holding an environmental identity. This is illustrated by data about the distribution of cooperative ties between organizations that differed in terms of their interest in environmental issues (Table 20.2) and in terms of holding

Table 20.1 Environmental identity and interest in environmental issues

	No environmental identity	Environmental identity	Total
No interest in environmental issues	59	3	62
	65%	7%	46%
Interest in environmental issues	32	40	72
	35%	93%	54%
	91	43	134
	100%	100%	100%
Pearson chi2(2) = 39.32; Pr = 0.000			

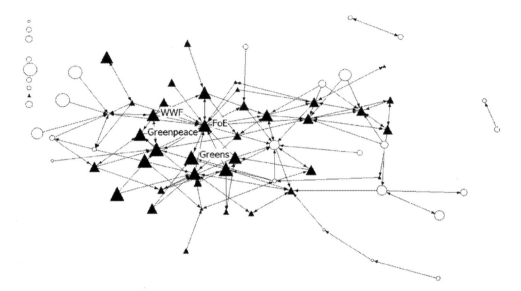

Figure 20.1   Bristol organizations with interest in environmental issues – all ties

Legend: black triangles (environmental identity); white circles (no environmental identity); size of nodes proportional to level of interest
Source: Figure created by the author

or not holding an environmental identity (Table 20.3). Whatever the criterion to define them, organizations close to the environmental perspective were more likely to exchange among themselves than with other organizations. However, the odds were much higher in the case of environmental identity, suggesting the presence of a distinctive field not kept together purely by convergent specific agendas.

We find the same general pattern, yet more pronounced, if we focus on multiplex ties. The role of multiplex ties, combining resources and symbolic exchanges, for our understanding of the structure of social movements has been repeatedly emphasized in several contexts. Some have focused on the online networks connecting organizations through their hyperlinks (Simpson, 2015), others

Table 20.2 Salience of interest in multiple environmental issues 262 ties; ratio observed/expected in brackets

	No interest	Interest
No interest in environmental issues	60 (1.08)	33 (0.50)
Interest in environmental issues	35 (0.53)	134 (1.78)

Odds ratio = 6.9
Significance = 0.000100

Table 20.3 Salience of environmental identity I 262 ties; ratio observed/expected in brackets

	No identity	Identity
No environmental identity	131 (1.09)	27 (0.47)
Environmental identity	18 (0.31)	86 (3.24)

Odds ratio = 34.772 (23.2)
Significance = 0.00010

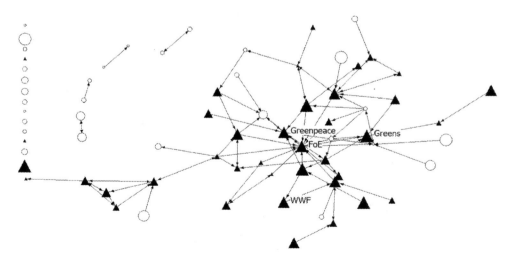

Figure 20.2 Bristol organizations with no occasional interest in environmental issues – multiplex ties

Legend: black triangles (environmental identity); white circles (no environmental identity); size of nodes proportional to level of interest
Source: Figure created by the author

Table 20.4 Salience of environmental interests Multiplex ties; 164 ties; ratio observed/expected in brackets

	No interest	*Interest*
No interest in environmental issues	35	14
	(1.01)	(0.34)
Interest in environmental issues	17	98
	(0.41)	(2.08)
Odds ratio = 11.869 (14.411)		
Significance = 0.00010000		

Table 20.5 Salience of environmental identity II Multiplex ties; 164 ties; ratio observed/expected in brackets

	No identity	*Identity*
No environmental identity	70	17
	(0.93)	(0.47)
Environmental identity	8	69
	(0.22)	(4.15)
Odds ratio = 75.469 (35.514)		
Significance = 0.00010		

on offline networks (Diani, 2015). Diani (2015) in particular has shown multiplex ties to provide the relational foundation to a specific "mode of coordination", peculiar to social movements. In the case of Bristol civil society, while the overall pattern is confirmed, the network based on multiplex ties shows a higher level of fragmentation, with a higher number of both isolates and small, dyadic components. (Check the left side of figure 20.2). As in the previous network, most organizations in these positions do not hold an environmental identity. However, the focus on the strongest ties reinforces the structuring power of identity. Looking at the distribution of the multiplex alliance ties also confirms the salience of both interests (Table 20.4) and identities (Table 20.5) in the multiplex network, yet with even stronger odds for homophily than in the previous situation. It is worth noting that this finding – namely, that both interests and identities shape the structure of fields, with identities playing the stronger role – is not a general rule; in fact, a comparison across British cities found identification with minority groups to shape organizational networks much less significantly than environmental identity (Diani and Pilati, 2011).

Individuals in civil society: linking associational types, frames, and practices

The relationship between concerned individuals and environmental organizations has been analyzed from a variety of perspectives. The most popular one has probably been the one emphasizing the role of pre-existing social networks in encouraging individuals to take action on environmental issues. Consistently with broader findings in social movement studies, several analysts of participation in environmental movements have commented on the network-action link, most notably David B. Tindall and his associates (Tindall, 2002, 2004, 2015; Tindall and Robinson, 2017). In contrast, there is far more limited attention to the role that individuals play in creating connections between organizations, thus contributing to the consolidation of environmental networks and/or the embeddedness of environmentalism in broader civil society networks. Here, the focus is on the action-networks link, meaning that, by being engaged in multiple organizations and/or communities of concerned people, environmental activists also create new networks or reinforce existing ones.

We can use this approach to explore the broader context in which environmental organizations are located by looking at the involvement of their members in other associations, as measured in standard survey data. A seminal exploration of this approach used data from the US General Social Survey to map the shifting position of US unions in relation to other organizations (Cornwell and Harrison, 2004). Following the same logic, and relying on European Value Survey data, Knoke et al. (2021, chap. 5) have shown that in Italy, in both 1990 and 2008, environmental groups' members have consistently held stronger connections to cultural and leisure time associations than to parties or other political groups. In contrast, in Germany in 1990, members of environmental groups had been more significantly active also in movement organizations on peace and human rights issues, moving later, as the 2008 data show, to more widespread joint memberships, without any link emerging as particularly strong. A more sophisticated approach, using survey data collected among participants in demonstrations rather than the general population, might explore the extent to which members of environmental associations are also involved in protest communities (i.e., sets of people regularly participating in local or national protest activities), thus creating connections between different social and political milieus. (See, for example, Diani, 2009, albeit with a focus on peace rather than environmental activism.)

Individuals play a broad role in environmental networks: concerned activists with a specific expertise may play a significant role in starting public debates and campaigns over controversial issues, steering collective action in specific directions, and engaging with "official" experts in a variety of ways (Bocking, 2004; Fischer, 2000). They also set up connections between voluntary organizations operating in civil society and other types of organizations interested in shaping environmental policy, whether as public agencies, interest groups, think tanks, etc. For example, some studies have used information on joint memberships to draw the boundaries of the environmental field. Hoffman and Bertels (2007) looked at 422 individuals who served on the boards of 54 major NGOs as well as in those of corporations or foundations between 2000 and 2005 (roughly 30% of the NGO board member sample). They identified different equivalent positions that they called portals, coordinators, members, and satellites. The last role was played by either purists (marginal by ideological choice) or fringe players (marginal by circumstances). Each position tended to correspond to specific identity mechanisms and specific styles of work, more or less confrontational/institutional (Bertels et al., 2014). Other studies have explored the role that individuals, occupying specific positions in public or private organizations, may play among members of associations in shaping the structure of alliances in specific conflicts. (See, e.g., Falcone et al., 2020 on actors involved in waste incineration issues in Campania, Italy.)

Conclusions

The core argument of this chapter may be summarized as follows. First, understanding environmental movements is not tantamount to assembling together all individuals claiming an interest in the state of the planet or all organizations promoting collective action on environmental issues or all the public events addressing local or global environmental crises. To the contrary, the nature of environmental movements is best captured by exploring the interactions and interdependencies between those elements. Second, the concept of field provides a useful framework to recognize the multiplicity of actors – individuals and organizations – engaged in environmental issues and bring them together without collapsing them under the indiscriminate and generic category of "movement". Finally, while valuable insights can be achieved through a range of research approaches, social network analysis may offer a distinctive contribution to explore the web of connections that make up environmental fields. The last section of this chapter has provided some illustration of how this can happen.

In future years, the study of network forms of organization in the environmental field would certainly profit from a refinement of its methodological tools as well as from the broadening of its territorial focus. On the methodological front, the growing attention to the study of multimodal networks (for an introduction: Knoke et al., 2021) should enable us to better analyze network patterns that consist of nodes of a various nature. Early studies tended to concentrate either on organizations, with a focus on alliance building (e.g., Ansell, 2003), or on interpersonal networks of activists, with a focus on recruitment processes (e.g., Tindall, 2002). Over time, increasing attention has been paid to the intersection of individuals and organizations (e.g., Diani, 2015); this should be expanded to also include non-agentic elements such as events or symbols. Whether of a protest or a less confrontational, civic nature, public events may be regarded as constitutive elements of environmental fields: they often represent the occasion through which groups and individuals, otherwise disconnected, may meet and find some common ground; conversely, looking at the multiple involvements of actors in events may enable us to identify more precisely the structure of environmental campaigns. Likewise, symbols play a significant role in movement networks: recognizing some symbols or messages as meaningful may create bonds even among actors that may not be interacting on a regular basis. Conversely, exploring the extent to which actors share some symbols may enable us to better explore the structure of environmental discourses (see also Diani and Kousis, 2014; Ingram et al., 2014).

In substantive terms, greater attention should be paid to the exploration of environmental networks in countries with unstable or non-existent democratic traditions. For example, environmental collective action in Eastern European countries attracted considerable attention, especially in the aftermath of the collapse of communism (Cisar, 2010; e.g., Pickvance, 1998). However, China probably represents the most interesting case in point due to the scale of its recent, spectacular economic growth as well as its massive environmental costs. Which has prompted the question, How does opposition to environmentally damaging projects develop under authoritarian regimes? While the presence of frequent and powerful political challenges at the strictly local level has long been documented (e.g., O'Brien, 2006), such protests extending beyond that level was usually deemed unlikely. Some recent studies, however, suggest the existence of forms of "networked contention" on environmental issues, with an intermediate structure between purely local action and full-blown, large-scale social movement dynamics (e.g., Bondes, 2019). More attention should also be paid to the interdependence of Indigenous and transnational actors. Looking at actors that do not have an explicitly contentious profile, such as most Northern NGOs, Yang (2013) found, for example, that their ability to attract local media coverage depended heavily on the quality of their connections to Indigenous NGOs. At the same time, the importance of the Chinese case should not divert analysts' attention away from other cases in which environmental threats are pursued in unsettled democracies like Bolsonaro's Brazil (de Area Leão Pereira et al., 2019; Ferrante and Fearnside, 2019) or even in supposedly established democracies when undermined by populist leaders such as Donald Trump (Bomberg, 2017).

References

Ackland, R., O'Neil, M., 2011. Online Collective Identity: The Case of the Environmental Movement. *Social Networks* 33, 177–190. https://doi.org/10.1016/j.socnet.2011.03.001

Ahrne, G., Brunsson, N., 2011. Organization Outside Organizations: The Significance of Partial Organization. *Organization* 18, 83–104. https://doi.org/10.1177/1350508410376256

Andrews, K.T., Edwards, B., 2005. The Organizational Structure of Local Environmentalism. *Mobilization* 10, 213–234.

Andrews, K.T., Edwards, B., Al-Turk, A., Hunter, A.K., 2016. Sampling Social Movement Organizations. *Mobilization: An International Quarterly* 21, 231–246. https://doi.org/10.17813/1086-671X-21-2-231

Ansell, C., 2003. Community Embeddedness and Collaborative Governance in the San Francisco Bay Area Environmental Movement, in: Diani, M., McAdam, D. (Eds.), *Social Movements and Networks*. Oxford University Press, Oxford, pp. 123–144.

Arrighi, G., Hopkins, T.K., Wallerstein, I., 1989. *Antisystemic Movements*. Verso, London.

Aydin, C.I., Ozkaynak, B., Rodríguez-Labajos, B., Yenilmez, T., 2017. Network Effects in Environmental Justice Struggles: An Investigation of Conflicts between Mining Companies and Civil Society Organizations from a Network Perspective. *PLoS ONE* 12. https://doi.org/10.1371/journal.pone.0180494

Barkan, S.E., 2004. Explaining Public Support for the Environmental Movement: A Civic Voluntarism Model. *Social Science Quarterly (Wiley-Blackwell)* 85, 913–937. https://doi.org/10.1111/j.0038-4941.2004.00251.x

Bertels, S., Hoffman, A.J., DeJordy, R., 2014. The Varied Work of Challenger Movements: Identifying Challenger Roles in the US Environmental Movement. *Organization Studies* 35, 1171–1210. https://doi.org/10.1177/0170840613517601

Bocking, S., 2004. *Nature's Experts: Science, Politics, and the Environment*. Rutgers University Press, New Brunswick, NJ.

Bomberg, E., 2017. Environmental Politics in the Trump Era: An Early Assessment. *null* 26, 956–963. https://doi.org/10.1080/09644016.2017.1332543

Bondes, M., 2019. *Chinese Environmental Contention: Linking Up against Waste Incineration*. Amsterdam University Press, Amsterdam.

Bourdieu, P., 1992. *An Invitation to Reflexive Sociology*. Polity Press, Cambridge.

Brulle, R., Turner, L., Carmichael, J., Jenkins, J., 2007. Measuring Social Movement Organization Populations: A Comprehensive Census of U.S. *Environmental Movement Organizations. Mobilization: An International Quarterly* 12, 255–270. https://doi.org/10.17813/maiq.12.3.j08421508773764m

Ciordia Morandeira, A., 2020. *Less Divided after ETA? Green Networks in the Basque Country between 2007 and 2017* (PhD Dissertation). Department of Sociology & Social Research, University of Trento, Trento.

Cisar, O., 2010. Externally Sponsored Contention: The Channelling of Environmental Movement Organisations in the Czech Republic after the Fall of Communism. *Environmental Politics* 19, 736–755. https://doi.org/10.1080/09644016.2010.508305

Cornwell, B., Harrison, J.A., 2004. Union Members and Voluntary Associations: Membership Overlap as a Case of Organizational Embeddedness. *American Sociological Review* 69, 862–881.

Crossley, N., 2015. *Networks of Sound, Style and Subversion. The Punk and Post – punk Worlds of Manchester, London, Liverpool and Sheffield, 1975–80*. Manchester University Press, Manchester.

Dalton, R., 1994. *The Green Rainbow: Environmental Groups in Western Europe*. Yale University Press, New Haven, CT.

de Area Leão Pereira, E.J., Silveira Ferreira, P.J., de Santana Ribeiro, L.C., Sabadini Carvalho, T., de Barros Pereira, H.B., 2019. Policy in Brazil (2016–2019) Threaten Conservation of the Amazon Rainforest. *Environmental Science & Policy* 100, 8–12. https://doi.org/10.1016/j.envsci.2019.06.001

de Moor, J., Marien, S., Hooghe, M., 2017. Why Only Some Lifestyle Activists Avoid State-Oriented Politics: A Case Study in the Belgian Environmental Movement. *Mobilization: An International Quarterly* 22, 245–264. https://doi.org/10.17813/10860-671X-22-2-245

Diani, M., 1992. The Concept of Social Movement. *Sociological Review* 40, 1–25.

Diani, M., 1995. *Green Networks. A Structural Analysis of the Italian Environmental Movement*. Edinburgh University Press, Edinburgh.

Diani, M., 2003. Leaders or Brokers? in: Diani, M., McAdam, D. (Eds.), *Social Movements and Networks*. Oxford University Press, Oxford/New York, pp. 105–122.

Diani, M., 2009. The Structural Bases of Protest Events. Multiple Memberships and Networks in the February 15th 2003 Anti-war Demonstrations. *Acta Sociologica* 52, 63–83.

Diani, M., 2012. Modes of Coordination of Collective Action: What Actors in Policy Making? in: Scotti, M., Vedres, B. (Eds.), *Networks in Social Policy Problems*. Cambridge University Press, Cambridge/New York, pp. 101–123.

Diani, M., 2015. *The Cement of Civil Society: Studying Networks in Localities*. Cambridge University Press, Cambridge/New York.

Diani, M., Kousis, M., 2014. The Duality of Claims and Events: The Greek Campaign Against the Troika's Memoranda and Austerity, 2010–2012. *Mobilization* 19, 387–404.

Diani, M., Lindsay, I., Purdue, D., 2010. Sustained Interactions, in: Van Dyke, N., McCammon, H. (Eds.), *Strategic Alliances: New Studies of Social Movement Coalitions*. University of Minnesota Press, Minneapolis, MN, pp. 219–238.

Diani, M., Pilati, K., 2011. Interests, Identities, and Relations: Drawing Boundaries in Civic Organizational Fields. *Mobilization* 16, 265–282.

Di Gregorio, M., 2012. Networking in Environmental Movement Organisation Coalitions: Interest, Values or Discourse? *Environmental Politics* 21, 1–25. https://doi.org/10.1080/09644016.2011.643366

DiMaggio, P., Powell, W.W., 1983. The Iron Cage Revisited: Institutional Isomorphism and Collective Rationality in Organizational Fields. *American Sociological Review* 48, 147–160.

Doherty, B., 2002. *Ideas and Actions in the Green Movement*. Routledge, London.

Doherty, B., Doyle, T., 2013. *Environmentalism, Resistance and Solidarity: The Politics of Friends of the Earth International*. Palgrave Macmillan, London. https://doi.org/10.1057/9781137316714_1

Ellingson, S., Woodley, V.A., Paik, A., 2012. The Structure of Religious Environmentalism: Movement Organizations, Interorganizational Networks, and Collective Action. *Journal for the Scientific Study of Religion* 51(2), 266–285. https://doi.org/10.1111/j.1468-5906.2012.01639.x

Falcone, P.M., D'Alisa, G., Germani, A.R., Morone, P., 2020. When all Seemed Lost. A Social Network Analysis of the Waste-related Environmental Movement in Campania, Italy. *Political Geography* 77, 102114. https://doi.org/10.1016/j.polgeo.2019.102114

Ferrante, L., Fearnside, P.M., 2019. Brazil's New President and 'Ruralists' Threaten Amazonia's Environment, Traditional Peoples and the Global Climate. *Environmental Conservation* 46, 261–263. https://doi.org/10.1017/S0376892919000213

Fischer, F., 2000. *Citizens, Experts, and the Environment: The Politics of Local Knowledge*. Duke University Press, Durham, NC/London.

Fligstein, N., McAdam, D., 2012. *A Theory of Fields*. Oxford University Press, Oxford/New York.

Giugni, M., Grasso, M.T., 2015. Environmental Movements in Advanced Industrial Democracies: Heterogeneity, Transformation, and Institutionalization. *Annual Review of Environment and Resources* 40, 337–361. https://doi.org/10.1146/annurev-environ-102014-021327

Hadden, J., 2015. *Networks in Contention. The Divisive Politics of Climate Change*. Cambridge University Press, New York/Cambridge.

Hadden, J., Jasny, L., 2019. The Power of Peers: How Transnational Advocacy Networks Shape NGO Strategies on Climate Change. *British Journal of Political Science* 49, 637–659. https://doi.org/10.1017/S0007123416000582

Hayes, G., Doherty, B., Saunders, C., 2020. A New Climate Movement? Extinction Rebellion's Activists in Profile [WWW Document]. http://publications.aston.ac.uk/id/eprint/41725/ (accessed 10.3.20).

Hervé, A., 2014. Roles of Brokerage Networks in Transnational Advocacy Networks. *Environmental Politics* 23, 395–416. https://doi.org/10.1080/09644016.2013.867163

Hoffman, A.J., Bertels, S., 2007. Organizational Sets, Populations and Fields: Evolving Board Interlocks and Environmental NGOs. *SSRN Journal*. https://doi.org/10.2139/ssrn.982886

Hopke, J.E., 2016. Translocal Anti-fracking Activism: An Exploration of Network Structure and Tie Content. *Environmental Communication* 10, 380–394. https://doi.org/10.1080/17524032.2016.1147474

Hutter, S., 2014. Protest Event Analysis and Its Offspring, in: della Porta, D. (Ed.), *Methodological Practices in Social Movement Research*. Cambridge University Press, Cambridge, pp. 335–367.

Ingram, M., Ingram, H., Lejano, R., 2014. What's the Story? Creating and Sustaining Environmental Networks. *Environmental Politics* 23, 984–1002. https://doi.org/10.1080/09644016.2014.919717

Knoke, D., Diani, M., Christopoulos, D.C., Hollway, J., 2021. *Multimodal Political Networks*. Cambridge University Press, Cambridge/New York.

Koopmans, R., 2004. Protest in Time and Space: The Evolution of Waves of Contention, in: Snow, D.A., Soule, S., Kriesi, H. (Eds.), *The Blackwell Companion to Social Movements*. Blackwell, Oxford, pp. 19–46.

Kriesi, H., Koopmans, R., Duyvendak, J.W., Giugni, M., 1995. *New Social Movements in Western Europe*. University of Minnesota Press, Minneapolis/London.

Levkoe, C.Z., 2014. The Food Movement in Canada: A Social Movement Network Perspective. *The Journal of Peasant Studies* 41, 385–403. https://doi.org/10.1080/03066150.2014.910766

Levkoe, C.Z., Wakefield, S., 2014. Understanding Contemporary Networks of Environmental and Social Change: Complex Assemblages within Canada's 'Food Movement'. *Environmental Politics* 23, 302–320. https://doi.org/10.1080/09644016.2013.818302

Loschi, C., 2019. Local Mobilisations and the Formation of Environmental Networks in a Democratizing Tunisia. *Social Movement Studies* 18, 93–112. https://doi.org/10.1080/14742837.2018.1540974

Luxton, I., Sbicca, J., 2020. Mapping Movements: A Call for Qualitative Social Network Analysis. *Qualitative Research* 1468794120927678. https://doi.org/10.1177/1468794120927678

Martinez-Alier, J., Temper, L., Bene, D.D., Scheidel, A., 2016. Is There a Global Environmental Justice Movement? *The Journal of Peasant Studies* 43, 731–755. https://doi.org/10.1080/03066150.2016.1141198

McPherson, M., Smith-Lovin, L., Cook, J.M., 2001. Birds of a Feather: Homophily in Social Networks. *Annual Review of Sociology* 27, 415–444.

Melucci, A., 1996. *Challenging Codes*. Cambridge University Press, Cambridge/New York.

Mertig, A.G., Dunlap, R.E., 2001. Environmentalism, New Social Movements, and the New Class: A Cross-national Investigation. *Rural Sociology* 66, 113–136.

Obach, B., 1999. The Wisconsin Labor-Environmental Network: A Case Study of Coalition Formation Among Organized Labor and the Environmental Movement. *Organization & Environment* 12(1), 45–74. https://doi.org/10.1177/1086026699121002

O'Brien, K.J., 2006. *Rightful Resistance in Rural China*. Cambridge University Press, Cambridge/New York.

O'Brien, T., 2013. Fragmentation or Evolution? Understanding Change Within the New Zealand Environmental Movement. *Journal of Civil Society* 9, 287–299. https://doi.org/10.1080/17448689.2013.818267

Oliver, P., 1989. Bringing the Crowd Back In: The Nonorganizational Elements of Social Movements. *Research in Social Movements, Conflict and Change* 11, 1–30.

Osa, M., 2003. *Solidarity and Contention. Networks of Polish Opposition*. University of Minnesota Press, Minneapolis, MN.

Park, S.S., Raridon, A., 2017. Survivor: Spectators and Gladiators in the US Environmental Movement, 2000–2010. *Social Movement Studies* 16, 721–734. https://doi.org/10.1080/14742837.2017.1331121

Pichardo, N.A., Sullivan-Catlin, H., Deane, G., 1998. Is the Political Personal? Everyday Behaviors as Forms of Environmental Movement Participation. *Mobilization* 3, 185–205. https://doi.org/10.17813/maiq.3.2.f1j01263w5623361

Pickvance, K., 1998. *Democracy and Environmental Movements in Eastern Europe*. Westview, Boulder, CO.

Robins, G.L., 2015. *Doing Social Network Research*. Sage, London.

Rudig, W., 1990. *Anti-nuclear Movements*. Longman, London.

Saunders, C., 2013. *Environmental Networks and Social Movement Theory*. Bloomsbury, London.

Simpson, C.R., 2015. Multiplexity and Strategic Alliances: The Relational Embeddedness of Coalitions in Social Movement Organisational Fields. *Social Networks* 42, 42–59.

Sommerfeldt, E.J., Yang, A., 2017. Relationship Networks as Strategic Issues Management: An Issue-stage Framework of Social Movement Organization Network Strategies. *Public Relations Review* 43, 829–839. https://doi.org/10.1016/j.pubrev.2017.06.012

Sumner, J., Wever, C., 2015. Cultivating Alliances: The Local Organic Food Co-ops Network. *Canadian Journal of Nonprofit and Social Economy Research* 6. https://doi.org/10.22230/cjnser.2015v6n2a204

Sun, Y., DeLuca, K.M., Seegert, N., 2017. Exploring Environmentalism amidst the Clamor of Networks: A Social Network Analysis of Utah Environmental Organizations. *Environmental Communication* 11, 332–352. https://doi.org/10.1080/17524032.2015.1094101

Temper, L., Demaria, F., Scheidel, A., Del Bene, D., Martinez-Alier, J., 2018. The Global Environmental Justice Atlas (EJAtlas): Ecological Distribution Conflicts as Forces for Sustainability. *Sustainability Science* 13, 573–584.

Tilly, C., Tarrow, S., 2007. *Contentious Politics*. Paradigm, Boulder, CO.

Tindall, D., 2002. Social Networks, Identification and Participation in an Environmental Movement: Low-medium Cost Activism within the British Columbia Wilderness Preservation Movement. *Canadian Review of Sociology & Anthropology* 39, 413–452.

Tindall, D., 2004. Social Movement Participation Over Time: An Ego-Network Approach to Micro-Mobilization. *Sociological Focus* 37, 163–184. https://doi.org/10.1080/00380237.2004.10571240

Tindall, D., 2015. Networks as Constraints and Opportunities, in: della Porta, D., Diani, M. (Eds.), *Oxford Handbook of Social Movements*. Oxford University Press, Oxford/New York, pp. 231–245.

Tindall, D., Robinson, J., 2017. Collective Action to Save the Ancient Temperate Rainforest: Social Networks and Environmental Activism in Clayoquot Sound. *Ecology and Society* 22. https://doi.org/10.5751/ES-09042-220140

Yang, A., 2013. When Transnational Civil Network Meets Local Context: An Exploratory Hyperlink Network Analysis of Northern/Southern NGOs' Virtual Network in China. *Journal of International and Intercultural Communication* 6, 40–60. https://doi.org/10.1080/17513057.2012.719632

21

ENVIRONMENTAL AND ANIMAL ORIENTED RADICALIZATION

Walking a different path?

Gerry Nagtzaam and Pete Lentini

Introduction

The emergence of modern environmental activism in the 1960s led to the development over several decades of radical environmental and animal liberation movements (hereafter REALMs), incorporating such groups as the Animal Liberation Front (ALF), Earth First! (EF!), the Earth Liberation Front (ELF), and the Sea Shepherd Conservation Society (SSCS) (Nagtzaam, 2017). Perceiving that mainstream political avenues of influence such as voting, protesting, and civil disobedience were either insufficient or ineffective to prevent states' and businesses' ever-increasing global environmental despoilation, these entities believed urgent and radical action on their part was needed to protect the environment (Vanderheiden, 2005: 445).

Such groups perceive themselves as "soldiers" for environmental and animal liberation against the prevailing, illegitimate social order and the political status quo that allows violence against other species (Liddick, 2006: 91). Their opponents brand them as "ecoterrorists", responsible for hundreds of millions of dollars in property damage (Monaghan, 1999: 164; Smith, 2008: 40). To their supporters they are "ecowarriors "committing *ecotage* – property damage with the aim of preventing activities considered harmful to the environment – on behalf of those species that lack voices of their own. Their stated endgame is to force those who exploit the environment – and occasionally their supporters – to end their destructive behavior or to make it financially harmful to them to continue their actions by using property damage, "economic sabotage", and other non-violent tactics (Mancuso-Smith, 2006: 332).

In this chapter, we address the issue of REALM actors' radicalization. We define radicalization here as the process of an individual or group making a commitment to realize substantial changes to one or more areas of either an individual society's or the global status quo. As what follows will demonstrate, this definition may well reflect what actually occurs within REALM organizations, but most scholarship to date on radicalization tends to focus on radicalization that leads to violence, especially in the form of terrorism.

Hence, this situation prompts us to pose two research questions: What is radicalization? And how, or to what extent, do REALM group radicalization patterns share similarities with or exhibit differences from other ideological forms of radical, extremist, and terrorist radicalization? We argue that REALM radicalization shares broad similarities with, for instance,

DOI: 10.4324/9780367855680-24

neo-jihadist (Lentini, 2013) and right-wing extremist and terrorist groups' radicalization patterns. However, they diverge significantly with respect to the ideological and tactical positions on the use of violence, the emphasis that they place on the value of life – human and nonhuman – and how social networks reinforce the values of life and non-violence as irrevocable in both theory and practice.

To address these questions, we start with a discussion of radicalism as a concept. Thereafter, we provide an overview of some of the key writings on radicalization and apply this theoretical material to the relevant REALM groups' experiences. This is followed by a general overview of these groups' ideologies and philosophies, in particular their attitudes toward the use of political violence, identifying both similarities and differences. We then include a brief examination of the most significant REALM groups of the last 50 years, with particular emphasis on their creation, structures, individual philosophies, and the particular strategies and tactics they adopted to achieve their stated goals. We conclude the chapter by reiterating our findings, explaining why such groups did not develop into a mass movement, and presenting an observation that the conditions for environmental radicalism have not disappeared and may well flare again.

Radicalization

Before proceeding to our discussion of REALM actors' radicalization, it is worth proposing that pro-environmental and pro-animal politics are, at their heart, radical (defined later in this chapter) philosophies and ideologies. Indeed, they contradict agrilogistics, which presupposes "the idea that humanity, its social and cultural institutions, and its artifacts are somehow separate and distinct from 'Nature'" (Morton cited in Rogers, 2018: 158).

This is manifest in at least two major domains: the socio-economic and the theological. Socio-economic philosophies and ideologies are radical within the context of two of the most significant manifestations of modernity: capitalism and communism. Both approaches are predicated on continuous progress and growth. Societal advancement is not possible without the exploitation of nature and the extraction of natural resources (Pellow, 2019: 114–115). On the theological side, the Book of Genesis (1:26) grants humans dominion over all other lifeforms and for some adherents, the earth is a fleeting entity to be fully utilized in the short time humans are here. Philosophies, ideologies, and organizations that critique, challenge, and seek to change these deeply embedded socio-political and theological premises, such as REALMs, are clearly radical from inception.

Also, before engaging with REALM actors' radicalization, it is necessary to address the notion of eco-terrorism itself, which is believed to be the endpoint of these processes. Opponents of environmental activism have affixed the label "ecoterrorism" to individuals and groups of the type we examine in this chapter since at least 1988, when private security firms used the term. Public relations offices have also been responsible for the spread of such a label: in 1991, the public relations firm Ketchum fomented a campaign accusing Greenpeace of being ecoterrorists over its chlorine phase-out campaign (Rowell, 1996: 150). By the mid-1990s the term had become so ubiquitous as to be the preferred nomenclature of the news media, law enforcement, politicians, and opponents of radical environmental action (Rosebraugh, 2004: 236). Some REALM groups have opposed their actions being labelled thusly (although Paul Watson, leader of the SSCS, has on occasion embraced the term), arguing that ecoterrorism better describes the activities of corporations (Eagen, 1996: 2).

The concept of "ecoterrorism", like terrorism, remains an essentially contested term with multiple competing definitions and understandings. Schwartz argues that the term is often uncritically accepted by academics, proponents, and opponents alike (1998: 484). For authors

311

like Karasick it is the "use of fear-inducing coercive tactics to the end of either protecting the environment or influencing those who may be affecting the environment to protect the environment (or at least cease affecting the environment)" (2009: 584).

However, the most cited definition was provided by Chief Jarboe of the US Federal Bureau of Investigation Counterterrorism Division, who defined "ecoterrorism" as:

> the use or threatened use of violence of a criminal nature against innocent victims or property by an environmentally-oriented, sub-national group for environmental-political reasons, or aimed at an audience beyond the target, often of a symbolic nature.
>
> (Amster, 2006: 289)

In light of these definitions of ecoterrorism, Michael Loadenthal's (2017) groundbreaking empirical research on the topic provides substantive evidence that the use of such a term is grossly misapplied to the overwhelming majority of REALM actors. He found (2017: 4–5, emphasis in original):

> Throughout more than 27,100 recorded attack incidents over a 38-year period, 98 per cent of attacks target *property* (i.e., not human beings). And 99.7 per cent cause no injury. These nonlethal attacks on property are designed to cause financial strain to targets through a campaign of economic sabotage and are *not* carried out to spread "anxiety" or "terror" among a population. The attacks carried out . . . are fundamentally not intended to provoke fear but instead to cause economic hardship to its targets, and thus, such actions fall short of traditional notions of what constitutes "terrorism".

Although he notes that 99.7% of all animal and environmental liberation movement actions in his database did not generate any casualties, Loadenthal acknowledges that such actors produced lethal outcomes on four occasions out of over 27,100 incidents. Unabomber Ted Kaczynski perpetrated three, and Volkert van der Graaf, who assassinated Dutch populist politician Pim Fortuyn, committed the other (Loadenthal, 2017: 17–18). Nonetheless, it is significant that both acted on their own, without the assistance or sanction of any established animal or environmental liberation movement groups. Moreover, the degree to which either of these individuals was associated with the broader movement is also debatable. There were indeed incidents in which REALM groups engaged in actions that resulted in serious injuries (on two occasions), and some individuals formed groups that did not adhere to established groups' non-violent philosophies. However, the perpetrators of the incidents recorded in his dataset nearly universally did not target persons.

As the following section suggests, most of our current understanding of radicalization presupposes that those who become radicalized do so in order to perpetrate violence. Therefore, with the aforementioned information on REALM incidents, we must query whether there are significant differences between how REALM actors and others such as neo-jihadists (Lentini, 2013) and right-wing extremists become radicalized.

Radicalization

It would seem safe to presume that radicalization should be represented in academic literature as the process of an individual or group making a commitment to realize substantial changes to one or more areas of either an individual society's or the global status quo – a definition that appears to be politically neutral and one that we prefer. There are, of course, scholars whose definitions of radicalization take a more neutral stance, reflecting it as a process that has as its end root-and-branch and/or comprehensive change. For Dalgaard-Nielsen (2010: 798), "[A] radical is understood as a person harboring a deep-felt desire for fundamental sociopolitical changes and radicalization is understood as a growing readiness to pursue and support far-reaching changes in society that conflict with, or pose a direct threat to, the existing order". Bartlett and Miller (2012: 2) note,

> [R]adicalization is simply the process by which, "individuals are introduced to an overtly ideological message and belief system that encourages movement from moderate, mainstream beliefs towards extreme views["]. . . . To be a radical is to reject the status quo, but not necessarily in a violent or even problematic manner. Some radicals conduct, support, or encourage terrorism, whilst many others do no such thing, and actively and often effectively agitate against it.

Lentini (2008: 9) maintains,

> [R]adicalization is a process in which individuals develop, adopt and embrace political attitudes and modes of behaviour which diverge substantially from those of any or all of the established . . . political, social, economic, cultural, and religious values, attitudes, institutions and behaviours which exist in a given society. . . . Regardless whether they personally use, condone or encourage the use of violence by those other than themselves – or even disavow using violence entirely – radicals advocate significantly disrupting, dislocating and ultimately destroying existing political, economic, social and cultural norms and structures. The result of this process is an eponymous radical departure from that which they seek to overturn.

Nonetheless, studies of radicalization, particularly for well over the past decade and a half, are inevitably linked with change facilitated by violence. Criticizing such work, Mark Sedgwick (2010: 479) has noted, "radicalization" is at present the standard term used to describe "what goes on before the bomb goes off". Although they acknowledge that radicalization can involve non-violent change, the authors of one of the most respected studies in the field write,

> Functionally, political radicalization is increased preparation for and commitment to intergroup conflict. Descriptively, radicalization means change in beliefs, feelings, and behaviours in directions that increasingly justify intergroup violence and demand sacrifice in defence of the ingroup.
>
> (McCauley and Moskalenko, 2008: 416)

Moreover, as much of the nearly two-decades-long war on terrorism has concentrated mostly on neo-jihadist political violence, it is not surprising that most of this literature addresses related themes. Some scholars have acknowledged that the term "radicalization" is pejorative and is too often linked with Islamist activities. They suggest that this fails to acknowledge that in Western contexts, for instance, individuals and groups also become mobilized to violence – including in reaction to Islamist violence and to retaliate against it – and suggest utilizing the term "militarization" instead (Haggerty and Bucerius, 2018). While their intentions to disentangle neo-jihadism (and, by extension, Islam and Muslims) from violence and to acknowledge the violent tendencies "among our own" are, indeed, noble, they too rely too heavily on the potential for engaging in lethality that is presupposed in such processes. Moreover, they tend to focus too much on one particular aspect of radicalization, largely those events that would lead to a willingness to engage in conflict and what might be considered the operational side of a terroristic or state-sanctioned act of violence.

Process theories are among several types of studies of radicalization, which also include social network approaches and meaning-of-life approaches. Process theories tend to address the various stages in which individuals and groups become radicalized. Their chief merit is that they demonstrate that radicalization, including radicalization that results in an act of violence like terrorism, is a fairly long-term process. Individuals and groups tend to go through various stages of political engagement and experience notable setbacks during this process before making the decision to enact violence.

Ehud Sprinzak's noted delegitimization model proposes that individuals and groups begin their journeys participating in legal activities such as writing letters and demonstrating against matters that disaffect them (crisis of confidence state). In circumstances in which they may not achieve their objectives, some disaffected members break from the main dissident group and escalate their activities to more intensive protest, largely targeted against agents of the state, and largely advocating non-violent, especially non-lethal, methods to implement their programs (conflict of legitimacy). In some cases in which these tactics also do not produce their intended results, an even smaller group may break away and form a smaller collective that considers lethal violence acceptable and preferable to meet its needs. In making this decision, they shift the targets of their protest from state agents to all those in the society who do not share their vision. At this stage, the group or individual has de-humanized such opponents to legitimate conducting violence against them. It is at this stage of the protest cycle that terrorism may occur (crisis of legitimacy) (Sprinzak, 1998).

There are other notable process theories, what we consider the "architectural approaches" to radicalization. These include Moghaddam's "staircase metaphor" (2005), which suggests that individuals and groups go through a five-stage process in which they increasingly go up the equivalent of a staircase in their radical views, which ultimately can lead to a terrorist attack. This approach involves an increase in commitment to ideology, to purpose, and to the group and a dwindling of attachments to broader society. McCauley and Moskalenko (2008) propose a pyramid model in which the mass of disaffected people is reflected in the structure's base, and the apex comprises those most aggrieved and willing to perpetrate violence to redress grievances.

Other studies emphasize that those with whom people associate are important in how both individuals and groups become radicalized. These social network approaches stress that in most circumstances, people's personal connections will be far more important than ideology in bringing them into radical movements. Indeed, it is only through trusted social networks that individuals feel the greatest sense of confidence exchanging ideas, including those that may involve criminal activity and risk their freedom and, in some cases, their lives. Hence, it is not surprising that much of the literature on contemporary terrorist cell activity notes the importance of friend and family connections during radicalization (Sageman 2004; Lentini, 2013).

Finally, a wave of scholarship on radical (and extremist) activities draws on or reflects themes in the psychological literature on ways that produce meaning in life, which Viktor Frankel pioneered in the early post-war period (Frankel 2008). These studies, many of which are based on interviews with former radicals, extremists, and terrorists, largely indicate that those people who were involved in such activities certainly possessed a set of grievances that they felt they could best redress by being involved in groups that sought to overturn the status quo, including engaging in violence or terrorism to do so. More importantly, these studies' findings tend to demonstrate that engaging in such activities gave the participants a sense of control over their lives; elevated their sense of self-esteem as they felt they were doing something to help alleviate their grievances; and, in many cases, made them feel somewhat exalted as they were engaged in activities about which others had lower levels of knowledge or that others were too afraid to pursue. Indeed, several scholars have noted that such participation offered people excitement. Moreover, such activities permitted these individuals with opportunities to revise their life narratives and recast themselves in the roles of heroes. This enabled them to transcend the mundane (Cottee and Hayward 2011; Ilardi 2013).

Such research not only provides enhanced understandings of different paths of radicalization broadly; it also facilitates nuanced insights into why individuals would risk their freedom or lives by choosing to pursue illegal and dangerous activities: being in a radical, extremist, or terrorist group or having such affiliation with them provides a sense of reward for these participants. Radicals, extremists, and terrorists clearly make choices that result in self-sacrifice, but they are not limited to those: they also receive something in return for their decisions to commit themselves to substantial societal and political change. The following section not only presents REALM groups' ideologies and eco- and animal-defense actions but also shows that processes, social networks, and gaining purpose and transcendence are as relevant to their participants' experiences of radicalization away from ENGOs or mainstream and progressive organizations as they are in those accounts that are recorded in the extant radicalization scholarship.

Active REALM groups

All the REALMs examined split off from mainstream environmental groups, arguing that they were not effective in protecting the environment (Doherty, Patterson and Seel, 2000: 1). Borrelli maintains that

> [P]articularly during the 1980s, many activists became increasingly disenchanted and alienated from mainstream environmental organizations. They were discouraged by the compromising attitude of mainstream groups, by the bureaucratization of the groups, by the professionalization of leaders and their detachment from the emerging concerns of grassroots supporters, and by the lack of success of mainstream organizations.
>
> (Devall, 2014: 55)

These failures led some frustrated activists to join REALMs in search of a "better" way to address environmental issues (della Porta and Rucht, 2002: 2). These processes reflect Sprinzak's (1998) crisis of confidence phase.

As opposed to mainstream ENGO groups, REALMs are willing to use direct action and occasionally risky or reckless actions to achieve their aims. Given their radical bent, it is not surprising that REALMs like EF!, the ELF, and ALF tend to be poorly resourced compared with mainstream ENGOs such as Greenpeace or the Sierra Club. Mainstream environmental groups tend to be hierarchically organized while, with the exception of the SSCS, which are run as a hierarchy with Paul Watson on top, REALMs tend to be organized in small, autonomous "affinity cells". Philosophically, mainstream ENGO groups adopt an anthropogenic approach, prioritizing the use of nature by present and future generations of humans, while REALMs all share biocentric beliefs toward nature (Silvaggio, 2005: 32–33).

What philosophically binds REALM groups together is the acceptance of the idea that protecting the environment is vital and that nature is intrinsically valuable in and of itself (an eco-centric perspective) and should be protected irrespective of its value to humanity. Such beliefs precipitated REALM participants' breaks from the ENGOs. For all the REALM groups:

> Nature is seen as benevolent and representative of a higher morality. In contrast, mere human morality is seen as tarnished or corrupt. As protesters are adhering to a higher morality – the preservation of the natural world – breaking human laws is deemed to be justifiable.
>
> (Hasbrouck, 2005: 1)

In order to fully understand the actions of radical environmentalists, it is thus necessary to realize that all such adherents are "driven by an intuitive *ecological consciousness* which serves as the movement's soul force" (Scarce, 1989: 7).

According to Manes, REALM actors realize that:

> The significance of radical environmentalism . . . is based on one simply but frightening realization: that our culture is lethal to the ecology that it depends on and has been so for a long time, perhaps from the beginning. The validity of the radical environmentalism movement rises or falls depending on the accuracy of this perception.
>
> (Manes, 1990: 22)

Another core belief that unites all radical environmental groups is the belief that an "environmental apocalypse is imminent" that requires immediate radical action to "hasten the downfall of modern civilization so as to realize a better world where man will live in harmony with the natural world" (Liddick, 2006: 3).

As opposed to other radical groups, REALMs do not have any "interest in a well-conceived philosophy or in any other explicit guideposts to tell them how to live their lives" (Scarce, 1989: 31). As David Barbarash, a former ALF spokesman, argued, "[W]e're very dangerous philosophically. Part of the danger is that we don't buy into the illusion that property is worth more than life. . . . [W]e bring that insane priority into the light, which is something the system cannot survive" (Best, 2006: 11).

Animal Liberation Front

To its adherents, the ALF, and its oft-times more violent offshoots the Animal Rights Militia, the Justice Department, and Stop Huntingdon Animal Cruelty, was willing to defend animals against the "vast industries [that] have built up around what Animal Liberators see as the 'exploitation' of non-human animals" at the risk of prison or worse (Scarce, 2006: 116). ALF grew out of the failure of more conservative groups such as the 1963 Hunt Saboteurs Association of the UK, whose activists utilized non-violent protest unsuccessfully against various forms of hunting. One member was a law student, Ronnie Lee, who had misgivings about the efficacy of a non-violent approach, preferring to meet "violence with violence" (Nagtzaam, 2017: 48). Lee argued that the hunts could be "sabotaged far more effectively, and foxes saved much more efficiently, if the hunt never reached the field in the first place" (Tester and Walls, 1996: 79).

Lee and others went to prison in 1975 for attempting to set a fire at the Oxford Laboratory Animal Colonies for the second time (Mann, 2008: 52). After serving his sentence in prison, Lee came out as the key leader of a nascent animal rights movement of approximately 30 people (Henshaw, 1989: 19). Lee had crafted a blueprint for a new organization while in prison, one that emphasized hit-and-run tactics, a diffuse cell structure (affinity cells) that was easily replicable, and a mass-media campaign to show the ongoing animal abuse (Henshaw, 1989: 208).

Lee and his 30 adherents created the ALF-UK in June 1976 (Arslan, 2008: 37). Those who joined did so out of a sense of frustration that animal suffering continued unabated and revolutionary action equating to warfare was needed (Best, 2006: 27). As Manne argues, ALF is best understood less as a group and more as "a title, an umbrella name, or a state of mind if you like – under which individuals and groups of people claim responsibility for illegal actions" (2008: 55. To this day, adherents operate in autonomous cells, choosing their own targets and methods to achieve their own goals (Monaghan, 1999: 164). As Henshaw explains, "[E]veryone knew who the targets were, so there seemed little point in having all operations directed from headquarters" (1989: 51).

Animal Liberation Front followers draw their beliefs from animal rights writings such as Singer and Regan as to the moral worth of animals, how they suffer, and how humans should interact with other species. As Eagan notes, the majority of environmental radicals believe that "human beings are just an ordinary member of the biological community, no more important than, say, a bear or a whale" (Young, 2004: 3). Building on the works of key writers on animals such as Bentham, Singer, and Regan, the fledgling ALF had "abolitionist objectives": to end all types of animal exploitation. They argued that animals are "bearers of rights – and particularly the right to life – we are not entitled to use them" (Garner, 1993: 337). Many adherents "described themselves and their activism in terms of either emotional attachments to animals or emotional reactions to animal abuse and exploitation" (Einwohler, 2002: 261).

The ALF strategy was to use methods of direct action (e.g., property damage, arson, liberation of animals) as an economic strategy to inflict unbearable losses on animal enterprises, with the goal of ending animal cruelty (Monaghan, 2006: 109; Walls, 2000: 86). For ALF members, only direct action was permissible based on "personal conviction and moral obligation: if you care about the animals it is no good hoping that someone else will carry out the required action – for, if everybody did that, there would be no direct action at all!" (Tester and Walls, 1996: 84). For example, between 1982 and 1988, ALF in Great Britain carried out campaigns against opponents utilizing letter and car bombs and product contamination threats. One notorious case publicizing that the confectionary Mars Bars had been adulterated led to the chocolate being removed from stores (it was later revealed to be a hoax) (Monaghan, 1997: 110).

Earth First! and Earth Liberation Front

The Earth First! movement was partly inspired by Edward Abbey's 1975 novel *The Monkey Wrench Gang*, which detailed activists travelling around the American Southwest damaging the property of "environmental despoilers" and culminates in an attempt to destroy the Glen Canyon Dam (Young, 2004: 26). In April 1980, Dave Foreman and four environmental activist friends: Ron Kezar (from the Sierra Club), Bart Koehler, Mike Roselle (from left-wing groups) and Howie Wolke went hiking in Mexico's Pinacate Desert. The activists had become disillusioned with the mainstream environmental movement, believing it was ineffective in the face of government and corporate opposition: for example, the inability to prevent the opening up of significant portions of US forests to resource extraction in 1979 (Nagtzaam, 2017: 121). That same year, Foreman started Earth First! because he wanted "a radical wing that would make the Sierra Club look moderate. Someone needs to say what needs to be said, and do what needs to be done, and take the strong actions to dramatize it" (Eagan, 1996: 6). To that end, they created what they called "a 'disorganization' with no official participants and no directors, and called themselves 'Earth First!'" (Lange, 1990: 479).

Rather than relying on the traditional "anthropocentric" view ("human is first, central, and dominant") of other environmental organizations, Earth First! adopted a "biocentric" belief system ("humans are only one species in the much grander scheme of things") as their philosophical underpinning. They also integrated into their belief system Aldo Leopold's land ethic that "a thing is right when it tends to preserve the integrity, stability, and beauty of the biotic community, and it is wrong when it tends otherwise" (Lange, 1990: 479).

They characterized themselves as a radical organization and sought to overcome the narrative that environmentalists were "wimps" compared to their rugged, more "macho" opponents. Instead, they offered a more empowering counter-narrative that stressed that "not all environmentalists are granola-crunching hippies. Some of us are rednecks and cowboys" (Short, 1991: 177). Earth First! started with only 13 participants and grew over time to more than 1,500 adherents (Manes, 2008: 76). They published a do-it-yourself guide, *The Earth First! Direct Action Manual*, as a guide to sabotage actions they dubbed "ecotage", which aimed to cause as much economic damage as possible to prevent the destruction of the environment, particularly by corporations. Drawing on the ALF model, believers were encouraged to form decentralized "affinity cells" in their localities to commit acts of civil disobedience in the "name" of the environment (Earth First! Direct Action Manual, 1997: ii).

However, several EF! members argued that its campaigns that only targeted "earth abusers" were hindering the speed of achieving their goal of a more "environmentally harmonious society" (Nagtzaam, 2017: 187). The argued that the tactics of "mass protest and civil disobedience is limited in its scope and sooner or later the legal system inevitably works in favor of the "earth rapist and environment destroyer" (Molland, 2006: 50. Drawing their inspiration from ALF, they wanted to undertake more radical actions against their perceived enemies to better "save the world" (Molland, 2006: 49–50).

In 1992 in Brighton, England, these adherents created the Earth Liberation Front. ELF saw itself as the physical manifestation of "the dying rage of the burning planet" with a mission to end the destruction of the global environment (Ziner, 2001: 17). Individuals and affinity cells were free to carry out illegal acts such as arson as their consciences dictated, but such choices were and "are not endorsed, encouraged, or approved of by the management and participants of [ELF]" (Joose, 2007: 354). These actions reflect what occurs in Sprinzak's (1998) conflict of legitimacy stage.

Both Earth First! and the ELF were influenced by anarchist writings, anti-capitalist and anti-technological approaches, misanthropic beliefs, and deep ecology, but they exhibited no overarching philosophy (Nagtzaam, 2017: 126–128). ELF believes that capitalist societies are to blame for "destroying all life on this planet" and to stop such wanton destruction requires Elves to "take the profit motive out of killing" (Pickering, 2007: 47). Pickering notes that for adherents, "[I]t is not enough to work solely on individual environmental issues; the capitalist state and its symbols of propaganda must also be targeted" (ibid: 44). Consequently, for Elves to realize their vision of a more perfect (ecological) world, current human civilizations need to collapse, and Elves should work to realize that goal (Hasbrouck, 2005: 140). Thus, ELF is not "seeking a place at any political table" since it would prefer to bring about the end of current political systems, paving the way for their "version" of society to be enacted (Castells, 2000: 693).

Participants were more willing to carry out ecotage, arguing it was a more effective tactic than legal protests. Significantly, Earth First! remained the public-facing side of the movement operating in plain sight while ELF members (or Elves) saw themselves as carrying out illegal activities under the cover of night. To some extent, the two entities operated separately without competition, and activists were free to choose the type of action that suited them (Leader and Probst, 2003, 38).

The Sea Shepherd Conservation Society

Since 1977 the SSCS has carried out its self-appointed task of protecting oceanic life and the aquatic realm they inhabit from human depredation (www.seashepherd.org). Founded by Paul Watson, an ex-merchant marine and early member of Greenpeace before he was expelled (according to Greenpeace; Watson claims he resigned) for violence against sealers in 1977, when Watson threatened Canadian sealers with their own clubs and threw their equipment and pelts into the sea. Watson maintained that Greenpeace's methods were ineffective, and radical direct action was required to save marine mammals (Nagtzaam, 2017: 208–209).

Determined to do more than "bear witness", he fashioned the SSCS into a radical group unafraid to use ecotage methods against those killing marine life" e.g., Japanese whalers, tuna and dolphin fishermen (Nagtzaam, 2017, p. 209, https://www.seashepherdglobal.org). From that time, it has grown from one ship protesting Canadian sealing to a global organization with multiple ships and the ability to confront those it deems despoilers globally. The SSCS mission is to "investigate violations; enforce laws; and protect global marine life summed up in three words "defend, conserve, protect" (www.seashepherd.org). For Paul Watson and the SSCS, the killing of whales equates to the murder of a human, and their continued slaughter is the moral equivalent of the Holocaust (Khatchadourian, 2007: 58).

Unlike the other REALMs' structures, which are democratic and decentralized, the SSCS structure is hierarchically organized. The group is predominantly run by volunteers and through donations. The SSCS support structure comprises both paid professionals and volunteer positions for their campaigns (www.seashepherd.org/get involved/crewing at sea). In Watson's view, he is the unquestioned leader since "[w]hen confrontation begins, the time for democratic discussion of strategy and tactics had ended. All decisions must then be entrusted to a recognized command" (Watson, 1993: 54).

To achieve its goals, the SSCS have crafted a multi-prong strategy that utilizes diplomacy and economic and direct actions against their opponents to a brilliant global media strategy designed to quickly highlight the "nefarious" campaigns of their opponents (Sea Shepherd, 1984: 3). Like EF! and ELF, the SSCS campaign strategy is to target property while humans are not to be considered legitimate targets. SSCS members must conform to five rules, based on Paul Watson's understanding of Gandhi's principle of non-violence:

> One is that we don't use firearms. Two, we don't utilize explosives. Three, we don't take any action where there is the possibility of injury to somebody. Four, we accept responsibility for what we do. And, five, we accept whatever moral or legal consequences will befall.
>
> (Scarce, 2006: 106)

Actions the SSCS have been accused of carrying out include ramming whaling vessels, sinking up to 10 whaling ships, attacking fishing boats, utilizing lasers to blind Japanese whalers, heaving butyric acid (rancid butter) at ships to disrupt the on-ship whale meat processing, fouling the propellers of ships, playing "chicken" with and/or harassing ships, and boarding Japanese whaling ships at sea (Bondaroff, 2011: 42–43; Caprari, 2010: 1508; Moffa, 2012: 209).

Despite multiple actions, Watson claims that no member or opponent has ever been injured or killed during a campaign (Darby, 2006: 15). Significantly, Watson argues he would prefer an effective enforcement agency take on the responsibility, but in its absence, he feels compelled to carry out vigilante acts against property to prevent ongoing marine mammal deaths (Scarce, 2006: 105–106; Nagtzaam and Lentini 2008).

Conclusion

The examples we provide in this chapter suggest strongly that on the whole, REALM groups' radicalizations followed patterns that are similar to those that other radicals, extremists, and terrorists experienced. Their interest in political activities began with legal forms of political participation and in what would be considered to be mainstream groups. Upon perceiving that such actions were not bringing about changes quickly enough or at all, some individuals decided to escalate their protests' intensity: some stayed within legal realms while others pursued illegal means. However, virtually no REALM participants engaged in any criminal activity that targeted individuals; such actions were more numerous amongst neo-jihadists and right-wing actors. Additionally, like neo-jihadist and right-wing radicals, extremist, and terrorists, REALM participants' radicalizations provided them with an exalted sense of self-esteem, gave them a sense of purpose and meaning, and made them feel that their actions set them apart from others within their respective movements and milieus who possessed grievances but did not have the fortitude or commitment to take further steps – including transgressing the law and potentially risking their lives and freedom to alleviate the source of that disaffection or suffering. Many participants clearly saw themselves as heroes. Additionally, social networks and ideology also played significant roles in all cases among neo-jihadist, right-wing, and REALM actors' radicalization.

Social networks and ideologies played different roles in REALM radicalization than what occurs in neo-jihadist and right-wing cases. In those ideological groupings that seek to cause change through violence and intimidation – such as neo-jihadists and right-wing extremists – there is much greater pressure and prestige to engage in violence, including that which can result in lethal action. There are also more incentives and rewards for individuals who do so. Additionally, there is internal competition within such cells and/or milieus, which encourages one-upmanship, which can, in turn, enhance the possibility of such actors engaging in activities that could inflict harm on and/or death to enemies to prove they have greater bravery, strength, leadership abilities, or commitment to the cause than others within their circles.

However, the situation is different among radicalized individuals who are members of organizations that profess non-violent objectives and are underpinned by non-violent philosophies and ideologies. In these circumstances, social networks and ideology serve as restraints to those within such circles from inflicting harm on others. Violence is antithetical to these groups' underpinning ideologies and philosophies, whereas in neo-jihadist and right-wing instances, engaging in violence is praiseworthy (presuming that it does not jeopardize an organization's goals or public standing). However, within the REALM groups, violence jeopardizes their objectives, damages group cohesion, and can result in ostracism and alienation. Moreover, such attitudes and consequences exhibit precedent and continuity from other ideological tendencies. During the Cold War, the US revolutionary left inflicted far fewer injuries and deaths on human targets than did their colleagues in Europe, notably the Red Brigades and Red Army Faction. This is related to the fact that the US left placed great pressure on organizations to resist lethal attacks on humans, and members would ostracize and alienate those groups or individuals who violated these taboos (Falciola 2016). As many REALM participants are active in the US, this is extremely noteworthy. Moreover, it is consistent with the overarching guidelines within REALM that operations must be conducted and change must occur without harm to human or non-human animals.

To date, none of the REALMs have developed into a mass movement. Most mainstream ENGO members were repelled by the actions against property or people (Vanderheiden, 2005: 436). Several factors explain why. In some cases, the ALF/ELF affinity cell model prevented members joining due to fears they were actually law enforcement. This fear prevented some potential adherents from starting their own cells. Further, the model inhibited the ability to share experiences and training. Law enforcement efforts were able to penetrate these cells regularly, and given there were only ever approximately 100 adherents in each grouping willing to commit ecotage or physical attacks, jailing entire cells disrupted group effectiveness and growth. Lastly, many of the environmental ideas REALMs promoted, such as vegetarianism, greater caring for the biosphere, and a decrease in animal testing have become mainstream ideas. This has reduced the "righteous anger" of most environmentalists who are not willing to use radical means and risk jail to save the environment when other methods appear to be currently working (Nagtzaam, 2017: 284).

The examined REALMs at this point in their history appear unsure as to how to proceed and are at a low ebb in terms of both members and actions carried out globally. Actions carried out by ALF and Elves still occur, but the number of actions is a mere trickle compared to their heyday of the 1980s and early 1990s. Many members have been imprisoned or left the organizations totally: e.g., Ronnie Lee. The SSCS's main goal of ending Japanese whaling in Antarctica appears to have occurred with Japan leaving the IWC and agreeing only to whale in its own waters. While REALM activities in the last few decades have declined, the inability of governments to act on pressing issues such as climate change and ongoing biodiversity loss may well see a resurgence of such activities by those concerned about their and the planet's future (Monaghan, 2013: 945). As Darryl Cherney of Earth First! warns, "As the Earth's condition gets worse, radical environmentalists will become more aggressive in defense of the planet" (Manes, 2008: 17), and the current political climate remains fertile ground for a resurgence of environmental radicalism. Groups like Extinction Rebellion are not yet fully radicalized; however, failure to achieve their goals could see them become so.

REALM and neo-jihadist and right-wing radical, extremist, and terrorist radicalization share some common processes, but they provide very different outcomes. In many cases, neo-jihadist and right-wing extremist and terrorist radicalization ends in loss of life and severe injuries to human targets – and even to the perpetrators themselves. REALM radicalization, in stark contrast, almost universally often ends up with no serious injuries or lethal violence and, in many instances, the saving of lives – especially of non-human animals. This chapter suggests that REALM radicalization constitutes new sets of experiences that can change the ways in which scholars understand and interpret this phenomenon.

References

Amster, R., 'Perspectives on Ecoterrorism: Catalysts, Conflations, and Casualties', *Contemporary Justice Review*, 9, September 2006, pp. 287–301.

Anonymous, *Earth First! Direct Action Manual*, DAM Collective, 1997.

Arslan, H. T., 'The Social and Operational Intersections of Environmental Extremism in North America and Europe' (PhD Dissertation, Sam Houston State University, Huntsville, TX, 2008).

Bartlett, Jamie and Carl Miller, 'The Edge of Violence: Towards Telling the Difference Between Violent and Non-Violent Radicalisation', *Terrorism and Political Violence*, vol. 24 (2012), pp. 1–21.

Best, Steven, 'Rethinking the Revolution: Animal Liberation, Human Liberation, and the Future of the Left', *International Journal of Inclusive Democracy*, vol. 2, no. 3 (2006), pp. 5–6.

Bondaroff, Teale Phelps, 'Sailing with the Sea Shepherds', *Journal of Military and Strategic Studies*, vol. 13, no. 3 (Spring 2011), pp. 1–55.

Caprari, Amanda M., 'Lovable Pirates? The Legal Implications of the Battle Between Environmentalists and Whalers in the Southern Ocean', *Connecticut Law Review*, vol. 42, no. 5 (2010), p. 1493.

Castells, Manuel, 'Toward a Sociology of the Network Society', *Contemporary Sociology*, vol. 29, no. 5 (2000), pp. 693–699.

Cottee, Simon and Keith Hayward, 'Terrorist (E)Motives: The Existential Attractions of Terrorism', *Studies in Conflict and Terrorism*, vol. 34 (2011), pp. 963–986.

Dalgaard–Nielsen, Anja 'Violent Radicalisation in Europe: What We Know and What We Do Not Know', *Studies in Conflict & Terrorism*, vol. 33 (2010), pp. 797–814.

Darby, A., 'Attack Plan on Japan's Whale Ships', *The Age* (27 December 2006).

della Porta, Donatella and Dieter Rucht, 'The Dynamics of Environmental Campaigns', *Mobilization: An International Journal*, vol. 7, no. 1 (2002), pp. 1–14.

Devall, Bill, 'Deep Ecology and Radical Environmentalism', in Riley E. Dunlop and Angela G. Mertig (eds.), *American Environmentalism: The U.S. Environmental Movement, 1970–1990*, London: Taylor & Francis, 2014.

Doherty, B., M. Patterson and B. Seel, *Direct Action in British Environmentalism*, London: Routledge, 2000.

Eagan, Sean P., 'From Spikes to Bombs: The Rise of Eco-terrorism', *Studies in Conflict & Terrorism*, vol. 19, no. 1 (1996), 1–18.

Einwohler, R. L., 'Bringing the Outsiders In: Opponents' Claims and the Construction of Animal Rights Activists' Identity', *Mobilization: An International Journal*, vol. 7, no. 3 (2002), pp. 253–268.

Falciola, Luca, 'A Bloodless Guerrilla Warfare: Why American Leftists Renounced Violence against People in the 1970s', *Terrorism and Political Violence*, vol. 28, no. 5 (2016), pp. 928–949.

Frankel, Viktor, E., *Man's Search For Meaning: The Classic Tribute to Hope from the Holocaust*. Ilse Lasch (trans. Part I). Sydney. Rider, 2008.

Garner, Robert, 'Political Animals: A Survey of the Animal Protection Movement in Britain', *Parliamentary Affairs*, vol. 46, no. 3 (1993).

Haggerty, Kevin D. and Sandra M. Bucerius, 'Radicalization as Martialization: Towards a Better Appreciation for the Progression to Violence', *Terrorism and Political Violence*, Located at: https://doi.org/10.10 80/09546553.2017.1404455 (2018).

Hasbrouck, J., 'Primitive Dissidents: Earth Liberation Front and the Making of a Radical Anthropology' (Thesis, University of Southern California, ProQuest Dissertations Publishing, 3219824, 2005).

Henshaw, David, *Animal Warfare: The Story of the Animal Liberation Front*. London: Fontana, 1989.

Ilardi, Gaetano Joe, 'Interviews With Canadian Radicals', *Studies in Conflict & Terrorism*, vol. 36, no. 9 (2013), pp. 713–738.

Joose, Paul, 'Leaderless Resistance and Ideological Inclusion: The Case of the Earth Liberation Front', *Terrorism and Political Violence*, vol. 19, no. 3 (2007), pp. 351–368.

Karasick, P. J., 'Curb Your Ecoterrorism: Identifying the Nexus Between State Criminalization of Eco-terror and Environmental Protection Policy', *Environmental Law and Policy Review*, vol. 33, no. 2 (Winter 2009).

Khatchadourian R., 'Neptune's Navy: Paul Watson's Wild Crusade to Save the Oceans', *The New Yorker* (5 November 2007).

Lange, Jonathan, 'Refusal to Compromise: The Case of Earth First!', *Western Journal of Speech Communication*, vol. 54, no. 4 (Fall 1990), pp. 473–494.

Leader, Stefan and Peter Probst, 'The Earth Liberation Front and Environmental Terrorism', *Terrorism and Political Violence*, vol. 15, no. 4 (2003), pp. 37–58.

Lentini, Pete, 'The Transference of Neojihadism: Towards a Process Theory of Transnational Radicalisation', in S. Khatab, M. Bakashmar and E. Ogru (eds.), *Radicalisation Crossing Borders: New Directions in Islamist and Jihadist Political, Intellectual and Theological Thought in Practice. Refereed Proceedings From the International Conference, 26–27 November 2008, Parliament House, Melbourne Victoria, 1–32*, www.monash.edu/__data/assets/pdf_file/0004/1677640/gtrec-proceedings-2008-01-pete-lentini.pdf

Lentini, Pete, *Neojihadism: Towards a New Understanding of Terrorism and Extremism?* Cheltenham: Edward Elgar. 2013.

Liddick, D.R., *Eco-Terrorism: Radical Environmental and Animal Liberation*. Westport, CT: Praeger, 2006.

Loadenthal, M., '"Eco-Terrorism": An Incident-Driven History of Attack (1973–2010)', *Journal for the Study of Radicalism*, vol. 11, no. 2 (2017), 1–34.

Mancuso-Smith, Chrystal, 'From Monkeywrenching to Mass Destruction: Eco-Sabotage and the American West', *26 Journal of Land Resources and Environmental Law* (2006), pp. 319–331.

Manes, Christopher, *Green Rage: Radical Environmentalism and the Unmaking of Civilization*. Boston, Toronto: Little Brown and Company, 1990.

Manes, K., *From Dusk 'til Dawn: An Insider's View of the Growth of the Animal Liberation Movement*, U.S.: Voice of The Voiceless, 2008.

Mann, Keith, *From Dusk 'til Dawn: An Insider's View of the Growth of the Animal Liberation Movement*, US: Voice of the Voiceless, 2008.

McCauley, Clark and Sophia Moskalenko, 'Mechanisms of Political Radicalisation: Pathways Toward Terrorism', *Terrorism and Political Violence*, vol. 20 (2008), pp. 415–433.

Molland, Noel, 'A Spark that Ignited a Flame: The Evolution of the Earth Liberation Front', in Steven Best and Anthony Nocella (eds.), *Igniting a Revolution: Voices in Defense of the Earth*. Oakland, CA: AK Press, 2006.

Moffa, Anthony L. I., 'Two Competing Models of Activism, One Goal: A Case Study of Anti-Whaling Campaigns in the Southern Ocean', *Yale Journal of International Law*, vol. 37, no. 201 (2012), pp. 201–213.

Moghaddam, F., 'The Staircase to Terrorism: A Psychological Exploration', *American Psychologist*, vol. 60, no. 2 (2005), pp. 161–169.

Monaghan, Rachel, 'Animal Rights and Violent Protest', *Terrorism and Political Violence*, vol. 9, no. 4 (1997), pp. 106–116.

Monaghan, Rachel, 'Terrorism in the Name of Human Rights', *Terrorism and Political Violence*, vol. 11, no. 4 (1999), pp. 159–169.

Monaghan, Rachel, 'Animal Rights and Violent Protest', in *Terrorism and Political Violence, Liberation*. Westport, CT: Praeger, 2006.

Monaghan, R., 'Not Quite Terrorism: Animal Rights Extremism in the United Kingdom', *Studies in conflict and Terrorism*, vol. 36, no. 11 (2013), pp. 933–951.

Nagtzaam, Gerry, *From Environmental Action to Ecoterrorism? Towards a Process Theory of Environmental and Animal Rights Oriented Political Violence*. Cheltenham, UK: Edward Elgar Press, 2017.

Nagtzaam, Gerry and Pete Lentini, 'Vigilantes on the High Seas: The Sea Shepherds and Political Violence', *Terrorism and Political Violence,* vol. 20, no. 1 (2008).

Pellow, David Naguib, 'Eco-Defense, Radical Environmentalism and Environmental Justice', in Ruth Kinna and Uri Gordon (eds.), *Routledge Handbook of Radical Politics*. London: Routledge, 2019, pp. 107–120.

Pickering, Leslie James, *The Earth Liberation Front: 1997–2002*. Portland, OR: Arissa Media Group, 2007.

Rogers, Nicole, 'Beyond Reason: Activism and Law in a Time of Climate Change', *Journal for the Study of Radicalism*, vol. 12, no. 2 (2018), pp. 157–182.

Rosebraugh, C., *Burning Rage of a Dying Planet: Speaking for the Earth Liberation Front*. New York: Lantern Books, 2004.

Rowell, A., *Green Backlash: Global Subversion of the Environment Movement*. London, New York: Routledge, 1996.

Sageman, Mark, *Understanding Terror Networks*. Philadelphia: University of Pennsylvania Press, 2004.

Scarce, R., *Eco-Warriors: Understanding the Radical Environmental Movement*. Chicago: Noble Press, 1989.

Scarce, Rik, *Eco-Warriors: Understanding the Radical Environmental Movement* (Updated Edition). Walnut Creek, CA: Left Coast Press, 2006.

Schwartz, D. M., 'Environmental Terrorism: Analyzing the Concept', *Journal of Peace Research*, vol. 35, no. 4 (1998), pp. 483–496.

Sea Shepherd Conservation Society Log, 'Campaigns from 1984–1986', *Sea Shepherd* (Summer 1984), on file with authors.

Sea Shepherd History, https://www.seashepherdglobal.org

Sedgwick, Mark, 'The Concept of Radicalisation as a Source of Confusion', *Terrorism and Political Violence*, vol. 22, no. 4 (2010), pp. 479–494.

Short, Brant, 'Earth First! and the Rhetoric of Moral Confrontation', *Communication Studies*, vol. 42, no. 2 (1991), pp. 172–188.

Silvaggio, A. V., 'The Forest Defense Movement, 1980–2005: Resistance at the Point of Extraction, Consumption, and Production' (PhD Dissertation, University of Oregon, Eugene, OR, 2005).

Smith, Rebecca K., "Ecoterrorism"? A Critical Analysis of the Vilification of Radical Environmental Activists as Terrorists', *Environmental Law*, vol. 38, no. 2 (2008), pp. 1–40.

Sprinzak, Ehud, 'The Psychopolitical Formation of Extreme Left Terrorism in a Democracy: The Case of the Weathermen', in Walter Reich (ed.), *Origins of Terrorism: Psychologies, Ideologies, Theologies, States of Mind*. Washington, DC: Woodrow Wilson Center Press, 1998, pp. 65–85.

Tester, Keith and John Walls, 'The Ideology and Current Activities of the Animal Liberation Front', *Contemporary Politics*, vol. 2, no. 2 (1996).

Vanderheiden, S., 'Eco-terrorism or Justified Resistance? Radical Environmentalism and the "War on Terror"', *Politics and Society*, vol. 22 (September 2005), pp. 425–447.

Wall, Derek, 'Snowballs, Elves and Skimmingtons? Genealogies of Environmental Direct Action', in B. Steel et al. (eds.), *Direct Action in British Environmentalism*. London: Routledge, 2000.

Watson, Paul, *Earthforce! An Earth Warrior's Guide to Strategy*. Los Angeles: Chaco Press, 1993.

Young, R. L., 'A Time Series Analysis of Eco-Terrorist Violence in the United States: 1993–2003' (PhD Dissertation, Sam Houston State University, Huntsville, TX, 2004).

Ziner, K. L., 'Burning Down the Houses', *E Magazine: The Environmental Magazine*, vol. 12, no. 3 (May/June 2001).

22

NEW FORMS OF ENVIRONMENTAL MOVEMENT INSTITUTIONALIZATION

Marketization and the politics of responsibility

Håkan Thörn

Introduction

While processes of institutionalization and anti-institutionalization (i.e., resistance against processes of institutionalization) have defined the environmental movement for almost half a century, I argue that recent developments associated with globalization, neoliberalism, and ecological modernization have transformed the field of environmental politics profoundly. These developments call for a re-conceptualization of movement institutionalization, which in previous research mainly has concerned national political contexts, particularly regarding movements' regularized access to policymakers. The focus and the main aim of this chapter is to provide new insights and revise existing conceptualizations of environmental movement institutionalization (and of social movement institutionalization more generally) in light of this changing structural context. I will demonstrate how the concepts of responsibilization and (de-)politicization provide accurate theoretical tools for grasping these changes, arguing that a key dimension of current climate activism affecting how institutionalization is shaped today is a politics of responsibility.

The chapter draws on empirical research on processes of the institutionalization in the context global climate governance and how these processes interacted with environmental movements in Sweden, using the US as a contrasting case (Cassegård et al. 2017).[1] Theoretically, it attempts to integrate theories on social movement institutionalization with governmentality analysis (Thörn 2016; Thörn and Svedberg 2016; Walters 2012). In the manner of previous research, it thus focuses on environmental movements based in the Global North: however, without making the assumption that this analytical framework could be applied to other contexts without re-conceptualization.

In the next section, as a point of departure, I briefly introduce key themes in the debate on social movement institutionalization in general and institutionalization of the environmental movement in particular. In the following section, I present a contribution to such a re-conceptualization of institutionalization, focusing on how marketization and responsibilization has transformed institutionalization and directed movement politics toward a new

 DOI: 10.4324/9780367855680-25

form of politics of responsibility. As already mentioned, social movement institutionalization has first and foremost been studied and theorized in a national context. And in those cases where it has been analyzed in a global context, it has most often been conceptualized as a "scale shift" from the national to the global level of politics (e.g., Van Der Heijden 2006; Betzold 2014). Much less attention has been paid to how processes of institutionalization may move from the global to the national. A highly significant example of this is how EMOs have promoted marketization strategies (such as carbon trading) following global developments originating in the Kyoto Protocol. To reverse the established mode of analysis, the third section discusses processes of (anti-)institutionalization in a global context while the fourth section takes a look at how global processes have affected and been translated to national contexts.

Classical perspectives on institutionalization

Going back to early twentieth-century classical sociology, institutionalization has always been a key theme in social movement theory (Blumer 1951; Michels 1915). The classical view emphasizes that institutionalization is defined by internal processes of formalization and professionalization, completed when a movement has become an integrated part of a society's organizational structure (della Porta and Diani 2006). Further, it has been argued that the institutionalization of a movement means that it loses its "charismatic" attraction and eventually declines as conflictive issues are translated into mainstream politics (Jamison et al. 1990; Coglianese 2001). This may, in turn, contribute to the emergence of new movement actors, reacting against the institutionalization of their predecessors with a radicalization of environmental politics. These developments produce movement cycles in which issue attention and intensified mobilization that involves radicalization are followed by periods of institutionalization and declining mobilization (e.g., Rüdig 1995).

In terms of the effects of institutionalization, the classical view implies that institutionalization brings social movements to an end as it "stops moving" because institutionalization is, in Alberoni's (1984, p. 83) words, "a way of channelling and conserving its tremendous energies". Other social movement scholars have challenged this view. In a study of the environmental movement, Diani and Donati (1999) showed how professionalization took place in parallel with the emergence of new radical actors (c.f. della Porta and Diani 2006: 151f). A survey of EMOs in 56 countries by Dalton et al. (2003) shows that confrontational action is more common among larger and better-staffed groups than among smaller, marginal groups. A similar debate concerns whether institutionalization involves actual political influence and/ or cooptation through "incorporation" (e.g., Dryzek et al. 2003). Importantly, declining mobilization in this context does not necessarily mean that membership in an institutionalized SMO decreases, or even stops increasing, but that active participation is replaced by passive membership. For example, in the context of the environmental movement, Greenpeace has continued to increase its entirely passive membership in periods of environmental movement institutionalization.

In connection with the so-called "new social movements", a number of scholars have argued that environmental movements have displayed particularly strong tendencies toward institutionalization: e.g., (Jamison et al. 1990; Rootes 1999). This research on the environmental movement has emphasized regularization of access to policy-makers as an important dimension of institutionalization. It should also be emphasized that this latter dimension of institutionalization mainly reflects developments in post-war capitalist democracies (Thörn and Svenberg 2016), partly changing the meaning of movement institutionalization in relation to the early twentieth-century political contexts that Michels and Blumer referred to. Regularized access to policy makers may be a result of a movement's strategy to influence policy (e.g., Dalton et al. 2003), but, as shown by Jamison (2001: 82), it may also be the result of external "incorporation pressures". For example, an important element of the Swedish model of welfare state capitalism was the creation of procedures for consulting movement representatives, recruiting movement leaders to government, and funding opportunities for movement groups, thus nurturing a culture of consensus (Thörn 2009).

This chapter recognizes and builds on previous research in the sense of understanding movement institutionalization in advanced capitalist societies as defined by three aspects: 1) formalization, 2) professionalization, and 3) regularization of access to policy makers. In the following, I will demonstrate how these three aspects come in new shapes in the context of advanced liberal governance.

Institutionalization and advanced liberal governance

Advanced liberal governance emerged under the influence of neoliberal discourse, involving policy networks with partnerships between state, market, and civil society, leading to more influence for business actors and the introduction of new regulations to support market mechanisms. In this context, new forms of institutionalization processes were again established, with processes of responsibilization among its key features. I would argue that established EMOs, by promoting marketization and engaging in responsibilization, once again displayed particularly strong tendencies also toward these new forms of institutionalization.

Importantly, I do not make a case for a qualitative shift from government to governance or argue that the new forms of institutionalization have completely replaced the old ones. Instead, I argue that advanced liberal governance has changed government and that the interlinked processes of responsibilization and marketization have added new forms of institutionalization, which have become increasingly dominant.

Politics of responsibility

I argue that in the context of advanced liberal – local, national, and global – governance, collective action by the environmental movement often takes the shape of a politics of responsibility, referring to conflict and struggle concerning responsibility. In the context of advanced liberal governance, the notion of a politics of responsibility implies a focus on how social movements may be involved in both negotiation and conflict around responsibilization and how this could be seen as a transformation of the dynamics of institutionalization as established during the era of welfare capitalism. Importantly, this involves establishing a discourse that combines an emphasis on moral agency and the rationality of marketization (Shamir 2008).

It should be noted that I do not claim that the politics of responsibility is an entirely new phenomenon. The struggle over responsibility has been a part of many modern political struggles, and the strategies used to hold governments responsible for their own actions have been numerous. In this sense, "politics of responsibility" is a broader concept than "responsibilization". However, as argued by Shamir (2008: 7),

> neo-liberal responsibilization is unique in ensuring an entrepreneurial disposition in the case of individuals and socio-moral authority in the case of institutions . . . a moral agency which is congruent with the attributed tendencies of economic-rational actors: autonomous, self-determined and self-sustaining subjects.

As my analysis will demonstrate, this new form of responsibilization has also reshaped the field of power and protest.

Responsibilization

The shift from welfare capitalism's social engineering to neoliberalism's advanced liberal governance (Scheller and Thörn 2018) involves a new political role of the state, affecting its relations to civil society and business. I will use "advanced liberal governance" to emphasize how contemporary liberal government, shaped under a strong influence of the political and economic philosophy of neoliberalism, does not necessarily imply less regulation or less politics as stipulated by neoliberal dogma. Rather, I argue that the field of environmental politics is a particularly relevant example of how advanced liberal governance involves a mix of de-regulations and re-regulations to support the introduction of market mechanisms.

Rose (1999: 174f.) has argued that advanced liberal governing involves a "double movement of autonomization and responsibilization". This implies that politics "is to be returned to society itself, but no longer in a social form: in the form of individual morality, organizational responsibility and ethical community". According to Burchell (1993: 275), this new form of responsibilization involves "encouraging" or "offering individuals or collectives active involvement in action to resolve the kind of issues hitherto held to be the responsibility of authorized governmental agencies" (ibid.: 275–276). There are, however, certain limitations to Rose's and Burchell's definitions of responsibilization and much of the research in which it is applied. While responsibilization does not appear as forced upon actors in their account, it still comes out as an overly unidirectional process. The approach presented here, which I call "politics of responsibility" (see further later in this chapter), recognizes these limitations and understands responsibilization as a process involving negotiation and/or struggle (Thörn 2016; Thörn and Svenberg 2016).

How then has responsibilization affected the dynamics of formalization, professionalization, and regularization of access to policymakers that define "classic" institutionalization processes? First, marketization comes with new modes of formalization of movement activities. For example, EMOs have engaged in carbon trading through a procedure of asking their members to buy carbon credits from the organization to compensate for their air travel (the EMOs then use that money to buy carbon credits in order to "lock them in") (Thörn and Svenberg 2016).

Second, the concept of responsibilization highlights how institutionalization in the sense of regularization of access to policy makers has changed with the introduction of advanced liberal governance. In this new context, EMOs participate in "policy networks" that may include government agencies and business, such as bodies set up to create "self- regulation". Based on a discourse of moral responsibility, such policy networks establish certain environmental codes or standards for businesses, which are meant to function as an alternative to state regulation through legislation (or to complement it).

Third, responsibilization changes both the meaning and content of professionalization. In the context of classical institutionalization, the professionalization of EMOs may be shaped and motivated by their "environmental expertise". However, new forms of professionalization of EMOs have emerged, and the status of professionals has changed in the context of advanced liberal governance. As argued by Power (1997) and Rose (1999), professionals are now subjected to new forms of accountability, involving a "technology of distrust" (Rose 1999: 154) linked to a heavy emphasis on (self-)evaluation and auditing. This further means that civil society organizations may need to acquire professional skills in business management. In the case of EMOs, skills in economics are also demanded by the emphasis on market mechanisms in processes of responsibilization. A significant example of this is the appointment of a leading Swedish professor of environmental economics (with a background as an activist in a Swedish EMO) to the US Environmental Defense Fund, which previously had interacted closely with the US administration on the construction of an international carbon-trading model in the run-up to Kyoto (Thörn et al. 2017a).

A transfer of responsibilities always involves de-responsibilization of another actor. It also means that agents can be responsibilized and de-responsibilized at the same time. For example, when the responsibility to participate in creating or implementing certain regulations (e.g., relating to carbon markets) is imposed on an EMO, it may also have the effect of de-responsibilizing the EMO in the sense of taking on a profound political responsibility in relation to climate change. In this case, (de)responsibilization thus involves de-politicization while, as will be demonstrated later, it may in other cases involve politicization. Finally, responsibilization does not in all cases involve a transfer of responsibility. Particularly in the case of environmental struggles, social movements may shoulder responsibilities that they feel no one is taking; for example, the Swedish EMO Nature and Youth addressed the politicians in the following way: "[W]e feel the responsibility that you shirk" (Thörn and Svenberg 2016).

(De-)politicization

The expanded conceptual understanding of institutionalization that I am proposing here offers a way to move beyond the debate on to what extent institutionalization means a loss of a movements' radical energies. Instead of working with the dichotomy of "institutionalization" versus "radicalization", I suggest that the concepts of politicization and de-politicization (e.g., Swyngedouw 2014; Chatterton et al. 2012; Jaeger 2007) provide better tools for analyzing the effects of movement institutionalization. De-politicization here refers to a process in which the (potential) articulation of social conflict is suppressed through (quasi-)consensus building between agents who are in a position of unequal dependency. Politicization refers to a process through which such conflicts are manifested (i.e., articulated and acted on in public). It may be argued that institutionalization per se implies that movement action is de-politicized, considering that formalization, professionalization, and regularization of access to policy makers are developments associated with consensus building and a technocratic, problem-solving approach to politics – and that responsibilization adds a moral discourse that transforms political subjectivity by turning political issues into moral responsibilities. However, while institutionalization historically often has involved de-politicization, I argue that the relation between the two processes is always an empirical question. Further, I will demonstrate how institutionalized and de-politicized EMOs have, in light of political disappointments and under the pressure of new, radical environmental actors, engaged in a re-politicization of their activities.

Institutionalization and globalization

How should one understand the relationship between institutionalization in a national and a global context? Writing in the mid-1990s, Rüdig (1995) linked the processes of institutionalization of the global environmental movement to two global issue attention cycles in environmental politics. The first emerged in the early 1970s as a new environmental movement demanded radical changes such as an end to economic growth. The second emerged around 1990, when new radical demands were made in connection with new global ecology issues, first and foremost global warming. Each of the two attention cycles lasted for roughly half a decade, and each was followed by a process of institutionalization of movement politics. But while the first cycle, according to Rüdig (1995: 2), was followed by an institutionalization of environmental policy at a national level, "the main institutional legacy of the second cycle" was at the global level. Further, writing in the late 1990s, Rootes (1999: 1–2) pointed to how environmental movements' regularized access to policy makers has been established in a global context:

> At a global level, NGOs that are part of or linked to environmental movements enjoy unprecedented status as interlocutors of the representatives of states as they attempt to grapple with the formation and implementation of policies and institutions to deal with global environmental problems.

This research, which concerns the new environmental movement during its first three decades, thus suggests a relatively straightforward development: radicalization is followed by a relatively rapid institutionalization in a movement process that is partly cyclical but also progresses in a scale shift from national to global. I challenge this narrative in two ways. First, I argue that the relationship between institutionalization in a national and a global context is not simply unidirectional and second, that the relation between institutionalization and anti-intuitionalist challenges is less straightforward than has been previously assumed. My starting point is research on the third cycle of attention in a global context: the build-up toward the Copenhagen COP15 in 2009 (Chatterton et al. 2012; Hadden 2015; Wahlström et al. 2013) and a fourth attention cycle: the build-up toward the Paris COP in 2015 and the developments following the Paris Agreement, including the emergence of new global environmental actors, such as Fridays for Future and Extinction Rebellion.

Advanced liberal global governance

The concept of global governance has been used to capture the political dimensions of contemporary globalization (Scholte 2005; Held and Koenig-Archibugi 2005), including global climate governance (e.g., Stevenson and Dryzek 2014), or redefined as "global governmentality" (Larner and Walters 2004). In globalization theory, "governance" is different from "government", as usually defined in political science and international relations. Governance is "defined by diverse sources of rule-making, political authority, and power" (Held and McGrew 2002: 9). Thus, nation-states may be strategic sites in global governance networks but do not constitute the center of political decision and strategy making as global governance processes can include a number of political layers (supra-state, nation-state, region, municipality) as well as various actors, including businesses and NGOs. Governance generally emphasizes social and political steering through self-organizing inter-organizational networks, of which public, private, and voluntary organizations can be part. In the governance literature, it is most often assumed that these networks are more open and flexible (i.e., less institutionalized) than the political structures of the nation-state and thus provide more opportunities for movement actors to have influence. However, as I will demonstrate later in this chapter, such networks hardly escape processes of institutionalization, and I thus consider them part of an institutionalized political milieu.

While the achievements of the UNFCCC in terms of contributing to the fight against climate change since its first Conference of the Parties (COP) in Berlin in 1995 have been too limited, there can be no doubt that it has become a key institution of global climate governance. At the 2015 COP21 in Paris, the largest gathering of national political leaders in history posed in front of the global media, with the corporations (some of them major funders) right behind them. The increasing globalization of EMOs in the 2000s is a process that has been spurred on by the emergence of the climate issue as the main theme of the environmental movement in the post-Kyoto process. This has also brought an institutionalization of EMOs through their participation in global climate policy networks, including not only political institutions but also businesses. For example, they participate in bodies set up either to solidify and implement objectives formulated by governments, supra-national political institutions, and corporations or to establish certain codes and standards meant to function as alternatives or complements to state regulation by legislation (e.g., Held and Koenig-Archibugi 2005; Scholte 2005). Next, I provide three examples of programs that have been launched in the context of global climate governance to address climate change. By establishing market mechanisms, these programs emphasize responsibilization of EMOs, private companies, and individuals. In this context, EMOs have been involved in both the construction of such regulatory frameworks and the actual implementation of programs. These examples also point to the heterogeneity, the ongoing struggle, and the internal reflexivity and change within the global environmental movement. While some actors were part of establishing the programs and have promoted them, others resisted them from the start, contributing to pressuring a few of the established actors to re-evaluate their original position.

1   *Emissions trading* has been the most important mechanism for achieving the Kyoto Protocol's target of reducing greenhouse gas emissions. Heavy corporate lobbying was behind the US proposal to the UN, which led to the adoption of the program in the Kyoto Protocol framework. As already mentioned, a major institutionalized EMO in the United States, the Environmental Defense Fund, interacted closely with the US administration in the process of constructing the carbon-trading model in the run-up to Kyoto (Thörn et al. 2017a). However, while market mechanisms were one of the key issues dividing the climate movement in Copenhagen in 2009, institutionalized EMOs re-evaluated emissions in the run-up to the Paris 2015 COP. Their approach to climate activism can still perhaps best be described as expressing ambivalence; on one hand, a criticism is articulated that dismisses the system, on the other hand there is a critique that mainly emphasizes its inefficiency, as for example in a report co-produced by Greenpeace and WWF (2012), titled 'Strengthening the EU emissions trading scheme and raising climate ambition'.

2   *REDD+* (reducing emissions from forest degradation and forest emission) is an example of global climate governance that involves development cooperation (e.g., Hermansen 2015) and includes the participation of EMOs in the implementation of its projects. The original REDD proposal was designed to reduce forest loss by including forests in a carbon-trading scheme. REDD+ also includes issues of conservation and sustainable forest management (cf. Hermansen 2015). REDD participation has been a highly contentious issue in the climate movement (Cassegård and Thörn 2017), especially among organizations based in the Global South. Certain NGOs based in resource-scarce areas in Asia and Africa, while being critical of how the program is designed, have still argued that REDD+ is what they have to work with, and their strategy is to try to change aspects of it "from within". At the same time, the NO REDD campaign has been highly visible in the context of the alternative spaces at the COP meetings, especially in Lima and in Paris.

3   *Forest Stewardship Council* is an international "multi-stakeholder organization", which has both corporate interests and environmental organizations as members. It aims to promote "responsible" management of the world's forests through self-regulation by creating certain standards for self-regulation. In Sweden, a country where 70% of the area is covered by forest, the participation of EMOs in FSC has been significant. For example the largest EMO, the Swedish Society for Nature Conservation (SSNC), claims to have taken the initiative to create the first Swedish standards for FSC certification in the 1990s, and in the first decade

of the 2000s, all the major Swedish EMOs were members of FSC. However, in 2010, the SSNC left the FSC after it had documented repeated violation of FSC standards by certified forest companies. Both WWF and Greenpeace have, however, remained members.

These programs are part of a global governance structure that has been theorized as a "hegemonic green carbon governmentality" (Methmann 2010; Oels 2005; Lövbrand and Stripple 2011; Luke 1999), which ultimately protects "business as usual". To paraphrase Methmann: the failure of these programs "is the success of a depoliticization of climate change politics" (Methmann 2010: 371). However this is not the whole story. Importantly, I would add that while certain EMOs are part of this game, I have also provided examples of resistance to such institutionalization in the shape of a politics of responsibility. Such resistance has, in the context of the global climate meetings, come in three forms, as movement actors have 1) rejected the offer to participate in policy-making processes, 2) redefined "moral agency" while accepting the premises of responsibilization by invoking a moral responsibility of corporations by "naming and shaming", and 3) criticized market solutions and instead demanded a re-responsibilization of political institutions (Cassegård et al. 2017). Such resistance represents a politicization of climate governance and provides reasons for questioning the narrative of a relatively straightforward movement trajectory, in which institutionalization per se implies de-politicization and even movement decline.

Importantly, with the globalization of the environmental movement, the more institutionalized EMOs in the Global North have had to adapt to the increasing presence and strength of voices from the Global South that are characteristic of global activism in the twenty-first century, a process that has thus undermined its US/Eurocentric character (Doherty 2002, 2006; Thörn et al. 2017b). As EMOs in the countries of the Global North have joined or become more active in global networks that have a strong representation of EMOs from the Global South, it has become difficult for them to avoid the fact that the issues of climate and social justice are inseparable in a global context. Instead, institutionalized EMOs have increasingly become engaged in politicizing environmental discourse by criticizing market mechanisms; calling for climate justice; and engaging in a politics of responsibility that calls on political leaders and local, national, regional, and global institutions to shoulder their political responsibility to take forceful action to fight climate change.

To sum up the global developments during the third and fourth global attention cycle in the 2000s: while new forms of institutionalization processes have clearly taken place in the context of global climate governance, we have also seen how highly institutionalized actors have redefined their previous approach by questioning the idea of businesses self-regulation and linked up with new and non-institutionalized actors, particularly from the Global South.

Institutionalization in national context

In this section, focusing on the example of Sweden and with the US as a contrasting case, I will focus on two aspects that have been under-emphasized in the main body of research on institutionalization, which has mainly been concerned with the context of the nation-state. (See also the chapter by de Moor and Wahlström in this volume.) First, I will demonstrate how institutionalization processes may vary depending on how capitalism is politically articulated in different national contexts and second, how processes of movement institutionalization in national contexts are affected by global processes (and not just vice versa).

Sweden belong to a group of states in the Global North characterized by "organized capitalism" (Hall and Soskice 2001), using a model of coordinated market economy (CME). This involves an active state and functional complementarity among institutions. A consensus-oriented political culture developed in Sweden during in the post-war era, involving policy networks with strong ties between government and big business. These developments also fostered close relationships between the government and civil society, including EMOs, and thus a high degree of movement institutionalization (Thörn 2009). This has facilitated active and highly coordinated environmental policies since the 1970s: e.g., supporting the development of energy-saving technologies or renewable energy (Thörn and Svenberg 2016).

However, beginning in 1991, a system shift brought changes to Swedish environmental movement strategy, as EMOs participated in a process of responsibilization. This involved responsibilizing the individual through the discourse of sustainable consumption, supporting green corporate responsibility and market solutions (e.g., carbon trading), and encouraging EMOs to take on regulatory functions by establishing certain codes or standards for corporations. Criticisms against these developments were voiced in connection with the build-up to Copenhagen COP15 as new actors emerged, criticizing the highly institutionalized EMOs for being co-opted into a political practice of business as usual and even greenwashing. In the wake of the post-Copenhagen disillusionment and in the build-up to COP21 in Paris, a more fundamental process of re-strategizing occurred among institutionalized Swedish EMOs, interacting with the emergence of new, anti-institutionalist actors in the global and national context. In this process, and particularly under the influence of developments in the global climate movement (Cassegård and Thörn 2017), climate justice became a discursive nodal point in the collective identity that unified the Swedish environmental movement, including new environmental actors and institutionalized actors, such as established EMOs, a number of Swedish NGOs that had previously focused entirely on global solidarity issues, and labor unions, which were also politicized in the process.

While this process thus provides an example of how a national social movement may transform when shifting to a global context, it also demonstrates how the articulation of a political issue by a social movement may change when shifting from the global to the national level and how it may involve new processes of institutionalization. While the establishing of climate justice as a unifying yet contested concept represented a politicization of previously politicized sections of the global climate movement, the case of Sweden demonstrates how climate justice does not unambiguously imply a politicization of the climate issue when translated into national politics. One of the interpretations of climate justice in the context of the COP meetings identified by Chatterton et al. (2012: 607) is an understanding of climate justice as "a struggle between global Northern and Southern states within the UNFCCC process". Swedish EMOs largely subscribed to this view, but their translation of the concept into the Swedish national context, particularly into an organizational form, needs to be seen in relation to a national history of state-civil society cooperation in the area of development aid. This meant that the climate justice discourse in the Swedish political context became embedded in institutionalized "partnerships" between EMOs based in Sweden and in countries of the Global South, selected by the Swedish governments as recipients of climate-related development aid. This cooperation involved a responsibilization of development aid (Thörn and Svenberg 2016) as Swedish EMOs channeled government funding from the Swedish International Development Agency (Sida) to NGOs in the Global South. As development aid has been organized in the mode of new public management, it has involved a de-politicization of civil society cooperation (Thörn 2016). At the same time, the climate justice framework has also been used to articulate anti-institutionalist approaches in the Swedish national context. For example, two leading EMOs linked climate justice to the issue of the restoration of poor Swedish suburbs (Thörn and Svenberg 2016).

The US case is distinct in several aspects. First, it belongs to the Anglo American variety of liberal market economies, which, in many respects, differs from the model of "organized capitalism" in Sweden (Hall and Soskice 2001). It involves more flexible and less coordinated institutions and policy networks that lack the consensual relationships between state and civil society that define climate politics in Sweden (and many other North European countries). Further, in contrast to Sweden, the environmental movement in the United States has never been formally institutionalized in terms of a more formalized regularized access to policy makers (Hadden 2017). On the other hand, the other dimension of institutionalization, professionalization, has been taken further by most established EMOs in the United States than in Sweden and in many other countries in the Global North (Thörn et al. 2017a). Further, the example mentioned earlier of how the EDF played an important part (together with the Clinton administration) in the co-construction of a model for carbon trading to be presented to the UNFCCC provides an example of a strong link between institutionalization at the national level in the United States and in the global context. This example, in fact, emphasizes how the hegemonic position of the US makes it substantially more globally influential than other countries.

In contrast to Sweden, "climate justice" has been more or less identical with politicizing developments in the US context in the 2010s. This must be understood in relation to the fact that "climate justice" in the US has emerged in connection with strong impulses from both local and global justice groups. Further, national mobilization, such as the struggle against the Keystone XL pipeline and the fossil fuel industry, politicized environmental discourse in the national arena during this period. These national mobilizations also had strong local dimensions, and links were created with the environmental justice movements that, since the 1980s, had mobilized around environmentally destructive facilities and waste located in poor minority communities, as well as Indigenous land rights issues.

Conclusion: beyond institutionalization versus radicalization

Drawing on empirical research on processes of movement institutionalization in the context global climate governance and how these processes interacted with environmental movements in the contrasting cases of Sweden and the US, this chapter has intended to make a contribution to a re-conceptualization of movement institutionalization. It has focused on how marketization and responsibilization have transformed institutionalization in both global and national contexts, processes involving both politicization and de-politicization of environmental activism. Further I have demonstrated that the relationship between institutionalization and anti-institutionalist approaches, and between institutionalization in a national and a global context, is less straightforward than what has been assumed in previous research.

As a point of departure, I referred to Rüdig's (1995) research on two attention cycles in environmental politics in the early 1970s and 1990s and his argument that the first cycle was followed by processes of institutionalization at a national level while the second's institutional legacy was at the global level. I have identified two further attention cycles (also lasting for half a decade each), representing an intensified globalization of environmental activism in the 2000s: the first beginning around 2005 (with an important mobilizing moment at the 2007 COP13 in Bali) and culminating with COP15 in Copenhagen and the second in the run-up to the 2015 COP21 in Paris and culminating in 2019 (after which it was brought to a halt by COVID-19). These attention cycles have been parallel to a continued globalization of advanced liberal governance and its emphasis on constructing a framework for transnational carbon markets. They were also accompanied by a continued globalization of environmental activism, which was part of the emergence of a broader climate movement. I have demonstrated how these interlocked processes of mobilization and institutionalization involved a complex pattern of interaction between national and global contexts. While in the environmental movement, institutionalization historically has often equaled a de-politicization of activism, recent developments in the 2000s have demonstrated how different articulations are possible as institutionalized EMOs have engaged in a politicizing environmental discourse by criticizing market mechanisms; calling for climate justice; and engaging in a politics of responsibility that calls on political leaders and local, national, regional, and global institutions to take on a political responsibility by forceful action to fight climate change.

Regarding processes of institutionalization in a national context, I argued that social movement institutionalization changed shape with the introduction of regularized access to policy makers in the context of democratic, post-war welfare capitalist societies and, in a corresponding manner, again with the introduction of advanced liberal governance. The latter has modified processes of institutionalization through the introduction of new practices of responsibilization, meaning active involvement by civil society and business in political responsibilities previously associated with state agencies – a development that has involved the introduction of new regulations to support market mechanisms. As in the context of welfare capitalism, this was a result of both the movement's active efforts to take part in policy making and the pressure/encouragement to do so by government institutions.

At the same time, the cases of the Swedish and the US environmental movements and their relation to ecological modernization have demonstrated that the shift to advanced liberal governance is defined by a great deal of continuity regarding movement institutionalization. Nevertheless, in both cases, advanced liberal responsibilization has reshaped the field of national environmental politics, and I have argued that the concept of responsibilization and the politics of responsibility provide accurate theoretical tools for grasping these changes.

This chapter has thus demonstrated that the assumption often made in previous research, that institutionalization of a movement automatically brings its decline in the sense of loss of radical energy and a de-politicization of the issues on which it acts, needs to be reformulated as a question open to empirical research. Movements are, in practice, never fully institutionalized, which means that activists and groups can remain outside government networks and formalized and professionalized modes of organization. Further, to account for the agency of institutionalized EMOs, we need pay attention to how they relate to criticism and resistance – from within (i.e., its own members) and from the outside (e.g., new and radical groups). The dynamics of this interaction means that institutionalized EMOs do not automatically "de-politicize" issues in the sense of suppressing conflicts with government institutions or corporations. Pressure from grassroots activists can bring about moments of re-politicization that lead to a breakdown of a consensual "big green" approach. Focusing on this interaction and its effects is a way to study the degree of stability of the dominant, advanced liberal governance of the environment.

Note

1 In addition to Sweden and the US, national cases in the project also included Denmark and Japan. This chapter primarily builds on two chapters and one article for which I was the main author: Thörn et al (2017a, 2017b) and Thörn and Svenberg (2016). I am grateful for the input from my colleagues in the project, particularly my co-editors and co-writers Carl Cassegård, Linda Sonderyd, Sebastian Svenberg, and Åsa Wettergren. Examples from the US environmental movement mainly build on Jennifer Hadden's (2017) contribution to our book.

Bibliography

Alberoni, Francesco (1984). *Movement and institution.* New York: Columbia University Press.

Betzold, Carola (2014). Responsiveness or influence? Whom to lobby in international climate change negotiations. *International Negotiation.* 1 (19), 35–61.

Blumer, Herbert (1951). Social movements. In: McClung Lee, A., ed. *Principles of sociology.* New York: Barnes and Nobles, 298–306.

Burchell, Graham (1993). Liberal government and techniques of the self. *Economy and Society.* 22 (3), 267–282.

Cassegård, Carl, Soneryd, Linda, Thörn, Håkan and Wettergren, Åsa (eds.) (2017). *Climate activism in a globalizing world: comparative perspectives on social movements in the global north.* New York: Routledge.

Cassegård, Carl and Thörn, Håkan (2017). Climate justice, equity and movement mobilization. In Thörn, H., Cassegård, C., Soneryd, L. and Åsa Wettergren, Å. eds. *Climate action in a globalizing world: Comparative perspectives on environmental movements in the global North.* New York: Routledge.

Cassegård, Carl and Thörn, Håkan (2018). Toward a postapocalyptic environmentalism? Responses to loss and visions of the future in climate activism. *Environment and Planning E: Nature and Space.* 1 (4), 561–578.

Chatterton, Paul, Featherstone, David and Routledge, Paul (2012). Articulating climate justice in Copenhagen: Antagonism, the commons, and solidarity. *Antipode.* 45 (3), 602–620.

Coglianese, Cary (2001). Social Movements, law, and society: The institutionalization of the environmental movement. *University of Pennsylvania Law Review.* 85 (150), 85–118.

Dalton, Russell J., Recchia, Steve, and Rohrschneider, Robert (2003). The environmental movement and the modes of political action'. *Comparative Political Studies.* 36 (7), 743–771.

della Porta, Donatella and Diani, Mario (2006). *Social movements – an introduction.* Second edition. Oxford: Blackwell.

Diani, Mario and Donati, Paolo (1999). Organizational change in Western European environmental groups: A framework for analysis. *Environmental Politics.* 8, 13–34.

Doherty, B. (2002). *Ideas and actions in the green movement.* New York: Routledge.

Doherty, B. (2006). Friends of the Earth International: Negotiating a transnational identity. *Environmental Politics.* 15 (5), 860–880.

Dryzek, John. S., Downes, David., Hunold, Christian., Schlosberg, David. w. Hernes, Hans-Kristian. (2003). *Green States and social movements: Environmentalism in the United States, United Kingdom, Germany & Norway.* Oxford: Oxford University Press.

Greenpeace and WWF (2012). Strengthening the EU emissions trading scheme and raising climate ambition: Facts, Measures and Implications. www.greenpeace.org/eu-unit/en/Publications/2012/ETS-report/. Downloaded 1 June 2015.

Hadden, Jennifer (2015). *Networks in contention: The divisive politics of climate change.* Cambridge: Cambridge University Press.

Hadden, Jennifer (2017). Learning from defeat: The strategic reorientation of the U.S. climate movement. In Thörn, H., Cassegård, C., Soneryd, L. and Åsa Wettergren, Å. eds. *Climate action in a globalizing world: Comparative perspectives on environmental movements in the global North.* New York: Routledge.

Hall, Peter A. and Soskice, David W. (2001). *Varieties of capitalism: The institutional foundations of comparative advantage.* Wiley Online Library.

Held, David and Koenig-Archibugi, Mathias (eds.) (2005). *Global governance and public accountability.* Oxford: Blackwell.

Held, David and McGrew, Anthony (eds.) (2002). *Governing globalization: Power, authority and global governance.* Malden; MA: Polity Press.

Hermansen, E.A. (2015). Policy window entrepreneurship: the backstage of the world's largest REDD+ initiative. *Environmental Politics.* 24 (6), 932–950.

Jaeger, Hans-Martin (2007). "Global civil society" and the political depoliticization of governance. *International Political Sociology.* 1 (3), 257–277.

Jamison, Andrew (2001). *The making of green knowledge: environmental politics and cultural transformation.* Cambridge: Cambridge University Press.

Jamison, Andrew, Eyerman, Ron, Cramer, Jacqueline and Læssøe, Jesper (1990). *The making of the new environmental consciousness: A comparative study of the environmental movements in Sweden, Denmark and the Netherlands.* Edinburgh: Edinburgh University Press.

Larner, W. and Walters, W. (eds.) (2004). *Global governmentality: Governing international spaces*. London: Routledge.

Lidskog, R., Soneryd, L. and Uggla, U. (2010). *Transboundary risk governance*. Abingdon: Earthscan.

Lövbrand, Eva and Stripple, Jonathan (2011). Making climate change governable: accounting for carbon as sinks, credits and personal budgets. *Critical Policy Studies*. 5 (2), 187–200.

Luke, Timothy W. (1999). Environmentality as Green governmentality. In: Darier, Éric, ed. *Discourses of the environment*. Oxford: Blackwell Publishers, 121–151.

Methmann, Chris Paul (2010). "Climate protection" as empty signifier: A discourse theoretical perspective on climate mainstreaming in world politics. *Millennium – Journal of International Studies*. 39 (2), 345–372.

Michels, Robert (1915). *Political parties: A sociological study of the oligarchial tendencies of modern democracy*. Glencoe. IL: Free Press.

Oels, Angela (2005). Rendering climate change governable: From biopower to advanced liberal government. *Journal of Environmental Policy and Planning*. 7 (3), 185–207.

Power, Michael (1997). *The audit society: Rituals of verification*. Oxford: Oxford University Press.

Rootes, Chris (1999). Environmental movements: From the local to the global. *Environmental Politics*. 8 (1), 1–12.

Rose, Nikolas (1999). *Powers of freedom: Reframing political thought*. Cambridge: Cambridge University Press.

Rüdig, W. (1995). Editorial. In: Rüdig, W., ed. *Green politics three*. Edinburgh: Edinburgh University Press, 1–8.

Scheller, David and Thörn, Håkan (2018). Governing 'sustainable urban development' through self-build groups and cohousing: The cases of Hamburg and Gothenburg". *International Journal for Urban and Regional Research*. 42 (5), 914–933.

Scholte, Jan A. (2005). *Globalization: A critical introduction*. Second edition. London: Macmillan.

Shamir, Ronen (2008). The age of responsibilization: On market-embedded morality. *Economy and Society*. 37 (1), 1–19.

Stevenson, H. and Dryzek, J. S. (2014). *Democratizing Global Climate Governance*. Cambridge: Cambridge University Press.

Swyngedouw, Eric (ed.) (2014). *The post-political and its discontents: Spaces of de-politicisation, spectres of radical politics*. Edinburgh: Edinburgh University Press.

Thörn, Håkan ((2009). *Anti-apartheid and the emergence of a global civil society*. Second edition. Basingstoke: Palgrave Macmillan.

Thörn, Håkan ((2016). Politics of responsibility: Governing distant populations through civil society in Mozambique, Rwanda and South Africa. *Third World Quarterly*. 37 (8), 1505–1523.

Thörn, Håkan, Cassegård, Carl, Soneryd, Linda and Wettergren, Åsa (eds.) (2017a). Climate action in a globalizing world: An introduction. In: Cassegård, C., Soneryd, L., Thörn, H., and Wettergren, Å., eds. *Climate action in a globalizing world: Comparative perspectives on environmental movements in the global north*. New York: Routledge.

Thörn, Håkan, Cassegård, Carl, Soneryd, Linda and Wettergren, Åsa (2017b). Hegemony and environmentalist strategy: Global governance, movement mobilization and climate justice. In: Cassegård, C., Soneryd, L., Thörn, H., and Wettergren, Å., eds. *Climate action in a globalizing world: Comparative perspectives on environmental movements in the global north*. New York: Routledge.

Thörn, Håkan and Svenberg, Sebastian (2016). "We feel the responsibility that you shirk": The politics of responsibility and the case of the Swedish environmental movement. *Social Movement Studies*. 15 (6), 593–609.

Van Der Heijden, H. A. (2006). Globalization, environmental movements, and international political opportunity structures. *Organization and Environment*. 19 (1), 28–45.

Wahlström, Mattias, Wennerhag, Magnus and Rootes, Chris. (2013). Framing "the climate issue": Patterns of participation and prognostic frames among climate summit protesters. *Global Environmental Politics*. 1 (4), 101–122.

Walters, W. (2012). *Governmentality: Critical encounters*. Abingdon: Routledge.

23

COMMERCIALIZATION

Environmentalism and the capitalist market

Philip Balsiger

Introduction

There can be no doubt today that the environmental cause has been commercialized to a great extent. To protect the environment, consumers can buy eco-friendly detergent, drive an electric car, choose furniture made from FSC-certified wood, make sustainable holidays on an organic farm, opt for renewable energies, and compensate their flight's emissions. Companies publish environmental reports, are evaluated according to environmental criteria, display their environmental accomplishments, and make partnerships with environmental NGOs to support conservation efforts. All these examples illustrate how markets, companies, and products are presented and act not as causes but as solutions to environmental problems. But what role did and does the environmental *movement* play in these processes? Are environmentalists at the origin of commercialization? Or has their cause been sold out, taken over by capitalist forces?

Commercialization (or related concepts such as marketization, economization, or commodification) is defined as a process through which life spheres, goods, or causes that were outside of markets enter the market sphere and become products or product qualities that are bought and sold in (capitalist) markets (Balsiger & Schiller-Merkens 2019; Çalışkan & Callon 2009; Hochschild 2003; Radin 1996). This chapter's aim is to describe the environmental movements' varied positions with regard to commercialization of the environmental cause and, more broadly, its views of capitalist markets at large.

Environmentalism as a whole identifies consumer culture and the globalized economy as a major cause of environmental hazards and climate change, but it disagrees as to whether or not environmental transformation is possible within a capitalist system and whether it can be or perhaps even should be pursued through the means of the market economy. Parts of the environmental movement see capitalism as a systemic cause of environmental degradation and global warming. They advocate radical and structural transformations through policies that severely limit capitalist firms, such as bans and strict regulations, and they are alarmed about the commercialization of the cause, which they have been criticizing for a long time. Yet another part of the movement has been a driving force behind this process. These environmentalists see actions of transnational companies as part of the solution to environmental problems. They develop and advocate market-based environmentalism such as partnerships with multinationals, certification, and green consumerism.

DOI: 10.4324/9780367855680-26

The chapter describes these different positions with regard to the role of capitalism and capitalist firms in the environmental cause and analyzes their evolution over time. It argues that while at least parts of the environmental movement have always considered commercial initiatives as one way to protect the environment, the role and place of firms in this process is contested within the movement, especially when it comes to big transnational companies. While market-based environmentalism has been on the increase since the 1990s, with the active support of many of the most powerful environmental NGOs, the past decade or so has seen renewed and growing criticism of this evolution within the environmental movement, in particular in light of the very limited results of past market-based efforts to fight climate change.

The chapter adopts a broad view of social movements as fields consisting of many different collective and individual actors sharing a common cause and broad goals but often disagreeing on the means to achieve these goals (Balsiger 2016b; Bereni 2019; Fillieule et al. 2010). The environmental movement is approached as a diversified field composed of both radical grassroots actors using confrontational tactics and seeing capitalism as the main cause of environmental degradation and reformist and often highly institutionalized actors lobbying and using market-based tactics – including professionalized NGOs, government officials, and sustainability officers in companies. The chapter's focus is by and large on the environmental movement in Western Europe and North America – it will not look at dynamics in specific countries but rather at the general evolution of the movement in this geographic sphere. It will also give limited attention to dynamics of the movement in countries from the Global South, where the turn to market-related action forms was generally less present, and the radical and anti-capitalist orientation of the environmental movement has been stronger (Dauvergne 2016).

The economy and the environmental movement

Many studies have discussed the diversity of the environmental movement and, in particular, its ideological divisions (Bernstein 2001; Felli 2008, 2021; Geels et al. 2015; Hajer 1995). Following in particular Felli (2021), I will distinguish here between an adaptive and a transformative pole of the movement. The former is pro-business, sees environmentalism as compatible with capitalism, and develops market-related actions that seek to make mainstream businesses greener through adaptation. The latter, meanwhile, is critical of mainstream businesses' involvement in environmentalism and seeks a transformation of society and the economy. It does so, in particular, by developing alternative forms of producing and consuming, sometimes clearly associated with anti-capitalist struggles, but often within a more diffuse ideology of a decentralized and small-scale alternative green economy. Not all initiatives and organizations can be clearly attributed to one side or the other, with pro-business NGOs often also supporting the development of alternative economic institutions and actors and initiatives from the alternative economy not necessarily opposed to, or collaborating with, profit-oriented businesses. But the distinction captures an essential fault line within the environmental movement and is required to understand its diverging positions on commercialization and the dynamics of these positions over time.

Adaptive environmentalism: saving the environment through green capitalism

The "adaptive" pole of environmentalism is at the core of the idea of sustainable development, which makes the pursuit of environmentalist goals such as environmental protection and the fight against global warming compatible with economic development. It also corresponds to what is referred to as "green capitalism", "green growth", or "green consumerism" (Akenji 2014). From this point of view, commercialization can indeed be a way of achieving environmental goals, if capitalism develops and implements green practices (Newell & Paterson 2010). It is important not to simply dismiss such concepts and ideological positions as forms of recuperation of the environmental movement by state actors and corporations. It is much more accurate to understand it as an evolution of the environmental movement, starting in the 1980s and becoming increasingly visible in the 1990s and 2000s. During this period, which also corresponds to the increased professionalization and institutionalization of environmentalism, reformist and pro-market positions gained increasing prominence in the movement and ended up becoming dominant (Mol 2000).

Actors pertaining to this position in the environmental movement would thus increasingly advocate market-based solutions to environmental problems. This includes sophisticated forms of carbon markets advocated by environmental economists, but also many other forms through which environmental policies will be implemented within markets. Commercialization means the integration of environmental or sustainability issues into the economy; criteria of environmental evaluation thus become part of the economy. Green technologies are marketized with the hope that they will be increasingly adopted by consumers. The idea is not to change society fundamentally – consumerism, for instance, is not seen as problematic as such. Rather, what counts is to orient production and consumption toward green values.

We can find many examples of this form of commercializing of the environmental movement since the 1990s. One of the earliest illustrations comes from the certification of sustainable forestry, with the development of the Forest Stewardship Council in the 1990s (Bartley 2003). Already in the late 1980s, the NGO Friends of the Earth had started to work on a system to recognize eco-friendly sources of tropical wood and had developed a "Good Wood Seal of Approval". At the same time, the NGO Rainforest Alliance developed its own initiative of independent certification, and some producers started partnerships with environmental NGOs. The FCS grew out of these industry-NGO networks (Bartley 2003, 2007). Actually, the turn of NGOs to such market-based solutions was partly a consequence of the incapacity of states to negotiate binding international treaties for environmental protection (Bernstein 2001). Bartley (2003) quotes a FCS employee stating that:

> FCS was a response to the failure of international organizations that ought to have had the remit to enforce, to implement and develop good forestry standards – International Tropical Timber Organization in particular . . . And FSC was set up to correct that failure.
>
> (p. 452)

The Forest Stewardship Council became one of the earliest examples of a wide range of such voluntary or private forms of regulation in environmental politics, driven sometimes merely by industry actors, but often in partnership with movement NGOs in so-called multi-stakeholder initiatives (Bartley 2018).

These certifications become visible as labels on consumer markets and therefore constitute examples of green product qualities. Eco-labels and eco-standards (Boström & Klintman 2008) are frequently developed through partnerships between NGOs and industry actors, sometimes also in collaboration with governments that have come to promote green consumerism as a preferred form of public policy (Balsiger et al. 2019; Dubuisson-Quellier 2016; Welch & Warde 2015). Eco-labels define and designate sustainable production, making it appear as a product quality on markets. They have multiplied over the past decades (Boström & Klintman 2008;

Reinecke et al. 2012), leading to the development of increasingly moralized markets (Balsiger 2021) where different labels and standards compete with each other (de Moor & Balsiger 2018; Reinecke et al. 2012). In parallel, environmental NGOs seek to establish new environmental criteria for product valuation, inciting consumers to take such criteria into account while at the same time trying to convince companies of a growing environmental demand and pushing them to offer more sustainable products (Balsiger 2010). Such "market mediation strategies" (Dubuisson-Quellier 2013) thus aim at encouraging firms to adopt eco-friendly supply practices.

While labels are often created by social movement organizations such as NGOs, the environmental movement also contributes directly to the emergence of green capitalism through green entrepreneurship. We can see green entrepreneurs as environmentalists building businesses around environmentally friendly forms of production. Green entrepreneurs are motivated at least in part by the environmental cause while developing ventures that are profit oriented (although not necessarily exclusively so) and seek to compete on capitalist markets (Jones 2017; Schaper 2010). Goals are thus multiple: on the one hand, it is about changing the way things are produced, toward production that protects the environment; on the other hand, this environmental change becomes a market opportunity to be seized and exploited with the goal of making a profit. Pioneers of green entrepreneurship (long before the term existed) can be found in the food and agriculture sector: for instance, around the rise of natural food at the turn of the twentieth century (Miller 2017) or around biodynamic and later organic agriculture in the first half of that decade (Jones 2017). Environmental goals and motivations were mixed with religious motifs and broader views of social change. These initiatives remained small and often were hardly viable from a business point of view, although some brands – for instance, the German firms Weleda (natural cosmetics) and Hipp (organic baby food) – still exist today.

Green entrepreneurship rose and expanded in the last decades of the twentieth century, often driven by "activist entrepreneurs" (Clark Davis 2017) shaped by the social movements of the 1960s and 1970s. Natural and organic foods, for example, found new customer bases among the European and American counterculture, and many small organic stores opened at this time (Miller 2017). One of them, founded in 1981 as "Safer Way" in Austin, Texas, would grow to become the supermarket chain Whole Foods, the largest organic supermarket in the US (Jones 2017), purchased by Amazon in 2017. A similar story is the organic yogurt brand Stoney Fields, founded by two environmental activists in 1983 in New Hampshire and eventually sold to the French food giant Danone in 2001 (ibid.). In Germany, the organic wholesaler Rapunzel has roots in the environmental movement (ibid.), as do many producers of organic milk (Suckert 2019), while the organic retailer Alnatura was founded by an entrepreneur inspired by anthroposophical ideology and wanting to create a counter-current model of business organization (Jones, 2017, pp. 184–185). Whereas all these business ventures started as small and alternative businesses in close proximity to social movement cultures, some of them would grow to become large profit-making businesses and sometimes went public (as in the case of the British Body Shop) or ended up being sold to conventional corporations. In the process, their commitment to environmental and social goals evolved, and they are often criticized as selling out to the market economy (see later in this chapter). Yet from the beginning, the characteristic of such green entrepreneurship was the idea of combining environmental goals with profit making or, from the opposite point of view, using the market to create environmental change.

Overall, the global green market of low-carbon environmental goods and services has an estimated size of US$4.2 trillion, according to information by the EU commission Single Market for Green Products Initiative. Of course, large parts of this market are strongly contested by (at least part of) the environmental movement, which frequently denounces so-called greenwashing practices. But this should not hide from view that a sizeable (although difficult to quantify) chunk of this green market is and has been developed in collaboration with actors from the environmental movement NGOs, who were often instigators of green products and product categories within big transnational firms, who are part of certification and labelling schemes, and who incite consumers to shop greener through campaigns.

Finally, the steepest form of environmental commercialization comes in the form of the creation of a tradeable product out of what economists call negative externalities: i.e., the environmental consequences of production processes such as pollution or carbon dioxide emissions (Felli 2015). In so-called cap-and-trade markets, states define amounts of pollution, and firms who want or need to pollute more than their allotted permit can buy these rights on a market. Such markets have become most prominent in the case of emissions trading and are a core (and highly controversial) achievement of the Kyoto Protocol. The first and, to this day, biggest of such markets is the EU emissions trading scheme, through which companies of emission-intense sectors buy or receive emission allowances, which they can trade with each other. The total amount of emissions is capped and reduced over time. In addition, through instruments such as the Clean Development Mechanism (Newell & Paterson 2010), companies or countries can also buy limited amounts of international credit from emission-savings projects around the world. In parallel to this, a voluntary market for carbon emissions has also emerged for companies that are not submitted to the EU emissions trading scheme but nonetheless want to reduce emissions through carbon trading.

Such markets are advocated by some environmental economists as the most efficient way of reducing emissions (Pestre 2016), but they are heavily criticized for their limited effects and for the possibility they give companies to buy carbon credits through compensation schemes. While most environmental NGOs have been critical of this instrument, they do not necessarily reject the principle. For instance, the environmental NGOs organized within the climate action network were not opposed to the market as such but asked for limits to the possibility of buying carbon credit (Valiergue 2019). In parallel, many environmental NGOs develop projects to limit emissions in the Global South and use the carbon markets as new ways of financing their projects, thus at least implicitly condoning it (ibid.).

The initiatives that I have discussed under the label of adaptive environmentalism are very diverse. Some of them – for instance, the FSC certification – are very demanding and lead to changes in systems of production and distribution, while others (for instance, CO_2 labels) are merely informative. While their potential for change is thus unequal, they all constitute market-based solutions to environmental problems. This rise of green or "climate" capitalism (Newell & Paterson 2010) is more than just a reaction of capitalist forces to the environmental movement or a domestication of the movement through which companies would recuperate the critique to commercialize it (Boltanski & Chiapello 2007; King & Busa 2017). Of course, such processes do happen; many green messages by businesses have little substance and deserve the "green-washing" label. But overall, green capitalism has risen in close proximity and often through cooperation with pro-business environmentalism, which became increasingly dominant in the 1990s and 2000s. There was a "corporate turn" of environmentalism at that time, for a series of reasons that I will come back to.

Transformative environmentalism: developing an alternative economy

On the other side of these market-related initiatives stands the part of the environmental movement that maintains that responding to the environmental crisis requires a profound transformation of economies and societies. Generally, this is meant to signify a systemic change, as capitalism, as a social system based on growth and extraction, is seen as the principal cause of global warming and environmental degradation. This is clearly opposed to the adaptive pole, which sees (reformed) capitalist institutions (firms and markets) as part of the solution. As a result, transformative environmentalists tend to reject market-related instruments and favor political and social change. In addition to asking for stricter regulations and limits to the capitalist economy (for instance, through taxes, bans, and strong environmental standards that increase the social and political control of the economy), proponents of this strand of environmentalism also seek to transform the dominant economic system through concrete social innovations: i.e., the development of alternative economic institutions such as contract farming, food cooperatives, farmer's markets, eco-villages, repair shops, sustainable purchasing groups, local currencies, social and solidarity economy, etc. Through the development of such alternative social and economic institutions, they hope to create forms of producing and consuming that are truly sustainable and undermine capitalist logics of property, profit, accumulation, and consumerism.

Transformative environmentalism comes in many shapes and draws on different ideologies, worldviews, and theories, whose relative importance have evolved over time. What they all have in common is the conviction that to fight against environmental destruction, it is necessary to strengthen alternative, non-capitalist forms of the economy. While this could mean a strengthening of the public sector, transformative environmentalists have often favored developing grassroots and decentralized alternative institutions (Felli 2008). This has to do with the critique of the productivist state and its institutions that established hierarchies of knowledge, an important aspect of 1970s political ecology (Felli 2008; Hajer 1995). Transformative environmentalism developed in close proximity to the emancipatory and anti-authoritarian stances of other new social movements of the era, with which it shared the goal of building an "alternative society" to bring about social and environmental change (Melucci 1996). Central to its discourse – besides the analysis of the ecological limits to economic growth and the damage done by certain forms of productivism and consumerism – is the idea of "small is beautiful" – the title of an influential book that pleads for developing an economy "where people matter" (Schumacher 1973). It translates to a preference for small and decentralized economic structures of production and exchange, which allow for autonomous and "convivial" (Ivan Illich) human relations, as opposed to the alienated consumers and dependent workers of capitalism (Felli 2008). Transformative environmentalism is thus explicit in its opposition to technocratic and adaptive forms of environmentalism (Felli 2008). For André Gorz, a particularly influential theorist of political ecology, ecology must not mean "a capitalism adapted to environmental constraints" but requires "a social, economic, and cultural revolution that abolishes the constraints of capitalism and, in so doing, establishes a new relationship between the individual and society and between people and nature" (Gorz 1980) (p. 4).

A myriad of local initiatives put into practice, more or less explicitly, the subordination of the economy to environmental limits as called for by transformative environmentalism (Seyfang 2009). Some of these forms have been short lived, such as many environmental communes in the 1960s and 1970s (although some still exist while others have been revived in the form of eco-villages). Others have built more long-lasting institutions. Examples of this can be found in the development of alternative food systems, such as local forms of contract agriculture in Europe, Australia, and the USA. The first such schemes were created in the 1970s. Since the 2000s, such alternative food networks have spread massively and, at the same time, diversified (Goodman et al. 2012). The example can illustrate the difficulty to classify institutions as "alternative" since they generally bring together both conventional forms of production and consumption, with clearly alternative forms (such as long-term commitments, imposed "choices", etc.). Another example of alternative institutions is the social and solidarity economy, an umbrella term with roots in the alternative left of the 1970s, used, for instance, in parts of

South America and in the French-speaking world. It designates economic institutions that are not profit driven and pursue social objectives – often associations or cooperatives active in different sectors of the economy (Laville 2016; Sahakian 2016). In the Italian context, Forno and Graziano (2014) speak of "sustainable community movement organizations" to designate organizations that focus on developing alternative forms of consumption and production.

The significance of the development of alternative economic institutions for transformative environmentalism could give the impression that commercialization is also present here. In alternative economic institutions, people also produce and consume goods, and imagining and developing alternative institutions to do so is core to the movement. Yet the forms of exchange and the property structures that are imagined and put into practice are in opposition to the capitalist model of commercialization. This commercialization takes place outside and at the margins of the capitalist economy, constituting alternatives to it. Profit making is not the ultimate goal and subordinated to social or ecological aims while growth and scaling up are seen as detrimental to the goal and thus not desirable; sharing and "commoning" (Asara 2020; De Angelis 2017) are privileged and commodification therefore limited; ownership structures are different; etc.

Probably the most prominent current of transformative environmentalism today is the degrowth movement (Kallis 2018). The origins of degrowth point to ecological economics and its critique of economic growth and the notion of development (Meadows et al. 1972); the term itself first started to be widely used in the early 2000s in France, where *décroissance* became a quite visible group and ideology around intellectuals such as Serge Latouche promoting sufficiency and criticizing consumerism and sustainable development (D'Alisa et al. 2014). It has become a diverse and influential political and academic movement bridging the environmental and global justice movements, activists and academic circles, for instance, around the bi-annual degrowth conference, first held in 2008 in Paris. Degrowth identifies economic growth as the main driver of environmental degradation and climate change, through the ever-growing extraction of limited natural resources and carbon emissions. As a consequence, to combat climate change, one has to stop the economy from growing by putting limits to certain forms of production and consumption. Degrowth explicitly condemns the process of consumerism and is here clearly opposed to the market-related actions of environmentalism, which use a consumerist dynamic to orient consumers toward "better" products. From the critical perspective of degrowth, this only displaces the problem and ultimately contributes to increased commodification and consumption. The downscaling of the economy is seen as necessary but must be done in a socially sustainable way. As other forms of transformative environmentalism, degrowth pleads for an encompassing change of lifestyles and the institutions of production around such ideas as work sharing, basic income, commons, and sufficiency (D'Alisa et al. 2014).

The consequences of commercialization

Transformative environmentalists see commercialization as a threat to alternative institutions, a view that is also supported by some sociological studies. It can be exemplified by Guthman's study of organic agriculture in California (Guthman 2004). Organic agriculture developed as an alternative environmentally friendly form of agricultural practice over the first half of the twentieth century (Jones 2017). With its growing success in the 1980s and 1990s, conventional firms increasingly entered the market and started producing and selling organic produce. In this process, the practice got "conventionalized": the small, alternative organic producers could not compete with the big industrial actors, and those who tried had to adapt their practices to continue to be competitive, thus diluting its core components such as their small scale or diversified production. For Guthman (2004), this process of conventionalization is built into the political economy of capitalism, where the force of the market will drive out alternatives.

Guthman's argument is reminiscent of other arguments on capitalist recuperation of critique and alternative practices, as developed in general by Boltanski and Chiapello (2007) or for the specific case of the environmental movement by Klein (2015) and Dauvergne (Dauvergne 2016; Dauvergne & Lister 2013). The goal of transformation gets undermined as the original pioneers grow in size and abandon core transformative principles for the sake of it or as they get marginalized in the face of powerful conventional competitors. This is particularly problematic because at the same time, the capitalist recuperation of alternative practices – in the form of product labels, for instance – gives the illusion that this conventional green consumerism constitutes a solution to environmental problems, whereas it is, in fact, counter to the goal of more profound and transformative change.

However, not all scholars take such a bleak view of the consequences of conventionalization. Some observers of organic agriculture, for instance, find that the entry of conventional businesses does not crowd out the more transformative initiatives but leads to a diversified market where a plurality of models coexist (Coombes & Campbell 1998). The conventionalization argument also neglects the expansionist movement actors who seek to develop market-related tactics in order to enroll conventional businesses to their cause: for instance, through the development of labels. Such actors are willing to take a more pragmatic stance to make a certification attractive, giving up certain principles but maintaining others in order to scale up (Balsiger 2021). Here, different conceptions of social change clash. The argument of adaptive actors is to say that commercialization (in the form of partnerships of movement actors with corporations) can help the cause, making smaller changes but at a much broader scale, and that this is ultimately more effective than transformative changes at a small scale. The argument of transformative actors, meanwhile, is to reject such compromises and to work toward the multiplication of small-scale transformative economic institutions. Again, we clearly see the opposition between the two views of environmentalism here: for adaptive environmentalists, the involvement of capitalist firms in green markets constitutes progress, whereas it is seen as undermining change by transformative environmentalists.

Beyond the issue of conventionalization and the change potential of alternative economic institutions, scholars have also analyzed the potential self-defeating effects of market-related tactics as they compete with other tactics seeking change through other means (Balsiger 2016a; Dauvergne 2016; Konefal 2013). Companies may use labels to sidestep (Balsiger 2018) more encompassing movement demands for environmental change, or they simply develop climate policies that are nothing but "business as usual" (Wright & Nyberg 2017). Dauvergne (2016) documents examples of corporations pursuing eco-business, including partnering with environmental NGOs, while at the same time pursuing aggressive market expansion, which ultimately leads to more, not less, polluting and carbon emissions. Worse, for the environmental NGOs that are in partnerships with such companies, their position often makes them unwilling to criticize them. Finally, it has also long been shown how industries voluntarily self-regulate in order to avoid more stringent state regulation (Walker & Rea 2014), and movements employing market-related tactics may play an inadvertent legitimizing role in such processes. Overall, scholars thus point at the power differential between movements and multinational corporations and the danger of cooptation this entails.

The rise (and fall?) of pro-market environmentalism

Most observers agree that environmentalism changed course in the late 1980s and the 1990s, increasingly embracing pro-business stances and market-related strategies and seeing environmental change as fundamentally compatible with a capitalist and neoliberal market economy. The environmental movement of the 1970s was radical and pursued fundamental social transformation or at least a very strong regulative state imposing strict environmental standards for pollution and waste management, for example. But toward the end of the century, both the transformative utopias and the calls for "command and control" methods of environmental management lost ground and gave way to an adaptive view of "liberal environmentalism" (Bernstein 2001). This does not mean that transformative environmentalists disappeared or all converted to the new ideology, but they were supplanted as the dominant force in the movement by the more reformist organizations (Felli 2008). In part, this reflects transformations that other "new social movements" of the 1960s and 1970s went through, such as the gay and lesbian and the so-called international solidarity movement (Armstrong 2002; Balsiger 2016b): transformative and revolutionary views of emancipatory struggle or structuralist theories of dependence gave way to a liberal discourse of rights (Whyte 2019). In addition to this broader change of the ideological context, scholars of the environmental movement point to the rise of ecological modernization theory and changes in the international context to explain this shift.

According to Hajer (1995), a new way of conceiving the environment emerged after the 1970s: the policy discourse of ecological modernization. Unlike the radical environmental movements, this view suggests that "environmental problems can be solved in accordance with the workings of the main institutional arrangements of society" (Hajer 1995, p. 3), and "economic growth and the resolution of the ecological problems can, in principle, be reconciled" (ibid.:24). The theory of ecological modernization, which was developed by environmental scientists in Germany in the early 1980s (Mol 2000), became influent also within the changing environmental movement at the time, offering pragmatic solutions to environmental problems to a movement characterized by increased professionalization and the ideological changes discussed earlier. According to Mol (2000, p. 48), writing at the turn of the century,

> a significant part of the ecological modernization ideas can be found back in the environmental movement's contemporary ideology. The dominant positions within the current environmental movement are rather oriented towards reforming and fine tuning the institutions of modernity in order to let them fulfil environmental goals.

In this evolution, the market actors that were strongly criticized for their capitalist orientation in the 1970s were now viewed as potential partners. The other important factor here is the changing international context, in which the ideology of free trade became more and more dominant as an international norm. In this context, environmentalism came to be pursued through instruments pertaining to the market – what Bernstein (2001) calls liberal environmentalism, which became increasingly dominant with the Brundtland report (WCED 1987) and then the Rio Earth summit of 1992 (Fuchs & Lorek 2005). While some businesses were strongly opposed to environmental regulation, others, such as those organized in the World Business Council for Sustainable Development, were more open to environmental issues (Bernstein 2001) – sometimes even more so than governments, which could often not agree on transnationally binding standards. Prominent environmentalists and environmental NGOs thus started to see businesses not as opponents but as potential partners in the environmental cause (Chartier & Deléage 1998). Although the Agenda 21 that came out of the Rio summit has been described as a moment of cooptation of parts of the environmental movement by the business community (Doyle 1998), the turn toward business solutions also reflected changed perceptions of activists, policy makers and businesses alike. From the point of view of activists, promoting business solutions was also a reaction to the difficulty of achieving efficient environmental regulation at the transnational level (Bernstein 2001). Again, this development mirrors what happened in other causes of social movements, such as transnational workers' rights within globalized supply chains, where activists turned to "voluntary regulation" in the form of certification, pressuring companies to comply and cooperating with "progressive" businesses in forms of voluntary standards (Balsiger 2016b).

To be sure, even at its heyday in the late 1990s and the 2000s, support of pro-business environmentalism varied widely within the environmental movement. Even NGOs that made partnerships with businesses continued at the same time to lobby for stricter transnational regulation and sometimes campaigned against businesses. The critique of pro-business stances was also widespread in environmental movements of countries from the Global South, where anti-corporate and anti-capitalist views tend to have remained the dominant force within the environmental movement (Dauvergne 2016; Doherty & Doyle 2018; Doyle 1998). Meanwhile, in the dominant capitalist countries, more radical organizations and voices of the environmental movement kept criticizing this corporate turn of some of the movement's biggest NGOs (Dauvergne & Lister 2013; Klein 2015).

Over recent years, the transformative pole of the environmental movement, critical of market-based action forms and advocating for limits to capitalist growth, has arguably regained some of the traction it had lost in the previous decades, potentially leading to a shift in the balance between the two poles. This shift is related on the one hand to the increased urgency of the climate change issue and the manifest evidence that the market-related, pro-business, voluntary measures taken have been unable to slow global warming. According to Dauvergne (2016, p. 4),

> the gains [of the dominant market-related tactics] are not adding up to anything approaching global sustainability. Resulting reforms are modest and incremental, rarely scaling up to improve global conditions as firms reinvest efficiency gains, as certification and regulation deflect production into new locations and sectors, as multinational corporations ramp up production in less-regulated markets, and as unsustainable consumption continues to rise.

The latest report by the intergovernmental panel on climate change (IPCC) even explicitly states that transformative social change is necessary to achieve the goal of limiting global warming to the 1.5°C set in the Paris accords.

On the other hand, the shift results from changes within the environmental movement itself, related to what happened in the broader social movement arena during the protest cycle of the global justice movement in the early 2000s and the following "square protests" (della Porta 2007, 2015). With their slogans of "another world is possible", their social forums, and later their encampments, these movements emphasized the importance of alternative institution building and prefigurative politics (Maeckelbergh 2011). It led to a renewal of anti-capitalist imaginaries (Monticelli 2018) and a rise of alternative forms of production and consumption (Forno and Graziano 2014). These protests and protest tactics became increasingly connected to the environmental cause and in particular the issue of climate change. For instance, during the anti-austerity occupations in Barcelona of 2011/2012, many initiatives took up environmental goals, linking them to ideas of autonomy and the commons (Asara 2020). Building also on longstanding radical actors in the global environmental movement, the protest cycles of the early twenty-first century thus led to a reinforcement of transformative views of environmentalism, coalescing under the "climate justice frame" (Wahlström et al. 2013). Climate justice renews the older term of "environmental justice" (Cole & Foster 2001) by bringing together the issue of the global justice movement and global warming and has increasingly also led to a reconsideration of claims and tactics within the largest and most influential environmental NGOs.

Doherty and Doyle (2018) have documented this evolution in the case of Friends of the Earth International. Starting in 2002, activists from FoE in Southern countries criticized activists from the North around "the degree of FoEI's critique of the dominant model of society, but especially over the nature of capitalism and corporate power, most Southern groups favouring a more explicit anti-capitalist and anti-corporate position than Northern groups" (p. 1064). The analysis shows the role played by movement crossover from the global justice movement, at first particularly influent in Latin America but later also shifting the views of the activists from the North. As a result of the internal dispute, FoE International came to embrace a more radical platform and in 2007 joined other groups (such as Via Campesina) in breaking with the Climate Action Network, a then-dominant coalition of more than 800 environmental NGOs. The main fault line between the newly formed Climate Justice Now group and the older Climate Action Network evolved around the role of insider tactics and technical solutions versus transformative policies criticizing capitalism and injustice.

The clash between these two poles became especially visible at the Copenhagen climate summit in 2008, where two distinct networks of environmentalists opposed each other (Hadden 2015): the transnational NGOs working inside the UN negotiations and the groups forming Climate Justice Now, which bridged climate change issues with issues from the global justice movement. Although the opposition formed around the issue of summit participation and not explicitly about the role of businesses in climate change policies (de Moor 2018), it did oppose adaptive/reform-oriented NGOs to transformative environmentalists, and, more importantly for the argument developed here, it showed the cracks in the dominance of the adaptive pole of the environmental movement. By the time of the COP21 summit in 2016, there was broad recognition within the environmental movement of the weakness of the UN conventions on climate change, which made it possible for the movement to unite in a single coordinated network this time. NGOs refused to participate in the summit and instead protested together – although divisions remained with regard to protest tactics and the degree to which the actual negotiations should be ignored (de Moor 2018).

Conclusion

Pro-market environmentalism has coexisted with transformative and often anti-capitalist environmentalism since the beginning of the environmental movement. The dominance of adaptive approaches in the late twentieth and early twenty-first centuries has led to a proliferation of market-related forms of environmentalism and to a widespread and diversified commercialization of the environmental cause. Yet over the past decade, the increasing climate urgency and the parallel observation of the incapacity of "environmental liberalism" to turn the trend of global warming has led to heightened critique of pro-market environmentalism and a certain reinforcement of transformative forces. The more recent youth movement of climate strikes and the parallel rise of the radical climate activism of Extinction Rebellion seem to confirm this trend. This current climate movement has been outspoken in its anti-corporate stance and, in particular, targets the fossil fuel industry and its creditors and shareholders. What seems most distinctive, however, about the latest iteration of the environmental movement is that their calls for developing, reinforcing, and supporting climate-friendly forms of production and consumption are addressed as much at the state as at individuals and their lifestyles (de Moor 2020). Restrictive standards and bans (such as of short distance flights) as well as investments in renewables and low-emissions infrastructures are advocated. In this sense, the call for massive government intervention is probably what distinguishes most the current environmental movement from its previous incarnations with regard to the role of markets. The movement remains diverse with regard to the capacity of reducing global warming within a capitalist system, between environmentalists advocating green growth (by decoupling economic growth from emissions growth through conversion to renewable energy) and others disputing this possibility and calling for degrowth or post-growth scenarios (Jackson 2017). Yet for most, the role of government policies of regulation and redistribution in order to force the economy to change course is essential. The proposals of "green new deal" legislation in the US or the EU go in this direction. They don't point toward a clear break with capitalism as such, nor do they resemble the market-related tactics and policies of the era of liberal environmentalism. If enacted, such programs would instead establish a new form of regulated green capitalism at the national and (in the case of the EU) the transnational level.

References

Akenji, Lewis 2014 'Consumer Scapegoatism and Limits to Green Consumerism' *Journal of Cleaner Production* 63:13–23.

Armstrong, Elizabeth A. 2002 *Forging Gay Identities: Organizing Sexuality in San Francisco, 1950–1994* Chicago: University of Chicago Press.

Asara, Viviana 2020 'Untangling the Radical Imaginaries of the Indignados' Movement: Commons, Autonomy and Ecologism' *Environmental Politics*. DOI:10.1080/09644016.2020.1773176

Balsiger, Philip 2010 'Making Political Consumers: The Tactical Action Repertoire of a Campaign for Clean Clothes' *Social Movement Studies* 9/3:311–329.

Balsiger, Philip 2016a 'Tactical Competition and Movement Outcomes on Markets' in L Bosi, M Giugni, & K Uba eds. *Consequences of Social Movements* Cambridge, UK: Cambridge University Press: 237–259.

Balsiger, Philip 2016b *The Fight for Ethical Fashion. The Origins and Interactions of the Clean Clothes Campaign* Abingdon, Oxforshire: Routledge.

Balsiger, Philip 2018 'Explaining Dynamic Strategies for Defending Company Legitimacy: The Changing Outcomes of Anti-Sweatshop Campaigns in France and Switzerland' *Business & Society* 57/4:676–705.

Balsiger, Philip 2021 'The Dynamics of 'Moralized Markets': A Field Perspective' *Socio-Economic Review* 19/1:59–82.

Balsiger, Philip & Schiller-Merkens, Simone 2019 'Moral Struggles In and Around Markets' in S Schiller-Merkens & P Balsiger eds. *The Contested Moralities of Markets* Bingley: Emerald Insight: 3–26.

Bartley, Tim 2003 'Certifying Forests and Factories: States, Social Movements, and the Rise of Private Regulation in the Apparel and Forest Products Fields' *Politics & Society* 31/3:433–464.

Bartley, Tim 2007 'Institutional Emergence in an Era of Globalization: The Rise of Transnational Private Regulation of Labor and Environmental Conditions' *American Journal of Sociology* 113/2:297–351.

Bartley, Tim 2018 'Transnational Corporations and Global Governance' *Annual Review of Sociology* 44/1:145–165.

Bereni, Laure 2019 'The Women's Cause in a Field: Rethinking the Architecture of Collective Protest in the Era of Movement Institutionalization' *Social Movement Studies* 0/0:1–16.

Bernstein, Steven 2001 *The Compromise of Liberal Environmentalism* New York: Columbia University Press.

Boltanski, Luc & Chiapello, Eve 2007 *The New Spirit of Capitalism* London: Verso.

Boström, Magnus & Klintman, Mikael 2008 *Eco-Standards, Product Labelling and Green Consumerism* London: Palgrave Macmillan.

Çalışkan, Koray & Callon, Michel 2009 'Economization, Part 1: Shifting Attention from the Economy Towards Processes of Economization' *Economy and Society* 38/3:369–398

Chartier, Denis & Deléage, Jean-Paul 1998 'The International Environmental NGOs: From the Revolutionary Alternative to the Pragmatism of Reform' *Environmental Politics* 7/3:26–41.

Clark Davis, Joshua 2017 *From Head Shops to Whole Foods. The Rise and Fall of Activist Entrepreneurs* New York: Columbia University Press.

Cole, Luke W & Foster, Sheila R 2001 *From the Ground Up: Environmental Racism and the Rise of the Environmental Justice Movement* New York: New York University Press.

Coombes, Brad & Campbell, Hugh 1998 'Dependent Reproduction of Alternative Modes of Agriculture: Organic Farming in New Zealand' *Sociologia Ruralis* 38/2:127–145.

D'Alisa, Giacomo; Demaria, Frederico & Kallis, Giorgos eds. 2014 *Degrowth: A Vocabulary for a New Era* Abingdon, Oxon, New York: Routledge.

Dauvergne, Peter 2016 *Environmentalism of the Rich* Cambridge, MA, London: The MIT Press

Dauvergne, Peter & Lister, Jane 2013 *Eco-Business: A Big-Brand Takeover of Sustainability* Cambridge: The MIT Press.

De Angelis, Massimo 2017 *Omnia Sunt Communia. On the Commons and the Transformation to Postcapitalism* London: Zed Books.

della Porta, Donatella ed. 2007 *The Global Justice Movement. Cross-national and Transnational Perspectives* Boulder, CO: Paradigm Publishers.

della Porta, Donatella 2015 *Social Movements in Times of Austerity: Bringing Capitalism Back Into Protest Analysis* Hoboken: John Wiley & Sons.

de Moor, Joost 2018 'The 'Efficacy Dilemma' of Transnational Climate Activism: The Case of COP21' *Environmental Politics* 27/6:1079–1100.

de Moor, Joost 2020 'New Kids on the Block: Taking Stock of the Recent Cycle of Climate Activism' *Social Movement Studies*:1–7.

de Moor, Joost & Balsiger, Philip 2018 'Political Consumerism in Northwestern Europe: Leading by Example?' in M Boström, M Micheletti, & P Oosterveer eds. *The Oxford Handbook of Political Consumerism* Oxford, New York: Oxford University Press: 435–456.

Doherty, Brian & Doyle, Timothy 2018 'Friends of the Earth International: Agonistic Politics, Modus Vivendi and Political Change' *Environmental Politics* 27/6:1057–1078.

Doyle, T 1998 'Sustainable Development and Agenda 21: The Secular Bible of Global Free Markets and Pluralist Democracy' *Third World Quarterly* 19/4:771–786.

Dubuisson-Quellier, Sophie 2013 'A Market Mediation Strategy: How Social Movements Seek to Change Firms' Practices by Promoting New Principles of Product Valuation' *Organization Studies* 34/5–6:683–703.

Dubuisson-Quellier, Sophie ed. 2016 *Gouverner les conduites* Paris: Presses de Sciences Po.

Felli, Romain 2008 *Les deux âmes de l'écologie. Une critique du développement durable* Paris: L'Harmattan.

Felli, Romain 2015 'Environment, Not Planning: The Neoliberal Depoliticisation of Environmental Policy by Means of Emissions Trading' *Environmental Politics* 24/5:641–660.

Felli, Romain 2021 The Great Adaptation. Climate, Capitalism, Catastrophe London: Verso.

Fillieule, Olivier; Agrikoliansky, Eric & Sommier, Isabelle eds. 2010 *Penser les mouvements sociaux. Conflits sociaux et contestations dans les sociétés contemporaines* Paris: La Découverte.

Forno, Francesca & Graziano, Paolo R 2014 'Sustainable Community Movement Organisations' F Forno & PR Graziano eds. *Journal of Consumer Culture* 14/2:139–157.

Fuchs, Doris A & Lorek, Sylvia 2005 'Sustainable Consumption Governance: A History of Promises and Failures | SpringerLink' *Journal of Consumer Policy* 28:261–288.

Geels, Frank W et al. 2015 'A Critical Appraisal of Sustainable Consumption and Production Research: The Reformist, Revolutionary and Reconfiguration Positions' *Global Environmental Change* 34:1–12.

Goodman, David E; Dupuis, Melanie & Goodman, Michael K 2012 *Alternative Food Networks: Knowledge, Practice, and Politics* Oxon, Canada, New York: Routledge.

Gorz, André 1980 *Ecology as Politics* Montreal: Black Rose Books Ltd.

Guthman, Julie 2004 *Agrarian Dreams. The Paradox of Organic Farming in California* Berkeley, Los Angeles, London: University of California Press.

Hadden, Jennifer 2015 *Networks in Contention. The Divisive Politics of Climate Change* Cambridge: Cambridge University Press.

Hajer, Maarten A 1995 *The Politics of Environmental Discourse Ecological Modernization and the Policy Process* Oxford: Clarendon Press.

Hochschild, Arlie Russell 2003 *The Commercialization of Intimate Life: Notes from Home and Work* Berkeley, Los Angeles, London: University of California Press.

Jackson, Tim 2017 *Prosperity without Growth: Foundations for the Economy of Tomorrow* New York, London: Routledge.

Jones, Geoffrey 2017 *Profits and Sustainability: A History of Green Entrepreneurship* 1 edition ed Oxford: Oxford University Press.

Kallis, Giorgos 2018 *Degrowth* Newcastle: Agenda Publishing.

King, Leslie & Busa, Julianne 2017 'When Corporate Actors Take over the Game: The Corporatization of Organic, Recycling and Breast Cancer Activism' *Social Movement Studies* 16/5:549–563.

Klein, Naomi 2015 *This Changes Everything: Capitalism vs. the Climate* New York: Simon & Schuster.

Konefal, J 2013 'Environmental Movements, Market-Based Approaches, and Neoliberalization: A Case Study of the Sustainable Seafood Movement' *Organization and Environment* 26/3:336–352.

Laville, Jean-Louis 2016 *L'Économie sociale et solidaire* Paris: Seuil.

Maeckelbergh, Marianne 2011 'Doing is Believing: Prefiguration as Strategic Practice in the Alterglobalization Movement' *Social Movement Studies* 10/1:1–20.

Meadows, Donella H et al. 1972 *The Limits to Growth* New York: Universe Books.

Melucci, Alberto 1996 *Challenging Codes: Collective Action in the Information Age* Cambridge: Cambridge University Press.

Miller, Laura J 2017 *Building Nature's Market. The Business and Politics of Natural Food* Chicago: The University of Chicago Press.

Mol, APJ 2000 'The Environmental Movement in an Era of Ecological Modernisation' *Geoforum* 31/1:45–56

Monticelli, Lara 2018 'Embodying Alternatives to Capitalism in the 21st Century' *tripleC: Communication, Capitalism & Critique* 16/2.

Newell, Peter & Paterson, Matthew 2010 *Climate Capitalism: Global Warming and the Transformation of the Global Economy* Cambridge: Cambridge University Press.

Pestre, Dominique 2016 'La mise en économie de l'environnement comme règle' *Ecologie politique* N° 52/1:19–44.

Radin, Margaret Jane 1996 *Contested Commodities* Cambridge, MA: Harvard University Press.

Reinecke, Juliane; Manning, Stephan & von Hagen, Oliver 2012 'The Emergence of a Standards Market: Multiplicity of Sustainability Standards in the Global Coffee Industry' *Organization Studies* 33/5–6:791–814.

Sahakian, Marlyne 2016 'The Social and Solidarity Economy: Why Is It Relevant to Industrial Ecology?' in 2016 *Taking Stock of Industrial Ecology* Cham: Springer, 205–227.

Schaper, Michael 2010 *Making Ecopreneurs: Developing Sustainable Entrepreneurship* Surrey: Gower.

Schumacher, Ernst F 1973 *Small Is Beautiful. Economics as if People Mattered.* London: Vintage.

Seyfang, Gill 2009 *The New Economics of Sustainable Consumption* New York: Palgrave Macmillan.

Suckert, Lisa 2019 'Playing the Double Game: How Ecopreneurs Cope with Opposing Field Logics in Moralized Markets' in S Schiller-Merkens & P Balsiger eds. *The Contested Moralities of Markets* Bingley: Emerald Publishing Limited: 107–126.

Valiergue, Alice 2019 'Relational Work as a Market Device: An Analysis of the Contested 'Voluntary' Carbon Offset Market' in S Schiller-Merkens & P Balsiger eds. *The Contested Moralities of Markets* Bingley: Emerald Publishing Limited: 49–66.

Wahlström, Mattias; Wennerhag, Magnus & Rootes, Christopher 2013 'Framing 'the climate issue'' *Global Environmental Politics* 13/4:101–122.

Walker, Edward T & Rea, Christopher M 2014 'The Political Mobilization of Firms and Industries' *Annual Review of Sociology* 40.

WCED 1987 *Our Common Future* New York, Oxford: World Commission on Environment and Development.

Welch, Daniel & Warde, Alan 2015 'Theories of Practice and Sustainable Consumption' in LA Reisch & J Thorgesen eds. *Handbook of Research on Sustainable Consumption* Cheltenham, UK, Northampton, MA: Edward Elgar Publishing: 84–100.

Whyte, Jessica 2019 *The Morals of the Market: Human Rights and the Rise of Neoliberalism* London: Verso.

Wright, Christopher & Nyberg, Daniel 2017 'An Inconvenient Truth: How Organizations Translate Climate Change into Business as Usual' *Academy of Management Journal* 60/5:1633–1661.

PART 4

Microstructural and social-psychological dimensions

24

SOCIAL CLASS AND ENVIRONMENTAL MOVEMENTS

Magnus Wennerhag and Anders Hylmö

Social movements often mobilize individuals from a specific social group or strata, basing their claims on the grievances, interests, and identity of this group. This description would, for instance, fit labor, women's, anti-racist, and LGBTI movements well. It would, however, be less obvious to describe environmental movements this way, as they often seek to mobilize individuals from different social groups for causes claimed to benefit humanity at large.

It has not been uncommon, however, to portray environmental activists as primarily middle class and well educated (Rootes and Brulle 2013), and at times, environmental movements' demands for natural preservation and ecological sustainability have been claimed to be in conflict with, or indifferent to, the interests of the working class. In recent decades, demands for "environmental justice" have, however, become more central for environmentalists, framing socio-economic inequalities such as class as intrinsically connected to today's environmental problems. These imageries, alleged tensions, and developments indicate that social class is a relevant dimension when analyzing environmental activism.

This chapter investigates the class composition of environmental movements, and previous research and data from environmental protests are used to discuss and analyze the social composition of various forms of environmental activism, both historically and today. We also discuss the possible causes and consequences of environmental movements' class composition. Studies of how socio-economic stratification affects individuals' political participation often focus only on educational level or income (see, e.g., Schlozman, Verba, and Brady 2012). In this chapter, we take a slightly different approach and discuss class mainly in terms of occupational class: i.e., the individual's position in the stratified labor market.

Previous empirical research about the actual class composition of environmental movements is quite scarce. While some literature discusses the idea of the middle class's dominance, or focuses on various aspects of class in relation to environmental activism, the use of statistical methods to investigate these movements' class composition is rarer. A few survey studies have, however, been conducted since the 1960s (see, e.g., Devall 1970; Cotgrove and Duff 1980; Kriesi 1989; Tranter 1996). Notably, surveys distributed to participants in protest events have recently been used more frequently for determining movements' socio-demographic profiles (see, e.g., van Stekelenburg *et al.* 2012; Hylmö and Wennerhag 2015; Giugni and Grasso 2019). In this chapter, protest survey data will be used for comparing the class composition of

DOI: 10.4324/9780367855680-28

environmental protests in a number of countries during the 2010s, including the 2019 Global Climate Strike protests.

This chapter has three main delimitations. First, we mainly discuss the social class of those being mobilized to environment-related political participation ("action mobilization") but not how class matters when environmental movements seek support for their views and claims ("consensus mobilization") (cf. Klandermans 1984). Second, we primarily discuss collective actions carried out by actors self-identifying as environmentalists, leaving out local or specific campaigns and mobilizations focusing on aspects of the environment (natural, urban, work-place, etc.) without framing this as part of an overall environmental struggle. Our main focus is thus the modern environmental movement, which since the 1960s has widened its scope from conservationism to issues like environmental pollution, nuclear energy, climate change, and environmental justice (Rootes and Brulle 2013). Third, we mainly discuss environmental move-ments in the Global North. The reason for this geographical delimitation is the lack (at least to our knowledge) of statistical data on environmental protesters' occupational class in other parts of the world. We will, however, use recent data from the World Values Survey (WVS) to analyze the class composition of members in environmental organizations in the Global South in order to briefly discuss class differences in environmental activism across the globe.

Social class and social movements

Conceptualizing social class

The classical sources for theories of social class are the writings of Karl Marx and Max Weber, who both saw the individual's employment situation as central to this type of social stratification (Wright 2009). Most subsequent conceptualizations of social class are indebted to their terms and perspectives. Marx's notion of class was central to his understanding of capitalist society, describing how conflicts between wage-laborers and the owners of the means of production over the organization and outcome of production determine the distribution of wealth and power. Weber, on the other hand, understood class primarily as a "market situation", through which competition on the labor market stratified the life chances of different groups of wage-laborers, a hierarchy-creating process in which education and other forms of qualifications played decisive roles.

The connection between social class and political action was elaborated by Marx when he distinguished wage-laborers only sharing an objective common situation ("class in itself") from those developing a political identity and agency connected to common class interests ("class for itself") (Marx 1846–1847/1975). While some of Marx's most well-known works describe the proletariat and the bourgeoisie as the main class protagonists (e.g., Marx and Engels 1848; Marx 1867/1990), others include more detailed analyses of the political role played by various intermediary classes (Marx 1852/1984). In contrast, Weber (1922/2019) distinguished "class" from both "social rank"/"status" (prestige, lifestyle, and honor) and "party" (power and politics) as analytically distinct forms of stratification without necessary interconnections.

During the twentieth century, the concepts and theories of Marx and Weber were developed further in various empirical studies of social class. In parallel, empirical research analyzing socio-economic stratification only in terms of educational level or income has been quite common. While these indicators tend to correlate with class positions, they are nevertheless conceptually different from class positions.

Much of the statistically oriented research on social classes that emerged since the 1960s has been based on Weber's conceptualization of class (e.g., Goldthorpe and Lockwood 1963; see also Wright 1979 for a model drawing inspiration from both Marx and Weber). These class schemes were based on different occupations' and managers' degree of control over the work process, resulting in a hierarchical classification of occupations allowing for empirical classification in survey-based research. A parallel development was the increasing attention paid to more multi-dimensional differences between class segments: for example, Gouldner's (1979) notion of the highly educated "new class" being divided into a technical intelligentsia and social-humanistic intellectuals. This has inspired the development of new class schemes for survey-based research, adding further dimensions to the traditional hierarchical division.

In this chapter's empirical analysis, we use the class scheme created by political sociologist Daniel Oesch (2006a; 2006b). Originally developed for studies about how social class affects political party preferences, Oesch's two-dimensional class scheme combines the Weberian idea of a hierarchically stratified labor market with a new horizontal dimension – namely, sector-wise differences within the labor market that arise due to different sectors' dominant "work logics".[1] Due to the expansion of the middle classes in developed economies, horizontal distinctions within these classes become increasingly important for understanding political preferences. While the traditional left–right division of the political spectrum often correlates with the hierarchical class division between manual workers and specialized employees, politics has become increasingly structured by conflicts over socio-cultural values (sometimes labelled green-alternative-libertarian versus traditional-authoritarian-nationalist values; see, e.g., Hooghe *et al.* 2002) that are not easily reduced to economic class interests.

Among wage-laborers, Oesch (2008) distinguishes between *organizational, technical,* and *interpersonal* work logics, while the work logic of the self-employed and employers is characterised as *independent.* (See Table 24.1.) The main idea of this two-dimensional class scheme is that political preferences and behaviors are shaped by both hierarchical stratification (due to different economic interests) and sector differences in work logics (due to predominant modes of social interaction and educational socialization into specific "work roles"). In his analysis, Oesch shows, for instance, that support for Green parties is much greater among specific sectors of the

Table 24.1 Oesch class scheme, 8-class version

Work logic	Employees			Self-employed and employers
	Interpersonal service work logic	*Technical work logic*	*Organizational work logic*	*Independent work logic*
Middle-class occupations	**Socio-cultural professionals and semi-professionals**	**Technical professionals and semi-professionals**	**Higher-grade and associate managers and administrators**	**Large employers and Self-employed professionals**
	Medical doctors, social workers, teachers, university researchers	*Software developers, architects, engineers, biologists, meteorologists*	*Financial managers, managers in small firms, public administrators*	*Business owners, managers, self-employed journalists, doctors and lawyers*
Working-class occupations	**Service workers**	**Production workers**	**Office clerks**	**Small business owners**
	Children's nurses, home helpers, cooks, waiters, telephone salespersons	*Assemblers, carpenters, machinery mechanics, bus drivers*	*Bank tellers, mail sorting clerks, secretaries, fire fighters*	*Farmers, hairdressers, shopkeepers, lorry drivers*

well-educated middle class (what he labels socio-cultural professionals and semi-professionals), while it is lowest among specific sectors of the working class (office clerks).

Class and movements within social movement theory

Early European theorizing about social movements during the late nineteenth and early twentieth centuries saw the mobilization of individuals into political action as deeply connected to class dynamics in society (von Stein 1850/1964; Sombart 1896/1968), and the concept of social movement almost exclusively denoted the labor movement. Class was, however, quite absent when North American scholars studied social movements and collective behavior during the early twentieth century (Park and Burgess 1921; Blumer 1939), with a few rare examples of studies of the connection between class and political mobilization among workers and farmers (Heberle 1951; Lipset 1950). Scholars studying the effects of socio-economic stratification on participation in protests and revolutions used concepts like "relative deprivation" or "strain", focusing on status change rather than on the role of occupational class (e.g., Geschwender 1968; Smelser 1962).

When a more coherent field of social movement studies emerged in Europe and North America from the 1960s and onward (della Porta and Diani 2015), the connection between class and social movements was an uncommon theme, with a few exceptions (e.g., Tilly 1978). The role of class for contemporary movements was, however, more thoroughly discussed by the "new social movement" theorists in Europe (Buechler 1995). This approach centered on the dynamics of the transformation from industrial to post-industrial societies and on the macro-level societal role of the protest wave of the late 1960s and early 1970s. Alain Touraine (1969/1971, 1978/1981), the original proponent of this approach, interpreted the protests of "Mai 68" as the harbinger of the demise of industrial society, but also as the weakening of the prominent socio-political role that the workers' movement and industrial workers had previously played during modernity. In contrast to the workers of the "old social movement", the activists of "the new social movement" were based in the more advanced and knowledge-oriented parts of the economy and belonged to a "new class", even though the movement had no collective identity grounded in existing class identities. As examples of new social movements, Touraine discusses the students' and women's movements – but also the environmental movement.

The idea that the class composition and collective identities of "new social movements" differed from the "old social movements" – and that this, more broadly, could be regarded as a sign of broader transformations of advanced capitalist societies – became important both for social movement studies and for social theory in general (see, e.g., Melucci 1980; Offe 1985; Kriesi 1989; Eder 1993; Rootes 1995; for an overview, see Buechler 1995). Some of these analyses were influenced by neo-Marxist theories, but also by studies about the growing importance of "post-materialist values" in Western societies (Inglehart 1977). A common theme was the notion that the main social base of "new social movements" was the middle classes. For instance, Offe (1985: 833–834) claimed that the main class bases of new social movements were the (highly educated) "new middle class", "the old middle class" (farmers, shop owners, etc.), and "decommodified groups" (students, the unemployed, housewives, and the retired). While the "new middle class" was "class aware" but engaged in "class-unspecific" and often universalistic demands, the "old middle class" was, according to Offe, more "premodern", or particularistic, in its demands, something that could create tensions within environmental movements and other new social movements.

Most of this literature on "new social movements" and social class is, however, mostly theoretically oriented. One exception is Kriesi's (1989) empirical analysis of the class composition of participants in "new social movements" (including the environmental movement), which was based on a large national election survey in the Netherlands. Kriesi distinguished hierarchically between workers, employees, and professionals but added a sectoral, or horizontal, dimension in order to get a more nuanced picture of "the new middle class". One result of that study is that "the new social movements" mobilize specific parts of "the new middle class" – in particular "social and cultural specialists": i.e., semi-professionals and professionals in health care, teaching, social work, arts, and media. Other parts of the "new middle class" – technical specialists (including engineers and natural scientists) or "administrative and commercial personnel" (including managers, lawyers, and economists) – were not overrepresented among the activists in relation to the general population, while working-class occupations were clearly underrepresented. Kriesi interprets this as an expression of a conflict within "the new middle class" between technocrats oriented toward an administrative and instrumental rationality and social and cultural specialists with a less instrumental attitude toward knowledge.

After the discussions about "new social movements" and "the new middle class" during the 1980s and early 1990s, questions about how class affects social movements became less central within the field of social movement studies, as did other questions about how the dynamics of capitalism affect protests (Hetland and Goodwin 2013). However, scholarly interest in such questions grew again in connection with the wave of protests of the late 2000s and early 2010s against austerity policies adopted in the aftermath of the financial crisis in 2008 (della Porta 2015; Giugni and Grasso 2015a). One of these studies (Hylmö and Wennerhag 2015) compared the class composition of 75 protest events (anti-austerity, May Day, and various new social movement protests such as environmental demonstrations) in eight European countries. In all types of protests, professionals and semi-professionals, especially socio-cultural and administrative professionals, were strongly overrepresented in comparison to the general population, while working-class occupations were clearly underrepresented. This overrepresentation of professionals did not, however, include the technical professionals, who roughly equalled their proportion in the general population. Interestingly, these overall patterns also stood for May Day marches and anti-austerity trade union demonstrations, with the exception that these protests mobilized a much higher proportion from the working class.

Research on the class composition of environmental movements

We know very little about the social composition of environmentalist movements and organizations prior to the emergence of the modern environmental movement during the 1960s and 1970s. A few accounts discuss the social class of leading movement intellectuals and organizers, but this tells us little about the movements' general social composition. For example, Taylor (1997) describes the early conservationist- and preservationist-oriented environmental movement in the US as dominated by the (white and male) middle class from the late nineteenth century to the 1950s. Although not based on any precise data for the movement's class composition, such accounts indicate that the idea of the middle class's domination of "new social movements" was already valid before the 1960s and thus does not represent a wholly new phenomenon.[2]

For the modern environmental movement since the late 1960s, one can, however, find some survey-based studies of the movement's participants, of participants in environmental protests, and of members of environmental organizations and Green parties. Table 24.2 summarizes these studies' main findings regarding the occupational class composition and educational level of individuals involved in different forms of environmental political participation. These studies show that the highly educated middle class both dominates and is overrepresented in relation to the general population, while the opposite is true for the working class. The same patterns can be found in conservationist, ecologist, anti-nuclear, and climate-related political participation.

It is furthermore specific segments of the well-educated middle class that are overrepresented in environment-related political participation, particularly what Kriesi (1989) labelled the social and cultural specialists, while technical specialists roughly tend to equal their proportion in the general population. The quite unanimous picture of the class composition of environmental movements, protests, organizations, and parties is well in line with Rootes and Brulle's (2013) summary of previous research on environmental activists – "disproportionately highly educated, employed in teaching, creative, welfare, or caring professions". It is, however, important to note that previous research has found the same patterns in other "new social movements", in anti-austerity protests, and even to some degree in demonstrations staged by "old social movements": for instance, May Day marches and trade union protests. The overrepresentation of the well-educated middle class is furthermore not only limited to protest politics, and similar, and often much stronger, patterns can be found in more routinized types of political participation connected to institutionalized forms of politics (Schlozman, Verba and Brady 2012).

One part of the explanation for why some social classes are overrepresented in environmental movements, organizations, and protests is that this has less to do with environmental issues as such and more to do with general patterns characterizing most forms of movement activism and political participation. Within social movement studies, the fact that the social composition of movements often differs from the general population has been explained by variance in activists' "biographical availability" (McAdam 1986), meaning that the potential costs and risks associated with activism differ between individuals in different social circumstances. The overrepresentation of well-educated middle-class individuals could then be seen as a result of their working conditions – characterized by greater autonomy and more flexible working hours – making it easier to take part in activism or their more secure employment contracts and overall higher status, which decrease the social risks involved in protesting controversial issues. Other social movement scholars have stressed the importance of "political engagement" – an interest in a specific political issue – and "structural availability" – a connection to social networks where activism is more common – when explaining why some individuals become engaged in social movements (Schussman and Soule 2005). In relation to class, this would imply that the well-educated middle class – and especially socio-cultural professionals – are in general more interested in environmental issues and are more likely to be parts of networks of colleagues, friends, and family in which activism around these issues is more common.

Some studies about environmental attitudes and environment-related political participation have discussed class-related differences in value orientation as an explanation for variation in attitudes and participation. One influential source for value-oriented explanations is Inglehart's (1977) theory about the growth of "postmaterialist values" in affluent countries, especially among younger generations. From such a perspective, support for and engagement in environmental issues are often seen as the result of less exposure to economic hardship (than the parents' generation) and thus less need to care about "materialist" concerns such as economic growth or full employment. This is also discussed by Inglehart (1981) in relation to the support of the "new class" for environmental causes.

As we can see in this overview of survey-based studies on the class composition of environmental activists, this research only concerns the Global North. On the basis of other types of studies, some scholars have characterised environmental activism in the Global South as being based in less-affluent social strata than in the North (see, e.g., della Porta and Rucht 2002). While not analyzing class as such, a study using WVS data (1990–1991) and country-level statistics on educational level found that a country's percentage of members in environmental organizations was strongly correlated to its population's overall level of education. This correlation was, however, strongest for OECD countries and weaker for less-developed countries (Dalton

Table 24.2 Previous research on the class composition of different forms of environment-related political participation

Study	Year of survey	Countries	Sampled group (sample size)	Survey method	Reference groups (sample size)	Class composition	Higher education
Devall 1970	1969	USA	Members of the Sierra Club (n = 907)	Mail survey	–	Male members: 49% higher professionals (physicians, lawyers, college professors, engineers), 21% lower professionals (school teachers, free-lance writers, artists), 5% working class.	74% at least 4 years' college, 39% advanced degree
Faich and Gale 1971	1971	USA	Members of the Sierra Club's Puget Sound local group (n ≈ 300)	Mail survey	–	74% professional occupations, 10% administrators, 3% clerical workers.	88% at least BA, of which 45% MA and 25% PhD
Cotgrove and Duff 1980	Probably 1979	UK	Members of Friends of the Earth and the Conservation Society (n = 441)	Not mentioned, probably a mail survey	General public (316), industrialists (220)	Professional/supervisory in industry/commerce 14% (14% within general public), clerical in industry/commerce 6% (12%), self-employed 10% (5%), service, welfare, and creative occupations 38% (12%), manual labour 5% (28%).	–
Kriesi 1989	1986	the Netherlands	Participants in the ecology movement (n = 133), within a sample of the general public (n = 1,130)	National election survey, probably by mail	Participants in peace (179), antinuclear (166), women's (45), and squatter's movements (25)	Social and cultural specialists 23% (12% within general population), administrative and commercial personnel 17% (17%), technical specialists 5% (6%), skilled workers 10% (14%), unskilled workers 5% (13%).	–

(Continued)

Table 24.2 (Continued)

Study	Year of survey	Countries	Sampled group (sample size)	Survey method	Reference groups (sample size)	Class composition	Higher education
Tranter 1996	1989, 1990 and 1993	Australia	Members of environmental groups (n = 173) and participants in environmental demonstrations (n = 80), within a sample of the general public (n = 1,779)	National social science survey, on three separate occasions	General public (n = 1,779)	Participation in environmental demonstrations: 8% of social and cultural professionals and human service professionals, 4% of technical professionals and workers. Members in environmental groups: 15–16% of all professionals, 6% of workers.	–
Eggert and Giugni 2012	2009–2010	Belgium, Denmark, Sweden	Participants in two climate protests (n = 516)	Protest survey	Participants in May Day marches (n = 559)	41% socio-cultural professionals, 13% managers, 10% technical professionals, 22% workers.	–
Wennerhag 2016	2009–2013	Belgium, Italy, Sweden, Switzerland, UK	Participants in environmental protests: 4 anti-nuclear energy, 3 climate, 1 conservationist (n = 2,480)	Protest survey	Participants in May Day marches (n = 2,336), trade union demonstrations (n = 1,830), pride parades (n = 919)	35% socio-cultural professionals, 17% associate managers/administrators, 7% technical professionals, 10% workers.	69% university
Saarinen, Koivula, Koiranen and Sivonen 2018	2016	Finland	Members of the Green League Party (n = 1,653)	Mixed internet and mail survey	Members of five other major Finnish political parties (n = 10,774)	17% high-grade technocrats (similar as other parties), 9% high-grade social and cultural specialists (higher), 10% low-grade technocrats (lower), 28% low-grade social and cultural specialists (17%).	49% MA (26%), 10% PhD (4%)

and Rohrschneider 2002). Another study using WVS data (1995–1997, 38 countries) found that highly educated individuals who were "satisfied" with their financial situation were more likely to be active members of environmental organizations and that inhabitants of developing countries were more likely to be active members than those in Western countries (Torgler, García-Valiñas and Macintyre 2011).

Questions about occupational class were only recently included in the WVS (2017–2020). These new data allow us to make a comparison of the class composition of members in environmental organizations vis-à-vis all respondents.[3] The results for 14 countries belonging to different economic strata in the world are shown in Table 24.3. For most countries, we can see an overrepresentation of professional and technical occupations and an underrepresentation of workers and those working in sales and service. These figures also give some support to previous characterizations of environmental movements in the Global South as being less dominated by the well-educated middle class than in the Global North. While a main reason for this is the strong variation in class structures between these parts of the world, we still find similar patterns of over- or underrepresentation of some classes. Table 24.3 also shows figures for the percentage of members of environmental organizations in each country and the percentage who think protecting the environment is more important than prioritizing economic growth and creating jobs. Quite interestingly, these figures do not show any obvious connection between the wealth of a country and support for and engagement in environmental issues. (For a more sophisticated statistical analysis showing similar results, see Dalton and Rohrschneider 2002).

This overview of previous research on the class composition of environmental movements has shown that the well-educated middle class tends to be overrepresented in various forms of environment-related political participation. Some of the studies also show that among this social stratum it is especially the socio-cultural professionals who tend to dominate, while technical professionals are not overrepresented. The possible reasons for this will be discussed in the following analysis of environmental protests of the 2010s.

Analyzing the class composition of contemporary environmental protests

In the following analysis, we use protest survey data from two international projects that employed a similar standardized method of sampling across countries and protest events. The data and methodology have been described in detail previously (van Stekelenburg *et al*. 2012; Peterson, Wahlström and Wennerhag 2018: Appendix; Walgrave and Verhulst 2011). The first dataset derives from the project Caught in the Act of Protest: Contextualizing Contestation and covers 95 protest events in 10 European countries and Mexico between 2009 and 2014 (N = 18,519). The second dataset derives from protest surveys distributed during the Global Climate Strike demonstrations in March, May, and September 2019 (de Moor *et al*. 2020; Wahlström *et al*. 2020) and covers 33 protest events in 16 European countries, the US, Mexico, and Australia (N = 5,542).

The class position of the participants was coded using a slightly modified version of Oesch's class scheme (e.g., 2006a; 2006b; for a detailed description, see Hylmö and Wennerhag 2012, Appendix C). Respondents' occupations were manually recoded using the latest international standard of occupations (ISCO-08). Diverging from Oesch (2006a), we extended the population coverage to not only cover respondents between age 20 and 65 currently in paid employment, and we also coded full-time students and retired and unemployed respondents. The unemployed and retired were coded according to their last paid employment while the relatively

Table 24.3 The class composition of members in environmental organizations, World Values Survey data (2017–2020).

	United States	Australia	Germany	Mexico	China	Brazil	Thailand	Iran	Indonesia	Bolivia	Philippines	Nigeria	Pakistan	Ethiopia
GDP/capita – in US$ (UN 2018)	62 918	58 393	47 514	9 695	9 532	8 921	7 274	5 783	3 893	3 549	3 103	2 154	1 330	735
WVS questions to all respondents (%)														
Agree that protecting the environment is more important than economic growth and creating jobs	51	68	66	56	69	64	53	65	73	73	67	41	43	47
Member of an environmental organisation	20	14	12	16	4	4	31	13	33	15	19	22	17	22
Class composition of members of environmental organisations (%)														
Professional and technical	41	39	22	20	16	20	4	32	5	16	7	10	3	10
Higher administrative	7	6	14	2	4	5	0	6	1	3	2	4	2	4
Clerical	10	14	23	4	11	13	1	19	4	7	7	6	3	5
Sales and Service	18	18	23	39	29	22	16	24	32	25	26	21	29	22
Workers (skilled, semi-skilled, and unskilled)	23	20	18	22	22	31	20	15	27	35	29	52	43	21
Farm worker	2	1	0	10	12	9	12	4	15	12	17	3	12	17
Farm owner, farm manager	0	1	1	3	6	0	46	1	16	3	13	4	7	21
Total (N)	217	226	165	204	90	55	418	139	811	275	199	185	175	213
Over or underrepresentation of different classes amongst members of environmental organisations														
Professional and technical	8	11	7	6	5	10	-1	9	0	4	4	2	-1	1
Higher administrative	0	0	6	0	2	3	0	1	0	0	1	2	0	2
Clerical	-3	-4	1	-2	3	0	-3	4	-1	0	3	0	-6	-4
Sales and Service	-6	-5	-3	-2	-2	-8	-11	5	1	-5	-7	-7	-3	-7
Workers (skilled, semi-skilled, and unskilled)	0	-2	-10	-6	-11	-6	-5	-16	1	-1	-8	6	13	1
Farm worker	1	0	-1	2	2	2	3	0	1	2	5	-1	1	6
Farm owner, farm manager	0	0	-1	2	2	0	18	-3	-2	1	3	-1	-4	1

large group of full-time students not in full-time employment were coded as an extra "class" of students added to our version of the Oesch 8-class scheme.

In our data, we can see the same overall patterns identified by previous research in the class composition of environmental movements and other new social movements. Table 24.4 shows the class composition of European environmental demonstrations (2009–2012), while Table 24.5 shows the class composition of climate strike demonstrations (2019). In line with previous research, we also see that environmental protests are dominated by the well-educated middle class. In both tables, around 77% of the protestors with an occupation (both employed and self-employed) are from the middle class, twice the share of the general populations in these countries (38%). Mirroring this, only around 15% have working-class occupations, less than a third of the national populations' corresponding figures (50%). We can furthermore see the predominance of socio-cultural professionals and semi-professionals at a percentage three times as high as the general population, which is also in line with previous research (see Table 24.2).

Although the overall patterns are very similar, a few striking differences can be noted between the protests of the two datasets, which were separated in time by about a decade. First, there is a much larger proportion of students among all protestors in the more recent dataset: 48% in the 2019 climate protests compared to 19% in previous demonstrations. This should not be surprising given the new framing of climate protests as "school strikes". Second, the share of self-employed professionals and large employers declined from 12% to 8% (but is still more than twice their 3% share in the national population). Third, and perhaps most striking, there is a distinctly higher proportion of technical professionals and technicians in the climate strikes. While only 7% of the participants belonged to this class in the 2009–2012 environmental demonstrations, equalling their share of the general population, their share has now almost doubled to 13%.[4]

Even if the share of highly educated technicians is still relatively small, the marked increase is intriguing. This increased participation by technical professionals can perhaps be attributed to how the climate issue was framed during the climate strikes: namely, the persistent message that politicians should "listen to the scientists". This "pro-science" framing has gained saliency in the public debate since the 2010s, not only in relation to the climate issue, but also when criticizing populist "fake news", conspiracy theories, and distrust in scientific facts. In some cases, this framing has been central for specific mobilizations; for instance, the first "March for Science" organized worldwide in more than 600 cities on 22 April 2017. A protest survey conducted in three major US cities showed that among the scientists participating in this march (54% of the total sample), 50% worked in biology and the medical sciences and 36% worked within other technical and natural science disciplines, while only 11% worked in the social and behavioral sciences (Ross, Struminger, Winking and Wedemeyer-Strombel 2018). It is thus not unreasonable to assume that technical professionals' higher degree of participation in climate protests is fuelled by a framing that politicizes the knowledge domains of natural scientists, engineers, and technologists – and that these occupations seek to defend their professional activities against anti-science sentiments in various polarized political conflicts.

This increasing participation by technical professionals could also be seen in the light of the historical relation of the environmental movement to science and technology. Since the movement gained political momentum in the 1960s, its core issues have often had to deal with the technological excesses of modern industrial society – the chemical industry, nuclear power, etc. With a critical stance toward science and technology's instrumental rationality and tendencies toward bureaucratization and formalization, a broad "environmental consciousness" created a common ground for the movement (Jamison *et al.* 1990). Although the critique of specific aspects of the dominance of science and technology also relied on scientific knowledge and

Table 24.4 The class composition of environmental demonstrations 2009–2012 (Caught in the Act of Protest: Contextualizing Contestation) and in the general population (ESS6, 2012), according to the Oesch-8 class scheme.

	Sweden	Switzer-land	Belgium	Czech Republic	Italy	United Kingdom	Nether-lands	Total (mean %/N)	National populations ESS6 (2012)
Self-employed									
Self-employed professionals and large employers	10	14	4	11	22	12	10	**12**	3
Small business owners	4	10	3	7	9	7	7	**7**	12
Employed: Middle-class occupations									
Associate managers and administrators	17	18	26	18	7	26	28	**20**	15
Technical professionals and technicians	6	8	9	4	3	11	8	**7**	7
Socio-cultural professionals and semi-professionals	44	40	47	32	43	34	32	**39**	13
Employed: Working-class occupations									
Office clerks	4	2	3	11	7	3	4	**5**	11
Production workers	3	3	4	4	7	3	4	**4**	19
Service workers	11	5	3	14	1	4	7	**6**	20
Total employees and self-employed, excl. students (N)	189	706	361	28	68	497	555	**2 404**	11 273
Students, not working (% of total)	21	9	12	39	31	9	9	**19**	–
Total, incl. students (N)	240	777	411	46	98	545	610	**2 727**	–

Table 24.5 The class composition of climate strike demonstrations in 2019 and in the general population (ESS9, 2018), according to the Oesch-8 class scheme.

	Sweden	Switzer-land	Belgium	Czech Republic	Italy	United Kingdom	Germany	Austria	Poland	United States	Australia	Total (mean %/N)	National populations ESS9 (2018)
Self-employed													
Self-employed professionals and large employers	6	6	3	17	12	14	4	7	7	11	5	**8**	3
Small business owners	7	6	5	7	12	8	8	11	2	25	8	**9**	12
Employed: Middle-class occupations													
Associate managers and administrators	17	15	24	17	6	16	16	18	16	20	34	**18**	15
Technical professionals and technicians	19	15	9	11	3	2	21	12	21	10	16	**13**	8
Socio-cultural professionals and semi-professionals	37	44	47	33	46	31	37	40	37	31	24	**37**	12
Employed: Working-class occupations													
Office clerks	5	6	7	4	4	8	6	2	5	2	8	**5**	11
Production workers	2	4	2	4	5	2	1	1	0	0	1	**2**	19
Service workers	6	4	3	7	12	18	8	9	12	2	4	**8**	20
Total employees and self-employed, excl. students (N)	563	336	224	54	100	49	335	178	43	61	141	**2 084**	16 902
Students, not working (% of total)	36	42	28	69	65	48	53	52	89	31	10	48	–
Total, incl. students (N)	874	580	312	177	287	94	707	370	389	88	157	**4 035**	–
Number of surveyed environmental demonstrations													
Climate protests	5	3	2	1	2	2	4	1	2	1	1	**24**	–

expertise, the broader movement engaged in the development of alternative forms of knowl-edge production, experimentation with alternative technologies, and the provision of coun-ter-expertise. However, parts of the movement's context have over time become increasingly professionalized and have contributed to the development of new areas of science and technol-ogy, such as climate science (Jamison 2006).

Today, the science of global environmental change that the climate strikes refer to in their calls to "listen to the scientists" is a well-established research field with high policy impact, not least through the UN's Intergovernmental Panel on Climate Change (IPCC). Although this scientific field's systemic perspectives include human dimensions, it is more closely related to formal natural science or technical engineering and tends to underemphasize perspectives from the humanities and social sciences, at least according to some observers (Castree *et al.* 2014). To some extent, the movement's earlier alternative "environmental consciousness" and critique against dominant forms of science and technology has thus been replaced by calls to adhere to established science, which today provides a much deeper and broader knowledge of systemic environmental issues. It is thus probable that technical professionals more easily recognize and align with such a framing than with the more radical and utopian views of the earlier environ-mental movement. The increasing deployment of environmental technologies – from renew-able energy and energy-saving technologies to electrified transportation – has probably also contributed to making technical solutions to decarbonization appear as increasingly important, not least for technical professionals.

While Kriesi (1989) previously explained the lower levels of environmental protest par-ticipation among technical specialists as a conflict within "the new middle class", between instrumentality-oriented "technocrats" and autonomy-oriented socio-cultural specialists, the framings of today's most dominant environmental protests around climate change seem to have made this conflict within the well-educated middle class less central. Whether this holds when explaining, at least partly, the increasing proportion of technical professionals in environmental protests in our still-quite-limited data and whether this is part of a broader trend remain to be explored. A deeper understanding of the relation between the environmental movement's class basis and the development of the movement would require an analysis of how different occupa-tional classes have varied in terms of motives, attitudes, and previous movement participation. Even though such an analysis would benefit significantly from data for non-participants in the general public, which we lack, our climate strike data can at least shed some light on whether there exist differences between classes among climate protestors.

The 2019 climate protest survey included one question regarding trust in modern science to solve environmental problems, as well as one about whether protecting the environment should be prioritized even if it leads to unemployment and reduced economic growth. Figure 24.1 shows differences between classes, including students, in their answers to these two questions. Overall, 55% of all respondents agreed that science could be trusted (only 18% disagreed, with the rest neither agreeing nor disagreeing). The highest numbers were among the technical professionals and the students. On the second question, 89% of all respondents agreed with prioritizing the environment over jobs and growth (only 3% disagreed). Here also, the techni-cal professionals scored highest, while the students scored the lowest. Even though this clearly indicates that climate protestors in the technical professions tend to be more pro-science and readier to prioritize the environment over jobs, it should be noted that the class differences do not deviate much from the figures for all climate protestors together. Figure 24.1 also shows the percentage having previous experience of climate change or environmental marches, indicating whether the group of "newcomers" differs between classes. While class differences are also rela-tively small here, one can note that the group of newcomers is slightly larger among technical

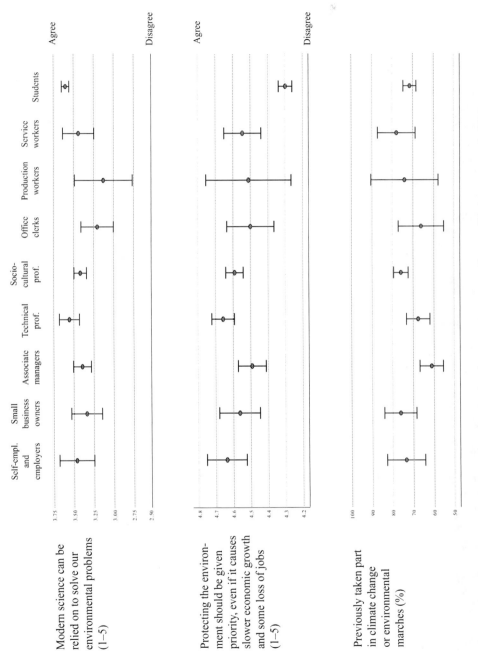

Figure 24.1 Differences between classes' attitudes and political participation among climate strike demonstrators in 2019

professionals than the average. Taken together, these analyses show small but interesting differences between classes, indicating that the group of technical professionals requires more attention when discussing the role of class in today's environmental movement.

Conclusion

This chapter started by arguing that environmental activists have often been portrayed as primarily belonging to the highly educated middle class, despite a lack of survey-based studies about environmental movements' class compositions. Our review of the very few empirical studies that can be found, and our own data from environmental protest surveys, showed that this widespread but often unsubstantiated assumption nevertheless was true. University-educated people with middle-class occupations are significantly overrepresented compared to their proportion in the general population within various forms of environmental political participation, while individuals with working-class occupations are significantly underrepresented. The same pattern can be seen in the Global North and the Global South. However, when compared with other social movements, "new" as well as "old", and with other forms of political participation, this pattern of middle-class overrepresentation within the environmental movement is nothing that stands out. The middle class tends to be overrepresented in other movements and other forms of political participation as well. It would therefore be far-fetched to conclude that this over- and underrepresentation primarily has to do with the environmental issue as such, claiming, for instance, that the working class is less interested in saving the environment. The fact that individuals with middle-class occupations are more likely to be mobilized by environmental movements obviously has more to do with more general social mechanisms surrounding all kinds of political activism. To talk about overrepresentation of certain social strata does not, however, contradict the fact that contemporary environmental movements still attract participants from various social classes, also those not part of "the new middle class" (cf. Giugni and Grasso 2015b).

In this chapter we furthermore highlight the fact that it has not been the middle class in general that has been overrepresented in environmental activism, but socio-cultural professionals in particular and not, for instance, technical professionals. This shows that analyses of the role of class within social movements must consider more aspects than just the hierarchical class stratification between middle-class and working-class occupations. Such studies should focus on the differences between occupational sectors and the roles of work-related interests other than those based on economic inequalities. Our finding that environmental protests during more recent years, in particular those focusing on climate change, tend to mobilize a higher proportion of technical professionals is an indication that sector-wise differences among occupations impact how classes are mobilized to environmental movements. Here, future research ought to investigate, for instance, the role of the resonance between the recent climate protests' pro-science framing and the knowledge interests of natural scientists and technologists, in order to see whether interests related to specific middle-class occupations contribute to these classes being mobilized in environmental movements.

Notes

1 Another standardized class scheme is the Goldthorpe-inspired European Socioeconomic Classification (ESeC), that only highlights the hierarchical stratification of occupations.
2 In a critical discussion about the real novelty of "new social movements", Calhoun (1993) argues that during the nineteenth century, the middle class already had an important role in many movements,

including the labor movement and early Socialist parties that also mobilized artisans, agricultural workers, white-collar workers, and small proprietors, and thus not only the industrial working class.

3 It should be noted that the occupational class categorization used in the WVS questionnaire differs from Oesch's and similar class schemes, for instance, in not making a distinction between employed and self-employed. However, the classes in the center of our discussion – the well-educated middle class and the working class – seem quite comparable.

4 The largest sub-groups of this class are science and engineering professionals (52%, including, e.g., engineers, architects, biologists, environmental protection professionals), ICT professionals (27%, including, e.g., software developers), and science and engineering technicians (11%). For socio-cultural professionals, the largest sub-group was teaching professionals (56%), which might also include university teachers and researchers in science and technology, something we unfortunately do not have any data on.

REFERENCES

Blumer, Herbert. 1939. Collective Behavior. In: Robert E. Park (Ed.). *An Outline of the Principles of Sociology*. New York: Barnes & Noble.

Buechler, Steven M. 1995. New Social Movement Theories. *The Sociological Quarterly* 36(3): 441–464.

Calhoun, Craig. 1993. "New Social Movements" of the Early Nineteenth Century. *Social Science History* 17(3): 385–427.

Castree, Noel, William M. Adams, John Barry, Daniel Brockington, Bram Büscher, Esteve Corbera, David Demeritt, *et al.* 2014. Changing the Intellectual Climate. *Nature Climate Change* 4(9): 763–768.

Cotgrove, Stephen and Andrew Duff. 1980. Environmentalism, Middle Class Radicalism and Politics. *Sociological Review* 28(2):333–351.

Dalton, Russell J. and Robert Rohrschneider. 2002. Political Action and the Political Context: A Multilevel Model of Environmental Activism. In: Dieter Fuchs, Edeltraud Roller and Bernhard Wessels (Eds.), *Bürger und Demokratie in Ost und West: Studien zur politischen Kultur und zum politischen Prozess*. Wiesbaden: Westdeutscher Verlag, pp. 333–350.

della Porta, Donatella. 2015. *Social Movements in Times of Austerity: Bringing Capitalism Back into Protest Analysis*. Cambridge: Polity Press.

della Porta, Donatella and Mario Diani. 2015. Introduction: The Field of Social Movement Studies. In: Donatella della Porta and Mario Diani (Eds.). *The Oxford Handbook of Social Movements*. Oxford: Oxford University Press, pp. 1–29.

della Porta, Donatella and Dieter Rucht. 2002. The Dynamics of Environmental Campaigns. *Mobilization: An International Journal* 7(1): 1–14.

de Moor, Joost, Katrin Uba, Mattias Wahlström, Magnus Wennerhag and Michiel De Vydt (Eds.) (2020). *Protest for a future II: Composition, mobilization and motives of the participants in Fridays For Future climate protests on 20–27 September, 2019, in 19 cities around the world*. Report. DOI 10.17605/OSF.IO/ASRUW

Devall, W. B. 1970. Conservation: An Upper-Middle Class Social Movement: A Replication. *Journal of Leisure Research* 2(2): 123–126.

Eggert, Nina and Marco Giugni. 2012. The Homogenization of "Old" and "New" Social Movements. *Mobilization: An International Journal* 17(3): 335–348.

Eder, Klaus. 1993. *New Politics of Class: Social Movements and Cultural Dynamics in Advanced Societies*. London: Sage.

Faich, Ronald G. and Richard P. Gale. 1971. The Environmental Movement: From Recreation to Politics. *The Pacific Sociological Review* 14(3): 270–287.

Geschwender, James A. 1968. Explorations in the Theory of Social Movements and Revolutions. *Social Forces* 47(2): 127–135.

Giugni, Marco and Maria T. Grasso (Eds.). 2015a. *Austerity and Protest: Popular Contention in Times of Economic Crisis*. Farnham: Ashgate.

Giugni, Marco and Maria T. Grasso. 2015b. Environmental Movements in Advanced Industrial Democracies: Heterogeneity, Transformation, and Institutionalization. *Annual Review of Environment and Resources* 40(1): 337–361

Giugni, Marco and Maria T. Grasso. 2019. *Street Citizens: Protest Politics and Social Movement Activism in the Age of Globalization*. New York: Cambridge University Press

Goldthorpe, John H. and David Lockwood. 1963. Affluence and the British Class Structure. *The Sociological Review* 11(2): 133–163.

Gouldner, Alvin. 1979. *The Future of Intellectuals and the Rise of the New Class*. London: Macmillan Education.

Heberle, Rudolf. 1951. *Social Movements: An Introduction to Political Sociology*. New York: Appleton-Century-Crofts.

Hetland, Gabriel and Jeffrey Goodwin. 2013. The Strange Disappearance of Capitalism from Social Movement Studies. In: Colin Barker, Laurence Cox, John Krinsky and Alf Gunvald Nilsen (Eds.). *Marxism and Social Movements*. Leiden: Koninlijke Brill NV, pp. 83–102

Hooghe, Liesbet, Gary Marks and Carol Wilson. 2002. Does Left/Right Structure Party Positions on European Integration? *Comparative Political Studies* 35(8): 965–989.

Hylmö, A. and Magnus Wennerhag. 2012. "Does Class Matter in Protests? Social Class, Attitudes towards Inequality, and Political Trust in European Demonstrations in a Time of Economic Crisis." Working Paper. http://www.protestsurvey.eu/index.php?page=publications&id=22

Hylmö, Anders and Magnus Wennerhag. 2015. Does Class Matter in Anti-Austerity Protests? Social Class, Attitudes towards Inequality, and Political Trust in European Demonstrations in a Time of Economic Crisis. In: Marco Giugni and Maria T. Grasso (Eds.). *Austerity and Protest: Popular Contention in Times of Economic Crisis*. Farnham: Ashgate, pp. 83–107.

Inglehart, Ronald. 1977. *The Silent Revolution: Changing Values and Political Styles among Western Publics*. Princeton, NJ: Princeton University Press.

Inglehart, Ronald. 1981. Post-Materialism in an Environment of Insecurity. *The American Political Science Review* 75(4): 880–900.

Jamison, Andrew. 2006. Social Movements and Science: Cultural Appropriations of Cognitive Praxis. *Science as Culture* 15(1): 45–59.

Jamison, Andrew, Ron Eyerman, Jacqueline Cramer and Jeppe Læssøe. 1990. *The Making of the New Environmental Consciousness: A Comparative Study of the Environmental Movements in Sweden, Denmark and the Netherlands*. Edinburgh: Edinburgh University Press.

Klandermans, Bert. 1984. Mobilization and Participation: Social-Psychological Expansions of Resource Mobilization. *American Sociological Review* 49(5): 583–600.

Kriesi, Hanspeter. 1989. New Social Movements and the New Class in the Netherlands. *American Journal of Sociology* 94(5): 1078–1116.

Lipset, Seymour Martin. 1950. *Agrarian Socialism: The Cooperative Commonwealth Federation in Saskatchewan: A Study in Political Sociology*. Berkeley: University of California Press.

McAdam, D. 1986. Recruitment to High-Risk Activism: The Case of Freedom Summer. *American Journal of Sociology* 92(1): 64–90.

Marx, Karl. 1846–1847/1975. *The Poverty of Philosophy: Answer to the "Philosophy of Poverty" by M. Proudhon*. Moscow: Progress Publishers.

Marx, Karl. 1852/1984. *The Eighteenth Brumaire of Louis Bonaparte*. Moscow: Progress.

Marx, Karl. 1867/1990. *Capital: A Critique of Political Economy. Volume I*. Harmondsworth: Penguin.

Marx, Karl, and Friedrich Engels. 1848. Manifesto of the Communist Party. In: Terrell Carver and James Farr (Eds.). 2015. *The Cambridge Companion to the Communist Manifesto*. New York: Cambridge University Press, pp. 237–260.

Melucci, Alberto. 1980. The New Social Movements: A Theoretical Approach. *Social Science Information* 19(2): 199–226.

Oesch, D. 2006a. *Redrawing the Class Map: Stratification and Institutions in Britain, Germany, Sweden, and Switzerland*. New York: Palgrave Macmillan.

Oesch, D. 2006b. Coming to Grips with a Changing Class Structure: An Analysis of Employment Stratification in Britain, Germany, Sweden and Switzerland. *International Sociology* 21(2): 263–88.

Oesch, D. 2008. The Changing Shape of Class Voting: An Individual-level Analysis of Party Support in Britain, Germany and Switzerland. *European Societies* 10(3): 329–55.

Offe, Claus. 1985. New Social Movements: Challenging the Boundaries of Institutional Politics. *Social Research* 52(4): 817–868.

Park, Robert E. and Ernest W. Burgess. 1921. *Introduction to the Science of Sociology*. Chicago: University of Chicago Press.

Peterson, Abby, Mattias Wahlström and Magnus Wennerhag. 2018. *Pride Parades and LGBT Movements: Political Participation in an International Comparative Perspective*. New York: Routledge.

Rootes, Christopher. 1995. A New Class? The Higher Educated and the New Politics. In: Louis Maheu (Ed.). *Social Movements and Social Classes: The Future of Collective Action*. London: Sage, pp. 220–235.

Rootes, Christopher and Robert Brulle. 2013. Environmental Movements. In: David A. Snow, Donatella della Porta, Bert Klandermans and Doug McAdam (Eds.). *The Wiley-Blackwell Encyclopedia of Social and Political Movements*. Chichester: Wiley-Blackwell.

Ross, Ashley D., Rhonda Struminger, Jeffrey Winking and Kathryn R. Wedemeyer-Strombel. 2018. Science as a Public Good: Findings From a Survey of March for Science Participants. *Science Communication* 40(2): 228–245.

Saarinen, Arttu, Aki Koivula, Ilkka Koiranen and Jukka Sivonen. 2018. Highly Educated but Occupationally Differentiated: The Members of Finland's Green League. *Environmental Politics* 27(2): 362–372.

Schlozman, Kay Lehman, Sidney Verba and Henry E. Brady. 2012. *The Unheavenly Chorus: Unequal Political Voice and the Broken Promise of American Democracy*. Princeton, NJ: Princeton University Press.

Schussman, Alan and Soule, Sarah A. 2005. Process and Protest: Accounting for Individual Protest Participation. *Social Forces* 84(2): 1083–1108.

Smelser, Neil J. 1962. *Theory of Collective Behavior*. London: Routledge & Kegan Paul.

Sombart, Werner. 1896/1968. *Socialism and the Social Movement*. New York: A.M. Kelley.

van Stekelenburg, Jacquelien, Stefaan Walgrave, Bert Klandermans and Joris Verhulst. 2012. Contextualizing Contention: Framework, Design, and Data. *Mobilization: An International Quarterly* 17(3): 249–262.

von Stein, Lorenz. 1850/1964. *The History of the Social Movement in France, 1789–1850*. Totowa, NJ: Bedminster Press.

Taylor, Dorceta E. 1997. American Environmentalism: The Role of Race, Class and Gender in Shaping Activism 1820–1995. *Race, Gender & Class* 5(1): 16–62.

Tilly, Charles. 1978. *From Mobilization to Revolution*. New York: Random House.

Torgler, Benno, Mariá García-Valiñas and Alison Macintyre. 2011. Participation in Environmental Organizations: An Empirical Analysis. *Environment and Development Economics* 16(5): 591–620.

Touraine, Alain. 1969/1971. *The Post-Industrial Society: Tomorrow's Social History: Classes, Conflicts and Culture in the Programmed Society*. New York: Random House.

Touraine, Alain. 1978/1981. *The Voice and the Eye: An Analysis of Social Movements*. Cambridge: Cambridge University Press.

Tranter, Bruce. 1996. The social bases of environmentalism in Australia. *The Australian & New Zealand Journal of Sociology* 32(2): 61–85.

Wahlström, Mattias, Piotr Kocyba, Michiel De Vydtand and Joost de Moor (Eds.), *Protest for a future: Composition, mobilization and motives of the participants in Fridays for Future climate protests on 15 March, 2019 in 13 European cities*. 2020. Report. DOI 10.17605/OSF.IO/XCNZH

Walgrave, Stefaan and Joris Verhulst. 2011. Selection and Response Bias in Protest Surveys. *Mobilization: An International Quarterly* 16(2): 203–222.

Weber, Max. 1922/2019. *Economy and Society. A New Translation*. Cambridge, MA: Harvard University Press.

Wennerhag, Magnus. 2016. Who Takes Part in May Day Marches? In: Abby Peterson and Herbert Reiter (Eds.). *The Ritual of May Day in Western Europe – Past, Present and Future*. Abingdon: Routledge, pp. 187–216.

Wright, Erik O. 1979. *Class Structure and Income Determination*. New York: Academic Press.

Wright, Erik O. 2009. Understanding Class: Towards an Integrated Analytical Approach. *New Left Review* 60: 101–116.

25

POLITICAL VALUES AND SOCIALIZATION IN ENVIRONMENTAL MOVEMENTS

David B. Tindall, Valerie Berseth, Marjolaine Martel-Morin, and Erick Lachapelle

Introduction

In this chapter we discuss key aspects of values and socialization pertaining to environmental movements. We first consider some ways in which the environmental movement can be mapped and examine how orientations vary within the movement. We then review several theoretical perspectives that focus on values and related concepts and examine how the different values, beliefs, and socialization processes we focus on are related to key environmental movement phenomena such as identification with the movement, environmental activism, and environmentally friendly behavior. In particular, we consider the post-materialist/materialist values distinction, the human exceptionalism/new ecological paradigm dimension, and liberalism-conservatism. We also consider a particular explanatory perspective in environmental sociology, the values-belief-norm (VBN) theory.

In exploring these perspectives, we draw upon empirical survey data collected by the authors on members/supporters of environmental movement organizations and the general public in Canada. Some results reported here have been previously published, and some are the result of new analyses undertaken for this chapter. Finally, we provide a critical discussion of key issues regarding conceptualizing, measuring, and modeling values in the context of the environmental movement.

While we make references to "the environmental movement" in this chapter, there are, in fact, many environmental movements. The multitude of movements vary in geographical location and scale; in terms of topics of concern, specialization, ideology, tactics and strategies; and in terms of critiques/accommodation of capitalism (Shabecoff 2012). As the authors of this chapter primarily work in Canada, our focus is North American–centric, though the Canadian case which we focus on is illustrative of the diversity in the environmental movement. Canada is an instructive case in that it is an economically advanced, Western, liberal democracy. It is relatively similar to other nation-states with these characteristics. It is a geographically large country, with an abundance of natural resources and "wilderness", which makes it similar to the United States, but it has a much smaller population than the US.

There have been several different waves of the environmental movement. These waves have focused more or less on different environmental and social issues, had varying demographic compositions, and had varying geographical scales. While we do not offer a temporal analysis of

DOI: 10.4324/9780367855680-29

the environmental movement, it is worth noting that the values that underlie environmentalism have been dynamic (for example, there is more emphasis given to equity and social justice issues in contemporary movements than in the early stages of the environmental movement).

There are a multitude of ways in which the environmental movement might be mapped out, including on dimensions such as anthropocentrism-biocentrism (Dunlap 2000), as captured by the HEP-NEP distinction, and in terms of orientations toward political-economic issues – such as the role of government intervention in the economy to protect environmental values (Gould et al. 1993; Schaiberg and Gould 1994; Klein 2015). We address this topic next.

Diversity within the movement

In this section, we consider some ways in which the environmental movement might be mapped – especially with regard to emphasizing individual behavior change versus broader systems change as a solution to environmental problems, views about technology, markets, capitalism and inequality, and orientations toward economic growth

Recently, Brulle and Norgaard (2019) have argued that the climate movement is divided into two camps: groups engaging in conventional advocacy ("reformists") and groups with a more contentious climate-justice approach ("radicals"). The former endorse a form of ecological modernization using technology, shifting investments, and market-based solutions; the latter identify environmental problems as structurally rooted in the global capitalist order that commodifies nature and ecosystems. This division is further complicated by other contemporary debates, between those advocating lifestyle change and those arguing for broader structural change (Shove 2010) and debates about degrowth (Kallis 2011). We explore aspects of these arguments next.

We present an example from a study led by the fourth author that draws on two online surveys conducted in Canada: data from environmental non-governmental organizations (n = 2,653) and data from collected from the general population (n = 3,458) in 2019. Using descriptive statistics, we examine the views of ENGO supporters on the question of how best to achieve environmental protection and dig deeper into what environmentally engaged citizens think about economic growth.

We first explore diversity among environmentally engaged citizens with respect to attitudes toward environmental solutions. Specifically, we look at the distribution of responses to the question, adapted from Dunlap and Gale (1972), "Which statement best describes your attitude regarding solutions to environmental problems in our society?" Response options included: 1) Environmental problems can be solved within our present political-economic system if enough people change their lifestyle; 2) Environmental problems can be solved only if significant changes are made in our present political-economic system; and 3) Environmental problems can be solved only if our present political-economic system is replaced by a radically different system. For simplicity, we refer to these attitudes as the lifestyle, institutional, and radical views, respectively.

Among the ENGO sample, results reveal that few (12%) agree with the lifestyle view that problems can be solved within the actual system if enough people change their lifestyle. Instead, about one in three environmental group supporters see radical systemic change as necessary to solving environmental problems, and about half the supporters surveyed believe that environmental problems can be solved if significant institutional changes are made to our present political-economic system.

Also noteworthy is that there are some striking differences in environmental solution orientations between the general public and supporters of environmental organizations. Whereas about one-third of environmental organization supporters share a radical view, this perspective remains marginal in the general population. In fact, environmental group members are almost three times more likely to share this view (32%) relative to the general population (12%). Conversely, the lifestyle view of social change is more popular in the general population (39%) than in the ENGO sample (12%). There are roughly similar levels of support for the more reformist, institutional view in both general population (49%) and ENGO supporter (56%) samples, respectively.

Next, we examine views about economic growth among environmental organization supporters. These data were obtained through survey questions adapted from Drews and van den Bergh (2016). Results show that beliefs about economic growth are less contentious than attitudes toward the solution of environmental problems. Most respondents either strongly disagree (37%) or disagree (30%) with the belief that "economic growth is good". Similarly, a vast majority of respondents agree (36%) or strongly agree (37%) that we need to set strict limits on production, consumption, and economic growth. In addition, most disagree (41%) or strongly disagree (34%) with the assumption that technology can solve all environmental problems associated with economic growth.

These results indicate that ENGO supporters are critical of the growth paradigm (i.e., growth at all costs) as well as of the consumer society on which it rests. This is in contrast with what is thought to be the prominent perspective within the general population, where growth is most often considered as natural and inherently good (Gustafsson 2013). This suggests that a non-trivial proportion of environmentally engaged citizens may be willing to challenge the economic growth paradigm.

As we have shown in this section, the environmental movement is far from homogenous, especially in terms of views about social change and economic growth. Yet beyond these divergences, members of the environmental movement have also been found to share some beliefs and values (Giugni and Grasso 2015).

Perspectives on values, socialization, and environmentalism

A variety of theoretical perspectives have been developed to explain the rise and dynamics of social movements. In this section, we will review several theoretical perspectives that focus on values and related phenomena as explanations for environmentalism and other forms of social movement activity.

One perspective that has been developed to explain contemporary social movements is the New Social Movement Theory (NSMT) (Larana et al. 1994). A key component of NSMT is an assertion that such movements arose in conjunction with a value shift in Western societies. Since the end of the 1960s, social movement scholars have focused much attention on "new" social movements, which are often juxtaposed with the "materialist" goals of the labor movement. According to Ronald Inglehart (1977, 1990), these movements emerged during a period of rising economic growth, social safety, and material well-being, leading people to shift their attention to realizing non-material goals like self-expression and protection of the environment. This account stresses the importance of culture, as exemplified by changing values, and suggests that one of the most profound changes in the second half of the twentieth century has been a shift in Western countries from materialist to post-materialist values among substantial segments of the population. While this shift occurred over time, it was thought that once such changes occurred, they would be relatively permanent.

Inglehart's post-materialist values argument draws upon, and parallels, the hierarchy of needs framework developed by the psychologist Abraham Maslow (1962). Maslow talked about the notion that at the level of the individual person, people have certain basic physiological needs they need to meet (such as safety needs and sustenance needs) before they can address higher order social and self-actualization needs, such as aesthetic and intellectual needs, belonging, and esteem. According to Inglehart, societies need to address issues like having a stable economy, economic growth, limiting inflation, having strong defense forces, fighting crime, and maintaining order (which correspond to "material values") before turning to embrace things like having a less impersonal society, having more say on the job, having more say in government, having beautiful cites and protecting nature, emphasizing the importance of ideas, and stressing freedom of speech (which correspond to "post-material values"). While scholars have debated various aspects of the post-materialist values thesis, versions of the post-materialist values scale have been used quite often in surveys, including to study the environmental movement.

Tindall's 2002 study obtained data that enables examination of the post-materialist values thesis (Inglehart 1990). The survey data are from a representative sample of participants in the wilderness preservation movement (Tindall 2002) in British Columbia, Canada, and a representative sample of the general public in British Columbia (Johnston 1988). Here we compare a few specific items in order to highlight the distinction between materialist and post-materialist values. Analysis shows that 46% of the BC public ranked the materialist value "maintaining a high rate of economic growth" highly (1st, 2nd, or 3rd), compared to only 6% of the wilderness preservation movement sample. By contrast, for the post-materialist value of "progress toward a society where ideas count more than money (PMV)", 57% of WPM members ranked this item highly, compared with only 26% of the general public. Overall, there was a statistically significant difference between the WPM movement and the general public in terms of scores on an index of post-materialist values t = 7.49, df = 279, p. .005. This supports the notion that support for post-materialist values distinguishes the environmental movement from the general public (Tindall 1994). While members of the WPM stream of the environmental movement are more likely to support post materialist values, how is this support associated with various aspects of environmentalism? To answer this question, zero order correlations were calculated among several variables, including support for post-materialist values, identification with the wilderness preservation movement, level of activism (Tindall 2002), and level of environmentally friendly behavior (Tindall et al. 2003) for members of the WPM sample. Results showed that the more strongly people support post-materialist values, the more strongly they identify with the environmental movement, the more active they are in the environmental movement, and the more they engage in environmentally friendly behavior. Results also show that these latter three variables are significantly intercorrelated. Of most theoretical importance, the more highly that people identify with the WPM stream of the environmental movement, the more active they are and the more they engage in environmentally friendly behavior. This provides some evidence that support for PMVs is correlated with various aspects of environmentalism.

One of the longest established frameworks in environmental sociology is the HEP-NEP continuum. Concerned with the lack of environmental focus in sociology, Catton and Dunlap (1978) argued that anthropocentrism and a binary view of nature/culture informs both the dominant Western worldview and mainstream sociology. They labelled this perspective the Human Exemptionalist Paradigm (HEP), comprising several core beliefs:

1   Humans have a cultural heritage in addition to genetic inheritance, which makes them unique among the earth's creatures.
2   Social and cultural factors (including technology) are the major determinants of human affairs.

3   Social and cultural environments are the crucial context of human affairs, and the biophysical environment is largely irrelevant.

4   Culture is cumulative, so progress can continue indefinitely, and all social problems are ultimately solvable.

Catton and Dunlap suggested that a growing eco-centric perspective, which they named the New Ecological Paradigm (NEP), presents a challenge to the dominant anthropocentrism. The NEP comprises four alternate beliefs:

1   Humans are exceptional but are one among many interdependent species.

2   Social life is also influenced by the biophysical environment, often as a reaction to human action.

3   Human action produces unintended effects for interconnections in the web of nature.

4   The world's finite resources impose physical and biological limits on economic growth and social progress.

To measure the existence and trajectory of the shift in paradigms, Dunlap and Van Liere (1978) proposed a 12-item scale, which asked respondents to respond to belief statements that correspond to three facets of the new ecological paradigm: disruptions to the balance of nature, limits to social and economic growth, and the right to rule over nature. The scale has since been expanded to 15-items that also address exceptionalism and the "ecocrisis" (Dunlap et al. 2000). Though it is not without critics (Hawcroft and Milfont 2010; Zhu and Lu 2017), the NEP scale has been used to measure environmental views worldwide (Dunlap 2008; Ogunbode 2013; Schultz and Zelezny 1999; Xiao et al. 2019). The NEP scale has also been used to measure other effects, such as gender and socialization (Zelezny et al. 2000) and rural-urban differences (Huddart Kennedy et al. 2009) on environmentalism.

The HEP-NEP continuum intersects with social movement research in a number of ways. As a measurement tool, the scale can be used to better understand how people become socialized toward either pro- or anti-environmental values. Though the values associated with HEP have been dominant in Western societies, several studies have found that pro-environmental values can be shaped through educational institutions, media, peers, and families (Ewert et al. 2005; Arcury et al. 1986; Villacorta et al. 2003). These findings intersect with social movement research, which similarly suggests that these factors, from education to social networks, contribute to levels of activism (Corrigall-Brown 2012; Passy 2001). They also point to possible targets for environmental activism, such as media coverage of protest events, though the movement-media relationship is notably asymmetrical (McCurdy 2012). While one might expect that environmental activists would exhibit higher NEP scores, there is also reason to expect diversity within the large umbrella of the "environmental movement".

Here we provide examples from a couple of studies that used the NEP scale. Tindall (Tindall and Piggot 2015) collected survey data on representative national level samples of the general public and of members/supporters of environmental movement organizations in Canada. Analyses reveal a significant difference between the general public and members of environmental groups, with the latter having more "pro-environmental" views. Zero order correlations among key variables were also obtained and reveal that members of environmental groups had more pro-environmental views (as measured by the NEP scale), identified more strongly with the environmental movement, were more active in the movement, and engaged in a greater number of environmentally friendly behaviors (EFBs). In terms of these variables, the NEP scale "behaves" similarly to the PMV scale. Though it should be noted that the zero order correlations between NEP and both identification and activism are larger than the respective correlations were between PMV index and these variables. Thus the NEP scale, which is more specifically tailored to environmental issues, has somewhat stronger predictive power.[1] Also noteworthy, but of less importance to the present discussion, is that identification, activism, and EFBs are all positively and significantly intercorrelated.

As distinct from values, other scholars have emphasized the role of political ideologies in shaping attitudes toward the environment and environmental protection. Defined here as a coherent set of beliefs and ideas held by groups of individuals that structure their attitudes and preferences on political issues, political ideologies cover preferences around stability and change, as well as the appropriate role of government in society, and interact with environmentalism in several respects (Carmines and D'Amico 2015). Theoretically, conservative political ideologies have been linked to system justification tendencies, or the tendency to more strongly support the maintenance of the status quo and resist social change (Jost, Nosek and Gosling 2008). Empirically, scholarship has also shown that those holding more conservative economic views (e.g., preference for the free market over government intervention) are less likely to support environmental protection (Dunlap and Van Liere 1984). In short, a large literature demonstrates that those on the political "left" are consistently more concerned about the environment and more likely to engage in pro-environmental behaviors than their "right-wing" counterparts (Dunlap et al. 2001; Eiser et al. 1990). It should be noted that the meanings and dynamics between liberalism and conservativism depend on social and cultural context and that the size of the liberal-conservative (or left-right) divide on environmental matters varies across contexts (Davidovic et al. 2020; Fairbrother 2016; Gillham 2008; Birch 2020). The empirical cases we discuss in this chapter are North American in origin, and so our engagement here is primarily with North American scholarship on political ideology, though we note that some scholars find a similar relationship between environmental attitudes and political ideologies in Western European countries as well (McCright et al. 2015). Traditionally, scholars have distinguished between liberalism and conservativism as ideologies underpinned by different philosophical principles against which alternative political futures are measured (Alexander 2015). These are not discrete identities or camps, but complex and multifaceted points of view. Broadly speaking, liberalism embraces an optimistic stance toward individual freedoms and, as a result, is more open to change and experiences (Graham et al. 2009). Conservativism is more closely aligned with stability and the constraints provided by social institutions, as well as a resistance to the changes proposed by those on the left of the spectrum (Feygina, Jost, and Goldsmith 2010; Jost et al. 2008).

These distinctions translate into environmental attitudes and behaviors. With respect to environmental concern, McCright and Dunlap (2011, 2013) find that conservative white American males are less concerned about environmental problems. This finding is partly explained by the particular political context of the United States, which has seen a concerted partisan effort by conservative politicians, think tanks, and funders to downplay environmental problems and reject claims made by the environmental movement, liberal politicians, and the scientific community since the 1990s (Jacques et al. 2008; McCright and Dunlap 2013). Similarly, Heath and Gifford's (2006) survey of people in Western Canada found that free-market ideology and techno-optimism were correlated with less environmental concern, while Lachapelle and colleagues (2012) find that supporters of the federal Conservative Party of Canada (CPC) are significantly less likely than supporters of all other federal political parties to believe in climate change (Lachapelle et al. 2012). Interestingly, this dynamic follows a similar pattern as that observed in the United States, with evidence that environmental (and in particular, climate change) attitudes of the Canadian public are responsive to elite partisan cues (Guntermann and

Lachapelle 2020). Recent work by Hochschild (2016) has also elucidated a number of other significant factors contributing to political polarization on environmental issues, including social networks, echo chambers, and distrust of liberal environmentalists.

The assertion that members of environmental movements tend to be more left-wing has been demonstrated empirically (Dietz et al. 1998; Olli et al. 2001). The same split occurs with respect to finding solutions to environmental problems. People with liberal ideologies express greater support for government regulations and economic interventions (e.g., environmental taxes) and greater trust in the science of environmental impacts (McCright et al. 2013), whereas conservatives (particularly fiscal conservatives) show more support for environmental provisions that align with neoliberal free-market principles, technological innovations, and minimal state regulation (Hess et al. 2015). Nevertheless, there are some conservatives who identify as environmentalists. As Pilbeam (2003) suggests, this is not paradoxical, but instead reflects some points of convergence between some elements of traditionalist conservativism and environmental ideologies: namely, a respect of natural limits, a skepticism towards scientific fundamentalism, and support for sustainable development, most closely aligning with ecological modernization. Nor is the pattern universal, with some cross-national studies suggesting that ideological polarization is mostly an issue in contexts in which left-wing parties have embraced environmentalism (Birch 2020).

Empirically, people who identify as more liberal/left wing (as opposed to conservative/right wing) and those who are affiliated with relatively more left-wing (as opposed to right-wing) political parties are more likely to support environmental protection and more likely to be affiliated with environmental movements. This is demonstrated in Tindall's (2002) study of the wilderness preservation movement in British Columbia, where 70% of these members reported having voted for the left-wing (NDP) or center-left party (Liberals), compared to only 21% who reported voting for one of the right-wing parties (the Progressive Conservatives or Reform Party) during the previous federal election. By contrast, for the national electorate overall, 52% of the general electorate had voted for one of the left-wing parties, while 43% had voted for the right-wing parties (LeDuc 1989).

Among a representative sample of the general public in British Columbia, another study's findings show that people who have more pro-environmental views as measured by the NEP scale tend to be more liberal (methodological details reported in Gates 2011). In this study, indexes measuring support for climate justice and support for climate change policies were also constructed. The NEP scale is relatively strongly and significantly correlated with both of these. Also of interest is that the liberalism-conservatism scale is also significantly associated with support for climate justice and support for climate change policies. However, the correlation between liberalism and support for CC policies is stronger than for climate justice, and both correlations are smaller than the correlations for the NEP scale with these variables. So liberalism-conservativism is correlated with key variables of interest in the climate justice movement and is also correlated with the NEP scale. However, the NEP scale is a stronger statistical predictor of support for the environmental policy outcome measures of interest.

The value-belief-norms (VBN) perspective asserts that there is a connection between the values that individuals hold, their perceptions of the environment and potential threats, and their decisions to take action (Dietz et al. 2005; Stern et al. 1999; Stern 2000).

The causal chain involved in the VBN theory model is illustrated in Figure 25.1. In its most basic form (Stern 2000), the VBN framework suggests that individuals adopt a given pro-environmental behavior (BAV) because they feel the moral obligation to behave pro-environmentally (personal norm, PN). This moral obligation is activated when individuals feel responsible (ascription of responsibility, AR) for the consequences of their behaviors on the environment

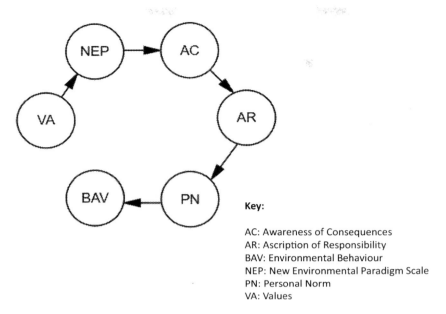

Key:

AC: Awareness of Consequences
AR: Ascription of Responsibility
BAV: Environmental Behaviour
NEP: New Environmental Paradigm Scale
PN: Personal Norm
VA: Values

Figure 25.1   VBN conceptual model

(awareness of consequences, AC). Finally, AC is influenced by pro-environmental beliefs (e.g., the new environmental paradigm, NEP), which are, in turn, influenced by values (VA, i.e., biocentric, altruistic, hedonic, or egoistic values).

In Figure 25.2, we present a structural equation model that sets out to test and illustrate key aspects of the VBN model. The data for this example was obtained from an online survey of Canadian ENGO supporters in 2019 mentioned earlier. For the purpose of structural equation modeling, cases with missing values were excluded from the analysis (n = 1,753).

The initial model included the hypothesized unidirectional path among the VBN variables reported in Figure 25.1. After preliminary data analyses, we decided to exclude egoistic and hedonic values from the model because their inclusion substantially worsened the fit indices. Moreover, we decided to include new paths based on the modification indices provided through the step-by-step model improvement process. The results of SEM analysis are shown in Figure 25.2. The goodness of fit is satisfactory. The number attached to each arrow indicates the effect of one variable in predicting another. Consistent with theoretical expectations, all the standardized path coefficients that lead the five causal paths hypothesized by the VBN theory were positive and statistically significant at p. < .001. We thus find evidence that the conceptual model provided by VBN provides a good fit to the data collected among environmental group supporters in Canada. The standardized coefficients suggest that the strongest direct predictors of pro-environmental behavior are values (VA, β =.49), followed by personal norms (PN, β =.29). Values, NEP, and awareness of consequences (AC) also have an indirect effect on pro-environmental behaviors via personal norms (β =.23, β =.22 and β =.22, respectively). Moreover, values (VA) have an indirect effect on behaviors via every other variable included in the model. Overall, our results indicate a strong positive direct path from values to behaviors and a smaller yet significant indirect effect through each of the outcome variables of the model. These results support the model developed using the VBN theory while also offering some insight into new pathways leading to environmental engagement. In particular, these results

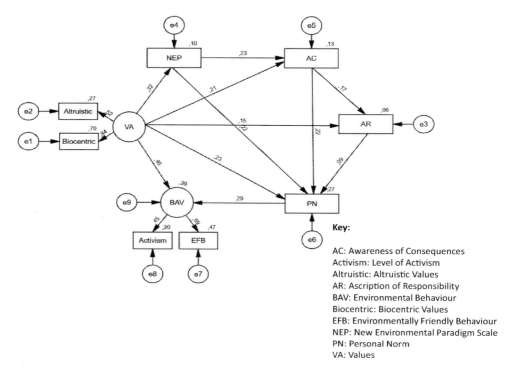

Figure 25.2   Structural equation model predicting level of activism and environmentally friendly behaviors

might suggest that the initial VBN model would underestimate the role of values in explaining pro-environmental behaviors among the most environmentally engaged citizens in Canada (i.e., ENGO supporters).

Political values and socialization: some critical considerations

In this penultimate section, we will describe some of the limitations of perspectives that focus on values and socialization for explaining environmentalism and also describe how values and socialization processes are part of a more complex model of micro-mobilization for environmental movement participation.

Despite the zero-order correlations between values and environmental activism that we have reviewed, structurally oriented scholars have argued that while support for particular values might be a necessary condition for social movement participation, it is not sufficient (McAdam 1986; Klandermans and Oegema 1987; Tindall 2002). Becoming mobilized as a social movement participant involves both socialization and social network ties. For example, as illustrated in Figure 3, people often learn about social movement campaigns through the media (Callison and Tindall 2017) or in the context of interpersonal networks (Tindall et al. forthcoming). Recruitment attempts are also often made in the context of organizational ties or interpersonal social network ties (Tindall 2002, 2015). For example, in Tindall's 2007 study (Tindall and Piggot 2015), over 60% of environmental movement organization respondents receive encouragement from others to participate in environmental movement organization activities. Further, while particular values such as post-materialism might distinguish environmental movement participants from the general public (see earlier examples), in multivariate models, evidence indicates that other variables have greater explanatory power. For example, Tindall in two separate studies of the environmental movement (Tindall 2002; Tindall and Robinson 2017) found that while PMV had significant zero order correlations with key variables such as level of activism, it was not significant in multivariate models. Tindall has suggested that other factors such as social network ties have more explanatory power for explaining differential activism once an individual becomes affiliated with an organization. Nevertheless, values may have indirect effects. Figure 25.3 illustrates some of these relationships.[2]

Statistically, at the zero order level, the NEP scale operates in a fashion similar to the PMV index, but it seems to be more strongly correlated with phenomena like environmental movement identification and environmental movement activism than does the PMV index. Also, unlike the PMV index, there is some evidence that NEP has a statistical effect on environmentalism net of other factors in multivariate models. For example, Tindall and Piggot (2015) found that NEP is positively associated with concern about climate change among the general public, controlling for social network ties to environmental organization members and other variables. Tindall and Howe (2018) found that the NEP scale has a positive association with environmental activism among environmental organization members in Canada, controlling for social network ties and other variables. The greater explanatory power of the NEP scale for explaining environmentalism is perhaps not surprising, given that it was developed specifically to measure concern about environmental issues.

Various critiques have been offered of both the post-materialist values thesis and the NEP scale. For example, some environmental sociologists have argued that economic wealth at the state level does not necessarily correlate with support for materialism versus post-materialism, and it is far from clear that people in lesser-developed countries and poorer neighborhoods are unconcerned or even less concerned about environmental issues. Some critics have pointed out that conceptually, desiring a high-quality environment would seem to be a materialist value. Also, in the current age of populist politics that favor domestic economic issues over other priorities, claims about the unidirectional shift to PMVs seem suspect (Inglehart and Norris 2017).

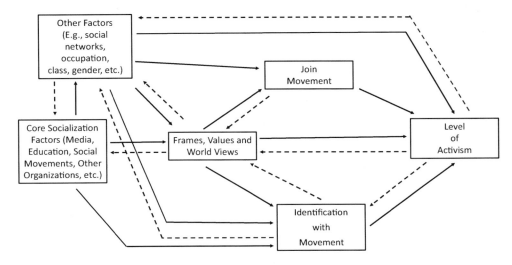

Figure 25.3   A simplified model of socialization, values, and activism

Regarding the NEP scale, some commentators have suggested that this measure has a liberal bias and that it tends to validate the views of upper-middle-class individuals with higher levels of education and may miss some of the environmental sensitivities of more conservative rural working-class people (Huddart Kennedy 2020). Similarly, while those who endorse liberalism are affiliated with environmentalism in greater numbers, there are some manifestations of conservative environmentalism than may be overlooked with such broad-stroke measures.

We would highlight that the results we have presented in this chapter do not necessarily validate the larger theoretical frameworks of these perspectives (e.g., such as changes at the macro level and their consequences at the macro level). Rather, we have provided some evidence that the measures associated with these perspectives have predictive validity at the individual level for statistically explaining phenomena that are thought to be indicators of environmentalism.

The analysis we have presented employing the value-behavior-norms (VBN) perspective extends insights presented about the NEP scale (and similar measures). In this framework, values are seen has having indirect effects on behavior through a variety of social psychological variables. Also, according to this framework, NEP is a measure of beliefs and is an intervening variable in the VBN model process. The structural equation model we present in this chapter analyzing survey data from supporters of environmental organizations is largely consistent with the VBN argument. Interestingly, empirical findings suggest that values have both direct and indirect effects on behavior, suggesting that values might have a larger overall impact than is detected in some past research. The model we present suggests that NEP is affected by values and has an indirect effect on environmental behavior.

Figure 25.3 illustrates some of the key factors involved in the socialization of pro-environmental values and other aspects of environmentalism (such as movement identity). Social movement organizations play an important role in the socialization of potential environmental movement participants through the framing of issues and by engagement in information campaigns (Cormier and Tindall 2005). Media are among the most important agents of socialization regarding environmental issues (Östman 2014; Callison and Tindall 2017). Various scholars have noted the role of educational institutions in affecting environmental values (Inglehart 1990; Jowett et al. 2014), with some finding evidence of reverse socialization: that is, children influencing their parents (Lawson et al. 2019). Occupations can also play an important role in the socialization of particular values (Brint 1984), as can social networks (Passy 2001; Tindall 2015). Various socio-demographic factors can also play a role in socialization of key values related to environmentalism, such as when a significant gender-based division of labor exists (Tindall et al. 2003). In some cases, it is not clear if values are the product of socialization or if selection processes explain correlations between values and environmentalism (as indicated by the reciprocal relations depicted in Figure 25.3). For example, does having ties to environmentalists influence individuals to become environmentalists themselves, or do those with pro-environmental values prefer to form social ties to like-minded others? Similar questions exist with regard to other correlations that are thought to provide evidence of socialization effects (e.g., education, urban-rural differences, occupation). In many cases, there are likely reciprocal causal paths (see Figure 25.3). Future research might explore this topic further.

We have focused our review on post-materialist values and the NEP scale (and, to a lesser extent, the liberal-conservative scale) because arguments have been made that these orientations underlie environmentalism (Inglehart 1990) and partly because measures associated with these perspectives have been relatively widely used. However, it might be argued that these conceptualizations and measures are inadequate for fully understanding contemporary environmental movements, and future research should explore the development of new measures that reflect contemporary dimensions of environmentalism.

Conclusion

Various commentators have asserted that associations exist between key values (and related phenomena such as beliefs and ideologies) and environmentalism. Here we have investigated: 1) post-materialism, 2) support for the new ecological paradigm (NEP), and 3) liberalism-conservatism. As our chapter demonstrates through empirical examples, there is correlational evidence for assertions that these constructs underlie environmentalism – at the individual level of analysis at least. That is, to use data on post-materialist values as an example, results show (in our examples) a significant correlation between holding post-materialist values and being affiliated with environmental SMOs. Further, there is also evidence that support for key values such as post-materialism is also associated with important phenomena such as identification with the environmental movement and engagement in environmental activism. (Similar correlations were found for support for the NEP scale and for liberalism-conservatism.)

As we describe, some commentators have noted distinctions between environmental movement organizations that focus on actions that promote lifestyle changes (or individual solutions) and those that endorse structural (or collective) solutions. Further, among those who are concerned about political and economic structures, as we have shown, there is a distinction between those who favor reforms and those who favor more radical restructuring of socio-political-economic structures. To some extent, we can think of this latter distinction as describing the difference between centrist and progressive perspectives.

We have presented results that demonstrate key differences in orientations between supporters of environmental organizations and the general public. The general public is much more likely to favor lifestyle changes as opposed to institutional change or radical change compared to environmental organization supporters. The findings reported here also show, somewhat in contrast with what we might expect for the general public, that among environmental organization supporters, a majority disagree with promoting economic growth at all costs and agree with curbing consumerism. Also, a majority disagree with the notion that technology can solve all problems. We conclude by recommending that future research on environmentalism should focus on developing common measures and collecting data using these validated metrics to examine these distinctions.

Notes

1 In the research methods literature, there are technical differences between scales and indexes. For practical purposes, however, in this chapter we are using the terms interchangeably, consistent with the term index.
2 The solid lines in Figure 3 are meant to illustrate causal relations between pairs of variables. The dashed lines indicate that many of these relationships involve reciprocal causation, or bidirectional causal influence.

References

Alexander, James. 2015. The major ideologies of liberalism, socialism and conservatism. *Political Studies*, **63**(5), 980–994.
Arcury, Thomas A., Timothy P. Johnson and Susan J. Scollay. 1986. Ecological worldview and environmental knowledge: The "New Environmental Paradigm". *Journal of Environmental Education*, **17**(4), 35–40.
Birch, Sarah. 2020. Political polarization and environmental attitudes: A cross-national analysis. *Environmental Politics*, **29**(4), 697–718.

Brint, S. 1984. "New-class" and cumulative trend explanations of the liberal political attitudes of professionals. *American Journal of Sociology*, **90**(1), 30–71.

Brulle, Robert J., and Kari Marie Norgaard. 2019. Avoiding cultural trauma: Climate change and social inertia. *Environmental Politics*, **28**(5), 886–908.

Callison, Candis and David B. Tindall. 2017. Climate change communication in Canada. In: *The Oxford Research Encyclopedia of Climate Science*. Oxford, UK: Oxford University Press.

Carmines, E. G. and N. J. D'Amico. 2015. The new look in political ideology research. *Annual Review of Political Science*, **18**, 205–216.

Catton Jr., William R. and Riley E. Dunlap. 1978. Environmental Sociology: A New Paradigm. *The American Sociologist*, **13**(1), 41–49.

Cormier, J. and D. B. Tindall. 2005. Wood frames: Framing the forests in British Columbia. *Sociological Focus*, **38**(1), 1–24.

Corrigall-Brown, Catherine. 2012. *Patterns of Protest: Trajectories of Participation in Social Movements*. Stanford, CA: Stanford University Press.

Davidovic, Dragana, Niklas Harring and Sverker C. Jagers. 2020. The contingent effects of environmental concern and ideology: Institutional context and people's willingness to pay environmental taxes. *Environmental Politics*, **29**(4), 674–696.

Dietz, Thomas, Amy Fitzgerald and Rachael Shwom. 2005. Environmental values. *Annual Review of Environmental Resources*, **30**, 335–372.

Dietz, Thomas, Paul C. Stern and Gregory A. Guagnano. 1998. Social structural and social psychological bases of environmental concern. *Environment and Behavior*, **30**(4), 450–471.

Drews, Stefan, and Jeroen CJM van den Bergh. 2016. Public views on economic growth, the environment and prosperity: Results of a questionnaire survey. *Global Environmental Change*, **39**, 1–14.

Dunlap, Riley E. 2008. The new environmental paradigm scale: From marginality to worldwide use. *The Journal of Environmental Education*, **40**(1), 3–18.

Dunlap, Riley E. and Richard P. Gale. 1972. Politics and ecology: A political profile of student eco-activists. *Youth and Society*, **2**, 379–397.

Dunlap, Riley E. and Kent D. Van Liere. 1978. The "new environmental paradigm": A proposed measuring instrument and preliminary results. *Journal of Environmental Education*, **9**(4), 10–19.

Dunlap, Riley E. and Kent D. Van Liere. 1984. Commitment to dominant social paradigm and concern for environmental quality. *Social Science Quarterly*, **65**, 1013–1065.

Dunlap, Riley E., Kent D. Van Liere, Angela G. Mertig, and Robert Emmet Jones. 2000. New trends in measuring environmental attitudes: measuring endorsement of the new ecological paradigm: A revised NEP scale. *Journal of Social Issues*, **56**(3), 425–442.

Dunlap, Riley E., Chenyang Xiao and Aaron M. McCright. 2001. Politics and environment in America: Partisan and ideological cleavages in public support for environmentalism. *Environmental Politics*, **10**(4), 23–48.

Eiser, J. Richard, Bettina Hannover, Leon Mann, Michel Morin, Joop van Der Pligt, and Paul Webley. 1990. Nuclear attitudes after Chernobyl: A cross-national study. Journal of *Environmental Psychology*, **10**(2), 101–110.

Ewert, Alan, Greg Place, and Jim Sibthorp. 2005. Early-life outdoor experiences and an individual's environmental attitudes. *Leisure Sciences*, **27**(3), 225–239.

Fairbrother, Malcolm. 2016. Trust and public support for environmental protection in diverse national contexts. *Sociological Science*, **3**, 359–382.

Feygina, Irina, John T. Jost, and Rachel E. Goldsmith. 2010. System justification, the denial of global warming, and the possibility of "system-sanctioned change". *Personality and Social Psychology Bulletin*, **36**(3), 326–338.

Gates, Jodie W. 2011. *Public Support for Climate Justice: A Survey of British Columbia Residents*. Vancouver, British Columbia. Unpublished Masters of Science Thesis. DOI: 10.14288/1.0105093

Gillham, Patrick F. 2008. Participation in the environmental movement: Analysis of the European Union. *International Sociology*, **23**(1), 67–93.

Giugni, Marco and Maria T. Grasso. 2015. Environmental movements in advanced industrial democracies: Heterogeneity, transformation, and institutionalization. *Annual Review of Environmental Resources*, **40**, 337–361.

Gould, Kenneth A., Adam S. Weinberg, and Allan Schnaiberg. 1993. Legitimating impotence: Pyrrhic victories of the modern environmental movement. *Qualitative Sociology*, **16**(3), 207–246.

Graham, Jesse, Jonathan Haidt, and Brian A. Nosek. 2009. Liberals and conservatives rely on different sets of moral foundations. *Journal of Personality and Social Psychology*, **96**(5), 1029–1046.

Guntermann, E. and E. Lachapelle. 2020. Canadian parties matter more than you think: Party and leader ratings moderate party cue effects. *Canadian Journal of Political Science/Revue canadienne de science politique*, **53**(4), 839–852.

Gustafsson, Anna W. 2013. The metaphor challenge of future economics: growth and sustainable development in Swedish media discourse. In: Benner, M. ed. *Before and Beyond the Global Crisis: Economics, Politics and Settlement*. Cheltenham: Edward Elgar Publishing Limited, pp. 197–217.

Hawcroft, Lucy J. and Taciano L. Milfont. 2010. The use (and abuse) of the new environmental paradigm scale over the last 30 years: A meta-analysis. *Journal of Environmental Psychology*, **30**(2), 143–158.

Heath, Yuko and Robert Gifford. 2006. Free-market ideology and environmental degradation: The case of belief in global climate change. *Environment and Behavior*, **38**(1), 48–71.

Hess, David J., Jonathan S. Coley, Quan D. Mai, and Lucas R. Hilliard. 2015. Party differences and Energy Reform: Fiscal Conservatism in the California legislature. *Environmental Politics*, **24**(2), 228–248.

Hochschild, Arlie R. 2016. *Strangers in Their Own Land: Anger and Mourning on the American Right*. New York: The New Press.

Huddart Kennedy, Emily. 2020. *Measuring Human-Environment Relationships: Introducing the 'Eco-Social Relationship' (ESR) Framework*. Unpublished manuscript.

Huddart Kennedy, Emily, Thomas M. Beckley, Bonita L. McFarlane, and Solange Nadeau. 2009. Rural-urban differences in environmental concern in Canada. *Rural Sociology*, **74**(3), 309–329.

Inglehart, Ronald. 1977. *The Silent Revolution: Changing Values and Political Styles among Western Publics*. Princeton, NJ: Princeton University Press.

Inglehart, Ronald. 1990. *Culture Shift in Advanced Industrial Society*. Princeton, NJ: Princeton University Press.

Inglehart, R. and P. Norris. 2017. Trump and the xenophobic populist parties: The silent revolution in reverse. *Perspectives on Politics*, **15**(2), 443–454.

Jacques, Peter J., Riley E. Dunlap, and Mark Freeman. 2008. The organisation of denial: Conservative think tanks and environmental scepticism. *Environmental Politics*, **17**(3), 349–385.

Johnston, Richard. Canadian National Election Study, 1988. Inter-university Consortium for Political and Social Research [distributor], 1992–03–05. https://doi.org/10.3886/ICPSR09386.v1

Jost, John T., Brian A. Nosek, and Samuel D. Gosling. 2008. Ideology: Its resurgence in social, personality, and political psychology. *Perspectives on Psychological Science*, **3**(2), 126–136.

Jowett, T., J. Harraway, B. Lovelock, S. Skeaff, L. Slooten, M. Strack, and K. Shephard. 2014. Multinomial-regression modeling of the environmental attitudes of higher education students based on the revised new ecological paradigm scale. *The Journal of Environmental Education*, **45**(1), 1–15.

Kallis, Giorgos. 2011. In defence of degrowth. *Ecological Economics*, **70**(5), 873–880.

Klandermans, Bert and Dirk Oegema. 1987. Potentials, networks, motivations, and barriers: Steps towards participation in social movements. *American Sociological Review*, **52**(4), 519–531.

Klein, Naomi. 2015. *This Changes Everything: Capitalism vs. the Climate*. New York: Simon and Schuster.

Lachapelle, Erick, Christopher P. Borick, and Barry Rabe. 2012. Public attitudes toward climate science and climate policy in federal systems: Canada and the United States compared. *Review of Policy Research*, **29**(3): 334–357.

Larana, Enrique, Hank Johnston, and Joseph R. Gusfield. 1994. *New Social Movements: From Ideology to Identity*. Philadelphia: Temple University Press.

Lawson, Danielle F., Kathryn T. Stevenson, M. Nils Peterson, Sarah J. Carrier, Renee L. Strnad and Erin Seekamp. 2019. Children can foster climate change concern among their parents. *Nature Climate Change*, **9**, 458–462.

LeDuc, L. (1989). The Canadian federal election of 1988. *Electoral Studies*, **8**(2), 163–167.

Maslow, Abraham H. 1962. *Toward a Psychology of Being*. New York: Van Nostrand.

McAdam, Doug. 1986. Recruitment to high-risk activism: The case of freedom summer. *American Journal of Sociology*, **92**(1), 64–90.

McCright, Aaron M. and Riley E. Dunlap. 2011. The politicization of climate change and polarization in the American public's views of global warming, 2001–2010. *The Sociological Quarterly*, **52**(2), 155–194.

McCright, Aaron M. and Riley E. Dunlap. 2013. Bringing ideology in: The conservative White male effect on worry about environmental problems in the USA. *Journal of Risk Research*, **16**(2), 211–226.

McCright, Aaron M., Riley E. Dunlap, and Sandra T. Marquart-Pyatt. 2015. Political ideology and views about climate change in the European Union. *Environmental Politics*, **25**(2), 338–358.

McCurdy, Patrick. 2012. Social movements, protest and mainstream media. *Sociology Compass*, **6**(3), 244–255.

Ogunbode, Charles A. 2013. The NEP scale: Measuring ecological attitudes/worldviews in an African context. *Environment, Development and Sustainability*, **15**(6), 1477–1494.

Olli, Eero, Gunnar Grendstad, and Dag Wollebaek. 2001. Correlates of environmental behaviors: Bringing back social context. *Environment and Behavior*, **33**(2), pp. 181–208.

Östman, J. 2014. The influence of media use on environmental engagement: A political socialization approach. *Environmental Communication*, **8**(1), 92–109.

Passy, Florence. 2001. Socialization, connection, and the structure/agency gap: A specification of the impact of networks on participation in social movements. *Mobilization: An International Quarterly*, **6**(2), 173–192.

Pilbeam, Bruce. 2003. Natural allies? Mapping the relationship between conservatism and environmentalism. *Political Studies*, **51**(3), 490–508.

Schnaiberg, Allan and Kenneth A. Gould. 1994. *Environment and Society: The Enduring Conflict*. New York: St. Martin's Press.

Schultz, P. Wesley and Lynnette Zelezny. 1999. Values as predictors of environmental attitudes: Evidence for consistency across 14 countries. *Journal of Environmental Psychology*, **19**(3), 255–265.

Shabecoff, P. 2012. *A Fierce Green Fire: The American Environmental Movement*. Washington: Island Press.

Shove, Elizabeth. 2010. Beyond the ABC: Climate change policy and theories of social change. *Environment and Planning*, **42**, 1273–1285.

Stern, Paul C. 2000. Toward a coherent theory of environmentally significant behavior. *Journal of Social Issues*, **56**(3), 407–424.

Stern, Paul C., Thomas Dietz, Troy Abel, Gregory A. Guagnano, and L. Kalof. 1999. A value-belief-norm theory of support for social movements: The case of environmentalism. *Human Ecology Review*, **6**(2), 81–97.

Tindall, David B. 1994. *Collective Action in the Rainforest: Personal Networks, Identity, and Participation in the Vancouver Island Wilderness Preservation Movement*. Unpublished doctoral dissertation, Department of Sociology University of Toronto, Toronto.

Tindall, David B. 2002. Social networks, identification, and participation in an environmental movement: Low-medium cost activism within the British Columbia wilderness preservation movement. *Canadian Review of Sociology and Anthropology*, **39**(4), 413–452.

Tindall, David B. 2015. Networks as constraints and opportunities. In della Porta, D. and Diani, M. eds. *Oxford Handbook of Social Movements*. Oxford, UK: Oxford University Press, pp. 231–245.

Tindall, David B., Scott Davies, and Céline Mauboulès. 2003. Activism and conservation behavior in an environmental movement: The contradictory effects of gender. *Society and Natural Resources*, **16**(10):909–932.

Tindall, David B. and Adam Howe. 2018. *Social Networking to Save the Planet: Social Networks and Participation in the Environmental Movement in Canada*. Unpublished paper presented at the Meetings of the International Network for Social Network Analysis (the Sunbelt Social Network Conference), Utrecht: Netherlands, June 30, 2018.

Tindall, David B. and Georgia Piggot. 2015. Influence of social ties to environmentalists on public climate change perceptions. *Nature Climate Change*, **5**(6), 546–549.

Tindall, David B. and Joanna L. Robinson. 2017. Collective action to save the ancient temperate rainforest: social networks and environmental activism in Clayoquot Sound. *Ecology and Society*, **22**(1), 40.

Tindall, David B., Mark C.J. Stoddart, John McLevey, Lorien Jasny, Dana R. Fisher, Jennifer Earl, and Mario Diani. Forthcoming. In Small, Mario L., Perry, Brea L., Pescosolido, Bernice, and Smith, Edward. eds. *Personal Networks: Classic Readings and New Directions in Ego-centric Analysis*. Cambridge, UK: Cambridge University Press.

Villacorta, Mark, Richard Koestner, and Natasha Lekes. 2003. Further validation of the motivation toward the environment scale. *Environment and Behavior*, **35**(4), 486–505.

Xiao, Chenyang, Riley E. Dunlap, and Dayong Hong. 2019. Ecological worldview as the central component of environmental concern: Clarifying the role of the NEP. *Society & Natural Resources*, **32**(1), 53–72.

Zelezny, Lynnette C., Poh-Pheng Chua, and Christina Aldrich. 2000. New ways of thinking about environmentalism: Elaborating on gender differences in environmentalism. *Journal of Social Issues*, **56**(3), 443–457.

Zhu, Xiaowen and Chuntian Lu. 2017. Re-evaluation of the new ecological paradigm scale using item response theory. *Journal of Environmental Psychology*, **54,** 79–90.

26

SOCIAL NETWORKS AND RECRUITMENT FOR ENVIRONMENTAL MOVEMENTS

Clare Saunders

Introduction

It is difficult to fathom how any social movement could exist without recruiting participants through some form of network linkage. Indeed, by now it is well established that networks are central to the recruitment of individual activists to social movement activity. As Snow et al. (1980: 798) famously put it: "[R]ecruitment cannot occur without prior contact with a movement agent. The potential participant has to be informed about and [be] introduced into a particular movement". Social networks matter for recruitment in a variety of ways, but they foster participation through two key mechanisms: structural availability and identity. Structural availability refers to the ways in which networks help put people in the right place at the right time for participation. Networks also foster a sense of collective identity that pulls potential recruits into association with a variety of ways of participating in movements. Moreover, networks play a function in sustaining participation over time through the same mechanisms.

There are three main ways in which networks generate structural availability and collective identity for social movement participation. These are 1) socialization through personal social networks such as family, friends, and acquaintances; 2) generation of social capital through participating in civic activities; and 3) being in receipt of the recruitment efforts of organizations. Of course, these three mechanisms for generating structural availability also overlap. In relation to personal networks, research has shown that being asked to and asked by others to participate in activism is a predictor of participation (Schussman and Soule 2005; Verba et al. 1994). Moreover, individuals with friends and relatives engaged in social movements are more likely to join themselves than those cut off from movement causes and activism. Passy and Giugni (2000) coined the concept of *life-spheres* as overlapping/interacting subjectively and objectively bound "regions" of belonging (2000: 120), including contacts in the family and at work. Frequently activated and overlapping life-spheres increase the sense of connection and importance to individuals of a collectivity and therefore become important at predicting not only recruitment into, but also sustainment of, activism.

Social capital is defined by its popularizer, Robert Putnam (1993: 35), as the "features of social organizations, such as networks, norms and trust that facilitate action and cooperation for mutual benefit". He was initially concerned that the loss of civic culture in the US since the 1960s had resulted in an erosion of trust and withdrawal from public life, resulting in worrying

DOI: 10.4324/9780367855680-30

levels of singleton bowlers: hence, the title of his famous tome – *Bowling Alone* (Putnam 1990). Civil associationism is important for helping people become aware of opportunities to engage in activism, but perhaps only if the associations in which people engage are themselves politically engaged or have among them politically engaged participants (Brown and Brown 2003).

The chances of being in receipt of social movement mobilization organizations' recruitment messages is increased by having (sometimes overlapping) organizational memberships. Established activists' structural availability is enhanced by their being party to closed information channels (i.e., organizational memberships or closed social media sites) that are not easily available to members of the public who lack these organizational connections (Saunders et al. 2012). Organizations can use what has become known as "bloc recruitment" to "recruit members and participants among groups of individuals already organized for some other purpose" (Oberschall 1993: 24). Some social movement organizations become "mesomobilization actors", which connect different groups together through joint actions and press materials as well as doing work to generate common senses of meaning (Gerhards and Rucht 1992). Thus, at least in the short term, once someone has been an activist, the chances of being reactivated are higher than the chances of someone who has never before been mobilized becoming active for the first time. In general, evidence suggests that denser networks are more likely to lead to social movement recruitment (Fernandez and McAdam 1988). However, some studies have shown that being active in multiple overlapping networks can also create competition for a potential recruit's time and that this therefore, at times, works against recruitment into participation (McAdam and Paulsen 1993; Stryker 2000).

Identity is developed not only through socialization, social capital, and the recruitment efforts of organizations, but also through framing mechanisms – such as when the message of a social movement organization reaches and resonates with an individual (Benford and Snow 2000) – and through interaction with others who share similar beliefs, which can result in solidarity and convergence of behaviors (Larana et al. 1994; Saunders 2008a). Van Stekelenburg and Klandermans (2019) call these types of identity formation deductive – when the identity of an organization is taken on board – and inductive when activists come together to shape their own identities. Whether inductive or deductive, networking is key to recruitment success, even if that is sometimes only through being in receipt of movement communications (Tindall 2002).

Although structural availability and identify formation are key recruitment factors across a variety of different movements, it is important to recognize that they play out differently across movements and even within movements, varying issue by issue and place by place. As I show in more detail as this chapter develops, many existing studies appear to assume generalizability across different types of movements. Among those that do not assume generalizability across movements, there tends to be an assumption that movements are homogenous, overlooking the different types of action within movements. But, as Giugni and Grasso (2015) note, environmental movements are very heterogeneous. Therefore, I use data in this chapter to illustrate the ways in which different types of environmental action in the UK might have different networking practices that encourage (or discourage) recruitment. I focus particularly on the role of networks in recruitment to climate change mobilizations and domestic energy-saving practices. I illustrate the ways in which the role of networks differs for climate change marches (Klandermans et al. 2009), school strikes (Doherty and Saunders, *Forthcoming*), movements using civil disobedience (e.g., Extinction Rebellion) (Saunders et al. 2020), and a study of pro-environmental behavior (Bardsley et al. 2019). I use the data to illustrate key points from existing literature on the relative importance of personal networks, indicators of social capital, and organizational memberships as recruitment tools in these four types of activism.

The chapter proceeds as follows. In the next section I, outline the role of networks in recruitment to environmental movements. Next, I briefly introduce the four data-sets used to illustrate what existing data shows. I then present data on personal networks, social capital in civic organizations, and organizational memberships (including closed mobilization channels). I end with some reflections on the importance of different types of networks to participation in environmental movement activism.

The role of networks in recruitment to environmental movements

The role of networks in generating the structural availability and identity formation that facilitate recruitment is, of course, considerably more complex than my introductory remarks allow. The role of networks in recruitment into activism varies across different stages of the recruitment process, across different issues, by the type of action undertaken, and as a result of the social and political environment in which the action takes place.

Structural availability and identity formulation matter to variable degrees at different stages of mobilization, which is a multi-stage process. Klandermans and Oegema (1987) draw attention to four stages of mobilization. First, there must be mobilization potential, which refers to individuals' attitudes towards a protest issue. To convert individuals to a cause, there needs to be a significant public awareness campaign that reaches the eyes, hearts, and minds of potential activists. Put differently, at this stage of recruitment, it is individuals' network links to a range of media sources that matters. Second, even if the media convinces people to be sympathetic to a cause, this sympathy alone is not enough to mobilize people into activism (McQuail 1993). Recruitment networks that consist of trustable messengers are what matters the most at this stage (Gerlach and Hine 1970). Motivation to participate must be achieved by convincing potential activists that their activism is worthwhile. In Klandermans and Oegma's model (1987), this stage of recruitment is deemed the responsibility of movement organizations. This might imply a movement leader communicating potential collective and solidarity incentives in a top-down manner. It is important to remember, though, that movements also communicate through subaltern networks – composed of grassroots networks – and, in quiet times between mobilizations, by abeyance structures. Abeyance structures, maintained by committed activists, are "a holding process through which movements sustain themselves in non-receptive political environments and provide continuity from one stage of mobilization to another" (Taylor 1989: 761). They may find themselves manifest in community organizing or radical bookshops, for instance. In my own field work in the early 2000s, the radical bookshop and social center 56a was such a space (Saunders 2014). The fourth and last stage of Klandermans and Oegma's (1987) step-wise process of mobilization is overcoming barriers to participation, which is more likely to be achieved when people have network links and a strong sense of identification with a particular identity (McAdam and Paulsen 1993). Most of the rest chapter and the illustrative data focus on the final stage of mobilization so as not to confuse across different stages, but I also illustrate how individuals have heard about the demonstration in which they participated (probably best represented by phase 2).

As I mentioned in the introduction, there is a tendency for scholars to assume generalizability across activism on different issues. Klandermans and Oegema (1987), for example, develop the theoretical approach that they apply to the empirical case of a Dutch anti-nuclear demonstration from other studies on a range of issues including anti-nuclear, peace, women's, disadvantaged people, workers, civil rights, the environment, and civil action. Such lumping might be dangerous because recent scholarly work reminds us to take seriously the different grievance contexts of activism that can affect participation in complex ways (Van Stekelenburg and Klandermans 2013, 2019). Snow et al. (1980) found in a summary of 10 pre-existing studies that networks are important for recruitment into activism in relation to most issues, except for the Catholic/Pentecostal movement. Jasper and Poulson (1995) found that animal rights activists are better motivated by moral shock than the personal networks that seem to activate participation in anti-nuclear movements. Any peculiarities in the illustrative data I use might be said to be a result of the specific mobilization context of climate change.

Moreover, some grievances relate to threats to personal safety, security, or well-being, others to more universalistic concerns (see Scott 1990). Networks drawing people into activism to fight for self-interested/particularistic concerns are likely to be narrower and more parochial than those that draw people into activism on a more universalistic issue (Carol and Ratner 1996). In relation to environmentalism, we might think about the contrast between not-in-my-backyard (NIMBY) activists and not-on-planet-earth (NOPE) activists. NIMBY activists will tend to rely on community networks as activists strive to protect their community against a locally unwanted land use. Activists against a high-speed railway (HSR) in the Susa Valley, Northwest Italy, for instance, reported "that a large number of people they knew in the community, such as relatives, friends, and acquaintances, were already involved in the mobilization" (Mannarini et al. 2009: 903). Formal community involvement (i.e., the mechanism through which social capital is derived) also positively predicted their probability of joining in the anti-HSR movement. NOPE activism of the sort expressed in the UK Camps for Climate Action (Saunders and Price 2009; Saunders 2012), in contrast, is more likely to stem from participation in countercultural networks developed, for example, among students, at festivals, in squats, and at resource centers (Plows 2008).

But it is not only the nature of grievances that matters. Also important is the extent of exclusivity – that is to say, the degree to which a movement requires immersion of the self and "total commitment" (Rochford 1982). Exclusive movements will attract participation from insiders in public places, whereas inclusive ones are more likely to invite participation from a wider network of interpersonal associations and networks (Snow et al. 1980). Let us now relate this to the environmental movement. In line with what Snow et al. (1980) suggest, the exclusive alternative rural secular intentional community participants that Metcalf (1986: 230) studied were recruited mainly through advertisements in "the alternative lifestyle press, or through health food shops, alternative technology and health centres, and local notice boards". Some of the larger groups also used alternative-lifestyle festivals as a recruitment avenue. Whereas a strong sense of movement identification might be required to join an exclusive (or high-risk) movement, it appears that for low-to-medium-risk activism, network ties – even when weak – can in some circumstances be sufficient to trigger participation. This supposition is supported by Tindall's (2002) research on the relationship between networks and recruitment to participation in British Columbian low-to-medium-risk activism. Mild social pressure from an acquaintance appears to be enough to convince those who have sympathy for a cause to join a low-risk environmental action, providing they have a "latitude of acceptance" (Tindal 2002: 440). In contrast, a much higher degree of pressure or a much stronger ideological connection is required for participation in an exclusive movement.

We can add to this two further levels of complexity. Not only do the networking factors and mechanisms that pull people into activist participation vary over time, but they also vary according to the type of activism, the issue of mobilization, and the regime in which they take place. Whereas a mass mailing (these days by email) might be able to encourage people to participate in low-risk activism – such as signing an online petition, especially when many others have already signed (Margetts et al. 2011) – it has been found less able to encourage people to participate in high-risk environmental activism (Klandermans and Oegema 1987). However, it seems misplaced to assume that a mass mailing has no role to play in recruiting people into high-risk environmental action. Those who participate in high-risk environmental activism often do so because they are disillusioned with their previous participation in more moderate organizations and actions (Saunders 2014). The mailing of communiques may, therefore, still be a starting point on a longer journey of recruitment into high-risk environmental activism.

The political and social environment also matters. In a repressive regime, social movements may turn insurgent or go underground (Boudreau 1996). The conditions for recruiting to a social movement organization in a repressive political environment are very different from those in a conducive political environment, not least due to the very high stakes of participation. Della Porta (1988: 157) identifies "tight-knit social networks" as a "very important precondition for joining clandestine organisations". Like the "exclusive" organizations that Snow et al. (1980) wrote about, organizations in repressive regimes will require total commitment and, therefore, some intense personal network ties. However, network links are not found to be sufficient to predict participation in clandestine organizations (della Porta 2006). Some of the more underground covert environmental actions require recruitment through and into similarly tight-knit affinity groups (Wall 2000).

What lessons can we learn from this when analyzing the role of networks in recruitment into environmental activism? First, we can learn that the importance of particular types of networks tends to vary across issues. In a study of recruitment into environmental activism that lumps together NIMBY activists (e.g., fighting against a local road) with climate change activists (who have a more universalistic concern), it might be a mistake to analyze these together because of the known differences between recruiting to universalist and localist concerns (Carol and Ratner 1996). Second, for similar reasons, it might also be a mistake to lump together high-risk and low-risk forms of environmental activism and those that are more and less exclusive (Snow et al. 1980). Third, the different political opportunity structures across countries (della Porta 1988; Boudreau 1996) might warrant a focus on a single country as a way of controlling for variation.

Overall, this brief review of the literature would lead us to expect that those who are engaged in environmental activism have significant network links but that these might vary according to the type of environmental activism in which activists engage. Those committing to individualized forms of action (such as pro-environmental behavior) may not require dense personal networks, social capital, or organizational memberships. For low-risk activism, in our case, engagement in a routinized climate change march, we might expect *some* network links, particularly at the organizational level, but perhaps fewer personal connects, for we expect low-risk/low-cost activism to require little immersion of the self. Organizational links are likely to be particularly important for climate change marches because these events are meso-mobilized. A series of established and smaller NGOs share responsibility for advertising climate marches, sometimes even for arranging transport for activists who are members of their organization (Saunders 2008b). For higher-risk activism (Fund Our Future and Extinction Rebellion), we expect to find that overlapping life-spheres (Passy and Giugni 2000) and intense personal networks are required to push activists into riskier forms of activism. These networks might be at the organizational and/or individual level. The organizational networks might be social movement organizations or community groups. We might, additionally, expect to find some differences related to political generations. Climate strike participants are generally younger and might, therefore, be more likely to be recruited through internet sources (Bakker and de Vreese 2011).

Illustrating recruitment into environmental activism

It is important to specify that an ideal research design would compare participants to non-participants. The rich data I use to illustrate how individuals are recruited to differential forms of environmental activism via networks is mostly on existing participants. However, differently from many studies that look at recruitment of participants only, we can build on existing knowledge about different types of network being important for different types of activism by illustrating recruitment processes via networks in recruitment to 1) pro-environmental behavior, 2) a routinized march, 3) a school strike, and 4) a London-based national Extinction Rebellion action. This approach has the additional advantage of avoiding confusion about the role of networks at different stages of the mobilization pathway.

The pro-environmental behavior data comes from the Community-based Initiatives in Energy Saving project (Bardsley et al. 2019), which asked 160 participants about their engagement in a range of pro-environmental behaviors, including turning electrical equipment off standby, only filling the kettle with as much water as is needed, turning the thermostat down to 18° Celsius or lower, switching lights off when no one else is in the room, and avoiding air travel. In particular, I focus on those questionnaire respondents who indicated that they did each of these things – separately – most of the time or always. I use answers to the survey question "Which of the following have influenced your energy use?" and examine the impact of partners, close family, other relatives, friends, colleagues, and members of an organization of which they are a part.

Participating in civil activities (as a way to get a handle on social capital) and social movement memberships are measured in similar ways across all data sets. Each survey has a version of the question "Of which of the following organizational types are you a member?" Organizations that are not social movement–based (e.g., church, professional organization, sport organization, or community organization) are presented as proxies for social capital because they involve participating in civic activities. Social movement organizations are used as a way to understand which types as well as the number of social movement organizations the environmental activists we examine are members of, to perhaps help us understand whether bloc recruitment has been successful (Oberschall 1973).

The data on climate marches comes from a survey of the climate march on 7 March 2015 in Central London. This march was called The People's Climate March. It processed from Lincoln's Inn Fields to Westminster where speakers, including Green Party Member of Parliament Caroline Lucas and the director of Greenpeace, John Sauven, addressed the crowd. The Caught in the Act of Protest (Klandermans et al. 2009) protest survey protocols were used to conduct the survey. These protocols were designed in order to maximize the chances of randomly allocating surveys to demonstrators and to allow research teams to approximate the extent of response rate bias. (For a fuller explanation, see Saunders and Schlomo 2020.) This data set has 278 respondents.

In addition to having questions on organizational membership comparable to those in the pro-environmental behavior change survey, the protest survey data (a version of which is used for the People's Climate March, Global Climate Strike, and Extinction Rebellion survey data) has questions about personal networks and channels through which respondents heard about the demonstration. The personal networks questions ask: 1) "Were you at this demonstration [with] . . . check as many as apply", and 2) "Which of the following people specifically asked you to take part in the demonstration?" The information channels question asks "How did you find out about the demonstration? Was it. . .?" The question proceeds to ask about open (radio, television, newspaper, online social networks) and closed (partner or family, friends of acquaintances, people at school or work, fellow organizational members, and an organization) information channels (Saunders et al. 2012).

In March 2019, I worked with Brian Doherty (Doherty and Saunders forthcoming) as part of an international team to survey participants in the Global Climate Strike in the UK cities of Manchester and Truro (see also Wahlström et al. 2019). For this survey (as well as the Extinction Rebellion one), we used an online approximation of the Caught in the Act of Protest survey protocols. Instead of handing out mail-back surveys, we instead handed out a leaflet that had a QR code and URL link to an online version of the questionnaire. Using this method, we received completed survey responses from a total of 100 respondents. There is one caveat to this data: in order to comply with research ethics obligations, it was not permissible for us to survey children under the age of 16 without consent of a parent. In many cases, a parent was not present. This, unfortunately, means that quite a few children who were present at the demonstrations were not included in the sample.

The Extinction Rebellion survey data was collected at the London rebellion actions in April and October 2019 (Saunders et al. 2020). A comparison of the more representative face-to-face interview data and online survey data reveals very few differences between the sub-samples, except for age. Online survey respondents are slightly older. Otherwise, we are confident of having achieved a relatively representative sample. In total, we have 103 responses from the April rebellion and 130 from the October rebellion. For convenience, I henceforth refer to the people recruited to different forms of environmental movement participation as pro-environmentalists (people who engage in pro-environmental behavior), marchers (participants in the 2015 climate march), strikers (participants in the Global Climate Strike) and rebels (participants in the Extinction Rebellion London rebellions).

Personal networks

Respondents to the pro-environmental behavior change survey were asked not only whether they engage in a series of pro-environmental behaviors, but also to rate the extent to which they consider that people in their personal networks influence their domestic energy use on a scale of 1 to 5, where 1 is not at all and 5 is very much so. The average (mean) influence of partners on domestic energy use is 3.3, of (other) close family members 2.3, of other relatives 1.7, of friends 2.2, of colleagues 2.2 and of fellow members of an organization 2.1. But how does this compare for those who engage frequently in pro-environmental behaviors to those who engage infrequently? Table 26.1 cross-tabulates mean scores for the influence of those in personal networks by those who engage in pro-environmental behavior sometimes or less frequently and those who engage in pro-environmental behavior very often or always. As expected, personal networks of energy use influence seem to have little effect on pro-environmental behavior. The mean scores are very similar across the two columns of Table 26.1. The only very notable exception is for avoiding flying, for which the mean score for influence of fellow members of an organization is significantly higher for those who engage in the pro-environmental behavior of avoiding air travel (2.7), compared to those who do not (1.9).

How important are personal networks for recruitment into the other types of environmental activism that we consider in this chapter? In Table 26.2, I show the company with whom demonstrators attended the three types of action (marches, climate strike, and a rebellion) and – where the data is available – who asked them to attend. The most popular company that our demonstration participants had is friends/relatives, with over 40% of marchers, strikers, and rebels claiming to have attended the demonstration with them. This is the highest for the

Table 26.1 Mean influence on energy use of those in personal networks (scale 1–5) and recruitment into pro-environmental behavior

	Engages in each pro-environmental behavior listed . . .	
	Sometimes or less frequently	Very often or always
Turns thermostat to < 19 degrees		
Partner	3.1	3.2
Family	2.4	2.3
Other relatives	1.7	1.6
Friends	2.2	2.2
Colleagues	2.2	2.2
Co-members	2.2	2.0
Only fills the kettle with as much water as needed		
Partner	2.8	3.2
Family	2.3	2.3
Other relatives	1.7	1.7
Friends	2.3	2.1
Colleagues	2.3	2.1
Co-members	1.8	2.2
Turns electrical equipment off standby		
Partner	2.9	3.3
Family	2.3	2.4
Other relatives	1.7	1.7
Friends	2.0	2.4
Colleagues	2.0	2.4
Co-members	2.0	2.0
Turns lights off when no one is in the room		
Partner	3.2	3.1
Family	2.2	2.4
Relatives	1.6	1.7
Friends	2.0	2.2
Colleagues	1.9	2.3
Co-members	2.1	2.1
Avoids air travel		
Partner	3.1	3.3
Family	2.3	2.4
Relatives	1.7	1.5
Friends	2.2	2.5
Colleagues	2.2	2.3
Co-members	1.9	2.7

climate strike participants (51% went with friends/relatives), where networks of solidarity may have needed to be strong, especially if the young people we surveyed (aged 16+, or younger with parental consent) were taking the day off school to participate. Co-members of an organization are the next most important "company" for all three types of demonstrators. A little more than one-third of marchers and rebels claimed to have attended with co-members. In contrast, only around one-fifth of the climate strikers attended with co-members. Acquaintances accompany rebels (39%) notably more than they do strikers (16%) and marchers (17%). Partners are fairly common company for marchers and rebels (just under one-third) but are much less common among strikers. We might assume that the strikers are generally younger and therefore less likely to have a partner.

Who, of these sources of company, asked our respondents to attend the demonstrations? Overall, the data suggests that relatively low proportions of people were "asked by" others to attend the demonstration, although this is markedly higher for the marchers (32% were asked by co-members) than for the strikers and rebels. In the Extinction Rebellion survey, we did not ask for details of who the rebels were asked by, only if they were asked. Only 18% were asked by someone else to attend. For the strikers, less than 10% were asked to attend by each of partner/family (5%), friends (9%), and colleagues/fellow students (4%). The marchers were slightly more likely to have been asked to attend by their partner/family (11%) and friends (16%) than the strikers. As a larger and lower-cost demonstration, larger numbers of people attended the 2015 Climate March (an estimated 20,000–40,000), which perhaps accounts for the higher numbers of people attending who has been asked by others to attend.

Open or closed mobilization channels?

Even if they were asked by others to attend the demonstration, our marchers, strikers, and rebels may have first heard about the demonstration from another source. How did they hear about it? Was it through personal networks or through open/closed mobilization channels? In Table 26.3, I show whether participants heard about the demonstration through personal networks, open channels, or closed channels. The table also indicates the most important channel overall. Looking first at personal networks, we can see that friends/acquaintances are the most popular group of people from whom demonstrators – across all three categories – hear about a demonstration. Proportionally, half the number of marchers heard about the climate march through friends or acquaintances (24%), compared to half for the climate strike (50%) and

Table 26.2 The role of personal networks in recruitment to a range of types of climate activism

	Climate march 2015 (%)	Climate strike 2019 (%)	Extinction Rebellion 2019 (%)
Attended the demonstration with. . .			
Partner	30.8 (86)	14 (14)	28.0 (65)
Children	12.2 (34)	–	–
Friends/relatives	41.9 (117)	51 (51)	44.0 (103)
Acquaintances	17.2 (48)	16 (16)	28.5 (66)
Co-members	38.0 (106)	20 (20)	36.2 (84)
Was asked to attend by. . .			–
Partner/family	10.7 (30)	5 (5)	–
Relatives	1.4 (4)	–	–
Friends	15.5 (43)	9(9)	–
Acquaintances	3.8 (11)	0 (0)	–
Colleagues/fellow students	4.0 (11)	4 (4)	–
Co-members	32.0 (89)	0 (0)	–
Someone	–	–	18.1 (37)

Note: Frequencies are shown in parenthesis; the sign "-" denotes lack of comparable data two-fifths for the Extinction Rebellion actions (16%). In general, personal contacts seem less important for the climate marchers than for the strikers and the rebels. Regarding open mobilization channels, online social networking sites seem to be the most important across all three types of action, but this is much higher for strikers (66%) than for rebels (48%) and marchers (38%). There are also interesting differences in relation to whether they heard about the action over the radio or television; only one marcher heard about the 2015 climate march in that way, compared to around one in ten of each of the strikers (12%) and rebels (9%). Newspapers and advertisements/flyers were each responsible for informing 10% to 14% of respondents across each category about the action in which they participated.

In relation to closed information channels, the patterns in the data are, perhaps quite surprisingly given the very different nature of the actions, rather similar for marchers and rebels. Around one-quarter heard about their action through alternative online media (25% for marchers, 27% for rebels), near to two-fifths heard from co-members (35% for marchers, 44% for rebels), and a similar number from an organization (42% for marchers, 36% for rebels). The patterns are very different for strikers. Only 3% of them heard from online media, and only 13% from an organization. Nearly one-quarter, though, had heard from co-members of an organization of which they are a member.

The most popular mobilization channel overall – across the categories of personal, open, and closed – is an organization for 27% of marchers and for 40% of strikers, but online networks for 23% of rebels. (See Table 26.3) In all cases, the most important channel as identified by aggregating respondents' answers to the question "Which *one* is the most important channel?" is the same as the one with the highest frequency for each type of action. Looked at both ways, what is most "striking" is the importance of social networking sites as a means to recruit strikers. The mobilization of individuals into the newer forms of environmental activism seems to be less dependent on conventional organizational forms. Part of this might be explained by increasing use of, and dependency upon, the internet over time.

Table 26.3 How did they hear about the demonstration?

	Climate march 2015 (%)	Climate strike 2019 (%)	Extinction Rebellion 2019 (%)
Personal networks			
Partner or family	8.3 (23)	16 (16)	16.4 (38)
Friends/acquaintances	24.1 (67)	50 (50)	41.8 (97)
School/work contacts	6.1 (17)	22 (22)	3.5 (8)
Open channels			
Radio or television	0.4 (1)	12 (12)	8.6 (20)
Newspaper	10.1 (28)	14 (14)	13.8 (32)
Advertisements/flyers	13.7 (38)	10 (10)	12.8 (53)
Online SNS	37.8 (105)	66 (66)	48.3 (112)
Closed channels			
Alternative online media	25.2 (70)	3 (3)	27.2 (63)
Co-members	34.9 (97)	24 (24)	44.4 (103)
Organization	42.1 (117)	13 (13)	35.8 (83)
Most important channel	An organization 26.9%	Online SNS 40%	Online SNS 22.8%

Notes: Frequencies are show in parenthesis. SNS stands for "social networking sites". "An organization" is shorthand for "An organization (magazine, meeting, website, mailing list . . .")". "Online SNS" is shorthand for "Online social networks" (e.g. Facebook, Twitter). "Co-members" is a truncation of "(Fellow) members of an organization or association". Note that participants could tick as many options as they wanted, which is why the columns add up to more than 100%.

Social capital

If it is true that civic engagement increases social capital, then we have some evidence, presented in Table 26.4, that social capital can be a vehicle through which people can be recruited into different forms of environmental activism. Membership in charity/welfare organizations seems particularly important for participation in marches, strikes, and rebellions, with over a quarter of strikers (26%), even more marchers (39%), and nearly half the rebels (49%) having such memberships. Generally, the pro-environmental behaviorists have fewer links to civic organizations and, perhaps consequently, less social capital. It is easy to make an argument that social capital matters a lot less for engaging in these relatively private acts "beyond the activist ghetto" (Saunders et al. 2014). However, churchgoing and sports/culture activity are relatively high among the pro-environmental behaviorists. These activities might be partially responsible for instilling values, if not collective action. And yet churchgoers are most prominent among the climate marchers. Churches have long been actively engaged in humanitarian and aid work and will have increasingly "turned green" (Saunders 2008b) as environmental organizations have "faced south" (Rootes 2007). Political partisanship is notably low among the pro-environmentalist behaviorists (only one from the sample); but surprisingly high for Extinction Rebellion activists, who are part of a network that had vowed to place itself "beyond politics" (Saunders et al. 2020). (See Table 26.4.)

Notes: Frequencies are in parenthesis. Respondents to the pro-environmental behavior survey are classified as engaging in pro-environmental behavior if they engage at least very often in three or more of the five pro-environmental behaviors analyzed for this chapter (any three of turning the thermostat to less than 19°, only putting the amount of water in the kettle that is required, turning electrical equipment off standby, turning off lights when no one is in the room, and avoiding air travel). The total *n* for those with these pro-environmental behavioral traits is 89.

Organizational memberships

In which types of social movement organizations (SMO) do our respondents have memberships? This question is answered in Table 26.4. For those engaged in pro-environmental behavior,

Table 26.4 Participation in civic activities

	Pro-environmental behavior (%)	Climate march 2015 (%)	Climate strike 2019 (%)	Extinction Rebellion 2019 (%)
Church or religious organization	13.5 (12)	19.2 (54)	10(10)	9.1 (23)
Political party	1.1 (1)	16.1 (120)	24 (24)	34.1 (79)
Sports/culture	19.1 (17)	12.9 (36)	19 (19)	17.2 (40)
Community/ neighborhood	14.6 (13)	26.1 (73)	12 (12)	–
Charity/welfare	6.7 (6)	38.9 (109)	26 (26)	49.1 (114)

Table 26.5 Memberships in social movement organizations

	Pro-environmental behavior (%)	Climate march 2015 (%)	Climate strike 2019 (%)	Extinction Rebellion 2019 (%)
Trade union	23.6 (21)	26.1 (73)	19 (19)	20.7 (38)
Women's	–	9.6 (27)	7 (7)	10.8 (25)
Environmental	14.6 (13)	66.8 (187)	37 (37)	69.4 (161)
LGBT	–	5.4 (15)	8 (8)	9.9 (23)
Global justice	7.9 (7)	35.0 (98)	14 (14)	34.1 (79)
Anti-racism	–	11.1 (31)	13 (13)	–
Human rights	6.7 (6)	26.4 (74)	13 (13)	30.6 (71)

Notes: Frequencies are in parenthesis; see explanation under Table 26.4 for an explanation of the sample in the first data column

trade unions are the most frequently mentioned SMO type (24%), but environmental organizations are the most common for rebels (69%); marchers (67%); and, albeit at a much lower level, for climate strikers (37%). The profile of SMO memberships for the marchers and rebels is very similar across the board and ranked here in order of their popularity: unions (26% marchers, 21% rebels); women's organizations (10% marchers, 11% rebels); LGBT+ (5%, 10% respectively); global justice (25%, 34%); and human rights (26%, 31%). Organizational memberships are generally less common – except for union membership among the pro-environmentalists – for the pro-environmental behaviorists and the strikers.

Conclusions

The illustrative data and the review of literature point in similar directions. First and foremost, networks of some description are vital as recruitment tools. Without some form of network link, one would not even hear about a demonstration. However, we have also learned that networks into recruitment have a variety of shapes and sizes, depending on the nature of the action (even when the action is on the same issue). Environmentalism is a particular type of grievance that is more universalistic than particularistic, which invites a broader range of networks to influence participation than, say, a labor demonstration. Certainly, a range of networks played a role in mobilizing people to participate in pro-environmental behavior, a routinized climate march, a climate strike, and an Extinction Rebellion action.

It has also been illustrated here – by both the literature and the illustrative data – how the role of networks in recruitment varies according to the type of action. Moderate- and low-risk actions are easier to participate in than high-risk actions and therefore are generally thought to rely less heavily on a set of values or degree of commitment, and weak networks might suffice. The data illustrated here shows that close contacts were actually quite important in recruitment to a routinized demonstration and less so for the higher-risk activism, which suggests that network links might be less important when commitment is high. This probably tells us something about the general acceptability of a routine protest compared to an action positioned deliberately to break the law. Even if it is not the case that more and more people are participating in protest, it is certainly the case that street demonstrations are increasingly viewed as part of the conventional repertoire of political participation (Saunders and Shlomo 2020), which perhaps makes them more likely to be talked about in everyday circles. In contrast, school strikes are shunned by some people, who think that children would better off spending the day in school

(Doherty and Saunders forthcoming), and Extinction Rebellion has its own critics who accuse it of stopping business as usual or of developing forms of action that are alienating to Black and minority ethnic sectors of the population (Saunders et al. 2020). Although existing literature would have us believe the opposite would have been true – that strong and tight personal network links to recruitment are important for high-risk activism and that low-risk activism might require acquaintances only – the central lesson is the same: the protest context really matters in understanding which types of networks are important and why.

Social capital and civic engagement – as shown by others, as well as hinted at in the illustrative data – is doubtless higher among environmental activists than those who are not participants in environmental activism. As the data illustrates, those engaging in the more individualized acts of pro-environmental behavior have less social capital than their protester counterparts. But still, no more than one-third of the environmental activists surveyed are members of civic associations across all categories. It is also notable that environmental organizational memberships are high for both marchers and rebels. But generally low levels of social capital do not equate straightforwardly with disengagement from environmental activism. This suggests that – although networking is important for recruitment – it takes more than networks to recruit people into activism. Networks alone are not sufficient to draw people into environmental activism. At least a "latitude of acceptance" (Tindall 2002) is required to pull people into activism, and as the case of participation in an Extinction Rebellion demonstration shows, deeper ideological commitment and/or moral outrage is required for higher-risk forms of activism. In this sense, there are similarities with recruitment into animal rights activism (Jasper and Poulsen 1995), but we must also remember the severity of the climate issue. It is now widely known that failure to reduce anthropogenic emissions will have calamitous effects, perhaps rendering networks less important for this issue than for an emergent issue.

Perhaps because of the threats that climate change poses to humanity, the new wave of climate activism expressed by Extinction Rebellion and the Global Climate Strikes have received unusual amounts of newspaper and television coverage for environmental activism. This brings us back to the point that the importance of networks for recruitment is conditioned by general mobilization contexts and the salience of issues. For the younger generations engaged in climate strikes, open mobilization channels – such as social networking sites – are the most important channel for hearing about a demonstration. This gives scholars an open invitation to update our understanding of recruitment into environmental activism by considering more closely the role of online networks.

Finally, to close, it is important to mention a key way in which this illustrative data could be improved. Ideally, as well as paying closer attention to online networks, we would have compared our recruitment data to a set of data on non-recruits. This is certainly a recommended step for future research.

References

Bakker, T.P. and de Vreese, C.H. (2011) 'Good news for the future? Young people, Internet use, and political participation', *Communication Research*, 38(4): 451–470.
Bardsley, N., Buechs, M., James, P., Papafragkou, A., Rushby, T., Saunders, C., Smith, G., Wallbridge, R., and Woodman, N. (2019) 'Domestic thermal upgrades, community action and energy saving: A three-year experimental study', *Energy Policy*, 127: 475–485.
Benford, R.D. and Snow, D.A. (2000) 'Framing processes and social movements: An overview and assessment', *Annual Review of Sociology*, 26(1): 611–639.
Boudreau, V. (1996) 'Northern theory, southern protest: Opportunity structure in cross-national perspective', *Mobilization*, 1(2): 175–189.

Brown, R.K. and Brown, R.E. (2003) 'Faith works: Church-based social capital resources an African American Political Activism', *Social Forces*, 82(8): 617–641.

Carroll, W.K. and Ratner, R.S. (1996) 'Master framing and cross-movement networking in contemporary social movements', *Sociological Quarterly*, 37(4): 601–625.

della Porta, D. (1988) 'Recruitment processes in clandestine political organizations', *International Social Movement Research*, 1: 155–169.

della Porta, D. (2006) *Social Movements, Political Violence and the State: A Comparative Analysis of Italy and Germany*. Cambridge: Cambridge University Press.

Doherty, B. and Saunders, C. *(forthcoming)* 'Global Climate Strike protesters and media coverage of the protests in Truro and Manchester', in J. Bessant, M. Mesinas, and S. Pickard (eds) *When Students Protest: Politics and Young People*.

Fernandez, R.M. and McAdam, D. (1988) 'Social networks and social movements: Multiorganizational fields and recruitment to Mississippi Freedom Summer', *Sociological Forum*, 3(3): 357–382.

Gerhards, J. and Rucht, D. (1992) 'Mesomobilization: Organising and framing in two protest campaigns in West Germany', *American Journal of Sociology*, 98(3): 555–596.

Gerlach, L.P. and Hine, V.H. (1970) *People, Power, Change: Movements of Social Transformation*. New York: Bobs-Merrill.

Giugni, M. and Grasso, M.T. (2015) 'Environmental movements in advanced industrial democracies: Heterogeneity, Transformation and Institutionalization', *Annual Review of Environment and Resources*, 40: 337–361.

Jasper, J. and Poulson, J.D. (1995) 'Recruiting strangers and friends: Moral shocks and social networks in animal rights and anti-nuclear movements', *Social Problems*, 42(4): 493–512.

Klandermans, B., Giugni, M., Peterson, A., Sabucedo, J.M., Saunders, C., and Walgrave, S. (2009) *Caught in the Act of Protest: Contextualising Contestation Survey Project*. ECRP Eurocores Project Funded by the ESF. Available online at: www.protestsurvey.eu.

Klandermans, B. and Oegema, D. (1987) 'Potentials, networks, motivations and barriers: Steps towards participation in social movements', *American Sociological Review*, 52(4): 519–531.

Larana, E., Johnston, H., and Gusfield, J.R. (1994) *New Social Movements: From Ideology to Identity*. Philadelphia, PA: Temple University Press.

Manarini, T., Coccato, M., Fedi, A., and Rover, A. (2009) 'Six factors fostering protest: Predicting movement participation in locally unwanted land uses movements', *Political Psychology*, 30(6): 895–920.

Margetts, H., John, P., Escher, T., and Reissfelder, S. (2011) 'Social information and political participation on the internet: an experiment,' *European Political Science Review: EPSR*, 3(3), p. 321.

McAdam, D. and Paulsen, R. (1993) 'Specifying the relationship between social ties and activism', *Social Forces*, 99: 640–663.

McQuail, D. (1993) *Mass Communication Theories*. London: Sage.

Metcalf, W.J. (1986) *Dropping Out and Staying in: Recruitment, Socialisation and Commitment Engenderment within Contemporary Alternative Lifestyles*, PhD thesis, School of Australian Environmental Studies, Griffith University, Australia. Available online at: https://research-repository.griffith.edu.au/handle/10072/365894. Last accessed 21/07/2020.

Oberschall, A. (1973) *Social Movements and Social Conflict*. Englewood Cliffs, NJ: Prentice-Hall.

Passy, F. and Giugni, M. (2000) 'Life-spheres, networks, and sustained participation in social movements: A phenomenological approach to political commitment', *Sociological Forum*, 15(1): 117–144.

Plows, A. (2008) 'Towards and analysis of the "success" of the UK green protests', *British Politics*, 3: 92–109.

Putnam. R. (1990) *Bowling Alone*. London: Simon and Schuster Ltd.

Putnam, R. (1993) 'The prosperous community', *The American Prospect*, 4(13): 35–42.

Rochford, E.B. (Jnr) (1982) 'Recruitment strategies, ideology, and organization in the Hare Krishna movement', *Social Problems*, 29(4): 399–410.

Rootes, C. (2007) 'Facing south? British environmental movement organisations and the challenge of globalisation', *Environmental Politics* 5: 768–786.

Saunders, C. (2008a) 'Double-edged swords? Collective identity and solidarity in the environment movement', *British Journal of Sociology*, 59(2): 227–253.

Saunders, C. (2008b) 'The stop climate chaos coalition: Climate change as a development issue', *Third World Quarterly*, 1509–1526.

Saunders, C. (2012) 'Reformism and radicalism in the Climate Camp in Britain: Benign coexistence, tensions and prospects for bridging', *Environmental Politics*, 21(5): 829–846.

Saunders, C. (2014) *Environmental Movements and Social Movement Theory*. London: Bloomsbury Academic Press.

Saunders, C., Büchs, M., Papafragkou, A., Wallbridge, R., and Smith, G. (2014) 'Beyond the activist ghetto: a deductive blockmodelling approach to understanding the relationship between contact with environmental organisations and public attitudes and behaviour', *Social Movement Studies*, 13(1): 158–177.

Saunders, C., Doherty, B., and Hayes, G. (2020) 'A new climate movement? Extinction Rebellion's activists in profile', *CUSP Working Paper*, 25: 1–39. Available at: https://cusp.ac.uk/themes/p/xr-study/. Last accessed 13th September 2021.

Saunders, C., Grasso. M., Olcese, C., Rainsford, E., and Rootes, C. (2012) 'Explaining differential protest participation: Novices, returners, repeaters and stalwarts', *Mobilization*, 17(3): 263–280.

Saunders, C. and Price, S. (2009) 'One person's eutopia, another's hell: Climate Camp as a heterotopia', *Environmental Politics*, 18(1): 117–122.

Saunders, C. and Shlomo, N. (2020) 'A new approach to assess the normalisation of differential rates of protest participation', *Quality and Quantity*, Online First doi: 10.1007/s11135-020-00995-7.

Schussman, A. and Soule, S.A. (2005) 'Process and protest: Accounting for individual protest participation', *Social Forces*, 84(2): 1093–1108.

Scott, A. (1990) *Ideology and the New Social Movements*. London: Unwin-Hyman.

Snow, D., Zurcher, L. Jnr and Ekland-Olson, E. (1980) 'Social networks and social movements: A micro-structural approach to differential recruitment', *American Sociological Review*, 45: 787–801.

Stryker, S. (ed) (2000) *Self, Identity and Social Movements*. Minneapolis, MN: University of Minnesota Press.

Taylor, V. (1989) 'Social movement continuity: The women's movement in abeyance', *American Sociological Review*, 54(5): 761–775.

Tindall, D.B. (2002) 'Social networks, identification and participation in an environmental movement: Low-medium cost activism within the British Columbia wilderness preservation movement', *Canadian Review of Sociology*, 39(4): 413–452.

Van Stekelenburg, J. and Klandermans, B. (2013) 'The social psychology of protest', *Current Sociology*, 61(5–6): 886–905.

Van Stekelenburg, J. and Klandermans, B. (2019) 'Identity formation in street demonstrations', in J.E. Stets and R.T Serpe (eds) *Identities in Everyday Life*. Oxford: Oxford University Press.

Verba, S., Lehman, S., Schlozman, L., and Brady, H.E. (1994) *Voice and Equality: Civic Voluntarism in American Politics*. Cambridge, MA: Harvard University Press.

Wahlström, M., Sommer, M., Kocyba, P., De Vydt, M., de Moor, J., Davies, S., Wouters, R., Wennerhag, M., van Stelekeburg, J., Uba, K., Saunders, C., Rucht, D., Mikecz, D., Zamponi, L., Lorenzini, J., Kotczynska, M.J., Haunss, G., Giugni., M., Gaidyte. T., Doherty, B. and Buzogany, A. (2019) 'Protest for a future: Composition, mobilization and motives of the participants in Fridays for Future climate protests on 15 March 2019 in 13 European cities'. Available online at: www.cusp.ac.uk/themes/p/protest-for-a-future-report/. Last accessed 22/07/2020.

Wall, D. (2000) 'Snowballs, elves and skimmingtons? Genealogies of environmental direct action', in B. See, P. Paterson, and B. Doherty (eds) *Direct Action in British Environmentalism*. London: Routledge, pp. 79–92.

27

FRAMING ENVIRONMENTAL ISSUES

Louisa Parks

Introduction

Framing approaches help us understand how meaning is created and contested. Though scholars often discuss frames, these are always analytical reconstructions – static snapshots of meanings assigned within a certain context and time that are the products of framing processes. These are the processes "by which people develop a particular conceptualization of an issue or reorient their thinking about an issue" (Chong and Druckman, 2007, p. 104). As such, framing approaches touch upon concepts in social psychology where the focus is on how an individual's "frames in thought" impact their understanding of some issue (ibid.). In political science and political sociology, attention is placed on the collective impact of framing processes on public opinion or on how political actors use framing processes in an attempt to shape public opinion or some section of it. The study of social movements is no exception. Studies that seek to understand how social movements frame issues are concerned with questions of how certain groups of people are convinced and motivated to act within a social movement or in line with its issue framings. These are the fundamental questions in the field – why do movement cycles or cycles of contention arise (Tarrow, 1998), why do they fade, and why do they have certain impacts (Giugni and Grasso, 2015, p. 348)?

The underlying constructivist assumption of framing processes is that the meaning we assign to issues, events, people, and the like can change, and, more importantly, this affects our actions. A fundamental part of politics, in that view, is about contests over meaning. Of course, not all social movements are exclusively political in outlook, but arguably, political change is included among their ultimate goals, even where the aim is to achieve this through cultural change. This is also the case for environmental movements – even those that aim to change individual consciousness envisage that this will eventually lead to political change (Dryzek, 2005).

This chapter will focus on framing approaches as applied to environmental movements. It will first provide the reader with an overview of the core concepts used in the field before exploring how these have been empirically applied. A broad distinction will be made here between studies of how social movements frame environmental issues and more internally oriented processes on the one hand and studies of how the issue framings of environmental movements match up with others at large in society.

DOI: 10.4324/9780367855680-31

The aim of the discussion presented in this chapter is not intended to be an exhaustive literature review, but rather an illustrative one. It seeks to be at once practical, providing a view of some recent empirical findings and the different methods at the disposal of scholars, and reflective, underlining the need for more introspective studies of framing to engage with broader discussions about how environmental movements could contribute to environmental democracy and vice versa. Indeed, at a time when some call for benign dictatorship to address the planetary crisis in light of the failures of multilateral environmental governance (see Dryzek and Stevenson, 2011), a more connected view is needed to describe how environmental movements can increase democratic deliberation about environmental issues and how to solve them. Reflecting on environmental movements' framing processes as complex moments of internal deliberation both within and between movements, as well as moments of engaging in meaning contestation in society more broadly, with impacts on politics and policies, reveals a view of how they play a crucial and integral part in driving innovation in environmental governance. Arguably, this is achieved in deliberative and thus substantively democratic ways.

Framing approaches and social movements: an overview and core concepts

Framing approaches rely on a range of concepts in an effort to uncover the ways in which meanings are built and attached to events, objects, or experiences (Snow, 2004, p. 384). Broadly, scholars interested in framing processes *within* social movements depart from an interest in three core framing tasks: diagnosis (how an issue is cast as problematic), prognosis (how that problem should be solved, and why collective action – including protest – is part of that), and mobilization (convincing people to take part in that collective action). Scholars interested in framing processes *outside* social movements (i.e., in how social movement frames challenge, change, and reflect the frames of other actors or those long established in broader society) use other concepts to understand how movement frames "fit". One useful feature of the framing approach in the study of social movements is that these concepts are generally widely shared and well defined. This provides a clear key to read and reflect on existing studies of framing in environmental movements and helps highlight areas where new research is needed as well as the broader argument in this chapter about reading the frames and framing processes of environmental movements together with those of other actors in order to build more fleshed-out models of environmental democracy. Although there are different ways of classifying these core concepts, recent work by Snow and colleagues provides a useful single source outlining all of these within a "conceptual architecture" (Snow, Vliegenthart and Ketelaars, 2019, p. 394).

Summarizing, they identify the following (ibid.):

1   *Collective action frames*, the broad concept used to refer to the frames that emerge from meaning work within social movements.
2   *Core framing tasks*, as already mentioned: identifying problems, solutions, and reasons to act. Frames that carry out these tasks are diagnostic, prognostic, and motivational, respectively.
3   *Master frames*, which are 'guiding frames' (ibid., p. 395) that provide broad scripts across a number of movements. The term is often applied to the environmental justice frame in the field of environmental movements.
4   *Frame crystallization*, in which frames become fixed and generally accepted or even dominant. Most studies of framing tend to concentrate on meaning contestation, leaving this phenomenon understudied.

5   *Discursive processes and framing mechanisms*, the processes through which frames are cre-
     ated and changed. Other concepts that refer to these processes include *frame articulation*
     (arranging information in compelling ways) and *frame elaboration* (selectively highlighting
     information).

6   *Frame alignment processes*, in which movements use frames to link themselves to potential
     and actual allies. These may be geared toward individuals, other movements, or other actors
     (Ketelaars, Walgrave and Wouters, 2014). Four strategies are identified: *bridging* (linking
     congruent frames), *amplification* (selectively highlighting to fit a broader frame to unite
     actors), *extension* (applying a frame to new constituencies), and *transformation* (changing
     perspectives entirely).

7   *Discursive fields and discursive opportunity structures* are the contexts in which framing processes
     unfold. The discursive field is the broadest of the two and includes "cultural materials"
     (Snow, Vliegenthart and Ketelaars, 2019, p. 398) while narrower discursive opportunity
     structures (e.g., Koopmans and Olzak, 2004) focus on political culture and actors. Both
     concepts point to the importance of situatedness: framing processes can only be fully
     understood in context.

8   *Frame resonance*, which refers to how far those targeted by a frame accept and adopt it. Similari-
     ties with the concept of alignment are clear (ibid., p. 401), but resonance can be thought of,
     perhaps, as a broader concept that takes into account factors beyond a social movement's initial
     strategizing, as suggested by the literature on the diffusion of movements and their frames
     (Strang and Soule, 1998; Snow and Benford, 2009). Key ideas here are *credibility* and *salience*.

9   *Framing hazards* are events and processes that threaten movement frames. "Ambiguous
     events", "errors or misframings", "frame disputes", and "frame shifts" are discussed as haz-
     ards (Snow, Vliegenthart and Ketelaars, 2019, pp. 403–404).

Scholars of social movement framing generally choose from among these concepts on the basis
of the questions they ask, with the choice often linked to an interest in more internal or external
aspects. Indeed, framing concepts can also be organized along these lines (Johnston and Noakes,
2005, p. 13). The illustration of literature on movements and the framing of environmental
issues here follows this broad approach. Nevertheless, it is worth recalling that this division
remains purely analytical: the internal framings and other dynamics within social movements
affect their actions and, ultimately, their impacts.

The following section discusses literature with a primary focus on dynamics internal to social
movements, while the fourth section continues the discussion with a focus on work, paying
attention predominantly to external aspects. Although not all the studies discussed use the concepts briefly outlined here explicitly, they remain relevant. In fact, strikingly similar arguments
and findings about framing (whether named as such or not) emerge across disciplinary divides
in the social sciences (Parks and Morgera, 2015). As the discussion shows, more recent work
has focused on alignment and the emergence of a master frame of environmental justice, as well
as on how environmental justice (comprising climate justice) frames affect the outcomes and
influence of social movements.

Framing environmental issues within social movements

For social movements, framing is crucial to mobilization.

> Mediating between opportunity, organization, and action are the shared meanings and
> cultural understandings that people bring to any instance of potential mobilization. At

a minimum, people need to feel both aggrieved about (or threatened by) some aspect of their lives and optimistic that by acting collectively they can begin to redress the problem.

(McAdam, 2017, p. 194)

Collective action frames thus allow social movements to problematize issues and convince would-be supporters to mobilize. Environmental movements are no exception. The collective action frames that environmental movements have formed have changed over time and vary within movements. Nevertheless, more or less distinct frames have been attributed to each major wave of environmentalism. The earliest campaigns relied on conservationist frames, often linked to the protection of specific areas or species via the creation of parks and other forms of protected areas (Dalton, 1994).[1] A more radical environmentalist wave linked environment and peace in the collective action frames of the anti-nuclear movement in particular (ibid.), and a third wave drew on the frame of sustainable development with the emergence of international institutions of global environmental governance (see Kaldor, 2003; Dryzek, 2005). A fourth wave – one whose framing forms the focus of scholars today – draws on the broadest frame yet: environmental justice.[2] The framing work behind this, as well as its other features, form the focus of the empirical literature discussed in this section.

Environmental justice, to the extent that it provides a broad script that leaves space to accommodate a number of movements related both to this most recent wave and to previous ones, has been described as a new master frame for environmental movements today (Giugni and Grasso, 2015). The environmental justice frame originated in movements against environmental racism, which referred at its origins to the disproportionate way that environmental damage affects people of color, and, indeed, on the basis of class divisions, in the United States. The frames of these movements rang true within climate change movements increasingly disaffected by the scant efficiency and ambition emerging from multilateral environmental agreements and diplomacy, culminating in the disappointing outcomes of the Fifteenth Conference of the Parties to the United Nations Framework Convention on Climate Change (UNFCCC) held in Copenhagen (Copenhagen COP) (della Porta and Parks, 2014; de Moor, 2020). Groups worked to fuse the local frames of environmental racism with the transnational framings of the global justice movement that had peaked in the first years of the new millennium. Environmental justice frames were then further extended to incorporate the struggles of various local communities and indigenous peoples. At present, framing is moving to incorporate new approaches including just sustainabilities, frames that account for the rights of non-human nature, and pessimistic or "collapsist" frames that focus on how to manage loss through adaptation (see, e.g., Pezzullo, this volume Schlosberg and Collins, 2014; Agyeman et al., 2016; Cassegård and Thörn, 2018). In terms of more internally oriented framing processes, the environmental justice frame can be understood as originating from meaning work that sought to align the frames of the more internationally or globally oriented organizations of third-wave environmental movement groups by extending them to include the collective action frames of environmental justice as first developed in local movements in the United States and those of global social justice as developed in the (many and varied) movement of the same name.

The resulting environmental justice collective action frame could thus be seen as ideationally closer to the original formulations of sustainable development, which sought to reconcile economic development, social justice, and environmental protection (Dryzek, 2005) and were convincing for third-wave groups. It answered increasing frustration with and unease about the failures of multilateralism (see, e.g., Stevenson, 2018) and the appetite to engage in more concrete environment-saving action by including local-level action frames from environmental racism, as well as global-level action frames from the global justice movement. The latter, in particular, built a core collective action frame around the idea that institutions of global governance needn't push a narrow view of economic development alone – another world, they argued, is possible. This description should not lead us to overlook longstanding overlaps between these movements, however. Environmentalism was a part of the global justice movement from the outset (Pleyers, 2010), and its very nature as a "movement of movements" springs from framing processes aimed at underlining common social justice aims among an array of social movements and cultivating multiple identities (della Porta, 2005). The framing shift from third- to fourth-wave environmentalism can also be seen as a response to this call. Overall, the argument for environmental justice as a new master frame clearly answers the description of creating spaces to gather different movements and actors in alliances beneath a broad ideational umbrella. In particular, the environmental justice master frame provides a response to the tensions between global governance processes and local action and effects that are particularly prominent in environmental politics (Jasanoff and Long Martello, 2004): it frames global governance as a framework that can and should allow for local struggles to be resolved in just and sustainable ways.

Recent literature on framing has discussed other aspects of this new master frame. Important findings have emerged in particular from the Caught in the Act of Protest-Contextualizing Contestation project (Wahlström, Wennerhag and Rootes, 2013; Ketelaars, Walgrave and Wouters, 2014). This project has produced quantitative findings using survey methods, focusing on the issue of frame alignment in particular, in a field in which studies have tended to be smaller scale and qualitative in terms of their data. Frame alignment refers not only to how social movements act to bridge their frames with those promoted by others (thus describing steps that may end in the emergence of master frames, as is argued in the case of environmental justice), but also to how movements' collective action frames convince and come to be shared by the individuals who support them and mobilize in protests and other actions. The assumption that underlies this is that to protest means to share a movement's collective action frame – yet the qualitative and small-scale nature of most research on framing processes has left this essentially untested (ibid.). By issuing surveys to participants at three large demonstrations in Brussels, London, and Copenhagen, all of which targeted the Copenhagen COP held in 2009 (when environmental justice frame extension processes were well underway and the master frame was emerging), Wahlström and his colleagues were able to test this theory by asking about the frames that motivated participation (Wahlström, Wennerhag and Rootes, 2013). Focusing on prognostic collective action frames, they found that protest participants in Brussels tended to describe solutions to environmental problems in terms of individual lifestyle changes, while in both London and Copenhagen, solutions were to be achieved via legislation and policy change, with individual change moving to second place. Though more of those demonstrating in Copenhagen made some mention of global justice frames, systemic change, and technology, the numbers were small given the discussion in the literature at that time and since about the clear emergence of an environmental justice frame (ibid., p. 113).

This raises several arguments: about the reality of the emergence of an environmental justice master frame that incorporates climate justice and about longstanding assumptions relating to the necessity of frame alignment processes for social movement mobilization. Regarding the first, the authors suggest that "announcements of the birth in 2009 of a transnational climate justice movement appear premature" (ibid., p. 120), given that the participants in the protests were not on the same page in terms of prognostic frames when compared to frames attributed to organizers. Regarding the second, their findings challenge the assumption of the necessity of frame alignment between organizers and protest participants and suggest that alignment might be a "matter of degree" rather than an absolute category (see Ketelaars, Walgrave and Wouters, 2014, on this point).

While the need to rethink frame alignment to some extent is clear, the wider story of the emergence of the environmental justice master frame suggests that movement organizers and participants may simply be grouped together despite expressing preferences for a range of different, but not incompatible, prognostic frames. The low extent to which frames of environmental justice were shared among the participants could, perhaps, be explained, or at least a different perspective gained, with reference to the discussion of the climate justice frame. Climate justice can be thought of as a sub-frame of environmental justice used to describe movements active on climate change: indeed, the story of the emergence of the environmental justice frame could be thought of as having been sparked by the reflections of global climate change movement organizations that worked to extend their collective action frames to include the locally rooted frames of environmental racism (della Porta and Parks, 2014). A focus on climate justice and transnational or global movements can obscure this very local side of the frame extension by emphasizing the concurrent move to link with the global justice movement. A broader reading of framing processes suggests that groups and individuals with different prognostic frames instead have enough alignment under the umbrella of a master frame to allow mobilization. Environmental justice as a master frame can allow individual change-oriented frames, local change-oriented frames, and global change-oriented frames to be understood as different approaches to a similar aim. With the same logic, what were first dismissed as NIMBY (not in my backyard) movements, later recast as LULU (locally unwanted land use) movements, can be understood within the environmental justice frame alongside NIABY (not in anyone's backyard) and even NOPE (not on planet earth) movements (Imperatore, 2020) and, indeed, food security movements, community-based natural resource management groups, and a host of others. The environmental justice master frame in this view underlines the potential global ideational reach of local and individual collective-action frames.

Yet the question of frame alignment and, perhaps alongside it, collective identity remains. If frames do not need to be closely aligned to allow mobilization, but only loosely organized within the boundaries of a master frame, what role does collective identity play in moments of mass mobilization? Its role in the long-term survival of social movements is known, but assumptions attributed to the concept of frame alignment, coupled with the view of framing processes as "also central to the development and resilience of collective identities" (Giugni and Grasso, 2015, p. 349), suggest there may be some of the sort of circular reasoning that Snow and colleagues attribute to frame resonance at work here (Snow, Vliegenthart and Ketelaars, 2019). If collective identity is necessary to the long-term existence of social movements and is built in shared experiences (like demonstrations) as well as common frames of understanding, and if frame alignment is considered necessary to mobilization, then perhaps the same problem of the existence of a mobilization being taken as evidence of aligned frames and, thus, collective identity persists and is challenged by the findings described on climate justice (Wahlström, Wennerhag and Rootes, 2013). Research on framing processes may then need to re-evaluate links between these, mobilization, and collective identity.

Questions of frames, mobilization, and collective identity are also suggested by the most famous of recent environmental movements: Fridays for Future, or the School Strikes for the Climate, begun by and closely associated with Greta Thunberg. The reason for the prominence of questions linked to mobilization potential and framing processes is the sheer numbers of people involved in this protest wave, particularly among the youngest cohorts. Fortunately, empirical data on the framings shared by participants in this social movement have been gathered using the same methodology applied in the previously mentioned Caught in the Act of

Protest-Contextualizing Contestation project (Wahlström et al., 2019). This rich data concerns participants in parallel protests held across Europe on 15 March 2019 in 13 cities. The information on frames expressed by participants generally matches the frame expressed by Thunberg herself: governments and other centers of power should act in line with the advice and knowledge shared by climate scientists, though trust in governments is rather low. Individuals (including adults) should also change their lifestyles, though the extent to which this is seen as the primary solution to environmental problems changes significantly in different national contexts (ibid., p. 17). Adults participating in the protests do so primarily in solidarity with younger protestors (ibid., p. 11).

This movement – and youth participants in particular – present a great opportunity for research on the links between collective action frames, frame alignment between individuals and social movements, and the shared concerns that contribute to the construction of collective identity. Young participants here are often engaging in protests and identifying with collective action frames and collective social movement identity for the first time. The potential for discovering what motivates them and how collective identity building fits into this is clear – many complex variables are somewhat simpler than usual: previous political experience is reduced; collective action frames might come for the most part from a single source in the figure of Thunberg. The case could also shed light on questions peculiar to environmental movements: not only the tension between prognostic frames of government and individual-led solutions explored in the research discussed, but also intergenerational justice, hope and pessimism about the future, and the need to listen to science (or at least the knowledge produced in the Enlightenment tradition of the scientific method (see, e.g., Jasanoff and Long Martello, 2004)). These are beyond the scope of this chapter, but work that situates the appeal of collective action frames within wider societal discourses – on the trustworthiness and perception of science and risk, on ideas of justice, on hopeful and pessimistic views of the future, and broadly on environmental politics and governance – seems well placed to provide explanations. Research that connects environmental movements and framing to particular discursive contexts is discussed in the next section.

Framing environmental issues in discursive context

Key concepts and studies of framing processes in social movements tend to relate primarily to either the internal actions of movements or how those movements fit into and try to affect a particular context. This section discusses some work on environmental movements in their discursive contexts (again, the aim is not to be exhaustive but indicative), before broadening the focus once more to take into account literature that is not directly concerned with the framing processes of social movements, but instead with the framing of environmental issues in wider societal discourses, how these shape movements, and vice versa. The links between literature on environmental discourses and environmental social movements, it is argued, can help us adopt perspectives that can contribute new questions in the field and reveal trends in civil society and environmental governance more generally.

What drives much research focusing on how environmental movements frame issues according to varying discursive contexts is the question of their influence. The literature on the outcomes of social movements has flourished in recent years and includes, but is not limited to, studies on how social movements influence political decision making: this can range from agenda setting, influence on specific policies or legislation and their implementation, and long-term cultural influence (see Bosi, Giugni and Uba, 2016, for further discussion). Framing processes are understood to affect social movements' chances of influencing decision making.

The concepts of frame resonance and the ideas of credibility and salience are essentially ways of explaining how social movement frames contribute to influence by being more convincing. To achieve credibility and salience, frames must be built with attention to the discursive fields and/ or discursive opportunity structures they exist in and try to avoid framing hazards. The framing processes that occur within social movements thus affect their chances of influencing actors and decisions external to them. In work that focuses on how civil society framing processes ultimately contribute to shape specific decisions, Allan and Hadden illustrate the links between internal framing and external influence (2017). The specific decision concerned is about loss and damage in the context of global climate governance, a matter discussed at the 2015 Paris COP of the UNFCCC and eventually included in the resulting Paris Agreement as a standalone clause, rather than being subsumed under the theme of adaptation without reference to liability and compensation. This outcome, given the deep splits between developed and developing nations prior to the COP, is seen as a partial victory for the developing nations and NGOs that pushed for this solution.

Following a process-tracing method, including a quantitative analysis of key documents, the authors reconstruct a shift in the frames used by NGOs away from legalistic and technical views and toward one of justice, a finding also in line with the story of environmental justice framing described earlier. This shift then had knock-on effects, widening the scope for coalition building among different types of NGOs, as well as between NGOs and like-minded states. Finally, using well-established tests for process-traced narratives (hoop tests and counterfactuals), the influence of NGOs on the adoption of the loss and damage clause is proven: moving into line with the master frame of environmental justice boosted NGO alliance building and, consequently, their ability to influence state parties via persuasion and coercion (ibid., 2017). This demonstrates the link between internal framing processes and influence on specific decisions using clear empirical evidence. Though they do not use a framing approach, Marion Suiseeya and Zanotti (2019) shed further light on how civil society groups – in this case, Indigenous people's groups – can influence decisions in global environmental governance. They follow a collective ethnography method and describe the different types of power groups wielded at the aforementioned Paris COP. In so doing, they provide insights on the channels through which movements' frames can seek influence. The different avenues of power they describe include online work, used to remind negotiators of their global audience of citizens in a logic of "virtual publics" (Garrido and Halavais, 2003); "revolving doors", where Indigenous people were also state party delegates; protests; and more conventional strategies, including press conferences and lobbying (Marion Suiseeya and Zanotti, 2019). Together, they argue, these actions contributed to the addition of Indigenous rights in Article 2 of the Paris Agreement, though hopes about their addition to the operational part of the treaty did not come to fruition (ibid.).

Thinking about the mechanisms by which social movement frames might be brought to the attention of powerful actors and potential allies points to studies that draw on the concept of diffusion, with the aim of shedding light on how movement frames travel and the extent to which they are taken up by different actors. The literature on framing processes discusses this with reference, above all, to transnational social movements. It suggests that frame diffusion can occur actively through the deliberate efforts of movement actors or passively through external channels, notably media channels (della Porta and Kriesi, 2009). Frames are most easily spread when both the transmitter and the receiver share some basic cultural or structural characteristics and are in some way linked, but in most cases in which this is not so, the crucial factor is the manipulation and interpretation of a frame so as to fit a new societal context (Snow and Benford, 2009). Thus, diffusion slots into the concept of resonance. Research building on this view has thus moved beyond attention to social movements and social movement actors alone to pay more attention to the frames and discourses of the powerful actors in the discursive fields they seek to influence.

In the field of environmental movements, arguably loosely united under the master frame of environmental justice, Parks (2020) notes the formidable structural barriers in place for less-organized local groups to influence global environmental governance – including those already noted with reference to NGOs and Indigenous peoples' groups (Allan and Hadden, 2017; Marion Suiseeya and Zanotti, 2019; see also Eastwood, 2019; Witter et al., 2015). This is particularly true for groups that are marginalized within their respective national political landscapes and thus more reliant on the opportunities for influence afforded at the international level (Keck and Sikkink, 1998). Seeking to understand the discursive barriers that may be faced by such groups, the study uses qualitative methods to identify some core shared frames related to the theme of benefit sharing, before turning the spotlight on the discursive field provided by the Convention on Biological Diversity (CBD) – the primary source of global rules for benefit sharing. Conducting a discursive analysis of the CBD's decisions concerning local communities and Indigenous peoples from its beginnings up to its meeting of the parties in 2018, she uncovers a particular emphasis on the recognition of these groups' contributions to the conservation of biodiversity, with an accompanying emphasis on their participation (Parks, 2020). An inductive frame analysis of texts referring to participation revealed a number of openings and opportunities (as well as closed-off areas) for the frames of local groups to make incursions into global decision making. In particular, local groups can join (should they wish) with NGOs to provide inputs regularly called for by the CBD and engage with global arenas by taking part in – and adapting – the implementation of their policies (ibid., 2020; see also Parks and Schröder, 2018).

To understand the discursive fields in which environmental movements move, attention to scholarship on discourses of environmental politics thus appears as necessary. If the master frame of environmental justice shows a turn in environmental movements toward reading apparently disparate struggles within a single logic that ultimately aims to right environmental wrongs, broad discourses of environmental politics as discussed by various scholars appear to be turning toward the view that disparate voices need to be listened to in order to find solutions. To take two prominent examples, Dryzek's seminal work on discourses of environmental politics ends in suggestions of ecological democracy based on the ideas of deliberative democratic theory (Dryzek, 2005), and more recent work emphasizes the need for environmental movements to provide innovative ideas and challenges to decision makers as they are unlikely to come up with much-needed radical ideas within the confines of their bureaucratic systems (Stevenson and Dryzek, 2014). In their work on global environmental politics in the field of climate governance, Bäckstrand and Lövbrand have convincingly argued that a discourse of civic environmentalism has emerged, in which stakeholder participation by civil society is regarded as the key to effective and fair policies (2006, 2019). The reasoning is that policies based on participation will take account of more points of view. The discourse builds on earlier ones of green governmentality (with a focus on planetary limits and the need for rational management by a professional bureaucracy) and ecological modernization (which admits the inherent complexity of environmental problems and, thus, the need for decentralized governance). In this vein, a recent special issue on ecological democracy brings scholars of movements, discourse, and democracy together to discuss the difficulties of reconciling movements that seek to achieve outcomes and institutions that seek inputs from "stakeholders" (Schlosberg, Bäckstrand and Pickering, 2019).

A discussion of these difficulties is beyond the remit of this chapter. The point for research on the framing of environmental issues is that a contribution to this debate could be made by linking work on framing processes, both within social movements and in their attempts to influence discursive fields and specific decisions. This is suggested by the emphasis in recent literature on environmental movements on the emergence of the environmental justice frame and the debates and consequences among diverse movements that led to and resulted from it on the one hand, and debates about participation, ecological democracy, and mitigation versus adaptation among scholars of environmental discourse on the other. To begin, such a broad reading of the "waves" of environmental movements, each characterized by a more or less dominant frame, suggests that these debates are linked since environmental movements and discourses of environmental politics are produced in a symbiotic relationship in which each reacts to and is shaped by the other: frames and discourse do not emerge in vacuums. This much is implied in the very idea of movement waves, in which moments of mobilization are followed by periods of latency during which parts of movements transform in different ways, including via institutionalization, as a normal response to the political (and discursive) opportunities available to them (Tarrow, 1998). Kaldor's discussion of global civil society sheds more light on the ways in which parts of social movements have, following periods of high mobilization, "tamed" in response to states and international organizations opening to their frames in response to claims made (Kaldor, 2003). "NGOization" arguments then provide a potential explanation for the re-emergence of mobilization. If (at least some) groups become aware that their institutionalization and professionalization has led to their depoliticization and demobilization (in other words, to their cooptation within a hegemonic system) (Choudry and Kapoor, 2013), then new impetuses for a protest wave can be imagined as a consequence.

A reading of the waves of environmental movement in this view looks beyond the frames that, *grosso modo*, characterize each of these. In this view, the second wave of environmental movements challenges the narrower, post-colonialist framings of the first wave by bridging environmental concerns with salient themes on peace flowing from global politics during the Cold War and the 1968 wave of new left movements. The third wave, in turn, includes the emergence of large numbers of international NGOs, institutionalizing in response to the development of the architecture of global environmental governance, and frames of sustainable development, changes that themselves responded to the post–Cold War climate, including independence movements against colonialism and the ideas of the new international economic order (Kaldor, 2003). The environmental justice "wave" bridges global justice, local justice, and sustainable development and pushes back against the perceived failure of multilateral diplomacy that emerged among NGOs in particular at and after the Rio +20 summit in 2002 (Stevenson, 2018) and in the field of climate governance after the Copenhagen COP (della Porta and Parks, 2014; de Moor, 2020). In such a view, the links between a push to seek new and inclusive ways of organizing both the governance of environmental issues and environmental social movements become clear.[1] Studies of framing processes in environmental movements understood in this longer-term view can reveal their deliberative democratic credentials. Though deliberation unaffected by structural power asymmetries is likely impossible (Young, 2004), studies of social movements have shown that they come closer than models developed and run by formal institutions (della Porta and Rucht, 2013) and have had more success in including marginalized voices (della Porta, 2020). Or it may be that framing studies reveal how individuals' opinions are easily manipulated (Chong and Druckman, 2007), thus pointing to the need for other kinds of solutions. Studies of framing processes in environmental movements can in both cases contribute to shed light on some of the vexed questions of ecological democracy. Theorization, after all, is one important factor in the diffusion of frames (Strang and Meyer, 1993). Equally, placing framing processes in this broader context may also shed light on questions of collective identity by leading scholars to reflect on the exchanges among diverse movements under the banner of environmental justice. In this vein, collective identity may also arise from the discussion of differences as well as in moments of shared experience, as seen in some aspects of the emergence of the environmental justice frame (Schlosberg, 2002).

Summary and conclusions

This chapter began with an overview of the key concepts used in the literature on framing processes in social movements. It noted that studies of framing often tend to focus either on those processes that take place within movements or on how movements use framing processes to seek to influence the discursive contexts they exist within, including the frames of decision makers. Two sections then described illustrative examples of recent literature on framing processes in environmental movements following these two perspectives. It is interesting to note that many of these studies drew on both quantitative and qualitative, or mixed, methods rather than the more traditional qualitative approaches often attributed to the field. Each section pointed to outstanding questions – on collective identity and its relation to framing processes and alignment in particular and on how framing processes necessarily relate to broader discursive shifts, respectively. Finally, it was suggested that reading framing processes in broader perspectives might contribute to these debates and, indeed, to the continued and crucial debate on inclusion and deliberation in a model of ecological democracy. Other important avenues for research on framing processes are hinted at in the chapter and have emerged forcefully from recent events. The frame of the responsibility to listen to science brought to prominence by the Fridays for Future movement now finds itself in a discursive field defined by the highly debated role of science and scientists in the COVID-19 pandemic, for example. Frames of environmental racism have received new attention in the media with the most recent wave of contention of the Black Lives Matter movement, which has directly raised how environmental inequalities contribute to higher death and serious illness rates among people of color in both the United States and Europe. Continued colonialism has been raised in the politics of vaccinations and their distribution, and the destruction of habitats linked to heightened risks from zoonotic diseases. Questions of how frames and collective identities are built online and how this may change the ways in which social movements function have also been pushed into the foreground.

Questions of inclusion and democracy underpin all these issues. Studying frames as processes of discursive contestation or arguments over meaning is crucial to resolving outstanding tensions in the field. The chapter pointed to some of these: the tension between movements seeking influence and institutions seeking stakeholder input and on justice between generations; between different views of expertise, science, and knowledge and how they should be integrated in environmental governance; and between calls for individual-level sensibility and behavioral change and the responsibilities of states and international organizations. All these also suggest some more fundamental tensions: about gradual change within existing systems versus radical systemic change, about how change can not only be achieved democratically but also with the urgency imposed by the planetary crisis, or whether we should instead be mobilizing around how to manage inevitable collapse. Though only one part of the equation, studies of framing have an important contribution to make. First, social movements and their framing processes are places of lively debate – they can bring agonistic politics back into a vision of environmental democracy based on deliberation that prominent thinkers such as Mouffe argue risks excluding radical politics through an emphasis on consensus. Second, framing studies can help us understand current power structures by unpacking their discursive bases and thus clarify what needs to change, where, and how quickly.

Notes

1 These earlier conservation movements tended to regard the presence of all humans as a threat to "wild" and "pristine" landscapes and fauna. In many areas of the world, beginning from the United States, this led to a model of "fortress conservation", in which this colonialist logic denied the agency of people over lands they had traditionally occupied for centuries. These frames thus contributed to a mistrust between some environmentalist causes and indigenous peoples that persists to this day. For a deeper discussion, see the chapters by Mertig and Etchart in this volume.

2 Though, of course, this view of "waves" is an overly simplistic reading of an extremely diverse movement (Schlosberg, 2002), the aim is to underline how placing this diversity within a broader view may contribute to some big questions in the field.

References

Agyeman, J. et al. (2016) "Trends and directions in environmental justice: From inequity to everyday life, community, and just sustainabilities," *Annual Review of Environment and Resources*, 41(1), pp. 321–340. doi: 10.1146/annurev-environ-110615-090052.

Allan, J. I. and Hadden, J. (2017) "Exploring the framing power of NGOs in global climate politics," *Environmental Politics*, 26(4). doi: 10.1080/09644016.2017.1319017.

Bäckstrand, K. and Lövbrand, E. (2006) "Planting trees to mitigate climate change: Contested discourses of ecological modernization, green governmentality and civic environmentalism," *Global Environmental Politics*. MIT Press Journals, pp. 50–75. doi: 10.1162/glep.2006.6.1.50.

Bäckstrand, K. and Lövbrand, E. (2019) "The road to Paris: contending climate governance discourses in the post-Copenhagen era," *Journal of Environmental Policy and Planning*, 21(5), pp. 519–532. doi: 10.1080/1523908X.2016.1150777.

Bosi, L., Giugni, M. and Uba, K. (eds.) (2016) *The Consequences of Social Movements*. Cambridge: Cambridge University Press. doi: 10.1017/CBO9781316337790.

Cassegård, C. and Thörn, H. (2018) "Toward a postapocalyptic environmentalism? Responses to loss and visions of the future in climate activism," *Environment and Planning E: Nature and Space*, 1(4). doi: 10.1177/2514848618793331.

Chong, D. and Druckman, J. N. (2007) "Framing theory," *Annual Review of Political Science*, 10(1), pp. 103–126. doi: 10.1146/annurev.polisci.10.072805.103054.

Choudry, A. and Kapoor, D. (2013) *NGOization: Complicity, Contradictions and Prospects*. London: Zed Books.

Dalton, R. J. (1994) *The Green Rainbow. Environmental Groups in Western Europe*. New Haven, CT: Yale University Press.

della Porta, D. (2005) "Multiple belongings, tolerant identities and the construction of 'another politics'," in della Porta, D. and Tarrow, S. (eds) *Transnational Protest and Global Activism*. New York: Rowman and Littlefield, pp. 175–202.

della Porta, D. (2020) *How Social Movements Can Save Democracy*. Cambridge: Polity.

della Porta, D. and Kriesi, H. (2009) "Social movements in a globalizing world: An introduction," in della Porta, D., Kriesi, H., and Rucht, D. (eds) *Social Movements in a Globalizing World*. Basingstoke: Palgrave Macmillan, pp. 3–22.

della Porta, D. and Parks, L. (2014) "Framing processes in the climate movement: From climate change to climate justice," in Dietz, M. and Garrelts, H. (eds) *Routledge Handbook of Climate Change Movements*. Abingdon: Routledge, pp. 19–30.

della Porta, D. and Rucht, D. (eds) (2013) *Meeting Democracy*. Cambridge: Cambridge University Press. doi: 10.1017/CBO9781139236034.

de Moor, J. (2020) "Alternative globalities? Climatization processes and the climate movement beyond COPs," *International Politics*. doi: 10.1057/s41311-020-00222-y.

Dryzek, J. S. (2005) *The Politics of the Earth. Environmental Discourses*. Second Edition. Oxford: Oxford University Press.

Dryzek, J. S. and Stevenson, H. (2011) "Global democracy and earth system governance," *Ecological Economics*, 70(11), pp. 1865–1874. doi: 10.1016/j.ecolecon.2011.01.021.

Eastwood, L. E. (2019) *Negotiating the Environment. Civil Society, Globalisation and the UN*. Abingdon: Routledge.

Garrido, M. and Halavais, A. (2003) "Mapping networks of support for the Zapatista movement: Applying social networks analysis to study contemporary social movements," in McCaughey, M. and Ayers, M. D. (eds) *Online Activism in Theory and Practice*. Oxon: Routledge, pp. 165–184.

Giugni, M. and Grasso, M. T. (2015) "Environmental movements in advanced industrial democracies: Heterogeneity, transformation, and institutionalization," *Annual Review of Environment and Resources*, 40(1), pp. 337–361. doi: 10.1146/annurev-environ-102014-021327.

Imperatore, P. (2020) "Territori e Protesta: La Relazione tra Opportunità Politiche e Mobilitazione nei Casi No TAP e No Grandi Navi," *Polis*, 34(3), pp. 621–644.

Jasanoff, S. and Long Martello, M. (eds) (2004) *Earthly Politics: Local and Global in Environmental Governance*. Cambridge, MA: MIT Press.

Johnston, H. and Noakes, J. A. (2005) *Frames of Protest: Social Movements and the Framing Perspective*. Basingstoke: Palgrave Macmillan.

Kaldor, M. (2003) *Global Civil Society: An Answer to War*. Cambridge: Polity Press.

Keck, M. E. and Sikkink, K. (1998) *Advocacy Networks in International Politics*. Cornell University Press. Available at: www.jstor.org/stable/10.7591/j.ctt5hh13f.

Ketelaars, P., Walgrave, S. and Wouters, R. (2014) "Degrees of frame alignment: Comparing organisers' and participants' frames in 29 demonstrations in three countries," *International Sociology*, 29(6), pp. 504–524. doi: 10.1177/0268580914548286.

Koopmans, R. and Olzak, S. (2004) "Discursive opportunities and the evolution of right-wing violence in Germany," *American Journal of Sociology*, 110(1), pp. 198–230. doi: 10.1086/386271.

Marion Suiseeya, K. R. and Zanotti, L. (2019) "Making influence visible: Innovating ethnography at the Paris climate summit," *Global Environmental Politics*, 19(2), pp. 38–60.

McAdam, D. (2017) "Social movement theory and the prospects for climate change activism in the United States," *Annual Review of Political Science*, 20(1), pp. 189–208. doi: 10.1146/annurev-polisci-052615-025801.

Parks, L. (2020) *Benefit-Sharing in Environmental Governance Local Experiences of a Global Concept*. Abingdon: Routledge.

Parks, L. and Morgera, E. (2015) "The need for an interdisciplinary approach to norm diffusion: The case of fair and equitable benefit-sharing," *Review of European, Comparative and International Environmental Law*, 24(3). doi: 10.1111/reel.12143.

Parks, L. and Schröder, M. (2018) "What we talk about when we talk about 'local' participation in international biodiversity law. The changing scope of indigenous peoples and local communities' participation under the Convention on Biological Diversity," *Participation and Conflict*, 11(3), pp. 743–785.

Pleyers, G. (2010) *Alter-Globalization: Becoming Actors in the Global Age*. Cambridge: Polity Press.

Schlosberg, D. (2002) *Environmental Justice and the New Pluralism: The Challenge of Difference for Environmentalism*. Oxford: Oxford University Press.

Schlosberg, D., Bäckstrand, K. and Pickering, J. (2019) "Reconciling ecological and democratic values: Recent perspectives on ecological democracy," *Environmental Values*, 28(1), pp. 1–8. doi: 10.3197/096327119X15445433913541.

Schlosberg, D. and Collins, L. B. (2014) "From environmental to climate justice: climate change and the discourse of environmental justice," *WIREs: Climate Change*, 5(3), pp. 359–374.

Snow, D. A. (2004) "Framing processes, ideology, and discursive fields," in Snow, D. A., Soule, S. A., and Kriesi, H. (eds) *The Blackwell Companion to Social Movements*. Oxford: Blackwell, pp. 380–412.

Snow, D. A. and Benford, R. D. (2009) "Alternative types of cross-national diffusion in the social movement arena," in Della Porta, D., Kriesi, H., and Rucht, D. (eds) *Social Movements in a Globalizing World*. Basingstoke: Palgrave Macmillan, pp. 23–39.

Snow, D. A., Vliegenthart, R. and Ketelaars, P. (2019) "The framing perspective on social movements: Its conceptual roots and architecture," in Snow, D. A. et al. (eds) *The Wiley Blackwell Companion to Social Movements*. Second. Oxford: Wiley Blackwell, pp. 392–410.

Stevenson, H. (2018) *Global Environmental Politics. Problems, Policy and Practice*. Cambridge: Cambridge University Press.

Stevenson, H. and Dryzek, J. S. (2014) *Democratizing Global Climate Governance*. Cambridge: Cambridge University Press.

Strang, D. and Meyer, J. W. (1993) "Institutional conditions for diffusion," *Theory and Society*, 22(4), pp. 487–511.

Strang, D. and Soule, S. A. (1998) "Diffusion in organizations and social movements: From hybrid corn to poison pills," *Annual Review of Sociology*, 24, pp. 265–290.

Tarrow, S. (1998) *Power in Movement*. Cambridge: Cambridge University Press. doi: 10.1017/CBO9780511813245.

Wahlström, Mattias, Piotr Kocyba, Michiel De Vydt and Joost de Moor (Eds.) (2019). *Protest for a future: Composition, mobilization and motives of the participants in Fridays For Future climate protests on 15 March, 2019 in 13 European cities*. doi: 10.17605/OSF.IO/XCNZH.

Wahlström, M., Wennerhag, M. and Rootes, C. (2013) "Framing 'the climate issue': Patterns of participation and prognostic frames among climate summit protesters," *Global Environmental Politics*, 13(4), pp. 101–122. doi: 10.1162/GLEP_a_00200.

Witter, R. et al. (2015) "Moments of influence in global environmental governance," *Environmental Politics*, 24(6), pp. 894–912.

Young, I. M. (2004) *Inclusion and Democracy*. Oxford: Oxford University Press.

28

GENDER AND ENVIRONMENTAL MOVEMENTS

Chie Togami and Suzanne Staggenborg

In this chapter, we show that gender dynamics are connected to several related processes in the mobilization of the environmental movement occurring at different levels (Tarrow 2011). Large-scale changes such as climate change and critical events such as oil spills and other environmental disasters create concern among potential supporters and draw attention to movement issues. Political and cultural opportunities, such as a sympathetic government and public, can also facilitate mobilization. At the meso level, mobilizing structures, including pre-existing networks and organizations and emergent movement organizations, are needed to recruit activists, devise strategies, and form coalitions. At the micro level, individuals become activists when they take on movement beliefs and collective identities, agree that collective action is needed, and develop solidarity with other participants. Individuals are more likely to be recruited to movements when they are biographically or structurally available, meaning that they lack barriers to recruitment, such as competing ties or responsibilities that will prevent their commitment to a movement (Snow et al. 1980). The framing of issues by movement organizations and activists is critical to their ability to connect the concerns of individuals to those of the movement. Tactics such as the climate marches held in cities around the world are essential for mobilizing participants.

Gender is frequently related to these processes of mobilization. While large-scale changes and critical events affect entire populations, perceptions of their impact vary by gender; men and women have different life experiences that alter their awareness of problems such as the impacts of pollution on children's health. Women also vary in their life experiences based on race or ethnicity and class, which affect their perceptions of political and cultural opportunity. At the organizational and interactional levels, women often participate in different settings, and have different networks than men. Once they become involved in movements, women's organizational experiences may lead them to develop new networks, solidarities, skills, and collective identities. Depending on their race or ethnic and class situations, as well as gender roles, women may be more or less structurally available than men for movement participation. As we describe, women's participation is likely to affect the strategies and tactics pursued by environmental movements, including the framing of issues. In the following sections, we examine the role of gender in environmental movement recruitment and participation, ideology and framing, and tactics. Our discussion draws heavily on research conducted in the United States, but we also note some global trends and studies.

DOI: 10.4324/9780367855680-32

Gender, recruitment, and participation in environmental movements

Participation in different types of environmental movements has varied by gender. (See Stover and Cable 2017 for an overview of American women's participation.) Mainstream environmental groups were male dominated through much of the twentieth century while women became the leaders of community-based movements (Gottlieb 2005). Men have directed many large environmental organizations, including professionalized "Big Green" organizations such as the Wilderness Society and media-savvy international groups such as Greenpeace. They have also been at the forefront of many radical environmental groups such as Earth First! and the Earth Liberation Front (ELF), which have engaged in controversial direct-action tactics like tree spiking and the vandalizing of logging equipment. Such groups often appealed to a certain form of male-centric machismo, with Earth First!'s founders even referring to themselves as "rednecks and cowboys for wilderness" (Shantz 2002:107). Women have not been absent from professional and radical direct-action groups, but they have often participated in less-visible capacities in these groups. One notable exception was Judi Bari, an Earth First! leader who organized Georgia Pacific sawmill workers in the late 1980s to form a radical labor-ecology union of IWW and Earth First! in Northern California. Bari's high-profile campaign to slow the harvest of redwood forests made her the target of a car bomb assassination attempt in May 1990, an attack that she miraculously survived. The attempt on Bari's life (which remains unsolved to this day) demonstrates the kind of "high-risk activism" (McAdam 1986) that environmentalists may need to undertake when confronting deeply vested economic interests. In the case of Earth First! and ELF, it is likely that machismo and sexism, coupled with the high-risk nature of their chosen tactics, acted as deterrents to many women taking on visible roles within the organizations.

In contrast, many community-based environmental justice campaigns have been led by women (Stover and Cable 2017:690). Numerous accounts highlight the role of women in fighting against contamination of schools and communities by air and water pollution, toxic waste, coal mining, and fracking for natural gas and oil, among other threats to health and environment. In explaining gender differences in recruitment and participation in the environmental movement, scholars frequently cite women's roles in families and communities, particularly as mothers concerned about their children's health. Women who have children also tend to be more aware of some types of environmental hazards, such as miscarriages and stillbirths caused by toxic exposure (Stover and Cable 2017:693). Mobilizing structures are also important insofar as women are usually more involved than men with childcare, and thus, they come into contact with other concerned women through institutions such as schools. Housewives and other women have often been more structurally available to participate in movements than men, resulting in their more extensive participation and leadership in environmental campaigns (Cable 1992). As they participated in local environmental organizations, women often used skills that they had learned through their experiences with their families, children's schools, and communities, and they developed "a new kind of movement identity" (Gottlieb 2005:277).

In the United States, scholars have documented gender differences in environmental movement activism in the conservation movement arising in the nineteenth century, in the Progressive Era of the early twentieth century, and in the contemporary movement emerging in the 1960s. In the nineteenth century (and earlier), the environmental consciousness and activity of both men and women were shaped by the rigid gender roles and ideology of the time, whereby men were expected to perform dangerous tasks, take risks, and pursue their own interests while women were supposed to selflessly nurture children and manage their households (Taylor 2016:22–23). Men who hunted worked to protect wildlife from excessive hunting in order to preserve game, and sportsmen's clubs served as mobilizing structures for the activities of largely wealthy men (2016:170–172). Many women became involved in protecting birds, which were endangered in part by the use of their feathers in women's hats, and upper-class women's clubs began collaborating with the Audubon Society after it was founded in 1886 (2016:192–194).

In the Progressive Era of the late nineteenth and early twentieth centuries in the United States, gender ideology continued to shape the participation of both men and women in the conservation movement. Women were heavily involved in advocating for environmental reforms such as the preservation of wilderness and wildlife, clean air and water in cities, public parks, and safe food (Mann 2011; Merchant 2007; Rome 2006). In line with the gender politics of the era, women often justified their activities as extensions of their traditional responsibilities for home and family and described their environmental activism as "municipal housekeeping" (Mann 2011:7). Men at the time exhibited anxiety about their masculinity, resulting from social and economic changes such as the growth of white-collar work and new demands from "the new woman" for suffrage and other rights (Rome 2006:448). This anxiety affected the willingness of some male environmental reformers to work on issues that were "strongly gendered" as feminine concerns, such as "beauty, health, [and] future generations" (Rome 2006:443).

Significantly, as Adam Rome (2006) argues, gender politics affected the organizations, campaigns, and coalitions of the environmental reform movement. The Sierra Club, founded in 1882, admitted women from its beginning and elected its first female president, Aurelia Harwood, in the 1920s (Berry 2015:162). Women's prominent participation in Sierra Club campaigns, such as the controversy over the Hetch Hetchy Valley in Yosemite National Park, was seized upon by opponents who famously published a political cartoon depicting John Muir dressed as a woman and holding a broom. As Rome argues, the Muir cartoon is symbolic of the ways in which gender was weaponized by environmental opponents in order to discredit the efforts of men and women engaged in environmental reform work during the Progressive Era (2006:442). Another prominent environmental organization of the time, the American Forestry Association, also experienced gender-based conflict. The group initially welcomed women but later excluded them in an effort "to professionalize the organization" and "to focus on the economic benefits of scientific management" rather than issues championed by women, such as the preservation of trees (Rome 2006:450–451). Gender politics affected movement campaigns and led to the marginalization of some issues, such as bird protection for its own sake; instead of "aesthetic and emotional arguments for bird protection", men advocated for the preservation of "useful birds", such as those that assisted farmers by eating agricultural pests (2006:452–453). In addition to changing the nature of campaigns, gender politics changed the ability to form cross-gender coalitions. Rome notes that campaigns such as the effort to ban interstate trade in bird feathers were supported by both men and women, and women were highly active in them. Eventually, however, the environmental campaigns of men and women became more segregated, in part due to the influence of organizations like the American Forestry Association (2006:454).

American environmental campaigns during the Progressive Era were also segregated by race, reflecting the segregated organizations and networks through which women were recruited. White middle-class women were mobilized through women's clubs to work on a wide variety of environmental issues, including the conservation of natural resources and public lands as well as increasingly urban issues such as air and water pollution, lack of sanitation in cities, and food safety. In addition to working through women's clubs, white women formed hundreds of conservation organizations in the early twentieth century (Unger 2012). Middle-class Black women were also highly active in Progressive Era reform activities through their own clubs and national federations such as the National Association of Colored Women (Stover and Cable 2017:688).

Given the rising concentration of Black residents in urban areas, African American activists were particularly involved in efforts to combat pollution and lack of sanitation leading to serious health issues in their neighborhoods (Mann 2011). Women's clubs segregated by race served as mobilizing structures for white and Black women, who were highly motivated to participate in the municipal housekeeping of the Progressive Era.

In the contemporary environmental movement that emerged in the 1960s, gender relations continued to influence women's recruitment and participation. In the late 1960s and early 1970s, the United States experienced a wave of "citizen environmentalism", consisting of increased local participation in environmental organizations, many of which were newly formed (Longhurst 2010). In his case study of the Group Against Smog and Pollution (GASP), which was founded in Pittsburgh in 1969, historian James Longhurst details the central role of women in the organization. He finds that histories of contemporary environmental organizations have typically neglected gender dynamics because they focus on national organizations rather than local activism (Longhurst 2010:86). In the case of GASP, Longhurst (2010:85) shows how "much of GASP's fund-raising, organization, and educational activities took place in what might be termed women's social space, through cookbooks, garden clubs, schools, and a network of women's social and civic groups". Although GASP did not identify as a women's group, and men as well as women held positions of leadership in the organization, Longhurst was able to observe "beneath the surface" GASP's "explicitly maternalistic rhetoric and female organizational base" (2010:86). The League of Women's Voters, for example, conducted training sessions for early organizers of GASP to prepare them for participation in public hearings in 1969 (2010:89). Women served as presidents and board members of GASP along with men, and they developed some of its most innovative and successful mobilizing tactics, such as cookbooks and bake sales, which funded the organization and helped educate people. They connected this "flour power" to a network of pre-existing women's organizations, which organized their members to bake cookies, using a GASP-supplied kit with a cookie cutter in the shape of GASP's mascot, a bird called "Dirtie Gertie" who called attention to air pollution. Longhurst reports that at least 42 different women's organizations recruited bakers for GASP as part of an extensive network that included church groups as well as other women's groups (2010:94). This linking of environmental advocacy with domestic pursuits, Longhurst argues, "echoes the rhetoric of Progressive Era municipal housekeeping", and "it also reflected the experiences and lives of the women of GASP, who were likewise blurring the lines of domestic and municipal responsibility" (2010:97). Like women in other local environmental groups, many GASP members were mothers who were concerned about the impacts of pollution on their children.

Beginning in the late 1970s, a growing movement of protests against toxic waste disposal became a central focus of women's environmental activism. Perhaps the most famous protest in the US occurred in Niagara Falls, New York, where the Hooker Chemical Company had used an abandoned canal project, Love Canal, as a chemical waste dump. A school and adjacent neighborhood were later built on top of the chemical waste site with disastrous health impacts for the community. Media coverage of the Love Canal calamity transformed the local issue into a national one (Szasz 1994:52), and working-class housewives such as Lois Gibbs became prominent leaders in the movement. Although mainstream environmental organizations were concerned about toxic waste disposal and had been supporting legislation to impose government regulations to deal with the growing problem, the community protests at Love Canal and elsewhere in the US brought effective new tactics and frames to the struggle (Gottlieb 2005:243–251). After a local newspaper reported on dangerous chemicals buried beneath Love Canal in 1978, Lois Gibbs came to understand that the health problems her children were experiencing were due to the toxic waste, and she found in talking to her neighbors that many others were also suffering from health problems. They organized a community group called the Love Canal Homeowners Association and began to engage in militant tactics, such as detaining EPA officials, to attract media attention and force the government to address their problems, eventually succeeding in getting the federal government to pay to evacuate the families who wanted to leave Love Canal (Shabecoff 2003: 228–229). Gender was important in the framing of the issues around children's health and the recruitment of many women to the cause. As Gottlieb (2005:280) argues, "The focus on community development, on place, on children, and on participation and access to power has provided a gender framework for the antitoxics movement and has created a different kind of language for environmental protest". The movement also created new types of community organizations, and Gibbs went on the found a national organization, the Citizens Clearinghouse for Hazardous Wastes (later the Center of Health, Environment and Justice), to advise other community groups dealing with toxic waste problems.

Studies show that women have provided the leadership and majority support for many campaigns against toxic waste. Krauss (1993) notes that toxic waste facilities are disproportionately sited in working-class or low-income communities and communities of color and that women motivated by their personal experiences often take leadership of grassroots organizations. Many of these women are mothers, who link their children's ill health to toxic hazards. Krauss finds that these women combine their strong concerns about home and children with resources such as extended family networks that help them spread information about toxic waste. The framing of these concerns varied by race and class as well as gender. In her interviews with women activists, Krauss found that white women tended to lose their faith in government as a result of their experiences. African American women viewed government with mistrust to begin with, employing the frame of "environmental racism" in considering toxic waste sites (1993:255). Native American women added genocide and colonialism to their narratives of environmental racism (1993:257). Krauss concludes that women used their experiences to "reshape traditional language and meanings into an ideology of resistance" and shows how issues of class and race alter women's analyses of environmental justice (1993:259).

Brown and Ferguson (1995) also find that women's caretaker roles in the family increase their awareness of the health problems associated with toxic waste. They review a number of case studies of toxic waste activism, which show similar patterns; women are often transformed from housewives to activists after their children experience health problems, and they discover a pattern in the community after talking to neighbors (1995:148). Brown and Ferguson show that women take advantage of the "image of a mother rising to the defence of her children" in their struggles against industry and government around toxic waste (1995:161). They also connect this "strategic use of motherhood as a basis for activism" with concerns about the "reproductive consequences of toxic exposure" (1995:162), thereby creating a powerful narrative. The participation of local women fuels a grassroots movement, but the authors contend that it is part of a global movement in which gender plays a central role (1995:168).

In the Global South, women have often been at the forefront of campaigns to protect their communities from the negative impacts of deforestation, resource extraction, and land grabbing. One notable example of this is the Green Belt Movement (GBM). Founded in 1977 by Wangari Maathai, the Green Belt Movement is a grassroots movement that, for decades, has taught and paid women a small sum to grow seedlings and plant trees in order to restore soil, retain rainwater, and alleviate the burden caused by scarcity of firewood. At the same time, the Green Belt movement has sought to empower women by hosting civic seminars that educate participants about the political, economic, and environmental circumstances leading to government and corporate mismanagement of natural resources. Over the years, this focus on democratic engagement, and accountability from national leaders has translated into campaigning against land grabbing (especially in and around Nairobi) and fighting the encroachment of livestock grazing on forests. As of 2020, it was estimated that the women of the Green Belt Movement have planted over 51 million trees in the highlands of Mount Kenya, the Aberdares, and the Mau Complex – three of the most important mountain ecosystems in Kenya (Maathai 2006; "Our History", greenbeltmovement.org).

Another important movement that has engaged women around environmental and social justice issues is La Via Campesina. Founded in 1993, Via Campesina is a transnational peasant movement comprising 182 organizations worldwide in 81 countries that advocates for "food sovereignty", a term that signifies the "rights of people to healthy and culturally appropriate food produced through ecologically sound and sustainable methods, and their right to define their own food and agriculture systems" (Via Campesina 2007). Rather than privileging the demands of markets and corporations, the concept of food sovereignty prioritizes the needs of those who produce, distribute and, consume food and seeks to shape food systems and policies that reflect this priority. As Vivas (2012:2) stresses, the quest for food sovereignty is inherently linked to issues of gender, given that in the Global South, women are responsible for 60% to 80% of food production but are often paid far less than their male counterparts and are more likely to experience hunger and malnutrition. As Desmarias (2007) explains, gender equity was not initially a central priority of Via Campesina (in fact, all the original regional coordinators elected at the first international conference of Via Campesina were men). However, since the inception of the movement, women have successfully fought to make Via Campesina into an explicitly feminist organization, with women occupying many leadership roles and continuing to visibly and actively take part in decision making. As Desmarias notes,

> In most countries, agricultural and rural organizations are dominated by men. The women of La Via Campesina refuse to accept these subordinate positions. While acknowledging the long and difficult road ahead, women accept the challenge with enthusiasm, and vow to carry out a major role shaping the Via Campesina as a movement committed to gender equality.
>
> (2007:265)

In the United States, women formed the backbone of many community-based environmental groups that continued to form in the 1980s and 1990s. Sherry Cable (1992) examines the recruitment and participation of women into the Yellow Creek Concerned Citizens (YCCC), a group organized in 1980 to stop the pollution of a creek by a tannery in southeastern Kentucky. The rural community was largely working class, and most women were housewives while men worked in the coal mines or other industries. Cable examines the role of grievances, structural availability, and social networks in the recruitment and participation of group members, demonstrating the critical role of gender in participation. Both men and women expressed similar grievances regarding the pollution of the creek, first as it interfered with lifestyle pursuits such as swimming and fishing and later as they discovered the pollution was connected to serious health problems. The real gender difference was related to structural availability and division of labor in the group, and this changed over time. In the early stage, men were the group leaders, and women performed tasks such as taking minutes of meetings and fundraising through activities like bake sales. Later, when the group turned to litigation and needed to raise money from nonprofit organizations, attend hearings, and make presentations, women gradually expanded their roles and learned new skills because they were more structurally available than the men to take on these responsibilities during working hours. Women also enlarged their social networks through their participation; thus, Cable finds "an extended effect of structural availability on the nature of participation and gender role behavior *after* initial recruitment" (1992:47).

Other work on environmental justice movements attempts to explain why women have played extensive roles in these movements while men dominate the mainstream environmental movement. In looking at environmental justice activism in the coalfields of Appalachia, Bell and Braun (2010) argue that gender identities shape the activism of men and women. While women's sense of duty and identity as mothers support their activism, the connection between masculine identity and coal mining makes it more difficult for men to participate. Despite the drastic decline in the coal industry, many men still feel an allegiance to coal mining that prevents them from criticizing its health and environmental impacts and, in the view of one male activist, "this silence is linked to peer pressure and the fear of losing status within the community" (Bell and Braun 2010:806). Thus, pre-existing ties and gender identities can either facilitate or hinder activism in the environmental justice movement, depending on their fit with the collective identity of the movement (2010:810). In her detailed study of the experiences of 12 women in the movement, Bell (2013) shows how women's activism is maintained as they are transformed by their personal experiences in the movement and as they develop new ties to other women activists and expanded feelings of responsibility beyond their own children and families for their communities and natural environment.

Grievances, ideology, and framing

Gender impacts the ways in which environmental movement groups understand, formulate, and articulate grievances. Historically, many environmental frames focused on male experiences and ignored women's issues, but movements such as the antitoxics movement, the women's health movement, and the broader feminist movement itself helped shift environmental frames (Gottlieb 2005). Among the important frameworks and ideologies influenced by these movements are environmental justice, maternalism, ecofeminism, and climate justice frames.

Environmental justice

In 1982, a group of civil rights activists organized a forceful and sustained campaign to prevent 120 million pounds of toxic, PCB-contaminated soil from being dumped in Warren County, a predominantly African American community in North Carolina. This highly publicized resistance mounted by residents and their allies propelled the notion of "environmental racism" into the national consciousness, and 40 years later, the struggle against the Warren County landfill is viewed as the beginning of the environmental justice (EJ) movement in the United States (Mohai et al. 2009). According to McGurty (2009:19–20), the Warren County activists created the environmental racism frame, which then led to the development of the broader environmental justice frame. The EJ movement has also been associated with the anti-toxics movement, and some scholars view anti-toxics and anti-environmental racism as two streams under the umbrella of environmental justice in the United States (Bell and Braun 2010; Buckingham and Kulcur 2009; Taylor 1997). In both cases, women have served as crucial leaders and participants.

In Warren County, Dollie Burwell, a local resident and veteran of the civil rights movement, was instrumental in organizing the support of churches to oppose the toxic landfill. Within a six-week period, Burwell and nearly 500 other individuals were arrested for acts of civil disobedience that included obstructing roads to prevent trucks from bringing in contaminated soil (Washington Post 1982). In 1992, Zulene Mayfield, a woman whose community was directly adjacent to the largest trash incinerator in the commonwealth of Pennsylvania, founded Chester

Residents Concerned for Quality Living (CRCQL) to oppose the practice of locating polluting industries in poor neighborhoods of color. Under her leadership, CRCQL launched the first environmental racism lawsuit in the United States, suing the Pennsylvania Department of Environmental Protection on the grounds that the high concentration of the county's waste facilities (60%) in a predominantly African American community reflected a racial bias (Foster 1998). Nicole Horseherder, a member of the Navajo Nation, witnessed her tribe's ancestral land desecrated by the activities of coal-mining companies and the effects of mining's toxic byproducts (mercury, selenium, arsenic, and lead) on the health of her community. In 2001, she formed the group Tó Nizhóní Ání (Beautiful Water Speaks), which successfully fought to shut down the Black Mesa mine and its slurry pipeline in 2005 (Wong 2019). The stories of each of these women provide a brief glimpse at the history of women's leadership in high-profile environmental justice initiatives. They also highlight an important observation: issues relating to gender and environmental justice have historically been bound up together. In fact, women of color and working-class women comprise the majority of the membership in many grassroots environmental justice groups (Di Chiro 1992).

The question of what explains the predominance of women's participation in environmental justice movements has garnered a significant amount of scholarly attention. Although structural availability is certainly part of the story, the literature on environmental justice also emphasizes women's lived experience of environmental degradation and the impact these experiences have in terms of stirring them to engage in activism. Women are often the first to experience the intrusion of environmental degradation into the private sphere of their homes. Their children may become ill, for example, which in turn may lead them to "expand their issue identification to locate their concerns within broader societal/structural contexts" (Kurtz 2007:412). Biologically, there is even evidence to suggest that female bodies are more susceptible to environmental toxins. For example, Buckingham and Kulcur (2009) cite a 2001 report by Physicians for Social Responsibility, which notes that certain groups of fat-soluble toxic chemicals (such as dioxins) more easily bio-accumulate in women who tend to have higher fat ratios than men. These toxins are then likely to be passed on to developing fetuses and babies through the placenta or breast milk. Such findings underscore the importance of differentiating between sex and gender (sex referring to physiological differences between males and females, and gender referring to the social and cultural meaning assigned to people based on their sex). As these authors contend, the notion that "this different experience registers biologically . . . does not equate with it being essentializing" (2009:666). Rather, it stands as a reminder of the complex relationship between biology and socially determined environmental conditions that can amplify or mitigate the impact of environmental harm.

Maternalism

One of the ways that some environmental campaigns, especially in the anti-toxics movement, have sought to gain respect in the male-dominated public sphere is by deploying aspects of maternalism. Maternalism is both an ideology and a philosophy that encompasses a variety of beliefs about women possessing certain "motherly wisdom" or strengths. It asserts that women have special purchase on morality, which makes them especially well suited to lead interventions in political affairs. In the context of environmental movements, maternalism is often used to explain why women have been drawn into environmental politics. Maternalistic narratives often play up the biological differences between men and women, portraying women as uniquely susceptible to the impacts of pollution, especially health problems related to childbearing, such as birth defects and miscarriage. Another common maternalistic narrative focuses on women's work as childcare providers and the narrative of mothers who come together to sound the alarm after noticing their children developing health problems caused by environmental toxicity (Moore 2018). A common critique of maternalistic framing in environmental movements is the tendency for women to be portrayed as either victims or saviors. By painting women as victims, maternalistic framings detract from the notion that women are also empowered individuals who hold politicians and corporations to account for their role in the creation of environmental suffering. The savior role can be equally problematic as it feeds into the already-overwhelming pressure women face to be "good" mothers who successfully protect their children from environmental harms. A study of the Argentinian shantytown of Flammable (a locale surrounded by a large petrochemical compound), for example, found that women with lead-poisoned children faced stigma and were often viewed in the neighborhood as "bad mothers" (Auyero and Swistun 2009:17). Similarly, as Sze (2004) underscores in her research on gender and the politics of childhood asthma, poor women and women of color who have children with asthma are often implicated in their children's illness when public health officials concentrate on indoor household triggers such as dust mites, cockroaches, and mice. This focus, in turn, leads to critiques of mothers' housekeeping rather than the corporate malfeasance, inadequate government regulations, and systemic failures that result in poor outdoor air quality (Sze 2004:185).

Ecofeminism

Another notable body of scholarship with ramifications for women and environmental mobilization focuses on ecofeminism (also known as ecological feminism), a branch of feminism with roots in the French tradition of feminist theory. Françoise d'Eaubonne (1920–2005), a French feminist author and activist, coined the term *l'eco-féminisme* in her book *Le Féminisme ou la Mort*, in which she argues that many parallels exist between the subjugation of women under patriarchal social systems and the destruction of the natural world. In the years since, numerous scholars have built upon d'Eaubonne's original argument to create a body of academic work known as ecofeminist theory. Generally speaking, ecofeminism emphasizes the connections between women and the natural world, arguing that the same patriarchal structures responsible for the domination of women are also heavily implicated in the destruction of the natural world. Thus, many ecofeminists assert that the solution to ecological destruction involves a turn away from a worldview that centers domination, extraction, and linear and mechanistic forms of thinking and toward one that centers the earth and its systems as sacred.

Ecofeminism first became an important perspective within alternative environmental groups in the early 1980s, when ecofeminist ideas helped inspire women's peace tactics like the marches on the Pentagon in the United States and the camp at Greenham Common in England (Gottlieb 2005:304). As Gottlieb (2005:305) notes, however, ecofeminists generally lacked connections to activists in the antitoxics movement, which was "one of the most dynamic forces shaping environmental politics in the 1980s and early 1990s", and women in antitoxic groups did not typically see themselves as feminists. Later, connections were forged between ecofeminists, environmental justice activists, indigenous movements, and some mainstream environmental groups as part of the global climate justice movement (Grosse 2019:185). Thus, ecofeminism remains an influential perspective, and many of its core tenets have been adopted by and integrated into environmental movements.

An example of this can be seen in the calls from leftist environmental groups for a radical restructuring of how humans relate to the natural world. For example, Extinction Rebellion, an international, non-violent, direct-action climate group, has called repeatedly for the transition to a "regenerative" society, one that ends domination of nature as well as other forms of domination and hierarchy. Similarly, Rising Tide, an international network of climate justice activists, echoes ecofeminist ideas regarding the connection between the oppression of humans and the earth in their statement of core principles:

> We believe climate change can only be addressed by exposing the intersections between the oppressions of humans and the earth. . . . The people hardest hit by climate-induced natural disasters have been and will continue to be those most disenfranchised by our society and least responsible for the emission of greenhouse gases: the poor, women, and people of colour.
>
> (Rising Tide North America 2007)

Together, these two groups exemplify the ways in which ecofeminism – while not launching a full-fledged mass mobilization – has significantly shaped other environmental groups, especially within the radical left wing of the broader environmental movement.

Climate justice

In recent years, the idea of environmental justice has been extended to the issue of climate change, with activists around the world arguing that large, developed nations must take responsibility for their historic and present carbon footprint. One way this has been emphasized by transnational climate movements is through the use of "climate justice" framing. Frames are forms of "cognitive schemata", which assist movement actors in making sense of situations by focusing attention, attributing blame, identifying solutions, and motivating participation (Benford and Snow 2000; Snow 2004, 2013). In the case of the climate movement, gravitation toward climate justice occurred in the wake of the perceived failure to achieve binding and sufficiently aggressive climate commitments at the 2009 United Nations Climate Change Summit in Copenhagen. According to della Porta and Parks (2014:7), making the notion of climate justice central had two main effects: first, it broadened the view of the problem and encouraged local action as opposed to a singular focus on international channels; second, the linking of climate to "justice" allowed the movement to bridge its concerns with other issues pertaining to social justice.

Framing climate change as a problem that requires primarily technical and economic solutions leaves little room for including gender equity issues. However, by drawing on the frame of climate justice, activists were able to foreground the gendered aspects of the climate crisis. There is little disagreement among scholars that women and girls – especially those who live in the Global South – are, and will continue to be, disproportionately impacted by climate change (Lambrou and Piana 2006; Neumayer and Plümper 2007). There are a myriad of reasons for this, which ultimately boil down to the reality that, cross culturally, women experience gendered inequities in access to land, livelihood, and security. This, in turn, increases their vulnerability during times of social disruption that may occur as a result of the impacts of climate change. One striking example of this is the case of the 2004 Asian tsunami. A survey of badly affected Indonesian villages found that between 70 and 80% of victims were female. The authors of the report explain this disparity by noting that women were more likely to have been at home when the tsunami hit. Moreover, their escape was likely slowed as they attempted to save their children and other dependents. Additionally, the report notes that women in the region were also much less likely to know how to swim (Oxfam International 2005). As climate change leads to such severe weather events, it is almost certain that women will fare worse than men. Such disparities are further exacerbated by unequal access to participation in climate-related planning and decision making (UNDP 2019). Against this backdrop, activists have increasingly called for the prioritization of gender justice under the umbrella of climate justice. At the movement level, mainstream organizations like 350.org and the Sierra Club have adopted the language of climate justice and are increasingly using that frame in tandem with a focus on gender equity.

Gender and movement tactics

Social movement tactics are the forms of collective action used by movements with the aim of "influencing and coercing one or more of opponents, the general public, and fellow movement activists" (Doherty 2013:652). Tactics are critical to the success of social movements, and women's presence in environmental movements has greatly shaped the tactics embraced by some of the most dynamic elements of the movement. For example, in the case of the Pittsburgh-based clean-air group GASP, women worked to mobilize their community by hosting events such as bake sales and cookbook fundraisers (Longhurst 2010). These events, reminiscent of the activities of other predominantly women-led volunteer groups such as parent-teacher associations, served as approachable, low-stakes gateways for engaging more people in the fight for better air quality. At the same time, women have also successfully deployed confrontational tactics such as marches, sit-ins, and occupations in order to compel concessions from their opponents and galvanize public support for environmental causes. Consider the example of Dollie Burwell, who helped lead six weeks of marches and blockades to stop the dumping of toxic waste at the Warren County landfill, or the case of Julia Butterfly Hill, who fought to stop the clear-cutting of redwood forests by establishing a tree sit lasting for 738 days.

Recently, young women have emerged as leaders of the transnational climate movement. Before August 2017, Greta Thunberg was just another teenager alarmed by the climate crisis and her government's failure to act appropriately. Today, she is one of the most recognized climate activists in the world. Her viral solo protest outside the Swedish Parliament served as inspiration for the grassroots school strike movement (Fridays for Future), a movement that has now spread internationally. During the week of 20 September 2019, it is estimated that close to six million people took part in climate strikes and school walkouts (Taylor et al. 2019). Around the world, children and youth walked out of school and into the streets to protest the failure of adults to adequately address the climate crisis. To some social movement scholars, this unprecedented level of youth protest activity signals a reinvigoration of civic engagement among young people. And importantly, there is a discernible gendered pattern to this activity. As Dana Fisher observed recently, "Something different is happening here. We have a new wave of contention in society that's being led by women. . . . And the youth climate movement is leading this generational shift" (quoted in Kaplan 2019). Fisher, who surveyed more than 100 US organizers of the 2019 climate strike found that 68% of organizers and 58% of strike participants identified as female. Additionally, her survey results indicated that more than a third of protesters identified as people of color – a proportion that reflects the racial makeup of the US population (Fisher 2019a).

As Fisher notes, the school strike tactic builds on a range of well-known tactics employed by social movements for decades (e.g., sit-ins, walkouts, strikes, and die-ins) (Fisher 2019b:430). So why has this tactic taken off in such a short amount of time? Perhaps one explanation has to do with young climate activists' ability to utilize social media platforms to share their activism with large numbers of people. The Sunrise Movement, another youth-based climate change movement, heavily emphasizes the use of technology to amplify the reach of protests through the use of live-streaming on platforms like Facebook, Instagram, and Twitter. Immediately after the US midterm elections in 2018, Sunrisers livestreamed a prolonged sit-in of House Speaker

Nancy Pelosi's office to demand that she and the rest of the Democratic leadership support a "Green New Deal". Here again, the sit-in tactic was well worn, but Sunrise's was able to reach thousands of young people through savvy social media messaging and secure the endorsement of high-profile individuals like Representative Alexandria Ocasio-Cortez. While more research is needed to understand how young women are being drawn into youth climate groups in higher numbers than their male counterparts, the representation of young women as founders and leaders of youth climate organizations – including Jamie Margolin (Zero Hour), Varshini Prakash (Sunrise Movement), and of course, Greta Thunberg (Fridays for Future) – is certainly an important factor.

Conclusion

As we demonstrate throughout this chapter, gender is relevant to all aspects of environmental movement dynamics. Over time, movement participation, framing, and choice of tactics have shifted in response to large-scale changes in the economy and gender roles. For example, many early environmental activists were housewives, a role that allowed for a certain level of biographical availability and lent itself to certain framing of environmental issues, especially as they related to home and the private sphere. As more women moved into the workforce, they extended this same concern for safety and well-being to the environmental hazards encountered at work. As new forms of participation become important, there will be new research questions, such as how early experiences with the climate movement will shape and transform the young female participants who are now becoming leaders and how this new generation of participants will continue to shape and transform the social bases of environmental movements (Giugni and Grasso 2015).

Gender politics affect organizations, campaigns, and coalitions as well. Issue framing is very relevant insofar as certain frames (particularly "justice" frames) provide greater opportunities for different groups to find common ground through issue linking. This, in turn, can contribute to a greater overlap of different movements and communities. Consider, for example, the influence of feminist ideas in the 1970s and early 1980s and the bringing together of peace, feminist, and environmental frames. In the 1990s, the environmental justice frame united various constituents, and the climate justice frame is today critical to the global movement. To be sure, coalitions face enormous challenges when it comes to organizing across race, class, and gender, but frames can play an important role in the facilitation of difficult alliances such as those between labor and environmentalist groups (Giugni and Grasso 2015:345). Future scholarship can examine the newest crop of emerging environmental movements with an eye to the ways in which gender dynamics play out in terms of participation, skill sharing, organization, and tactics.

References

Auyero, Javier and Swistun, Débora Alejandra. 2009. *Flammable*. Oxford: Oxford University Press.
Bell, Shannon. 2013. *Our Roots Run Deep as Ironweed: Appalachian Women and the Fight for Environmental Justice*. Urbana, Chicago and Springfield: University of Illinois Press.
Bell, Shannon and Braun, Yvonne A. 2010. Coal, Identity, and the Gendering of Environmental Justice Activism in Central Appalachia. *Gender & Society*, 24(6), pp. 794–813.
Benford, Robert D. and Snow, David A. 2000. Framing Processes and Social Movements: An Overview and Assessment. *Annual Review of Sociology*, 26(1), pp. 611–639.
Berry, Evan. 2015. *Devoted to Nature: The Religious Roots of American Environmentalism*. Oakland: University of California Press.

Brown, Phil and Ferguson, Faith T. 1995. 'Making a Big Stink': Women's Work, Women's Relationships, and Toxic Waste Activism. *Gender and Society*, 9(2), pp. 145–172.

Buckingham, Susan and Kulcur, Rakibe. 2009. Gendered Geographies of Environmental Injustice. *Antipode*, 41(4), pp. 659–683.

Cable, Sherry. 1992. Women's Social Movement Involvement: The Role of Structural Availability in Recruitment and Participation Processes. *The Sociological Quarterly*, 33(1), pp. 35–50.

della Porta, Donatella and Parks, Louisa. 2014. Framing Processes in the Climate Movement: From Climate Change to Climate Justice. In: M. Dietz and H. Garrelts, eds., *The Routledge Handbook of the Climate Change Movement*. Abingdon: Routledge, pp. 19–30.

Desmarais, Annette. 2003. The Via Campesina: Peasant Women at the Frontiers of Food Sovereignty. *Canadian Woman Studies*, 23(1), pp. 140–145.

Desmarais, Annette. 2007. *La Vía Campesina: Globalization and the Power of Peasants*. Ann Arbor, MI: Pluto Press.

Di Chiro, Giovanna. 1992. Defining Environmental Justice: Women's Voices and Grassroots Politics. *Socialist Review*, 22(4), pp. 93–130.

Doherty, Brian. 2013. Tactics. In: D. Snow, D. della Porta, B. Klandermans and D. McAdam eds., *The Blackwell Encyclopedia of Social and Political Movements*. Malden, MA: Blackwell Publishing Ltd.

Fisher, Dana. 2019a. *American Resistance: From the Women's March to the Blue Wave*. New York: Columbia University Press.

Fisher, Dana. 2019b. The Broader Importance of #Fridaysforfuture. *Nature Climate Change*, 9(6), pp. 430–431.

Foster, S. 1998. Justice from the Ground Up: Distributive Inequities, Grassroots Resistance, and the Transformative Politics of the Environmental Justice Movement. *California Law Review*, 86(4), p. 775.

Giugni, M. and Grasso, M.T. 2015. Environmental Movements in Advanced Industrial Democracies: Heterogeneity, Transformation, and Institutionalization. *Annual Review of Environment and Resources*, 40(1), pp. 337–361.

Gottlieb, Robert. 2005. *Forcing the Spring: The Transformation of the American Environmental Movement*. Revised and Updated Edition. Washington, DC: Island Press.

Green Belt Movement. 2020. Our History | The Green Belt Movement. *Greenbeltmovement.org* [online]. Available at: https://greenbeltmovement.org/who-we-are/our-history [Accessed 5 May 2020].

Grosse, Corrie. 2019. Ecofeminism and Climate Justice. In: J. Reger, ed., *Nevertheless, They Persisted: Feminisms and Continued Resistance in the U.S. Women's Movement*. New York: Routledge, pp. 185–203.

Kaplan, Sarah. 2019. Teen Girls Are Leading the Climate Strikes and Helping Change the Face of Environmentalism. *Washington Post* [online]. Available at: www.washingtonpost.com/science/2019/09/24/teen-girls-are-leading-climate-strikes-helping-change-face-environmentalism/ [Accessed 13 May 2020].

Krauss, Celene. 1993. Women and Toxic Waste Protests: Race, Class and Gender as Resources of Resistance. *Qualitative Sociology*, 16(3), pp. 247–262.

Kurtz, Hilda E. 2003. Scale Frames and Counter-Scale Frames: Constructing the Problem of Environmental Injustice. *Political Geography*, 22(8), pp. 887–916.

Kurtz, Hilda E. 2005. Alternative Visions for Citizenship Practice in an Environmental Justice Dispute. *Space and Polity*, 9(1), pp. 77–91.

Kurtz, Hilda E. 2007. Gender and Environmental Justice in Louisiana: Blurring the Boundaries of Public and Private Spheres. *Gender, Place & Culture*, 14(4), pp. 409–426.

Lambrou, Yianna and Piana, Grazia. 2006. *Gender: The Missing Component of the Response to Climate Change*. Rome: Food and Agriculture Organization of the United Nations.

Longhurst, James. 2010. *Citizen Environmentalists*. Medford, MA: Tufts University Press.

Maathai, Wangari. 2006. *The Green Belt Movement*. New York: Lantern Books.

Mann, Susan A. 2011. Pioneers of US Ecofeminism and Environmental Justice. *Feminist Formations*, 23(2), pp. 1–25.

McAdam, Doug. 1986. Recruitment to High-Risk Activism: The Case of Freedom Summer. *American Journal of Sociology*, 92(1), pp. 64–90.

McGurty, Eileen. 2009. *Transforming Environmentalism: Warren County, PCBs, and the Origins of Environmental Justice*. New Brunswick, NJ: Rutgers University Press.

Merchant, Carolyn. 2007. *American Environmental History: An Introduction*. New York: Columbia University Press.

Mohai, Paul, Pellow, David and Roberts, J. Timmons. 2009. Environmental Justice. *Annual Review of Environment and Resources*, 34(1), pp. 405–430.

Moore, Niamh. 2018. Refiguring Motherhood and Maternalism in Ecofeminism. In: T. Marsden ed., *The Sage Handbook of Nature: Three Volume Set*. London: Sage Publications Ltd, pp. 780–794.

Neumayer, Eric and Plümper, Thomas. 2007. *The Gendered Nature of Natural Disasters: The Impact of Catastrophic Events on the Gender Gap in Life Expectancy, 1981–2002. Annals of the Association of American Geographers*, 97(3), pp. 551–566.

Oxfam International. 2005. *The Tsunami's Impact on Women*. Oxfam Briefing Note. Oxfam International, pp. 1–14 [online]. Available at: https://oxfamilibrary.openrepository.com/bitstream/handle/10546/115038/bn-tsunami-impact-on-women-250305en.pdf?sequence=1&isAllowed=y#:~:text=Many%20women%20also%20lost%20their,with%20them%20at%20the%20time.&text=Figures%20collated%20by%20Oxfam%20for,in%20the%20worst%20affected%20districts [Accessed 5 March 2020].

Rising Tide North America. 2007. *Principles* [online]. Available at: https://risingtidenorthamerica.org/features/principles/ [Accessed 4 June 2020].

Rome, Adam. 2006. 'Political Hermaphrodites': Gender and Environmental Reform in Progressive America. *Environmental History*, 11(3), pp. 440–463.

Shabecoff, Philip. 2003. *A Fierce Green Fire*. Revised Edition. Washington, DC: Island Press.

Shantz, Jeffrey. 2002. Judi Bari and 'The Feminization of Earth First!': The Convergence of Class, Gender and Radical Environmentalism. *Feminist Review*, 70(1), pp. 105–122.

Snow, David A. 2004. Framing Processes, Ideology, and Discursive Fields. In: D. Snow, S. Soule and H. Kriest, eds., *Blackwell Companion to Social Movement*. Oxford: Blackwell, pp. 380–412.

Snow, David A. 2013. Framing and Social Movements. In: D. Snow, D. della Porta, B. Klandermans and D. McAdam, eds., *Wiley-Blackwell Encyclopedia of Social and Political Movements*. Oxford: Wiley-Blackwell, pp. 70–475.

Snow, David A., Zurcher, Louis and Ekland-Olson, Sheldon. 1980. Social Networks and Social Movements: A Microstructural Approach to Differential Recruitment. *American Sociological Review*, 45(5), pp. 787–801.

Stover, Kayla and Cable, Sherry. 2017. American Women's Environmental Activism. In: H. McCammon, V. Taylor, J. Reger and R. Einwohner, eds., *Oxford Handbook of US Women's Social Movement Activism*. New York: Oxford University Press, pp. 685–707.

Szasz, Andrew. 1994. *Ecopopulism: Toxic Waste and the Movement for Environmental Justice*. Minneapolis: University of Minnesota Press.

Sze, Julie. 2004. Gender, Asthma Politics, and Urban Environmental Justice Activism. In: R. Stein, ed., *New Perspectives on Environmental Justice: Gender, Sexuality, and Activism*. London: Rutgers University Press, pp. 177–190.

Tarrow, Sidney. 2011. *Power in Movement: Social Movements and Contentious Politics*. Revised and Updated Third Edition. New York: Cambridge University Press.

Taylor, Dorceta E. 1997. Women of Color, Environmental Justice, and Ecofeminism. In: K. J. Warren, ed., *Ecofeminism: Women, Culture, Nature*. Bloomington: Indiana University Press.

Taylor, Dorceta E. 2016. *The Rise of the American Conservation Movement: Power, Privilege, and Environmental Protection*. Durham, NC: Duke University Press.

Taylor, Matthew, Watts, Jonathan and Bartlett, John. 2019. Climate Crisis: 6 Million People Join Latest Wave of Global Protests. *The Guardian* [online]. Available at: www.theguardian.com/environment/2019/sep/27/climate-crisis-6-million-people-join-latest-wave-of-worldwide-protests [Accessed 29 April 2020].

UNDP. 2019. *Human Development Report 2019: Beyond Income, Beyond Averages, Beyond Today: Inequalities in Human Development in the 21st Century*. United Nations Development Programme. Available at: http://hdr.undp.org/en/content/human-development-report-2019 [Accessed 5 April 2020].

Unger, Nancy. 2012. *Beyond Nature's Housekeepers: American Women in Environmental History*. New York: Oxford University Press.

Via Campesina. 2007. *Nyéléni Declaration*. Sélingué: Forum for Food Sovereignty [online]. Available at: www.foodandwaterwatch.org/world/global-trade/NyeleniDeclaration-en.pdf/view [Accessed 15 February 2020].

Vivas, Esther. 2012. Without Women There Is No Food Sovereignty. *International Viewpoint*. Available at: https://esthervivas.com/english/without-women-there-is-no-food-sovereignty/ [Accessed 28 January 2020].

Washington Post. 1982. Dumping on the Poor. *Washington Post* [online]. Available at: www.washingtonpost.com/archive/politics/1982/10/12/dumping-on-the-poor/bb5c9b8c-528a-45b0-bd10–874da288cd59/ [Accessed 10 April 2020].

Wong, K. 2019. Beautiful Water Speaks. *Sierra Club*, 2 November [online]. Available at: www.sierraclub.org/sierra/2019-6-november-december/faces-clean-energy/how-be-stewards-land [Accessed 14 March 2019].

29

ENVIRONMENTAL ACTIVISM AND EVERYDAY LIFE

Francesca Forno and Stefan Wahlen

Introduction

Environmental activism is traditionally associated with specific environmental movement organizations (EMOs). It is generally agreed that there were surges of environmental protest in the 1970s and especially in the late 1980s and that these fed the rise of EMOs and other environmental NGOs. Over the last few decades, much scholarly attention has been devoted to what has become known as the institutionalization of environmentalism as well as to the formation of new groups and to the development of new forms of protest (Rootes, 2003; Giugni & Grasso, 2015). Along with these changes, and more recently, however, we have also witnessed the spread of a number of everyday environmental practices that appear to challenge traditional conceptualizations of environmental collective action. While some environmental movement organizations have remained focused on national or supranational policy battles, others have increasingly become involved in actions that appear to bypass policy-oriented activism, focusing instead on the idea of a self-changing society as part of the politics of everyday life (Schlosberg & Craven, 2019). Broadly stated, environmental activism has expanded its repertoire of actions, increasingly taking place through informal groups and networks, which promote individualized-collective actions (Micheletti, 2003) such as boycott, buycott, and alternative/sustainable lifestyles.

The growing importance of such forms of action is also reflected by an increasing number of studies that focus on different forms of everyday activism emerging from people's concerns associated to the unsustainability of contemporary consumption and production patterns (Haenfler et al., 2012; Stolle & Micheletti, 2013; Forno & Graziano, 2014; Schlosberg & Coles, 2015; Wahlen & Laamanen, 2015; de Moor, 2017; Schlosberg & Craven, 2019). Although collective action research has usually focused more on "visible" forms of mobilizations and major social changes (Melucci, 1989), scholarly debates and empirical research increasingly identify rather invisible "everyday life" practices as significant to understand contemporary citizens' political involvement. Scholars of social movements and collective action are more and more acknowledging everyday life as an important "locus for change" from which to understand contemporary mobilization and politicization. Forms of environmental activism embedded in daily life include different variants of individual market-based actions such as "political consumerism" (Micheletti, 2003; Bostrom, 2019) and lifestyles choice (e.g., being vegan) (Jallinoja et al., 2019)

DOI: 10.4324/9780367855680-33

as well as more communal ecological practices such as urban gardening, permaculture, alternative food networks, and community energy and housing projects (Forno & Graziano, 2014; Monticelli & della Porta, 2019; Schlosberg & Coles, 2015).

This chapter focuses on the interplay between everyday life and environmental activism. We start by discussing how environmental everyday activism politicizes three key facets of everyday life: time, space, and modality (Felski, 1999) to enlace individualized-collective action. After this more general and introductory part, we will discuss through the lens of social movement theory *why*, *how*, and *when* everyday practices started to be increasingly utilized as a way to address environmental problems. Following, we will exemplify two different paths that everyday environmental activism has taken in the attempt to set up alternative structures for new material flows (Schlosberg & Craven, 2019). The chapter concludes by discussing the potentials as well as the limits of everyday environmental activism.

Environmental activism and the time, space, and modality facets of everyday life

Everyday life is often understood as an inconspicuous "private sphere". This might have confined everyday actions as a rather residual theme within environmental activism for a long time. Yet interest in the role of daily practices in (re-)producing environmental problems has grown considerably among social movement organizations over the last decades. Social movement actors promoting everyday environmental activism share the idea of the need to abandon ecologically destructive practices of consumption and production to favor more sustainable ways of living. Such a perspective claims everyday life activities coming across not only in individual or symbolic dimensions but also in a material one, as they silently contribute to making up the world. Increasing awareness of the social and environmental consequences (what is often defined as the "true cost") of ordinary daily actions such as shopping, cooking and eating, travelling, etc. represents for an increasing number of environmental movement organizations a necessary step to (re)engage people to challenge the status quo and act in favor of the environment. In other words, the unsustainability of contemporary society should not be a phenomenon solely associated with the political arena or corporate strategies, trade, and investment but also with everyday life.

Undoubtedly, such development goes hand in hand with policies of economic liberalization (including privatization, deregulation, globalization, free trade, austerity, and reductions in government spending), which advocate for an increase in the role of the private sector in the economy and society and which are often supported by individualist theorizing (e.g., economist or psychological) that emphasizes individual consumers responsibility (Wahlen, 2012). As critics of everyday forms of activism have often highlighted (Bluhdorn, 2014; Maxton-Lee, 2020), by supporting the idea that citizens, in their role of consumers, have to take over responsibilities for their (economic) action toward more green or sustainable development, discourses promoting changes toward sustainability in everyday life appear, in fact, very much in line with certain neoliberal conceptualizations of the role of the state, market, and society. Indeed, instead of controlling companies' operations, many institutions such as nation-states, international organization, and local administrative bodies are today very keen to promote changes toward sustainability in everyday life, such as recycling, reducing energy and water consumption in households, waste reduction, ecological models of transportation, adoption of "sustainable diets", etc.

In contrast to top-down interventions, in which institutions set goals and implement strategies, bottom-up efforts do not just aim at increasing "consumer sovereignty" and responsibility. Bottom-up initiatives advocate for a profound criticism about how life is organized in advanced capitalist societies (Dal Gobbo, 2022). Such argumentation considers a transformation of every-day life by increasing commodification and privatization as progressively limiting the autonomy of people to choose the lives they want to live by spreading economic insecurity, fragmentation, disengagement, and lower levels of well-being and physical health (Forno & Wahlen, 2022). By putting everyday actions at the center of their discourses, environmental activists recognize that present ecological problems need to be understood as the outcome of a complex system of relations that find their support on a broadly accepted and institutionally secured "imperial mode of living" (Brand & Wissen, 2012): an unsustainable way of life that is embedded and embodied in everyday interactions among peoples and between people and nature. The construction of discourses and narratives able to enhance individualized-collective actions to support the establishment of new networks of everyday social (and economic) relations is a central activity for actors promoting everyday forms of activism. In such efforts, lots of work is devoted to re-signifying the often-taken-for-granted routine and invisible everydayness of "the quotidian" reworking the three facets of everyday life (Felski, 1999): time (routine temporality), space (spatial ordering). and modality (habits) (Figure 29.1).

Time

The way time relates to the environment, economy, and society holds a central position in the discourses and practices of environmental activism. As Felski has argued (1999: 81), the "every-day" is linked to the temporality, rhythm, and repetition of people's daily actions. It comprises activities such as sleeping, eating, working, commuting, etc. Currently, a growing number of grassroots initiatives promote a more conscious use of time and slower lifestyles, claiming that the unsustainability of contemporary societies needs to be linked to the way in which people use their time. Such a perspective stresses time as inextricably interrelated with peoples' lived experience and modes of social reproduction. The time use of individuals has several environmental consequences. Contemporary accelerated society (Rosa, 2003) has produced a *modus vivendi* that demands an increasing use of energy and water while producing enormous amounts of waste. Time has been reduced to an economic resource in line with modern thinking toward progress and accumulation in contemporary society. Rethinking time, it is claimed, is fundamental to building an effective response to sustainability challenges. Therefore, in putting time at the center of their discourses and actions, everyday activists emphasize the need to slow down and to reverse the trend toward increasing acceleration of everyday activities that are seen as connected with the economic growth imperative (Latouche, 2009) and not compatible with the need to stay within planetary boundaries. Examples are the slow food, slow fashion, simplicity, downsizing and degrowth movements, which are all promoting individualized collective actions such as slow travelling, slow eating, and slow living in order to promote sustainability. In all these efforts, everyday life is propagated to change toward a mode of living that does not harm the environment for current as well as for future generations. As Parkins and Craig (2006) explain, slowness is also used as a means of critiquing or challenging dominant narratives or values that characterize contemporary modernity.

Space

Everyday life inevitably takes place in social contexts that are constructed and reproduced through everyday activities. Everyday environmental activism has highlighted how processes of commodification and privatization have increasingly invaded important aspects of social reproduction (Hochschild, 2012). Individual choices are ever more dependent on economic resources. In such a context, micro-social activities such as sharing, bartering, DIY, growing food together in a public garden, etc. are interpreted and promoted as a sort of everyday form of resistance to regain autonomy while re-engaging with the material quality of places (Blanc, 2019). Moreover, when used collectively, such practices help give rise to and support "experimental laboratories" (Melucci, 1996) for collective learning and bottom-up democracy (Meyer & Kersten, 2016; Schlosberg & Coles, 2015). Within everyday environmental activism discourses, the home is a space of particular importance. The home is often recognized as the place where, for example, food culture and related competences of choosing, preparing and tasting food are transmitted and preserved. All these activities have important consequences with regard to sustainability and the use of resources such as nutrients, water, electricity, etc. Here, by acknowledging the political character of often-disregarded household activities, everyday environmentalism aims to stimulate actions such as "buycotting" ("positive buying") to build new alliances in order to (re)connect environmentalism to the wider community. Choosing the food to buy from a local farmer or even growing your own food with the aim to "take back the economy" (Gibson-Graham et al., 2014) are currently types of actions increasingly adopted by social movement organizations to promote more sustainable practices of consumption or production (Pelenc et al., 2019). In other words, by (re)appropriating and (re)signifying the residues of work and time through "subterranean practices" (in the sense of not being immediately visible), everyday environmentalism aims to forge alternative, productive, and sustainable flows of resources (Schlosberg & Craven, 2019). To this type of activism, thus, "the everyday" affords the space in which individuals can not only regain control over their lives but also start to build alternatives that oppose "environmental bads" by promoting "environmental goods" (de Moor et al., 2021).

Modality

Everyday life also manifests in habitual behavior as modality. Habit refers to both action and attitude. Everyday environmentalism aims to directly impact detrimental material flow by creating and supporting the adoption of sustainable alternative practices. This is an interesting contrast to earlier environmental mobilization, which used to engage in conflict through contentious action. Contemporary everyday environmentalism's efforts at changing people's actions and attitude come across on three levels of action: cultural, economic, and political (Forno & Graziano, 2014). On a cultural level, everyday environmentalism promotes alternative values practices (Centemeri, 2018) to oppose consumerism as an economic order that encourages the endless consumption of finite resources in the name of exponential economic growth. Actors in everyday environmentalism promote and create "new social imaginaries" (Asara, 2020) through the organization of various activities such as festivals, conferences, guided visits to local producers, farmers' markets, and a skillful use of new and old media. All these activities appear fundamental in order to generate, sustain, and spread not only alternative projects but also a different conception of what has to be understood as "good life". On an economic level, these experiences encourage greater economic self-sufficiency as well as attempt to facilitate the construction and sustainability of alternative economic circuits. They favor services and products that respect certain ethical and environmental standards, such as fair trade and recycled goods, and the consumption of local, seasonal, fresh, traditional, and often organic produce. Attention is also paid to supporting supplies from renewable energy sources to reduce reliance on fossil fuels (insulation, efficient appliances, carpooling, and community transport). In so doing, the aim is to bring different collectives together to help them develop alternative socio-economic systems in which the overriding object of profit maximization is substituted with cooperation,

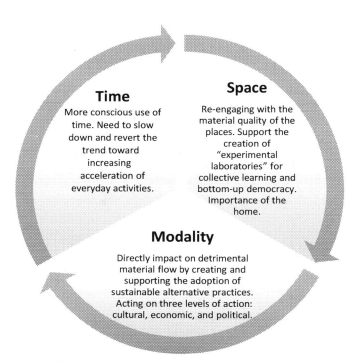

Time

More conscious use of time. Need to slow down and revert the trend toward increasing acceleration of everyday activities.

Space

Re-engaging with the material quality of the places. Support the creation of "experimental laboratories" for collective learning and bottom-up democracy. Importance of the home.

Modality

Directly impact on detrimental material flow by creating and supporting the adoption of sustainable alternative practices. Acting on three levels of action: cultural, economic, and political.

Figure 29.1   Time, space, and modality facets of everyday activism

solidarity, and mutualism. The alternative economic networks set in place are important to facilitate both the circulation of resources (information, tasks, money, and goods) and the construction of common interpretations of reality, thus simultaneously providing a framework for collective action and enabling the actual deployment of alternative lifestyles (Forno et al., 2015). Everyday environmental activism aims to develop and sustain innovative models of environmental regulatory governance through the promotion of political consumerism and sustainable lifestyles and based on citizen participation in bottom-up processes. Even though organizations do not mobilize and structure their claims primarily through contentious activities, to a certain extent, the contentious dimension of these networks can be seen as embedded in their social and economic networking modalities. Put differently, it is through solidarity exchanges that these organizations support strategies of "direct action" (Bosi & Zamponi, 2015).

Mobilizing everyday life to save the planet: why, when, and how

The fact that social movement organizations choose their tactics and organizational structures according to the desired end and by considering the system of opportunities characterizing the external environment within which they find themselves operating has been long acknowledged (Wahlstrom & Peterson, 2006). Mobilization is the outcome of a complex process of interactions that involve different types of actors. Social movement actions are, in fact, conditioned (facilitated or hindered) by a variety of factors (Giugni & Grasso, 2020). To explain mobilization, its characteristics, and its dynamics, scholars of social movements consider different influences by focusing both on exogenous factors, such as main socio-economic alterations or shifts having occurred in the configuration of power, and on endogenous factors, considering challengers' resources and framing capacities. In order to better grasp the characteristics and growing importance of everyday activism within pro-environmental mobilization, we will, in what follows, use social movement theory to pose three questions to better understand mobilization of and in everyday life by environmental activism: *why*, *when*, and *how*.

Why mobilize everyday life?

The modern repertoire of protest continues to be part of strategies widely utilized in conflict situations. Forms of mobilization tend to remain stable over time (Tilly, 1984, 1986); however, sustainable practices of consumption and lifestyles are increasingly thought of as a way to bring about pro-environmental change. Such a shift can be read as a further adaptation to the changing balance of opportunities and constraints contemporary movements are confronted with (Balsiger, 2014; Forno & Graziano, 2014). In particular, processes of globalization, commoditization, individualization, and privatization have led to significant changes in the way people construct their personal identities, often described as "liquid" (Bauman, 2000), as well as the material world they need to confront (Beck & Gernsheim, 2009). Some forms of protest (such as the strike) have become less effective with the greater ease in the movement of goods and services as well as increased economic competition, while limiting the political and redistributive capacity of nation-states. The transformation of traditional channels of interest mediation (especially political parties and trade unions) and the end of the great ideological narratives of the twentieth century (the traditional ideologies of left and right) have made collective action more difficult to organize and sustain. This shift seems to have pushed social movement organizations toward the identification of new sites and forms of pressure and a greater use of everyday forms of actions.

There are at least two possible yet interrelated reasons *why* environmental movement actors are increasingly instigating people to take action in their everyday lives. The first relates to the fact that in order to be effective, social movements' strategies need to be emotionally and morally salient in people's lives (Jasper, 1997) and to the role played in advanced capitalist societies by consumption and lifestyles in the definition of people's identities (Bauman, 1991; Beck, 1992; Giddens, 1991). From this point of view, it can be argued that given the centrality taken on by consumption in late capitalist societies, it should not be a surprise that many contemporary social movement organizations have increasingly started to appeal to individuals in their role as consumers. The second reason can be found in environmental actors' frustration and the difficulties of bringing about environmental change. In other words, everyday environmental activism should be understood as a way for contemporary environmental movement organizations to face two challenges: firstly, (re)building social bonds of solidarity and cooperation necessary for collective action in a highly individualized society (D'Alisa et al., 2015; Forno & Graziano, 2014), and secondly, confronting institutions that are less able (or willing) to mediate new demands for social and environmental justice. It is in this context that everyday life actions as politically inspired acts of consumption and lifestyle choices have become an important component of contemporary environmental movements' repertoire of actions.

The facets of everyday environmental activism assist us in fully grasping the peculiarities and potentials of such repertoire shifts. More specifically, the *modus operandi* of sustainable practices of consumption (including so-called anti-consumption practices: e.g., reusing, recycling/upcycling, DIY, making things last, etc.) can be distinguished from other forms of protest as they not only move the locus of conflict from the state and street to market and the everyday but also incorporate the three logics of protest of the modern repertoire of action at the same time: the logics of numbers, damage, and bearing witness (della Porta & Diani, 2020). By practicing certain values and actions, everyday environmental activism aims to resocialize wrongdoers aiming to change (or substitute) business activities through the "power of numbers" (DeNardo, 1985). Everyday environmentalism incorporates the logic of numbers, for example, through boycotts. Transnational activists have been able to publicize grievances and build new transnational awareness across borders to pressure corporations. While globalization has stretched the distances between workers and consumers, boycotts have helped individuals consider the conditions under which goods are produced in an increasingly global market (Collins, 2003; Micheletti et al., 2006). In response to boycotts, some major corporations have made efforts to improve working conditions or their environmental standards, either because they feared that transnational campaigns might blemish their image and hurt their sales or because they recognized the validity of activists' concerns (Spar & La Mure, 2003). Moreover, both boycott and buycott campaigns can empower participants by spreading a sense of belonging to a community (Stolle & Micheletti, 2013).

In addition to the logic of numbers, everyday environmentalism also adds to the logic of material or commercial damage (or, alternatively, advantage). By pushing citizens to make use of their purchasing power, for example, environmental movement organizations seek to inflict as much damage as possible on their opponents in a way that is reminiscent of the strike. As when workers block production through strike action to damage the employer and force negotiation, by choosing whether to buy or not to buy a given good or brand, citizens in their role as consumers can damage or encourage producers to change their production policies. Through the strategy of naming and shaming, environmental actors have put the spotlight on the abuse of several multinational companies that were considered "enemies" (Boström, 2019). Among the most famous boycotts in recent years were those against Shell, criticized for polluting the North Sea and the Niger River; Nike, accused of subcontracting production to small enterprises in Indonesia and Vietnam that use child labor; Novartis, condemned for denying life-saving treatment to millions of (poor) people who needed it; and McDonald's, picked out for supposedly using the meat of animals raised extensively on antibiotics (Friedman, 1999; Seidman, 2007). Finally, everyday environmentalism also incorporates the logic of bearing witness. As della Porta and Diani argue, by politicizing everyday actions, grassroots organizations stress "the central role of individuals in taking responsibility for the common goods in their everyday life" (della Porta and Diani, 2020). Moreover, by practicing certain values, social movement activists aim to demonstrate that everyday activities can be important not only as instruments of political protest but also to prefigure and experiment with an alternative and desirable ecological, sustainable society (Goodman et al., 2012; Veron, 2016; Yates, 2015; Pelenc et al., 2019). After all, it is ultimately in the unofficial networks of everyday social relations and activities that new meaning and identities are formed, providing a basis for the politics of opposition (Melucci, 1989). As Alberto Melucci (1989) has emphasised, the everyday life in contemporary society is never far removed from collective action and social change, and the unofficial sphere of everyday life is where processes of social change might begin.

When did everyday actions become mobilized?

Everyday environmental actions are not new. Boycotts in particular were used frequently by environmental movement in the past (Rootes, 2003; Dubuisson-Quellier, 2013). The role of environmental movement organizations was particularly important in the development of buycotts, especially with regard to green labels that, in some countries, date back to the 1980s and even earlier. Particularly in countries such as Austria, Sweden, Germany, the Netherlands, the United Kingdom, and the Nordic countries, environmental organizations were, in fact, crucial in the development of labelling and certification for everyday consumption and also in other sectors, such as forestry (Boström and & Klintman, 2011; Stolle and & Micheletti, 2013). Traditionally, such initiatives have been more widespread in North America and Northern Europe (de Moor & Balsiger, 2019; Katz, 2019). Since the mid-1990s, political consumerism and lifestyle actions have, however, started to grow in contexts in which they had long been a niche phenomenon (Forno & Ceccarini, 2006; Koos, 2012; Ferrer-Fons & Fraile, 2013; Lekakis & Forno, 2019). The spread of everyday forms of environmental activism was strongly influenced by the events that followed the so-called Battle of Seattle (the demonstration against the WTO in 1999 that took place in Seattle, Washington). By identifying the market as a privileged arena for political activism, the Global Justice Movement opened up space for experimentation with consumerist action (della Porta, 2006; Micheletti, 2003). Moreover, the success of some boycott campaigns, as well as of certain movements such as fair trade and the organic movement (Krier, 2006; Wilkinson, 2007), signaled the growing willingness of citizens to act politically in their role as consumers. It was during these years that, for example, the term "political consumerism" became increasingly important both among social movement actors and in academic debate.

The growth of such types of activism in the second half of the 1990s confirms the existence of a close connection between the spread of new forms of action and cycles of mobilization (Freeman & Johnson, 1999; Kriesi et al., 1995; McAdam, 1995; Tarrow, 1998; Traugott, 1995). Cycles of protest are rapid expansions of social movement action on a geographical scale, the diversity of social groups participating, and the amount of disruptive activity. These special "moments of madness" (Tarrow, 1998) occur when multiple social movements or social groups engage in sustained protest clustered over time and spanning a wide geographical boundary (e.g., on a national scale). Although cycles of protest have an irregular frequency and may vary with regard to their duration, studies that have analyzed the temporal evolution of mobilization have often shown that these moments are characterized by 1) the rapid spread of the protest from the more mobilized to less mobilized, 2) the territorial expansion of the conflict, 3) the emergence of new social movement organizations and the re-activation of those more established, 4) the creation of new, dominant interpretive schemes, and 5) the invention of new forms of collective action (Tarrow, 1995). By participating as co-organizers in major social events and protests, from Seattle to Genoa, from the Social Forum to the Marches for Peace, since the late 1990s, the movement organizations involving in boycott and buycott actions increased their centrality among organizations involved in the global justice movement. The joint action in the campaigns and counter-summits of the various organizations active in protests against neoliberal globalization has clearly favored the exchange of content and experiences, on the one hand, and the fertilization of forms of protest among different actors on the other (della Porta, 2003; Diani, 2005). Economic activism appeared to be not only a way to contrast neoliberalization and economic globalization but also an efficient response to the growing interest in global issues as it represented a means to address issues the scope of which is not confined to territorial or national boundaries (Diani, 2005), particularly with regard to the environment.

The cross-fertilization (della Porta & Mosca, 2007) of the repertoires of actions among different SMOs was one of the key features of the anti-globalization mobilization cycle. The diffusion of everyday forms of activism was made possible by the socialization of practices that occurred during the various gatherings that also continued into the 2000s. During this period, practices such as political consumerism began to extend to an increasingly large number of people and actors. After Seattle, political consumerism, in fact, also began to be incorporated in the repertoire of actions by a variety of environmental groups (Micheletti & McFarland, 2011).

However, the global justice movement was rather short lived (della Porta & Mosca, 2007). The lack of institutional allies, the internal and problematic differentiation among the various components of the movement, the violence with which certain demonstrations were repressed, and the disappointment of activists in the negative outcome of the great popular mobilization against the war in Iraq in 2003 led to a rapid decline in transnational mobilization. Nevertheless, the protest cycle developed throughout the 1990s left significant changes in the culture and practices of many social movement organizations and of society at large. Furthermore, when mobilization declined, many activists brought back to their territories not only a different worldview but also a new arsenal of tactics.

The end of the cycle, which scholars date between 2003 and 2005 (della Porta & Mattoni, 2015), took a substantial re-repositioning of some social movement organizations from the global to the local scale of action (Forno & Graziano, 2014). At the local level, everyday activism has continued to spread and expand through initiatives aiming at raising awareness regarding the need for more sustainable lifestyles and for new systems of material flows capable of optimizing production processes so that materials and energy are used more efficiently (Schlosberg & Craven, 2019). In other words, from the beginning of the new century, everyday actions have started to be increasingly utilized not only by environmental movements calling citizens' attention to problems in the global supply chains in order to put pressure on international corporations but also by several community-based initiatives.

How is the organizational structure of everyday activism manifesting?

The spread of everyday forms of activism experienced in the 1990s came across with the development and use among wider sectors of the population of new technologies of communication. A number of successful boycotts during these years were initiated via email and the internet. Particularly well known is the Nike ID sweatshop email controversy, in which an email exchange with a customer pointing toward working conditions was the key example for culture jamming. Through boycotts, transnational activists have publicized grievances and built new transnational awareness across borders to step up pressure on corporations. The use of the internet is particularly important since it has progressively allowed a faster dissemination of detailed information and easier coordination among the various initiatives put forward by different political organizations (Rosenkrands, 2004). Furthermore, between the old and new century, there has also been an incredible increase in the number of published books, manuals, and magazines (both printed and online), webpages, and apps that presented critical assessments of various products, easily increasing information available to consumers about different issues and campaigns.

After the end of the GJM wave of protest, along with more individualized-collective forms of engagement, everyday activism also went beyond the idea of "individual responsibility taking", which is typical of political consumerism (Stolle & Micheletti, 2013) to take more collectivistic forms. This is the case, for example, of new consumer-producer cooperatives, community gardens, eco-communities, solidarity purchasing groups, etc. In all these experiences, everyday actions started to be used as tools to construct collective, citizenship-driven alternative styles of provisioning (Grasseni, 2013) based on a more locally based, collective approach to boycotting, which ultimately aims to search for a comprehensive strategy for social change, in the name of the common good and sustainability (Gibson-Graham, 2006; Conill et al., 2012; Cembalo et al., 2012; Graziano and & Forno, 2012). In other words, rather than being an end in itself, sustainable practices of consumption started to be utilized as a means through which to construct and reinforce solidarity ties in order to implement more collective/communitarian actions around distinct political projects (Diani, 2019).

The re-repositioning of some social movement organizations from the global to the local scale of action observed after the downturn of the GJM can be read in the light of the latency-visibility model (Melucci, 1996). According to this model, networks and activities do persist even when movements are not mobilizing, and it is during these latent phases that new meanings and identities are often forged, and new repertoires of action are put to the test. As Melucci (1985) argues, visibility and latency are mutually constructive. It is, in fact, during the phase of latency that solidarity ties and new cultural frameworks are often created, in turn becoming essential resources for further mobilization and new cycles of contention. To capture such "movement-building dynamics" as well as to better grasp the interaction between various political cultural elements that help sustain such more locally based politicization of the everyday, scholars have used different names: sustainable community movement organizations (Forno & Graziano, 2014), sustainable materialism (Schlosberg & Craven, 2019), alternative actions organizations (Kousis, 2017), and lifestyles movement organization (de Moor, 2017; Haenfler et al., 2012). By politicizing the everyday, such grassroots initiatives create new economic and cultural spaces for civic learning and environmental actions.

Going against some expectations about everyday environmental activism being closely associated with higher levels of wealth, the mushrooming of organizations supporting socially and culturally alternative ways of practicing sustainable economic exchanges observed during the 2007–08 crisis (Conill et al., 2012; Guidi & Andretta, 2015; D'Alisa et al., 2015; Kousis, 2017; Forno & Graziano, 2019) somehow demonstrated that hard times represent a favorable environment for such actions. Everyday environmentalism finds expression in day-to-day activity: for example, buying food directly from producers, going to local markets or swapping food in an urban warehouse, living in an eco-ecovillage, or taking part in a swap group. Such activities seem to represent not only a way to respond to a search for a meaningful life but also a means to help mobilize individuals toward environmental collective action (Kousis, 2017).

Different paths of everyday environmental activism

Everyday environmentalism that acknowledges temporality, space, and modality of day-to-day action might provide novel vistas of how social movement organizations consider their tactics and opportunities. The turn to locally based projects can be seen as a cyclical feature for social movements linked to the declining phase of mobilization after the global justice movement (Forno & Graziano, 2014). After all, the same dynamic was observed after period of mass mobilization as in the 1970s after the 1968 movement (Bosi & Zamponi, 2015). However, as seen before, projects of everyday environmentalism represent a new strategic direction for an environmental movement that worries about the ability of the states and other institutions to solve environmental crises (de Moor et al., 2021). Additionally, the spread of digitalization and new media technologies mean new means available to grassroots actors to communicate not only about environmental causes but also about their day-to-day activities. On the one hand, new social media can assist in mobilizing individuals and, on the other hand, thanks to their bidirectional character, can allow individuals to show how they implement strategies of environmental activity in daily life. In other words, social media facilitate individuals staying connected and, in their individuality, acting together as a dispersed collective. Hence, also thanks to new media infrastructure, everyday environmentalism offers a do-it-yourself approach that does not rely solely on the state or other actors (Stolle & Micheletti, 2013).

As argued by Wahlen and Laamanen (2015), practices of everyday life can give rise and support different forms of mobilization on individual as well as collective levels and across different scales. (See Table 29.1.) Everyday environmental mobilization may refer to more individualist variants such as political consumerism, in which individual actors use their consumption as a political tactic (the so-called "vote with your dollar") or single out people who decide to change their lifestyles by living a "small life" or turn to veganism and freeganism for a given environmental or social reason. Sustainable practices of consumption, however, can also be at the base of more collective activities. In the more collectivistic version, everyday environmental activism expands from products to places (Discetti, 2021), as in the case of people working together and collectively sharing the produce grown in an urban garden or dividing the workload to set up and run community-supported agriculture (CSA) or a solidarity purchasing group to combat global warming associated with industrialized food production. Moreover, individualistic and collectivistic versions of everyday environmentalism seem to implement different strategies for diffusion, even though distinct forms of mobilization might overlap.

Individualist environmental activism generally tries to advance more environmentally friendly behavior, experimenting and setting in place strategies aimed at creating a critical, reflexive moral consciousness on the part of the citizen/consumer. This is the case, for example, of fair trade and environmental labelling schemes and remodeling choice architectures and other specific regulatory systems, as well as green branding partnerships, specific advertising campaigns, and all sorts of creative events such as dedicated fairs and festivals. Considering the three facets of everyday life, individualist activism focuses on mobilization, which is associated with activity and individual behavior. In this sense, individualist environmental activism is often enhanced to promote more efficient practices and linked to regulation that promotes shopping for a difference.

In contrast, collectivist environmental activism often evolves in place-based multisector coalitions, which may or may not involve local authorities. This is, for example, the case in social and solidarity economy networks and food policy councils (FPCs), which are grassroots networks contrasting economic insecurity connected with precarious and low-paid jobs as well as growing environmental problems. By placing questions of production and consumption at the center of their action and engaging people through their everyday life activities, place-based multisector coalitions promote initiatives aiming, on the one hand, to raise awareness regarding the need for a more sustainable lifestyle and, on the other hand, to construct alternative systems of exchange and material flow paths, which are good for workers, the health of consumers, and the environment (Schlosberg & Craven, 2019). In all cases, either in the more individualistic, collectivistic, or even blended variants, the forms of mobilization that emerge in the interplay

Table. 29.1 Types of experiences that emerged in interplay between everyday life and environmentalism

	Forms	*Strategies for diffusion*
Individual	Political consumerism (boycott and buycott), voluntary simplicity, veganism, freeganism, etc.	Fair trade and eco-labelling schemes, green branding partnerships, advertising campaign, fairs and festivals
Collective	Community supported agriculture (CSA), solidarity consumer groups, community gardens, etc.	Place-based multi-sector coalition initiatives such as social and solidarity economy networks, food policy councils, etc.

between everyday life and environmentalism appear to work through a process of horizontal diffusion based on random connectivity rather than patterns and structure, which has been often described as "viral" (Randall, 2013) or "rhizome-like" (Feola & Butt, 2017; Forno & Weiner, 2020).

Conclusion

Environmental activism has for a long time remained centered on macro-level dynamics. Moreover, as many scholars have stressed, environmental movements have undergone a process of institutionalization (Rootes, 2003; Giugni & Grasso, 2015). However, as discussed in this chapter, along with this change, an increasing number of grassroots groups and organizations have recently started promoting practice-based actions emphasizing how micro-actions have macro-results. The focal point lies in the inconspicuousness of everyday life that lays the foundation for social relations and unsustainable (re)production. In order to understand the interplay of environmental activism and everyday life, we need to recognize the facets of everyday life in their political dimensions.

As argued, beyond its different variants, everyday environmental activism shares some common traits. All these experiences start out from a critique of the individualized consumerist lifestyle and support sustainable ways of production and consumption, often based on simpler and more sober lifestyles. Here it is often pointed out that the current standards of consumption damage the environment, contribute to climate change, and unsustainably use up resources. These experiences also tend to share a common understanding that attention is paid excessively to the price of products. This development has undermined the guarantee of labor standards and accentuated exploitation of workers, with the aim of reducing the overall unitary cost of labor. The experiences may differ in many respects; however, they share the idea of the need to abandon ecologically destructive economic systems in favor of more sustainable forms of production based on the valorization and revitalization of the local economy. Modern industrial economies and agricultural systems are accused of damaging both the environment and society, and the solution is to re-reorganize consumption and production in terms of new provisioning systems based on principles of participation and solidarity. Finally, rather than seeking to change the agenda of policy makers, everyday environmental activism mainly aims (both in its more individualists and collectivist variants) to implement value and alternatives, starting from the experience of daily life in the local community and through the network and organizations they set in place.

The everyday as site for environmental action, however, has also faced a number of criticisms. In particular, the focus on self-determination and self-changing strategies was criticized as diverting civic action from real economic and social problems (the so-called "crowding out" thesis), promoting political-ideological formulas that channel social discontent away from the targets, such as national and international institutions. Based on the example of alternative food networks, Goodman et al. (2012) have stressed the limits of lifestyle practices in terms of their transformative potential and efficacy. As often highlighted, proponents of such practices have shown in some cases to be scarcely politicized and more interested in preserving their own health and identity, as well as social status. Similarly, it has been argued that sustainable consumption and lifestyles encounter the risk of remaining a niche phenomenon at the edge of the market, with limited or no impact on how society functions because they can be easily co-opted by corporate marketing strategies (Dubuisson-Quellier, 2019). Yet several reflections on everyday environmental activism have highlighted the speed with which capitalism is able to absorb critiques and demands, transforming them into further commodities to be sold on the market for profit.

With regard to these criticisms, empirical research has shown that alternative ways of living and consuming do not displace other forms of engagement (Adams & Raisborough, 2010). Those engaged in alternative consumption and lifestyles tend to be more active in other forms of political participation. This was also proven true in more collective practices of sustainable procuring and provisioning, as in the case of solidarity-based consumer groups (Forno et al., 2015; Guidi & Andretta, 2015). As the example of new food movements has revealed, building new circulations of localist food economies does not mean abandoning lobbying and protesting as means to push national and transnational reforms of food policy systems. As Schlosberg and Coles (2015) argued: "one form of political engagement does not simply replace other; new materialist political action is not a zero-sum or an either/or" (p. 174). Nevertheless, if empirical research does not support the "crowding out" thesis, the question of whether these practices have the potential to change society or are only a shallow form of participation able at best to give rise to niche communities reinforcing traditional class structures remains open. While suggesting that more conceptual work is needed to understand the political nuances of everyday practices that may still appear as "apolitical", it seems important to recognize that such types of actions are of foremost importance to enhance people's prefigurative power and resistance, especially in an increasingly globalizing and unsustainable consumer society. In other words, everyday practices can be the site where new meanings and identities emerge, which, in turn, might support more visible actions and mobilization in the future. An avenue for future research would be, for example, to interrogate how much of the discourses and practices experimented with in the "new environmentalism of everyday life" are present in the recent wave of climate activism, in particular for activists taking part in large mobilizations by Extinction Rebellion and the Fridays for Future school climate strikes.

References

Adams, Matthew and Raisborough, Jayne (2010) Making a Difference: Ethical Consumption and the Everyday, *British Journal of Sociology*, 61(2): 256–274.

Asara, Viviana (2020) Untangling the Radical Imaginaries of the Indignados' Movement: Commons, Autonomy and Ecologism, *Environmental Politics*, doi:10.1080/09644016.2020.1773176

Balsiger, Philip (2014) Between Shaming Corporations and Promoting Alternatives: The Politics of an 'Ethical Shopping Map', *Journal of Consumer Culture*, 14(2): 218–235.

Bauman, Zygmunt (1991) *Modernity and Ambivalence*, Cambridge: Polity Press.

Bauman, Zygmunt (2000) *Liquid Modernity*, Cambridge: Polity Press.

Beck, Ulrich (1992) *Risk Society: Towards a New Modernity*, London: Sage.

Beck, Ulrich and Beck-Gernsheim, Elisabeth (2009) *Individualization*, London: Sage.

Blanc, Nathalie (2019) From Ordinary Environmentalism to the Public Environment: Theoretical Reflections Based on French and European Empirical Research, *Ecology and Society*, 24(3): 33.

Blühdorn, Ingolfur (2014) Post-Ecologist Governmentality: Post-Democracy, Post-Politics and the Politics of Unsustainability, in *The Post-Political and Its Discontents: Spaces of Depoliticisation, Spectres of Radical Politics*, edited by E. Swyngedouw and J. Wilson, 146–166, Edinburgh: Edinburgh University Press.

Bosi, Lorenzo and Zamponi, Lorenzo (2015) Direct Social Actions and Economic Crises: The Relationship Between Forms of Action and Socio-Economic Context in Italy, *Partecipazione e Conflitto [Participation and Conflict]*, 8(2).

Boström, Magnus (2019) Rejecting and Embracing Brands in Political Consumerism, in *The Oxford Handbook of Political Consumerism*, edited by Magnus Boström, Michele Micheletti and Peter Oosterveer, 205–225, Oxford: Oxford University Press.

Boström, Magnus and Klintman, Mikael (2011) *Eco-Standards, Product Labelling and Green Consumerism*, Houndmills and Basingstoke: Palgrave Macmillan.

Brand, Ulrich and Wissen, Markus (2012) Global Environmental Politics and the Imperial Mode of Living: Articulations of State – Capital Relations in the Multiple Crisis, *Globalizations*, 9(4): 547–560.

Cembalo, Luigi, Migliore, Giuseppina and Schifani, Giorgio (2012) Consumers in Postmodern Society and Alternative Food Networks: The Organic Food Fairs Case in Sicily, *New Medit*, 11(3): 41–49.

Centemeri, Laura (2018) Commons and the New Environmentalism of Everyday Life: Alternative Value Practices and Multispecies Commoning in the Permaculture Movement, *Rassegna italiana di Sociologia*, 64(2): 289–313.

Collins, Jane L. (2003) *Threads: Gender, Labor, and Power in the Global Apparels Industry*. Chicago: University of Chicago Press.

Conill, Joana, Castells, Manuel, Cardenas, Amalia and Servon, Lisa (2012) Beyond the Crisis: The Emergence of Alternative Economic Practices, in *Aftermath: The Cultures of the Economic Crisis*, edited by Manuel Castells, João Caraça and Gustavo Cardoso, 210–250, New York: Oxford University Press.

Dal Gobbo, Alice (2022) Engaging the Everyday: Sustainability, Practices, Politics, in *Handbook of Critical Environmental Politics*, edited by Luigi Pellizzoni, Emanuele Leonardi and Viviana Asara, London: Elgar.

D'Alisa, Giacomo, Forno, Francesca and Maurano, Simon (2015) Grassroots (Economic) Activism in Times of Crisis: Mapping the Redundancy of Collective Actions, *PaCo*, 8(2): 328–342.

della Porta Donatella (2003) *I new global*. Bologna: il Mulino.

della Porta, Donatella (2006) *Globalization from Below: Transnational Activists and Protest Networks*, Minneapolis: University of Minnesota Press.

della Porta, Donatella and Diani, Mario (2020) *Social Movements: An Introduction*, New York: John Wiley & Sons.

della Porta, Donatella and Mattoni, Alice (2015) *Spreading Protest: Social Movements in Times of Crisis*, Colchester: ECPR Press.

della Porta, Donatella and Mosca, Lorenzo (2007) In Movimento: 'Contamination' in Action and the Italian Global Justice Movement, *Global Networks*, 7(1): 1–27.

de Moor, Joost (2017) Lifestyle Politics and the Concept of Political Participation, *Acta Politica*, 52(2): 179–197.

de Moor, Joost and Balsiger, Philip (2019) Political Consumerism in North Western Europe: Leading by Example?, in *The Oxford Handbook of Political Consumerism*, edited by Magnus Boström, Michele Micheletti and Peter Oosterveer, 435–456, New York: Oxford University Press.

de Moor, Joost, Catney, Philip and Doherty, Brian (2021) What Hampers 'Political' Action in Environmental Alternative Action Organizations? Exploring the Scope for Strategic Agency Under Post-Political Conditions, *Social Movement Studies*, 20(3): 312–328.

DeNardo, James (1985) *Power in Numbers: The Political Strategy of Protest and Rebellion*, Princeton, NJ: Princeton University Press.

Diani, Mario (2005) Cities in the World: Local Civil Society and Global Issues in Britain, in *Transnational Protest and Global Activism*, edited by D. della Porta and S. Tarrow, 45–70, Lanham, MD: Rowman & Littlefield.

Diani, Mario (2019) Modes of Coordination in Political Consumerism, in *The Oxford Handbook of Political Consumerism*, edited by Magnus Boström, Michele Micheletti and Peter Oosterveer, 89–109, Oxford: Oxford University Press.

Discetti, Roberta (2021) Campaigning for Sustainable Food: Sustainably Certified Consumer Communities, *British Food Journal*, 123(3): 958–973.

Dubuisson-Quellier, Sophie (2013) *Ethical Consumption*, Winnipeg: Fernwood Publishing.

Dubuisson-Quellier, Sophie (2019) From Moral Concerns to Market Values: How Political Consumerism Shapes Markets, in *The Oxford Handbook of Political Consumerism*, edited by Magnus Boström, Michele Micheletti and Peter Oosterveer, 813–832, New York: Oxford University Press.

Felski, Rita (1999) The Invention of Everyday Life, *New Formations*, 39: 15–31.

Feola, Giuseppe and Butt, Anisa (2017) The Diffusion of Grassroots Innovations for Sustainability in Italy and Great Britain: An Exploratory Spatial Data Analysis, *Geographical Journal*, 183: 16–33, doi:10.1111/geoj.12153

Ferrer-Fons, Mariona and Fraile, Marta (2013) Political Consumerism and the Decline of Class Politics in Western Europe, *International Journal of Comparative Sociology*, 54(5–6): 467–489.

Forno, Francesca, Grasseni, Cristina and Signori, Silvana (2015) Italy's Solidarity Purchase Groups as 'Citizenship Labs', in *Putting Sustainability into Practice: Advances and Applications of Social Practice Theories*, edited by E. Huddart Kennedy, M. J. Cohen and N. Krogman, 67–88, Cheltenham: Edward Elgar.

Forno, Francesca and Graziano, Paolo R. (2014) Sustainable Community Movement Organisations, *Journal of Consumer Culture*, 14(2): 139–157.

Forno, Francesca and Graziano, Paolo R. (2019) From Global to Glocal. Sustainable Community Movement Organisations (SCMOs) in Times of Crisis, *European Societies*, 21(5): 729–752.

Forno, Francesca and Luigi, Ceccarini (2006) From the Street to the Shops: The Rise of New Forms of Political Actions in Italy, *South European Society and Politics*, 11(2): 197–222.

Forno, Francesca and Wahlen, Stefan (2022) Prefiguration in Everyday Practices, in *The Future Is Now: An Introduction to Prefigurative Politics*, edited by L. Monticelli, Bristol: Bristol University Press.

Forno, Francesca and Weiner, Richard (2020) *Sustainable Community Movement Organizations: Solidarity Economies and Rhizomatic Practices*, London: Routledge.

Freeman, Jo and Johnson, Victoria (1999) *Waves of Protest: Social Movements Since the Sixties*, Lanham, MD: Rowman & Littlefield.

Friedman, Monroe (1999) *Consumer Boycotts*, New York: Routledge.

Gibson-Graham, J.K. (2006) *A Postcapitalist Politics*, Minneapolis: University of Minnesota Press.

Gibson-Graham J.K., Cameron, Jenny and Healy, Stephen (2013) *Take Back the Economy: An Ethical Guide for Transforming Our Communities*, Minneapolis: University of Minnesota Press.

Giddens, Anthony (1991) *Modernity and Self-Identity – Self and Society in Late Modern Age*, Stanford, CA: Stanford University Press.

Giugni, Marco, Grasso Maria (2015) Environmental Movements: Heterogeneity, Transformation, and Institutionalization, *Annual Review of Environment and Resources*, 40: 337–361.

Giugni, Marco and Grasso, Maria (2020) Social Movements, in *The Palgrave Encyclopedia of Interest Groups, Lobbying and Public Affairs*, edited by P. Harris, A. Bitonti, C. Fleisher, A. Skorkjær Binderkrantz, Cham: Palgrave Macmillan.

Goodman, Michael, DuPuis, Melanie and Goodman, David (2012) *Alternative Food Networks: Knowledge, Practice and Politics*, London: Routledge.

Grasseni, Christina (2013) *Beyond Alternative Food Networks: Italy's Solidarity Purchase Groups*, London: Bloomsbury.

Graziano, Paolo R. and Forno, Francesca (2012) Political Consumerism and New Forms of Political Participation: The Gruppi di Acquisto Solidale in Italy, *The Annals of the American Academy of Political and Social Science*, 644(1): 121–133.

Guidi, Riccardo and Andretta, Massimiliano (2015) Between Resistance and Resilience: How Do Italian Solidarity Based Purchase Groups Change in Times of Crisis and Austerity? *Partecipazione e conflitto*, 8(2): 443–447.

Haenfler, Ross, Johnson, Brett and Ellis, Jones (2012) Lifestyle Movements: Exploring the Intersection of Lifestyle and Social Movements, *Social Movement Studies*, 11(1): 1–20.

Hochschildt, Arlie (2012) *The Managed Heart Commercialization of Human Feeling*, third edition, Los Angeles: University of California Press.

Jallinoja, Piia, Vinnari, Markus and Niva, Mari (2019) Veganism and Plant-Based Eating: Analysis of Interplay Between Discursive Strategies and Lifestyle Political Consumerism, in *The Oxford Handbook of Political Consumerism*, edited by Magnus Boström, Michele Micheletti and Peter Oosterveer, 157–179, New York: Oxford University Press.

Jasper, James M. (1997) *The Art of Moral Protest: Culture, Biography, and Creativity in Social Movements*. Chicago: University of Chicago Press.

Katz, Meredith A. (2019) Boycotting and Buycotting in Consumer Cultures: Political Consumerism in North America, in *The Oxford Handbook of Political Consumerism*, edited by Magnus Boström, Michele Micheletti and Peter Oosterveer, New York: Oxford University Press.

Koos, Sebastian (2012) What Drives Political Consumption in Europe? A Multi-Level Analysis on Individual Characteristics, Opportunity Structures and Globalization, *Acta Sociologica*, 55(1): 37–57.

Kousis, Maria (2017) Alternative Forms of Resilience Confronting Hard Economic Times: A South European Perspective, *PaCo: Partcipazione e conflitto*, 10(1).

Kriesi, Hanspeter, Koopmans, Ruud, Duyvendak, Jain Willem and Giugni, Marco (1995) *New Social Movements in Western Europe*. London: UCL Press.

Krier, Jean-Marie (2006) *Fair Trade in Europe 2005: Facts and Figures on Fair Trade in 25 European Countries*, Brussels: Fair Trade Advocacy Office.

Latouche, Serge (2009) *Farewell to Growth*, London: Polity Press.

Lekakis, Eleftheria and Forno, Francesca (2019) Political Consumerism in Southern Europe, in *The Oxford Handbook of Political Consumerism*, edited by Magnus Boström, Michele Micheletti and Peter Oosterveer, 457–478, New York: Oxford University Press.

Maxton-Lee, Bernice (2020) Activating Responsible Citizens: Depoliticized Environmentalism in Hegemonic Neoliberalism, *Democratization*, 27(3): 443–460.

McAdam, Doug (1995) 'Initiator' and 'Derivative' Movements: Diffusion Processes in Protest Cycles, in *Repertoires and Cycles of Collective Action*, edited by Mark Traugott, 217–239, Durham, NC: Duke University Press.

Melucci, Alberto (1985) The Symbolic Challenge of Contemporary Movements, *Social Research*, 52(4): 789–816.

Melucci, Alberto (1989) *Nomads of the Present: Social Movements and Individual Needs in Contemporary Society*, London: Century Hutchinson.

Melucci, Alberto (1996) *Challenging Codes: Collective Action in the Information Age*, Cambridge: Cambridge University Press.

Meyer, J.M. and Kersten, J. (eds.). (2016) *The Greening of Everyday Life: Challenging Practices, Imagining Possibilities*, Oxford: Oxford University Press.

Micheletti, Michele (2003) *Political Virtue and Shopping: Individuals, Consumerism and Collective Action*, London: Palgrave Macmillan.

Micheletti, Michele, Follesdal, Andrew and Stolle, Dietlind (2006) *Politics, Products, and Markets: Exploring Political Consumerism Past and Present*, New Brunswick, NJ: Transaction Press.

Micheletti, Michele and McFarland, Andrew (eds.). (2011) *Creative Participation: Responsibility Taking in the Political World*, Boulder, CO and London: Paradigm.

Monticelli, Lara and della Porta, Donatella (2019) The Successes of Political Consumerism as a Social Movement, in *The Oxford Handbook of Political Consumerism*, edited by Magnus Boström, Michele Micheletti and Peter Oosterveer, 773–792. New York: Oxford University Press.

Parkins, Wendy and Craig, Geoffrey (2006) *Slow Living*, Oxford: Berg.

Pelenca, Jérôme, Wallenborn, Grégoire, Milanesi Julien, Sébastien, Léa, Vastenaekels, Julien, Lajarthe Fany, Ballet, Jérôme, Cervera-Marzal, Manuel, Carimentrandg, Aurélie, Merveillei, Nicolas and Frèrek, Bruno (2019) Alternative and Resistance Movements: The Two Faces of Sustainability Transformations? *Ecological Economics*, 159: 373–378.

Randall, Bob (2013) Culture, Permaculture, and Experimental Anthropology in the Houston Foodshed, in *Environmental Anthropology Engaging Ecotopia: Bioregionalism, Permaculture, and Ecovillages*, edited by Joshua Lockyer and James R. Veteto, 146–162, New York and Oxford: Berghahn Books.

Rootes, Christopher (2003) *Environmental Protest in Western Europe*, Oxford: Oxford University Press.

Rosa, Harmut (2003) Social Acceleration: Ethical and Political Consequences of a Desynchronized High – Speed Society, *Constellations*, 10(1): 3–33, doi:10.1111/1467-8675.00309

Rosenkrands, Jacob (2004) Policing Homo Economicus: Analysis of Anti-Corporate Websites, in *Cyberprotest: New Media, Citizens and Social Movements*, 57–76, London and New York: Routledge.

Schlosberg, David and Coles, Romand (2015) The New Environmentalism of Everyday Life: Sustainability, Material Flows, and Movements, *Contemporary Political Theory*, 15(2): 160–181.

Schlosberg, David and Craven, Luke (2019) *Sustainable Materialism: Environmental Movements and the Politics of Everyday Life*, Oxford: Oxford University Press.

Seidman, Gay W. (2007) *Beyond the Boycott: Labor Rights, Human Rights and Transnational Activism*, New York: Russell Sage Foundation.

Spar, Deborah and La Mure, Lane (2003) The Power of Activism: Assessing the Impact of NGOs on Global Business, *California Management Review*, 45(3): 78–101.

Stolle, Dietlind and Micheletti Michele (2013) *Political Consumerism: Global Responsibility in Action*, Cambridge: Cambridge University Press.

Tarrow, Sidney (1995) Cycles of Collective Action: Between Movements and Madness and the Repertoire of Contention, in *Repertoires & Cycles of Collective Action*, edited by M. Traugott, 89–116, Durham, NC: Duke University Press.

Tarrow, Sidney (1998) *Power in Movement*, Cambridge: Cambridge University Press.

Tilly, Charles (1984) Social Movements and National Politics, in *Statemaking and Social Movement*, edited by C. Bright and S. Harding, 297–317, Ann Arbor: University of Michigan Press.

Tilly, Charles (1986) *The Contentious French*, Cambridge, MA: Harvard University Press.

Traugott, Mark (ed.). (1995) *Repertoires and Cycles of Collective Action*, Durham, NC: Duke University Press.

Veron, Ophelie (2016) (Extra)ordinary Activism: Veganism and the Shaping of Hemerotopias, *International Journal of Sociology and Social Policy*, 36(11–23): 756–773.

Wahlen, Stefan (2012) *Governing Everyday Consumption*, Helsinki: National Consumer Research Centre.

Wahlen, Stefan and Laamanen, Mikko (2015) Consumption, Lifestyle and Social Movements, *International Journal of Consumer Studies*, 39(5): 397–403.

Wahlström, Mattias and Peterson, Abby (2006) Between the State and the Market, *Acta Sociologica*, 49: 363–377.

Wilkinson, John (2007) Fair Trade: Dynamic and Dilemmas of a Market Oriented Global Social Movement, *Journal of Consumer Policy*, 30(3): 219–239.

Yates, Luke (2015) Rethinking Prefiguration: Alternatives, Micropolitics and Goals in Social Movements, *Social Movement Studies*, 14(1): 1–21.

PART 5

Consequences and outcomes

30

POLICY AND LEGISLATIVE OUTCOMES OF ENVIRONMENTAL MOVEMENTS

Erik W. Johnson and Jon Agnone

Introduction

Over the past 50 years, "the environment" has become a prominent and persistent feature of legislative politics in Western democracies and much of the world (Meyer et al 1997). In this chapter, we examine the role of environmental movements in helping shape legislative attention and action. In part one, our focus is the broad types of political outcomes that environmental movements pursue. They seek substantive change, of course, but they also pursue what social scientists refer to as regular access to legitimate avenues of political influence (Tilly 1978). Across Europe, Green Parties are significant and established players in many Parliamentary systems. In other contexts, environmental activism is strongly linked to broader movements for democratic reform or the rights of marginalized populations.

In part two, we apply a "staged" model of the policy-making process to conceptualize various points of potential access and influence. In this model, movements help set legislative agendas, influence the content of laws – perhaps, ultimately, their passage – and then how they are implemented. Environmental movements, at least in the Global North, often diverge from classic academic conceptions of social movements in that they are heavily integrated into the policy-making apparatus of nation-states. In addition to changing broad cultural understandings of and language around issues of ecology, environmental movements work directly with conventional political actors to influence legislative agendas, may be heavily involved in helping craft the text of legislation, and increasingly participate in the implementation and enforcement of environmental laws. The evidence of direct effects on the incidence of law passage, however, is decidedly mixed. Research instead highlights the many other factors central to policy making generally, including the actions of legislators and opposition interests, public opinion, and dynamics in the larger political system.

In part three, we examine how environmental movements go about exerting influence: by building organizational capacity, conducting disruptive protest, and participating in governance structures. We suggest here that diversity of form and function is a strength of environmental movements. In the United States, radical ecologists engage in direct action (e.g., tree sitting and forest road lockdowns) to conserve wilderness. Sports groups focus on the conservation of wilderness in more formally structured "public interest" organizations (e.g., Ducks Unlimited, Boone and Crocket Club). Civil rights and Indigenous people's movements increasingly

DOI: 10.4324/9780367855680-35

promote environmental issues as linked to social justice and community sovereignty and development. Scientists promote environmental protection both in dedicated interest groups (e.g., Union of Concerned Scientists) and in professional fields that are often documenting rapid and concerning changes in the relationship between social and natural systems. A small group of coordinating groups has fostered a distinct wave of large-scale direct-action protests around climate change and climate justice. There is, we think, ample research suggesting the importance of uniting divergent environmental interests to make policy advancements.[1]

We conclude with a case study of federal climate policy in the United States, which we see as poised for change. This is a particularly relevant topic as we've seen the weakening of environmental policy in the US during the Trump presidency and continued inaction on climate in particular. Globally, the US has abdicated leadership on climate to China and the EU block. Domestically, the US environmental movement has increasingly centered its focus on climate change, drawn media and public attention to the issue, and built significant energy for transformation across localities and pockets of industry. There is a compounding understanding of the human-centered nature of the problem and what levers of remediation and timing are needed to pull back the climate impact. *The Guardian*, a global news outlet with tremendous reach, announced a ban on fossil fuel advertisements in early 2020. Even more astounding is the once unthinkable: carbon-based energy producers such as BP (announced in February 2020) and Shell (announced in April 2020) and major financial powers such as Blackrock and Citigroup (Atkin 2020a, 2020b) began to divest from oil exploration and investment, pushing carbon-neutral solutions as their aim to be carbon neutral themselves. Such organizations embracing scientific research in response to public opinion and environmental movement activity, among other factors, is key as actors within the US government move in the opposite direction. This is very similar to what happened with earlier and more targeted anti-coal corporate actions by Berkshire Hathaway in the 1980s and 1990s (e.g., Nace 2010: Chapter 9).

What political outcomes?

We follow Gamson (1975) in dividing the political outcomes of environmental movements into two broad categories: acceptance, whereby the movement obtains greater routinized access to the levers of political power, and new advantages that are realized. Two defining elements of classic social movement theory are that 1) movements are composed primarily of populations that exist on the fringes of a state polity, and 2) they act outside institutional channels to exert pressure on the political system. In the West, environmental movements have by and large gained acceptance to political systems, with access often institutionalized in Green political parties and parliamentary politics, especially in Northern and Western Europe, where environmental associations actively and regularly participate in both the development and implementation of environmental policy (Van Koppen and Markham 2007; Rootes 2007). In Britain, the US, Australia, and Canada, environmentalists operate in policy systems that provide relatively ample opportunities for the participation of organized citizens groups.

In other parts of the world, environmentalism is tightly intertwined with broader movements for political acceptance. One of the most basic forms of acceptance is access to the vote, and environmental movements were important components of movements for democratic reform across various former Soviet nations (Jancar-Webster 1998; Podoba 1998). In China, environmental movements experience more political space to operate than most other citizens' movements and are increasingly able to effectively work with state actors (Zhang 2018). Environmental issues, from oil pipelines to forest degradation, are integral to movements for Indigenous sovereignty across the world (Estes 2019). In Latin America, environmental issues are often represented within broader peasant and urban popular movements where demands for greater participatory democracy are central (Garcia-Guadilla and Blauert 1992; Lewis 2016). Environmental movements seek to change state policy, but a seat at the table remains an important goal and precursor to such change in many parts of the world.

New advantages

To better conceptualize the various points of the policy process that environmentalists may potentially access, we apply a staged model that begins with the setting and framing of public agendas. For the American environmental movement, it was a fundamental reframing of the issue of pesticides from an economic good to a major threat to human and ecological health that was critical to the legislative successes of the 1970s (Bosso 1987; Baumgartner and Jones 1993). More generally, the rise of new scientific and public discourse of ecology after World War II spurred new ways of thinking about human-nature dynamics in the West. These fundamental cognitive changes in how humans think about "the environment" ultimately undergird any legislative progress on environmental issues.

In legislative terms, the setting of agendas occurs through things like holding hearings, introducing bills, and submitting questions of the prime minister. It is a stage at which environmental movements may have significant impact. In the United States, where access to policy agendas is an important precursor to policy adoption, the environmental movement plays an important role in influencing national political agendas (Johnson 2008; Johnson et al 2010; Olzak and Soule 2009). Sparse congressional attention to climate in the US both demonstrates the importance of setting agendas in the US system, and presents a strong counterpoint to the influence of environmental movements when confronted by the concerted opposition of powerful special interests and political actors (McCright and Dunlap 2003). In other nations like Denmark, which have fewer points of access available to special interests and were much slower to incorporate environmental issues on legislative agendas initially, legislative attention at the agenda-setting stage has been more sustained with the incorporation of Green politics into the larger system of institutionalized partisan conflict (Green-Pedersen and Wolfe 2009).

The second stage in the policy-making process is specifying the content of policy proposals, and legislators often draw heavily from the technical, scientific, and subject-specific expertise of special interests. There is a general consensus that environmental movements play a perhaps uniquely important role in helping specify the content of policy proposals in both Europe and the United States. At least in part, this is because scientific and technical expertise is a strength and even defining feature of many environmental movement organizations (EMOs) (Bosso 2005; Chalmers 2013; Gottlieb 1993; Rootes 2007). Ganz and Soule (2019), for example, conclude that high scientific expertise relative to other organized interests explains EMO's participating in US Congressional hearings focused on proposed legislation (rather than non-legislative tasks such as gathering information or conducting an investigation) at uniquely high rates. At the same time, however, and reflecting the larger need to account for a diversity of factors in the policy process, the relative effect of environmental movements in crafting public policy may be viewed as suspect when compared to the much larger corporate interests to whom they are often opposed (Lund 2013).

The third stage of the legislative policy process, the passage of legislation, is the most obvious outcome of interest and perhaps the most commonly studied. It is also perhaps the area for which findings about the relevance of social movements are most in question (Burstein 2020). Quantitative assessments collectively highlight the rather limited direct impact of environmental movements on the passage of new laws, the highly contingent nature of law passage more generally, and the interactions between movements and other related causal factors, such as public opinion, national partisan political dynamics, the characteristics and actions of political allies and other interest groups (e.g., Agnone 2007; Giugni 2007; Johnson 2008; Johnson et al 2010; Olzak and Soule 2009; Olzak et al 2016). Environmental movements may sometimes directly influence the passage/failure of legislation, but on the whole, their direct impact appears to be quite limited within legislative policy-making systems that involve great complexity and contingency as well as multiple actors, not just social movements and countermovements but industrial and commercial interests, political parties, public opinion, and other factors that likely exert causal influence on the processes of political change. This does not mean environmental movements do not matter in the passage of law, however. Environmental movements clearly effect precursor steps to policy passage, and they may have numerous indirect effects operating through broader changes movements exert on public opinion, on broader cultural norms and beliefs, and helping facilitate the creation of "green" industries that can serve as powerful allies in future legislative tussles.

The history of environmental legislation in the US illustrates the importance of more general political dynamics and what political scientists refer to as a punctuated equilibrium model of policy change (Baumgartner and Jones 1993). The punctuated equilibrium model builds on the observation that, most of the time, new legislation in any particular issue arena is sparse and incremental in nature. Sometimes, though, when the conceptual framing of issues undergoes significant change and/or new actors are brought into policy sub-systems, there can be brief periods of punctuated policy activity marked by significant change before policy systems once again stabilize. In the United States, it was both the growing awareness of a new concept of ecology and political gamesmanship between the Republican President Richard Nixon and a Democratic Congress at the close of the 1960s/start of the 1970s that spurred a massive period of policy change widely referred to as a "golden era" in environmental policy making. The punctuated equilibrium model allots an important role for social movements and interest groups, but broader national political dynamics remain center stage when explaining national policy developments over time.

Across most Western Democracies, environmental movements are widely accepted as important stakeholders at the final policy implementation stage. National governments increasingly promote the development of "collaborative governance regimes" (Emerson and Nabatchi 2015; Scott 2015), which actively solicit the participation of civil society actors in implementing policy and which are widely promoted as offering great potential for civic participation and local democratic governance. Place-based collaborative management of natural resources (e.g., forests, watersheds, fisheries) are particularly established as a focus in governance literatures (Emerson and Nabatchi 2015; Weber 2000). In France, the establishment of public consultative procedures around large development projects invites democratic participation and that participation is dominated by spokespersons of associations (Claeys-Mekdade and Jacqué 2007). In Denmark and other corporatist states, the participation of environmental interests is more routinized but with environmental interest groups again playing central roles. A primary question about collaborative governance arrangements has been the extent to which acceptance in the policy arena has resulted in new advantages versus cooptation of movement goals. Collaborative governance requires that movement actors engage simultaneously in sustained collaboration, and confrontation, with government and industry (Pellow 1999). In the process, movement actors are simultaneously exposed to opportunities to advance their agenda and to threats of cooptation.

How do environmental movements effect policy and legislative outcomes?

A classic debate in social movement literature is about the relative advantages of movements conducting disruptive protest versus building organizations to marshal resources and embracing institutionally approved tactics (i.e., lobbying and crafting policy). The dichotomy is false, both because the presence of social movement organizations may facilitate protest (Minkoff 1997) and because, as the existence of the debate implies, both approaches to movement development can be productive avenues for influencing legislative processes. We think there are multiple advantages to movements adopting diverse strategies of organizational and tactical development, which we outline in this section. Most obviously, a movement with diverse constituencies, including in the case of environmentalism wealthy wildlife/nature conservation groups as well as groups anchored in "rights" movements of disadvantaged populations, can tap a greater diversity of resource pools. Diverse coalitions also expose movement actors to a greater diversity of tactical innovations that they may adopt (Soule and Roggeband 2020).

The outcomes of movements and the tactics they adopt are highly contingent on larger political conditions, however, and a key explanation of a movement's relative success is the match between tactics and political opportunities (Amenta 2006; Giugni 2007; see chapter 18 of this volume for more on the critical area of political opportunity structures). A diversity of movement tactics, both lobbying lawmakers and protesting in the streets, increases the likelihood of environmental movement success (Johnson et al 2010; Woodhouse 2018), likely in part because it maximizes the potential of finding a fit between movement strategy and the larger political environment. A key collective action problem for movement actors is that political opportunities are often shrouded in ambiguity and difficult to identify or properly interpret. Political opportunity "windows" are not only opaque, but they also may open suddenly and for a limited duration. Because protests and organizational capacity cannot typically be ramped up on short notice, movements that are continuously pursuing both have greater optionality when windows do open and maximize the potential for fortuitous matching with political opportunities.

Intra-movement diversity also increases opportunities for more synergistic and/or radical flank effects (Haines 1988), where more militant movement activists expand the room available for the operation of mainstream activists whose demands come to be seen as relatively moderate by comparison. Qualitative-historical analyses support the notion that one key to the 1970s golden era in legislative activity in the United States was that the environmental movement managed to mobilize not just liberal constituencies, but also conservative "hook and bullet" or "rod and gun" sectors of the movement (Bosso 2005; Gottlieb 1993). Campaigns against toxic dumping in the United States and Superfund legislation that responds to these concerns were spurred through grassroots protest movements disproportionately composed of women, the working class, and people of color, working in alliance with large national EMOs that provide scientific expertise and experience with national legislative politics (Szasz 1994). In a period of general retrenchment for the environmental movement, the 1980s wilderness movement successfully pushed for the implementation of major legislation by combining militant actions by groups like Earth First! with more conventional politics in an important push-pull on wilderness policy (Woodhouse 2018).

Environmental movements may also help create political opportunities, either directly or indirectly, by changing broader cultural understanding. Environmental movements do not restrict their focus to fomenting political change; they are centrally focused on educating the citizenry by evoking lifestyle change and improving the public's understanding and language around various phenomena (e.g., pesticides). In doing so, they can have tremendous impacts on legislation that goes beyond the types of measures that necessarily populate quantitative social science models (e.g., counts of people attending a protest or the size of environmental organizations). A fundamental aspect of most legislative policy-making models is that causes of change are highly multi-dimensional and contingent. While EMOs may directly impact legislative processes, they are part of a much broader and multi-dimensional policy-making system in which industrial actors are often the more dominant special interest. The advantage that social movements have, and what makes them unique actors and the environmental movement uniquely successful, is that they may operate across a wide variety of social institutions and create broader change that may impact policy systems in indirect ways. The environmental movement is composed of the traditional student protestor but also strongly tied to scientific institutions and scientists. Ironically, many of the best scientists are funded in whole or part by US government sources such as the NSF, NIH, or NICHD, which is a stark contrast to the political opinions and directions coming from the executive branch and federal agencies under the Trump administration. One feature of social movements that complicates attempts to model direct influence on legislation is that their most important influences are often indirect, resulting from changes they make to things like the attitudes and behaviors of individuals and the culture at large. A political process perspective, with strong roots in political science and emphasizing the way social movements impact state policies through extra-institutional channels, has dominated the field of social movement studies over the past 40 years. At the same time, however, a chorus of scholars have consistently argued that the true significance of social movements lies not in their direct effects on state policy but in the larger cultural changes that they may engender (e.g., Eyerman and Jamison 1991).

In their classic article, McCarthy and Zald (1977) describe the primary goal of social movements as shifting sentiment pools to convert bystander publics to adherents and adherents to constituents who actively contribute to a movement. There are obvious political implications of shifting sentiment pools that make the attainment of social movement political goals more probable and synergistic benefits to movement political activities when there are sympathetic publics that back their demands (Agnone 2007; Giugni 2007). Public opinion is the subject of chapter 31 in this volume, and so we do not consider it in more depth here, but to make one observation and speculation. While public support for environmental issues in the US is generally widespread, opinions on the environment are not generally deeply held and are superseded by other political criteria (Guber 2003; Johnson and Schwadel 2019). Public opinion on its own, then, is unlikely to spur legislative change; the actions of relevant political actors are important components in achieving desired political outcomes.

The indirect effects of environmental movements on legislative processes also act through effects on business. Industrial interests are a high priority for legislative bodies and often powerful opponents of environmental movements. In the US at the end of 2019, the consistently strong opposition of an industry-funded countermovement is notable for its success in blunting federal climate legislation. Industry can also be an important ally in legislative politics, and nation-states with stronger "green" industries are more likely to adopt pro-environmental policies (Aklin and Urpelainen 2013; Meckling et al 2015).

Environmental movements seek to alter the private sector not just through legislation but by altering the culture and practices of existing producers and by creating entirely new markets. Hoffman (2001) shows how protecting the environment went *From Heresy to Dogma* in chemical and petroleum industries in the US. A number of studies describe how activists and industrial actors work together to redefine and build markets for things like sustainably harvested lumber (Bartley 2007) and seafood (Konefal 2013; Oosterveer and Spaargaren 2011). Similarly, expansion in the wind industry has received critical assistance from alternative energy advocates (Pacheco et al 2014). A common refrain in business schools today is the importance of companies advancing a "triple bottom line" that prizes not just economic profits but social and environmental concerns. Similarly, several high-profile companies have publicly acknowledged commitments to divest or stop investing in carbon-based energy extraction. For example, as Emily Atkin (2020a) notes, "Citigroup – the third largest bank in the US – announced a commitment to never invest in new oil and gas projects in the Arctic" and, further, "follows similar decisions by Goldman Sachs, JPMorgan Chase, and Wells Fargo" (Atkin 2020a). This follows Blackrock's January 2020 decision, also reported by Atkin (2020b), to pivot away from fossil fuel–oriented stocks. The implications for legislative outcomes of change within industry are understudied but may be profound.

A more proximate mechanism of movement influence on policy is the critical role played by policy entrepreneurs (Beeri et al 2020), actors that play crucial roles in framing public issues, linking problem definitions and solutions, and more generally pulling together the different "process streams" that must align in order to develop new public policy (Kingdon 2011). Environmental policy entrepreneurs are often employed within governments but may also be social movement actors who play central roles in knitting together allied interests to build new fields of action. The role of these actors is often hidden but crucial in developing or blocking new environmental initiatives (Huitema and Meijerink 2010).

The case of climate change in the US

Climate legislative activity

Enacted in 2015, the Paris Agreement was to date the crowning achievement of global alignment around climate change, with nearly every nation acknowledging the underlying issues related to greenhouse gas emissions and pledging to take steps toward ameliorating the underlying causes. The commitment, as the NRDC notes, was to limit global temperature increases to 2° Celsius, while making every effort to limit that increase to 1.5° by cutting greenhouse gas emissions (Denchak 2018). The United States played a leadership role in securing the convention (Parker and Karlsson 2018) but has since been a notable laggard. As promised in his campaign, President Trump proclaimed in the summer of 2017 that the US would pull out of the Paris Agreement. While this is not an immediate impact – the US is unable to formally walk away until November 2020 – the symbolic impact of the global leader on economic and peace-keeping efforts is loud and clear: the US is not interested in leading the world on climate change (Denchak 2018). It is also reflective of a domestic political system on which climate change barely registers on official agendas.

To get a sense of the (dis)engagement within the US federal policy-making system around issues of climate change in the US over time, we relied on various data collections from the Comparative Agendas Project (CAP) (Adler and Wilkerson 2016). For the legislative data from the CAP, each of the data sources rely on a normalized coding system, with climate change issues covered within the subcode 705, which includes all air pollution issues, climate change, and noise pollution.[2] Data from 1989 to 2019, with some missing years due to the limitations of the various data sources, are summarized in Table 30.1.

There were 513 legislative hearings on air pollution and/or climate change from 1989 through 2017 in the US, which comprised just over 1% of the total number of environment-related hearings and a tenth of a percent of all legislative hearings held over that time. Though the level of hearings held generally increased over time, with an average of nearly 20 per year since 2000, there is a stark drop in legislative agenda-setting activities after 2010. The congressional election that year resulted in the highest losses for a party in a midterm election since 1938, returning control of the House of Representatives to a Republican party whose policies have been driven by a highly influential climate countermovement.

The low level of hearings focused, broadly, on issues related to climate change is reflected in the low number of bills introduced by Congress and ultimately passed into law. From 1989 to 2018, a total of 736 out of the nearly 131,000 bills brought before Congress focused on air pollution (a rate of 0.6%). Fourteen out of the more than 6,600 laws passed from 1989 to 2018, less than .2%, focused on air pollution. As a final confirmation on the lack of federal political engagement with climate change policy, we also looked at data from the Congressional Quarterly Almanac (2017) from 1989 to 2015. Of the nearly 3,700 articles in the almanac – which covers bills and laws – only 10, or .2%, touched on climate change, broadly defined.

Climate change mobilization

Despite the lack of federal policy attention to date, we think (and hope) the US is poised for major action on climate change. We see signs for optimism in 1) the increased engagement with, and tactical diversity around, issues of climate in the US environmental movement, and 2) change that is already occurring within the larger socio-political landscape, much of which represents indirect influences of the movement on the policy process. There is also the ecological reality that, in the words of Greta Thunberg: "Change is coming whether you like it or not". Political change may well not occur quickly enough to prevent some of the worst impacts of a heating world, but the US government is facing significant pressures from both above (at the level of international institutions) and below (from domestic political advocacy groups) to address climate change, and national political actors have begun to take the issue seriously (see the Green New Deal.) When change does occur, the policy implications of climate change are so far reaching that we are cautiously optimistic of at least a small "punctuated" period of policy development as the venues in which climate policy is enacted move beyond legislative committees focused on energy and the environment.

As we see it, climate change presents important similarities to movement dynamics around pesticides, except even more amplified, in that it has a unique ability to draw across all the different elements of the movement: groups focused on pollution, wildlife and wildlands conservationists, social justice–focused organizations, and often more politically conservative hook-and-bullet groups. The growing salience of climate change across the US environmental movement is palpable. We draw from the Encyclopedia of Associations (EA) for a rough estimate on the timing of this growing interest. (See Figure 30.1, with the 2010 to 2017 period of heightened climate change organizational activity highlighted.) The EA offers the advantage of categorizing a broad range of nationally organized and oriented citizens' associations in the US, including EMOs. Limitations include the fact that it is both slow to change (Bevan et al 2013) and that brief organizational summaries highlight only the central organizing interests that an organization articulates. Our approach, relying exclusively on these summaries to identify climate change as a central organizational focus, vastly underestimates the level of attention within the US EMO population. In addition to the temporal delay, these data do not account for the many EMOs focusing on related issues (e.g., the group Vote Solar Initiative) but lacking concise climate-related frames of their work. Still, the increased focus on issues of climate is palpable, with just over 1% of EMOs identifying climate as a central organizing issue in 1990, and more than 10% doing so after 2010. This increased interest is driven by the founding of an entirely

Table 30.1 Environmental movement protests, climate change protests, and legislative activity, 1989 to 2019

Year	Environmental Protests	Non-Climate Change Protests	Climate Change Protests	Climate Change in NYT	Climate Change Hearings Held	Climate change subcommittee Hearings Held	Climate Change Bills Passed	Climate Change Laws Passed	Climate Change Articles in CQ	EMOs indicating climate change as central focus	EMOs not indicating climate change as central focus
1989	2	2	0		42	0	57	1	3	0	95
1990	17	7	0		9	0	5	1	2	10	615
1991	3	3	0		5	0	3	2	0	10	630
1992	10	0	0		3	0	7	0	0	1	35
1993	11	1	0		3	1	8	0	0	1	41
1994	4	4	0		10	0	16	0	0	11	
1995	5	5	0		5	2	1	1	0	1	54
1996	8	8	0	5	4	0	0	1	0	1	61
1997	7	7	0	4	0	3	6	0	1	3	67
1998	4	4	0	0	8	3	13	1	0	17	670
1999	15	5	2	4	4	4	47	1	0	20	667
2000	21	9	0	0	1	6	17	0	0	22	666
2001	12	2	0	15	9	1	6	0	0	22	656
2002	11	1	0	11	2	2	2	1	0	25	663
2003	4	4	1	10	1	4	6	0	1	30	659
2004	5	4	2	4	4	1	6	0	0	6	46
2005	11	9	1	12	11	4	5	0	0	8	49
2006	3	2	1	9	10	2	4	0	0	5	46
2007	5	4	4		61	2	58	0	1	56	651
2008	8	4	4		3	1	3	2	0	2	49
2009	6	4	2		3	1	7	0	1	9	50
2010	7	6	1		1	1	3	1	0	0	25
2011	14	8	6		6	1	5	0	0	2	03
2012	4	1	3		3	0	5	1	0	4	96

(*Continued*)

Table 30.1 (Continued)

Year	Environmental Protests	Non-Climate Change Protests	Climate Change Protests	Climate Change in NYT	Climate Change Hearings Held	Climate change subcommittee Hearings Held	Climate Change Bills Passed	Climate Change Laws Passed	Climate Change Articles in CQ	EMOs indicating climate change as central focus	EMO's not indicating climate change as central focus
2013	10	2	8		2	1	3	0	0	6	86
2014	7	0	7		7	3	9	1	1	7	79
2015	10	1	9		7	2	4	0	0	7	66
2016	11	2	9		4	1	0	0		5	61
2017	10	2	8		5	0		0		6	59
2018	7	0	7					0			
2019	15	0	5					0			
Grand Total	**287**	**201**	**86**	**124**	**513**	**46**	**736**	**14**	**10**	**1,137**	**18,289**

462

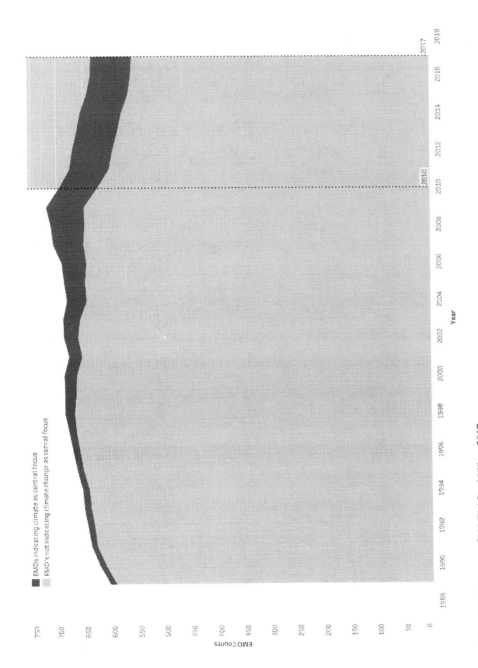

Figure 30.1 Counts of US EMOs, 1989 to 2017

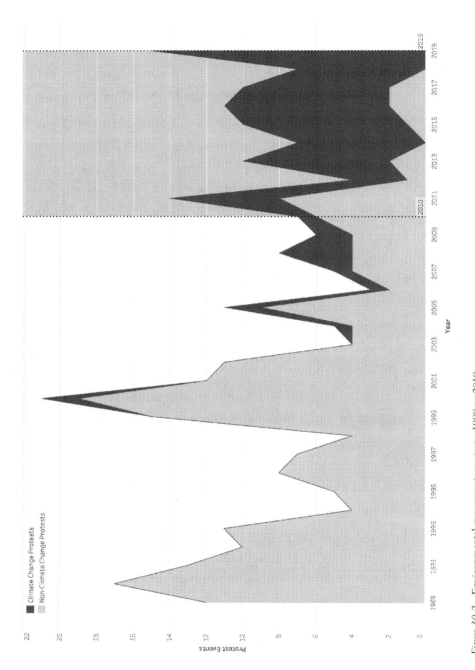

Figure 30.2 Environmental movements protests, 1989 to 2019

new set of climate-focused organizations, including influential groups like 350.org and Rising Tide that are helping drive direct-action protests. Of 220 groups in our data that were founded after 2001, fully 63% are focused on the issue of climate change. Additionally, these data reflect the embrace of climate by "Big 10" groups like Greenpeace, World Wildlife Fund, and the Environmental Defense Fund.

The orienting power of climate within the environmental movement is, again, vastly underestimated in the organizational data presented here.[3] Climate issues are also integrally tied to related movements for social justice and worker rights in ways that are qualitatively different than the issue of pesticides. In the 1970s, national environmental groups' solution to the issue of pesticides often involved legislation that moved the risk of pesticides from the consumers onto the poor and disproportionally immigrant workers who produce it (Pulido and Peña 1998). Today environmental groups are, while still notorious laggards (Taylor 2014), increasingly attentive to issues of social justice as well as forging blue-green alliances (Mayer 2008).

Importantly, environmentalists have also increasingly pushed for action around climate change both through institutional channels and, in recent years, in the streets through protests that often emphasize the social justice dimensions of a changing climate. To codify the level of political engagement around climate change and related issues, we pull together environmental protest data from the *New York Times* from 1989 through 2019, following the coding conventions set forth by the Dynamics of Collective Action (DCA) project (McAdam et al 2009) and breaking out climate change protests. (See Figure 30.2.) The first climate change protest we identify occurred in 2000, tied to anti-globalization protests in the wake of the virulent World Trade Organization (WTO) events in Seattle the prior year. In the 2010s, climate-oriented direct action became a larger proportion of environmental movement protest activity so that climate change represents the entirety of environmental protest covered by the *New York Times* – all 15 environmental-focused protests were centered on issues related to climate change. Between 2000 and the end of 2009 climate-oriented protest accounted for 15% of the 86 direct-action events, compared to 77% of the 95 events from 2010 to the end of 2019 (See Figure 30.2, with the 2010 to 2019 period of heightened climate change protest activity highlighted.) Beyond their frequency, recent climate protests have been notable for their large scale and nationwide geographic dispersion.

In addition to efforts aimed at political actors, environmental movements are pressing (with more success) for change across various other institutions, creating indirect pressures on the federal policy system. Corporate actors are increasingly attentive to climate issues, in significant part because of the direct pressures placed on them by environmentalists who take a variety of approaches, such as seeking to limit emissions at individual facilities (Grant and Vasi 2017) and promoting carbon divestment strategies (Ayling and Cunningham 2017). The EA includes numerous policy-oriented EMOs focused on climate, as well as direct-action groups like Rising Tide North America and numerous organizations like the Climate Group that work directly with corporations to develop CO_2 emissions plans.

Working against the entrenched skeptics movement, environmentalists have drawn substantial media attention to the issue of climate. In the policy process, public opinion and media attention are key to moving the policy agenda of Congress, given representatives reliance on the polity for reelection and maintaining their jobs. While public opinion is a topic covered in Chapter 31 of this volume, we briefly touch on available media attention data. One way to get a glimpse into media attention to climate change issues is to examine the content in the *New York Times*. A recent analysis of the full *New York Times* corpus by Romps and Retzinger (2019) confirms the minimal attention to issues of climate prior to 2015, after which there is a dramatic surge in coverage that both lags behind increased movement attention to the issue and is a possible leading indicator of coming change in the US congressional agenda. This increased pattern of coverage is clearly visible in the coverage of several major US news outlets, including the *New York Times*, from 2000 through July 2020 via the University of Colorado's Media and Climate Change Observatory (Boykoff et al 2020). Their data is presented in Figure 30.3, with a spike in coverage notable starting in January 2007, December 2009, and then a steady increase in coverage over the decade from 2010 to 2020 – particularly due to the *New York Times*.

Perhaps one of the strongest pressures for federal change that we see is reflected in the activity that is already going on at different levels of scale. In light of the federal government abdicating global leadership on climate, state and local governments within the US have had the burden shifted to them if they are interested in moving the needle (see Klyza and Sousa 2008). The C40 Cities, a collaboration among climate-conscious global cities, is among the latest examples by which local action on climate change is being federated through the US (C40 Cities 2020). This particular group is intent on holding their municipalities to the 1.5° global heating increase originally set by the Paris Agreement, among other climate-related pledges. Analyses of a similar effort during the 1990s, called the Cities for Climate Protection program, highlight the importance of what social movement scholars might call "scale shift" and the ways in which international context is significant even at the level of individual cities (Vasi 2007).

The very states' rights that undergird the federated nature of US national-level politics is the bedrock of the most classic example of states leading on climate change impacts: California's well-known leadership on automobile fuel efficiency and exhaust standards, originally authorized under the Clean Air Act that allowed California to set its own standard via a waiver process. In 2019, the Trump administration directed the NTSB and EPA to revoke that waiver and effectively remove California as the standard bearer for nationwide fuel efficiency standards (Dennis and Eilperin 2019). In May of 2020, California and 22 other states filed a lawsuit "arguing that the move is based on erroneous science, and endangers public health" (Tabuchi 2020).

The international context for climate action is a clear and strong pressure on the US, both because of diffuse legitimation pressures and the implications for geopolitical politics. A convincing argument has been made that geopolitics – particularly the pressure of the Cold War whereby the Soviet Union was utilizing images of Black protestors being brutalized by the white police and citizens as an example of the greater equality possible within communist regimes – played a crucial role in the Johnson administration's support for the 1965 Voting Rights Act (McAdam 1982). One externality of the US government's disengagement with the Paris Agreement is the possibility of China stepping into the global leadership void. China has been yearning to lead globally in all aspects of supra-national politics, and the US stepping aside from the Paris Agreement provides an opportunity to step into the void and project global leadership. Whether the US leads from a policy and reputational perspective is second to the fact that China is the global leader in CO_2 emissions and the nation that most needs to change its current energy allocations in order to achieve the global targets set by the Paris Agreement (Ma 2019). As several scholars and public intellectuals have noted, "As the world's manufacturing hub, China is in a unique position to change the course of global emissions. In most industrial sectors, 75% of greenhouse-gas emissions are produced from the supply chains" (e.g., Tollefson 2019). Abject inaction on the part of the US government in recent years is perceivably wreaking on a global scale, creating opportunities for geopolitical competitors and more strong pressure for legislative change following in the near future.

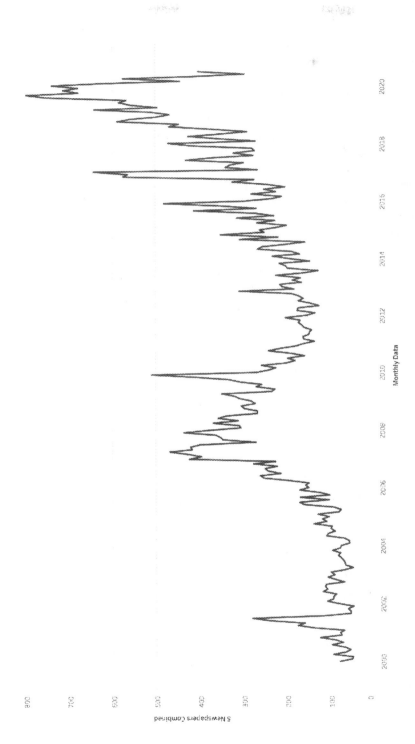

Figure 30.3 United States newspaper coverage of climate change or global warming, 2000–2020

Conclusion

Environmental movements around the world pursue a variety of goals, including substantive policy change and increased access to institutionalized political systems. Environmental movements help set national political agendas, are often important players in specifying the content of legislation, at least occasionally have direct impact on the passage of legislation, and, at least in Western democracies, are important participants in policy implementation. Environmental movements are perpetually relevant due to their sustained mobilization and because they go beyond formal "movement" organizations to include an expansive coalition of, among others, business entrepreneurs, scientists, civic activists, and churches. The modern environmental movement, in the words of this volume's editors (Giugni and Grasso 2015), have profoundly transformed since the 1960s, are notably heterogeneous in terms of actors and issues addressed as well as strategies and effects, and have generally become increasingly institutionalized and a "constitutive part of contemporary societies" (355). The heterogeneity within environmental movements is, we think, a major source of strength.

Political change on issues of climate is, based on our research herein, on the near horizon in the United States. The physical reality of mass ecological change is going to require a (political) response across not just the "environment" proper but business, education, military, health care, food production, and water distribution. Clearly, the US environmental movement is increasingly focused on climate change as an overarching issue that impacts energy and transportation systems, the preservation of wildlife and their habitats, and social justice. We posit that in the aftermath of the Trump administration – whether in 2021 or 2025 – the US will see a policy backlash against the egregious anti-environment stances and (loosely used) regulations in light of the clear current and future impacts based on scientific research and lived experiences. Additionally, we expect to see a drastic increase in global alignment and leadership from the US that spans the political, business, and nonprofit sectors. The policy response may not be as successful as 1970s-era anti-pollution legislation, but the well-being of human society in the coming decades will hinge on it.

Notes

Thank you to Azdren Coma and Annika Johnson for assistance in assembling data on environmental protests and organizations used in this chapter.

1 The circumstances that may foster the building of effective coalitions in diverse movements are the subject of a related and now large literature that is beyond our focus here. (See Van Dyke and Amos 2017 for a review.)

2 The one exception from the data we are leveraging is the hearing data, which has more detailed subcommittee codes. For climate change, we rely on 20735 (Climate Change) and 20914 (Clean Air and Climate Change, as well as Nuclear Safety).

3 We also went to the websites of these organizations in August and September of 2020: 28% of groups indicate climate as a central organizing issue. This is indicative of the central nature of climate but not suitable for temporal comparison as it reflects some combination of growing interest in climate over time, as well as the lag in EA updating (Bevan et al 2013) and the more detailed coding available in a website format.

References

Adler, E. Scott, and John Wilkerson. 2016. *Congressional Bills Project: (1947–2016), NSF 00880066 and 00880061. The Views Expressed Are Those of the Authors and Not the National Science Foundation.* Cambridge: Cambridge University Press.

Agnone, Jon. 2007. "Amplifying Public Opinion: The Policy Impact of the U.S. Environmental Movement." *Social Forces* 85(4): 1593–1620.

Aklin, Michael, and Johannes Urpelainen. 2013. "Political Competition, Path Dependence, and the Strategy of Sustainable Energy Transitions." *American Journal of Political Science* 57(3): 643–658.

Amenta, Edwin. 2006. *When Movements Matter*. Princeton, NJ: Princeton University Press.

Atkin, Emily. 2020a, April 21. "Citigroup Dumps Arctic Oil." https://heated.world/p/citigroup-dumps-arctic-oil

Atkin, Emily. 2020b, January 15. "BlackRock Who?" https://heated.world/p/blackrock-who

Ayling, Julie, and Neil Gunningham. 2017. "Non-State Governance and Climate Policy: The Fossil Fuel Divestment Movement." *Climate Policy* 17(2): 131–149.

Bartley, Tim. 2007. "How Foundations Shape Social Movements: The Construction of an Organizational Field and the Rise of Forest Certification." *Social Problems* 54(3): 229–255.

Baumgartner, Frank R., and Bryan D. Jones. 1993. *Agendas and Instability in American Politics*. Chicago: University of Chicago Press.

Beeri, Itai, Nissim Cohen, and Neomi Frisch-Aviram. 2020. "Entrepreneurship in the Policy Process: Linking Behavior and Context Through a Systematic Review of the Policy Entrepreneurship Literature." *Public Administration Review* 80(2): 188–197. doi:10.1111/puar.13089

Bevan, Shaun, Frank R. Baumgartner, Erik W. Johnson, and John D. McCarthy. 2013 "Understanding Selection Bias, Time-Lags and Measurement Bias in Secondary Data Sources: Putting the Encyclopedia of Associations Database in Broader Context." *Social Science Research* 42(6): 1750–1764.

Bosso, Christopher J. 1987. *Pesticides & Politics: The Life Cycle of a Public Issue*. Pittsburgh, PA: University of Pittsburgh Press.

Bosso, Christopher J. 2005. *Environment, Inc.: From Grassroots to Beltway*. Lawrence: University Press of Kansas.

Boykoff, M., Daly, M., McNatt, M., and Nacu-Schmidt, A. 2020. *United States Newspaper Coverage of Climate Change or Global Warming, 2000–2020*. Media and Climate Change Observatory Data Sets, Cooperative Institute for Research in Environmental Sciences. Boulder: University of Colorado. doi:10.25810/jck1-hf50

Burstein, Paul. 2020. "Testing Theories About Advocacy and Public Policy." *Perspectives on Politics* 1–12. doi:10.1017/S1537592719004663

C40 Cities. 2020, July 15. "Mayors Launch a Green and Just COVID-19 Recovery Plan & Demand National Governments End Fossil Fuel Subsidies." www.c40.org/press_releases/mayors-launch-a-green-and-just-covid-19-recovery-plan-demand-national-governments-end-fossil-fuel-subsidies?utm_medium=email&utm_source=govdelivery

Chalmers, A. W. 2013. "Trading Information for Access: Informational Lobbying Strategies and Interest Group Access to the European Union." *Journal of European Public Policy* 20(1): 39–58.

Claeys-Mekdade, Cécilia and Marie Jacqué. 2007. "Nature Protection Associations in France." Pp. 63–86 in C.S.A (Kris) Van Koppen and William T. Markham (eds.) *Protecting Nature: Organizations and Networks in Europe and the USA*. North Hampton, MA: Edward Elgar Publishing.

Congressional Quarterly Almanac. 2017. "Hearings." Laws: The Policy Agendas Project at the University of Texas at Austin. www.comparativeagendas.net. Accessed May 26, 2020.

Denchak, Melissa. 2018, December 12. "Paris Climate Agreement: Everything You Need to Know." *National Resource Defense Council*. www.nrdc.org/stories/paris-climate-agreement-everything-you-need-know#:~:text=The%20Paris%20Agreement%20is%20a,change%20and%20its%20negative%20impacts.&text=The%20agreement%20includes%20commitments%20from,strengthen%20those%20commitments%20over%20time

Dennis, Brady, and Juliet Eilperin. 2019, November 15. "California and Nearly Two Dozen Other States Sue Trump Administration for the Right to Set Fuel-Efficiency Standards." *Washington Post*. www.washingtonpost.com/climate-environment/2019/11/15/california-nearly-two-dozen-other-states-sue-trump-administration-right-require-more-fuel-efficient-cars

Emerson, Kirk, and Tina Nabatchi. 2015. *Collaborative Governance Regimes*. Washington, DC: Georgetown University Press.

Estes, Nick. 2019. *Our History Is the Future: Standing Rock Versus the Dakota Access Pipeline, and the Long Tradition of Indigenous Resistance*. New York: Verso.

Eyerman, Ron, and Andrew Jamison. 1991. *Social Movements: A Cognitive Approach*. State College: Penn State University Press.

Gamson, William A. 1975. *The Strategy of Social Protest*. Homewood, IL: Dorsey Press.

Ganz, Scott C., and Sarah A. Soule. 2019. "Greening the Congressional Record: Environmental Social Movements and Expertise-Based Access to the Policy Process." *Environmental Politics* 28(4): 685–706.

Garcia-Guadilla, Maria Pilar, and Jutta Blauert. 1992. "Environmental Social Movements in Latin America and Europe: Challenging Development and Democracy." *International Journal of Sociology and Social Policy* 12(4–7): 1–274.

Giugni, Marco. 2007. "Useless Protest? A Time-Series Analysis of the Policy Outcomes of Ecology, Antinuclear, and Peace Movements in the United States, 1977–1995." *Mobilization* 12(1): 53–77.

Giugni, Marco, and M. T. Grasso. 2015. "Environmental Movements: Heterogeneity, Transformation, and Institutionalization." *Annual Review of Environment and Resources* 40. doi:10.1146/annurev-environ-102014-021327

Gottlieb, Robert. 1993. *Forcing the Spring: The Transformation of the American Environmental Movement.* Washington, DC: Island Press.

Grant, Don, and Ion Bogdan Vasi. 2017. "Civil Society in an Age of Environmental Accountability: How Local Environmental Nongovernmental Organizations Reduce U.S. Power Plants' Carbon Dioxide Emissions." *Sociological Forum* 32(1): 94–115.

Green-Pedersen, Christoffer, and Michelle Wolfe. 2009. "The Institutionalization of Environmental Attention in the United States and Denmark: Multiple- Versus Single- Venue Systems." *Governance: An International Journal of Policy, Administration, and Institutions* 22(4): 625–646.

Guber, Deborah Lynn. 2003. *The Grassroots of a Green Revolution: Polling America on the Environment.* Cambridge, MA: MIT Press.

Haines, Herbert H. 1988. *Black Radicals and the Civil Rights Mainstream, 1954–1970.* Knoxville: University of Tennessee Press.

Hoffman, Andrew J. 2001. *From Heresy to Dogma: An Institutional History of Corporate Environmentalism.* Stanford, CA: Stanford Business Books.

Huitema, Dave, and Sander Meijerink. 2010. "Realizing Water Transitions: the Role of Policy Entrepreneurs in Water Policy Change." *Ecology and Society* 15(2): 26.

Jancar-Webster, Barbara. 1998. "Environmental Movement and Social Change in the Transition Countries." *Environmental Politics* 7(1): 69–90.

Johnson, E. W. 2008. "Social Movement Size, Organizational Diversity and the Making of Federal Law." *Social Forces* 86(3): 967–993.

Johnson, Eric W., J. Agnone, and J. D. McCarthy. 2010. "Movement Organizations, Synergistic Tactics and Environmental Public Policy." *Social Forces* 88(5): 2267–2292.

Johnson, Erik W., and Philip Schwadel. 2019. "Political Polarization and Long-Term Change in Public Support for Environmental Spending." *Social Forces* 98(2): 915–941.

Jun, Ma. 2019, September 12. "How China Can Truly Lead the Fight Against Climate Change." https://time.com/5669061/china-climate-change/

Kingdon, John. 2011. *Agendas, Alternative and Public Policies: Updated Second Edition.* New York: Longman.

Klyza, Christopher M., and David Sousa. 2008. *American Environmental Policy, 1990–2006: Beyond Gridlock.* Cambridge, MA: MIT Press.

Konefal, Jason. 2013. "Environmental Movements, Market-Based Approaches, and Neoliberalization: A Case Study of the Sustainable Seafood Movement." *Organization & Environment* 26(3): 336–352.

Lewis, Tammy L. 2016. *Ecuador's Environmental Revolutions: Ecoimperialists, Ecodependents, and Ecoresisters.* Cambridge, MA: MIT Press.

Lund, Emma. 2013. "Environmental Diplomacy: Comparing the Influence of Business and Environmental NGOs in Negotiations on Reform of the Clean Development Mechanism." *Environmental Politics* 22(5): 739–759.

Mayer, Brian. 2008. *Blue-Green Coalitions: Fighting for Safe Workplaces and Healthy Environments.* Ithaca, NY: Cornell University Press.

McAdam, Doug. 1982. *Political Process and the Development of Black Insurgency, 1930–1970.* Chicago: University of Chicago Press.

McAdam, Doug, John D. McCarthy, Susan Olzak, and Sarah Soule. 2009. "Dynamics of Collective Action Dataset." *New York Times.*

McCarthy, John D., and Mayer N. Zald. 1977. "Resource Mobilization and Social Movements: A Partial Theory." *American Journal of Sociology* 82(6): 1212–1241.

McCright, Aaron M., and Riley E. Dunlap. 2003. "Defeating Kyoto: The Conservative Movement's Impact on U.S. Climate Change Policy." *Social Problems* 5(3): 348–373.

Meckling, Jonas, Nina Kelsey, Eric Biber, and John Zysman. 2015. "Winning Coalitions for Climate Policy." *Science* 349(6253): 1170–1171.

Meyer, John W., David John Frank, Ann Hironaka, Evan Schofer, and Nancy Brandon Tuma. 1997. "The Structuring of a World Environmental Regime, 1870–1990." *International Organization* 51(4): 623–651.

Minkoff, Debra C. 1997. "The Sequencing of Social Movements." *American Sociological Review* 779–799.

Nace, Ted. 2010. *Climate Hope: On the Front Lines of the Fight Against Coal.* San Francisco: Coal Swarm Press.

Olzak, Susan, and Sarah A. Soule. 2009. "Cross-Cutting Influences of Environmental Protest and Legislation." *Social Forces* 88(1): 201–225. doi:10.1353/sof.0.0236

Olzak, Susan, Sarah A. Soule, Marion Coddou, and John Muñoz. 2016. "Friends or Foes? How Social Movement Allies Affect the Passage of Legislation in the U.S. Congress." *Mobilization* 21(2): 213–230.

Oosterveer, Peter, and Gert Spaargaren. 2011. "Organizing Consumer Involvement in the Greening of Global Food Flows: The Role of Environmental NGOs in the Case of Marine Fish." *Environmental Politics* 20(1): 97–114.

Pacheco, Desirée F., Jeffrey G. York, and Timothy J. Hargrave. 2014. "The Coevolution of Industries, Social Movements, and Institutions: Wind Power in the United States." *Organization Science* 25(6): 1609–1632.

Parker, Charles F., and Christer Karlsson. 2018. "The UN Climate Change Negotiations and the Role of the United States: Assessing American Leadership from Copenhagen to Paris." *Environmental Politics* 27(2): 1–22.

Pellow, David N. 1999. "Negotiation and Confrontation: Environmental Policymaking Through Consensus." *Society & Natural Resources* 12(3): 189–203.

Podoba, Juraj. 1998. "Rejecting Green Velvet: Transition, Environment and Nationalism in Slovakia." *Environmental Politics* 7(1): 129–144. doi:10.1080/09644019808414376

Pulido, Laura, and Devon Peña. 1998. "Environmentalism and Positionality: The Early Pesticide Campaign of the United Farm Workers' Organizing Committee, 1965–71." *Race, Class & Gender* 6(1): 33–50.

Romps, David M., and Jean P. Retzinger. 2019. "Climate News Articles Lack Basic Climate Science." *Environmental Research Communications* 1(8).

Rootes, Christopher. 2007. "Environmental Movements." Pp. 608–640 in D. A. Snow, Sarah A. Soule, and Hanspieter Kriesi (eds.) *The Blackwell Companion to Social Movements.* Oxford: Blackwell.

Scott, Tyler. 2015. "Does Collaboration Make Any Difference? Linking Collaborative Governance to Environmental Outcomes." *Journal of Policy Analysis and Management* 34(3): 537–566.

Soule, S. A., and C. Roggeband. 2020. "Diffusion Processes Within and Across Movements." In D. A. Snow, S. A. Soule, H. Kriesi, and H. J. McCammon (eds.) *The Wiley Blackwell Companion to Social Movements.* Hoboken, NJ: Blackwell. doi:10.1002/9781119168577.ch13

Szasz, Andrew. 1994. *Ecopopulism: Toxic Waste and the Movement for Environmental Justice. Vol. 1. Social Movements, Protest, and Contention.* Minneapolis: University of Minnesota Press.

Tabuchi, Hiroko. 2020, May 27. "States Sue to Block Trump From Weakening Fuel Economy Rules." *New York Times.* www.nytimes.com/2020/05/27/climate/lawsuit-fuel-economy-climate.html

Taylor, Dorceta. 2014. *The State of Diversity in Environmental Organizations: Mainstream NGOs, Foundations, Government Agencies.* Green 2.0 and the Raben Group. Ann Arbor: University of Michigan.

Tilly, Charles. 1978. *From Mobilization to Revolution.* Reading, MA: Addison-Wesley.

Tollefson, Jeff. 2019, September 18. "The Hard Truths of Climate Change – by the Numbers." www.nature.com/immersive/d41586-019-02711-4/index.html

Van Dyke, Nella, and Bryan Amos. 2017. "Social Movement Coalitions: Formation, Longevity, and Success." *Sociology Compass* 11(7): e12489.

Van Koppen, C. S. A. (Kris), and William T. Markham (Eds.). 2007. *Protecting Nature: Organizations and Networks in Europe and the USA.* Northampton, MA: Edward Elgar.

Vasi, Ion Bogdan. 2007. "Thinking Globally, Planning Nationally and Acting Locally: Nested Organizational Fields and the Adoption of Environmental Practices." *Social Forces* 86(1): 113–136.

Weber, Edward P. 2000. "A New Vanguard for the Environment: Grass-Roots Ecosystem Management as a New Environmental Movement." *Society & Natural Resources* 13: 237–259.

Woodhouse, Keith Makoto. 2018. *The Ecocentrists: A History of Radical Environmentalism.* Columbia University Press.

Zhang, Yang. 2018. "Allies in Action: Institutional Actors and Grassroots Environmental Activism in China." *Research in Social Movements, Conflicts and Change* 42: 9–38.

31

INFLUENCE OF ENVIRONMENTAL MOVEMENTS ON PUBLIC OPINION AND ATTITUDES

Do people's movements move the people?

Joanna K. Huxster

Introduction

It is generally accepted that messages developed by environmental organizations within the movement influence the attitudes and behaviors of individual members of the public (Brulle, 1996), and much historical and theoretical work operates under this assumption, but little empirical work exists on the topic. Given that much of the environmental movement is focused on shifting public opinion, it is vital to understand the relationship between these two variables. In this chapter, I explore existing empirical and theoretical research to explain how public opinion might be moved by environmental movements, given the dearth of data. Much of the most recent and relevant work on these issues has focused on the United States public. For this reason, I use the US as a case study to outline the potential avenues of and barriers to shifting environmental attitudes that relate to the actions of environmental movements. I include a call for research at the end of this chapter, in which I outline some additional avenues of further study.

In writing with a US focus, I must acknowledge the immense diversity of subjects and issues tackled by the environmental movement writ large and the vast differences in environmental values between cultures. Scholars studying environmental movements and public opinion in international contexts cite early US environmental thinkers as pioneers of modern environmental movements across the globe (Dryzek *et al.*, 2003; Torkar and Bogner, 2019), the effects of which are often considered strongest in the US and Western Europe (Mertig and Dunlap, 2001). Still, the environmental movement is not one entity but comprises many disparate communities and discourses (Brulle, 2008). Environmental justice, "wilderness" preservation, climate change activism, biodiversity and conservation biology, Indigenous environmental activism, and the anti-fracking movement, for example, may have overlapping themes but often have different goals, audiences, and strategies. Occasionally, these sub-movements may even be at odds with one another, particularly when we compare them internationally. These movements also have differences in their capacity to influence public opinion. The size of a movement, the locality of the issue, and the individual's perception of efficacy affect how much the public can be swayed (Gifford and Nilsson, 2014; Stoknes, 2015). The climate movement stands out for its variance

DOI: 10.4324/9780367855680-36

from the rest of environmental movement. Public opinion on climate, for myriad reasons, behaves differently (Shum, 2009; Stoknes, 2015). Some of the generalizations I make in this chapter, therefore, may not apply to all aspects of the environmental movement within the US and will not apply across all cultures and nations. My US focus is not meant to be representative of the international public. It does, however, serve as a critical case study, given its prominence in the creation of the modern environmental movement and as an industrialized, democratic nation with intense politicization of the environment.

US environmentalism, public opinion, and environmental attitudes

Before examining the drivers of public opinion and how they might relate to the actions of the environmental movement in the United States, it is necessary to understand the current state of US environmental opinions and attitudes. Gallup poll data show that in 2018, 42% of Americans considered themselves environmentalists. This percentage has been continuously declining since Gallup first asked this question in 1989, when 76% of Americans identified as environmentalists (Gallup, 2020). One possible explanation for this decline is in the definition of the term "environmentalist" itself. The label has likely evolved to become associated with radical environmental action more than commonplace individual responsibilities like recycling and energy conservation (Jones, 2016). A quick glance at these declining numbers could give the impression that the environmental movement is losing the battle for public participation and identification with the cause, but an interpretation that points to a shifting definition of "environmentalism" might actually reveal the opposite view. If the bar for environmentalism is active movement participation, then 42% of Americans identifying with this term is a sizable percentage.

Asking directly about individual identification with the environmental movement could be another means of gauging influence. Figure 31.1 shows percentages of participants indicating they are active in, sympathetic to, or unsympathetic to the environmental movement from 2000 through 2017 (Gallup, 2020). Just over half of Americans identify as either active in or sympathetic to the environmental movement. Sympathy toward the movement may be one of the clearer indications that the movement has had significant effect on public opinion, although it does not tell *what* the public thinks and is not a direct comparison of movement output to public opinion.

The political polarization of the environment in the US contributes to the overall decline in environmentalist identity over time. Republican identification as environmentalist has declined considerably. In 1991, 78% of both parties identified as environmentalists, but in 2018, only 27% of Republicans, compared to 56% of Democrats, thought of themselves in the same way. (See Figure 31.2.)

Although some differences in levels of concern are seen by race, education level, income level, and gender on various environmental issues (Leiserowitz, 2006; Liu *et al.*, 2014; McCright and Xiao, 2014; van der Linden *et al.*, 2015), the greatest predictor of environmental concern in the United States is political affiliation (Cruz, 2017; Liu *et al.*, 2014). Gender is a less significant but very consistent determinant, with higher levels of concern in women across all environmental issues (Liu *et al.*, 2014; McCright and Xiao, 2014). In the United States, non-whites tend to have higher levels of environmental concern than whites, but education level is not a consistent determinant of environmental concern between studies (Liu *et al.*, 2014).

Survey results from the Pew Research Center in early 2020 (prior to the global coronavirus pandemic, which is likely to have significantly influenced public concerns and opinions) found that the environment has risen as a priority in the US; however, the gap between Republican

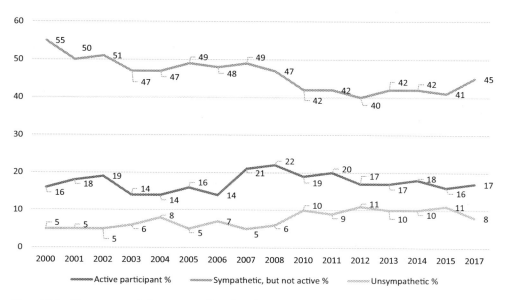

Figure 31.1   Percentages of those responding that they are an active participant; sympathetic, but not active; and unsympathetic when asked "Do you think of yourself as an active participant in the environmental movement; sympathetic toward the movement, but not active; neutral; or unsympathetic toward the environmental movement?"

Source: Gallup Poll 2020, graphed for this chapter by the author

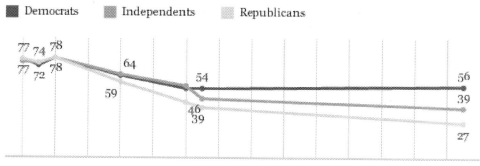

Figure 31.2   Gallup Poll data for self-identification as an environmentalist in the United States from 1989 to 2018

and Democrat prioritization is substantial; 85% of Democrats indicated that the environment should be a top priority for the president and Congress, in contrast with only 39% of Republicans. This gap is mirrored in the same question asked with the words "climate change" rather than "the environment". The increasing polarization in public concern over climate change has been well documented (Carmichael *et al.*, 2017; Dunlap *et al.*, 2016; Huxster *et al.*, 2014; McCright and Dunlap, 2011; Zhou, 2016) and can be seen in Figure 31.3 from Carmichael *et al.*'s aggregated policy mood score analysis for climate change concern, the CCTI (2017). This polarization provides anecdotal evidence that the environmental movement, at least on the issue of climate, has been unable to break through political biases in the United States to influence public opinion.

Measurement of environmental public opinion in the US has often ignored the views and experiences of marginalized communities, including those of Black, Latin, and Native Americans. These communities experience vast differences in privilege, access, and political power compared to white communities, disparate and disproportionate effects from environmental degradation, and unequal access to, and attention from, the environmental movement (Taylor, 2016).

Among marginalized communities in the US, the environmental attitudes, behaviors, and concerns of Black Americans are most studied. Despite current and historic barriers to Black American involvement in the environmental movement (Parker and McDonough, 1999; Taylor, 2014), Black Americans are as concerned, if not more so, than whites about the environment (Gifford and Nilsson, 2014b; Lazri and Konisky, 2019; Parker and McDonough, 1999). The most recent empirical work finds that people of color (POCs) are significantly more likely than white Americans to be concerned about air pollution, water pollution, and other issues that affect their immediate surroundings (Lazri and Konisky, 2019). Issues associated with environmental justice are most important to the Black American community, but people of color are as concerned as whites about global issues as well. Lazri and Koninsky posit that the emergence

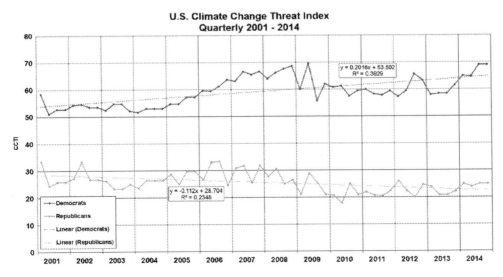

Figure 31.3 Climate Change Threat Index (CCTI) by political party, 2001–2014

Source: Carmichael et al., 2017

and strengthening of the environmental justice movement in the 1980s coincides with Black Americans and other POCs challenging the dominant discourses about their perceived ambivalence toward environmental issues (2019). The few studies examining the environmental values, attitudes, and concerns of Latin American and Hispanic communities in the US point to strong environmental concern, particularly for issues of environmental justice (Lazri and Konkinsy, 2019; Burger and Greenberg, 2006). I hypothesize, therefore, that the environmental movement and the environmental justice movement have had strong influences on public opinion in the Black and Latin American communities.

Despite a near fetishization of Native American culture as a "natural" and environmentally conscious way of life in US environmental discourses, little empirical research exists on the environmental concerns of Indigenous US peoples. A 2012 analysis of data from four waves of the General Social Survey finds no difference between Native American–identified participants and other ethnicities in connection to or concern for the environment (Sage, 2012). Some evidence exists that Native American communities are more informed and concerned than others regarding local issues (Biondo, 2018). Indigenous US populations have played crucial roles in recent environmental activism, particularly in protests against the construction of major oil pipelines, Keystone XL and Dakota Access (Healy, 2016). Historically, Native Americans have suffered immensely from injustices affecting their environment in the United States (Pasternak, 2011) and from the environmental movement itself (Taylor, 2016). High levels of concern in this community have likely grown independently of the US modern environmental movement, with more recent connections to the environmental justice movement. Significantly more research is needed on this front.

Drivers of public opinion

Environmental risk perception

Individual-level risk perception is one of the better-studied aspects of environmental concern and attitudes in the US and a potential avenue through which environmental movements might influence the public. Global environmental issues, such as climate change, are not likely to raise our individual risk alarms. Generally, we are more likely to perceive situations as risky if they are spectacular (like a plane crash or a natural disaster), personal, often discussed, immediate, sudden, and unfamiliar (Leiserowitz, 2005; Spence and Pidgeon, 2010; Weber and Stern, 2011). Although spectacular events are becoming increasingly common, these disasters are fleeting, punctuating a landscape of generally slow and almost imperceptible increases in global temperatures. They do little to affect long term risk perceptions. (Kahn, 2013). Global-level environmental issues like climate are rarely personal, sudden, or immediate. Most move slowly, are not new, and affect people in developing countries and marginalized communities much more than they do most US citizens.

These theories of risk perception can be applied to explain why members of the US public are more concerned about air and water pollution. These issues are often local and personal – the individuals and communities near polluted water and breathing polluted air are personally affected and therefore are likely to perceive high levels of risk (Stoknes, 2015). However, they have to be cognizant that the pollution is present, is causing the health effects they are experiencing, and is perpetrated by some person or industry (Pezzullo and Cox, 2017). Increasing risk awareness is another way in which the environmental movement and environmental advocacy have influenced public opinion. It is apparent that environmental justice groups have been at least partially responsible for public awareness of risks and hazards in local communities.

Drivers of aggregate public opinion trends

Media coverage is well documented as a driver of US public opinion on climate change (Hoyos, 2014; Painter and Gavin, 2016; Tan and Weaver, 2009). Scholars have also studied elite political cues (Brulle *et al.*, 2012), temperature changes and weather events (Howe and Leiserowitz, 2013; Krosnick *et al.*, 2006; McCright *et al.*, 2014; Spence *et al.*, 2011; Weber and Stern, 2011), and scientific literacy (Bauer *et al.*, 2007; Reynolds *et al.*, 2010; Weber and Stern, 2011) as drivers of public environmental opinion and concern. Media often works as an amplification of these other factors – bringing the information about political discourse, scientific reports, and weather events to the public (Carmichael and Brulle, 2017). Schafer et al. find that activism can increase levels of media coverage on social issues, pointing to media as an avenue by which the environmental movement has influenced public opinion (2014). Advocacy groups attempt to influence the content and amount of media coverage on environmental issues, in addition to providing information directly to the public (Agnone, 2007; Carmichael *et al.*, 2012).

Carmichael and Brulle's 2017 study of the effects of various factors on aggregate public climate concern is one of the only peer-reviewed, empirical measurements of the effects of advocacy efforts on public opinion. The study uses a macro-political perspective with a national-level time series to examine relationships between advocacy efforts, political discourses, media coverage, and public opinion. The design of the study allows for examination of both the direct and indirect effects of each of the different factors on aggregate public climate change concern (Carmichael and Brulle, 2017). They find that the strongest predicter of public concern about climate change is media coverage and that media coverage is most strongly predicted by elite political cues. One important takeaway from this work is that although individuals may be affected by direct contact with climate advocacy, media attention is the primary way in which the climate movement is able to sway aggregate public opinion. A second key takeaway is that environmental movement activity is also a significant predictor of media coverage, but only by about half as much as political elite activity (2017). One conclusion to draw from this is that environmental advocates may sway public opinion through swaying political leaders rather than vice versa. This study does not measure the ways in which elite cues may be *directly* affected by climate advocacy, which could then affect public opinion through the media. If this is the pathway of influence, then the importance of targeting public opinion may be diminished.

Potential avenues to shifting public opinion

Despite minimal empirical evidence of the relationship between the environmental movement and public environmental attitudes, there exist historical, qualitative, and theoretical perspectives that have explanatory potential. Applications of issue-specific work on climate change attitudes and an understanding of media effects on public opinion can help illuminate the relationship between the movement and environmental attitudes.

Theoretical influences in the US from discourse analysis and the constructivist perspective

Historical shifts in public support for environmental policies and causes corresponding with the creation and activity of the US environmental movement point to clear connections, particularly in the early decades of the movement. The sudden interest in measuring public opinion in the 1960s can be seen as an indication that the blossoming modern movement was perceived as affecting environmental attitudes. Further evidence exists in the aftermath of the environmental protests marking the first Earth Day in 1970 (which included around 20 million participants) and the creation of new environmental NGOs within the same time frame. The discourse of the modern environmental movement and the popular ecological paradigm shift are often credited with the subsequent enactment of some of the boldest environmental legislation in the United States, including the National Environmental Policy Act, the creation of the US Environmental Protection Agency, and the Clean Air Act (Inglehart, 1995). Similarly, one can easily argue that the rise of the environmental justice movement, which eventually led President Bill Clinton to pass an executive order on the inclusion of environmental justice considerations in federal agency missions in 1994, influenced public awareness and attitudes toward environmental racism and classism in the United States (Pezzullo and Cox, 2017).

Discourse analysis of the environmental movement and organizations offers theoretical perspectives on how the US movement has shaped public opinion in over 120 years of collective action. Brulle, who defines discourses as "term(s) used to describe the historically specific world-views that serve as the basis for formulation of collective action" (p. 60), analyzes the origins and historical influences of the most prominent and widely agreed-upon environmental discourses in the United States (1996). Brulle pairs preservationism, conservationism, ecocentrism, political ecology, deep ecology, and ecofeminism with the movement organizations that espouse them and the social events each discourse defined (1996). The connections between environmental discourses, the movement, and policy making offer a compelling argument that the environmental movement shape public attitudes. Brulle explains that environmental degradation does not create collective action on its own but that new discourses must be created to generate public support, and social movements "play a major role in the development and transmission of these alternative ideas" (1996, p. 80).

The creation of new discourses, and even of names and terms within those environmental discourses, can also be examined from rhetorical and constructivist perspectives. One of the key rhetorical tools for categorizing parts of nature is the act of naming, and part of this act is defining environmental conditions or events as "issues" or "problems" (Pezzullo and Cox, 2017). Movement organizations are found to be strategic and attentive to how the public receives their rhetoric and framing (Banaszak and Ondercin, 2016). The constitutive power of communication on environmental conditions and ideas helps create and enforce social constructions. Cronan famously describes the social construction of "wilderness" and idea that comes from the early founders of the preservationist branch of environmental movement and the problems that have arisen from this construct (1995), but the environmental movement has also been responsible for bringing numerous environmental conditions from the realm of ivory-tower science to socially recognized "issues" (Taylor, 2000). From the constructivist perspective, the identification and naming of various environmental situations as problems worthy of public concern is an obvious contribution to public awareness and opinion. Before Rachel Carson identified pesticide use as a problem, naming it as such and using apocalyptic rhetoric and metaphors to war (1962), DDT was seen as a societal boon. Recent examples regarding public awareness of plastic pollution in the oceans, the decline of pollinating bee species, and the sharp increase in species extinction are cases in which outcry and outreach from environmental advocates and organizations have clearly impacted public awareness and concern, even if these influences have not yet been measured. The naming and identification of issues dangerous to human and ecological well-being, I would argue, have been the most obvious and substantial influences of the environmental movement, and actors within it, on public opinion.

Protests and public opinion

Public demonstrations, marches, and other forms of public protest are key tactics in many social movements, including the environmental and environmental justice movements (Lester and Cattle, 2015). The turning point of the modern environmental movement in the US and the spark for the country's most far-reaching and strongest environmental legislation was the protest on the first Earth Day in 1970 (Inglehart, 1995). Environmental protests can now be seen in nations throughout the world, and global protests with participants in many countries at once have become increasingly common for both local and global issues (Lester and Cattle, 2015).

Achieving large turnouts for public environmental demonstrations and marches obviously requires that those in attendance are of environmentally like mind, and the number of protesters is often estimated and broadcast to show the strength of a movement. Given that they are generally conducted with the goal of generating a specific change, usually in legislation, scholars have asked how public demonstrations affect legislative activity (for an example, see Agnone, 2007). Some protests are also aimed at gaining further public support (Banaszak and Ondercin, 2016). Banaszek and Ondercin find that for the women's rights movement, public events and demonstrations significantly influence public attitudes toward gender equality (2016). There is reason for caution when applying these findings to all aspects of the environmental movement, however. Given the well-documented boomerang effects on public opinion observed on the particularly polarized issue of climate change when media covers the issue (Zhou, 2016), I would posit that protests on climate may actually be more polarizing in the United States, although they could be effective for other issues.

Media attention and effects

Media plays a vital role in environmental movement groups' abilities to convey their concerns and demands to the public and decision makers as these groups usually lack direct channels to their intended audiences (Cox and Schwarz, 2015). Environmental scholars have noted that environmental groups use multiple means to attract media attention. One of the most common and older techniques is what scholars call "earned media": attention earned through public actions meant to fulfill requirements of newsworthiness such as conflict, oddity, and emotional impact (Cox and Schwarz, 2015; Pezzullo and Cox, 2017). Protests, sit-ins, ecotage, and acts of civil disobedience all fit into this category. These tactics for attracting media attention often are initially successful but lose their potency over time and have the additional disadvantage of giving mainstream media the opportunity to frame groups as radical or extremist (Cox and Schwarz, 2015). A second and newer technique groups use to bring their causes and names into the media is to act as researchers and information providers for the already time-taxed news professionals and journalists. This type of media participation may lead to more sustained coverage and attention (Cox and Schwarz, 2015).

Media effects theories postulate the ways in which media content and frequency affect the attitudes of the intended audience(s) (Pezzullo and Cox, 2017). The theory of agenda setting is frequently studied and cited as relevant to environmental news coverage. It is also highly relevant to the ways in which the environmental movement has, indirectly through media, affected public attitudes and concern toward environmental issues. For decades, scholarly work has confirmed that the amount of attention the media pays to an issue correlates with the public's subsequent perceptions of the importance of that issue to the nation (Cox and Schwarz, 2015; Kenix, 2000; Pezzullo and Cox, 2017). Agenda setting and other media effects are likely the clearest paths by which the environmental movement affects public opinion. News cycles, the shrinking space available in traditional news media, shifts from "old" to new media, media political economy, and numerous other factors all play a role in how much and how often environmental movement groups are able to gain the media attention necessary to keep their issues on the public agenda. (For a full analysis of the ways in which coverage of environmental actions are framed in the media, see Cox and Schwarz, 2015).

Messengers and elites

The effectiveness of different messengers for conveying information across various forms of traditional, visual, audio, and social media is a growing field of social scientific study. One might consider the "elites" whose "cues" are significantly tied to aggregate public opinion on climate change (Carmichael *et al.*, 2017; Carmichael and Brulle, 2018, 2017) as one messenger type. Recent decades have seen a dramatic increase in the number of celebrities acting as environmental messengers, and online activists have become a new type of international celebrity (see Greta Thunberg as an example) (Abidin *et al.*, 2020). With their massive online followings on social media platforms, celebrity and activist messengers have the potential for significant influence on public opinion. It is possible that some celebrities only pick up social causes like environmentalism because they are already popular. Although a great deal of work has been done documenting the rise of celebrities as environmental communicators, continued research is needed to assess their impact on public attitudes and concerns.

Kahan et al.'s research on more traditional climate change messengers (i.e., scientists) finds that individuals' trust in a communicator has more to do with the message than the credentials of the messenger (2011). The authors find that cultural cognition of risk, or the tendency for individuals to perceive risk as it aligns with their values, influences how they perceive scientific consensus. Consequentially, individuals only believe that scientific elites are trustworthy and knowledgeable if the elite's stated beliefs match up with their own (Kahan *et al.*, 2011). If these findings are true with highly educated (hypothetical) messengers, I think it reasonable to assume that individuals can easily dismiss celebrities or young adults like Thunberg as being unknowledgeable and wrong if they disagree with those messengers' assertions. Although climate change is the most politicized and polarized of current environmental issues, the increasing polarization on the environment in the US may amplify this tendency. Continuing to examine and research the credibility and efficacy of movement messengers will be critical to understanding their influence on public opinion.

Clicktivism and social media

The internet and social media have influenced and shaped the environmental movement and its ability to reach the public to an extent that cannot be fully described here. I have woven some of the avenues by which social media has contributed to and changed the landscape of the movement throughout this chapter, but there is much more to be said and studied on this front. Transnational environmental movements, actions, and protests would not be possible on their current scale without the aid of the internet and social media. The platforms through which celebrities advocate, and even the types of celebrities who can advocate, are all centered online. A new breed of celebrity, the "influencer", who only exists because of social media, can now advocate for environmental causes.

Social and digital media also allow for new ways to engage publics on issues. Anyone can "bear witness" to an act of environmental destruction by filming it on their cellphone and sharing it on the web (Pezzullo and Cox, 2017). Viral videos and images are closely tied to the amplification of the movement to ban single-use plastics, for example, and citizen documentation and dissemination of damage from the BP oil spill while formal press was blocked from the area would not have been possible without digital and social media (Pezzullo and Cox, 2017). Anecdotal evidence suggests that these types of communications have been highly influential on public opinion and concern.

The environmental movement's shift to internet-based activism has also made signature and donation collection easier. Online petitions for environmental causes abound, and digitally signing them is incredibly simple. These acts of "clicktivism" usually do not result in long-term engagement with an issue (Pezzullo and Cox, 2017). Recent criticism of virtue signaling and performative activism has also been leveled against support for social movements displayed on social media. Long-term studies of the connections between public participation in activism on social media, public attitudes and concern, and continued engagement with real-world activism would help further illuminate the efficacy of digital media for the environmental movement.

Barriers and room for improvement

Attitude-behavior gap

Scholars studying environmental attitudes and concerns have long been aware of a persistent disconnect between pro-environmental attitudes and actions, often called the "attitude-behavior gap". Participation in the environmental movement or environmental activism is usually characterized as different from more general pro-environmental behavior such as acts of conservation, transportation choices, recycling, and household consumption choices (Dono *et al.*, 2010). Although strong environmental attitudes and values are necessary for both types of participation, they are not sufficient for increasing pro-environmental behavior (Bamberg, 2003). This may be because concern is an important *indirect* determinant of behavior, but concerned individuals' behavior choices are *directly* affected by their perceptions of the efficacy of their actions and their expectations of what others are doing (Bamberg, 2003). The implications for connections between the environmental movement and public opinion are multiple. First, measurements of public action, like participation in specific behaviors, clearly cannot be used as proxies for the influence of the movement on public opinion. People's recycling habits, for example, do not indicate whether or not the movement has moved the public on environmental issues. Second, the attitude-behavior gap brings up a relevant question about whether public opinion is necessary for moving forward environmental causes. The third implication concerns perceptions of efficacy and how they influence behavior. The efficacy of individual-level action is questionable at best, which means we must now examine mainstream environmental groups' focus on these types of actions.

Room for improvement: Limits of individual action and the deficit model

Although there are many environmental organizations working for systemic and political change, the push for individuals to take actions like recycle their plastic bottles and paper, change their lightbulbs from incandescent to CFLs, take shorter showers, and turn off the lights is prominent in the messaging from mainstream environmental organizations. Yet these actions and the "if everyone just does their part, we can save the world!" mentality championed by these groups are minimally effective. Worse yet, most individuals have some sense that changing their lightbulbs isn't going to solve the problem (in this case, climate change), even if everyone does it (Stoknes, 2015). If the mainstream contingent of the environmental movement continues to push for actions that individuals don't see as effective, it's unlikely that even those with concern will act. It's even possible that people actually will become *less* concerned, as individuals are more likely to be concerned about something they feel they can be personally effective to counteract (Gifford and Nilsson, 2014b; Hart and Feldman, 2016). Mainstream environmental groups promoting individual-level actions in an attempt to make people feel they can "do something about it" may actually be losing ground in increasing public attention and activism. A better approach may be more vocal advocacy for systemic or political change.

Plenty of recent empirical research exists on the failings of a particular form of science communication termed "the deficit model" in which mismatches between scientific evidence and public opinion are assumed to be products of an uninformed public. Those following the deficit model attempt to remedy the mismatch by giving the public more facts and scientific information through one-way communication, with the assumption that this will change their beliefs and attitudes toward an issue (Cortassa, 2016; Kahan, 2010; Simis *et al.*, 2016). Despite a body of social scientific research that contradicts these assumptions (see, for example, Kahan, 2016; Kahan *et al.*, 2012), the deficit model still persists in much of the communication about environmental issues like climate change put forth by science communicators (Simis *et al.*, 2016), including environmental organizations. A great deal of research on effective environmental and climate communication exists, and some of the movement has begun to use this work to their advantage. Ignoring that work will surely be a barrier to moving public opinion, particularly in the face of the active efforts of the anti-environmental movement to sway the public (Dryzek, 2013; Lewandowsky *et al.*, 2019; Miller and Dinan, 2015; Oreskes and Conway, 2011).

Does the movement need public opinion?

In the United States, the biggest policy victories occurred early in the modern environmental movement, and many scholars have questioned why further meaningful policy has stalled while public concern has increased (Kenix, 2000). Meanwhile, other democratic nations are moving ahead with much stronger environmental policies (Dryzek *et al.*, 2003). The relationship between public concern and meaningful environmental policy differs by country and culture and depends a great deal on the politics of the nation in question, but there are reasons to wonder if the political climate in the United States is such that shifting public opinion should be the main goal of the environmental movement. Dryzek points out that in capitalist democratic societies, politics are often influenced by interests with large financial resources and power, and these interests, like the fossil fuel industry for example, are often able to steer the outcomes of policy making (2013). The space for the public to influence policy is small in a capitalist market economy that affords considerable privilege to business.

There are tactical indications that some organizations have realized they don't need the entire public on their side to move policy forward. There is still evidence that public opinion and environmental policy move together in democratic nations like the US, but Carmichael *et al.*'s findings that aggregate public opinion is moved by political elite cues, not the other way around, raise questions about the directionality of these relationships (Carmichael *et al.*, 2017). Ultimately, I think the movement does need public opinion, even if just to reinforce environmental social norms and ease future transitions to more sustainable energy sources and practices. These questions warrant further investigation.

Conclusion and call for research

Even a cursory historical view of the environmental movement and environmental public opinion shows that the two are clearly connected, and, as with all social movements, influencing the attitudes and concerns of the public has been a primary concern for environmental organizations and activists throughout the world. Yet, as this chapter has highlighted, many questions remain on the nature and strength of this relationship, and considerably more empirical work is needed to move past the theoretical and observational. The United States, the case study for this chapter and the country in which the modern environmental movement is said to have originated, is exceptional in its polarization and politicization of environmental attitudes (McCright *et al.*, 2016). Although little or no empirical work directly examines the relationship between the environmental movement and public opinion, this chapter has explored the various ways in which other documented drivers might hypothetically connect the environmental movement and the attitudes and concerns of the US public. I outlined here some of the known effects on public opinion of tactics, like protests and media attention, as I believe they are another key piece of the puzzle. In addition, I highlighted some contradictions and barriers to increasing public environmental concern that I believe the movement has encountered.

As I have reiterated throughout, considerably more empirical research is needed to fully answer the key question of this chapter. Measuring the output, efforts, and work of the environmental movement will be a difficult exercise, but it is not insurmountable, and it must be done if we are to truly understand how the movement has influenced and will continue to influence public opinion on environmental issues. Further, more data are needed from developing countries, countries outside of North America, Europe, and Australia, and Indigenous and minority populations within nations, to better understand drivers of public opinion, environmental behaviors, and environmental activism in various cultural and political contexts. Finally, there are some very interesting questions about the directional relationship between political elites' cues, policy, and public opinion on the environment in the United States, and likely other capitalist democracies, that require further research.

The significance of environmental movements at local, national, and international levels is unquestionable. As Giugni and Grasso assert in the introduction to this *Handbook* and elsewhere (2015), the environmental movement is heterogeneous, transforming, and institutionalizing. It is composed of a wide variety of peoples, interests, and actors with the potential for far-reaching influence tailored to specific audiences. It has evolved over time from the days of conservationism through eras of direct action and political lobbying, showing great plasticity and capacity for change. The movement has played a constitutive role in contemporary societies' view of environmental problems, and international movements surrounding global environmental crises, organized and amplified by social and digital media, are only likely to grow as the issues themselves become more dire. For these reasons and more, it is vital to more clearly understand the impact of environmental movements on public opinion.

References

Abidin, C., Brockington, D., Goodman, M.K., Mostafanezhad, M., Ann Richey, L., 2020. The Tropes of Celebrity Environmentalism. *Annu. Rev. Environ. Resour.* 45. https://doi.org/10.1146/annurev-environ-012320-081703

Agnone, J., 2007. Amplifying Public Opinion: The Policy Impact of the U.S. Environmental Movement. *Soc. Forces.* 85, 1593–1620.

Bamberg, S., 2003. How Does Environmental Concern Influence Specific Environmentally Related Behaviors? A New Answer to an Old Question. *J. Environ. Psychol.* 23, 21–32. https://doi.org/10.1016/S0272-4944(02)00078-6

Banaszak, L.A., Ondercin, H.L., 2016. Public Opinion as a Movement Outcome: The Case of the U.S. Women's Movement. *Mobilization Int. Q.* 21, 361–378. https://doi.org/10.17813/1086-671X-21-3-361

Bauer, M.W., Allum, N., Miller, S., 2007. What Can We Learn from 25 Years of PUS Survey Research? Liberating and Expanding the Agenda. *Public Underst. Sci.* 16, 79–95. https://doi.org/10/dpn6sd

Biondo, A., 2018. Poll Shows Indigenous People More Aware of Great Lakes Threats [WWW Document]. *Great Lakes Echo.* https://greatlakesecho.org/2018/10/26/poll-shows-indigenous-people-more-aware-of-great-lakes-threats/ (accessed 6.17.2020).

Brulle, R.J., 2008. The US Environmental Movement. In: Gould, K., Lewis, T. (Eds.), *20 Lessons in Environmental Sociology.* Oxford University Press, New York, pp. 14–18.

Brulle, R.J., 1996. Environmental Discourse and Social Movement Organizations: A Historical and Rhetorical Perspective on the Development of U.S. Environmental Organizations. *Sociol. Inq.* 66, 58–83. https://doi.org/10.1111/j.1475-682X.1996.tb00209.x

Brulle, R.J., Carmichael, J., Jenkins, J.C., 2012. Shifting Public Opinion on Climate Change: An Empirical Assessment of Factors Influencing Concern Over Climate Change in the U.S., 2002–2010. *Clim. Change.* 114, 169–188. https://doi.org/10.1007/s10584-012-0403-y

Burger, J., Greenberg, M., 2006. Ethnic Differences in Ecological Concerns: Spanish-Speaking Hispanics Are More Concerned Than Others. *Environ. Res.* 102, 36–45. https://doi.org/10.1016/j.envres.2005.12.009

Carmichael, J.T., Brulle, R.J., 2018. Media Use and Climate Change Concern. *Int. J. Media Cult. Polit.* 14, 243–253. https://doi.org/10/gg4367

Carmichael, J.T., Brulle, R.J., 2017. Elite Cues, Media Coverage, and Public Concern: An Integrated Path Analysis of Public Opinion on Climate Change, 2001–2013. *Environ. Polit.* 26, 232–252. https://doi.org/10.1080/09644016.2016.1263433

Carmichael, J.T., Brulle, R.J., Huxster, J.K., 2017. The Great Divide: Understanding the Role of Media and Other Drivers of the Partisan Divide in Public Concern Over Climate Change in the USA, 2001–2014. *Clim. Change.* 1–14. https://doi.org/10/f92vzp

Carmichael, J.T., Jenkins, J.C., Brulle, R.J., 2012. Building Environmentalism: The Founding of Environmental Movement Organizations in the United States, 1900–2000. *Sociol. Q.* 53, 422–453. https://doi.org/10.1111/j.1533-8525.2012.01242.x

Carson, R., 1962. *Silent Spring.* Houghton Mifflin Company, Boston.

Cortassa, C., 2016. In Science Communication, Why Does the Idea of a Public Deficit Always Return? The Eternal Recurrence of the Public Deficit. *Public Underst. Sci.* 25, 447–459. https://doi.org/10/gg4342

Cox, R., Schwarz, S., 2015. The Media/Communication Strategies of Environmental Pressure Groups and NGOs. In: *The Routledge Handbook of Environment and Communication.* Routledge, Taylor & Francis Group, New York.

Cronon, W., 1995. The Trouble with Wilderness: Or, Getting Back to the Wrong Nature. *Environ. Hist.* 1, 7. https://doi.org/10.2307/3985059

Cruz, S.M., 2017. The Relationships of Political Ideology and Party Affiliation with Environmental Concern: A Meta-Analysis. *J. Environ. Psychol.* 53, 81–91. https://doi.org/10.1016/j.jenvp.2017.06.010

Dono, J., Webb, J., Richardson, B., 2010. The Relationship Between Environmental Activism, Pro-Environmental Behaviour and Social Identity. *J. Environ. Psychol.* 30, 178–186. https://doi.org/10.1016/j.jenvp.2009.11.006

Dryzek, J.S., 2013. *The Politics of the Earth: Environmental Discourses,* 3rd ed. Oxford University Press, Oxford.

Dryzek, J.S., Downes, D., Hunold, C., Schlosberg, D., Hernes, H.-K., 2003. *Green States and Social Movements: Environmentalism in the United States, United Kingdom, Germany, and Norway, Green States and Social Movements.* Oxford University Press, Oxford.

Dunlap, R.E., McCright, A.M., Yarosh, J.H., 2016. The Political Divide on Climate Change: Partisan Polarization Widens in the U.S. *Environ. Sci. Policy Sustain. Dev.* 58, 4–23. https://doi.org/10.1080/00139157.2016.1208995

Gallup, 2020. In Depth: Environment [WWW Document]. *Gallup.com.* https://news.gallup.com/poll/1615/Environment.aspx (accessed 6.16.2020).

Gifford, R., Nilsson, A., 2014. Personal and Social Factors That Influence Pro-Environmental Concern and Behaviour: A Review. *Int. J. Psychol.* 49, 141–157. https://doi.org/10.1002/ijop.12034

Giugni, M., Grasso, M.T., 2015. Environmental Movements in Advanced Industrial Democracies: Heterogeneity, Transformation, and Institutionalization. *Annu. Rev. Environ. Resour.* 40, 337–361.

Hart, P.S., Feldman, L., 2016. The Influence of Climate Change Efficacy Messages and Efficacy Beliefs on Intended Political Participation. *PLoS One.* 11, e0157658. https://doi.org/10.1371/journal.pone.0157658

Healy, J., 2016. Occupying the Prairie: Tensions Rise as Tribes Move to Block a Pipeline. *New York Times*.

Howe, P.D., Leiserowitz, A., 2013. Who Remembers a Hot Summer or a Cold Winter? The Asymmetric Effect of Beliefs About Global Warming on Perceptions of Local Climate Conditions in the U.S. Glob. *Environ. Change.* 23, 1488–1500. https://doi.org/10.1016/j.gloenvcha.2013.09.014

Hoyos, G., 2014. No More Great Expectations: Media Response to Obama's Climate Action Plan. *Interact. Stud. Commun. Cult.* 5, 93–106. https://doi.org/10.1386/iscc.5.1.93_1

Huxster, J.K., Carmichael, J.T., Brulle, R., 2014. A Macro Political Examination of the Partisan and Ideological Divide in Aggregate Public Concern over Climate Change in the U.S. Between 2001 and 2013. *Environ. Manag. Sustain. Dev.* 4, 1. https://doi.org/10/gg433w

Inglehart, R., 1995. Public Support for Environmental Protection: Objective Problems and Subjective Values in 43 Societies 17. *Polit. Sci. Polit.* 28, 1.

Jones, J.M., 2016. Americans' Identification as "Environmentalists" Down to 42% [WWW Document]. *Gallup.com.* https://news.gallup.com/poll/190916/americans-identification-environmentalists-down.aspx (accessed 6.16.2020).

Kahan, D., 2010. Fixing the Communications Failure. *Nature.* 463, 296–297.

Kahan, D., 2016. "Ordinary Science Intelligence": A Science-Comprehension Measure for Study of Risk and Science Communication, with Notes on Evolution and Climate Change. *J. Risk Res.* 1–22. https://doi.org/10/gg433s

Kahan, D., Jenkins-Smith, H., Braman, D., 2011. Cultural Cognition of Scientific Consensus. *J. Risk Res.* 14, 147–174. https://doi.org/10/bdrqf6

Kahan, D., Peters, E., Wittlin, M., Slovic, P., Ouellette, L.L., Braman, D., Mandel, G., 2012. The Polarizing Impact of Science Literacy and Numeracy on Perceived Climate Change Risks. *Nat. Clim. Change.* 2, 732–735. https://doi.org/10/gc3fs6

Kahn, B., 2013. Hurricane Sandy Hasn't Shifted Climate Narrative [WWW Document]. *Climatecentral.org.* www.climatecentral.org/news/sandy-didnt-change-a-thing-16669 (accessed 6.17.2020).

Kenix, L.J., 2000. The Modern Environmental Movement: Public Opinion, Media Coverage, and the Importance of Visual Information. *J. Egypt. Pub. Op. Res.* 1, 1–49.

Krosnick, J.A., Holbrook, A.L., Lowe, L., Visser, P.S., 2006. The Origins and Consequences of Democratic Citizens' Policy Agendas: A Study of Popular Concern About Global Warming. *Clim. Change.* 77, 7–43. https://doi.org/10.1007/s10584-006-9068-8

Lazri, A.M., Konisky, D.M., 2019. Environmental Attitudes Across Race and Ethnicity. *Soc. Sci. Q.* 100, 1039–1055. https://doi.org/10.1111/ssqu.12626

Leiserowitz, A.A., 2005. American Risk Perceptions: Is Climate Change Dangerous?: American Risk Perceptions. *Risk Anal.* 25, 1433–1442. https://doi.org/10.1111/j.1540-6261.2005.00690.x

Leiserowitz, A.A., 2006. Climate Change Risk Perception and Policy Preferences: The Role of Affect, Imagery, and Values. *Clim. Change.* 77, 45–72. https://doi.org/10.1007/s10584-006-9059-9

Lester, L., Cattle, S., 2015. Transnational Protests, Publics, and Media Participation (in and Environmental Age). In: *The Routledge Handbook of Environment and Communication.* Routledge, Taylor & Francis Group, New York.

Lewandowsky, S., Pilditch, T.D., Madsen, J.K., Oreskes, N., Risbey, J.S., 2019. Influence and Seepage: An Evidence-Resistant Minority Can Affect Public Opinion and Scientific Belief Formation. *Cogn.* 188, 124–139. https://doi.org/10.1016/j.cognition.2019.01.011

Liu, X., Vedlitz, A., Shi, L., 2014. Examining the Determinants of Public Environmental Concern: Evidence from National Public Surveys. *Environ. Sci. Policy* 39, 77–94. https://doi.org/10.1016/j.envsci.2014.02.006

McCright, A.M., Dunlap, R.E., 2011. The Politicization of Climate Change and Polarization in the American Public's Views of Global Warming, 2001–2010. *Sociol. Q.* 52, 155–194. https://doi.org/10/bgr783

McCright, A.M., Dunlap, R.E., Marquart-Pyatt, S.T., 2016. Political Ideology and Views About Climate Change in the European Union. *Environ. Polit.* 25, 338–358. https://doi.org/10.1080/09644016.2015.1090371

McCright, A.M., Dunlap, R.E., Xiao, C., 2014. The Impacts of Temperature Anomalies and Political Orientation on Perceived Winter Warming. *Nat. Clim. Change.* 4, 1077–1081. https://doi.org/10.1038/nclimate2443

McCright, A.M., Xiao, C., 2014. Gender and Environmental Concern: Insights from Recent Work and for Future Research. *Soc. Nat. Resour.* 27, 1109–1113. https://doi.org/10.1080/08941920.2014.918235

Mertig, A.G., Dunlap, R.E., 2001. Environmentalism, New Social Movements, and the New Class: A Cross-National Investigation. *Rural Sociol.* 66, 113–136. https://doi.org/10.1111/j.1549-0831.2001.tb00057.x

Miller, D., Dinan, W., 2015. Resisting Meaningful Action on Climate Change: Think Tanks, "Merchants of Doubt" and the "Corporate Capture" of Sustainable Development. In: *The Routledge Handbook of Environment and Communication.* Routledge, Taylor & Francis Group, New York, pp. 86–99.

Oreskes, N., Conway, E.M., 2011. *Merchants of Doubt: How a Handful of Scientists Obscured the Truth on Issues from Tobacco Smoke to Climate Change*, reprint ed. Bloomsbury Publishing, New York.

Painter, J., Gavin, N.T., 2016. Climate Skepticism in British Newspapers, 2007–2011. *Environ. Commun.* 10, 432–452. https://doi.org/10.1080/17524032.2014.995193

Parker, J.D., McDonough, M.H., 1999. Environmentalism of African Americans: An Analysis of the Subculture and Barriers Theories. *Environ. Behav.* 31, 155–177. https://doi.org/10.1177/00139169921972047

Pasternak, J., 2011. *Yellow Dirt: A Poisoned Land and the Betrayal of the Navajos*, reprint ed. Free Press, New York.

Pezzullo, P.C., Cox, R., 2017. *Environmental Communication and the Public Sphere*, 5th ed. Sage Publications, Los Angeles, CA.

Reynolds, T.W., Bostrom, A., Read, D., Morgan, M.G., 2010. Now What Do People Know About Global Climate Change? Survey Studies of Educated Laypeople: Now What Do People Know About Global Climate Change? *Risk Anal.* 30, 1520–1538. https://doi.org/10/cb53s9

Sage, Franklin. 2012. *Comparing the Environmental Attitudes and Behaviors of Native Americans and Non-Native Americans.* UND Scholarly Commons. Theses and Dissertations. University of North Dakota 1031. https://commons.und.edu/theses/1031

Schafer, M.S., Ivanova, A., Schmidt, A., 2014. What Drives Media Attention for Climate Change? Explaining Issue Attention in Australian, German and Indian Print Media from 1996 to 2010. *Int. Commun. Gaz.* 76, 152–176.

Shum, R.Y., 2009. Can Attitudes Predict Outcomes? Public Opinion, Democratic Institutions and Environmental Policy. *Environ. Policy Gov.* 19, 281–295. https://doi.org/10.1002/eet.518

Simis, M.J., Madden, H., Cacciatore, M.A., Yeo, S.K., 2016. The Lure of Rationality: Why Does the Deficit Model Persist in Science Communication? *Public Underst. Sci.* 25, 400–414. https://doi.org/10/gfv8gg

Spence, A., Pidgeon, N., 2010. Framing and Communicating Climate Change: The Effects of Distance and Outcome Frame Manipulations. *Glob. Environ. Change*, 20th Anniversary Special Issue 20, 656–667. https://doi.org/10.1016/j.gloenvcha.2010.07.002

Spence, A., Poortinga, W., Butler, C., Pidgeon, N.F., 2011. Perceptions of Climate Change and Willingness to Save Energy Related to Flood Experience. *Nat. Clim. Change.* 1, 46–49. https://doi.org/10.1038/nclimate1059

Stoknes, P.E., 2015. *What We Think About When We Try Not To Think About Global Warming: Toward a New Psychology of Climate Action.* Chelsea Green Publishing, White River Junction, VT.

Tan, Y., Weaver, D.H., 2009. Local Media, Public Opinion, and State Legislative Policies: Agenda Setting at the State Level. *Int. J. Press.* https://doi.org/10.1177/1940161209336225

Taylor, D.E., 2000. The Rise of the Environmental Justice Paradigm: Injustice Framing and the Social Construction of Environmental Discourses. *Am. Behav. Sci.* 43. https://doi.org/10.1177/0002764200043004003

Taylor, D.E., 2014. *The State of Diversity in Environmental Organizations.* Green 20 Work Group, Green 2.0 192, Ann Arbor, MI.

Taylor, D.E., 2016. *The Rise of the American Conservation Movement: Power, Privilege, and Environmental Protection.* Duke University Press Books, Durham, NC.

Torkar, G., Bogner, F.X., 2019. Environmental Values and Environmental Concern. *Environ. Educ. Res.* 25, 1570–1581. https://doi.org/10.1080/13504622.2019.1649367

van der Linden, S.L., Leiserowitz, A.A., Feinberg, G.D., Maibach, E.W., 2015. The Scientific Consensus on Climate Change as a Gateway Belief: Experimental Evidence. *PLoS One* 10, e0118489. https://doi.org/10/f68jv2

Weber, E.U., Stern, P.C., 2011. Public Understanding of Climate Change in the United States. *Am. Psychol.* 66, 315–328. https://doi.org/10/dg82vr

Zhou, J., 2016. Boomerangs Versus Javelins: How Polarization Constrains Communication on Climate Change. *Environ. Polit.* 25, 788–811. https://doi.org/10.1080/09644016.2016.1166602

32

ENVIRONMENTAL MOVEMENTS AND SCIENTIFIC, TECHNOLOGICAL, AND INDUSTRIAL CHANGE

David J. Hess

Introduction

The goals of environmental movements frequently include industrial change. On a small scale, local environmental justice struggles often seek to stop an unwanted source of environmental risk, such as pollution from a local industrial site, or to gain some other kind of remediation. Environmental movements can also involve grassroots efforts to build alternative forms of industrial processes, technologies, and organizations. In doing so, they bring together industrial innovation and social movement goals, again often at a local level. On a broader scale, environmental movements can help to motivate more widespread changes in science, technology, and industry (STI) that are guided by public policy and shifts in consumer tastes and organizational strategy. This chapter reviews environmental movements that include among their goals STI change. The review will develop the argument that attention to this topical area has implications not only for the study of environmental movements but also for the study of social movements more generally, and research in this area can help to identify new perspectives that may otherwise tend to receive less attention from theories developed for other types of movements. The new questions and analytical perspectives are broadly "sociotechnical" in the sense that they enable a clearer understanding of ways of thinking about the material and epistemic dimensions of environmental mobilizations and outcomes. (For a broad overview of sociotechnical perspectives, see Hess and Sovacool 2020.)

Research that focuses on the study of environmentally related changes in STI can be viewed as part of the broader literature on the outcomes of social movements. These outcomes can include state-oriented policy change, but they also include economic outcomes, such as direct effects on markets and consumer preferences, and they can include cultural changes in values and identities (Giugni and Grasso 2018; Earl 2004). This chapter focuses on environmentally oriented change and explores the potential of using a sociotechnical perspective that brings attention to technology, products, material culture, and knowledge. The chapter begins with some potential implications for general social movement studies, then it examines three ways of thinking that are related to the three areas of science, technology, and industry.

DOI: 10.4324/9780367855680-37

Definitions and theoretical categories

Categories such as "social movements" or "environmental movements" are constructed by researchers to define a terrain of inquiry in which results from one study may be helpful for informing research in another study and for developing middle-level, generalizable, social scientific knowledge. Frequently, definitions of social movements and the study of social movements focus on mobilizations that utilize some type of extra-institutional repertoires of action such as street protest and strikes. However, when the focus of attention is on STI change, this definitional scope may become limiting. Frequently, there are mobilizations by coalitions of challengers who either do not rely exclusively on protest and unruly action or who avoid such repertoires in favor of institutionalized approaches. Although many social movements utilize a mixture of extra-institutional and institutional repertoires of action, in the area of STI, the emphasis may be on building coalitions for reforming government policies, changing the strategy of corporations, inventing new technologies, designing new organizational forms, creating job opportunities, providing low-income access to industrial goods and avoidance of bads, and bringing about changes in the practices and goals of an occupation (e.g., Frickel and Gross 2005; Hess 2007; Hoffman 1989). Thus, the study of STI and environmental movements requires a broad conceptualization of a social movement as a sustained mobilization by challengers who have met with resistance from incumbents in a social field. If researchers prefer to keep the definition restricted to extra-institutional action, then some other term might be used, such as "mobilized public" or "mobilization".

The focus on STI and outcomes in the study of social movements has several implications for general social movement theory. For example, the middle-range structural perspective represented by research on the political opportunity structure tends to become broadened by STI questions. (For a background on the political opportunity concept, see Giugni and Grasso 2015; McAdam 1996; Meyer and Minkoff 2004.) One example of broadening is the parallel concept of the industry opportunity structure, which can include a range of levels from the firm to global industries (Schurman 2004; Soule 2012). When the goal is regulatory reform or other kinds of policy changes, there is also an epistemic dimension to the opportunity structure because of differences in scientific evaluations of risk and the volume of available scientific research (Hess 2016). In some cases, policy changes must also await the technological dimension of opportunities because new technologies are not yet market ready and require more research and development (Elzen et al. 2011).

Another example of how inquiry into STI-related goals and outcomes may have implications for general social movement theory is research on the strategic symbolic dimensions of mobilizations. Again, there is a long and distinguished tradition of research on collective action frames and the dynamics of framing and counter-framing in social movement studies (Benford and Snow 2000; Esacove 2004). But a subsequent literature suggests that in the context of environmental and STI research, attention needs to be paid to the broader visions and imaginaries of interwoven technological, institutional, and industrial futures (Smith and Tidwell 2016; Zilliox and Smith 2018). Likewise, work on scientization suggests the need to examine how framing activities involve conflicts over defining problems and solutions as merely technical and not political or vice-versa (Kinchy 2012; Levidow 2013).

Even very basic definitional questions such as stratification, agency, and societal inequality may undergo a shift. For example, when defining inequality and actors, should non-human species be included? These questions emerge particularly in the study of animal rights and deep ecology movements, in which the study of STI and environmental justice meets the challenges of human-centered social theory (Pellow 2014). Sociotechnical perspectives sometimes also examine how human agency becomes delegated to technology within sociomaterial networks or ensembles, thus endowing "things" with a kind of agency, and how scientific theories and models have a "performative" or world-making dimension when used to construct new social institutions such as energy markets (MacKenzie et al. 2007).

In summary, part of the motivation for examining the STI dimensions of environmental movements is that this area of research may have some significant implications for general social movement studies and theory. The remainder of this review will examine three concepts that provide examples of these implications: industrial transition movements, the politics of design, and undone science.

Industrial transition movements

Environmental movements can involve some type of STI change as an outcome, but STI change is only one of multiple possible types of outcomes. For example, consumption-oriented environmental movements may involve changes in consumer practices without significant STI outcomes, but they can also become the basis of changes in consumer preferences that have implications for STI. Arguably, some environmental countermovements do not involve STI change if the primary goal is to maintain the status quo against proposed changes (Hess and Brown 2017; Jacques et al. 2008), and likewise, some environmental mobilizations may also attempt to preserve a pro-environmental status quo against roll-back attempts. However, if an environmental movement involves STI change as a goal, it can be considered an industrial transition movement: a type of social movement that has the goal of bringing about a substantial change in an industry, generally with implications for scientific research and technology development (Hess 2016). ITMs do not always have environmental change as a goal; they may instead target other types of industrial change, such as industrial concentration, privacy rights, consumer safety, equitable access, or public health risks.

Social movement researchers have long studied environmentally oriented ITMs that operate in a protest mode, such as the anti-nuclear energy movement of the 1970s and 1980s (Kitschelt 1986). Likewise, researchers have also recognized the generative potential of movements that have helped to spur industrial innovation. Examples include the role of grassroots mobilizations in the development of the organic foods industry (Obach 2015), the recycling industry (Lounsbury et al. 2003), and the wind industry (Vasi 2011). Although researchers have long studied ITMs, the systematic comparative analysis across industries is much less developed. One of the benefits of using the category of ITMs is that it provides a framework for thinking about the social movement mobilizations that have a goal of STI change.

The use of the concept of goals, which are understood here as articulated and intended outcomes of a mobilization, is difficult, but it is necessary to define the category of ITMs. Goals are not always congruent with outcomes, movements can have multiple and not always coherent sets of goals, and outcomes can be unintended and unanticipated (Giugni 1998). There are often disagreements within the movement over goals, and internal divisions can affect the likelihood of achieving the goals. However, thinking about movements in terms of goals can facilitate an analysis that examines movement strategy in relationship to consequences. Advocates and activists in movements often seek to answer this question; however, with a few exceptions (Jasper 2008), researchers in social movement studies have not explored the topic with the same attention that is found for other research questions in the field.

A synthesis of previous work on ITMs (Hess 2016) has identified two main types of goals: sociotechnical or design goals, which focus on the material and organizational dimensions of industrial sectors (with the understanding that design changes may require policy or political change in additional to scientific and technological change and changes in industrial strategy) and societal change goals, which focus more on the connections between industrial change and broader agendas of societal reform. Within each of these two broad categories are two subcategories:

1 Sociotechnical or design change

    a   Sunsetting or opposing unwanted industrial processes, technologies, side effects, or technological systems (industrial opposition)

    b   Supporting alternative industrial processes, technologies, or technological systems (alternative industrial development)

2 Societal change

    a   Addressing problems of equality such as access to material products and safe employment

    b   Changing the organizational form of industrial production and the governance of industry and technology in more democratic directions

In some cases, it is possible to demarcate a movement that focuses on one aspect of industrial change, such as a green jobs equity movement, which can be studied apart from other movements occurring in the same social and political space at the same time. In other cases, the movement or mobilization of interest is an amalgam of various types.

This approach helps with the problem of classifying the vast research on social movements and industrial change in order to compare studies across industries and sectors. Among the most salient industrial sectors for environmental movements are the built environment and transportation, energy, finance, food and agriculture, the media, waste and materials, and water. Examples of research from the substantial literature for four broad industrial sectors are provided in Table 32.1. For example, oppositional movements include mobilizations against highways and land development; fossil fuels and nuclear energy; pesticides, genetically modified food, and confined animal feeding; and chemical toxicity and landfills. But these movements also have a "pro" counterpart, sometimes in the form of occupational reform movements. Corresponding examples include support for human-powered transportation and urban density; renewable energy and energy efficiency; organic food and plant-based diets; and green chemistry, recycling, and zero waste. Moreover, movements can also address sector-specific inequality: affordable housing and transportation; affordable electricity and heating; hunger and food deserts; and unequal access to clean or nontoxic air, land, products, and water. These movements may also be connected with demands for access to green jobs. Finally, movements can attempt to build alternative organizations and institutions or advocate for more democratic governance processes. Examples include public transit and vehicle-sharing programs, community-controlled or publicly owned energy, food cooperatives and community gardens, and eco-parks and industrial ecology. The last category can include both the development of new organizational forms (public agencies, cooperatives, B corporations, local ownership and control, etc.) and new processes of governance (public oversight, transparency improvements, public engagement mechanisms, etc.).

Thinking about environmental movements and industrial change in this way opens up the possibility of comparative social science analysis that seeks to find patterns in strategies and outcomes across movements. For example, consistent with the broad sociological literature on routinization and cooptation, the industrial opposition movements frequently begin with a goal of a full moratorium on a technology or industrial process, but the outcomes are often modified to involve STI design changes and a partial moratorium on some aspects of the industrial

Table 32.1 Examples of industrial transition movements for specified sectors and goals

	Built environment and transportation	Energy	Food and agriculture	Waste and chemicals
Industrial opposition (sunsetting)	Infrastructure (Mohl 2014)	Infrastructure and fossil fuels (McAdam and Boudet 2012; Vasi et al. 2015)	Industrial agriculture (Ansell et al. 2006; Schurman 2004)	Waste and toxics (Pellow 2007; Sherman 2011)
Alternative industrial development	Sustainable transportation (Golub et al. 2016; Hess 2007) Urban design reform (Bullard et al. 2007; Talen 2005)	Wind energy development (Mey and Diesendorf 2018; Vasi 2011)	Sustainable food (Cherry 2006; Jaffee and Howard 2010; Obach 2015)	Recycling (Lounsbury et al. 2003) Green chemistry (Iles 2013; Woodhouse and Breyman 2005)
Inequality remediation, distributive justice	Transit access (Bullard et al. 2004)	Energy access (Fuller and McCauley 2016), green jobs (Nugent 2011)	Food access (Alkon and Agyeman 2011; Sbicca 2013)	Clean water access (Krings et al. 2019)
Democracy, procedural justice	Urban planning reform (Bailey et al. 2011; Gengs 2002)	Energy governance reform (e.g., Hess and Lee 2020)	Food governance reform (Andrée et al. 2019; Goodman et al. 2012; Schneiberg et al. 2008)	Toxics governance reform (Chilvers and Burgess 2008; Howell et al. 2019)

technology. Likewise, alternative industrial movements often end up losing the original aspirations of local ownership and community control as the technologies (e.g., solar, organic agriculture, recycling) are scaled up and incorporated into industrial regimes, which nevertheless undergo changes in response to the absorption process. Equity-oriented movements sometimes become routinized as organizations gain acceptance for their demands and shift into a service-provisioning, nonprofit model. The comparative analysis of the movements can point to common pitfalls and challenges that movements face as they gain partial concessions from the state and industrial incumbents (Hess 2007).

Another way to use this approach is to develop a "multi-coalition perspective" on environmental social movements. Unlike the broad comparative project outlined in the previous paragraph, this approach studies the divergences and convergences of related forms of mobilization in a demarcated space and time. For example, energy-related environmental mobilizations in New York State during the first two decades of the twenty-first century were diverse but also interconnected (Hess 2018). With respect to the goal of industrial opposition, a prominent industrial opposition movement related to energy transitions was the statewide movement against natural gas fracturing (fracking) technologies (Dodge and Lee 2017). The extensive movement ultimately led to a positive outcome (for the movement) of a state government decision not to proceed with fracking, and the movement advocates and activists subsequently moved on to opposition to natural-gas pipelines and liquid natural-gas terminals.

This more visible and classic type of oppositional, protest-based environmental movement is not the only type that was active in New York State during the two-decade period. With respect to the goal of alternative industrial development, a group of mostly different environmental organizations played a significant role, along with partners from the private sector, in building support for the policy framework for a statewide energy transition (Raymond 2016). In the first decade, they helped build support for the state government's decision to embrace the Regional Greenhouse Gas Initiative, which put in place a cap-and-trade system in the region, and they were active in subsequent policy reforms. With respect to the goal of equity, another group of organizations, located more in community-based organizations and the labor movement, advocated successfully for a green jobs law that was also connected with low-income weatherization and energy affordability (Hess 2018). With respect to the goal of democratizing energy governance, as the energy-transition and energy-equity policies became institutionalized, another mobilization emerged to promote a more just and democratic energy transition in the state, with goals that included those of the other three mobilizations but also procedural changes in the state government's decision-making process and support for community-based and community-controlled renewable energy. The energy-democracy coalitions could count some significant, albeit partial, victories, such as a climate justice component of a law approved in 2019 (Assembly Bill 1564, Senate Bill 2385; NYRenews 2019).

In summary, with either a cross-industry perspective or a multi-coalition perspective within a region, the comparative analysis of ITMs helps identify research questions and new perspectives with respect to the study of outcomes and consequences of environmental movements:

1   From a comparative perspective, what are the general tendencies for industries to adopt, transform, and deflect proposals for the sunsetting of some technologies and organizational forms and the sunrising of others?
2   When goals are broadened from sociotechnical change (e.g., ending nuclear power or fossil fuels for electricity) to societal change (e.g., improved equity or democracy), under what conditions does this broadening improve or worsen the achievement of goals?
3   What is the structure of coalitions or networks for a range of related environmental ITM mobilizations in a demarcated space and time? Under what conditions do the mobilizations occur as silos, and under what conditions are broad coalitions formed? How does the organizational composition and framing change as broader coalitions are formed?
4   What is the role of private- and public-sector actors in these different mobilizations, and where are the divisions within private-sector, public-sector, and civil-society actors? How are the mobilizations connected with internal conflicts within companies and industries over strategy and change?

Technological change and the politics of design

Environmentally related industrial change involves the complex interweaving and co-construction of cultural, organizational, political, and material dimensions. The sociotechnical perspective views these dimensions as connected and mutually constituting, but it also views the design of the material dimensions of social life as a site for politics. A broad term for this approach is the "politics of design". Long used in the design professions, the first use of the term in the science and technology studies (STS) literature is probably by Donald MacKenzie in his essay "Marx and the Machine" (MacKenzie 1984). In the essay, MacKenzie rejected a technological determinist reading of Marx and instead argued that Marx viewed technological changes and social changes as deeply interconnected. MacKenzie then shifted from the discussion of technology in Marx to the politics of design: that is, the idea that technological design "reflects the social relations within which it develops" (1984: 499). Although he argued that Marx equivocated on the issue, MacKenzie turned to work in the history and philosophy of technology that pointed to how the design of technological systems could reflect social and political choices.

Other researchers were also developing a similar sociotechnical perspective. For example, Noble (1978) showed how choices over machine tool design emerged in the context of the labor movement and labor-capital struggles, and the decisions reflected the desire of industry owners and managers to wrest control of the machine from workers and shift it to management. Winner (1986) discussed how decisions about highway design reflected racist values, and he drew Mumford's analysis of democratic and authoritarian technics to argue that artifacts have politics (Mumford 1934, 1964). Similarly, Wajcman (1991) and other feminist technology researchers pointed to the political implications of design choices for gender relations in the workplace, domestic, and reproductive technologies (Layne et al. 2010).

Much of this research recognizes the role of social movements (labor, civil rights, environmental, feminist) in developing alternative views or frames for understanding design choices. Thus, the politics of design perspective does not just explain design outcomes as the result of structural conflicts in society; it also draws attention to how the design of technological systems and material culture more generally can change as the result of political contestation. To broaden MacKenzie's analysis somewhat, the "politics of design" perspective includes how the political and technical orders (or the social and material orders) are coconstituted through relations of cooperation and conflict. The design of technological systems is constantly modified, reproduced, and contested, and at any given point in time, the design represents a sociomaterial settlement (such as an imposition or a compromise). Technology, especially at the scale of large technological systems such as infrastructure, is coconstituted with social structures, fields, and networks. In Winner's phrase, "technology is legislation" (2007).

From this perspective, technology is not merely a black-boxed prop or instrument in movement struggles, such as the study of how activists use information technologies to support mobilizations. Likewise, technology is not just a black-boxed object of contestation (e.g., movements that advocate for or against some kind of material change, such as a ban on natural-gas fracking or tuna fishing with nets). These approaches to technology should be considered in an analysis, but a sociotechnical perspective also views the design of the material world as a complicated negotiation with multiple possibilities and positions. The design focus implies that choices, options, or alternatives are both imaginable and possible. Technology is not a backdrop or prop for politics but a site for political contestation and mobilization, which often involves mobilizations in the political field and may also involve changes focused on industrial innovation, consumer use and redesign, and upstream scientific research.

Design conflicts can be broken down into various subtypes. "Object conflicts" are a subset that focuses on existential questions (Should the pipeline be built? Can we close the landfill?) or more complex questions of remediation (Can we reroute the powerline or put it underground? What are the political implications of gas, clean diesel, or electric buses for our city?). But design conflicts can also erupt over large-scale technological systems, such as the restructuring of a country's power grid. These conflicts can include the design of the technological governance – that is, the procedures by which decisions are made and public accountability is strengthened – and the design of systems of remediation or resettlement (such as for hydroelectric dams). In turn, the politics of design shades into the more general politics of democratic accountability and power. Easily misconstrued to mean that the focus on STI involves acceptance of private-sector governance and becomes compromised by an implicit neoliberalism, instead, the "politics of design" perspective suggests continuity with questions raised by Marx. The design of sociotechnical systems is politics by other means, just as the development of technology policy is engineering by other means. One of the tasks of researchers is to show how the framing of technological, scientific, industrial, and infrastructure policy as guided merely by technical criteria (cost, efficacy, efficiency) can itself be a maneuver to shift power to more easily controlled, scientized, technocratic, decision-making fora.

Of great significance in twenty-first century environmental politics is the politics of design of the electricity system and, increasingly, the electrified transportation system. These industrial transitions involve myriad sites of political conflict that include how organizations, practices, devices, and infrastructure are configured. Does solar take the form of large-scale, utility-controlled energy, or can it be reimagined as enabling greater local control and democratic accountability? Are smart meters configured in wireless or wired mode, with detailed monitoring of real-time household energy use or with aggregated data that offers better privacy protections? Do utility programs that require time-of-use pricing have negative implications (by gender, race, and class) for households with second- and third-shift workers? These conflicts take place in the political field and can be conceptualized in traditional ways, but they also take place in the guise of politically neutral, "technical" choices that may require the mobilization of counter-expertise even to identify the political valences and societal implications of emergent forms of design.

In summary, the "politics of design" perspective opens up the study of environmental movements and industrial change to a series of questions, such as the following:

1   What is the material and technological dimension of the environmental movement's goals, and what is the range of design changes that are in play?
2   What are the political valences of the various design proposals in play in the field of contention? What groups benefit or lose from the proposals, and how are the proposals related to coalition composition and framing?
3   How are the object conflicts (the materially focused design conflicts) connected to the design conflicts over arrangements of governance and remediation?

Epistemic change and undone science

Scientific research and environmental movements come together in various ways, and the mutual shaping of the two can be classified using the different goal types outlined previously. Where the goal is industrial opposition, the movement often needs research that documents risk or harm. Such research can be used to expand frames to include public health concerns and to build coalitions between environmentalists, public health leaders, and community groups. The frame expansion can contribute to improved chances of a mitigation outcome. Where the goal is building alternative industrial technologies or industries, the focus is more on innovation and the role of scientific research in contributing to the development of new technologies or to making existing ones more economically and environmentally viable. Social science research can also be valuable for documenting unequal distributions of goods and bads and for developing a better understanding of new modes of governance and industrial organization.

Again, the epistemic dimensions of social movements have long been recognized, but the sociotechnical perspective adopted here argues for a more systematic approach to the topic. For example, scientists play a role in shaping social movements, such as opposition to wars and weapons research (Moore 2013), not only by providing research but also by defining the epistemic ground of the movement. Scientists can also embrace the goals of social movements by altering their research agendas, such as by working with social movements in an advisory capacity or by providing research in citizen-science alliances and shadow mobilizations (Brown 2007; Frickel et al. 2015; Lubitow 2013; McCormick 2006, 2007), and they can also develop new research fields in response to articulations of research needs by social movements, such as environmental toxicology (Frickel 2004). Scientists also sometimes engage in participatory and community-based research, where their research programs are more directly an outcome of social negotiation with publics (Allen 2018; Cordner et al. 2019). The relationships between, on the one hand, activists, advocates, and communities and, on the other hand, scientists and scientific research are not always easy and smooth. Scientists have their own priorities and may negotiate with the activists and advocates, and likewise participatory, community-based research can be associated with projects that lack symbolic capital in the scientific field. Sometimes the resulting research does not document the effects that activists and advocates wanted to have demonstrated (Yearley 1992, 2005).

Social movements themselves can also be sources of grassroots research and innovation. The topic of citizen science has gained popularity in recent years, partly in response to the failure of governments to address research needs that social movements and public-interest civil-society organizations have identified (Jalbert et al. 2017; Kimura and Kinchy 2019; Ottinger 2017). When movements are institutionalized and have large organizations, sometimes the organizations have the means to hire scientists or otherwise to fund scientific research directly, as occurs with some of the large environmental organizations (Hess 2009). Social movements and civil-society organizations can also provide laboratories of grassroots innovation, where ideas for new technologies are translated into prototypes and tested (Smith et al. 2016). The early history of the Danish wind industry or the organic food industry in the Northeastern US are examples (Mey and Diesendorf 2018; Obach 2015). These experiments can also be sites for the development of new organizational forms (e.g., community renewable energy and community-supported agriculture) and for political organizing for "stretch and transform" policy changes (Smith and Raven 2012).

By developing a politics of knowledge similar to and in parallel with the politics of design, social movements participate in the social shaping of science but at a level quite different from the processes of social construction identified in the STS programs of the 1980s, which focused on how networks of scientists negotiated the transformation of knowledge claims into consensus knowledge in their specialty fields (Knorr-Cetina and Mulkay 1983). Instead, the focus is less on the construction of credibility for scientific claims within research fields and more on the construction of research agendas and priorities.

Attention to the construction of research agendas and priorities also entails identifying areas in which research is needed and not yet completed. In other words, the science aspect of STI outcomes involves identifying areas of scientific ignorance. The study of scientific ignorance – both within the scientific field and in the broader social spaces in which scientific knowledge is valued, rejected, vetted, and interpreted – has become a topic of growing interest (Gross and McGoey 2015). Within the broad range of interdisciplinary inquiries and conceptualizations of ignorance, one type that is relevant to social movements, and especially movements related to health and the environment, is undone science (Hess 2016). This type of scientific ignorance focuses on non-knowledge specified from the standpoint of a social movement, public interest group, or community that is mobilizing to protect its health, welfare, and environment. These mobilizations identify not only goals of political, technological, and industrial change but also the need for new or different types of research, and they identify the knowledge that is missing, in insufficient quantity, or inconclusive. The absence or low volume of research is defined oppositionally, especially in contrast with research that is conducted or funded by industry. Often, industry can produce research at a higher level of volume and visibility in the public sphere to support its view that an industrial site, technology, process, or infrastructure does not present a public risk and that regulation is not needed (Frickel et al. 2010; Hess 2016).

Undone science is systematically produced because the lack of knowledge is beneficial to powerful actors such as industries that generate risk from toxic exposure and pollution. (Again, it is helpful to remember Marx, whose development of an alternative political economy was also a kind of sociology of scientific ignorance.) Dominant actors in industrial and political fields can exert systematic influence on funding flows to tilt the contours of research agendas in directions favorable to the more environmentally harmful industrial processes and technologies so that the relevant research remains in an ongoing state of doubt and inconclusiveness. In turn, the funding agendas send signals of what is valued to research fields, and these signals become internalized as "habitus" (Jeon 2019). When scientists set out to address undone science, and especially when they have results that are unfavorable to industry, and they circulate the results in the media, then industry (and sometimes government) have a range of techniques of suppression that they can use to maintain doubt and ignorance in the public. The suppression of environmental science is widespread, and the exemplary tales can cause other scientists to think twice before entering the fray (Kempner et al. 2011; Martin 2007; Oreskes and Conway 2010). Likewise, if industry funds research that ends up documenting unwanted health or environmental risk, it will engage in internal processes of suppression that lead to the "sequestering" of knowledge to keep it hidden from the public (Richter et al. 2018).

The situation of undone science is not necessarily a permanent condition, and thus, one of the outcomes of a social movement can be to get the undone science done, as some of the studies mentioned earlier recognized. However, often the project of getting undone science done is challenging, and this outcome, like other outcomes of environmental movements, can become ambiguous. For example, even if advocates and activists are successful in convincing either funding agencies to support the research or scientists to take on such research projects as pro-bono work, undone science can re-emerge in a second-order form. This situation occurs when research is conducted to address the undone science, but it is configured methodologically in ways that the original research questions are not answered directly or fully, or the methods are set up in ways that bias results toward inconclusiveness that legitimates further policy inaction (Allen et al. 2017; Kleinman and Suryanarayanan 2013).

Moreover, the epistemic battles also involve the interpretation of scientific knowledge in the public sphere. The public relations machinery that industry has developed and the rise of right-wing populism, fake news, and political polarization can make it difficult for independent scientists to maintain credibility and visibility in the public sphere and, likewise, for social movements to get the knowledge to the public (Bray 2017; Cordner 2015; Dunlap and McCright 2011). Thus, even a consensus around "done science" may be undone by the mechanisms of politicized attacks and the circulation of claims on social media without vetting.

In summary, just as the politics of design leads to a conceptualization of environmental movements as sociotechnical projects with sociotechnical outcomes, so the focus on epistemic politics and undone science leads to a conceptualization of sociotechnical change as also epistemic change. A set of corresponding research questions then emerges:

1   What are the mechanisms by which undone science is produced and maintained, and likewise, what are the mechanisms by which this form of scientific ignorance is addressed?
2   Under what conditions do other forms of scientific ignorance occur and again, through what mechanism, and how are they combatted?
3   Under what conditions are scientific research and the epistemic dimension of environmental movements important to outcomes (such as achieving an environmental justice remediation or gaining broad policy support for industrial transition policies), and under

what conditions is this dimension relatively unimportant in comparison with other forms of mobilization and contestation (e.g., protest, litigation, coalition expansion)?

Conclusion

The study of STI outcomes and environmental movements can be more than a small subfield that is, in turn, positioned in the subfield of research on environmental movements. Rather, as this chapter has argued, research on STI outcomes requires a sociotechnical perspective that can contribute to thinking about fundamental concepts in social movement studies.

Longstanding definitions and understandings in social movement theory may come to be viewed in a new light that emerges at the nexus of science and technology studies (STS) and social movement studies (reviewed in Hess 2016). For example, the concept of political opportunity structures becomes broadened to opportunity structures in other social fields (industry, research), but even the concept of political opportunities takes on a new, epistemic hue. The concept of a frame becomes broadened to include sociotechnical visions and the ways in which technological systems and the criteria upon which they are evaluated come to frame the limits of the imaginable. The concept of agency may be extended to include non-human agency such as animals, delegations of agency to objects, and the world-making capacity of scientific knowledge. The concept of mobilizing structures is broadened to include scientific and intellectual movements, scientist activists, citizen-science alliances, and citizen science.

Moreover, the nexus of STS and social movement studies may help to open up new kinds of empirical research problems and questions. The nexus contributes to ongoing thinking in social movement studies that has diversified the understanding of the target of social change from the state to industry and cultural practices. In doing so, new categories such as the industrial transition movement may be helpful for establishing an object of comparative or quantitative analysis that can be the source of new generalizations. Attention to the politics of design may help sharpen thinking about the political effects of technical decisions and choices but also how existing systems frame and limit the imagination. Likewise, concepts in the study of scientific ignorance, such as undone science, point to the important role of systematic absences of knowledge and to the increasingly important role of the construction of disinformation and science denialism. These sections ended with lists of more specific questions that can emerge from a sociotechnical perspective.

Finally, the sociotechnical perspective may help activists and advocates find new sites for political contestation. Where political opportunities are partially or highly closed, they may find that targeting other sites such as research fields, industrial innovation, and consumer practices may help create broader awareness that can reopen political opportunities. Attention to the ways in which technological design choices and the prioritization of research agendas are a form of politics by other means may help avoid lock-in when new projects are under development and to find ways to integrate technical, epistemic, and political change. In a world that is increasingly mediated by technology and cyber-infrastructure, it will be increasingly important to pay attention to how the patterns of the co-constitution of the material and symbolic orders are themselves crucial to the generation, maintenance, and transformation of what Bourdieu (1991) termed "symbolic power".

References

Alkon, Alison, and Julian Agyeman (eds.). 2011. *Cultivating Food Justice: Race, Class, and Sustainability.* Cambridge, MA: The MIT Press.

Allen, Barbara. 2018. Strongly participatory science and knowledge justice in an environmentally contested region. *Science, Technology, & Human Values* 43(6), 947–971.

Allen, Barbara, Yolaine Ferrier, and Alison Cohen. 2017. Through a maze of studies: Health questions and "undone science" in a French industrial region. *Environmental Sociology* 3(2), 134–144.

Andrée, Peter, Jill Clark, Charles Levkoe, and Kristen Lowitt (eds.). 2019. *Civil Society and Social Movements in Food System Governance*. London: Routledge.

Ansell, Christopher, and David Vogl (eds.). 2006. *What's the Beef? The Contested Governance of European Food Safety*. Cambridge, MA: MIT Press.

Bailey, Keiron, Benjamin Blandford, Ted Grossardt, and John Ripy 2011. Planning, technology, and legitimacy: Structured public involvement in integrated transportation and land-use planning in the United States. *Environment and Planning B: Planning and Design* 38(1), 447–467.

Benford, Robert, and David Snow 2000. Framing processes and social movements: An overview and assessment. *Annual Review of Sociology* 26(1), 611–639.

Bourdieu, Pierre. 1991. *Language and Symbolic Power*. Cambridge, MA: Harvard University Press.

Bray, Laura. 2017. Media and "undone science" in West Virginia's Elk River chemical spill. *Environmental Sociology* 3(4), 359–369.

Brown, Phil, 2007. *Toxic Exposures: Contested Illnesses and the Environmental Health Movement*. New York: Columbia University Press.

Bullard, Robert Doyle (ed.). 2007. *Growing Smarter: Achieving Livable Communities, Environmental Justice, and Regional Equity*. Cambridge, MA: MIT Press.

Bullard, Robert Doyle, Glenn Steve Johnson, and Angel O. Torres (eds.). 2004. *Highway Robbery: Transportation Racism and New Routes to Equity*. Boston: South End Press.

Cherry, Elizabeth. 2006. Veganism as a cultural movement: A relational approach. *Social Movement Studies* 5(2), 155–170.

Chilvers, Jason, and Jacquelin Burgess. 2008. Power relations: The politics of risk and procedure in nuclear waste governance. *Environment and Planning A* 40(3), 1881–1900.

Cordner, Alissa. 2015. Strategic science translation and environmental controversies. *Science, Technology, & Human Values* 40(6), 915–938.

Cordner, Alissa, Lauren Richter, and Phil Brown 2019. Environmental chemicals and public sociology: Engaged scholarship on highly fluorinated compounds. *Environmental Sociology* 5(4), 339–351.

Dodge, Jennifer and Jeongyoon Lee. 2017. Framing dynamics and political gridlock: The curious case of hydraulic fracturing in New York. *Journal of Environmental Policy & Planning*, 19(1), 14–34.

Dunlap, Riley, and Aaron McCright. 2011. Organized climate change denial. In John Dryzek, Richard Norgaard, and David Schossberg (eds.), *The Oxford Handbook of Climate Change and Society*. Oxford: Oxford University Press, 144–160.

Earl, Jennifer. 2004. The cultural consequences of social movements. In David Snow, Sarah Soule, and Hanspeter Kriesi (eds.), *The Blackwell Companion to Social Movements*. Hoboken, NJ: Blackwell Publishing, 508–530.

Elzen, Boele, Frank Geels, Cees Leeuwis, and Barbara Van Mierlo. 2011. Normative contestation in transitions "in the making": Animal welfare concerns and system innovation in pig husbandry. *Research Policy* 40(2), 263–275.

Esacove, Anne. 2004. Dialogic framing: The framing/counterframing of "partial-birth" abortion. *Sociological Inquiry* 74(1), 70–101.

Frickel, Scott. 2004. *Chemical Consequences: Environmental Mutagens, Scientist Activism, and the Rise of Genetic Toxicology*. New Brunswick, NJ: Rutgers University Press.

Frickel, Scott, Sahra Gibbon, Jeff Howard, Joanna Kempner, Gwen Ottinger, and David J. Hess. 2010. Undone science: Charting social movement and civil society challenges to research agenda setting. *Science, Technology, & Human Values* 35(4), 444–473.

Frickel, Scott, and Neil Gross. 2005. A general theory of scientific/intellectual movements. *American Sociological Review* 70(2), 204–232.

Frickel, Scott, Rebekah Torcasso, and Annika Anderson. 2015. The organization of expert activism: Shadow mobilization in two social movements. *Mobilization: An International Quarterly* 20(3), 305–323.

Fuller, Sara, and Darren McCauley. 2016. Framing energy justice: Perspectives from activism and advocacy. *Energy Research & Social Science* 11, 1–8.

Giugni, Marco, and Maria Grasso. 2015. Environmental movements in advanced industrial democracies: Heterogeneity, transformation, and institutionalization. *Annual Review of Environment and Resources* 40, 337–361.

Giugni, Marco, and Maria Grasso. 2018. Economic outcomes of social movements. In David Snow, Sarah Soule, Hanspieter Kriesi, and Holly McCammon (eds.), *The Wiley Blackwell Companion to Social Movements*. Oxford: Oxford University Press, 466–481.

Giugni, Marco. 1998. Was it worth the effort? The outcomes and consequences of social movements. *Annual Review of Sociology* 24(1), 371–393.

Golub, Aaron, Melody Hoffmann, Adonia Lugo, and Gerardo Sandoval (eds.). 2016. *Bicycle Justice and Urban Transformation: Biking for All?* London: Routledge.

Goodman, David, E. Melanie DuPuis, and Michael Goodman. 2012. *Alternative Food Networks: Knowledge, Practice, and Politics*. New York: Routledge.

Grengs, Joe. 2002. Community-based planning as a source of political change: The transit equity movement of Los Angeles' bus riders union. *Journal of the American Planning Association* 68(2), 165–178.

Gross, Matthias, and Linsey McGoey (eds.). 2015. *Routledge International Handbook of Ignorance Studies*. London: Routledge.

Hess, David. 2007. What is a clean bus? Object conflicts in the greening of urban transit. *Sustainability: Science, Practice and Policy* 3(1), 45–58.

Hess, David. 2009. The potentials and limitations of civil society research: Getting undone science done. *Sociological Inquiry* 79(3), 306–327.

Hess, David, 2016. *Undone Science: Social Movements, Mobilized Publics, and Industrial Transitions*. Cambridge, MA: MIT Press.

Hess, David. 2018. Energy democracy and social movements: A multi-coalition perspective on the politics of sustainability transitions. *Energy Research & Social Science* 40, 177–189.

Hess, David, and Kate Brown. 2017. Green tea: Clean-energy conservatism as a countermovement. *Environmental Sociology* 3(1), 64–75.

Hess, David, and Dasom Lee. 2020. Energy decentralization in California and New York: Conflicts in the politics of shared solar and community choice. *Renewable and Sustainable Energy Reviews* 121, 109716.

Hess, David, and Benjamin Sovacool. 2020. Sociotechnical matters: Reviewing and integrating science and technology studies with energy social science. *Energy Research and Social Science* 70, 101617.

Hoffman, Lily. 1989. *The Politics of Knowledge: Activist Movements in Medicine and Planning*. Albany, NY: SUNY Press.

Howell, Sharon, Michael D. Doan, and Ami Harbin. 2019. Detroit to Flint and back again: Solidarity forever. *Critical Sociology* 45(1), 63–83.

Iles, Alastair. 2013. Greening chemistry: Emerging epistemic political tensions in California and the United States. *Public Understanding of Science* 22(4), 460–478.

Jacques, Peter, Riley Dunlap, and Mark Freeman. 2008. The organisation of denial: Conservative think tanks and environmental scepticism. *Environmental Politics* 17(3), 349–385.

Jaffee, Daniel, and Philip Howard. 2010. Corporate cooptation of organic and fair trade standards. *Agriculture and Human Values* 27(4), 387–399.

Jalbert, Kirk, Samantha Rubright, and Karen Edelstein. 2017. The civic informatics of fractracker alliance: Working with communities to understand the unconventional oil and gas industry. *Engaging Science, Technology, and Society* 3, 528–559.

Jasper, James. 2008. *Getting Your Way: Strategic Dilemmas in the Real World*. Chicago: University of Chicago Press.

Jeon, Jeon. 2019. Rethinking scientific habitus: Toward a theory of embodiment, institutions, and stratification of science. *Engaging Science, Technology, and Society* 5, 160–172.

Kempner, Joanna, Jon F. Merz, and Charles L. Bosk. 2011. Forbidden knowledge: Public controversy and the production of nonknowledge. *Sociological Forum* 26(3), 475–500.

Kimura, Aya, and Abby Kinchy. 2019. *Science by the People: Participation, Power, and the Politics of Environmental Knowledge*. New Brunswick, NJ: Rutgers University Press.

Kinchy, Abby. 2012. *Seeds, Science, and Struggle: The Global Politics of Transgenic Crops*. Cambridge, MA: MIT Press.

Kitschelt, Herbert. 1986. Political opportunity structures and political protest: Anti-nuclear movements in four democracies. *British Journal of Political Science* 16(1), 57–85.

Kleinman, Daniel, and Sainath Suryanarayanan. 2013. Dying bees and the social production of ignorance. *Science, Technology, & Human Values* 38(4), 492–517.

Knorr-Cetina, Karin, and Michael Mulkay (eds.). 1983. *Science Observed: Perspectives on the Social Study of Science*. Beverly Hills, CA: Sage Publications.

Krings, Amy, Dana Kornberg, and Erin Lane. 2019. Organizing under austerity: How residents' concerns became the flint water crisis. *Critical Sociology* 45(4–5), 583–597.

Layne, Linda, Sharra Vostral, and Kate Boyer (eds.). 2010. *Feminist Technology* (Vol. 4). Champaign: University of Illinois Press.

Levidow, Les. 2013. E.U. criteria for sustainable biofuels: Accounting for carbon, depoliticising plunder. *Geoforum* 44, 211–223.

Lounsbury, Michael, Mark Ventresca, and Paul Hirsch. 2003. Social movements, field frames and industry emergence: A cultural – political perspective on US recycling. *Socio-Economic Review* 1(1), 71–104.

Lubitow, Amy. 2013. Collaborative frame construction in social movement campaigns: Bisphenol-A (BPA) and scientist – activist mobilization. *Social Movement Studies* 12(4), 429–447.

MacKenzie, Donald F. 1984. Marx and the machine. *Technology and Culture* 25(3), 473–502.

MacKenzie, Donald, F. Muniesa, and L. Siu (eds.). 2007. *Do Economists Make Markets? On the Performativity of Economics.* Princeton, NJ: Princeton University Press.

Martin, Brian. 2007. *Justice Ignited: The Dynamics of Backfire.* Lanham, MD: Rowman and Littlefield.

McAdam, Doug. 1996. Conceptual origins, current problems, future directions. In D. McAdam, J. McCarthy, and M. Zald (eds.), *Comparative Perspectives on Social Movements.* Cambridge: Cambridge University Press, 23–40.

McAdam, Doug, and Hilary Boudet. 2012. *Putting Social Movements in Their Place: Explaining Opposition to Energy Projects in the United States, 2000–2005.* Cambridge: Cambridge University Press.

McCormick, Sabrina. 2006. The Brazilian anti-dam movement: Knowledge contestation as communicative action. *Organization & Environment* 19(3), 321–346.

McCormick, Sabrina. 2007. The governance of hydro-electric dams in Brazil. *Journal of Latin American Studies* 39(2), 227–261.

Mey, Franziska, and Mark Diesendorf. 2018. Who owns an energy transition? Strategic action fields and community wind energy in Denmark. *Energy Research & Social Science* 35, 108–117.

Meyer, David, and Debra Minkoff. 2004. Conceptualizing political opportunities. *Social Forces* 82(4), 1457–1492.

Mohl, Raymond. 2014. Citizen activism and freeway revolts in Memphis and Nashville: The road to litigation. *Journal of Urban History* 40(5), 870–893.

Moore, Kelly. 2013. *Disrupting Science: Social Movements, American Scientists, and the Politics of the Military, 1945–1975* (Vol. 39). Princeton, NJ: Princeton University Press.

Mumford, Lewis. 1934. *Technics and Civilization.* London: Routledge and Kegan Paul.

Mumford, Lewis. 1964. Authoritarian and democratic technics. *Technology and Culture* 5(1), 1–8.

Noble, David. 1978. Social choice in machine design: The case of automatically controlled machine tools, and a challenge for labor. *Politics and Society* 8(3–4), 313–347.

Nugent, James. 2011. Changing the climate: Ecoliberalism, green new dealism, and the struggle over green jobs in Canada. *Labor Studies Journal* 36(1), 58–82.

NYRenews. 2019. *NY Renews Statement on Governor Cuomo Signing the Environmental Justice Bill.* www.nyrenews.org/news/2019/12/23/ny-renews-statement-on-governor-cuomo-signing-the-environmental-justice-bill.

Obach, Brian. 2015. *Organic Struggle: The Movement for Sustainable Agriculture in the United States.* Cambridge, MA: MIT Press.

Oreskes, Naomi, and Michael Conway. 2010. *Merchants of Doubt.* New York: Bloomsbury.

Ottinger, Gwen. 2017. Crowdsourcing undone science. *Engaging Science, Technology, and Society* 3, 560–574.

Pellow, David. 2007. *Resisting Global Toxics: Transnational Movements for Environmental Justice.* Cambridge, MA: MIT Press.

Pellow, David. 2014. *Total Liberation: The Power and Promise of Animal Rights and the Radical Earth Movement.* Minneapolis: University of Minnesota Press.

Raymond, Leigh. 2016. *Reclaiming the Atmospheric Commons: The Regional Greenhouse Gas Initiative and a New Model of Emissions Trading.* Cambridge, MA: MIT Press.

Richter, Lauren, Alissa Cordner, and Phil Brown. 2018. Non-stick science: Sixty years of research and (in)action on fluorinated compounds. *Social Studies of Science* 48(5), 691–714.

Sbicca, Joshua. 2013. The need to feed: Urban metabolic struggle of actually existing radical projects. *Critical Sociology* 40(6), 817–834.

Schneiberg, Marc, Marissa King, and Thomas Smith. 2008. Social movements and organizational form: Cooperative alternatives to corporations in the American insurance, dairy and grain industries. *American Sociological Review* 73(4), 635–667.

Schurman, Rachel. 2004. Fighting "frankenfoods": Industry opportunity structures and the efficacy of the anti-biotech movement in Western Europe. *Social Problems* 51(4), 243–268.

Sherman, Daniel. 2011. *Not Here, Not There, Not Anywhere: Politics, Social Movements, and the Disposal of Low-Level Radioactive Waste*. Washington, DC: RFF Press.

Smith, Adrian, and Rob Raven. 2012. What is protective space? Reconsidering niches in transitions to sustainability. *Research Policy* 41(6), 1025–1036.

Smith, Adrian, Mariano Fressoli, Dinesh Abrol, Elisa Arond, and Adrian Ely. 2016. *Grassroots Innovation Movements*. London: Routledge.

Smith, Jessica, and Abraham Tidwell. 2016. The everyday lives of energy transitions: Contested sociotechnical imaginaries in the American West. *Social Studies of Science* 46(3), 327–350.

Soule, Sarah. 2012. Targeting organizations: Contentious and private politics. *Research in the Sociology of Organizations* 34, 261–285.

Talen, Emily. 2005. *New Urbanism and American Planning: The Conflict of Cultures*. New York: Routledge.

Vasi, Ion Bogdan. 2011. *Winds of Change: The Environmental Movement and the Global Development of the Wind Energy Industry*. New York: Oxford University Press.

Vasi, Ion Bogdan, Edward Walker, John Lohnson, and Hui Tan. 2015. "No fracking way!" Documentary film, discursive opportunity, and local opposition against hydraulic fracturing in the United States, 2010 to 2013. *American Sociological Review* 80(5), 934–959.

Wajcman, Judy. 1991. *Feminism Confronts Technology*. University Park, PA: Penn State Press.

Winner, Langdon. 1986. *The Whale and the Reactor*. Chicago: University of Chicago Press.

Winner, Langdon. 2007. Is there a right shape to technology? *Argumentos de Razón Técnica* 10, 199–213.

Woodhouse, Edward, and Steve Breyman. 2005. Green chemistry as a social movement? *Science, Technology, and Human Values* 32(3), 199–222.

Yearley, Steven. 1992. Green ambivalence about science: Legal-rational authority and the scientific legitimation of a social movement. *British Journal of Sociology* 43(4), 511–532.

Yearley, Steven. 2005. *Cultures of Environmentalism: Empirical Studies in Environmental Sociology*. London: Palgrave Macmillan.

Zilliox, Skylar, and Jessica Smith. 2018. Colorado's fracking debates: Citizen science, conflict and collaboration. *Science as Culture* 27(2), 221–241.

33

BIOGRAPHICAL CONSEQUENCES OF ENVIRONMENTAL ACTIVISM

Sara Vestergren and John Drury

We get daily reports of people taking collective action against injustice, inequality, and oppression: for example, the current environmental movement with groups like Extinction Rebellion (XR), activists like Greta Thunberg, and events such as Earth Day. The main part of news reports on personal consequences focus on the negative effects of participation in activism, such as activists getting imprisoned and sometimes losing their lives. However, these horrific events are only a small part of environmental activism and only include a small number of activists. What happens to the other activists? How does moderate environmental activism, such as participating in rallies and being part of an environmental campaign, affect the everyday participants?

Collective action has been defined as action that aims to improve the ingroup's status (Wright, Taylor & Moghaddam, 1990) or actions in solidarity with other groups (Becker, 2012). We argue that environmental activism does not easily fit into the standard definition of collective action. In most environmental collective action, there is no distinct disadvantaged group to increase status for, nor is there a distinct group to fight in solidarity with. However, it could be argued that the consequences of climate change disproportionately affect already disadvantaged groups (e.g., Islam & Winkel, 2017) and that participation in environmental movements and actions could be conducted in solidarity with these disadvantaged groups or future generations.

This chapter describes and discusses biographical consequences of participation in environmental activism that could emerge through participation in, for example, Standing Rock (Elbein, 2017), Fridays for Future (Fridays for Future, 2020), or the Gezi Park Protests (e.g., Uluğ & Acar, 2016, 2018, 2019). More specifically, we suggest that participation in activist campaigns can have profound consequences (both good and bad) for the activists' personal lives. However, we argue that not all the biographical consequences identified in previous research will emerge through environmental activism. Environmental activists are expected to change in line with the norms of their activist group – that is, consequences are related to identity-relevant content – and in order to understand and conceptualize the biographical consequences of activism, we need a self-categorization perspective. We demonstrate how biographical consequences emerge through interaction with other groups (such as the police) and with their own group. We draw upon our own research within environmental campaigns (e.g., Drury & Reicher, 2000; Vestergren, Drury & Hammar Chiriac, 2018) and develop a theory of self and self-change based on change in four dimensions: content (who we are), boundaries (who counts as ingroup

 DOI: 10.4324/9780367855680-38

"we", and who counts as outgroup "them"), legitimacy (what actions, both by self and others, count as legitimate or illegitimate), and power (what actions/behaviors "we" see as possible, connected to the restraining power of outgroups/others).

Some scholars have made the case for environmental identity being too vague and environmental issues too shifting to create a strong sense of collective identity and movement (Kahan, 2015; McAdam, 2017; McCright & Dunlap, 2011). McAdam (2017) argues, founded on a review of social science literature on climate change, that for most people, the identity vagueness leads to other identities becoming salient as environmental issues are too big and vague to serve to create a salient self-concept as an environmentalist. However, based on our interviews with environmental activists (e.g., Drury & Reicher, 2000; Vestergren, Drury & Hammar Chiriac, 2019), we argue that environmental activists, through their involvement and interactions with other groups as well as their own group, develop an environmental identity that affects their lives within and outside the campaign and, for some, has long-lasting effects. We show that continued interaction with other activists is crucial for the biographical changes to sustain. Lastly, this chapter makes the case for the need for a self-categorization perspective on change (e.g., Drury & Reicher, 2000; Reynolds & Branscombe, 2014; Vestergren, Drury & Hammar Chiriac, 2018) to describe and explain the emergence and endurance of biographical changes through environmental activism. In this chapter, we start by outlining a typology of biographical consequences through participation in activism in general, before moving on to focusing on biographical consequences for environmental activists. This is followed by discussing the process of biographical change, developing a theory of identity change along four dimensions, and the endurance of these biographical changes.

Typology of biographical consequences in activism

Researchers on collective action and social movement participation have an extensive body of work behind them; however, the focus on biographical consequences through such participation remains small (e.g., Giugni & Grasso, 2016; McAdam, 1989; Vestergren, Drury & Hammar Chiriac, 2017). Previous research on activism and collective action participation has identified a range of biographical changes (Vestergren, Drury & Hammar Chiriac, 2017), such as changes in attitudes and behaviors related to consumption (Stuart, Thomas, Donaghue & Russell, 2013) and well-being (Vestergren, Drury & Hammar Chiriac, 2019). The range of various biographical consequences can be organized into changes in what we say that we do (objective changes) and changes in how we see ourselves (subjective changes) (Vestergren, Drury & Hammar Chiriac, 2017).

Objective changes – changes in what we do

Participation in activism in general can change our relationships with others and how we behave within those relationships. Some studies suggest that participation in activism can lead to new relationships forming (e.g., Cherniss, 1972; Passy & Monsch, 2020), and former relationships can come under strain and break due to becoming part of an activist community (Cherniss, 1972). Several studies suggest that participation in activism changes the relationship to work and education (e.g., Braungart & Braungart, 1990; Fendrich, 1974; Fendrich & Tarleau, 1973; Nassi & Abramowitz, 1979), such as activists' tendency to change career more often throughout life than non-activists (McAdam, 1989; Sherkat & Blocker, 1997). The perceived activism context and issue of concern can change from local to global as participation in one campaign can lead to extended participation in other campaigns (e.g., Drury, Reicher & Stott, 2003;

Fendrich & Lovoy, 1988; McAdam, 1989; Sherkat & Blocker, 1997; Shriver, Miller & Cable, 2003; Van Dyke & Dixon, 2013). Furthermore, activists have been seen to make changes in their consumption patterns (Stuart, Thomas, Donaghue & Russell, 2013). In their study of activists against whaling in the Sea Shepherd Conservation Movement, Stuart and colleagues (2013) found that some anti-whaling activists changed their diet to exclude or decrease their intake of meat.

Subjective changes – changes in how we see ourselves

Previous research has also identified changes in how participants see themselves. For example, activists and protesters change their views of what they can change and achieve – a change in empowerment (e.g., Blackwood & Louis, 2012; Drury, Cocking, Beale, Hanson & Rapley, 2005; Shriver, Miller & Cable, 2003; Tausch & Becker, 2012). Hence, through participation in collective action, participants change their view of their ability to reshape the world and its existing power relations. Furthermore, it has been suggested that participants become more liberal or progressive, or even more radical in their beliefs and behaviors, after becoming involved in collective action campaigns (e.g., Adamek & Lewis, 1973, 1975; Drury & Reicher, 2000; Hirsch, 1990; McAdam, 1989; Nassi, 1981; Simon & Klandermans, 2001; Thomas, McGarty & Louis, 2014).

Additionally, what participants view as legitimate or illegitimate action can change through participation in activism (e.g., Drury & Reicher, 2000; Marwell, Aiken & Demerath, 1987). For example, during the Kent State sit-in, protesters became more willing to participate in, and view, civil disobedience as legitimate action (Adamek & Lewis, 1975). Activists may also shift in their view of the legitimacy of actions taken by the outgroup, such as the police (e.g., Drury & Reicher, 2000). One of the most commonly observed biographical consequences of participation is sustained commitment (e.g., Macgillivray, 2005; Profitt, 2001; Whittaker & Watts, 1971). For example, Marwell and colleagues (1987) found that 1960s activists were committed to their activism and ideology 20 years after participation. Furthermore, in their study of six different protest contexts, Jasko, Szastok, Grzymala-Moszczynska, Maj, and Kruglanski (2019) found that radical left-wing, pro-democratic, feminist, environmental, and labor and health-care rights activists became more radical and willing to self-sacrifice both their health and financially.

There are also consequences related to mental health and well-being reported. Some scholars point to the risk of decreasing mental health caused by burnout (Downton & Wehr, 1998; Einwohner, 2002; Lawson & Barton, 1980), whereas others have identified an increase in well-being through both online activism (Foster, 2015) and offline activism (Boehnke & Wong, 2011; Klar & Kasser, 2009). Engagement in activism can increase participants' positive feelings about themselves (Becker, Tausch & Wagner, 2011) and their sense of belonging (Bäck, Bäck & Knapton, 2015), consequently making them feel fulfilled and giving them a sense of personal significance (Kruglanski, Jasko, Chernikova, Dugas & Webber, 2017; Molinario et al., 2019). Relatedly, self-esteem has been demonstrated to increase as a consequence of participation in, for example, the women's movement (Cherniss, 1972), and increased self-confidence has been observed for women activists involved in the Gulf Illness Movement (Shriver, Miller & Cable, 2003). Former student activists have been found to change in their personality characteristics, "traits", such as scoring higher on cognitive flexibility, autonomy, and impulse expression (Whittaker & Watts, 1971). There are also some reports of anti-war activists (Sherkat, 1998) and free speech activists (Nassi, 1981) transforming in their religious beliefs. Sherkat (1998) found that eight years after participation in protests, former activists had less religious participation than non-activists in the same cohort.

Activism can lead to transformations in more practical ways, such as gaining skills in organization and how to manage a household and increased knowledge in various areas. Among others, activists in the AFL-CIO Union Summer program developed skills in organizing, which subsequently could be applied in other contexts (van Dyke & Dixon, 2013). Skills obtained through activism engagement can come to use in activists' everyday lives, such as managing the household economy (e.g., Beckwith, 2016; Cable, 1992; Shriver, Miller & Cable, 2003). The protest and movement context offers a platform for acquiring new or developed knowledge (e.g., Klandermans, van der Toorn & van Steklenburg, 2008; Lawson & Barton, 1980). Most studies on biographical changes through activism mentioned here have focused on political activism or 1960s activists. However, some studies have identified one or a few biographical consequences through engagement environmental campaigns (e.g., Cable, 1992; Drury & Reicher, 1999, 2005; Jasko, Szastok, Grzymala-Moszczynska, Maj & Kruglanski, 2019 [study 5]; Molinario et al., 2019; Passy & Monch, 2020).

Changes through participation in environmental activism

Environmental awareness has existed for over 5,000 years, through individuals such as Hippocrates and civilizations such as Mohenjo Darro (Weyler, 2018). One of the earliest environmental protest campaigns could be argued to be the Hindu group Bishnoi. Members of the Bishnoi protested, and some gave their lives, to hinder deforestation in India in the 1730s (Temper, 2017). Environmental movements and actions such as Zero Hour, Extinction Rebellion (XR), Fridays for Future, and Earth Day gather millions of people acting together globally for the climate and environment. Some researchers have explored how such participation affects participants and identified various biographical changes emerging through their participation. During a protest to save a piece of land from becoming a motorway, the No M11 link road campaign, campaign participants changed in their view of what actions were legitimate to use during the protest (Drury & Reicher, 2000). Furthermore, the participants were found to change in their view of the police as a whole, from being perceived as a legitimate force to becoming seen as an illegitimate force. Jasko and colleagues (2019) identified that the biographical changes were more intense for participants who had direct involvement in radical actions in the Białowieza forest camp than for activists engaged outside the camp. Along with changes in the legitimacy of actions, they found changes in radicalism, commitment to the cause, and well-being (Jasko, Szastok, Grzymala-Moszczynska, Maj & Kruglanski, 2019). Additionally, in the Yellow Creek Concerned Citizens movement, Cable (1992) found that participants became empowered and consequently started to challenge power structures in their everyday lives.

In a longitudinal study of environmental activists in Sweden, 11 types of biographical consequences relating to the participants' involvement in the collective action were identified (Vestergren, Drury & Hammar Chiriac, 2019): (ill)legitimacy of action, radicalization, empowerment, confidence, well-being, skills, knowledge, personal relationships, career, extended involvement, and consumer behavior. For example, participants changed careers or areas of study, reduced or stopped their consumption of meat and dairy products to hold a diet more in line with the environmentally friendly ideology, or experienced reduced pain and depressive symptoms. Some of the biographical consequences, such as an increase in well-being, can seem unrelated to the activist participation; however, the participants reported between 4 and 11 changes each that they related to the environmental direct action and activist identity (Vestergren, Drury & Hammar Chiriac, 2019). The participants related the changes to their shared identity as environmental activists and discussed them based on a framework of fairness related to environmental and human rights (Vestergren, Drury & Hammar Chiriac, 2019).

Vestergren and colleagues' study (2019) demonstrates that many of the previously identified biographical consequences can occur in one activist campaign, related to identity-relevant content. Hence, environmental activists will change their beliefs, relationships, and behaviors in line with the values and meanings attached to the relevant environmental activism ideology and identity.

How do these biographical consequences come about?

In this part, we discuss how biographical consequences emerge through activism, based on a theory of self and self-change. First, we summarize previous findings and highlight the two most prevalent processes: between-group and within-group interaction. Second, we suggest a model of emergence for environmental activists that combines the two, related to a theory of self and self-change.

Interaction with an outgroup

The first type of interaction for biographical changes to emerge is interaction with other groups. This interaction is mainly reported as a conflictual relationship with an outgroup, most often the police (e.g., Adamek & Lewis, 1973, 1975; Jasko, Szastok, Grzymala-Moszczynska, Maj & Kruglanski, 2019; Unsworth & Fielding, 2014). This type of interaction could, for example, be seen in the environmental campaign to save the Hambach forest in Germany, where, after a six-year-long battle and occupation of the forest, the police forcefully evicted and arrested activists from the camp (e.g., Vonberg & Schmidt, 2018). Adamek and Lewis (1973) compared students present at a protest against the Vietnam war in 1970 to students who were not present. During the protest, the National Guard opened fire and killed nine students. Students present at the protest, who had experienced police violence, had stronger ideological beliefs, were more likely to participate in future protests, and held stronger anti-government orientation (Adamek & Lewis, 1973). Additionally, by surveying the protesters' beliefs and behaviors before and after the protest, they found that the intentions to participate in civil disobedience almost doubled, and the willingness to participate in violent confrontations with the police increased by 83% (Adamek & Lewis, 1975). Similarly, Jasko and colleagues (2019, study 5) noted that participants who had been involved in the more radical actions in the environmental protest camp, such as blocking logging machines, reported higher levels of self-sacrifice and future protest intentions than participants who had engaged in the protest by moderate actions, such as signing a petition. These studies serve as examples of how between-group interactions, especially of a conflictual nature, can change participants in both beliefs and behaviors along the lines of extended activism, radicalization, legitimacy of their own actions, and illegitimacy of other's actions.

Interaction within the group

The second type of interaction that contributes to activists' biographical changes is interaction within the group. This type of interaction is usually referred to as "discussions" (e.g., Hirsch, 1990; Klandermans, 1997; Klar & Kasser, 2009; McAdam, 1989; Thomas, McGarty & Louis, 2014). For example, several Black Lives Matter activists reported that they had learned how to be activists through participation and interaction with others in the school climate strikes or XR (Murray & Mohdin, 2020). The activists highlighted how participation and engagement in the environmental protests through interaction within the group had empowered them to continue their activism in other groups. Through discussions within the group, activists get a sense of support for their new views and beliefs and a sense of a shared worldview (Passy & Monsch, 2014, 2020; Shriver, Miller & Cable, 2003). For example, a union (Unia) activist explained how interpersonal discussions enhanced and developed their working-class consciousness and how they acquired deeper understanding of issues (Passy & Monsch, 2020). Passy and Monsch (2020) argue that through conversations with other group members, the group culture becomes integrated within the mind. Along with interpersonal discussions, organized interaction such as workshops or seminars contribute to activists' biographical changes (e.g., Van Dyke & Dixon, 2013). Passy and Monsch (2020) describe how activists in Greenpeace talk about the knowledge they obtain in terms of both understanding and behavioral actions. For example, one Greenpeace activist described how group training sessions, pre-action meetings, exchanges with external actors and professionals, and interpersonal discussions affected their knowledge, understanding, sense of self, and worldview.

Combining between- and within-group interaction for emergence of biographical change

While interaction has been identified as crucial to explain the emergence of biographical consequences through activism and movement participation, the two types of interaction, between- and within-group, are mainly separate from each other and discussed in isolation (Dovidio, 2013). Dovidio (2013) emphasizes the importance of including both types of interaction as they are likely to affect each other.

In his study of the No M11 link road campaign, Drury (e.g., Drury, Reicher & Stott, 2003; Drury & Reicher, 2000, 2005) analyzed how the two interaction types interrelated to change participants. The participants engaged in direct action almost every day by, for example, occupying green areas; they faced resistance and violent force from both security companies and police (Drury, Reicher & Stott, 2003). Similarly, Vestergren and colleagues (2019) used the elaborated social identity model (ESIM) framework, developed by Drury and colleagues (Drury & Reicher 2000, 2005; Drury, Reicher & Stott, 2003; Reicher, 1996; Stott & Reicher, 1998), to understand the processes of participants' biographical changes in the environmental campaign in Sweden. In their efforts to save a piece of forest from becoming a limestone quarry, locals had engaged in resistance through legal processes and raising public awareness for almost 10 years. In the summer of 2012, a group of youth environmental activists set up camp in the forest and occupied it to hinder the deforestation machines carrying out their work. This was the starting point of a month filled with both within-group and between-group interaction that subsequently led to all participants reporting various biographical changes (Vestergren, Drury & Hammar Chiriac, 2019).

To explore the interrelated process between between-group and within-group interaction, we need to explore the sequence of events in the forest in more detail (see Vestergren, Drury & Hammar Chiriac, 2018, 2019). As in many environmental campaigns, the campaign as a whole involved a variety of people – some living in the area, some having traveled there – from children to pensioners, women and men, and various societal classes. The youth activists spent their days in the forest camp, sitting in trees and in front of deforestation machines to hinder the preparation work for the quarry. At this point, most of the locals supported the activists from afar, afraid to be labelled by the community if they partook in the direct actions. The police arrived with reinforced numbers (the local police force is very small) and started to physically remove the activists from the area. The introduction of force from an outgroup (the police) made the locals reposition their identities and, starting to see themselves as activists, joined the direct actions in the forest. Hence, the interaction with the outgroup created more unity and support within the activist group, which now included more participants. Participants explained that through the campaigners coming together, in opposition to the police and the quarry company, they became empowered and changed in their worldviews, which affected their behavior. Many environmental campaigns and collective actions follow the same pattern as the forest campaign in Sweden and the No M11 campaign in the UK. It can be suggested that participants in the Standing Rock, Hambach forest, Gezi Park, Quidong, and Roşia Montană protests; Fridays for Future; and other environmental campaigns changed in similar ways, driven by the same processes.

Biographical consequences for environmental activists along four identity dimensions

Many of the biographical changes, such as empowerment, legitimacy, and radicalization (e.g., Drury, Reicher & Stott, 2003; Drury & Reicher, 2000, 2018) could be conceptualized as changes in identity. Some studies refer to a change in identity or self as a separate consequence without exploring further dimensions (e.g., Beckwith, 2016; Klandermans, Sabucedo, Rodriguez & de Weerd, 2002; Profitt, 2001). For example, in studies of women unionists involved in the British miners' strike in the 1980s, Beckwith (2016) found that during their involvement, a political and feminist identity emerged. We argue that the identity construction or reconstruction is of importance for biographical changes to emerge through activist and movement participation. The basis for this argument is that we transform in ways that are relevant to our social collective identity. Hence, some changes may not be relevant for certain groups, or the content of the change might differ. For example, it was relevant for the 1960s activist identity to challenge family power relations, such as the nuclear family. However, in many contemporary societal contexts, this type of change content is no longer relevant. The relevance of the identity content is apparent when focusing on environmental activists and movement participation.

Based on our own studies and previous research, we suggest that the identity process of biographical change for environmental activists follow the four-dimension model (e.g., Drury, Reicher & Stott, 2003; Drury & Reicher, 2000, 2005, 2018). The first dimension relates to what it means to be an environmental activist (content). "Environmental activists" have been defined as "people who intentionally engage in the most difficult ecological behaviors" (Séguin, Pelletier & Hunsley, 1998, p. 631). Molinario and colleagues (2019) extend this by explaining that this includes actions beyond recycling for their own home, such as actively encouraging and promoting environmentally friendly behaviors. Hence, being an environmental activist means acting upon the values and beliefs attached to the environmental identity. For example, for the activists in Vestergren and colleagues' study (2018, 2019), this meant changing their consumption to exclude or decrease meat and dairy and to reduce their use of petrol, diesel, and plastic. Furthermore, the activists explained changes in their career and academic focus on the basis of what they had learned and come to understand as important to their new activist identity. Similarly, many participants gained new knowledge and skills, such as growing their own vegetables, related to components seen as part of the environmental activist identity (Vestergren, Drury & Hammar Chiriac, 2019).

Biographical consequences of participation in environmental activism are also related to changes in social relationships, in who is considered as "us" and "them" (identity boundaries). Both in the No M11 link road campaign (e.g., Drury, Reicher & Stott, 2003) and the Swedish forest campaign (Vestergren, Drury & Hammar Chiriac, 2019), participants changed in who they saw as a member of their group. In the initial phase of the environmental forest campaign, the youth activists and the locals did not see each other as part of the same category. However, through the events in the forest, they became united under a shared activist category. This activist category subsequently became even broader to include activists globally, such as environmentalists in Latin America (Vestergren, Drury & Hammar Chiriac, 2019). The changes in identity boundaries were also found to generate extended involvement as activists perceived other campaigns to be part of the same struggle, such as engagement in anti-mining protests in the north of Sweden. This type of change can be seen in several environmental movements – for example, the local campaign started by Greta Thunberg in 2018, which rapidly came to include more issues and more participants globally. The changes in identity boundaries also define and redefine who "they" are. After repositioning themselves as activists, and through the interaction with the police, the environmental activists defined the police as an outgroup, with whom they would not interact within or outside the campaign. They also included other state actors in the new categorization of "them" and became opposed to both the police and the state (Vestergren, Drury & Hammar Chiriac, 2019), which can also be seen in, for example, some areas of the XR movement (Extinction Rebellion, 2020).

Related to the repositioning of "us" is the change in perceived legitimacy of the actions taken by "us". This repositioning of who we are, for example from locals to activists, affects our own actions and beliefs, such as changing aims and becoming tactical about non-violent direct action. Most environmental movements work on the basis of non-violent action. For example, both Greenpeace and XR have a core of non-violent direct action. However, as the collective action context changes, so do the aims and what is seen as appropriate and legitimate action (e.g., Hayes, 2020). The change in what is perceived as legitimate and illegitimate action affects the participants in what can be understood as radical change, consequently resulting in more radical methods, for example minor public-order offences that activists get arrested for, such as gluing themselves to doors or trespassing. For example, participants in the environmental campaign to save a piece of forest in Sweden became more willing to participate in actions such as blocking roads, destroying deforestation machines, and, in a few cases, even breaking the law (Vestergren, Drury & Hammar Chiriac, 2019).

Finally, we suggest that environmental activists change as a consequence of a shift in the perception of possible actions in relation to the restraining powers of other groups (power). Through becoming united and sharing a sense of community under a shared identity, environmental activists come to expect that other group members share their beliefs and will support their actions (Drury & Reicher, 2005, 2009; Vestergren, Drury & Hammar Chiriac, 2019). Hence, they become empowered and perceive that the collective can successfully challenge the existing power relationships. The empowerment and sense of support have a positive effect on environmental activists' well-being. Environmental activists gain more confidence in their beliefs and actions within the campaign, and these changes can be brought to other areas of their lives, such as during job interviews (Vestergren, Drury & Hammar Chiriac, 2019).

We suggest that environmental activists change in ways that are relevant to their environmental identity, based on the social relationships and context relevant to the campaign or protest. It should be noted that we suggest the same four dimensions for activists in general; however, change in the content of the dimensions will be identity specific. For example, changing to a vegan diet makes sense for environmental activists; however, for right-wing anti-immigration activists, it would make more sense to change to a diet that only include nationally produced products rather than excluding meat and dairy. Furthermore, as with most protests and activist campaigns, the majority of environmental protests and campaigns do not include a physical conflictual relationship with an outgroup such as the police. We argue, in line with self-categorization theorists (Turner, Hogg, Oakes, Reicher & Wetherell, 1987), that to categorize yourself as a member of a group, you need to make a differentiation between who is in your group and who is not. This categorization is cognitive and conceptual and does not necessarily require a visible physical group in close proximity. Hence, for environmental activists such as Greenpeace or Fridays for Future participants, the outgroup could be large polluting companies, the fracking industry, the government, and so forth, and through categorizing themselves in opposition to outgroups, biographical changes emerge in line with the salient environmental identity. In contexts such as the Swedish forest campaign, where there was a physical conflictual relationship with an outgroup, the biographical changes will likely emerge faster and possibly more intensely, which could explain the difference in intensity of change Jasko and colleagues (2019) found in their sample of environmental activists who had participated in the camp compared to taking moderate actions such as signing a petition. Taken together, the theory could help explain why some environmental protests, such as the 2015 climate talks in Paris or the anti-fracking campaign Barton Moss, go from non-violent direct action to more radical actions and how participants sustain activist commitment from campaigns such as school climate strikes to Black Lives Matter. Furthermore, it helps us understand the importance of a theory of the self in explaining both participation in environmental movements and action outside the movement, such as recycling and diet behavior.

Do the biographical consequences of participation in environmental activism endure?

In this third and last part, we discuss how biographical consequences can be sustained or discontinued. We discuss the available findings and the importance of within-group interaction and shared environmental identity.

The main research conducted on endurance of biographical consequences through activism has focused on left-wing activist groups. Various studies have demonstrated profound long-term implications for the 1960s activists in terms of their views of themselves and the world (e.g., Braungart & Braungart, 1990; Fendrich, 1974; Marwell, Aiken & Demerath, 1987; McAdam, 1989; Nassi, 1981). Similar implications have been identified for the 1980s activists (e.g., Boehnke & Boehnke, 2005; Boehnke & Wong, 2011) and in more contemporary data (e.g., Giugni & Grasso, 2016).

However, most of the studies on biographical consequences of participation in activism lack a psychological account of how the changes are sustained over time. Some scholars suggest that biographical consequences are sustained by the outcome of the collective action (Becker & Tausch, 2015; Louis et al., 2017), whereas others highlight the context of collective action as a space where activists can re-assess themselves and their worldviews, which can lead to future engagement (van Zomeren, Leach & Spears, 2012). Similarly, Thomas, McGarty, and Mavor (2009) argue that a shared identity needs to be created with identity-relevant norms, which, in turn, create a system of understanding that forms the sustained activism commitment. Passy and Giugni (2000) suggest that there is a need to create a link between the activist sphere and the personal sphere. Hence, the social becomes personal when the activist identity become relevant to the life outside the campaign. Furthermore, characteristics of social networks have been suggested to influence the sustained commitment to activism. For example, the larger the network size, the more likely we are to generalize the activist identity, consequently increasing the likelihood of commitment to other campaigns (Louis, Amiot, Thomas & Blackwood, 2016; Thomas, McGarty & Louis, 2014). The connection between interaction, identity, and sustained biographical consequences in environmental movements can shed some further light on the endurance of the biographical consequences of participation in environmental activism.

Intragroup interaction and support to sustain biographical consequences over time

In our own research (e.g., Drury, Reicher & Stott, 2003; Drury & Reicher, 2000; Vestergren, Drury & Hammar Chiriac, 2018, 2019), we have observed a relationship in which intragroup processes mediate the effect of intergroup dynamics on sustained biographical consequences for environmental activists. More specifically, contradiction in the way activists expect the police to behave, to be on "the right side", and the way activists experience the police behavior, treating them all like criminals and physically removing them from the area, leads to a stronger unity among the activists (Vestergren, Drury & Hammar Chiriac, 2018). In the anti-fracking campaign in the UK, environmental campaigners highlight issues such as human health and their right to protest to justify their actions alongside environmental issues. In many of these campaigns, the police are accused of being excessively violent, threatening and dangerous and using labels such as "domestic extremists" in reference to the activists (e.g., Jackson, 2019), creating a perceived contradiction. The contradiction makes activists reposition the "self" and re-assess the identity boundaries, which, in turn, creates more support and discussions within the activist group. The new relationships within the group facilitate the endurance of biographical consequences and make activists more open to new arguments from within the group, as they now see themselves as part of a shared identity. Biographical consequences will sustain, or further increase, only when environmental activists perceived themselves to be part of the group (Vestergren, Drury & Hammar Chiriac, 2018). The level of interactive activity with other group members predicted the endurance of the participants' biographical consequences (Vestergren, Drury & Hammar Chiriac, 2018). Hence, perceived within-group interaction is crucial for the endurance of biographical consequences as it allows the activist to keep the environmental self salient and sustain the social values as personal values. Conversely, where the interaction with other participants discontinues, so do the beliefs and behaviors attached to the relevant environmental identity and self. In a few cases, where the within-group interaction had discontinued, there was a notable decline in the biographical consequences: for example, from being a vegan to eating meat (Vestergren, Drury & Hammar Chiriac, 2018). We expect the same relationship for other environmental activist campaigns, such as anti-fracking camps and protests and more large-scale protests such as the XR movement. Environmental activists will change or strengthen their beliefs and behaviors in accordance with the emerging and salient environmental identity. This repositioning of the self and identity will stay with the activists as long as they perceive themselves to be part of the environmental movement.

Conclusions

In this chapter, we have overviewed research describing the range of biographical consequences in relation to environmental activism. We have explored and suggested a theory of self and self-change for environmental activists along four dimensions: content, boundaries, legitimacy, and power. Through interaction with other environmental activists and interaction with perceived outgroups (such as the police or fracking companies), biographical consequences relevant to the shared identity can emerge. Even though the heterogeneity in environmental movements is often emphasized (e.g., Giugni & Grasso, 2015) – for example, heterogeneity was emphasized by some of the No M11 link interviewees who denied that there was a shared identity (Drury, Reicher & Stott, 2003), however, other evidence suggested they did share identity – the shared identity can explain the homogeneity in beliefs, actions, etc. in environmental movements and campaigns.

We have also made the case for the importance of sustained interaction with other environmental activists for the biographical consequences and the shared environmental identity to endure. Hence, to explain emergence and endurance of biographical consequences through participation in activism, we need to adopt a self-categorization perspective.

We argue that the advantage in researching biographical consequences relates to two areas. First, movement participation has a profound impact on the personal lives of activists. Activism can benefit participants in various areas, such as personal health and future job prospects, along with contributing to socialization processes within society. Second, understanding the processes of emergence and endurance of an environmental identity can help the environmental movement in creating a salient shared identity around environmental issues. Furthermore, understanding the process of endurance of environmental identity can help the environmental movement keep participation and extend participation to similar campaigns and causes, both of which have been argued by scholars to be issues for environmental activists (Kahan, 2015; McAdam, 2017; McCright & Dunlap, 2011). In line with Giugni and Grasso (2015), this chapter has emphasised the importance of local activism both for individual activists in terms of biographical changes and for larger campaigns and movements in relation to sustained commitment and pro-environmental behaviors.

References

Adamek, Raymond and Lewis, Jerry. 1973. Social control violence and radicalizations: The Kent State case. *Social Forces.* **51**, 342–347.

Adamek, Raymond and Lewis, Jerry. 1975. Social control violence and radicalization: Behavioral data. *Social Problems.* **22**, 663–674.

Bäck, Emma, Bäck, Hanna and Knapton, Holly. 2015. Group belongingness and collective action: Effects of need to belong and rejection sensitivity on willingness to participate in protest activities. *Scandinavian Journal of Psychology.* **56**, 537–544.

Becker, Julia. 2012. Virtual special issue on theory and research on collective action in the European journal of social psychology. *European Journal of Social Psychology.* **42**, 19–23.

Becker, Julia and Tausch, Nicole. 2015. A dynamic model of engagement in normative and non-normative collective action: Psychological antecedents, consequences, and barriers. *European Review of Social Psychology.* **26**, 43–92.

Becker, Julia, Tausch, Nicole and Wagner, Ulrich. 2011. Emotional consequences of collective action participation: Differentiating self-directed and outgroup-directed emotions. *Personality and Social Psychology Bulletin.* **37**, 1587–1598.

Beckwith, Karen. 2016. All is not lost: The 1984–85 British miners' strike and mobilization after defeat. In: Bosi, L., Giugni, M. and Uba, K. (eds.), *The Consequences of Social Movements.* Cambridge: Cambridge University Press, 41–65.

Blackwood, Leda and Louis, Winnifred. 2012. If it matters for the group then it matters to me: Collective action outcomes for seasoned activists. *British Journal of Social Psychology.* **51**, 72–92.

Boehnke, Klaus and Boehnke, Mandy. 2005. Once a peacenik – always a peacenik? Results from a German six-wave, twenty-year longitudinal study. *Peace and Conflict: Journal of Peace Psychology.* **11**(3), 337–354.

Boehnke, Klaus and Wong, Becky. 2011. Adolescent political activism and long-term happiness: A 21-year longitudinal study on the development of micro- and macrosocial worries. *Personality and Social Psychology Bulletin.* **37**(3), 435–447.

Braungart, Margaret and Braungart, Richard. 1990. The life-course development of left- and right-wing youth activist leaders from the 1960s. *Political Psychology.* **11**(2), 243–282.

Cable, Sherry. 1992. Women's social movement involvement: The role of structural availability in recruitment and participation processes. *The Sociological Quarterly.* **33**(1), 35–50.

Cherniss, Cary. 1972. Personality and ideology: A personological study of women's liberation. *Psychiatry.* **35**(2), 109–125.

Dovidio, John. 2013. Bridging intragroup processes and intergroup relations: Needing the twain to meet. *British Journal of Social Psychology.* **52**, 1–24.

Downton, James and Wehr, Paul. 1998. Persistent pacifism: How activist commitment is developed and sustained. *Journal of Peace Research.* **35**(5), 531–550.

Drury, John, Cocking, Christopher, Beale, Joseph, Hanson, Charlotte and Rapley, Faye. 2005. The phenomenology of empowerment in collective action. *British Journal of Social Psychology.* **44**, 309–328.

Drury, John and Reicher, Stephen. 1999. The intergroup dynamics of collective empowerment: Substantiating the social identity model of crowd behavior. *Group Processes & Intergroup Relations.* **2**(4), 381–402.

Drury, John and Reicher, Stephen. 2000. Collective action and psychological change: The emergence of new social identities. *British Journal of Social Psychology.* **39**, 579–604.

Drury, John and Reicher, Stephen. 2005. Explaining enduring empowerment: A comparative study of collective action and psychological outcomes. *European Journal of Social Psychology.* **35**, 35–58.

Drury, John and Reicher, Stephen. 2009. Collective psychological empowerment as a model of social change: Researching crowds and power. *Journal of Social Issues.* **65**, 707–725.

Drury, John and Reicher, Stephen. 2018. The conservative crowd? How participation in collective events transforms participants' understandings of collective action. In: Wagoner, B., Moghaddam, F., and Valsiner, J. (eds). *The Psychology of Radical Social Change. From Rage to Revolution.* Cambridge: Cambridge University Press, 11–28.

Drury, John, Reicher, Stephen and Stott, Clifford. 2003. Transforming the boundaries of collective identity: From the 'local' anti-road campaign to 'global' resistance? *Social Movement Studies.* **2**, 191–212.

Einwohner, Rachel. 2002. Motivational framing and efficacy maintenance: Animal rights activists' use of four fortifying strategies. *The Sociological Quarterly.* **43**(4), 509–526.

Elbein, Saul. 2017. The youth group that launched a movement at standing rock. *The New York Times,* 31 January. Available at: www.nytimes.com/2017/01/31/magazine/the-youth-group-that-launched-a-movement-at-standing-rock.html (Accessed 24 August 2020).

Extinction Rebellion. 2020. Statement on Extinction Rebellion's relationship with the police. *Extinction Rebellion,* 1 July. Available at: https://extinctionrebellion.uk/2020/07/01/statement-on-extinction-rebellions-relationship-with-the-police/ (Accessed 24 August 2020).

Fendrich, James. 1974. Activists ten years later: A test of generational unit continuity. *Journal of Social Issues.* **30**(3), 95–118.

Fendrich, James and Lovoy, Kenneth. 1988. Back to the future: Adult behaviour of former student activists. *American Sociological Review.* **53**(5), 780–784.

Fendrich, James and Tarleau, Alison. 1973. Marching to a different drummer: Occupational and political correlates of former student activists. *Social Forces.* **52**(2), 245–253.

Foster, Mindi. 2015. Tweeting about sexism: The well-being benefits of a social media collective action. *British Journal of Social Psychology.* **54**, 629–647.

Fridays for Future. 2020. Available at: https://fridaysforfuture.org (Accessed 23 August 2020).

Giugni, Marco and Grasso, Maria. 2015. Environmental movements in advanced industrial democracies: heterogeneity, transformation, and institutionalization. *Annual Review of Environment and Resources.* **40**, 337–361.

Giugni, Marco and Grasso, Maria. 2016. The Biographical Impact of Participation in Social Movement Activities: Beyond Highly Committed New Left Activism. In: Bosi, L., Guigni, M. and Uba, K. (eds.), *The Consequences of Social Movements.* Cambridge: Cambridge University Press, 85–105.

Hayes, Graeme. 2020. XR and the problem of accountability: Reflections on the September rebellion. *Centre for the Understanding of Sustainable Prosperity,* 7 September. Available at: www.cusp.ac.uk/themes/p/blog-gh-xr-september-2020/ (Accessed 7 September 2020).

Hirsch, Eric. 1990. Sacrifice for the cause: Group processes, recruitment, and commitment in a student social movement. *American Sociological Review.* **55**(2), 243–254.

Islam, Nazrul and Winkel, John. 2017. *Climate Change and Social Inequality.* UN Department of Economic and Social Affairs (DESA) Working Papers, 152. New York: UN.

Jackson, Will. 2019. Fracking: How the police response is threatening the right to protest. *Each Other,* 11 November. Available at: https://eachother.org.uk/fracking-right-to-protest/ (Accessed 23 August 2020).

Jasko, Katarzyna, Szastok, Marta, Grzymala-Moszczynska, Joanna, Maj, Marta and Kruglanski, Arie. 2019. Rebel with a cause: Personal significance from political activism predicts willingness to self-sacrifice. *Journal of Social Issues.* **75**(1), 314–349.

Kahan, Dan. 2015. Climate-science communication and the measurement problem. *Political Psychology.* **36**(1), 1–43.

Klandermans, Bert. 1997. *The Social Psychology of Protest.* Oxford: Blackwell.

Klandermans, Bert, Sabucedo, Jose, Rodriguez, Mauro and De Weerd, Marga. 2002. Identity processes in collective action participation: Farmers' identity and farmers' protest in the Netherlands and Spain. *Political Psychology*. **23**(2), 235–251.

Klandermans, Bert, van der Toorn, Jojanneke and van Steklenburg, Jaquelien. 2008. Embeddedness and identity: How immigrants turn grievances into action. *American Sociological Review*. **73**, 992–1012.

Klar, Malte and Kasser, Tim. 2009. Some benefits of being an activist: Measuring activism and its role in psychological well-being. *Political Psychology*. **30**, 755–777.

Kruglanski, Arie, Jasko, Katarzyna, Chernikova, Marina, Dugas, Michelle and Webber, David. 2017. To the fringe and back: Violent extremism and the psychology of deviance. *American Psychologist*. **72**, 217–230.

Lawson, Ronald and Barton, Stephen. 1980. Sex roles in social movements: A case study of the tenant movement in New York City. *Signs*. **6**(2), 230–247.

Louis, Winnifred, Amiot, Catherine, Thomas, Emma and Blackwood, Leda. 2016. The "activist identity" and activism across domains: A multiple identities analysis. *Journal of Social Issues*. **72**, 242–263.

Louis, Winnifred, Thomas, Emma, McGarty, Craig, Amiot, Catherine, Moghaddam, Fathali, Rach, Timothy, Davies, Grace and Rhee, Joshua. 2017. *Predicting Variable Support for Conventional and Extreme Forms of Collective Action After Success and Failure*. Paper presented at 18th General Meeting of the European Association of Social Psychology, Granada, July.

MacGillivray, Ian. 2005. Shaping democratic identities and building citizenship skills through student activism: México's first gay-straight alliance. *Equity & Excellence in Education*. **38**(4), 320–330.

Marwell, Gerald, Aiken, Michael and Demerath, Nicholas. 1987. The persistence of political attitudes among 1960s civil rights activists. *Public Opinion Quarterly*. **51**(3), 359–375.

McAdam, Doug. 1989. The biographical consequences of activism. *American Sociological Review*. **54**, 744–760.

McAdam, Doug. 2017. Social movement theory and the prospects for climate change activism in the United States. *Annual Review of Political Science*. **20**(1), 189–208.

McCright, Aaron and Dunlap, Riley. 2011. The politicization of climate change and the polarization in the American public's views of global warming. *The Sociological Quarterly*. **52**(2), 155–194.

Molinario, Erica, Kruglanski, Arie, Bonaiuto, Flavia, Bonnes, Mirilia, Cicero, Lavinia, Fornara, Ferdinando, Scopelliti, Massimiliano, Admiraal, Jeroen, Beringer, Almut, Dedeurwaerdere, Tom, DeGroot, Wouter, Hiedanpää, Juha, Knights, Paul, Knippenberg, Luuk, Ovdenden, Chris, Polajnar Horvat, Katarina, Popa, Florin, Porras-Gomez, Carmen, Smrekar, Aleš, . . . Bonaiuto, Marino. 2019. Motivations to act for the protection of nature biodiversity and the environment: A matter of "significance". *Environment & Behavior*. 1–31.

Murray, Jessica and Mohdin, Aamna. 2020. "It was empowering": Teen BLM activist learning the ropes at school climate strikes. *The Guardian*, 11 August. Available at: www.theguardian.com/world/2020/aug/11/school-strikes-were-empowering-teen-black-lives-matter-activists-on-their-environmental-awakening-extinction-rebellion (Accessed 11 August 2020).

Nassi, Alberta. 1981. Survivors of the sixties: Comparative psychosocial and political development of former Berkeley student activists. *American Psychologist*. **36**(7), 753–761.

Nassi, Alberta and Abramowitz, Stephen. 1979. Transition or transformation? Personal and political development of former Berkeley free speech movement activists. *Journal of Youth and Adolescence*. **8**(1), 21–35.

Passy, Florence and Giugni, Marco. 2000. Life-spheres, networks, and sustained participation in social movements: A phenomenological approach to political commitment. *Sociological Forum*. **15**(1), 117–144.

Passy, Florence and Monsch, Gian-Andrea. 2014. Do social networks really matter in contentious politics?. *Social Movement Studies*. **13**(1), 22–47.

Passy, Florence and Monsch, Gian-Andrea. 2020. *Contentious Minds: How Talk and Ties Sustain Activism*. New York: Oxford University Press.

Profitt, Norma Jean. 2001. Survivors of woman abuse: Compassionate fires inspire collective action for social change. *Journal of Progressive Human Services*. **11**(2), 77–102.

Reicher, Stephen. 1996. "The battle of Westminster": Developing the social identity model of crowd behaviour in order to explain the initiation and development of collective conflict. *European Journal of Social Psychology*. **26**, 115–134.

Reynolds, Katherine and Branscombe, Nyla. 2014. *Psychology of Change: Life Contexts, Experiences, and Identities*. London: Psychology Press.

Séguin, Chantal, Pelletier, Luc and Hunsley, John. 1998. Toward a model of environmental activism. *Environment and Behavior*. **30**, 628–652.

Sherkat, Darren. 1998. Counterculture or continuity? Competing influences on baby boomers' religious orientations and participation. *Social Forces.* **76**(3), 1087–1115.

Sherkat, Darren and Blocker, Jean. 1997. Explaining the political and personal consequences of protest. *Social Forces.* **75**(3), 1049–1076.

Shriver, Thomas, Miller, Amy and Cable, Sherry. 2003. Women's work: Women's involvement in the Gulf War illness movement. *The Sociological Quarterly.* **44**(4), 639–658.

Simon, Bernd and Klandermans, Bert. 2001. Politicized collective identity: A social psychological analysis. *American Psychologist.* **56**(4), 319–331.

Stott, Clifford and Reicher, Stephen. 1998. Crowd action as intergroup process: Introducing the police perspective. *European Journal of Social Psychology.* **26**, 509–529.

Stuart, Avelie, Thomas, Emma, Donaghue, Ngaire and Russell, Adam. 2013. "We may be pirates, but we are not protesters": Identity in the Sea Shepherd conservation society. *Political Psychology.* **34**, 753–777.

Tausch, Nicole and Becker, Julia. 2012. Emotional reactions to success and failure of collective action as predictors of future action intentions: A longitudinal investigation in the context of student protests in Germany. *British Journal of Social Psychology.* **52**(3), 525–542.

Temper, Leah. 2017. Globalizing environmental justice: Radical and transformative movements past and present. In: Holifield, R., Chakraborty, J. and Walker, G. (eds.), *The Routledge Handbook of Environmental Justice.* London: Routledge, 490–503.

Thomas, Emma, McGarty, Craig and Louis, Winnifred. 2014. Social interaction and psychological pathways to political engagement and extremism. *European Journal of Social Psychology.* **44**, 15–22.

Thomas, Emma, McGarty, Craig and Mavor, Kenneth. 2009. Aligning identities, emotions, and beliefs to create commitment to sustainable social and political action. *Personality and Social Psychology Review.* **13**, 194–218.

Turner, John, Hogg, Michael, Oakes, Penelope, Reicher, Stephen and Wetherell, Margaret. 1987. *Rediscovering the Social Group: A Self-Categorization Theory.* Oxford: Blackwell.

Uluğ, Özden Melis and Acar, Yasemin Gülsüm. 2016. 'We are more than alliances between groups': a social psychological perspective on the Gezi Parl protesters and negotiating levels of identity. In: David, I. and Tokham, K.F. (eds.), *'Everywhere Taksim': Sowing the Seeds for a New Turkey at Gezi.* Amsterdam: Amsterdam University Press, 121–136.

Uluğ, Özden Melis and Acar, Yasemin Gülsüm. 2018. What happens after the protests? Understanding protest outcomes through multi-level social change. *Journal of Peace Psychology.* **24**(1), 44–53.

Uluğ, Özden Melis and Acar, Yasemin Gülsüm. 2019. 'Names will never hurt us': A qualitative exploration of çapulcu identity through the eyes of Gezi Park protesters. *British Journal of Social Psychology.* **58**(3), 714–729.

Unsworth, Kerrie and Fielding, Kelly. 2014. It's political: How the salience of one's political identity changes climate change beliefs and policy support. *Global Environmental Change.* **27**, 131–137.

Van Dyke, Nella and Dixon, Marc. 2013. Activist human capital: Skills acquisition and the development of commitment to social movement activism. *Mobilization: An International Journal.* **18**, 197–212.

Van Zomeren, Martijn, Leach, Colin Wayne and Spears, Russell. 2012. Protesters as "passionate economists": A dynamic dual pathway model of approach coping with collective disadvantage. *Personality and Social Psychology Review.* **16**, 180–199.

Vestergren, Sara, Drury, John and Hammar Chiriac, Eva. 2017. The biographical consequences of protest and activism: A systematic review and a new typology. *Social Movement Studies.* **16**, 203–221.

Vestergren, Sara, Drury, John and Hammar Chiriac, Eva. 2018. How collective action produces psychological change and how that change endures over time – a case study of an environmental campaign. *British Journal of Social psychology.* **57**(4), 855–877.

Vestergren, Sara, Drury, John and Hammar Chiriac, Eva. 2019. How participation on collective action changes relationships, behaviours, and beliefs: An interview study of the role of inter- and intragroup processes. *Journal of Social and Political Psychology.* **7**(1), 76–99.

Vonberg, Judith and Schmidt, Nadine. 2018. Activists clash with police in Germany over occupation of ancient forest. *CNN*, 13 September. Available at: https://edition.cnn.com/2018/09/13/europe/germany-hambach-forest-police-intl/index.html (Accessed 23 August 2020).

Weyler, Rex. 2018. A brief history of environmentalism. *Greenpeace*, 5 January. Available at: www.greenpeace.org/international/story/11658/a-brief-history-of-environmentalism/ (Accessed 23 August 2020).

Whittaker, David and Watts, William. 1971. Personality characteristics associated with activism and dis-affiliation in today's college-age youth. *Journal of Counselling Psychology.* **18**(3), 200–206.

Wright, Stephen, Taylor, Donald and Moghaddam, Fathali. 1990. Responding to membership in a disad-vantaged group: From acceptance to collective protest. *Journal of Personality and Social Psychology.* **58**(6), 994–1003.

PART 6

Environmental movements in the twenty-first century

34

YOUTH AND ENVIRONMENTAL ACTIVISM

Sarah Pickard, Benjamin Bowman, and Dena Arya

Introduction

Young people's activism within environmental movements is a significant political phenomenon around the world today. Youth participation in social movements and, more specifically, environmental activism is not new. However, the current wave of environmental protest mobilizing the young generation across the globe is unprecedented in its scale and longevity. Since 2018, a large and growing critical mass of young environmental activists is calling for radical systemic change to bring about climate and social justice. They are adopting, adapting, and expanding the repertoire of contention used by former generations of environmental protesters. Offline and online, as part of a global movement, the contemporary young generation of environmental activists emphasizes the importance of non-violent direct action and peaceful civil disobedience, reflecting their aims and hopes for a fairer and kinder world. The current wave of environmental activism is also significant because youth from primary school age through to young adults are dissenting about issues that are not "youth-centered". Political reactions to this young generation of environmental activists, their demands, and their protest actions emphasize the age and life stage of the protesters.

In this chapter, we analyze the specificities of young people's involvement in contemporary environmental movements. The chapter draws on a series of interviews we carried out with school climate strikers participating in the Fridays for Future (FFF) movement and young Extinction Rebellion (XR) activists in Britain and France, as part of a research project on young people and environmental movements.[1] The face-to-face interviews took place before and during two crucial protest periods. First, the "Global Week for Future", from 20 to 27 September 2019, when "more than 7.6 million people took part in a week of climate strikes in 185 countries" (Amnesty International 2019a). The biggest school strike was on Friday 20 September 2019, involving "two million people walking out of schools and workplaces" around the world, according to FFF. Second, the "International Rebellion" from 7 to 19 October 2019, when Extinction Rebellion and "allied movements" organized an intergenerational "global uprising" fortnight to "continue to rebel against the world's governments" and bring an end to "ecological breakdown" (Extinction Rebellion 2019), which drew an estimated 20,000 people in London (Lavender 2019). We intentionally interviewed a wide age range of young people from those beginning secondary education through to those departing young adulthood. The

 DOI: 10.4324/9780367855680-40

eldest participants were 34 years old, while the youngest participants were aged 11: i.e., they were born in the year of the global financial crisis.

Through the voices of contemporary young environmental activists and concepts in scholarly work, we explain why and how young people today are engaging in environmental activism. We posit the specific period of young people's political socialization, marked by a series of crises, has impinged adversely on the quality of their lives in particular. At the same time, this generation of young people has certain capitals that also sets them apart from former young generations, as well as older generations today. The historical period of their political socialization has clearly shaped their political values, attitudes, and behavior. These and other multiple intersecting and overlapping factors outlined in the chapter have contributed to making the young generation more aware of and concerned about environmental issues and more likely to hold powerholders to account through protest actions than previous generations of young people. Crucially, these factors have provided the young generation with the forum, scope, motivation, and opportunity to use their agency to "do something" to make politicians in the older generation "do something" substantial and urgently about the climate crisis and situated injustices.

The concept of Do-It-Ourselves (DIO) political participation (Pickard 2019a) can be helpful to understand the current wave of young people's environmental activism, which is particular to their age, life stage, and generation. Thus, we suggest, due to a period effect − "distinct historical events that leave a lasting impression" (Norris 2004, p. 10) − young people around the world are part of a global generational unit (Mannheim 1952). Despite certain media and political representations, it should be noted that not all young people are activists in environmental movements, and those who are do not constitute a homogeneous cohort, as there are significant intragenerational differences at national and international levels.

The chapter first outlines the salience of youth as a life stage and status with regards to political socialization, political participation, and especially activism in protest movements. This leads to an analysis of the factors involved in why young people are turning to DIO politics and taking an active part in environmental movements. Young people's participation in environmental movements is then analyzed: i.e., demands, structures, and repertoire of contention (protest actions). Last, political reactions to young environmental activists are discussed in relation to their age, status, and generation. Throughout the chapter, we draw on our interviews with young environmental activists.

Youth, young people, the young generation, and political participation

Crucial to understanding this young generation's activism in environmental movements are the specificities of youth as a life stage and the status of young people, in combination with the political life cycle and the period of their political socialization. This section outlines their relevance and makes the link between the young generation in the twenty-first century and its propensity to adopt DIO politics and protest actions, especially in collective environmental activism.

There is no universal definition of "youth" beyond it being a life stage between childhood and adulthood. For Bourdieu (1978, 1993), "youth" is a social construct, and it is intimately linked to power relations (see Bessant, Pickard and Watts 2019). It is also important to take into account that over the past decades, for a variety of reasons, transitions from childhood to adulthood have become less linear and more extended (see Furlong 2013, 2017; Cuzzocrea 2020), as young lives have become more complex and precarious (Bessant, Farthing and Watts 2017).

These factors are helpful in understanding young people's environmental activism today due to sentiments of belonging to a generation let down by powerholders in older generations.

Moreover, children and young people hold an ambiguous status in society. There are no fixed ages when someone enters or exits youth or when someone starts or stops being a young person. Legislation is inconsistent regarding the status of young people – their rights and responsibilities – as thresholds vary and are often contradictory even within one nation. This is important in relation to the perceived legitimacy of the political engagement of young people, some of whom are not old enough to vote in parliamentary elections but are protesting on the streets and on social media about environmental justice.

In this chapter, the young people we refer to are mostly between the ages of 11 and 34.[2] There are obviously enormous intragenerational differences across the world that we cannot explore in this chapter. However, it is mainly during these two ages when most political socialization takes place, as young people become increasingly in contact (offline and online) with people outside the family and school, developing and asserting their own political values, opinions, attitudes, and behavior.

Young people around the world today have been and are being politically socialized during a period of diverse crises (financial, economic, political, constitutional, environmental, etc.) (Pickard and Bessant 2017). These multiple and overlapping crises have a detrimental effect, particularly on the young, especially the global financial crisis of 2008, the ensuing economic crisis (Cammaerts 2018) or "Great Recession", followed by austerity measures introduced by governments in many countries (Bessant, Farthing and Watts 2017), and now the COVID-19 pandemic (Beatfreeks 2020). The resulting precarity experienced by many in the current young generation differentiates them from older generations (who did not endure such levels of precarity when young and do not experience them today). This has had an impact on how young people feel about elected politicians, which is reflected in higher levels of disappointment and distrust (European Social Survey 2018; Hansard Society 2019).

But young people today have been and are being politically socialized into a world where they also have certain social, material, social, and cultural capital (Bourdieu 1986) not experienced by previous young generations.

First, young people are staying in school longer as mandatory education has been lengthened, and a greater proportion are entering tertiary education (although rates are much higher in the Global North and more affluent countries). Those with higher levels of educational attainment (i.e., those continuing after post-obligatory schooling age) are more politically active both electorally and non-electorally for diverse reasons, including civic skills, political knowledge, and social networks (Persson 2015).

Second, there has been a shift in values among young people toward more socially liberal, open, "outward looking" (Sloam 2020) and "cosmopolitan" outlooks (Sloam and Henn 2018; Keating 2021). This is especially the case among those going into tertiary education and particularly young women. Academics note a shift in young people's values from materialist to more post-materialist values (Inglehart 1977, 1997), resulting in a "cultural backlash" among generations (Norris and Inglehart 2019). However, it is fair to point out that this applies more to young people in the Global North than the Global South as a driver for young people seeking political change (Doyle and Chaturvedi 2010). Furthermore, in our interviews in Britain and France, we observed and consider that much of young people's environmental activism is also linked to materialist values – due to their generation's precarity – but also a wider concern with the very material impact of environmental degradation around the world, especially in poorer countries.

Third, the young generation has access to digital technologies and are digitally connected (Bessant 2014; Collin 2015) like never before, giving them greater and wider access to information and other young people around the globalized world. Being digitally connected increases young people's political participation (Boulianne and Theocharis 2018). Interviewees spoke of watching documentaries on YouTube, finding out most information online, receiving alerts, sharing material, and creating content.

Together, these specificities of the current young generation living in a globalized world make them more aware of and concerned about environmental issues. These generational factors provide political agency to young people in general terms and specifically in relation to political participation and environmental activism. Young people are placing the environment high up on or at the very top of their list of concerns, and they do so more than older cohorts (Sloam and Henn 2018). In an Amnesty International (2019b) survey, a majority of young people said climate change is the "most important issue facing the world". This is reflected in their electoral participation, with young people voting more for Green parties than in the past and more than older cohorts.

Despite greater support for Green parties in the twenty-first century around the world, young people's involvement in electoral and institutional political participation (for example, political party membership and turnout rates in elections) has tended to decrease and be lower than both older members of the electorate and previous generations of young people. Rather than adhering to traditional political ideologies, the young generation tends to be more inclined to mobilize around issue politics – for example, MeToo, March for Our Lives and Black Lives Matter (BLM) – than traditional political ideologies leading to paid-up political party membership and votes. Conversely, young people's non-electoral political participation (for example, lifestyle choices and protest actions) has increased (Grasso 2016, 2017; Sloam 2018). Overall, the young generation tends to vote less and protest more than older generations and previous young generations, meaning there are significant intergenerational differences in political participation.

It has been argued that young people are more "predisposed" to contest and take part in protests due to biological, psychological, or social characteristics of adolescence; their age; or life stage. (For an overview, see Pickard 2019a; Bessant 2021.) But the heterogeneity of young people as a demographic group and their diverse grammars of political activity, as well as competing perspectives both among young people and in wider society about what counts as "political", make it vital not to consider young people as a monolith or a homogeneous group or generation in a deterministic way.

Moreover, it can be suggested that young people, especially students and the unemployed, are at a life stage when they tend to have fewer commitments and responsibilities but more leisure and free time. It follows that they are thus more available than older citizens to participate in protest actions, especially forms of direct action that require more engagement in "cost" terms of time and effort. From this perspective, it is "easier" for young people to "do" certain forms of dissent – for example, occupations and climate camps – that have been key protest actions in environmental movements.

Young people have been at the forefront of activism in social movements encompassing civil rights and socio-economic justice around the world since the 1960s "wave of protest" (Barker 2008). Much academic work has focused on tertiary students and the effect of being in further or higher education on mobilization (Watts 2021). Less documented is the involvement of secondary school students in various protest actions. (For an overview, see Cunningham and Lavalette 2016; Bessant, Mejia Mesinas and Pickard 2021.) But the current wave of environmental activism is youth driven, especially the school climate strikes. This should be cautioned by the fact that as well as studying, many students are obliged to work to earn money – protesting depends on "biographical availability" (Prendergast, Hayward et al. 2021). Moreover, there are also those young people, particularly from lower socio-economic backgrounds, who, despite supporting protest actions such as the climate strikes, are unable to engage due to educational pressures that are vital to their future social mobility (Dorling 2019). In this way, Walker (2020, p. 13) highlights the importance of research taking into consideration less "high-profile" young people who are not involved in youth climate strikes as key contributors to the "generationally positioned" concerns of young people affected by the environmental crisis.

Last, the contemporary young generation is increasingly turning to DIO politics. They are taking the initiative to do politics themselves and doing it together: i.e., they are acting politically collectively outside formal political institutions (e.g., political parties, trade unions) while trying to influence politicians and other powerholders (Pickard 2019a). This produces feelings of belonging, agency, and self-efficacy.

These are some of the reasons young people are increasingly engaged in protest actions. The next section examines in more detail why the current young generation is concerned about the environment and how they are protesting in environmental movements.

Young people and environmental activism

Young people in particular have been involved in the current wave of global environmental movements for further multiple and interlinked reasons. This section addresses the demands, structures, and repertoire of young environmental activists, referring to what young participants said to us and our observations.

Historical youth environmental activism

Young people's environmental activism in a not a new phenomenon. School pupils and older youth have been involved in environmental movements around the world for decades in various ways. Historical environmental activism encompasses a wide range of issues, including globalization, social justice, and peace, in combination with more specific environmental issues, such as the hole in the ozone layer, road building, pollution, oil pipelines, airport expansion, shale extraction (fracking), animal protection, and consumption.

The environmental movement that emerged during the late 1960s and 1970s as part of the rise of new social movements is well documented in other chapters of this volume (see also Giugni and Grasso 2015). It was the time when radical environmental advocacy groups (such as Earth First!) were formed, involving mostly young adults. Secondary school students would also become engaged in environmental activism. For example, in Australia, "throughout the 1970s and 1980s secondary students were on record as being among those most concerned about the destruction of the environment" (Adamson 1993, p. 26; see also Fals Borda 1992).

Environmental activism gained traction during the 1990s. At that time, the "green movement" attracted considerable support from younger generations (Byrne 1997, p. 162), with young people "playing increasingly important roles in investigating, planning, monitoring and managing the environments of their own communities" (Hart 1994, p. 77). For example, at the 1992 United Nations Earth Summit in Rio de Janeiro, Brazil (the Rio Summit), 12-year-old Severn Cullis-Suzuki from Canada spoke out about environmental degradation and the responsibility of older generations.

During the same period, there was "a dramatic rise in the amount of direct activism" (Seel, Paterson and Doherty 2000, p. 1) in various countries (Rootes 2003), with young environmental activists engaging in radical direct action, adopting and adapting the repertoire of contention from the previous generation of young environmental activists and the civil rights movement. For example, in Britain, activists protested at ecological sites where road building was planned or taking place (Rootes 2000, 2003). Dissent included treetop protests over several weeks, tunnelling, and lock ons, as well as "eco-sabotage", such as the "monkey-wrenching" of equipment (Pickard 2020). In 1996, media attention focused on tunnelling "eco-warrior" Daniel Hooper, a.k.a. "Swampy", then in his early 20s (see Paterson 2000).

The 1990s also saw growing hostility to neoliberalism, capitalism, and globalization, while "democracy, social justice, and a better world were championed" (Kahn and Kellner 2004), with young people at the forefront of protest actions. For example, in 1999, the World Trade Organization's (WTO) new millennial round of trade negotiations saw substantial street protests involving young people in Seattle (USA). At this time, the study of young environmentalist activism, as one facet of the broader trend of young people's politics toward championing systems change for a better world, gained momentum. Studies of young environmental activism explored how young people were "playing increasingly important roles in investigating, planning, monitoring and managing the environments of their own communities" (Hart 1994, p. 77). They examined the particular role in activism played by young people in the Global South, where young people "are the worst-affected victims of resource degradation and environmental pollution" (Bajracharya 1994, p. 91). Scholars also identified the characteristic feature of young people's environmental activism, which is that it diverges from mainstream environmentalism in its focus on "international solidarity and grassroots democracy" and being "overtly critical" of socioeconomic and political macro-structures (Järvikoski 1995, p. 84).

The intersections of environmental problems with an unequal and deleterious global status quo has, as Fals Borda (1992) writes, historically attracted young people across the world to environmental activism as a project "to bring about a new ethos, a better kind of society and social relations in which unity may coexist with diversity" (in Haynes 1999, p. 223). In the twenty-first century, young people's environmental activism broadly continues in this historical vein. Young people are a marginalized group, and their environmental activism has deep roots in long-lived global and local movements, among marginalized people, for environmental justice.

For this reason, young people's activism in the form of environmental justice activism is distinguishable from mainstream environmentalist approaches that "largely continue to frame the goals of the environmental movement in narrowly constructed, technocratic, and dehistoricized ways" (Curnow and Helferty 2018, p. 149). The environmentalism of young people is characteristically oriented toward intersectional approaches that address "a system of interlocking oppressions" (Roberts 2012, p. 240). It is also closely linked to lived experiences of pollution, resource degradation, access to green spaces and open areas, environmental racism, and so forth. As young people's environmental activism tends to be framed in terms of social and economic justice more often than mainstream adult environmentalism, it is more frequently aligned to "cycles of protest" (Tarrow, 1998; Castells 2012) in reaction to various crises and coalesces around anti-capitalism and anti-austerity protests around the world.

The "circulation of protest framework" (Cammaerts 2018, p. 9) about anti-austerity protests is a useful way to understand discourse, collective identity, communication practices, media representations, and reception of the movement and the media discourse by non-activists. There has been a circulation of grievances and hopes, as well as repertoire of contention (Tilly 1995). Thus, "young people from different parts of the world are engaging in redemptive actions that are regenerating politics" (Pickard and Bessant 2017, p. 7). Environmentalism is one way they are doing this.

The historical context of young people's environmental activism provides some explanation for the facets of young activism today. As a subaltern group, young people's environmentalist activism is characteristically justice oriented and transformative in its scope (Bowman, 2020). Young people's activism is historically more about building a better society than advocating technocratic measures for sustaining society as it is. Young environmental activism, for these reasons, is often closely aligned to broader campaigns and causes for social and economic justice (Arya and Henn 2021).

Youth activism in environmental movements since 2018

From political opportunity and resource mobilization social movements theoretical perspectives, there were two crucial triggers that both came toward the end of 2018 that led to substantial youth involvement in environmental movements. First, 15-year-old Greta Thunberg started her school strike for climate (*Skolstrejk för klimatet*) in Sweden in August 2018 that would become the worldwide FFF movement (Camerini 2019). Second, Extinction Rebellion (XR) was officially launched in England in October 2018 by members of RisingUp!, previously involved in other environmental and social movements.

These two movements, in combination with key young figures, especially Greta Thunberg, have harnessed and developed young people's concern for environmental and social justice (Balsiger and Lorenzini 2019; Collin and Matthews 2021). They have acted as a catalyst for young "standby citizens" (Amnå and Ekman 2014), concerned about the environment but previously lacking the forum to express it. The young environmental activists taking part in climate strikes and Extinction Rebellion protests talked to us about feelings of "belonging" and "finding a home" for their values and concern for the environment. In particular, many said that they no longer felt solitary in their quest.

The young activists also spoke of feelings of "joy" and "solidarity" at protesting with like-minded young people, but also alongside older protesters in Extinction Rebellion affinity groups and as part of the climate strikes. It is noteworthy that participants in school climate strikes are not all primary or secondary school students (Wahlström et al 2019). Sometimes parents are in attendance, alongside their children or at a distance. Some young adult environmental activists are present "in solidarity" with younger ones to "support them" or be "an extra person" to help add to the critical mass. Some act as stewards, marshals, or legal observers. Conversely, some young adult activists in Extinction Rebellion commented that they deliberately did not get involved in the climate strikes, in order to leave school students their own "special space".

There is thus both intragenerational and intergenerational sharing of protest actions, which is construed as a positive experience for young environmental activists, as well as a source of uplifting emotions. Likewise, the sheer number of young people and older people protesting creates feelings of hope for the young environmental activists.

Beyond the place of positive emotions, such as joy and hope, when taking part in collective protest actions in general (Jasper 1998; Berman and Montgomery 2017; Pickard and Bessant 2018), the role of other emotions in the current environment movement is clearly huge for the young activists. Greta Thunberg and other key figures involved in the climate strikes and Extinction Rebellion use highly emotive data, narratives, and language ("emergency", "crisis", "breakdown"), which mobilize young people to protest. The young activists interviewed referred frequently to the emotional consequences of the current context ("anger", "despair", "grief", "mourning") and were often emotional when speaking to us about their activism.

Thus, a whole range of emotions were at play while the urgency and scale of climate change as it is depicted in environmental movements is a mobilizing force for young people calling for radical change (Pickard 2021).

DIO politics demanding systemic change in horizontal networks

The demands for radical change from powerholders made by FFF, other youth-led environmental networks, and Extinction Rebellion are centered on bringing about "system change not climate change". Young environmentalism is characteristically oriented toward imagining and constructing a new world, rather than just policy changes that can sustain the current one. They have a "symbolic representation of the kind of peaceful society they wish to create in the future" (Giddens 1990). System change is typically proposed in ways that are global in their implications and intergenerational in their timescale. There is nothing new about such radical demands, but today the urgency is more immediate, and the number of young environmental activists of all ages calling for it is more sizeable (Pickard, Bowman and Arya 2020). Moreover, this young generation's environmental activism is more complex with personal and institutional changes, combined with local and structural levels, as illustrated in Table 34.1.

At the same time, part of the appeal for young people to get involved in the school climate strikes, Extinction Rebellion, and other movements is their structure. Young activists are attracted to the fluid environmental advocacy networks that aspire to internal democracy and horizontalism. The appeal is especially the case because they are viewed as being structurally different from traditionally hierarchical political parties or trade unions with paid membership

Table 34.1 Orientation compass for young environmental activism, comparing institutional vs personal changes to global vs local structural levels

	Oriented toward institutional change	
Challenging the local status quo	• Protest messages directed at lawmakers and politicians • Petitioning local authorities • Writing to government officials • Youth councils and organizations • Green political parties • Pressure on schools, colleges, universities • Online activism oriented toward policy change at local, national, and international levels • Being inspired by friends, acquaintances, and family • Working to change opinions among friends, acquaintances, and family • Building friendship groups • Attending protests with others • Advocating for the participation of young people in public action • Making space for babies, young children, and their families • Taking time to volunteer locally • Bearing witness to environmental racism • Critiquing and intervening in adult-oriented and dominated groups	• Protest messages directed at mass media coverage and global audiences • Protest messages directed at banks and global corporations • Advocacy through international organizations • Global movement building and organizing • Online activism oriented toward policy change at the global level • Critiquing capitalism • Being inspired by global influencers like Greta Thunberg • Changing lifestyle: e.g., avoiding car and air transport; veganism • Critiquing mainstream, adult environmentalism • Bearing witness to environmental racism at a global level • Conceptualizing positions of marginalization in an intersectional way • Critiquing mainstream, adult environmentalism |**Challenging the global status quo**
	Oriented toward personal change	

and top-down organization, leaving relatively little autonomy to members or supporters. Thus, in environmental movements, activists can and are encouraged to take initiative and "do" protest actions freely and together without having to follow directives from above while being guided.[3]

Within these environmental movements, young environmental activists are adopting and adapting the existing repertoire of contention centered on non-violent direct action (NVDA). Young environmental activists are learning by doing protests, building on repertoires of previous generations of activism and what "works" or not, as well as developing their own protest skills along with other younger and older activists.

Many interviewees taking part in school climate strikes and Extinction Rebellion protests spoke of how individual acts of environmentalism were insufficient to bring about significant change of environmental degradation. Recycling, adopting a plant-based diet or going vegan, boycotting, buycotting (ethical consumption), and avoiding private transport, as well as contacting and lobbying politicians, were not considered enough to influence political decisions about the environment.

Thus, young people previously living their environmentalism through private individual lifestyle DIO politics have found a collective arena in current environmental movements to express their values and hopes. Collective protest actions, such as walkouts, rallies, marches, and occupations were considered by these activists as more effective means to bring about change by being part of a critical mass.

Creative and artistic forms of performative protest actions are also fundamental to the popularity of the environmental movements among young people. We asked climate strikers to talk about their placards: how they made them, with whom, from what, why, etc. The replies revealed much care and thought about the design, materials, depictions, words, and pictures, as well as what the climate strikers were planning to do with them afterward. In Extinction Rebellion, protest actions such as swarming, supergluing, funeral marches, die-ins, fake blood, and the Red Army were frequently described by young activists as enjoyable and effective – the most effective ways to draw media, public, political, and peer attention.

Notably, young activists in Extinction Rebellion spoke of the importance of being "disruptive" in their protest actions, including being an "arrestable". Indeed, much media attention about young environmental activism has tended to focus on the more spectacular and "newsworthy", disruptive direct action and civil disobedience repertoires of contention employed by Extinction Rebellion activists, seemingly involving only a tiny minority of youth. But the more numerous school strikers in the FFF movement are also being disruptive because they are breaking school rules (often leading to an unauthorized absence).

One other fundamental characteristic stands out in our interviews regarding the repertoire of protest actions: many young environmental activists insisted on the importance for them of engaging in non-violent direct action (NVDA) in harmony with their values. This was expressed explicitly and implicitly through statements such as "we act in peace" and "we are radical in our kindness" (see Pickard, Bowman and Arya 2020).

We think the combination of all the factors mentioned here have crucially provided young people with the forum and scope to "do something" about climate change. The concept of DIO political participation can be helpful to understand the increase in young people's environmentalism. It refers to citizens taking politics into their own hands and acting individually, but mostly collectively, in order to bring about change together in an empowering way. School climate strikers and young Extinction Rebellion activists spoke repeatedly about politicians not "doing" anything about the climate crisis and their own feelings of needing, as young people, to "do" something beyond individual acts.

In this way, environmental movements and prominent young environmental activists and their peers have provided young people with the structures for collective protest actions as DIO politics to demand radical change from politicians.

Political reactions and outcomes of young people's environmental activism

Reactions from political figures to young environmental activists and their protest actions as DIO politics is a key aspect of young people's engagement in environmental movements. This last section addresses the two main responses from politicians that stand out regarding the school climate strikers in general and Greta Thunberg in particular: criticisms and congratulations. The young environmental activists we interviewed were very aware of these polarized reactions.

First, for young people as environmental activists, their demands and protest actions are met with criticism and derision. Much of the condemnation is based on their age or life stage and linked to the status of children and young people (Bessant 2021). Young environmental protesters are portrayed as immature, naive, manipulated, irrational, idealistic, unrealistic, ill informed, misinformed, and at times extremist. They are also accused of not being genuinely interested in the issues at stake and merely participating in climate strikes to follow a trend, just to look cool or skip school.

Australian Prime Minister Scott Morrison (Liberal Party) exemplifies age-based criticism of young environmental activists. For example, on 26 November 2018, he yelled in Parliament, "What we want is more learning in schools and less activism in schools" and that kids should remain in school and not protest about things that "can be dealt with outside of school": i.e., by politicians. This is obviously "age based prejudice, that young people cannot and should not be political" (Young-Bruel 2012), founded on the notion that they cannot act rationally, responsibly, or reasonably.

Greta Thunberg, as a young person on the autism spectrum, has been derided and vilified by multiple (mostly male) politicians around the world. Brazilian president Jair Bolsonaro called her "a little brat" (*pirralha*) in December 2019, while Donald Trump mocked her on Twitter and elsewhere several times. For example, the young environmental activist spoke at the World Economic Forum in Davos (Switzerland), on 22 January 2020, lamenting politicians' lip service and inertia on climate change in the following terms:

> You say children shouldn't worry. You say: "Just leave this to us. We will fix this, we promise we won't let you down. Don't be so pessimistic". And then . . . nothing. Silence. Or something worse than silence. Empty words and promises which give the impression that sufficient action is being taken.
>
> (Thunberg 2020)

Trump, the then President of the United States of America retorted in a media interview: "How old is she?" Clearly, for these hostile politicians, Greta Thunberg's age is an issue. As well as her age, her gender also seems to be a challenge for some. For example, on 21 July 2019, when the then-16-year-old was about to address the Assemblée Nationale in Paris, Julien Aubert, the deputy general secretary of the right-wing Les Républicains (LR) political party, tweeted that he would not be applauding a "female prophet in short trousers".[4] When asked about the criticisms aimed at her, Thunberg commented:

> Those attacks are just funny because they obviously don't mean anything. . . . I guess of course it means something: they are terrified of young people bringing change

which they don't want. But that is just proof that we are actually *doing* something and that they see us as some kind of threat.

(Thunberg 2019, emphasis added)

By publicly reproving young environmental activists, their demands, and their actions on the basis of their life stage or age, politicians seem to be attempting to delegitimize and dismiss what young people are doing as irrelevant. Politicians use the age or life stage of protesters as an excuse or a justification to ignore them, their demands, and their hopes for significant change toward the better world that was promised to the young generation. Politicians thus remove their own responsibility, obligation, necessity to "do" something. It is also a way to sideline young people who are not acknowledged to be citizens with valid concerns or interest in the future.

Second, young environmental activists – especially school climate strikers – have been congratulated by politicians (both on the left and right). Sometimes, the compliments come in ambivalent ways, and it is impossible to disentangle the semiotics. It is often unfeasible to evaluate with any certainty whether such comments constitute genuine admiration of young people and their environmental activism or a real interest in the environmental issues at stake. We cannot know the extent to which young activists in environmental movements are being praised, patronized, and manipulated by politicians endearing themselves to stave off further protest and for electoral purposes: i.e. being treated as naive future vote fodder through hypocritical and sycophantic lip service, greenwashing, "youth-washing" "youth-bait", and "youth-glossing" (Pickard 2019a) or "cool hunting" (Farthing 2010). For example, when Greta Thunberg spoke at Westminster, London, in June 2019, Michael Gove (Conservative MP) declared:

Your voice – still, calm and clear – is like the voice of our conscience. . . . When I listened to you, I felt great admiration, but also responsibility and guilt. I am of your parents' generation, and I recognise that we haven't done nearly enough to address climate change and the broader environmental crisis that we helped to create.

(Gove 2019)

The emphasis on "generation" here, from the then-Minister for Agriculture and the Environment, highlights the dichotomy about whether young people lack maturity and the capacity to act politically in an informed and responsible way. It is also linked to the debate in several countries around the world about votes at 16 (see Eichhorn and Bergh 2020).

The sustained environmental movement is all the more perplexing and disconcerting for politicians because it is not about a youth-centered issue per se, such as education (conditions, teachers, schooling). It is beyond the sphere of the everyday, and thus, children's interest in it challenges conventional conceptions of childhood: i.e., children cannot think for themselves and should not have opinions, let alone demands that interfere with the status quo and hold politicians to account (Bessant and Lohmeyer 2021). Young environmental activists we interviewed gave reflexive and reasoned explanations for their activism and said they were not immature (see Arya, Bowman and Pickard 2019). In turn, this is part of the reason Greta Thunberg frequently states: "Listen to the science".

Criticizing and condemning young environmental protesters is also, from a functionalist perspective, a way to regulate and sanction young people and "keep them in their place" (Pickard, Nativel and Portier 2012) as a form of social control. School climate strikers are faced with an "unauthorized absence" on their school records that affects their end-of-school-year assessments. The policing of environmental movements' protest actions is another form of social control and repression (Grasso and Bessant 2019; Pickard 2019b).

However, beyond the ambiguity of potential gesture politics, demagogy, electioneering, spin, soundbites, and hyperbole, we can document official reactions to young environmental activists – i.e., governmental declarations and positions – and whether they have been followed through on with actual policy implementation and any discrepancies (for example, acknowledgment of environmental emergency, creation of citizen assemblies, adherence to the 2016 Paris Agreement), which is addressed in other chapters of this volume (see also Henn and Pickard 2021; Sloam, Pickard and Henn 2021). Certainly, young environmental activism has attracted media, public, and political attention, as shown by official statements and policy announcements from politicians, which shows that the protest actions are having some impact.

Conclusion

In this chapter, we have shown, through what young activists engaged in environmental movements said to us and through theoretical work, why and how this current generation of young environmental activists are protesting. We have pointed out that since 2018 they have been mobilized in an unprecedented way and scale due to the specific set of circumstances they have lived and are living through, in combination with crucial changes to society compared to previous generations.

Young people around the world have been and are being politically socialized during a period of diverse crises that affect them negatively, in particular because they are a subaltern and marginalized group. The outlook for young environmental activism may depend on how young people develop generational forms of capital, such as higher levels of education and digital connectivity on a global scale, as well as the evolution of their shift in values toward more socially liberal, open, cosmopolitan outlooks, especially among students. Together, these have made digitally connected young people more aware of and concerned about environmental and social justice, as well as less trusting of politicians and more likely to hold powerholders to account. We suggest, with caution, that the combination of environmental awareness, inclusivity of others, and ability to organize online and offline indicates that young people may be able to continue to mobilize in ways that can affect policy as well as public debate.

In particular, we identify a characteristic tendency toward DIO politics in young people's personal and collective environmental activism. This includes a commitment to performative or creative non-violent direct action. In addition, young people are attracted to fluid environmental advocacy networks that aspire to internal democracy and horizontalism. We consider that if young environmental activism is to influence social change, it will depend on the extent to which young people's democratic, inclusive, and horizontal structures can adapt to climate change, an issue that is dominated by top-down and hierarchical approaches to knowledge and action, and gain leverage on elected representatives, democratic institutions, and, perhaps, private corporations.

Diversity, plurality, and horizontalism offer many opportunities for young environmental activists, but they also offer challenges. Although we can identify a global movement in the process of navigating its diversity, this wave of activism is still in the process of developing solidarities. Some of these solidarities, as Curnow and Helferty write, are contradictory (2018): structural inequalities, not least enduring global economic and racial inequalities, intersect the movement in its diversity. There are inequalities in which young people are considered activists, which would call themselves activists, and which have the privilege to take direct action, for instance. We neither infer that all young people care about the environmental crisis and are out on the streets nor that it is only white, middle-class youth in the Global North who are protesting. We recognize the complexity of the global movement and the challenges it faces as a generally horizonalist movement that is nevertheless bound up with global inequalities. More research is required to understand how young people across the world perceive the nature of their environmentalism with respect to such inequalities.

We also urge caution among those who would celebrate the gathering influence of young environmental activism. Politicians may or may not act convincingly on calls for action on climate change; accordingly, young people may become disillusioned with or inspired by elected politicians. Their DIO politics and repertoires of contention may become more creative. Environmental activism among young people may dissipate, generalize, or intensify. Police responses to young political action may escalate, and a crackdown may have wide-ranging effects. For whatever reasons, protesters and protest actions may become more radical. Indeed, some prominent figures in Extinction Rebellion have been calling for more radical actions (hunger strikes and arrests); our most recent interviews with environmental activists in Paris show a growing radicalization of a small number of young activists (under 18) who have gone from school climate strikes to XR activism to anarchic and black bloc activism in the space of a year.[5] It remains to be seen whether what we identify as the generational unit of young environmental activists experiencing an historical period effect will take forward their environmentalism through the political life cycle as a cohort, resulting in a generational effect through generational replacement.

However, the contemporary young environmentalist movement evolves, we have illustrated that young people of all ages have values, views, voice, and agency. Young people are agents of change, and they are having an impact on public perception and political policy regarding environmental issues. The global movement of the young has diverse and important potential consequences in the short and long term. The unprecedented global scale and longevity of young environmental activists' protest actions have "forced climate change onto the agenda . . . and shown politicians they can't ignore young people" (Zoé, 22, XR activist, Sheffield, September 2019).

Notes

1 This chapter is based on 60 semi-structured interviews we carried out in Edinburgh, London, Manchester, Nottingham, Sheffield, and Paris. Participants signed ethical consent forms prior to the interviews, and for interviewees under the age of 16, signed parental consent was given. We would like to thank all the young environmental activists interviewed as part of our research project and Lee Phillips.
2 Young people of primary school age are also taking part in climate strikes, but they are not the focus of this study.
3 Despite aspirations of horizontalism and internal democracy there are internal hierarchies of power in these movements.
4 Julien Aubert @JulienAubert84, 21 July 2019, "@GretaThunberg a été invitée à l'Assemblée nationale pour la séance. Je respecte la liberté de penser . . . mais ne comptez pas sur moi pour applaudir une prophétesse en culottes courtes, " Prix Nobel de la peur ". La planète, oui. Le greenbusiness, non".
5 For analysis of radical environmental activists, see work by Heather Alberro (2020).

References

Adamson, Greg. 1993. *25 Years of Secondary School Revolt: 1968–1993*. Sydney: Resistance.

Alberro, Heather. 2020. *Ecotopia Rising: An Ecocritical Analysis of Radical Environmental Activists as Ecotopian Expressions Amid Anthropocene Decline*. PhD thesis. Nottingham Trent University, Nottingham, 17 December.

Amnå, Erik and Ekman, Joakim. 2014. Standby citizens: Diverse faces of political passivity. *European Political Science Review*. 6(2), 261–281.

Amnesty International. 2019a. *Protests Around the World Explained*, 25 October (www.amnesty.org/en/latest/news/2019/10/protests-around-the-world-explained)

Amnesty International. 2019b. *Climate Change Ranks Highest as Vital Issue of Our Time – Generation Z Survey*. Amnesty International, 10 December (www.amnesty.org/en/latest/news/2019/12/climate-change-ranks-highest-as-vital-issue-of-our-time)

Arya, Dena, Bowman, Benjamin and Pickard, Sarah. 2019. *Young Climate Strikers Are Neither Immature Nor Ill-Informed*. London School of Economics – LSE Politics and Policy Blog, 21 October 2019 (https://blogs.lse.ac.uk/politicsandpolicy/britains-young-climate-strikers)

Arya, Dena and Henn, Matt. 2021. COVID-ized ethnography: Challenges and opportunities for young environmental activists and researchers. *Societies*. 11(12), 58. (https://doi.org/10.3390/soc1102 0058)

Bajracharya, Deepak. 1994. Primary environmental care for sustainable livelihood: A UNICEF perspective. *Childhood*. 2(1–2), 41–55.

Balsiger, Philip and Lorenzini, Jasmine. 2019. *Generation Climate*. Paper. Euryka International Scientific Conference, Monte Verità, Switzerland, 10 May.

Barker, Colin. 2008. Some reflections on student movements of the 1960s and early 1970s. *Revista Crítica de Ciências Sociais*. 81, 43–91.

Beatfreeks. 2020. A national youth trends report understanding the impact of coronavirus on young people in the UK. *National Youth Trends Take the Temperature* (www.beatfreeksyouthtrends.com)

Berman, Carla and Montgomery, Nick. 2017. *Joyful Militancy: Building Thriving Resistance in Toxic Times*. London: AK Press.

Bessant, Judith. 2014. *Democracy Bytes: New Media and New Politics and Generational Change*. London: Palgrave Macmillan.

Bessant, Judith. 2021. *Making Up Young People: Youth, Truth and Politics*. London and New York: Routledge.

Bessant, Judith, Pickard, Sarah and Watts, Rob. 2019. **Translating Bourdieu into youth studies.** *Journal of Youth Studies*. 23(1), 76–92. (https://doi.org/10.1080/13676261.2019.1702633)

Bessant, Judith and Lohmeyer, Ben. 2021. Politics of naming and recognition: Student protest. In: Bessant, J., Mejia Mesinas, A. and Pickard, S., eds. *When Students Protest: Secondary and High Schools*. Washington, DC: Rowman and Littlefield, 37–54.

Bessant, Judith, Farthing, Rys and Watts, Rob. 2017. *The Precarious Generation: A Political Economy of Young People*. London and New York: Routledge.

Bessant, Judith, Mejia Mesinas, Analicia and Pickard Sarah. 2021. Introductory essay: What it means when secondary and high school students protest. In: Bessant, J., Mejia Mesinas, A. and Pickard, S., eds. *When Students Protest. Volume One: When Students Protest. Secondary and High Schools*. Lanham, MD: Rowman and Littlefield, 1–18.

Boulianne, Shelley and Theocharis, Yannis. 2018. Young people, digital media, and engagement: A meta-analysis of research. *Social Science Computer Review*. 38(2), 111–127.

Bourdieu, Pierre. 1978. La jeunesse n'est qu'un mot. Entretien avec Anne-Marie Métailié. In: Métailié, A.M. and Thiveaud, J.M., eds. *Les jeunes et le premier emploi*. Paris: Association des Ages, 520–530.

Bourdieu, Pierre. 1986. The forms of capital. In: Richardson, J., ed. *Handbook of Theory and Research of the Sociology of Education*. New York: Greenwood, 241–258.

Bourdieu, Pierre. 1993. 'Youth' is just a word. In: Bourdieu, P., ed. *Sociology in Question*. Thousand Oaks, CA: Sage, 94–102.

Bowman, Benjamin. 2020. 'They don't quite understand the importance of what we're doing today': The young people's climate strikes as subaltern activism. *Sustainable Earth*. 3, 16 (https://doi.org/10.1186/s42055-020-00038-x)

Byrne, Paul. 1997. *Social Movements in Britain*. London and New York: Routledge.

Camerini, Valentina. 2019. *Greta's Story: The Schoolgirl Who Went on Strike to Save the Planet*. Translated by Moreno Giovannoni. London: Simon & Shuster.

Cammaerts, Bart. 2018. *The Circulation of Anti-Austerity Protest*. London: Palgrave Macmillan.

Castells, Manuel. 2012. *Networks of Outrage and Hope. Social Movements in the Internet Age*. Second edition. Cambridge: Polity Press.

Collin, Philippa. 2015. *Young Citizens and Political Participation in a Digital Society*. London: Palgrave Macmillan.

Collin, Philippa and Matthews, Ingrid. 2021. School strike for climate: Australian students renegotiating citizenship. In: Bessant, J., Mejia Mesinas, A. and Pickard, S., eds. *Volume One: When Students Protest: Secondary and High Schools*. Washington, DC: Rowman and Littlefield, 125–144.

Cunningham, Steve and Lavalette, Michael. 2016. *Schools Out! The Hidden History of Britain's School Student Strikes*. London: Bookmark Publications.

Curnow, Joe and Helferty, Anjali. 2018. Contradictions of solidarity: Whiteness, settler coloniality, and the mainstream environmental movement. *Environment and Society*. 9(1), 141–163.

Cuzzocrea, Valentina. 2020. A place for mobility in metaphors of youth transitions. *Journal of Youth Studies*. 23(1), 61–75.

Dorling, Danny. 2019. *Report Forward: The Influence of Place Geographical Isolation and Progression to Higher Education*. London: The Bridge Group (www.dannydorling.org/wpcontent/files/dannydorling_publication_id7134.pdf)

Doyle, Timothy and Chaturvedi, Sanjay. 2010. Climate territories: A global soul for the global South? *Geopolitics*. 15(3), 516–535.

Eichhorn, Jan and Bergh, Johannes. 2020. *Lowering the Voting Age to 16: Learning for Real Experiences Worldwide*. London: Palgrave Macmillan.

European Social Survey. 2018. (www.europeansocialsurvey.org)

Extinction Rebellion. 2019. *Extinction Rebellion Website* (https://rebellion.earth)

Fals Borda, Orlando. 1992. Social movements and political power in Latin America. In: Escobar, A. and Alvarez, S.E., eds. *The Making of Social Movements in Latin America: Identity Strategy and Democracy*. London and New York: Routledge, 303–316.

Farthing, Rys. 2010. The politics of youthful antipolitics: Representing the 'issue' of youth participation in politics. *Journal of Youth Studies*. 13(2), 181–195.

Furlong, Andy. 2013. *Youth Studies. An Introduction*. London and New York: Routledge.

Furlong, Andy. 2017. *Routledge Handbook of Youth and Young Adulthood*. Second edition. London and New York: Routledge.

Giddens, Anthony. 1990. *The Consequences of Modernity*. Stanford, CA: Stanford University Press.

Giugni, Marco and Grasso, Maria. 2015. Environmental movements: Heterogeneity, transformation, and institutionalization. *Annual Review of Environment and Resources*. 40 (https://doi.org/10.1146/annurev-environ-102014-021327)

Gove, Michael. 2019. UK parliament. In: Watts, J., ed. The Greta Thunberg effect. *The Guardian*, 23 April (www.theguardian.com/environment/2019/apr/23/greta-thunberg)

Grasso, Maria, T. 2016. *Generations, Political Participation and Social Change in Western Europe*. London and New York: Routledge.

Grasso, Maria, T. 2017. Young people's political participation in Europe in times of crisis. In: Pickard, S. and Bessant, J., eds. *Young People Re-Generating Politics in Times of Crises*. London: Palgrave Macmillan, 179–196.

Grasso, Maria, T. and Bessant, Judith., eds. 2019. *Governing Youth Politics in the Age of Surveillance*. London and New York: Routledge.

Hansard Society. 2019. *Audit of Political Engagement 16: The 2019 Report*. The Annual Health Check on Attitudes Towards Politics in Great Britain. London: Hansard Society.

Hart, Roger. 1994. Children's role in primary environmental care. *Childhood*. 2(1–2), 103–110.

Haynes, Jeff. 1999. Power, politics and environmental movements in the third world. *Environmental Politics*. 8(1), 222–242.

Henn, Matt and Pickard, Sarah, eds. 2021. *Youth Activism in Environmental Politics*. Frontiers political participation special issue (www.frontiersin.org/research-topics/12319/youth-activism-in-environmental-politics).

Inglehart, Ronald. 1977. *The Silent Revolution: Changing Values and Political Styles Among Western Publics*. Princeton, NJ: Princeton University Press.

Inglehart, Ronald. 1997. *Modernization and Postmodernization: Cultural, Economic, and Political Change in 43 Societies*. Princeton, NJ: Princeton University Press.

Järvikoski, Timo. 1995. Young people as actors in the environmental movement. *Young*. 3(3), 80–93.

Jasper, James. 1998. The emotions of protest: Affective and reactive emotions in and around social movements. *Sociological Forum*. 13(3), 397–424.

Kahn, Richard and Kellner, Douglas. 2004. New media and internet activism: From Battle of Seattle to blogging. *New Media and Society*. 6(1), 87–65.

Keating, Avril. 2021. Mobility for me but not for others: The contradictory cosmopolitan practices of contemporary White British youth. *Sociology* (https://doi.org/10.1177/0038038521999565).

Lavender, Andy. 2019. Theatricalizing protest: The chorus of the commons. *Performance Research: A Journal of the Performing Arts.* 24(8), 4–11.

Mannheim, Karl. 1952. The problem of generations. In: Kecskemeti, P., ed. *Essays on the Sociology of Knowledge.* London and New York: Routledge and Kegan Paul, 276–320.

Norris, Pippa. 2004. *The Evolution of Election Campaigns: Eroding Political Engagement?* Paper. Conference on Political Communications in the 21st Century. University of Otago, New Zealand.

Norris, Pippa and Inglehart, Ronald. 2019. *Cultural Backlash: Trump, Brexit, and Authoritarian Populism.* Cambridge: Cambridge University Press.

Paterson, Matthew. 2000. Swampy Fever: Media Constructions and Direct Action Politics. In: Doherty, B. and Paterson, M., eds. *Direct Action in British Environmentalism.* London and New York: Routledge, 151–166.

Persson, Mikael. 2015. Education and political participation. *British Journal of Political Science.* 45(3), 689–703.

Pickard, Sarah. 2019a. *Politics, Protest and Young People: Political Participation and Dissent in 21st Century Britain.* London: Palgrave Macmillan (https://10.1057/978-1-137-57788-7).

Pickard, Sarah. 2019b. Excessive force, coercive policing and criminalisation of dissent: Repressing young people's protest in twenty-first century Britain. *Revista Internacional de Sociología.* 77(4), e319.

Pickard, Sarah. 2020. The nature of environmental activism among young people in Britain in the twenty-first century. In: Prendiville, B. and Haigron, D. eds. *Political Ecology and Environmentalism in Britain.* Newcastle: Cambridge Scholars, 89–109.

Pickard, Sarah. 2021. 'You are stealing our future in front of our very eyes': The representation of climate change, emotions and the mobilization of young environmental activists in Britain. *E-Rea.* 18(2).

Pickard, Sarah and Bessant, Judith, eds. 2017. *Young People Re-Generating Politics in Times of Crises.* London: Palgrave Macmillan.

Pickard, Sarah and Bessant, Judith. 2018. France's #Nuit Debout social movement: Young people rising up and moral emotions. *Societies* (8)4 (https://doi.org/10.3390/soc8040100).

Pickard, Sarah, Bowman, Benjamin and Arya, Dena. 2020. 'We are radical in our kindness': The political socialisation, motivations, demands and protest actions of young environmental activists in Britain. Muxel, A., ed. Special Issue: Protest, extremism and radicalization. *Youth and Globalization.* 2(2), 250–279.

Pickard, Sarah, Nativel, Corinne and Portier, Fabienne. 2012. *Les politiques de jeunesse au Royaume-Unis et en France: Désaffection, répression et accompagnement à la citoyenneté.* Paris: Presses Sorbonne Nouvelle.

Prendergast, Kate, Hayward, Bronwyn, et al. 2021. Youth attitudes and participation in climate protest: An international cities comparison. *Frontiers in Political Science Special Issue: Youth Activism in Environmental Politics* (https://doi.org/10.3389/fpos.2021.696105)

Roberts, Dorothy. 2012. Race, gender, and the political conflation of biological and social issues. *Du Bois Review: Social Science Research on Race.* 9(1), 235–244.

Rootes, Christopher. 2000. Environmental protest in Britain 1988–1997. In: Seel, B., Paterson, M. and Doherty, B., eds. *Direct Action in British Environmentalism.* London and New York: Routledge, 25–61.

Rootes, Christopher. 2003. *Environmental Protest in Western Britain.* Oxford: Oxford University Press (OUP).

Seel, Benjamin, Paterson, Michael and Doherty, Brian., eds. 2000. *Direct Action in British Environmentalism.* London and New York: Routledge.

Sloam, James. 2020. Young Londoners, sustainability and everyday politics: The framing of environmental issues in a global city. *Sustainable Earth.* 3(14) (https://doi.org/10.1186/s42055-020-00036-z)

Sloam, James and Henn, Matt. 2018. *Youthquake: The Rise of Young Cosmopolitans in Britain.* London: Palgrave Macmillan.

Sloam, James, Pickard, Sarah and Henn, Matt, eds. 2021. Young people and environmental activism: The transformation of democratic politics and youth engagement. Special issue, *Journal of Youth Studies,* forthcoming.

Tarrow, Sydney. 1998. *Power in Movement: Social Movements and Contentious Politics.* Cambridge: Cambridge University Press.

Thunberg, Greta. 2019. Today Programme, Radio 4. *BBC,* 30 December.

Thunberg, Greta. 2020. *Our House Is Still on Fire and You're Fuelling the Flames,* Speech. World Economic Forum, Davos, Switzerland, 21 January.

Tilly, Charles. 1995. *Popular Contention in Great Britain 1758–1934.* Cambridge: Cambridge University Press.

Wahlström, Mattias, Kocyba, Piotr, De Vydt, Michiel and de Moor, Joost., eds. 2019. *Protest for a Future: Composition, Mobilization and Motives of the Participants in Fridays for Future Climate Protests on 15 March 2019 in 13 European Cities* (https://gup.ub.gu.se/publication/283193)

Walker, Catherine. 2020. Uneven solidarity: The school strikes for climate in global and intergenerational perspective. *Sustainable Earth*. 3(5) (https://doi.org/10.1186/s42055-020-00024-3)

Watts, Rob. 2021. Making sense of the student voice: Theorizing student protest in the neoliberal university. In: Côté, J. and Pickard, S., eds. *Routledge Handbook of the Sociology of Higher Education*. Second edition. London and New York: Routledge, 19–36.

Young-Bruel, Elisabeth. 2012. *Childism: Confronting Prejudice Against Children*. New Haven, CT: Yale University Press.

35

ENVIRONMENTAL MOVEMENTS AND DIGITAL MEDIA

Anastasia Kavada and Doug Specht

Introduction

The rise of mainstream environmental movements can be traced back to the 1950s and 60s when organizations began to alert the wider public to the dangers of pollution and environmental degradation (Maantay, 2002). These early movements, much like those that followed them, focused on effecting environmental justice by combining local, experiential, and other knowledges to bring about concrete policy actions or to influence environmental policy debates (Ottinger et al., 2017). To achieve their aims, environmental movements have long employed new communication technologies to raise awareness, mobilize participation, and organize their activities (Hansen 2010: 59). Yet in recent years, digital media have emerged as a pivotal tool, transforming the practices and potential of environmental movements.

Digital tools offer a way of connecting the dots between a wide range of environmentally damaging activities and allow environmental movements to engage in a wide range of communication activities to provoke reactions in relation to activism and environmental justice (Cable 2014). They also help environmental movements connect with numerous audiences and leverage the power of data and local knowledge to envisage different futures (Klenk 2018) and address complex problems (Lenette 2017).

This chapter examines the role of digital media in environmental activism by focusing on processes of organization and the rapid formation of collectives. It also explores social media and visual communication, including genres and formats that are native to the internet, such as memes and livestreaming, as well as the effects of spectacular images of protest. The chapter further reflects on the potential and limitations of digital mapping technologies for telling stories of environmental justice and for bringing local knowledges of environmental degradation to bear on campaigning about these issues. We illustrate this analysis with examples of contemporary environmental movements, including #FridaysForFuture, Extinction Rebellion, and the Dakota Access Pipeline protests.

Hashtags and organization

In recent years, an increasing number of social movements are emerging with the help of social media. From #OccupyWallStreet in 2011 to #BlackLivesMatter in 2013 to #metoo in 2017 to

DOI: 10.4324/9780367855680-41

#FridaysForFuture in 2018, many contemporary movements include a hashtag in their name, a feature that points to the key role of social media. Yet far from being simply Twitter or Facebook mobilizations, as some initial accounts of these mobilizations had proclaimed, these movements are employing a wide range of media platforms, including face-to-face communication, to organize their activities and mobilize people to participate.

Digital media facilitate the emergence of such movements in various ways. First, they are allowing the quick consolidation of public feeling around important issues, particularly if these are already on the media agenda. They thus enable the formation of "affective publics" (Papacharissi 2015) and "insurgent communities" (Castells 2012) and the creation of a sense of belonging. This helps accelerate the speed of mobilization waves that follow the equally fast rhythm of the news cycle.

Processes of mobilization and organization can now be undertaken more easily by loose and informal groups or even by individual activists, while already established organizations may either take a back seat in the organizing process or be absent from it altogether (Bennett & Segerberg 2013). For Bennett and Segerberg (2013), social media are facilitating a new type of self-organized "connective action" that revolves around the circulation of personalized frames on social media. In such mobilizations, social media platforms serve as organizing mechanisms of the crowd, eliminating the need for social movements to develop sustainable and hierarchical organizations. Thus, digital media are considered to facilitate networked forms of organization (Kavada 2014), in which entrepreneurial activists have greater freedom to take initiative and act outside the confines of traditional organizations.

Yet research in contemporary movements has also shown that, with time, such movements do develop common practices and an organizing structure, however loose and informal. What is more, social media are connected with processes of leadership and power asymmetries as they allow the administrators of such channels to play the role of "connective leaders" (Poell et al. 2016) or "choreographers of assembly" by mobilizing participation in street protests and "scripting" or choreographing the movement of participants in physical space (Gerbaudo 2012). At the same time, pre-existing networks of activists, which may be based on previous experiences of organizing and their shared affiliation to other groups and organizations, are crucial for the emergence of new waves of protest. More hybrid networks are also in evidence, in which different types of organizations and individuals temporarily come together around the coordination of events or the promotion of specific causes.

And while social media may be allowing the aggregation of individuals and the circulation of personalized frames of action, more collective processes of decision making and discussion, also taking place through face-to-face communication, help in the production of collective subjectivity (Juris 2012). However broad, inclusive, and flexible the definition of that group may be, a movement's social media channels also need to invent a collective voice, with activists developing guidelines about what the collective should sound like (Kavada 2015). In other words, digital media are related not only with dynamics of personalization and dispersion but also with processes of building the collective.

These organizational trends are also evident in contemporary environmental movements. #FridaysForFuture is a case in point. Emerging from the actions of a single protester, the then-16-year-old Greta Thunberg, #FridaysForFuture has become a defining youth movement against climate change. It began in August 2018 when Greta Thunberg decided to hold a protest in front of the Swedish parliament every Friday, urging politicians to take more decisive action around climate change. Clasping a now-iconic sign with the slogan "*Skolstrejk för klimatet*", meaning "School strike for climate", Greta Thunberg inspired a generation of students her age, helping place the issue of climate emergency in the spotlight. Soon the movement grew, starting to organize international climate strike events attended by millions of people. The first one took place on 15 March 2019 and attracted 1.4 million protesters across 128 countries (Carrington 2019). According to the movement's website, #FridaysForFuture is now present in 75,000 cities on all continents and includes more than 13 million people (Fridays For Future 2020a).

The movement revolves around the coordination of climate strikes without the presence of a single formal organization. Instead, its mobilization infrastructure comprises multiple social media accounts in different countries and languages and an initially rudimentary website that has recently received an overhaul. Survey research of 1,905 participants in the 15th March Climate Strike in 13 European cities has demonstrated the important role of social media in mobilization. The study found that "34.4% of school students and 31.6% of adults indicate having learnt about the protest through social media like Facebook, Twitter or Instagram" (Walstrom et al. 2019: 13). Attracting predominantly younger protesters, many of them of school age, #FridaysForFuture thus relies on communication media used by this generation of activists.

However, social media provide everyone with the capacity to create an account with the name #FridaysForFuture and assume to speak in the movement's collective voice. This leads social media audiences to disperse across different accounts, social media platforms, and languages. It also means that the message of the movement may become confused as a cacophony of voices speaking on behalf of #FridaysForFuture may cloud the movement's narrative. At the same time, the high number of social media administrators, each controlling a different account, may complicate processes of coordination and decision making.

What seems to bring this movement together is the use of the #FridaysForFuture hashtag, which also acts as the name of the movement. This helps coordinate the exchange of information on disparate social media accounts and place them together under the same umbrella. The movement also has a central website (fridaysforfuture.org), providing information and contact details about the movement's national chapters and their social media accounts (Fridays For Future 2020b). The main role of the central website is to provide a clear narrative about the movement and a first port of call for people looking for information while local activists have the freedom to set up their own groups and register them with the international website. In other words, the movement seems to operate as a decentralized online organization, with an international hub and autonomous local units.

However, web organizations of the loose and informal kind may find it difficult to engage with the authorities and undertake certain organizing tasks that require them to be a legal entity, such obtaining permits for demonstrations. The support of already-existing organizations may be crucial in this respect. #FridaysForFuture has been endorsed by various environmental NGOs such as Friends the Earth, Greenpeace, and 350.org, as well as trade unions and Amnesty International. The 350.org hosts the website globalclimatestrike.net to support the climate strike movement, while Greenpeace has organized "Street Classrooms" to help students prepare for the uncertain future of climate change (Greenpeace 2020).

This network of organizations and local chapters is also brought together by Greta Thunberg, who serves as the movement's figurehead, becoming a global icon of youth activism. Since 2018, she has made numerous high-profile speeches and media appearances and was *Time*'s Person of the Year in 2019. Thunberg operates as the movement's ambassador and "travelling evangelist" (Gerlach & Hine 1970). Her well-publicized travel itinerary in 2019 took her from addressing climate-strike events in Europe to the United Nations Climate Action meeting in New York. Thus, by gravitating around the figure of Thunberg, the movement's moral center and charismatic leader, #FridaysForFuture can bring together the narratives of its autonomous chapters and make its message more coherent. However, Thunberg's celebrity has also made her a target for the ire and ridicule of various politicians, including Donald Trump, and the subject of horrific online abuse. Yet attempts to delegitimize the movement by attacking its charismatic leader do not seem to have succeeded as Thunberg's popularity and authority remain undiminished.

Visual communication, memes, and livestreaming

In recent years, television and digital media have transformed the public sphere into the "public screen" (Delicath & Deluca 2003: 329), making images a crucial aspect of political communication. Yet visuals have also become central in environmental discourse (Doyle 2007) as photographs and videos can be more eye catching, engaging, and persuasive for audiences.

Social media have accentuated the centrality of visuals for environmental communication (Highfield & Leaver 2016). Images can now be quickly shared on platforms like Facebook and Twitter or on applications like Instagram that are designed specifically for visual communication. Research has shown that posts and tweets with spectacular images are circulated more widely and are more noticeable within the social media attention economy (Pang & Law 2017). Environmental movements can reach an international audience more easily and shift the scale of the protest from the local to the global as images can surpass linguistic and cultural barriers (Clancy & Clancy 2016).

The participatory affordances of digital media, which allow lay users to create and circulate their own images and videos, can further benefit environmental movements (Wang et al. 2018). Activists can now obtain images from a variety of sources that may offer a fresher and more authentic perspective on the issue. This can increase the audience's engagement with environmental issues (Corner et al. 2016: 5) as it allows environmental movements to go beyond common visual depictions of environmental problems, which often include majestic but abstract images of environmental catastrophe or specific icons, such as the use of polar bears to depict climate change (Doyle 2007).

Local witnessing of environmental destruction also adds a personal perspective that places everyday people, rather than politicians or environmental activists, at the center of the action. Visuals can depict how specific localities are affected, making the issue more tangible and accessible for audiences and increasing their emotional engagement. Furthermore, as research on the media coverage of COP21 has shown (Leon & Erviti 2016 in Wang et al. 2018: 3), these more authentic, informal, and grounded images can have a greater appeal for news outlets that are native to the internet, such as Vice and the Huffington Post.

Environmental movements increasingly employ genres of visual communication that are native to the digital environment, such as memes (Esteves & Meikle 2015). Broadly defined as "context-bound viral texts that proliferate on mutation and replication" (Denisova 2019: 10), memes can change meaning as they circulate in different contexts. Memes are primarily visual as they usually comprise images overlaid by text. They also tend to be based on humor and in-jokes and invite the participation of the audience to make their own meaning out of suggestive but incomplete slogans and messages (Denisova 2019; Esteves & Meikle 2015). Yet memes also "go viral based on their ability to articulate commonly shared beliefs and ideas" (Hinzo & Clark 2019: 796), rendering them powerful tools of environmental communication.

Research on the Dakota Access Pipeline protests offers a case in point. The construction of the pipeline, which transfers crude oil from North Dakota to Illinois, was opposed by the Sioux and Lakota tribes as the pipeline violated US treaties around the sacred lands of Native American tribes (Hinzo & Clark 2019). The protests received widespread media attention in April 2016, when the tribes founded the "Sacred Stone Camp" at Standing Rock, "a site of cultural preservation and spiritual resistance to the proposed construction of the Dakota Access Pipeline" (Presley & Crane 2018: 305). Soon the protest attracted diverse activists who arrived at the camp to help draw attention to the cause. Rather than calling themselves "protesters", activists used the term "water protectors" to signal the "prayerful and ceremonial, reflective, and sacred" (Presley & Crane 2018: 306) character of the protest that emerges out of feelings of love and respect for nature. #NoDAPL protestors thus tried to challenge mainstream depictions of protest in general and of Indigenous people in particular as angry and aggressive (Presley & Crane 2018).

Memes were part of this strategy. Activists employed memes to challenge the marginalization of the protest in the mainstream news media (Hinzo & Clark 2019), which followed a broader pattern of erasing Indigenous voices from media representations. At the same time, Standing Rock water protectors also drew on Indigenous epistemologies, such as the Ho-Chunk Tricksters Wak'djunk'aga and Wašjingéga, to infuse their memes with irony in line with a long Indigenous tradition of using humor as a form of resistance to colonialism (Hinzo Clark 2019: 793). The memes studied by Hinzo and Clark (2019) brought to the fore different narratives around Native American identity and the "sacrality of land and water" (p. 804) in juxtaposition with settler colonialist values.

The #NoDAPL protests also used livestreaming to great effect (Martini 2018). Livestreaming involves the broadcasting of live video through mobile phones and laptops. Viewers can watch and comment on the livestream both synchronously and asynchronously once the video is recorded and archived (Kavada & Treré 2019). Livestreaming is characterized by immediacy, rawness, liveness, and an embedded/embodied perspective (Kavada & Treré 2019), characteristics that render it emotionally engaging and believable for audiences (Martini 2018; Thorburn 2017). Live video is immediate as it is focused on the direct and simultaneous transmission of happenings on the ground. It also tends to be unedited and unstaged, which adds to its rawness and sense of immediacy (Andén-Papadopoulos 2013). Livestreaming further tends to be shot from the perspective and eye level of the livestreamer, who is embedded in the action on the ground (Gregory 2015).

Where livestreaming truly differs from other types of online video is in its liveness, a feature that, prior to the advances of mobile technologies, tended to be very costly as it required a significant technological capacity. Yet in recent years, livestreaming has gone mainstream. Live video was used by the social movements of the Arab Spring in 2011 and popularized with the "movements of the squares", such as Occupy and the Spanish Indignados, during the same year (Costanza-Chock 2012). Livestreamers initially relied on platforms and applications offered by start-up companies such as Ustream and Livestream, but in the ensuing years, major social media platforms such as Facebook and Instagram have started to provide this capacity to their users.

In the Dakota Access Pipeline protests, livestreaming was used to broadcast the action on the ground and to counter the "blackout" of the mainstream media. Standing Rock is a remote location that media crews could not access easily. There were also accusations that the police tried to silence protesters and radical media, since celebrities such as the actor Shailene Woodley and high-profile journalists like Amy Goodman were arrested (Levin 2016). Goodman was charged with rioting for filming the police using dogs and pepper spray against protesters and broadcasting the video on Facebook Live (Levin 2016). However, live video allowed protesters and journalists to bypass this police repression as livestreaming is difficult to censor. Indigenous journalists also established their own alternative media channels, on which livestreaming had a central place. For instance, the Digital Smoke Signals Facebook page, founded by Myron Dewey, became "one of the most widely followed information outlets of the NO

DAPL movement" (Martini 2018: 4037), with some of his videos attracting more than 2.5 million views (Martini 2018).

Apart from recording police violence, live communication also provided coverage of unexpected and surprising moments, allowing activists to engage audiences in actions unfolding on the ground. One such instance was when a herd of buffalo appeared at the protest site (Ecowatch 2016). Buffalo are sacred to Native Americans, who consider them a symbol of both sacrifice and sovereignty. As a valuable source of food and clothing, the preservation of buffalo herds and their freedom to roam are thought to strengthen the sovereignty of Native American tribes (Ecowatch 2016). Thus, the sighting of wild buffalo during the protest was a moment of highly symbolic value that was captured on live video in all its unexpectedness and emotional intensity.

However, livestreaming can also operate as a form of self-surveillance (Kavada & Treré 2019), providing the authorities with visual evidence of the transgressions not only of the police but also of protesters themselves. This has caused controversy and intense debates within social movements and has given rise to guidelines about livestreaming to safeguard the identity of protesters.

Furthermore, livestreaming cannot be easily used to portray environmental destruction. Its emphasis on liveness, on the spectacular here and now, means that it cannot depict longstanding and slow processes of environmental degradation. This compounds a broader problem of visuals when it comes to environmental communication: that by the time movements obtain visual evidence of environmental destruction, it is too late to take preventative action (Doyle 2007). Therefore, livestreaming is a form of visual communication that is more suited to placing people at the center of environmental action in the present moment rather than to portraying long-term environmental catastrophe.

As the preceding analysis shows, online communication feeds off the creation of spectacular images created offline, whether they are majestic photographs of environmental destruction or spectacular images of protest. This logic may be affecting the design and organization of street protest so that it conforms to the visual dictates of the media. Extinction Rebellion is exemplary in this respect as it has used visuals effectively in its communication strategy by putting together street action with high aesthetic value. According to its website, "Extinction Rebellion is an international movement that uses non-violent civil disobedience in an attempt to halt mass extinction and minimise the risk of social collapse" (Extinction Rebellion 2020). The movement appeared in 2018, with a "Rebellion Day" organized on 17 November 2018. This was followed by different protest events, including 10 days of rebellion in April 2019 and an International Rebellion, unfolding in 60 cities around the world (Extinction Rebellion 2019) in October 2019. These events have attracted extensive media attention, which has focused particularly on mass arrests for civil disobedience, strengthening Extinction Rebellion's message that in a climate emergency, people are willing to take urgent and disruptive action to address the problem.

However, during these events, Extinction Rebellion also drew on performance theater and artistic practices to organize spectacular stunts. The activities of the Red Brigade are exemplary in this respect. Created by the Bristol street theatre company Invisible Circus (Drewett 2019), the Red Brigade performances include a silent procession of protestors dressed in red robes with white-painted faces. According to its Facebook page, "The Red Brigade symbolises the common blood we share with all species, that unifies us and makes us one" (XR Invisible Theatre – Red Rebel Brigades 2020: n.p.). By generating striking images, the Red Brigade has ensured widespread attention on both social media and mainstream news outlets.

Extinction Rebellion is evidently not the first environmental group to engage in such tactics. Organizations such as Greenpeace and Earth First! are well known for their coordination of what Delicath and Deluca (2003) call "image events": "staged acts of protest designed for media dissemination" (p. 315). Such image events allow movements that are normally marginalized or excluded from the public sphere to gain a footing in the news agenda (Delicath & Deluca 2003). The act of protest itself operates as a strong visual message (Doerr et al. 2013) and as "critique performed through spectacle" (Delicath & Deluca 2003: 321).

Social media algorithms seem to be fueling this emphasis on the spectacular (Poell & van Dijck 2015). Posts with powerful images garner more "likes" and go viral more easily as they are favored by the algorithm. Yet this reliance on the spectacular may limit the effectiveness of environmental communication. Spectacular images and live videos of protest tend to focus on events, rather than on the structural conditions underlying the issues that movements are protesting about. They are thus reinforcing the dominant tendency for events-based reporting, which is also evident in the mainstream news media (Doyle 2007). Such "tactics do not enable the communication of long term and accumulative (non-visible) environmental problems" (Doyle 2007: 133). This adaptation to the requirements of both social media platforms and mainstream news media outlets thus constrains environmental movements from using the internet in innovative ways (Lester & Hutchins 2009) and from sustaining a narrative about enduring issues and effects.

However, for groups like Extinction Rebellion, putting forward spectacular "image events" is a core of their media strategy. According to Roger Hallam, one of the founders of Extinction Rebellion, "If thousands of people get arrested, it'll be a major political event, like the civil rights movement of the 1960s" (Fawbert 2019: para 5). In this respect, Extinction Rebellion aimed to highlight the urgency of climate change and people's commitment to addressing it, using spectacle to shatter political inertia around this issue. Their emphasis was less on raising awareness since scientific information about climate change has been widely shared for decades.

Therefore, visual communication and digital media are in a mutually reinforcing relationship. Digital media strengthen the capacity of environmental movements for visual communication, which occurs also through new formats and genres such as memes and livestreaming. At the same time, social media platforms increase the activists' reliance on visuals, as posts with images and videos attract more attention and circulate more widely.

Digital maps and participatory storytelling

Maps have a long history of use in environmental justice campaigns. Following their employment in development work as a way of bringing voices to the fore, maps lend themselves well to storytelling that embodies personal experiences of the environment and to the exploration of deep understandings of places and injustice (Maantay 2002; Caquard 2013; Rossetto 2015). Maps, and the cartographic practices through which they are created, have shifted from being merely a tool of representation with static features toward a philosophy of action that seeks to reveal spatial associations. This renders mapping an invaluable tool for environmental movements and wider political participation (Rossetto 2015; Yuan et al. 2015; Crampton 2009).

While notions of spatial storytelling and spatial narratives are not yet fully agreed-upon terms (Caquard 2013; Harris 2015), it is clear that digital mapping practices are able to express complex spatial information in a way that tells stories which are rapidly and intuitively interpreted in relation to environmental activism (Harris 2015). Furthermore, the ubiquity of maps, along with the pervasiveness of digital cartographic devices such as smartphones, makes them widely acknowledged and readable (Rossetto 2015). However, maps are not without their risks and disadvantages, and while they have become increasingly prevalent in the environmental justice community, maps remain selective in their arrangement of events and information (Maantay 2002; Harris 2015).

It is now easier than ever for any internet user to create their own maps or add their own narrative to maps through the proliferation of cheap or free online mapping tools (Caquard 2013). The development of web mapping and mobile mapping means that users are no longer restricted to static media. Instead, anyone with an internet connection can build stories on environmental issues on interactive, multimedia, and detailed base maps (Lu et al. 2017). This ease of map creation has come about not only because of the lower financial barriers to production but also because of the way maps are now seen as part of everyday practice (Dodge et al. 2011), facilitating a move toward fluid and liberating spaces of engagement that allow for collaborative constructions of meaning and memories around environmental concerns (Rossetto 2015; Bonacini et al. 2018).

These maps can be individual, collective, and deeply political (Caquard 2013). What they share is that when used for environmental campaigning, these maps draw extensively on the local knowledge of communities, storing and recalling information that helps build up images of the complexities of the environment (Harris 2015) and allows for a broadly inclusive sharing and integration of memory (Klaebe et al. 2007). Furthermore, citizen sensors – such as GPS in a smartphone – or more active engagements of measuring and providing voluntary geographic information (VGI) – means that there is a wealth of data being generated to help create deeper narratives through these mapping practices (Harris 2015).

It is important, however, not to disavow the power of maps. This power can be used to imply authenticity to the advantage of the map maker (Harris 2015), but it is also crucial to remember that maps have long been used to marginalize and exclude (Sletto 2012). The field of critical cartographies has exposed the hidden, and sometime hideous, narratives and agendas smuggled into maps and their metanarratives (Caquard 2013; Crampton 2009). These agendas are often transferred into digital mapping projects without the awareness of the maker or the community (Specht & Feigenbaum 2018). Mapmaking is still steeped in an extensive praxis of design aesthetics, science, and technology that ostensibly seeks to model only certain aspects of reality and knowledge (Harris 2015).

Despite these concerns, there are numerous positive examples of mapping environmental justice stories from around the world, operating at a range of scales and with a plethora of goals. Perhaps some of the earliest can be traced to the Detroit Geographic Expedition, a 1970s project that aimed to skill inner-city Black students to create their own maps of injustice. Its most provocative output was a map of "Where Commuters Run Over Black Children" (D'Ignazio 2015). Rudé's 1964 volume, *The Crowd in History: A Study of Popular Disturbances in France and England 1930–1848*, also brought to the fore the importance of spatially locating environmental and economic degradation and the protests that emerged around it (Rudé 1964).

The digital age has allowed many more to follow. Landsat imagery is now regularly used to monitor environmental impacts (Paull et al. 2006). *Observatorio de Conflictos Mineros de America Latina* (OCMAL) in Latin America maps injustices related to mining projects (Martinez-Alier et al. 2016). *An Architektur* in Germany produces maps that highlight the uneven distribution of abuses (Walters 2008). *Funambulist* has also long been documenting the interactions between space, bodies, and the environment through maps. The Humanitarian OpenStreetMap Team (HOTOSM), while still primarily a crisis-response organization, has also tried its hand at longer-term mapping of environmental justice. Many organizations have also made mapping a part of their practice, using various online tools. MapCollaging, for example, allows lay persons to build complex multimedia maps with ease (Lu et al. 2017). Manpo, originally designed for creating digital walking tours, has also been appropriated for the task. Paid-for products such as MapBox are also used to create deep maps of environmental issues.

Perhaps the best-known project is the EJolt Altas, which maps ecological distribution conflicts around the world, seeking not only to map injustices but also to highlight moments of resistance, aiming to foster global solidarity. The atlas draws sources from communities, "activist knowledge" (Escobar 2008), and academics and now comprises over 1,600 cases of environmental conflict, making it a rich source for the exploration of such issues (Martinez-Alier et al. 2016). This mapping activity draws events to the fore and allows for a quick reference point of environmental conflicts. The map can be used to see what is happening around the world, as well as who is involved. This provides a sense of solidarity but, more importantly, can allow activist groups to engage with each other across national and transnational boundaries, potentially creating a more united front in the fight for environmental justice.

Despite their lofty aims, these projects are not without their problems. Maps are fleeting and have little ontological security (Crampton 2009). Each forms nothing more than a representation to be interpreted by the readers' experiences and worldview (Harris 2016). The majority of these mapping activities rely on projections, symbols, and base maps that are determined by global entities such as Google, Esri, and Microsoft, all of which are steeped in politics and none of which has interest in supporting environmental justice (Lu et al. 2017). These products are the same as those used by mining and oil companies (Paull et al. 2006), and while there is something poetic about attempting to use their own tools against them, it is more common that environmental activist mapping projects become warped by the tools they are using, creating maps that erase rather than highlighting local knowledge through the use of hegemonic symbology and cartographic practice. Once a symbol is placed somewhere and another is left blank, then an inference is made that the blank space is not a site of concern (Charlesworth 2017). Furthermore, issues such as the modifiable area unit problem (MAUP), created through the aggregation of data often seen in choropleth maps, means the same data can produce diametrically opposed representations (Maantay 2002). Maps then can be a great aid in storytelling about environmental actions, but they must be used with the same caution as any image, data, or text, or even more, because of their embodied "authority".

It is then important to look at mapping for environmental justice through the lens that no map can ever be a neutral, objective embodiment of the real world. These maps are just as susceptible to subjective assumptions as the more overtly colonial maps of old (Walters 2008; Maantay 2002; Caquard 2013; Specht & Feigenbaum 2018). Questions should be raised especially around the use of tools such as Google or even OpenStreetMap, both of which embed their own politics into the base maps, and the mapping platforms used by environmental movements (Caquard 2013). We must remember to question who the maps and diagrams are intended for and what their overt and hidden narratives are (Walters 2008).

The map does though remain a powerful tool for storytelling and sharing of environmental knowledge (Harris 2015), and by mapping the environment and the knowledges of environmental (in)justice, the landscape itself becomes a library of information in the struggle for rights (Davis 2012). Rather than map environmental justice or projects around it, the map itself must become the site of protest and political commentary, not just a way of reporting on those events (Crampton 2009).

Coda: digital media and environmental movements in times of COVID-19

At the time of writing this chapter in the spring of 2020, the coronavirus pandemic is spreading around the world. As country after country is imposing lockdowns and social distancing rules, environmental movements are abandoning street protest in favor of digital tactics that are safer to practice in times of COVID-19.

In a tweet on 11 March 2020, Greta Thunberg urged #FridaysForFuture protesters to "unite behind experts and science" as they did for the climate crisis and "avoid big public gatherings". Instead, participants could join a #DigitalStrike every Friday by posting photographs of themselves holding signs on Twitter, Instagram, and other social media platforms.

Groups like Extinction Rebellion have also shifted their tactics online to cope with the pandemic. In a newsletter published in the end of May 2020, the group noted that while mass street action has been very successful, "Covid has brought that tactic to a temporary, yet possibly lengthy, close" (XR Newsletter 2020). Thus, XR chapters moved their strategy of civil disobedience and mass disruption to the online realm. For instance, XR Denmark "recently launched an online blockade of top CO_2 emitters by designing 'a web browser add-on . . . to overwhelm selected polluters with a barrage of web requests" (XR Newsletter 2020), an action that is the equivalent of an online "sit-in". In Australia, 100 XR activists "'swarmed' every social post made by Australia's four major banks, pointing out how they fund climate destruction" (Extinction Rebellion 2020), managing to create online disruption with limited means.

There were also cases in which activists engaged in highly symbolic street action, involving a low number of participants but generating powerful visuals. "Shoe protests" fall within this category. Activists from Extinction Rebellion placed empty shoes in London's Trafalgar Square, demanding that government commit to a green recovery when addressing the coronavirus crisis (XR Newsletter 2020). Activists in the Netherlands put shoes in front of the Dutch parliament to oppose the bailout of polluters such as KLM (XR Newsletter 2020) while similar actions were organized in other cities like Zurich (Shields 2020). The tactic of "shoe protests" was first used during the COP21 meeting in Paris in November 2015 where street action was banned as Paris was still in a state of emergency after the terrorist attacks a couple of weeks before the meeting.

As more restrictions are imposed on street protest due to the coronavirus crisis, the emphasis on online tactics is expected to continue in the foreseeable future. This will strengthen some of the trends and patterns identified in this chapter – the quick formation of "insurgent communities" (Castells 2012) through social media and the importance of online visual communication and spectacular action, as well as the crucial role of digital storytelling practices, including digital mapping, in environmental protest. Whether and to what extent this move to the digital will leave a permanent mark on the strategies and tactics of environmental movements remains to be seen. What seems certain is that the COVID-19 crisis is acting as a catalyst for the maturing of online tactics and practices and their widespread use by environmental movements.

Conclusion

Environmental movements have long had to negotiate a diverse range of other forces and actors. They are rarely just fighting to highlight environmental issues, but instead, as has been noted elsewhere (see Giugni & Grasso 2015), are working against the status quo that allows for the destruction of the planet. Capitalism, corporate greed, greenwashing in the form of corporate social responsibility, misinformation, and criminal domestic and international politics all fall within the sphere of environmental activism. To fight these, diverse groups of people and actors are called upon, from grassroots movements, Indigenous land defenders, national and multi-national NGOs, and even some corporations. This complex battlefield is highlighted in the myriad ways in which environmental movements engage with digital media. The broad array of actors and targets means that a wide range of tools is needed in order to disrupt the status quo with a view to creating environmental justice for all.

As this chapter has demonstrated, activists and environmental movements have utilized social media, digital maps, memes, and other kinds of visual communication and leveraged the affordances of these tools in the fight for the environment. While the examples provided offer a range of success stories, the continually warming planet that is leading us toward a tipping point of irreversible climate change might lead us to question if the fight is really being won. What is clear, though, is that these tools, for all their limitations, do have an ability to bring people together around a shared idea of environmental justice, to galvanize movements, and to provide capacity for change. Digital media cannot do this alone, but they remain an important part of the environmental activists' toolkit.

References

Andén-Papadopoulos, K. (2013). Media witnessing and the 'crowd-sourced video revolution'. *Visual Communication*. 12(3), 341–357. https://doi.org/10.1177/1470357213483055

Bennett, W. L. and Segerberg, A. (2013). *The Logic of Connective Action: Digital Media and the Personalization of Contentious Politics*. New York: Cambridge University Press.

Bonacini, E., Tanasi, D. and Trapani, P. (2018, October). *Participatory Storytelling, 3D Digital Imaging and Museum Studies: A Case Study from Sicily*. 2018 3rd Digital Heritage International Congress (Digital-HERITAGE) Held Jointly with 2018 24th International Conference on Virtual Systems & Multimedia (VSMM 2018), 1–4, IEEE.

Cable, J. (2014). More than an electronic soapbox: Activist web presence as a collective action frame, newspaper source and police surveillance tool during the London G20 protests in 2009. In: D. Trottier and C. Fuchs (eds). *Social Media, Politics and the State: Protests, Revolutions, Riots, Crime and Policing in the Age of Facebook, Twitter and YouTube*. New York and Abingdon: Routledge, 143–160.

Caquard, S. (2013). Cartography I: Mapping narrative cartography. *Progress in Human Geography*. 37(1), 135–144.

Carrington, D. (2019). School climate strikes: 1.4 million people took part, say campaigners. *The Guardian*, 19 March [Accessed 14 July 2020]. Available from: www.theguardian.com/environment/2019/mar/19/school-climate-strikes-more-than-1-million-took-part-say-campaigners-greta-thunberg

Castells, M. (2012). *Networks of Outrage and Hope: Social Movements in the Internet Age*. Cambridge and Malden, MA: Polity Press.

Charlesworth, A. (2017). *An Atlas of Rural Protest in Britain 1548–1900*. Abingdon and New York: Routledge.

Clancy, K. A. and Clancy, B. (2016). Growing monstrous organisms: The construction of anti-GMO visual rhetoric through digital media. *Critical Studies in Media Communication*. 33(3), 279–292.

Corner, A., Webster, R. and Teriete, C. (2016). *Climate Visuals: Seven Principles for Visual Climate Change Communication (Based on International Social Research)*. Oxford: Climate Outreach. Available from: https://climatevisuals.org/sites/default/files/2018-03/Climate-Visuals-Report-Seven-principles-for-visual-climate-change-communication.pdf

Costanza-Chock, S. (2012). Mic check! Media cultures and the occupy movement. *Social Movement Studies*. 11(3–4), 375–385.

Crampton, J. W. (2009). Cartography: Performative, participatory, political. *Progress in Human Geography*. 33(6), 840–848.

Davis, D. K. (2012). Reading landscapes and telling stories: Geography, the humanities and environmental history. In: S. Daniels, D. DeLyser, J. N. Entrikin, J. N. and D. Richardson (eds). *Envisioning Landscapes, Making Worlds: Geography and the Humanities*. London and New York: Routledge.

Delicath, J. W. and Deluca, K. M. (2003). Image events, the public sphere, and argumentative practice: The case of radical environmental groups. *Argumentation*. 17(3), 315–333.

Denisova, A. (2019). *Internet Memes and Society: Social, Cultural, and Political Contexts*. New York and London: Routledge.

D'Ignazio, C. (2015). What would feminist data visualization look like. *MIT Center for Civic Media*. 20.

Dodge, M., Kitchin, R. and Perkins, C. (Eds.). (2011). *Rethinking Maps: New Frontiers in Cartographic Theory*. New York and London: Routledge.

Doerr, N., Mattoni, A. and Teune, S. (2013). Toward a visual analysis of social movements, conflict, and political mobilization. In: N. Doerr, A. Mattoni and S. Teune (eds). *Advances in the Visual Analysis of Social Movements*. Bingley: Emerald Group, xi–xxvi.

Doyle, J. (2007). Picturing the clima(c)tic: Greenpeace and the representational politics of climate change communication. *Science as Culture*. 16(2), 129–150.

Drewett, Z. (2019). Who are the red brigade who silently appear at extinction rebellion protests?. *Metro*, 7 October [Accessed 14 July 2020]. Available from: https://metro.co.uk/2019/10/07/red-brigade-silently-appear-extinction-rebellion-protests-10875730/

Ecowatch. (2016). *Standing Rock: Thousands of Wild Buffalo Appear Out of Nowhere* [Accessed 14 July 2020]. Available from: www.youtube.com/watch?v=fetub0FvEwk

Escobar, A. (2008). *Territories of Difference: Place, Movements, Life, Redes*. Durham, NC, and London: Duke University Press.

Esteves, V. and Meikle, G. (2015). "Look @ This Fukken Doge": Internet Memes and Remix Cultures. In: Atton, C. (ed). *The Routledge Companion to Alternative and Community Media*. Abingdon and New York Routledge, 561–570.

Extinction Rebellion. (2019). *This Monday – The International Rebellion Continues in More Than 60 Cities Around the World* [Accessed 15 July 2020]. Available from: https://rebellion.earth/2019/10/04/this-monday-the-international-rebellion-continues-in-more-than-60-cities-around-the-world/

Extinction Rebellion. (2020). *About Us* [Accessed 15 July 2020]. Available from: https://rebellion.earth/the-truth/about-us/

Fawbert, D. (2019). My six months with extinction rebellion. *BBC*, 19 July [Accessed 14 July 2020]. Available from: www.bbc.co.uk/bbcthree/article/66227e29-405e-44c1-bd6c-5ac33308cca0

Fridays For Future. (2020a). *What We Do* [Accessed 13 July 2020]. Available from: https://fridaysforfuture.org/

Fridays For Future. (2020b). *Contact Us* [Accessed 13 July 2020]. Available from: https://fridaysforfuture.org/what-we-do/contact-us/

Gerbaudo, P. (2012). *Tweets and the Streets: Social Media and Contemporary Activism*. London: Pluto Press.

Gerlach, L. P. and Hine, V. H. (1970). *People, Power, Change: Movements of Social Transformation*. Indianapolis and New York: The Bobbs-Merrill Company.

Giugni, M. and Grasso, M. T. (2015). Environmental movements: Heterogeneity, transformation, and institutionalization. *Annual Review of Environment and Resources*. 40. doi:10.1146/annurev-environ-102014-021327

Greenpeace. (2020). *Be a Part of the Street Classrooms!* [Accessed 14 July 2020]. Available from: www.greenpeace.org/international/act/global-climate-school-strike/

Gregory, S. (2015). Ubiquitous witnesses: Who creates the evidence and the live (d) experience of human rights violations ? *Information, Communication & Society*. 18(11), 1378–1392.

Hansen, A. (2010). *Environment, Media and Communication*. London and New York: Routledge.

Harris, T. M. (2015). Deep geography – deep mapping: spatial storytelling and a sense of place. In: D. J. Bodenhamer, J. Corrigan and T. M. Harris (eds). *Deep Maps and Spatial Narratives*. Bloomington and Indianapolis: Indiana University Press, 28–53.

Harris, T. M. (2016). From PGIS to participatory deep mapping and spatial storytelling: An evolving trajectory in community knowledge representation in GIS. *The Cartographic Journal*. 53(4), 318–325.

Highfield, T. and Leaver, T. (2016). Instagrammatics and digital methods: Studying visual social media, from selfies and GIFs to memes and emoji. *Communication Research and Practice*. 2(1), 47–62.

Hinzo, A. M. and Clark, L. S. (2019). Digital survivance and Trickster humor: Exploring visual and digital Indigenous epistemologies in the #NoDAPL movement. *Information Communication and Society*. 22(6), 791–807.

Juris, J. S. (2012). Reflections on #Occupy everywhere: Social media, public space, and emerging logics of aggregation. *American Ethnologist*. 39(2), 259–279.

Kavada, A. (2014). Transnational civil society and social movements. In: K. G. Wilkins, T. Tufte and R. Obregon (eds). *Handbook of Development Communication & Social Change*. Chichester: Wiley-Blackwell, 357–375.

Kavada, A. (2015). Creating the collective: Social media, the occupy movement and its constitution as a collective actor. *Information, Communication & Society*. 18(8), 872–886.

Kavada, A. and Treré, E. (2019). Live democracy and its tensions: Making sense of livestreaming in the 15M and occupy. *Information, Communication & Society*. DOI:10.1080/1369118X.2019.1637448

Klaebe, H. G., Foth, M., Burgess, J. E. and Bilandzic, M. (2007). *Digital Storytelling and History Lines: Community Engagement in a Master-Planned Development*. Proceedings of the 13th international conference on virtual systems and multimedia: Exchange and experience in space and place, VSMM 2007. Australasian Cooperative Research Centre for Interaction Design Pty, Limited. https://dspace.flinders.edu.au/xmlui/handle/2328/14011

Klenk, N. (2018). Adaptation lived as a story: Why we should be careful about the stories we use to tell other stories. *Nature and Culture*. 13(3), 322–355.

Lenette, C. (2017). *Using Digital Storytelling in Participatory Research with Refugee Women*. Sage Research Methods Cases in Health. London: Sage Publications Ltd.

Leon, B., & Erviti, M. C. (2016). A climate summit in pictures. *Something old, something new: Digital media and the coverage of climate change*, 63–72.

Lester, L. and Hutchins, B. (2009). Power games: Environmental protest, news media and the internet. *Media, Culture & Society*. 31(4), 579–595.

Levin, S. (2016). Judge rejects riot charges for journalist Amy Goodman after oil pipeline protest. *The Guardian*, 17 October [Accessed 14 July 2020]. Available from: www.theguardian.com/us-news/2016/oct/17/amy-goodman-north-dakota-oil-access-pipeline-protest-arrest-riot

Lu, M., Si, R., Arikawa, M. and Kaji, H. (2017, November). *User-Generated Storytelling Based on Analog Maps with Local and Dynamic Georeferencing*. 2017 Pacific Neighborhood Consortium Annual Conference and Joint Meetings (PNC), 134–141, IEEE, Washington, DC.

Maantay, J. (2002). Mapping environmental injustices: Pitfalls and potential of geographic information systems in assessing environmental health and equity. *Environmental Health Perspectives*. 110(suppl 2), 161–171.

Martinez-Alier, J., Temper, L., Del Bene, D. and Scheidel, A. (2016). Is there a global environmental justice movement?. *The Journal of Peasant Studies*. 43(3), 731–755.

Martini, M. (2018). Online distant witnessing and live-streaming activism: Emerging differences in the activation of networked publics. *New Media & Society*. 20(11), 4035–4055.

Ottinger, G., Barandiarán, J. and Kimura, A. H. (2017). Environmental justice: Knowledge, technology, and expertise. In: U. Felt, R. Fouché, C. A. Miller and L. Smith-Doerr (eds). *Handbook of Science and Technology Studies*. Cambridge, MA and London: MIT Press, 1029–1058.

Pang, N. and Law, P. W. (2017). Retweeting #WorldEnvironmentDay: A study of content features and visual rhetoric in an environmental movement. *Computers in Human Behavior*. 69, 54–61.

Papacharissi, Z. (2015). *Affective Publics: Sentiment, Technology, and Politics*. Oxford and New York: Oxford University Press.

Paull, D., Banks, G., Ballard, C. and Gillieson, D. (2006). Monitoring the environmental impact of mining in remote locations through remotely sensed data. *Geocarto International*. 21(1), 33–42.

Poell, T. and van Dijck, J. (2015) Social Media and Activist Communication. In: C. Atton (ed). *The Routledge Companion to Alternative and Community Media*. Abingdon and New York: Routledge, 527–537.

Poell, T., Abdulla, R., Rieder, B. and Woltering, R. (2016) Protest leadership in the age of social media. *Information, Communication & Society*. 19(7), 994–1014.

Presley, R. and Crane, J. (2018). Sonic colonizations, sound coalitions: Analyzing the aural landscape of standing rock's No-DAPL movement. *Argumentation and Advocacy*. 54(4), 305–322.

Rossetto, T. (2015). The map, the other and the public visual image. *Social & Cultural Geography*. 16(4), 465–491.

Rudé, G. (1964). *The Crowd in History: A Study of Popular Disturbances in France and England, 1730–1848* (Vol. 3). New York: Wiley.

Shields, M. (2020). Shoes replace protesters as Swiss climate activists obey virus curbs. *Reuters*, 24 April [Accessed 14 July 2020]. Available from: https://uk.reuters.com/article/us-health-coronavirus-swiss-climatechang/shoes-replace-protesters-as-swiss-climate-activists-obey-virus-curbs-idUKKCN226206

Sletto, B. (2012). Indigenous rights, insurgent cartographies, and the promise of participatory mapping. *Portal*. 7, 12–15.

Specht, D. and Feigenbaum, A. (2018). From the cartographic gaze to contestatory cartographies. In: P. Bargués-Pedreny, D. Chandler and E. Simon (eds). *Mapping and Politics in the Digital Age*. New York and London: Routledge, 39–55.

Thorburn, E. D. (2017). Social reproduction in the live stream. *TripleC*. 15(2), 423–440.

Walstrom, M., Kocyba, P., De Vydt, M. and de Moor, J. (2019). *Protest for a Future: Composition, Mobilization and Motives of the Participants in Fridays For Future Climate Protests on 15 March, 2019 in 13 European Cities*. Available from: https://protestinstitut.eu/wp-content/uploads/2019/07/20190709_Protest-for-a-future_GCS-Descriptive-Report.pdf

Walters, W. (2008). Acts of demonstration: Mapping the territory of (non-) citizenship. In: E. Isin and G. Neilson (eds). *Acts of Citizenship*. London: Zed Books, 182–207.

Wang, S., Corner, A., Chapman, D. and Markowitz, E. (2018). Public engagement with climate imagery in a changing digital landscape. *Wiley Interdisciplinary Reviews: Climate Change*. 9(2), 1–18.

XR Invisible Theatre – Red Rebel Brigades. (2020). *About Us* [Accessed 15 July 2020]. Available from: www.facebook.com/groups/1518920178239149/about

XR Newsletter. (2020). *Global Newsletter #39*, 20 May [Accessed 14 July 2020]. Available from: https://rebellion.earth/2020/05/20/global-newsletter-39/

Yuan, M., Mcintosh, J. and Delozier, G. (2015). GIS as a narrative generation platform. In: D. J. Bodenhamer, J. Corrigan and T. M. Harris (eds). *Deep Maps and Spatial Narratives*. Bloomington and Indianapolis: Indiana University Press, 179–202.

36

GREEN DEMOCRACY

Political imaginaries of environmental movements

Amanda Machin

Read Earth First!, get ideas, be creative, and do something!

(EF! 1981: 4)

[O]ne could even argue that the future of democratic governance itself will depend upon our ability to meet the ecological challenge by imagining ways to construct and practice new forms of democracy.

(Fischer 2017: 3)

The word "democracy" is at once a solution and a problem.

(Rosanvallon 2019: 27)

Introduction

A recurring feature within green movements is the emphasis on democracy (Doherty 2002: 3). But there is no necessary connection here. As scholars have long noticed, democratic means may not produce environmental ends (Goodin 1992; Machin 2018; Saward 1996; Wong 2016). If anything, conventional liberal democratic mechanisms seem not simply unresponsive to environmental concerns (Hay 1996) but actually more adept at "sustaining the unsustainable" (Blühdorn 2011) and might actually be part of the problem (Fischer 2017: 3). Still, the form of democracy that is envisaged within green movements is hardly a conventional form of democracy. The political expectations of these movements are not limited to voting for representatives every four years but more commonly involve a potentially more radical form of democracy, one that aligns with the demand for a decentered and egalitarian society that is in harmony with nature (Giugni and Grasso 2015: 340) and involves grassroots participation (Eckersley 2004: 11; Doherty 2002: 67).

What, then, do greens mean when they speak about democracy? Is there a definition or set of principles on which greens agree? How do they delineate what is and what is not democratic? I argue here that although there is no precise formula for "green democracy", there are nevertheless some general normative understandings that enable and shape discussions of democracy between greens, without any explicit definitive consensus. What constitutes a legitimate

DOI: 10.4324/9780367855680-42

political practice is therefore not something that certain necessary features can be ticked off against, but is rather something that fits within widely shared images and ideals of democracy.

This is why, borrowing particularly from Charles Taylor (2002, 2004) and Benedict Anderson (1991), I use the term "imaginary" to consider the discussions of democracy in green movements. What I refer to here as "green democracy" can usefully be understood as a "political imaginary" that resonates within and across green movements, although it is not restricted to them. The aim of this chapter, therefore, is to tentatively delineate a "green democratic imaginary" by referring to various green movements (in particular Earth First!, Extinction Rebellion, and Fridays for Future). These "green movements" all fit within the broader category of "environmental" movements, which encompasses heterogeneous networks of organizations and individuals whose actions vary in form and intensity (Giugni and Grasso 2015; Rootes 2004: 610). In contrast to more reformist environmentalists, "green movements" can be understood as those characterized by the demand for radical social transformation (Doherty 2002). These movements are interesting for democratic theorists because, by mobilizing large numbers of human bodies into the political realm, they are already providing a pertinent reminder of alternatives to the emaciated visions of democracy that arguably dominate today.

I start by explaining further the concept of "green imaginaries" and providing some background to the green movements, before exploring the "green democratic imaginary" in more detail by considering its six dimensions: decentralization, inclusion, participation, protest, passion and rupture. I point out that although these dimensions are clearly evident in green movements, they do not feature uniformly across them, nor do they always fit comfortably together. I compare the green democratic imaginary to the prevailing liberal democratic imaginary, and I conclude by considering its potential to provoke a political and socio-economic transformation. The aim of this contribution is to provide a theoretical framework of "green democracy" that can be tested and refined through further research and to make it easier to both get a grasp on the democratic designs of environmental movements and to seize their potential.

Green imaginaries

What is a green imaginary? Charles Taylor describes an imaginary as "that largely unstructured and inarticulate understanding within which particular features of our world become evident" (2002: 107). He explains that "if the understanding makes the practice possible, it is also true that the practice largely carries the understanding" (2002: 107). For Taylor, an imaginary is the general background that makes sense of the world and our place in it; it is what tells us how we live together and how we *ought* to live together; it is what enables us to act and interact (2002: 91). When these forms of imaginary become dominant, or hegemonic, they affect the way we see the world, ourselves, and each other (Taylor 2004: 2). Benedict Anderson attends to the way that nations emerged as "imagined communities" to powerfully alter modern consciousness (1991), and Taylor explains that it is our sense of belonging to such "imagined communities" that underpins our belief in the legitimacy of democratic decision making (2004: 190). It is important to realize that imaginaries cannot be easily imposed or manipulated by those in power; they rather are "co-constitutive" of society and therefore emerge, transform, and splinter beyond conscious control (Komárek 2015: 786).

Following these theories, scholars have recently attended more closely to political imaginaries to consider how the political realm is formed and transformed (Brown 2019; Browne and Diehl 2019: 394). Likewise, I use the term "imaginary" here to refer to the taken-for-granted background to our political interaction, which makes our political practices possible and is reproduced by them. Taylor explains that democracy can only function because of a shared imaginary that incorporates our expectations of one another and helps us identify what is *not* democratic; what constitutes an illegitimate "misstep" or a "foul" (2002: 106): "[T]his confidence that we and other human beings can sustain a democratic order together, that it is within our range of possibilities, is based on images of moral order through which we understand human life and history" (2002: 110). At the same time as facilitating democratic interaction, political imaginaries configure the political realm to support or declaim hierarchy (Brown 2019: 399) and to construct communities through including some and excluding "others" (McAfee 2017: 917). Working at an unconscious level, "political imaginaries delineate who the key actors, groups and deliberators are; the norms according to which agents interact; the grievances they have; and the kinds of power they employ" (McAfee 2017: 919). I suggest that distinct to the conventional understandings of liberal democracy is a different democratic imaginary that reimagines the political community, shapes environmental politics, and is performed within environmental movements. Social movements in general have often advocated and practiced alternative conceptions of democracy (della Porta 2013: 1).

Imaginaries are important in environmental politics because they produce a common orientation for complex issues such as climate change and anchor expectations about collective social life in a changing world (Whiteley et al. 2016). For Timothy W. Luke, the "climate change imaginary" draws together "complex clusters of signs, symbols, and stories" (2015: 281), whereas for Levy and Spicer there is not one climate change imaginary but several evolving and competing imaginaries that each offer "a shared sense of meaning, coherence and orientation" (Levy and Spicer 2013: 660) and connect with popular interests and identities (675). Different climate imaginaries contain distinct visions of nature, of the future, and of the required degree of socio-economic change (Levy and Spicer 2013: 662). I argue that imaginaries of democracy also offer specific images of what constitutes political participation and who is allowed to participate.

In this chapter, I map out what I refer to as the "green democratic imaginary" by exploring the characteristics and contradictions of its six dimensions. To do this, I draw on various types of literature: theoretical accounts presented under various labels such as "environmental democracy" and "ecological democracy" and academic research on environmental movements, as well as material written and disseminated by the green movements themselves.

Green movements

Which green movements shape, and are shaped by, the green democratic imaginary? Although I draw on various examples, I focus particularly on three movements: Earth First!, Fridays for Future, and Extinction Rebellion. All three fit within what Brian Doherty calls "the green movement", which he defines as comprising "western environmentalists who believe that radical political and social changes are necessary to deal with the ecological crisis" (2002: 1). Although Doherty refers to the green movement (singular), I refer to them as separate green movements (plural) here. This is because they are distinct in many ways, and all exemplify the dimensions of the green democratic imaginary in different ways and to varying degrees.

Earth First! (EF!), a green movement spanning at least three decades, was founded in the United States in 1980 with the memorable slogan "No compromise in defense of mother earth!" Labelled "eco-terrorists" who employed tactics such as sabotage and "monkeywrenching", Earth First!ers combined their eco-centrism with the belief that democracy had been weakened and corrupted by corporate power and wealth.[1] The *EF! Journal* is a rich source for discourse analysis on radical green environmentalism.[2]

In contrast, Extinction Rebellion (XR) was launched only a few years ago as a "grassroots activist climate movement" in October 2018, although it has quickly drawn significant national and international attention (Slaven and Heydon 2020). It makes three demands of government: 1) to tell the truth, 2) to act now to reduce carbon emissions, and 3) to create a citizens assembly. Formed in the UK, it currently has a presence in 45 countries, with about 650 groups globally (Gunningham 2019: 5).

Fridays for Future (FFF) is described on its website as a "global movement" that is part of "a hopeful new wave of change".[3] Beginning as a singular "school strike" undertaken by the movement's icon, Greta Thunberg, it has mobilized millions of school children to "strike for the climate" on Fridays. Commentators have suggested that it has promoted climate change onto the political agenda (Marquardt 2020: 14). According to a report on the FFF protests on 15 March 2019, the movement is "unique in its tactics, global scope and appeal to teenage school students" (Wahlström et al. 2019: 5), and "it is creating a new cohort of citizens who will be active participants in democracy" (Wahlström et al. 2019: 44).

There is a multiplicity of perspectives and beliefs held by the individuals who are part of these movements, which may not be fully represented by their media communication (Saunders 2012: 830). They each contain "ideological divides" and "internal tensions, conflicts and ambiguities" (Marquardt 2020: 2). I do not claim that there is homogeneity or consensus between or within these movements, but I do suggest that they are connected by various themes and that distinctive "imaginaries" subsist across them, including a "green democratic imaginary". This imaginary, I propose, appears in environmental politics outside and beyond these movements, which only reinforces the value in studying it. Next, I tease out six interconnected dimensions.

1 Decentralization

The first dimension of the green democratic imaginary that I delineate here is the aspect of decentralization. Decentralization and the "return to the local" (Fischer 2017: 13) are familiar features in environmentalism in general, echoed, for example, in the call to take the control of technology away from centralized government and put it instead in the hands of the community (Carter 2001: 49) and the formular "think globally, act locally" (Giugni and Grasso 2015: 350). Environmentalists – both scholars and activists – call for localization as an idealized "strategy for sustainability" that is sometimes depoliticized (Kenis and Mathijs 2014: 174). As Alan Carter puts it: "[M]any environmentalists argue on straightforward environmental grounds that moving from large-scale, urban communities to small-scale decentralised ones is essential if we are to reduce our environmental impact" (Carter 1999: 239). This is paralleled by an emphasis on political decentralization, too, in which negotiations and decision making also take place at a local, grassroots level (Carter 1999: 241).

Democratic decentralization is explicitly advocated by Frank Fischer, who recommends that democratic values might be best preserved and promoted through a re-orientation away from "larger political-institutional structures" and toward "specific local environmental projects" (2017: 90), such as eco-villages, transition towns and eco-neighborhood movements: "face-to-face relations have long been recognized as the foundation of authentic democratic self-governance" (Fischer 2017: 14) and "decentralized grassroots democracy has indeed long been considered a requirement for achieving sustainability" (Fischer 2017: 16).

This political "return to the local" is definitely evident in green movements, which emphasize that "decisions should be taken at the lowest level possible" (Doherty 2002: 72). The EF! proclaims itself as essentially local: "Local groups are the backbone of the Earth First! movement" (EF! 1981). The XR movement has a preference for "devolved decision-making involving groups connected in a complex web" (Gunningham 2019: 6), and its website describes it as "a decentralised, international and politically non-partisan movement" that is both "global" and "grassroots".[4]

And yet, significantly, this decentralization tendency is more ambiguous in recent climate movements; XR and FFF both noticeably urge state governments to take action and therefore, in a way, reinforce rather than challenge the authority of the center. While FFF urges action from the grassroots, their aim is "to put moral pressure on policymakers, to make them listen to the scientists, and then to take forceful action to limit global warming".[5] Researchers highlight the contradiction that FFF protestors "believe that government should take responsibility for combatting climate change, yet there is little trust in their respective government's approach to the problem" (Wahlström et al. 2019: 17).

Localized or decentralized decision making is a common taken-for-granted feature of democracy as imagined by the green movement, although it is in tension with the counter-orientation toward the centralized authority. It is important to notice, however, that localized or decentralized decision making is not necessarily more democratic, but that it is simply a significant feature of the green democratic imaginary.

2 Inclusion

While the first dimension of decentralization recommends the reduction of the scale of politics toward the local, the second dimension of the green democratic imaginary works toward the expansion of opportunities to participate in democratic discussion and decision making (Müller and Walk 2014). Here, the aim is to include the conventionally excluded, such as non-human nature and future generations as part of the demos (Lepori 2019: 78).

Robyn Eckersley, for example, recommends an "ecological extension of the familiar idea of a democracy of the affected" in which "the opportunity to participate or *otherwise be represented in* the making of risk-generating decisions should literally be extended to *all* those potentially affected, regardless of social class, geographic location, nationality, generation, or species" (2004: 112; emphasis in original). Similarly, Terence Ball, promotes a "greatly expanded democracy", or what he calls "biocracy" (2006: 139). In this "democracy of the affected", the boundaries of the community are widened to include animals, ecosystems, and future generations. It is not that these new members are actually given voting rights, but rather that their interests are represented, perhaps by designated positions for spokespeople in legislative bodies (2006: 144). The idea of the representation of non-human nature and future generations raises difficult questions: most obviously, "Who has the authority to speak on nature's behalf? And does the representation perspective replicate the human/nature dualism that ecologists are trying to overcome?" (Lepori 2019: 79).

Certainly, the emphasis on inclusion is also clearly found within green movements. XR proclaims "We welcome everyone and every part of everyone".[6] Perhaps most significantly, FFF demands the expansion of the demos to include children and future generations. Their website states that their movement "knows no borders", and "Everyone is welcome. Everyone is needed. No one is too small to make a difference".[7] (As I explain more later, by challenging the conventional political boundaries of the demos in this way, FFF disrupts the political realm.)

More ambiguous, however, is the rhetoric of EF!, whose "Introductory Guide" states, "[W]e never envisaged Earth First! as being a mass movement. . . . Either decide you can handle the militancy or find your environmental group elsewhere" (EF! 1981). And yet the movement illustrates its inclusiveness in a different way: by connecting up the human to the non-human; contemporary "fragmented" lives are lamented, and individuals are embedded into ecology:

> all forms of life are vitally connected. Removing even a single strand from the web of life produces a widening ripple of catastrophe. On a more spiritual level, Earth First!ers understand that we can never be the healthy humans that we were meant to be in a world without wilderness, clean air and the howling of wolves under the moon.[8]

The demos that appears in the green democratic imaginary, then, is not populated by atomistic individuals or by delegates who rationally communicate the interests of their constituents, but rather by embodied human creatures who care about the community and environment they live within. "Nature" is brought into green democracy not only through the extension of rights of representation but through the construction of participants themselves as individuals who are situated within their particular socio-ecological conditions.

3 Participation

In line with the decentralized and inclusive dimensions of the green democratic imaginary that together expand the possibilities of political interaction at the local level, environmentalism has traditionally been associated with an emphasis on direct participation (Carter 2001; Wall 2010), either alongside or in lieu of the delegation of decision making to representatives (della Porta 2013). As Doherty describes, greens are commonly in favor of "extending participation of democracy" (2002: 3). But participation beyond elections can take different forms, such as petitions, referendums, and citizens' initiatives (Hammond and Smith 2017). For example, FFF has set up a European Citizens Initiative that, if it receives one million signatures, will call on the European Commission to "adjust its goals under the Paris Agreement to an 80% reduction of greenhouse gas emissions by 2030".[9]

Many environmentalists advocate specifically deliberative participation (della Porta 2009). A dominant ideal in democratic theory, deliberation is seen as particularly suited for allowing citizens to exchange perspectives and knowledge, to learn about complex topics, and to become more socially and ecologically aware (Smith 2003; Smith and Machin 2014). Theorists and activists therefore advocate the institutionalization of forums that offer citizens the chance to reflect on environmental issues such as climate change and that will generate more environmentally sensitive conclusions (Smith 2009).

One of the three demands of XR, for example, is that "government must create and be led by the decisions of a Citizens Assembly".[10] Deliberation is indeed seen as a providing a route for debate and involvement in sustainability concerns (Peters 2019: 133).

Some are concerned, however, that forums such as citizenship assemblies do not encourage opposition to the prevailing social order, but will, on the contrary, shore it up (Böker 2017). The emphasis on deliberation has also been criticized for impeding the emergence of political alternatives (Machin 2013: 67–87; Machin 2020). As with decentralization, therefore, it should be mentioned that deliberation is not inherently democratic, but that it nevertheless increasingly features within the imaginary of green democracy.

4 Protest

A different form of participation that particularly characterizes the green democratic imaginary is one of embodied protest and direct action that has, to a certain extent, been normalized in recent years (Giugni and Grasso 2019: 3). Alongside their promotion of citizens assemblies, XR also explicitly advocates non-violent direct action and civil disobedience.[11] The aim of XR has been to carry out civil disobedience to sustain disruption "for days on end" in full public view (Gunningham 2019: 5).

Civil disobedience, direct action, and embodied protest featured in the anti-nuclear and anti-roads movements of earlier decades (see Machin 2021, chapter 5; Milder 2015) and continue to be practiced today. The numerous actions of civil disobedience by EF! span three decades (Taylor 2018). EF! explains its tactic of "monkeywrenching" as "a step beyond civil disobedience. . . . The final step in the defense of the wild, the deliberate action taken by the Earth defender when all other measures have failed" (1981). The *Earth First! Journal* unambiguously states: "When the law won't fix the problem, we put our bodies on the line to stop the destruction".[12]

In more recent years, there have been countless examples of embodied protest, particularly in relation to climate change (Garrelts and Dietz 2014). The campaign "Sing for the Climate" in 2012, for example, involved around 400,000 people raising their voices to "Let world leaders know, hear and feel that citizens want serious measures"[13] (Pepermans and Maeseele 2014: 224). Civil disobedience has taken the form of occupations of runways (Plane Stupid) and coalmines (Ende Gelände) and the sabotage of pipelines (Standing Rock). FFF explicitly recommends "non-violent civil disobedience".[14] Climate Camp also aimed to facilitate "direct action against targets deemed responsible for contributing to climate change" (Saunders 2012: 829) and involves "audacious, dramatic, nonviolent direct action", which is seen as "taking democracy into one's own hands" (Bergman 2014: 342; McGregor 2015).

In short, political participation, for many environmental movements, involves embodied occupation, striking, and marching. One important dimension of the green democratic imaginary, therefore, is protest. And yet, as we saw earlier, inclusion of the affected seems to demand representation of certain groups that cannot speak for themselves, as well as careful and respectful deliberation. It is worth considering whether there is an inevitable contradiction between these different dimensions or if indirect representation, circumscribed deliberation, and direct protest work to complement each other in the green democratic imaginary.

5 Passion

To notice that protest constitutes an important part of the green democratic imaginary, is to notice that politics in this imaginary is not always rational, calm, and deliberate but is often extremely emotional and passionate. Indeed, imaginaries are not rationally calculated but persist by engaging the imagination through aesthetic practices and emotional appeals. The green democratic imaginary not only engages at an emotional level but also incorporates affects and passions into political participation.

The politics of green movements is highly affective. Participation is motivated not solely by economic self-interest but by political affects, and the rhetoric used does not consist of strategic bargaining so much as emotional appeals. As XR warns: "[I]f we don't succeed in uniting to protect our planet, everyone will be impacted – you, your family, everyone and everything you hold dear".[15] The value and role of passion are explicitly realized by green movements. "It's time to be passionate", states EF! (Foreman et al. 1980). "We are emotional, passionate and angry. And we have a sense of humor" (EF! 1981).

The FFF protestors declare both "instrumental" and "expressive" motivations (Wahlström et al. 2019: 15). And the climate strikes they undertake are indeed highly passionate. Speakers rage and weep into their microphones and make emotional appeals.[16] Something that seems to be crucial in the FFF movement, actually, is the emotional interplay between the lone(ly) individual and the group. The narrative of FFF inevitably begins with the singular figure of Greta Thunberg sitting, alone yet determined, outside the Swedish parliament. This trope is picked up by other under-eighteen-year-old activists, who promote their loneliness and their vulnerability. And yet this solitude is juxtaposed with the growing numbers and increasing strength of the movement: "Every day there are more of us and together we are strong".[17] As this implies, passions circulate between bodies in such protests, creating a sense of identity and belonging. For Sara Ahmed, emotions perform a crucial role in the formation of collectivities. She argues that emotions should not be regarded as being contained within individual subjects but rather as arising through the bodily interaction that takes place between them. Emotions – which, she notes, both move us and attach us – (re)shape the space between bodies: "emotional responses to others involve the alignment of subjects with and against other others"(Ahmed 2004: 32). Collective bodies, Ahmed notes, are "surfaced" through the emotional encounter with others; the "skin" of a collective body is formed through the touch of the other (Ahmed 2004: 27). Passions, then, are part of the green democratic imaginary, facilitating an emotional connection with others and potentially reinforcing the strong collective identifications that appear in green movements.

6 *Rupture*

Finally, a key dimension of the green democratic imaginary is the emphasis on rupture with the existing socio-economic and political order. Through the civil disobedience and direct action described briefly in this chapter, green movements aim to disrupt unsustainable institutions and lifestyles. XR notoriously caused much disruption in London by supergluing themselves to trains, blocking Oxford Circus, and planting trees in Parliament Square (Gunningham 2019). This constitutes an attempt at socio-economic disruption.

However, green movements potentially disrupt political conventions, too, and in this way, create political rupture. What is so striking about the FFF climate strikes in particular is that (young) activists and protestors who are so highly politicized, so active and passionate, cannot vote. This means that by simply speaking in the public realm, they are disordering the established order, which demarcates who can speak and who cannot, who is counted and who is not. This is what constitutes a radical democratic moment in Jacques Rancière's sense: "Spectacular or otherwise, political activity is always a mode of expression that undoes the perceptible divisions of the police order" (1999: 30). Whereas the "police" order bodies into their assigned places, for Rancière, politics demonstrate the contingency of that order in an attempt to achieve equality and freedom: "[P]olitical activity is whatever shifts a body from the place assigned to it. . . . It makes visible what had no business being seen" (1999: 30). And it is this disruption of the prevailing order – by the demands that are made by those who count themselves as part of the demos – that constitutes democracy (1999: 99).

The question that arises here is whether the rupture that is part of the green democratic imaginary is able to provoke substantive change. Would it encourage political debate and the emergence of real alternatives, (re)politicize environmental governance, and disorder the unsustainable status quo? To where would this rupture lead?

(Re)imagining democracy

To summarize, the green democratic imaginary as I have mapped it here involves decentralized decision making, taken by an inclusive demos, who passionately participates in politics through direct action in order to disrupt unsustainable conventions. This is not a formula but an imagined understanding of democracy that persists, I contend, across green movements at least the three I have focused on here. And it does not dictate the specificity of political interaction but rather orientates it. This green democratic imaginary comprises various interconnecting and contradicting dimensions. But how distinctive is this imaginary, and how does it contrast and conflict with other democratic imaginaries?

All democratic imaginaries circle around the values of equality and freedom, but they construct these values in different ways. Arguably, the dominant imaginary of democracy today is the liberal democratic one: modern democracy developed in a particular liberal form (Eckersley 2004: 106). The liberal democratic imaginary is characterized by equal freedom for citizens, the protection of minorities, and equal rights. The state plays a crucial role here, and democratic participation mainly consists of voting.

The green democratic imaginary differs from this liberal democratic one in several ways, but particularly in the dimension of *rupture*. It apparently involves a struggle over taken-for-granted boundaries, identities, and practices. Take the example of the climate strikes of FFF, in which children without a vote nevertheless make political demands and shape political debates (Marquardt 2020: 3). Green democracy therefore potentially involves a transformation of the demos, a reordering of public spheres, and a reinvention of political parties and practices. But if this rupture is not a matter of simple revision, nor is it outright revolution. As Eckersley argues, the central ideas of the imaginary of liberal democracy do not necessarily have to be abandoned in order to permit the rethinking of politics and the reimagining of institutions along more ecological lines (2004).

This leaves us with many questions about the potential of the green democratic imaginary: is it able to facilitate the expression of radical and valid alternatives to the prevailing socio-economic order and enable distinct conceptions of the meaning of "sustainability"? Could it offer a point of resistance to the prevailing tendency to preclude the political negotiation of climate change and instead to solve it through the "green economy" (Kenis and Lievens 2015)? Can it overcome its various contradictions and tensions in order to prevent the evacuation of dissent and critique from environmental politics and (re)install "a genuine political space of disagreement" (Swynegedouw 2010: 227–228)? Might impassioned activists and environmentally minded citizens cooperate through renewed democratic practices to provoke social transformation? Finally, what might promote the consolidation of a new democratic imaginary?

Some suggest that the dominant neoliberal order is fracturing and urge the emergence of new political imaginaries, in which citizens around the world imagine themselves as empowered communities (McAfee 2017). But the question of how this shift might occur and what might make this shift more likely is a difficult one to answer. Scholars emphasize that massive social and technological transformations occur alongside changes in social and political imaginaries. For Benedict Anderson, the emergence of the technology of the printing press and the consolidation of print languages underpinned the emergence of "imagined communities" (Anderson 1991). We might ask, therefore, whether a changing climate and the concomitant ecological, agricultural, economic, social, and demographic problems it creates can provoke a shift in our social imaginaries. If the "climate crisis" itself represents a disruption of the established social order (Methmann 2010), could it usher in a new democratic imaginary?

Conclusion

Although many theorists agree that democracy is an aspect of environmental movements, it is hard to get a grip on what is meant when democracy is spoken about by these movements. In this chapter, I have used the concept of an "imaginary" to consider "green democracy", which is, I suggest, envisaged and performed within green movements.

The green democratic imaginary I have outlined calls for more decentralization and inclusion, deepened participation in the form of deliberation and protest, passionate engagement, and profound rupture. Its different dimensions do not fit together neatly, they sometimes complement each other and at others compete. This is because the imaginary is not a formula or a set of rules; rather, it provides a background assumption and normative orientation to the actors, practices, and discourses of green movements.

Different green movements carry certain features of the green democratic imaginary more than others. The persistence and resilience of certain movements and the way they morph over time and space will alter the imaginary itself, to affect our expectations of democratic politics and ourselves as political actors.

It is difficult to measure the power and persistence of the green democratic imaginary and its ability to guide ongoing structural change. The rise and demise of our social imaginaries cannot be predicted, and democratic moments often come when they are least expected. But the very existence of alternative imaginaries that offer to reconfigure and revive democratic life is perhaps what matters most in driving the social and political transformation sought by environmental movements.

Notes

1 For more on EF!, see Taylor (2018).
2 The *EF! Journal* (from 1980–2012) is available at www.environmentandsociety.org/mml/collection/11571.
3 See the FFF website, available at https://fridaysforfuture.org/what-we-do/who-we-are/.
4 See the XR website, available at https://rebellion.earth/join-us/.
5 See the FFF website, available at https://fridaysforfuture.org/what-we-do/who-we-are/.
6 See the XR website, available at https://rebellion.global/about-us/.
7 See the FFF website, available at https://fridaysforfuture.org/what-we-do/who-we-are/.
8 See the *EF! Journal*, available at https://earthfirstjournal.org/about/.
9 See FFF "Actions on Climate Emergency" webpage, available at https://eci.fridaysforfuture.org/en/.
10 https://rebellion.global/about-us/.
11 https://rebellion.global/about-us/.
12 https://earthfirstjournal.org/about/.
13 See the "About" page of the "Sing for the Climate" campaign website, available at https://singfortheclimate.com/about/.
14 https://fridaysforfuture.org/take-action/how-to-strike/.
15 https://rebellion.global/why-rebel/.
16 see https://fridaysforfuture.org/what-we-do/activist-speeches/.
17 https://fridaysforfuture.org/what-we-do/who-we-are/.

References

Ahmed, Sara. 2004. "Collective Feeling or, the Impression Left by Others" *Theory, Culture and Society*. 21 (2): 25–42.
Anderson, Benedict. 1991. *Imagined Communities*. Second Edition. London and New York: Verso.
Ball, Terence. 2006. "Democracy" In A. Dobson and R. Eckersely (eds) *Political Theory and the Ecological Challenge*. Cambridge and New York: Cambridge University Press.
Bergman, Noam. 2014. "Climate Camp and Public Discourse of Climate Change in the UK" *Carbon Management*. 5 (4): 339–348.
Blühdorn, Ingolfur. 2011. "The Sustainability of Democracy on Limits to Growth, the Post-Democratic Turn and Reactionary Democrats" *Eurozine*. Available at: www.eurozine.com/the-sustainability-of-democracy/

Böker, Marit. 2017. "Justification, Critique and Deliberative Legitimacy: The Limits of Mini-Publics" *Contemporary Political Theory*. 16: 19–40.

Brown, Craig. 2019. "The Modern Political Imaginary and the Problem of Hierarchy" *Social Epistemology*. 33 (5): 398–409.

Browne, Craig and Paula Diehl. 2019. "Conceptualising the Political Imaginary: An Introduction to the Special Issue" *Social Epistemology*. 33 (5): 393–397.

Carter, Alan. 1999. *A Radical Green Political Theory*. London and New York: Routledge.

Carter, Neil. 2001. *Politics of the Environment*. Cambridge and New York: Cambridge University Press.

della Porta, Donatella. (ed) (2009) *Democracy in Social Movements*. London: Palgrave Macmillan.

della Porta, Donatella. 2013. "Democracy and Social Movements" In David A. Snow, Donatella della Porta, Bert Klandermans, and Doug McAdam (eds) *The Wiley-Blackwell Encyclopedia of Social and Political Movements*. London: Blackwell Publishing.

Doherty, Brian. 2002. *Ideas and Actions in the Green Movement*. London and New York: Routledge.

Eckersley, Robyn. 2004. *The Green State: Rethinking Democracy and Sovereignty*. Cambridge and London: MIT Press.

EF! 1981. *Earth First!* Introductory Guide. Available at: www.environmentandsociety.org/mml/earth-first-introductory-guide-1981

Fischer, Frank. 2017. *Climate Crisis and the Democratic Prospect: Participatory Governance in Sustainable Communities*. Oxford: Oxford University Press.

Foreman, Dave, et al. (eds). 1980. *Earth First* 1 (1). Republished by the Environment & Society Portal, Multimedia Library. Available at: www.environmentandsociety.org/node/5251

Garrelts, Heiko and Matthias Dietz. 2014. "Introduction: Contours of the Transnational Climate Movement – Conception and Contents of the Handbook" In Heiko Garrelts and Matthias Dietz (eds) *Routledge Handbook of the Climate Change Movement*. London: Routledge.

Giugni, Marco and Maria T. Grasso. 2015. "Environmental Movements: Heterogeneity, Transformation, and Institutionalization" *Annual Review of Environment and Resources* 40: 337–361. DOI:10.1146/annurev-environ-102014-021327

Giugni, Marco and Maria T. Grasso. 2019. *Street Citizens: Protest Politics and Social Movement Activism in the Age of Globalization*. Cambridge: Cambridge University Press.

Goodin, Robert E. 1992. *Green Political Theory*. Cambridge and Oxford: Polity Press.

Gunningham, Neil. 2019. "Averting Climate Catastrophe: Environmental Activism, Extinction Rebellion and Coalitions of Influence" *King's Law Journal*. 30 (2).

Hammond, Marit and Graham Smith. 2017. *Sustainable Prosperity and Democracy – A Research Agenda*. CUSP Working Paper No 8. Guildford: University of Surrey. Available at: www.cusp.ac.uk/themes/p/no08/

Hay, Colin. 1996. "From Crisis to Catastrophe: The Ecological Pathologies of the Liberal-Democratic State" *Innovation*. 9 (4): 421–434.

Kenis, Anneleen and Matthias Lievens. 2015. *The Limits of the Green Economy: From Reinventing Capitalism to Repoliticising the Present*. London and New York: Routledge.

Kenis, Anneleen and Erik Mathijs. 2014. "(De)politicising the Local: The Case of the Transition Towns Movement in Flanders (Belgium)" *Journal of Rural Studies*. 34: 172–183.

Komárek, Jan. 2015. "Europe's Democratic Imaginary: Government by the People, for the People and of the People?" *Maastricht Journal of European and Comparative Law*. 22 (6): 784–787.

Lepori, Matthew. 2019. "Towards a New Ecological Democracy: A Critical Evaluation of the Deliberation Paradigm Within Green Political Theory" *Environmental Values*. 28: 75–99.

Levy, David L. and André Spicer. 2013. "Contested Imaginaries and the Cultural Political Economy of Climate Change" *Organization*. 20 (5): 659–678.

Luke, Timothy W. 2015. "The Climate Change Imaginary" *Current Sociology Monograph*. 63 (2): 280–296.

Machin, Amanda. 2013. *Negotiating Climate Change: Radical Democracy and the Illusion of Consensus*. London: Zed Books.

Machin, Amanda. 2018. "Green Democracy" In Noel Castree, Mike Hulme and James Proctor (eds) *The Companion to Environmental Studies*. London and New York: Routledge, 184–187.

Machin, Amanda. 2020. "Democracy, Disagreement, Disruption: Agonism and the Environmental State" *Environmental Politics*. 29 (1): 155–172.

Machin, Amanda. 2021. *Bodies of Democracy: Modes of Embodied Politics*. Bielefeld: Transcript [forthcoming].

Marquardt, Jens. 2020. "Fridays for Futures' Disruptive Potential: An Inconvenient Youth Between Moderate and Radical Ideas" *Frontiers in Communication*. 5: 48. DOI:10.3389/fcomm.2020.00048

McAfee, Noëlle. 2017. "Neo-Liberalism and Other Political Imaginaries" *Philosophy and Social Criticism*. 43(9): 911–931.

McGregor, Callum. 2015. "Direct Climate Action as Public Pedagogy: The Cultural Politics of the Camp for Climate Action" *Environmental Politics*. 24 (3): 343–362.

Methmann, Chris Paul. 2010. "Climate Protection as Empty Signifier: A Discourse Theoretical Perspective on Climate Mainstreaming in World Politics" *Millennium*. 39 (2): 345–372.

Milder, Stephen. 2015. "Between Grassroots Protest and Green Politics" *German Politics and Society*. 33 (4): 25–39.

Müller, Melanie and Heike Walk. 2014. "Democratizing the Climate Negotiations System Through Improved Opportunities for Participation" In H. Garrelts and M. Dietz (eds) *Routledge Handbook of the Climate Change Movement*. London: Routledge.

Pepermans, Yves and Pieter Maeseele. 2014. "Democratic Debate and Mediated Discourses on Climate Change: From Consensus to De/politization" *Environmental Communication*. 8 (2): 216–232.

Peters, Michael. 2019. "Can Democracy Solve the Sustainability Crisis? Green Politics, Grassroots Participation and the Failure of the Sustainability Paradigm" *Educational Philosophy and Theory*. 51 (2): 133–141.

Rancière, Jacques. 1999. *Disagreement: Politics and Philosophy*. Translated by Julie Rose. Minneapolis: University of Minnesota Press.

Rootes, Christopher. 2004. "Environmental Movements" In David A. Snow, Sarah A. Soule and Hanspeter Kriesi (eds) *The Blackwell Companion to Social Movements*. London: Blackwell.

Rosanvallon, Pierre. 2019. "The Political Theory of Democracy" In Oliver Flügel-Martinsen et al. (eds) *Pierre Rosanvallon's Political Thought Interdisciplinary Approaches*. Bielefeld: Bielefeld University Press.

Saunders, Clare. 2012. "Reformism and radicalism in the Climate Camp in Britain: Benign Coexistence, Tensions and Prospects for Bridging" *Environmental Politics* 21 (5): 829–846.

Saward, Michael. 1996. "Must Democrats Be Environmentalists?" In B. Doherty and M. de Geus (eds) *Democracy and Green Political Thought: Sustainability, Rights and Citizenship*. London and New York: Routledge.

Slaven, Mike and James Heydon. 2020. "Crisis, deliberation and Extinction Rebellion" *Critical Studies on Security*. 8 (1).

Smith, Graham. 2003. *Deliberative Democracy and the Environment*. London: Routledge.

Smith, Graham. 2009. *Democratic Innovations: Designing Institutions for Citizen Participation*. Cambridge: Cambridge University Press.

Smith, Graham and Amanda Machin. 2014. "Means, Ends, Beginnings: Environmental Technocracy, Ecological Deliberation or Embodied Democracy?" *Ethical Perspectives*. 21 (1): 47–72.

Swynegedouw, Erik. 2010. "Apocalypse Forever? Post-political Populism and the Spectre of Climate Change" *Theory, Culture and Society*. 27(2–3): 213–232.

Taylor, Bron. 2018. "Radical Environmentalisms Print History: From Earth First! to Wild Earth" *Environment & Society*. 1. Available at: www.environmentandsociety.org/exhibitions/radical-environmentalisms-print-history/third-decade-and-beyond-radical-environmentalism

Taylor, Charles. 2002. "Modern Social Imaginaries" *Public Culture*. 14 (1): 91–124.

Taylor, Charles. 2004. *Modern Social Imaginaries*. Durham and London: Duke University Press.

Wahlström, Mattias, Piotr Kocyba, Michiel De Vydt and Joost de Moor (eds) 2019. *Protest for a Future: Composition, Mobilization and Motives of the Participants in Fridays For Future Climate Protests on 15 March, 2019 in 13 European Cities*. Available at: https://protestinstitut.eu/wp-content/uploads/2019/07/20190709_Protest-for-a-future_GCS-Descriptive-Report.pdf

Wall, Derek. 2010. *The No-Nonsense Guide to Green Politics*. Oxford: New Internationalist.

Whiteley, Andrea, Angie Chiang and Edna Einsiedel. 2016. "Climate Change Imaginaries? Examining Expectation Narratives in Cli-Fi Novels" *Bulletin of Science, Technology and Society*. 36 (1): 28–37.

Wong, James K. 2016. "A Dilemma of Green Democracy" *Political Studies*. 64 (15): 136–155.

37

NEOLIBERALISM AND SOCIAL-ENVIRONMENTAL MOVEMENTS IN THE AFTERMATH OF THE 2008 FINANCIAL CRASH

Linking struggles against social, spatial, and environmental inequality

Elia Apostolopoulou

Introduction

The era following the 2008 financial crash has been characterized by the entrenchment of neoliberal policies in the form of fiscal and prolonged austerity; privatizations of public space and public property, land and natural resources; deregulation and market-friendly re-regulation of a wide range of policies; cuts in public health and public education; and an ignorance of the infrastructures of social reproduction. From mining, fracking, infrastructure megaprojects, waste disposal, and land grabbing in rural locations to shrinking access and loss of public green spaces, uneven gentrification and urban regeneration policies, and housing precarity in urban areas, public spaces and socionatures within and beyond cities are being appropriated, privatized, commoditized, transformed, and degraded with the aim of overcoming recession and boosting economic growth. The increasing neoliberalisation of nature and space manifests new enclosures and reterritorializations aiming to control land and resources by creating new forms of access and exclusion, disregarding in the process local experiences, traditions, and meanings. The exclusion of community groups, the increasing role of non-elected and unaccountable institutions, and the governmental suppression of social struggles, along with the further shrinking of the welfare state, has exposed the fact that the consensus-driven neoliberal rhetoric has been increasingly lapsing into undemocratic and even authoritarian governance (Apostolopoulou et al., 2014) in an era of a harsh global capitalist crisis. In response, various social-environmental movements have emerged with the purpose of opposing social, environmental, and spatial inequality and the undemocratic character of socio-spatial and socio-environmental changes often preventing the relentless exploitation of people and nature by capital: the protests against pipelines in Canada and the US; the opposition to gold mining in Romania, Turkey, and Greece; the anti-fracking struggle in the UK; and the school climate strikes, as well as anti-privatization struggles across the globe are among the many examples.

This chapter explores the emergence of social-environmental movements and struggles in the aftermath of the 2008 financial crash by linking it to the entrenchment of neoliberal policies across the globe. It approaches the latter as part of a wider attack on the working class and marginalized social groups and the collapse of the (remaining) welfare state. In particular, in what follows, I discuss the origins of neoliberalism and what constitutes the neoliberalization of nature and space to explain why its intensification entails the loss of rights for the social majority. I conclude by highlighting the need to bring together struggles for social, environmental, and spatial justice by linking struggles for the right to the city with struggles for the right to nature.

Neoliberalism and the neoliberalization of nature and space

Neoliberalism is a theory of political economic practices that proposes that human well-being can be best advanced by liberating individual entrepreneurial freedoms and skills within an institutional framework characterized by strong private property rights, free markets, and free trade (Harvey, 2005). The role of the state is to create and preserve an institutional framework appropriate to such practices and to set up the necessary structures and functions to secure private property rights and guarantee, by force if needed, the proper functioning of markets (ibid.). Expressions of neoliberal ideology have been evident from the end of the Second World War, but, as Harvey (2005) explains, existing neoliberalism can be better understood as a political-economic project that emerged during the 1970s – initially in the US and the UK, later in continental Europe and gradually across the globe – with the key aim of re-establishing, renewing, and expanding the conditions for capital accumulation. Various developments are linked with the rise of neoliberalism, including events surrounding the crisis of the dollar and policies enacted during dictatorships in Latin America in the 1970s (notably, the 1973 coup in Chile), as well as the 1973 oil crisis, during which the members of the Organization of Arab Petroleum Exporting Countries proclaimed an oil embargo. For many, neoliberalism has been identified with the policies of Margaret Thatcher, who was elected prime minister of Britain in 1979, and Ronald Reagan, who was elected president of the United States in 1980.

The period when neoliberalism emerged is not coincidental. The corporate capitalist class felt threatened both politically and economically toward the end of the 1960s and into the 1970s and made the strategic choice to launch a political project that would curb the increasing power of labor (Harvey, 2016). Despite these aspirations, neoliberalism has not been as effective as expected in revitalizing global capital accumulation, but it has nonetheless succeeded in restoring class power and the power of economic elites (Duménil and Lévy, 2004). As Duménil and Lévy (2001) have shown, neoliberalization was from the beginning a remarkable illustration of the class contradictions of capitalism: after the implementation of neoliberal policies in the late 1970s, the share of national income of the top 1% of income earners in the US soared to reach 15% by the end of the century. Neoliberalism expressed the strategy of the capitalist classes in alliance with upper management, intending to strengthen and expand their hegemony (Duménil and Lévy, 2013). Consequently, the overall dynamics of capitalism under neoliberalism have been determined by new class objectives that worked to the benefit of the highest income brackets, capitalist owners, and the upper fractions of management (ibid.; see also Apostolopoulou, 2020).

If we consider that in neoliberalism, economic elites seek to increase their wealth, income, and political and economic freedom and flexibility primarily by rolling back the redistributive reforms of the mid-twentieth century, we then see that neoliberalism is a counter-revolutionary project that intensifies social inequality (Harvey, 2016; Heynen et al., 2007). Key expressions of the latter include the new configurations of income distribution, the direct political assault on organized labor and anti-corporate reforms to disempower labor, the creation of various bubbles in the asset market, the pressure on workers to restore profit rates, and the attempt to cover the gap between declining wages and increasing effective demand by pushing the debt economy to its limits (Harvey, 2012), as well as the extensive deregulations, market-friendly re-regulations and privatizations. Importantly, the aggregate purpose and cumulative effect of neoliberal reforms has not been to roll back the state in general but to roll back and restructure a particular kind of state that, in most of the advanced capitalist countries, has been translated to attacks against the Keynesian welfare state. This has been followed by the rollout of new state forms, modes of regulation, and regimes of governance, attempting to consolidate and manage the increasing expansion of markets (ibid.). In the case of the UK, as Peck and Tickell (2007) explain, this included the restoration of a unilateral "right to manage" that presupposed the decapitation of the labor movement; the shift to market-oriented economic policies and the abolition of corporatist institutions; the privatization of nationalized industries, together with the deregulation of key sectors; the extension of financial markets, which entailed the transformation and internationalization of the City of London; and the intensification of competitive relations in the labor market, which were predicated on the erosion of social entitlements and workplace protections.

The relationships between nature, society, and space have not remained immune from neo-liberalism. As Heynen et al. (2007, p. 10) explain, the relationship between neoliberal reform and environmental politics, governance, and change has been inherent in the imperative that runs through the history of neoliberalization: namely, "to expand opportunities for capital investment and accumulation by re-working state-market-civil society relations to allow for the stretching and deepening of commodity production, circulation and exchange". The latter has been combined with an emphasis on individual rights and freedoms and a clear support for private property rights (ibid.). Importantly, even in cases in which neoliberal measures were not primarily aiming at expanding opportunities for capital accumulation, or failed to do so, they still brought about new ways of "locking up" surplus capital in the form of socio-natural (Heynen et al., 2007, pp. 11–12) and socio-spatial fixes. The pervasive influence of neoliberalism on non-human nature has been expressed well in the new terms that have emerged to describe neoliberal-driven transformations in nature-society relationships: these include the "neoliberali-zation of nature"; "neoliberal" or "capitalist natures"; and, more recently, "neoliberal conserva-tion" (see, e.g., Büscher et al., 2012; Corson et al., 2013; Igoe et al., 2010). These terms have been increasingly used to describe nature-society relationships under neoliberal capitalism and led to the formation of an expanding critical literature which, inter alia, explores what exactly constitutes the neoliberalization of nature (e.g., Apostolopoulou et al., 2014; Apostolopoulou and Adams, 2015; Bakker, 2010; Birch et al., 2010; Heynen and Robbins, 2005; Heynen et al., 2007; McCarthy and Prudham, 2004). For example, Castree (2008a, 2008b, 2010), in a very influential publication, offers six generic elements of neoliberal thought and practice that characterize the neoliberalization of nature: privatization, marketization, deregulation, market-friendly re-regulation, the adoption of market proxies in the residual public sector, and the construction of flanking mechanisms in civil society.

Neoliberalism has been also crucial in reinforcing and normalizing transurban tendecies toward reflexive and entrepreneurial city governance already indentified from the early 2000s (Peck and Tickell, 2002). This has been expressed in imposing a "growth-first" approach on urban development, at least during the last three decades, reconsituting social-welfarist arrangments as anticompetitive costs and rendering issues of social investment and redistribution as antagonistic to economic development (ibid.). As Peck and Tickell (2002) further explain, neoliberalism has not only promoted lean governments, deregulations, and privatizations but has also undermined or even completely foreclosed alternative paths of urban development based on social redistribution, economic rights, and public investment, producing a neoliberal "lock-in" of public-sector austerity and growth-chasing economic development.

Neoliberal austerity and social, spatial, and environmental inequality in the aftermath of the 2008 financial crash

Since the global financial crisis of 2008 began to unfold, the state of neoliberalism has been at the epicenter of important debates. In 2008, Neil Smith argued that neoliberalism was "dead but dominant",[1] in a "state of atrophy" but with its economic and military power continuing to have devastating consequences both for the environment and for people. In 2009, Eric Hobsbawm[2] argued that while it was not yet known how serious and lasting the effects of the economic crisis would be, they would certainly mark the end of the kind of free-market capitalism that had dominated the world in the years that followed the governments of Margaret Thatcher and Ronald Reagan. At the same time, David Harvey[3] questioned whether the crisis would mark the end of neoliberalism, suggesting that we should not easily jump to conclusions.

Today, in many parts of the world, neoliberalism remains more alive than ever, despite increasingly losing its legitimacy (Apostolopoulou and Cortes-Vazquez, 2019; Harvey, 2019). But how did we get to where we are today? After the financial crisis of 2008 and when the immediate need to rescue the banks ended, the crisis shifted from a financial crisis of the banking sector to a fiscal crisis of the state. The purpose of this shift was to protect the interests of banks, major bondholders, and powerful sections of capital (Lapavitsas et al., 2011). This has led to a sharp deterioration in public finances and profound changes at all levels of government and in all policy areas in many countries around the world, with the indicative example of Southern Europe. As Lapavitsas et al. (2010) explain, the "rescue" packages for the peripheral economies of the EU (by the EU and the International Monetary Fund [IMF]) were guided by neoliberal ideology and blind faith in fiscal austerity both as a cure and as a prevention of financial crises. The crisis, of course, was not limited to Southern Europe; strict austerity programs became widespread after 2008 in many countries across the globe (see Apostolopoulou and Adams, 2015; Cahill, 2011; Calvário et al., 2017). Overall, and despite some initial concerns and some stimulus measures, most governments, in a classic neoliberal way, imposed draconian austerity (Harvey, 2011; Lapavitsas et al., 2011). This was reflected in the drastic reduction of public spending, the increase in indirect taxes, cuts in wages and pensions, and the collapse of the (remaining) welfare state, accompanied by extensive deregulations and privatizations of public space and public property, land, and natural resources.

It is important to note that these reforms took place within the broader context of the domination of austerity policies that, as Gray and Barford (2018) explain, reshaped the relationship between central and local government by transferring, inter alia, the fiscal crisis to local governments (see also Peck, 2012), deepening the inequality between local governments and spatial injustice. As Harvey (2011) explains, austerity is a class policy that leads to the restructuring of society and the appropriation of the commons. This has been expressed since 2008 through the implementation of a set of policies that led to major cuts in social spending,[4] including education, health care, and environmental protection; reduced public investment; increased the privatization of public services and key sectors of the economy; and reduced wages,[5] pensions, and social rights, while transferring the responsibility for social reproduction to individuals and charities (Apostolopoulou and Adams, 2015; Harvey, 2011; Gray and Barford, 2018; Karaniko-los et al., 2013; Lipman, 2015).

These changes were accompanied by a more revanchist phase of neoliberal development (Peck, 2012; Harvey, 2019), which became apparent, inter alia, in the neoliberal restructuring of cities, which often took the form of neoliberal urban austerity (Theodore et al., 2011). This was expressed in the extensive privatizations of urban space, the reduction in public spending and projects to support social reproduction, and quality of life in the city, as well as in the deepening neoliberalization of both urban space and urban socionatures (Apostolopoulou et al., 2014; Apostolopoulou and Adams, 2015), with huge consequences for city dwellers (Peck, 2012; Harvey, 2012). To these we must add the deregulation of a number of environmental, land, and spatial planning regulations and the extensive privatization of public space, land, and natural resources (Apostolopoulou and Adams, 2015; Apostolopoulou and Cortes-Vazquez, 2019; Cortes-Vazquez and Apostolopoulou, 2019). The use of the debt trap as a primary means of accumulation also played a crucial role, confirming that the creation of crises and their management on the world stage reflect the intensification of uneven geographical development (Harvey, 2007).

A key new element in changing socio-spatial and socio-environmental conditions, which marks the intensification of the neoliberalization of space and nature in the post-2008 era, is the coexistence of, and sometimes even the symbiotic relationship between, processes of green and "ungreen" grabbing. The term "green grabbing" is used to describe the ways in which land and natural resources are appropriated for environmental purposes and can be understood as part of the broader discussion on land grabbing (Fairhead et al., 2012; Borras et al., 2012). Typical examples are biofuel policies, payments for ecosystem services, ecotourism, and biodiversity/carbon offsetting. Green grabbing has its roots in the colonial and neo-colonial expropriation of land and resources while, at the same time, introducing new dimensions to the exploitation of nature through the extensive expropriation of land for "green" purposes and the radical restructuring of the rules for access to natural resources and ecosystems. Ungreen grabbing, on the other hand, refers to the exploitation of nature and space without any green or environmentally friendly argumentation (Apostolopoulou and Adams, 2015) and has been a key part of the infrastructure rush (Tooze, 2018) that has characterized the post-2008 era, signalling the emergence of an infrastructure-led development paradigm worldwide (Schindler and Kanai, 2019). The latter includes major infrastructure projects, with the emblematic example of China's Belt and Road Initiative (Apostolopoulou, 2021a, 2021b). Hilyard and Sol (2017) characterize this period as the era of extreme infrastructure that is remaking places and socionatures to establish capital-friendly tradescapes and mega-corridors.

The parallel spread of green and ungreen grabbing has led to a situation in which strategies for creating markets for biodiversity, water, and carbon coexist with the overthrow of historic environmental regulations to facilitate economic growth. Thus, together with neoliberal optimism about the ability of the green economy (i.e., green capitalism) to "save nature", we see the reluctance of strong sections of capital to commit to a more sustainable development path as manifested in important international meetings and UN summits on environment and climate change in the decade 2010 to 2020. At the same time, at the national level, governmental responses to the economic crisis focused mainly on the deregulation of key political and economic regulations (McCarthy, 2012). These developments have been visible in Europe, the USA, and Australia but also in many other countries around the world where governments have used the economic crisis as a "Trojan horse" to facilitate the further neoliberalization of nature and space (Apostolopoulou and Cortes-Vazquez, 2019; Cortes-Vazquez and Apostolo-poulou, 2019).

These changes were accompanied, as expected, by fundamental changes in governance arrangements toward a deeper neoliberal direction. Central to these has been the shift to new networked arrangements between the state, the market, and the civil society, the strengthening of which has been a central element of neoliberalism (Harvey, 2005). In the aftermath of the 2008 financial crash, in the broader context of prolonged austerity (i.e., the constant and extensive cutting of government budgets) (Gray and Barford, 2018), the decentralization of state powers to regions and municipalities was accompanied not only by a further withdrawal of the state from key provisions of the welfare state but also by an increasing delegation of state responsibilities to non-governmental organizations (NGOs) and consultants (Apostolopoulou et al., 2014). Typical is the example of England, where the shift toward the decentralization of central and regional power led to a new form of localism strongly shaped by policies of prolonged austerity (the so-called "austerity localism" (see Apostolopoulou and Adams, 2019; Apostolopoulou, 2020). This meant that only those who had the resources, knowledge, and appropriate connections to the market and the government had the power to shape local policies and participate in decision making (Apostolopoulou et al., 2014; Featherstone et al., 2012). Many local communities and activists have strongly criticized their severely limited ability to intervene in local initiatives and actions and their reduced participation in public hearings and consultation processes due to their critical attitude toward the market, government policies, and private-public partnerships. Indeed, severe cuts in state funding and staff reductions in a number of government services have coincided with increased public-private partnerships, the promotion of market-based policy tools, and the intensification of economic exploitation or privatization of land for the purpose of profitability in the tourism and real estate sectors. Changes in governance have also manifested in the upgraded role of international organizations, such as the International Monetary Fund (IMF), which since the 1980s have become key agents of neoliberalization (Apostolopoulou and Adams, 2015; Swyngedouw, 2004). The combinations of public, private, and "hybrid" governance (Hodge and Adams, 2012) reflect a dynamic deconstruction and reconstruction of the scale of governance, which, of course, is not politically neutral. Changes in governance are shaped by and express power relations (Apostolopoulou and Paloniemi, 2012) and lead to the introduction of mechanisms of exclusion of specific social groups and classes (Swyngedouw, 2000), with the remarkable example of the consolidation of the power of private interests, which entails the loss of rights for the social majority. An indicative example here is the suppression of social and environmental struggles in many countries, with such emblematic examples in Europe as the suppression of struggles against fracking in England; against mining in Greece (Skouries), Romania, and Finland; and against the mobilizations in Gezi Park in Turkey.

It is important to point out here that neoliberal austerity has marked both a reduction in public spending on environmental and social welfare and the emergence and consolidation of new forms of capitalist accumulation by privatizing and/or expropriating natural resources (e.g., metals, forests, parks) and affecting access to public, safe green spaces; housing rights; public health; the sense of belonging; and daily security. The economic crisis has thus signaled a simultaneous intensification of the economic exploitation of nature and a deterioration in the living and reproductive conditions of the social majority, making it clear that environmental policy cannot be seen in isolation from other aspects of social policy. Perhaps the most indicative example of the latter has been the loss of public spaces and ecosystems that has occurred during the last decade in parallel with the attack on citizens' labor and social rights. In England, for example, a recent survey recorded a loss of 22,000 hectares of green space between 2006 and 2012, an area twice the size of Liverpool, which was converted into "artificial surfaces", mostly homes. This included the loss of more than 7,000 hectares of forest, 14,000 hectares of agricultural land, and 1,000 hectares of wetlands (Mathiesen, 2015). This loss coincided with the imposition of harsh austerity measures that worsened the quality of life of the lower-income classes, leading to social struggles across the country against the social, spatial, and ecological implications of the economic exploitation of public spaces and ecosystems inside and outside the city and ongoing urban sprawl (Apostolopoulou, 2020).

Social movements under capitalism in crisis: grassroots resistance to uneven socio-spatial and socio-environmental change

These developments show that, in the last decade, local and national governments, under the direct influence of large industries, corporate lobbies and strong capitalist interests, have supported and promoted the further neoliberalization of nature and space, ignoring the consequences of crisis-driven socio-spatial and socio-environmental transformation; the unequal distribution of environmental costs and benefits; and the social, economic, and cultural links between local communities, non-human nature, and place. This has resulted in numerous communities seeing their rights to clean water and clean air; access to nature, decent housing, and safe public green spaces; and quality of life in the areas where they live and work threatened or completely lost. This marked a new era in which governments have been taking back planning and environmental regulations that have been influenced by competition between different sections of capital but have been primarily won by social and environmental movements and class struggle. (For the latter, see Harvey, 2005; Vlachou, 2005.) Moreover, and importantly, in many cases, excluding local community groups from the decisions that affect their lives has occured in parallel with upgrading the role of unelected institutions and suppressing social struggles. The latter, together with the further collapse of the (remaining welfare) state, shows well that the neoliberal rhetoric has become increasingly anti-democratic and accompanied by a shift toward authoritarian forms of governance (Apostolopoulou et al., 2014; Swyngedouw, 2005).

The increase in socio-environmental conflicts, especially in the period following the outbreak of the global economic crisis, highlights in the most obvious way the intensification of socio-environmental and socio-spatial inequality during the last decade due to these developments (Apostolopoulou and Cortes-Vazquez, 2019) and reflects the inherent inability of capitalism to articulate a positive pathway out of the crisis. Indeed, grassroots activism and community struggles in the post-2008 era have risen in parallel to increasing food and housing precarity, poverty, governmental neglect for public spaces, urban and rural marginality, and the deepening of social and spatial inequality in relation to the accessibility and use of open and safe public spaces along lines of class, race, ethnicity, and gender (Anguelovski, 2014; Madanipour, 2010). Based on the data provided in the Environmental Justice Atlas, a collaborative map of socio-environmental conflicts around the world (Temper et al., 2018), conflicts are unequally distributed around the world, confirming that unequal geographical development is an inherent feature of capitalism (Smith, 2010) but nonetheless is spread across the globe. The scale and diversity of emerging struggles across the Global South and North have also been reflected in a recently published volume focusing on what we call the "Right to Nature" (see Apostolopoulou and Cortes-Vazquez, 2019). In this volume, fights against the social, spatial, and ecological impacts of extractive industries in Colombia, Ecuador, and Russia; the Keystone oil pipeline in Nebraska and American oil and gas companies in Africa; gold mining in Greece and Romania; and fracking in England met with struggles against water privatization in Egypt, food justice struggles in Mozambique and Latin America, protests against the Rio Olympic Games and the consequences of urban gentrification in Brooklyn, and campaigns against major infrastructure projects (megaprojects) across Europe.

These cases, as well as a series of other struggles that have emerged in the last decade, show rather clearly that unequal geographical development intensifies social and spatial injustice and requires building solidarity networks (Soja, 2010; Hadjimichalis, 2011). Indeed, in parallel with the outbreak of conflicts, new socio-environmental movements have been emerging to formulate a critical response to neoliberalism and defend radically different socio-spatial and socio-natural relationships, often directly challenging capitalist logic (Temper et al., 2018). Examples of such movements and radical demands from below include 1) the occupation of public spaces, the establishment of squats, and the creation of resistance camps as a means of protest against mining activities, the privatization of land and natural resources, the housing crisis, and the neo-liberalization of public space and nature; 2) the creation of free, cooperative, innovative grass-roots initiatives, solidarity networks, and cooperatives based on the ethics of care and solidarity as a way of achieving social, spatial, and environmental justice and socio-ecologically sustainable practices and address the impacts of austerity policies, particularly for marginalized social groups, 3) alternative, low-energy consumption practices and low-impact living as an answer to the interconnected housing, food, and energy crises. These practices offer valuable ideas (e.g., community and local food growing, local renewable energy sources, housing alternatives, and co-ownership) of what social/public housing could look like in the twenty-first century and are important tools for challenging property relationships; 4) cases of community gardening and self-managed farms, socially and environmentally sustainable agricultural production, and edible landscapes that not only aim at addressesing the uneven impacts of the food crisis but also have the potential to strengthen the ability of local communities, including Indigenous communities, to achieve and maintain territorial autonomy and cooperative, community-based production practices; and 5) formulation of popular assemblies based on the principles of direct democracy as a response to the inability or unwillingness of elected representatives to address the needs of their communities and prevent the privatization of public land and natural resources and the dispossession of the commons and the deterioration of everyday lives.

At least three observations are crucial here. Firstly, as is clear from these examples, many movements that have emerged in the last decade place at the center of their demands and claims a number of distinct but interrelated issues of social, spatial, and environmental inequality, showing that the various crises of capitalism (housing, energy, food, public health, environmental) are deeply interrelated. Thus, struggles to defend the right of access to public green or open spaces within and beyond cities or to preserve the countryside are directly linked to struggles for the right to housing or opposition to infrastructure projects without any social benefits. Secondly, these movements often try not only to counter the consequences of the interconnected crises of capitalism but also to openly discuss ways of transition to post-capitalist societies. Thirdly, the expansion of urbanization beyond the boundaries of the traditional city has created the conditions for urban struggles within cities to be linked, both analytically and politically, to mobilizations against land expropriations, processes of accumulation by dipossession, privatizations, and large-scale infrastructure projects (dams, highways, pipelines, mines) in rural or even seemingly remote areas (see also Brenner and Schmid, 2015) in diverse places across the Global South and North.

A final note is important here. In most socio-environmental movements, attachment to place proves a key factor that relates to the need to oppose the dispossession of the commons. Place-based struggles by exploring ways to bring about social change through solidarity, cooperation, self-governance, egalitarianism, and democracy make certain commons sites of radical grassroots innovation and resistance. As Chatterton (2010, p. 626) points out, the common is "made real through the practice of communing", which reflects dynamic socio-spatial practices that have the potential to form alternative politics when common wealth (e.g., land, soil, water, seeds, air, food, biodiversity, cultural and social practices) that supports social and physical well-being is faced with enclosure. The common, then, becomes a political byword for resistance (Chatterton, 2010), particularly within the context of prolonged crisis and austerity that has led to a revanchist phase of capitalist development and growth evident in the profound and unequal social, spatial, economic, and environmental consequences of the post-2008 neoliberal policies (Apostolopoulou and Cortes-Vazquez, 2019; Harvey, 2012; Peck, 2012).

The right to nature and the right to the city as key social rights: linking environmental to social and spatial justice

The origins of the environmental justice movement are usually traced to the United States in the early 1980s, with the emblematic example of the protest against a toxic waste facility in a low-income community in Warren County, North Carolina. This movement, which had significant roots in the civil rights movement, defended the right of people to resist the unequal distribution of environmental hazards. Today, the environmental justice movement is gaining momentum worldwide and is often severely repressed due to its potential to obstruct capitalist development and, therefore, put barriers to capital accumulation. This movement was born out of the struggles around the world against the extraction of fossil fuels; the creation of huge mines, plantations, and monocultures; the construction of dams and nuclear power plants; the disposal of waste; and the increase of pollution in socially and environmentally sensitive areas, disproportionally affecting people across lines of gender, race, and class.

The concept of the "right to nature", as we have shown extensively elsewhere (Apostolopoulou and Adams, 2019; Apostolopoulou and Cortes-Vazquez, 2019; Apostolopoulou, 2019; Cortes-Vazquez and Apostolopoulou, 2019), has the potential to signal a radically different understanding of environmental struggles, emphasizing the need for collective action to achieve social, spatial, and environmental justice and the need to realize and co-create an alternative way of organizing social production and reproduction. The right to nature is inspired by the legacy of the Right to the City (Lefebvre, 1968, 1996; Harvey, 2008, 2012), which has been defined as the right to intervene in a fundamental and radical way in the process of urbanization (Harvey, 2012), and both are inextricably linked to claims concerning the relations between society, nature, and space. Placing both the right to nature and the right to the city on the agenda of critical research and radical practice, as research objects and as political demands, requires creating new conceptual and methodological tools. It can create important strategic links between the spatial, social, and environmental aspects of emerging social movements in the post-2008 era as it raises the question of who controls the link between economic exploitation, urbanization, and accumulation redefining the debate about who defines the production of nature and space and which class interests this production serves. The right to nature and the right to the city are political and activist positions that are oriented toward the future, approaching environmental struggles as social struggles and vice versa and fighting for radically different social relations. As collective rights, they emphasize the need to deepen and extend existing rights, including property rights, not as liberal democratic rights guaranteed by the state, but as political demands of mobilized groups (Apostolopoulou, 2020; Lefebvre, 2003; Purcell and Tyman, 2015), recognizing that environmental justice is impossible without social and spatial justice (and vice versa).

Establishing these links within but most importantly beyond academia could open pathways for radical demands that would put forward the need for social and environmental policies that would focus on the material interests of the vast majority of the working class and marginalized groups, who are forced to experience environmental degradation and the deterioration of their quality of life along with wage cuts, rising debts, job insecurity, and unequal access to health and education. A socio-environmental program with a clear class orientation against capital and in favor of the working class and the oppressed should also focus on combating perpetual austerity by claiming the right of people to meet the basic reproductive needs of their lives (e.g., their food needs, energy, housing, health care, love, leisure, and social relationships) (Huber, 2019). Such a program requires building a movement that will make clear that solutions to a range of crises (climate, energy, health care, and housing) require action against the industries that are not only responsible for these crises but also benefit from them.

What this also shows is that a political ecology that aims at not only understanding but also transforming uneven socio-spatial and socio-natural relations has to embrace the non-urban as constitutive of the urban and understand how the former is related to the latter (Apostolopoulou, 2020; Apostolopoulou and Adams, 2019). Similarly, urban geography should also embrace the rural as constitutive of the urban. This requires understanding how struggles for the city and for nature in dense city cores and in seemingly "remote" areas are often deeply interrelated. In the Marxist tradition, environmental and urban struggles are usually construed as being about issues of reproduction rather than production and therefore not about class and thus dismissed as devoid of revolutionary potential or significance (Harvey, 2012). However, given that urbanization is crucial in the history of capital accumulation and perceives increasing importance in the context of planetary or generalized urbanization, struggles against its uneven reworking and its materialization are political and class struggles, whether or not they are explicitly recognized as such, and must, therefore, be placed at the forefront of any radical political action.

Linking the right to nature to the right to the city and seeing both as fundamental social rights clearly shows the need to organize social struggles not only around the workplace but also around the living conditions of the working class and the marginalized in order to recreate everyday lives and eradicate poverty; catastrophic environmental degradation; urban marginality; and social, spatial, and environmental inequality (see also Apostolopoulou and Kotsila, 2021). Such a program for the future should be openly anti-capitalist and would have the challenging task of seeking unity from within the diversity of fragmented social spaces and locations. The iconic socio-environmental struggles of the last decade, from resistance to pipelines in the US and anti-fracking struggles in the UK to the emblematic anti-mining struggle in the village of Skouries in Greece, along with emerging global mobilizations for climate, food, energy, and housing justice, show that socio-environmental movements can stand against the hegemonic narratives that describe an apocalyptic future. What is urgently needed, particularly within the context of the COVID-19 pandemic that has already exarcebated existing inequalities and disproportionately affected the most vulnerable (Rose-Redwood et al., 2020), is to realize that the protracted global crisis of capitalism will not cease to produce revanchist and dystopian policies unless a radical, anti-capitalistic program dominates.

Notes

1 www.berghahnjournals.com/view/journals/focaal/2008/51/focaal510113.xml.
2 http://banmarchive.org.uk/collections/mt/pdf/98_11_04.pdf.
3 www.counterpunch.org/2009/03/13/is-this-really-the-end-of-neoliberalism/.
4 www.theguardian.com/business/2012/may/08/austerity-europe-what-does-it-mean; https://thepresspro ject.gr/mnimonio-3-genikeusi-tis-ftoxeias-me-antallagma-tin-paramoni-stin-eurozoni/.
5 According to the International Labour Office (ILO, www.ilo.org), the economic crisis led to a significant reduction in wages at a global scale.

References

Anguelovski, I. (2014). *Neighborhood as refuge: Community reconstruction, place remaking, and environmental justice in the city.* MIT Press.

Apostolopoulou, E. (2021a). Tracing the links between infrastructure-led development, urban transformation, and inequality in China's belt and road initiative. *Antipode* 53(3), 831–858.

Apostolopoulou, E. (2021b). A novel geographical research agenda on Silk Road urbanisation. *The Geographical Journal*, https://doi.org/10.1111/geoj.12412.

Apostolopoulou, E. (2020). Beyond post-politics: Offsetting, depoliticization and contestation in a community struggle against executive housing. *Transactions of the Institute of British Geographers* 45, 345–361.

Apostolopoulou, E. (2020). *Nature swapped and nature lost: Biodiversity offsetting, urbanization and social justice.* Springer-Palgrave Macmillan.

Apostolopoulou, E., Adams, W.M. (2015). Neoliberal capitalism and conservation in the post-crisis era: The dialectics of green and ungreen grabbing in Greece and the UK. *Antipode* 47, 15–35.

Apostolopoulou, E., Adams, W.M. (2019). Cutting nature to fit: Urbanization, neoliberalism and biodiversity offsetting in England. *Geoforum* 98, 214–225.

Apostolopoulou, E., Bormpoudakis, D., Paloniemi, R., Cent, J., Grodzińska-Jurczak, M., Pietrzyk-Kaszyńska, A., Pantis, J.D. (2014). Governance rescaling and the neoliberalization of nature: The case of biodiversity conservation in four EU countries. *International Journal of Sustainable Development and World Ecology* 21, 481–494.

Apostolopoulou, E., Cortes-Vazquez, J.A. (2019). *The right to nature: Social movements, environmental justice and neoliberal natures.* Routledge-Earthscan.

Apostolopoulou, E., Kotsila, P. (2021). Community gardening in Hellinikon as a resistance struggle against neoliberal urbanism: Spatial autogestion and the right to the city in post-crisis Athens, Greece. *Urban Geography*, https://doi.org/10.1080/02723638.2020.1863621.

Apostolopoulou, E., Paloniemi, R. (2012). Frames of scale challenges in Finnish and Greek biodiversity conservation. *Ecology & Society* 17(4).

Bakker, K. (2010). The limits of 'neoliberal natures': Debating green neoliberalism. *Progress in Human Geography* 34, 715–735.

Birch, K., Levidow, L., Papaioannou, T. (2010). Sustainable capital? The neoliberalization of nature and knowledge in the European 'knowledge-based bio-economy'. *Sustainability* 2, 2898–2918.

Borras S.M., Franco, J.C., Gómez, S., Kay, C., Spoor, M. (2012). Land grabbing in Latin America and the Caribbean. *The Journal of Peasant Studies* 39, 845–872.

Brenner, N., Schmid, C. (2015). Towards a new epistemology of the urban? *City* 19, 151–182.

Büscher, B., Sullivan, S., Neves, K., Igoe, J., Brockington, D. (2012). Towards a synthesized critique of neoliberal biodiversity conservation. *Capitalism Nature Socialism* 23, 4–29.

Cahill, D. (2011). Beyond neoliberalism? Crisis and the prospects for progressive alternatives. *New Political Science* 33, 479–492.

Calvário, R., Velegrakis, G., Kaika, M. (2017). The political ecology of austerity: An analysis of socio-environmental conflict under crisis in Greece. *Capitalism Nature Socialism* 28, 69–87.

Castree, N. (2008a). Neoliberalising nature: The logics of deregulation and reregulation. *Environment and Planning A* 40, 131–152.

Castree, N. (2008b). Neoliberalising nature: Processes, effects, and evaluations. *Environment and Planning A* 40, 153–173.

Castree, N. (2010). Neoliberalism and the biophysical environment: A synthesis and evaluation of the research. *Environment and Society* 1, 5–45.

Chatterton, P. (2010). Seeking the urban common: Furthering the debate on spatial justice. *City* 14, 625–628.

Corson, C., MacDonald, K.I., Neimark, B. (2013) Grabbing "green": Markets, environmental governance, and the materialization of natural capital. *Human Geography* 6, 1–15.

Cortes-Vazquez, J.A., Apostolopoulou, E. (2019). Against neoliberal natures: Environmental movements, radical practice and "the right to nature". *Geoforum* 98, 202–205.

Duménil, G., Lévy, D. (2001). Costs and benefits of neoliberalism: A class analysis. *Review of International Political Economy* 8, 578–607.

Duménil, G., Lévy, D. (2004). *Capital resurgent: Roots of the neoliberal revolution.* Harvard University Press.

Duménil, G., Lévy, D. (2013). *The crisis of neoliberalism.* Harvard University Press.

Fairhead, J., Leach, M., Scoones, I. (2012) Green grabbing: A new appropriation of nature? *Journal of Peasant Studies* 39, 237–261.

Featherstone, D., Ince, A., Mackinnon, D., Strauss, K., Cumbers, A., 2012. Progressive localism and the construction of political alternatives. *Transactions of the Institute of British Geographers* 37, 177–182.

Gray, M., Barford, A. (2018). The depths of the cuts: The uneven geography of local government austerity. *Cambridge Journal of Regions, Economy and Society* 11, 541–563.

Hadjimichalis, C. (2011). Uneven geographical development and socio-spatial justice and solidarity: European regions after the 2009 financial crisis. *European Urban and Regional Studies* 18, 254–274.

Harvey, D. (2005). *A brief history of neoliberalism.* Oxford University Press.

Harvey, D. (2007). Neoliberalism as creative destruction. *The Annals of the American Academy of Political and Social Science* 610, 21–44.

Harvey, D. (2008). The right to the city. *New Left Review* 53, 23–40.

Harvey, D. (2011). Crises, geographic disruptions, and the uneven development of political responses. *Economic Geography* 87, 1–22.

Harvey, D. (2012). *Rebel cities: From the right to the city to the urban revolution.* Verso.

Harvey, D. (2016). Neoliberalism is a political project. *Jacobin,* www.jacobinmag.com/2016/07/david-harvey-neoliberalism-capitalism-labor-crisis-resistance/.

Harvey, D. (2019). *The neoliberal project is alive but has lost its legitimacy,* https://mronline.org/2019/02/16/the-neoliberal-project-is-alive-but-has-lost-its-legitimacy-david-harvey/.

Heynen, N., McCarthy, J., Prudham, S., Robbins, P. (eds). 2007. *Neoliberal environments: False promises and unnatural consequences.* Routledge.

Heynen, N., Robbins, P. (2005). The neoliberalization of nature: Governance, privatization, enclosure, and valuation. *Capitalism Nature Socialism* 16, 5–8.

Hildyard, N., Sol, X. (2017). *How infrastructure is shaping the world: A critical introduction to infrastructure megacorridors.* Counter Balance.

Hodge, I.D., Adams, W.M. (2012). Neoliberalisation, rural land trusts, and institutional blending. *Geoforum* 43, 472–482.

Huber, M. (2019). *Climate change is class struggle,* https://jacobinmag.com/2019/12/on-fire-naomi-klein-review-climate-change.

Igoe, J., Neves, K., Brockington, D. (2010). A spectacular eco-tour around the historic bloc: Theorising the convergence of biodiversity conservation and capitalist expansion. *Antipode* 42, 486–512.

Karanikolos, M., Mladovsky, P., Cylus, J., et al. (2013). Financial crisis, austerity, and health in Europe. *The Lancet* 381(9874), 1323–1331.

Lapavitsas, C., Kaltenbrunner, A., Labrinidis, G., Lindo, D., Meadway, J., Michell, J., Painceira, J.P., Pires, E., Powell, J., Stenfors, A., Teles, N. (2010). *The Eurozone between austerity and default, research on money and finance (RMF).* Occasional Report, September, www.researchonmoneyandfinance.org/.

Lapavitsas, C., Kaltenbrunner, A., Lindo, D., Meadway, J., Michell, J., Painceira, J.P., Pires, E., Powell, J., Stenfors, A., Teles, N., Vatikiotis, L. (2011). *Breaking up? A route out of the eurozone crisis, research on money and finance (RMF).* Occasional Report 3, November, www.researchonmoneyandfinance.org/.

Lefebvre, H. (1968). *Le Droit à la Ville.* Anthropos.

Lefebvre, H. (1996). *Writings on cities,* vol. 63(2). Blackwell.

Lefebvre, H. (2003) [1990]. From the social pact to the contract of citizenship. In Elden, S., Lebas, E., Kofman, E., eds. *Henri Lefebvre: Key Writings.* Continuum.

Lipman, P. (2015). Capitalizing on crisis: Venture philanthropy's colonial project to remake urban education. *Critical Studies in Education* 56(2), 241–258.

Madanipour, A., ed. (2010) *Whose public space? International case studies in urban design and development.* Routledge.

Mathiesen, K. (2015). *How and where did UK lose city-sized area of green space in just six years?,* www.theguardian.com/environment/2015/jul/02/how-where-did-uk-lose-green-space-bigger-than-a-city-six-years.

McCarthy, J. (2012). The financial crisis and environmental governance "after" neoliberalism. *Tijdschrift Voor Economische en Sociale Geografie* 103, 180–195.

McCarthy, J., Prudham, S. (2004). Neoliberal nature and the nature of neoliberalism. *Geoforum* 35, 275–283.

Peck, J. (2012). Austerity urbanism: American cities under extreme economy. *City* 16, 626–655.

Peck, J., Tickell, A. (2002). Neoliberalizing space. *Antipode* 34(3), 380–404.

Peck, J., Tickell, A. (2007). Conceptualizing neoliberalism, thinking Thatcherism. *Contesting Neoliberalism: Urban Frontiers* 26, 50.

Purcell, M., Tyman, S.K. (2015). Cultivating food as a right to the city. *Local Environment* 20, 1132–1147.

Rose-Redwood Kitchin, R., Apostolopoulou, E., Rickards, L., Blackman, T., Crampton, J., Rossi, U., Buckley, M. (2020). Geographies of the COVID-19 pandemic. *Dialogues in Human Geography* 10(2), 97–106.

Schindler, S., Kanai, J.M. (2019). Getting the territory right: Infrastructure-led development and the re-emergence of spatial planning strategies. *Regional Studies*, https://doi.org/10.1080/00343404.2019.16 61984.

Smith, N. (2010). *Uneven Development* (3rd edn). Verso.

Soja, E. (2010). *Seeking Spatial Justice*. University of Minnesota Press.

Swyngedouw, E. (2000). Authoritarian governance, power, and the politics of rescaling. *Environment Planning D* 18, 63–76.

Swyngedouw, E. (2004). Globalisation or 'glocalisation'? Networks, territories and rescaling. *Cambridge Review of International Affairs* 17, 25–48.

Swyngedouw, E. (2005). Governance innovation and the citizen: The Janus face of governance-beyond-the-state. *Urban Studies* 42, 1991–2006.

Temper, L., Demaria, F., Scheidel, A., et al. (2018). The global environmental justice atlas (EJAtlas): Ecological distribution conflicts as forces for sustainability. *Sustainability Science* 13, 573–584.

Theodore, N., Peck J., Brenner N. (2011). Neoliberal urbanism: Cities and the rule of markets. In Bridge, G., Watson, S., eds. *The new Blackwell companion to the city*, Wiley-Blackwell.

Tooze, A (2018). *How a decade of financial crises changed the world*. Allen Lane.

Vlachou, A. (2005). Environmental regulation: A value-theoretic and class-based analysis. *Cambridge Journal of Economics* 29, 577–599.

38

THE FUTURE OF ENVIRONMENTAL MOVEMENTS[1]

Carl Cassegård

To start with, here are four snapshots that highlight some directions in which the environmental movement is developing today. In 2015, Greenpeace and many other leading environmental organizations lauded the outcome of COP21, the UN-led climate summit in Paris at which world leaders agreed to limit global warming to "well below 2°C above pre-industrial levels" and to pursue this "in the light of equity and the best available science". A few months later, members of the Standing Rock Sioux tribe announced their intention to oppose the planned Dakota Access pipeline to "protect the water". Meanwhile, the British Dark Mountain collective was issuing biannual anthologies and holding festivals, workshops, and courses in which participants sought to invent new languages for mourning the losses that would accompany the approaching end of civilization. Finally, in Stockholm, 15-year-old Greta Thunberg initiated a school strike in 2018, which soon spread globally, declaring to the world's politicians that they should listen to the science and act, and that she preferred them to feel panic rather than hope.

Rather than trying to predict the future of this multifarious and rapidly changing movement, the aim of this chapter is to chart some prominent trends and suggest certain scenarios and dimensions of change that may be useful when gauging possible future developments. Since movements always develop in relation to a larger context, I start in the first section by briefly outlining three scenarios that build on how society will react to the environmental crises facing it today. The scenarios are those of radical transformation, business as usual, and collapse. The first stands for a future in which movements pressure powerholders to carry out swift and massive changes to the present system in order to stave off environmental threats, even at the cost of going against elite interests. The second stands for a future characterized by reformist changes within the framework set by existing institutions and prevailing practices. The third stands for the breakdown of important social functions due to environmental factors and/or accompanying political and social crises. These scenarios do not just help us envision the possibly shifting conditions for the movement in the future but are also of heuristic value since different currents in today's environmental movement orient themselves to different scenarios.

In the second section, I survey some of these currents and distinguish three separate dimensions along which the movement may change: social justice, post-apocalypse, and emergency action. I exemplify them with developments taking place today and argue that they all represent challenges to the far-reaching institutionalization that the environmental movement has gone

 DOI: 10.4324/9780367855680-44

through in many countries in recent decades. I will use examples mostly from climate- or energy-related environmental activism, considering their prominence in recent decades. I also discuss how these developments contribute to a politicization of the climate issue and how they also carry with them the seeds of their own distinctive varieties of depoliticization.

In the final section, I return to the three scenarios and make some suggestions about how they may affect the surveyed movement currents and about the dimensions of change that appear especially relevant in relation to each of them.

Three scenarios

While environmental destruction does not automatically translate into movement activity, it would be foolhardy to neglect the former when considering the possible future development of the environmental movement. Global warming, resource depletion, species loss, and pollution are all examples of ongoing catastrophic changes, caused or dramatically exacerbated by industrial capitalism. Unprecedented efforts have now become necessary to limit global warming to the presumably safe limit of 1.5°C above pre-industrial levels, and as the Intergovernmental Panel on Climate Change (IPCC) made clear in a 2018 report, even that would still result in a heightened risk of species reduction, loss of ecosystems, and widespread poverty. Making the picture even bleaker, problems such as resource depletion and habitat destruction are likely to continue at a brisk pace, even if greenhouse gas emissions are curbed, or at least as long as the capitalist economy continues to grow.

Depending on how governments and societies at large respond to global warming and other environmental threats, three scenarios of how society and its relationship with nature may change in the future seem possible.[2]

1   *Radical transformation*: This scenario implies a break with the socio-economic system as it has functioned for centuries. Politicians and society at large, in both the Global North and the Global South, respond in a swift, resolute, and coordinated fashion, giving us a chance of breaking with the pathway towards catastrophe. Destructive practices are curbed, and massive investments are channeled into alternatives. As a result, global warming is kept within tolerable limits. However, this scenario is hard to combine with the consumerism, growth ideology, and pursuit of endless accumulation characteristic of capitalism. Mass protests can be expected if the transition is carried out without consideration for the material interests of ordinary people. The transition must therefore be eased by massive transfers of wealth both domestically and globally in order to prevent social disruption, further socio-economic justice, and "democratize survivability" (Hamilton 2010: 223). Resistance from elites with vested interests in the existing system will certainly be fierce. This scenario therefore requires the presence of strong social movements and a public opinion committed to ecological concerns and socio-economic justice.

2   *Business as usual*: This response involves stepped-up efforts to manage climate change and other environmental threats within a framework set by existing institutions and prevailing practices. The efforts are gradualist and pragmatic since environmental problems are viewed as secondary to the imperative of accommodating powerful interests. Drastically raising energy prices or imposing other burdens on ordinary people is avoided out of fear of mass protests. A large redistribution of wealth from elites is also avoided since elites are too powerful to be challenged. Income gaps as well as the gap between the Global North and the Global South are maintained. While this scenario is plausible, the measures it outlines fail to address the causes of the crisis and therefore risk leading to the third scenario.

3   *Collapse*: Meaning that important social functions break down. This can happen directly
    through environmental factors such as global warming affecting agriculture, water sup-
    ply, contagion, extreme weather, or rising sea levels. It can also happen indirectly, through
    escalating political and social crises such as a breakdown of the global international order,
    political turmoil, and social unrest. This, too, will involve far-reaching transformations of
    the socio-economic order but in a largely uncontrolled way. Scarcity of energy and other
    resources will lead to a reduction of social complexity (Tainter 1988), with diminishing trade,
    de-urbanization, and an increasing need for local self-sufficiency as likely consequences.

These scenarios are ideal-typical simplifications. Real developments may well involve a mixture of tendencies as well as regional variations. The scenarios also simplify since they focus on
government responses to environmental developments, omitting many other factors. The time
horizon of the scenarios is deliberately left vague due to the complex nature of the processes
referred to – such as the difficulty of predicting developments that involve feedback loops. They
do, however, introduce a qualified determinism based on the notion of natural limits. While
refraining from predicting any particular future, they indicate that change *will* come, whether
we like it or not, since the present system is unsustainable. Acknowledging the possibility of real
developments switching from one scenario to another is important since it alerts us to the fact
that we cannot make predictions by simply extrapolating from existing trends.

Despite the uncertainty of the future, I suggest that these scenarios are useful points of reference when considering possible future developments of the environmental movement. Each
scenario suggests vastly different conditions for it. Since different groups and organizations
prepare for different scenarios, the scenarios are useful not only for thinking about the future
but also for understanding present-day trends in environmental activism. The scenarios are thus
linked to future orientations embodied in movements that are already active today. Ann Mische
(2014) usefully points out that future imaginaries can be studied via their externalizations in
attitudes, narratives, performance, and material forms, which make them accessible to empirical
study, and she especially singles out social movements as fruitful objects of study.

The first scenario is most emphatically endorsed in radical, left-leaning currents, such as
the climate justice movement (e.g., Klein 2014; Malm 2020), in certain versions of the New
Green Deal (e.g., Aronoff et al 2019), and in radical demands such as "keep it in the ground" or
"system change, not climate change". In the appeal to urgency, there is an affinity for the recent
wave of protests associated with groups such as Extinction Rebellion (XR) and Fridays for
Future (FFF). The second scenario is in line with actors proposing green capitalism and is acted
out by mainstream, institutionalized environmental organizations. The idea of a compatibility
of sustainability and economic growth is thus central to the carbon trading institutionalized
through the Kyoto Protocol, widely endorsed by many established environmental organizations
in the wake of the 1997 climate summit in Kyoto (see, e.g., Reitan & Gibson 2012: 402f),
as well as more recent attempts to valuate nature in terms of natural capital and ecoservices.
Preparing for the third scenario is more difficult but includes organizing at the grassroots level,
engaging in community building, and local experiments in small-scale resilient living, as can be
seen in the transition movement.

Predicting the likelihood of each scenario is hard since social, political, and cultural factors
all influence the future. More useful than attempts at prediction, it seems to me, is to identify
the dimensions that are most useful when considering ongoing and possible changes within the
environmental movement. Next, I will turn to this task, before returning in the concluding
section to the question of how these dimensions of change of the movement may be related to
the futures envisioned in the scenarios.

Institutionalization and its challengers: three dimensions of change

In what follows, I will introduce three significant dimensions of change within the environmental movement and exemplify them with contemporary movement currents. I will argue that each of these currents represents a challenge to a prominent characteristic of the environmental movement of the Global North in recent decades: namely, a high degree of institutionalization in the sense of increasing regularization of access to policy makers (e.g., Brand 1999; Coglianese 2001; Dalton et al. 2003; Giugni & Grasso 2015; Jamison 2001; Jimenez 1999; Rootes 2003, 2007; see also the chapter by Thörn in this volume).

Why is it important to focus on institutionalization? Three reasons can be mentioned. Firstly, it has been a prominent trend that has come to define established environmentalism and that has been especially important in relation to how governments have attempted to govern or manage the climate issue. Secondly, contestation around institutionalization is central to the dynamics of movement development. At least since the environmental movement's "second cycle" of institutionalization, which started in the 1990s (Rüdig 1995), the tendency toward increasing institutionalization has been propelled to a large extent by the climate issue, the urgency of which is today also fueled by increasing popular mobilization. The result is a situation in which the movement's development is likely to be determined by the dynamic tension generated by the competition between institutionalization and popular mobilization.

A final reason for the importance of focusing on institutionalization is its frequent link to depoliticization. These two processes are analytically distinct. While institutionalization indicates a change in social relations, depoliticization is a discursive process that naturalizes consensus and covers up conflict lines (Kenis 2018). It is thus an empirical question whether institutionalization entails depoliticization (Doyle 2005: 156f; Rootes 2003, 2007; see also Thörn's chapter in this volume). Pressure from non-institutionalized actors can lead institutionalized organizations to adopt a more politicized language. Conversely, non-institutionalized currents, too, carry with them risks for depoliticization that will be exemplified later in this chapter.

The dimensions to which I will now turn – those of social justice, post-apocalypse, and emergency action – are analytical constructs. Even if a movement current can exemplify several dimensions of change at the same time, the dimensions should be kept conceptually distinct since they refer to changes that do not necessarily go hand in hand.

The first challenge: social justice

The first dimension of change concerns the degree to which social justice is included as a central issue in the environmental movement, as, for instance, when focus is put on how environmental problems are entwined with exploitation, oppression, and discrimination. In contrast to older forms of environmentalism in the Global North, such as wilderness preservation, such inclusion implies a recognition that the impacts of environmental destruction are not equally distributed but reflect social hierarchies. It also implies a recognition that any measure to "save the earth" must not be taken at the expense of workers, minorities, or other subordinate groups, whose responsibility for environmental destruction is often negligible. Implicit in the idea of justice is a critique of the depoliticizing discourse of humanity in the abstract – the global collective "we" often invoked in mainstream environmentalism – which disregards that only a small portion of humanity, above all the capitalist elite, is responsible.

Stressing justice is not new per se in the environmental movement. An "environmentalism of the poor" – i.e., mobilizing in defense of environments on which people depend for their livelihood and often their traditional lifestyles – has deep historical roots and has been especially prominent in the Global South where environmental movements have seldom been as institutionalized as in the North (Guha & Martinez-Alier 1997; Doyle 2005). Another part of this current is the environmental justice movement that originated in the US in the 1980s and has mobilized around the concentration of pollution and environmentally destructive facilities to poor African American communities and around Indigenous land right issues (Agyeman et al. 2016; Schlosberg & Collins 2014).

Activists organizing under the call for climate justice have perhaps posed the major challenge to the institutionalized wing of the environmental movement in recent decades. Climate justice activism gathered force in the years before the climate summit in Copenhagen in 2009, fueled by the strength of environmental groups from the Global South and the influx of activists from the global justice movement (Hadden 2014, 2015). The result was a visible split in Copenhagen between climate justice activists and the institutionalized organizations of the Climate Action Network (CAN) (Chatterton et al. 2012; Reitan & Gibson 2012). The split reflected the clash between the market-friendly solutions promoted by CAN and the far more capitalism-critical stance of the climate justice groups (Bond & Dorsey 2010). By bringing these groups together in a single global arena, the climate summit helped visualize the widespread dissatisfaction with the strategy of the institutionalized wing of the movement that existed both in the Global South and among radical activists in the Global North (Cassegård et al. 2017).

The years after the Copenhagen summit were marked not only by disillusionment with the summit negotiations among many environmental organizations, but also by attempts to learn from failure (de Moor & Wahlström 2019; Hadden 2017). One result was that major institutionalized environmental organizations adopted the climate justice slogan, which went from having a divisive to a unifying function and contributed to healing the rift that had appeared in Copenhagen. The new movement unity was first manifested in the joint walk-out from the summit negotiations at the Warsaw summit in 2013, in which major CAN-affiliated organizations such as the World Wide Fund for Nature (WWF), Greenpeace, and Oxfam participated, along with justice-oriented groups such as the Third World Network and Jubilee South. It became even more evident during the Paris summit in 2015 when the climate justice slogan was ubiquitous and conspicuously displayed, not least by institutionalized organizations like the WWF, which decorated the metro with gigantic posters that sported its logo animal, the panda, standing on the barricades in imitation of Eugène Delacroix's famous painting *Liberty Leading the People*. The fresh impetus of climate justice activism at the time of Copenhagen thus both provoked conflict and pushed institutionalized organizations to adopt a more confrontational stance, thereby building up momentum for the Paris summit as well as other climate manifestations, such as the 2014 People's Climate March in New York (Cassegård & Thörn 2017; Gach 2019; Hadden 2017).

The question arises whether this mainstreaming of climate justice may have led to its dilution. At the Paris summit, the term was also adopted by establishment actors outside the environmental movement, such as the French president Francois Hollande, who used it in the speech that inaugurated the summit, and the term is also mentioned in the agreement text. When used in these contexts, the term becomes dissociated from anti-capitalist connotations and loses much of its critical edge. On the other hand, the justice wing of the environmental movement has continued to yield radical challenges to the fossil industry also in the post-Paris period, as exemplified by the opposition to the Dakota Access pipeline at Standing Rock in the US and the Ende Gelände civil disobedience actions to shut down lignite coal mines in Germany. In this sense, climate justice is still a politicizing notion associated with a system-critical impetus. Significantly, these campaigns signal a return of climate justice activism from the global arena of the UN summits to local resistance. The Ende Gelände campaign, which attracted thousands of participants from all over Europe, successfully retained momentum in transnational mobilization after Paris while breaking away from the UN climate summits as focal points of activism (de Moor 2018, 2020; de Moor & Wahlström 2019; Thörn et al. 2017). The combination of translocal solidarity (Routledge 2011) and place-based politics was also significant in Standing Rock, where social media helped draw worldwide attention to the struggle of the Standing Rock Sioux to defend their ancestral land and the web of life connected to it (Streeby 2018: 38–44).

The second challenge: the post-apocalypse

A further dimension of change concerns how activists relate to the apocalypticism that has long been a mainstay of the environmental movement. Do they view environmental catastrophes as future events that can be averted or as ongoing or inevitable events that must be accepted as premises of political action? As Thörn points out, the environmental movement has long stood out through its "future-oriented pessimism": utopia has been less important as a mobilizing tool than the coming catastrophe or collapse (Thörn 1997: 322, 372). We should note that the apocalyptic discourse of mainstream environmentalism is typically conditional – it is meant as a warning about what will happen *unless* we act. With Rachel Carson's often-used metaphor, it envisages humanity as standing at a "crossroads". In insisting that it is still not too late to act, it is paradoxically infused with hope.

The apocalyptic discourse in the environmental movement received renewed strength with the ascendancy of the climate issue in the 2000s. Apocalyptic imagery of melting polar caps and other disasters was regularly invoked by environmentalist establishment figures such as Al Gore, leading to a situation in which this apocalypticism was increasingly criticized for having lost oppositional force and for disregarding the real catastrophic changes that were already happening, especially in the Global South (Methmann & Rothe 2012; Swyngedouw 2010). Its compatibility with technocratic optimism became visible in the UN-led climate negotiations, where carbon markets and geo-engineering were promoted precisely as measures needed to avert future catastrophic warming. In the period leading up to the 2015 Paris summit, this optimism was also bolstered for strategic reasons by several environmental organizations that felt that hopeful messages were needed to mobilize support (Thörn et al. 2017).

Counterintuitively, the most far-reaching challenge to the apocalypticism of mainstream environmentalism comes not from technocratic optimism, but from a completely different direction, through what has been referred to as a post-apocalyptic environmentalism taking form primarily among non-institutionalized actors disillusioned with the inadequacy of official climate measures (Cassegård & Thörn 2018). These currents are nourished by the experience of catastrophic loss as *already* occurring or inevitable, rather than as a future risk. As illustrated by the increasing frequency of extreme weather as well as by the "slow violence" that takes the form of an erosion of the environmental conditions for certain cultures and ways of life (Nixon 2011), climate-related catastrophes have already arrived and are becoming the new normal. Environmental currents that have arisen in response to these experiences include, for example, the Dark Mountain collective (Cassegård & Thörn 2018: 569ff), the network of "deep adaptation" groups initiated by Jem Bendell, and the "collapsology" network in France (Tasset 2019), as well as artistic initiatives such as the Bureau of Linguistical Reality (n.d.), which arranges field studies and salons where people come together in search of words to express feelings, thoughts, and experiences related to the ongoing environmental disruptions for which language is felt to be lacking. Viewing catastrophes as already occurring or inevitable, these currents all stress the need to bid farewell to the belief in progress and mentally prepare for the decline, depletion, chaos, and hardships that will accompany the continuing environmental degradation.

Since the post-apocalyptic currents typically see little meaning in summit protesting and campaigning, they have an affinity to more local and prefigurative forms of activism, something which is visible in the transition movement, which was founded in 2006 with the first "transition town" in the UK. Engaging in activities like permaculture and do-it-yourself energy generation, it aims at constructing resilient local communities to adopt to a future of diminishing resources and climate change. Practical activities are seen as a way to produce hope where no hope can be discerned through a purely intellectual diagnosis of the situation. Common to these groups is that they view the catastrophe as a fact that must be accepted rather than as a future that can still be averted. Hence the emphasis on resilience, the construction of systems capable of absorbing shocks without ceasing to function. The predominant emotions concern the necessity of bidding farewell to present lifestyles, mourning or working through losses, and finding new meaning on that basis (a process referred to as "inner transition" by transition activists). Only by doing so can hope and possibilities for meaningful action be regained. Emotionally, post-apocalyptic currents offer a striking contrast to mainstream environmentalism's customary reliance on a mixture of future-oriented hope and fear as mobilizing emotions (Kleres & Wettergren 2017; Ojala 2011). Post-apocalyptic environmentalism is instead more centered on the experience of loss (Elliot 2018) and involves a larger element of mourning, anger, guilt, and despair, along with a rediscovery of new kinds of hope.

Much post-apocalyptic environmentalism can appear apolitical through its stress on introspection and mourning and its preference for prefigurative practical activities over eye-catching street demonstrations. At the same time, these currents often represent a radical rejection and distrust of current mainstream institutions. As in the transition movement, the awareness that the activities aim to bring about a radically different society means that politicization is always latently present (Kenis 2018; Schlosberg & Coles 2016). Furthermore, postapocalyptic environmentalism is not per se inimical to public protest. This is evident in cases in which it merges with climate justice activism, which is often driven by grief and outrage at catastrophes that are already happening rather than by fear of future catastrophes. The activism of the Sami people and other Indigenous peoples, which often concerns processes that are already now eroding their traditional lifestyles, is a case in point. Another example of how the post-apocalyptic rhetoric can be staged in public manifestations is the International Rights of Nature Tribunals, mock tribunals that have been set up by activists who treat cases such as polluted water, oil spills, displacement caused by dam construction, murdered anti-mining activists, and so on. Common to the cases is their focus on suffering that is already happening and that is calling out for justice – a message condensed in the image of a suffering mother earth, who "is calling out to us and our hearts are breaking" (quoted in Cassegård & Thörn 2018: 572). A final example of how post-apocalyptic sentiments can go hand in hand with public protest is the powerful anti-nuclear power movement that erupted in Japan in the wake of the 2011 Fukushima nuclear disaster. Again, it was anger at a catastrophe that had already happened that overwhelmingly fueled the protests and that found expression in demands to "restore" destroyed communities and the living of those who had been displaced (Cassegård 2014: 233–256).

Whereas the re-orientation of energies from trying to avert future threats has been criticized as defeatism (see, e.g., Kingsnorth & Monbiot 2009), the post-apocalyptic stance is not per se inimical to conflict and struggle. Indeed, almost all well-known waves of protest that have infused fresh anti-institutional energy in the environmental movement in recent years seem to be nourished by already ongoing rather than future catastrophes. This also holds for youth activism, to which we will now turn.

The third challenge: emergency action

A third challenge to institutionalized environmentalism comes from activists who call for a break with conventional politics, driven by the urgency of the climate crisis and despairing at the gradualism of official climate policy. While the message of these new radical initiatives is often congruent with what is preached by institutionalized environmental organizations – namely, that politicians should listen to the science and decarbonize as quickly as needed to keep dangerous warming at bay – they differ in the means they employ to drive home this message. Rather than working through conventional channels, they emphasize the need for civil disobedience and mass mobilization to bring irresistible pressure to bear on the political system. The decisive difference to institutionalized environmentalism is thus the insistence that the "emergency brake" must be pulled, even at the cost of disrupting the prevailing system.

The radicalism of stressing emergency thus consists in prioritizing the climate over what is possible within the framework of the status quo. As expressed by Greta Thunberg, realism in the sense of political pragmatism is woefully insufficient when nature is considered: "Until you start focusing on what needs to be done rather than what is politically possible, there's no hope" (2019: 16). This attitude, it has been pointed out, expresses a reversal of the customary definition of realism: "'realism' becomes utopian while the utopian fringe becomes the new realism" (Rosewarne et al. 2014).

Many of these radical initiatives are based in youth constituencies. Although some arose in the period before the 2015 Paris summit – such as the divestment movement initiated by 350. org in the US – it is only in the post-Paris period that they have become a global mass movement (Gunningham 2019). In contrast to the movement depression that followed the 2009 Copenhagen summit, the Paris summit was a steppingstone for the recent wave of activism, not least through what appeared to be the appalling weakness of the agreement – even if all countries kept to their pledges, the world would still be headed for above 3° of warming this century. Desperation was given an added boost by a grim IPCC report in 2018, which helped ignite the rise of Fridays for Future (FFF) and Extinction Rebellion (XR), the two most spectacular climate movement initiatives to have arisen in recent years. The school strike has become the signature form of direct action for FFF, while XR advocates mass civil disobedience, aiming for prolonged blockades of capital cities meant to make traffic grind to a halt and exert real economic pressure (see, e.g., de Moor et al. 2018; Gunningham 2019).

In these initiatives, several of the dimensions of change we have discussed so far come into play. A post-apocalyptic streak is rhetorically present in both XR and FFF, as can be seen in the *mise-en-scène* of grief, mourning rituals, and funeral marches and in the dismissal of false hope (de Moor 2021). Yet, at the same time, both groups clearly do their utmost to make politicians curb warming – pressuring them to "listen to the science", to "tell the truth", and to declare a "climate emergency". In that sense, both groups are close to the apocalyptic discourse of mainstream environmentalism, although with an added sense of urgency – a sense which is also expressed in the "defence of panic" penned by the eco-Marxist scholar Andreas Malm (2018: 219). In terms of emotions, the stress is neither on passive hope nor despair, but on desperation, courage, anger, and the need to rise to the occasion. "I don't want you to be hopeful", as Thunberg said. "I want you to panic. . . . And then I want you to act" (2019: 24). XR and FFF also offer a contrast to the typical post-apocalyptic groups by squarely putting the emphasis on highly visible forms of public protest and direct action, targeting national governments and global elites (de Moor et al. 2020: 4). To these activists, the urgency of the climate threat leaves no time for slowly spreading prefigurative forms of action.

Paradoxically, the very success of these groups in mobilizing a worldwide protest wave may have been bought at the cost of a certain form of depoliticization – one that easily occurs in broad, popular mobilizations and that is often particularly visible in single-issue movements when movements attempt to gather supporters from all sides of the political spectrum. Here, the best example might be XR, which explicitly aims for a movement for the climate beyond right and left. Furthermore, both XR and FFF stand out through their appeal to science, a seemingly politically neutral framing that they share with many established, institutionalized environmental organizations (de Moor et al. 2020; Zulianello & Ceccobelli 2020). The narrow focus on decarbonization has also invited the criticism that XR neglects justice-related issues such as class, racism, and the gap between the Global South and North (de Moor et al. 2018; Slaven & Heydon 2020), although it needs to be added that XR is clearly making efforts to remedy its insensitivity to these issues (see Kinniburgh 2020; also several contributions to Farrell 2019). Climate justice appears to be more foregrounded in FFF (see, e.g., Thunberg 2019: 3, 15), showing that nothing per se makes climate emergency and climate justice activism incompatible.

Final remarks about an open future

In the previous sections, I have identified three dimensions of change – those of social justice, post-apocalypse, and emergency action – and exemplified them with currents in today's environmental movement. How can these dimensions and currents be connected to the three scenarios of revolutionary transition, business as usual, and collapse?

As sketched in the scenarios, the future of the environmental movement will to a considerable degree depend on how governments and social elites respond to environmental problems and to movement demands. Since the responses can, in turn, be influenced by movement mobilizations and since many other factors can also be expected to play in, predictions are difficult indeed. Adding to the difficulty is that the relation between the envisioned futures and movement trends is two way: while different futures create different conditions for movement activity, movements influence which future should come into being. Nevertheless, the scenarios are helpful in at least two respects. Firstly, they visualize the huge differences that exist between possible futures. Secondly, they caution us against simply extrapolating present trends, since shifts between these futures are possible.

In addition to helping us envision the future, the scenarios also throw light on orientations that are already present in today's environmental movement. They help us understand the sense of urgency, the need for grieving and coping with loss, the need to protest injustices and fight for system change; the desire to cooperate with authorities that animate different currents within the movement; and how these needs contribute to shaping their strategies and tactics. Clearly, different movement currents have different degrees of fit with the different scenarios. The viability of the strategy of many institutionalized environmental organizations thus appears to depend on how effectively environmental problems can be managed through the gradualist approach envisaged in the business-as-usual scenario. However, if the activists associated with the new radical groups like XR or FFF are right, this gradualist strategy will be woefully insufficient. "It is plain that climate-nemesis is coming our way on a business as usual pathway", as activist scholar and XR spokesperson Rupert Read (2019) points out. The call of these radical groups for an "emergency" instead aims at bringing about another scenario, that of radical transformation. The viability of this current depends heavily on the possibility of mass mobilizations and strong support from the public, without which the power of vested interests may well prove unsurmountable. While the urgency of the required measures appears likely to lend energy to this current in the coming years, it may well be a weakness in the longer run since it is hard to imagine how it might survive for long as a movement current without transforming itself. A contrast is offered by the post-apocalyptic current, which prepares itself for a third scenario, that of collapse. Here we find activists who focus their energies on ecological farming, community building, and honing practical do-it-yourself skills suitable for a low-energy future, as well as artistical activities meant to help participants come to terms with ecological loss, grief, and anxiety. "Once false hopes are shrugged off, once we stare into the darkness that surrounds us, we can see new paths opening up; new forms; new words", as the editors of a Dark Mountain anthology put it (Du Cann et al. 2017: 2). This current's orientation to a future of diminished resources and a more disaster-prone climate may offer good chances of long-term viability if the third scenario becomes unavoidable, perhaps along the lines of existing environmental groups in the Global South. However, the tendency among several groups belonging to this current in the Global North to focus on present needs for mourning and introspection may conceivably become less urgent as environmental disasters become a new, routinized normal.

Of the surveyed currents, climate justice activism alone appears likely to play an important role in all three scenarios. Fighting socio-economic inequality and vested interests is bound to remain relevant regardless of whether the movement focuses on trying to bring about the radical transformation scenario or on preparing for the struggles that can be expected to dominate a post-apocalyptic world. As pointed out by Clive Hamilton (2010: 218), fighting for an egalitarian society is necessary not just to prevent a collapse, but also for a humane society to remain possible if a collapse occurs. Unless we create a society in which "survival is democratized", climate change is likely to bring about a brutal future in which the ruthless and the wealthy protect themselves while large swaths of humanity (as well as non-human nature) perish.

The capacity of movements to bring this about, however, depends on their ability to politicize issues forcefully when necessary. Several of the currents we have been looking at have contributed to politicizing environmentalist discourse by emphasizing urgency, socio-economic injustice, and ongoing catastrophes. At the same time, at least three different variants of depoliticization can be discerned in today's environmental movement. Firstly, environmental organizations that are institutionalized or that aspire to institutionalization may choose to downplay conflict in order to preserve or create good relations with policy makers. This form of depoliticization can be pragmatically justified to the extent that the gradualist approach associated with the business-as-usual scenario is capable of effectively dealing with environmental problems, but it can also fetter the movement if it prevents it from orienting itself toward other scenarios, thereby limiting its freedom of action. A second form of depoliticization arises in grassroots groups that only partially operate in the public sphere, either because they are still groping about for an ideological position or because they prefer to focus on practical activities such as permaculture or the mental reorientation needed to adapt to climate change. Certain variants of post-apocalyptic environmentalism appear to exemplify this form of depoliticization. Thirdly, depoliticization can occur because of the aspiration to mobilize a broad, popular movement beyond left and right, as seen in groups stressing emergency action. In the latter case, a highly public conflict is staged, but it is usually centered on a single conflictual issue at the expense of disregarding or downplaying other conflict lines. Clearly, these different forms of depoliticization occur for different reasons. Although they can all appear justified, depending on the situation, they all carry with them the risk of incapacitating the movement when it becomes necessary for it to engage in conflict: for instance, when powerful interests block its aspirations or demands.

As for future research, it will certainly be important to see how the environmental movement will respond in coming years to the environmental destruction that unfortunately appears likely to continue. The coming decade may well be crucial, not only for the possibility of steering the planet away from the collapse scenario, but also for the future shape of the environmental movement. Important questions to focus on will no doubt include both to what extent the urgency of environmental problems will contribute to a further institutionalization of this movement and to what extent this institutionalization will be challenged by counteracting currents such as the ones surveyed in this chapter – currents emphasizing social justice, ongoing catastrophes, and the need for emergency action.

By way of ending, I want to stress that predictions are tricky not just because of the complexity of the subject matter. They are also questionable since they presuppose an objectification of future developments that disregards our agency, the very quality that is absolutely crucial considering the gravity of today's environmental crises. Today crises are multiplying, but how crises will play out is always determined to some extent by how we act.

Notes

1 The author would like to thank the participants at the CSM-RESIST workshop at the University of Gothenburg in May 2021 for helpful comments.
2 The scenarios draw on and combine insights from many sources. The massive state intervention outlined in the first scenario is aligned with visions in, e.g., Wainwright and Mann (2018) and also with powerful demands advanced within the environmental movement: e.g., Malm (2020) or Aronoff et al. (2019). Regarding the need for rapid decarbonization, I rely on uncontroversial science (as outlined in, e.g., the 2018 IPCC special report on the impacts of global warming of 1.5°C). The incompatibility of such decarbonization with a growing economy in the Global North is stressed by, e.g., Hickel and Kallis (2019). The second scenario is best expressed in eco-modernist writings (e.g., the Breakthrough Institute). The third scenario can find support in works like Servigne and Stevens (2020) and Oreskes and Conway (2014).

References

Agyeman, Julian, Schlosberg, David, Craven, Luke, and Matthews, Caitlin. 2016. Trends and directions in environmental justice: From inequity to everyday life, community, and just sustainabilities. *Annual Review of Environment and Resources*. 41, 321–340.

Aronoff, Kate, Battistoni, Alyssa, Cohen, Daniel Aldana, and Riofrancos, Thea. 2019. *A Planet to Win: Why We Need a Green New Deal*. London: Verso.

Bond, Patrick, and Dorsey, Michael K. 2010. Anatomies of environmental knowledge and resistance: Diverse climate justice movements and waning eco-neoliberalism. *Journal of Australian Political Economy*. 66(66), 286–316.

Brand, Karl-Werner. 1999. Dialectics of institutionalization: The transformation of the environmental movement in Germany. *Environmental Politics*. 8(1), 35–58.

Bureau of Linguistical Reality. n.d. http://bureauoflinguisticalreality.com/ (accessed 2021, February 3).

Cassegård, Carl. 2014. *Youth Movements, Trauma, and Alternative Space in Contemporary Japan*. Leiden: Global Oriental.

Cassegård, Carl, and Thörn, Håkan. 2017. Climate justice, equity and movement mobilization. In: Cassegård, C., Soneryd, L., Thörn, H., and Wettergren, Å. eds. *Climate Action in a Globalizing World: Comparative Perspectives on Environmental Movements in the Global North*. New York: Routledge, 33–56.

Cassegård, Carl, and Thörn, Håkan. 2018. Toward a postapocalyptic environmentalism? Responses to loss and visions of the future in climate activism. *Environment and Planning E: Nature and Space*. 1(4), 561–578.

Cassegård, Carl, Thörn, Håkan, Soneryd, Linda, and Wettergren, Åsa., eds. 2017. *Climate Action in a Globalizing World: Comparative Perspectives on Environmental Movements in the Global North*. New York: Routledge.

Chatterton, Paul, Featherstone, David, and Routledge, Paul. 2012. Articulating climate justice in Copenhagen: Antagonism, the commons, and solidarity. *Antipode*. 45(3), 602–620.

Coglianese, Cary. 2001. Social movements, law, and society: The institutionalization of the environmental movement. *University of Pennsylvania Law Review.* 150(85), 85–118.

Dalton, Russell J., Reccia, Steve, and Rohrschneider, Robert. 2003. The environmental movement and the modes of political action. *Comparative Political Studies.* 36(7), 743–771.

de Moor, Joost. 2018. The 'efficacy dilemma' of transnational climate activism: The case of COP21. *Environmental Politics.* 27(6), 1079–1100.

de Moor, Joost. 2020. Alternative globalities? Climatization processes and the climate movement beyond COPs. *International Politics.* https://doi.org/10.1057/s41311-020-00222-y

de Moor, Joost. 2021. Postapocalyptic narratives in climate activism: Their place and impact in five European cities. *Environmental Politics.* https://doi.org/10.1080/09644016.2021.1959123

de Moor, Joost, De Vydt, Michiel, Uba, Katrin, and Wahlström, Mattias. 2020. New kids on the block: taking stock of the recent cycle of climate activism. *Social Movement Studies.* https://doi.org/10.1080/14742837.2020.1836617

de Moor, Joost, Doherty, Brian, and Hayes, Graeme. 2018. The 'new' climate politics of extinction rebellion? *Open Democracy,* November 27. www.opendemocracy.net/joost-de-moor-brian-doherty-graeme-hayes/new-climate-politics-of-extinction-rebellion (accessed 2018, November 30).

de Moor, Joost, and Wahlström, Mattias. 2019. Narrating political opportunities: Explaining strategic adaptation in the climate movement. *Theory and Society* 48, 419–451.

Doyle, Timothy. 2005. *Environmental Movements in Minority and Majority Worlds: A Global Perspective.* New Brunswick, NJ: Rutgers University Press.

Du Cann, Charlotte, Hine, Dougald, Hunt, Nick, and Kingsnorth, Paul. 2017. Uncentring Our Minds. In: Du Cann, C., Hine, D., Hunt, N., and Kingsnorth, P. eds. *Walking on Lava: Selected Works for Uncivilised Times.* White River Junction, VT: Chelsea Green Publishing, 1–3.

Elliott, Rebecca. 2018. The sociology of climate change as a sociology of loss. *European Journal of Sociology.* 59(3), 301–337.

Farrell, Clare, Green, Alison, Knights, Sam Knights, and Skeaping, William, eds. 2019. *This Is Not a Drill: An Extinction Rebellion Handbook.* London: Penguin.

Gach, Evan. 2019. Normative shifts in the global conception of climate change: The growth of climate justice. *Social Sciences* 8(1), 1–18.

Giugni, Marco, and Grasso, Maria T. 2015. Environmental movements in advanced industrial democracies: Heterogeneity, transformation, and institutionalization. *Annual Review of Environment and Resources.* 40, 337–361.

Guha, Ramachandra, and Martinez-Alier, Joan. 1997. *Varieties of Environmentalism: Essays North and South.* London: Earthscan.

Gunningham, Neil. 2019. Averting climate catastrophe: Environmental activism, extinction rebellion and coalitions of influence. *King's Law Journal.* 30(2), 194–202.

Hadden, Jennifer. 2014. Explaining variation in transnational climate change activism: The role of inter-movement spillover. *Global Environmental Politics.* 14(2), 7–25.

Hadden, Jennifer. 2015. *Networks in Contention: The Divisive Politics of Climate Change.* New York: Cambridge University Press.

Hadden, Jennifer. 2017. Learning from defeat: The strategic reorientation of the U.S. climate movement. In: Thörn, H., Cassegård, C., Soneryd, L., and Wettergren, Å. eds. *Climate Action in a Globalizing World: Comparative Perspectives on Environmental Movements in the Global North.* New York: Routledge, 143–164.

Hamilton, Clive. 2010. *Requiem for a Species: Why We Resist the Truth About Climate Change.* London: Earthscan.

Hickel, Jason, and Kallis, Giorgos. 2019. Is green growth possible?. *New Political Economy.* 25(4), 469–486.

Jamison, Andrew. 2001. *The Making of Green Knowledge: Environmental Politics and Cultural Transformation.* Cambridge: Cambridge University Press.

Jimenez, Manuel. 1999. Consolidation through institutionalisation? Dilemmas of the Spanish environmental movement in the 1990s. *Environmental Politics.* 8(1), 149–171.

Kenis, Anneleen. 2018. Post-politics contested: Why multiple voices on climate change do not equal politicisation. *Environment and Planning C: Politics and Space.* 37(5), 831–848.

Kingsnorth, Paul, and Monbiot, George. 2009. Is there any point in fighting to stave off industrial apocalypse? *The Guardian,* August 17. www.theguardian.com/commentisfree/cif-green/2009/aug/17/environment-climate-change (accessed 2018, January 25).

Kinniburgh, Colin. 2020. Can extinction rebellion survive? *Dissent.* 67(1), 125–133.

Klein, Naomi. 2014. *This Changes Everything: Capitalism vs. the Climate.* New York: Simon & Schuster.

Kleres, Jochen, and Wettergren, Åsa. 2017. Fear, hope, anger, and guilt in climate activism. *Social Movement Studies*. 16(5), 507–519.

Malm, Andreas. 2018. *The Progress of This Storm: Nature and Society in a Warming World*. London: Verso.

Malm, Andreas. 2020. *Corona, Climate, Chronic Emergency: War Communism in the Twenty-First Century*. London: Verso.

Methmann, Chris, and Rothe, Delf. 2012. Politics for the day after tomorrow: The logic of apocalypse in global climate. *Security Dialogue*. 43(4), 323–344.

Mische, Ann. 2014. Measuring futures in action: Projective grammars in the Rio+20 debates. *Theory & Society*. 43, 437–464.

Nixon, Rob. 2011. *Slow Violence and the Environmentalism of the Poor*. Cambridge, MA: Harvard University Press.

Ojala, Maria. 2011. Hope and climate change: The importance of hope for environmental engagement among young people. *Environmental Education Research*. 18(5), 1–18.

Oreskes, Naomi, and Conway, Erik M. 2014. *The Collapse of Western Civilization: A View from the Future*. New York: Columbia University Press.

Read, Rupert. 2019. Climate change and deep adaptation. *The Ecologist*, February 8. https://theecologist. org/2019/feb/08/climate-change-and-deep-adaptation (accessed 2021, February 3).

Reitan, Ruth, and Gibson, Shannon. 2012. Climate change or social change? Environmental and leftist praxis and participatory action research. *Globalizations*. 9(3), 395–410.

Rootes, Christopher, ed. 2003. *Environmental Protest in Western Europe*. Oxford: Oxford University Press.

Rootes, Christopher. 2007. Environmental movements. In: Snow, D.A., Soule, S.A., and Kriesi, H. eds. *The Blackwell Companion to Social Movements*. Oxford: Blackwell, 608–640.

Rosewarne, Stuart, Goodman, James, and Pearse, Rebecca. 2014. *Climate Action Upsurge: The Ethnography of Climate Movement Politics*. Abingdon: Routledge.

Routledge, Paul. 2011. Translocal climate justice solidarities. In: Dryzek, J.S., Norgaard, R.B., and Schlosberg, D. eds. *The Oxford Handbook of Climate Change and Society*. Oxford: Oxford University Press, 384–398.

Rüdig, Wolfgang. 1995. Editorial. In: Rüdig, W. ed. *Green Politics Three*. Edinburgh: Edinburgh University Press, 1–8.

Schlosberg, David, and Coles, Romand. 2016. The new environmentalism of everyday life: Sustainability, material flows and movements. *Contemporary Political Theory*. 15, 160–181.

Schlosberg, David, and Collins, Lisette B. 2014. From environmental to climate justice: Climate change and the discourse of environmental justice. *WIREs Climate Change*. 5, 359–374, May–June.

Servigne, Pablo, and Stevens, Raphaël. 2020. *How Everything Can Collapse: A Manual for Our Times*. Cambridge: Polity.

Slaven, Mike, and Heydon, James. 2020. Crisis, deliberation, and extinction rebellion. *Critical Studies on Security*. 8(1), 59–62.

Streeby, Shelley. 2018. *Imagining the Future of Climate Change: World-Making Through Science Fiction and Activism*. Oakland: University of California Press.

Swyngedouw, Erik. 2010. Apocalypse forever? Post-political populism and the spectre of climate change. *Theory Culture & Society*. 27(2–3), 213–232.

Tainter, Joseph A. 1988. *The Collapse of Complex Societies*. Cambridge: Cambridge University Press.

Tasset, Cyprien. 2019. Les 'effondrés anonymes'? S'associer autour d'un constat de dépassement des limites planétaires. *La Pensée écologique*. 1(3), 53–62.

Thörn, Håkan. 1997. *Rörelser i det moderna: Politik, modernitet och kollektiv identitet i Europa 1789–1989*. Stockholm: Tiden Athena.

Thörn, Håkan, Cassegård, Carl, Soneryd, Linda, and Wettergren, Åsa. 2017. Hegemony and environmentalist strategy: Global governance, movement mobilization and climate justice. In: Cassegård, C., Soneryd, L., Thörn, H., and Wettergren, Å. eds. *Climate Action in a Globalizing World: Comparative Perspectives on Environmental Movements in the Global North*. New York: Routledge, 219–244.

Thunberg, Greta. 2019. *No One Is Too Small to Make a Difference*. London: Penguin.

Wainwright, Joel, and Mann, Geoff. 2018. *Climate Leviathan: A Political Theory of Our Planetary Future*. London: Verso.

Zulianello, Mattia, and Ceccobelli, Diego. 2020. Don't call it climate populism: On Greta Thunberg's technocratic ecocentrism. *The Political Quarterly*. 91(3), 623–631.

INDEX

Page numbers in *italics* refer to figures, those in **bold** indicate tables.

Index

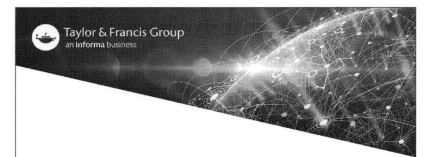

Printed in the United States
by Baker & Taylor Publisher Services